Map pages south

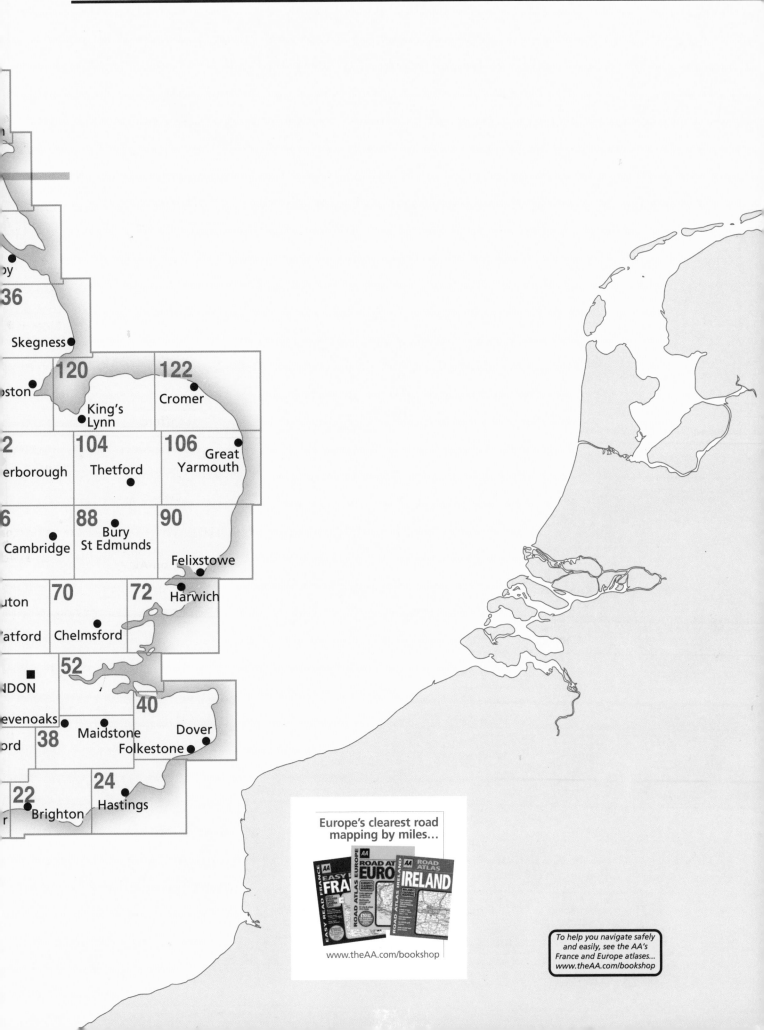

36

Skegness

120

122

King's Lynn

Cromer

oston

104

106

Great Yarmouth

erborough

Thetford

88

90

Cambridge

Bury St Edmunds

Felixstowe

70

72

Harwich

uton

atford

Chelmsford

52

NDON

40

evenoaks

38

Maidstone

Dover

ord

Folkestone

24

22

Hastings

Brighton

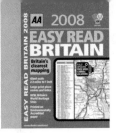

Atlas contents

Scale 1:148,000 or 2.34 miles to 1 inch

Map pages south	inside front cover
Route planner	II–VII
Atlas symbols	VIII–1
Road maps 1:148,000 scale	2–283
Channel Islands 1:100,000 scale	9
Isle of Man 1:200,000 scale	154
Orkney Islands 1:450,000 scale	275
Shetland Islands 1:450,000 scale	281
Western Isles 1:480,000 scale	282–283

Restricted junctions	284–285
Index to place names	286–368
County, administrative area map	286–287
Map pages north	inside back cover

8th edition June 2007

© Automobile Association Developments Limited 2007
Original edition printed 2000.

Cartography:
All cartography in this atlas edited, designed and produced by the Mapping Services Department of AA Publishing (A03298).

This product includes mapping data licensed from Ordnance Survey® with the permission of the Controller of Her Majesty's Stationery Office. © Crown copyright 2007. All rights reserved. Licence number 100021153.

Publisher's notes:
Published by AA Publishing (a trading name of Automobile Association Developments Limited, whose registered office is Fanum House, Basing View, Basingstoke, Hampshire RG21 4EA, UK. Registered number 1878835).

ISBN-13: 978 0 7495 5264 0
ISBN-10: 0 7495 5264 6

A CIP catalogue record for this book is available from The British Library.

Disclaimer:
The contents of this atlas are believed to be correct at the time of the latest revision, it will not contain any subsequent amended, new or temporary information including diversions and traffic control or enforcement systems. The publishers cannot be held responsible or liable for any loss or damage occasioned to any person acting or refraining from action as a result of any use or reliance on material in this atlas, nor for any errors, omissions or changes in such material. This does not affect your statutory rights. The publishers would welcome information to correct any errors or omissions and to keep this atlas up to date. Please write to the Atlas Editor, AA Publishing, The Automobile Association, Fanum House, Basing View, Basingstoke, Hampshire RG21 4EA, UK. E-mail: *roadatlasfeedback@theaa.com*

Acknowledgements:
AA Publishing would like to thank the following for their assistance in producing this atlas:

RoadPilot Information on fixed speed camera locations provided by RoadPilot
© Copyright RoadPilot® Driving Technology. English Nature, Forestry Commission, Johnsons, National Trust and National Trust for Scotland, RSPB, Scottish Natural Heritage, The Countryside Agency, The Countryside Council for Wales.

Printer:
Printed in Spain by Graficas Estella, Estella.
This book has been printed with a PEFC paper.
Certificate nb: 14-33-00002-B.
Paper: 90gsm Matt Coated paper.

SPEED READING

Speed camera locations

Speed camera locations provided in association with RoadPilot Ltd

RoadPilot is the developer of one of the largest and most accurate databases of speed camera locations in the UK and Europe*. It has provided the speed camera information in this atlas. RoadPilot is the UK's pioneer and market leader in GPS (Global Positioning System) road safety technologies.

MicroGo (pictured right) is RoadPilot's latest in-car speed camera location system. It improves road safety by alerting you to the location of accident black spots, fixed and mobile camera sites. RoadPilot's MicroGo does not jam police lasers and is therefore completely legal. RoadPilot's database of fixed camera locations has been compiled with the full co-operation of regional police forces and the Safety Camera Partnerships.

For more information on RoadPilot's GPS road safety products, please visit **www.roadpilot.com** or telephone 0870 240 1701

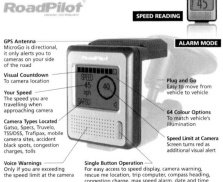

GPS Antenna
MicroGo is directional, it only alerts you to cameras on your side of the road

Visual Countdown
To camera location

Your Speed
The speed you are travelling when approaching camera

Camera Types Located
Gatso, Specs, Truvelo, TSS/DSS, Trafipax, mobile camera sites, accident black spots, congestion charges, tolls

Voice Warnings
Only if you are exceeding the speed limit at the camera

Plug and Go
Easy to move from vehicle to vehicle

64 Colour Options
To match vehicle's illumination

Speed Limit at Camera
Screen turns red as additional visual alert

Single Button Operation
For easy access to speed display, camera warning, rescue me location, trip computer, compass heading, congestion charge, max speed alarm, date and time

*European database included

DUBLIN

Dún Laoghaire

To help you navigate safely
and easily, see the AA's
Ireland atlases...
www.theAA.com/bookshop

REPUBLIC
OF
IRELAND

Rosslare
Harbour

(Summer only)

Holyhead

Anglesey

Bangor
Caernarfon
Bethesda
Betws-y-Coed

Llandudno
Colwyn Bay
Rhyl
Abergele
Holywell
Denbigh
Mold
Ruthin

Conwy

A55

A548

A55

A5

A4086

A525

A494

A55

Queensferry

Ellesmere Port

Chester

A51

Crewe

Nantwich

Newcastle-under-Lyme

Whitchurch

Market Drayton

Wrexham

Llangollen

Oswestry

Shrewsbury

Telford

WOLVERHAMPTON

Bridgnorth

Stourbridge
Halesowen

Kidderminster

Bromsgrove

Pwllheli
Porthmadog
Abersoch

Bala

Barmouth
Dolgellau

Cardigan Bay

Machynlleth

Newtown

Welshpool

Church Stretton

Ludlow

Knighton

Leominster

Worcester

Great Malvern

Ledbury

Tewkesbury

Aberystwyth

A44

Llangurig

Rhayader

Llandrindod Wells

Kington

Aberaeron

Tregaron

Lampeter

Builth Wells

Hay-on-Wye

Hereford

Ross-on-Wye

Gloucester

Cardigan

Newcastle Emlyn

Fishguard

St David's

Haverfordwest

Milford Haven
Pembroke Dock
Pembroke

Carmarthen

St Clears

Tenby

Llandeilo

Llandovery

Brecon

Abergavenny

Monmouth

Chepstow

Llanelli

Swansea
Neath
Port Talbot

Merthyr Tydfil

Ebbw Vale

Pontypridd

Cwmbran

Newport

CARDIFF

Cardiff

Bridgend

Avonmouth

BRISTOL

Bristol

Bath

Clevedon

Weston-super-Mare

Cheddar

Wells

Shepton Mallet

Frome

Bristol Channel

Lundy

Ilfracombe

Lynton

Minehead

Barnstaple

Bridgwater

Glastonbury

Bideford

Great Torrington

South Molton

Taunton

Wincanton

Bude

Hatherleigh

Tiverton

Ilminster

Yeovil

Sherborne

Holsworthy

Crediton

Honiton

Chard

Crewkerne

Blandford Forum

Okehampton

Exeter

Axminster

Bridport

Launceston

Tavistock

Buckfastleigh

Newton Abbot

Lyme Regis

Dorchester

Wadebridge

Bodmin

Liskeard

Plymouth

Totnes

Torquay

Paignton

Weymouth

Fortuneswell

Newquay

St Austell

Saltash

Torpoint

Dartmouth

Kingsbridge

Redruth

Truro

Lostwithiel

Guernsey
Jersey
St Malo

Camborne

Falmouth

Penzance

Helston

Land's End

Lizard

Cork (Ringaskiddy)
(Suspended until 2008)

Santander
(Summer only)

Roscoff

ENGLISH

WALES

LIVERPOOL
Birkenhead
Widnes
Runcorn
Northwich

Bolton
Bury
Wigan
St Helens
Warrington

Formby
Ormskirk
Skelmersdale
Crosby

John Lennon

Knutsford

Exmouth
Dawlish
Teignmouth

Route planner

Legend:

- Motorway
- Toll motorway
- Primary route dual carriageway
- Primary route single carriageway
- Other A roads
- Vehicle ferry
- Vehicle ferry - fast catamaran

To help you navigate safely and easily, see the AA's France and Europe atlases... www.theAA.com/bookshop

Scale:
0 10 20 30 miles
0 10 20 30 40 kilometres

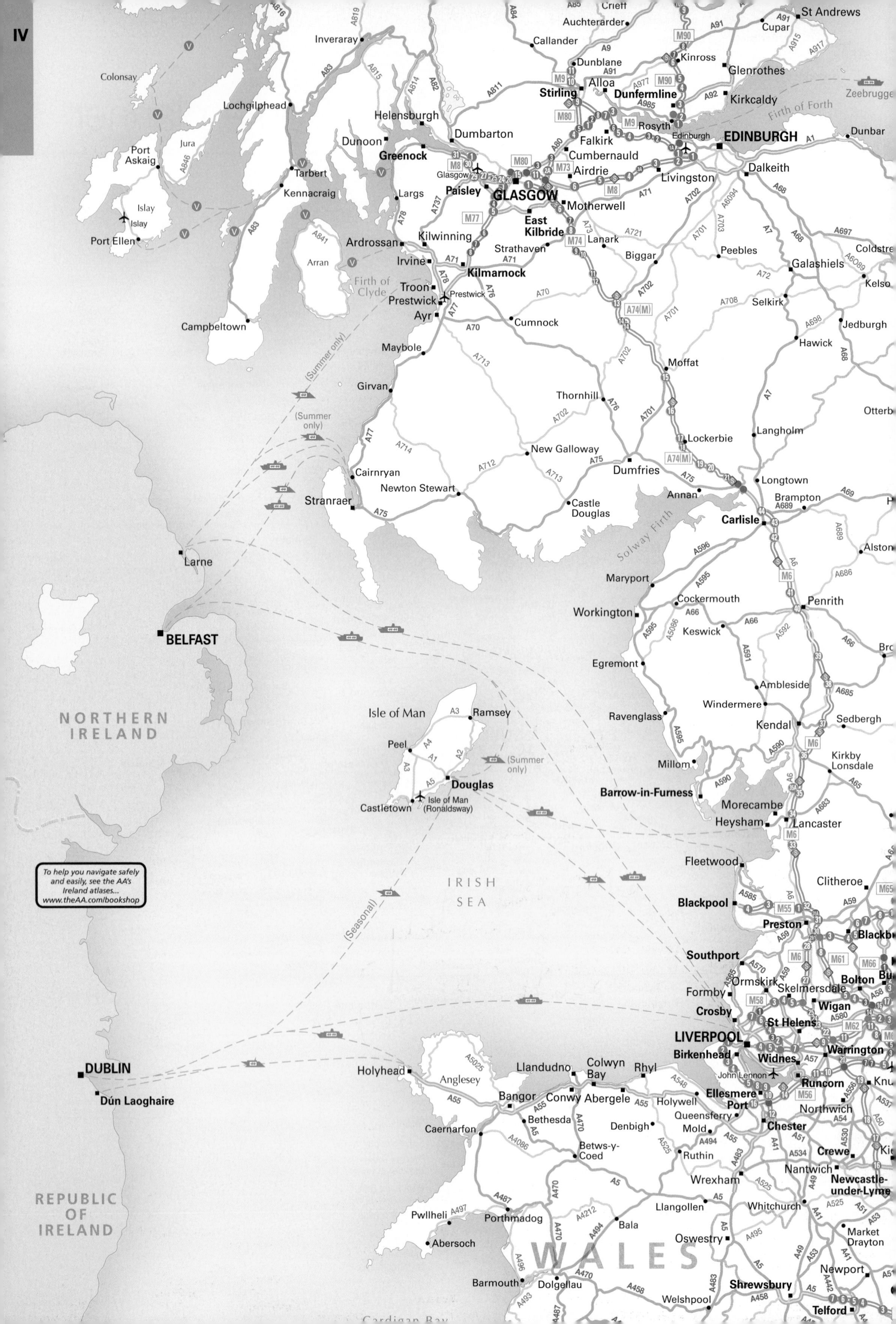

Colonsay

Inveraray

St Andrews

Crieff

Auchterarder

Cupar

Callander

M90

Kinross

Glenrothes

Dunblane

Alloa

Kirkcaldy

Zeebrugge

Stirling

Dunfermline

Helensburgh

Rosyth

Dunbar

Lochgilphead

Dumbarton

Edinburgh

EDINBURGH

Dunoon

Falkirk

A1

Greenock

Cumbernauld

Livingston

Dalkeith

Port Askaig

Airdrie

Paisley

GLASGOW

Motherwell

Peebles

Largs

East Kilbride

Lanark

Galashiels

Islay

Ardrossan

Kilwinning

Strathaven

Biggar

Kelso

Port Ellen

Irvine

Selkirk

Arran

Kilmarnock

Jedburgh

Troon

Prestwick

Hawick

Firth of Clyde

Ayr

Cumnock

Otterb

Campbeltown

Maybole

Moffat

Girvan

Thornhill

Langholm

Cairnryan

New Galloway

Lockerbie

Longtown

Newton Stewart

Dumfries

Brampton

Larne

Stranraer

Annan

Carlisle

Alston

Castle Douglas

Solway Firth

NORTHERN IRELAND

Maryport

Penrith

BELFAST

Cockermouth

Workington

Keswick

Bro

Isle of Man

Ramsey

Keswick

Egremont

Ambleside

Peel

Ravenglass

Windermere

Sedbergh

Kendal

Millom

Kirkby Lonsdale

Douglas

Castletown

Isle of Man (Ronaldsway)

Barrow-in-Furness

Morecambe

To help you navigate safely and easily, see the AA's Ireland atlases... www.theAA.com/bookshop

Heysham

Lancaster

IRISH SEA

Fleetwood

Clitheroe

Blackpool

Preston

Blackb

Southport

Ormskirk

Skelmersdale

Bolton

Bu

Formby

Wigan

Crosby

St Helens

LIVERPOOL

Warrington

DUBLIN

Birkenhead

Dún Laoghaire

Widnes

Runcorn

Knu

Holyhead

Llandudno

Colwyn Bay

Rhyl

John Lennon

Anglesey

Bangor

Conwy

Abergele

Holywell

Ellesmere Port

Northwich

REPUBLIC OF IRELAND

Caernarfon

Bethesda

Denbigh

Mold

Chester

Queensferry

Ruthin

Crewe

Betws-y-Coed

Nantwich

Pwllheli

Porthmadog

Bala

Llangollen

Whitchurch

Newcastle-under-Lyme

Barmouth

Dolgellau

Oswestry

Abersoch

WALES

Welshpool

Shrewsbury

Newport

Telford

NORTH

SEA

Eyemouth

Berwick-upon-Tweed

Wooler

Alnwick

Amble

Ashington

Morpeth

Newcastle

Corbridge
m
Gateshead

Consett

Durham

Bishop Auckland

Barnard
Castle

Darlington

Richmond

Leyburn

Ripon

Harrogate

Otley

Keighley

BRADFORD LEEDS
Leeds
Bradford

Halifax

rnley

Huddersfield

ndale

Oldham

MANCHESTER

Stockport

Glossop

SHEFFIELD

Stafford

Rugeley

STOKE-ON-TRENT

DERBY

Buxton

Bakewell

Matlock

Leek

ongleton
rove

Uttoxeter

Ashbourne

Ilkeston

NOTTINGHAM

Long
Eaton

Loughborough

Nottingham
East
Midlands

LEICESTER

Stone

Lichfield

M6 Toll

nock

North Shields

Tynemouth

NEWCASTLE UPON TYNE

South Shields

SUNDERLAND

Chester-le-Street

Hartlepool

Stockton-
on-Tees

Middlesbrough

Durham
Tees Valley

Scotch
Corner

Guisborough

Whitby

Northallerton

Thirsk

Helmsley

Pickering

Easingwold

Malton

York

Wetherby

Selby

Market
Weighton

Beverley

Scarborough

Filey

Bridlington

Driffield

KINGSTON UPON HULL

Goole

Pontefract

Wakefield

Thorne

Scunthorpe

Immingham

Grimsby

Cleethorpes

Humberside

Barnsley

Doncaster

Robin Hood
Doncaster Sheffield

Rotherham

Bawtry

Brigg

Worksop

Retford

Gainsborough

Market
Rasen

Louth

Mablethorpe

Chesterfield

Mansfield

Lincoln

Horncastle

Skegness

Alfreton

Newark-
on-Trent

Sleaford

Boston

The
Wash

Sheringham

Cromer

Hunstanton

North Walsham

Aylsham

Grantham

Spalding

Bourne

King's
Lynn

Fakenham

Dereham

Norwich

Caister-
on-Sea

Melton Mowbray

Oakham

Stamford

Wisbech

Swaffham

Great
Yarmouth

Downham

Burton upon
Trent

Stockport

ENGLAND

Motorway

Toll motorway

Primary route
dual carriageway

Primary route
single carriageway

Other A roads

Vehicle ferry

Vehicle ferry -
fast catamaran

Stavanger, Haugesund
Bergen, Kristiansand
Göteborg

IJmuiden

Rotterdam
(Europoort)
Zeebrugge

0   10   20   30 miles
0   10   20   30   40 kilometres

Western
Isles

Port Nis
(Port of Ness)

Scourie

A857

A894

Steornabhagh
(Stornoway)

Stornoway

A859

Isle of
Lewis

The Minch

Outer Hebrides

Taransay

Ullapool

Tairbeart
(Tarbert)

A835

Harris

A832

Gairloch

A832

Uibhist a Tuath
(North Uist)

Sound of Harris

Kinlochewe

Achnash

A832

Loch nam Madadh
(Lochmaddy)

Uig

A87

A890

Beinn na Faoghla
(Benbecula)

Benbecula

Dunvegan

A850

Portree

Uibhist a Deas
(South Uist)

A865

Isle
of
Skye

Kyle of
Lochalsh

A87

A87

Inver

Loch Baghasdail
(Lochboisdale)

A887

Barra

Sound of Barra

Armadale

A87

Invergarry

Barraigh
(Barra)

Rùm

Mallaig

A830

Eigg

Inner Hebrides

A82

Coll

Fort Willia

A861

Tobermory

Ballachulish

A884

Tiree

Lochaline

A828

Craignure
Isle of Mull

Oban

A85

Fionnphort

A849

A816

A819

Inveraray

Colonsay

A83

A815

A814

Lochgilphead

Helensbur

Jura

Dunoon

Port
Askaig

Greenock

Tarbert

Largs

A846

Kennacraig

A78

Islay

Islay

A83

Ardrossan

Irvine

Port Ellen

A841

Arran

Troo

Firth of
Clyde

Prestwi
Ay

Campbeltown

Summer only

Maybole

Legend

	Motorway
	Toll motorway
	Primary route dual carriageway
	Primary route single carriageway
	Other A roads
🚢 or V	Vehicle ferry
🚢	Vehicle ferry - fast catamaran

0 10 20 30 miles

0 10 20 30 40 kilometres

Orkney
Islands
Stromness
Kirkwall
Kirkwall
Lerwick

St Margaret's
Hope

Gills
John o'Groats
Scrabster
Melvich
Thurso
A836
A9
Tongue
A836
A882
Wick
Wick
A99

Altnaharra
A897
A9
Helmsdale

Lairg
A837
A839

Bonar
Bridge
A949
A836
Tain
Alness
A9
Lerwick
Dingwall
A832
Cromarty
Nairn
Cullen
Banff
Fraserburgh
A98
A90
Elgin
A98
Keith
A95
Turriff
A952
Peterhead
Inverness
(Dalcross)
Forres
A96
A941
A96
Inverness
A9
A940
Aberlour
Huntly
A947
hadrochit
A82
Grantown-
on-Spey
A95
Oldmeldrum
Ellon
A90
ston
A938
Tomintoul
Inverurie
Aberdeen
Aviemore
A929
A96
Aberdeen
Newtonmore
A9
Kingussie
Braemar
Ballater
Banchory
A93
A86
A889
A93
Stonehaven
A92

S C O T L A N D

A9
Pitlochry
Brechin
Montrose
A90
Aberfeldy
Blairgowrie
Forfar
A827
A826
A94
A9
A90
A92
Arbroath
Killin
Coupar Angus
Carnoustie
yndrum
A85
Lochearnhead
Dundee
A85
Crieff
Newport-on-Tay
Crianlarich
Perth
A92
St Andrews
A84
Auchterarder
A91
Cupar
A91
A915
A917
Callander
A9
M90
Dunblane
Kinross
Zeebrugge
Dunblane
A91
Glenrothes
N O R T H
M9
Alloa
A977
M90
S E A
Stirling
Dunfermline
A92
Kirkcaldy
M80
A985
Rosyth
Firth of Forth
Dumbarton
A811
M9
Falkirk
Edinburgh
Dunbar
A80
Cumbernauld
EDINBURGH
A1
M80
M73
Airdrie
Livingston
Eyemouth
M8
lasgow
M8
A71
Dalkeith
GLASGOW
Motherwell
A71
A702
A68
A6094
Berwick-upon-Tweed
M77
East
Kilbride
Lanark
A721
A701
A703
A7
A68
A697
Coldstream
A698
A1
nning
Strathaven
A71
Biggar
Peebles
Galashiels
A6089
A71
M74
A72
Kelso
Kilmarnock
A70
A702
Selkirk
A698
Wooler
Prestwick
A78
A76
A74(M)
A701
A708
Jedburgh
Cumnock
A70
Hawick
A68
Alnwick
A697
A713
Moffat
A1
A1068
Amble

Atlas symbols

Motoring information

Motorway with number	Speed camera site (fixed location)
Toll motorway with toll station	Section of road with two or more fixed speed cameras
Motorway junction with and without number	Average speed camera (SPECS™)
Restricted motorway junctions	Road toll
Motorway service area	Distance in miles between symbols
Motorway and junction under construction	Vehicle ferry
Primary route single/dual carriageway	Vehicle ferry - fast catamaran
Primary route junction with and without number	Railway line/in tunnel
Restricted primary route junctions	Railway station and level crossing
Primary route service area	Tourist railway
Primary route destination	Airport, heliport, international freight terminal
Other A road single/dual carriageway	24-hour Accident & Emergency hospital
B road single/dual carriageway	Park and Ride (at least 6 days per week)
Minor road more than 4 metres wide, less than 4 metres wide	City, town, village or other built-up area
Roundabout	Spot height in metres
Interchange/junction	Pass
Narrow primary/other A/B road with passing places (Scotland)	Sandy beach
Road under construction	National boundary
Road tunnel	County, administrative boundary
Steep gradient (arrows point downhill)	Page continuation number

Touring information

Before visiting check opening times, to avoid disappointment.

	Tourist Information Centre		RSPB site		Show jumping/equestrian circuit
	Tourist Information Centre (seasonal)		National Nature Reserve (England, Scotland, Wales)		Motor-racing circuit
	Visitor or heritage centre		Local nature reserve		Air show venue
	Abbey, cathedral or priory		Forest drive		Ski slope – natural
	Ruined abbey, cathedral or priory		National trail		Ski slope – artificial
	Castle		Viewpoint	NT	National Trust property
	Historic house or building		Picnic site	NTS	National Trust for Scotland property
	Museum or art gallery		Hill-fort		Other place of interest
	Industrial interest		Roman antiquity		Boxed symbols indicate attractions within urban areas
	Aqueduct or viaduct		Prehistoric monument		World Heritage Site (UNESCO)
	Garden		Battle site with year		National Park
	Arboretum		Steam centre (railway)		National Scenic Area (Scotland)
	Vineyard		Cave		Forest Park
	Country park		Windmill		Heritage coast
	Agricultural showground		Monument		Major shopping centre
	Theme park		Golf course	IKEA	IKEA store
	Farm or animal centre		County cricket ground	BURGER KING	Welcome Break or Moto Burger King
	Zoological or wildlife collection		Rugby Union national stadium	KFC	Kentucky Fried Chicken at Welcome Break
	Bird collection		International athletics stadium		
	Aquarium		Horse racing		

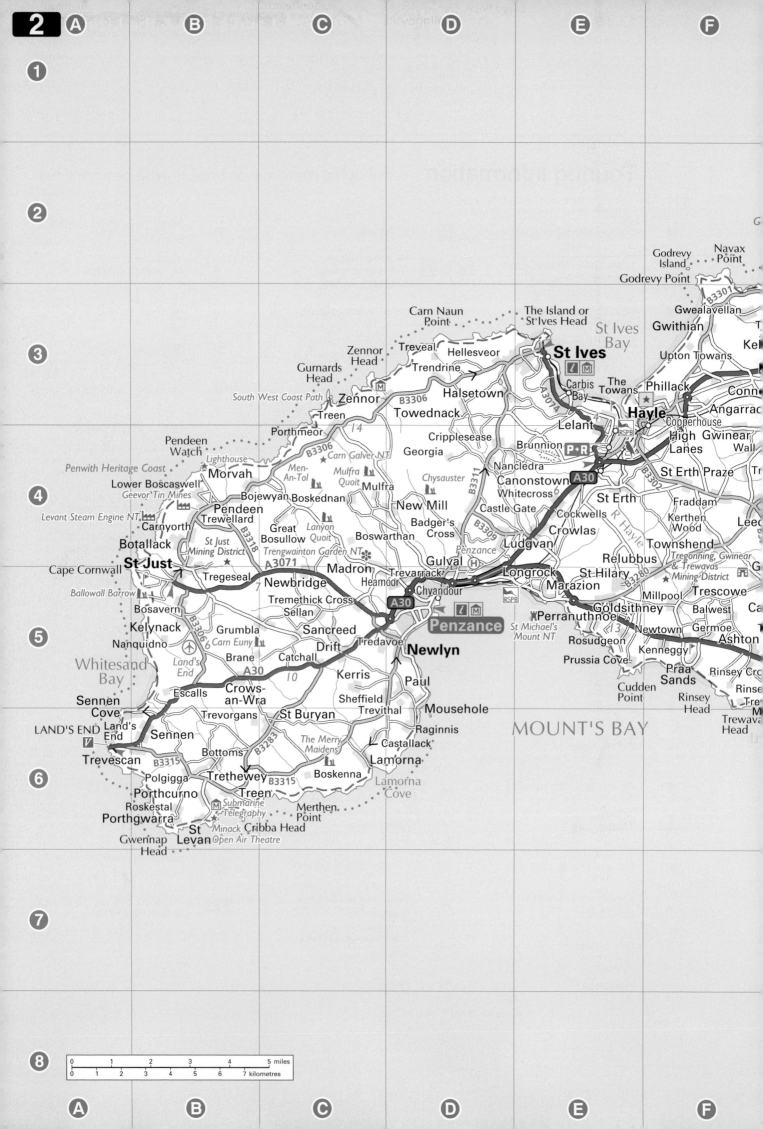

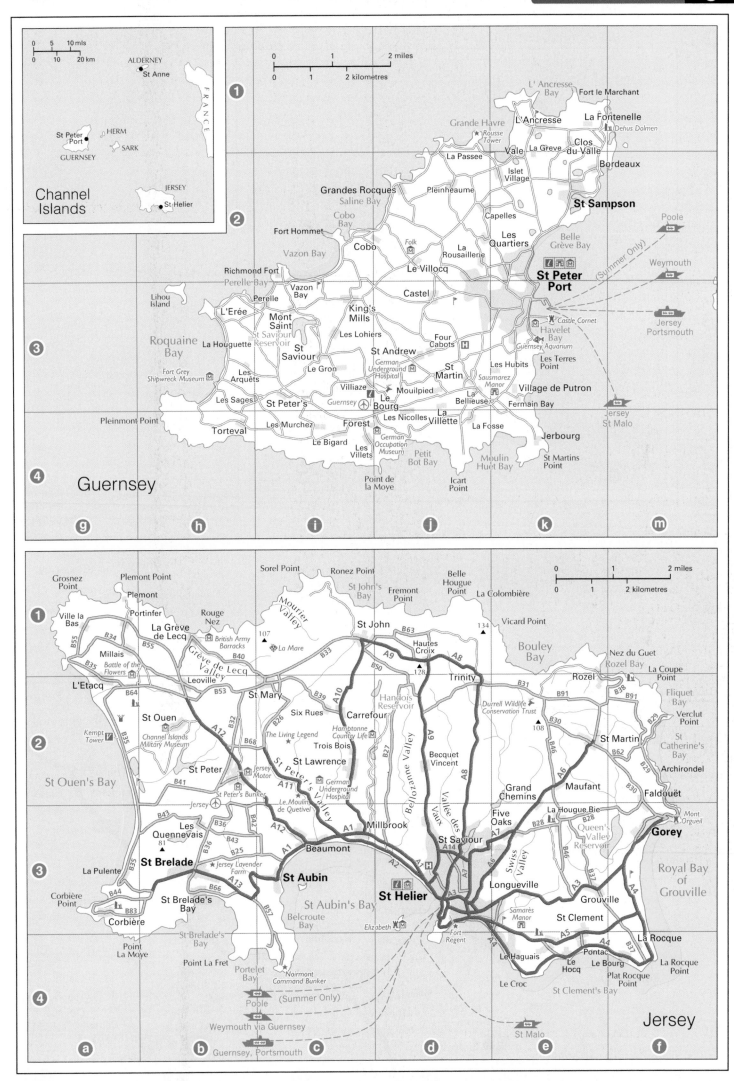

Channel Islands

ALDERNEY
St Anne

FRANCE

St Peter Port
HERM
SARK
GUERNSEY

JERSEY
St Helier

0 5 10 mls
0 10 20 km

Guernsey

0 1 2 miles
0 1 2 kilometres

1

L' Ancresse Bay
Fort le Marchant
Grande Havre
Rousse Tower
L'Ancresse
La Greve
La Fontenelle
Dehus Dolmen
Vale
La Passee
Clos du Valle
Islet Village
Bordeaux

2

Grandes Rocques
Saline Bay
Pleinheaume
Capelles
St Sampson
Cobo Bay
Fort Hommet
Folk
La Rousaillerie
Les Quartiers
Belle Greve Bay
Poole
Cobo
Le Villocq
St Peter Port
Weymouth
Vazon Bay
Castel
(Summer Only)

3

Richmond Fort
Perelle Bay
Vazon Bay
Castle Cornet
Jersey Portsmouth
Lihou Island
Perelle
King's Mills
Havelet Bay
Guernsey Aquarium
L'Erée
Mont Saint
Les Lohiers
Four Cabots
Roquaine Bay
St Saviour Reservoir
La Houguette
St Saviour
St Andrew
Les Hubits
Les Terres Point
Fort Grey Shipwreck Museum
Les Arquêts
Le Gron
German Underground Hospital
St Martin
Sausmarez Manor
Village de Putron
Les Sages
Villiaze
Mouilpied
La Bellieuse
Fermain Bay
St Peter's
Guernsey
Le Bourg
Jersey St Malo

4

Pleinmont Point
Torteval
Les Murchez
Forest
Les Nicolles
La Villette
La Fosse
Jerbourg
Le Bigard
German Occupation Museum
Les Villets
Petit Bot Bay
Moulin Huet Bay
St Martins Point
Point de la Moye
Icart Point

g   h   i   j   k   m

Jersey

0 1 2 miles
0 1 2 kilometres

1

Grosnez Point
Plemont Point
Sorel Point
Ronez Point
Belle Hougue Point
La Colombière
Plemont
Mourier Valley
St John's Bay
Fremont Point
Portinfer
Rouge Nez
107
Vicard Point
Ville la Bas
La Grève de Lecq
La Mare
St John
134
Bouley Bay
B55
B34
British Army Barracks
B63
Nez du Guet
Rozel Bay
Millais
B55
Grève de Lecq Valley
B40
Hautes Croix
B33
A9
A8
La Coupe Point
Battle of the Flowers
Leoville
B50
Trinity
B31
Rozel

2

L'Etacq
B35
B64
B53
St Mary
B39
A10
128
B91
B38 B91
Fliquet Bay
St Ouen
B26
Handois Reservoir
Durrell Wildlife Conservation Trust
Verclut Point
Kempt Tower
Channel Islands Military Museum
Six Rues
Carrefour
30
St Martin
St Catherine's Bay
B35
A12
B32
B68
The Living Legend
Hamptonne Country Life
108
B46
B62
Archirondel
St Peter
Trois Bois
B27
Becquet Vincent
A9
A6
B30
Faldouët

3

St Ouen's Bay
Jersey Motor
St Lawrence
A8
Grand Chemins
Maufant
Mont Orgueil
A11
German Underground Hospital
Vallée des Vaux
La Hougue Bie
B28
St Peter's Bunker
Le Moulin de Quetivel
A9
B28
Jersey
A12
B41
Five Oaks
Queen's Valley Reservoir
B43
Millbrook
A7
B36
Les Quennevais
B42
A1
St Saviour
Swiss Valley
Royal Bay of Grouville
81
B25
Beaumont
A14
A6
St Brelade
B35
Jersey Lavender Farm
A2
Longueville
A3
Grouville
La Pulente
St Aubin
A1
H
A7
La Hougue Bie
A3
B66
St Helier
Corbière Point
B44
A13
St Aubin's Bay
A3
Samarès Manor
St Clement
A4
Corbière
B83
St Brelade's Bay
Belcroute Bay
Elizabeth
Fort Regent
A4
La Rocque
Point La Moye
B57
St Brelade's Bay
Le Haguais
Le Bourg
Pontac
La Rocque Point

4

Point La Fret
Portelet Bay
Noirmont Command Bunker
Le Croc
Le Hocq
Plat Rocque Point
Poole
(Summer Only)
St Clement's Bay
Weymouth via Guernsey
St Malo
Guernsey, Portsmouth

Jersey

a   b   c   d   e   f

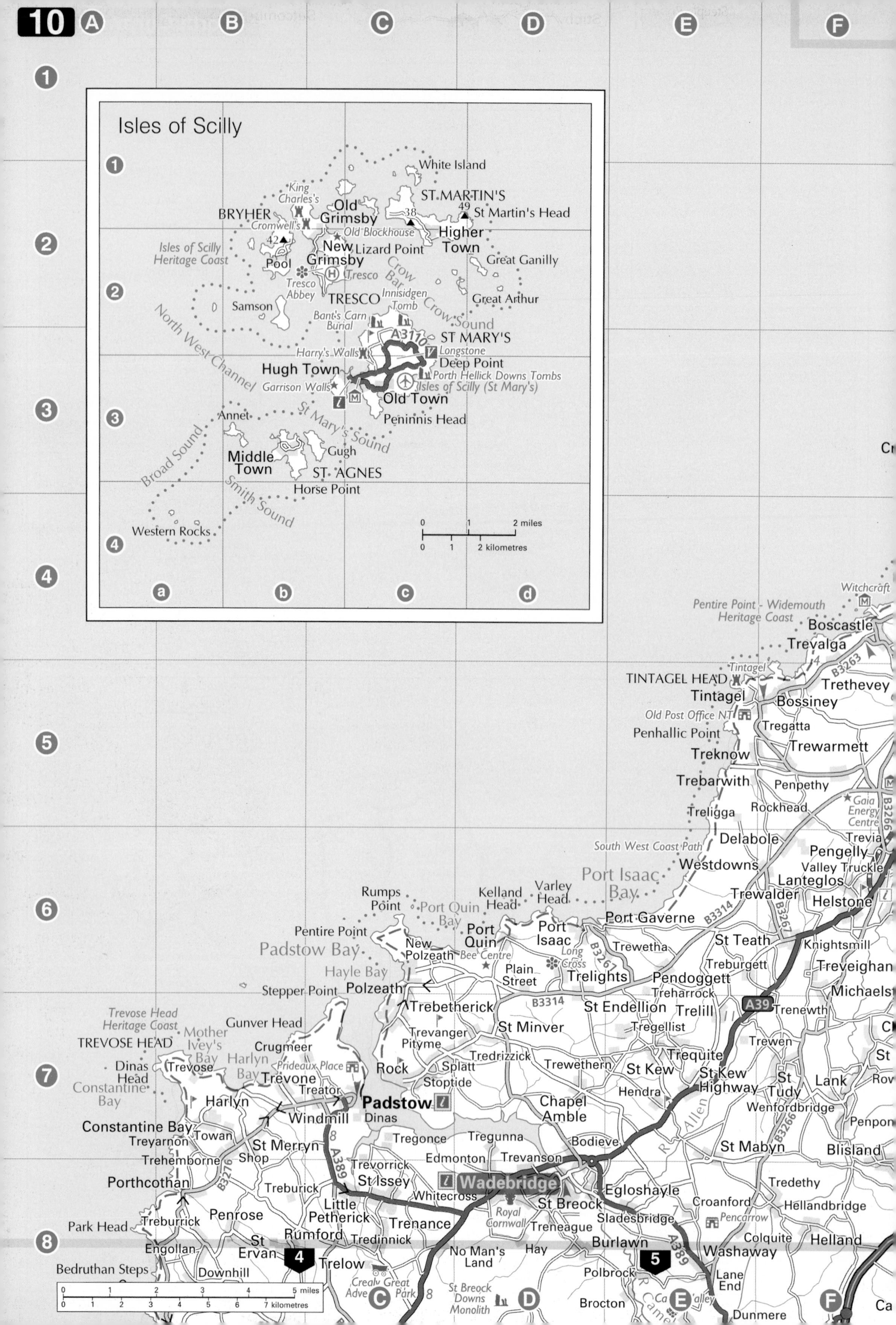

A   B   C   D   E   F

1

Isles of Scilly

1

White Island

King
Charles's

ST MARTIN'S

BRYHER
Cromwell's
Old
Grimsby
38   49   St Martin's Head
Old Blockhouse
Higher
Town

2

42

Isles of Scilly
Heritage Coast
New
Grimsby   Lizard Point
Crow
Bar

Pool   (H) Tresco
Great Ganilly

2
Tresco
Abbey   **TRESCO**   Innisidgen
Tomb   Crow
Sound
Great Arthur

Samson   Bant's Carn
Burial

A3110
ST MARY'S

Harry's Walls   Longstone
Deep Point

3

Hugh Town   Porth Hellick Downs Tombs
Garrison Walls   Isles of Scilly (St Mary's)

Old Town

Annet   **Old Town**   Peninnis Head

3
Gugh

**Middle
Town**   **ST AGNES**
Horse Point

North West Channel

Broad Sound

St Mary's Sound

Smith Sound

4

Western Rocks

0   1   2 miles

0   1   2 kilometres

4

a   b   c   d

Witchcraft

Pentire Point - Widemouth
Heritage Coast   **Boscastle**
Trevalga

B3263

TINTAGEL HEAD   Tintagel   **Trethevey**
Tintagel   **Bossiney**
Old Post Office NT   **Tregatta**

Penhallic Point   **Trewarmett**

5

Treknow

Trebarwith   Penpethy

Treligga   Rockhead   Gaia
Energy
Centre

South West Coast Path   **Delabole**   **Trevia**

Port Isaac   **Pengelly**
Bay   **Westdowns**   Valley Truckle   **Lanteglos**
Helstone

Rumps   **Trewalder**
Point   Kelland   Varley
Head   Head   **Port Gaverne**   B3314
Port Quin   B3267
Bay   Port
Quin   Port
Isaac   **St Teath**

6

New
Polzeath   Trewetha   Knightsmill
Padstow Bay   Bee Centre   **Treviighan**
Plain   Long   Treburgett
Street   Cross
Pentire Point   Trelights   **Pendoggett**   A39   **Michaels**
Hayle Bay   Treharrock   Trenewth
Stepper Point   **Polzeath**   **Trebetherick**   B3314   **St Endellion**   **Trelill**   **Trequite**
Trevose Head   Gunver Head   Trevanger   **St Minver**   Tregellist   **Trewen**   **St
Heritage Coast**   Mother   Pityme   **St Kew**   **Lank**
TREVOSE HEAD   Ivey's   Crugmeer   Tredrizzick   Trewethern   Highway   **St
Bay   Prideaux Place   **Rock**   Splatt   Trewethern   **St Kew**   **Tudy**   **Penpon**

7

Dinas   Harlyn   Treyone   Stoptide   Hendra   Wenfordbridge
Head   Bay   **Trevone**   **Padstow**   Chapel
Constantine   Harlyn   Windmill   Dinas   Amble   R. Allen   **St Mabyn**   **Blisland**
Bay   **Constantine Bay**   Towan   Tregonce   Tregunna   Bodieve   **Tredethy**
Treyarnon   Shop   **St Merryn**   Trevorrick   Edmonton   Trevanson   Croanford   Hellandbridge
Trehemborne   Treburick   **St Issey**   Pencarrow   Colquite   **Helland**
Porthcotha   Little   Trenance   **Wadebridge**   **Egloshayle**   Polbrock
Penrose   Petherick   Tredinnick   Whitecross   **St Breock**   **Sladesbridge**   Lane
Park Head   Treburrick   Rumford   Royal   Treneague   **Burlawn**   A389   **Washaway**
Cornwall   Hay

8

Bedruthan Steps   Engollan   **St
Ervan**   **4**   **Trelow**   No Man's
Land   **5**   Brocton   **E**   **F**
Downhill   Crealy Great   St Breock   Polbrock   Dunmere

0   1   2   3   4   5 miles

0   1   2   3   4   5   6   7 kilometres

C   D

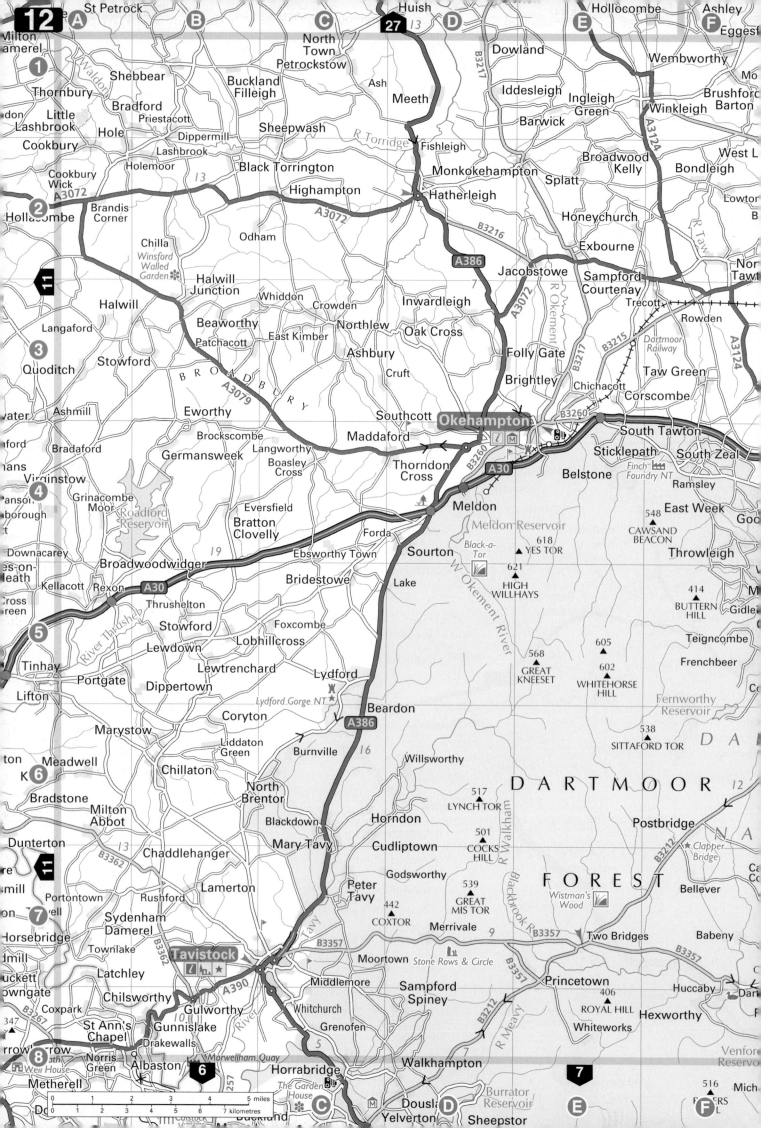

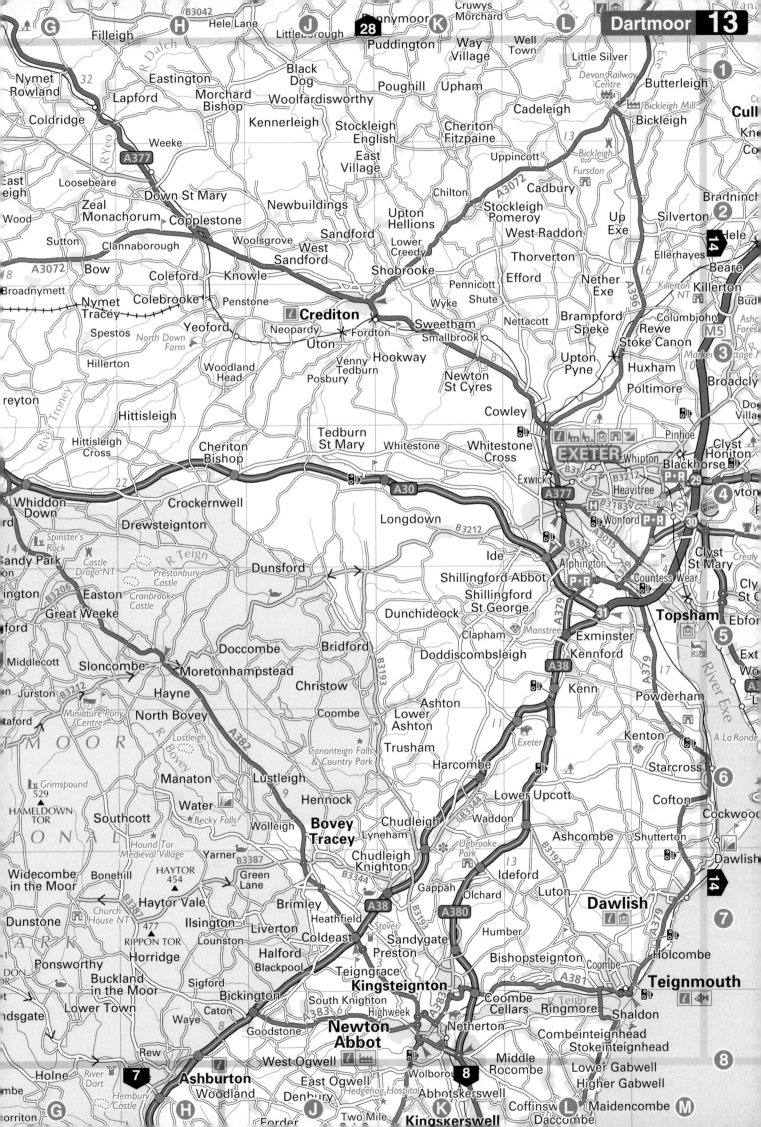

LYME BAY

★ Jurassic Coast
World Heritage Site

★ Jurassic Coast
World Heritage Site

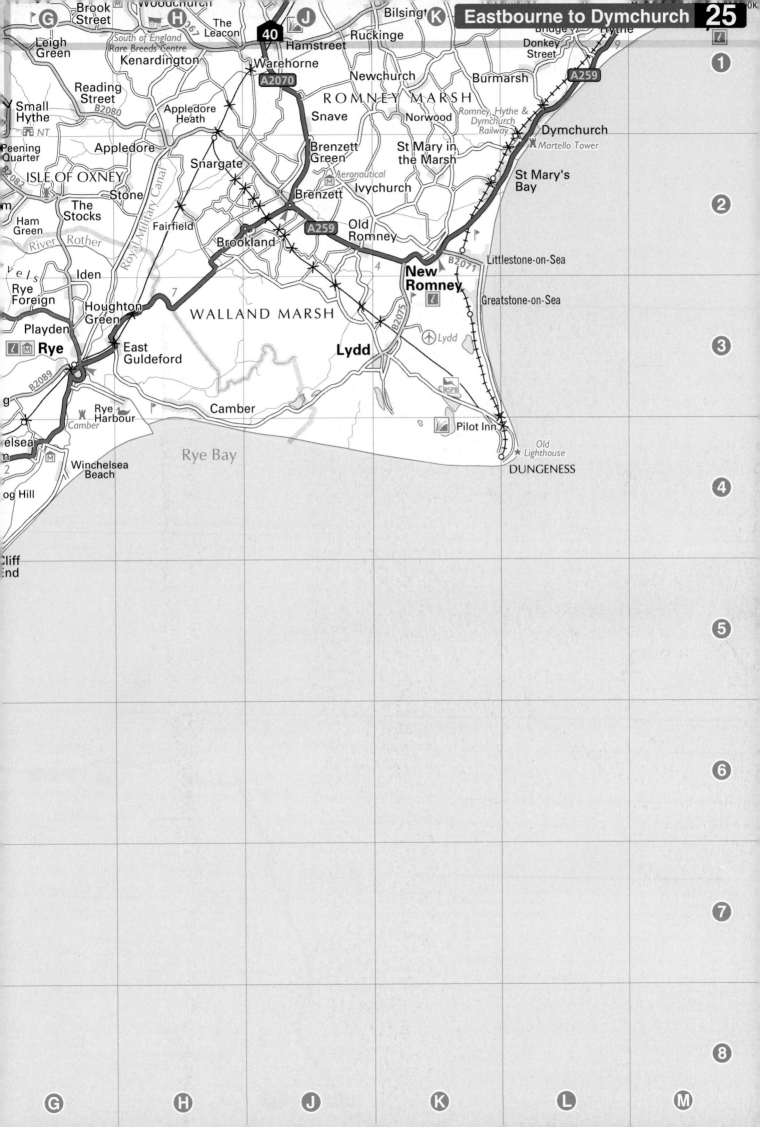

Brook Street
Woodchurch
Leigh Green
G
H
The Leacon
Bilsingt
K
J
40
Hamstreet
Ruckinge
Bridge
Hythe
9
Donkey Street
Kenardington
South of England Rare Breeds Centre
Warehorne
Newchurch
Burmarsh
A259
A2070
Reading Street
B2080
Appledore Heath
ROMNEY MARSH
Romney, Hythe & Dymchurch Railway
Dymchurch
Small Hythe
NT
Appledore
Snave
Norwood
Martello Tower
Peening Quarter
Snargate
Brenzett Green
St Mary in the Marsh
St Mary's Bay
ISLE OF OXNEY
Stone
Brenzett
Ivychurch
Aeronautical
Fairfield
A259
Old Romney
Ham Green
The Stocks
Brookland
4
New Romney
Littlestone-on-Sea
River Rother
B2071
B2082
Iden
Greatstone-on-Sea
v e l s
Rye Foreign
7
WALLAND MARSH
B2075
Playden
Houghton Green
Lydd
Lydd
Rye
East Guldeford
RSPB
og Hill
Rye Harbour
Camber
Pilot Inn
Camber
Old Lighthouse
elsea
2
Winchelsea Beach
Rye Bay
DUNGENESS
Cliff End

1
2
3
4
5
6
7
8

G **H** **J** **K** **L** **M**

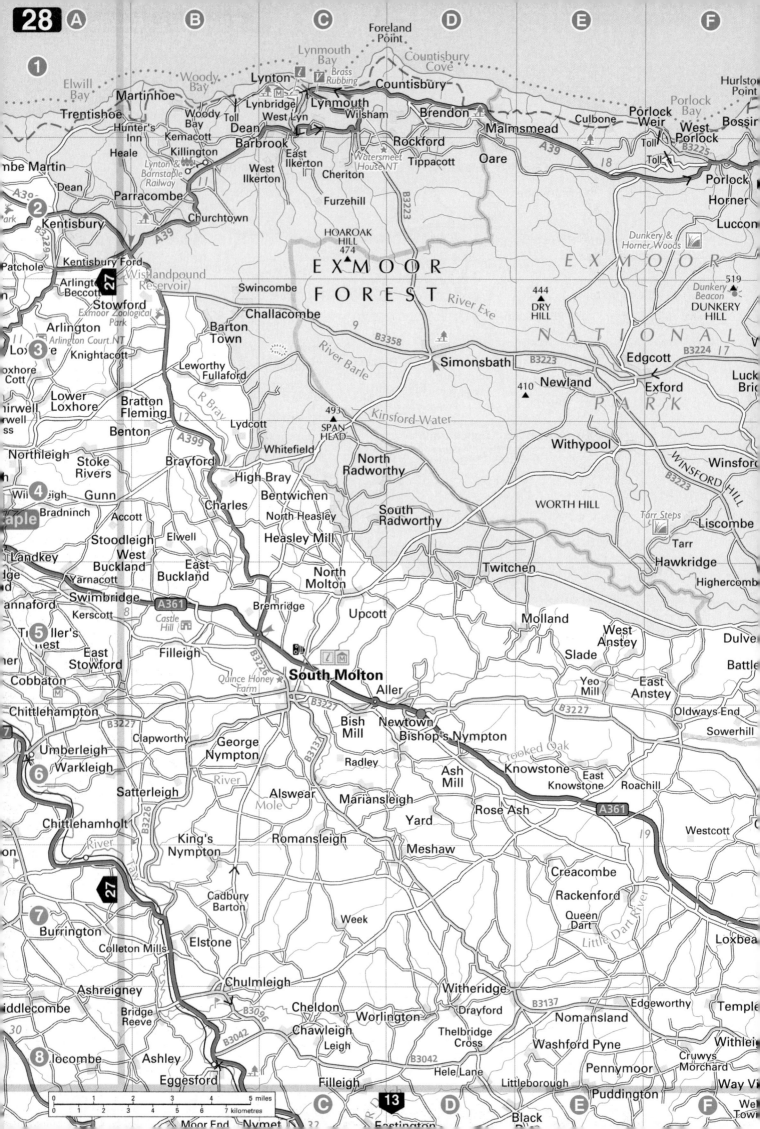

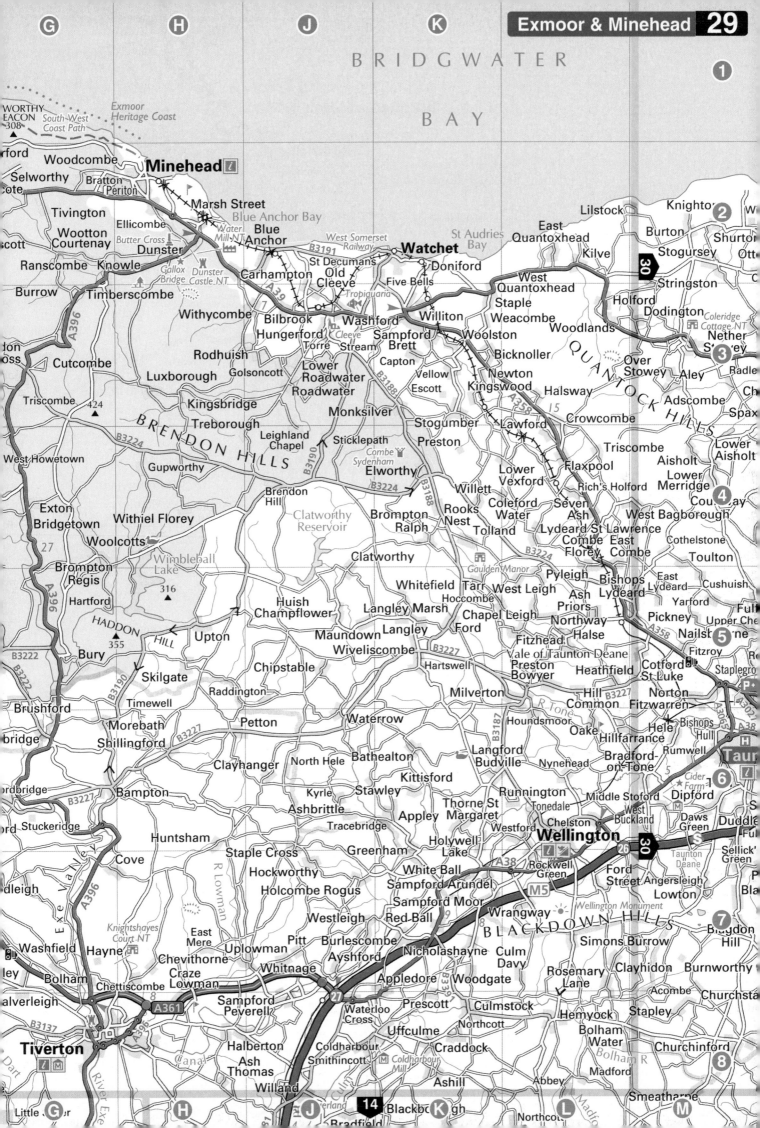

G H J K

1

B R I D G W A T E R

B A Y

WORTHY
EACON
308
*South West
Coast Path*
*Exmoor
Heritage Coast*

Woodcombe
Minehead ℹ️

Selworthy
cote
Bratton
Periton
Marsh Street
Blue Anchor Bay
Lilstock
Knighto

2

Burton
Shurtor

Tivington
Ellicombe
Butter Cross
Water Mill NT
Blue
Anchor
B3191
*West Somerset
Railway*
St Audries
Bay
Watchet
Doniford
East
Quantoxhead
Kilve
Stogursey
Stringston

Wootton
Courtenay
Dunster
Carhampton
St Decumans
Old
Cleeve
Five Bells
West
Quantoxhead
Staple
Holford
Dodington
*Coleridge
Cottage NT*

3

Nether
S
Over
Stowey
Aley
Radle
Ch

Ranscombe
Knowle
*Gallox
Bridge*
*Dunster
Castle NT*
A39
7
Bilbrook
Washford
Tropiquaria
Willitor
Woolston
Weacombe
Woodlands

Burrow
Timberscombe
Withycombe
Hungerford
Cleeve
Sampford
Brett
Bicknoller

A396
Torre
Stream
Capton
Newton
Kingswood
Halsway
Crowcombe

Cutcombe
Rodhuish
Golsoncott
Lower
Roadwater
Roadwater
Yellow
Escott
A358
15
Adscombe
Spax

Triscombe
424
Luxborough
Kingsbridge
Monksilver
Stogumber
Preston
Lawford
Triscombe
Lower
Aisholt

Treborough
B3224
Leighland
Chapel
Sticklepath
*Combe
Sydenham*
Elworthy
Flaxpool
Aisholt
Lower
Merridge

West Howetown
BRENDON HILLS
Gupworthy
B3190
Brendon
Hill
B3224
B3188
Willett
Lower
Vexford
Rich's Holford
Seven
Ash
West Bagborough
Cou ay

Exton
Bridgetown
Withiel Florey
*Clatworthy
Reservoir*
Brompton
Ralph
Rooks
Nest
Coleford
Water
Lydeard St Lawrence
Combe
Florey
East
Combe
Cothelstone
Toulton

Woolcotts
27
*Wimbleball
Lake*
316
Clatworthy
Tolland
B3224
Gaulden Manor
Pyleigh
Bishops
Lydeard
East
Lydeard
Cushuish

Brompton
Regis
Hartford
Huish
Champflower
Whitefield
Tarr
Hoccombe
West Leigh
Ash
Priors
Northway
Yarford
Pickney
Ful
Upper Che

HADDON
HILL
355
Upton
Langley Marsh
Langley
Chapel Leigh
Ford
Fitzhead
Halse
Nailsne

Bury
B3222
Maundown
Wiveliscombe
B3227
Hartswell
Vale of Taunton Deane
Preston
Bowyer
Heathfield
Cotford
St Luke
Fitzroy
Staplegro
P

Skilgate
Chipstable
Raddington
Milverton
Hill
Common
B3227
Norton
Fitzwarren
Tau
ℹ️

Brushford
Timewell
Waterrow
B3187
Houndsmoor
Oake
Hillfarrance
Hele
Bishops
Hull
Rumwell
H
A38

Morebath
Shillingford
B3227
Petton
North Hele
Bathealton
Langford
Budville
Nynehead
Bradford-
on-Tone
5
*Cider
Farm*
6
ℹ️

bridge
Clayhanger
Kyrle
Kittisford
Stawley
Runnington
Tonedale
Middle Stoford
West
Buckland
Dipford
Daws
Green
Duddle
Ful

rdbridge
Bampton
Ashbrittle
Appley
Thorne St
Margaret
Westford
Chelston
Wellington
Taunton
Deane
S
Sellick
Green

Stuckeridge
Huntsham
Tracebridge
Holywell
Lake
Holywell
Lake
Rockwell
Green
A38
M5
Ford
Street
Angersleigh
Lowton

Cove
Staple Cross
Greenham
White Ball
26
30
Wellington
Monument
BLACKDOWN HILLS
7
Bla

dleigh
*Knightshayes
Court NT*
Hockworthy
Sampford Arundel
Sampford Moor
Wrangway
Simons Burrow
Bagdon
Hill

Washfield
Hayne
Holcombe Rogus
Westleigh
Red Ball
9
8

ley
Bolham
Chevithorne
Craze
Lowman
East
Mere
Pitt
Uplowman
Burlescombe
Ayshford
Nicholashayne
Culm
Davy
Woodgate
Rosemary
Lane
Clayhidon
Burnworthy

alverleigh
Chettiscombe
8
27
Whitnage
Appledore
Prescott
Acombe
Churchsta

B3137
A361
A396
Sampford
Peverell
Waterloo
Cross
Uffculme
Culmstock
Hemyock
Bolham
Water
Stapley

Tiverton
ℹ️
Halberton
Ash
Thomas
Coldharbour
Smithincott
*Coldharbour
Mill*
Northcott
Craddock
Churchinford

River Exe
Willand
14
Bolham R
8

G H J K L M

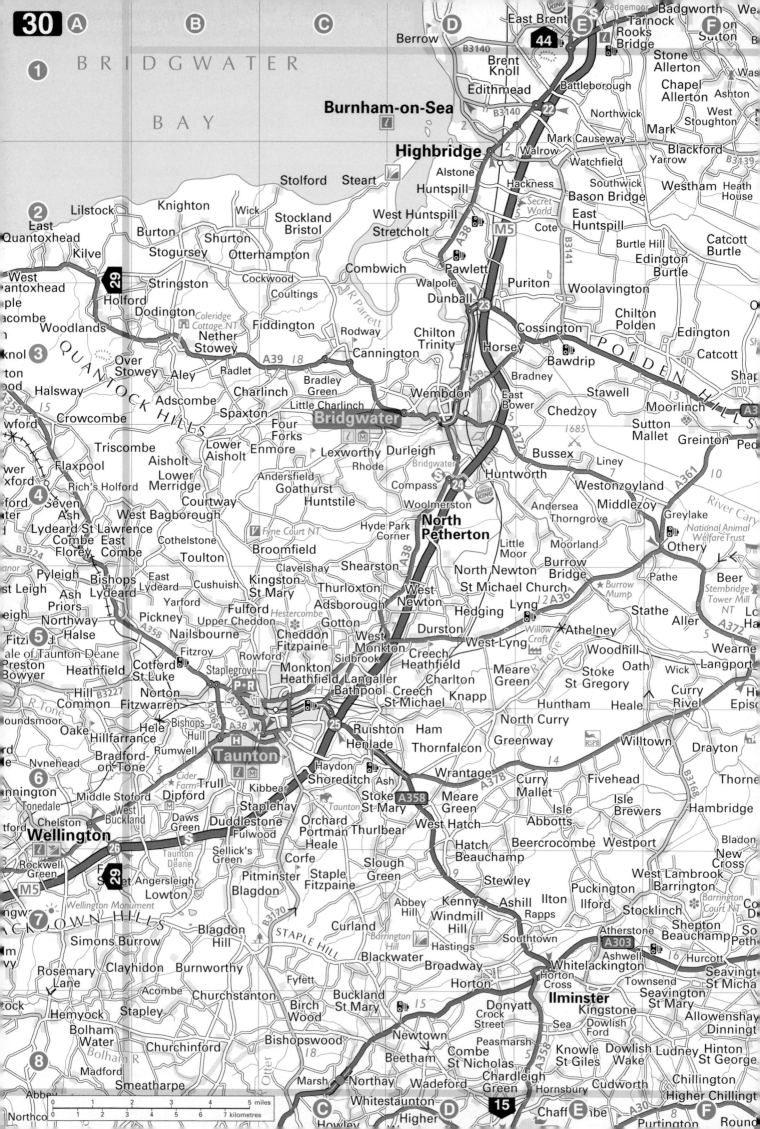

Cheddar · Chewton Mendip · Bathway · Easton · Clapton · Chilcompton · Stratton-on-the-Fosse · Babington · Kilmersdon

Draycott · East Water · Emborough · Downside · Newbury · Upper Vobster · Mells

Priddy · Green Ore · Gurney Slade · Holcombe · Highbury · Vobster · Little

Clewer · Old Ditch · Binegar · Nettlebridge · Ham · Coleford · Whatley

Cocklake · Rodney Stoke · Westbury-sub-Mendip · Wookey Hole · West Horrington · Ashwick · Oakhill · Leigh upon Mendip · Chantry · Little Elm

Wedmore · Latcham · Theale · Easton · Lower Milton · Walcombe · South Horrington · East Horrington · Downside · Stoke St Michael · East End · Downhead

Bagley · Panborough · Henton · Wookey · Burcott Mill · Dulcote · Dinder · Darshill · Doulting · Leighton · Cloford · Trudox

Bleadney · Yarley · Worth · Coxley Wick · **Wells** · Croscombe · **Shepton Mallet** · Charlton · Dean · East Cranmore · Wanstrow

Lower Godney · Upper Godney · Polsham · Coxley · Southway · Worminster · North Town · West Compton · West Horrington · Cranmore · Chesterblade · Higher Alham · Town

Westhay Moss · Godney · North Wootton · Westholme · Pilton · East Compton · Prestleigh · Stoney Stratton · Westcombe · Batcombe · Upton Noble

Meare · Stileway · Northload Bridge · Brindham · West Pennard · Street on the Fosse · Pylle · Royal Bath and West Showground · Evercreech · Milton Clevedon · North Brewham

Glastonbury · Glastonbury Tor NT · Havyatt · West Bradley · East Pennard · Hembridge · Wraxall · Ditcheat · Lamyatt · South Brewham · King Alfred's Tower NT

Northover · Edgarley · Woodland Street · Coxbridge · Parbrook · Huxham Green · Stone · Alhampton · West End · Bruton · Hardway

Walton · Asney · **Street** · Butleigh Wootton · West Town · Tilham Street · Four Foot · Hornblotton Green · Clanville · Wyke Champflower · Cole · Redlynch · Stoney Stoke

Overleigh · Baltonsborough · Gosling Street · Catsham · Southwood · West Lydford · East Lydford · Alford · Lovington · Ansford · Pitcombe · Shepton Montague · Charlton Musgrove

Compton Dundon · Butleigh · Silver Street · Wheathill · Castle Cary · Bratton Seymour · Bayford

Dundon · Barton St David · Kingweston · Lydford · Foddington · Galhampton · Hadspen · Yarlington · Wincanton

Littleton · Keinton Mandeville · Charlton Mackrell · Babcary · North Barrow · South Barrow · Brookhampton · Woolston · **Wincanton** · Lattiford

Somerton · Pitney · Midney · Charlton Adam · Haynes Motor Museum · North Cadbury · Blackford · Holton · Compton Pauncefoot · Maperton · North Cheriton · South Cheriton · Horsington · Abbas Combe

Upton · South Hill · Catsgore · Kingsdon · Downhead · Sparkford · Little Weston · South Cadbury · Templecombe · Yenston

Pibsbury · Long Sutton · Knole · Podimore · West Camel · Queen Camel · Wales · Sutton Montis · Charlton Horethorne · Stowell · Milborne Wick

Little Load · Long Load · Ilchester · Bridgehampton · Chilton Cantelo · Marston Magna · Corton Denham · Sandford Orcas · Milborne Port

Muchelney Ham · Northover · RNAS Yeovilton · Fleet Air Arm · Yeovilton · Limington · Ashington · Rimpton · Adber · Poyntington · Hensridge Ash

Milton · Witcombe · Ash · Draycott · West Mudford · Mudford · Trent · Nether Compton · Oborne · Henstridge · Purse Caundle

Martock · Treasurer's House NT · Tintinhull NT · Chilthorne Domer · Yeovil Marsh · Mudford Sock · Up Mudford · Poyntington · Goathill · Stalbridge Weston

Hurst NT · Stoke sub Hamdon · Thorne · **Yeovil** · Over Compton · Stallen · Stourton Caundle

Montacute · Montacute House NT · Odcombe · Preston Plucknett · Worldwide Butterflies · **Sherborne** · North Wootton · Allweston · Bishop's Caundle

Norton sub Hamdon · Little Norton · Brympton · West Coker · Barwick · Bradford Abbas · Haydon · Folke · Caundle Marsh · Holwell

Wigborough · Chiselborough · East Chinnock · Burton · Thornford · Lillington · Longburton · Knighton · Crouch Hill · Packers Hill

Middle Chinnock · Hardington Mandeville · Hardington Moor · Sutton Bingham · East Coker · Beer Hackett · Stoford · Leweston · King's

Crewkerne · North Perrott · Haselbury Plucknett · Pendomer · Ryme Intrinseca · Yetminster · Boys Hill · Sandhills · East Pulham

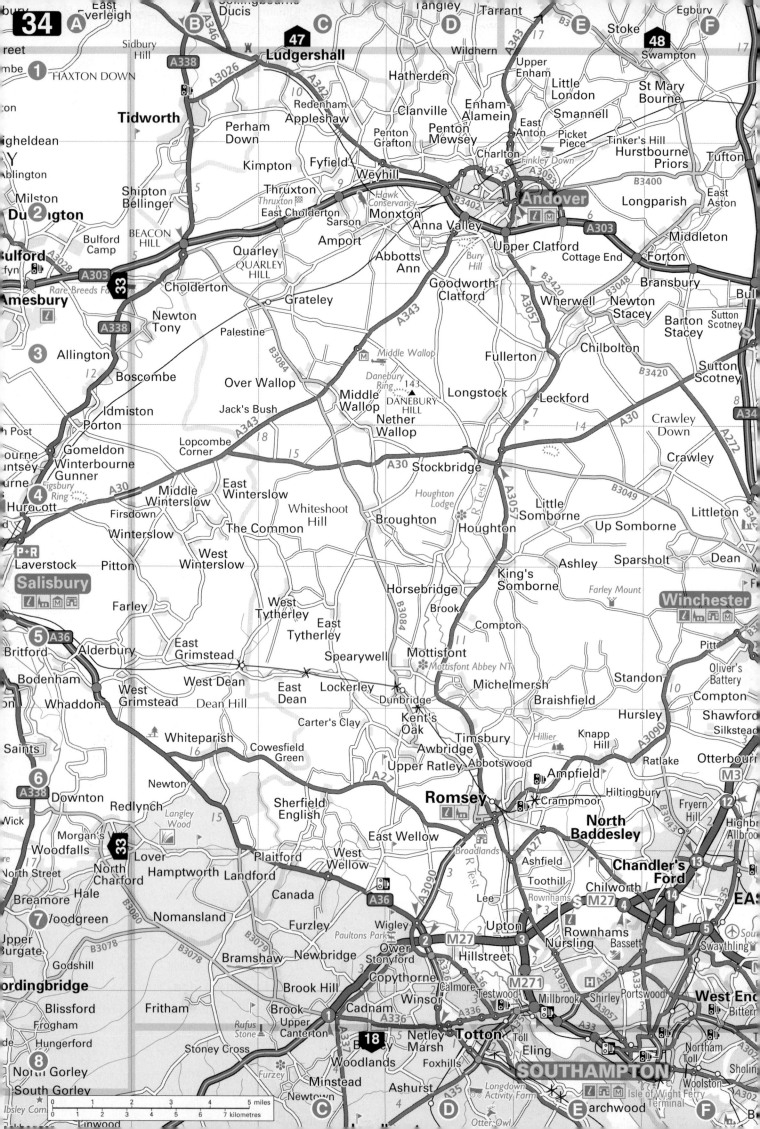

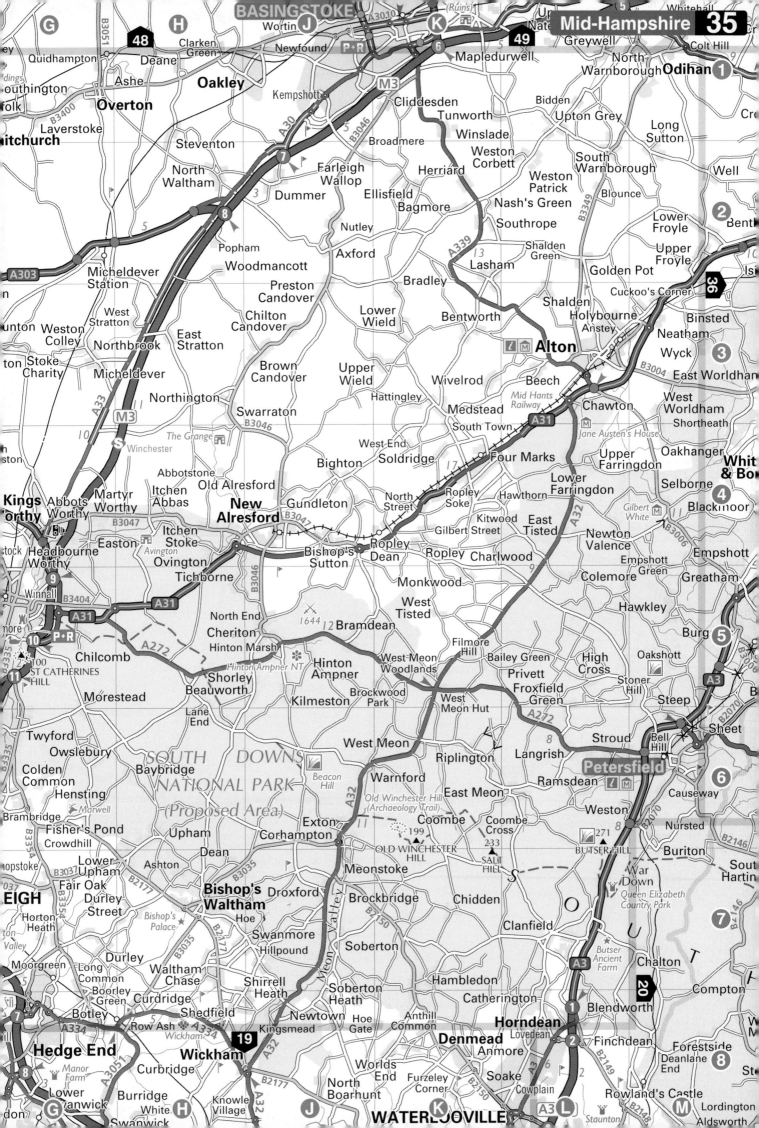

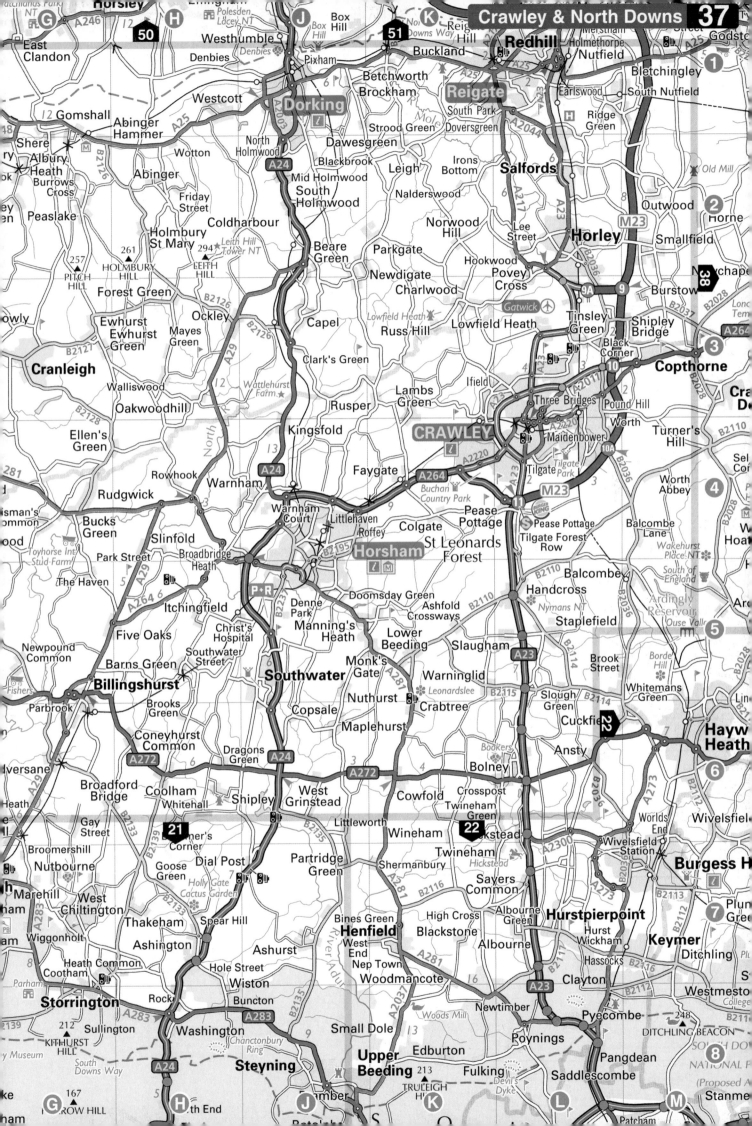

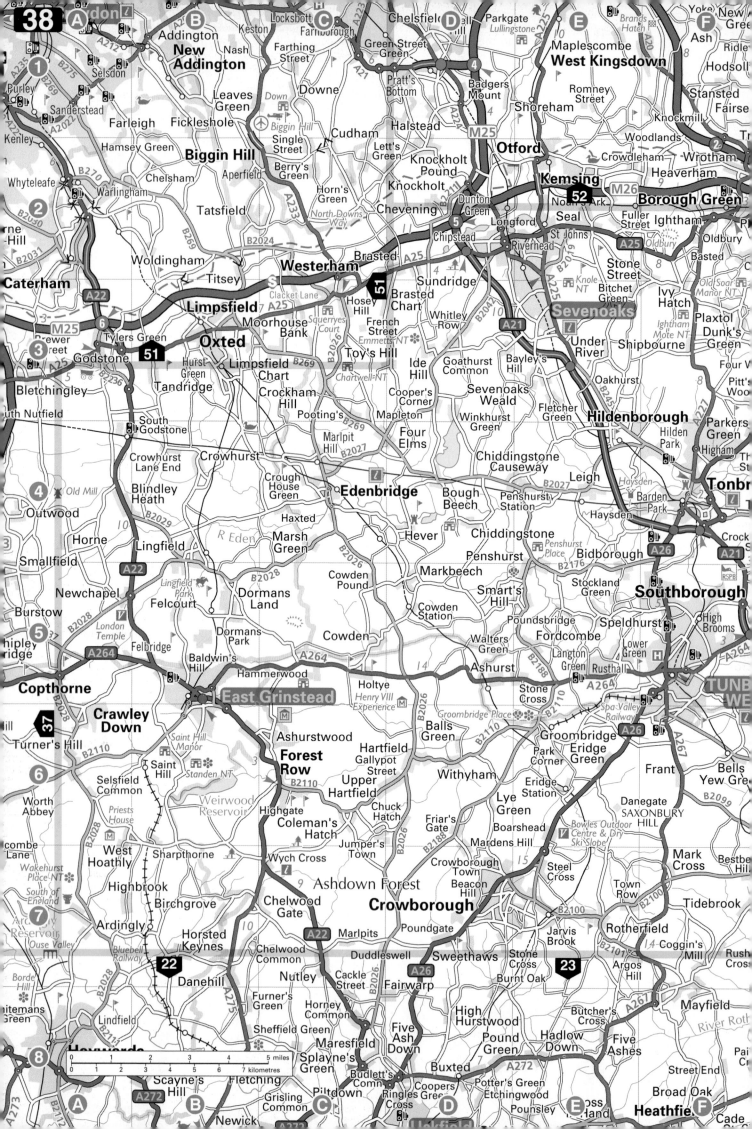

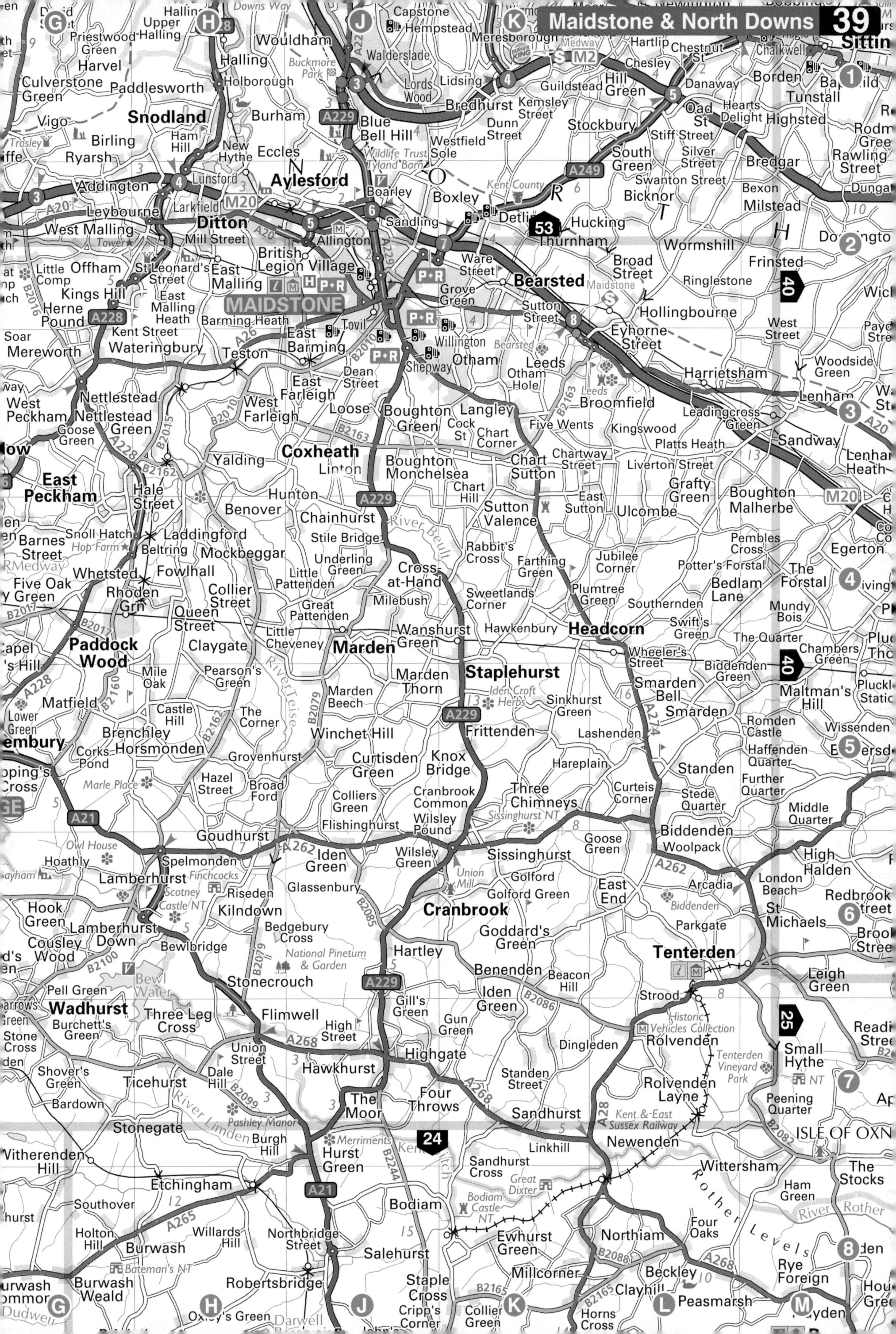

Downs Way
Priestwood Halling
Harvel
Upper Halling
Culverstone Green
Paddlesworth
Vigo
Trosley
Birling
Ryarsh
Snodland
Ham Hill
Holborough
Burham
Eccles
New Hythe
Aylesford
Blue Bell Hill
Wildlife Trust
Tyland Barn
Boarley
Boxley

Wouldham
Buckmore Park
Lords Wood
Walderslade
Bredhurst
Knox Wood

Capstone
Hempstead
Meresborough
Burger King
Hartlip
Chestnut St
Chesley
Borden
Tunstall
Chalkwell
Danaway
Hearts Delight
Highsted
Bexon
Milstead

Lidsing
Guildstead Green
Kemsley Street
Dunn Street
Westfield Sole
Stockbury
South Green
Silver Street
Swanton Street
Bicknor
Bredgar

Addington
Leybourne
West Malling
Ditton
Larkfield
Mill Street
Allington
Sandling

Snodland
Aylesford
Wildlife Trust Tyland Barn
Boxley
Kent County

Hucking
Thurnham
Wormshill
Ringlestone
Frinsted
Doddington

Little Offham Comp
St Leonard's Street
East Malling
Barming Heath
Kings Hill
Herne Pound
Kent Street
Wateringbury
Teston
East Barming
Dean Street
Tovil
Willington
Otham
Grove Green
Sutton Street
Leeds
Broomfield
Bearsted
Hollingbourne
West Street
Harrietsham
Woodside Green
Lenham

MAIDSTONE

East Farleigh
West Farleigh
Loose
Boughton Green
Langley Green
Cock St
Chart Corner
Five Wents
Kingswood
Platts Heath
Leadingcross Green
Sandway
Lenham Heath

West Peckham
Nettlestead
Nettlestead Green
Goose Green
Yalding
Coxheath
Linton
Boughton Monchelsea
Chart Sutton
Chartway Street
Liverton Street
Grafty Green
Boughton Malherbe

East Peckham
Hale Street
Hunton
Benover
Chainhurst
Stile Bridge
Chart Hill
Sutton Valence
East Sutton
Ulcombe
Pembles Cross
Egerton
The Forstal

Snoll Hatch
Hop Farm
Beltring
Laddingford
Mockbeggar
Underling Green
Little Pattenden
Cross-at-Hand
Milebush
Great Pattenden
Rabbit's Cross
Farthing Green
Jubilee Corner
Plumtree Green
Southernden
Swift's Green
Mundy Bois
Bedlam Lane

Whetsted
Fowlhall
Collier Street
Queen Street
Little Cheveney
Marden
Wanshurst Green
Hawkenbury
Headcorn
Wheeler's Street
Biddenden Green
The Quarter
Chambers Green

Five Oak Green
Rhoden Grn
Claygate
Paddock Wood
Mile Oak
Pearson's Green
Marden Thorn
Staplehurst
Iden Croft Herbs
Sinkhurst Green
Smarden Bell
Smarden
Maltman's Hill
Pluckley Station

Matfield
Castle Hill
The Corner
Marden Beech
Winchet Hill
Frittenden
Lashenden
Romden Castle
Wissenden

Brenchley
Horsmonden
Corks Pond
Hazel Street
Broad Ford
Grovenhurst
Curtisden Green
Knox Bridge
Hareplain
Standen
Curteis Corner
Stede Quarter
Further Quarter
Middle Quarter

Marle Place
Colliers Green
Flishinghurst
Cranbrook Common
Wilsley Pound
Three Chimneys
Sissinghurst NT
Goose Green
Biddenden
Woolpack
High Halden

Owl House
Goudhurst
Spelmonden
Finchcocks
Iden Green
Glassenbury
Wilsley Green
Union Mill
Sissinghurst
Golford
Golford Green
East End
Arcadia
Biddenden
London Beach
St Michaels
Redbrook Street

Hoathly
Lamberhurst
Scotney Castle NT
Riseden
Kilndown
Bedgebury Cross
Cranbrook
Goddard's Green
Parkgate
Tenterden

Hook Green
Cousley Wood
Lamberhurst Down
Bewlbridge
National Pinetum & Garden
Hartley
Benenden
Beacon Hill
Historic Vehicles Collection
Rolvenden
Strood
Leigh Green

Wadhurst
Burchett's Green
Three Leg Cross
Stonecrouch
Flimwell
High Street
Gill's Green
Iden Green
Gun Green
Dingleden
Rolvenden Layne
Tenterden Vineyard Park
Small Hythe
Reading Street

Pell Green
Ticehurst
Union Street
Dale Hill
Hawkhurst
Highgate
Standen Street
Kent & East Sussex Railway
Peening Quarter
Isle of Oxn

Shover's Green
Bardown
Stonegate
The Moor
Four Throws
Sandhurst
Newenden
Northiam
Wittersham
Ham Green
The Stocks

Vitherenden Hill
Etchingham
Burgh Hill
Hurst Green
Merriments
Bodiam
Sandhurst Cross
Great Dixter
Bodiam Castle NT
Linkhill
Four Oaks
Rother Levels
River Rother

Holton Hill
Burwash
Willards Hill
Northbridge Street
Salehurst
Ewhurst Green
Millcorner
Clayhill
Beckley
Rye Foreign

Bateman's NT
Burwash Weald
Robertsbridge
Staple Cross
Cripp's Corner
Collier Green
Horns Cross
Peasmarsh

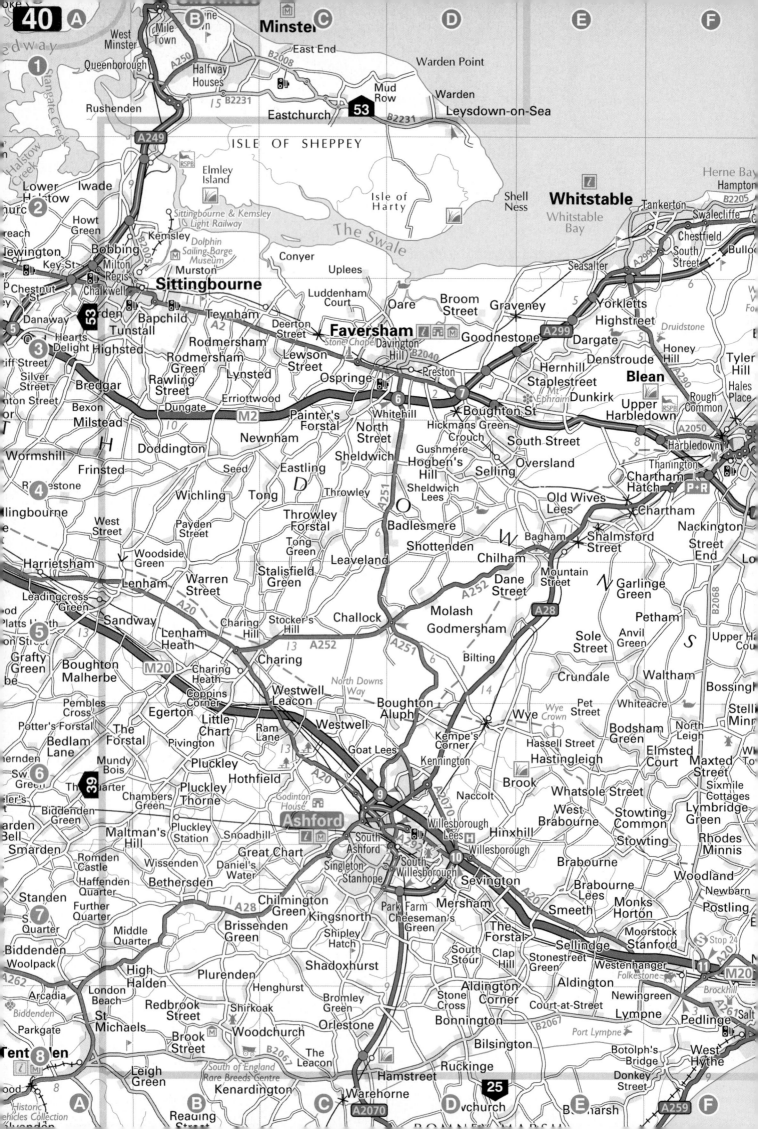

G   H   J   K   L   M

1
2
3
4
5
6
7
8

MARGATE
Foreness Point
Cliftonville
Kingsgate
B2051
B2052
Northdown
NORTH FORELAND
Westgate on Sea
Westbrook
Reading Street
Lighthouse
Minnis Bay
Minnis Bay
Birchington
Salmestone Grange
Garlinge
St Peter's
Broadstairs
Herne Bay
Bishopstone
Reculver
Hillborough
Potten Street
Brooks End
Lydden
Westwood
Dumpton
Hereson
Beltinge
Eddington
Broomfield
Highstead
Acol
ISLE OF THANET
Haine
Manston
St Lawrence
Ramsgate
Herne
A299
B2048
B2190
Kent International
Herne Common
St Nicholas at Wade
Boyden Gate
A28
Monkton Way
A299
A253
Sarre
Chislet
Hoo
Durlock
Cliffsend
Pegwell
Maypole
Gore Street
Plucks Gutter
Minster
St Augustine's Cross
Viking Ship 'Hugin'
Pegwell Bay
Oostende
Hoath
Upstreet
West Stourmouth
R Stour
A28
Grove
East Stourmouth
Westmarsh
Paramour Street
Goldstone
Richborough
Prince's
Sandwich Bay
Westbere
Stodmarsh
Preston Street
Elmstone
Cop Street
Cooper Street
Great Stonar
A256
Fordwich
Wickhambreaux
Preston
Walmestone
Hoaden
Weddington
Sandwich
Canterbury
Old Town Hall
Littlebourne
Shatterling
Ash
A257
Stone Cross
Royal St George's
Ickham
Seaton
Durlock
Guilton
Marshborough
Toll
A257
Wingham
Barnsole
Woodnesborough
Howletts
Bekesbourne Hill
Bramling
Twitham
Staple
Statenborough
Worth
Bekesbourne
B2046
Goodnestone
Eastry
Ham
Hacklinge
Patrixbourne
Heronden
West Street
Finglesham
Adisham
Ratling
Chillenden
Knowlton
Marley
A258
The Downs
Higham Park
Nonington
Betteshanger
Northbourne
Sholden
Deal
Kingston
Aylesham
Easole Street
Great Mongeham
Upper Deal
North Downs Way
Elmstead
Womenswold
Holt St
Tilmanstone
Little Mongeham
Ripple
Walmer
Barham
Frogham
Elvington
Sutton
Marley
Woolage Village
Barfrestone
Lower Eythorne
East Studdal
Ringwould
Derringstone
Woolage Green
Eythorne
Kingsdown
East Kent Railway
Ashley
Sutton Downs
Breach
Shepherdswell
West Langdon
Martin
A258
Bladbean
North Downs Way
Denton
Lydden
Coldred
Wootton
A2
Whitfield
Guston
East Langdon
St Margaret's at Cliffe
North Elham
Selsted
A256
St Margaret's Bay
Swingfield Minnis
Ewell Minnis
Temple Ewell
A2
West Cliffe
SOUTH FORELAND
Kearsney
Chilton
River
A256
Pines
Lighthouse NT
Swingfield Street
Wolverton
Buckland
A258
South Foreland Heritage Coast
Densole
Alkham
St Radigund's
Gateway to the White Cliffs NT
Hawkinge
South Alkham
Maxton
Ridge Row
Drellingore
West Hougham
DOVER
Calais
Dunkerque
Upper Standen
Lower Standen
Farthingloe
B2011
Battle of Britain
Capel-le-Ferne
Satmar
A20
Boulogne
Channel Tunnel Terminal
Peene
Samphire Hoe
Dover - Folkestone Heritage Coast
Channel Tunnel (Rail)
Cheriton
Morehall
East Wear Bay
Horn Street
FOLKESTONE
Sandgate
A259
Seabrook
Hythe

0   1   2   3   4   5 miles
0   1   2   3   4   5   6   7 kilometres

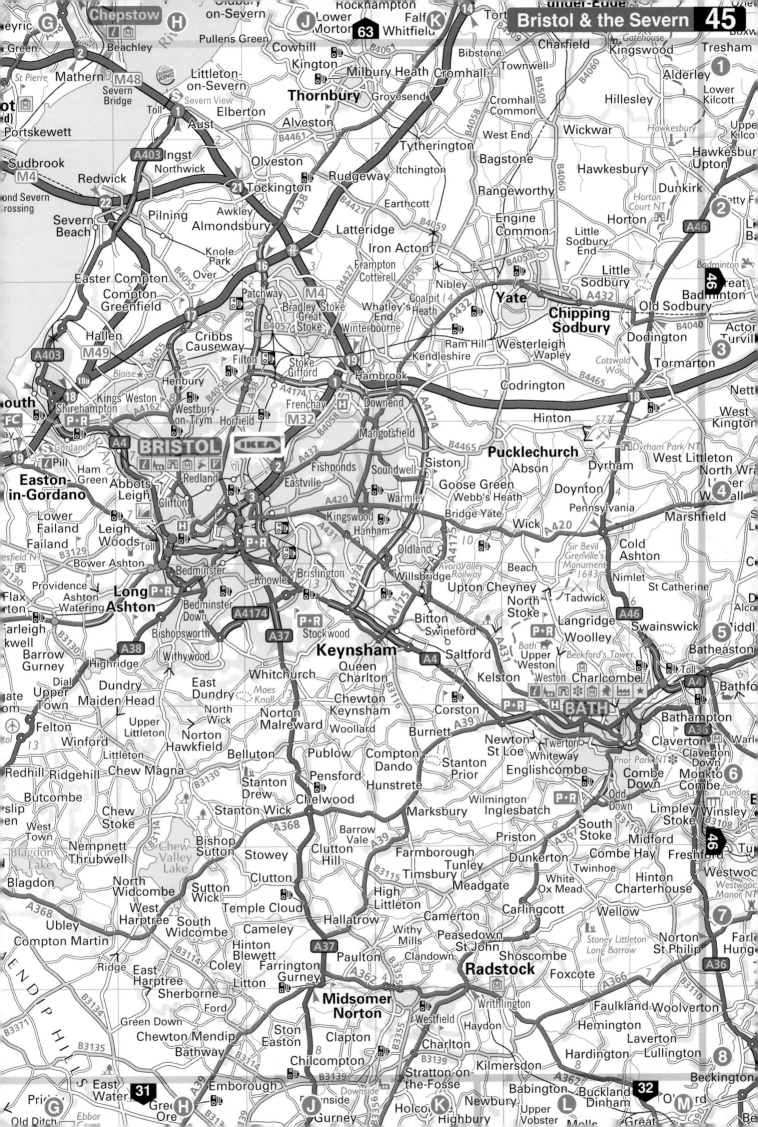

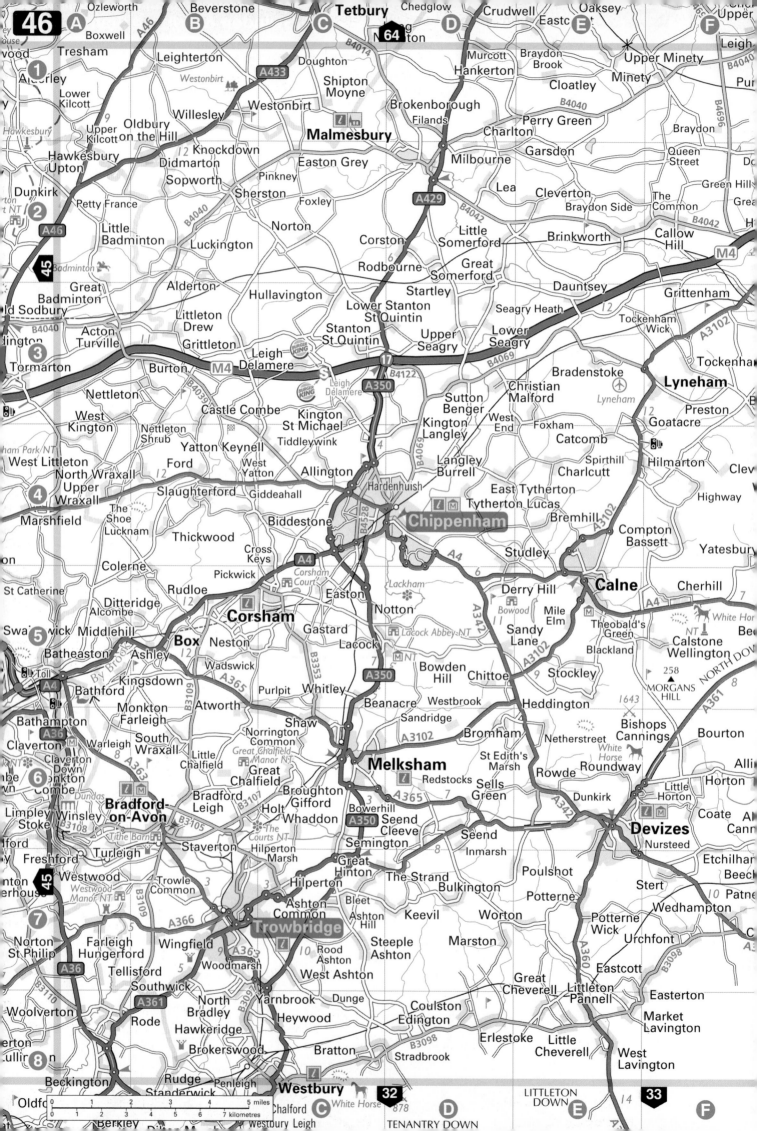

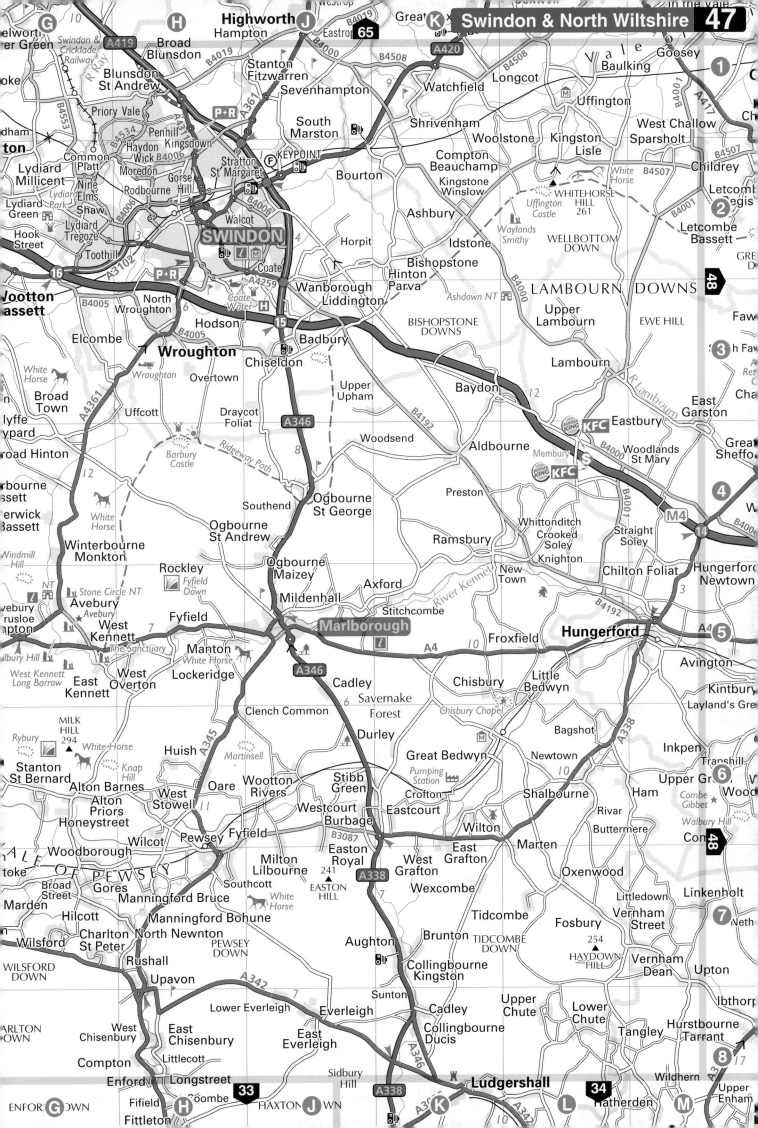

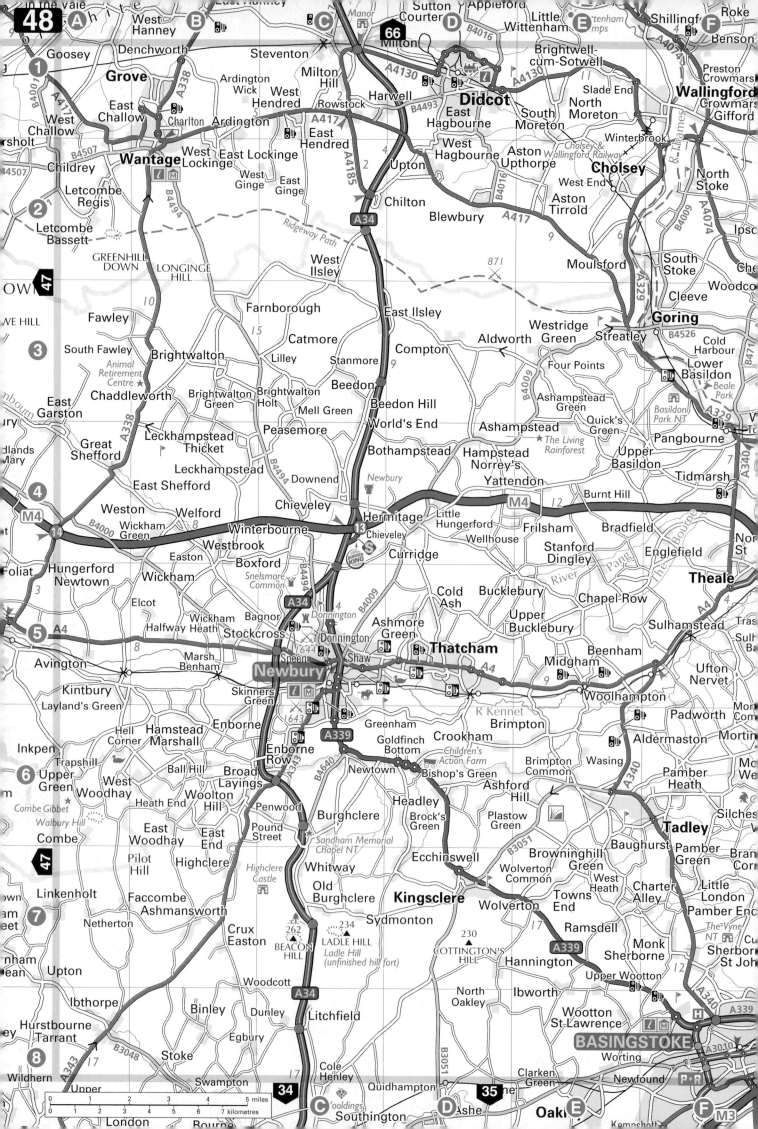

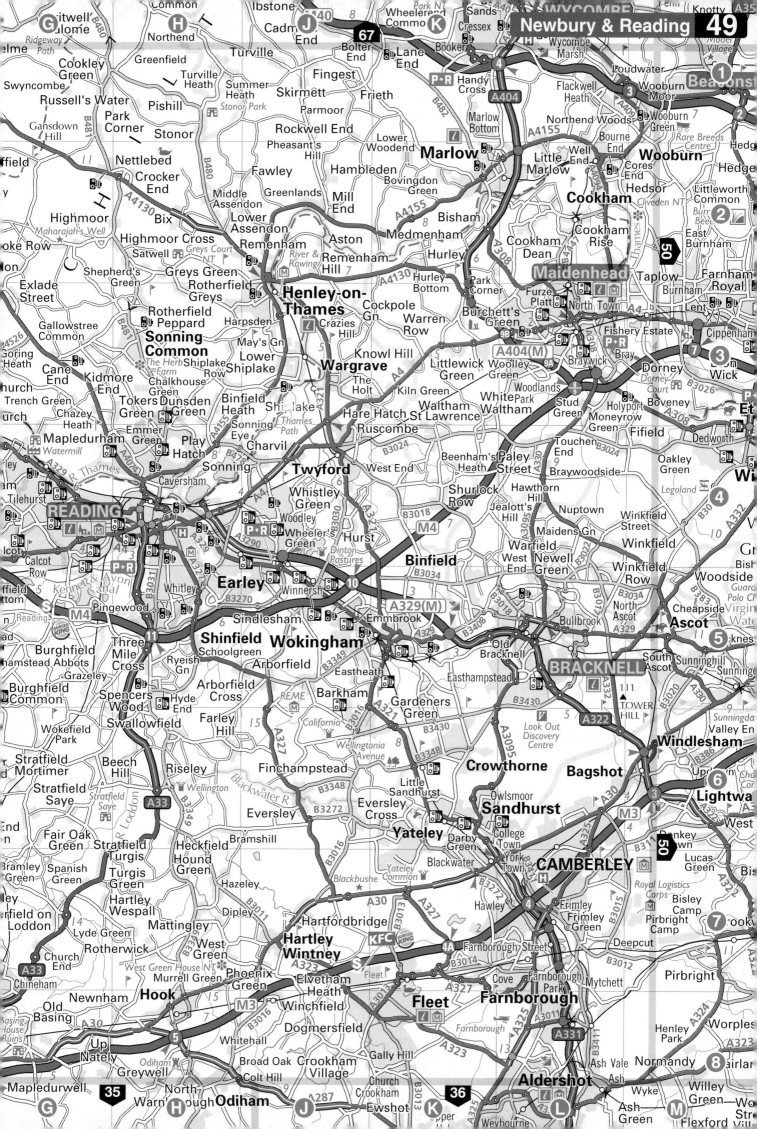

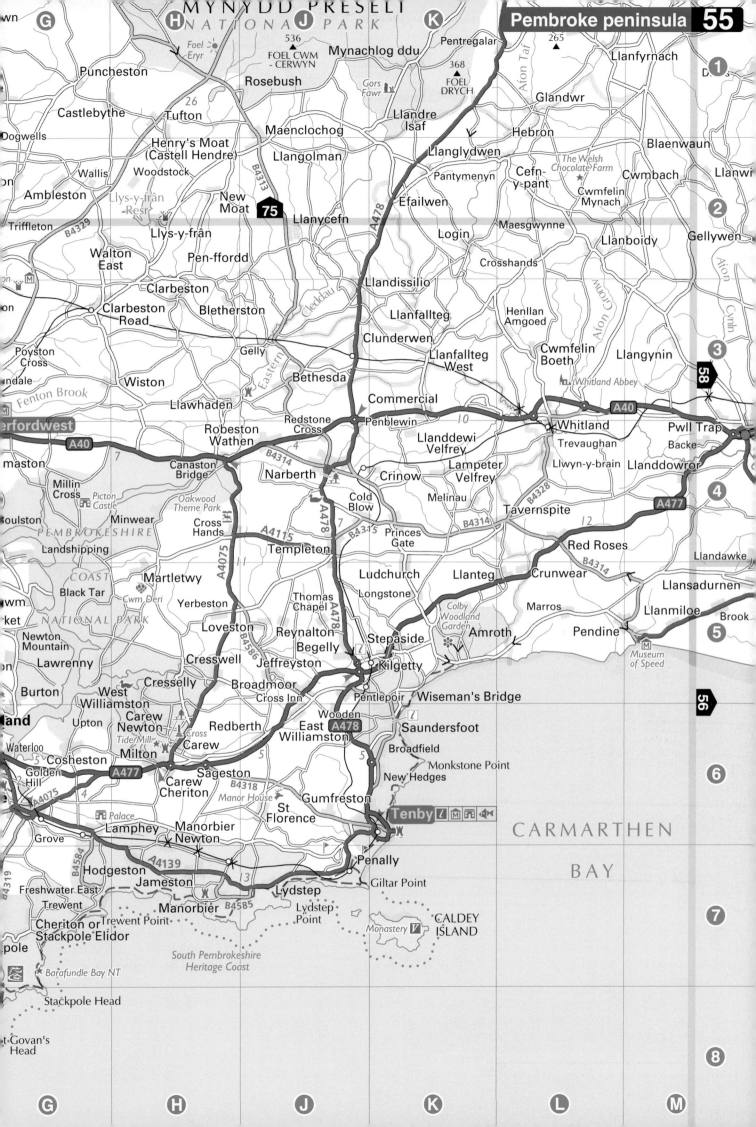

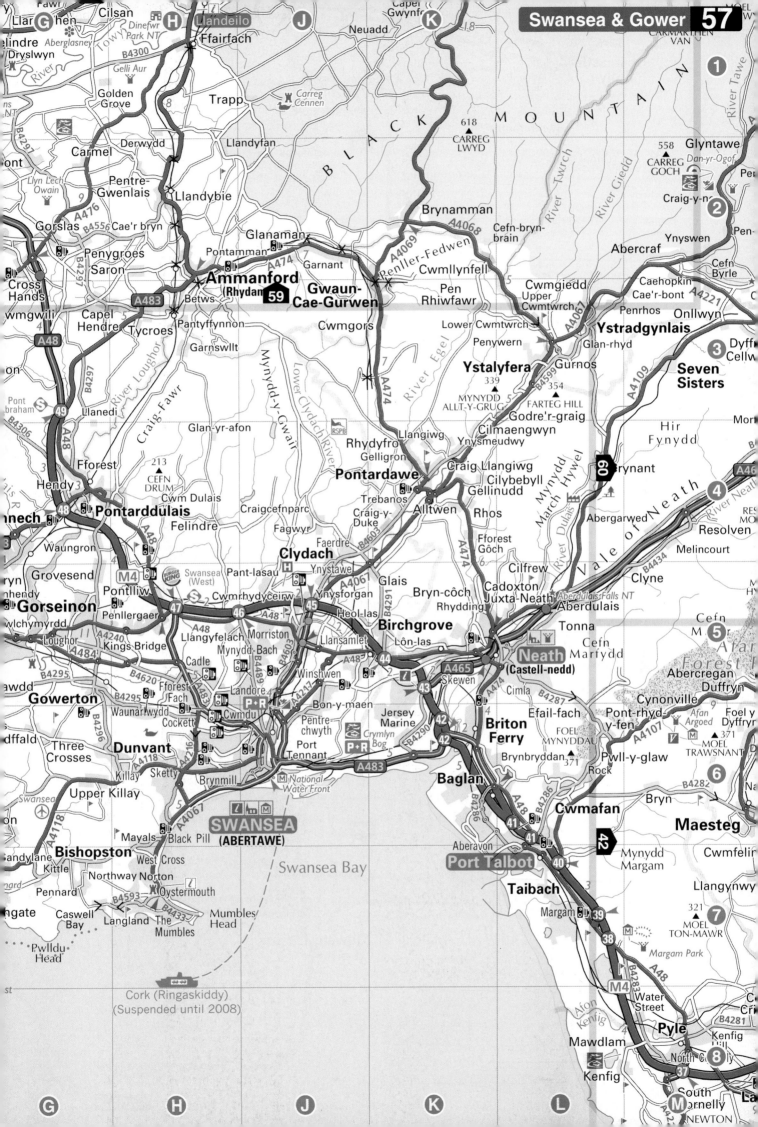

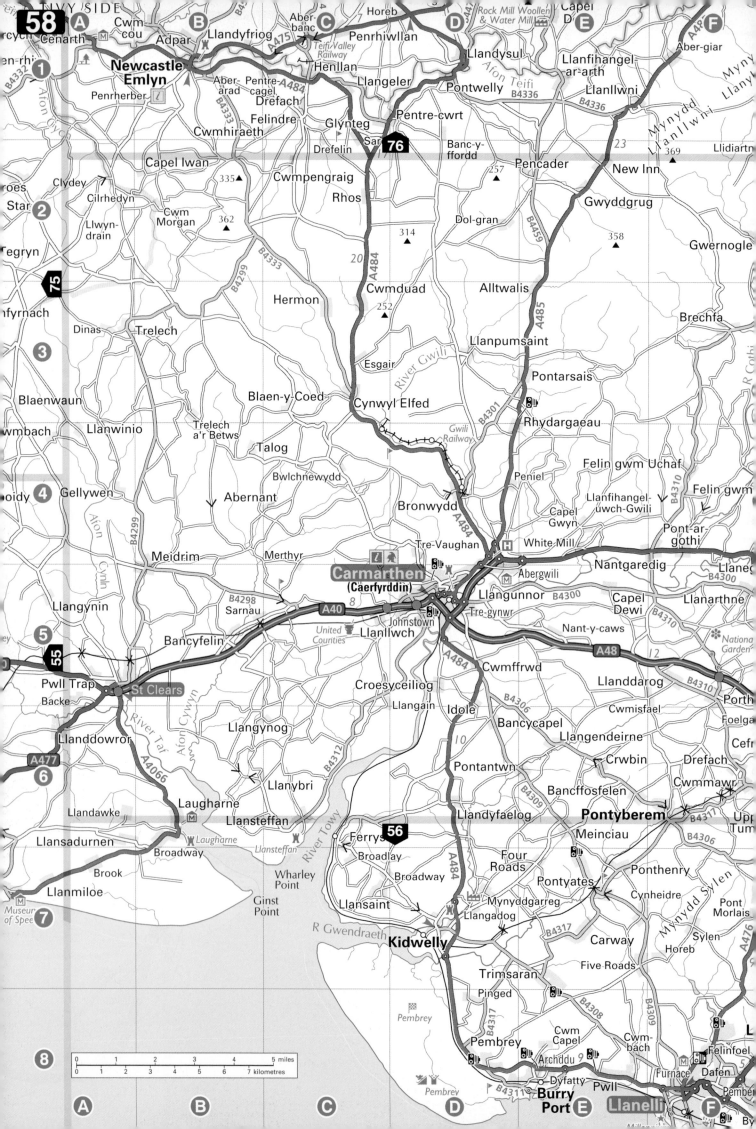

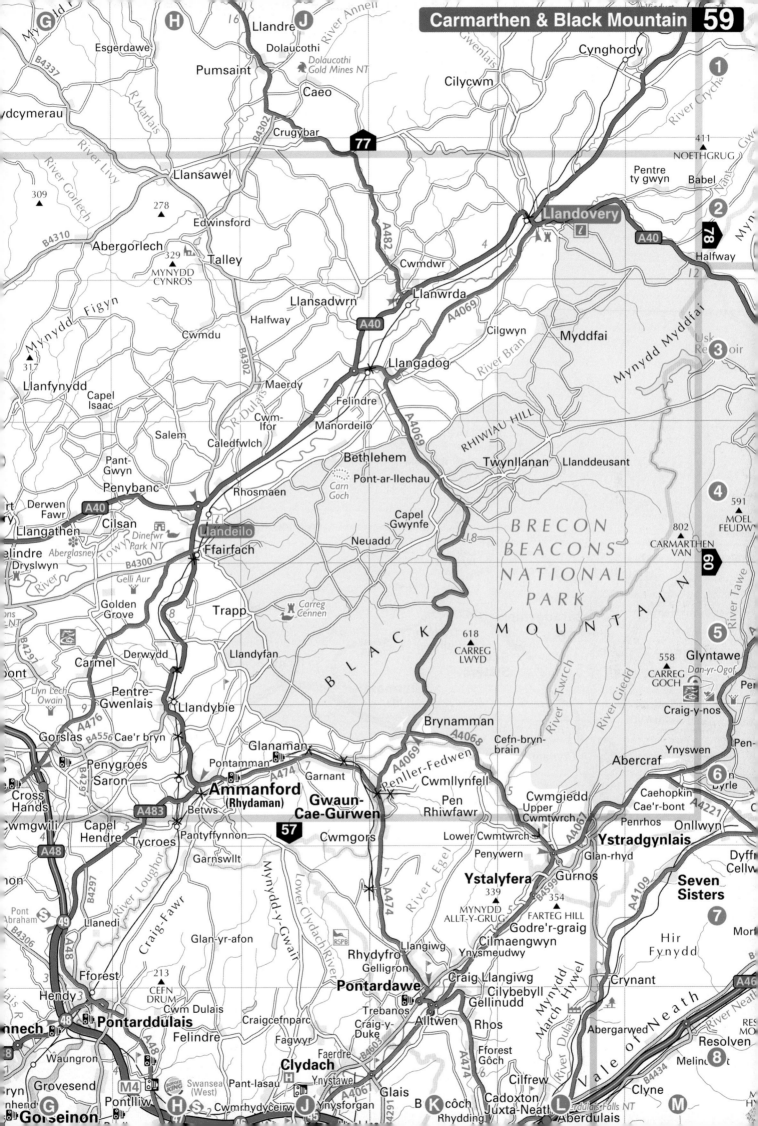

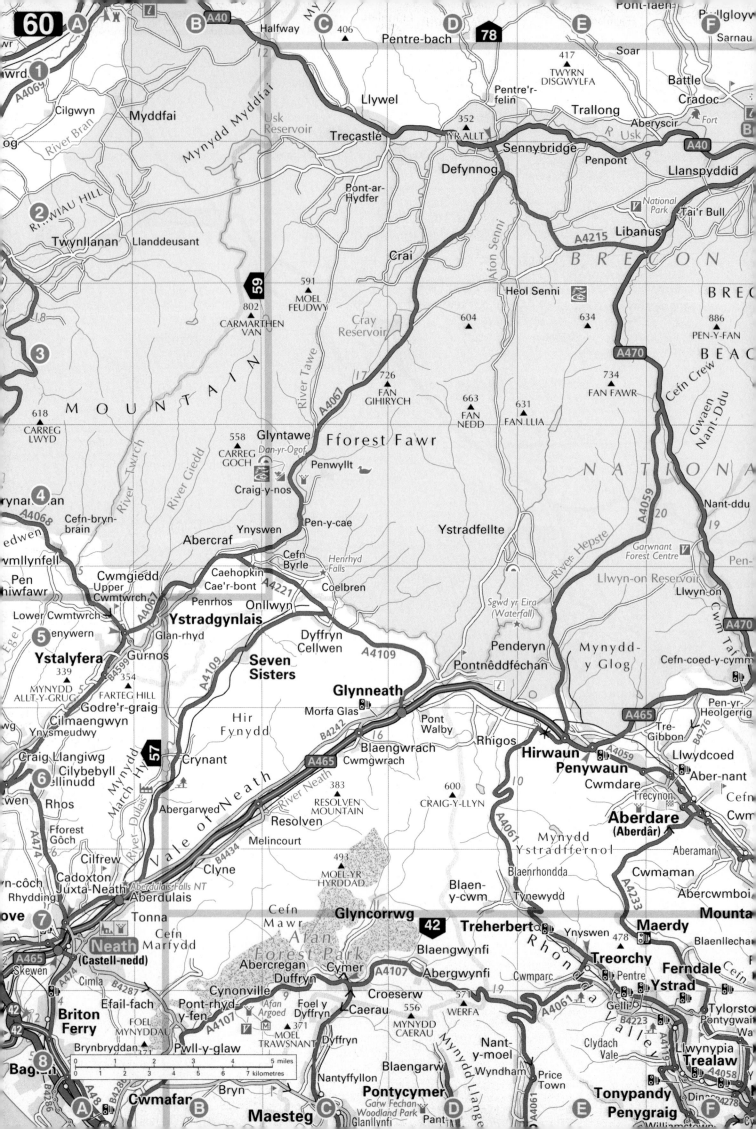

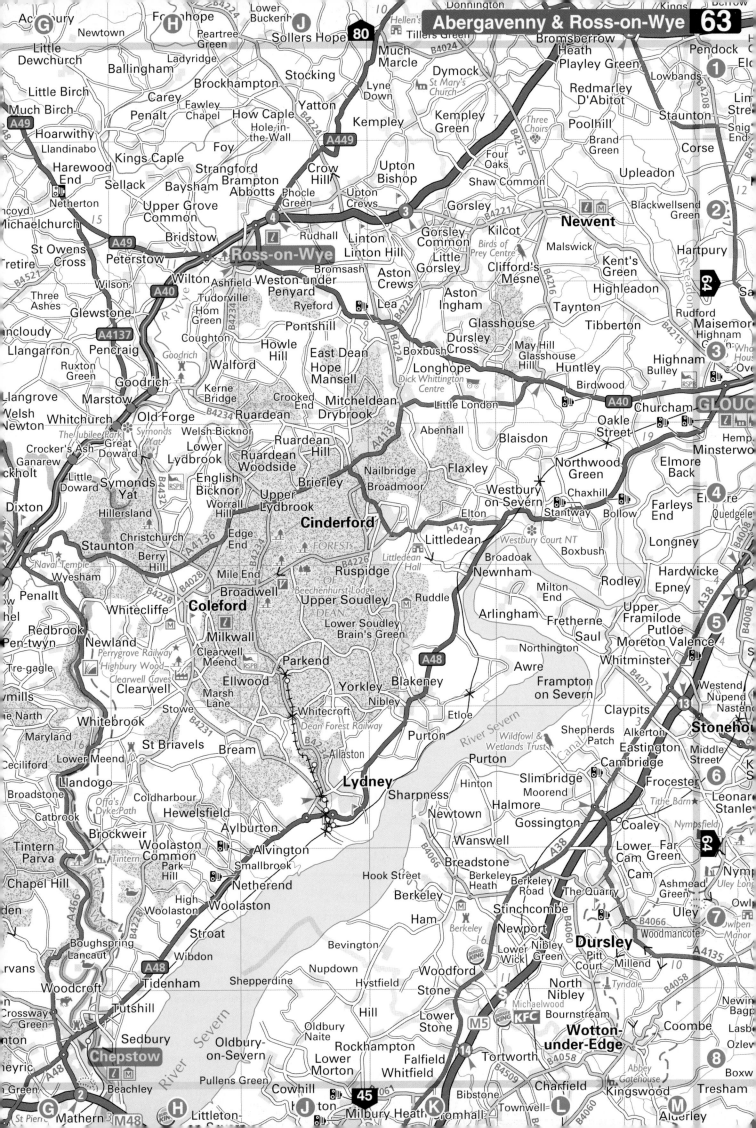

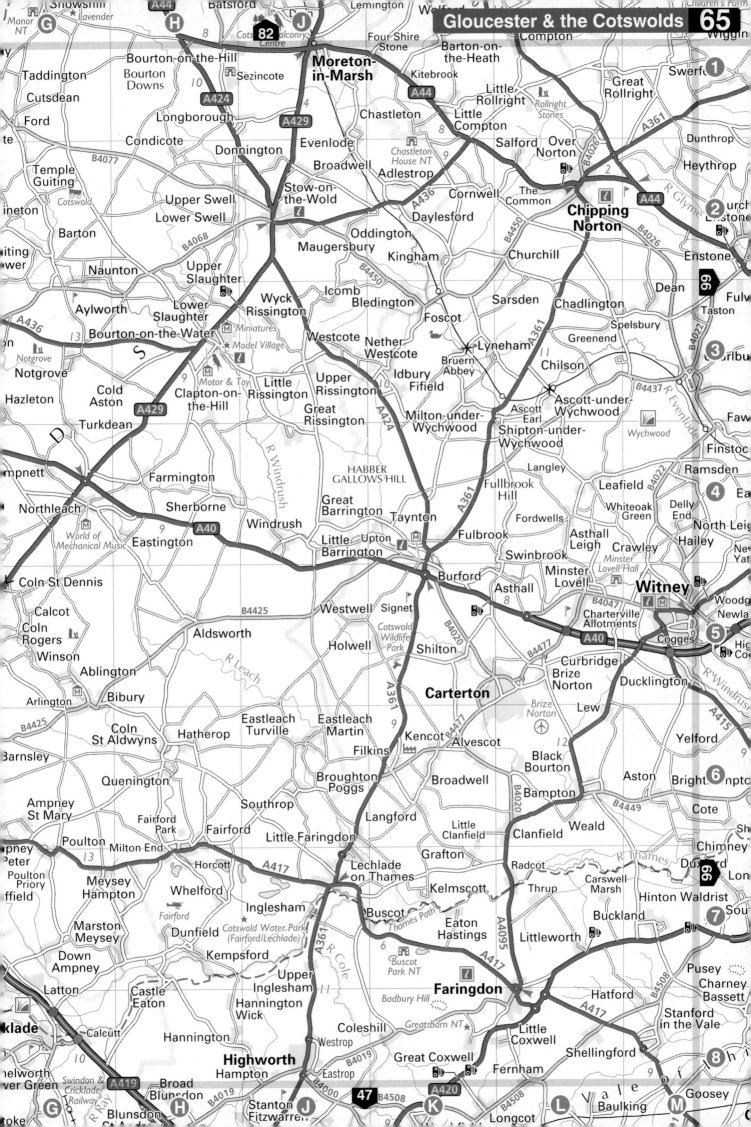

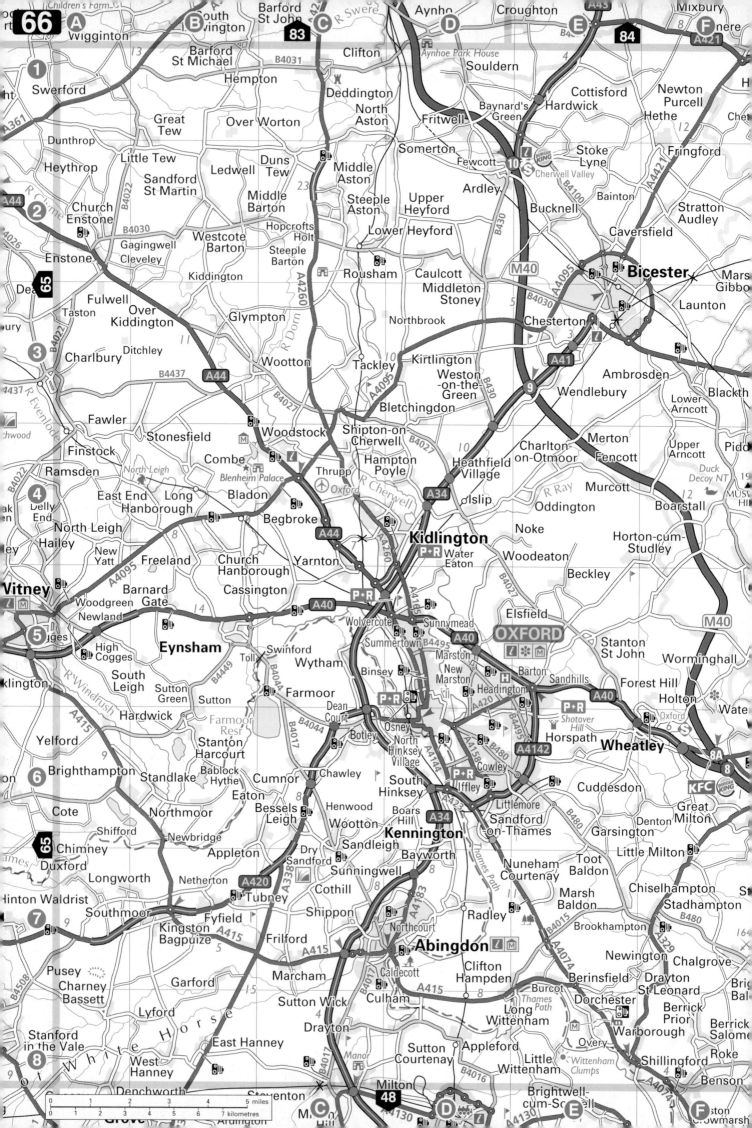

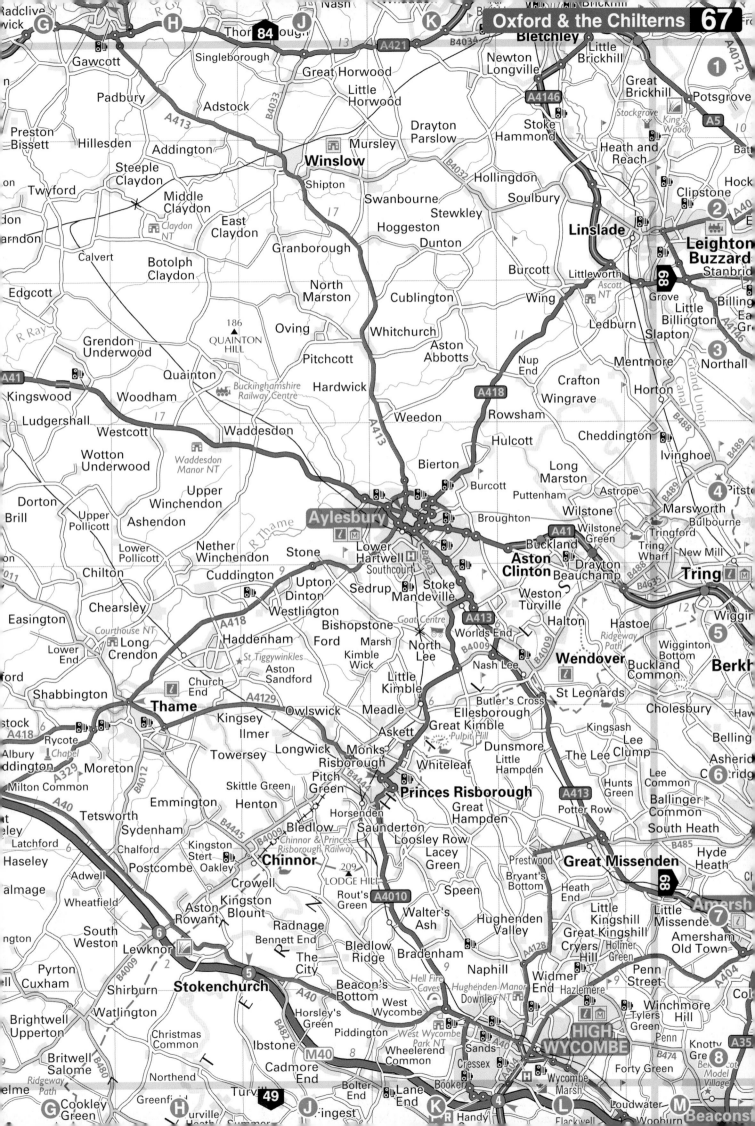

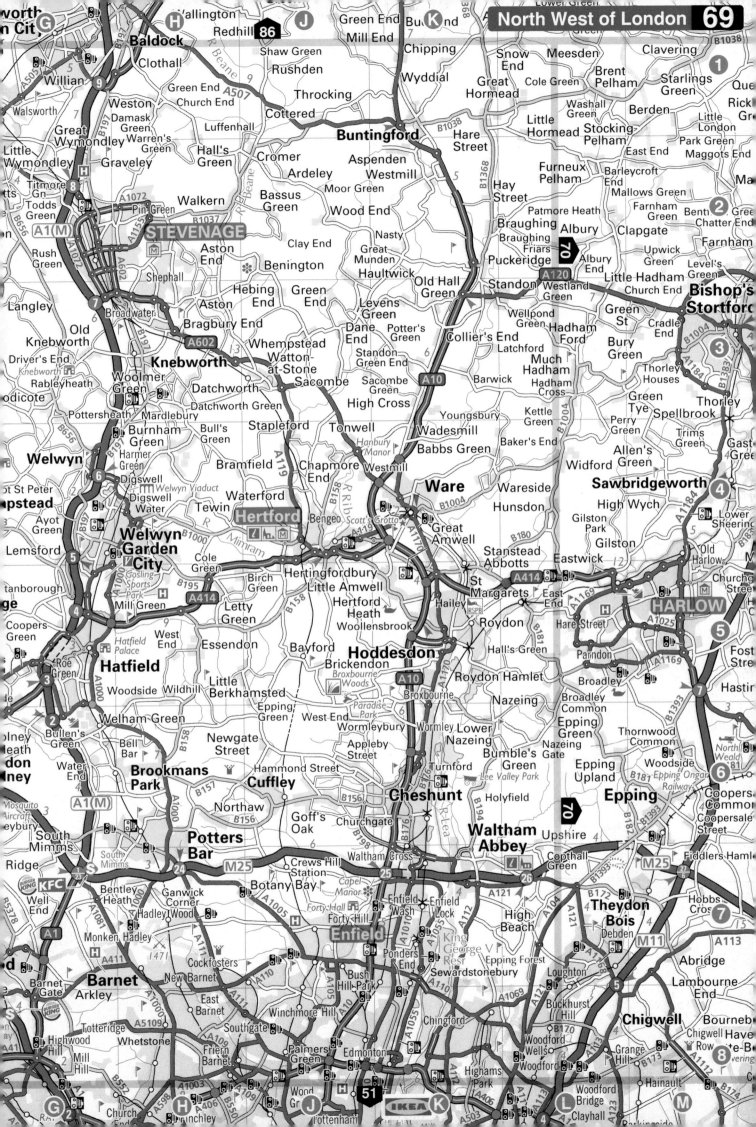

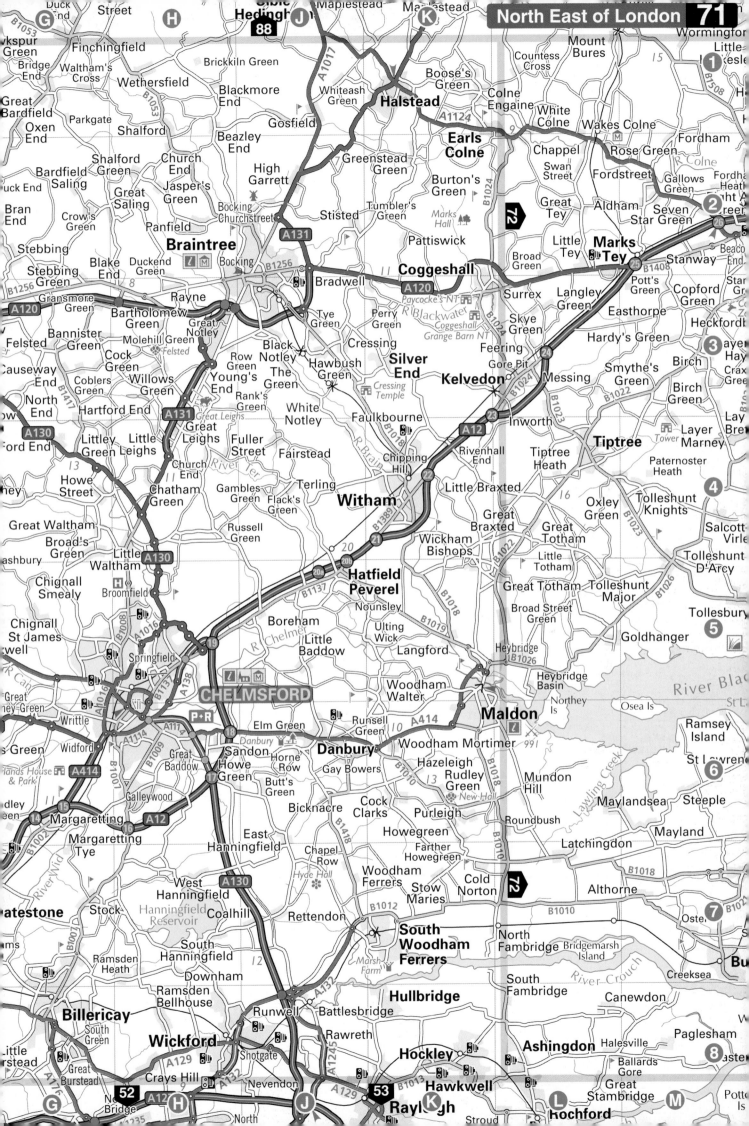

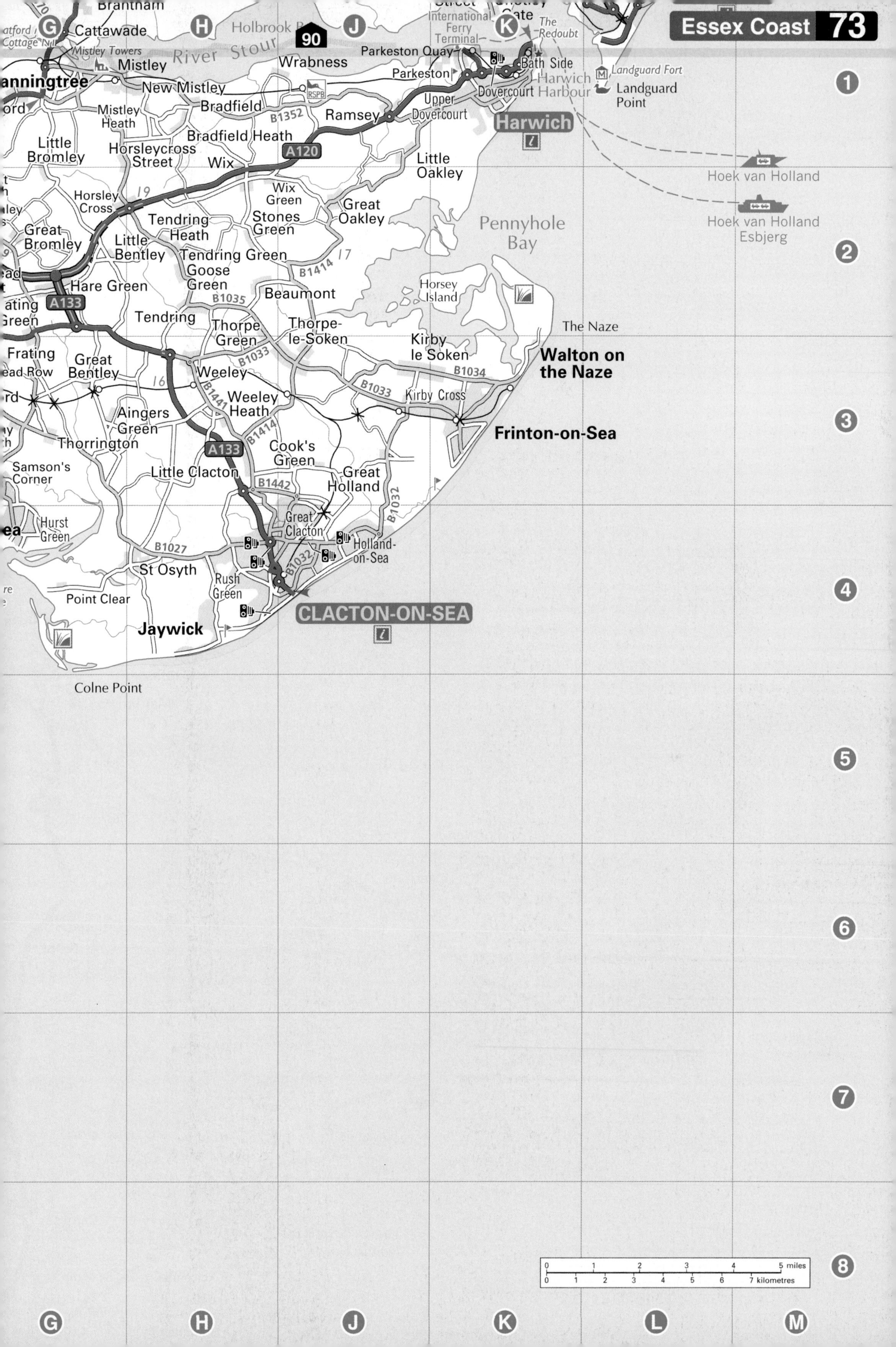

Brantham
Cattawade
Holbrook
River Stour
Mistley Towers
Mistley
Wrabness
Parkeston Quay
90
anningtree
New Mistley
Parkeston
International Ferry Terminal
Bath Side
Landguard Fort
Landguard Point
Mistley Heath
Bradfield
Ramsey
Upper Dovercourt
Dovercourt
Harwich Harbour
B1352
Harwich
Bradfield Heath
A120
Little Oakley
Little Bromley
Horsleycross Street
Wix
Horsley Cross
19
Wix Green
Great Oakley
Stones Green
Pennyhole Bay
Tendring Heath
Little Bentley
Tendring Green
B1414 17
Great Bromley
Goose Green
Horsey Island
ead
A133
Hare Green
B1035
Beaumont
The Naze
ating Green
Tendring
Thorpe Green
Thorpe-le-Soken
Kirby le Soken
Walton on the Naze
Frating
Great Bentley
B1033
Weeley
B1441
B1033
B1034
Kirby Cross
rd
16
Aingers Green
Weeley Heath
Kirby Cross
Frinton-on-Sea
Thorrington
A133
B1414
Cook's Green
Samson's Corner
Little Clacton
B1442
Great Holland
B1032
Hurst Green
Great Clacton
ea
B1027
Holland-on-Sea
St Osyth
B1032
Point Clear
Rush Green
CLACTON-ON-SEA
Jaywick
Colne Point

RSPB

Hoek van Holland
Hoek van Holland
Esbjerg

0 1 2 3 4 5 miles
0 1 2 3 4 5 6 7 kilometres

G H J K L M

1 2 3 4 5 6 7 8

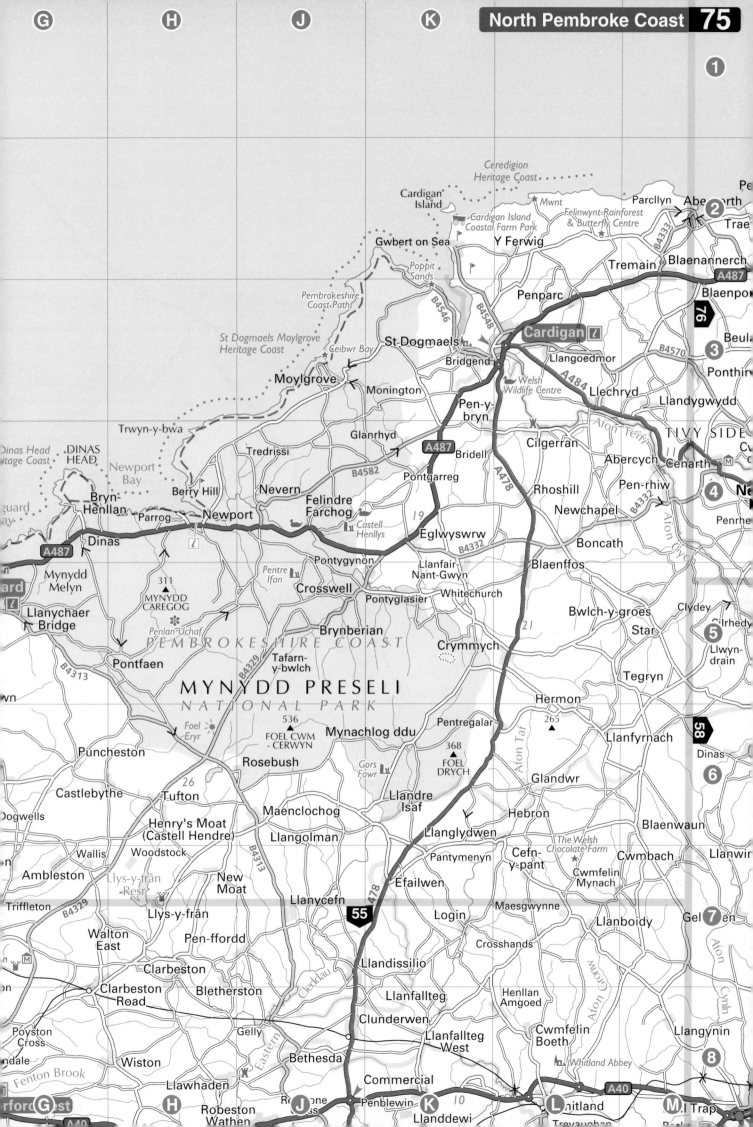

G · H · J · K

1

2

76

3

4

5

58

6

7

8

Ceredigion Heritage Coast

Cardigan Island

Mwnt

Felinwynt-Rainforest & Butterfly Centre

Parcllyn

Abe—orth

Trae—

Cardigan Island Coastal Farm Park

Gwbert on Sea

Y Ferwig

Tremain

Blaenannerch

A487

Poppit Sands

Penparc

Blaenpo—

Pembrokeshire Coast Path

B4546

B4548

Cardigan ℹ

Beul—

St Dogmaels Moylgrove Heritage Coast

Ceibwr Bay

St-Dogmaels

Bridgend

Llangoedmor

B4570

Ponthir—

Moylgrove

Monington

Pen-y-bryn

Welsh Wildlife Centre

A484

Llechryd

Llandygwydd

Trwyn-y-bwa

Glanrhyd

A487

Bridell

Cilgerran

Afon Teifi

TIVY SIDE

Dinas Head —itage Coast

DINAS HEAD

Newport Bay

Tredrissi

Nevern

Pontgarreg

Rhoshill

Abercych

Cenarth

C—

Berry Hill

A478

Newchapel

Pen-rhiw

B4332

N—

Bryn-Henllan

Felindre Farchog

19

Castell Henllys

Eglwyswrw

B4332

Boncath

Penrhe—

—guard —ay

Parrog

Newport

ℹ

Pontygynon

Llanfair-Nant-Gwyn

Blaenffos

Dinas

A487

Pentre Ifan

Crosswell

Pontyglasier

Whitechurch

Bwlch-y-groes

Clydey

Cilrhedy—

—ard ℹ

Mynydd Melyn

311

Penlan-Uchaf

Brynberian

Star

5

Llwyn-drain

Llanychaer Bridge

MYNYDD CAREGOG

PEMBROKESHIRE COAST

Crymmych

21

Tegryn

B4313

Pontfaen

Tafarn-y-bwlch

Hermon

265

58

Foel Eryr

MYNYDD PRESELI

Llanfyrnach

NATIONAL PARK

536

FOEL CWM -CERWYN

Mynachlog ddu

Pentregalar

Dinas

6

Puncheston

Rosebush

Gors Fawr

368 FOEL DRYCH

Glandwr

Castlebythe

26

Tufton

Llandre Isaf

Hebron

Blaenwaun

Llanwir—

—ogwells

Henry's Moat (Castell Hendre)

Maenclochog

Llanglydwen

The Welsh Chocolate Farm

Cwmbach

Wallis

Woodstock

Llangolman

B4313

Pantymenyn

Cefn-y-pant

Cwmfelin Mynach

Ambleston

Llys-y-frân Resr

New Moat

Efailwen

—rifeton

B4329

Llanycefn

55

Login

Maesgwynne

Llanboidy

Gel—

7

—en

Llys-y-frân

478

Crosshands

—dale

Walton East

Pen-ffordd

Llandissilio

Henllan Amgoed

Llangynin

Poyston Cross

Clarbeston

Clarbeston Road

Bletherston

Llanfallteg

Afon Cynin

Afon —

—rdale

Wiston

Gelly

Clunderwen

Llanfallteg West

Cwmfelin Boeth

—rford —st

Gelly

Bethesda

Llanfalltej

Whitland Abbey

8

Fenton Brook

Llawhaden

Robeston Wathen

Commercial

A40

Penblewin

10

Llanddewi

—hitland

—l Trap—

G · H · J · K · L · M

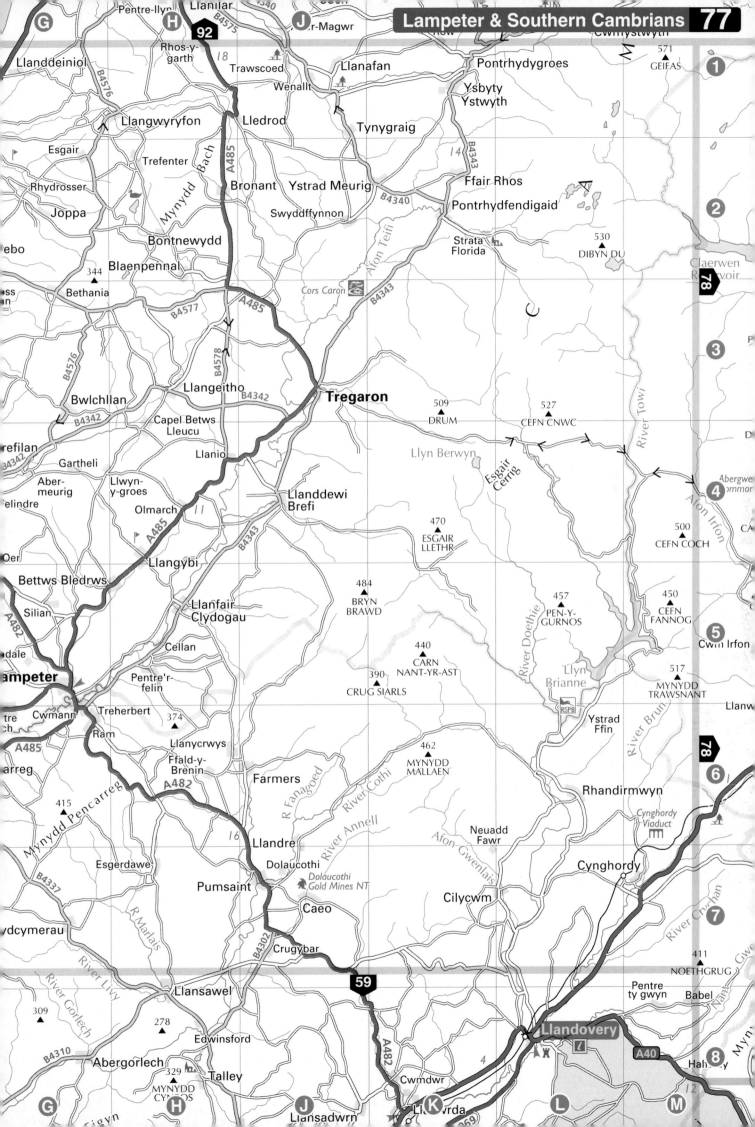

G   H   J

Pentre-llyn   Llanilar   92   B4575   -Magwr   B4340

Llanddeiniol   Rhos-y-garth   Trawscoed   Wenallt   Llanafan   Pontrhydygroes   Ysbyty Ystwyth   Cwmystwyth   571 ▲ GEIFAS   **1**

Llangwyryfon   Lledrod   Tynygraig   Ffair Rhos   **2**

Esgair   Trefenter   Bronant   Ystrad Meurig   14   B4343

Rhydrosser   Swyddffynnon   Pontrhydfendigaid   B4340

Joppa   Bontnewydd   B4577   B4343   Strata Florida   530 ▲ DIBYN DU   Claerwen Reservoir   **78**

Blaenpennal   344 ▲   Cors Caron   **3**

Bethania   Afon Teifi

B4576   A485   B4578

Bwlchllan   B4342   Llangeitho   B4342   Tregaron   509 ▲ DRUM   527 ▲ CEFN CNWC   River Towi

Capel Betws Lleucu   Llyn Berwyn   **4**

refilan   B4342   Llanio   Esgair Cerrig   Abergwe mmor   Afon Irfon

Gartheli   Llwyn-y-groes   Aber-meurig   Olmarch   11   Llanddewi Brefi   470 ▲ ESGAIR LLETHR   500 ▲ CEFN COCH

A485   B4343   Oer   Llangybi   484 ▲ BRYN BRAWD   457 ▲ PEN-Y-GURNOS   450 ▲ CEFN FANNOG   Cwm Irfon   **5**

Bettws Bledrws   Silian   Llanfair Clydogau   440 ▲ CARN NANT-YR-AST   River Doethie   Llyn Brianne   517 ▲ MYNYDD TRAWSNANT   Llanw

Cellan   390 ▲ CRUG SIARLS   RSPB   Ystrad Ffin   River Brun

ampeter   A482   Pentre'r-felin   Treherbert   374 ▲   462 ▲ MYNYDD MALLAEN   **78**

Cwmann   Ram   Llanycrwys   Rhandirmwyn   **6**

arreg   A485   Ffald-y-Brenin   A482   Farmers   R Fanagoed   RiverCothi   Cynghordy Viaduct

415 ▲   Mynydd Pencarreg   16   Llandre   River Annell   Neuadd Fawr   Afon Gwenlais   Cynghordy

Esgerdawe   Dolaucothi   Dolaucothi Gold Mines NT   Cilycwm   River Crichan   **7**

B4337   R Marlais   Pumsaint   Caeo   Afon Gwe   411 ▲ NOETHGRUG

ydcymerau   Crugybar   Pentre ty gwyn   Babel

309 ▲   River Gorlech   Llansawel   59   A482   Llandovery   A40   **8**

B4310   278 ▲   Edwinsford   Cwmdwr   Hah   12   Myn

Abergorlech   329 ▲   Talley   Llansadwrn   969

G   H   MYNYDD CYN OS   J   K   L   M

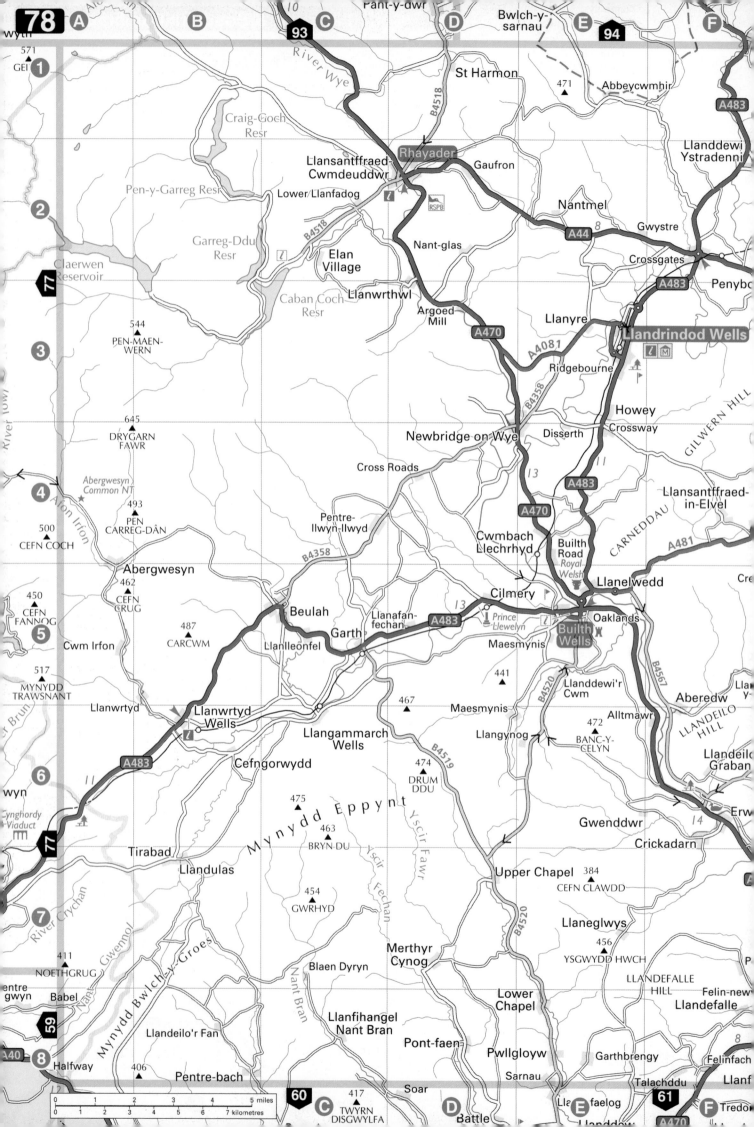

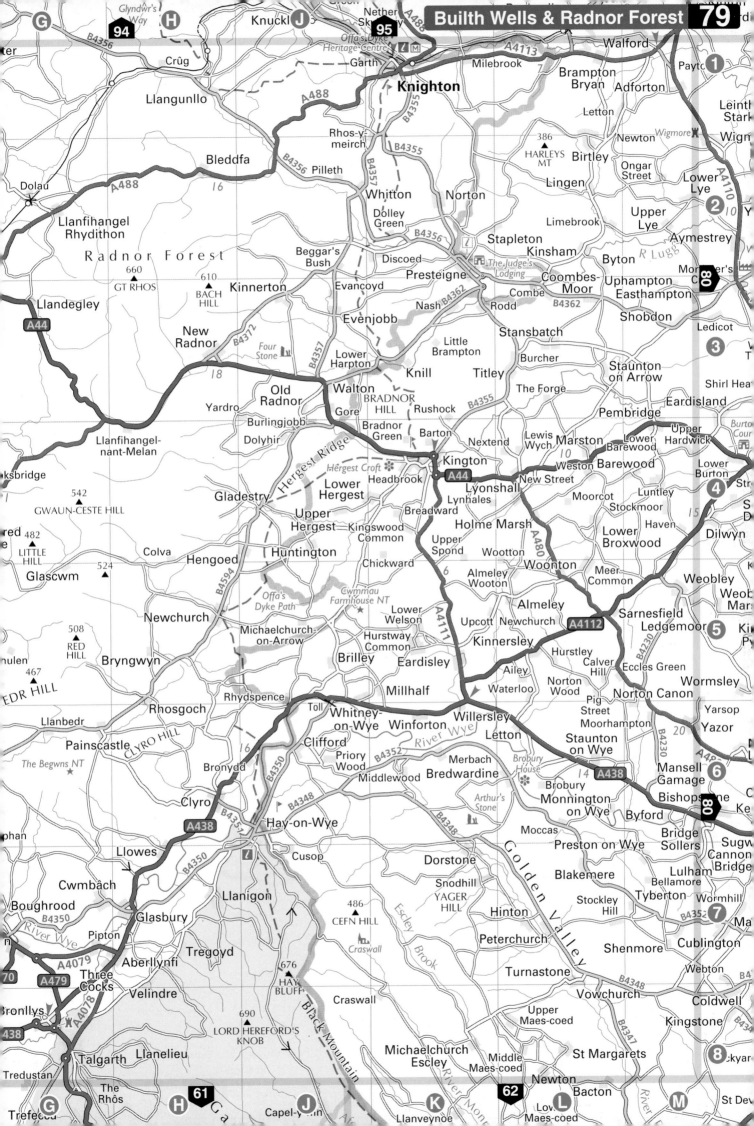

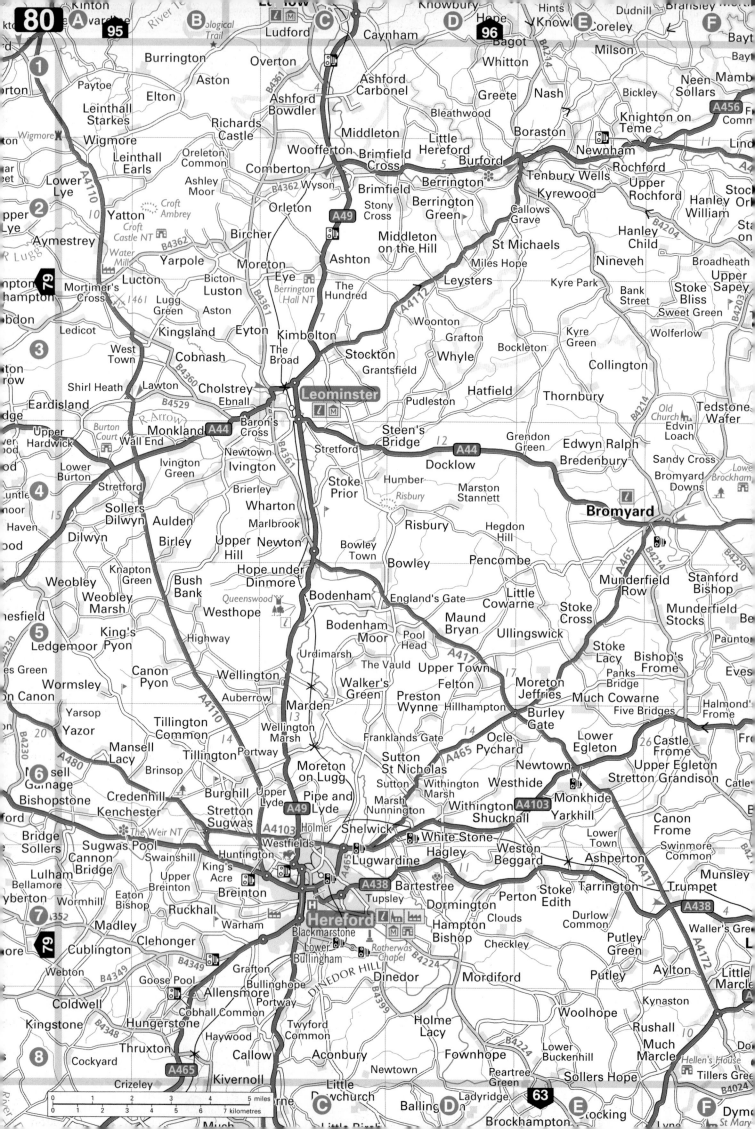

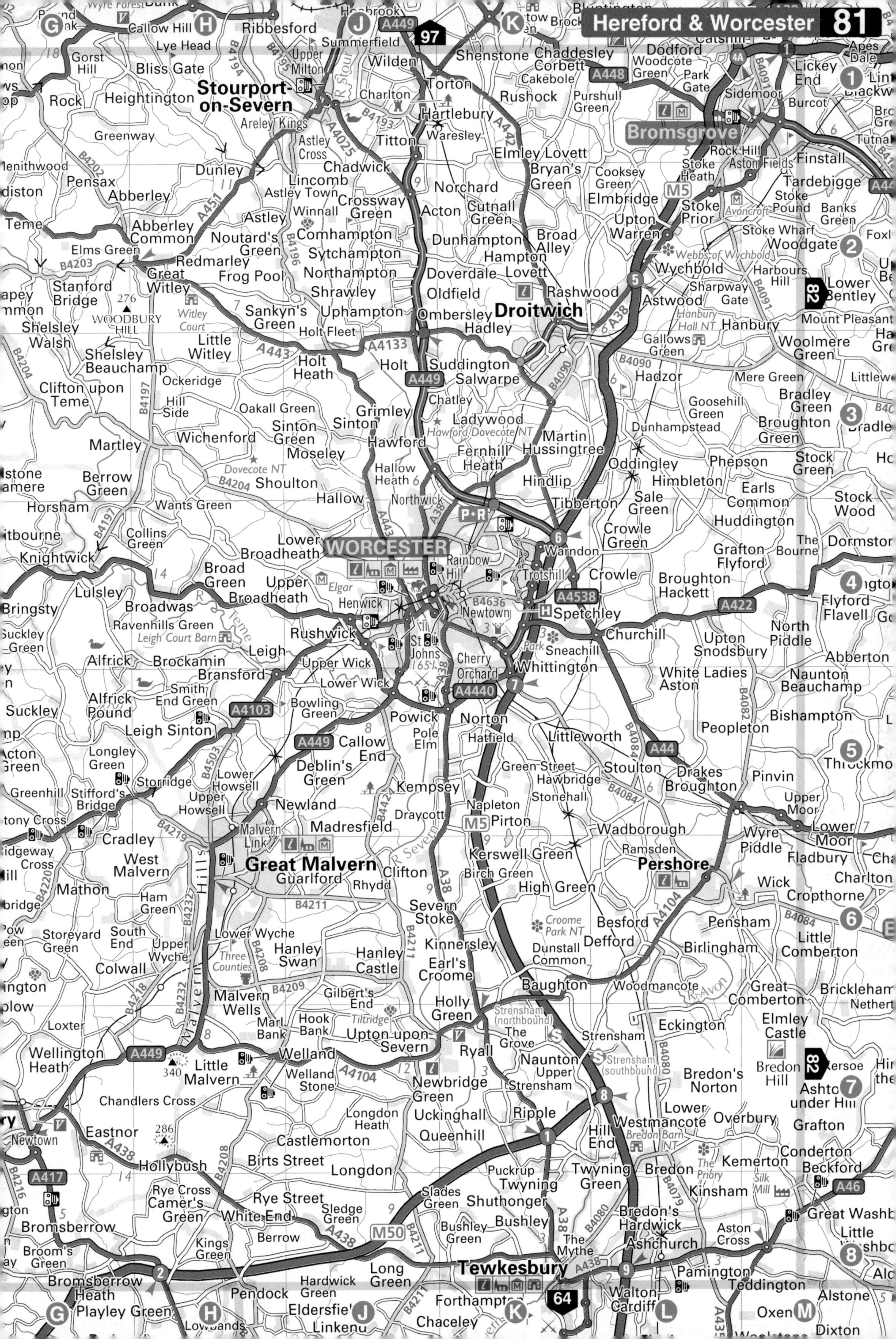

Wyre Forest

A449

97

Stourport-on-Severn

Bromsgrove

1

M5

82

Droitwich

Abberley

Great Witley

Stanford Bridge

Shelsley Walsh

Clifton upon Teme

Martley

WORCESTER

2

Great Malvern

Malvern Link

Malvern Wells

3

Pershore

4

5

Upton-upon-Severn

6

82

7

Welland

Little Malvern

Eastnor

A438

A417

M50

Bromsberrow

Tewkesbury

64

8

A38

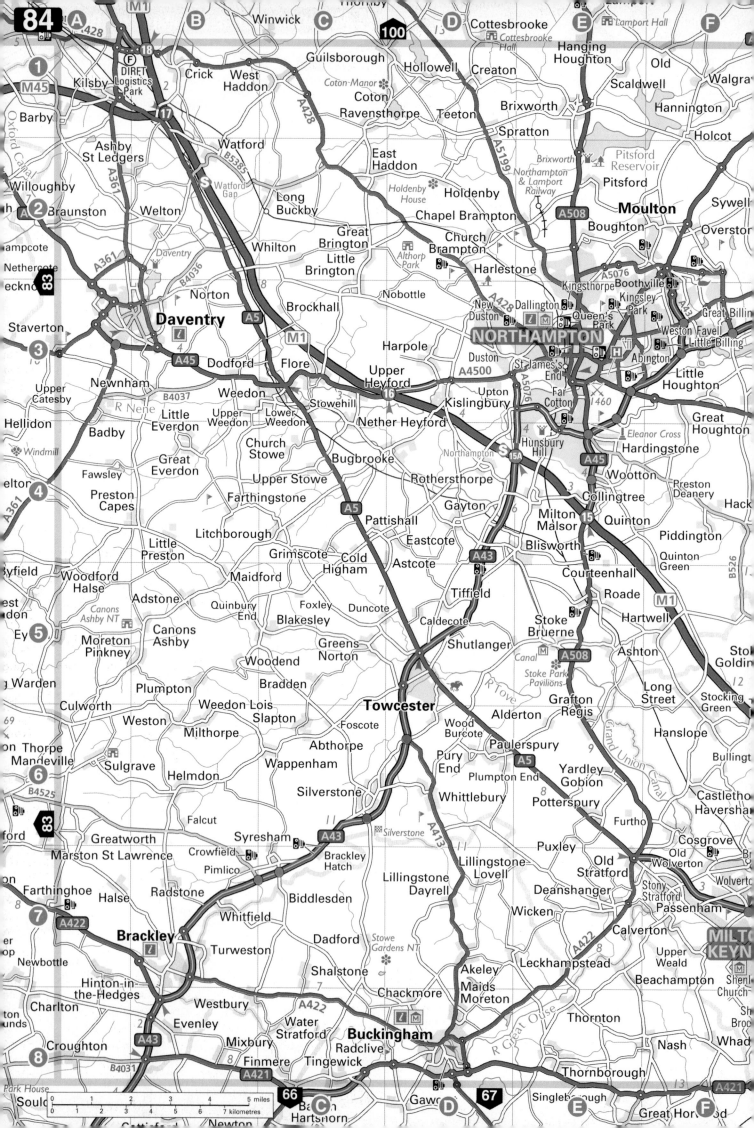

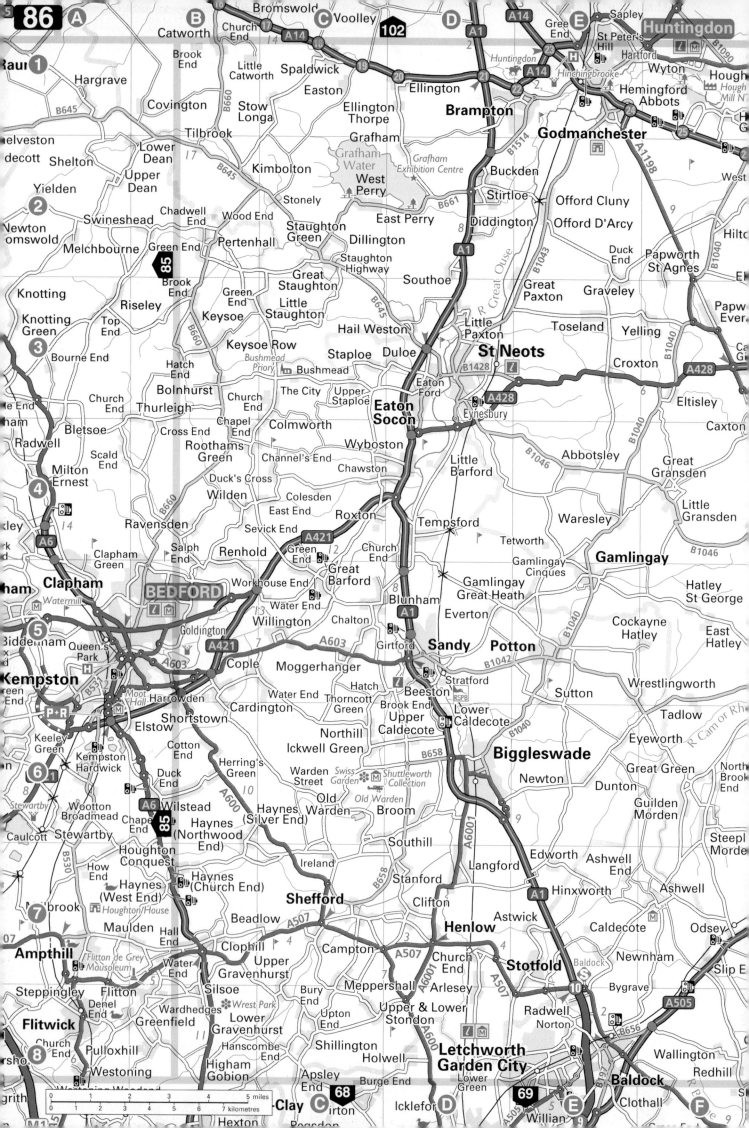

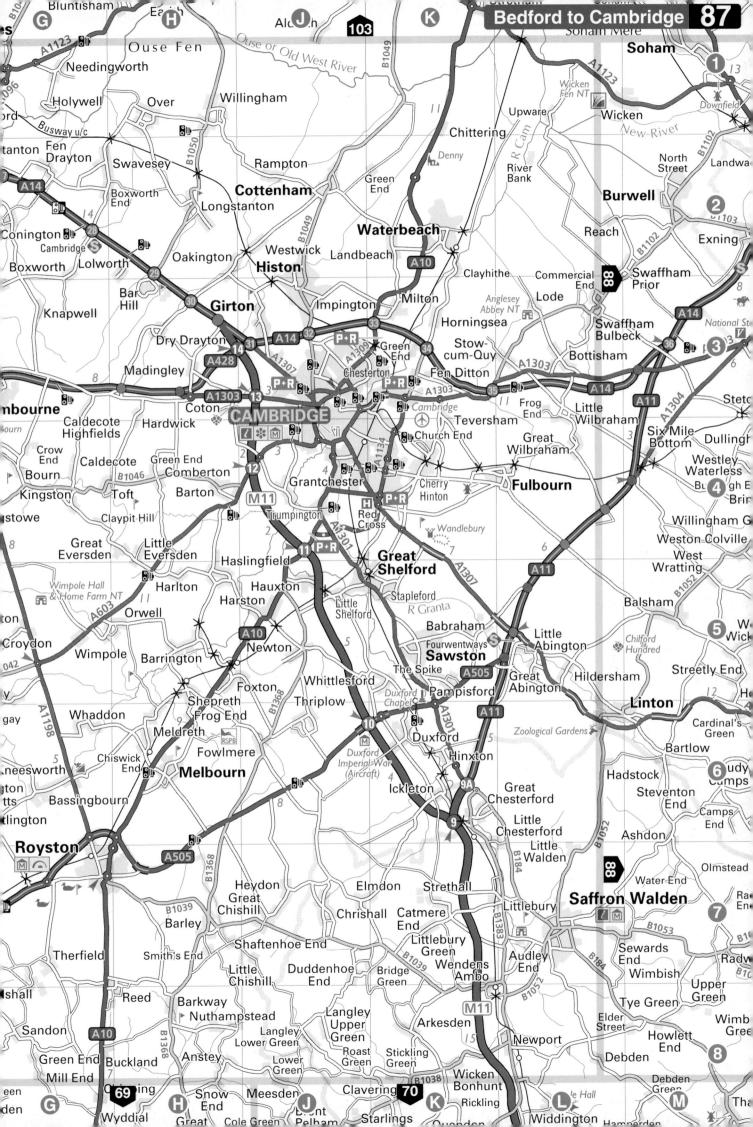

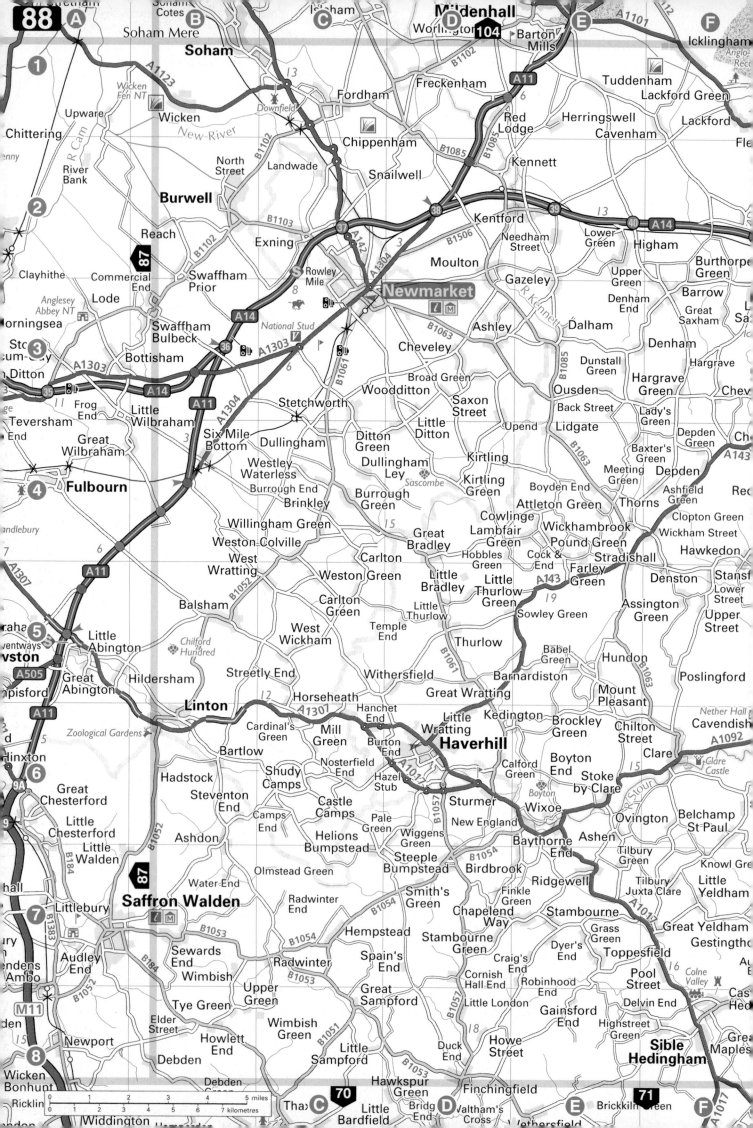

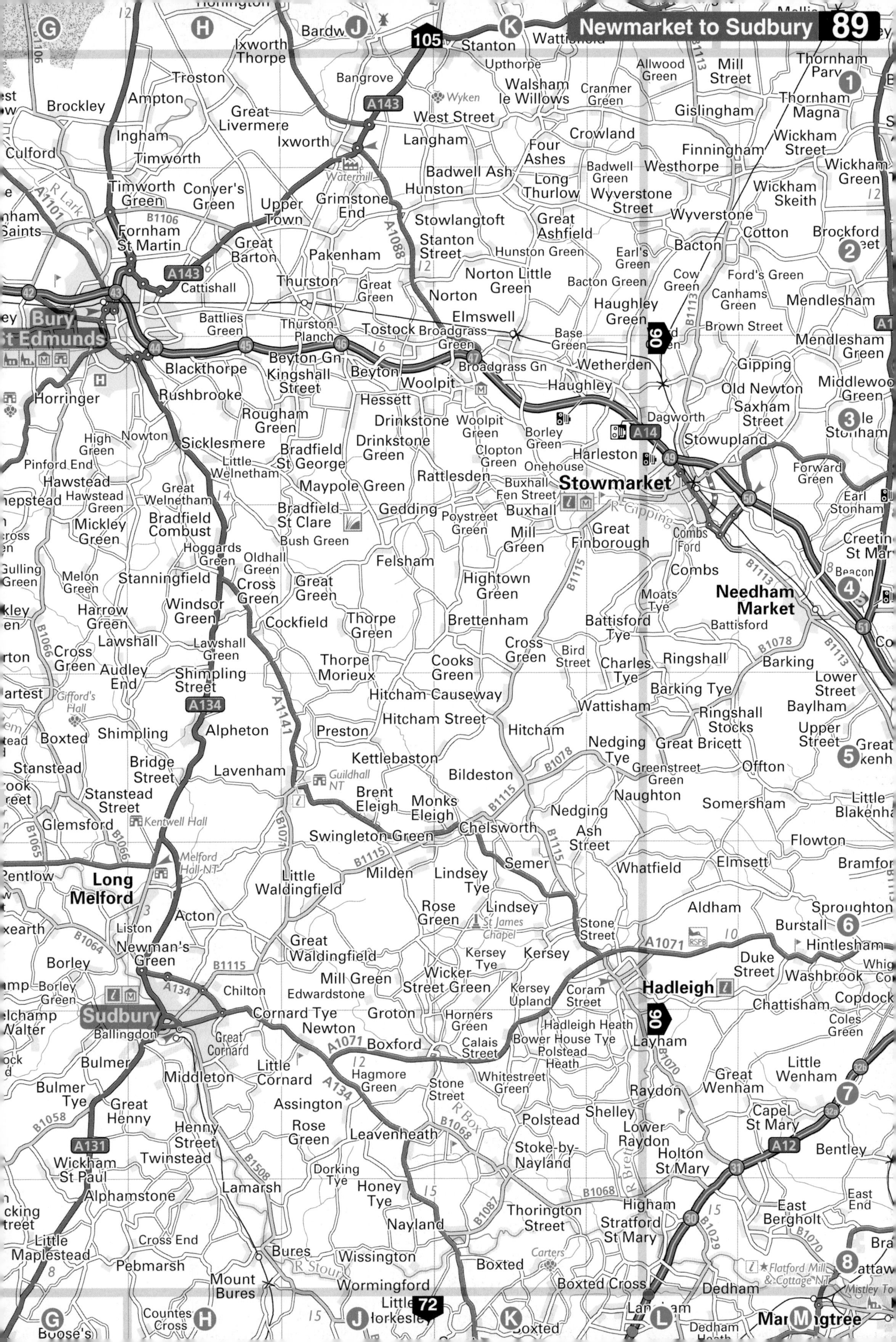

Thornham Parva
Thornham Magna
Wickham Street
Wickham Green
Ixworth Thorpe
Bardwell
J
Stanton
Wattisfield
K
Allwood Green
Mill Street
Bangrove
Upthorpe
Walsham le Willows
Cranmer Green
Gislingham
Finningham
Westhorpe
Wickham Skeith
Brockford
Troston
Ampton
Great Livermere
Wyken
West Street
Four Ashes
Crowland
Badwell Green
Wyverstone Street
Wyverstone
Cotton
Brockley
Ingham
Ixworth
Langham
Badwell Ash
Long Thurlow
Great Ashfield
Earl's Green
Bacton
Bacton Green
Cow Green
Ford's Green
Canhams Green
Mendlesham
Culford
Timworth
Upper Town
Grimstone End
Hunston
Stowlangtoft
Stanton Street
Hunston Green
Norton Little Green
Haughley Green
Brown Street
Mendlesham Green
Timworth Green
Conyer's Green
Pakenham
Thurston
Great Green
Norton
Elmswell
Base Green
Wetherden
Gipping
Old Newton
Middlewood Green
Fornham St Martin
Great Barton
Cattishall
Battlies Green
Thurston Planch
Tostock
Broadgrass Green
Haughley
Dagworth
Saxham Street
Stowupland
le Stonham
Bury St Edmunds
Blackthorpe
Beyton Gn
Kingshall Street
Beyton
Broadgrass Gn
Woolpit
Harleston
Stowmarket
Forward Green
Earl Stonham
Horringer
Rushbrooke
Rougham Green
Hessett
Drinkstone
Woolpit Green
Borley Green
Onehouse
Creeting St Mary
Beacon
High Green
Nowton
Sicklesmere
Bradfield St George
Drinkstone Green
Rattlesden
Clopton Green
Buxhall Fen Street
Buxhall
Great Finborough
Combs Ford
Combs
Needham Market
Hawstead
Hawstead Green
Mickley Green
Little Welnetham
Maypole Green
Gedding
Poystreet Green
Mill Green
Barking
Bradfield Combust
Hoggards Green
Oldhall Green
Bush Green
Felsham
Hightown Green
Battisford Tye
Battisford
Ringshall
Lower Street
Baylham
Melon Green
Stanningfield
Windsor Green
Cross Green
Great Green
Brettenham
Cross Green
Bird Street
Charles Tye
Barking Tye
Ringshall Stocks
Upper Street
Harrow Green
Lawshall
Lawshall Green
Cockfield
Thorpe Green
Cooks Green
Wattisham
Nedging Tye
Great Bricett
Offton
Cross Green
Audley End
Shimpling Street
Thorpe Morieux
Hitcham Causeway
Greenstreet Green
Somersham
Little Blakenham
Boxted
Shimpling
Alpheton
Preston
Hitcham Street
Hitcham
Naughton
Flowton
Bridge Street
Lavenham
Kettlebaston
Bildeston
Nedging
Elmsett
Bramford
Stanstead
Stanstead Street
Brent Eleigh
Monks Eleigh
Ash Street
Whatfield
Glemsford
Kentwell Hall
Swingleton Green
Chelsworth
Semer
Aldham
Sproughton
Long Melford
Melford Hall
Little Waldingfield
Milden
Lindsey Tye
Lindsey
Stone Street
Burstall
Acton
Liston
St James Chapel
Rose Green
Hintlesham
Duke Street
Washbrook
Newman's Green
Great Waldingfield
Kersey Tye
Kersey
Hadleigh
Chattisham
Copdock
Borley
Borley Green
Chilton
Mill Green
Wicker Street Green
Kersey Upland
Coram Street
Coles Green
Sudbury
Ballingdon
Great Cornard
Edwardstone
Groton
Horners Green
Hadleigh Heath
Bower House Tye
Polstead Heath
Layham
Bulmer
Cornard Tye
Newton
Boxford
Calais Street
Whitestreet Green
Raydon
Great Wenham
Little Wenham
Bulmer Tye
Middleton
Little Cornard
Hagmore Green
Stone Street
Polstead
Shelley
Lower Raydon
Capel St Mary
Great Henny
Assington
Rose Green
Leavenheath
Stoke-by-Nayland
Holton St Mary
Bentley
Wickham St Paul
Henny Street
Twinstead
Dorking Tye
Honey Tye
Thorington Street
Higham
Stratford St Mary
East Bergholt
East End
Alphamstone
Lamarsh
Nayland
Boxted
Boxted Cross
Dedham
Little Maplestead
Cross End
Bures
Wissington
Wormingford
Flatford Mill & Cottage NT
Mistley
Boose's
Countess Cross
Mount Bures
Little Horkesley
Boxted
Langham
Manningtree

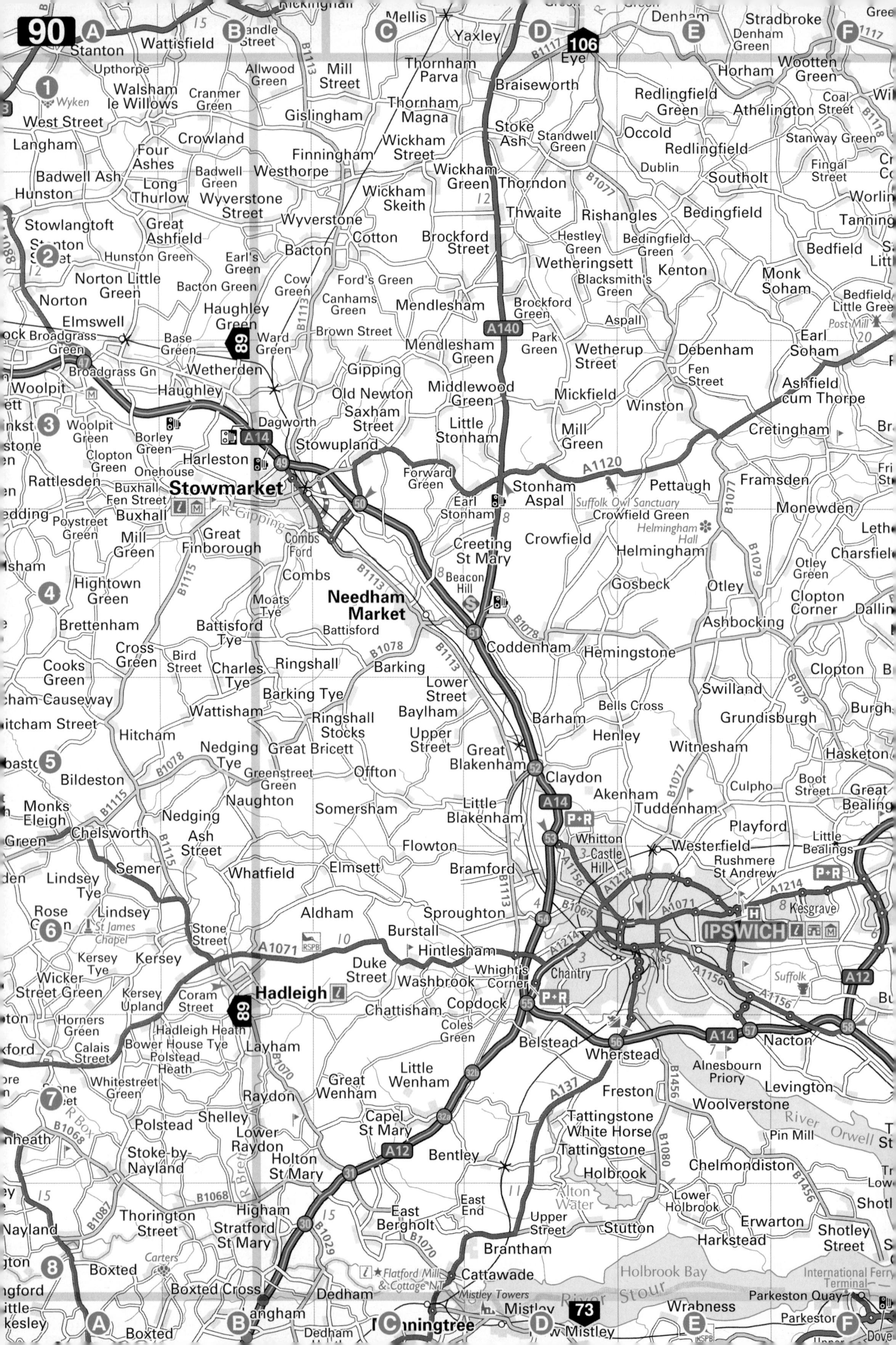

A · B · C · D · E · F

Stanton · Wattisfield · Bandle Street · Mellis · Yaxley · Denham · Stradbroke · Gree

1

Wyken · Upthorpe · Walsham le Willows · Cranmer Green · Allwood Green · Mill Street · Thornham Parva · Braiseworth · Horham · Denham Green · Wootten Green
West Street · Gislingham · Thornham Magna · Redlingfield Green · Athelington Street · Stanway Green · Coal · Wi
Langham · Crowland · Finningham · Wickham Street · Stoke Ash · Standwell Green · Occold · Redlingfield · Fingal Street · Worlin · 1118

2

Four Ashes · Badwell Green · Westhorpe · Wickham Skeith · Wickham Green · Thorndon · Dublin · Southolt · Tanning
Badwell Ash · Long Thurlow · Wyverstone Street · Wyverstone · Cotton · Brockford Street · Thwaite · Rishangles · Bedingfield · Bedfield · Li
Hunston · Great Ashfield · Bacton · Hestley Green · Bedingfield Green · Kenton · Monk Soham · Bedfield Little Gree
Stowlangtoft · Earl's Green · Wetheringsett · Blacksmith's Green · Earl Soham · Post Mill · 20
St Stanton · Hunston Green · Bacton Green · Cow Green · Canhams Green · Mendlesham · Aspall · Park Green · Aspall · Debenham
Norton Little Green · Haughley Green · Ford's Green · Mendlesham Green · Brockford Green · A140 · Wetherup Street · Fen Street · Ashfield cum Thorpe

3

Norton · Elmswell · Base Green · Ward Green · Brown Street · Gipping · Middlewood Green · Mickfield · Winston · Cretingham · Br
Broadgrass Green · 89 · Wetherden · Old Newton · Little Stonham · Mill Green · Fr
Broadgrass Gn · Haughley · Saxham Street · Forward Green · Stonham Aspal · Pettaugh · Framsden · Monewden · Leth
Woolpit · Dagworth · Stowupland · Earl Stonham · Crowfield Green · Suffolk Owl Sanctuary · Charsfiel
Woolpit Green · A14 · Harleston · 49 · Creeting St Mary · Crowfield · Helmingham Hall · Otley · Clopton Corner · Dallin
Clopton Green · Onehouse · Stowmarket · 50 · Beacon Hill · Helmingham · Gosbeck · Otley Green · Ashbocking
Rattlesden · Borley Green · Combs Ford · Coddenham · Hemingstone · Clopton

4

Buxhall Fen Street · Great Finborough · Combs · Needham Market · Barking · Lower Street · Barham · Bells Cross · Swilland · Burgh
Poystreet Green · Buxhall · Mill Green · Moats Tye · Battisford · Ringshall · Baylham · Henley · Witnesham · Grundisburgh
Hightown Green · Battisford Tye · Bird Street · Charles Tye · Barking Tye · Upper Street · Great Blakenham · Akenham · Tuddenham · Hasketo
Brettenham · Cross Green · Ringshall Stocks · Great Bricett · 52 · Claydon · Culpho · Boot Street · Great Bealing

5

Cooks Green · Wattisham · Nedging Tye · Greenstreet Green · Offton · A14 · Whitton · Playford · Little Bealings
ham Causeway · Hitcham · Naughton · Somersham · Little Blakenham · 53 · Castle Hill · Westerfield · Rushmere St Andrew · P+R
itcham Street · Bildeston · Nedging · Flowton · Bramford · Sproughton · A1156 · A1214 · Kesgrave
Monks Eleigh · Ash Street · Whatfield · Elmsett · Aldham · Burstall · IPSWICH · H

6

Chelsworth · Lindsey Tye · Semer · Stone Street · A1071 · RSPB · Hintlesham · Wight's Corner · Chantry · A1214 · A12
Rose G · Lindsey · St James Chapel · Duke Street · Washbrook · Copdock · 55 · Suffolk · A1156
Kersey Tye · Kersey · Coram Street · Chattisham · Coles Green · Belstead · 56 · Wherstead · A14 · 57 · Nacton · 58

7

Wicker Street Green · Kersey Upland · 89 · Layham · Little Wenham · Copdock · Alnesbourn Priory · Levington
Horners Green · Calais Street · Hadleigh Heath · Bower House Tye · Polstead Heath · Great Wenham · Capel St Mary · Freston · Woolverstone · River Orwell
xford · Whitestreet Green · Raydon · Shelley · Lower Raydon · Bentley · Tattingstone White Horse · Tattingstone · Chelmondiston · Pin Mill · St
tone · Polstead · Holton St Mary · East End · Holbrook · Lower Holbrook · Erwarton
ore · B1068 · A12 · East Bergholt · Upper Street · Stutton · Shotley Street · Shot

8

Nayland · Thorington Street · Higham · Stratford St Mary · Brantham · Alton Water · Harkstead
gton · Boxted · B1087 · 30 · Carters · Flatford Mill & Cottage N. · Cattawade · Holbrook Bay · River Stour · International Ferry Terminal
little · Boxted · Boxted Cross · Dedham · ngham · Mistley Towers · Mistley · 73 · Wrabness · Parkeston Quay

A · B · C · D · E · F

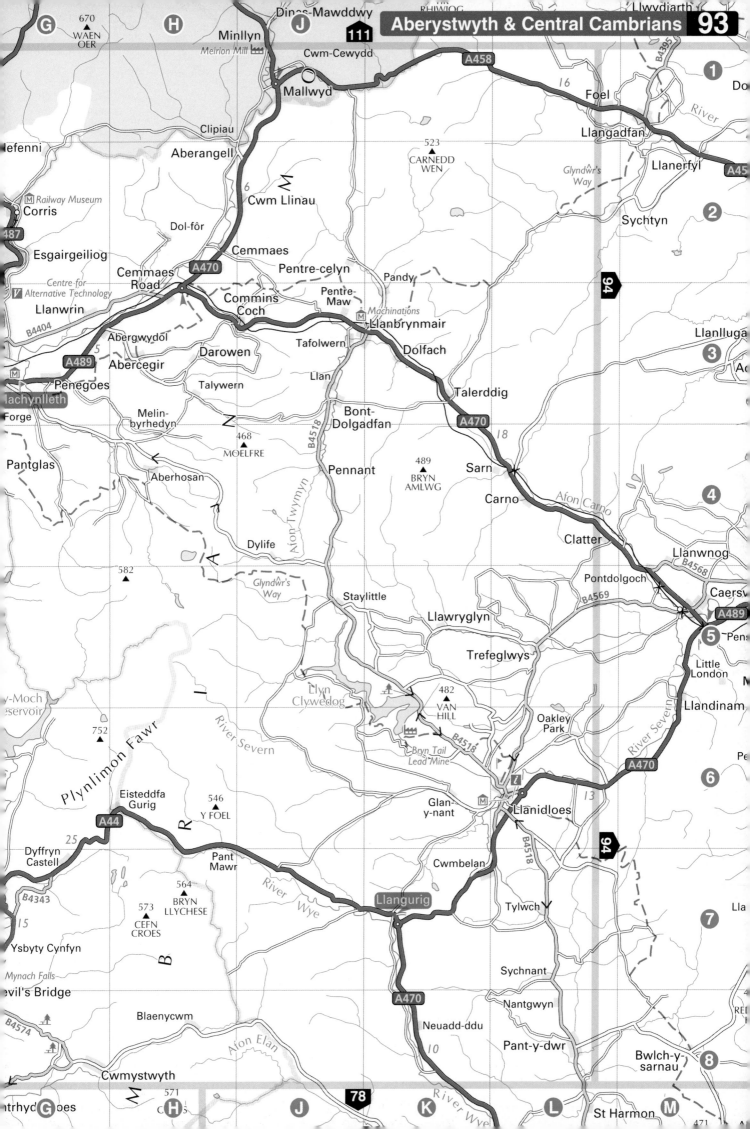

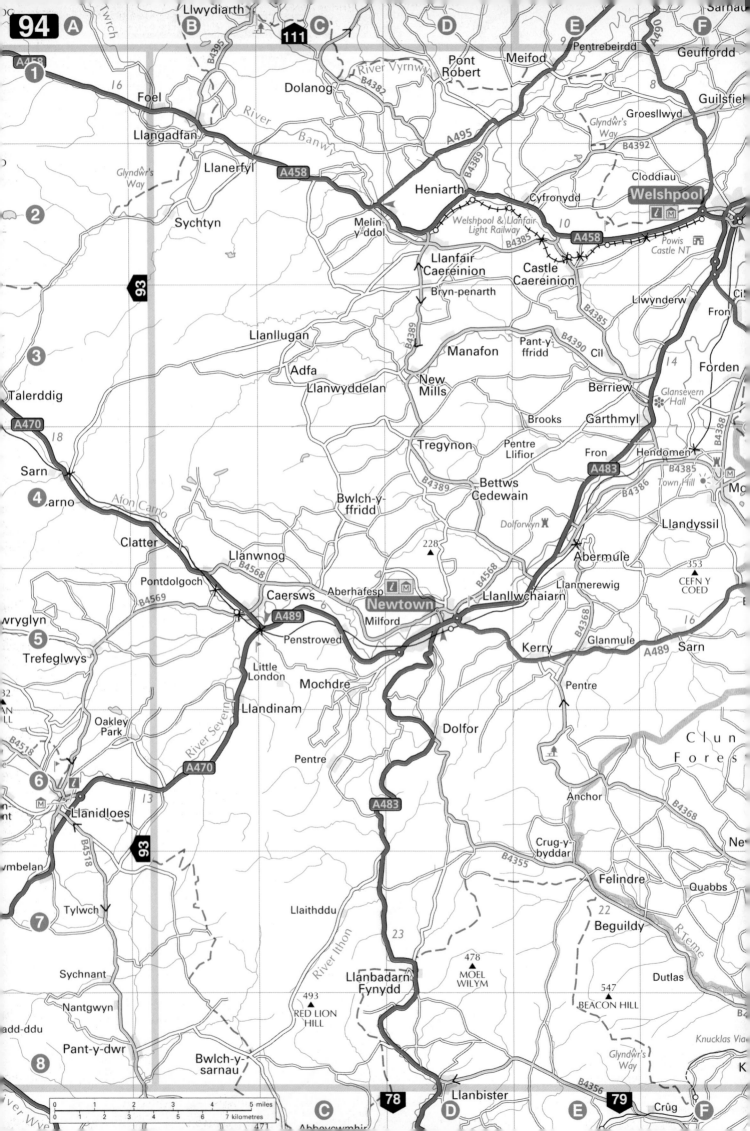

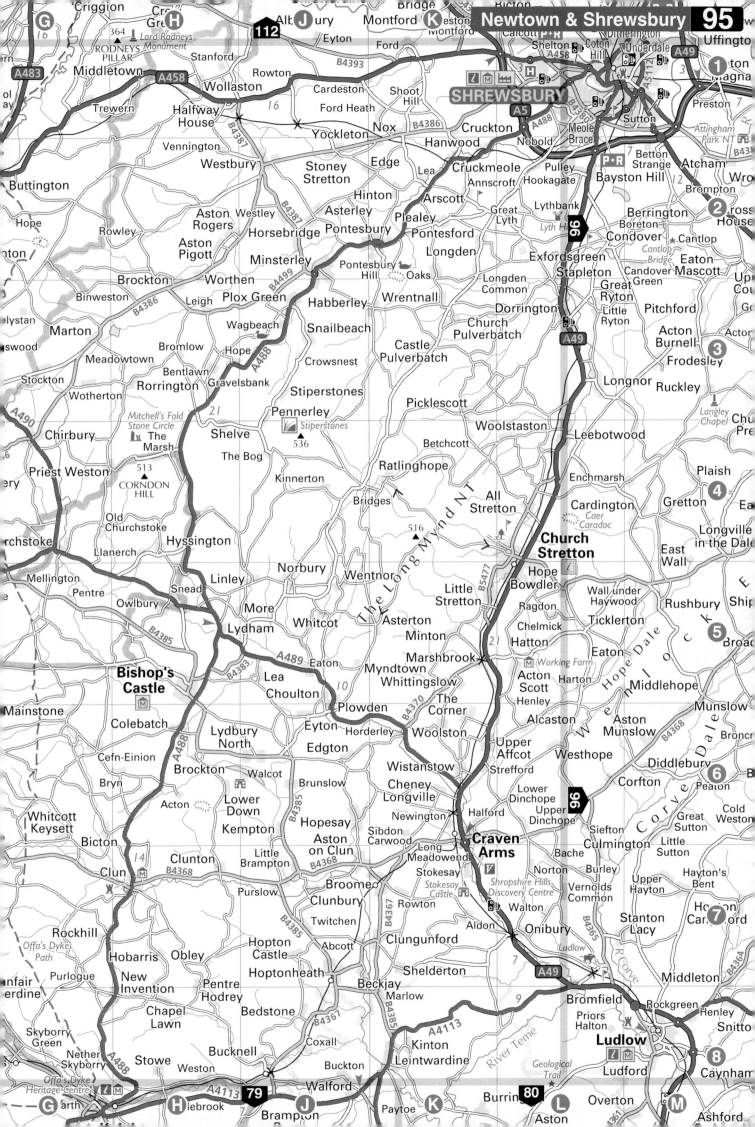

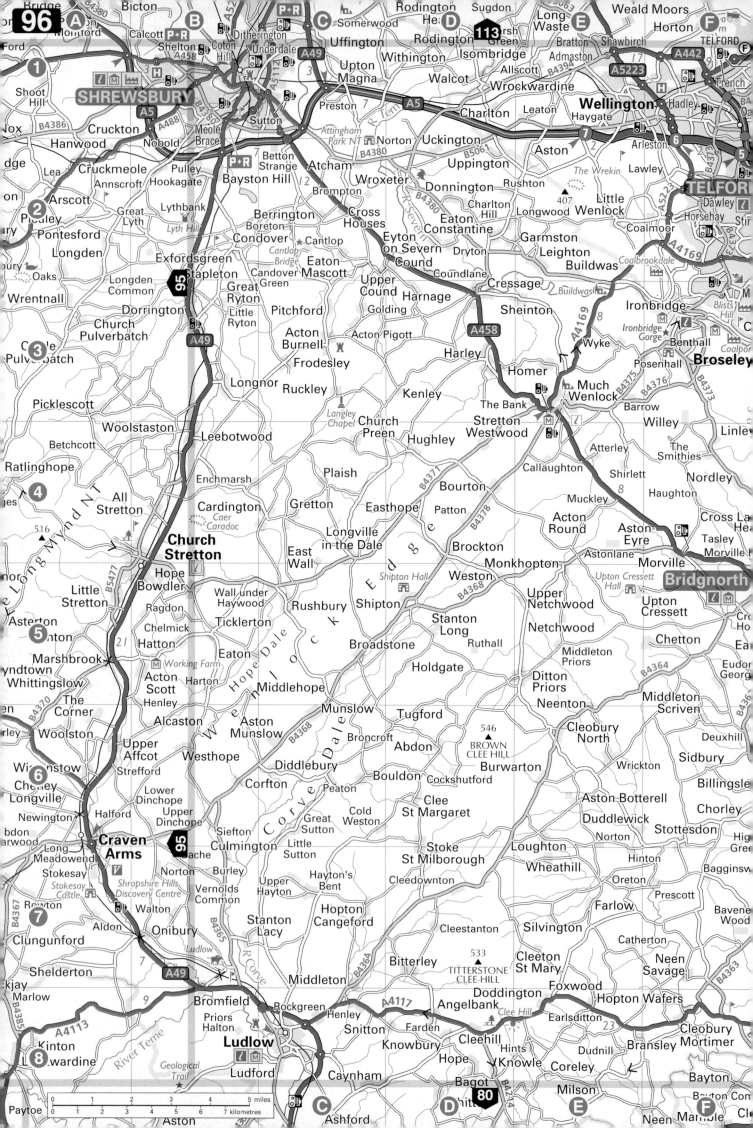

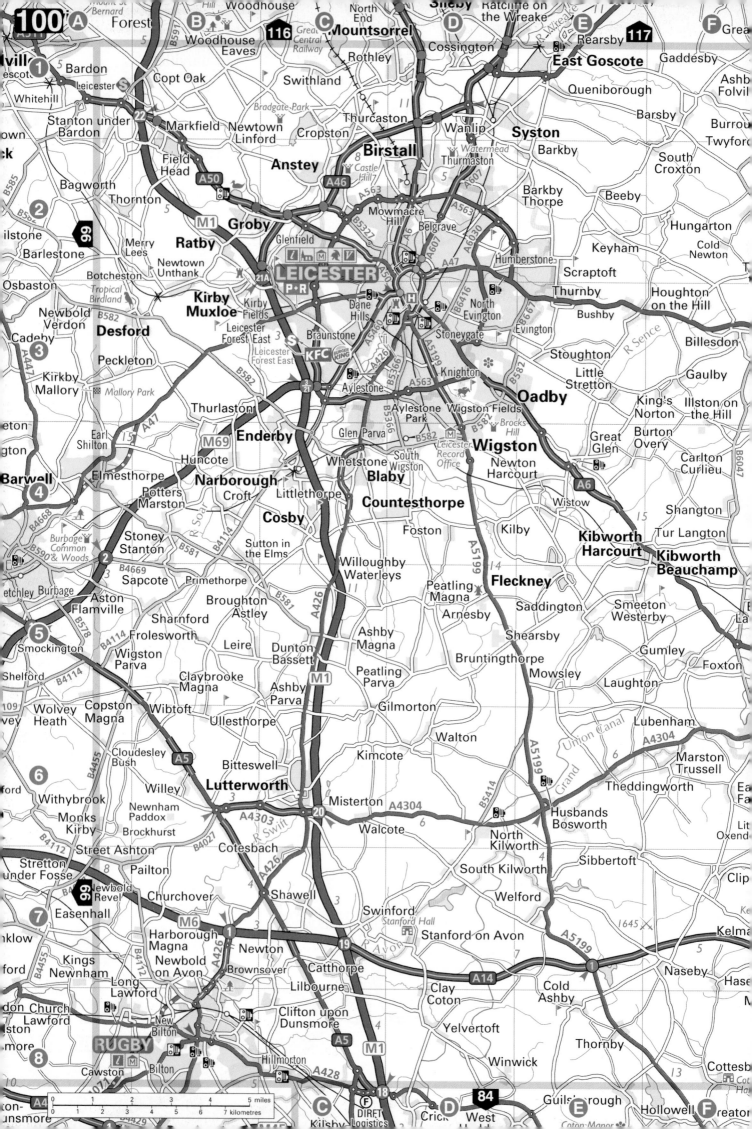

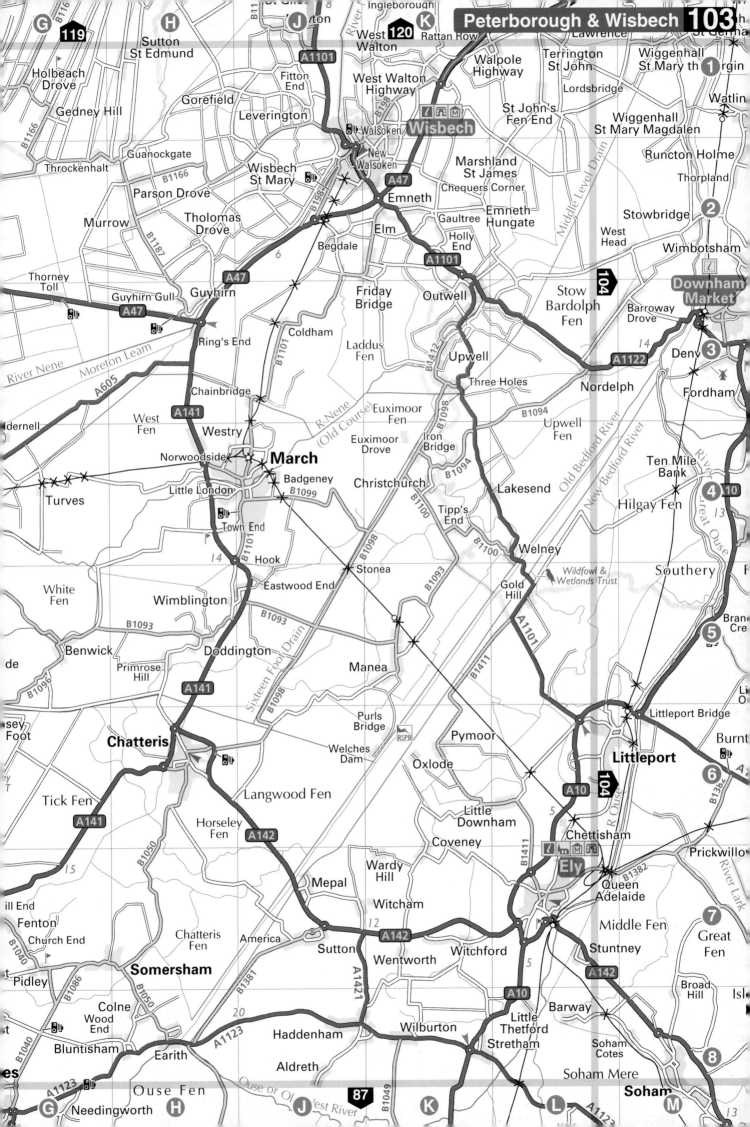

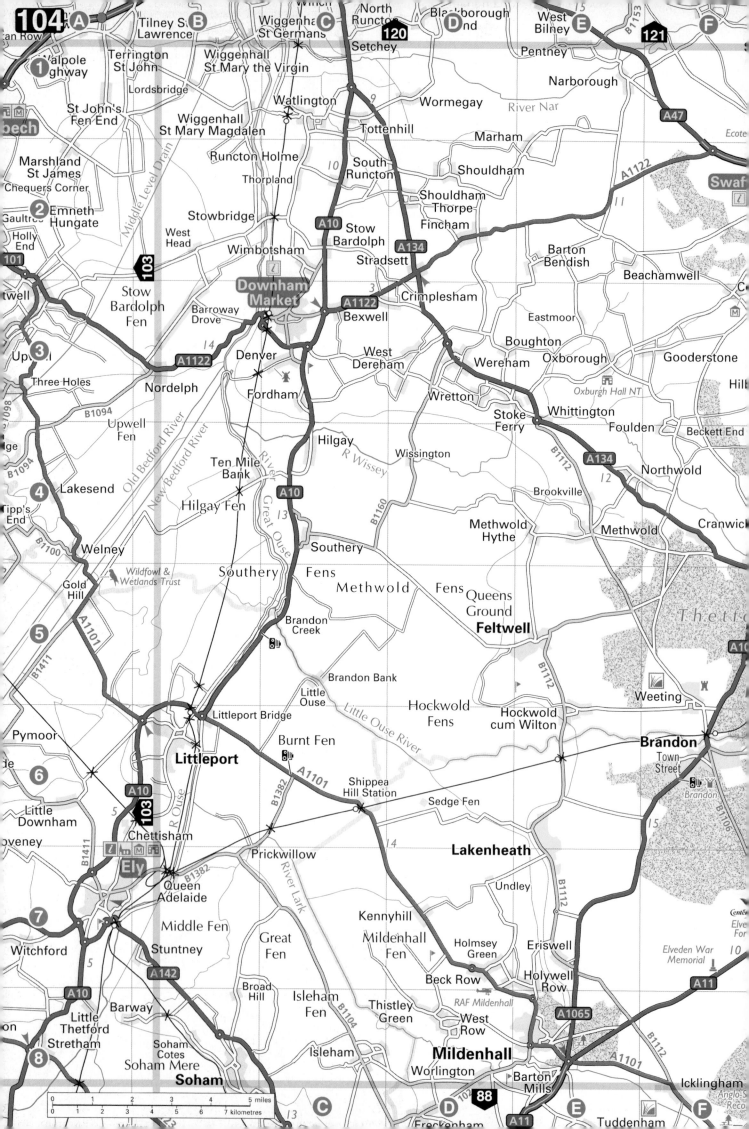

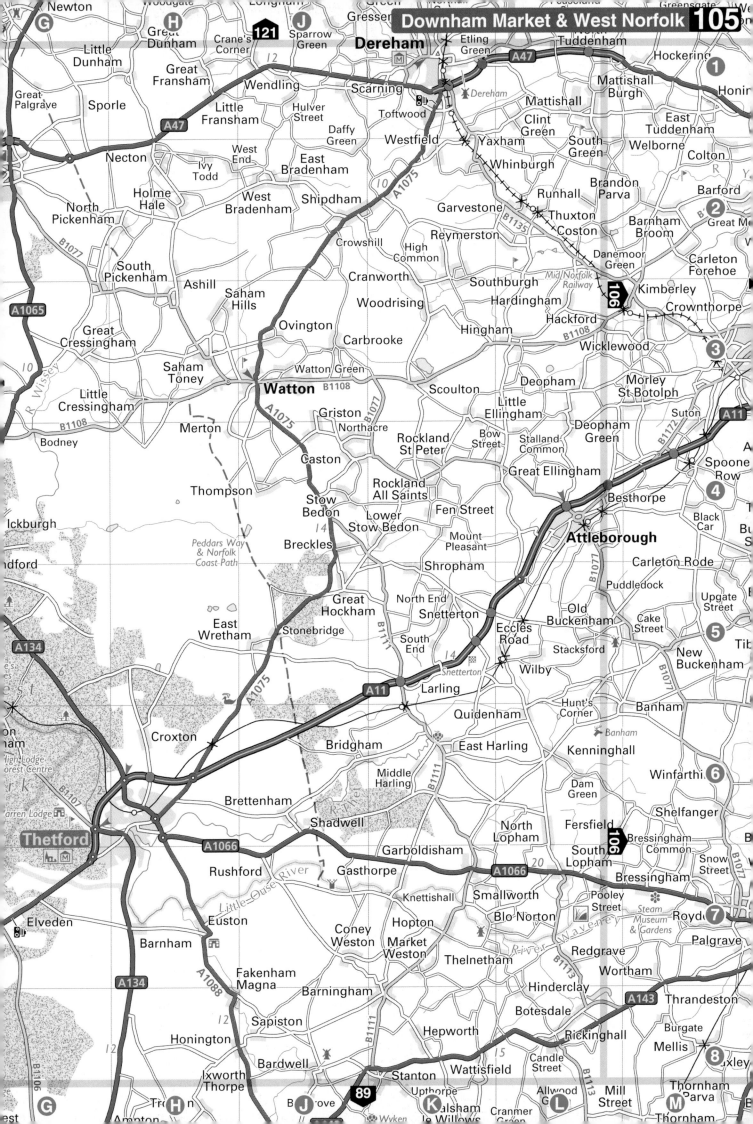

G **H** **J** **K**

Ranworth
house
Panxworth

Broadland
Conservation Centre
Pilson
Green

Thurne
Clippesby **123**
Cargate
Green

B..gh St
..garet Ormesby
St Michael

Caister-on-Sea

Billockby

The Village

Filby

Mautby

West End

West Caister

Thrigby
Thrigby Hall

Caister

1

Town
Green
..ield
..ath

South
Walsham
Burlingham
Green

Upton
Acle

Stokesby
Runham

A149

Hemblington
North
Burlingham

Damgate

2

..on
Blofield
Lingwood
Beighton
Tunstall
A47
9
THE BROADS
River Yare
Runham
Southtown
GREAT YARMOUTH
RSPB
..all
..umpshaw

South
Burlingham
Moulton
St Mary
Halvergate
Gorleston on Sea

RSPB
Buckenham
Freethorpe
Wickhampton
Burgh
Castle
Berney
Arms
Fort
Bradwell

3
..ngham
Hassingham
Southwood
Freethorpe
Common
Belton
Browston Green
Hobland Hall
H
10
Rockland
St Mary
Cantley
Limpenhoe
Witton Green
Fritton
Fritton Lake
Countryworld
Hopton on Sea
..ellington
..by
..ary
Carleton
St Peter
Langley
Street
Hardley
Street
Nogdam End
Reedham
St Olaves
Lound
Somerleyton Hall
& Gardens
A12
Corton
Mill Common
Chedgrave
Lower
Thurlton
Herringfleet
Somerleyton
4
Thurton
Loddon
Norton
Subcourse
Thurlton
Thorpe
A143
Blundeston
B1074
Pleasurewood Hills
Gunton
Mundham
Hales
B1136
Haddiscoe
Somerleyton
Oulton
Seething
Raveningham
13
Maypole
Green
Toft Monks
A146
Kirby Cane
Wheatacre
Burgh
St Peter
Oulton
Broad
LOWESTOFT
Lowestoft Ness
5
..waite
..ary
Stockton
A143
Bull's
Green
Aldeby
Kirkley
..gay
..n
Ellingham
Kirby Row
Gillingham
River Waveney
Pakefield
Wainford
Geldeston
9
A146
A1145
Shipmeadow
B1062
Worlingham
Barnby
Carlton Colville
Mile End
Mettingham
Barsham
Ringsfield
Beccles
North
Cove
Gisleham
Broome
..he Otter Trust
Ilketshall
St Andrew
Ingate
Place
Mutford
Rushmere
6
..xton
..Aviation
Ilketshall
St John
Ilketshall
St Margaret
Ringsfield
Corner
Winter
Flora
Ellough
Hulver
Street
Henstead
Black
Street
Kessingland
Suffolk
Wildlife
Park
Kessingland
Beach
..rgaret
..lmham
St Michael
South Elmham
Redisham
Sotterley
14
Benacre
Benacre Ness
..ll Saints
..h Elmham
Ilketshall
St Lawrence
Stone
Street
Cox
Common
Shadingfield
A12
Wrentham
B1127
A145
..James
..h Elmham
Rumburgh
Mill
Common
Stoven
Church
Street
South Cove
Covehithe
7
Spexhall
Brampton
Frostenden
Cove Bottom
Suffolk Heritage Coast
Wissett
Westhall
Uggeshall
Barnaby Green
..stead
..rva
Chediston
Green
Broadway
Holton
Wangford
B1126
Reydon
Sole
Bay
..atfield
Cheshire
91
Halesworth
Cookley
Mells
Wenhaston
Blyford
A1095
Lighthouse
Southwold
..ntingfield
Blackheath
Blythburgh
B1123
8
Walpole
Bramfield
Thorington
B1387
Walberswick
..leveningham
91
A12
Suffolk
Coast
..Ubbeston

G **H** **J** **K** **L** **M**

A · B · C · D · E · F

1

CAERNARFON

2

BAY

Lleyn Heritage
Coast

Trefor

Trwyn y
Grolech

564
YR EIFL

3

Carreg Ddu

Porth
Nefyn

B4417

Llithfa

Morfa
Nefyn

Pistyll

Llwy

Porth Dinllaen
Groesffordd

Nefyn

Fron B43

Edern

Bodfuan

Porth Ysgaden

4

Rhos-y-llan

Tudweiliog

A497

7

Llann

LLEYN

Efailnew

Porth
Colman

Dinas
371
Carn
Fadrum

B4415

Denio

Pen-y-graig

Bryn-
mawr

Llaniestyn

Garnfadryn

Rhyd-y-clafdy

A499

14

B4417

Meyllteyrn

7

Penrhos

Llangwnnadl

Sarn

Botwnnog

Llanbedrog

5

17

B4413

Nanhoron

B4413

Mynytho

Bryncroes

Trwyn Llanbedro

Porthoer

Llandegwning

Rhydlios

Rhoshirwaun

St Tudwal's
Road

Plas-Yn-
Rhiw-NT

Llangian

Anelog

B4413

Abersoch

Penycaerau

Y Rhiw

Llanengan

Uwchmynydd

Aberdaron

Llanfaelrhys

Porth
Ysgo

Porth Neigwl

Bwlchtocyn

Sarn Bach

Marchros

St Tudwal's
Island East

6

St Tudwal's
Island West

Aberdaron
Bay

Porth
Geiriad

Lleyn Heritage
Coast

Bardsey Sound

St Mary's

7

BARDSEY ISLAND

G

H

J

Llandwrog
Groeslon
Moel
Tryfan
Glynllifon
Carmel **125**
Cilgwyn
Fron
Nantlle
MYNYDD MAWR
B4418
698

Cwellyn
1085
SNOWDON
pass
Llyn
Llydaw

1

Penygroes
Talysarn
Rhyd-Ddu
A4085
747
YR
ARAN
Hafod y
Llan NT
Glanaber
A498
Llyn
Gwynant
12

2

Pontlyfni
Aberdesach
Llanllyfni
655
Nebo
Nasareth
Llywelyn
Cottage NT
Beddgelert
Sygun
Copper Mine
Nant Gwynant
Gelli Iago NT

Rhiwbryfd
Tan-y-grisiau

nog-fawr
-gôch
Capeluchaf
Pant
Glas
782
MOEL
HEBOG
Nantmor
Croesor **110**
770
MOELWYN MAWR
711
MOELWYN
BACH
Powers
Tan-y-Gri

522
GYRN-DDU
A487
Bryncir
Garn-
Dolbenmaen
Llanfihangel-
y-pennant
552
MOEL
DDU
A498
A4085
8
B4410
Rhyd
Ffestiniog
Railway
Tan-y-sarn
yd-
y-sarn

3

Llanaelhaearn
Glan-Dwyfach
Dolbenmaen
Golan
Prenteg
Garreg
7
Afon Glaslyn
Llanfrothen
Tan-y-Bwlch
Tan-y-
Bwlch
Maentwrog
A496

PENINSULA
21
St Cybi's
Well
Llangybi
Rhoslan
Penmorfa
Tremadog
A487
Penrhyndeudraeth
Gellilydan

Pencaenewydd
Y Ffor
B4354
Llanarmon
Pentrefelin
Wern
Porthmadog
Welsh Highland
Railway
3
Minffordd
Toll
Llandecwyn

Trawsfy

4

erch
R Erch
Pennarth
Fawr
Llanystumdwy
Chwilog 13
Criccieth
Morfa
Bychan
Borth-
y-Gest
Ffestiniog
Railway
Portmeirion
9
Bryn-bwbach
Talsarnau
Llyn
rawsfy

Pen-ychain
Traeth Bach
Harlech
Point
Llanfihangel-
y-traethau
Morfa
Harlech
A496
624
MOEL YSGYFARNOGOD

5

Tremadog
Bay
Harlech
B4573
Harlech
Castle
SNOWDONIA
NATIONAL

Llanfair
PARK
720
RHINOG FAWR

6

Mi
Llandanwg
Llanbedr
Pentre Gwynfryn
754
Y LLETHR

Shell
Island
Maes Artro
Centre
Morfa Dyffryn
11
589
MOELFRE
750
DIFFWYS

Coed Ystumgwern
Llanenddwyn
Afon Ysgethin

7

Dyffryn Ardudwy
Burial
Cors-y-
Gedol
Tal-y-bont **110**
Bontddu
RSPB

Llanddwywe
Caerdeon
Penmaenpool

Llanaber
10
A493

8

Cutiau
A496
Afon Mawddach

Barmouth
Barmouth Bridge
Fairbourne &
Barmouth
Steam Railway
Arthog

Barmouth
Bay
Fairbourne

G

H

J

92

K

L

M

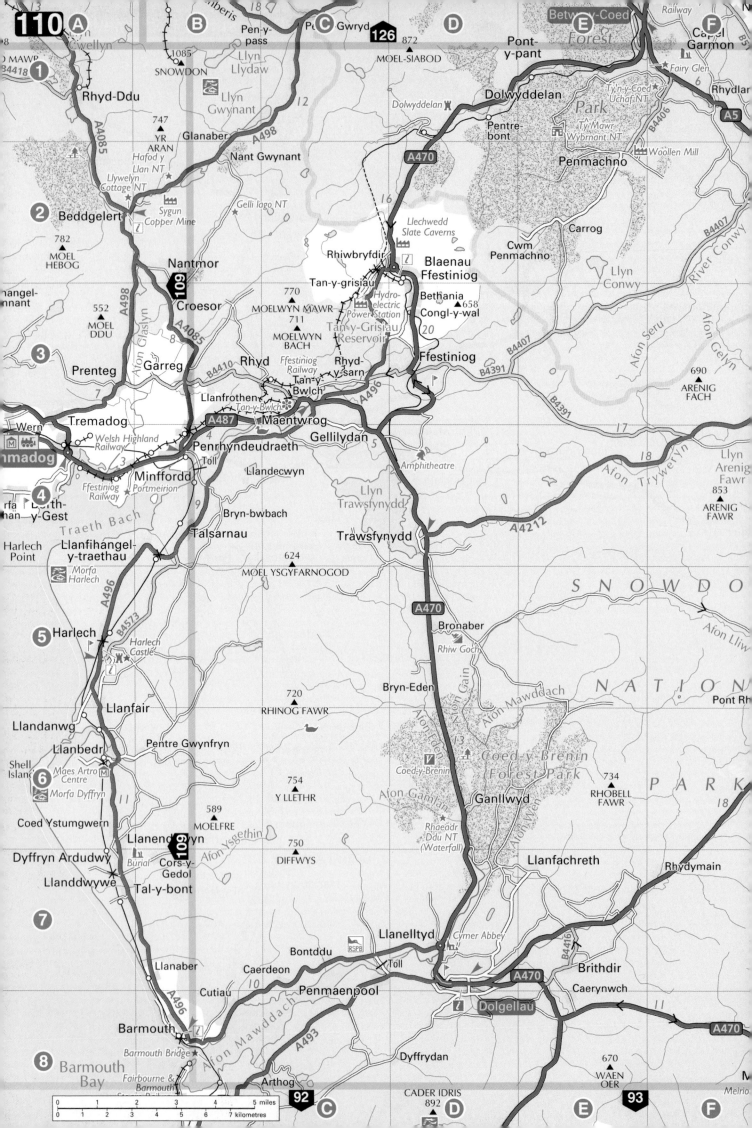

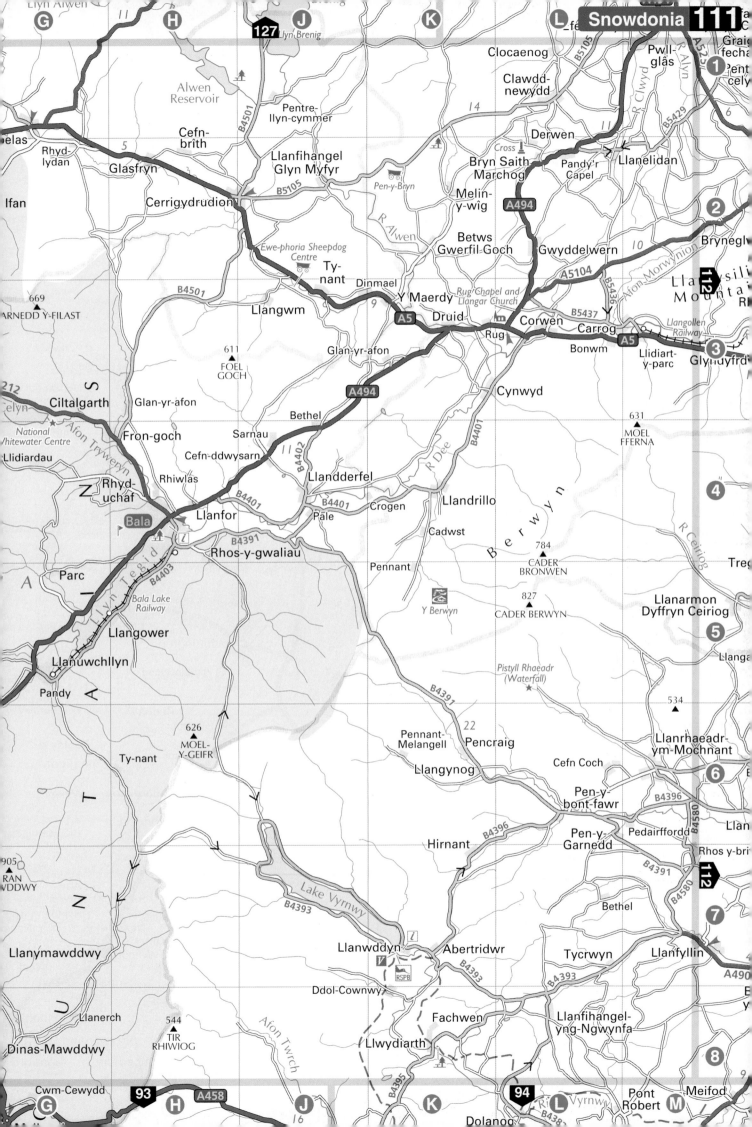

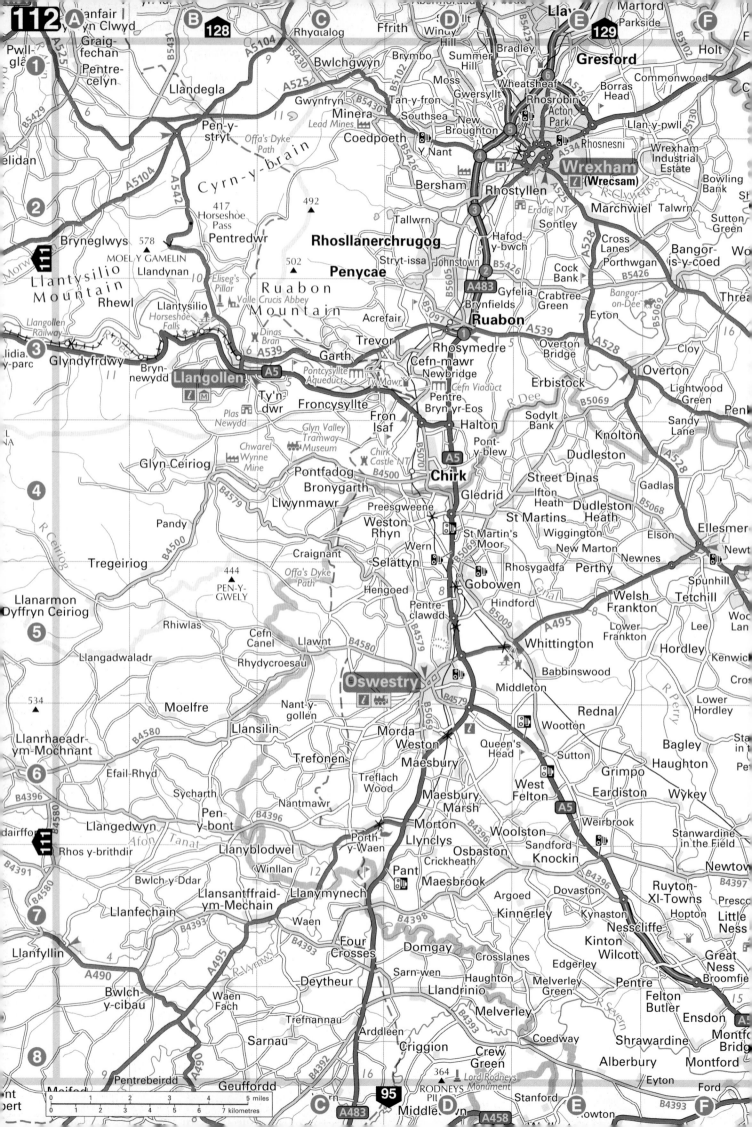

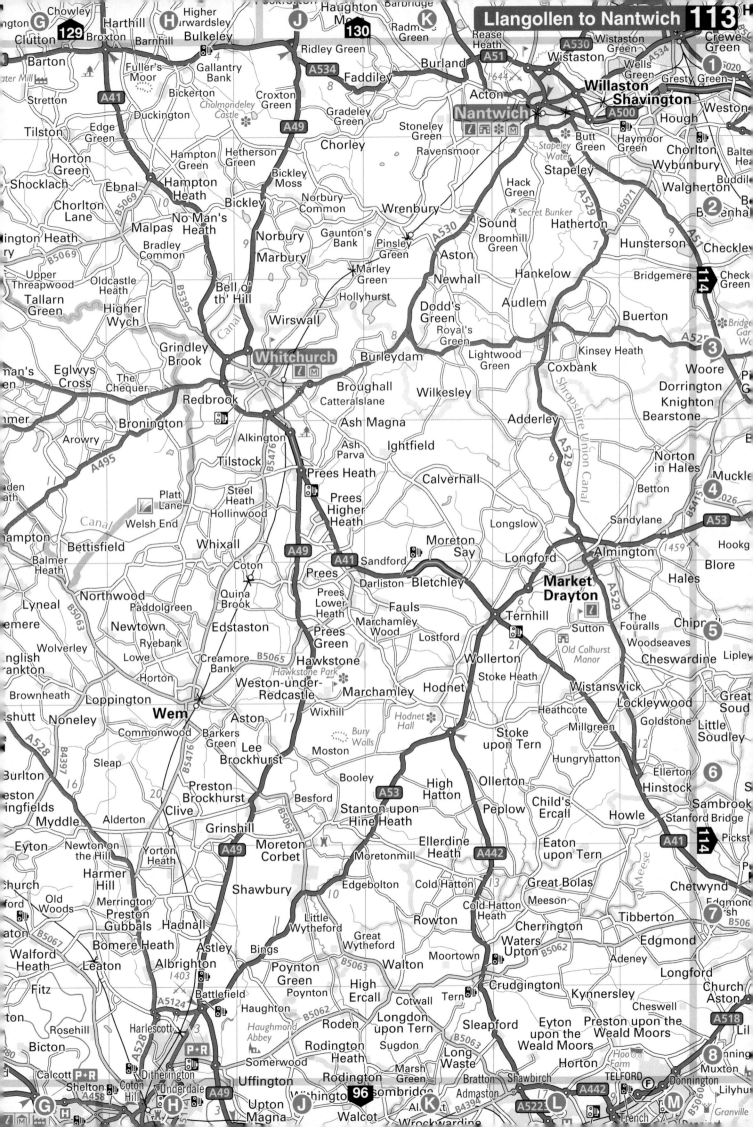

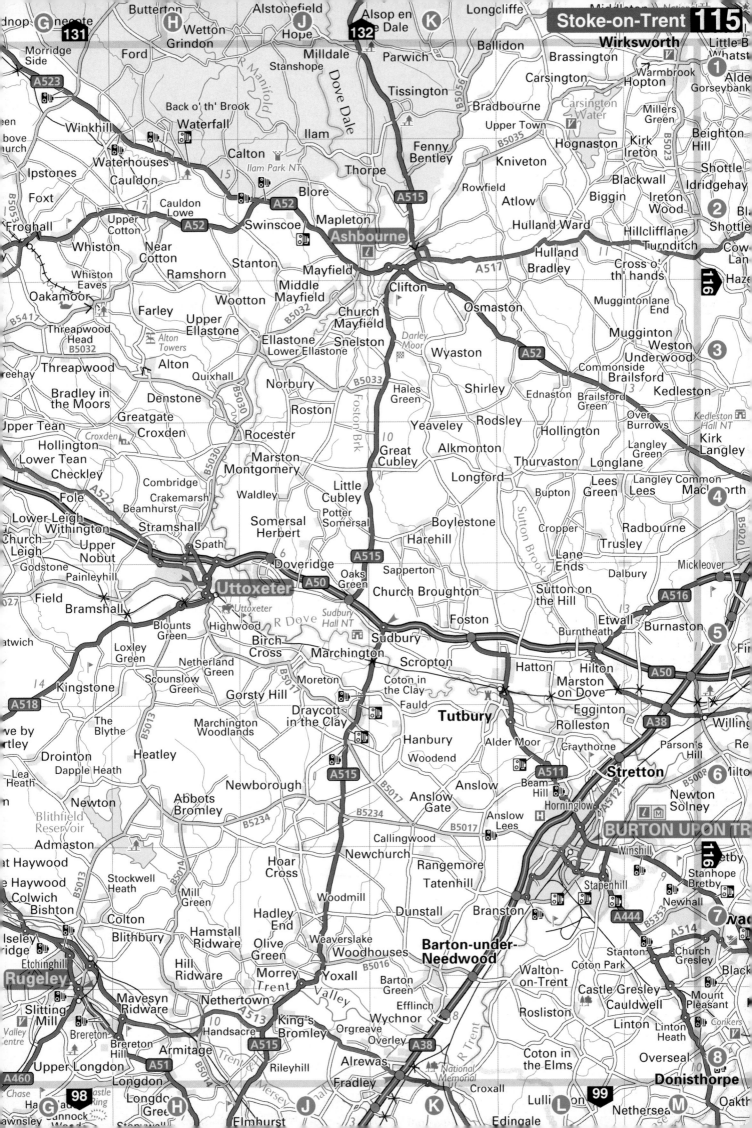

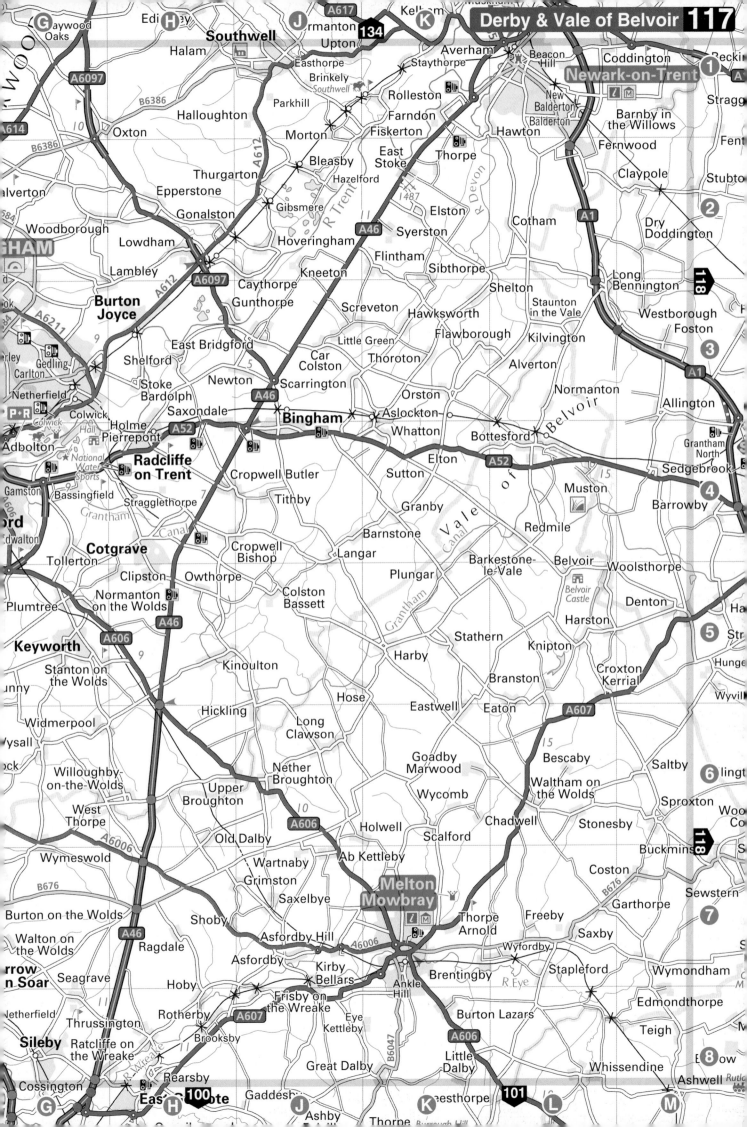

Newark-on-Trent

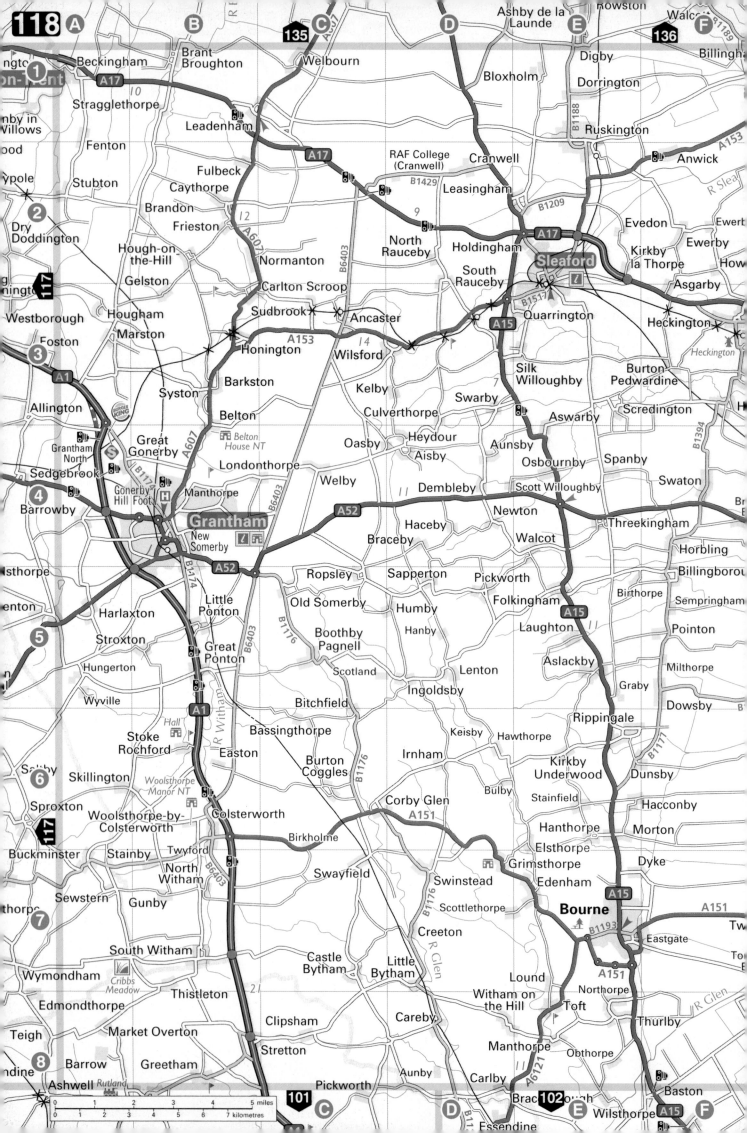

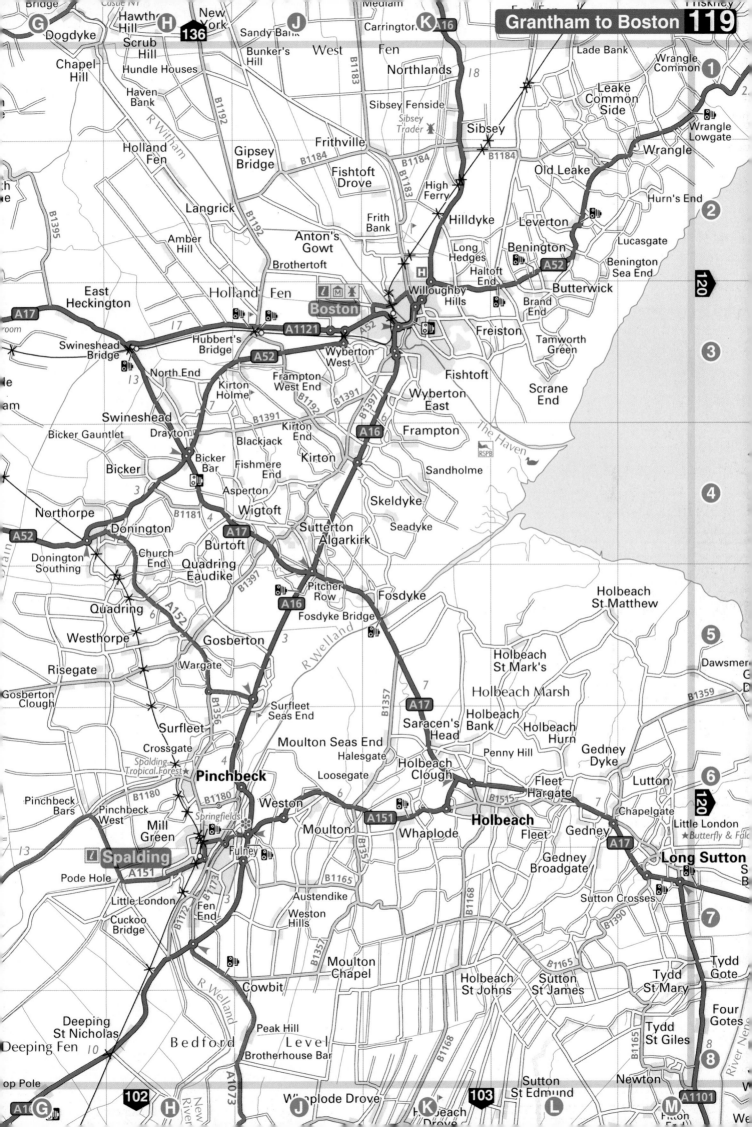

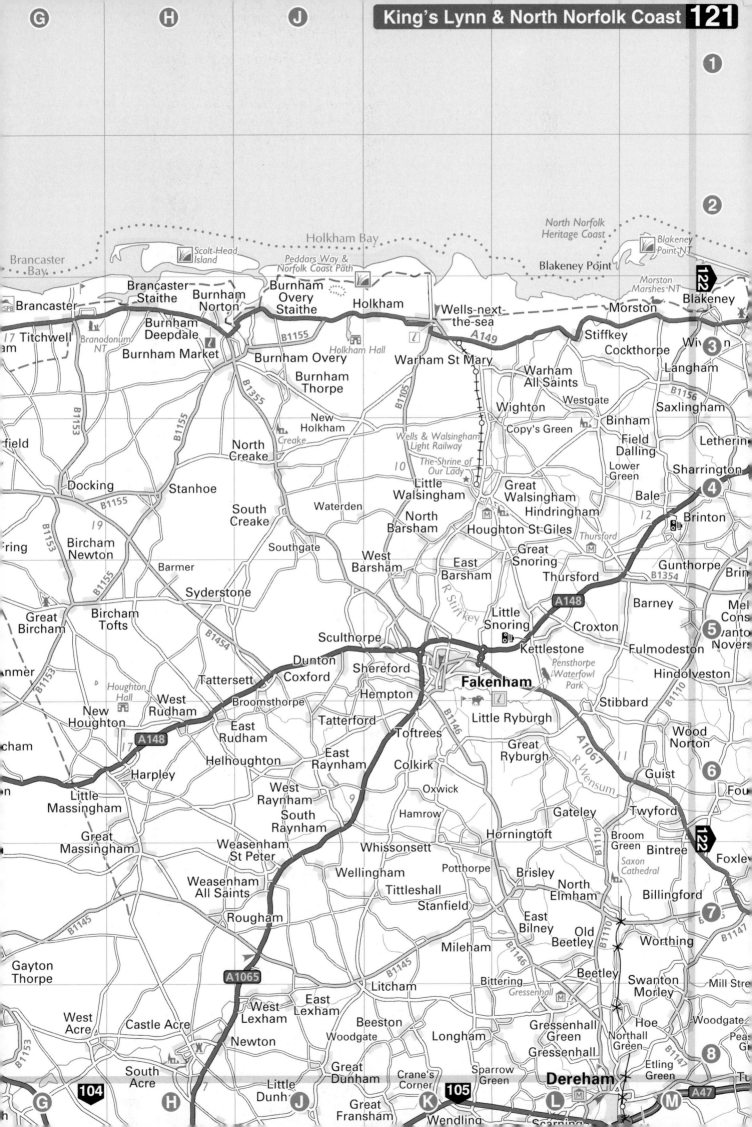

G   **H**   **J**

Brancaster Bay

North Norfolk Heritage Coast

Holkham Bay

Scolt-Head Island

Peddars Way & Norfolk Coast Path

Blakeney Point NT

Blakeney Point

Morston Marshes NT

Brancaster Staithe

Brancaster

SPB

Burnham Norton

Burnham Overy Staithe

Holkham

Wells-next-the-sea

A149

Morston

Blakeney

122

Titchwell
ham
17

Branodonum NT

Burnham Deepdale

Burnham Market

B1155

Holkham Hall

Warham St Mary

Stiffkey

Cockthorpe

Wiv n

Langham

3

Burnham Overy

Warham All Saints

Westgate

Saxlingham

Letherin

B1156

B1355

Burnham Thorpe

New Holkham

B1105

Wighton

Copy's Green

Binham

Field Dalling

field

Creake

Wells & Walsingham Light Railway

B1153

North Creake

Lower Green

Sharrington

4

Docking

Stanhoe

10

The Shrine of Our Lady

Little Walsingham

Great Walsingham

Hindringham

Bale

Brinton

B1155

South Creake

Waterden

North Barsham

Houghton St-Giles

Thursford

12

Brin

19

Southgate

West Barsham

East Barsham

Great Snoring

Gunthorpe

Barney

5

Bircham Newton

Barmer

R Stiffkey

Thursford

B1354

B1153

Syderstone

A148

Little Snoring

Croxton

Fulmodeston

Mel Cons anto Novers

Great Bircham

Bircham Tofts

B1454

Sculthorpe

Kettlestone

Hindolveston

B1110

nmer

Dunton

Shereford

Fakenham

Penthorpe Waterfowl Park

Stibbard

Tattersett

Coxford

Hempton

Little Ryburgh

A1067

Wood Norton

New Houghton

Houghton Hall

West Rudham

Broomsthorpe

Tatterford

Great Ryburgh

R Wensum

Guist

6

A148

East Rudham

East Raynham

B1146

11

cham

Harpley

Helhoughton

Colkirk

Oxwick

Gateley

Twyford

122

Little Massingham

West Raynham

South Raynham

9

Hamrow

Horningtoft

Broom Green

Bintree

Foxle

Great Massingham

Weasenham St Peter

Whissonsett

Wellingham

Potthorpe

Brisley

Saxon Cathedral

Billingford

7

Weasenham All Saints

Tittleshall

Stanfield

North Elmham

B1110

B1141

Rougham

Mileham

East Bilney

Old Beetley

Worthing

Gayton Thorpe

A1065

Bittering

Gressenhall

Beetley

Swanton Morley

Mill Stre

West Acre

West Lexham

East Lexham

Beeston

Woodgate

Longham

Gressenhall Green

Gressenhall

Hoe

Northall Green

Woodgate

8

Castle Acre

Newton

B1145

B1147

Woodgate

Pea G

B1153

South Acre

104

Little Dunh

J

Great Dunham

Crane's Corner

105

Sparrow Green

Dereham

A47

M

Great Fransham

Wendling

Scarning

Tu

G   **H**   **J**   **K**   **L**   **M**

G · H · J · K · L · M

1 · 2 · 3 · 4 · 5 · 6 · 7 · 8

Mundesley
tow Mill
Paston
B1159
gthorpe
Bacton
Walcott
Pollard
Street
rpe
Happisburgh
Witton
Ridlington
Ridlington
Street
Crostwight
Whimpwell Green
Happisburgh
Common
Eccles on Sea
oning
Hempstead
Lessingham
Ingham
Corner
Sea Palling
riggate
East
Ruston
B1159
Ingham
Waxham
tead
Stalham
Calthorpe
Street
Dilham
Stalham
Green
Hickling
rt
Low
Street
A149
Horsey Corner
lburgh
Sutton
Hickling Green
Horsey
Pennygate
Barton
Turf
Wood
Street
Hickling
Heath
Hill Common
Horsey Windpump NT
d
Barton
Broad
Catfield
Hickling
Broad
Neatishead
Catfield
Common
East
Somerton
eet
Irstead
Sharp
Green
West
Somerton
Threehammer
Common
Potter
Heigham
Winterton-on-Sea
Hoveton
Ludham
Martham
A1062
Johnson's
Street
Bastwick
Cess
Hemsby
Hemsby
Hole
pper
reet
R Thurne
Newport
Horning
Upper Street
Repps
Ormesby
Broad
Scratby
Bure
Marshes
Rollesby
9
Ormesby
St Margaret
astwick
Thurne
B1152
Burgh St
Margaret Ormesby
California
hous
Broadland
Conservation Centre
Clippesby
St Michael
Ranworth
Pilson
Green
Cargate
Green
Billockby
9
Caister-on-
Sea
140
Fairhaven
R Bure
107
A149
Pan
G
rth
South
Walsham
H
Green
J
The Village
Filby
K
L
M
Town
1064
Thrigby
Mautby

A **B** **C** **D** **E** **F**

1 **2** **3** **4** **5** **6** **7** **8**

The Skerries

Wylfa Head   Cema Bay

North Anglesey Heritage Coast

Cemlyn Bay   Cemaes

Hen Borth   NT

CARMEL HEAD   Tregele

Llanfairynghornwy   Llanfechell

17   Llanfflewyn

Holyhead Bay   Llanrhyddlad   Llanba

Church Bay   Llanfaethlu

Dublin   Llanddeusant   Elim

Dublin Dun Laoghaire   Stryd-y-Facsen   Llantrisant

Porth Tywynmawr   Llanfwrog   Pen-llyn   Llyn Llywena

North Stack   Breakwater Quarry   i   Llanfachraeth   Llanfigael

Gogarth Bay   Holyhead Mountain Hut Group   Holyhead (Caergybi)   Penrhos

South Stack   Llaingoch   3   B5109

Holyhead Mountain Heritage Coast   RSPB   Penrhos-Feilw   1   Llanynghenedl   Bodedern

South Stack   Kingsland   2   A5   Valley   A5025

Penrhyn Mawr   Porth Dafarch NT   Trefignath   A55   Caergeiliog   Bryngw

Treaddur Bay   B4545   3   4

HOLY ISLAND   Four Mile Bridge   Llanfihangel yn Nhowyn   5

Llanfair-yn-Neubwll   Llechylched   A4080

Rhoscolyn   Plas Cymyran   RSPB   Capel Gwyn   10   Pencar

Rhoscolyn Head   Ty Newydd   Llanfaelog

Cymyran Bay   Bryn Du

Rhosneigr   A4080

Barclodiad y Gawres

Porth Trecastell   Llang

Aberffraw   Llang

Aberffraw Bay

Aberffraw Bay Heritage Coast   Malltrae

Llanddwyn

C A E R N A R F O N

B A Y

0   1   2   3   4   5 miles
0   1   2   3   4   5   6   7 kilometres

A · B · C · D · E · F

1

2

Seawatch Centre

Moelfre
Llanallgo
Marian-glas
Benllech
Red Wharf Bay
Red Wharf Bay
Glan-yr-afon
Penmon Priory
Puffin Island
Black Point
Caim Toll
Penmon
Great Orme Heritage Coast
GREAT ORMES HEAD
Conwy Bay
Llandudno
Llanrhos
Pen
Deganwy
A546 B5115 A470
Llanddona
Llangoed
17
Tywyn
Pentraeth
Llanfaes
Dwygyfylchi
16A 16
Conwy
Conwy Castle
RSPB
A5025 B5109
Gaol & Courthouse
Beaumaris Castle
Penmaenmawr
15A
Penmaenan
Capelulo
18
A47
Beaumaris
Llanfairfechan
15 14
Garizim
Henryd
Llansadwrn
A55
Nant-y-pandy
Llandegfan
14
Gorddinog
SNOWDONIA
610 TAL-Y-FAN
Rowen
B5106
Menai Bridge
A545
13
Abergwyngregyn
Ty'n-y-Groes
Bangor
Afon Anafon
Caerhun
Anglesey Column
Penrhyn NT
NATIONAL
Castell
Vale of Conwy
G
Llandygai
Afon
580
Aber Waterfall
Llanbedr-y-Cennin
Tal-y-Con
Britannia Bridge
Penrhos garnedd
12
Tal-y-bont
MOEL WINION
Tal-y-Bont
16
Plas Newydd NT
9 11
A55
11
Llanllechid
757
942
Dolgarrog
Capel-y-graig
3
Rachub
Y DROSGL
FOEL-FRAS
Waen-wen
Glasinfryn
Afon Dullyn
Pont Dolgarrog
Y Felinheli
Rhyd-y-groes
Gerlan
Afon Caseg
Llyn Eigiau
Maena
Seion
Pentir
Tregarth
Bethesda
Sling
Ogwen Bank
P A R K
Afon Ddu
Bethel
Waen-pentir
B4409
Llanddeiniolen
12
Rhiwlas
Mynydd Llandygai
1062
Greenwood Centre
Saron
CARNEDD LLEWELYN
Trefriw Woollen Mill
Trefriw
Penisarwaun
Rhiwen
125
Llyn Cowlyd
Llanrug
Deiniolen
1044
Pont-rug
Clwt-y-bont
CARNEDD DAFYDD
Gallt-y-foel
Llanrhychwyn
Llanrwst
Cwm-y-glo
Brynrefail
923
Pont Pen-y-benglog
Gwydir Castle
Caeathro
Padarn
Llyn Padarn
Llyn Ogwen
Llyn Crafnant
Gwydir
Uchaf Chap
442
Llanberis Lake Railway
Groeslon
Dinorwic
ELIDIR FAWR
946
Y GARN
Gwydyr
Llanberis
Welsh Slate
917
Y Stablau
Electric Mountain
Dolbadarn
Y TRYFAN
Llyn Geirionydd
Waunfawr
Llyn Peris
Nant Peris
National Mountain Centre
Capel Curig
Forest
Betws Garmon
726
Gwastadnant
999
994
A5
MOEL EILIO
Snowdon Mountain Railway
GLYDER FAWR
GLYDER FACH
A4086
Pont Cyfyng
Y Stablau
Rhosgadfan
Penyffridd
Pass of Llanberis
698
Pen-y-pass
Pen-y-Gwryd
872
Pont-y-pant
Moel
Llyn Cwellyn
1085
MOEL-SIABOD
Betws-y-Coed

0 1 2 3 4 5 miles
0 1 2 3 4 5 6 7 kilometres

B · C · D · E · F

110
125

G H J

1

2

128

Prestatyn

RSPB

Gronant

Gwes

3

Llanasa

Picton

e Ormes Head

Penrhyn
Bay

Rhyl

Meliden

Gwaenysgor

Trelog

Rhôs-on-Sea

Kinmel
Bay

Abergele Roads

Kinmel Bay

Trelawnyd

Berth

Axton

Walwer

Colwyn Bay
(Bae Colwyn)

Towyn

Dyserth

12

ndrillo-
n-Rhos

20

A547

Old
Colwyn

7

A55

23

23A Pensarn

A547

Cwm

4

Mochdre

21

22

Abergele

24

Rhuddlan

Rhuallt

29

30

udno
ction

Llanddulas

A547

St George

24A

25

A55

26

27A

28

Pen-

Llanelian-
yn-Rhôs

Llysfaen

Rhyd-
y-foel

Pengwern

Bodelwyddan

27

St Asaph

ffraid
nwy

Bryn-
y-Maen

Dolwen

Bodelwyddan

Tremeirchion

Caerwys

Graig

5

41

Glascoed

Sodom

Afon-w

Groesffordd
Marli

Trofarth

Dawn

Betws-
yn-Rhos

Pentre Isaf

Trefnant

Bodfari

Llanfair
Talhaiarn

Llannefydd

River Elwy

Cefn
Berain

Henllan

Green

6

langw

Hafodunos

Llangernyw

Fron

Kilford

Waen

Brook
House

Llandyrnog

Denbigh

Llwyn

Ff

Llansannan

Rhydgaled

Groes

Llanynys

Pandy
Tudur

Tan-y-
fron

Pentre
Llanrhaeadr

A543

A544

B5435

Bylchau

Waen

Peniel

Prion

Pentre

7

Rhewl

Gwytherin

Nantglyn

Pant-
pastynog

Pentre
Saron

128

Rut

Llanfwrog

Llyn
Aled

B4501

Archaeological
Trail

Y Gyffylliog

Bontuchel

467
MOEL SEISIOG

448
MOEL LLYN

Llyn
Brenig

A49

Nebo

Llyn Alwen

Mynydd
Hiraethog

8

Efenechty

Llyn Brenig

Clocaenog

gl

G **111** H J K L M

1

2

3

4

5

6

7

8

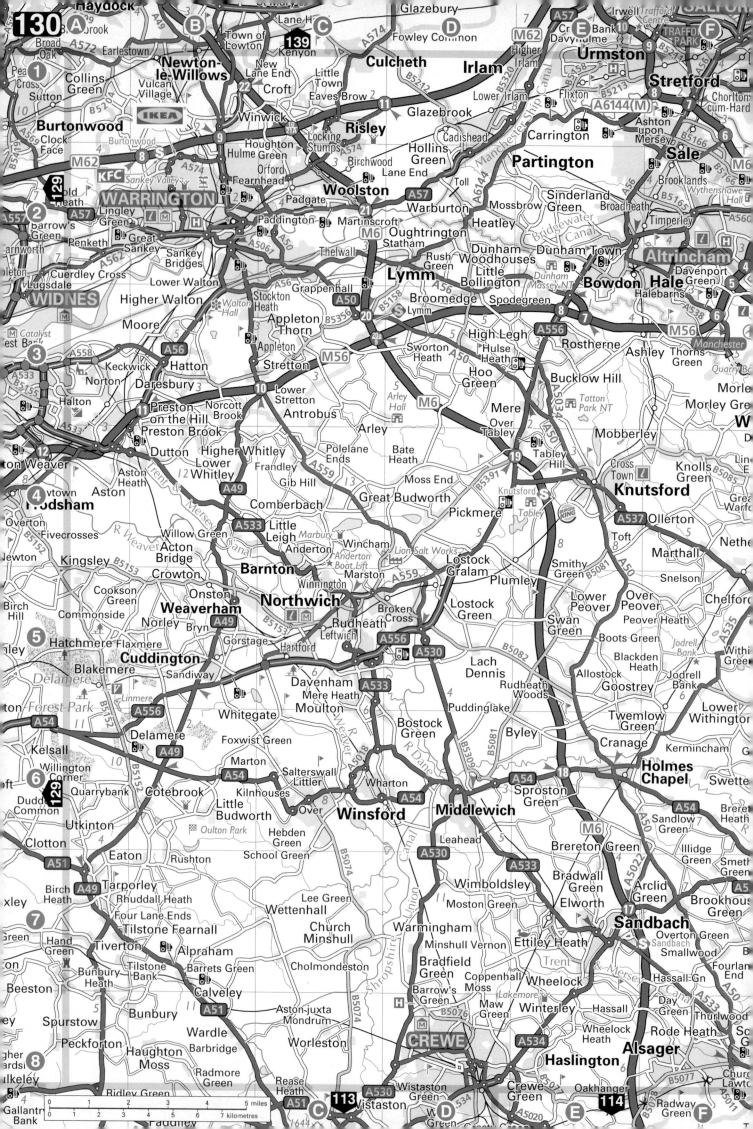

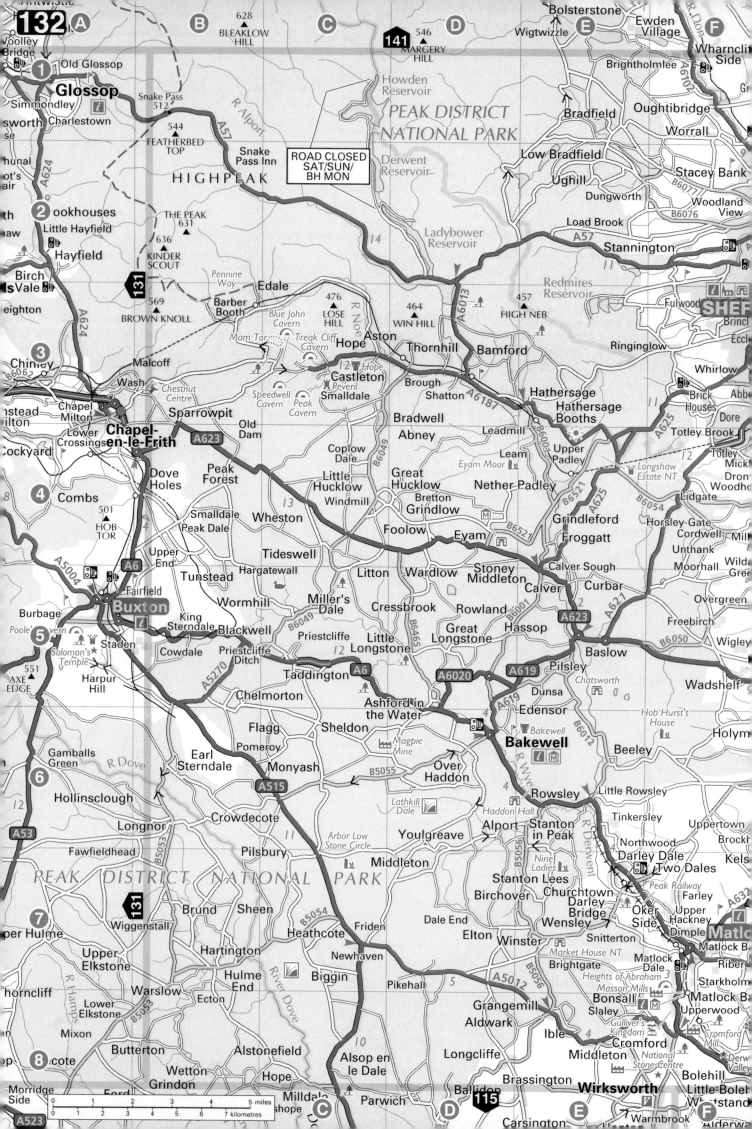

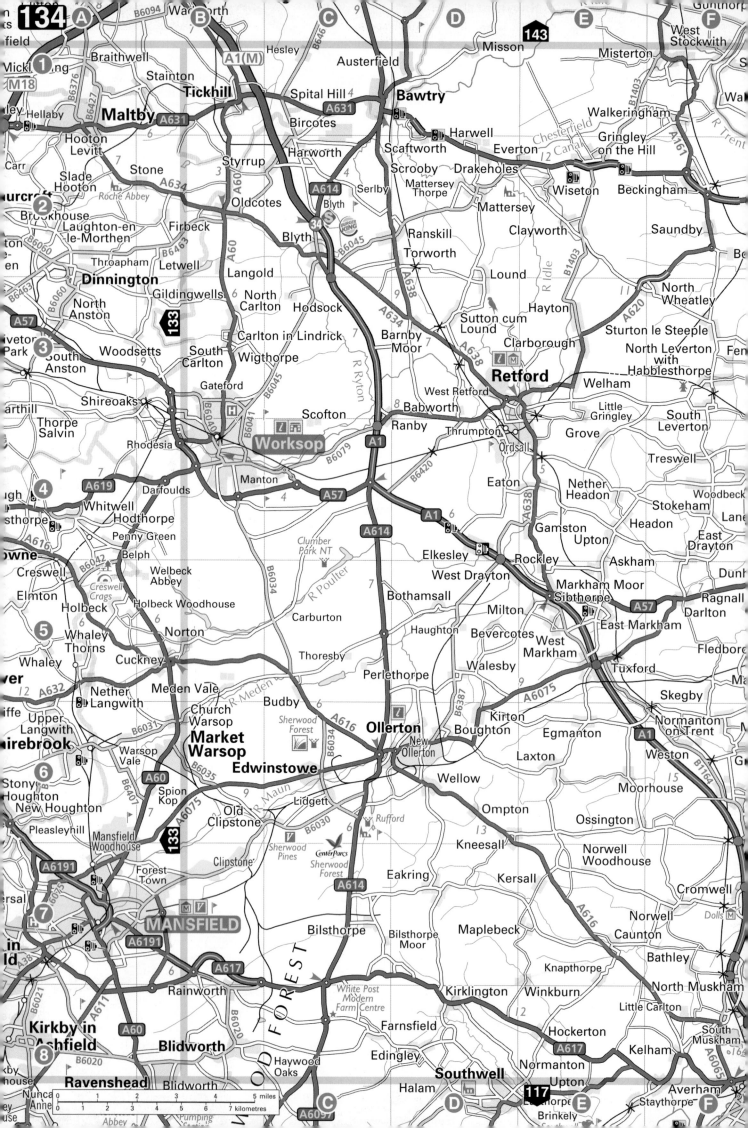

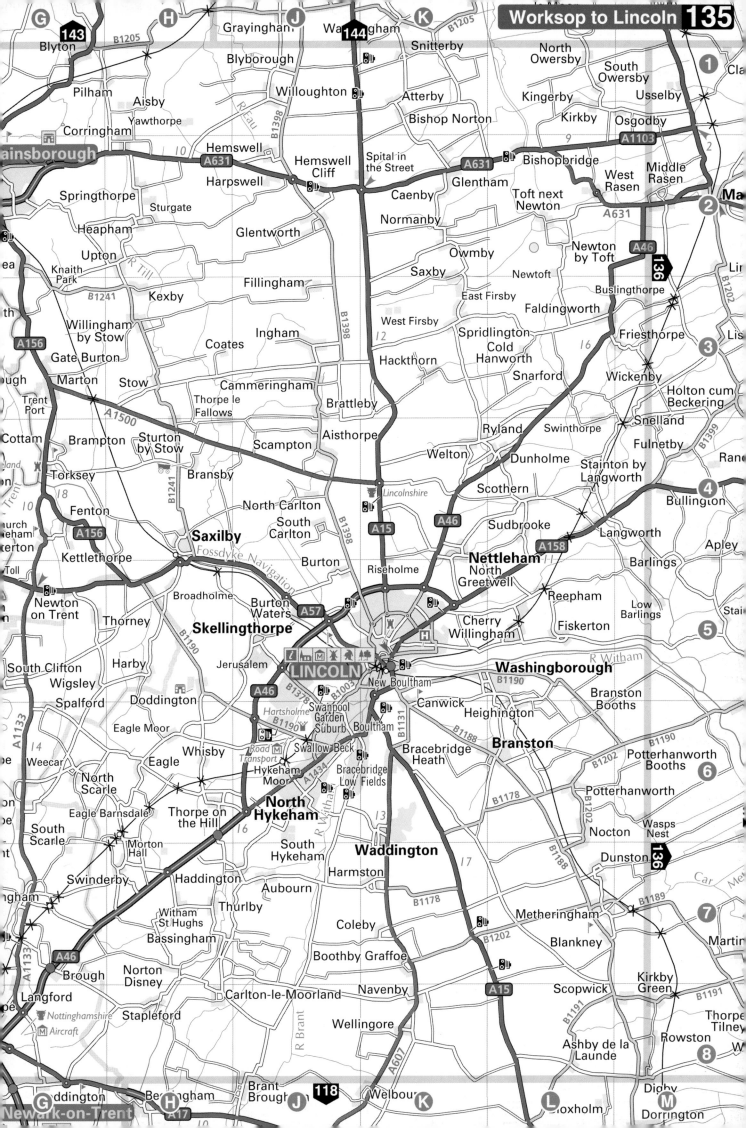

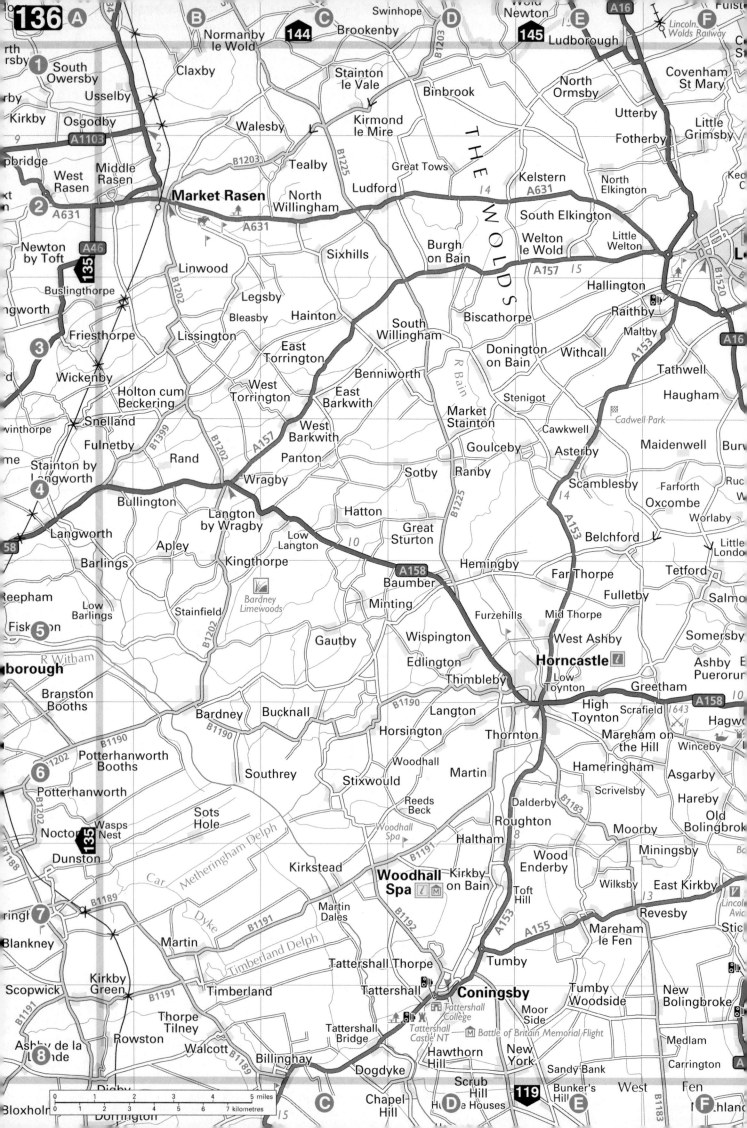

Cholme
G
H
J

145
Church
End
Skidbrooke
North End
Saltfleet
mew
South
Somercotes
Skidbrooke
rgh
ingham
North
Cockerington
North End
Saltfleetby
St Clement
ton
South
Cockerington
Saltfleetby
All Saints
Saltfleetby
St Peter
Theddlethorpe
St Helen
Grimoldby
B1200
tewton
Theddlethorpe
All Saints
A1031
Mablethorpe
Manby
Little
Carlton
Great
Carlton
Great Eau
Legbourne
North
Reston
A157
Gayton
le Marsh
A1104
Trusthorpe
Thorpe
Sutton on Sea
A52
rpe
South
Reston
Strubby
Maltby
le Marsh
Sandilands
ton
Withern
Tothill
B1373
Hagnaby
A1111
Hannah
Authorpe
Woodthorpe
Beesby
Saleby
Markby
Asserby
Belleau
Claythorpe
★ Watermill &
Wildfowl Gardens
Thoresthorpe
Asserby
Turn
Huttoft
White
Pit
Swaby
Aby
South
Thoresby
Ailby
Bilsby
Thurlby
Calceby
Haugh
Alford
B1449
Anderby Creek
Rigsby
Anderby
Brinkhill
Driby
A1104
Farlesthorpe
Mumby
Authorpe
Row
rington
Well
B1196
Cumberworth
Chapel Point
Sutterby
Mawthorpe
Helsey
**Chapel
St Leonards**
Langton
A1028
Ulceby
Bonthorpe
Hogsthorpe
ardby
Dalby
Claxby
Willoughby
Slackholme
End
Sausthorpe
5
Skendleby
Hasthorpe
Sloothby
Fantasy Island
m
Grebby
Habertoft
Addlethorpe
Ingoldmells
Raithby
Partney
Scremby
Welton
le Marsh
Ingoldmells
Point
by
A16
Spilsby
Ashby by
Partney
Gunby
Candlesby
Orby
A52
Hundleby
Monksthorpe
Winthorpe
New Spilsby
Halton
Holegate
Great
Steeping
Burgh le Marsh
est
Toynton All
Saints
Northcote
Halton
Fenside
B1195
Bratoft
A158
al
East
Keal
Toynton
St Peter
Little
Steeping
Firsby
Irby in the Marsh
Skegness
Keal
Cotes
Toynton
Fen Side
Croft
Seacroft
Thorpe St Peter
Wainfleet
Haven
Gibraltar
New
Leake
Fendike
Corner
Wainfleet
Bank
Wainfleet
All Saints
Gibraltar Point
Midville
Eastville
Wainfleet
St Mary
A52
East Fen
Friskney
Friskney Eaudike
119
G
Lade Bank
H
'rangle
mmon
J
120
K
L
M

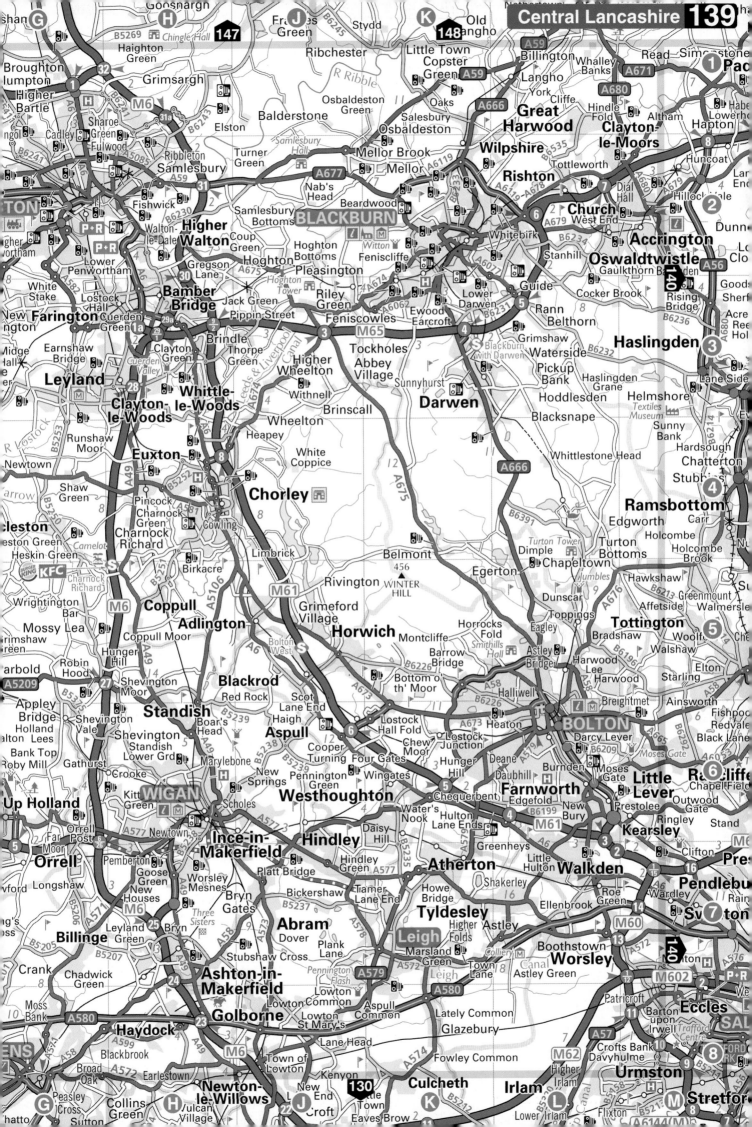

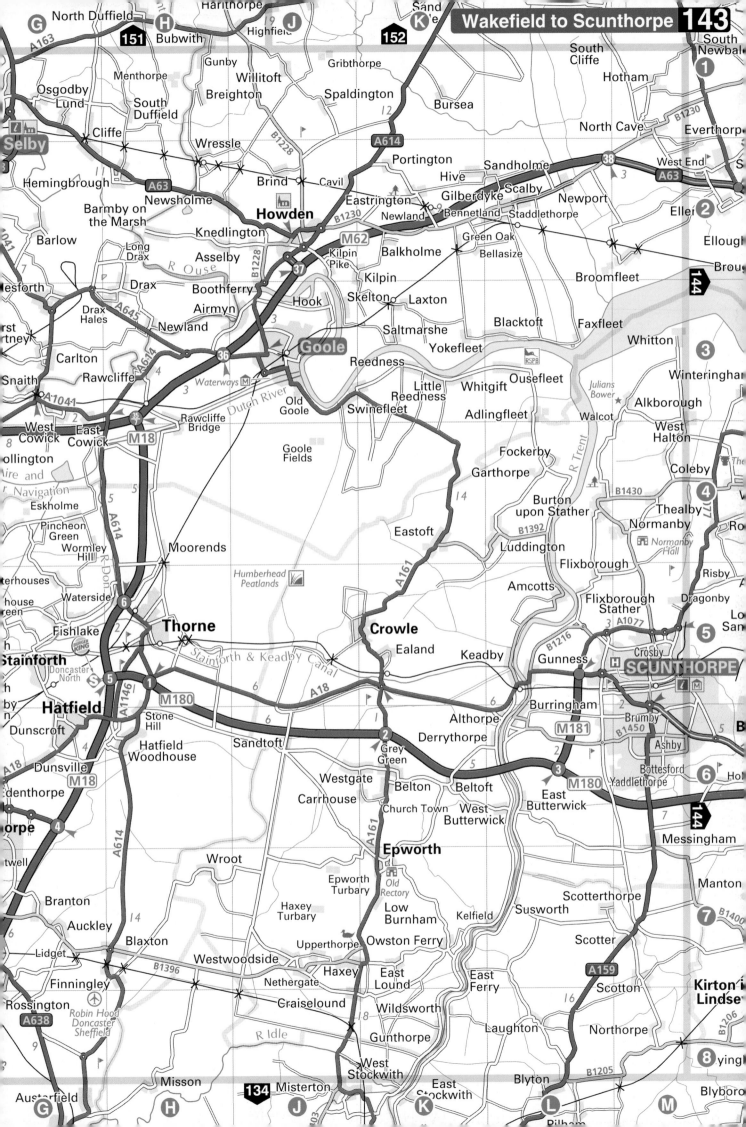

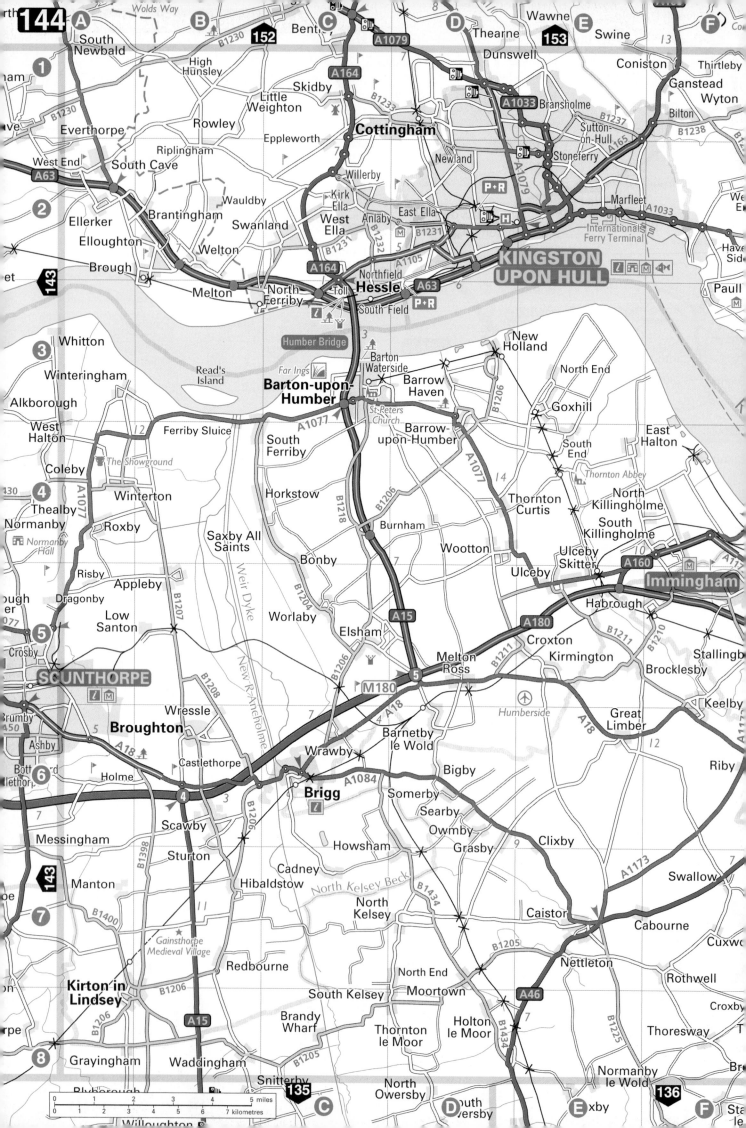

G   H   J   1

2

3

4

5

6

7

8

Flintc
B1238 B1242 Newton
153 Garton
oatley Grimston
Humbleton Fitling
ley Hilston
R Owstwick
Elstronwick Danthorpe North End
t End Burton Tunstall
ton Pidsea Roos Waxholme
E B1242
B1362 Rimswell Owthorne
West End B1362 **Withernsea**
don Burstwick East End
Thorngumbald Halsham S Hollym
A1033 Keyingham S 4
Ryehill 16 Winestead Holmpton
Ottringham A1033 Patrington
Out Newton
Patrington Haven
Welwick
Sunk Island Weeton B1445 Easington
Skeffling South End

Spurn Heritage Coast

Kilnsea

mingham
ck

Kilnsea

Spurn Heritage Coast

A180
B1210 **GRIMSBY**
SPURN HEAD

ealing
Great Coates West Marsh
ylesby A1136 Little Coates A180 **Cleethorpes**
6 Nunsthorpe A46 Thrunscoe
Rotterdam (Europoort)
Zeebrugge

Bradley Scartho A1098 _The Jungle_
Laceby B1203 Pleasure Island
by upon **Humberston**
umber **Waltham** New Waltham
Barnoldby _Waltham Windmill_ Holton le Clay
le Beck Brigsley A1031
Beelsby A18 North End RSPB
Hatcliffe Ashby cum Fenby Tetney Lock
Waithe Tetney North Cotes
West Grainsby Marshchapel
Ravendale North Thoresby Eskham
East B1201 West End Grainthorpe
Ravendale Churchthorpe 29 North Somercotes
y Wold Newton 15 Fulstow Conisholme A1031
hope _Lincolnshire Wolds Railway_ Church End Skidbrooke North End
B1203 A16 Ludborough Covenham Saltf
136 St Bartholomew
Covenham South Somercotes
St Mary

G   H   J   K   L   M

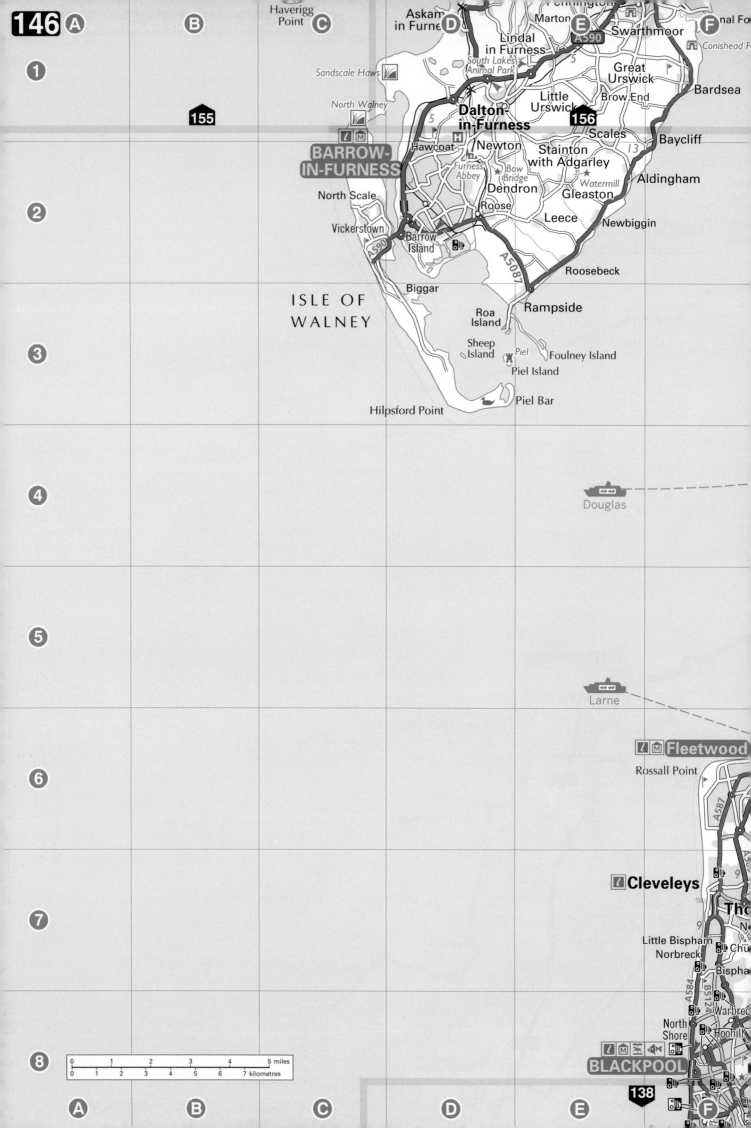

A   B   Haverigg Point C   Askam in Furness D   Marton E   Final Fo F

Swarthmoor

A590

Conishead P

1

Sandscale Haws

Lindal in Furness

South Lakes Animal Park

Great Urswick

5

Little Urswick

Brow End

Bardsea

North Walney

155

Dalton-in-Furness

156

Scales

Baycliff

13

BARROW-IN-FURNESS

Hawcoat

H

Newton

Stainton with Adgarley

Aldingham

2

North Scale

Furness Abbey

Bow Bridge

Watermill

Dendron

Gleaston

Vickerstown

A590

Roose

Leece

Newbiggin

Barrow Island

A5087

Roosebeck

ISLE OF WALNEY

Biggar

Rampside

Roa Island

3

Sheep Island

Piel

Foulney Island

Piel Island

Hilpsford Point

Piel Bar

4

Douglas

5

Larne

Fleetwood

Rossall Point

6

Cleveleys

Th

7

Little Bispham

Norbreck

Ch

Bispha

A584

B512

North Shore

Hoohil

Warbre

8

BLACKPOOL

138

A   B   C   D   E   F

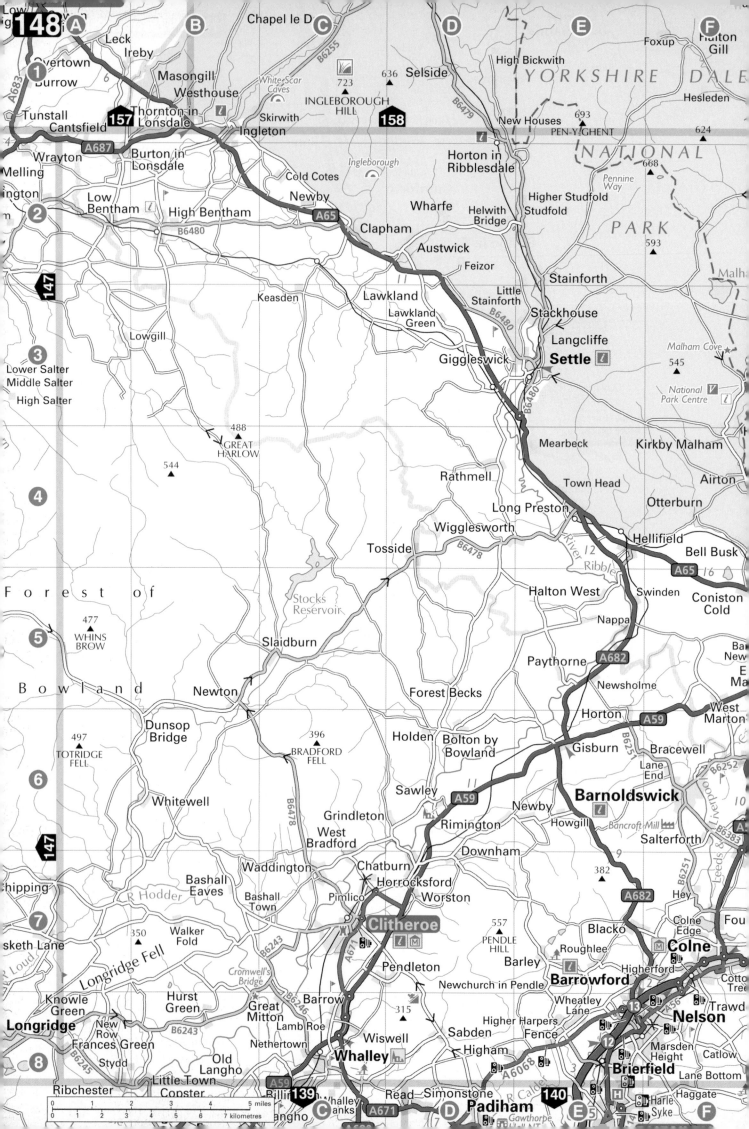

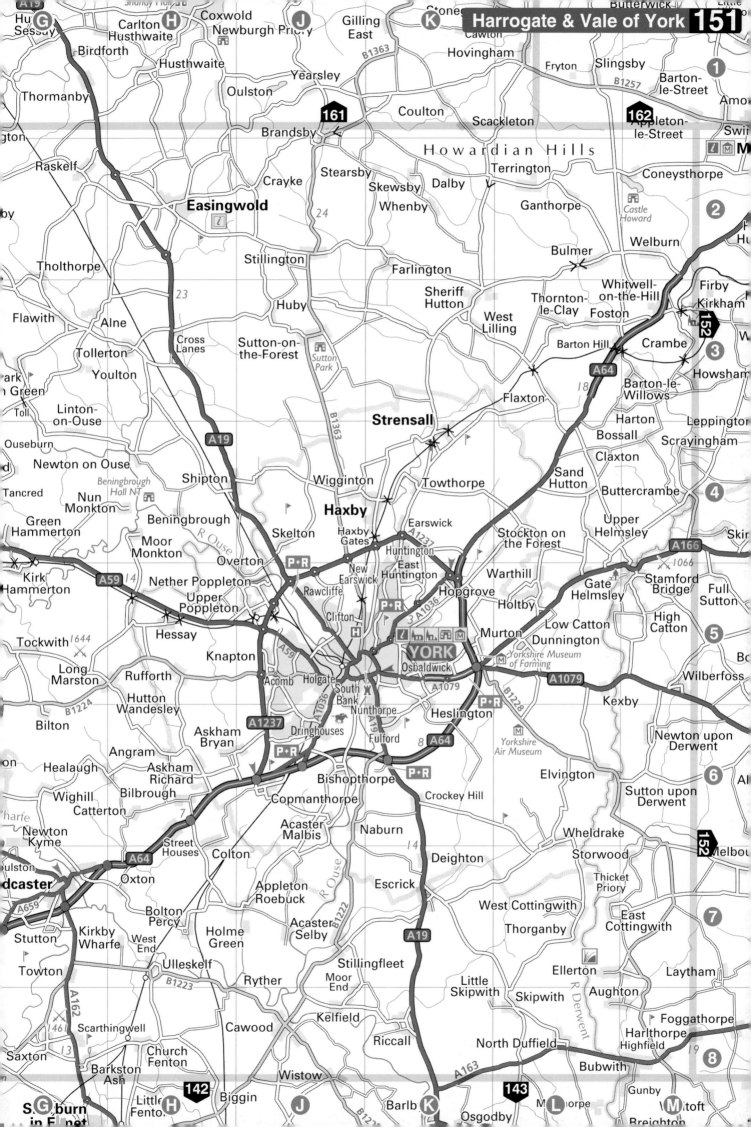

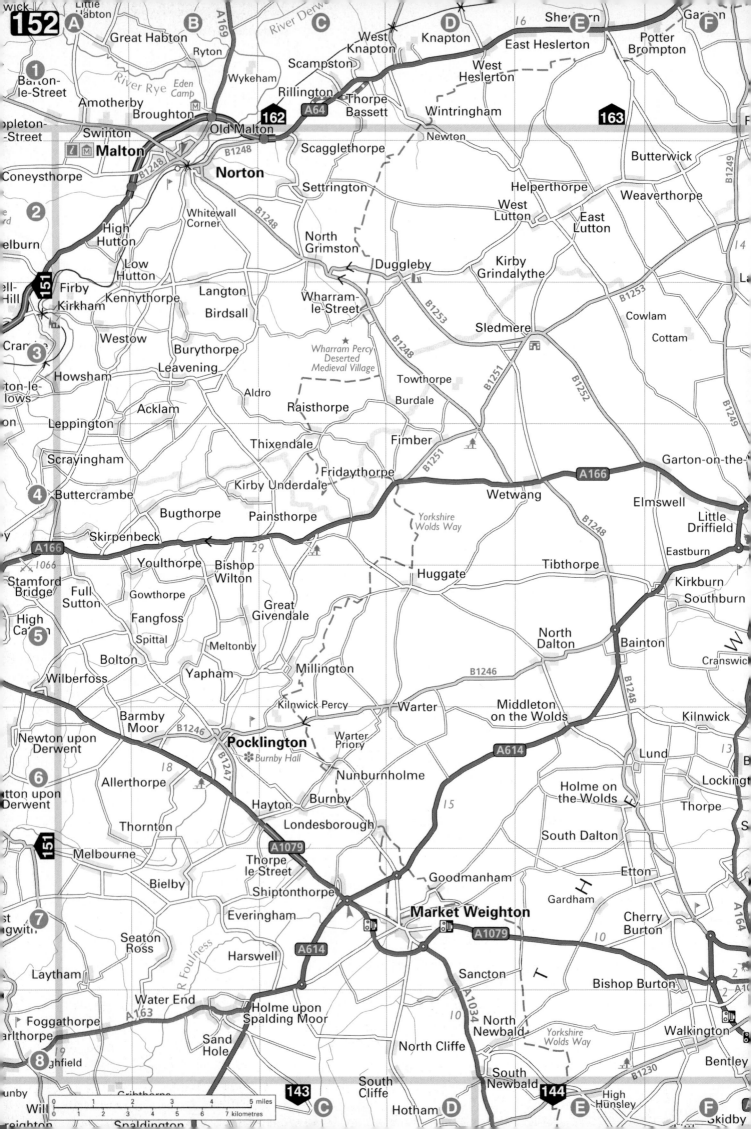

G **Hunmanby** H J

1

Fordon
Reighton
Speeton
Flamborough Head
Heritage Coast
Thornwick
Bay

Wold
Newton
Burton
Fleming
B1229
163
RSPB
Buckton
Bempton
North Landing

Thwing
Grindale
A165
B1229
Marton
B1259
Selwicks
Bay
FLAMBOROUGH
HEAD
Lighthouse

2

11
Sewerby
B1255
Flamborough

B1253
Boynton
A1038
Bondville
Miniature Village
BRIDLINGTON
BAY

Rudston
Monolith
Bessingby
Bridlington

Carnaby
Hilderthorpe

Kilham
Haisthorpe
Thornholme

3

Burton Agnes
Norman
Manor House
S
A165

Ruston Parva
Harpham
D
Fraisthorpe

A614
Lowthorpe
Little Kelk
Gransmoor
Barmston

field
Nafferton
Great Kelk
Lissett
B1242

4

Wansford
Gembling
16
Ulrome

R Hull
Cruckley
Animal Farm
Foston on
the Wolds
Dringhoe
Skipsea

Skerne
Beeford
Skipsea
Brough

Brigham
B1249
Upton

North
Frodingham
Dunnington

5

on
wick
Rotsea
A165
Atwick

n
Hempholme
Bewholme
B1242

Nunkeeling
Honeysuckle
Farm
Hornsea
Mere
Hornsea

6

Burshill
Brandesburton
Seaton

Aike
B1244
6
Sigglesthorne
Goxhill
Rolston

ough
Arram
Leven
Catwick
Mappleton

field
Little
Catwick
Little
Hatfield
Great
Hatfield
B1242
Mappleton Sands

7
erley
A1035
Routh
7
Long
Riston
B1243
Rise
Great
Cowden

Tickton
H
Arnold
North End
Withernwick
Aldbrough

roft
Meaux
O
Skirlaugh
New
Ellerby
Marton
17
East
Newton

Weel
L
Old
Ellerby
West
Newton
Etherdwick
B1238
B1242

8
Woodmansey
A1174
R Hull
D
Burton
Constable Hall
Flinton
Garton

Wawne
A165
Swine
13
E
Grimston

Thearne
Coniston
Thirtleby
Sproatley
145
Humbleton
Hilston

A1079
Dunswell
144
J
nstead
Wyton
K
L
M

G 144 H J K L M

POINT OF AYRE

Rue Point
Ayres
Port Cranstal
The Lhen
A10
Cranstal
Bride
A19
A16
A17
Jurby Head
Andreas
Shellag Point
Jurby
A14
B3
A9
A10
Sandygate
B14
Ballachurry Fort
Regaby
St Jude's
A13
Rural Life
Ramsey Bay
The Cronk
A10
Sulby
A13
Sulby R.
Ramsey
Ballaugh
A3
Churchtown
Manx Electric Railway
Orrisdale
Cronk Sumark
Glen Auldyn
Port e Vullen
Orrisdale Head
Ravensdale
A14
Block Eary
A18
Dreemskerry
Maughold
Kirk Michael
ISLE
561
NORTH BARRULE
Maughold Head
TT Circuit
620 SNAEFELL
Corrany
Ballajora
488
Sulby Reservoir
OF
Glen Mona
Ballafayle
Barregarrow
545
462 SLIEAU LHEAN
Cashtal yn Ard
Knocksharry
R Nebb
The Bungalow
BEINN Y PHOTT
Snaefell Mountain Railway
Dhoon Bay
Cronk-y-Voddy
B10
Laxey Wheel
St Patrick's Isle
487
MAN
Laxey
King Orry's Grave
Peel
COLDEN
Millennium Way
Ballalheannagh
Old Laxey
Laxey Head
Corrins Folly
A20
479
Laxey Bay
Contrary Head
A1
SLIEAU RUY
B22
8
B12
Patrick
A30 Tynwald Hill
Greeba
Cregny Baa
Baldrine
St John's
TT Circuit
Baldwin
B21
Manx Electric Railway
Waterfall
Glen Maye
Lower Foxdale
Crosby
A1
Glen Vine
A23
Cloven Stones
Niarbyl
Dalby
Foxdale
Strang
Onchan
Clay Head
A24
Eairy
B35
Union Mills
Groudle Glen Railway
Niarbyl Bay
A27
Norse Houses
B32
Cronkbourne
Onchan Head
16
Round Table
A11
483
Braaid
A24
DOUGLAS
Belfast
SOUTH BARRULE
Closeclark
Brough Fort
Douglas Bay
437
B39
St Marks
A37
Douglas Head
CRONK NY ARREY LAA
Ballamodha
Millennium Way
B33
Heysham
A36
B41
A5
10
Grenaby
B26
Santon
A25
Liverpool
Fleshwick Bay
Ballakilpheric
Ballakelly
Port Soderick
Milners Tower
Ballafesson
Colby
A27
Silverdale Glen
Isle of Man Steam Railway
Bradda Head
A7
Ballabeg
Santon Head
Port Erin
Rushen
Ballasalla
Cronk ny Merriu
Dublin
Marine Interpretation Centre
Howe
A5
B52
Meayll Circle
A31
Castletown
Isle of Man (Ronaldsway)
CALF OF MAN
Port St Mary
Derbyhaven
Cregneash
Close ny Chollagh
Scarlett
Hango Hill
Derby Fort
Spanish Head
Scarlett Point
Castletown Bay
Herring Tower
Caigher Point
Dreswick Point

scale: 0 1 2 3 4 5 miles
0 1 2 3 4 5 6 7 kilometres

G
H
J
K
L

1
2
3
4
5
6
7
8

Wilton
Florence Mine
Carleton
Haile
Coulderton
Middletown
Nethertown
Blackbeck
Beckermet
Braystones
Calder Bridge
Ponsonby
Sellafield Visitor Centre
Cross
Wellington
Gosforth
B5343
Santon
Santon Bridge
Eskdale Green
Beckfoot
Nether Wasdale
Seascale
Drigg
Holmrook
Muncaster Mill
Ravenglass and Eskdale Railway
River Esk Railway
Saltcoats
Ravenglass
Bath House
Muncaster
Newbiggin
Broad Oak
Lane End
Waberthwaite
Corney
Loganbeck
Hycemoor
Selker Bay
Hyton
Bootle
Swinside Stone Circle
Annaside
600
BLACK COMBE
Gutterby Spa
Whitbeck
The Green
Whicham
Silecroft
Kirksanton
Steel Green
Haverigg
Haverigg Point
Askam in Furness
Sandscale Haws
North Walney
North Scale
Vickerstown
BARROW-IN-FURNESS
Hawcoat
Worm Gill
River Bleng
691
SEATALLAN
Wasdale Head
KIRK FELL
GREAT
899
GABLE
West Water
964
SCAFELL
Burnmoor Tarn
Boot
Hardknott Fort
ESKDALE
Devoke Water
LAKE DISTRICT
Hall Dunnerdale
Ulpha
NATIONAL
573
WHITFELL
PARK
Beckfoot
Duddon Bridge
Lower Hawthwaite
Broughton Mills
A595
Lady Hall
Foxf
Hallthwaites
Arnaby
Bridge End
The Hill
Sand Si
Souterg
Millom
Borwick Rails
RSPB
A5093
164
A595
156
146
155

0 1 2 3 4 5 miles
0 1 2 3 4 5 6 7 kilometres

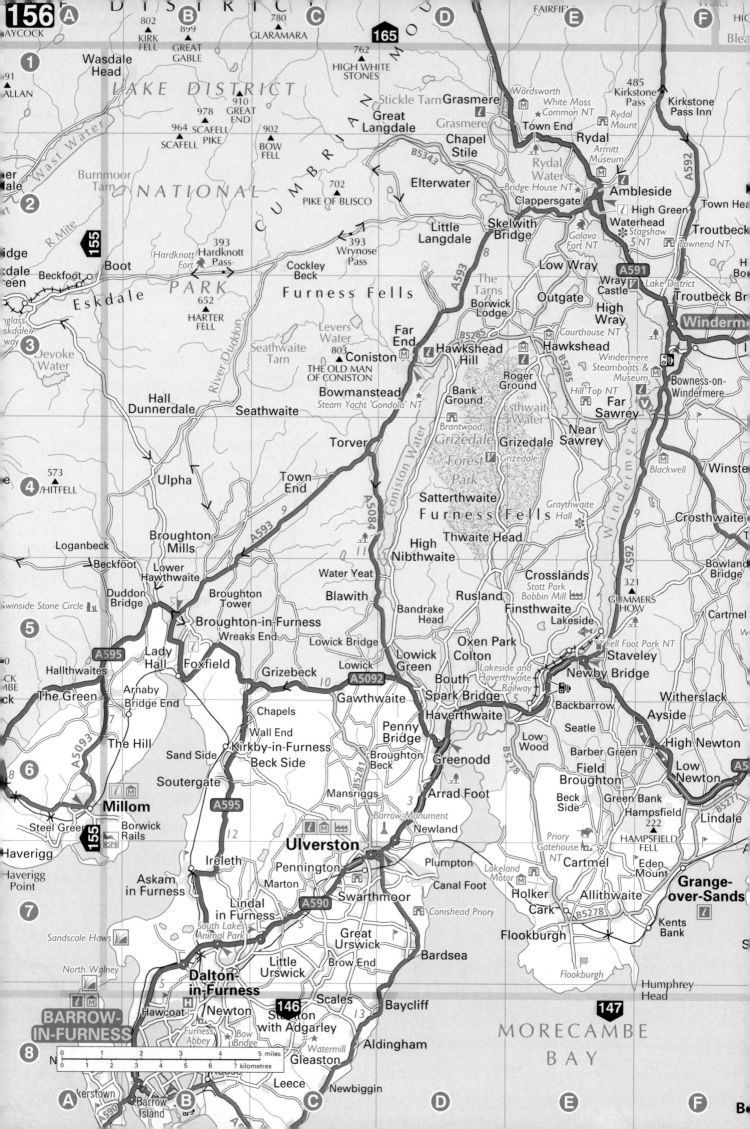

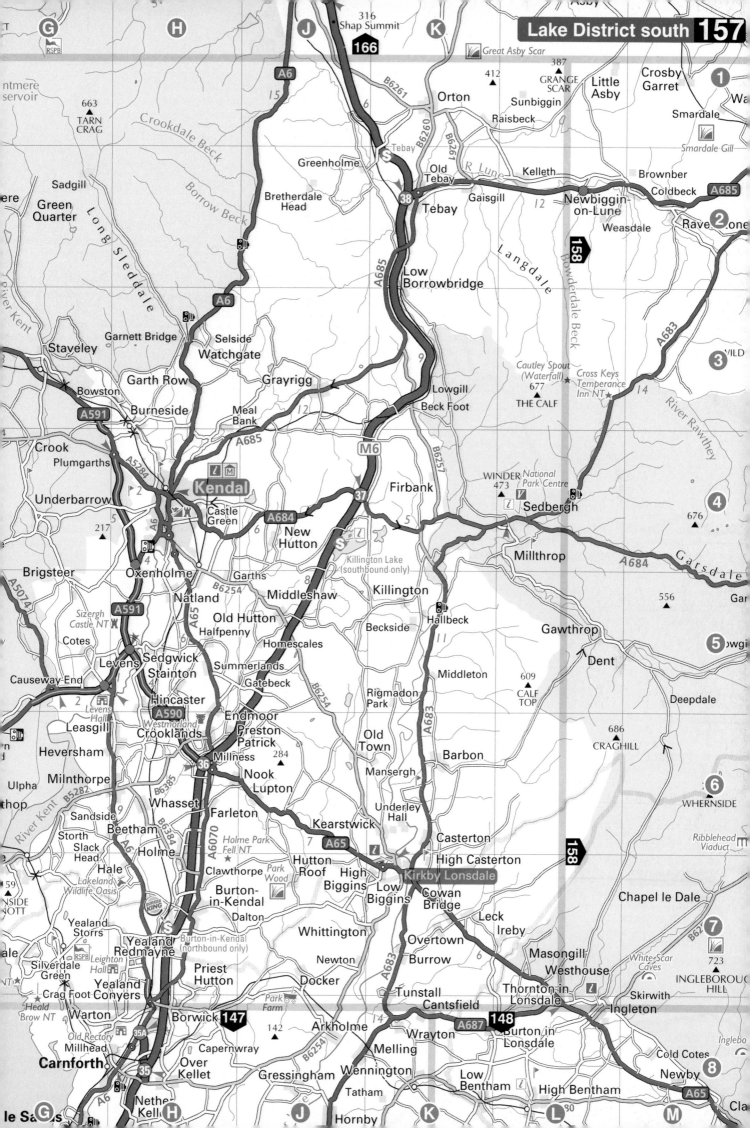

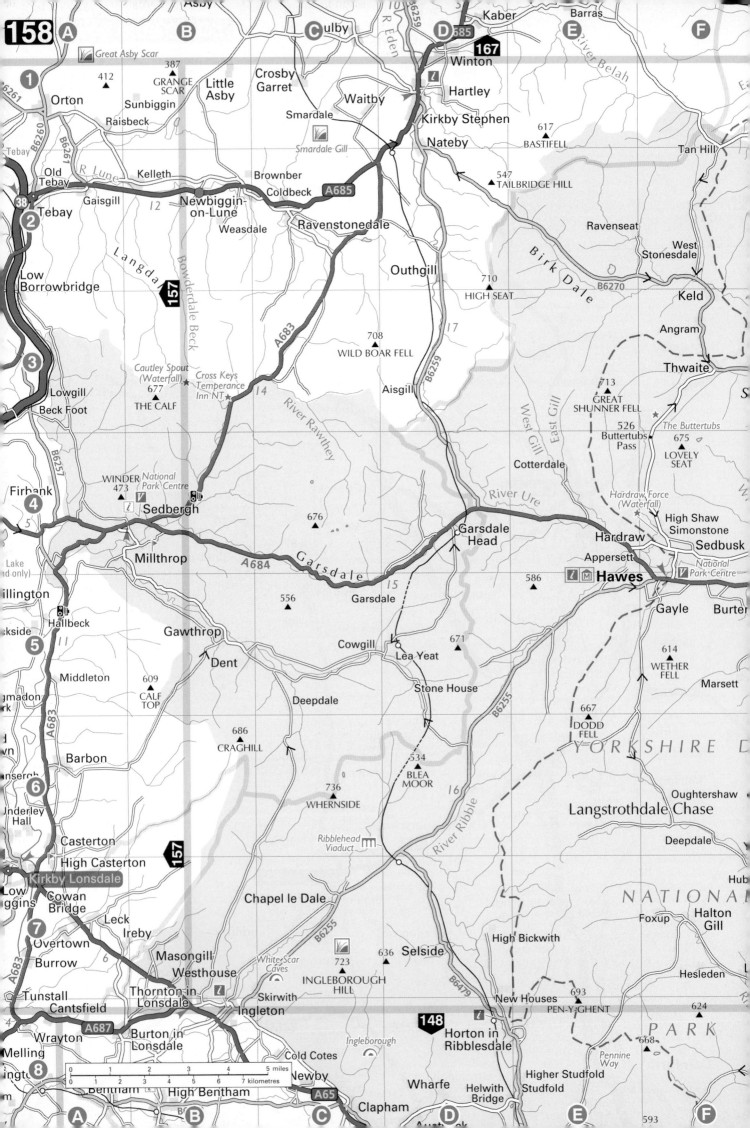

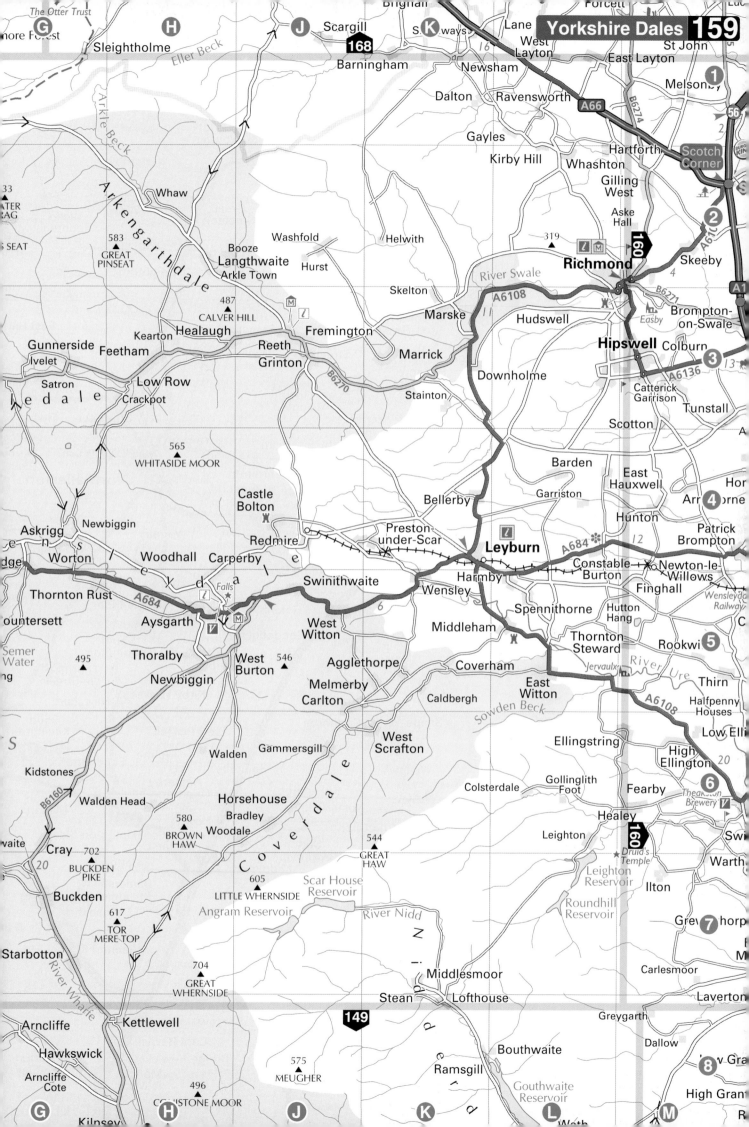

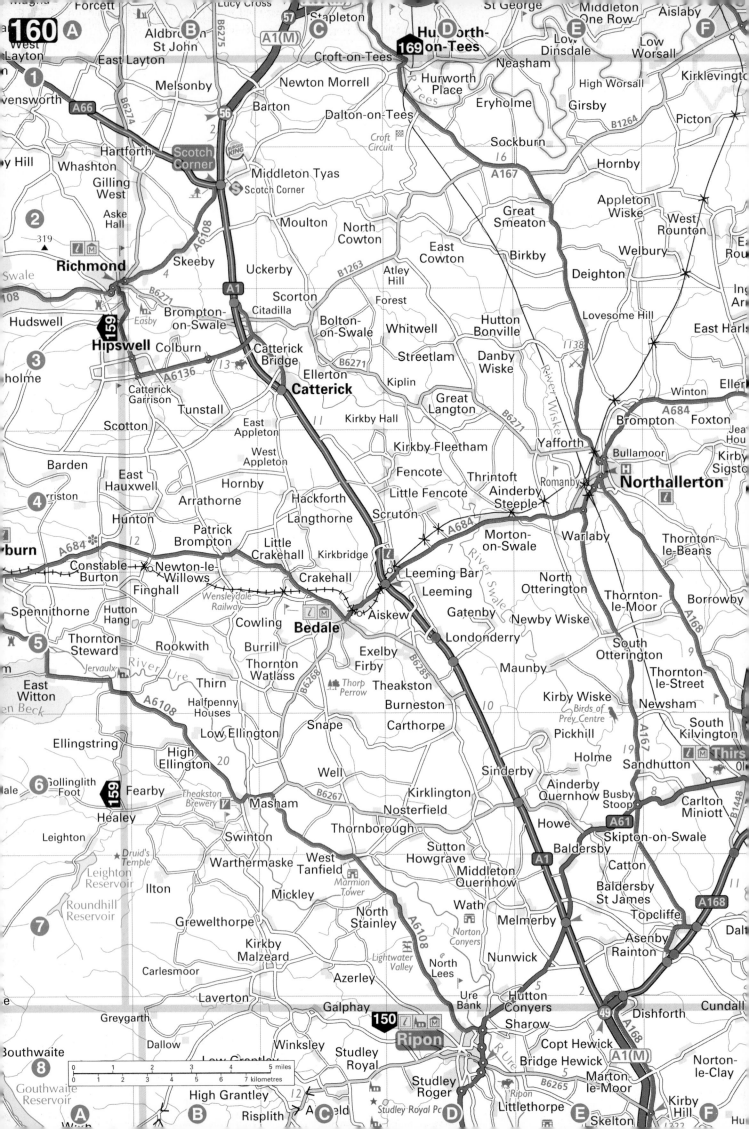

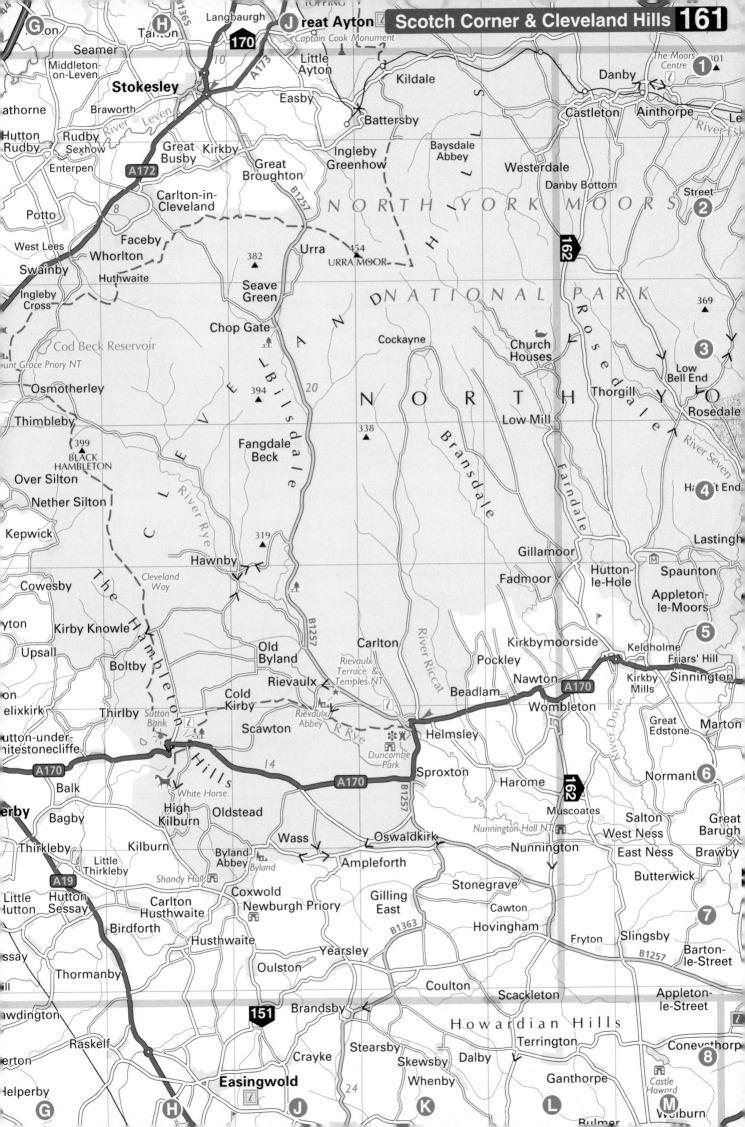

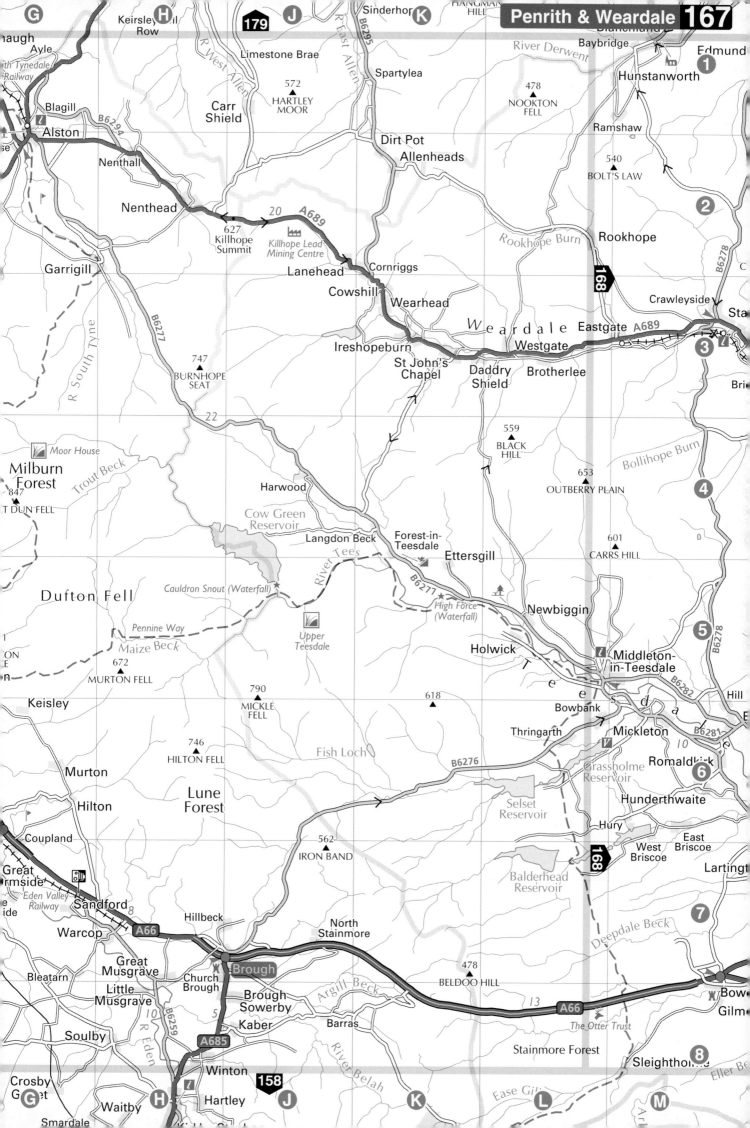

G   H   J **179**   K   Sinderhope   HANGMAN HILL

Keirsley Hill
Keirsley Row

Limestone Brae

Spartylea

River Derwent   Baybridge

Edmund

Hunstanworth

1

Ayle

haugh
th Tynedale
Railway

Blagill

Carr
Shield

572
HARTLEY
MOOR

478
NOOKTON
FELL

Ramshaw

B6294

Alston

540
BOLT'S LAW

2

se

Nenthall

Dirt Pot
Allenheads

Rookhope Burn   Rookhope

Nenthead

20   A689

627
Killhope
Summit

Killhope Lead
Mining Centre

Cornriggs

Lanehead

Cowshill

Wearhead

Weardale   Eastgate   A689

Crawleyside

Sta

3

B6278

Garrigill

B6277

R South Tyne

747
BURNHOPE
SEAT

22

Ireshopeburn

St John's
Chapel

Westgate

Daddry
Shield   Brotherlee

Bri

559
BLACK
HILL

Bollihope Burn

4

653
OUTBERRY PLAIN

Moor House

Milburn
Forest

847
T DUN FELL

Trout Beck

Harwood

Cow Green
Reservoir

Langdon Beck

River Tees

Forest-in-
Teesdale

Ettersgill

601
CARRS HILL

B6277

5

B6278

Cauldron Snout (Waterfall)

Dufton Fell

Pennine Way

Maize Beck

672
MURTON FELL

Upper
Teesdale

High Force
(Waterfall)

Newbiggin

Holwick

Tees

Middleton-
in-Teesdale

B6282

Hill

Keisley

746
HILTON FELL

790
MICKLE
FELL

618

Fish Loch

Bowbank

Thringarth

Mickleton

e   e   s   d   a

B6281

10

Romaldkirk

6

Murton

Hilton

Lune
Forest

562
IRON BAND

B6276

Grassholme
Reservoir

Hunderthwaite

Coupland

Selset
Reservoir

Hury

168

West
Briscoe

East
Briscoe

Lartingt

Great
rmside

Eden Valley
Railway

Sandford   8

Hillbeck

Balderhead
Reservoir

Deepdale Beck

7

Warcop   A66

North
Stainmore

478
BELDOO HILL

Bow

Gilm

Great
Musgrave

Bleatarn

Little
Musgrave

Church
Brough

Brough

Brough
Sowerby

Kaber

13   A66

The Otter Trust

8

Soulby

B6259

Barras

Argill Beck

Crosby
G   et

A685

Winton   158

Hartley

Stainmore Forest

Sleightho

Waitby

G   H   J   K   River Belah   L   Ease Gi   M

Smardale

Eller Be

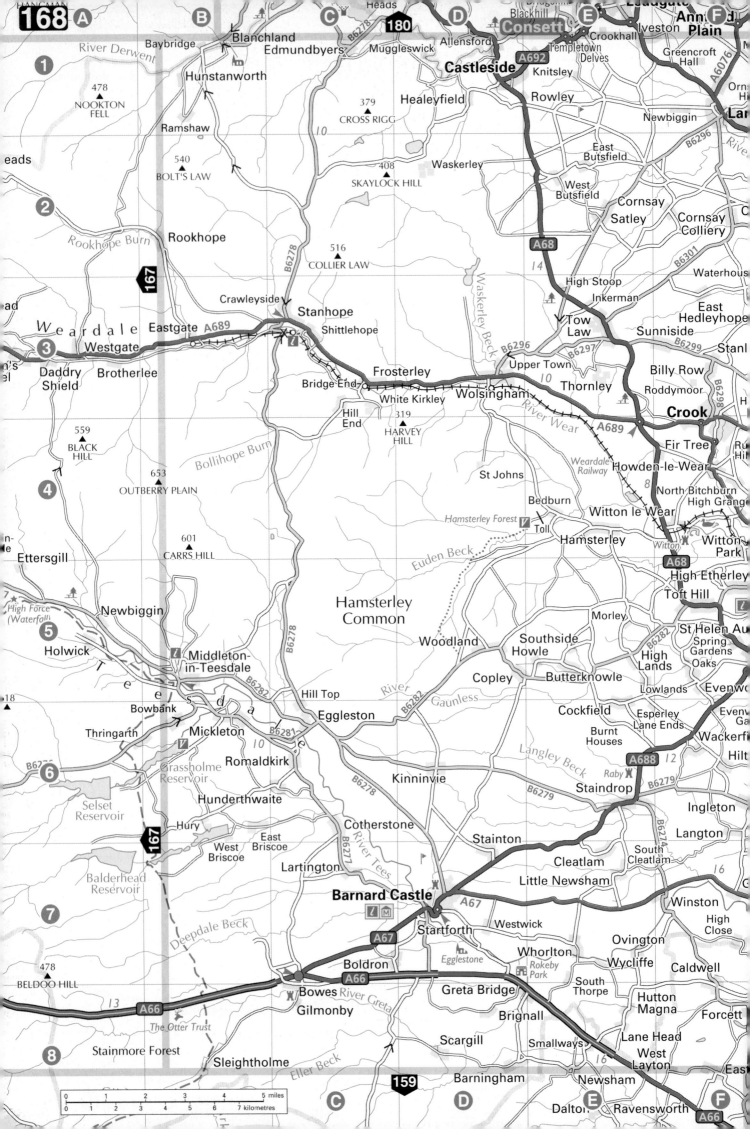

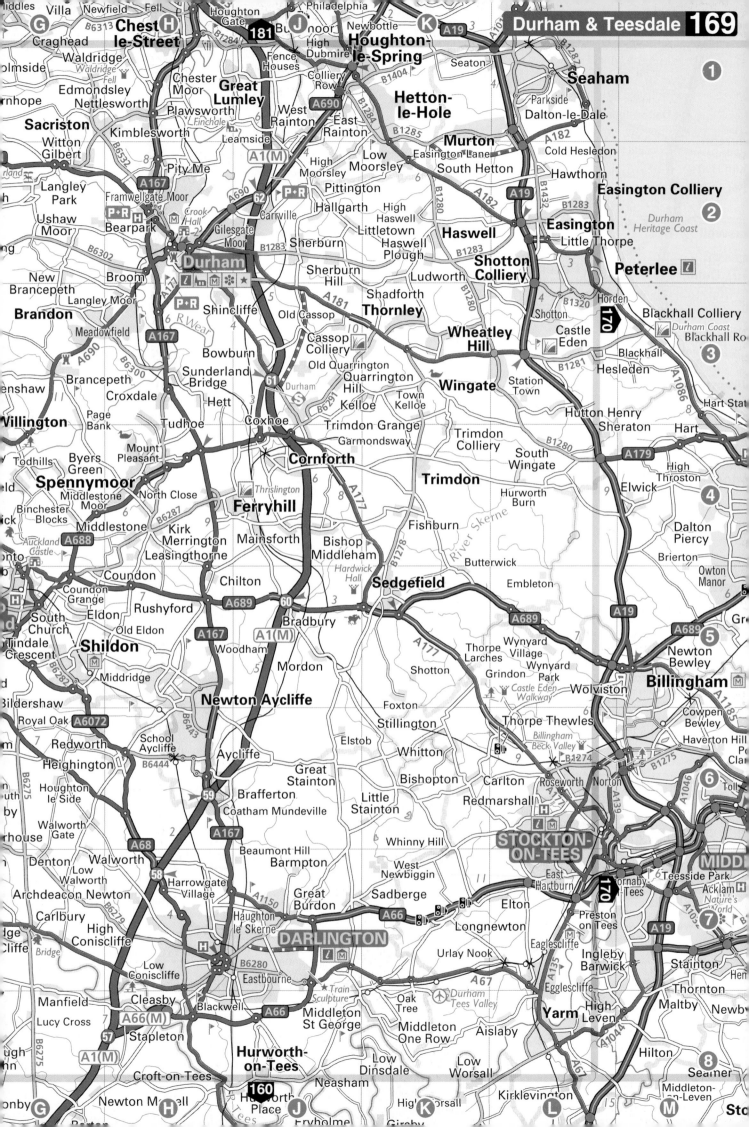

G H J

1

2

3

4

5

6

uugglers

w Brotton

Carlin
How   Skinningrove   Hummersea Scar

ton   Upton   Boulby

Loftus   Staithes

Dalehouse   Heritage Centre

tton   Easington   16   Port Mulgrave

Liverton
rpe   Mines   Hinderwell

erton   Handale   Roxby   Newton   Runswick   Runswick
                              Mulgrave   Bay

Borrowby   Kettleness   Goldsborough

Ellerby   Overdale
                                           Wyke

sholm   Scaling   B1266   A174   Lythe

Gerrick   Sandsend   Sandsend
                                                           Wyke

            Scaling   Mickleby   **Whitby**
            Dam   East
by   West   Barnby
            Ugthorpe   Barnby   Raithwaite

                                   Dunsley   Saltwick
The Moors   Newholm   Bay
Centre   301

by   G   Stongre   H   162   J   Hutton   K   riggswath   L acre   M
                                            Mulgrave
                                   A171   Aislaby   High

North Yorkshire and
Cleveland Heritage Coast

7

8

Ruswarp   St

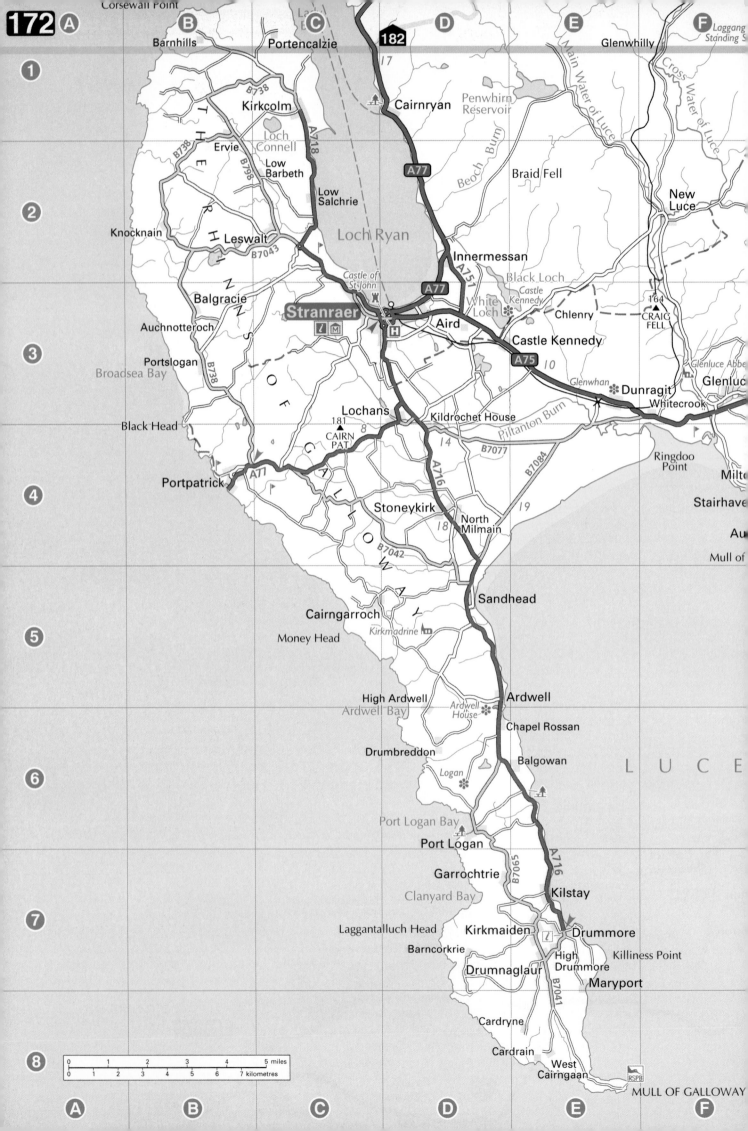

G | H | J
K

Knowe | 183

River Bladnoch

G A L L O W A Y

184 ▲
URRALL FELL

271 ▲
-ARTFIELD FELL

Black Burn

Carseriggan

Challoch

R. Cree

Penkill Burn

Minnigaff

RSPB

710 ▲
CAIRNSMORE OF FLEET

1

Barfad

214 ▲
CULVENNAN FELL

Loch Ronald

Shennanton

15

B735

B733

Craighlaw

A75

Kirkcowan

R Bladnoch

B733

Clugston

Dernaglar Loch

Tarf Water

Fell Loch

B7052

Newton Stewart

Creebridge

A714

Baltersan

174

Causeway End

Torhouse Stone Circle

B733

Palnure

A75

Kirroughtree

Gem Rock

Creetown

18

Kirkmabreck

Carsluith

Carsluith

Cairnholy Chambered Ca-

2

3

4

Castle Loch

Mochrum Loch

Water of Malzie

B7005

T H E

M A C H A R S

Wigtown

Bladnoch

Kirwaugh

Braehead

Kirkinner

Orchardton Bay

Ravenshall Point

-alg

A747

-s

Auchenmalg Bay

B7005

Culshabbin

Chapel Finian (ruin)

A747

13

Elrig

Barrachan

Druchtag Mottel

B7085

12

B7052

B7085

Whauphill

Little Airies

11

Sorbie

A746

B7004

Pouton

Culscadden

B7052

Garlieston

Cruggleton Bay

Wi

5

6

B A Y

Mochrum

Port William

Drumtrodden Cup & Ring

Drumtrodden Standing Stones

Big Balcraig

'Wren's Egg' Standing Stones

Barsalloch Fort

Barsalloch Point

Monreith

Point of Leg

A747

10

Drummoddie

Broughton Mains

B7021

174

Priory

Whithorn Cradle of Christianity

Rispain Camp

A746

Whithorn

Portyerrock

B7004

B7063

Glasserton

St Ninian's Cave

Kidsdale

B7004

Isle of Whithorn

St Ninian's Chapel (ruin)

Cutcloy

BURROW HEAD

7

8

G | H | J | K | L | M

A **B** **C** **D** **E** **F**

1

G A L L O W A Y

Carseriggan

Challoch

Minnigaff

GARLICK
HILL

Galloway Deer Range

402
ROUND
FELL

471
FELL OF FLEET

R Cree

RSPB

Penkill Burn

208
AUCHENCLOY HILL

2

arfad

Newton
Stewart

Creebridge

Palnure

A714

Loch
Grannoch

Loch
Fleet

710
CAIRNSMORE
OF FLEET

Kirroughtree

Big Water of Fleet

Little Water of Fleet

Big Water of Fleet

Lo
Ske

173

Baltersan

A75

hennanton

B735

3

Kirkcowan

Clugston

B733

R Bladnoch

Causeway
End

7

335
WHITE TOP
OF CULREACH

Gem Rock

Creetown

Upper
Ruscoe

B796

Fleet
Valley

Skyre Burn

Anwoth

Gate

Torhouse
Stone Circle

B733

Wigtown

18

2

Kirkmabreck

455
CAIRNHARROW

Cardoness

THE

4

Bladnoch

Kirwaugh

B7052

B7005

Carsluith

Carsluith

Cairnholy
Chambered Cairns

Girthon

Malzie

M A C H A R S

Braehead

Kirkinner

Orchardton
Bay

Ravenshall
Point

Mossyard

Fleet
Bay

Lennox
Plunton

B7005

B7052

B7085

B7004

Margrie

5

Eng

Barrachan

Whauphill

Little
Airies

11

A746

Culscadden

Islands
of Fleet

Kirkandrews

Druchtag
Motte

B7085

12

Sorbie

B7052

Wigtown Bay

Mochrum

Drumtrodden
Cup & Ring

Drummoddie

Pouton

Garlieston

Cruggleton
Bay

Borness

Drumtrodden
Standing Stones

Broughton
Mains

B7004

Ringdoo Point

6

William

'Wren's Egg'
Standing Stones

Monreith

B7021

173

Priory

B7063

Barsalloch Fort

Whithorn Cradle
of Christianity

Barsalloch Point

Point of Leg

A747

10

Rispain
Camp

A746

Whithorn

Portyerrock

7

Glasserton

St Ninian's
Cave

Kidsdale

B7004

Isle of Whithorn

St Ninian's
Chapel
(ruin)

Cutcloy

BURROW HEAD

8

A **B** **C** **D** **E** **F**

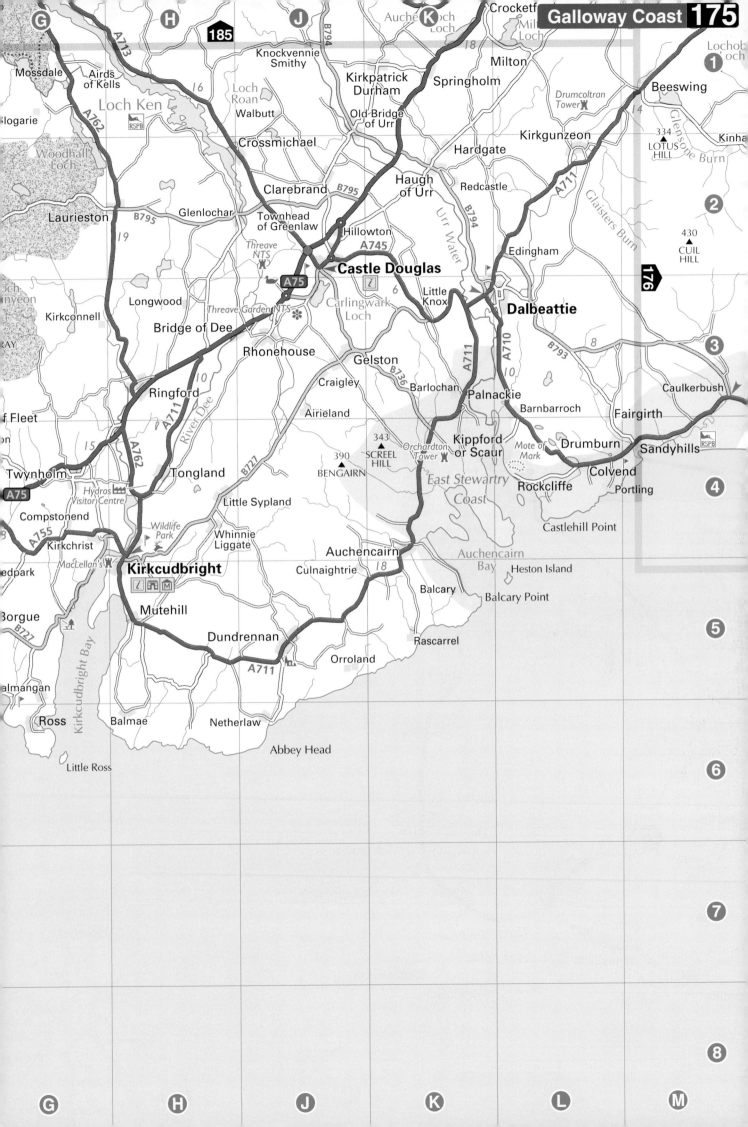

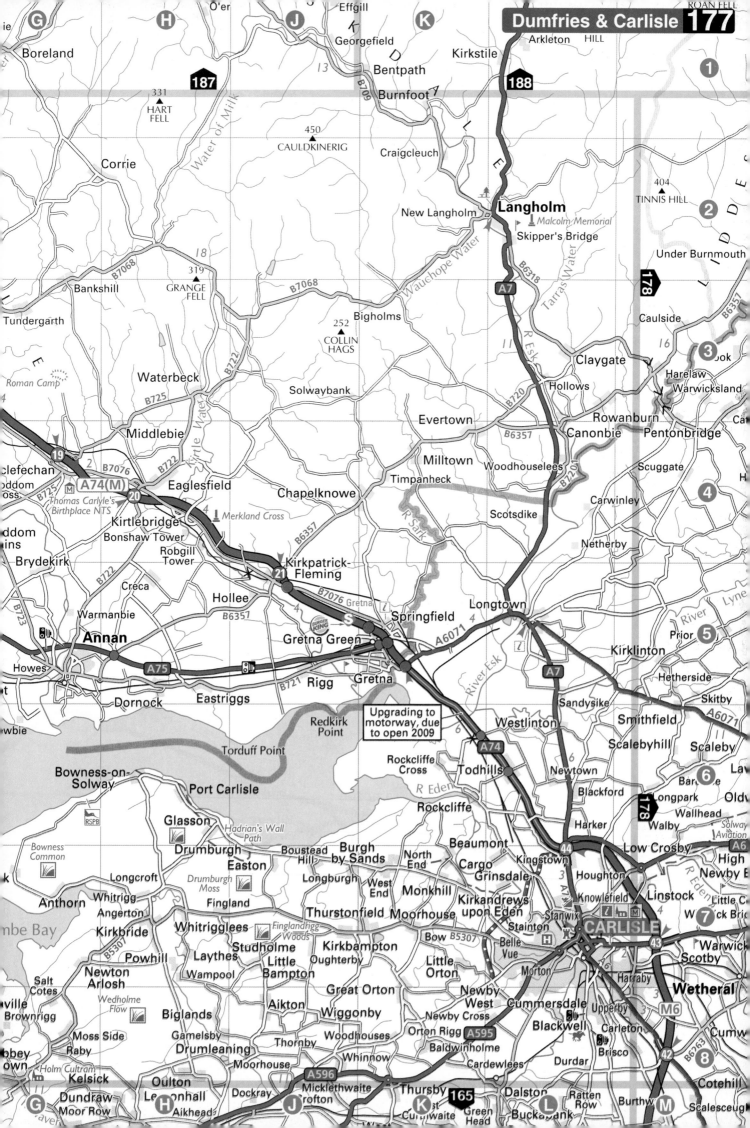

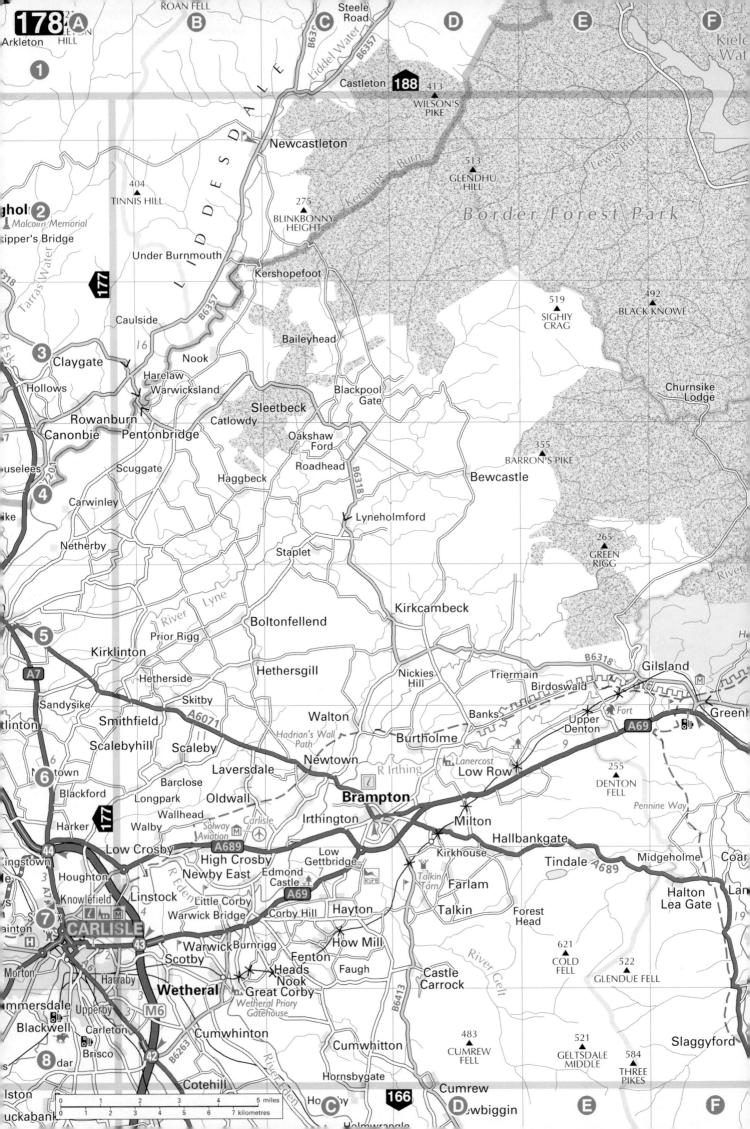

G · H · J · K · L · M

1 · 2 · 3 · 4 · 5 · 6 · 7 · 8

A1068
Ellington
Lynemouth
A189
191 Beacon Point
Woodhorn
A197
Woodhorn Demesne
M
Hirst
North Seaton
H
B1334
Newbiggin-by-the-Sea
Wansbeck Riverside
pwash
North Seaton Colliery
Stakeford
ide Post
West Sleekburn
cotland Gate
Bomarsund
Cambois
4
East Sleekburn
North Blyth
ington
A193
Cowpen
Blyth
B1331
Bebside
Newsham
A189
New Delaval
East Hartford
B1505
A192
Shankhouse
A1061
New Hartley
A193
Seaton Sluice
A192
East Cramlington
Seaton Hartley
B1326
Seaton Delaval
Seghill
A190
Holywell
St Mary's Lighthouse
Annitsford
B1325
Dudley
B1322
Burradon
A192
Earsdon
A1148
Whitley Bay
de en
Camperdown
Backworth
Monkseaton
Cullercoats
1056
Killingworth
B1317
Shiremoor
Murton
Tynemouth
A191
Forest Hall
A191
New York
A1058
A193
A189
Rising Sun
A19
Bergen
Göteborg
Haugesund
IJmuiden
Kristiansand
Stavanger
Longbenton
North Shields
A187
SOUTH SHIELDS
Jesmond
A1058
Willington Quay
Wallsend
Heaton
Int. Ferry Terminal
M
Toll
Tyne Tunnel
A187
Jarrow
A185
Westoe
Harton
Marsden Bay
A183
Walker
B1313
Hebburn
Monkton
Marsden
Souter Lighthouse NT
Felling
A184
Wardley
A194
A19
A1300
H
Cleadon
Souter Point
GATESHEAD
Boldon Colliery
West Boldon
B1298
A183
Whitburn
Low Fell
H
B1288
A184
B1299
Whitburn Bay
Bowes Railway & Museum
A167
A194(M)
East Boldon
A184
A1018
Springwell
Usworth
A195
A1290
A19
Fulwell
Southwick
Roker
Seaburn
Monkwearmouth
Birtley
Portobello
65
A1231
Castletown
WASHINGTON
S
Washington
64
Ouston
A167
BURGER KING
A195
Offerton
Penshaw NT
Penshaw
A183
A690
South Hylton
Grindon
Wildfowl & Wetlands Trust
B1405
H
A183
SUNDERLAND
erkinsville
A693
Fatfield
Penshaw
A183
Herrington
High Newport
New Silksworth
Hendon
Grangetown
Shiney Row
New Herrington
Silksworth
B1286
Tunstall
Ryhope
Durham Heritage Coast
hester-Street
63
A183
Houghton Gate
Philadelphia
B1284
Burnmoor
Newbottle
A19
A1018
Fe Ho
High Dubmire
Houghton-le-Sprir
169
Colliery
B1404
Seaton
Seaham

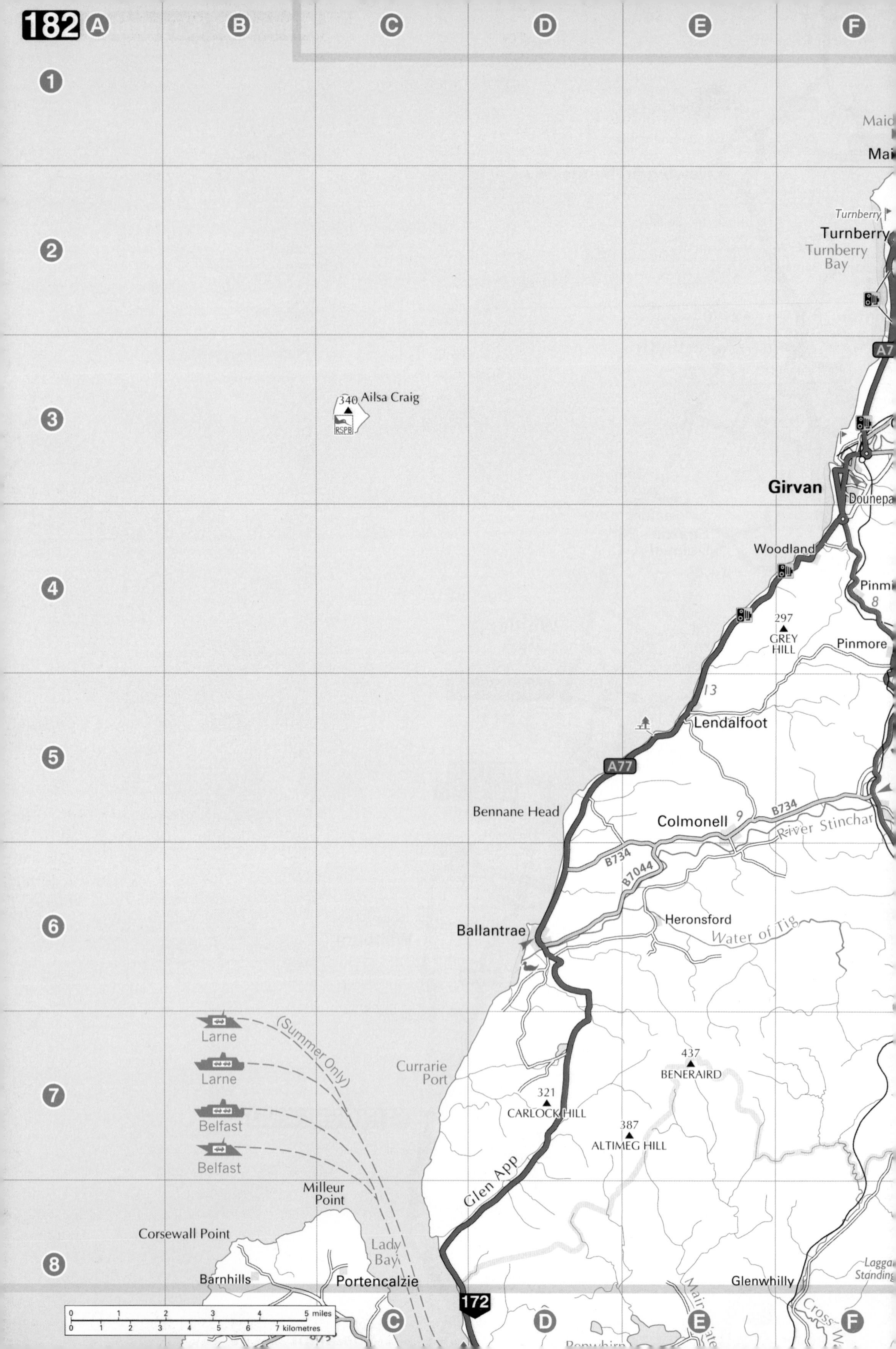

A   B   C   D   E   F

1

2

Maid
Mai

Turnberry
Turnberry
Turnberry
Bay

A7

340 Ailsa Craig
▲
RSPB

Girvan
Dounepa

Woodland

Pinmi
8

297
▲
GREY
HILL

Pinmore

13

Lendalfoot

A77

Bennane Head

Colmonell 9   B734

River Stinchar

B734

B7044

Heronsford

Water of Tig

Ballantrae

Larne

Larne

(Summer Only)

Currarie
Port

437
▲
BENERAIRD

321
▲
CARLOCK HILL

Belfast

387
▲
ALTIMEG HILL

Belfast

Milleur
Point

Glen App

Corsewall Point

Lady
Bay

Lagga
Standing

Glenwhilly

8

Barnhills   **Portencalzie**

172

Cross

0   1   2   3   4   5 miles
0   1   2   3   4   5   6   7 kilometres

C   D   E   F

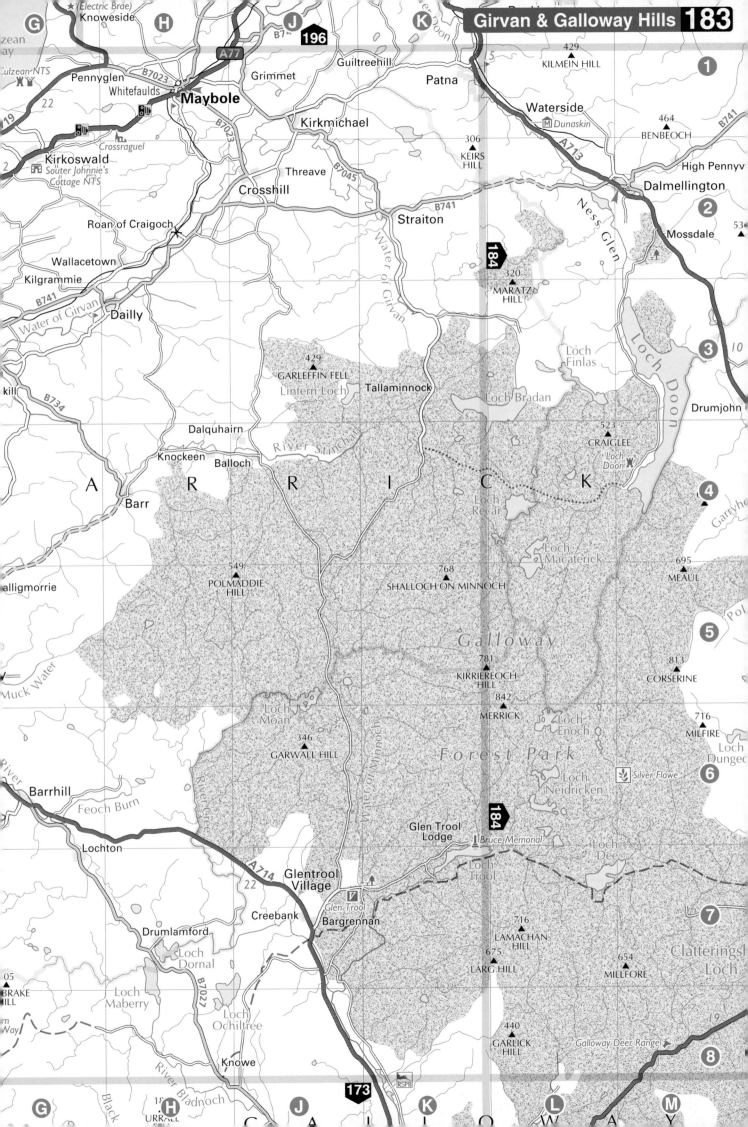

G H J K

(Electric Brae)
Knoweside

B7_

196

A77

Guiltreehill

Patna

1

zean ay

Culzean NTS

Pennyglen
Whitefaulds

B7023

Grimmet

Maybole

Kirkmichael

Waterside

Dunaskin M

429
KILMEIN HILL

464
BENBEOCH

22

19

Kirkoswald

Souter Johnnie's
Cottage NTS

Crossraguel

B7023

Threave

B7045

Crosshill

B741

Straiton

306
KEIRS
HILL

A713

Dalmellington

High Pennyv

B741

2

Roan of Craigoch

184

320
MARATZ
HILL

Mossdale

53

Ness Glen

Wallacetown

Kilgrammie

B741

Water of Girvan

Dailly

Water of Girvan

429
GARLEFFIN FELL

Linfern Loch

Tallaminnock

Loch Bradan

Loch
Finlas

Loch Doon

Loch Doon

3

Drumjohn

kill

B734

Dalquhairn

River Stinchar

523
CRAIGLEE

Loch
Doon

Knockeen

Balloch

A R R I C K

Loch
Recar

Loch
Macaterick

695
MEAUL

4

Barr

549
POLMADDIE
HILL

768
SHALLOCH ON MINNOCH

Galloway

813
CORSERINE

Pol

alligmorrie

Muck Water

781
KIRRIEREOCH
HILL

842
MERRICK

Loch
Enoch

716
MILFIRE

5

Loch
Moan

346
GARWALL HILL

Forest Park

Loch
Neidricken

Silver Flowe

Loch
Dunge

6

Barrhill

Feoch Burn

River Cree

Water of Minnoch

184

Bruce Memorial

Loch
Trool

Loch
Dee

Lochton

A714

Glen Trool
Lodge

7

Clatteringsh
Loch

22

Glentrool
Village

Creebank

Glen Trool

Bargrennan

716
LAMACHAN
HILL

654
MILLFORE

Drumlamford

Loch
Dornal

675
LARG HILL

05

BRAKE
HILL

Loch
Maberry

B7027

440
GARLICK
HILL

Galloway Deer Range

8

rn Way

Loch
Ochiltree

Knowe

River Bladnoch

173

RSPB

G H J K L M

URRALL

18

C A L L O W A Y

G **H** **J**

197 Kirkconnel
Kelloholm
A76
Newtown
Sanquhar

594 ▲ HARE HILL
Blackcraig

700 ▲ BLACKCRAIG

Kello Water

Ulzieside

Mennock

Euchan Water

450 ▲ CLOUD HILL

Polgown

478 ▲

475 ▲ COUNTAM

554 ▲ CAIRNKINNA HILL

Cleuchhead

598 ▲ COLT HILL

Big Carlae

Old Auchenbrack
Auchenhessnane

Benbuie

Shinnel Water

Scaur Water

532 ▲ CORNHARROW HILL

Water of Ken

Southern Upland Way

337 ▲ BENNAN

Stenhouse

Tynron

Moniaive

Kirkland

B729

15

Glencrosh

Craigneston

385 ▲ WETHER HILL

Black Water

A702

13

Loch Urr

Loch Howie

quhairn

Bogue

A713

B7075

Balmaclellan

A712

281 ▲ LARGLEAR HILL

Ironmacannie

Corsock

25

Knockvennie Smithy

B794

175

Kirkpatrick Durham

G **H** **J** **K**

Airds of Kells

16

Loch

Springholm

GREEN LOWTHER

725 ▲ LOWTHER HILL

Nether Fi...nd

1

17

Dalveen

Enterkin Burn

River Nith

23

Durisdeermill

69 ▲

BALLENC... LA...

2

Enterkinfoot

186

A76

A702

Durisdeer

Gateslack

East Morton

Drumlanrig

Morton Loc...
Morton

3

Carronbridge

Tibbers

Burnhead
Penpont

Thornhill

B731

Closeburnmill

4

Keir Mill

Closeburn

Cample

Claughrie Burn

Breckonside

Maxwelton

Keir Hills

Kirkpatrick

Park

5 ...ligh ...dgirth

Blackwood

Auldgirth

Dals...

431 ▲ BOGRIE HILL

Skelston

Sundaywell

Snade

Lag

A76

15

Dunscore

Throughgate

B729

17

6

Upper Stepford

176

Holyw...

392 ▲ SKEOCH HILL

Drumpark

Twelve Ap...

Newb...

Shawhead

7

Te...les

Shawhead

Cargen W...

Lochfoot

Cargen...

A71

A75

Eastlands

Crocketford

Lochrutton Loch

Auchenreoch Loch

Milton Loch

8

Milton

175

Springholm

Lochobe... Loch

K **L** **M**

Beeswing

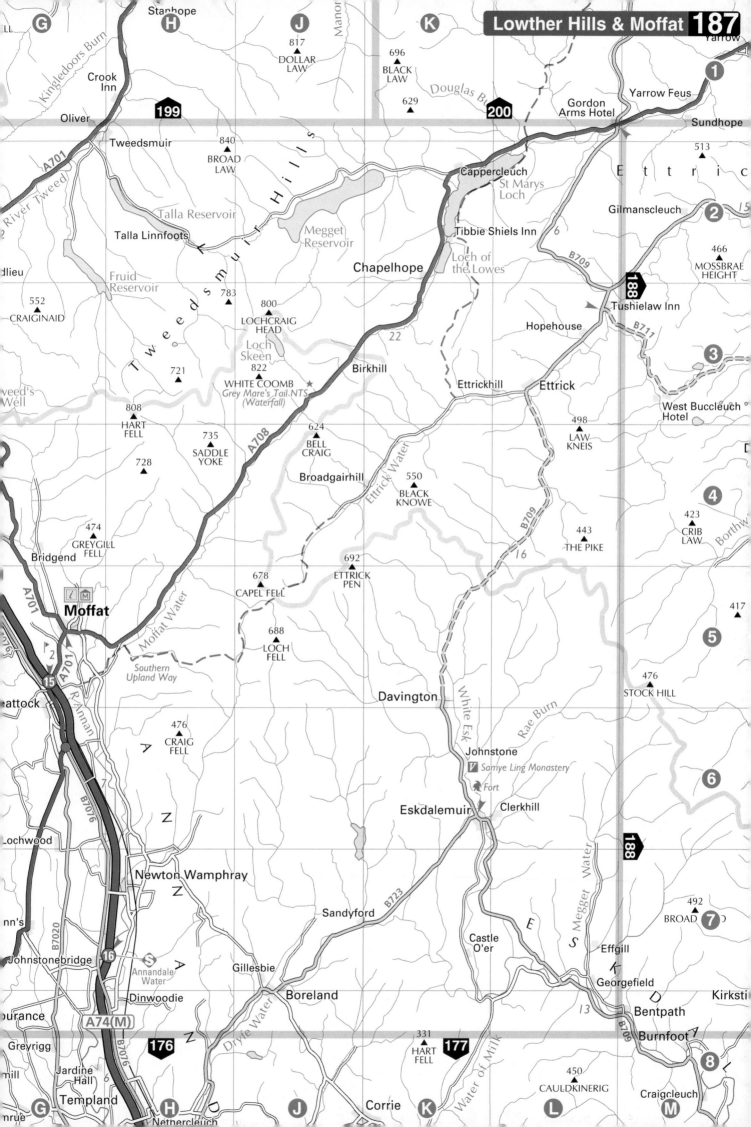

G H J K

Stanhope

Kingledoors Burn

Crook Inn

Oliver

199

Manor

817
▲
DOLLAR LAW

696
▲
BLACK LAW

629
▲

Douglas Burn

200

Yarrow

1

Yarrow Feus

Gordon Arms Hotel

Sundhope

A701

Tweedsmuir

840
▲
BROAD LAW

Talla Reservoir

Megget Reservoir

Cappercleuch

St Marys Loch

513
▲

Ettric

River Tweed

Talla Linnfoots

Tibbie Shiels Inn

6

B709

Gilmanscleuch

2

15

dlieu

Fruid Reservoir

Chapelhope

Loch of the Lowes

466
▲
MOSSBRAE HEIGHT

552
▲
CRAIGINAID

783
▲

800
▲
LOCHCRAIG HEAD

22

188

Tushielaw Inn

Hopehouse

eed's Well

Loch Skeen

721
▲

822
▲
WHITE COOMB
★
Grey Mare's Tail NTS
(Waterfall)

Birkhill

Ettrickhill

Ettrick

B711

3

West Buccleuch Hotel

808
▲
HART FELL

A708

624
▲
BELL CRAIG

Ettrick Water

498
▲
LAW KNEIS

735
▲
SADDLE YOKE

Broadgairhill

550
▲
BLACK KNOWE

B709

443
▲
THE PIKE

423
▲
CRIB LAW

4

Borthw

728
▲

474
▲
GREYGILL FELL

678
▲
CAPEL FELL

692
▲
ETTRICK PEN

16

417
▲

5

Bridgend

Moffat Water

688
▲
LOCH FELL

476
▲
STOCK HILL

A701

ℹ M

Moffat

Southern Upland Way

Davington

White Esk

Rae Burn

6

188

B7076

A74(M)

A701

R. Annan

2

A701

15

476
▲
CRAIG FELL

Johnstone

V Samye Ling Monastery

🏛 Fort

eattock

Eskdalemuir

Clerkhill

Lochwood

B7020

Newton Wamphray

Z

Z

A

B723

Sandyford

E

S

Megget Water

492
▲
BROAD

7

Effgill

Johnstonebridge

16

S

Annandale Water

Gillesbie

Castle O'er

Georgefield

B709

Kirksti

nn's

Boreland

13

Bentpath

ourance

Dinwoodie

Dryfe Water

Burnfoot

Greyrigg

A74(M)

176

Z

Water of Milk

177

331
▲
HART FELL

450
▲
CAULDKINERIG

8

A

Jardine Hall

6

Craigcleuch

mill

G

Templand

H

Nethercleuch

J

Corrie

K

L

M

nrue

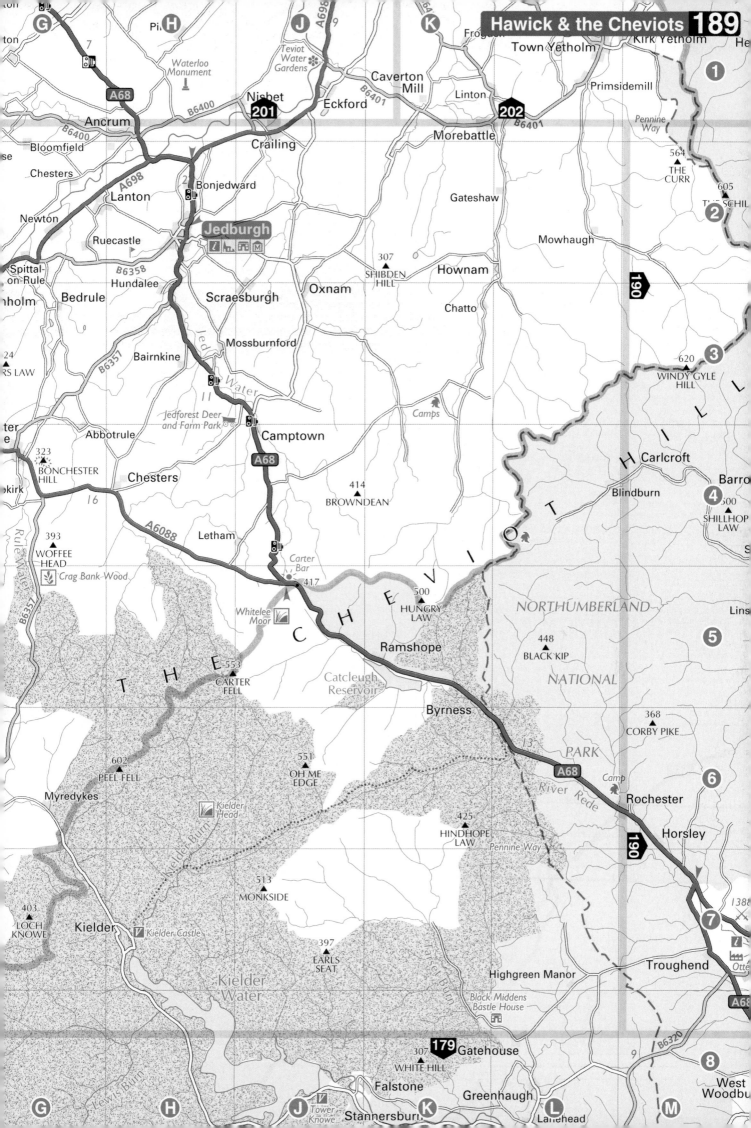

G
H
Pi
J
A698
9
K
Frog
Town Yetholm
Kirk Yetholm
He

7

A68

Waterloo
Monument

Teviot
Water
Gardens

Caverton
Mill

Linton

Primsidemill

1

Pennine
Way

Nisbet

Eckford

B6401

564
THE
CURR

B6400

201

Ancrum

Crailing

Morebattle

202
B6401

605
THE SCHIL
2

Bloomfield

A698

Gateshaw

Chesters

B6400

Lanton

B6400

Bonjedward

Mowhaugh

Newton

Jedburgh
ℹ 🏰 📷 Ⓜ

Ruecastle

Spittal-
on-Rule

B6358

Hundalee

Scraesburgh

Oxnam

307
SHIBDEN
HILL

Hownam

190

Bedrule

Chatto

holm

B6357

Bairnkine

Mossburnford

Camps

620
WINDY GYLE
HILL
3

Jedforest Deer
and Farm Park

Camptown

Carlcroft

Abbotrule

Chesters

A68

Blindburn

Barro

323
BONCHESTER
HILL

414
BROWNDEAN

500
SHILLHOP
LAW
4

kirk

16

A6088

Letham

393
WOFFEE
HEAD

Crag Bank Wood

Carter
Bar

417

Whitelee
Moor

CHEVIOT

NORTHUMBERLAND

Lins

500
HUNGRY
LAW

448
BLACK KIP

5

Ramshope

Catcleugh
Reservoir

NATIONAL

B6357

THE

553
CARTER
FELL

Byrness

13

368
CORBY PIKE

PARK

602
PEEL FELL

551
OH ME
EDGE

A68

368
CORBY PIKE

Camp

6

Myredykes

Kielder
Head

Kielder Burn

River Rede

Rochester

425
HINDHOPE
LAW

Horsley

403
LOCH
KNOWE

513
MONKSIDE

Pennine Way

190

Kielder

Kielder Castle

397
EARLS
SEAT

1388

7

ℹ

Kielder
Water

Highgreen Manor

Troughend

Ott

Black Middens
Bastle House

A68

307
WHITE HILL

179
Gatehouse

B6320

9

Lewis Burn

Tower
Knowe

Falstone

Greenhaugh

West
Woodbu

Stannersburn

G
H
J
K
Lanehead
L
M

G   Warenford   Newham   H   J   Beadnell   K

1

Swinhoe
Beadnell Bay
Newstead   Chathill   Tughall
Ellingham
Preston   203   Brunton   Newton-by-the-Sea
Preston Pele Tower   Christon Bank
Brownieside   Doxford   Embleton   2
North Charlton   Falloden   Embleton Bay
Dunstan Steads   Dunstanburgh NT
Ditchburn   South Charlton
Eglingham   Dunstan   Craster
Rock
Rennington   Stamford   Howick
Howick Hall   Cullernose Point   3
Broxfield   Littlehoughton
East Bolton   Longhoughton
River Aln   Denwick   Boulmer
Abberwick   Alnwick   Seaton Point
Broome Park   Hawkhill   Lesbury   4
Bilton   Hipsburn
Bilton Banks   Alnmouth
Edlingham   High Buston   Alnmouth Bay
Shilbottle   Low Buston
A1068
260   8
GLANTLEES HILL   Birling
Newton-on-the-Moor   Warkworth Castle & Hermitage   Warkworth
A697   Amble   5
Guyzance   Gloster Hill   Coquet Island
Swarland Estate   Togston   High Hauxley
Swarland   Acklington   Radcliffe
North End   Broomhill
amlington   Felton   South Broomhill   East Chevington   6
East Thirston   Red Row   Chevington Drift   Druridge Bay
Pauperhaugh   West Thirston   Eshott
Brinkburn   Weldon Bridge   West Chevington   Druridge   Druridge Bay
Todburn   Helm   Stobswood   Widdrington   North Northumberland Heritage Coast
Wingates   Causey Park   8
Longhorsley   Causey Park Bridge   Widdrington Station   Cresswell   7
8   Earsdon   A1068
Tritlington   Ulgham   Ellington
Fenrother   Linton   Lynemouth
A697   Stanton   Hebron   A189   Beacon Point
A1   Longhirst   180   Woodhorn
River Font   Pigdon   Pegswood   Ashington   Woodhorn Demesne   8
Newton Underwood   A197   Hirst   North Seaton   Newbiggin-by-the-Sea
Meld   Throphill   Bothal   Wansbeck Rive   B1334
Park   Sheepwash   North Seaton Colliery
G   H   J   Morpeth   K   L   M

Muasdale

Glenacardoch
Point

Belloch

Barr Water

Glenbarr

MacAlister Clan

BEINN AN TUIRC
454

Tor

319

Cleongart

408
BORD
MOR

N

Bellochantuy Bay

Bellochantuy

194

Sadd

396
SGREADAN
HILL

Ugadale

Tangy Loch

Glen Lussa

Kilkenzie

Peninver

Ardnac
Bay

A83

Kilmichael

B842

Machrihanish
Bay

Campbeltown

Campbeltown

Island Da

Machrihanish

Campbeltown
Loch

6
B843

Drumlemble

Kilkerran

Kildalloig

Earadale Point

352
BEINN GHUILEAN

Achinhoan

385
THE
STATE

446
CNOC
MOY

10

Dalsmeran

Ru

Glen Breakevre

Conie Glen

Glen Kerran

Strone Glen

Cattadale

Polliwilline Bay

BEINN NA LICE

Macharioch

428

Carskey

Southend

MULL
OF
KINTYRE

Dunaverty

Carskey Bay

Sanda Sound

Borgadalemore Point

Sheep Island

Sanda Island

205

0 1 2 3 4 5 miles
0 1 2 3 4 5 6 7 kilometres

G Carradale
B879
Carradale House
Carradale Point
Carradale Bay

dell ay

K I L B R A N N A

H Balliekine
J
792 BEINN NUIS
K
Glen Rosa
Brodick NTS
Merkland Point
1

Iorsa Water

A R R A N

Brodick Bay
Brodick
Strathwhillan
Corriegills

Machrie Bay
Auchagallon Stone Circle
Machrie
Machrie Moor Stone Circles
Moss Farm Road Stone Circle
Tormore

B880
512 A'CHRUACH

M
A841
4
Clauchlands Point
2

Balmichael
503 BEINN BHREAC
Balmichael

Margnaheglish
Lamlash
Lamlash Bay
Holy Island

Torbeg
Shiskine

Cordon

Blackwaterfoot

Auchencairn
Kingscross
Knockenkelly
3

Drumadoon Bay
Kilpatrick
Kilpatrick Dun

Glen Scorrodale
Carn Ban

Whiting Bay
Whiting Bay

194 Brown Head

A841

Glen Ashdale
Largymore

Corriecravie
Sliddery

Kilmory Water

Largybeg
Dippen Head
4

Torr a' Chaisteal Fort

16

Kilmory
Lagg
Torrylin Cairn
Bennan

Dippen
Kildonan

Bennan Head
Pladda

195
5

6

7

340 Ailsa Craig
RSPB

8

G   H   J   K   L   M

G

H

Ga____ty

J

207

K

Arran & Firth of Clyde

B784

B780

1

Garroch Head

Little
Cumbrae
Island

Fairlie R____

Hunterston
Power Station

12

Crosbie

Blackshaw

Drakemyre

Hi___

Dalry

B780

Portencross

B7048

Munnoch

B781

B780

A737

Farland Head

**West
Kilbride**

Dalgarven
Mill

Seamill

B7047

C

U

N

B780

B714

Dalgarven

7

Kilwinning

B778

A78

A78

A738

nox

Corrie

Ardrossan

A738

A738

Stevenston

B77

A841

Horse Isle

B780

Ardeer

B779

Saltcoats

196

3

6

Merkland Point

Irvine

Maritime

Brodick
Bay

V

V

The Big Idea

Ful___

Strathwhillan

Irvine
Bay

G

Corriegills

F I R T H

4

Clauchlands Point

O F

Bara

Margnaheglish

4

Lamlash
Bay

Holy Island

C L Y D E

Cordon

(Summer Only)

Troon

chencairn

Kingscross

5

Roya

Knockenkelly

4

Larne

Whiting
Bay

hiting Bay

0

Ashdale

6 Ayr
Bay

Largymore

Largybeg

i M A

Dippen

Dippen Head

196

Kildonan

da

Heads
of Ayr

Doonfo

Heads of Ayr

Burns Cott_

A719

7

All_

Fisherton

De

Dunure

Culroy

Drumshang

Croy Brae
(Electric Brae)

Knoweside

8

G

H

182

J

K

Culzean
Bay

L

Pennyglen

Culzean __ TS

M

A

Whitefaulas

Mayb_

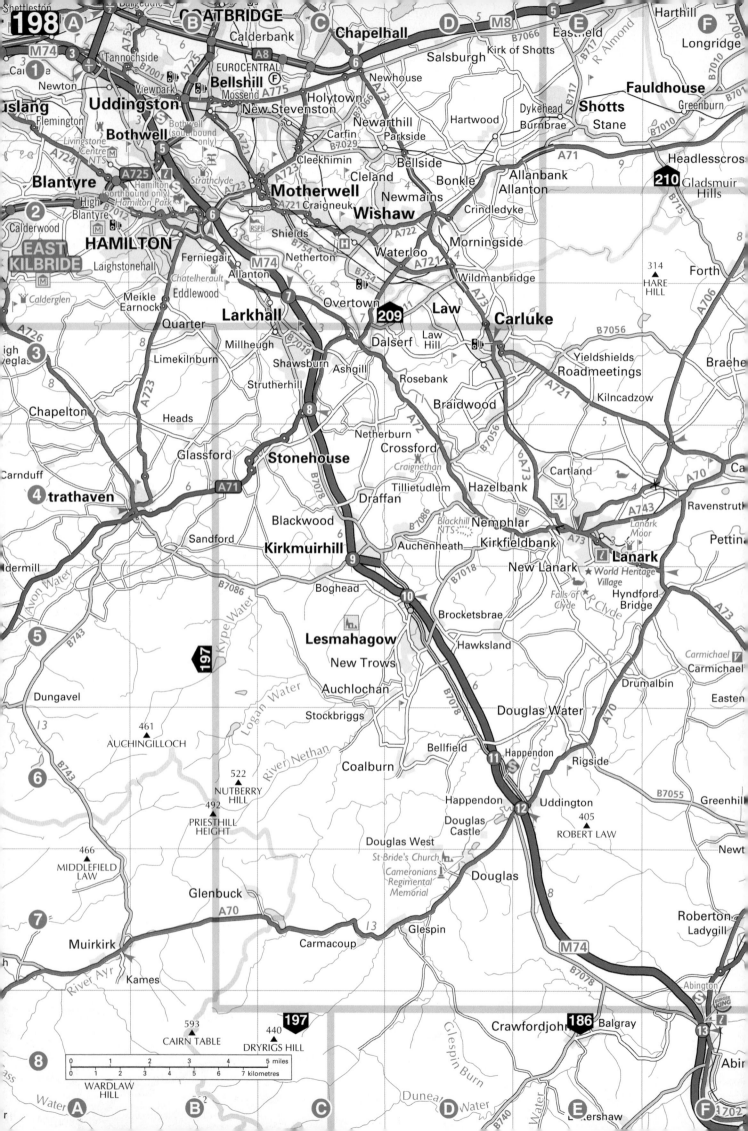

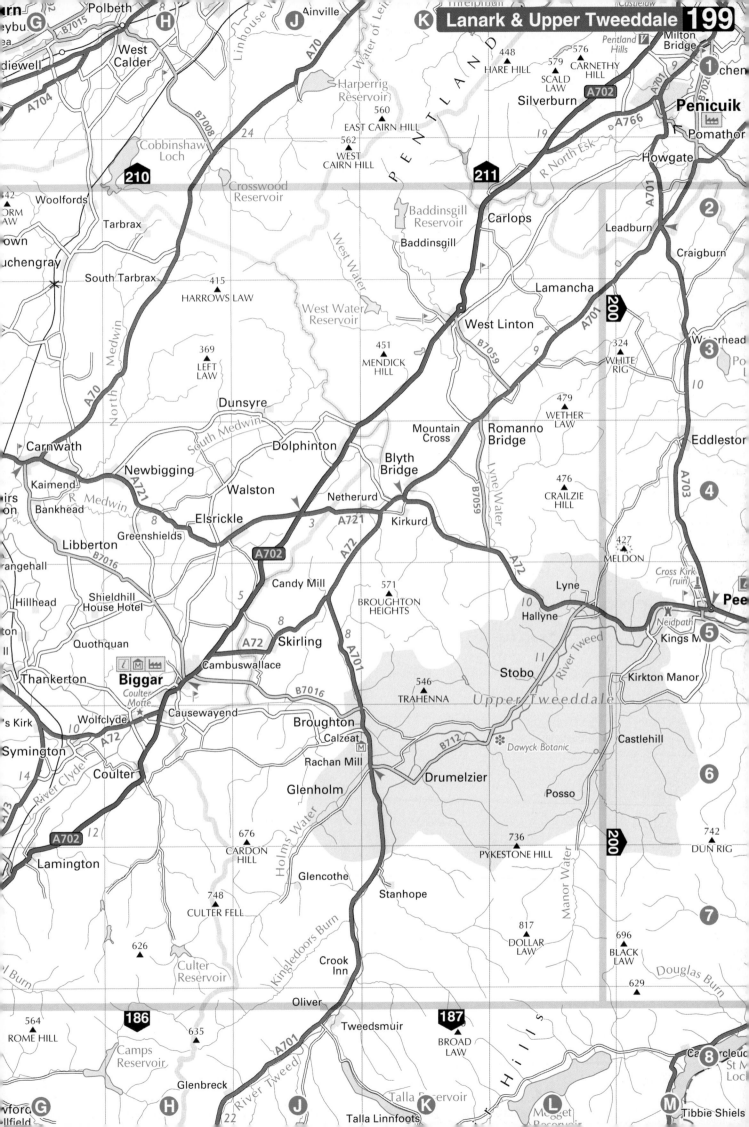

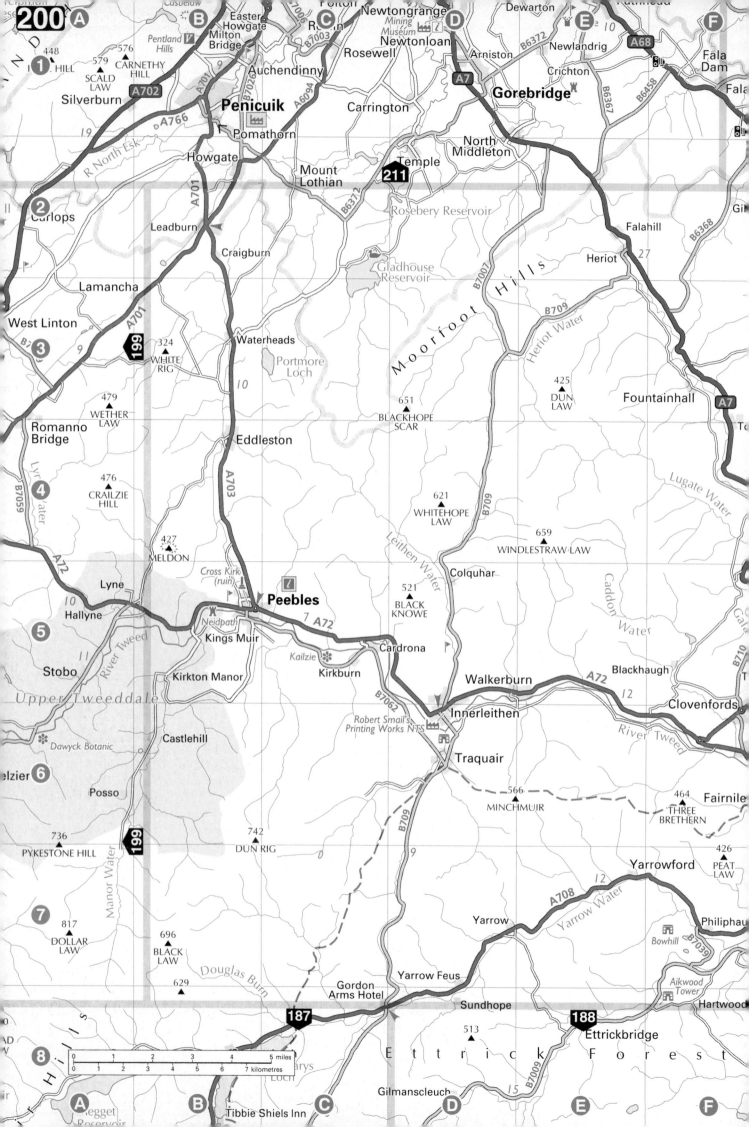

G   H   J   K   N St A

1

Blegbie
Blythe

528 ▲ LAMMER LAW

MEIKLE SAYS LAW

533 ▲

Whiteadder Reservoir

Cranshaws

Abbey St Bathar

Ellemford

Edin Hall B

1

509 ▲ CRIB LAW

513 ▲ SEENES LAW

467 ▲ MEIKLE LAW

Whitchester

Longformacus

325 ▲ COCKBURN LAW

Primroseh

495 ▲ HUNT LAW

212

Southern Upland Way

399 ▲ DIRRINGTON GREAT LAW

2

68

Oxton

Carfraemill

14

Soonhope Burn

Wedderlie Burn

202

Gavinton

A697

383 ▲ COLLIE LAW

17

Thirlestane

Lauder

Blythe

Spottiswoode

Westruther

B6456

Polwarth

Fogo

3

Thornydykes

A697

8

A6105

Greenlaw

Blackadder Water

B6460

Cha

4

B6362

Thirlestane

Boon

A6089

Houndslow

5

Bassendean

Greenlaw

B6362

Nether Blainslie

Legerwood

6

Greenknowe Tower

Gordon

Middlethird

Hume

Lambden

Eccles

B6364

Threepwood

A6105

B6397

Gordon

B6460

Stichill

Nenthorn

Ednam

Hendersyde Park

West Morriston

Fans

Mellerstain

9

6

B6461

Bi

5

A68

Earlston

B6356

Redpath

Smailholm

A6089

Kelso

Kelso

6

Galashiels

Langlee

Priorwood Garden NTS

3

Gattonside

B6360

Newstead

Scott's View

Smailholm Tower

B6397

Floors

Border Union

Sprou

Tweedbank

A6091

Darnick

Melrose

B6361

Trimontium

Eildon and Leaderfoot

Wallace Monument

Mertoun

Clintmains

Manorhill

Kelso

202

Abbotsford

422 ▲

EILDON HILLS

Newtown St Boswells

2

Dryburgh

10

River Tweed

A699

Roxburgh

Heiton

B6352

A7

B6398

St Boswells

Maxton

Rutherford

A698

B6436

Selkirk

A699

Bowden

Camieston

7

Pirnie

Teviot Water Gardens

Caverton Mill

7

Midlem

B6359

Longnewton

Ale Water

A68

Waterloo Monument

Nisbet

Eckford

B6401

Linton

Lilliesleaf

Riddell

Belses

188

Greenhouse

Bloomfield

Chesters

Ancrum

189

Crailing

Morebattle

B6400

Harelaw

B6359

Minto

276 ▲

N on

A698

Lanton

Bonjedward

Jedburgh

Gateshaw

8

G   H   J   K   L   M

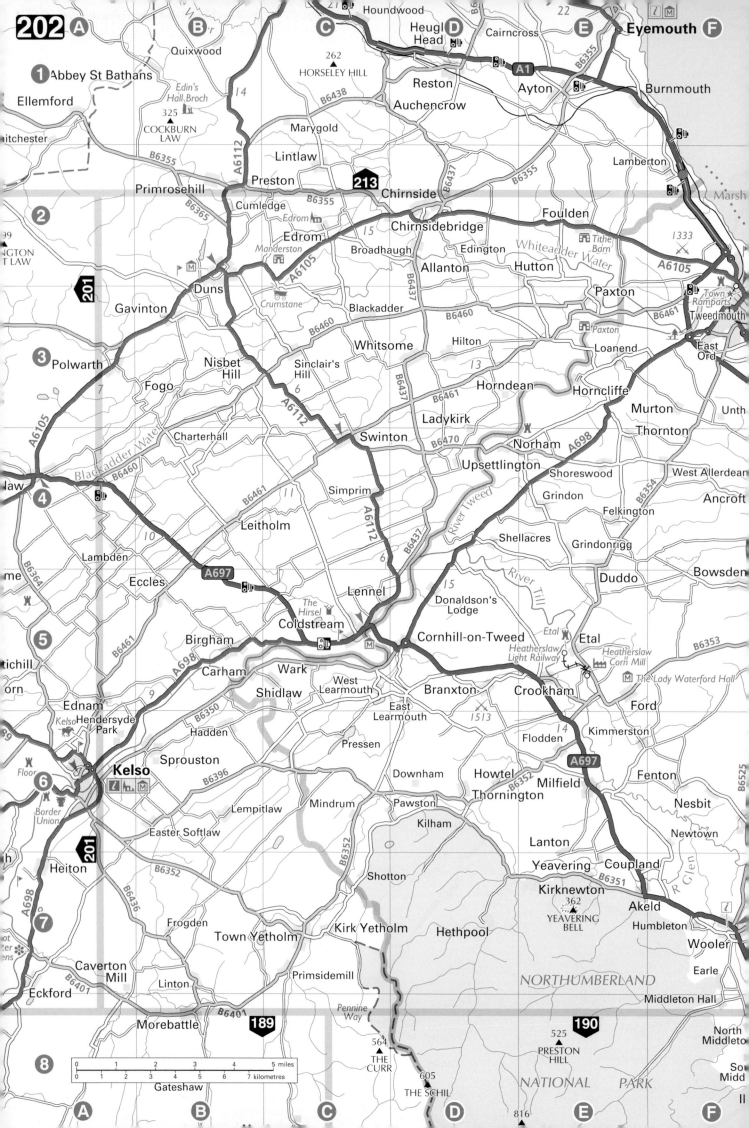

1

2

3

4

5

6

7

8

G   H   J   K   L   M

vs Bay

Northumberland Heritage Coast

ck-upon-Tweed

Huds
lead
nerston

Cheswick

Goswick

Haggerston

Beal

Fenham

Holy
Island

HOLY ISLAND

Lindisfarne
Priory

Lindisfarne NT

Castle Point

Guile Point

Longstone
Lighthouse

NT

FARNE
ISLANDS

West
Kyloe

owick

Fenwick

Buckton

Smeafield

Elwick

Ross

Staple
Sound

Inner
Sound

North Northumberland
Heritage Coast

Holburn

St Cuthbert's
Cave NT

Detchant

Middleton

Low
Middleton

Easington

Budle
Bay

Bamburgh

Bamburgh

Hetton
Steads

Belford

Outchester

Waren
Mill

Budle

B1342

B1340

New
Shoreston

North
Hazelrigg

Spindlestone

Burton

South
Hazelrigg

B6349

Bradford

Seahouses

Bellshill

Warenton

Lucker

Elford

North Sunderland

East
Horton

Adderstone

B6348

Warenford

Newham

Beadnell

Chatton

Newstead

Chathill

Tughall

Swinhoe

Beadnell
Bay

River Till

Ros
Castle NT

Newstead

Ellingham

Preston

Newton-by-the-Sea

ewtown

Chillingham

Wild Cattle
Park

190

Hepburn

Preston
Pele Tower

191

Brunton

Christon
Bank

Embleton

Embleton
Bay

A697

CATERAN
HILL

267

Old Bewick

Brownieside

North
Charlton

Doxford

Falloden

Dunstan
Steads

Dunstanburgh
NT

A1

B6346

Ditchbur

South
Charlton

B347

B1339

Dunstan

G · H · J · K · 215

Jura Forest

506
▲ SCRINADLE

398
▲ BEINN
TARSUINN

Loch a'
Chnuic Bhric

784
▲ BEINN
AN OIR

Paps of Jura

734
▲

24

J U R A

Jura

560
▲ GLASS BHEINN

529
▲ DUBHA
BHEINN

Keils

Small
Isles

342
▲ BRAT
BHEINN

Craighouse

Rudha na Gaillich

Feolin Ferry

Cabrach

Am Fraoch
Eilean

Rudha na Tràille

Brosdale
Island

A846

McArthur's
Head

NAM
ANN

Port Askaig - Kennacraig

GEIR

Rudha Liath

Ardtalla

Claggain
Bay

Kintour

Ardmore
Point

Kildalton
Cross

Eilean
a' Chuirn

Port Ellen - Kennacraig

Rudha na
Gainmhich

Kinerarach

Tarbert

GIGHA

Ardminish

Achamore

Cara

Danna
Island

St Cormacs
Chapel

Kilmory Knap
Chapel

Kilmory Bay

Ellary

Kilmory

Point of Knap

206

C henga

Coulaghai

Kilberry
Sculptured
Stones ★

Kilberry

Kilberry Head

Keppoch Point

Tiretigan

213
▲ CRUACH A

Loch Stornoway

Ard

Rona n Poin

Sound of Gigha

Rhunahaorine
Point

Rhunahaorine

38

Tayinloan

194

A83

Muasdale

Glenacardoch
Point

Belloch

Barr Water

Gl barr

G · H · J · K · L · M

214 · 215 · 192

1 · 2 · 3 · 4 · 5 · 6 · 7 · 8

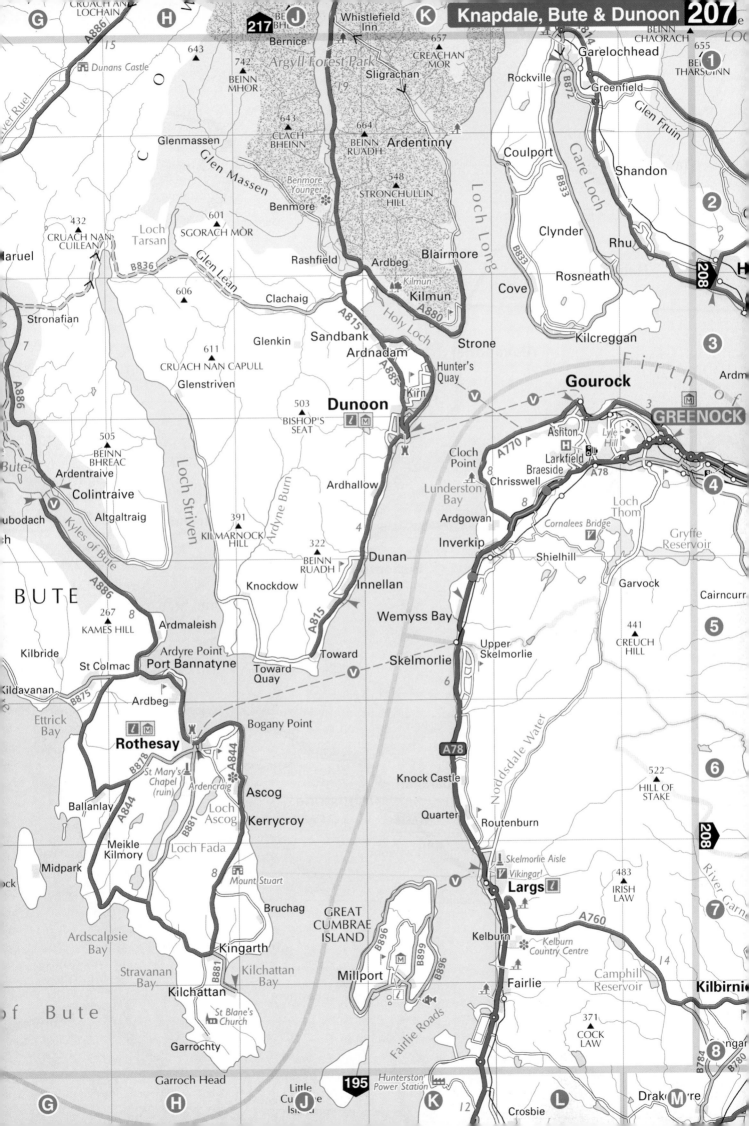

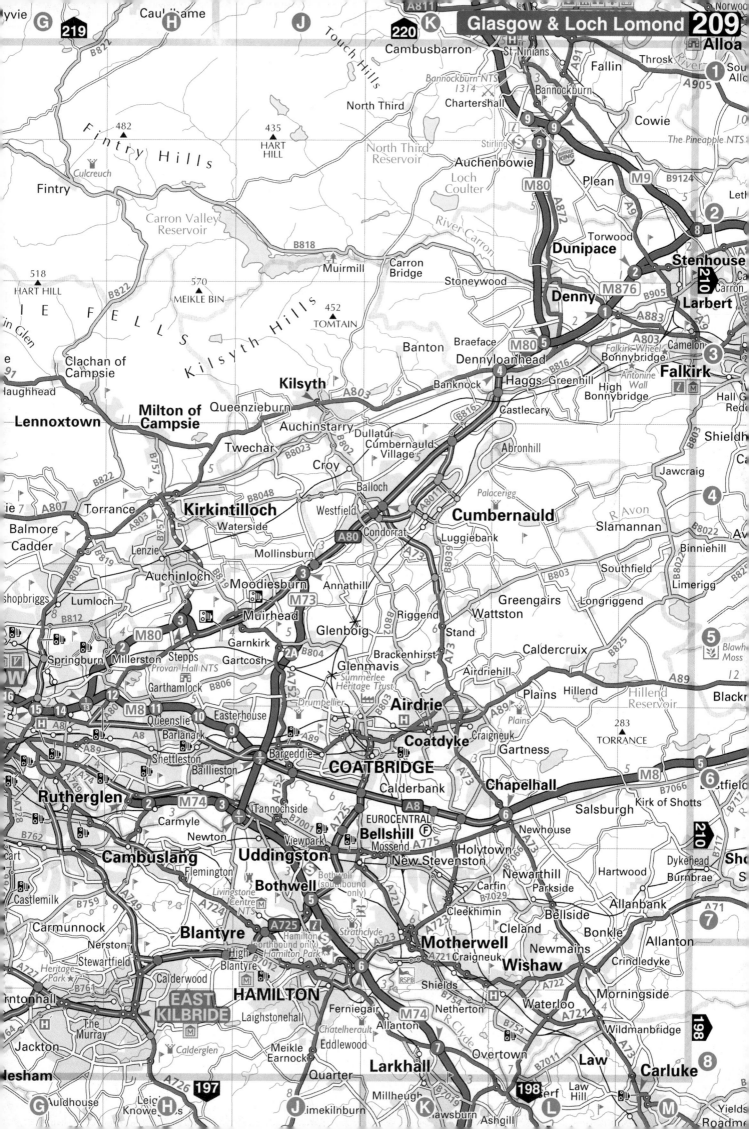

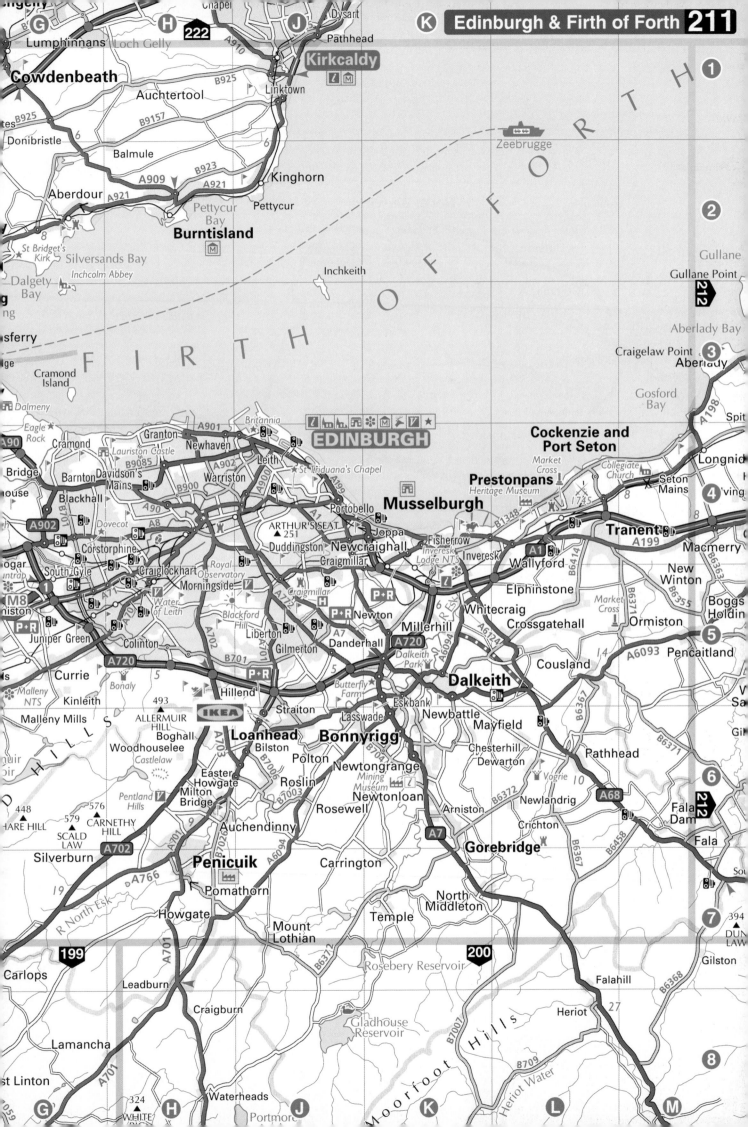

G   H   J

1

2

3

4

Chapel Point

Thorntonloch

owhill

Reed
Point

Cove   Pease
Bay   Siccar
Point

Collegiate Church

Cockburnspath

ks

Ecclaw

Southern
Upland Way

Grantshouse

Butterdean

Eye Water

Quixwood

Bathans

Edin's
Hall Broch

14

325
▲
COCKBURN
LAW

B6355

Primrosehill

B6365

Cumledge

Edrom

Duns

Gavinton

Manderston

Crumstane

A6105

A6112

Preston

Lintlaw

Marygold

B6438

262
▲
HORSELEY HILL

Reston

Auchencrow

15

Edrom

Chirnside

Chirnsidebridge

202

Broadhaugh

Allanton

Blackadder

B6437

Whitsome

Nisbet
Hill

Sinclair's
Hill

13

A1107

Fast Castle Head

196
▲
BROWN
RIG

Coldingham
Loch

ST ABB'S HEAD

St Abbs

Coldingham
Bay

Grantshouse

Houndwood

21

Heugh
Head

Cairncross

B6438

A1107

22

Eyemouth

A1

Ayton

B6355

Burnmouth

Lamberton

B6355

B6437

Foulden

Whiteadder Water

Tithe
Barn

1333

North Northumberl

Marshall Meadows Bay

Edington

Hutton

Paxton

Paxton

Hilton

Loanend

A6105

Berwick-upon

Town
Ramparts

Barracks

H

Tweedmouth

East
Ord

Spittal

Huds
Head

Scremerston

G   H   J   K   L   M

5

6

7

8

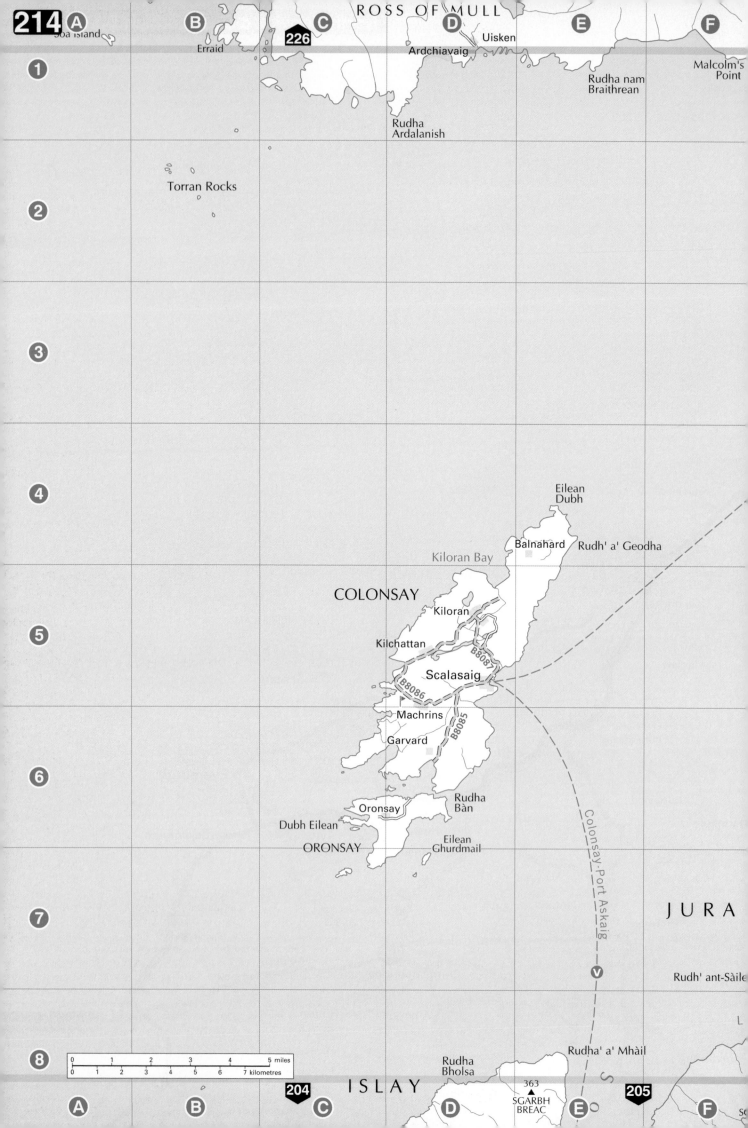

A B C D E F

ROSS OF MULL

226

Soa Island

Erraid

Uisken

Ardchiavaig

Malcolm's Point

1

Rudha nam Braithrean

Rudha Ardalanish

Torran Rocks

2

3

4

Eilean Dubh

Balnahard

Rudh' a' Geodha

Kiloran Bay

COLONSAY

Kiloran

B8087

5

Kilchattan

Scalasaig

B8086

Machrins

B8085

Garvard

6

Rudha Bàn

Oronsay

Dubh Eilean

ORONSAY

Eilean Ghurdmail

JURA

7

Colonsay–Port Askaig

Rudh' ant-Sàile

V

8

0 1 2 3 4 5 miles
0 1 2 3 4 5 6 7 kilometres

Rudha Bholsa

Rudha' a' Mhàil

204

ISLAY

363
SGARBH BREAC

205

A B C D E F

Dubh

G   H   J   K

227

Insh
Island

Clachan-Seil

SEIL

Ellanbeich   Easdale

Balvicar

1

Easdale   B844

Cuan Ferry Village   V   B8003

Cullipool
House   Torsay
Island   Degnish   2   Loch Melfor

Garbh Eileach

Eilean
Dubh Mòr   LUING   Arduaine
Garden NTS   Arduaine

GARVELLACHS   ★ Monastery & Beehive Cells   Toberonochy   SHUNA   3   Cra
Have

Eileach
an Naoimh   **LUNGA**   Sound of Luing   Craigdhu

Scarba, Lunga   Shuna Sound   Shuna
Point   Ardfern   Kin

and the   B8002   En Mhi

Garvellachs   En Ri

SCARBA   448
▲   Aird   4

CRUACH SCARBA

Gulf of Corryvreckan   Island
Macaskin   Slockavull

Temple Wood
Stone Circle

Craignish Point   Ri Cruin

Glengarrisdale
Bay   295
▲   Poltallo

CRUACH NA
SEILCHEIG   5

Loch Crinan

Glendebadel Bay   **Crinan**

Kilmahumaig

364
▲   Lealt Burn   B8025   Bellanoch   B841

BEN
GARRISDALE   Crinan

Lussa River   Barnluc   6

466
▲   Glen Grundale   V

Corpach Bay   BEINN
BHREAC   Taynish

Carsaig Bay   Tayvallich   206   Achnamara

453
▲   Ardlussa   *Knapdale*   Kilmichael of Inverlus

n-Bay   RAINBERG MÒR   Loch Sween   7   331
▲
BEIN
BHEA

Loch
gh Mòr   A846   Lussa
Point   466
▲
CRUACH
LUSACH

B8025

Keills Chapel

arbert   Kilbride   *Sween*

Danna
Island   Lochead   8

205   Loch na Cille   chahoish

G   H   J   K   L   M

G   H   **229**   J   K   1

River Noe

Glen Str

BEINN UDLAIDH 771

1

ve Ironworks

Inverawe

1124
BEN
CRUACHAN

988
BEINN EUNAICH

648
BEINN
DONACHAN

River Orchy

B8074

River Lochy

Tyndru

Glen Lochy

12

River Awe

Pass of Brander

B8077

Cruachan
Reservoir

Kilchurn

Stronmilchan

Inverlochy

A85

20

Lochawe

Cruachan
Power Station

Upper
Kinchrackine

Dalmally

2

1130
BEN LUI

1028
BEN OSS

977
BEINN
DUBHCHR

B845
B840

Ardanaiseig

Ardanaiseig Hotel

Hayfield

A819

6

636

218

739

*LOCH LOMOND AND
THE TROSSACHS
NATIONAL PARK*

3

renan

Taychreggan
Hotel

Cladich

7

We

Portsonachan
Hotel

*Lochan
Shira*

Glen Aray

A82

Glen Shira

947
BEINN
BHUIDHE

Glenfyne
Lodge

Glen Fyne

645
MAOL BREAC

A'llui

4

589
CRUACH
MHOR

A819

658
CLACHAN
HILL

942
BEN
VORLICH

*Loch
Sloy*

ghour

Bell Tower

Ardkinglas
Woodland
Garden

Cairndow

5

Inver glas

Loch Shira

Glen Kinglas

1011
BEN IME

Douglas Water

Inveraray Castle

Inveraray

Inveraray Jail

Ardno

Loch Fyne

10

St Catherines

Argyll
Wildlife Park

A815

565
CRUACH
NAN CAPULL

B839

B828

912
BEINN AN
LOCHAIN

11

Rest and be thankful

925
BEINN NARNAIN

881
THE
COBBLER

Succoth

416
CRUACH
TAIRBEIRT

6

A83

Glen
Croe

Arrochar

2

Auchindrain
Township

Furnace

A886

Strachur

River Cur

845
BEN
DONICH

River Gallt

Ardgartan

218

Argyll Forest Park

Lochgoilhead

A83

661
BEN
REACH

Newton

Balliemore

Glenbranter

Invernoaden

A815

779
BEINN
BHEULA

Corrow

Douglas Pier

Loch Goil

Glen Doug

A814

10

734
DOUNE
HILL

7

480
CRUACH
NAN CAPULL

A886

A

*Loch
Eck*

Carrick Castle

Portincaple

Arddarroch

702
BEINN EICH

Edentaggart

8

505
CRUACH AN
LOCHAIN

A886

15

Dunans Castle

G   H

618
BEINN
BHEAG

207

742

est Park

Sligachan

Whistlefield
Inn

A815

J

657
CREA
M

K

Whistlefield

A814

713
BEINN
CHAORACH

arelochhead

L

55
NN
THARSUINN

M

LOCH L

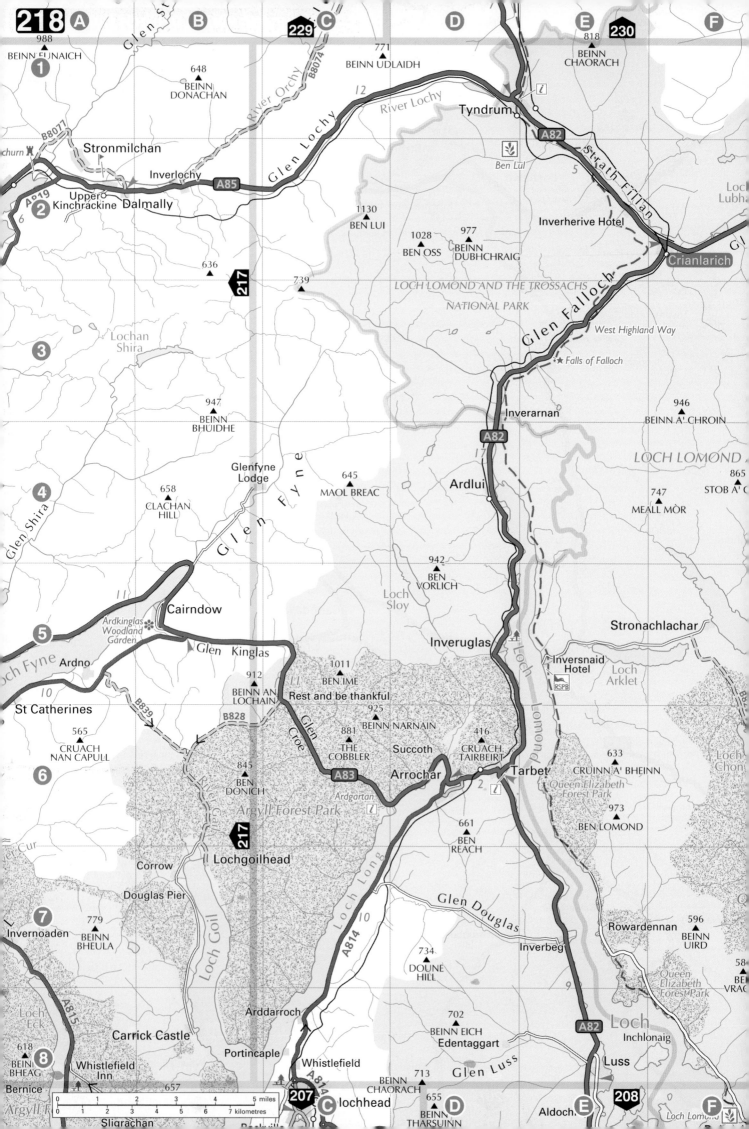

A **B** **C** 229 **D** **E** 230 **F**

988
BEINN EUNAICH
1

648
BEINN DONACHAN

771
BEINN UDLAIDH

818
BEINN CHAORACH

B8077
Stronmilchan
Inverlochy
A85
Glen Lochy
12
River Lochy
Tyndrum
i
A82
Strath Fillan
Loch Lubh

churn
Upper
Kinchrackine Dalmally
A819
6
2
Ben Lui

Inverherive Hotel
5
Crianlarich

636
217
739
1130
BEN LUI

1028
BEN OSS
977
BEINN DUBHCHRAIG

LOCH LOMOND AND THE TROSSACHS
NATIONAL PARK
Glen Falloch

West Highland Way
Falls of Falloch

Lochan Shira
3

947
BEINN BHUIDHE

Glenfyne Lodge

Inverarnan
A82
17
946
BEINN A' CHROIN
LOCH LOMOND

658
CLACHAN HILL
4

645
MAOL BREAC
Ardlui

865
STOB A' C
747
MEALL MÒR

Glen Shira
Glen Fyne

Cairndow
11
Ardkinglas Woodland Garden
5

942
BEN VORLICH
Loch Sloy

Inveruglas
Inversnaid Hotel
RSPB
Stronachlachar
Loch Arklet
B

ch Fyne
Ardno
10
St Catherines

Glen Kinglas
912
BEINN AN LOCHAIN
1011
BEN IME
Rest and be thankful
925
BEINN NARNAIN
881
THE COBBLER
Succoth
416
CRUACH TAIRBEIRT
Tarbet
633
CRUINN A' BHEINN
Loch Chon

565
CRUACH NAN CAPULL
6
B839
B828
Glen Croe
A83
Arrochar
i
2
Queen Elizabeth Forest Park
973
BEN LOMOND

River Goil
217
Argyll Forest Park
Ardgartan
i
661
BEN REACH
845
BEN DONICH

Corrow
Lochgoilhead

Loch Long
Glen Douglas
Inverbeg

Douglas Pier

596
BEINN UIRD
7
779
BEINN BHEULA
Invernoaden

A814
10
734
DOUNE HILL
Rowardennan
9
A82
Loch
58
BE
VRAC

Loch Eck
A815

Arddarroch
702
BEINN EICH
Edentaggart
Queen Elizabeth Forest Park

Carrick Castle
Portincaple
Whistlefield
Glen Luss
Inchlonaig
Luss

618
BEIN BHEAG
8
Whistlefield Inn
657
713
BEINN CHAORACH
655
BEINN THARSUINN
Aldoch
208
Loch Lomon

Bernice
Argyll F
Slighrachan
207
lochhead

0 1 2 3 4 5 miles
0 1 2 3 4 5 6 7 kilometres

A **B** **C** **D** **E** **F**

G 230 H J 231

EATHAICH

Finlarig
Killin
Falls of Dochart ★
Breadalbane
Folklore Centre

879
CREAG
UCHDAG

682
RUADH MHEALL

Loch
Lednock

1

Auchlyne

B R E A D

River Dochart

671
SRON
MHOR

85 Dochart A85

2

Glen Beich

St Fillans A85

Glen

778
▲MEALL AN
FHIODHAIN

Dalveich

Lochearnhead

A84

Ardvorlich

Loch Earn

220

River Earn

Balquhidder

Auchtubh

Kingshouse
Hotel

Glen Vorlich

985
▲BEN VORLICH

Dalchruin

3

Craigruie

Loch Voil

Loch
Doine

975
▲STUC A' CHROIN

HE TROSSACHS NATIONAL PARK

Ballimore

Strathyre

Ardchullarie
More

630
▲MEALL
ODHAR

4

818
▲BENVANE

Queen Elizabeth
Forest Park

14

Loch
Lubnaig

671
▲MEALL
CALA

876
▲BEN LEDI

Katrine

Glen Finglas
Reservoir

Kilmahog
Woollen Mill

5

The
Trossachs

Falls of Leny ★

Kilmahog

SS Sir
Walter Scott

Coilantogle

Callander

Upper
Drumbane

6

Trossachs Pier

Brig o'Turk

729
▲BEN
VENUE

700
▲BEINN
BHREAC

Loch
Achray

10

A821

Rob Roy
and Trossachs

A81

A84

Queen Elizabeth
Forest Park

Lendrick

Loch Venachar

Drumvaich

Burn of
Cambus

Buchany

Altskeith
Hotel

Loch
Drunkie

Menteith Hills

427
▲BEINN
DEARG

B822

B8032

Dour
Deanston

chard

Loch Ard

Milton

Queen Elizabeth
Forest Park

4 A81

Port of
Menteith

Ruskie

Thornhill

B826

Doune
Meldrum

7

abeth
Park

Duchray Water

Aberfoyle

Inchmahome

Goodie Water

Lake of
Menteith

Dykehead

Flanders Moss

B8031

A873

13

B8075

208
▲ELRIG

Cunninghame Graham
Memorial NTS

Gartmore

River
Forth

B8034

B822

19

Dalmary

A81

B835

Arnprior

B8037

Kippen

Cauldhame

Gargunnock

8

West Highland
Way

Milto
Buchanan

Auchentroig

A811

Buchlyvie

209

B822

Touch Hills

G H J K L M

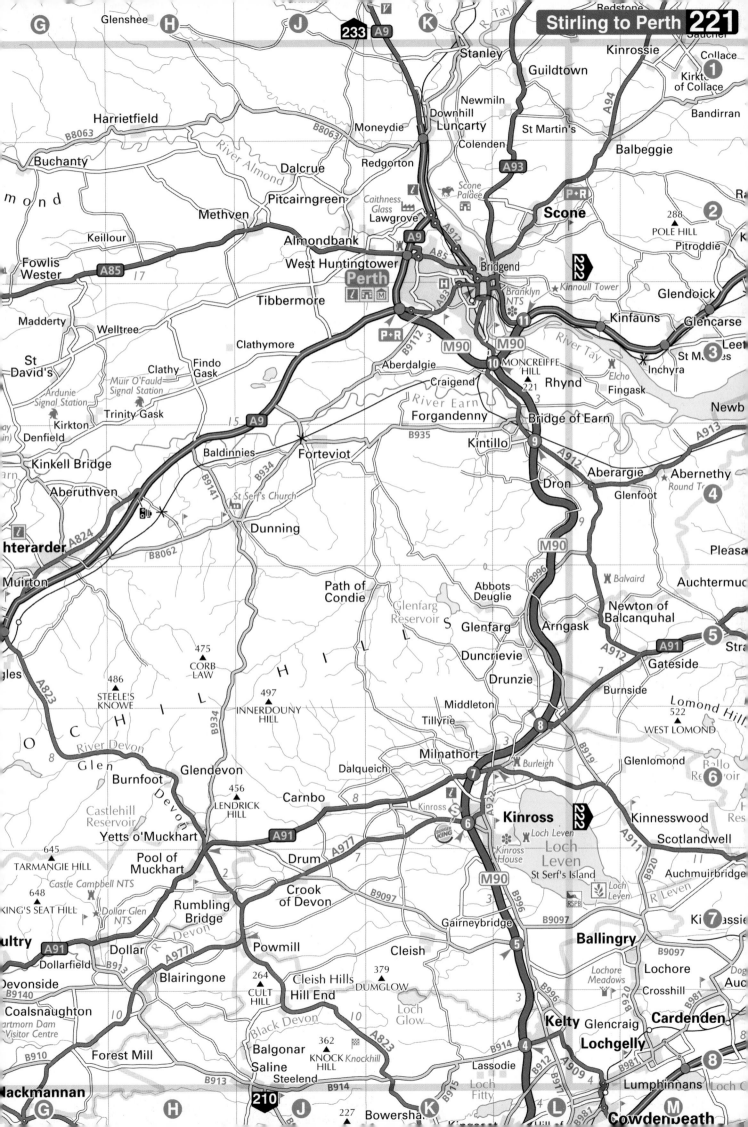

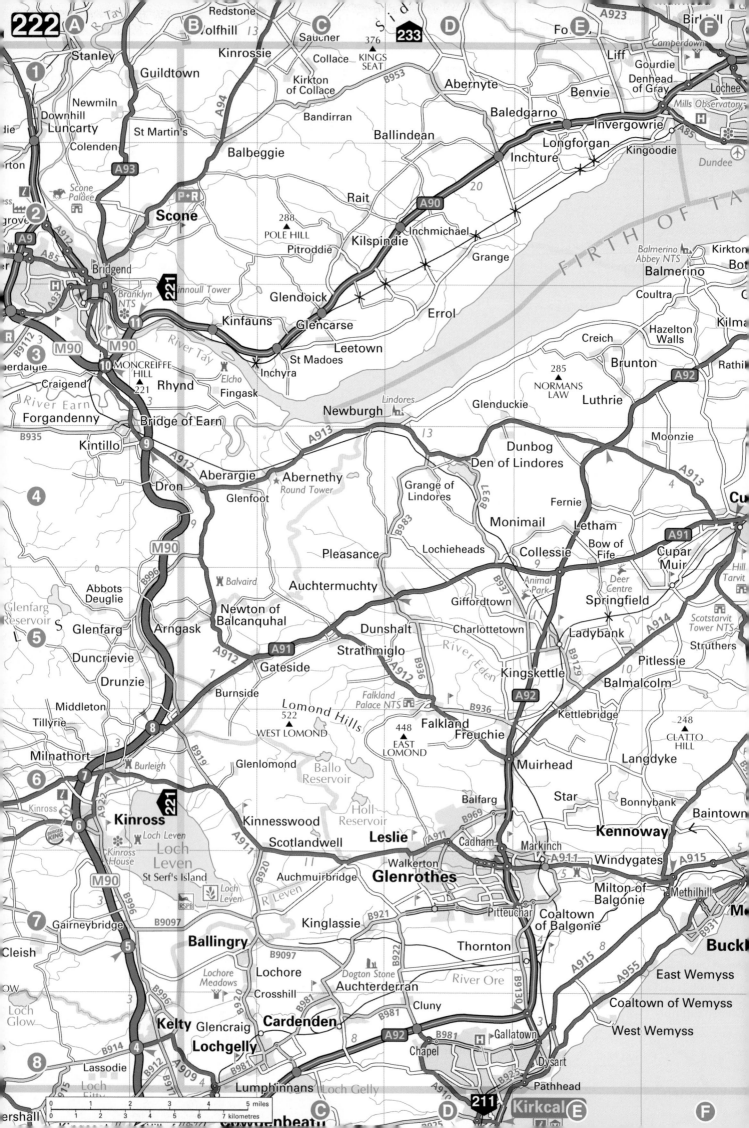

G H J K L M

1
2
3
4
5
6
7
8

Burnside of Duntrune
Douglas and Angus
Baldovie
Monifieth
Barnhill
Broughty Ferry
Broughty
North Carr Lightship
DUNDEE
Toll
A92 Tay Bridge
HM Frigate 'Unicorn'
Newport-on-Tay
Tayport
Wormit

Barry
Carnoustie
Buddon
West Haven
Carnoustie
Buddon Ness
BUDDON NESS

Scottish National Golf Centre
Tentsmuir Point
Tentsmuir Point

ST ANDREWS BAY

Leuchars
RAF Leuchars
Balmullo
Guardbridge
River Eden
Kincaple
St-Andrews
A91
St Andrews

Strathkinness
Kemback
Blebocraigs
Botanic Gardens
Craigtoun
Brownhills
A917
Boarhills
Stravithie

B939
Denhead
Pitscottie
Ceres
Baldinnie
B940
Cameron Reservoir
Radernie
Dunino
Kingsbarns
Balcomie Links
FIFE NESS

Peat Inn
New Gilston
Woodside
Lathones
Largoward
Kingsmuir
Lochty
B940
Scotland's Secret Bunker
Carnbee
B9171
Easter Pitkierie
A917
Crail

Upper Largo
A915
Colinsburgh
B942
Arncroach
Kellie Castle NTS
Newton of Balcormo
Wester Pitkierie
B9131
Kilrenny
Cellardyke
Anstruther

Lundin Mill
Drumeldrie
A917
Kilconquhar
B941
B942
Fisheries
Pittenweem
St Monans
Lower Largo
Lundin Links
Largo Bay
Earlsferry
Elie

Isle of May

234
A92
B962
A930
B961
B959
B960
A946
A914
B945
A919
A914
A915
B939
B941

Gris
Clabhac

Hogh Bay   Bally

Totron

Feall
Bay   Arileod   Ac
Uig

RSPB

Calgary Point   Crossapol
Bay   Rud
Fàsac

Gunna   Loch Breachacha

Rudha Port   Caoles   Rudha Dubh
Bhiosd   Clachan
Mor   Balephetrish   B8069
Loch   Bay   B8068   Ruaig
Haugh   Bhàsapoll
Bay   Ballevullin   Cornoigmore   Kenovay   Gott
Bay
B8068   Tiree   Scarinish
Kilkenneth
Moss   Heylipoll   B8065
Middleton   Crossapoll   TIREE
B8065   Hynish Bay
Barrapoll
Loch a'   B8067   Balemartine
Phuill
Mannel
Rinn   Hynish
Thorbhais   Balephuil
Bay

0   1   2   3   4   5 miles
0   1   2   3   4   5   6   7 kilometres

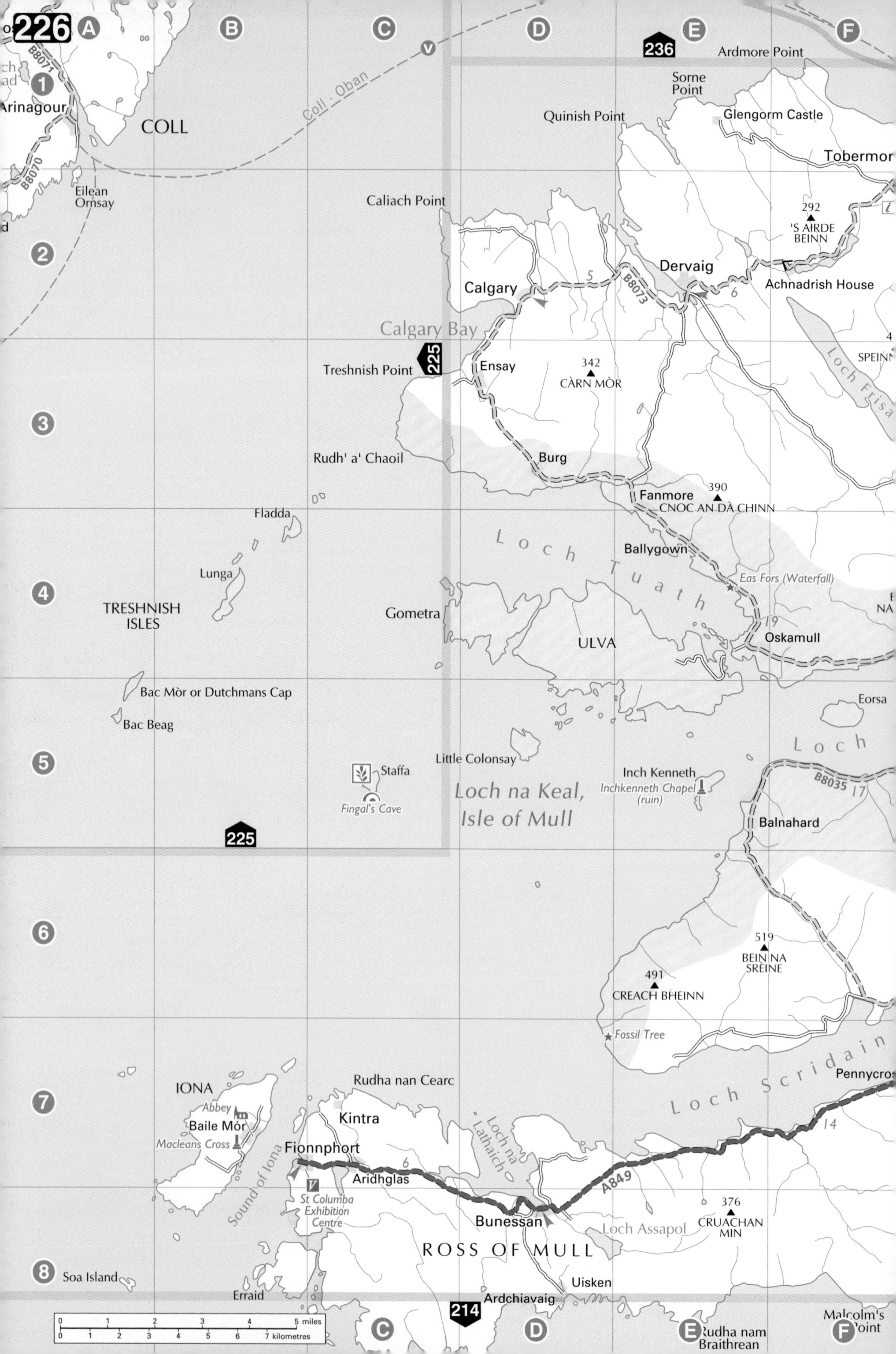

A B C D E F

1

236

Arinagour

COLL

Eilean
Ornsay

2

Caliach Point

Ardmore Point

Sorne
Point

Quinish Point

Glengorm Castle

Tobermor

292 ▲
'S AIRDE
BEINN

Calgary

Dervaig

B8073

Achnadrish House

5

6

Loch Frisa

SPEIN

Calgary Bay

Treshnish Point 225

Ensay

342 ▲
CÀRN MÒR

3

Rudh' a' Chaoil

Burg

Fanmore

390 ▲
CNOC AN DÀ CHINN

Loch Tuath

Ballygown

Eas Fors (Waterfall) ★

19

NA

Fladda

4

Lunga

TRESHNISH
ISLES

Gometra

ULVA

Oskamull

Eorsa

Bac Mòr or Dutchmans Cap

Bac Beag

Little Colonsay

Inch Kenneth

Inchkenneth Chapel
(ruin)

L o c h

B8035

17

5

Staffa

Loch na Keal,
Isle of Mull

Balnahard

Fingal's Cave

225

6

519 ▲
BEIN NA
SREINE

491 ▲
CREACH BHEINN

★ Fossil Tree

Loch Scridain

Pennycros

7

IONA

Rudha nan Cearc

Abbey

Baile Mór

Kintra

Macleans Cross

Fionnphort

Loch na Lathaich

A849

14

Sound of Iona

Aridhglas

6

St Columba
Exhibition
Centre

Bunessan

Loch Assapol

376 ▲
CRUACHAN
MIN

8

Soa Island

ROSS OF MULL

Uisken

Erraid

Ardchiavaig

Malcolm's
Point

214

Rudha nam
Braithrean

Point

C D E F

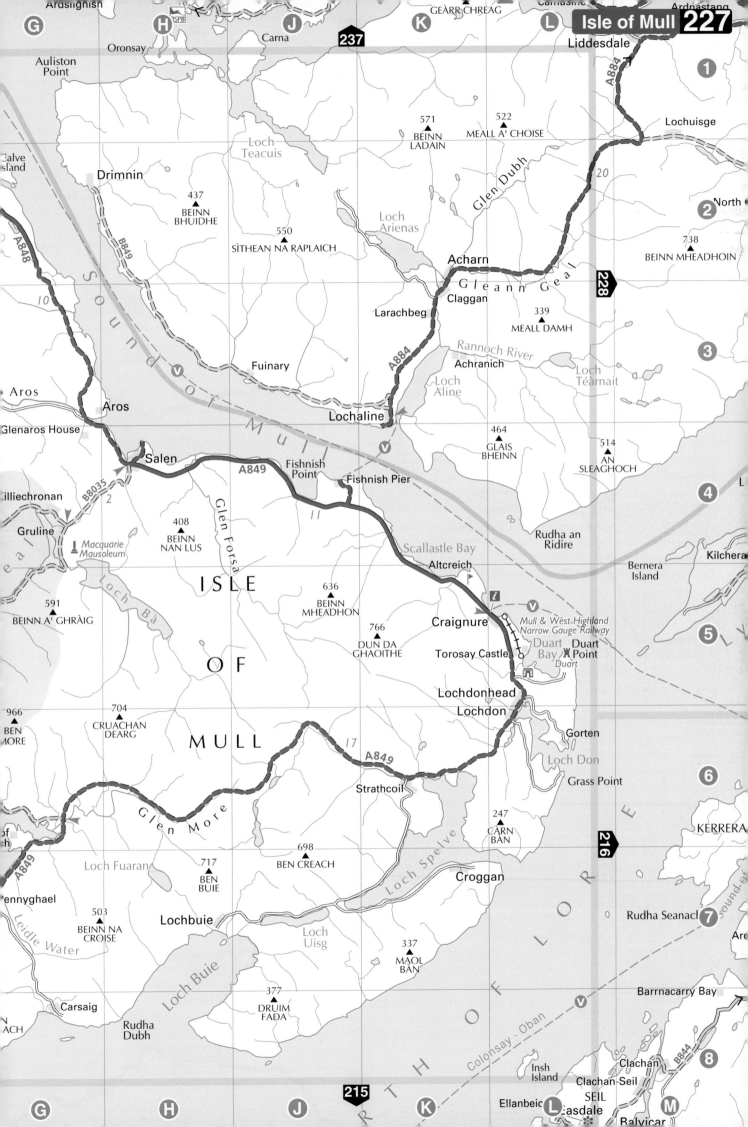

Aràslighish

Carna

GEÀRR CHREAG

Camasine

Ardnastang

G **H** RSPB **J** 237 **K** **L** Liddesdale **227**

Oronsay

A884

1

Auliston
Point

Drimnin

Calve
Island

Loch
Teacuis

571
BEINN
LADAIN

522
MEALL A' CHOISE

Lochuisge

Glen Dubh

20

2 North

437
BEINN
BHUIDHE

Loch
Arienas

738
BEINN MHEADHOIN

550
SÌTHEAN NA RAPLAICH

Acharn

Gleann Geal

228

B849

Larachbeg

Claggan

339
MEALL DAMH

3

Sound of Mull

Fuinary

A884

Rannoch River

Achranich

Loch
Téarnait

Aros

Aros

Lochaline

Loch
Aline

464
GLAIS
BHEINN

514
AN
SLEAGHOCH

4

Glenaros House

A849

Salen

Fishnish
Point

Fishnish Pier

Killiechronan

B8035
2

408
BEINN
NAN LUS

Glen Forsa

11

Scallastle Bay

Rudha an
Ridire

Bernera
Island

Kilchera

Gruline

Macquarie
Mausoleum

ISLE

Altcreich

i

Mull & West Highland
Narrow Gauge Railway

5

591
BEINN A' GHRÀIG

Loch Bà

636
BEINN
MHEADHON

OF

766
DUN DA
GHAOITHE

Craignure

Duart
Bay

Duart
Point

Duart

966
BEN
MORE

704
CRUACHAN
DEARG

MULL

Torosay Castle

Lochdonhead

Lochdon

Gorten

Loch Don

6

Glen More

A849

17

Strathcoil

247
CARN
BAN

Grass Point

216

KERRERA

Loch Fuaran

717
BEN
BUIE

698
BEN CREACH

Loch Spelve

Croggan

7

Rudha Seanach

Pennyghael

A849

Leidle Water

503
BEINN NA
CROISE

Lochbuie

Loch
Uisg

337
MAOL
BAN

NORTH OF FLORE

Barrnacarry Bay

B844

Carsaig

Rudha
Dubh

Loch Buie

377
DRUIM
FADA

Colonsay - Oban

Insh
Island

Clachan

8

G 215 **H** **J** 215 **K** **L** Easdale Ellanbeic SEIL **M** Balvicar

Clachan-Seil

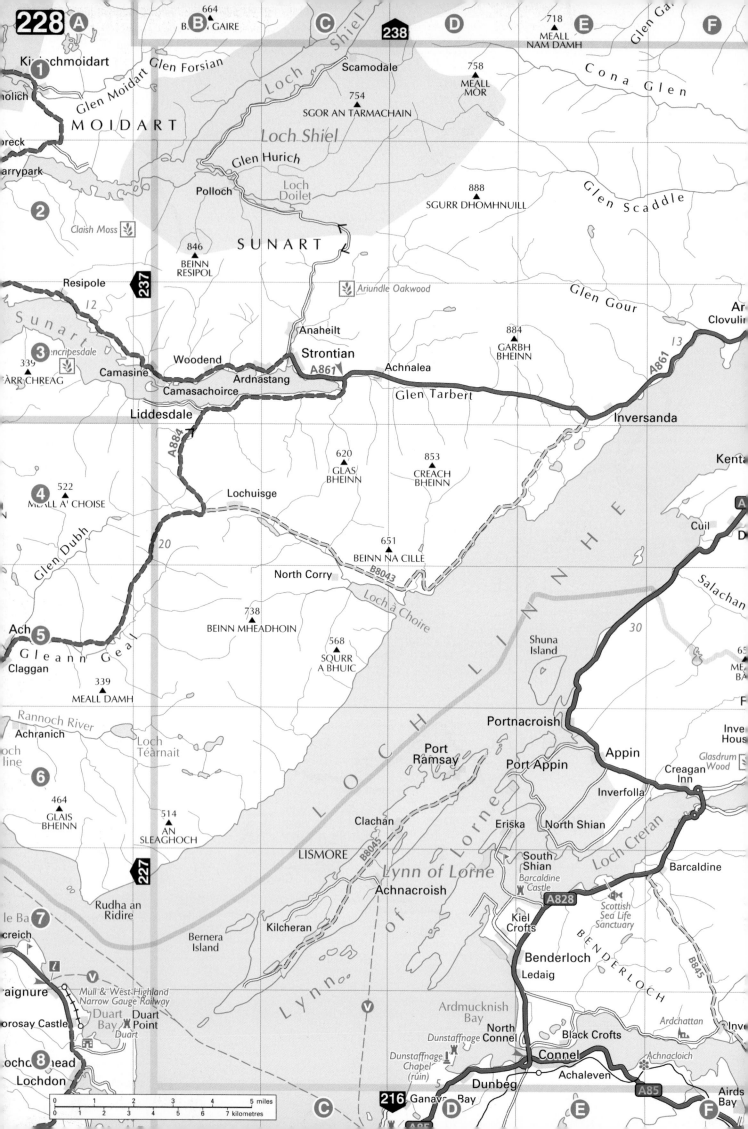

A B C D E F

228

1 Kinlochmoidart
Glen Moidart
Glen Forsian
MOIDART
664
B. B. GAIRE
Scamodale
Loch Shiel
238
Glen Ga...
Glen Gu...
718
MEALL
NAM DAMH
MEALL
NAM DAMH
Cona Glen
nolich
breck
arrypark
754
SGOR AN TARMACHAIN
Loch Shiel
758
MEALL
MÒR
2 Claish Moss
Glen Hurich
Polloch
Loch
Doilet
SUNART
888
SGURR DHOMHNUILL
Glen Scaddle
846
BEINN
RESIPOL
237
Resipole
Ariundle Oakwood
Glen Gour
Ar
Clovulin
12
Sunart
encripesdale
3 339
ÀRR CHREAG
Camasine
Woodend
Anaheilt
Strontian
A861
Achnalea
884
GARBH
BHEINN
13
A861
Camasachoirce
Ardnastang
Glen Tarbert
Inversanda
Liddesdale
A884
Kenta
4 522
MEALL A' CHOISE
Lochuisge
620
GLAS
BHEINN
853
CREACH
BHEINN
Cuil
D
A
Glen Dubh
20
651
BEINN NA CILLE
B8043
North Corry
Salachan
30
65
ME
BÀ
5 Ach
Gleann Geal
Claggan
738
BEINN MHEADHOIN
568
SQURR
A BHUIC
Loch a Choire
Shuna
Island
LOCH   LINNHE
339
MEALL DAMH
Rannoch River
Achranich
och
line
Loch
Téarnait
Portnacroish
6 464
GLAIS
BHEINN
Port
Ramsay
Appin
Creagan
Inn
Glasdrum Wood
Inver
Hous
514
AN
SLEAGHOCH
Port Appin
Inverfolla
227
Clachan
Eriska
North Shian
Loch Creran
le Ba
creich
7 Rudha an
Ridire
Bernera
Island
Kilcheran
LISMORE
B8045
Lynn of Lorne
Achnacroish
South
Shian
Barcaldine Castle
A828
Barcaldine
Scottish
Sea Life
Sanctuary
B845
BENDERLOCH
i
aignure
V
Mull & West Highland
Narrow Gauge Railway
orosay Castle
Duart
Bay
Duart
Point
Duart
Kiel
Crofts
Benderloch
Ledaig
Ardchattan
8 Loch...head
Lochdon
Lynn of Lorne
V
Ardmucknish
Bay
North
Connel
Black Crofts
Achnacloich
Inve
Dunstaffnage
Dunstaffnage
Chapel
(ruin)
Connel
Achaleven
A85
216 Ganava Bay
Dunbeg
Airds
Bay

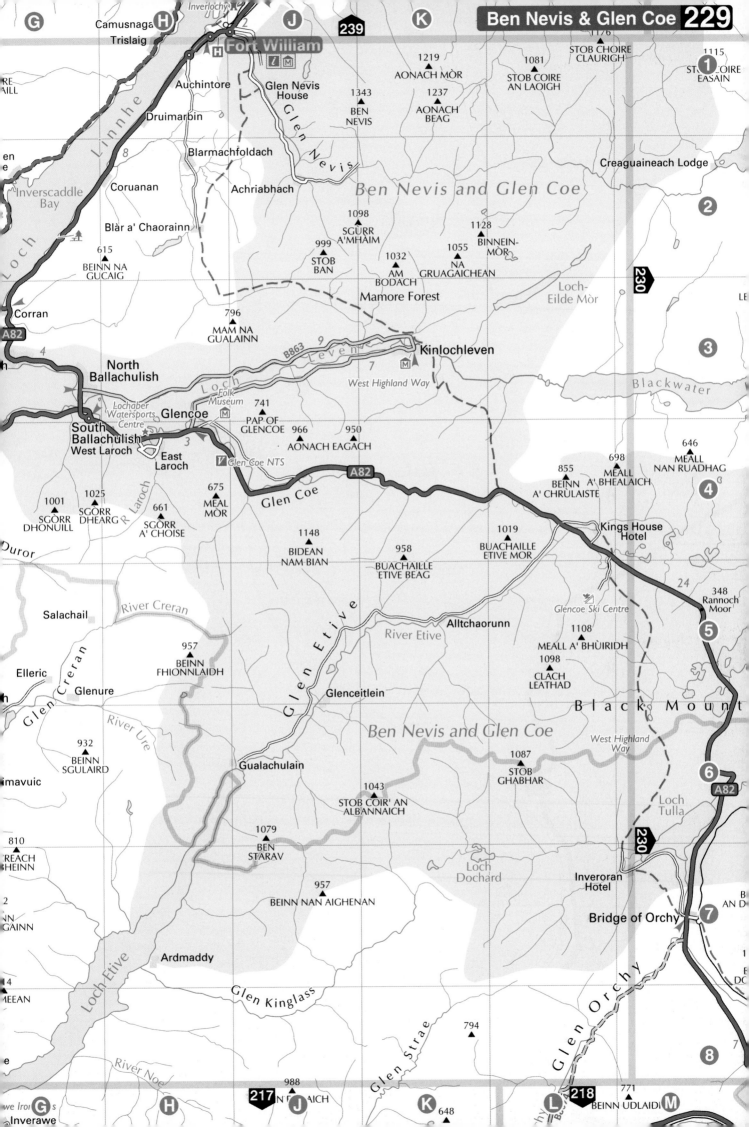

G
H
Camusnagaul
Trislaig
Inverlochy
J
239
K
1176
STOB CHOIRE
CLAURIGH
1115
STOB COIRE
EASAIN
1

Fort William
1219
AONACH MÒR
1081
STOB COIRE
AN LAOIGH

Auchintore
Glen Nevis
House
1343
BEN
NEVIS
1237
AONACH
BEAG

Druimarbin
Glen Nevis

Blarmachfoldach
Creaguaineach Lodge

Ben Nevis and Glen Coe
2

Coruanan
Achriabhach
1098
SGÙRR
A'MHÀIM
1128
BINNEIN-
MÒR
230

Inverscaddle
Bay
Blàr a' Chaorainn
999
STOB
BAN
1032
AM
BODACH
1055
NA
GRUAGAICHEAN

615
BEINN NA
GUCAIG
Mamore Forest
Loch-
Eilde Mòr
3

Corran
796
MAM NA
GUALAINN
B863
9
Leven
7
Kinlochleven
West Highland Way
Blackwater

A82
4
North
Ballachulish
Loch
Folk
Museum
741
PAP OF
GLENCOE
966
AONACH EAGACH
950

Lochaber
Watersports
Centre
Glencoe
646
MEALL
NAN RUADHAG

South
Ballachulish
West Laroch
East
Laroch
Glen Coe NTS
675
MEAL
MÒR
A82
Glen Coe
855
BEINN
A' CHRÙLAISTE
698
MEALL
A' BHEALAICH
4

1001
SGÒRR
DHONUILL
1025
SGÒRR
DHEARG
R Laroch
3
661
SGÒRR
A' CHOISE
1148
BIDEAN
NAM BIAN
958
BUACHAILLE
ETIVE BEAG
1019
BUACHAILLE
ETIVE MOR
Kings House
Hotel

Duror
River Creran
Glencoe Ski Centre
24
348
Rannoch
Moor
5

Salachail
Glen Etive
Alltchaorunn
River Etive
1108
MEALL A' BHÙIRIDH

Elleric
Glenure
957
BEINN
FHIONNLAIDH
Glenceitlein
1098
CLACH
LEATHAD

Glen Creran
River Ure
Black Mount

932
BEINN
SGULAIRD
Ben Nevis and Glen Coe
West Highland
Way

imavuic
Gualachulain
1087
STOB
GHABHAR
6
A82

810
REACH
HEINN
1043
STOB COIR' AN
ALBANNAICH
Loch
Tulla

1079
BEN
STARAV
Loch
Dochard
Inveroran
Hotel
230

957
BEINN NAN AIGHENAN
Bridge of Orchy
7

Ardmaddy
Glen Kinglass

Loch Etive
Glen Strae
Glen Orchy

MEAN
River Noe
988
217
J
K
648
794
218
L
771
BEINN UDLAIDH
M

G
H
Inverawe

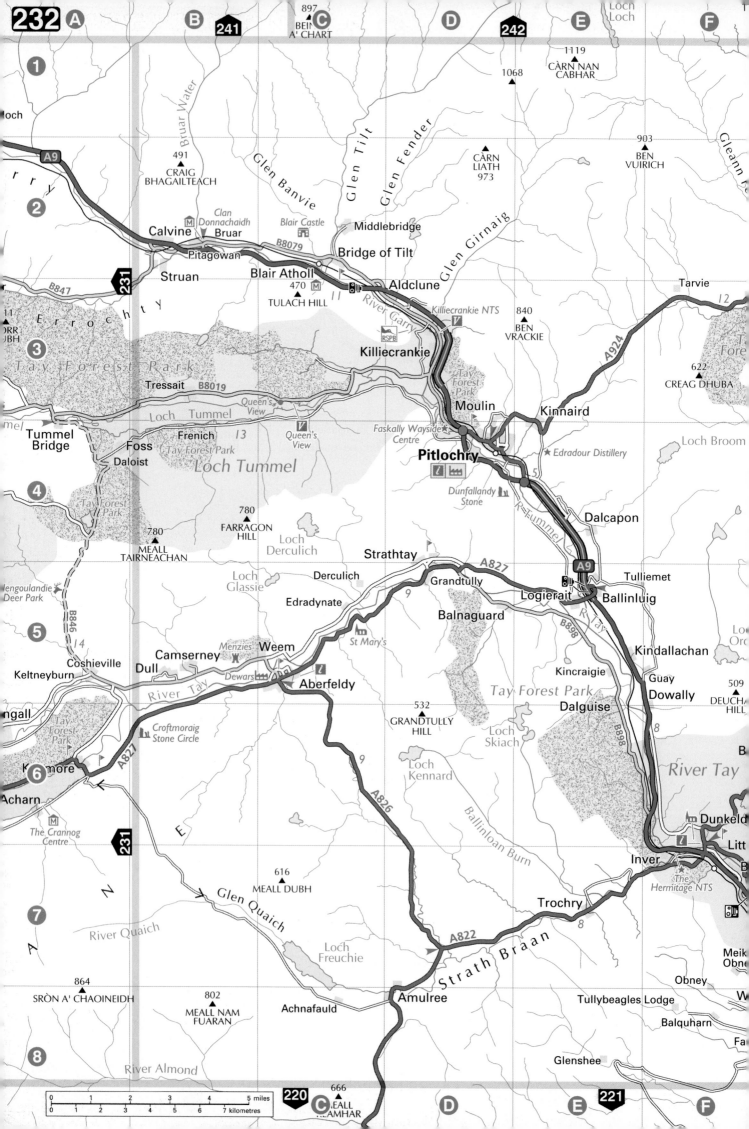

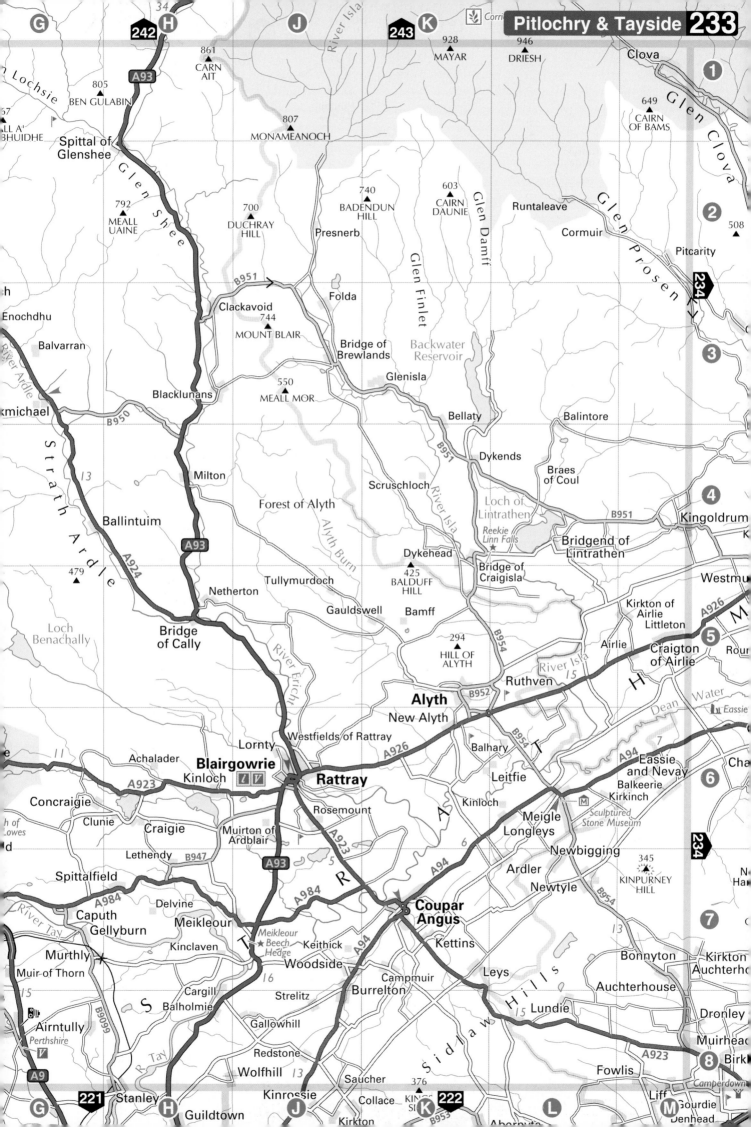

G **242** H J K **243** K Clova

1

928 ▲ MAYAR
946 ▲ DRIESH

Glen Clova

Corri

River Isla

861 ▲ CARN AIT

805 ▲ BEN GULABIN

LL A' BHUIDHE

Spittal of Glenshee

Glen Lochsie

A93

807 ▲ MONAMEANOCH

649 ▲ CAIRN OF BAMS

2

508 ▲

Pitcarity

Cormuir

Runtaleave

234

792 ▲ MEALL UAINE

700 ▲ DUCHRAY HILL

740 ▲ BADENDUN HILL

603 ▲ CAIRN DAUNIE

Glen Damff

Glen Prosen

Enochdhu

Balvarran

Presnerb

Glen Finlet

Glen Shee

B951

Clackavoid
744 ▲ MOUNT BLAIR

Folda

Bridge of Brewlands

Backwater Reservoir

3

River Ardle

kmichael

B950

Blacklunans

550 ▲ MEALL MOR

Glenisla

Bellaty

Balintore

B951

Dykends

Braes of Coul

4

Milton

Forest of Alyth

Loch of Lintrathen

Reekie Linn Falls

Bridgend of Lintrathen

Kingoldrum

B951

Strath Ardle

13

Ballintuim

A93

Alyth Burn

Dykehead

425 ▲ BALDUFF HILL

Bridge of Craigisla

Kirkton of Airlie Littleton

Westmu

A926

479 ▲

A924

Netherton

Tullymurdoch

Gauldswell

Bamff

294 ▲ HILL OF ALYTH

Airlie

Craigton of Airlie

5

Loch Benachally

Bridge of Cally

River Ericht

Ruthven

River Isla 15

H

Dean Water

Eassie

Alyth
New Alyth

B952

A926

Westfields of Rattray

Lornty

Balhary

Leitfie

B954

A94

Eassie and Nevay

Balkeerie Kirkinch

6

e 11

Achalader

Blairgowrie
Kinloch i V

Rattray

Kinloch

A

T

7

Concraigie

Rosemount

Sculptured Stone Museum

M

Meigle
Longleys

Clunie

Craigie

A93

A923

A94

6

Newbigging

345 ▲ KINPURNEY HILL

N Ha

234

h of Lowes

Muirton of Ardblair

5

R

Ardler

Newtyle

B954

Lethendy B947

Spittalfield

A984

Delvine

Meikleour

Coupar Angus

Kettins

13

7

A984

Caputh

Gellyburn

Meikleour Beech Hedge

Keithick

Leys

Bonnyton

Kirkton Auchterho

River Tay

16

Kinclaven

Woodside

Campmuir

Sidlaw Hills

Lundie

Auchterhouse

Murthly

Muir of Thorn

Cargill

Balholmie

Strelitz

Burrelton

15

Dronley

Muirhe

15

B9099

Airntully

Perthshire
V

Gallowhill

Redstone

Saucher

376 ▲

A923

Liff

Fowlis

8

Birk

A9

Stanley

Wolfhill 13

Kinrossie

Collace

KING'S SE

B953

Gourdie

Camperdown

G **221** H Guildtown J K **222** L M Denhead

Aberny

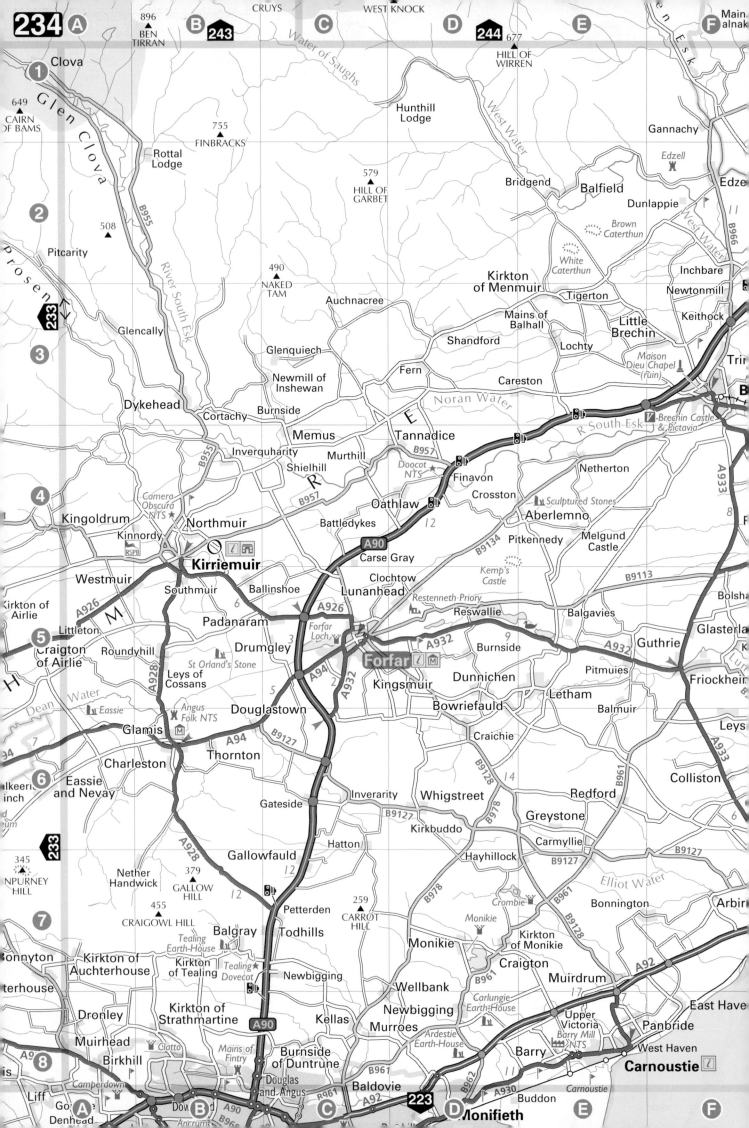

G

H

J

K

244

245

Pittarrow

edmyre

1

Mains of
Haulkerton

Inverbervie

Bervie
Bay

B9120

Laurencekirk

Gourdon

gmuir

B9120

Sauchieburn

Redford

Dykelands

Benholm

2

hermuir

13

A937

Johnshaven

A90

B974

Marykirk

Bush

Milton Ness

North Esk

Hospital

Craigo

Lochside

St Cyrus

Logie Pert

Logie

Morphie

Morphie

3

Hillside

A92

Dun

House of
Dun NTS

9 A935

ian

Montrose

Montrose

i M

Barnhead

Basin

Scurdie Ness

Maryton

Ferryden

4

A934

Craig

Westerton

Usan

Boddin Point

Braehead

Lunan

5

Lunan Bay

Inverkeilor

Red Head

13

pelton

Cauldcots

6

A92

Marywell

eans

Auchmithie

Carlingheugh
Bay

The Deil's
Head

7

Arbroath

i M

G

H

J

K

L

M

A   B   C   246   D   E   Ru...a na Roinne   F

1   A Bhrideanach   570 ORVAL   Kinloch   Loch Scresort

RÙM

810 ASKIVAL

2   The Small Isles   763 SGÙRR NAN GILLEAN

Rudha nam Meirleach   Sound of Rum

Bay of Laig   Cleadale

3   Rudha an Fhasaidh   Laig   299 AN CRUACHAN

EIGG   Kildo

393 AN SGÙRR   Sandavo

4   Eilean nan Each   MUCK   Sound of Eigg   Eilean Chathastail

Port Mor

5

6   Sanna Point   Sanna Bay   Sanna Bay   Achnaha
Portuairk
Ardnamurchan Point   MEAL
Achosnich

7   Eilean Mòr   Bagh a Chaisteil (Castlebay)   Loch Baghasdail (Lochboisdale)   B8007
Rudha Mòr   Rudha Sgor-innis   225   342 BEINN NA SEILG   Kil
Bousd   Sorisdale   Ormsaigmor
Cliad Bay   B8072   COLL   Coll - Oban

8   0 1 2 3 4 5 miles / 0 1 2 3 4 5 6 7 kilometres
...ost   B8071   Ardmore Point
...och ...iad   Sorne P...   226
Arinagour   A   B   C   D   E   Glengorm Castle   F
Quinish Point

KNOYD

Sleat

G   H   J   V   K   and

Ard
Thurinish

247

Point
of Sleat

Inverie
Bay

1

Rudha
Raonuill

Courteachan

Mallaigvaig

BEINN

Mallaig

CÀRN A'GHOBHAIR
547

V   i

Glasnacardoch Bay

Loch an
Nostaire

437

Stoul

SGURR BHUIDHE

Beoraidbeg

Morar

Loch Nevis

Bracora

Bracorina

2   lesn

Tarbet

238   Swordland

Glenancross

Loch   Morar

Lettermorar

B8008   A830

Meoble

Bunacaimb

CÀRN A'
MHÀDAIDH-RUAIDH
503

3

MEITH

Eilean Ighe

River Meoble

Back of
Keppoch

SIDHEAN
MÒR
600

Luinga Mhòr

Arisaig

Loch nan Ceall

Prince Charlie's
Cairn

10

Rudh' Arisaig

103

Druimindarroch

Arisaig
House

CRUACH
DOIRE

Kinlochnanuagh

Loc

Loch nan Uamh

Polnish

Lochailort

Loch
4

Sound of Arisaig

Ardnish

Inverailort

Loch Eilt

Rudha
Choalais

Peanmeanach

Loch Ailort

A861

ROIS-BHEINN
877

Smearisary

Glenuig

712

5

21

BEINN GAIRE
664

Eilean
Shona

Rudha Aird
Druimnich

Loch Moidart

Kinlochmoidart

Glen Forsian

Ockle
Point

Tioram

Glen Moidart

MOIDART

6

Morar, Moidart and
Ardnamurchan

239

Ardmolich

Loch

Glen Hurich

mory

Ockle

Ardtoe

Shielfoot

BEINN
BHREAC

Dalnabreck

228   Polloch

Branault

356

Kentra

B8044

Blain

Mingarrypark

Loc
Doil

BEINN
BHREAC

Arevegaig

SUNAR

ARDNAMURCHAN

437

Acharacle

Claish Moss

846

BEINN
RESIPOL
7

Loch
Mudle

A861

Salen

Resipole

527

BEN
HIANT

Glenbeg

512

B8007

Loch Sunart

12

BEN
LAGA

Glencripesdale

Woodend

Glenborrodale

Laga

339

Camasine

Ardslignish

Carna

GEÀRR CHREAG

Ardnastang

RSPB

Camasachoirce

Oronsay

8

Auliston
Point

Liddesdale

227

A884

G   H   J   K   L   M

A   B   C   D   E   F

1

2

3

4

5

6

7

8

BEINN NA
S▲MRAIG

Loch na Dal

lemc

rnsay

Ornsay

Sandaig
Island

Rudha
Buidhe

Rudh' Ard
Slisneach

SOUND OF SLEAT

Loch Hourn

Glen Beag
Gleneig
Brochs

Buirvaid

974
▲
BEINN
SGRITHEAL

773
▲
BEINN NAN CAORACH

1011
▲
THE SADDLE

945
▲
SGURR
NA SGINE

Arnisdale

Glen Arnisdale

Corran

614
▲

709
▲
DRUM
FADA

Kinloch
Hourn

STERS

Glen Shiel

Glen FHUAR

SGU
FHUAR

SG
MHAC

247

Airor

Inverguseran

Glen Guseran

784
▲
BEINN NA
CAILLICH

Barrisdale
Bay

518
▲
DRUIM NA
CLUAIN-AIRIDHE

1019
▲
LADHAR
BHEINN

Knoydart

KNOYDART

Sandaig

Sandaig Bay

Inverie

Inverie
Bay

Loch Nevis

Loch-an
Dubh-Lochain

940
▲
LUINNE BHEINN

Rudha
Raonuill

M▲igvaig

547
▲
CÀRN A'GHOBHAIR

Loch an
Nostaire

437
▲
SGÙRR BHUIDHE

praidbeg

orar

Bracora

Bracorina

Stoul

854
▲
BEINN BHUIDHE

Carnoch

1039
▲
SGURR NA CICHE

1003
▲
SGURR MÒR

Kylesmorar

859
▲
SGURR NAH-AIDE

Glen Dessarry

ross

Tarbet

Swordland

723
▲
SGARR BREAC

Loch   Morar

Lettermorar

Glen Pean

503
▲
CÀRN A'
MHÀDAIDH-RUAIDH

River Meoble

Meoble

716
▲
AN STAC

949
▲
SGURR NAN COIREACHAN

964
▲
SGURR
THUILM

600
▲
SIDHEAN
MÒR

237

710
▲
MEITH BHEINN

10

Prince Charlie's
Cairn

Arisaig
House

Kinlochnanuagh

Loch Beoriad

633
▲

796
▲
SGURR
AN UTHA

Glen Finnan

Gleann Dubhlighe

Gleann Fionnligh

Loch nan Uamh

Polnish

Lochailort

A830

14

M

Glenfinnan

Glenfinnan NTS

Kinlocheil

Ardnish

Peanmeanach

Inverailort

Loch
Eilt

Glenfinnan
Monument NTS

Drimsallie

dha
alais

Loch Ailort

A861

877
▲
ROIS-BHEINN

882
▲
BEINN
ODHAR BHEAG

Garvan

Glen Garvan

uig

712
▲

664
▲
BEINN GAIRE

718
▲
MEALL
NAM DAMH

Glen Shiel

228

758
▲

Con

Scamodale

0   1   2   3   4   5 miles
0 1 2 3 4 5 6 7 kilometres

C   D   E   F

G H J K

249

1

2

240

3

4

5

6

240

7

8

1030
SQÙRR A'BHEALAICH

33

CISTE DHUBH

1120
A'CHRALAIG

1108
SGURR NAN CONBHAIREAN

A87

i

Cluanie Inn

Cluanie Lodge

Loch Cluanie

Ceannacroc Lodge

Tomchrasky

Dalchreichart

Glen

Du

671
CEANN A'MHAIN

787
MEALL DUBH

1019
AONACH AIR CHRITH

947
CREAG A'MHAIM

1035
GLEOURAICH

996
SPIDEAN MIALACH

Glenquoich Forest

Loch Loyne

Glen Loyne

Glen Garry

A87

13

Glen Garry

Loch Garry

Inve

Inchlaggan

Tomdoun

Greenfield

Mandally

A

919
GAIRICH

D Quoich

Glen Kingie

River Kingie

River

Garry

556
GLAS BHEINN

901
BEN TEE

Glengarry Forest

Kilfinnan

Lag

879
SGURR HURLAGAIN

Loch Blair

656
MEALL BLÀIR

821
MEALL COIRE NAN SAOBHAIDH

935
SRON A'CHOIRE GHAIRBH

Corriegour Lodge Hotel

803
BEINNIARU

33

VAIN

Caonich

Loch Arkaig

Ardechive

Gleann Cia-aig

Letterfinlay Lodge Hotel

Loch Lochy

15

Glen Gloy

723

Clunes

Inverloy

772
MEALL A' PHÙBUILL

Glen Mallie

Achnacarry

M

Bunarkaig

B8005

796
BEINN BHAN

Great Glen Way

Glenfintaig Lodge

654
COIRE CEIRSLE

Glen Roy

Glen Loy

Gairlochy

B8004

Stronenaba

Spean Bridge

Inverroy

Bohuntine

738
STOB A' GHRIANAIN

B8004

Brackletter

228

Commando Memorial

Killiechonate

River Spean

Roy Bridge

Mor Fe

DRUM FADA

Strone

Muirshearlich

River Lochy

A82

The Cour

714
BEINN CHLIANAIG

Fassfern

11

A830

Corpach

Neptune's Staircase (Locks)

Torcastle

Nevis Range

River Lundy

662
SGÙRR-FINNISG-AIG

och Eil

A861

Blaich

Banavie

B8006

Caol

Inverlochy

i M

Fort William

229

1219
AONACH MÒR

1081
STOB COIRE

1176
STOB CHOIRE CLAURIG

Camusnagaul

Trislaig

G H J K L M

ky

7

STOB COIRE

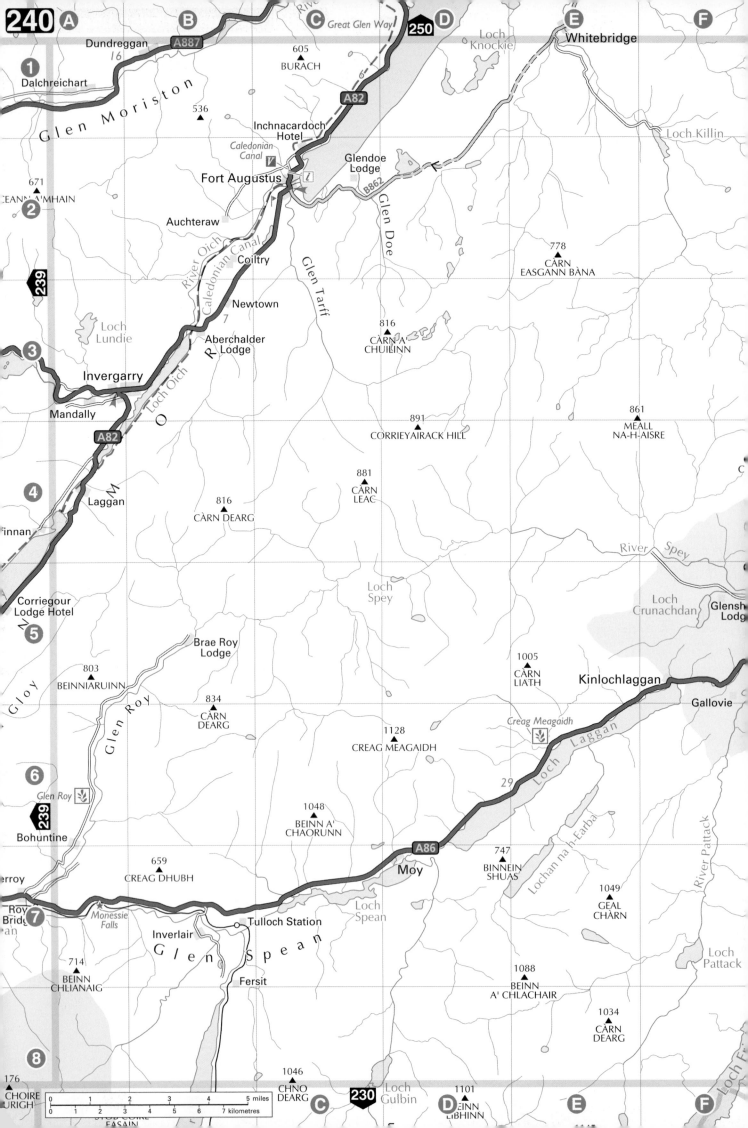

A   B   C   D   E   F

1

Dundreggan
Dalchreichart
A887
16

Glen Moriston

Great Glen Way
6

Loch
Knockie

Whitebridge

Loch Killin

605
▲
BURACH

A82

2

536
▲

Inchnacardoch
Hotel

Caledonian Canal

Glendoe
Lodge

671
▲
CEANN A'MHAIN

Fort Augustus

Auchteraw

Glen Doe

B862

778
▲
CÀRN
EASGANN BÀNA

River Oich

Coiltry

Glen Tarff

239

Newtown

816
▲
CÀRN A'
CHUILINN

861
▲
MEALL
NA-H-AISRE

3

Loch
Lundie

Aberchalder
Lodge

891
▲
CORRIEYAIRACK HILL

Invergarry

Loch Oich

881
▲
CÀRN
LEAC

River Spey

Mandally

A82

4

M
O

Laggan

816
▲
CÀRN DEARG

Loch
Spey

Loch
Crunachdan

Glensh
Lodge

Finnan

Corriegour
Lodge Hotel

5

N

Brae Roy
Lodge

1005
▲
CÀRN
LIATH

Kinlochlaggan

Gallovie

803
▲
BEINN IARUINN

Glen Roy

834
▲
CÀRN
DEARG

Creag Meagaidh

1128
▲
CREAG MEAGAIDH

Loch Laggan

6

Glen Roy

Gloy

29

239

Bohuntine

1048
▲
BEINN A'
CHAORUNN

A86

747
▲
BINNEIN
SHUAS

Lochan na h-Earba

River Pattack

1049
▲
GEAL
CHÀRN

659
▲
CREAG DHUBH

Moy

Roy
erroy
Bridg
an

7

*Monessie
Falls*

Inverlair

Tulloch Station

Loch
Spean

Glen Spean

714
▲
BEINN
CHLIANAIG

Fersit

1088
▲
BEINN
A' CHLACHAIR

Loch
Pattack

1034
▲
CÀRN
DEARG

8

176
▲
CHOIRE
URIGH

STOB COIRE
EASAIN

1046
▲
CHNO
DEARG

230

Loch
Gulbin

1101
▲
BEINN
EIBHINN

Loch F

0   1   2   3   4   5 miles
0   1   2   3   4   5   6   7 kilometres

A   B   C   D   E   F

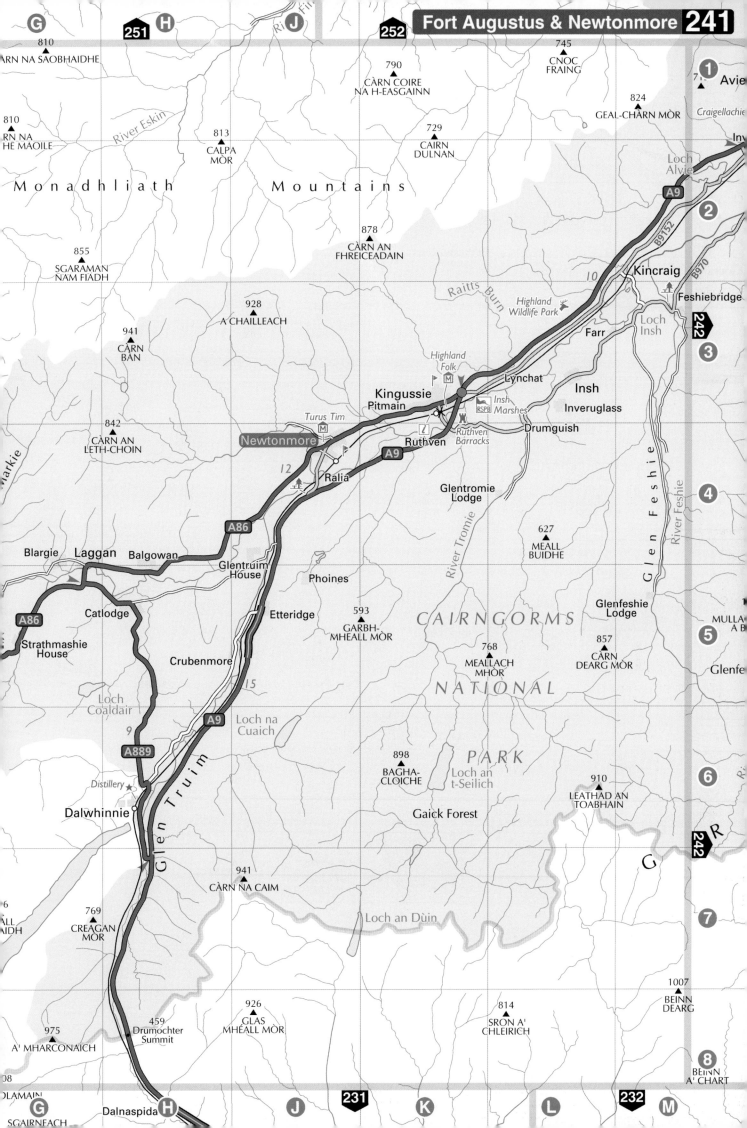

G
251 H
J
252

810
▲ CÀRN NA SAOBHAIDHE

810
RN NA HE MAOILE

River Eskin

Monadhliath Mountains

790
▲ CÀRN COIRE NA H-EASGAINN

745
▲ CNOC FRAING

824
▲ GEAL-CHÀRN MÒR

1
Avie

813
▲ CALPA MÒR

729
▲ CAIRN DULNAN

Loch Alvie

A9

B9152

Inv

855
▲ SGARAMAN NAM FIADH

878
▲ CÀRN AN FHREICEADAIN

Raitts Burn

Highland Wildlife Park

Kincraig

B970

Feshiebridge

928
▲ A CHAILLEACH

Highland Folk M

Loch Insh

242

941
▲ CÀRN BAN

Farr

Lynchat

Insh

Inveruglass

3

Highland Folk M

Kingussie

Pitmain

RSPB Insh Marshes

Drumguish

842
▲ CÀRN AN LETH-CHOIN

Turus Tim M

Newtonmore

Ruthven Barracks

i

Ruthven

Glen Feshie

River Feshie

4

A9

Glentromie Lodge

12

Ralia

627
▲ MEALL BUIDHE

CAIRNGORMS

Glenfeshie Lodge

5

MULLA A B

Blargie Laggan Balgowan

A86

Glentruim House

Phoines

River Tromie

857
▲ CÀRN DEARG MÒR

Glenfe

Catlodge

Etteridge

593
▲ GARBH-MHEALL MÒR

768
▲ MEALLACH MHÒR

NATIONAL

Crubenmore

Strathmashie House

15

Loch Coaldair

A9

Loch na Cuaich

PARK

898
▲ BAGHA-CLOICHE

Loch an t-Seilich

910
▲ LEATHAD AN TOABHAIN

6

9

A889

Glen Truim

Gaick Forest

242

Distillery ★

Dalwhinnie

G

R

941
▲ CÀRN NA CAIM

7

1007
▲ BEINN DEARG

6

ALL AIDH

769
▲ CREAGAN MÒR

Loch an Dùin

926
▲ GLAS MHÉALL MÒR

814
▲ SRON A' CHLEIRICH

975
▲ A' MHARCONAICH

459
Drumochter Summit

8
BEINN A' CHART

DLMAIN
08

A   B   253   C   D   E   254   F

Straanruie

River Spey

1

712 ▲ **Aviemore**

24 ▲
ARN MÒR

Craigellachie

Glenmore
Forest Park

MEALL A' BHUACHAILLE

809 ▲

821 ▲
GEAL CHÀRN

803 ▲
CARN BHEADHAIR

606 ▲
CARN
TUADHAM

River Nethy

Inverdruie

Rothiemurchus

Coylumbridge

Glenmore

*Reindeer
Centre*

Glen More

730 ▲
MAIM
SUIM

Loch
Alvie

A9

2

B9152

241

Glenmore Lodge

*Loch
Morlich*

C A I R N G O R M S

Glen A

Kincraig

Rothiemurchus
Lodge

*Cairngorm
Ski Area*

713 ▲
THE
BRUACH

Feshiebridge

N A T I O N A L

Loch
Insh

3

1245 ▲
CAIRN
GORM

117 ▲
BEN
AVO

Glen Feshie

C a i r n g o r m

1083 ▲
BEINN A
CHAORRUINN

1196 ▲
NORTH
TOP

1108 ▲
SGÒR AN
DUBH MÒR

Lochan
Buidhe

P A R K

River Feshie

1295 ▲
BRAERIACH

Lairig Ghru

M o u n t a i n s

1084 ▲
CARN
EÀS

Loch
Einich

1309 ▲
BEN
MACDHUI

4

1049 ▲
CARN
BAN MOR

1293 ▲
CAIRN
TOUL

930 ▲
BEINN
BHREAC

1177 ▲
SOUTH
TOP

Glen Derry

M O

shie

1017 ▲
MULLACH CLACH
A BHLÀIR

1157 ▲
BEINN
BHROTAIN

River Dee

813 ▲
SGÒR
MÒR

Glen Lui

Linn of Dee

Quoich Water

Allanaquoich

B

5

Glenfeshie   Forest

Glen Dee

A N

River Eldart

Inverey

859 ▲
MORR
HIL

816 ▲
CARN
LIATH

6

River Feshie

M P I

241

G R A

999 ▲
CARN
EALAR

1006 ▲
AN
SGARSOCH

919 ▲
CARN BHAC

Glen Ey

886 ▲
SGOR
MOR

7

Tarf Water

Baddoch Burn

Glens
Ski A

1007 ▲
BEINN
DEARG

River Tilt

Gleann Mòr

9

T
CAIR

1050 ▲
GLAS
TULAICHEAN

34

8

897 ▲
BEINN
A' CHART

Loch
Loch

Glen Loc

805

0	1	2	3	4	5 miles
0	1	2 3 4	5	6	7 kilometres

068

C   1119 ▲
N NAN
CABHAR   232   D   E   233   F
A9

G Blairnamarrow

H

254

J 718
▲ THE SOCACH

Glenbuchat

Glenkindie 1

637 Lecht Summit
Lecht Ski Area

Bellabeg
Strathdon
Roughpark
Forbestown

Towie

792 ▲ CARN EALASAID

710 ▲ CRAIG VEANN

Heughhead

Boltenstone

Garchory

A944

Milltown

8

Cock Bridge
Corgarff
Corgarff

A97

9

749 ▲ MONA GOWAN

Migvie 2

244

Corrach

Loch Buildg

829 ▲ BROWN COW HILL

744 ▲ CARN A' BHACAIN

A939

12

872 ▲ MORVEN

Logie Coldstone

3

River Gairn

S

Candacraig

Muir of Dinnet

Loch

Loch

Cambus o' May

B9119

8

900 ▲ CULARDOCH

B976

743 ▲ GEALLAIG HILL

Coilacriech

Bridge of Gairn

B972

Milton of Tullich

4 Tilly

River

Balmoral Castle

Crathie

Dee

Ballater

Pannanich Wells Hotel

B976

River Avon

n

A

618 ▲ MEALL GORM

17

Easter Balmoral

Littlemill

B976

531 ▲ BLACK CRAIG

N

T

Inver

Balnacroft

Birkhall

Water of Tanar

Keiloch

A93

600 ▲ CREAG NAN GALL

Glen Gelder

596 ▲ THE COYLES OF MUICK

699 ▲ CAIRN LEUCHAN

5 7 CLACHAN YELL

Balmoral Forest

River Muick

Glen Muick

938 ▲ MOUNT KEEN

6

1154 ▲ LOCHNAGAR

Loch Callater

1045 ▲ CAIRN TAGGART

720 ▲ FASHEILACH

244

Loch Muick

Spittal of Glenmuick

Glen Mark

unie
e

996 ▲ BROAD CAIRN

832 ▲ EASTERBALLOCH

Inverm

7

1018 ▲ CÀRN AN TUIRC

Glen Lee

Loch Lee

Glen Doll

831 ▲ LAIR OF ALDARARIE

1067 ▲ GLAS MAOL

739 ▲ CRUYS

8

River Isla

Corrie Fee

G H

928 ▲ MAYAR

233

946 ▲ DRI

J

896 ▲ BEN TIRRAN

K Clova

L 234

M

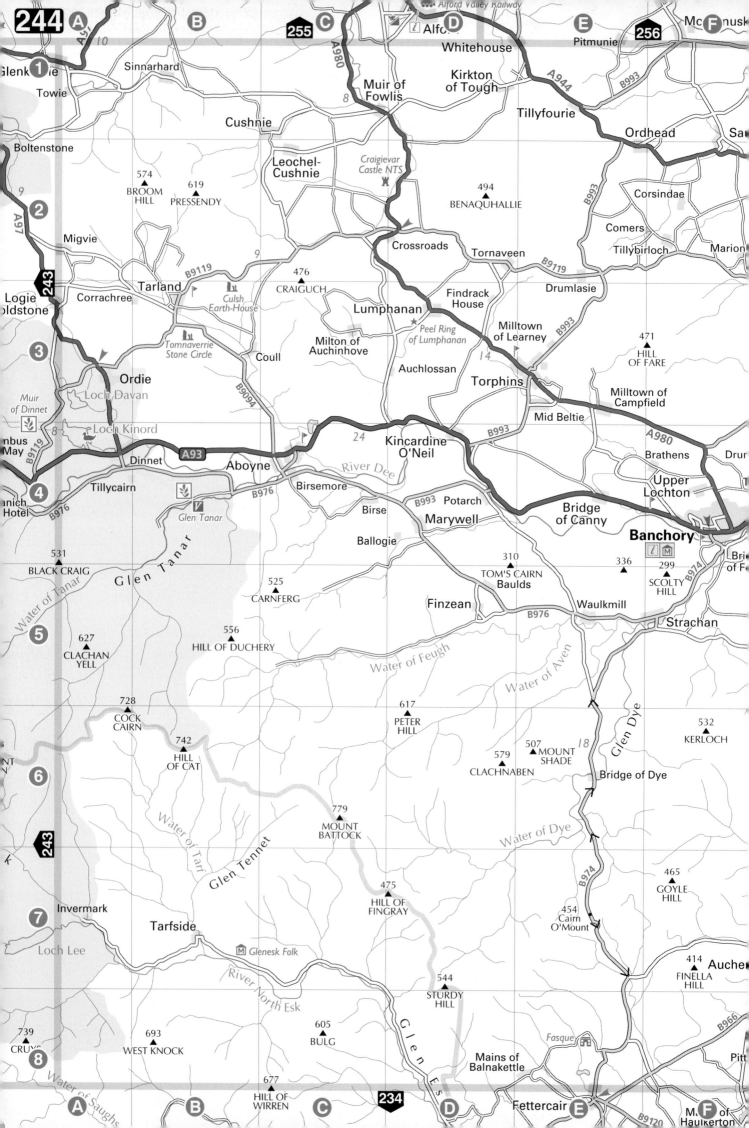

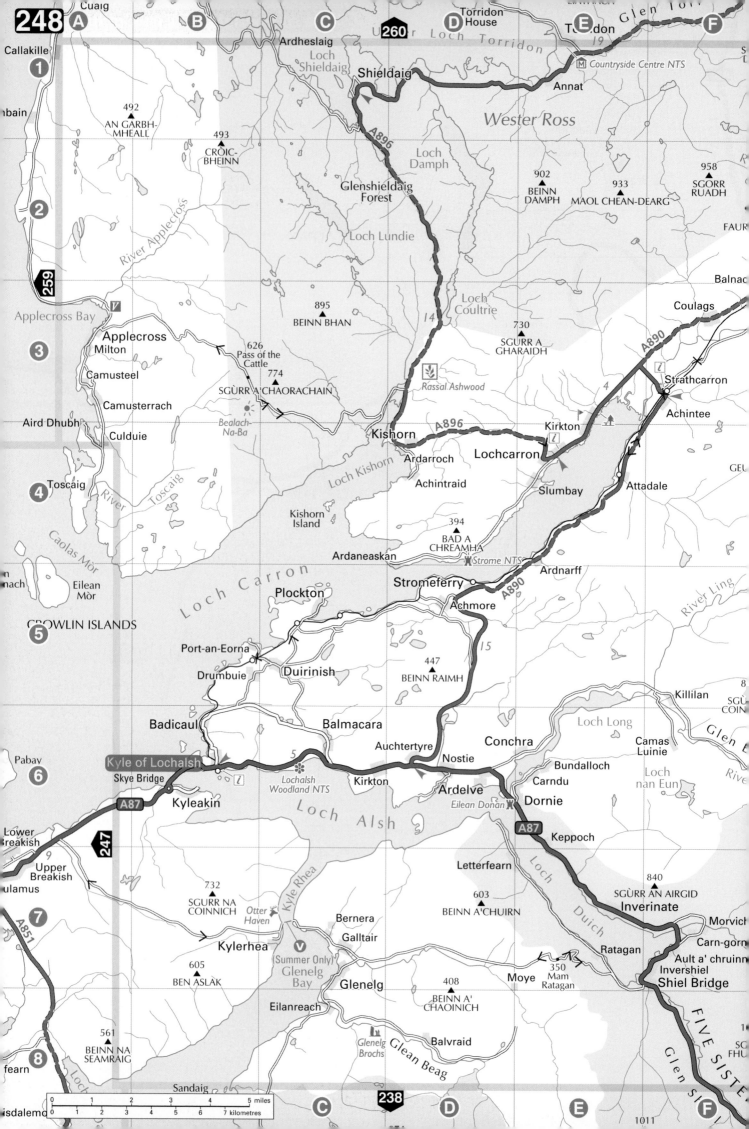

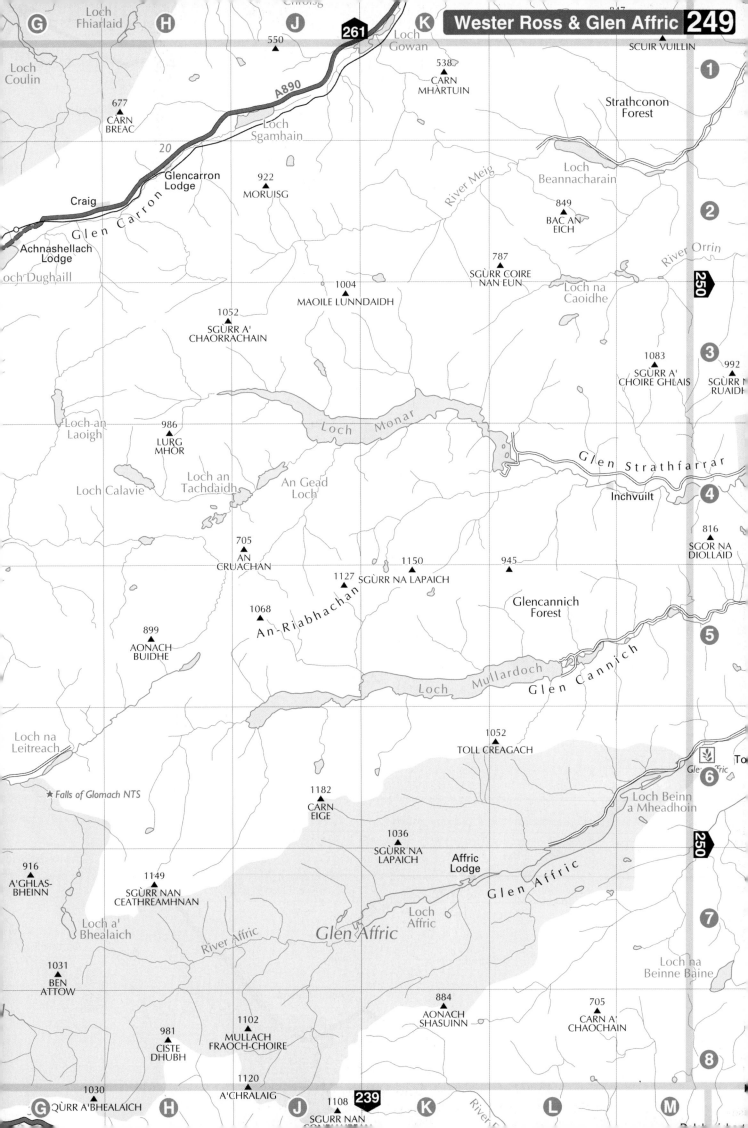

Loch Chroisg

847

SCUIR VUILLIN ▲

1

Loch Gowan

550 ▲

538 ▲
CARN
MHÀRTUIN

Strathconon
Forest

Loch Coulin

A890

677 ▲
CARN
BREAC

20

Glencarron
Lodge

Loch
Sgamhain

922 ▲
MORUISG

River Meig

Loch
Beannacharain

849 ▲
BAC AN
EICH

River Orrin

2

Craig

Glen Carron

Achnashellach
Lodge

och Dughaill

787 ▲
SGURR COIRE
NAN EUN

Loch na
Caoidhe

250

1004 ▲
MAOILE LUNNDAIDH

1052 ▲
SGÙRR A'
CHAORRACHAIN

1083 ▲
SGÙRR A'
CHOIRE GHLAIS

992 ▲
SGÙRR N
RUAIDH

3

Loch-an
Laoigh

986 ▲
LURG
MHOR

Loch Monar

Glen Strathfarrar

Loch Calavie

Loch an
Tachdaidh

An Gead
Loch

Inchvuilt

4

816 ▲
SGOR NA
DIOLLAID

705 ▲
AN
CRUACHAN

1150 ▲
SGÙRR NA LAPAICH

945 ▲

1127 ▲

1068 ▲

An-Riabhachan

Glencannich
Forest

899 ▲
AONACH
BUIDHE

5

Loch Mullardoch

Glen Cannich

Loch na
Leitreach

1052 ▲
TOLL CREAGACH

Gle   ric

6

★ Falls of Glomach NTS

1182 ▲
CARN
EIGE

Loch Beinn
a Mheadhoin

To

250

1036 ▲
SGÙRR NA
LAPAICH

Affric
Lodge

Glen Affric

916 ▲
A'GHLAS-
BHEINN

1149 ▲
SGÙRR NAN
CEATHREAMHNAN

Loch
Affric

7

Loch a'
Bhealaich

River Affric

Glen Affric

Loch na
Beinne Baine

1031 ▲
BEN
ATTOW

884 ▲
AONACH
SHASUINN

705 ▲
CARN A'
CHAOCHAIN

981 ▲
CISTE
DHUBH

1102 ▲
MULLACH
FRAOCH-CHOIRE

8

1030 ▲
SGÙRR A'BHEALAICH

1120 ▲
A'CHRALAIG

1108 ▲
SGURR NAN

239

River

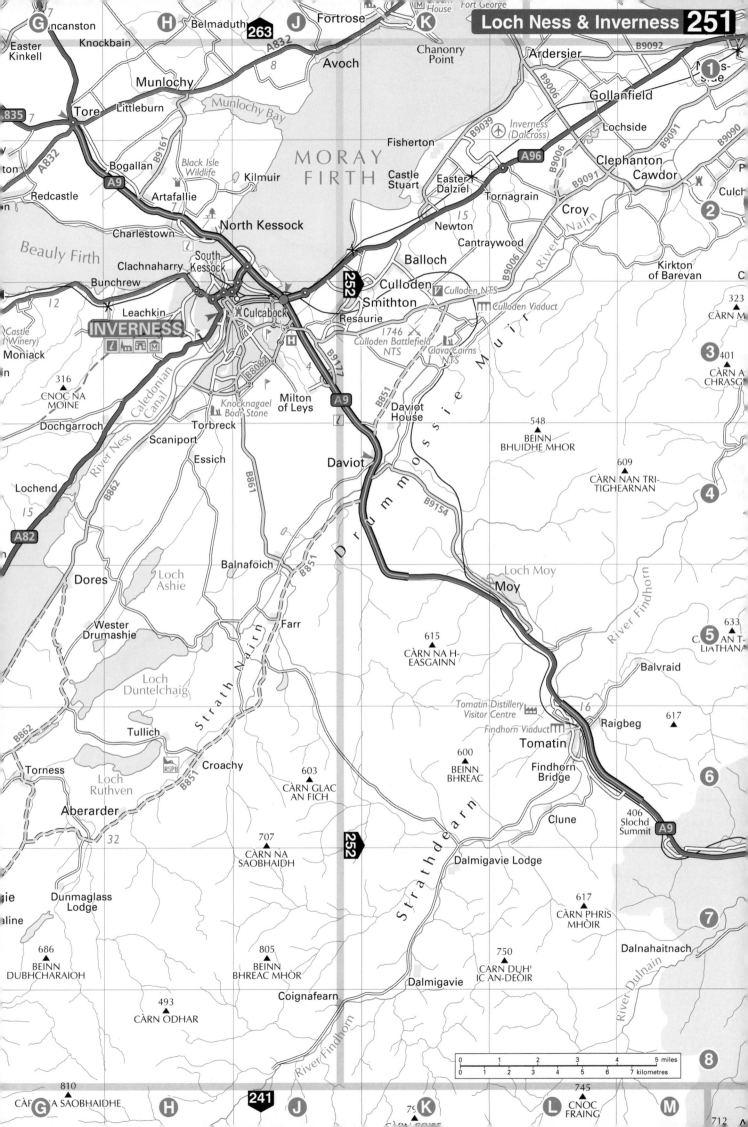

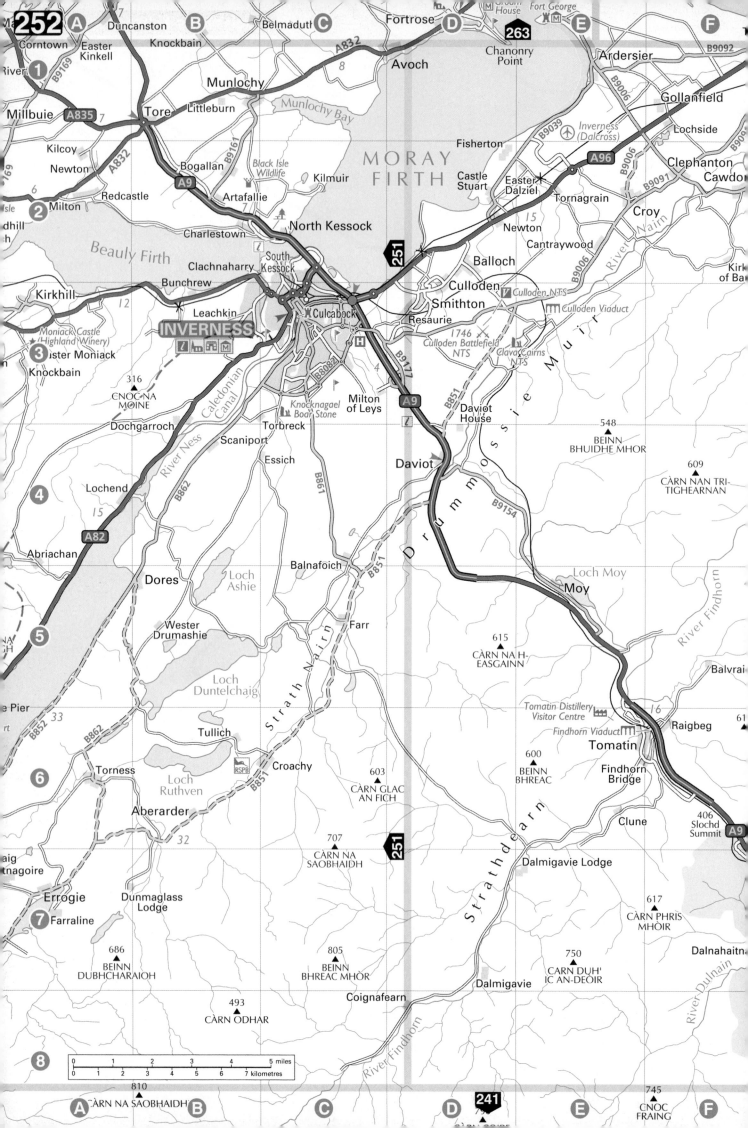

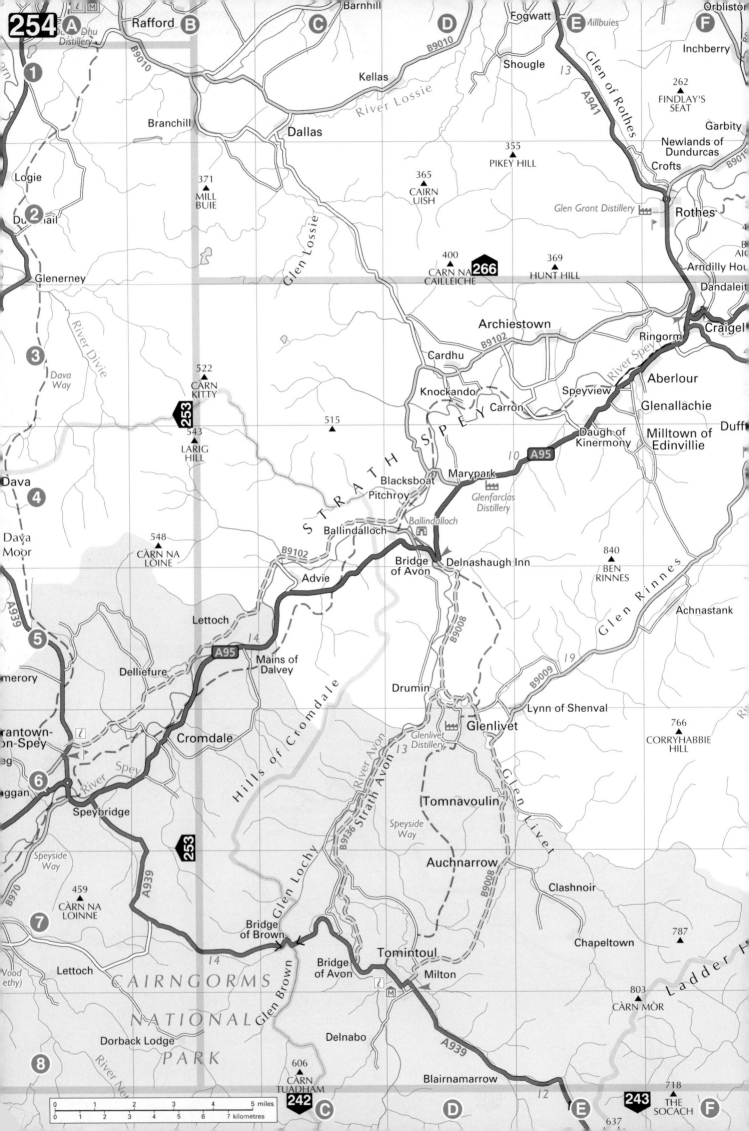

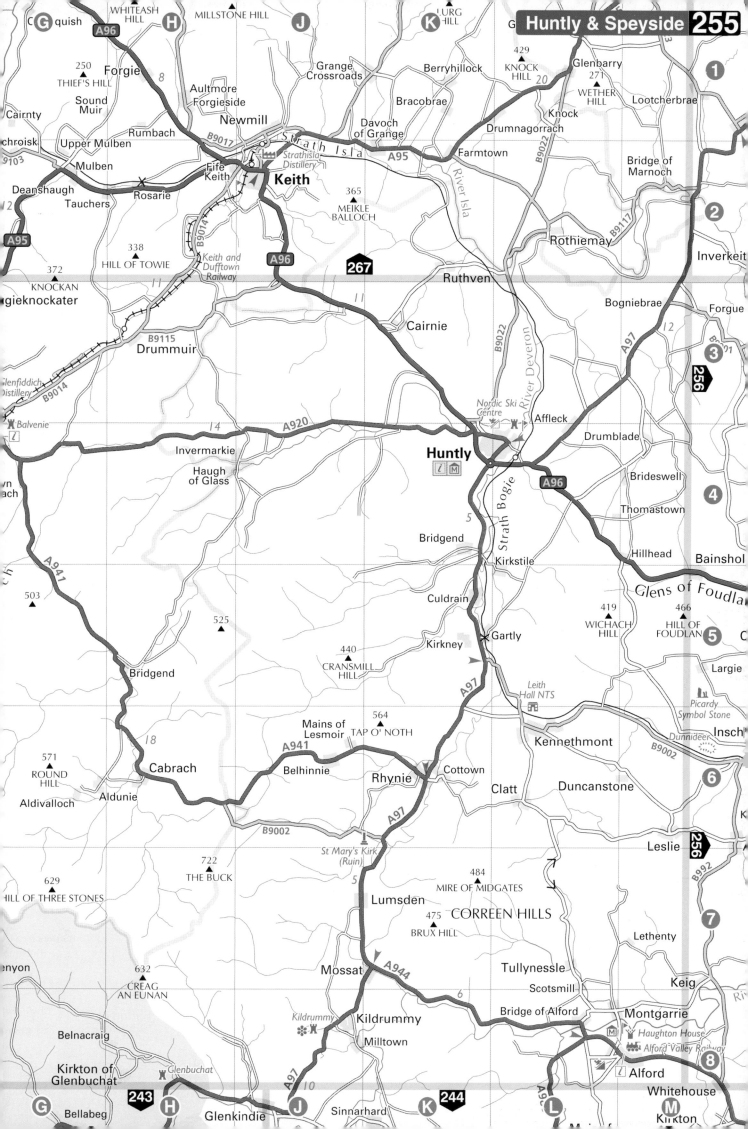

C**G**quish

WHITEASH HILL **H**

MILLSTONE HILL **J**

K LURG HILL

1

A96

250
THIEF'S HILL

Forgie

8

Aultmore
Forgieside

Grange
Crossroads

Berryhillock

Glenbarry

429
KNOCK
HILL

271
WETHER
HILL

Lootcherbrae

Sound
Muir

Cairnty

Newmill

B9017

Davoch
of Grange

Bracobrae

Drumnagorrach

20

Knock

B9022

chroisk

Rumbach

Upper Mulben

Strath Isla

A95

Farmtown

Bridge of
Marnoch

2

B9103

Mulben

Strathisla
Distillery

River Isla

Deanshaugh
Tauchers

Fife
Keith

Rosarie

Keith

365
MEIKLE
BALLOCH

Rothiemay

B9117

Inverkeit

A95

372
KNOCKAN

338
HILL OF TOWIE

Keith and
Dufftown
Railway

A96

267

Ruthven

Bogniebrae

Forgue

gieknockater

11

11

Cairnie

B9022

A97

12

B9001

3

256

B9115

Drummuir

River Deveron

Glenfiddich
Distillery

B9014

Nordic Ski
Centre

Affleck

Drumblade

Balvenie

A920

14

Invermarkie

Huntly

Brideswell

4

Haugh
of Glass

5

Strath Bogie

Thomastown

Bridgend

Hillhead

Bainshol

A941

Kirkstile

Glens of Foudla

503

Culdrain

419
WICHACH
HILL

466
HILL OF
FOUDLAN

5

525

440
CRANSMILL
HILL

Kirkney

Gartly

Leith
Hall NTS

Largie

Picardy
Symbol Stone

Insch

564
TAP O' NOTH

Mains of
Lesmoir

A941

Kennethmont

B9002

Dunnideer

6

571
ROUND
HILL

18

Cabrach

Belhinnie

Rhynie

Cottown

Clatt

Duncanstone

Aldunie

A97

Aldivalloch

B9002

St Mary's Kirk
(Ruin)

Leslie

256

722
THE BUCK

5

484
MIRE OF MIDGATES

B992

629
HILL OF THREE STONES

Lumsden

475
BRUX HILL

CORREEN HILLS

Lethenty

7

enyon

632
CREAG
AN EUNAN

Mossat

A944

Tullynessle

Keig

6

Scotsmill

Bridge of Alford

Montgarrie

Haughton House

Belnacraig

Kildrummy

Kildrummy

Milltown

A97

Alford Valley Railway

8

Kirkton of
Glenbuchat

Glenbuchat

10

Alford

Whitehouse

G
Bellabeg

243

H
Glenkindie

J
Sinnarhard

244 **K**

L

M
Kirkton

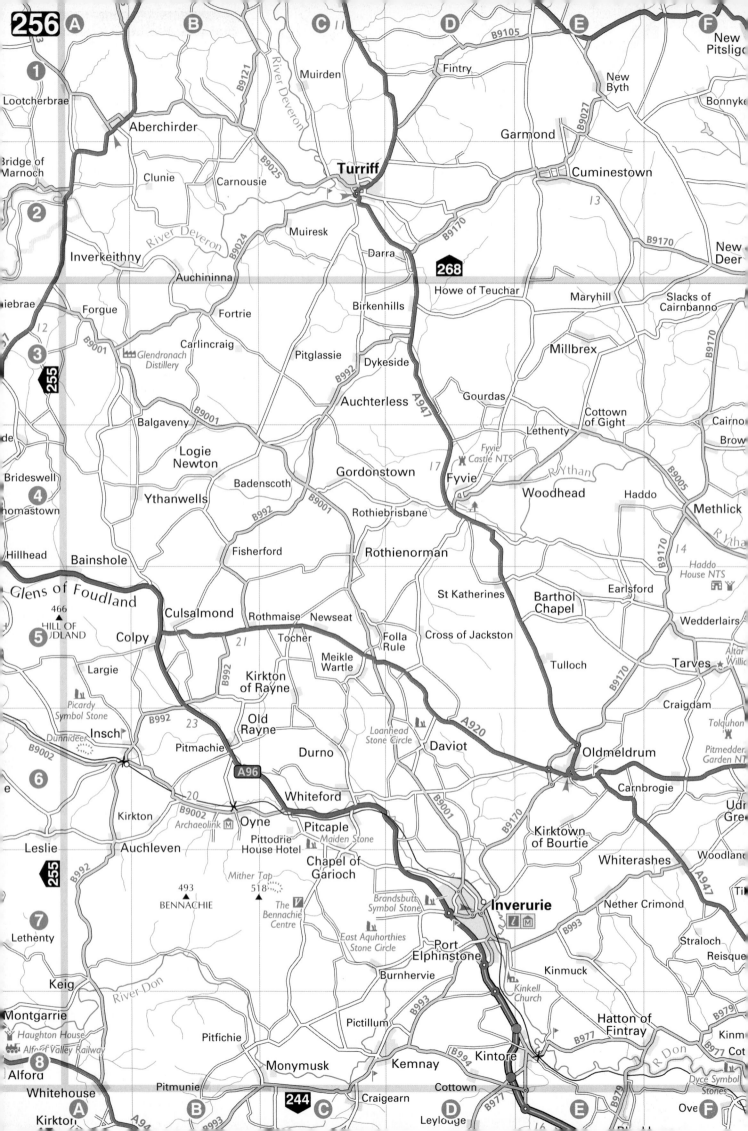

G
H
J
K

Strathbeg

WAUGHTON HILL

Strichen

Crimond

Blackhill

18

New Leeds

B9093

B9093

Leys

Denhead

Backfolds

Kirktown

St Fergus

Fetterangus

Rora

A90

A952

A981

A950

6

Deer Abbey

Dunshillock

River Ugie

Inverugie

Buchanhaven

Peterhead

Maud

B9106

Aden

Mintlaw

Longside

A950

B9029

Old Deer

269

Peterhead Bay

Blackhill of Clackriach

Inverquhomery

9

Burnhaven

B9029

Stuartfield

Drymuir

Bulwark

Millbreck

Nether Kinmundy

Hillhead of Cocklaw

Buchan Ness

Boddam

B9028

Clola

Little Dens

Blackhill

Stirling

uchnagatt

Kinnadie

Lendrum Terrace

12

Kinknockie

B9030

Inkhorn

Ardallie

Longhaven

A952

A90

Bullers of Buchan

Coldwells

Hatton

Auchiries

North Haven

A948

Arthrath

Muirtack

14

Slains

Cruden Bay

17

Ythanbank

Bogbrae

Chapel Hill

Bay of Cruden

uchedly

Birness

A975

Whinnyfold

The Skares

Kinharrachie

Artrochie

Ellon

P+R

Kirkton of Logie Buchan

Kirktown of Slains

Esslemont

B9005

Colliesston

A920

10

medden

Logierieve

B9000

Forvie

32

ousieside

B9000

Udny Station

A90

Newburgh

Cultercullen

Foveran

A975

Delfrigs

machar

17

Causeyend

B979

Balmedie

hitecairns

Belhelvie

Balmedie

B999

B977

B977

Potterton

245

B999

G
H
J
K
L
M

khill use

Blackdog

0   1   2   3   4   5 miles
0 1 2 3 4 5 6 7 kilometres

1
2
3
4
5
6
7
8

G H J K L

1
2
3
4
5
6
7
8

260

248

247

n Trodday

North
Duntulm
Kilmaluag
Flodigarry
useum
d Life
Eilean Flodigarry
Poldorais
542
MEAL NA
SUIREAMACH
Digg
Staffin
Bay
Staffin Island
Brogaig
17
Stenscholl
Staffin
464
BIODA
BUIDHE
Trotternish
Kilt Rock Waterfall
Ellishader
Marishader
Valtos
River Conon
611
BEINN
EDRA
Garros
Rudha nam Brathairean
Culnaknock
Lealt
Tote
einlich
608
CREAG A' LAIN
nisdal
451
BEINN
A' SGA
A855
Loch a' Bhràige
Ob
Chuaig
Re
Poi
Rudha
na Fearn

RONA
uaig
Callakille

River Romesdal
Old Man
719 of Storr
THE
STORR
esdal
Eilean
Tigh
Lonbain
Kensaleyre
River Haulton
Loch
Leathan
16
Loch
Fada
Eilean
Fladday
Umachan
l Carbost
Borve
Manish
Point
Loch
Arnish
Torran
Drumuie
Glengrasco
A855
312
Arnish
Torvaig
Brochel
Portree
Seafield
i
417
BEINN NA
GREINE
Penifiler
412
BEN
TIANAVAIG
Glenmore
Glenvarragill
444
DUN CAAN
RAASAY

SOUND OF RAASAY

INNER SO

Applecross Bay
Milton
Camu
Aird Dhu
Ca

G Mugeary A87 H Camastianav J Oskaig K Rudha na' Leac L M Toscaig
Tianavaig
Bay

A B C D E F

270

1

Rudha Beag
Stattic Point
Mellon
Udrigle
GRUINARD
ISLAND
Badlu

Foura

Cove

2

Rudha Reidh

Laide
Gruinard
Bay
Mellon
Charles
Ormiscaig
Gruinard
Aultbea

296
AN
CUAIDH

B8057

Little Gruinard River

A832

Melvaig

ISLE
OF EWE

Loch
Fada

CRE
MHEAL

3

Aultgrishin

Loch Ewe

Inverasdale

293
CNOC
BREAC

Naast

681
BEINN A'
CHAISGEIN B

North Erradale

Inverewe
Garden NTS

13

250
MEALL NA MEINE

B8021

Londubh

Poolewe

Fionn

Weste

Big Sand

4

A832

Strath

Smithstown

Auchtercairn

Lonemore

Longa
Island

Gairloch

Heritage
Museum

Loch
Gairloch

Charlestown

421
MEALL AN
DOIREIN

791
BEINN
AIRIDH CHARR

Loch

Eilean
Horrisdale

5

Port
Henderson

Badachro

B8056

Opinan

South Erradale

Loch Bad
an Sgalaig

Loch
Maree
Hotel

Letterewe

B

Talladale

19

A832

Maree

Redpoint

6

Red
Point

Loch Ghaineamhach

Loch na
A-Oidhche

259

Loch a'
Ghobhainn

875
BAOSBHEINN

855
BEINN
AN EOIN

724

619
BEINN BHREAC

Loch a'
Bhealaich

7

Rudha
na Fearn

Loch
Torridon

Craig River

Lower
Diabaig

985
BEINN
ALLIGIN

914
BEINN DEARG

1009
RUADH-
STAC MÒR

Fearnmore

Òb
Chuaig

Fearnbeg

Loch
Diabaig

1024
LIATHACH

1053

BEINN

Arrina

Inveralligin

8

Cuaig

Kenmore

Alligin Shuas

Glen Torridon

Torridon
House

Torridon

19

Callakille

Ardheslaig

Upper Loch Torridon

248

Countryside Centre NTS

Shieldaig

0 1 2 3 4 5 miles
0 1 2 3 4 5 6 7 kilometres

C D E F

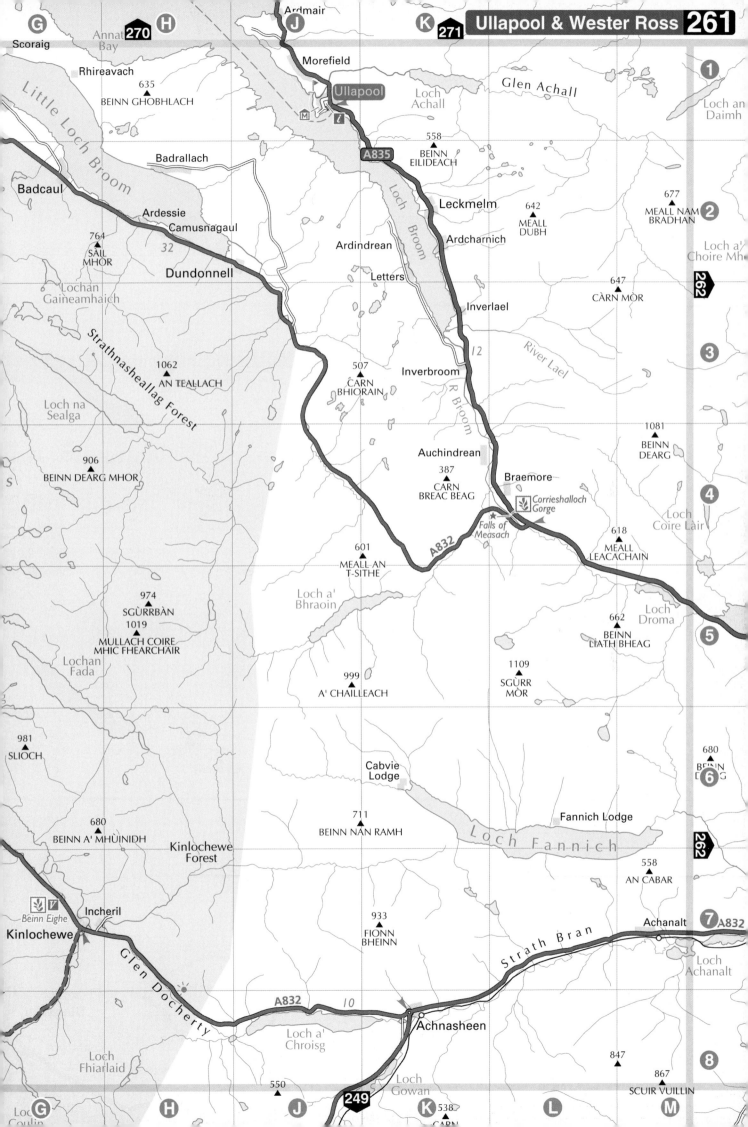

Scoraig

Annat Bay

Rhireavach

635 ▲
BEINN GHOBHLACH

Ardmair

Morefield

Ullapool

Glen Achall

Loch Achall

Loch an Daimh

Badrallach

Badcaul

Ardessie

Camusnagaul

32

764 ▲
SÀIL MHÓR

Dundonnell

Lochan Gaineamhaich

Loch na Sealga

1062 ▲
AN TEALLACH

Strathnasheallag Forest

906 ▲
BEINN DEARG MHÓR

A835

558 ▲
BEINN EILIDEACH

Leckmelm

Ardcharnich

642 ▲
MEALL DUBH

677 ▲
MEALL NAM BRADHAN

Loch a' Choire Mh

262

Ardindrean

Letters

Inverlael

R Broom

River Lael

647 ▲
CÀRN MÓR

507 ▲
CARN BHIORAIN

Inverbroom

1081 ▲
BEINN DEARG

Auchindrean

387 ▲
CARN BREAC BEAG

Braemore

Corrieshalloch Gorge

Falls of Measach

A832

618 ▲
MEALL LEACACHAIN

Loch Coire Làir

974 ▲
SGÙRRBÀN

1019 ▲
MULLACH COIRE MHIC FHEARCHAIR

Lochan Fada

601 ▲
MEALL AN T-SITHE

Loch a' Bhraoin

662 ▲
BEINN LIATH BHEAG

Loch Droma

5

981 ▲
SLIOCH

999 ▲
A' CHAILLEACH

1109 ▲
SGÙRR MÓR

680 ▲
BEINN DEARG

6

Cabvie Lodge

680 ▲
BEINN A' MHÙINIDH

Kinlochewe Forest

711 ▲
BEINN NAN RAMH

Fannich Lodge

Loch Fannich

262

558 ▲
AN CABAR

Beinn Eighe

Incheril

Kinlochewe

Glen Docherty

933 ▲
FIONN BHEINN

Strath Bran

Achanalt

7 A832

Loch Achanalt

A832

10

Achnasheen

Loch a' Chroisg

847 ▲

867 ▲
SCUIR VUILLIN

8

Loch Fhiarlaid

Loch Gowan

550 ▲

249

538 ▲

A B C D E F

271 272

1

Loch an Daimh

412
CREAG LOISGTE

BEINN ULBHAIDH

463
BREAC BHEINN

506
MEALL DHEIRGIDH

Brealangwell Lodge

Strathcarron

677
MEALL NAM BRADHAN

2

Loch a' Choire Mhòir

701
CARN A' CHOIN DEIRG

Croik

River Carron

Giasha Burn

Strath Mulzie

261

842
CARN BAN

Glencalvie Forest

634
CÀRN BHREN

3

Gleann Beag

628

710
BEINN THARSUINN

Crom Loch

838
CÀRN CHUINNEAG

1081
BEINN DEARG

602
CÀRN CAS NAN GABHAR

4

Loch Coire Làir

771
MEALL A' GHRIANAIN

Loch a' Chaorunn

Loch Morie

742
BEINN NAN EUN

E A

742
TOM BÀN MÒR

Loch Vaich

737
MEALL MOR

Loch Droma

Strathkvaich Forest

Loch Glascarnoch

Loch Glass

5

Aultguish Inn

20

A835

Glen Gla

600

Inchbae Lodge Hotel

1045
BEN WYVIS

680
BEINN DEARG

479

Ben Wyvis

6

Corriemoille Forest

261

439
CÀRN NA DUBH CHOILLE

761
LITTLE WYVIS

558
N CABAR

Lochluichart

Corriemoille

484
CLOCH MHÒR

Gorstan

Strath Garve

7

Ach It

A832

16

Loch Luichart

Garve

Loch Garve

Auchterneed

7

A834

579
SGÙRR MARCASAIDH

Rogie Falls

Strathpeffer

Highland Museum of Childhood

Gower

Dingwall

Keithtown

8

536

Little Scatwell

Loch Achilty

Contin

Jamestown

Loch Ussie

Conon Brid

Ma

867
CUIR VUILLIN

Loch Meig

R Conon

G H J K L

1

2

3

4

5

266

Branderburgh
Stotfield
B9040
Lossiemouth

Burghead Well
Hopeman
Burnside
Burghead
Kinneddar
Duffus
St Peter's Kirk & Parish Cross
Cummingston
B9012
B9135
6
B9013
Roseisle
Duffus
Loch Spynie
B9012
6
Burghead Bay
College of Roseisle
A941
Stonewells
Spynie Palace
B9103
Kir on
Findhorn
B9089
Quarrywood
Viewfield
Lochill
Hempriggs
Newton
Bishopmill
Calcots
B9011
Kinloss
Coltfield
A96
Elgin
Innesmill
Findhorn Bay
Glen Moray Distillery
Urquhart
7
ncorth House
266
Alves
H
New Elgin
Lhanbryde
The Lochs
Grange Hall
Kilbuiack
12
Linkwood
9
ueno's Stone
Mosstodlo
row
Forres
Muir of Miltonduff
Crofts of Dipp
Califer
Pluscarden
Clackmarras
B9103
Dallas Dhu Distillery
Rafford
Barnhill
Longmorn
Orbl on
8
253
B9010
Fogwatt
Millbuies
Inchberry
B9015
G H J K L M
Kellas
Shougle
Glen
263

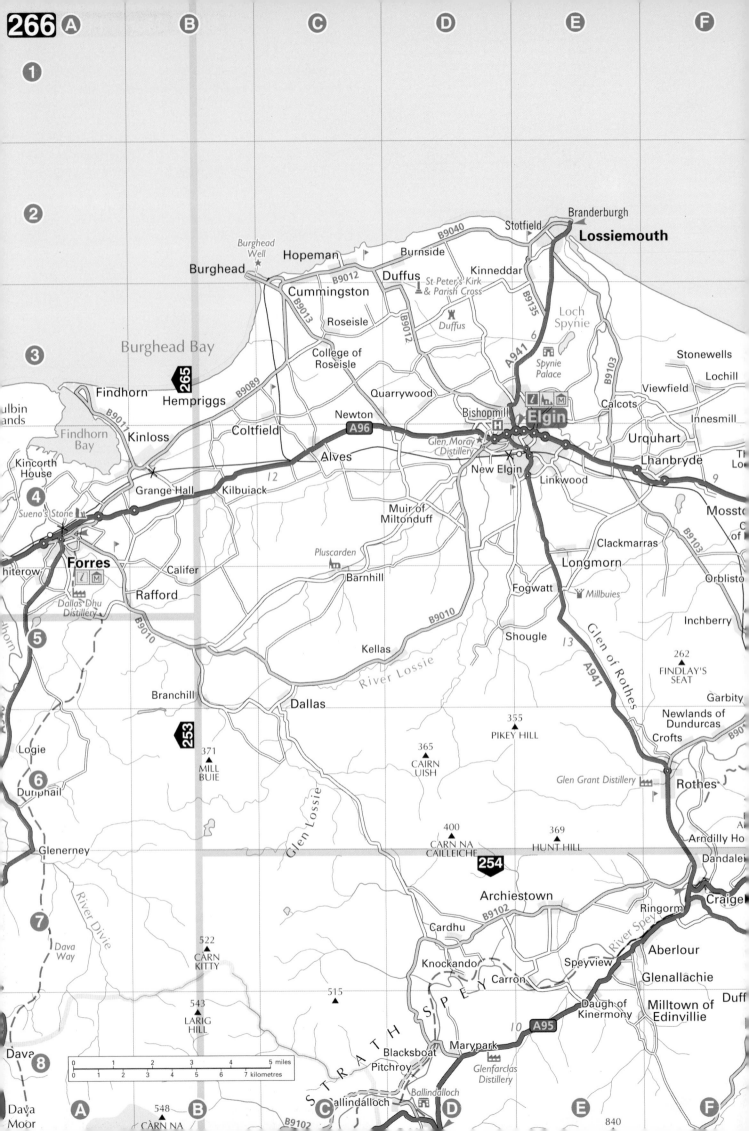

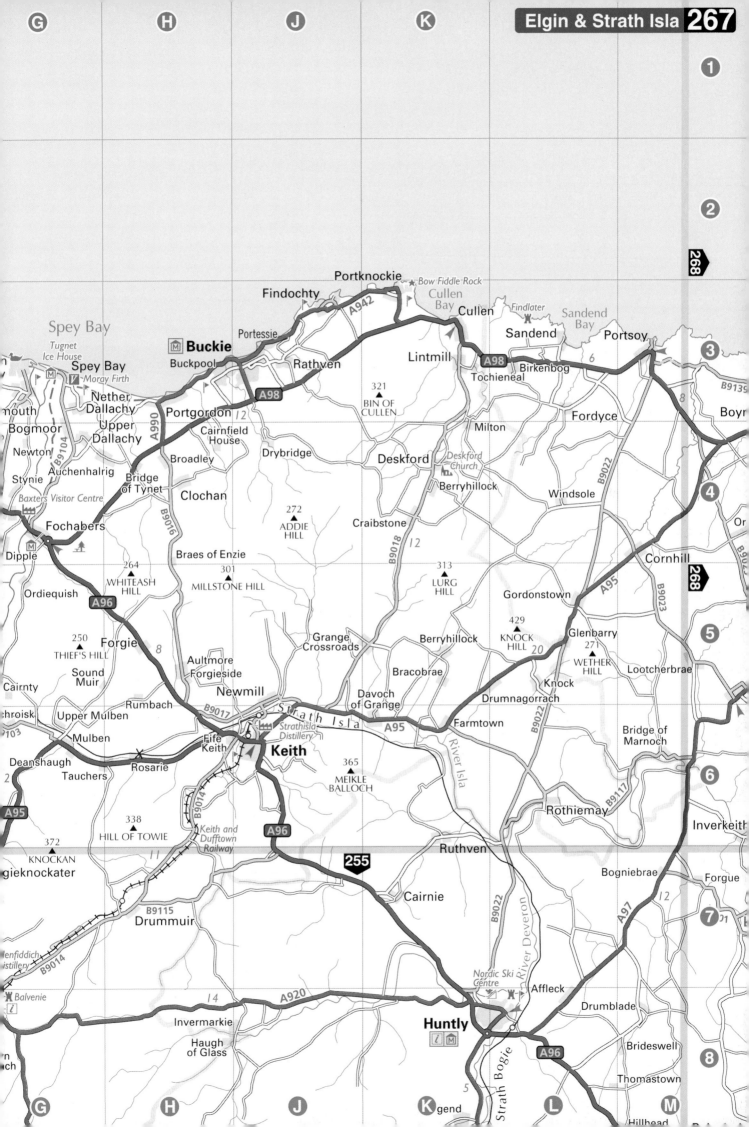

G H J K

1

2

268

Portknockie
Bow Fiddle Rock
Findochty
Cullen
Bay
Cullen
Findlater
Sandend
Bay
Portessie
Sandend
Portsoy
Spey Bay
A942
Tugnet
Ice House
Buckie
Buckpool
Rathven
Lintmill
A98
Birkenbog
6
3
Spey Bay
Moray Firth
A98
Tochieneal
8
B9139
Nether
Dallachy
Portgordon
12
321
BIN OF
CULLEN
Milton
Fordyce
Boyr
mouth
A990
Cairnfield
House
Drybridge
Deskford
Deskford
Church
Bogmoor
Upper
Dallachy
Broadley
Berryhillock
Windsole
4
Newton
B9104
Clochan
Craibstone
B9018
Cornhill
Stynie
Auchenhalrig
Bridge
of Tynet
272
ADDIE
HILL
12
268
Baxters Visitor Centre
B9016
313
LURG
HILL
A95
B9023
Fochabers
264
WHITEASH
HILL
Braes of Enzie
301
MILLSTONE HILL
Gordonstown
Glenbarry
Dipple
A96
Ordiequish
429
KNOCK
HILL
20
271
WETHER
HILL
Lootcherbrae
5
250
THIEF'S HILL
Forgie
8
Grange
Crossroads
Berryhillock
Knock
Cairnty
Sound
Muir
Aultmore
Forgieside
Bracobrae
Drumnagorrach
Bridge of
Marnoch
chroisk
Upper Mulben
Rumbach
Newmill
B9017
Strath Isla
Davoch
of Grange
A95
Farmtown
B9022
9103
Mulben
Fife
Keith
Strathisla
Distillery
Keith
Rothiemay
B9117
6
Deanshaugh
Tauchers
Rosarie
365
MEIKLE
BALLOCH
River Isla
Inverkeith
A95
338
HILL OF TOWIE
B9014
Keith and
Dufftown
Railway
A96
Ruthven
Bogniebrae
Forgue
372
KNOCKAN
255
Cairnie
12
7
gieknockater
B9115
Drummuir
B9022
A97
01
nfiddich
istillery
B9014
Nordic Ski
Centre
Affleck
Drumblade
Balvenie
14
A920
Invermarkie
Haugh
of Glass
Huntly
Brideswell
8
Strath Bogie
A96
Thomastown
G H J K gend L M
5
Hillhead

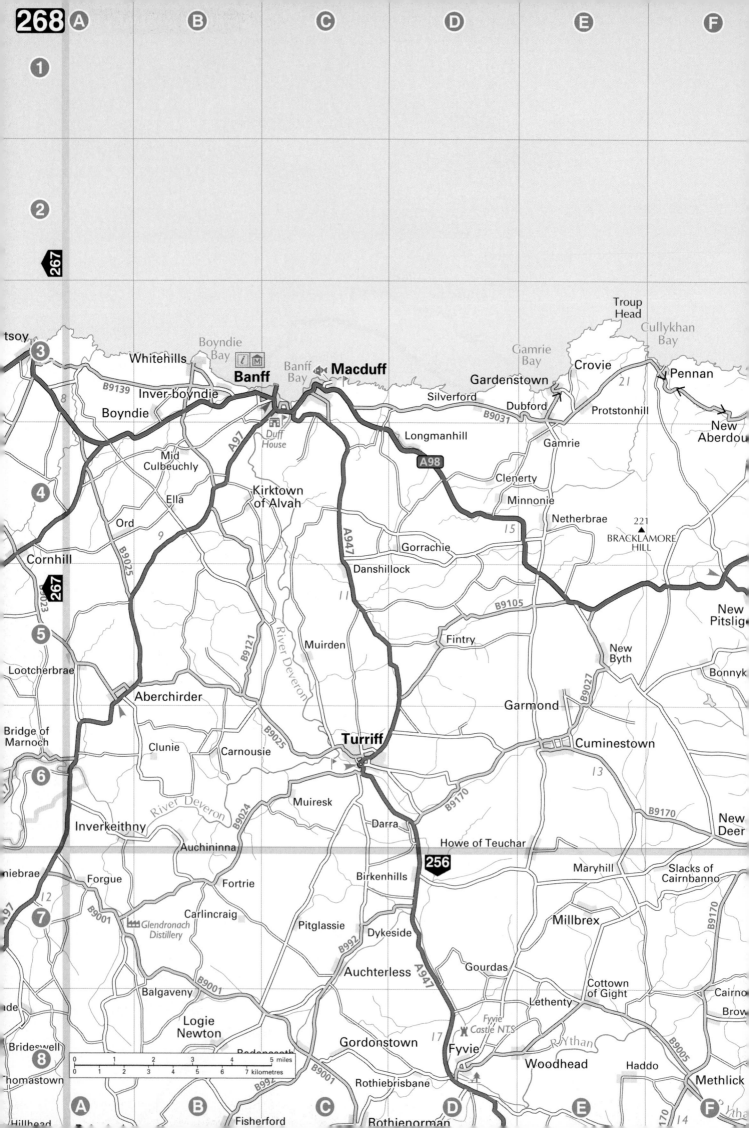

A B C D E F

1

Point of Stoer

OLDANY ISLAND

Eddrach Bay

Old Man of Stoer

Culkein

Culkein Drumbeg

Clashnessie Bay

Oldany

Drumbeg

Achnacarnin

Nedd

2

Clashmore

Clashnessie

Loch Poll

Stoer

Loch Beannac

Clachtoll

B869

3

Bay of Clachtoll

Rhicarn

Achmelvich Bay

A837

Achmelvich

Baddidarrach

i

Lochinver

Soyea Island

Loch Inver

Strathan

Assy

Inverkirkaig

4

River Kirkaig

Fionn Loch

Rhu Coigach

Eilean Mòr

Enard Bay

Rubha Mòr

Reiff

5

Achnahaird

Loch Sionasc

Altandhu

Eilean Mullagrach

Loch Osgaig

Isle Ristol

612
▲
STAC POLLAIDH

Polbain

769
▲
CUL BE

Glas-leac Mòr

6

SUMMER ISLES

Achiltibuie

Loch Lurgainn

Tanera Beg

Badentarbat Bay

Polglass

V

Steornabhagh (Stornoway)

Tanera Mòr

C O I G A C H

Glas-leac Beag

Horse Island

Horse Sound

652
▲
BEN MORE COIGACH

Achduart

Eilean Dubh

7

Culnacraig

Strathcanai

Priest Island

Strath

Greenstone Point

Leac Dhonn

Isle Martin

A835

Cailleach Head

Ardmair

8

Rudha Beag

tic Point

C

261

D

E

Mo F ld

Scoraig

Annat Bay

Rhireavach

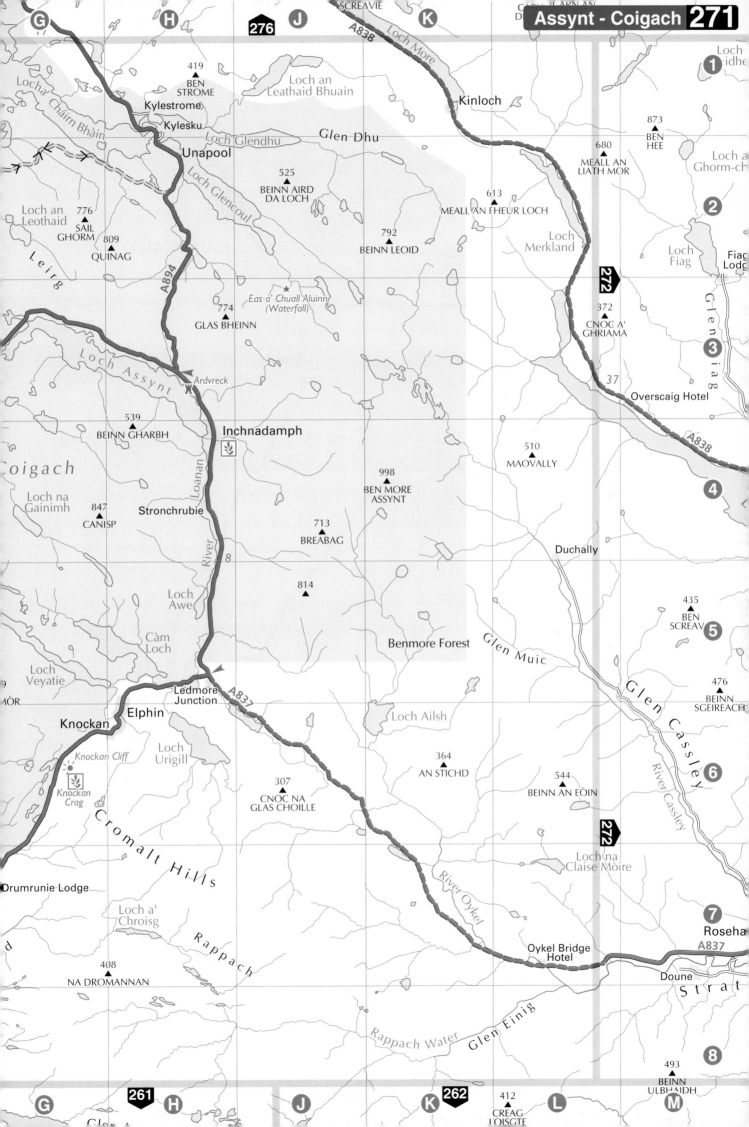

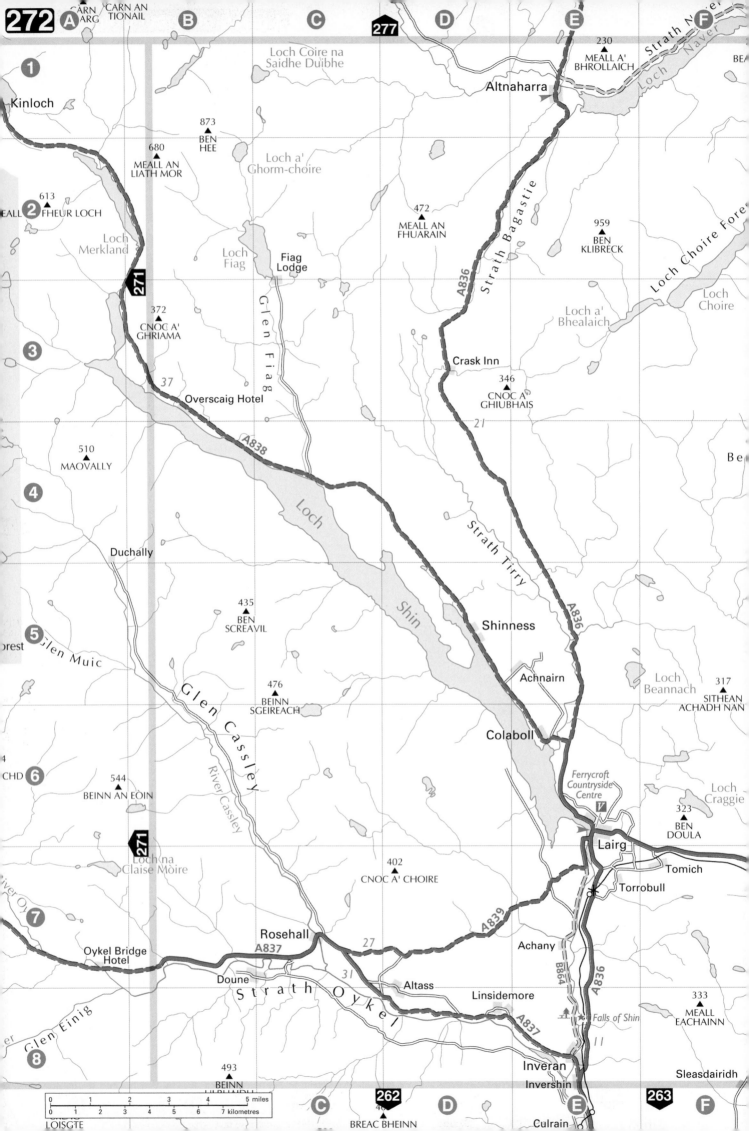

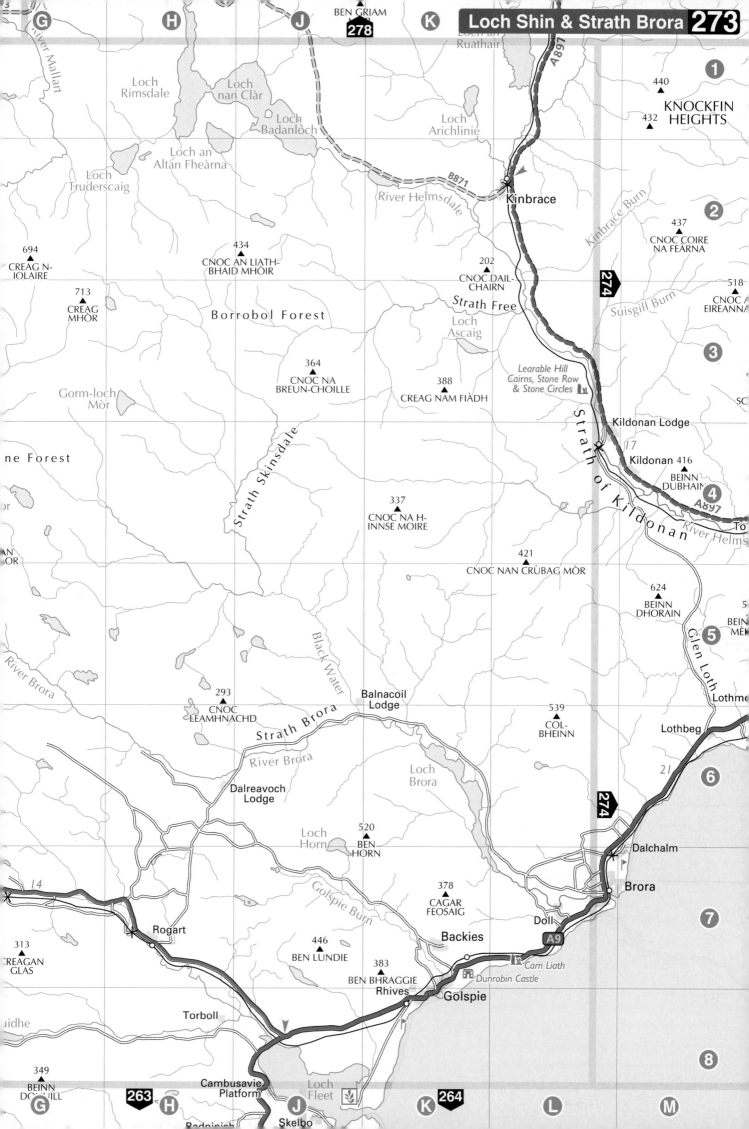

G   H   J   BEN GRIAM **278**   K   **1**

440 ▲
432 ▲   KNOCKFIN
HEIGHTS

Loch Rimsdale   Loch nan Clàr   Loch an Altán Fheàrna   Loch Badanlòch   Loch Arichlinie   Lochan Ruathair   A897

River Mallart   **2**   437 ▲   CNOC COIRE NA FEÀRNA

River Helmsdale   B871   Kinbrace

Loch Truderscaig   **274**   518 ▲   CNOC EIREANNA

694 ▲   CREAG N-IOLAIRE   434 ▲   CNOC AN LIATH-BHAID MHÒIR   202 ▲   CNOC DAIL-CHAIRN   Strath Free   Suisgill Burn   Kinbrace Burn

713 ▲   CREAG MHÒR   Borrobol Forest   Loch Ascaig   **3**   SC

Gorm-loch Mòr   364 ▲   CNOC NA BREUN-CHOILLE   388 ▲   CREAG NAM FIÀDH   Learable Hill Cairns, Stone Row & Stone Circles   Kildonan Lodge

ne Forest   Strath Skinsdale   Strath of Kildonan   17   Kildonan   416 ▲   BEINN DUBHAIN   **4**   A897

337 ▲   CNOC NA H-INNSE MOIRE   To   River Helms

421 ▲   CNOC NAN CRÙBAG MÒR   624 ▲   BEINN DHORAIN   BEIN MÈ   **5**

AN ... OR   River Brora   Glen Loth

293 ▲   CNOC LEAMHNACHD   Balnacoil Lodge   Black Water   Lothm   Lothbeg   **6**

Strath Brora   River Brora   539 ▲   COL-BHEINN   21

Dalreavoch Lodge   Loch Brora

14   Loch Horn   520 ▲   BEN HORN   **274**   Dalchalm

Rogart   378 ▲   CAGAR FEOSAIG   Brora   **7**

313 ▲   CREAGAN GLAS   446 ▲   BEN LUNDIE   Golspie Burn   Backies   Doll   A9

383 ▲   BEN BHRAGGIE   Rhives   Carn Liath   Dunrobin Castle

Torboll   Golspie   **8**

349 ▲   BEINN DO ... ILL   **263**   Cambusavie Platform   **264**   L   M

G   H   J   Skelbo   Loch Fleet   K

Radni ...

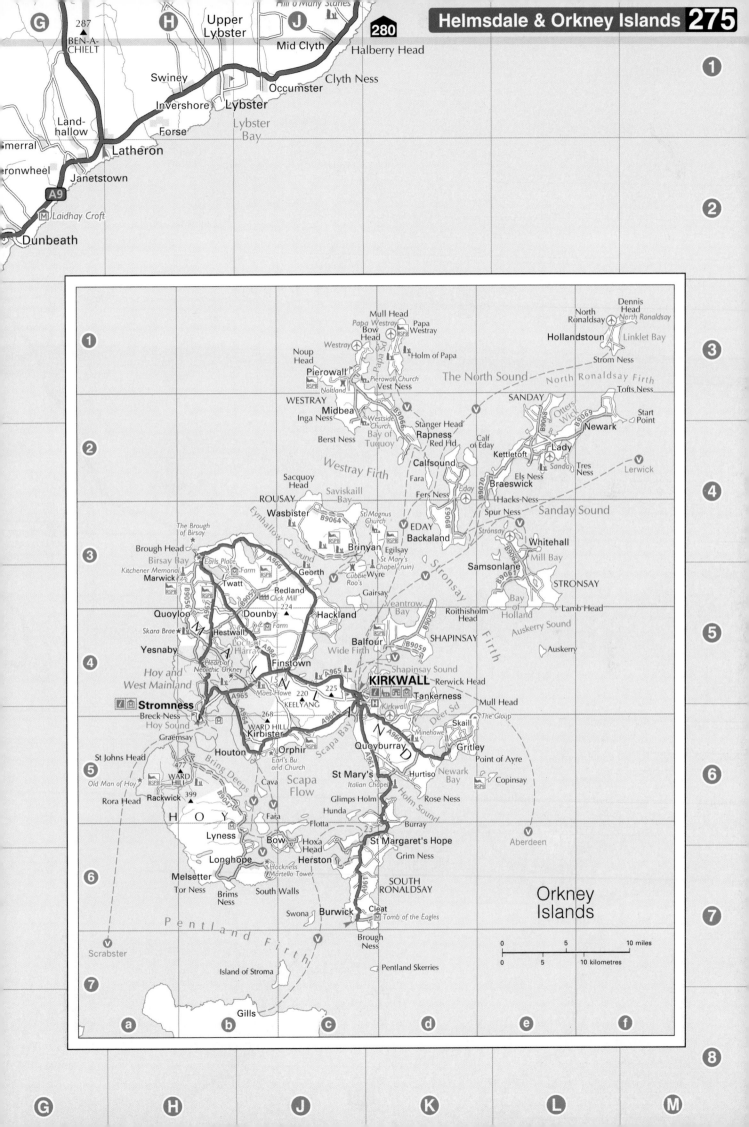

A
B
C
D
E
F
1
2
3
4
5
6
7
8
CAPE WRATH
Cléit Dhubh
Faraid Head
371
SGRIBHIS-BHEINN
297
CNOC A GHIUBHAIS
300
MAOVALLY
Balnakeil Bay
Balnakeil
Durness
Sangomo
THE PARPH
457
FASHVEN
Loch Airigh na Beinne
Keold
Kyle of Durness
Sandwood Bay
Sandwood Loch
485
CREAG RIABACH
468
BEINN DEARG MHÒR
464
MEALL NA MÒINE
Rudh' an Fhir Leithe
Strath Shinary
331
GHLAS-BHEINN
A838
Sheigra
Balchreick
Blairmore
19
Oldshoremore
521
FARVEALL
489
MEALL NA CRÀ
355
AN SOCACH
773
BEINN SPIONNAIDH
Kinlochbervie
Loch Clash
Badcall
801
CRANSTACKIE
B801
Strath Dionard
Achriesgill
Loch Inchard
River Dionard
Strath Beag
Rhiconich
Loch na Claise Càrnaich
Rudha Ruadh
908
FOINAVEN
Skerricha
Fanagmore
Loch Laxford
Tarbet
A838
HANDA ISLAND
Foindle
North-west Sutherland
Loch na Tuadh
786
ARKLE
Laxford Bridge
River Laxford
7
Scourie Bay
A894
Scourie
Scourie More
Loch Stack
729
SÀBHAL BEAG
721
BEN STACK
Badcall
Strath Stack
Badcall Bay
Loch a' Mhuilinn
386
BEN AUSKAIRD
Achfary
333
BEN SCREAVIE
800
796
CÀRN DEARG
757
CARN A TIONA
Rudh' a' Mhucard
17
A838
Loch More
0 1 2 3 4 5 miles
0 1 2 3 4 5 6 7 kilometres
271
419
NY

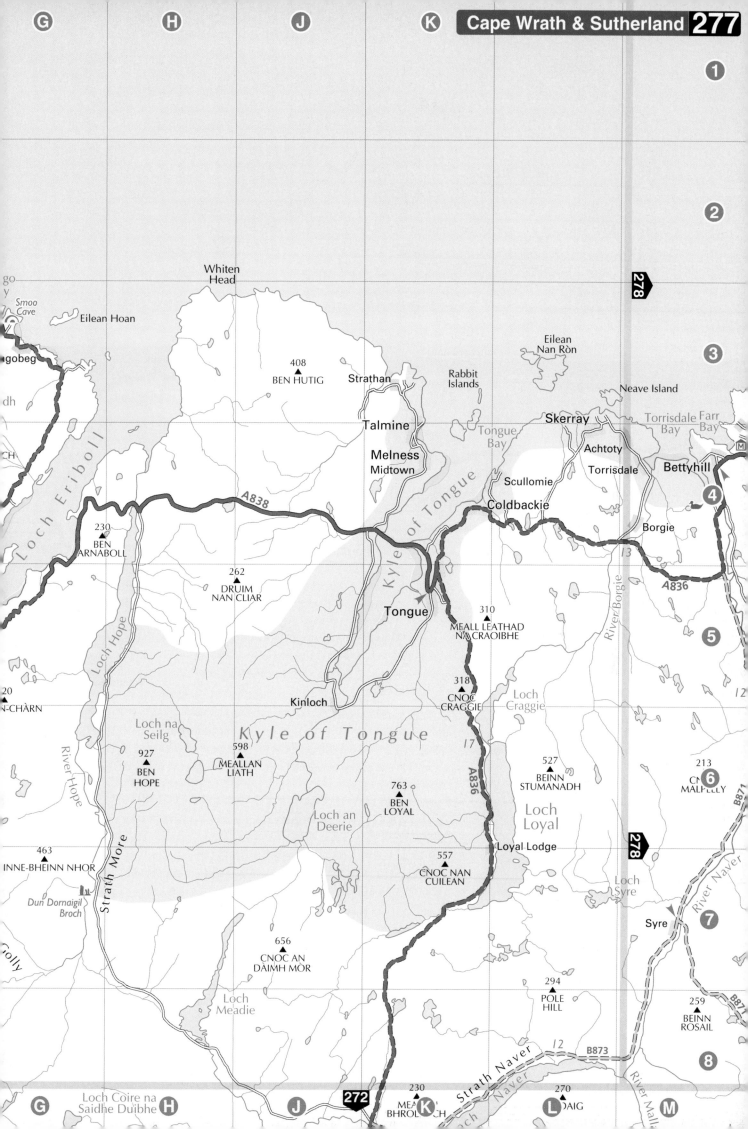

G
H
J
K

1

2

278

3

Whiten Head

Smoo Cave

Eilean Hoan

gobeg

dh

goy

CH

408 ▲ BEN HUTIG

Strathan

Rabbit Islands

Eilean Nan Ròn

Neave Island

Torrisdale Farr Bay Bay

Talmine

Skerray

Tongue Bay

Achtoty

Torrisdale

Bettyhill

M

Melness

Midtown

Scullomie

Coldbackie

4

A838

Loch Eriboll

230 ▲ BEN ARNABOLL

Borgie

13

A836

262 ▲ DRUIM NAN CLIAR

Kyle of Tongue

Tongue

310 ▲ MEALL LEATHAD NA CRAOIBHE

River Borgie

5

20

N-CHÀRN

Loch Hope

Loch na Seilg

Kinloch

318 ▲ CNOC CRAGGIE

Loch Craggie

12

17

Kyle of Tongue

927 ▲ BEN HOPE

598 ▲ MEALLAN LIATH

763 ▲ BEN LOYAL

A836

527 ▲ BEINN STUMANADH

Loch Loyal

213 ▲ CN MALFELLY

6

463 ▲ INNE-BHEINN NHOR

Strath More

Loch an Deerie

557 ▲ CNOC NAN CUILEAN

Loyal Lodge

278

B871

Dun Dornaigil Broch

Loch Syre

Syre

River Naver

7

olly

656 ▲ CNOC AN DÀIMH MÒR

294 ▲ POLE HILL

259 ▲ BEINN ROSAIL

Loch Meadie

Strath Naver

12

B873

River Mall

B871

8

G
Loch Coire na Saidhe Duibhe
H
J
272
230 ▲ MEA BHROL CH
K
270 ▲ AIG
L
M

Loch Naver

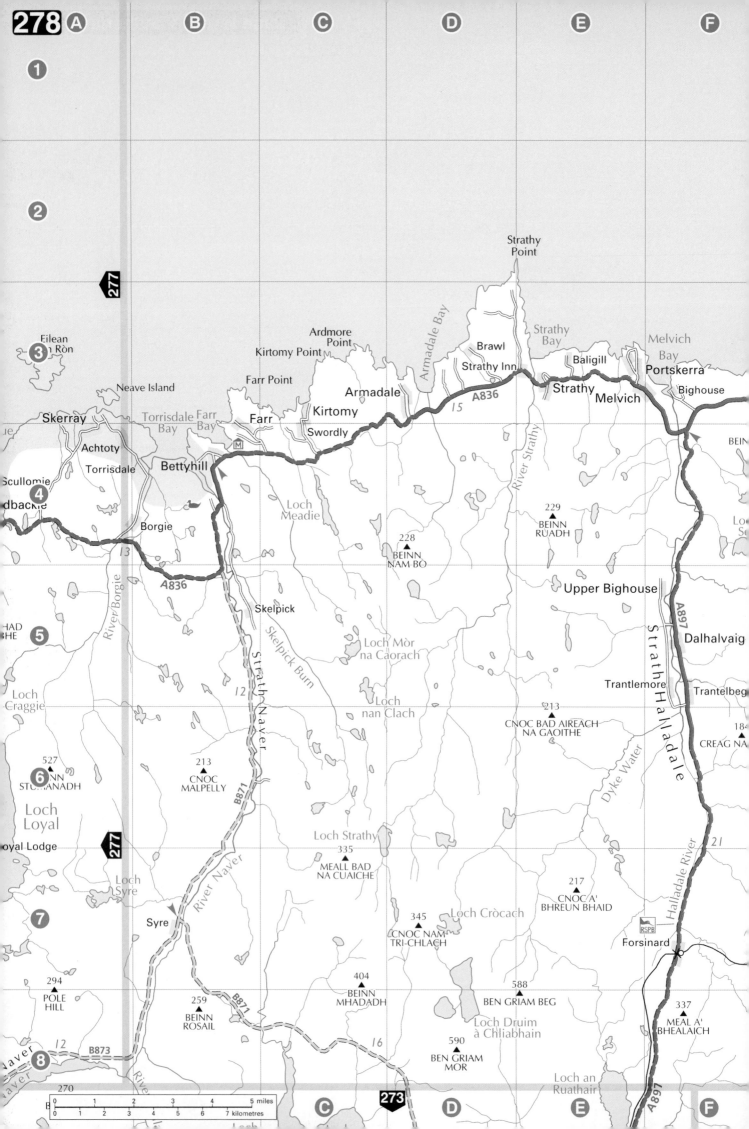

G H J K

1

DUNNET HEAD
▲127

Briga Head

▲121
DUNNET HILL

Brough

St John Loch

West Dunnet

Dunnet

Dunnet Bay

2 Dunnet

B855

Stromness
Ⓥ

Holborn Head

Brims Ness

St Mary's Chapel (ruin)

Crosskirk

Scrabster

A9

Thurso Bay

ⓘ Ⓜ

Thurso

stlehill

280

A836

Murkle

Castletown

3

Tai

B876

16

Bridge of Forss

A836

5

Buldoo

Skiall

Lythmore

B874

Achreamie

Cnoc Freiceadain Long Cairns

Glengolly

A9

Weydale

Olrig House

Upper Dounreay

Forss Water

Shebster

Westfield

Hilliclay

Bower

Isauld

Reay

Sandside Bay

▲242
BEINN RATHA

Broubster

Loch Calder

Sordale

Knockdee

Roadside

4 Halc

Clayock

Gillock

B874

Shurrery

B870

Halkirk

Loch Scarmclate

Shurrery Lodge

Loch Scye

Dorrery

Scotscalder Station

21

Loch Watten

▲290
BEIN NAM BAD MHOR

176
▲SPITTAL HILL

Harpsdale

5 Watten

▲243
CNOC AN
DARAIN BHÀIN

160
▲BRAIGH FÉITH HEMIGAL

Loch Shurrery

River Thurso

Spittal

B870

Backlass

Mybster

Loch of Toftingall

132
▲DRUIM A' CHRACAIRNIE

Loch Tuim Ghlais

Loch Caluim

Westerdale

23

6

▲203
CNOC PREAS A'MHADAIDH

200
▲CNOC BEUL NA FAIRE

Strath Beg

136
▲BEINN CHÀITEAG

280

Altnabreac Station

A9

75
▲OC GALL

Strathmore Water

Loch More

Loch Ruard

Achavanich

Loch Stemster

7 BALL H

Rumsdale Water

Loch an Thulachan

Loch Sand

248
▲STEMSTER HILL

Glutt Water

Dalnawillan Lodge

Loch Rangag

226
▲COIRE NA BEINN

348
▲BEN ALISKY

Gl Lodge

274

CNOCAN

287
▲BEN-A-CHIELT

280

8

Swiney

G H J K L M

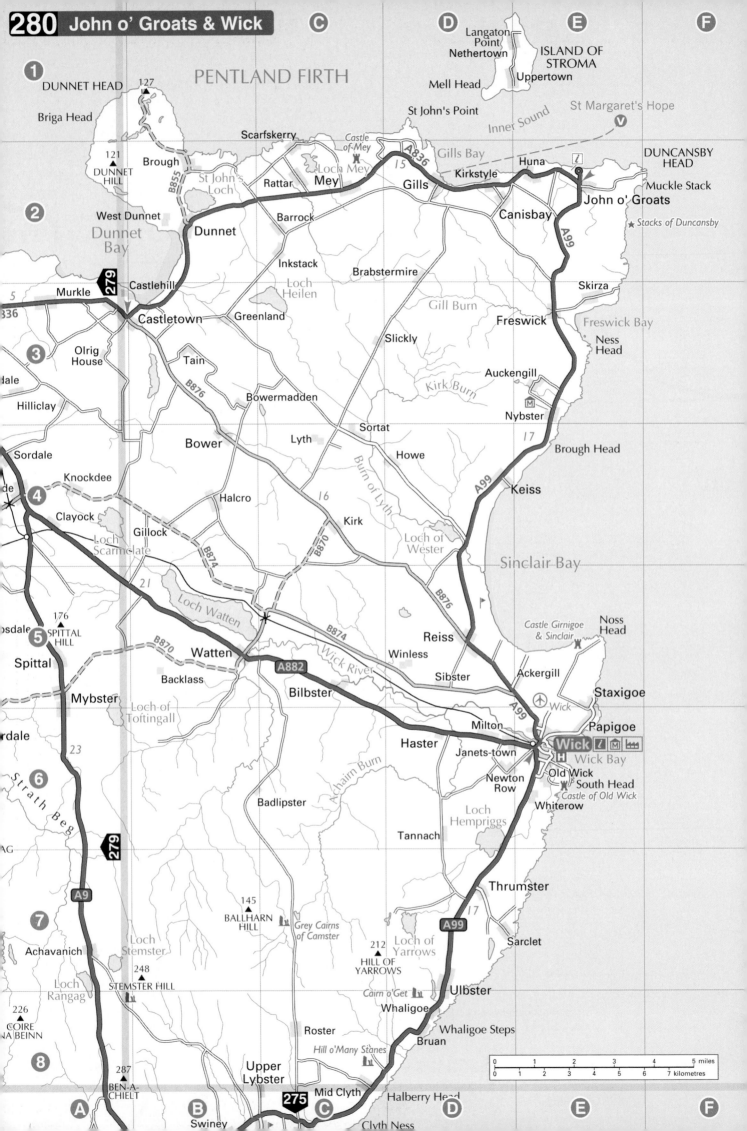

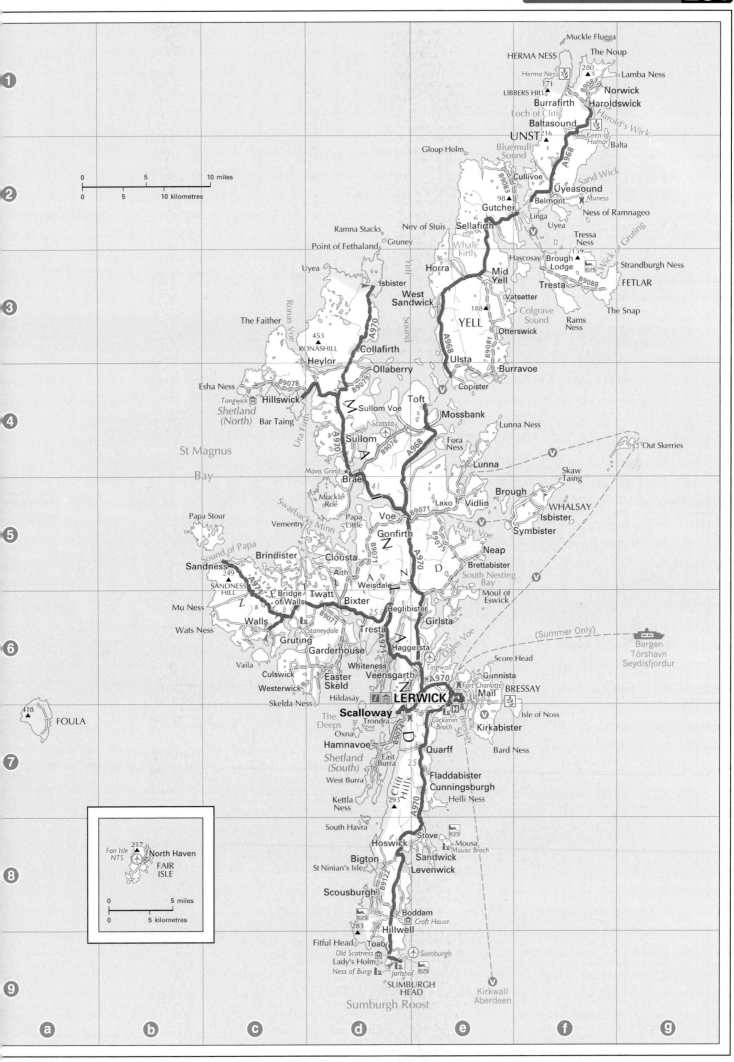

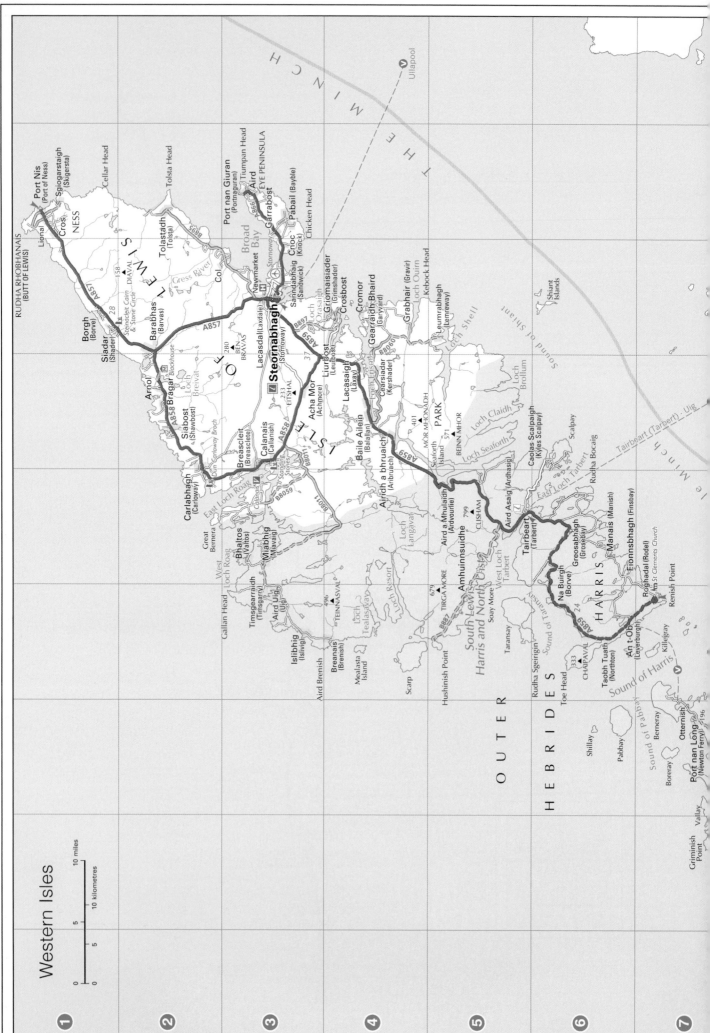

Western Isles

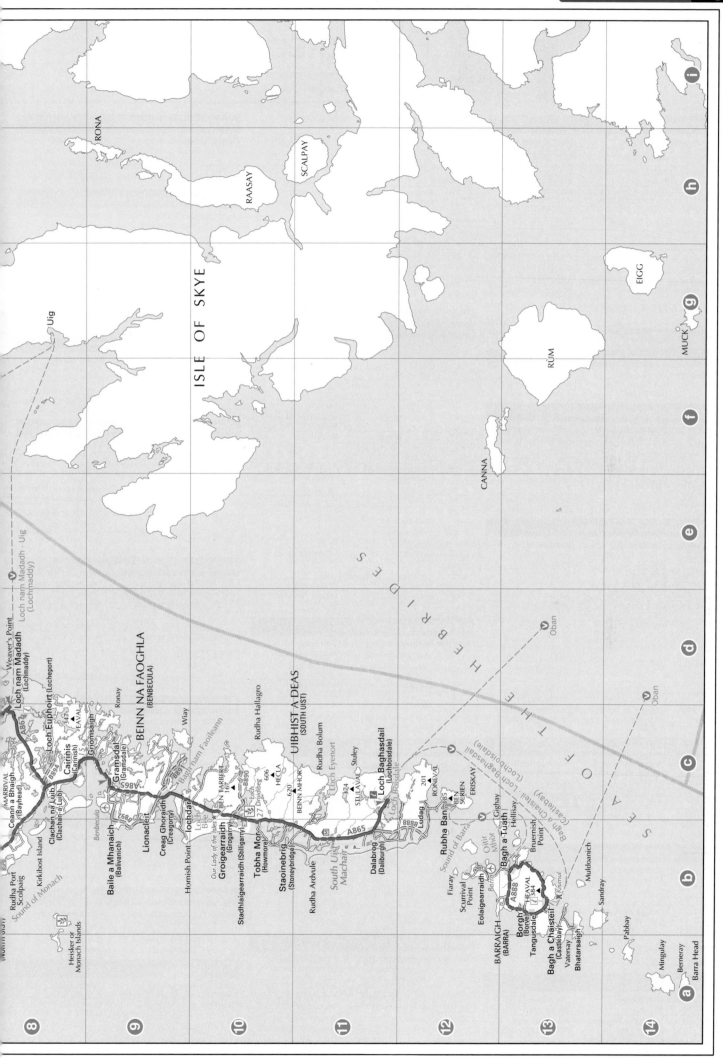

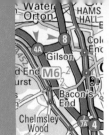

Restricted junctions

Motorway and Primary Route junctions which have access or exit restrictions are shown thus ⬦3⬦ , ⬦5B⬦ on the map pages.

M1 London - Leeds

Junction	Northbound	Southbound
2	Access only from A1 (northbound)	Exit only to A1 (southbound)
4	Access only from A41 (northbound)	Exit only to A41 (southbound)
6A	Access only from M25 (no link from A405)	Exit only to M25 (no link from A405)
7	Access only from M10	Exit only to M10
17	Exit only to M45	Access only from M45
19	Exit only to northbound M6	Access only from M6
21A	Exit only to A46	Access only from A46
23A	Access only from A42	Exit only to A42
24A	Access only from A50	Exit only to A50
35A	Exit only to A616	Access only from A616
43	Exit only to M621	Access only from M621
48	Exit only to A1(M) (northbound)	Access only from A1(M) (southbound)

M2 Rochester - Faversham

Junction	Westbound	Eastbound
1	Exit only to A289 (eastbound)	Access only from A289 (westbound)

M3 Sunbury - Southampton

Junction	Southwestbound	Northeastbound
8	Exit only to A303	Access only from A303
10	Access only from Winchester & A31	Exit only to Winchester & A31
13	Access only to M27 (westbound) & A33	No restriction
14	Exit only to M27 (eastbound) & A33	Access only

M4 London - South Wales

Junction	Westbound	Eastbound
1	Access only from A4 (westbound)	Exit only to A4 (eastbound)
4A	No exit to A4 (westbound)	No restriction
21	Exit only to M48	Access only from M48
23	Access only from M48	Exit only to M48
25	Exit only to B4596	Access only from B4596
25A	Exit only to A4042	Access only from A4042
29	Exit only to A48(M)	Access only from A48(M)
38	Exit only to A48	No restriction
39	Access only from A48	No access/exit
42	Staggered junction; follow signs - exit only to A483	Staggered junction; follow signs - access only from A483

M5 Birmingham - Exeter

Junction	Southwestbound	Northeastbound
10	Exit only to A4019	Access only from A4019
11A	Exit only to A417 (eastbound)	Access only from A417 (westbound)
18A	Access only from M49	Exit only to M49
29	Access only from A30 (westbound)	No restriction

M6 Toll Motorway

Junction	Northbound	Southbound
T1	Access only	No access or exit
T2	No access or exit	Exit only
T3	Staggered junction; follow signs - access only from A38	Staggered junction; follow signs - no restriction
T5	Access only from A5127 (southbound)	Exit only to A5148 (northbound)
T7	Exit only	Access only
T8	Exit only	Access only

M6 Rugby - Carlisle

Junction	Northbound	Southbound
3A	Exit only	Access only
4	No access from M42 (southbound). No exit to M42 (northbound)	No access from M42 (southbound). No exit to M42
4A	Access only from M42 (southbound)	Exit only to M42

5	Exit only to A452	Access only from A452
10A	Exit only to M54	Access only from M54
11A	Access only	Exit only
20A (with M56)	No restriction	No access from M56 (westbound)
20	Access only from A50	No restriction
24	Access only from A58	Exit only to A58
25	Exit only	Access only
29	No direct access, use adjacent slip road to jct 29A	No direct exit, use adjacent slip road from jct 29A
29A	No direct exit, use adjacent slip road from jct 29	No direct access, use adjacent slip road to jct 29
30	Access only from M61	Exit only to M61
31A	Exit only	Access only

M8 Edinburgh - Bishopton

Junction	Westbound	Eastbound
8	No access from M73 (southbound) or from A8 (eastbound) & A89	No exit to M73 (northbound) or to A8 (westbound) & A89
9	Access only	Exit only
13	Access only from M80 (southbound)	Exit only to M80 (northbound)
14	Access only	Exit only
16	Exit only to A804	Access only from A879
17	Exit only to A82	No restriction
18	Access only from A82 (eastbound)	Exit only to A814
19	No access from A814 (westbound)	Exit only to A814 (westbound)
20	Exit only	Access only
21	Access only	Exit only to A8
22	Exit only to M77 (southbound)	Access only from M77 (northbound)
23	Exit only to B768	Access only from B768
25	No access or exit from or to A8	No access or exit from or to A8
25A	Exit only	Access only
28	Exit only	Access only
28A	Exit only to A737	Access only from A737

M9 Edinburgh - Dunblane

Junction	Northwestbound	Southeastbound
1A	Exit only to A8000	Access only from A8000
2	Access only	Exit only
3	Exit only	Access only
6	Access only from A904	Exit only to A905
8	Exit only to M876 (southwestbound)	Access only from M876 (northeastbound)

M10 St Albans - M1

Junction	Northwestbound	Southeastbound
with M1 (jct 7)	Exit only to M1 (northbound)	Access only from M1 (southbound)

M11 London - Cambridge

Junction	Northbound	Southbound
4	Access only from A406	Exit only to A406
5	Exit only to A1168	Access only from A1168
9	Exit only to A11	Access only from A11
13	Exit only to A1303	Access only from A1303
14	Exit only to A14 (eastbound)	Access only from A14

M20 Swanley - Folkestone

Junction	Southeastbound	Northwestbound
2	Staggered junction; follow signs - exit only to A227	Staggered junction; follow signs - access only from A227
3	Access only from M26 (eastbound)	Exit only to M26 (westbound)
5	For access follow signs - exit only to A20	Access only from A20
6	For exit follow signs	No restriction
11A	Exit only	Access only

M23 Hooley - Crawley

Junction	Southbound	Northbound
7	Access only from A23 (southbound)	Exit only to A23 (northbound)
10A	Exit only to B2036	Access only from B2036

M25 London Orbital Motorway

Junction	Clockwise	Anticlockwise
1B	No direct access, use slip road to Jct 2. Exit only to A296	Access only from A296. No exit - use jct 2
5	No exit to M26	No access from M26
19	Exit only to A41	Access only from A41
21	Access only from M1 (southbound). Exit only to M1 (northbound)	Access only from M1 (southbound). Exit only to M1 (northbound)
31	No exit (use slip road via jct 30)	For access follow signs

M26 Sevenoaks - Wrotham

Junction	Eastbound	Westbound
with M25 (jct 5)	Access only from anticlockwise M25 (eastbound)	Exit only to clockwise M25 (westbound)
with M20 (jct 3)	Exit only to M20 (southeastbound)	Access only from M20 (northwestbound)

M27 Cadnam - Portsmouth

Junction	Eastbound	Westbound
4	Staggered junction; follow signs - access only from M3 (southbound). Exit only to M3 (northbound)	Staggered junction; follow signs - access only from M3 (southbound). Exit only to M3 (northbound)
10	Access only from A32	Exit only to A32
12	Staggered junction; follow signs - access only from M275 (northbound)	Staggered junction; follow signs - exit only to M275 (southbound)

M40 London - Birmingham

Junction	Northwestbound	Southeastbound
3	Exit only to A40	Access only from A40
7	Exit only to A329	Access only from A329
8	Exit only to A40	Access only from A40
13	Exit only to A452	Access only from A452
14	Access only from A452	Exit only to A452
16	Access only from A3400	Exit only to A3400

M42 Bromsgrove - Measham

Junction	Northeastbound	Southwestbound
1	Access only from A38	Exit only to A38
7	Exit only to M6 (northwestbound)	Access only from M6 (northwestbound)
7A	Exit only to M6 (southeastbound)	No access or exit
8	Access only from M6 (southeastbound)	Exit only to M6 (northwestbound)

M45 Coventry - M1

Junction	Eastbound	Westbound
unnumbered (Dunchurch)	Exit only to A45 & B4429	Access only from A45 & B4429
with M1 (jct 17)	Exit only to M1 (southbound)	Access only from M1 (northbound)

M53 Mersey Tunnel - Chester

Junction	Southeastbound	Northwestbound
11	Access only from M56 (westbound). Exit only to M56 (eastbound)	Access only from M56 (westbound). Exit only to M56 (eastbound)

M54 Telford

Junction	Westbound	Eastbound
with M6 (jct 10A)	Access only from M6 (northbound)	Exit only to M6 (southbound)

M56 North Cheshire

Junction	Westbound	Eastbound
1	Access only from M60 (*westbound*)	Exit only to M60 (*eastbound*) & A34 (*northbound*)
2	Exit only to A560	Access only from A560
3	Access only from A5103	Exit only to A5103 & A560
4	Exit only	Access only
9	Exit to M6 (*southbound*) via A50 interchange	Access from M6 (*northbound*) via A50 interchange
15	Exit only to M53	Access only from M53

M57 Liverpool Outer Ring Road

Junction	Northwestbound	Southeastbound
3	Access only from A526	Exit only to A526
5	Access only from A580 (*westbound*)	Exit only to A580

M58 Liverpool - Wigan

Junction	Eastbound	Westbound
1	Access only	Exit Only

M60 Manchester Orbital

Junction	Clockwise	Anticlockwise
2	Access only from A560	Exit only to A560
3	No access from M56 (*northbound*)	Access only from A34 (*northbound*)
4	Access only from A34 (*northbound*). Exit only to M56	Access only from M56 (*eastbound*). Exit only to A34 (*southbound*)
5	Access and exit only from and to A5103 (*northbound*)	Access and exit only from and to A5103 (*southbound*)
7	No direct access, use slip road to jct 8. Exit only to A56	Access only from A56. No exit - use jct 8
14	Access from A580 (*eastbound*)	Exit only to A580 (*westbound*)
16	Access only from A666	Exit only to A666
20	Exit only to A664	Access only from A664
22	No restriction	Exit only to A62
25	Exit only to A6017	No restriction
26	No restriction	No access or exit
27	Access only from A626	Exit only to A626

M61 Manchester - Preston

Junction	Northwestbound	Southeastbound
3	No access or exit	Exit only to A666
with M6 (jct 30)	Exit only to M6 (*northbound*)	Access only from M6 (*southbound*)

M62 Liverpool - Kingston upon Hull

Junction	Eastbound	Westbound
23	Exit only to A640	Access only from A640

M65 Preston - Colne

Junction	Northeastbound	Southwestbound
1	Access and exit to M6 only	Access and exit to M6 only
9	Exit only to A679	Access only from A679
11	Access only	Exit only

M66 Bury

Junction	Southbound	Northbound
with A56	Access only from A56 (*southbound*)	Exit only to A56 (*northbound*)
1	Access only from A56	Exit only to A56

M67 Hyde Bypass

Junction	Eastbound	Westbound
1	Exit only to A6017	Access only from A6017
2	Access only	Exit only to A57
3	No restriction	Exit only to A627

M69 Coventry - Leicester

Junction	Northbound	Southbound
2	Access only from B4669	Exit only to B4669

M73 East of Glasgow

Junction	Northbound	Southbound
2	No access from or exit to A89. No access from M8 (*eastbound*).	No access from or exit to A89. No exit to M8 (*westbound*)
3	Exit only to A80 (*northeastbound*)	Access only from A80 (*southwestbound*)

M74 and A74(M) Glasgow - Gretna

Junction	Southbound	Northbound
2	Access only from A763	Exit only to A763
3	Exit only	Access only
7	Exit only to A72	Access only from A72
9	Exit only to B7078	No access or exit
10	Access only from B7078	No restrictions
11	Exit only to B7078	Access only from B7078
12	Access only from A70	Exit only to A70
18	Access only from B723	Exit only to B723
21	Exit only to B6357	Access only from B6357
with B7076	Access only	Exit only
Gretna Green	Exit only	Access only
with A75	Access only from A75	Exit only to A75
with A6071	Exit only to A74 (*southbound*)	Access only from A74 (*northbound*)

M77 South of Glasgow

Junction	Southbound	Northbound
with M8 (jct 22)	No access from M8 (*eastbound*)	No exit to M8 (*westbound*)
4	Exit only	Access only
with A77	Exit only to A77 (*southbound*)	Access only from A77 (*northbound*)

M80 Stepps Bypass

Junction	Northeastbound	Southwestbound
1	Access only	No restriction
3	Exit only	Access only

M80 Bonnybridge - Stirling

Junction	Northbound	Southbound
5	Exit only to M876 (*northeastbound*)	Access only from M876 (*southwestbound*)

M90 Forth Road Bridge - Perth

Junction	Northbound	Southbound
2A	Exit only to A92 (*eastbound*)	Access only from A92 (*westbound*)
7	Access only from A91	Exit only to A91
8	Exit only to A91	Access only from A91
10	No access from A912. No exit to A912 (*southbound*)	No access from A912 (*northbound*). No exit to A912

M180 Doncaster - Grimsby

Junction	Eastbound	Westbound
1	Exit only A18	Access only from A18

M606 Bradford Spur

Junction	Northbound	Southbound
2	Exit only	No restriction

M621 Leeds - M1

Junction	Clockwise	Anticlockwise
2A	Access only	Exit only
4	Exit only	No restriction
5	Access only	Exit only
6	Exit only	Access only
with M1 (jct 43)	Exit only to M1 (*southbound*)	Access only from M1 (*northbound*)

M876 Bonnybridge - Kincardine Bridge

Junction	Northeastbound	Southwestbound
with M80 (jct 5)	Access only from M80 (*northbound*)	Exit only to M80 (*southbound*)
2	Exit only to A9	Access only from A9
with M9 (jct 8)	Exit only to M9 (*eastbound*)	Access only from M9 (*westbound*)

A1(M) South Mimms - Baldock

Junction	Northbound	Southbound
2	Exit only to A1001	Access only from A1001
3	No restriction	Exit only to A414
5	Access only	No access or exit

A1(M) East of Leeds

Junction	Northbound	Southbound
44	Access only from M1 (*northbound*)	Exit only to M1 (*southbound*)

A1(M) Scotch Corner - Newcastle upon Tyne

Junction	Northbound	Southbound
57	Exit only to A66(M) (*eastbound*)	Access only from A66(M) (*westbound*)
65	No access Exit only to A194(M) & A1 (*northbound*)	No exit Access only from A194(M) and A1 (*southbound*)

A3(M) Horndean - Havant

Junction	Southbound	Northbound
1	Exit only to A3	Access only from A3
4	Access only	Exit only

A48(M) Cardiff Spur

Junction	Westbound	Eastbound
29	Access only from M4 (*westbound*)	Exit only to M4 (*eastbound*)
29A	Exit only to A48 (*westbound*)	Access only from A48 (*eastbound*)

A66(M) Darlington Spur

Junction	Eastbound	Westbound
with A1(M) (jct 57)	Access only from A1(M) (*northbound*)	Exit only to A1(M) (*southbound*)

A194(M) Newcastle upon Tyne

Junction	Northbound	Southbound
with A1(M) (jct 65)	Access only from A1(M) (*northbound*)	Exit only to A1(M) (*southbound*)

A12 M25 - Ipswich

Junction	Northeastbound	Southwestbound
13	Access only from B1002	No restriction
14	Exit only	Access only
20A	Exit only to B1137	Access only from B1137
20B	Access only B1137	Exit only to B1137
21	No restriction	Access only from B1389
23	Exit only to B1024	Access only from B1024
24	Access only from B1024	Exit only from B1024
27	Exit only to A113	Access only from A113
unnumbered (with A120)	Exit only A120	Access only from A120
29	Access only from A120 and A1232	Exit only to A120 and A1232
unnumbered	Exit only	Access only

A14 M1 - Felixstowe

Junction	Eastbound	Westbound
With M1/M6 (jct19)	Access only from M6 and M1 (*southbound*)	Exit only to M6 and M1 (*northbound*)
4	Access only from B669	Exit only to B669
31	Access only from A428 & M11. Exit only to A1307	Exit only to A428 & M11. Access only from A1307
34	Exit only to B1047	Access only from B1047
unnumbered	No access from or exit to A1303	Access only from A1303
36	Access only from A11	Exit only to A11
38	Exit only to A11	Access only from A11
39	Access only from B1506	Exit only to B1506
49	Exit only to A1308	Access only from A1308
61	Exit only to A154	Access only from A154

A55 Holyhead - Chester

Junction	Eastbound	Westbound
8A	Access only from A5	Exit only to A5
23A	Exit only	Access only
24A	No access or exit	Exit only
33A	No access from or exit to B5126	Exit only to B5126
33B	Access only from A494	Exit only to A494
35A (west)	Exit only A5104	Access only from A5104
35B (east)	Access only from A5104	Exit only to A5104

Index to place names

This index lists places appearing in the main-map section of the atlas in alphabetical order. The reference before each name gives the atlas page number and grid reference of the square in which the place appears. The map shows counties, unitary authorities and administrative areas, together with a list of the abbreviated name forms used in the index.

England

BaNES	**Bath & N E Somerset (18)**
Barns	**Barnsley (19)**
Beds	**Bedfordshire**
Birm	**Birmingham**
Bl w D	**Blackburn with Darwen (20)**
Bmouth	**Bournemouth**
Bolton	**Bolton (21)**
Bpool	**Blackpool**
Brad	**Bradford (22)**
Br & H	**Brighton and Hove (23)**
Br For	**Bracknell Forest (24)**
Bristl	**City of Bristol**
Bucks	**Buckinghamshire**
Bury	**Bury (25)**
C Derb	**City of Derby**
C KuH	**City of Kingston upon Hull**
C Leic	**City of Leicester**
C Nott	**City of Nottingham**
C Pete	**City of Peterborough**
C Plym	**City of Plymouth**
C Port	**City of Portsmouth**
C Sotn	**City of Southampton**
C Stke	**City of Stoke**
Calder	**Calderdale (26)**
Cambs	**Cambridgeshire**
Ches	**Cheshire**
Cnwll	**Cornwall**
Covtry	**Coventry**
Cumb	**Cumbria**
Darltn	**Darlington (27)**
Derbys	**Derbyshire**
Devon	**Devon**
Donc	**Doncaster (28)**
Dorset	**Dorset**
Dudley	**Dudley (29)**
Dur	**Durham**
E R Yk	**East Riding of Yorkshire**
E Susx	**East Sussex**
Essex	**Essex**
Gatesd	**Gateshead (30)**
Gloucs	**Gloucestershire**
Gt Lon	**Greater London**
Halton	**Halton (31)**
Hants	**Hampshire**
Hartpl	**Hartlepool (32)**
Herefs	**Herefordshire**
Herts	**Hertfordshire**
IoS	**Isles of Scilly**
IoW	**Isle of Wight**
Kent	**Kent**
Kirk	**Kirklees (33)**
Knows	**Knowsley (34)**
Lancs	**Lancashire**
Leeds	**Leeds**
Leics	**Leicestershire**
Lincs	**Lincolnshire**
Lpool	**Liverpool**
Luton	**Luton**
M Keyn	**Milton Keynes**

Manch	**Manchester**
Medway	**Medway**
Middsb	**Middlesbrough**
NE Lin	**North East Lincolnshire**
N Linc	**North Lincolnshire**
N Som	**North Somerset (35)**
N Tyne	**North Tyneside (36)**
N u Ty	**Newcastle upon Tyne**
N York	**North Yorkshire**
Nhants	**Northamptonshire**
Norfk	**Norfolk**
Notts	**Nottinghamshire**
Nthumb	**Northumberland**
Oldham	**Oldham (37)**
Oxon	**Oxfordshire**
Poole	**Poole**
R & Cl	**Redcar and Cleveland**
Readg	**Reading**
Rochdl	**Rochdale (38)**
Rothm	**Rotherham (39)**
Rutlnd	**Rutland**
S Glos	**South Gloucestershire (40)**
S on T	**Stockton-on-Tees (41)**
S Tyne	**South Tyneside (42)**
Salfd	**Salford (43)**
Sandw	**Sandwell (44)**
Sefton	**Sefton (45)**
Sheff	**Sheffield**
Shrops	**Shropshire**
Slough	**Slough (46)**
Solhll	**Solihull (47)**
Somset	**Somerset**
St Hel	**St Helens (48)**
Staffs	**Staffordshire**
Sthend	**Southend-on-Sea**
Stockp	**Stockport (49)**
Suffk	**Suffolk**
Sundld	**Sunderland**
Surrey	**Surrey**
Swindn	**Swindon**
Tamesd	**Tameside (50)**
Thurr	**Thurrock (51)**
Torbay	**Torbay**
Traffd	**Trafford (52)**
W & M	**Windsor & Maidenhead (53)**
W Berk	**West Berkshire**
W Susx	**West Sussex**
Wakefd	**Wakefield (54)**
Warrtn	**Warrington (55)**
Warwks	**Warwickshire**
Wigan	**Wigan (56)**
Wilts	**Wiltshire**
Wirral	**Wirral (57)**
Wokham	**Wokingham (58)**
Wolves	**Wolverhampton (59)**
Worcs	**Worcestershire**
Wrekin	**Telford and Wrekin (60)**
Wsall	**Walsall (61)**
York	**York**

Scotland

Abers	**Aberdeenshire**
Ag & B	**Argyll & Bute**
Angus	**Angus**
Border	**Borders**
C Aber	**City of Aberdeen**
C Dund	**City of Dundee**
C Edin	**City of Edinburgh**
C Glas	**City of Glasgow**
Clacks	**Clackmannanshire (1)**
D & G	**Dumfries & Galloway**
E Ayrs	**East Ayrshire**
E Duns	**East Dunbartonshire (2)**
E Loth	**East Lothian**
E Rens	**East Renfrewshire (3)**
Falk	**Falkirk**
Fife	**Fife**
Highld	**Highland**
Inver	**Inverclyde (4)**
Mdloth	**Midlothian (5)**
Moray	**Moray**
N Ayrs	**North Ayrshire**
N Lans	**North Lanarkshire (6)**
Ork	**Orkney Islands**
P & K	**Perth & Kinross**
Rens	**Renfrewshire (7)**
S Ayrs	**South Ayrshire**
Shet	**Shetland Islands**
S Lans	**South Lanarkshire**
Stirlg	**Stirling**
W Duns	**West Dunbartonshire (8)**
W Isls	**Western Isles**
W Loth	**West Lothian**

Wales

Blae G	**Blaenau Gwent (9)**
Brdgnd	**Bridgend (10)**
Caerph	**Caerphilly (11)**
Cardif	**Cardiff**
Carmth	**Carmarthenshire**
Cerdgn	**Ceredigion**
Conwy	**Conwy**
Denbgs	**Denbighshire**
Flints	**Flintshire**
Gwynd	**Gwynedd**
IoA	**Isle of Anglesey**
Mons	**Monmouthshire**
Myr Td	**Merthyr Tydfil (12)**
Neath	**Neath Port Talbot (13)**
Newpt	**Newport (14)**
Pembks	**Pembrokeshire**
Powys	**Powys**
Rhondd	**Rhondda Cynon Taff (15)**
Swans	**Swansea**
Torfn	**Torfaen (16)**
V Glam	**Vale of Glamorgan (17)**
Wrexhm	**Wrexham**

Channel Islands & Isle of Man

Guern	**Guernsey**
Jersey	**Jersey**
IoM	**Isle of Man**

ORKNEY
ISLANDS

SHETLAND
ISLANDS

WESTERN

ISLES

HIGHLAND

MORAY

S C O T L A N D

Aberdeen

ABERDEENSHIRE

ANGUS

PERTH &
KINROSS

Dundee

ARGYLL
& BUTE

STIRLING

FIFE

1

4
8
7
2
FALK
W
LOTH
6
3
5

Edinburgh

E LOTH

Glasgow

5

NORTH
AYRSHIRE

S LANS

BORDERS

E AYRS

S AYRS

DUMFRIES &
GALLOWAY

NORTHUMBERLAND

Newcastle
upon Tyne
36
30
42

Sunderland

IoM

CUMBRIA

DURHAM

32
27
41
R & CL

Middlesbrough

NORTH YORKSHIRE

Blackpool

LANCASHIRE

22

26

York

EAST RIDING
OF YORKSHIRE

Kingston
upon Hull

Leeds

54

20

33

19

N LINCS

N E
LINCS

45
56
34
57
31

21 25 38
48 37
43 50
55 52
49

Manchester

28

39

Sheffield

Liverpool

IoA

CONWY

FLINTS

CHESHIRE

DERBYS

NOTTS

LINCOLNSHIRE

DENBGS

WREXHAM

Stoke-on-
Trent

Derby

Nottingham

GWYNEDD

STAFFS

LEICS

RUTLAND

NORFOLK

60

Leicester

Peterborough

CERDGN

POWYS

SHROPSHIRE

59 61
29 44

Birmingham

Coventry

47

NHANTS

CAMBS

SUFFOLK

WORCS

WARWKS

Milton
Keynes

BEDS

PEMBKS

CARMTH

HEREFS

W A L E S

E N G L A N D

Luton

HERTS

ESSEX

12 9
13
15 11
10
17

MONS
16
14

GLOUCS

OXON

BUCKS

Reading

53 46

GREATER
LONDON

51

Southend-
on-Sea

Swansea

Cardiff

40

Swindon

58 24

MEDWAY

Bristol

35
18

W BERKS

SURREY

KENT

WILTSHIRE

HAMPSHIRE

W SUSX

E SUSX

SOMERSET

23

DEVON

DORSET

Southampton
Portsmouth

CORNWALL

Bournemouth
Poole

IoW

Plymouth

Torbay

CHANNEL
ISLANDS

Guernsey

Jersey

IoS

A

32 B6 **Abbas Combe** Somset
81 H2 **Abberley** Worcs
81 G2 **Abberley Common** Worcs
72 E3 **Abberton** Essex
82 A4 **Abberton** Worcs
191 G3 **Abberwick** Nthumb
70 E5 **Abbess Roding** Essex
29 L8 **Abbey** Devon
78 E1 **Abbeycwmhir** Powys
132 F3 **Abbeydale** Sheff
62 D1 **Abbey Dore** Herefs
131 J8 **Abbey Green** Staffs
30 D7 **Abbey Hill** Somset
213 G6 **Abbey St Bathans** Border
147 L5 **Abbeystead** Lancs
177 G8 **Abbey Town** Cumb
139 J3 **Abbey Village** Lancs
52 A3 **Abbey Wood** Gt Lon
189 G4 **Abbotrule** Border
27 G8 **Abbots Bickington** Devon
115 H6 **Abbots Bromley** Staffs
16 A5 **Abbotsbury** Dorset
131 K2 **Abbot's Chair** Derbys
221 K5 **Abbots Deuglie** P & K
27 G5 **Abbotsham** Devon
8 C1 **Abbotskerswell** Devon
68 E6 **Abbots Langley** Herts
8 B5 **Abbotsleigh** Devon
45 G4 **Abbots Leigh** N Som
86 E4 **Abbotsley** Cambs
82 B4 **Abbots Morton** Worcs
102 E7 **Abbots Ripton** Cambs
82 C5 **Abbot's Salford** Warwks
35 H4 **Abbotstone** Hants
34 D6 **Abbotswood** Hants
35 G4 **Abbots Worthy** Hants
34 D2 **Abbotts Ann** Hants
17 J2 **Abbott Street** Dorset
95 J7 **Abcott** Shrops
96 D6 **Abdon** Shrops
63 K4 **Abenhall** Gloucs
76 E3 **Aberaeron** Cerdgn
60 F7 **Aberaman** Rhondd
93 J2 **Aberangell** Gwynd
76 B7 **Aber-arad** Carmth
251 H6 **Aberarder** Highld
222 B4 **Aberargie** P & K
76 E3 **Aberarth** Cerdgn
57 K7 **Aberavon** Neath
76 C7 **Aber-banc** Cerdgn
61 J7 **Aberbargoed** Caerph
61 K6 **Aberbeeg** Blae G
61 G6 **Abercanaid** Myr Td
43 K3 **Abercarn** Caerph
74 D5 **Abercastle** Pembks
93 H3 **Abercegir** Powys
240 B3 **Aberchalder Lodge** Highld
268 A5 **Aberchirder** Abers
61 H3 **Aber Clydach** Powys
59 M6 **Abercraf** Powys
42 C2 **Abercregan** Neath
60 F7 **Abercwmboi** Rhondd
75 M4 **Abercych** Pembks
43 G3 **Abercynon** Rhondd
221 K3 **Aberdalgie** P & K
60 F6 **Aberdare** Rhondd
108 C6 **Aberdaron** Gwynd
245 L2 **Aberdeen** C Aber
109 G1 **Aberdesach** Gwynd
211 G2 **Aberdour** Fife
57 L5 **Aberdulais** Neath
92 D4 **Aberdyfi** Gwynd
78 F6 **Aberedw** Powys
74 C6 **Abereiddy** Pembks
109 G4 **Abererch** Gwynd
61 G7 **Aberfan** Myr Td
232 C5 **Aberfeldy** P & K
124 F6 **Aberffraw** IoA
92 E7 **Aberffrwd** Cerdgn
150 F8 **Aberford** Leeds
219 H7 **Aberfoyle** Stirlg
42 D5 **Abergarw** Brdgnd
60 B6 **Abergarwed** Neath
62 C4 **Abergavenny** Mons
127 J4 **Abergele** Conwy
76 F7 **Aber-giar** Carmth
59 G2 **Abergorlech** Carmth
78 A4 **Abergwesyn** Powys
58 D5 **Abergwili** Carmth
93 G3 **Abergwydol** Powys
42 D3 **Abergwynfi** Neath
126 C5 **Abergwyngregyn** Gwynd
92 E2 **Abergynolwyn** Gwynd
94 C5 **Aberhafesp** Powys
93 H4 **Aberhosan** Powys

42 D5 **Aberkenfig** Brdgnd
212 A3 **Aberlady** E Loth
234 E4 **Aberlemno** Angus
93 G2 **Aberllefenni** Gwynd
79 H7 **Aberllynfi** Powys
254 E3 **Aberlour** Moray
92 E8 **Aber-Magwr** Cerdgn
77 G4 **Aber-meurig** Cerdgn
129 G8 **Abermorddu** Flints
94 E4 **Abermule** Powys
58 C2 **Abernant** Carmth
60 F6 **Aber-nant** Rhondd
222 C4 **Abernethy** P & K
222 D1 **Abernyte** P & K
76 A5 **Aberporth** Cerdgn
108 E6 **Abersoch** Gwynd
62 B6 **Abersychan** Torfn
42 F6 **Aberthin** V Glam
61 K6 **Abertillery** Blae G
43 H4 **Abertridwr** Caerph
111 K7 **Abertridwr** Powys
61 H6 **Abertysswg** Caerph
221 H4 **Aberuthven** P & K
60 F1 **Aberyscir** Powys
92 C7 **Aberystwyth** Cerdgn
66 C7 **Abingdon** Oxon
37 H2 **Abinger** Surrey
37 G2 **Abinger Hammer** Surrey
84 F3 **Abington** Nhants
186 D2 **Abington** S Lans
86 F6 **Abington Pigotts** Cambs
117 J7 **Ab Kettleby** Leics
82 B5 **Ab Lench** Worcs
65 G5 **Ablington** Gloucs
33 K2 **Ablington** Wilts
132 D4 **Abney** Derbys
115 G2 **Above Church** Staffs
244 C4 **Aboyne** Abers
139 J7 **Abram** Wigan
250 F4 **Abriachan** Highld
70 C7 **Abridge** Essex
209 L4 **Abronhill** N Lans
45 L4 **Abson** S Glos
84 C6 **Abthorpe** Nhants
137 H4 **Aby** Lincs
151 J6 **Acaster Malbis** York
151 J7 **Acaster Selby** N York
27 M4 **Accott** Devon
139 M2 **Accrington** Lancs
224 F4 **Acha** Ag & B
206 B3 **Achahoish** Ag & B
233 H6 **Achalader** P & K
228 E8 **Achaleven** Ag & B
282 f3 **Acha Mor** W Isls
261 M7 **Achanalt** Highld
263 H5 **Achandunie** Highld
272 E7 **Achany** Highld
237 K7 **Acharacle** Highld
227 K2 **Acharn** Highld
231 L6 **Acharn** P & K
279 L7 **Achavanich** Highld
270 D7 **Achduart** Highld
276 D8 **Achfary** Highld
246 C7 **A'Chill** Highld
270 D6 **Achiltibuie** Highld
192 F5 **Achinhoan** Ag & B
248 F3 **Achintee** Highld
248 D4 **Achintraid** Highld
270 E3 **Achmelvich** Highld
248 D5 **Achmore** Highld
282 f3 **Achmore** W Isls
270 D2 **Achnacarnin** Highld
239 K6 **Achnacarry** Highld
247 J6 **Achnacloich** Highld
250 D8 **Achnaconeran** Highld
228 C7 **Achnacroish** Ag & B
226 F2 **Achnadrish House** Ag & B
232 C8 **Achnafauld** P & K
263 J6 **Achnagarron** Highld
236 F6 **Achnaha** Highld
270 D5 **Achnahaird** Highld
272 E5 **Achnairn** Highld
228 C3 **Achnalea** Highld
206 B2 **Achnamara** Ag & B
261 K8 **Achnasheen** Highld
249 G2 **Achnashellach Lodge** Highld
254 F5 **Achnastank** Moray
236 E7 **Achosnich** Highld
227 K3 **Achranich** Highld
279 H3 **Achreamie** Highld
229 J2 **Achriabhach** Highld
276 D5 **Achriesgill** Highld
277 M4 **Achtoty** Highld
102 A6 **Achurch** Nhants
263 J1 **Achvaich** Highld
280 E5 **Ackergill** Highld
170 C7 **Acklam** Middsb

152 B3 **Acklam** N York
97 H4 **Ackleton** Shrops
191 J6 **Acklington** Nthumb
142 C3 **Ackton** Wakefd
142 C4 **Ackworth Moor Top** Wakefd
107 H1 **Acle** Norfk
98 E6 **Acock's Green** Birm
41 J2 **Acol** Kent
179 L5 **Acomb** Nthumb
151 J5 **Acomb** York
30 B8 **Acombe** Somset
80 C8 **Aconbury** Herefs
140 B3 **Acre** Lancs
112 D3 **Acrefair** Wrexhm
113 K1 **Acton** Ches
17 J6 **Acton** Dorset
51 G3 **Acton** Gt Lon
95 H6 **Acton** Shrops
114 C3 **Acton** Staffs
89 H6 **Acton** Suffk
81 J2 **Acton** Worcs
80 F5 **Acton Beauchamp** Herefs
130 B4 **Acton Bridge** Ches
96 C3 **Acton Burnell** Shrops
81 G5 **Acton Green** Herefs
112 E1 **Acton Park** Wrexhm
96 C3 **Acton Pigott** Shrops
96 E4 **Acton Round** Shrops
95 L5 **Acton Scott** Shrops
114 F7 **Acton Trussell** Staffs
46 A3 **Acton Turville** S Glos
114 B6 **Adbaston** Staffs
31 K6 **Adber** Dorset
117 G4 **Adbolton** Notts
83 L8 **Adderbury** Oxon
113 L3 **Adderley** Shrops
203 J7 **Adderstone** Nthumb
210 C6 **Addiewell** W Loth
149 K6 **Addingham** Brad
67 H2 **Addington** Bucks
51 K6 **Addington** Gt Lon
52 E7 **Addington** Kent
51 J5 **Addiscombe** Gt Lon
50 D6 **Addlestone** Surrey
50 D6 **Addlestonemoor** Surrey
137 K6 **Addlethorpe** Lincs
113 M7 **Adeney** Wrekin
68 D5 **Adeyfield** Herts
94 C3 **Adfa** Powys
79 M1 **Adforton** Herefs
41 H4 **Adisham** Kent
65 K2 **Adlestrop** Gloucs
143 L3 **Adlingfleet** E R Yk
131 H4 **Adlington** Ches
139 J5 **Adlington** Lancs
115 G7 **Admaston** Staffs
96 E1 **Admaston** Wrekin
82 E6 **Admington** Warwks
76 B7 **Adpar** Cerdgn
30 D7 **Adsborough** Somset
30 B3 **Adscombe** Somset
67 H1 **Adstock** Bucks
84 B5 **Adstone** Nhants
131 H2 **Adswood** Stockp
37 G6 **Adversane** W Susx
254 C5 **Advie** Highld
141 K2 **Adwalton** Leeds
67 G7 **Adwell** Oxon
142 E6 **Adwick Le Street** Donc
142 D7 **Adwick upon Dearne** Donc
176 C1 **Ae** D & G
176 D2 **Ae Bridgend** D & G
139 M5 **Affetside** Bury
255 L4 **Affleck** Abers
16 F4 **Affpuddle** Dorset
249 K7 **Affric Lodge** Highld
128 D5 **Afon-wen** Flints
8 C2 **Afton** Devon
18 E6 **Afton** IoW
159 K5 **Agglethorpe** N York
129 J2 **Aigburth** Lpool
153 G6 **Aike** E R Yk
166 B1 **Aiketgate** Cumb
165 H1 **Aikhead** Cumb
177 J8 **Aikton** Cumb
137 H4 **Ailby** Lincs
79 L5 **Ailey** Herefs
102 C4 **Ailsworth** C Pete
160 E6 **Ainderby Quernhow** N York
160 E4 **Ainderby Steeple** N York
73 G3 **Aingers Green** Essex
138 C5 **Ainsdale** Sefton
138 C5 **Ainsdale-on-Sea** Sefton
166 C2 **Ainstable** Cumb
139 M5 **Ainsworth** Bury
162 C1 **Ainthorpe** N York
138 D8 **Aintree** Sefton

210 F6 **Ainville** W Loth
216 B7 **Aird** Ag & B
172 D3 **Aird** D & G
282 h3 **Aird** W Isls
282 e5 **Aird a Mhulaidh** W Isls
282 e5 **Aird Asaig** W Isls
248 A4 **Aird Dhubh** Highld
216 F1 **Airdeny** Ag & B
227 G6 **Aird of Kinloch** Ag & B
247 J8 **Aird of Sleat** Highld
209 K6 **Airdrie** N Lans
209 K5 **Airdriehill** N Lans
216 F1 **Airds Bay** Ag & B
175 G1 **Airds of Kells** D & G
282 d3 **Aird Uig** W Isls
282 f4 **Airidh a bhruaich** W Isls
175 J3 **Airieland** D & G
233 M5 **Airlie** Angus
143 J3 **Airmyn** E R Yk
233 G8 **Airntully** P & K
247 M7 **Airor** Highld
210 B2 **Airth** Falk
148 F4 **Airton** N York
118 D4 **Aisby** Lincs
135 H1 **Aisby** Lincs
158 D3 **Aisgill** Cumb
7 K3 **Aish** Devon
8 C3 **Aish** Devon
30 B4 **Aisholt** Somset
160 C5 **Aiskew** N York
162 D5 **Aislaby** N York
162 F1 **Aislaby** N York
169 L8 **Aislaby** S on T
135 J4 **Aisthorpe** Lincs
281 d5 **Aith** Shet
202 E7 **Akeld** Nthumb
84 D7 **Akeley** Bucks
90 D5 **Akenham** Suffk
12 A8 **Albaston** Cnwll
112 E8 **Alberbury** Shrops
22 C4 **Albourne** W Susx
22 C4 **Albourne Green** W Susx
97 H3 **Albrighton** Shrops
113 H7 **Albrighton** Shrops
106 F6 **Alburgh** Norfk
70 B2 **Albury** Herts
67 G6 **Albury** Oxon
37 G2 **Albury** Surrey
70 B2 **Albury End** Herts
37 G2 **Albury Heath** Surrey
122 D5 **Alby Hill** Norfk
263 G8 **Alcaig** Highld
95 L6 **Alcaston** Shrops
82 C4 **Alcester** Warwks
98 D7 **Alcester Lane End** Birm
23 H6 **Alciston** E Susx
46 A5 **Alcombe** Wilts
102 D8 **Alconbury** Cambs
102 D7 **Alconbury Weston** Cambs
150 F3 **Aldborough** N York
122 D5 **Aldborough** Norfk
47 K4 **Aldbourne** Wilts
153 L8 **Aldbrough** E R Yk
169 G8 **Aldbrough St John** N York
68 B4 **Aldbury** Herts
147 J4 **Aldcliffe** Lancs
232 D3 **Aldclune** P & K
91 K4 **Aldeburgh** Suffk
107 J5 **Aldeby** Norfk
68 F7 **Aldenham** Herts
33 L5 **Alderbury** Wilts
116 D2 **Aldercar** Derbys
122 C7 **Alderford** Norfk
33 K8 **Alderholt** Dorset
45 M1 **Alderley** Gloucs
131 G4 **Alderley Edge** Ches
99 K6 **Aldermans Green** Covtry
48 E6 **Aldermaston** W Berk
82 F5 **Alderminster** Warwks
115 L6 **Alder Moor** Staffs
129 K8 **Aldersey Green** Ches
36 C1 **Aldershot** Hants
82 B8 **Alderton** Gloucs
84 E6 **Alderton** Nhants
113 H6 **Alderton** Shrops
91 H7 **Alderton** Suffk
46 B2 **Alderton** Wilts
116 A1 **Alderwasley** Derbys
150 C2 **Aldfield** N York
129 K7 **Aldford** Ches
101 L3 **Aldgate** Rutlnd
72 D2 **Aldham** Essex
90 B6 **Aldham** Suffk
20 F5 **Aldingbourne** W Susx
146 E2 **Aldingham** Cumb
40 E8 **Aldington** Kent
82 C6 **Aldington** Worcs
40 E7 **Aldington Corner** Kent

255 G6 **Aldivalloch** Moray
208 B1 **Aldochlay** Ag & B
95 K7 **Aldon** Shrops
164 F1 **Aldoth** Cumb
103 J8 **Aldreth** Cambs
98 D3 **Aldridge** Wsall
91 K3 **Aldringham** Suffk
152 B3 **Aldro** N York
65 H5 **Aldsworth** Gloucs
20 C5 **Aldsworth** W Susx
255 G6 **Aldunie** Moray
132 E8 **Aldwark** Derbys
151 H4 **Aldwark** N York
20 E7 **Aldwick** W Susx
101 M7 **Aldwincle** Nhants
48 E3 **Aldworth** W Berk
208 C3 **Alexandria** W Duns
30 B3 **Aley** Somset
26 E8 **Alfardisworthy** Devon
14 D3 **Alfington** Devon
36 F4 **Alfold** Surrey
36 F4 **Alfold Bars** W Susx
36 F4 **Alfold Crossways** Surrey
255 M8 **Alford** Abers
137 H4 **Alford** Lincs
31 K4 **Alford** Somset
133 H8 **Alfreton** Derbys
81 H4 **Alfrick** Worcs
81 G5 **Alfrick Pound** Worcs
23 H6 **Alfriston** E Susx
119 J4 **Algarkirk** Lincs
31 K4 **Alhampton** Somset
143 M3 **Alkborough** N Linc
63 M6 **Alkerton** Gloucs
83 J6 **Alkerton** Oxon
41 H6 **Alkham** Kent
113 H4 **Alkington** Shrops
115 K4 **Alkmonton** Derbys
8 B4 **Allaleigh** Devon
242 F5 **Allanaquoich** Abers
209 M7 **Allanbank** N Lans
202 D2 **Allanton** Border
209 M7 **Allanton** N Lans
209 K8 **Allanton** S Lans
63 J6 **Allaston** Gloucs
34 F6 **Allbrook** Hants
46 F6 **All Cannings** Wilts
179 J7 **Allendale** Nthumb
98 F4 **Allen End** Warwks
167 K2 **Allenheads** Nthumb
168 D1 **Allensford** Dur
70 C4 **Allen's Green** Herts
80 B8 **Allensmore** Herefs
116 B5 **Allenton** C Derb
28 D5 **Aller** Devon
30 F5 **Aller** Somset
164 E3 **Allerby** Cumb
14 B3 **Allercombe** Devon
28 F2 **Allerford** Somset
162 F6 **Allerston** N York
152 B6 **Allerthorpe** E R Yk
141 H1 **Allerton** Brad
263 K6 **Allerton** Highld
129 J2 **Allerton** Lpool
142 C2 **Allerton Bywater** Leeds
150 F4 **Allerton Mauleverer** N York
99 J7 **Allesley** Covtry
116 B4 **Allestree** C Derb
4 C5 **Allet Common** Cnwll
101 H3 **Allexton** Leics
131 J6 **Allgreave** Ches
53 H3 **Allhallows** Medway
53 H3 **Allhallows-on-Sea** Medway
260 D8 **Alligin Shuas** Highld
114 D7 **Allimore Green** Staffs
15 K4 **Allington** Dorset
53 G7 **Allington** Kent
117 M3 **Allington** Lincs
33 L3 **Allington** Wilts
46 C4 **Allington** Wilts
46 F6 **Allington** Wilts
156 E7 **Allithwaite** Cumb
220 F8 **Alloa** Clacks
164 E2 **Allonby** Cumb
130 E5 **Allostock** Ches
196 C7 **Alloway** S Ayrs
30 D8 **Allowenshay** Somset
107 G7 **All Saints South Elmham** Suffk
97 G4 **Allscott** Shrops
96 E1 **Allscott** Wrekin
95 L4 **All Stretton** Shrops
129 G6 **Alltami** Flints
229 K5 **Alltchaorunn** Highld
78 F6 **Alltmawr** Powys
58 E3 **Alltwalis** Carmth
57 K4 **Alltwen** Neath
76 F6 **Alltyblaca** Cerdgn

31 L8 **Allweston** Dorset
90 B1 **Allwood Green** Suffk
79 L5 **Almeley** Herefs
79 L5 **Almeley Wooton** Herefs
17 H3 **Almer** Dorset
142 F6 **Almholme** Donc
113 M4 **Almington** Staffs
20 D7 **Almodington** W Susx
221 J2 **Almondbank** P & K
141 J5 **Almondbury** Kirk
45 J2 **Almondsbury** S Glos
151 G3 **Alne** N York
90 E7 **Alnesbourn Priory** Suffk
263 H6 **Alness** Highld
190 E4 **Alnham** Nthumb
191 J4 **Alnmouth** Nthumb
191 H3 **Alnwick** Nthumb
50 F2 **Alperton** Gt Lon
89 H8 **Alphamstone** Essex
89 H5 **Alpheton** Suffk
13 L4 **Alphington** Devon
106 F3 **Alpington** Norfk
132 D6 **Alport** Derbys
130 B7 **Alpraham** Ches
72 F3 **Alresford** Essex
115 K8 **Alrewas** Staffs
130 F8 **Alsager** Ches
114 C2 **Alsagers Bank** Staffs
132 C8 **Alsop en le Dale** Derbys
167 G2 **Alston** Cumb
15 G2 **Alston** Devon
82 A8 **Alstone** Gloucs
30 D2 **Alstone** Somset
132 C8 **Alstonefield** Staffs
114 D7 **Alstone Green** Staffs
44 E8 **Alston Sutton** Somset
28 C6 **Alswear** Devon
140 E7 **Alt** Oldham
270 C5 **Altandhu** Highld
11 J6 **Altarnun** Cnwll
272 D8 **Altass** Highld
227 K5 **Altcreich** Ag & B
207 G4 **Altgaltraig** Ag & B
140 A1 **Altham** Lancs
72 D7 **Althorne** Essex
143 L6 **Althorpe** N Linc
279 H7 **Altnabreac Station** Highld
216 C2 **Altnacraig** Ag & B
272 E1 **Altnaharra** Highld
142 B3 **Altofts** Wakefd
133 G6 **Alton** Derbys
35 L3 **Alton** Hants
115 H3 **Alton** Staffs
33 K2 **Alton** Wilts
47 G6 **Alton Barnes** Wilts
16 D2 **Alton Pancras** Dorset
47 G6 **Alton Priors** Wilts
130 E2 **Altrincham** Traffd
219 G6 **Altskeith Hotel** Stirlg
220 F7 **Alva** Clacks
129 L5 **Alvanley** Ches
116 C5 **Alvaston** C Derb
82 B1 **Alvechurch** Worcs
99 H3 **Alvecote** Warwks
33 G6 **Alvediston** Wilts
97 G6 **Alveley** Shrops
27 J6 **Alverdiscott** Devon
19 K4 **Alverstoke** Hants
19 K6 **Alverstone** IoW
141 M3 **Alverthorpe** Wakefd
117 L3 **Alverton** Notts
266 C4 **Alves** Moray
65 K6 **Alvescot** Oxon
45 J1 **Alveston** S Glos
82 F4 **Alveston** Warwks
137 G2 **Alvingham** Lincs
63 J7 **Alvington** Gloucs
102 C4 **Alwalton** C Pete
190 C5 **Alwinton** Nthumb
150 C7 **Alwoodley** Leeds
150 D7 **Alwoodley Gates** Leeds
233 K5 **Alyth** P & K
116 B1 **Ambergate** Derbys
119 H2 **Amber Hill** Lincs
64 B6 **Amberley** Gloucs
21 H4 **Amberley** W Susx
133 G8 **Amber Row** Derbys
23 K5 **Amberstone** E Susx
191 K5 **Amble** Nthumb
97 K6 **Amblecote** Dudley
141 H2 **Ambler Thorn** Brad
156 E2 **Ambleside** Cumb
75 G7 **Ambleston** Pembks
66 F3 **Ambrosden** Oxon
143 L5 **Amcotts** N Linc
103 J7 **America** Cambs
68 B7 **Amersham** Bucks
68 B7 **Amersham Common** Bucks

68 B7 **Amersham Old Town** Bucks
68 B7 **Amersham on the Hill** Bucks
114 F6 **Amerton** Staffs
33 K3 **Amesbury** Wilts
282 d5 **Amhuinnsuidhe** W Isls
99 G3 **Amington** Staffs
176 D2 **Amisfield Town** D & G
125 H1 **Amlwch** IoA
59 H6 **Ammanford** Carmth
162 C7 **Amotherby** N York
34 E6 **Ampfield** Hants
161 J7 **Ampleforth** N York
64 F6 **Ampney Crucis** Gloucs
65 G6 **Ampney St Mary** Gloucs
65 G6 **Ampney St Peter** Gloucs
34 C2 **Amport** Hants
85 K7 **Ampthill** Beds
89 H1 **Ampton** Suffk
55 K5 **Amroth** Pembks
232 D8 **Amulree** P & K
68 F4 **Amwell** Herts
228 C3 **Anaheilt** Highld
118 C3 **Ancaster** Lincs
94 E6 **Anchor** Shrops
202 E6 **Ancroft** Nthumb
189 H1 **Ancrum** Border
21 G6 **Ancton** W Susx
137 K4 **Anderby** Lincs
30 E4 **Andersea** Somset
30 C4 **Andersfield** Somset
17 G3 **Anderson** Dorset
130 C4 **Anderton** Ches
6 E4 **Anderton** Cnwll
34 D2 **Andover** Hants
64 F3 **Andoversford** Gloucs
154 f2 **Andreas** IoM
108 B6 **Anelog** Gwynd
51 J5 **Anerley** Gt Lon
129 J1 **Anfield** Lpool
2 F3 **Angarrack** Cnwll
3 K4 **Angarrick** Cnwll
96 D8 **Angelbank** Shrops
30 B7 **Angersleigh** Somset
177 H7 **Angerton** Cumb
54 D6 **Angle** Pembks
21 H6 **Angmering** W Susx
151 H6 **Angram** N York
158 F3 **Angram** N York
3 H7 **Angrouse** Cnwll
179 L5 **Anick** Nthumb
264 C5 **Ankerville** Highld
117 K7 **Ankle Hill** Leics
144 C2 **Anlaby** E R Yk
121 G5 **Anmer** Norfk
19 L1 **Anmore** Hants
177 G5 **Annan** D & G
155 H5 **Annaside** Cumb
248 E1 **Annat** Highld
209 J5 **Annathill** N Lans
34 D2 **Anna Valley** Hants
196 E6 **Annbank** S Ayrs
116 E1 **Annesley** Notts
116 E1 **Annesley Woodhouse** Notts
180 E8 **Annfield Plain** Dur
208 F5 **Anniesland** C Glas
181 G4 **Annitsford** N Tyne
95 L2 **Annscroft** Shrops
138 D2 **Ansdell** Lancs
31 L4 **Ansford** Somset
99 J5 **Ansley** Warwks
115 L6 **Anslow** Staffs
115 K6 **Anslow Gate** Staffs
115 K6 **Anslow Lees** Staffs
36 D4 **Ansteadbrook** Surrey
35 L3 **Anstey** Hants
87 H8 **Anstey** Herts
100 D2 **Anstey** Leics
223 K6 **Anstruther** Fife
37 L6 **Ansty** W Susx
99 L6 **Ansty** Warwks
33 L6 **Ansty** Wilts
16 E2 **Ansty Cross** Dorset
19 L1 **Anthill Common** Hants
50 C6 **Anthonys** Surrey
177 G7 **Anthorn** Cumb
122 E5 **Antingham** Norfk
282 d6 **An t-Ob** W Isls
119 J2 **Anton's Gowt** Lincs
6 D4 **Antony** Cnwll
130 C3 **Antrobus** Ches
3 G5 **Antron** Cnwll
11 M2 **Anvil Corner** Devon
40 E5 **Anvil Green** Kent
118 F2 **Anwick** Lincs
174 F4 **Anwoth** D & G

51 L7 **Aperfield** Gt Lon
82 A1 **Apes Dale** Worcs
102 A4 **Apethorpe** Nhants
114 D7 **Apeton** Staffs
136 B5 **Apley** Lincs
133 H4 **Apperknowle** Derbys
64 B2 **Apperley** Gloucs
150 B8 **Apperley Bridge** Brad
180 C7 **Apperley Dene** Nthumb
158 A1 **Appersett** N York
228 E6 **Appin** Ag & B
144 B5 **Appleby** N Linc
166 F6 **Appleby-in-Westmorland** Cumb
99 J2 **Appleby Magna** Leics
99 J2 **Appleby Parva** Leics
69 J6 **Appleby Street** Herts
248 A3 **Applecross** Highld
27 H5 **Appledore** Devon
29 K7 **Appledore** Devon
25 H2 **Appledore** Kent
25 H1 **Appledore Heath** Kent
66 D8 **Appleford** Oxon
176 F2 **Applegarth Town** D & G
142 A5 **Applehaigh** Wakefd
34 C1 **Appleshaw** Hants
165 J5 **Applethwaite** Cumb
129 M2 **Appleton** Halton
66 C6 **Appleton** Oxon
130 B3 **Appleton** Warrtn
162 C5 **Appleton-le-Moors** N York
162 C7 **Appleton-le-Street** N York
151 J7 **Appleton Roebuck** N York
130 C3 **Appleton Thorn** Warrtn
160 F2 **Appleton Wiske** N York
188 F3 **Appletreehall** Border
149 J4 **Appletreewick** N York
29 K6 **Appley** Somset
139 G2 **Appley Bridge** Lancs
19 J7 **Apse Heath** IoW
86 C8 **Apsley End** Beds
20 D6 **Apuldram** W Susx
264 C5 **Arabella** Highld
234 F7 **Arbirlot** Angus
264 D3 **Arboll** Highld
49 H5 **Arborfield** Wokham
49 J5 **Arborfield Cross** Wokham
133 G3 **Arbourthorne** Sheff
235 G7 **Arbroath** Angus
245 H8 **Arbuthnott** Abers
39 L6 **Arcadia** Kent
56 E4 **Archddu** Carmth
169 H7 **Archdeacon Newton** Darltn
208 C3 **Archencarroch** W Duns
254 E3 **Archiestown** Moray
9 f2 **Archirondel** Jersey
130 F7 **Arclid Green** Ches
257 J4 **Ardallie** Abers
217 H2 **Ardanaiseig Hotel** Ag & B
248 D4 **Ardaneaskan** Highld
248 D4 **Ardarroch** Highld
204 F7 **Ardbeg** Ag & B
207 H5 **Ardbeg** Ag & B
207 K2 **Ardbeg** Ag & B
261 K2 **Ardcharnich** Highld
214 D1 **Ardchiavaig** Ag & B
216 F5 **Ardchonnel** Ag & B
219 K4 **Ardchullarie More** Stirlg
218 C8 **Arddarroch** Ag & B
112 C8 **Arddleen** Powys
239 J5 **Ardechive** Highld
196 B3 **Ardeer** N Ayrs
69 J2 **Ardeley** Herts
248 D6 **Ardelve** Highld
208 B2 **Arden** Ag & B
82 D4 **Ardens Grafton** Warwks
216 C2 **Ardentallen** Ag & B
207 K2 **Ardentinny** Ag & B
207 G4 **Ardentraive** Ag & B
231 J8 **Ardeonaig** Stirlg
252 E1 **Ardersier** Highld
261 H2 **Ardessie** Highld
216 C6 **Ardfern** Ag & B
263 G2 **Ardgay** Highld
229 G3 **Ardgour** Highld
207 L4 **Ardgowan** Inver
207 K4 **Ardhallow** Ag & B
282 e5 **Ardhasig** W Isls
260 C8 **Ardheslaig** Highld
261 K2 **Ardindrean** Highld
38 A7 **Ardingly** W Susx
48 B1 **Ardington** Oxon
48 B1 **Ardington Wick** Oxon
206 F6 **Ardlamont** Ag & B
72 F1 **Ardleigh** Essex
72 F1 **Ardleigh Heath** Essex
233 L7 **Ardler** P & K

66 D2 **Ardley** Oxon
70 D4 **Ardley End** Essex
218 D4 **Ardlui** Ag & B
215 J6 **Ardlussa** Ag & B
229 H7 **Ardmaddy** Ag & B
270 F8 **Ardmair** Highld
207 H5 **Ardmaleish** Ag & B
205 L6 **Ardminish** Ag & B
237 K6 **Ardmolich** Highld
208 A3 **Ardmore** Ag & B
263 J3 **Ardmore** Highld
207 K3 **Ardnadam** Ag & B
250 F2 **Ardnagrask** Highld
248 E4 **Ardnarff** Highld
228 B3 **Ardnastang** Highld
217 J5 **Ardno** Ag & B
206 B7 **Ardpatrick** Ag & B
206 D2 **Ardrishaig** Ag & B
263 H5 **Ardross** Highld
195 L3 **Ardrossan** N Ayrs
142 B6 **Ardsley** Barns
141 M3 **Ardsley East** Leeds
237 H8 **Ardslignish** Highld
205 G5 **Ardtalla** Ag & B
237 J6 **Ardtoe** Highld
216 B5 **Arduaine** Ag & B
263 G7 **Ardullie** Highld
247 K7 **Ardvasar** Highld
219 K3 **Ardvorlich** P & K
282 e5 **Ardvourlie** W Isls
172 D5 **Ardwell** D & G
140 C8 **Ardwick** Manch
81 H1 **Areley Kings** Worcs
237 J7 **Arevegaig** Highld
36 B3 **Arford** Hants
61 J7 **Argoed** Caerph
112 E7 **Argoed** Shrops
78 D3 **Argoed Mill** Powys
23 J2 **Argos Hill** E Susx
282 f4 **Aribruach** W Isls
226 C7 **Aridhglas** Ag & B
224 F4 **Arileod** Ag & B
225 G4 **Arinagour** Ag & B
216 D2 **Ariogan** Ag & B
237 J3 **Arisaig** Highld
237 K4 **Arisaig House** Highld
150 E4 **Arkendale** N York
87 K8 **Arkesden** Essex
147 L2 **Arkholme** Lancs
164 F3 **Arkleby** Cumb
188 C7 **Arkleton** D & G
159 H2 **Arkle Town** N York
69 G7 **Arkley** Gt Lon
142 F6 **Arksey** Donc
133 H5 **Arkwright Town** Derbys
64 D2 **Arle** Gloucs
164 D7 **Arlecdon** Cumb
83 J5 **Arlescote** Warwks
86 D7 **Arlesey** Beds
96 F1 **Arleston** Wrekin
130 C3 **Arley** Ches
99 H5 **Arley** Warwks
63 L5 **Arlingham** Gloucs
27 L3 **Arlington** Devon
23 J5 **Arlington** E Susx
65 G5 **Arlington** Gloucs
27 L3 **Arlington Beccott** Devon
247 K7 **Armadale** Highld
278 D3 **Armadale** Highld
210 B5 **Armadale** W Loth
164 F5 **Armaside** Cumb
166 C2 **Armathwaite** Cumb
106 E3 **Arminghall** Norfk
115 H8 **Armitage** Staffs
141 H5 **Armitage Bridge** Kirk
141 L1 **Armley** Leeds
82 F6 **Armscote** Warwks
114 E2 **Armshead** Staffs
102 B6 **Armston** Nhants
143 G6 **Armthorpe** Donc
225 G3 **Arnabost** Ag & B
156 A5 **Arnaby** Cumb
149 G2 **Arncliffe** N York
149 G2 **Arncliffe Cote** N York
223 J6 **Arncroach** Fife
266 F6 **Arndilly House** Moray
17 J5 **Arne** Dorset
100 D5 **Arnesby** Leics
221 L5 **Arngask** P & K
238 D2 **Arnisdale** Highld
259 K7 **Arnish** Highld
211 K6 **Arniston** Mdloth
282 f2 **Arnol** W Isls
153 H7 **Arnold** E R Yk
117 G2 **Arnold** Notts
219 K8 **Arnprior** Stirlg
157 G7 **Arnside** Cumb
227 G3 **Aros** Ag & B

113 G4 **Arowry** Wrexhm
156 D6 **Arrad Foot** Cumb
153 G7 **Arram** E R Yk
160 B4 **Arrathorne** N York
19 J6 **Arreton** IoW
260 B8 **Arrina** Highld
87 G5 **Arrington** Cambs
218 D6 **Arrochar** Ag & B
82 C4 **Arrow** Warwks
98 C8 **Arrowfield Top** Worcs
95 K2 **Arscott** Shrops
251 H2 **Artafallie** Highld
150 C6 **Arthington** Leeds
101 G7 **Arthingworth** Nhants
110 C8 **Arthog** Gwynd
257 H4 **Arthrath** Abers
150 E8 **Arthursdale** Leeds
257 J5 **Artrochie** Abers
21 G5 **Arundel** W Susx
164 E6 **Asby** Cumb
207 J6 **Ascog** Ag & B
50 A5 **Ascot** W & M
83 H8 **Ascott** Warwks
65 L3 **Ascott Earl** Oxon
65 L3 **Ascott-under-Wychwood** Oxon
160 F7 **Asenby** N York
117 J7 **Asfordby** Leics
117 J7 **Asfordby Hill** Leics
118 F3 **Asgarby** Lincs
136 F6 **Asgarby** Lincs
8 C5 **Ash** Devon
12 C1 **Ash** Devon
32 E8 **Ash** Dorset
41 J4 **Ash** Kent
52 D6 **Ash** Kent
30 D6 **Ash** Somset
31 G6 **Ash** Somset
36 D1 **Ash** Surrey
48 E4 **Ashampstead** W Berk
48 E3 **Ashampstead Green** W Berk
90 E4 **Ashbocking** Suffk
115 K2 **Ashbourne** Derbys
29 J6 **Ashbrittle** Somset
24 C4 **Ashburnham Place** E Susx
13 H8 **Ashburton** Devon
12 C3 **Ashbury** Devon
47 K2 **Ashbury** Oxon
143 M6 **Ashby** N Linc
137 H6 **Ashby by Partney** Lincs
145 H7 **Ashby cum Fenby** NE Lin
135 L8 **Ashby de la Launde** Lincs
116 B8 **Ashby-de-la-Zouch** Leics
100 F1 **Ashby Folville** Leics
100 C5 **Ashby Magna** Leics
100 C5 **Ashby Parva** Leics
136 F5 **Ashby Puerorum** Lincs
84 B2 **Ashby St Ledgers** Nhants
107 G3 **Ashby St Mary** Norfk
81 L8 **Ashchurch** Gloucs
13 L6 **Ashcombe** Devon
44 C6 **Ashcombe** N Som
31 G3 **Ashcott** Somset
88 B6 **Ashdon** Essex
35 H1 **Ashe** Hants
72 E6 **Asheldham** Essex
88 E6 **Ashen** Essex
67 H4 **Ashendon** Bucks
68 B6 **Asheridge** Bucks
34 E7 **Ashfield** Hants
63 H7 **Ashfield** Herefs
220 D6 **Ashfield** Stirlg
90 F3 **Ashfield cum Thorpe** Suffk
88 F4 **Ashfield Green** Suffk
106 F8 **Ashfield Green** Suffk
37 K5 **Ashfold Crossways** W Susx
7 K5 **Ashford** Devon
27 J4 **Ashford** Devon
40 D6 **Ashford** Kent
50 D4 **Ashford** Surrey
80 C1 **Ashford Bowdler** Shrops
80 C1 **Ashford Carbonel** Shrops
48 E6 **Ashford Hill** Hants
132 D5 **Ashford in the Water** Derbys
198 C3 **Ashgill** S Lans
36 D1 **Ash Green** Surrey
99 J6 **Ash Green** Warwks
29 K8 **Ashill** Devon
105 H3 **Ashill** Norfk
30 D7 **Ashill** Somset
72 C8 **Ashingdon** Essex
181 G1 **Ashington** Nthumb
17 K3 **Ashington** Poole
31 J6 **Ashington** Somset
21 K4 **Ashington** W Susx
188 E2 **Ashkirk** Border
19 G3 **Ashlett** Hants

64 A2 **Ashleworth** Gloucs
64 B2 **Ashleworth Quay** Gloucs
88 D3 **Ashley** Cambs
130 F3 **Ashley** Ches
28 B8 **Ashley** Devon
18 A3 **Ashley** Dorset
64 D8 **Ashley** Gloucs
18 C4 **Ashley** Hants
34 E4 **Ashley** Hants
41 J5 **Ashley** Kent
101 H5 **Ashley** Nhants
114 B4 **Ashley** Staffs
46 B5 **Ashley** Wilts
68 B6 **Ashley Green** Bucks
17 M2 **Ashley Heath** Dorset
80 B2 **Ashley Moor** Herefs
113 J4 **Ash Magna** Shrops
48 B7 **Ashmansworth** Hants
26 F7 **Ashmansworthy** Devon
63 M7 **Ashmead Green** Gloucs
11 M3 **Ashmill** Devon
28 D6 **Ash Mill** Devon
32 F7 **Ashmore** Dorset
48 D5 **Ashmore Green** W Berk
83 G4 **Ashorne** Warwks
133 G7 **Ashover** Derbys
133 G7 **Ashover Hay** Derbys
83 H1 **Ashow** Warwks
113 J4 **Ash Parva** Shrops
80 E7 **Ashperton** Herefs
8 B3 **Ashprington** Devon
29 L5 **Ash Priors** Somset
27 L8 **Ashreigney** Devon
89 K6 **Ash Street** Suffk
50 F7 **Ashtead** Surrey
29 H8 **Ash Thomas** Devon
102 B2 **Ashton** C Pete
129 L6 **Ashton** Ches
2 F5 **Ashton** Cnwll
13 K5 **Ashton** Devon
35 H7 **Ashton** Hants
80 C2 **Ashton** Herefs
207 L4 **Ashton** Inver
84 E5 **Ashton** Nhants
102 B5 **Ashton** Nhants
30 F1 **Ashton** Somset
46 C7 **Ashton Common** Wilts
46 C7 **Ashton Hill** Wilts
139 H7 **Ashton-in-Makerfield** Wigan
64 F8 **Ashton Keynes** Wilts
82 A7 **Ashton under Hill** Worcs
140 E7 **Ashton-under-Lyne** Tamesd
130 F1 **Ashton upon Mersey** Traffd
45 G5 **Ashton Watering** N Som
18 E2 **Ashurst** Hants
38 D5 **Ashurst** Kent
21 L4 **Ashurst** W Susx
38 B6 **Ashurstwood** W Susx
49 L8 **Ash Vale** Surrey
11 M3 **Ashwater** Devon
86 F7 **Ashwell** Herts
101 J1 **Ashwell** Rutlnd
30 E7 **Ashwell** Somset
86 E7 **Ashwell End** Herts
106 C4 **Ashwellthorpe** Norfk
31 K1 **Ashwick** Somset
120 F7 **Ashwicken** Norfk
97 K5 **Ashwood** Staffs
156 B7 **Askam in Furness** Cumb
160 B2 **Aske Hall** N York
142 F5 **Askern** Donc
15 M4 **Askerswell** Dorset
67 K6 **Askett** Bucks
166 C6 **Askham** Cumb
134 E5 **Askham** Notts
151 H6 **Askham Bryan** York
151 H6 **Askham Richard** York
206 E1 **Asknish** Ag & B
159 G4 **Askrigg** N York
149 L6 **Askwith** N York
118 E5 **Aslackby** Lincs
106 D5 **Aslacton** Norfk
117 K3 **Aslockton** Notts
31 G3 **Asney** Somset
90 E2 **Aspall** Suffk
164 F2 **Aspatria** Cumb
69 K2 **Aspenden** Herts
131 K2 **Aspenshaw** Derbys
119 J4 **Asperton** Lincs
114 C5 **Aspley** Staffs
85 J8 **Aspley Guise** Beds
85 H8 **Aspley Heath** Beds
82 C1 **Aspley Heath** Warwks
139 J6 **Aspull** Wigan
139 J8 **Aspull Common** Wigan
143 H2 **Asselby** E R Yk
137 J4 **Asserby** Lincs

137 J4 **Asserby Turn** Lincs
89 J7 **Assington** Suffk
88 F5 **Assington Green** Suffk
131 G7 **Astbury** Ches
84 D4 **Astcote** Nhants
136 E4 **Asterby** Lincs
95 J2 **Asterley** Shrops
95 K5 **Asterton** Shrops
65 L5 **Asthall** Oxon
65 L4 **Asthall Leigh** Oxon
263 K2 **Astle** Highld
142 B2 **Astley** Leeds
113 H7 **Astley** Shrops
99 J5 **Astley** Warwks
139 L7 **Astley** Wigan
81 H2 **Astley** Worcs
96 F4 **Astley Abbots** Shrops
139 L5 **Astley Bridge** Bolton
81 J1 **Astley Cross** Worcs
139 L7 **Astley Green** Wigan
81 H2 **Astley Town** Worcs
98 D5 **Aston** Birm
113 K2 **Aston** Ches
130 A4 **Aston** Ches
132 D3 **Aston** Derbys
129 G6 **Aston** Flints
80 B1 **Aston** Herefs
80 B3 **Aston** Herefs
69 H3 **Aston** Herts
65 M6 **Aston** Oxon
133 J3 **Aston** Rothm
97 H5 **Aston** Shrops
113 H6 **Aston** Shrops
114 B3 **Aston** Staffs
114 D6 **Aston** Staffs
114 E5 **Aston** Staffs
49 J2 **Aston** Wokham
96 E2 **Aston** Wrekin
67 K3 **Aston Abbotts** Bucks
96 E6 **Aston Botterell** Shrops
82 D3 **Aston Cantlow** Warwks
67 L4 **Aston Clinton** Bucks
63 K3 **Aston Crews** Herefs
81 L8 **Aston Cross** Gloucs
69 H2 **Aston End** Herts
96 E4 **Aston-Eyre** Shrops
81 M2 **Aston Fields** Worcs
100 A5 **Aston Flamville** Leics
130 A4 **Aston Heath** Ches
63 K3 **Aston Ingham** Herefs
130 C8 **Aston juxta Mondrum** Ches
96 E4 **Astonlane** Shrops
83 L5 **Aston le Walls** Nhants
82 E8 **Aston Magna** Gloucs
96 C6 **Aston Munslow** Shrops
95 J7 **Aston on Clun** Shrops
95 H2 **Aston Pigott** Shrops
95 H2 **Aston Rogers** Shrops
67 H7 **Aston Rowant** Oxon
67 J5 **Aston Sandford** Bucks
82 B7 **Aston Somerville** Worcs
82 D7 **Aston Subedge** Gloucs
48 E2 **Aston Tirrold** Oxon
116 C5 **Aston-upon-Trent** Derbys
48 E2 **Aston Upthorpe** Oxon
83 L7 **Astrop** Nhants
67 L4 **Astrope** Herts
86 E7 **Astwick** Beds
133 J6 **Astwith** Derbys
85 J5 **Astwood** M Keyn
81 L2 **Astwood** Worcs
82 B3 **Astwood Bank** Worcs
118 E4 **Aswarby** Lincs
137 G5 **Aswardby** Lincs
96 C2 **Atcham** Shrops
82 B5 **Atch Lench** Worcs
16 E4 **Athelhampton** Dorset
90 F1 **Athelington** Suffk
30 E5 **Athelney** Somset
212 C4 **Athelstaneford** E Loth
19 G7 **Atherfield Green** IoW
27 L6 **Atherington** Devon
21 G6 **Atherington** W Susx
30 F7 **Atherstone** Somset
99 J4 **Atherstone** Warwks
82 F5 **Atherstone on Stour** Warwks
139 K7 **Atherton** Wigan
160 D2 **Atley Hill** N York
115 L2 **Atlow** Derbys
248 E4 **Attadale** Highld
116 E5 **Attenborough** Notts
135 K1 **Atterby** Lincs
133 G2 **Attercliffe** Sheff
96 E5 **Atterley** Shrops
99 K4 **Atterton** Leics
105 L4 **Attleborough** Norfk
99 K5 **Attleborough** Warwks

122 C8 **Attlebridge** Norfk
88 E4 **Attleton Green** Suffk
153 K5 **Atwick** E R Yk
46 B6 **Atworth** Wilts
80 C6 **Auberrow** Herefs
135 J7 **Auburn** Lincs
257 G2 **Auchedly** Abers
244 F7 **Auchenblae** Abers
209 L2 **Auchenbowie** Stirlg
175 K4 **Auchencairn** D & G
176 C2 **Auchencairn** D & G
195 G5 **Auchencairn** N Ayrs
213 J7 **Auchencrow** Border
211 H6 **Auchendinny** Mdloth
199 G2 **Auchengray** S Lans
267 H4 **Auchenhalrig** Moray
198 D4 **Auchenheath** S Lans
185 K4 **Auchenhessnane** D & G
206 F4 **Auchenlochan** Ag & B
196 C2 **Auchenmade** N Ayrs
173 G4 **Auchenmalg** D & G
196 D2 **Auchentiber** N Ayrs
219 J8 **Auchentroig** Stirlg
261 K4 **Auchindrean** Highld
268 B6 **Auchininna** Abers
197 G6 **Auchinleck** E Ayrs
209 H5 **Auchinloch** N Lans
209 J4 **Auchinstarry** N Lans
229 H1 **Auchintore** Highld
257 K4 **Auchiries** Abers
245 K4 **Auchlee** Abers
256 A6 **Auchleven** Abers
198 D5 **Auchlochan** S Lans
244 D3 **Auchlossan** Abers
219 H1 **Auchlyne** Stirlg
197 G5 **Auchmillan** E Ayrs
235 G6 **Auchmithie** Angus
222 C7 **Auchmuirbridge** Fife
234 C3 **Auchnacree** Angus
257 G3 **Auchnagatt** Abers
254 D7 **Auchnarrow** Moray
172 B3 **Auchnotteroch** D & G
267 G6 **Auchroisk** Moray
221 G4 **Auchterarder** P & K
240 B2 **Auchteraw** Highld
253 H7 **Auchterblair** Highld
260 C4 **Auchtercairn** Highld
222 C8 **Auchterderran** Fife
233 M7 **Auchterhouse** Angus
256 C3 **Auchterless** Abers
222 D5 **Auchtermuchty** Fife
262 E7 **Auchterneed** Highld
211 H1 **Auchtertool** Fife
248 D6 **Auchtertyre** Highld
219 J3 **Auchtubh** Stirlg
280 E3 **Auckengill** Highld
143 G7 **Auckley** Donc
140 D8 **Audenshaw** Tamesd
113 L3 **Audlem** Ches
114 C2 **Audley** Staffs
87 L7 **Audley End** Essex
89 G7 **Audley End** Essex
89 G4 **Audley End** Suffk
114 C7 **Audmore** Staffs
97 K6 **Audnam** Dudley
165 H3 **Aughertree** Cumb
151 L8 **Aughton** E R Yk
138 E6 **Aughton** Lancs
147 L2 **Aughton** Lancs
133 J2 **Aughton** Rothm
47 K7 **Aughton** Wilts
138 E6 **Aughton Park** Lancs
253 H1 **Auldearn** Highld
80 B4 **Aulden** Herefs
176 B2 **Auldgirth** D & G
197 J1 **Auldhouse** S Lans
248 F7 **Ault a' chruinn** Highld
260 D2 **Aultbea** Highld
260 B3 **Aultgrishin** Highld
262 B6 **Aultguish Inn** Highld
133 J6 **Ault Hucknall** Derbys
267 H5 **Aultmore** Moray
250 F7 **Aultnagoire** Highld
263 J4 **Aultnamain Inn** Highld
118 D8 **Aunby** Lincs
14 B2 **Aunk** Devon
118 D2 **Aunsby** Lincs
45 H1 **Aust** S Glos
119 J7 **Austendike** Lincs
134 D1 **Austerfield** Donc
140 E6 **Austerlands** Oldham
142 B1 **Austhorpe** Leeds
141 H6 **Austonley** Kirk
99 J2 **Austrey** Warwks
148 D2 **Austwick** N York
137 G3 **Authorpe** Lincs
137 K5 **Authorpe Row** Lincs
47 G5 **Avebury** Wilts

47 G5 **Avebury Trusloe** Wilts
52 C3 **Aveley** Thurr
64 C7 **Avening** Gloucs
117 K1 **Averham** Notts
7 K5 **Aveton Gifford** Devon
242 B1 **Aviemore** Highld
48 A5 **Avington** W Berk
251 J1 **Avoch** Highld
18 A4 **Avon** Hants
210 B4 **Avonbridge** Falk
83 K5 **Avon Dassett** Warwks
45 G3 **Avonmouth** Bristl
7 K3 **Avonwick** Devon
34 D6 **Awbridge** Hants
45 H2 **Awkley** S Glos
14 D2 **Awliscombe** Devon
63 L5 **Awre** Gloucs
116 E3 **Awsworth** Notts
97 J7 **Axborough** Worcs
44 E8 **Axbridge** Somset
35 J2 **Axford** Hants
47 K5 **Axford** Wilts
15 G3 **Axminster** Devon
14 F4 **Axmouth** Devon
128 D4 **Axton** Flints
169 H6 **Aycliffe** Dur
180 B5 **Aydon** Nthumb
63 J6 **Aylburton** Gloucs
167 G1 **Ayle** Nthumb
14 B4 **Aylesbeare** Devon
67 K4 **Aylesbury** Bucks
145 G6 **Aylesby** NE Lin
52 F7 **Aylesford** Kent
41 H5 **Aylesham** Kent
100 C3 **Aylestone** C Leic
100 D3 **Aylestone Park** C Leic
122 D4 **Aylmerton** Norfk
122 D6 **Aylsham** Norfk
80 F7 **Aylton** Herefs
65 G3 **Aylworth** Gloucs
80 A2 **Aymestrey** Herefs
83 L8 **Aynho** Nhants
69 G4 **Ayot Green** Herts
69 G4 **Ayot St Lawrence** Herts
69 G4 **Ayot St Peter** Herts
196 C6 **Ayr** S Ayrs
159 H5 **Aysgarth** N York
29 J7 **Ayshford** Devon
156 F6 **Ayside** Cumb
101 J3 **Ayston** Rutlnd
70 E4 **Aythorpe Roding** Essex
213 K6 **Ayton** Border
160 C7 **Azerley** N York

B

8 D2 **Babbacombe** Torbay
116 E3 **Babbington** Notts
112 E5 **Babbinswood** Shrops
69 K4 **Babbs Green** Herts
31 J5 **Babcary** Somset
59 M2 **Babel** Carmth
88 E5 **Babel Green** Suffk
128 E5 **Babell** Flints
12 F7 **Babeny** Devon
32 B1 **Babington** Somset
66 B6 **Bablock Hythe** Oxon
87 K5 **Babraham** Cambs
134 D3 **Babworth** Notts
125 H3 **Bachau** IoA
95 L7 **Bache** Shrops
94 F5 **Bacheldre** Powys
24 F5 **Bachelor's Bump** E Susx
275 d3 **Backaland** Ork
156 E5 **Backbarrow** Cumb
58 A5 **Backe** Carmth
269 J5 **Backfolds** Abers
129 J5 **Backford** Ches
129 J5 **Backford Cross** Ches
273 K7 **Backies** Highld
280 B5 **Backlass** Highld
237 J3 **Back of Keppoch** Highld
115 H1 **Back o' th' Brook** Staffs
88 E3 **Back Street** Suffk
44 F5 **Backwell** N Som
181 H4 **Backworth** N Tyne
98 F6 **Bacon's End** Solhll
122 C4 **Baconsthorpe** Norfk
62 D1 **Bacton** Herefs
123 G5 **Bacton** Norfk
90 C2 **Bacton** Suffk
90 B2 **Bacton Green** Suffk
140 C3 **Bacup** Lancs
260 C5 **Badachro** Highld
47 J3 **Badbury** Swindn
84 A3 **Badby** Nhants
276 B7 **Badcall** Highld

276 C5 **Badcall** Highld
261 G2 **Badcaul** Highld
114 E1 **Baddeley Edge** C Stke
114 E1 **Baddeley Green** C Stke
82 F1 **Baddesley Clinton** Warwks
99 H4 **Baddesley Ensor** Warwks
270 E3 **Baddidarrach** Highld
199 K2 **Baddinsgill** Border
256 C4 **Badenscoth** Abers
255 G7 **Badenyon** Abers
11 J5 **Badgall** Cnwll
103 J4 **Badgeney** Cambs
97 H3 **Badger** Shrops
2 D4 **Badger's Cross** Cnwll
52 B6 **Badgers Mount** Kent
64 C3 **Badgeworth** Gloucs
44 E8 **Badgworth** Somset
11 J5 **Badharlick** Cnwll
248 B6 **Badicaul** Highld
91 G2 **Badingham** Suffk
40 D4 **Badlesmere** Kent
187 G2 **Badlieu** Border
280 B6 **Badlipster** Highld
261 G1 **Badluachrach** Highld
263 K1 **Badninish** Highld
261 H2 **Badrallach** Highld
82 C6 **Badsey** Worcs
36 C1 **Badshot Lea** Surrey
142 D5 **Badsworth** Wakefd
89 K2 **Badwell Ash** Suffk
89 K2 **Badwell Green** Suffk
32 C8 **Bagber** Dorset
161 G6 **Bagby** N York
136 F5 **Bag Enderby** Lincs
64 E5 **Bagendon** Gloucs
96 F7 **Bagginswood** Shrops
165 G2 **Baggrow** Cumb
283 b13 **Bagh a Chaisteil** W Isls
40 E4 **Bagham** Kent
283 b13 **Bagh a Tuath** W Isls
128 F4 **Bagillt** Flints
99 K8 **Baginton** Warwks
57 K6 **Baglan** Neath
141 K1 **Bagley** Leeds
112 F6 **Bagley** Shrops
31 G2 **Bagley** Somset
35 K2 **Bagmore** Hants
114 E1 **Bagnall** Staffs
48 C5 **Bagnor** W Berk
96 D8 **Bagot** Shrops
49 M6 **Bagshot** Surrey
47 L6 **Bagshot** Wilts
45 K2 **Bagstone** S Glos
116 D1 **Bagthorpe** Notts
99 M2 **Bagworth** Leics
62 F2 **Bagwy Llydiart** Herefs
149 L7 **Baildon** Brad
149 L7 **Baildon Green** Brad
282 f4 **Baile Ailein** W Isls
283 c9 **Baile a Mhanaich** W Isls
226 B7 **Baile Mor** Ag & B
35 K5 **Bailey Green** Hants
178 C3 **Baileyhead** Cumb
141 J3 **Bailiff Bridge** Calder
209 H6 **Baillieston** C Glas
147 J4 **Bailrigg** Lancs
159 G4 **Bainbridge** N York
256 A5 **Bainshole** Abers
102 B2 **Bainton** C Pete
152 E5 **Bainton** E R Yk
66 E2 **Bainton** Oxon
222 F6 **Baintown** Fife
189 H3 **Bairnkine** Border
69 L4 **Baker's End** Herts
52 D3 **Baker Street** Thurr
132 D6 **Bakewell** Derbys
111 H4 **Bala** Gwynd
282 f4 **Balallan** W Isls
250 D5 **Balbeg** Highld
222 B1 **Balbeggie** P & K
250 E3 **Balblair** Highld
263 J6 **Balblair** Highld
142 E7 **Balby** Donc
175 K5 **Balcary** D & G
250 F3 **Balchraggan** Highld
276 B4 **Balchreick** Highld
37 M5 **Balcombe** W Susx
37 M4 **Balcombe Lane** W Susx
223 L5 **Balcomie Links** Fife
160 E7 **Baldersby** N York
160 E7 **Baldersby St James** N York
139 J1 **Balderstone** Lancs
140 D5 **Balderstone** Rochdl
117 L1 **Balderton** Notts
4 C6 **Baldhu** Cnwll
223 G3 **Baldinnie** Fife
221 J4 **Baldinnies** P & K
86 E8 **Baldock** Herts

234 C8 **Baldovie** C Dund
154 f5 **Baldrine** IoM
24 E4 **Baldslow** E Susx
154 e6 **Baldwin** IoM
177 K8 **Baldwinholme** Cumb
114 B3 **Baldwin's Gate** Staffs
38 B5 **Baldwin's Hill** W Susx
121 M4 **Bale** Norfk
222 D1 **Baledgarno** P & K
224 C7 **Balemartine** Ag & B
211 G5 **Balerno** C Edin
222 D6 **Balfarg** Fife
234 E2 **Balfield** Angus
275 d4 **Balfour** Ork
208 F1 **Balfron** Stirlg
256 B4 **Balgaveny** Abers
234 E5 **Balgavies** Angus
221 J8 **Balgonar** Fife
172 E6 **Balgowan** D & G
241 H4 **Balgowan** Highld
258 F3 **Balgown** Highld
172 B3 **Balgracie** D & G
234 B7 **Balgray** Angus
186 C2 **Balgray** S Lans
51 H4 **Balham** Gt Lon
233 L6 **Balhary** P & K
233 H8 **Balholmie** P & K
278 E3 **Baligill** Highld
233 L4 **Balintore** Angus
264 D5 **Balintore** Highld
263 K5 **Balintraid** Highld
283 c9 **Balivanich** W Isls
161 G6 **Balk** N York
233 M6 **Balkeerie** Angus
143 K2 **Balkholme** E R Yk
154 c7 **Ballabeg** IoM
154 b7 **Ballafesson** IoM
154 g4 **Ballajora** IoM
154 b7 **Ballakilpheric** IoM
154 c7 **Ballamodha** IoM
207 G6 **Ballanlay** Ag & B
182 D6 **Ballantrae** S Ayrs
72 C8 **Ballards Gore** Essex
99 H5 **Ballards Green** Warwks
154 c7 **Ballasalla** IoM
243 L4 **Ballater** Abers
154 d3 **Ballaugh** IoM
263 K5 **Ballchraggan** Highld
212 B3 **Ballencrieff** E Loth
224 B6 **Ballevullin** Ag & B
114 D1 **Ball Green** C Stke
131 K8 **Ball Haye Green** Staffs
48 B6 **Ball Hill** Hants
115 K1 **Ballidon** Derbys
194 D3 **Balliekine** N Ayrs
217 H7 **Balliemore** Ag & B
183 G5 **Balligmorrie** S Ayrs
206 E2 **Ballimore** Ag & B
219 H4 **Ballimore** Stirlg
254 D4 **Ballindalloch** Moray
222 D2 **Ballindean** P & K
89 H7 **Ballingdon** Suffk
67 M6 **Ballinger Common** Bucks
63 H1 **Ballingham** Herefs
222 B7 **Ballingry** Fife
232 E5 **Ballinluig** P & K
234 B5 **Ballinshoe** Angus
233 G4 **Ballintuim** P & K
252 D2 **Balloch** Highld
209 K4 **Balloch** N Lans
220 E3 **Balloch** P & K
183 J4 **Balloch** S Ayrs
208 C3 **Balloch** W Duns
244 D4 **Ballogie** Abers
36 E5 **Balls Cross** W Susx
38 D6 **Balls Green** E Susx
64 B7 **Ball's Green** Gloucs
226 E4 **Ballygown** Ag & B
204 F3 **Ballygrant** Ag & B
224 F4 **Ballyhaugh** Ag & B
248 C6 **Balmacara** Highld
185 G7 **Balmaclellan** D & G
175 H6 **Balmae** D & G
208 C1 **Balmaha** Stirlg
222 E5 **Balmalcolm** Fife
175 G5 **Balmangan** D & G
257 H8 **Balmedie** Abers
113 G4 **Balmer Heath** Shrops
222 F2 **Balmerino** Fife
18 D3 **Balmerlawn** Hants
194 E5 **Balmichael** N Ayrs
209 G4 **Balmore** E Duns
264 D4 **Balmuchy** Highld
234 E5 **Balmuir** Angus
211 H2 **Balmule** Fife
223 G3 **Balmullo** Fife
273 J5 **Balnacoil Lodge** Highld
248 F3 **Balnacra** Highld

243 J5 **Balnacroft** Abers
251 J4 **Balnafoich** Highld
232 D5 **Balnaguard** P & K
214 E4 **Balnahard** Ag & B
226 E5 **Balnahard** Ag & B
250 D5 **Balnain** Highld
276 F3 **Balnakeil** Highld
264 B6 **Balnapaling** Highld
142 F4 **Balne** N York
232 F8 **Balquharn** P & K
219 H3 **Balquhidder** Stirlg
99 G8 **Balsall Common** Solhll
98 D6 **Balsall Heath** Birm
99 G8 **Balsall Street** Solhll
83 J6 **Balscote** Oxon
88 B5 **Balsham** Cambs
281 f1 **Baltasound** Shet
114 B2 **Balterley** Staffs
114 B2 **Balterley Green** Staffs
114 B2 **Balterley Heath** Staffs
174 C3 **Baltersan** D & G
31 J4 **Baltonsborough** Somset
233 G3 **Balvarran** P & K
216 B4 **Balvicar** Ag & B
248 D8 **Balvraid** Highld
252 F5 **Balvraid** Highld
2 F5 **Balwest** Cnwll
139 H3 **Bamber Bridge** Lancs
70 E3 **Bamber's Green** Essex
203 K6 **Bamburgh** Nthumb
233 K5 **Bamff** P & K
132 D3 **Bamford** Derbys
140 C5 **Bamford** Rochdl
166 C7 **Bampton** Cumb
29 G6 **Bampton** Devon
65 L6 **Bampton** Oxon
166 C7 **Bampton Grange** Cumb
239 J8 **Banavie** Highld
83 K7 **Banbury** Oxon
58 E6 **Bancffosfelen** Carmth
244 F4 **Banchory** Abers
245 K3 **Banchory-Devenick** Abers
58 D6 **Bancycapel** Carmth
58 B5 **Bancyfelin** Carmth
76 D7 **Banc-y-ffordd** Carmth
222 C1 **Bandirran** P & K
156 D5 **Bandrake Head** Cumb
268 C3 **Banff** Abers
125 K5 **Bangor** Gwynd
112 F2 **Bangor-is-y-coed** Wrexhm
11 H3 **Bangors** Cnwll
138 D6 **Bangor's Green** Lancs
89 J1 **Bangrove** Suffk
106 B6 **Banham** Norfk
18 D2 **Bank** Hants
176 D5 **Bankend** D & G
233 G8 **Bankfoot** P & K
197 H8 **Bankglen** E Ayrs
156 D3 **Bank Ground** Cumb
245 K2 **Bankhead** C Aber
199 G4 **Bankhead** S Lans
148 F5 **Bank Newton** N York
209 K3 **Banknock** Falk
178 D6 **Banks** Cumb
138 E4 **Banks** Lancs
82 A2 **Banks Green** Worcs
177 G3 **Bankshill** D & G
80 E3 **Bank Street** Worcs
141 H3 **Bank Top** Calder
139 G6 **Bank Top** Lancs
122 E5 **Banningham** Norfk
71 G3 **Bannister Green** Essex
209 L1 **Bannockburn** Stirlg
51 H7 **Banstead** Surrey
7 K6 **Bantham** Devon
209 K3 **Banton** N Lans
44 E7 **Banwell** N Som
40 B3 **Bapchild** Kent
33 G3 **Bapton** Wilts
282 g2 **Barabhas** W Isls
196 C4 **Barassie** S Ayrs
263 K5 **Barbaraville** Highld
132 B3 **Barber Booth** Derbys
156 F6 **Barber Green** Cumb
196 E7 **Barbieston** S Ayrs
157 K6 **Barbon** Cumb
130 B8 **Barbridge** Ches
28 C2 **Barbrook** Devon
84 A1 **Barby** Nhants
228 F7 **Barcaldine** Ag & B
83 G7 **Barcheston** Warwks
178 B6 **Barclose** Cumb
22 F4 **Barcombe** E Susx
23 G4 **Barcombe Cross** E Susx
149 J8 **Barcroft** Brad
159 L4 **Barden** N York
38 F4 **Barden Park** Kent
70 F1 **Bardfield End Green** Essex

71 G2 **Bardfield Saling** Essex
136 B6 **Bardney** Lincs
99 M1 **Bardon** Leics
179 H6 **Bardon Mill** Nthumb
209 G4 **Bardowie** E Duns
39 G7 **Bardown** E Susx
208 B4 **Bardrainney** Inver
156 D7 **Bardsea** Cumb
150 E7 **Bardsey** Leeds
140 D7 **Bardsley** Oldham
105 J8 **Bardwell** Suffk
147 J3 **Bare** Lancs
3 K5 **Bareppa** Cnwll
79 M4 **Barewood** Herefs
173 J2 **Barfad** D & G
106 C2 **Barford** Norfk
83 G3 **Barford** Warwks
83 K8 **Barford St John** Oxon
33 J4 **Barford St Martin** Wilts
83 K8 **Barford St Michael** Oxon
41 H5 **Barfrestone** Kent
116 B2 **Bargate** Derbys
209 J6 **Bargeddie** N Lans
61 J7 **Bargoed** Caerph
183 J7 **Bargrennan** D & G
102 C8 **Barham** Cambs
41 G5 **Barham** Kent
90 D5 **Barham** Suffk
87 H3 **Bar Hill** Cambs
102 B1 **Barholm** Lincs
100 E2 **Barkby** Leics
100 E2 **Barkby Thorpe** Leics
113 H6 **Barkers Green** Shrops
117 K4 **Barkestone-le-Vale** Leics
49 J5 **Barkham** Wokham
51 L2 **Barking** Gt Lon
90 C4 **Barking** Suffk
51 L1 **Barkingside** Gt Lon
90 C5 **Barking Tye** Suffk
141 G4 **Barkisland** Calder
4 B5 **Barkla Shop** Cnwll
118 B3 **Barkston** Lincs
151 G8 **Barkston Ash** N York
87 H8 **Barkway** Herts
209 H6 **Barlanark** C Glas
114 D4 **Barlaston** Staffs
21 J4 **Barlavington** W Susx
133 J4 **Barlborough** Derbys
143 G1 **Barlby** N York
99 L2 **Barlestone** Leics
87 H7 **Barley** Herts
148 E7 **Barley** Lancs
70 B2 **Barleycroft End** Herts
142 B8 **Barley Hole** Rothm
101 J2 **Barleythorpe** Rutlnd
53 K1 **Barling** Essex
135 M5 **Barlings** Lincs
175 K3 **Barlochan** D & G
133 G5 **Barlow** Derbys
180 E6 **Barlow** Gatesd
143 G2 **Barlow** N York
152 B6 **Barmby Moor** E R Yk
143 H2 **Barmby on the Marsh** E R Yk
121 H5 **Barmer** Norfk
39 J2 **Barming Heath** Kent
194 C2 **Barmollack** Ag & B
109 L8 **Barmouth** Gwynd
169 J7 **Barmpton** Darltn
153 J4 **Barmston** E R Yk
107 K7 **Barnaby Green** Suffk
216 F8 **Barnacarry** Ag & B
102 B2 **Barnack** C Pete
99 K6 **Barnacle** Warwks
168 D7 **Barnard Castle** Dur
66 D3 **Barnard Gate** Oxon
88 E5 **Barnardiston** Suffk
175 L3 **Barnbarroch** D & G
142 D7 **Barnburgh** Donc
107 K5 **Barnby** Suffk
142 F6 **Barnby Dun** Donc
117 M1 **Barnby in the Willows** Notts
134 B4 **Barnby Moor** Notts
172 D7 **Barncorkrie** D & G
52 B4 **Barnehurst** Gt Lon
51 G4 **Barnes** Gt Lon
39 G4 **Barnes Street** Kent
69 H7 **Barnet** Gt Lon
144 D6 **Barnetby le Wold** N Linc
69 G8 **Barnet Gate** Gt Lon
121 M5 **Barney** Norfk
105 H7 **Barnham** Suffk
20 F6 **Barnham** W Susx
106 B2 **Barnham Broom** Norfk
235 G4 **Barnhead** Angus
223 H1 **Barnhill** C Dund
113 H1 **Barnhill** Ches

266 C5 **Barnhill** Moray
182 B8 **Barnhills** D & G
168 D8 **Barningham** Dur
105 K8 **Barningham** Suffk
145 G7 **Barnoldby le Beck** NE Lin
148 F6 **Barnoldswick** Lancs
142 D5 **Barnsdale Bar** Donc
37 H5 **Barns Green** W Susx
142 A6 **Barnsley** Barns
65 G6 **Barnsley** Gloucs
97 G5 **Barnsley** Shrops
41 J4 **Barnsole** Kent
27 K4 **Barnstaple** Devon
70 F3 **Barnston** Essex
129 G3 **Barnston** Wirral
117 J4 **Barnstone** Notts
98 C8 **Barnt Green** Worcs
211 G4 **Barnton** C Edin
130 C7 **Barnton** Ches
102 A6 **Barnwell All Saints** Nhants
102 A6 **Barnwell St Andrew** Nhants
64 B3 **Barnwood** Gloucs
80 B4 **Baron's Cross** Herefs
13 G2 **Barons Wood** Devon
166 C2 **Baronwood** Cumb
183 H4 **Barr** S Ayrs
173 J5 **Barrachan** D & G
224 B6 **Barrapoll** Ag & B
167 J8 **Barras** Cumb
179 L4 **Barrasford** Nthumb
154 d4 **Barregarrow** IoM
130 B7 **Barrets Green** Ches
208 E7 **Barrhead** E Rens
183 G6 **Barrhill** S Ayrs
87 H5 **Barrington** Cambs
30 F7 **Barrington** Somset
3 G3 **Barripper** Cnwll
196 D1 **Barrmill** N Ayrs
216 C3 **Barrnacarry Bay** Ag & B
280 C2 **Barrock** Highld
64 C2 **Barrow** Gloucs
148 C8 **Barrow** Lancs
118 A8 **Barrow** Rutlnd
96 E3 **Barrow** Shrops
32 B4 **Barrow** Somset
88 F3 **Barrow** Suffk
104 B3 **Barroway Drove** Norfk
139 K5 **Barrow Bridge** Bolton
190 B4 **Barrow Burn** Nthumb
118 A4 **Barrowby** Lincs
101 L3 **Barrowden** Rutlnd
148 E7 **Barrowford** Lancs
45 G5 **Barrow Gurney** N Som
144 D3 **Barrow Haven** N Linc
133 H4 **Barrow Hill** Derbys
146 D2 **Barrow-in-Furness** Cumb
146 D2 **Barrow Island** Cumb
138 F7 **Barrow Nook** Lancs
130 D8 **Barrow's Green** Ches
129 M2 **Barrow's Green** Halton
32 D5 **Barrow Street** Wilts
144 D4 **Barrow-upon-Humber** N Linc
116 F8 **Barrow upon Soar** Leics
116 B6 **Barrow upon Trent** Derbys
45 J7 **Barrow Vale** BaNES
234 E8 **Barry** Angus
43 H7 **Barry** V Glam
43 H8 **Barry Island** V Glam
100 F1 **Barsby** Leics
107 H5 **Barsham** Suffk
99 G7 **Barston** Solhll
80 D7 **Bartestree** Herefs
256 E5 **Barthol Chapel** Abers
71 H3 **Bartholomew Green** Essex
114 B1 **Barthomley** Ches
18 D1 **Bartley** Hants
98 C7 **Bartley Green** Birm
88 B6 **Bartlow** Cambs
87 H4 **Barton** Cambs
113 G1 **Barton** Ches
65 G2 **Barton** Gloucs
79 K4 **Barton** Herefs
138 D6 **Barton** Lancs
147 K8 **Barton** Lancs
160 C1 **Barton** N York
66 E5 **Barton** Oxon
8 D2 **Barton** Torbay
82 D5 **Barton** Warwks
104 E2 **Barton Bendish** Norfk
64 B7 **Barton End** Gloucs
115 K7 **Barton Green** Staffs
66 F1 **Barton Hartshorn** Bucks
151 L3 **Barton Hill** N York
116 E5 **Barton in Fabis** Notts
99 L2 **Barton in the Beans** Leics
68 D1 **Barton-le-Clay** Beds
162 C7 **Barton-le-Street** N York

151 M3 **Barton-le-Willows** N York
104 E8 **Barton Mills** Suffk
18 C5 **Barton-on-Sea** Hants
83 G8 **Barton-on-the-Heath** Warwks
31 J4 **Barton St David** Somset
101 J7 **Barton Seagrave** Nhants
34 F3 **Barton Stacey** Hants
28 B3 **Barton Town** Devon
123 G7 **Barton Turf** Norfk
115 K7 **Barton-under-Needwood** Staffs
144 C3 **Barton-upon-Humber** N Linc
140 A8 **Barton upon Irwell** Salfd
144 C3 **Barton Waterside** N Linc
141 M6 **Barugh** Barns
141 M6 **Barugh Green** Barns
282 g2 **Barvas** W Isls
103 L8 **Barway** Cambs
99 L4 **Barwell** Leics
12 E1 **Barwick** Devon
69 K3 **Barwick** Herts
31 J8 **Barwick** Somset
150 F8 **Barwick in Elmet** Leeds
112 F7 **Baschurch** Shrops
83 J3 **Bascote** Warwks
83 J3 **Bascote Heath** Warwks
89 L3 **Base Green** Suffk
114 F1 **Basford Green** Staffs
148 B7 **Bashall Eaves** Lancs
148 C7 **Bashall Town** Lancs
18 C4 **Bashley** Hants
52 F1 **Basildon** Essex
48 F8 **Basingstoke** Hants
132 E5 **Baslow** Derbys
30 E2 **Bason Bridge** Somset
44 B2 **Bassaleg** Newpt
201 K4 **Bassendean** Border
165 H4 **Bassenthwaite** Cumb
34 F7 **Bassett** C Sotn
87 G6 **Bassingbourn** Cambs
117 G4 **Bassingfield** Notts
135 H7 **Bassingham** Lincs
118 C6 **Bassingthorpe** Lincs
69 J2 **Bassus Green** Herts
38 F2 **Basted** Kent
102 C1 **Baston** Lincs
123 J8 **Bastwick** Norfk
44 C7 **Batch** Somset
68 D8 **Batchworth** Herts
68 D8 **Batchworth Heath** Herts
16 B2 **Batcombe** Dorset
31 M3 **Batcombe** Somset
130 D4 **Bate Heath** Ches
68 F4 **Batford** Herts
45 L6 **Bath** BaNES
45 M5 **Bathampton** BaNES
29 K6 **Bathealton** Somset
45 M5 **Batheaston** BaNES
46 A5 **Bathford** BaNES
210 C5 **Bathgate** W Loth
134 F7 **Bathley** Notts
11 K7 **Bathpool** Cnwll
30 C5 **Bathpool** Somset
73 K1 **Bath Side** Essex
210 B5 **Bathville** W Loth
45 H8 **Bathway** Somset
141 K3 **Batley** Kirk
82 E8 **Batsford** Gloucs
7 L7 **Batson** Devon
161 K1 **Battersby** N York
51 H4 **Battersea** Gt Lon
7 H5 **Battisborough Cross** Devon
90 C4 **Battisford** Suffk
89 L4 **Battisford Tye** Suffk
24 D4 **Battle** E Susx
60 F1 **Battle** Powys
30 E1 **Battleborough** Somset
64 D3 **Battledown** Gloucs
234 C4 **Battledykes** Angus
113 H8 **Battlefield** Shrops
71 J8 **Battlesbridge** Essex
68 B2 **Battlesden** Beds
29 G5 **Battleton** Somset
89 H2 **Battlies Green** Suffk
18 E4 **Battramsley Cross** Hants
36 B3 **Batt's Corner** Hants
141 J4 **Battyeford** Kirk
81 K6 **Baughton** Worcs
48 E7 **Baughurst** Hants
244 D5 **Baulds** Abers
47 L1 **Baulking** Oxon
136 D5 **Baumber** Lincs
64 E6 **Baunton** Gloucs
96 F7 **Baveney Wood** Shrops
33 H4 **Baverstock** Wilts
106 D2 **Bawburgh** Norfk

22 A7 **Bawdeswell** Norfk
50 E3 **Bawdrip** Somset
91 H7 **Bawdsey** Suffk
20 E7 **Bawsey** Norfk
34 C1 **Bawtry** Donc
40 A2 **Baxenden** Lancs
99 H4 **Baxterley** Warwks
38 E4 **Baxter's Green** Suffk
58 D6 **Bay** Highld
82 h3 **Bayble** W Isls
35 H6 **Baybridge** Hants
68 B1 **Baybridge** Nthumb
46 F2 **Baycliff** Cumb
47 L3 **Baydon** Wilts
59 J5 **Bayford** Herts
52 B5 **Bayford** Somset
83 b8 **Bayhead** W Isls
47 K5 **Bay Horse** Lancs
58 D3 **Bayley's Hill** Kent
90 C5 **Baylham** Suffk
56 E1 **Baynard's Green** Oxon
61 K1 **Baysdale Abbey** N York
53 H2 **Baysham** Herefs
96 B2 **Bayston Hill** Shrops
38 E6 **Baythorne End** Essex
96 F8 **Bayton** Worcs
81 G1 **Bayton Common** Worcs
56 D6 **Bayworth** Oxon
45 L5 **Beach** S Glos
34 E7 **Beachampton** Bucks
04 E2 **Beachamwell** Norfk
45 H1 **Beachley** Gloucs
14 E2 **Beacon** Devon
72 D2 **Beacon End** Essex
38 D7 **Beacon Hill** E Susx
39 K6 **Beacon Hill** Kent
17 L1 **Beacon Hill** Notts
36 C3 **Beacon Hill** Surrey
67 J8 **Beacon's Bottom** Bucks
50 B1 **Beaconsfield** Bucks
61 L5 **Beadlam** N York
36 C7 **Beadlow** Beds
03 L7 **Beadnell** Nthumb
27 K7 **Beaford** Devon
42 E3 **Beal** N York
03 H4 **Beal** Nthumb
6 D2 **Bealbury** Cnwll
11 L7 **Bealsmill** Cnwll
15 L6 **Beam Hill** Staffs
15 H4 **Beamhurst** Staffs
15 L2 **Beaminster** Dorset
80 F8 **Beamish** Dur
49 K5 **Beamsley** N York
52 C4 **Bean** Kent
46 C5 **Beanacre** Wilts
90 F3 **Beanley** Nthumb
12 C5 **Beardon** Devon
39 K2 **Beardwood** Bl w D
14 A2 **Beare** Devon
37 J2 **Beare Green** Surrey
32 E3 **Bearley** Warwks
32 E3 **Bearley Cross** Warwks
92 G2 **Bearpark** Dur
08 F4 **Bearsden** E Duns
39 K2 **Bearsted** Kent
14 A4 **Bearstone** Shrops
98 C6 **Bearwood** Birm
17 L3 **Bearwood** Poole
87 G6 **Beattock** D & G
70 E5 **Beauchamp Roding** Essex
32 F3 **Beauchief** Sheff
82 E2 **Beaudesert** Warwks
61 J5 **Beaufort** Blae G
18 F3 **Beaulieu** Hants
18 E2 **Beaulieu Road Station** Hants
50 F2 **Beauly** Highld
26 B4 **Beaumaris** IoA
77 K7 **Beaumont** Cumb
73 H2 **Beaumont** Essex
9 c3 **Beaumont** Jersey
69 J7 **Beaumont Hill** Darltn
82 F1 **Beausale** Warwks
35 J5 **Beauworth** Hants
12 B3 **Beaworthy** Devon
71 H1 **Beazley End** Essex
29 H3 **Bebington** Wirral
81 G3 **Bebside** Nthumb
07 J5 **Beccles** Suffk
38 F3 **Becconsall** Lancs
97 H3 **Beckbury** Shrops
51 K5 **Beckenham** Gt Lon
55 J1 **Beckermet** Cumb
04 F4 **Beckett End** Norfk
55 L3 **Beckfoot** Cumb
56 B5 **Beckfoot** Cumb
57 K3 **Beck Foot** Cumb
64 E1 **Beckfoot** Cumb

82 A8 **Beckford** Worcs
47 G5 **Beckhampton** Wilts
162 E2 **Beck Hole** N York
118 A1 **Beckingham** Lincs
134 F2 **Beckingham** Notts
46 A8 **Beckington** Somset
95 J7 **Beckjay** Shrops
24 F3 **Beckley** E Susx
18 C4 **Beckley** Hants
66 E5 **Beckley** Oxon
104 D7 **Beck Row** Suffk
149 J6 **Becks** Brad
156 B6 **Beck Side** Cumb
156 E6 **Beck Side** Cumb
157 K5 **Beckside** Cumb
51 L3 **Beckton** Gt Lon
150 C5 **Beckwithshaw** N York
52 A2 **Becontree** Gt Lon
9 d2 **Becquet Vincent** Jersey
160 C5 **Bedale** N York
168 E4 **Bedburn** Dur
32 E7 **Bedchester** Dorset
43 G4 **Beddau** Rhondd
109 L2 **Beddgelert** Gwynd
23 G5 **Beddingham** E Susx
51 J6 **Beddington** Gt Lon
51 H5 **Beddington Corner** Gt Lon
90 F2 **Bedfield** Suffk
90 F2 **Bedfield Little Green** Suffk
85 L5 **Bedford** Beds
39 H6 **Bedgebury Cross** Kent
36 F6 **Bedham** W Susx
20 A5 **Bedhampton** Hants
90 E2 **Bedingfield** Suffk
90 E2 **Bedingfield Green** Suffk
150 C3 **Bedlam** N York
39 M4 **Bedlam Lane** Kent
181 G3 **Bedlington** Nthumb
61 H6 **Bedlinog** Myr Td
45 H5 **Bedminster** Bristl
45 H5 **Bedminster Down** Bristl
68 E6 **Bedmond** Herts
114 F7 **Bednall** Staffs
189 G3 **Bedrule** Border
95 J8 **Bedstone** Shrops
43 J4 **Bedwas** Caerph
61 J7 **Bedwellty** Caerph
99 K6 **Bedworth** Warwks
99 K6 **Bedworth Woodlands** Warwks
100 D4 **Beeby** Leics
35 L3 **Beech** Hants
114 D4 **Beech** Staffs
49 G6 **Beech Hill** W Berk
47 G7 **Beechingstoke** Wilts
48 C3 **Beedon** W Berk
48 C3 **Beedon Hill** W Berk
153 H5 **Beeford** E R Yk
132 E6 **Beeley** Derbys
145 G7 **Beelsby** NE Lin
48 E5 **Beenham** W Berk
49 K4 **Beenham's Heath** W & M
11 G4 **Beeny** Cnwll
14 F4 **Beer** Devon
30 F4 **Beer** Somset
30 D6 **Beercrocombe** Somset
31 K8 **Beer Hackett** Dorset
8 B6 **Beesands** Devon
137 J4 **Beesby** Lincs
8 B6 **Beeson** Devon
86 D5 **Beeston** Beds
129 M7 **Beeston** Ches
141 L2 **Beeston** Leeds
121 K8 **Beeston** Norfk
116 E4 **Beeston** Notts
122 D3 **Beeston Regis** Norfk
176 A5 **Beeswing** D & G
157 H6 **Beetham** Cumb
30 D8 **Beetham** Somset
121 L8 **Beetley** Norfk
43 K5 **Began** Cardif
66 C4 **Begbroke** Oxon
103 J2 **Begdale** Cambs
55 J5 **Begelly** Pembks
141 L3 **Beggarington Hill** Leeds
79 J2 **Beggar's Bush** Powys
94 F7 **Beguildy** Powys
107 H2 **Beighton** Norfk
133 J3 **Beighton** Sheff
115 M1 **Beighton Hill** Derbys
208 B8 **Beith** N Ayrs
41 G4 **Bekesbourne** Kent
41 G4 **Bekesbourne Hill** Kent
122 F7 **Belaugh** Norfk
97 L7 **Belbroughton** Worcs
16 F1 **Belchalwell** Dorset
16 F1 **Belchalwell Street** Dorset
88 F6 **Belchamp Otten** Essex

88 F6 **Belchamp St Paul** Essex
89 G7 **Belchamp Walter** Essex
136 E4 **Belchford** Lincs
203 H6 **Belford** Nthumb
100 D2 **Belgrave** C Leic
212 E3 **Belhaven** E Loth
257 H8 **Belhelvie** Abers
255 J6 **Belhinnie** Abers
243 K1 **Bellabeg** Abers
79 M7 **Bellamore** Herefs
216 B8 **Bellanoch** Ag & B
143 K2 **Bellasize** E R Yk
233 K3 **Bellaty** Angus
69 H6 **Bell Bar** Herts
148 F4 **Bell Busk** N York
137 G4 **Belleau** Lincs
97 L7 **Bell End** Worcs
159 K4 **Bellerby** N York
12 F7 **Bellever** Devon
177 L7 **Belle Vue** Cumb
142 A4 **Belle Vue** Wakefd
186 E2 **Bellfield** S Lans
198 D6 **Bellfield** S Lans
97 L7 **Bell Heath** Worcs
35 M6 **Bell Hill** Hants
68 B6 **Bellingdon** Bucks
179 J2 **Bellingham** Nthumb
192 D1 **Belloch** Ag & B
192 D2 **Bellochantuy** Ag & B
113 H2 **Bell o' th' Hill** Ches
33 J8 **Bellows Cross** Dorset
90 D5 **Bells Cross** Suffk
209 J7 **Bellshill** N Lans
203 J7 **Bellshill** Nthumb
209 L7 **Bellside** N Lans
210 D6 **Bellsquarry** W Loth
38 F6 **Bells Yew Green** E Susx
45 J6 **Belluton** BaNES
263 H8 **Belmaduthy** Highld
102 A2 **Belmesthorpe** Rutlnd
139 K4 **Belmont** Bl w D
51 H6 **Belmont** Gt Lon
196 C7 **Belmont** S Ayrs
281 f2 **Belmont** Shet
255 H8 **Belnacraig** Abers
4 F3 **Belowda** Cnwll
116 B2 **Belper** Derbys
116 B2 **Belper Lane End** Derbys
133 L4 **Belph** Derbys
180 D3 **Belsay** Nthumb
201 J8 **Belses** Border
7 L3 **Belsford** Devon
68 D7 **Belsize** Herts
90 D7 **Belstead** Suffk
12 E4 **Belstone** Devon
139 L3 **Belthorn** Lancs
41 G2 **Beltinge** Kent
179 H6 **Beltingham** Nthumb
143 K6 **Beltoft** N Linc
116 D7 **Belton** Leics
118 B3 **Belton** Lincs
143 K6 **Belton** N Linc
107 K3 **Belton** Norfk
101 H3 **Belton** Rutlnd
39 H4 **Beltring** Kent
52 B3 **Belvedere** Gt Lon
117 L5 **Belvoir** Leics
19 L6 **Bembridge** IoW
33 K5 **Bemerton** Wilts
153 K2 **Bempton** E R Yk
107 K6 **Benacre** Suffk
185 H4 **Benbuie** D & G
228 D7 **Benderloch** Ag & B
39 K6 **Benenden** Kent
180 D8 **Benfieldside** Dur
122 F6 **Bengates** Norfk
69 J4 **Bengeo** Herts
82 B6 **Bengeworth** Worcs
91 J3 **Benhall Green** Suffk
91 H3 **Benhall Street** Suffk
235 K2 **Benholm** Abers
151 H4 **Beningbrough** N York
69 J2 **Benington** Herts
119 L2 **Benington** Lincs
119 L2 **Benington Sea End** Lincs
125 J3 **Benllech** IoA
207 J2 **Benmore** Ag & B
11 K4 **Bennacott** Cnwll
193 K4 **Bennan** N Ayrs
166 B6 **Bennet Head** Cumb
143 L2 **Bennetland** E R Yk
67 J7 **Bennett End** Bucks
136 D3 **Benniworth** Lincs
39 H4 **Benover** Kent
149 L6 **Ben Rhydding** Brad
196 C2 **Benslie** N Ayrs
66 F8 **Benson** Oxon
70 D2 **Bentfield Green** Essex

96 F3 **Benthall** Shrops
64 C4 **Bentham** Gloucs
245 H3 **Benthoul** C Aber
95 H3 **Bentlawn** Shrops
142 E6 **Bentley** Donc
152 F8 **Bentley** E R Yk
36 A2 **Bentley** Hants
90 D7 **Bentley** Suffk
99 H4 **Bentley** Warwks
69 H7 **Bentley Heath** Herts
98 F8 **Bentley Heath** Solhll
28 B4 **Benton** Devon
188 B8 **Bentpath** D & G
28 C4 **Bentwichen** Devon
35 K3 **Bentworth** Hants
222 E1 **Benvie** Angus
15 M2 **Benville** Dorset
103 G5 **Benwick** Cambs
82 C1 **Beoley** Worcs
237 K2 **Beoraidbeg** Highld
20 D3 **Bepton** W Susx
70 C1 **Berden** Essex
74 C6 **Berea** Pembks
6 E2 **Bere Alston** Devon
6 E2 **Bere Ferrers** Devon
3 G6 **Berepper** Cnwll
17 G3 **Bere Regis** Dorset
106 F3 **Bergh Apton** Norfk
31 G4 **Berhill** Somset
66 E7 **Berinsfield** Oxon
63 K7 **Berkeley** Gloucs
63 K7 **Berkeley Heath** Gloucs
63 L7 **Berkeley Road** Gloucs
68 C5 **Berkhamsted** Herts
32 D1 **Berkley** Somset
99 H7 **Berkswell** Solhll
51 J3 **Bermondsey** Gt Lon
99 K5 **Bermuda** Warwks
248 C7 **Bernera** Highld
207 J1 **Bernice** Ag & B
258 F6 **Bernisdale** Highld
66 F8 **Berrick Prior** Oxon
66 F8 **Berrick Salome** Oxon
274 F3 **Berriedale** Highld
165 L5 **Berrier** Cumb
94 E3 **Berriew** Powys
202 F4 **Berrington** Nthumb
96 C2 **Berrington** Shrops
80 D2 **Berrington** Worcs
80 D2 **Berrington Green** Worcs
44 C8 **Berrow** Somset
81 H8 **Berrow** Worcs
81 H3 **Berrow Green** Worcs
141 H5 **Berry Brow** Kirk
27 H7 **Berry Cross** Devon
27 K2 **Berry Down Cross** Devon
63 H4 **Berry Hill** Gloucs
75 H4 **Berry Hill** Pembks
267 K4 **Berryhillock** Moray
267 K5 **Berryhillock** Moray
27 K2 **Berrynarbor** Devon
8 B3 **Berry Pomeroy** Devon
51 L7 **Berry's Green** Gt Lon
112 D2 **Bersham** Wrexhm
128 D4 **Berthengam** Flints
23 H6 **Berwick** E Susx
47 G4 **Berwick Bassett** Wilts
180 E4 **Berwick Hill** Nthumb
33 J3 **Berwick St James** Wilts
32 F6 **Berwick St John** Wilts
32 F4 **Berwick St Leonard** Wilts
202 F3 **Berwick-upon-Tweed** Nthumb
117 L6 **Bescaby** Leics
138 E5 **Bescar** Lancs
113 J6 **Besford** Shrops
81 L6 **Besford** Worcs
142 F7 **Bessacarr** Donc
66 C6 **Bessels Leigh** Oxon
140 B6 **Besses o' th' Barn** Bury
153 J3 **Bessingby** E R Yk
122 D4 **Bessingham** Norfk
38 F7 **Bestbeech Hill** E Susx
106 B4 **Besthorpe** Norfk
135 G6 **Besthorpe** Notts
116 F2 **Bestwood Village** Notts
152 F6 **Beswick** E R Yk
95 K4 **Betchcott** Shrops
37 K1 **Betchworth** Surrey
77 G3 **Bethania** Cerdgn
110 D3 **Bethania** Gwynd
111 J4 **Bethel** Gwynd
125 J6 **Bethel** Gwynd
125 G5 **Bethel** IoA
111 L7 **Bethel** Powys
40 B7 **Bethersden** Kent
126 C6 **Bethesda** Gwynd
55 J3 **Bethesda** Pembks

294 Bethlehem - Blackley

59 J4 **Bethlehem** Carmth
51 K2 **Bethnal Green** Gt Lon
114 B2 **Betley** Staffs
52 D4 **Betsham** Kent
41 J5 **Betteshanger** Kent
15 J2 **Bettiscombe** Dorset
113 G4 **Bettisfield** Wrexhm
113 M4 **Betton** Shrops
96 C2 **Betton Strange** Shrops
44 C1 **Bettws** Newpt
77 H5 **Bettws Bledrws** Cerdgn
94 D4 **Bettws Cedewain** Powys
76 B5 **Bettws Evan** Cerdgn
62 D6 **Bettws-Newydd** Mons
278 B4 **Bettyhill** Highld
42 D4 **Betws** Brdgnd
59 H6 **Betws** Carmth
125 K8 **Betws Garmon** Gwynd
111 K2 **Betws Gwerfil Goch** Denbgs
126 F8 **Betws-y-Coed** Conwy
127 H5 **Betws-yn-Rhos** Conwy
76 B6 **Beulah** Cerdgn
78 C5 **Beulah** Powys
22 E6 **Bevendean** Br & H
134 D5 **Bevercotes** Notts
153 G7 **Beverley** E R Yk
64 B8 **Beverstone** Gloucs
63 K7 **Bevington** Gloucs
165 H4 **Bewaldeth** Cumb
178 D4 **Bewcastle** Cumb
97 H8 **Bewdley** Worcs
149 L3 **Bewerley** N York
153 J6 **Bewholme** E R Yk
39 H6 **Bewlbridge** Kent
24 D5 **Bexhill** E Susx
52 B4 **Bexley** Gt Lon
52 A4 **Bexleyheath** Gt Lon
36 D6 **Bexleyhill** W Susx
53 J7 **Bexon** Kent
104 C3 **Bexwell** Norfk
89 J3 **Beyton** Suffk
89 J3 **Beyton Green** Suffk
282 e3 **Bhaltos** W Isls
283 b13 **Bhatarsaigh** W Isls
45 K1 **Bibstone** S Glos
65 G5 **Bibury** Gloucs
66 E3 **Bicester** Oxon
99 G7 **Bickenhill** Solhll
119 H4 **Bicker** Lincs
119 H4 **Bicker Bar** Lincs
119 H4 **Bicker Gauntlet** Lincs
139 J7 **Bickershaw** Wigan
138 F7 **Bickerstaffe** Lancs
113 H1 **Bickerton** Ches
8 B7 **Bickerton** Devon
151 G5 **Bickerton** N York
190 E6 **Bickerton** Nthumb
114 D8 **Bickford** Staffs
13 J7 **Bickington** Devon
27 J4 **Bickington** Devon
7 G2 **Bickleigh** Devon
13 M1 **Bickleigh** Devon
27 J5 **Bickleton** Devon
113 J2 **Bickley** Ches
51 L5 **Bickley** Gt Lon
163 G4 **Bickley** N York
80 E1 **Bickley** Worcs
113 J2 **Bickley Moss** Ches
71 J6 **Bicknacre** Essex
29 K3 **Bicknoller** Somset
53 J7 **Bicknor** Kent
33 K8 **Bickton** Hants
80 B2 **Bicton** Herefs
95 G6 **Bicton** Shrops
113 G8 **Bicton** Shrops
38 E5 **Bidborough** Kent
35 L1 **Bidden** Hants
39 L5 **Biddenden** Kent
39 M5 **Biddenden Green** Kent
85 K5 **Biddenham** Beds
46 B4 **Biddestone** Wilts
44 D8 **Biddisham** Somset
84 C7 **Biddlesden** Bucks
190 D4 **Biddlestone** Nthumb
131 H7 **Biddulph** Staffs
131 H8 **Biddulph Moor** Staffs
27 H5 **Bideford** Devon
82 D5 **Bidford-on-Avon** Warwks
129 G2 **Bidston** Wirral
152 B7 **Bielby** E R Yk
245 K3 **Bieldside** C Aber
19 H8 **Bierley** IoW
67 K4 **Bierton** Bucks
173 K6 **Big Balcraig** D & G
7 K5 **Bigbury** Devon
7 J6 **Bigbury-on-Sea** Devon
144 D6 **Bigby** Lincs
185 G3 **Big Carlae** D & G
146 D3 **Biggar** Cumb
199 H5 **Biggar** S Lans
115 L2 **Biggin** Derbys
132 C7 **Biggin** Derbys
142 E1 **Biggin** N York
51 L7 **Biggin Hill** Gt Lon
86 D6 **Biggleswade** Beds
177 K3 **Bigholms** D & G
278 F3 **Bighouse** Highld
35 J4 **Bighton** Hants
177 H8 **Biglands** Cumb
21 G4 **Bignor** W Susx
164 D8 **Bigrigg** Cumb
260 B4 **Big Sand** Highld
281 d8 **Bigton** Shet
116 E3 **Bilborough** C Nott
29 J3 **Bilbrook** Somset
97 K3 **Bilbrook** Staffs
151 H6 **Bilbrough** N York
280 C5 **Bilbster** Highld
169 G6 **Bildershaw** Dur
89 K5 **Bildeston** Suffk
11 J4 **Billacott** Cnwll
71 G8 **Billericay** Essex
100 F3 **Billesdon** Leics
82 D4 **Billesley** Warwks
118 F5 **Billingborough** Lincs
139 G7 **Billinge** St Hel
106 D7 **Billingford** Norfk
121 M7 **Billingford** Norfk
170 B6 **Billingham** S on T
136 C8 **Billinghay** Lincs
142 C6 **Billingley** Barns
37 G5 **Billingshurst** W Susx
96 F6 **Billingsley** Shrops
68 B3 **Billington** Beds
148 C8 **Billington** Lancs
114 D7 **Billington** Staffs
107 J1 **Billockby** Norfk
168 F3 **Billy Row** Dur
147 K7 **Bilsborrow** Lancs
137 J4 **Bilsby** Lincs
21 G6 **Bilsham** W Susx
40 D8 **Bilsington** Kent
134 C7 **Bilsthorpe** Notts
134 C7 **Bilsthorpe Moor** Notts
211 J6 **Bilston** Mdloth
98 B4 **Bilston** Wolves
99 K2 **Bilstone** Leics
40 D5 **Bilting** Kent
144 F1 **Bilton** E R Yk
150 D4 **Bilton** N York
151 G6 **Bilton** N York
191 J4 **Bilton** Nthumb
100 B8 **Bilton** Warwks
191 J4 **Bilton Banks** Nthumb
136 D1 **Binbrook** Lincs
169 G4 **Binchester Blocks** Dur
16 D5 **Bincombe** Dorset
31 K1 **Binegar** Somset
21 L3 **Bines Green** W Susx
49 K4 **Binfield** Br For
49 H3 **Binfield Heath** Oxon
180 A4 **Bingfield** Nthumb
117 J3 **Bingham** Notts
16 E2 **Bingham's Melcombe** Dorset
149 K7 **Bingley** Brad
113 J7 **Bings** Shrops
121 L4 **Binham** Norfk
99 K7 **Binley** Covtry
48 B8 **Binley** Hants
99 L7 **Binley Woods** Warwks
17 G5 **Binnegar** Dorset
209 M4 **Binniehill** Falk
36 E2 **Binscombe** Surrey
66 C5 **Binsey** Oxon
19 K5 **Binstead** IoW
36 A3 **Binsted** Hants
21 G5 **Binsted** W Susx
82 D4 **Binton** Warwks
121 M7 **Bintree** Norfk
95 H3 **Binweston** Shrops
72 D3 **Birch** Essex
140 C6 **Birch** Rochdl
121 G5 **Bircham Newton** Norfk
121 G5 **Bircham Tofts** Norfk
70 D3 **Birchanger** Essex
17 G2 **Birch Close** Dorset
115 J5 **Birch Cross** Staffs
141 H4 **Birchencliffe** Kirk
80 B2 **Bircher** Herefs
98 D5 **Birchfield** Birm
72 D3 **Birch Green** Essex
69 J5 **Birch Green** Herts
81 K6 **Birch Green** Worcs
43 J5 **Birchgrove** Cardif
57 K5 **Birchgrove** Swans
38 B7 **Birchgrove** W Susx
130 A7 **Birch Heath** Ches
129 M5 **Birch Hill** Ches
41 J2 **Birchington** Kent
99 H4 **Birchley Heath** Warwks
99 H3 **Birchmoor** Warwks
85 J8 **Birchmoor Green** Beds
132 E7 **Birchover** Derbys
131 K2 **Birch Vale** Derbys
30 C8 **Birch Wood** Somset
130 C2 **Birchwood** Warrtn
134 C2 **Bircotes** Notts
88 E7 **Birdbrook** Essex
161 G7 **Birdforth** N York
20 D6 **Birdham** W Susx
83 K2 **Birdingbury** Warwks
64 D4 **Birdlip** Gloucs
178 E5 **Birdoswald** Cumb
152 B3 **Birdsall** N York
141 K6 **Birds Edge** Kirk
70 E5 **Birds Green** Essex
97 H6 **Birdsgreen** Shrops
15 J2 **Birdsmoorgate** Dorset
89 K5 **Bird Street** Suffk
142 A7 **Birdwell** Barns
63 L3 **Birdwood** Gloucs
202 B5 **Birgham** Border
263 K2 **Birichin** Highld
139 H5 **Birkacre** Lancs
160 D2 **Birkby** N York
138 C5 **Birkdale** Sefton
267 L3 **Birkenbog** Abers
129 H2 **Birkenhead** Wirral
256 D3 **Birkenhills** Abers
141 K2 **Birkenshaw** Kirk
243 K5 **Birkhall** Abers
234 A8 **Birkhill** Angus
187 J3 **Birkhill** D & G
118 C6 **Birkholme** Lincs
142 E2 **Birkin** N York
141 L2 **Birks** Leeds
179 H5 **Birkshaw** Nthumb
80 B4 **Birley** Herefs
133 G1 **Birley Carr** Sheff
52 E6 **Birling** Kent
191 K5 **Birling** Nthumb
23 J8 **Birling Gap** E Susx
81 L6 **Birlingham** Worcs
98 D6 **Birmingham** Birm
232 F7 **Birnam** P & K
257 H5 **Birness** Abers
244 C4 **Birse** Abers
244 C4 **Birsemore** Abers
141 K3 **Birstall** Kirk
100 D2 **Birstall** Leics
150 B4 **Birstwith** N York
118 E5 **Birthorpe** Lincs
181 G7 **Birtley** Gatesd
79 L2 **Birtley** Herefs
179 K3 **Birtley** Nthumb
81 H7 **Birts Street** Worcs
101 J3 **Bisbrooke** Rutlnd
136 D3 **Biscathorpe** Lincs
5 H4 **Biscovey** Cnwll
49 K2 **Bisham** W & M
82 A5 **Bishampton** Worcs
28 C6 **Bish Mill** Devon
169 G5 **Bishop Auckland** Dur
135 L2 **Bishopbridge** Lincs
209 G5 **Bishopbriggs** E Duns
152 F7 **Bishop Burton** E R Yk
169 J4 **Bishop Middleham** Dur
266 E3 **Bishopmill** Moray
150 D3 **Bishop Monkton** N York
135 K1 **Bishop Norton** Lincs
41 G5 **Bishopsbourne** Kent
46 F6 **Bishops Cannings** Wilts
95 H5 **Bishop's Castle** Shrops
32 B8 **Bishop's Caundle** Dorset
64 D2 **Bishop's Cleeve** Gloucs
80 F5 **Bishop's Frome** Herefs
50 B5 **Bishops Gate** Surrey
70 F3 **Bishop's Green** Essex
48 D6 **Bishop's Green** Hants
30 B6 **Bishops Hull** Somset
83 J4 **Bishop's Itchington** Warwks
29 M5 **Bishops Lydeard** Somset
64 B2 **Bishop's Norton** Gloucs
28 D6 **Bishop's Nympton** Devon
114 B5 **Bishop's Offley** Staffs
70 C3 **Bishop's Stortford** Herts
35 J4 **Bishop's Sutton** Hants
83 H3 **Bishop's Tachbrook** Warwks
27 K5 **Bishop's Tawton** Devon
13 L7 **Bishopsteignton** Devon
34 F7 **Bishopstoke** Hants
57 G7 **Bishopston** Swans
67 J5 **Bishopstone** Bucks
23 G7 **Bishopstone** E Susx
80 A6 **Bishopstone** Herefs
41 G2 **Bishopstone** Kent
47 K2 **Bishopstone** Swindn
33 J5 **Bishopstone** Wilts
32 E2 **Bishopstrow** Wilts
45 H7 **Bishop Sutton** BaNES
35 H7 **Bishop's Waltham** Hants
30 C8 **Bishopswood** Somset
97 J2 **Bishop's Wood** Staffs
45 H5 **Bishopsworth** Bristl
150 C3 **Bishop Thornton** N York
151 J6 **Bishopthorpe** York
169 K6 **Bishopton** Darltn
208 D5 **Bishopton** Rens
82 E4 **Bishopton** Warwks
152 B5 **Bishop Wilton** E R Yk
44 D2 **Bishton** Newpt
115 G7 **Bishton** Staffs
64 C6 **Bisley** Gloucs
50 B7 **Bisley** Surrey
50 B7 **Bisley Camp** Surrey
146 F7 **Bispham** Bpool
138 F5 **Bispham Green** Lancs
3 K3 **Bissoe** Cnwll
18 A3 **Bisterne** Hants
38 E3 **Bitchet Green** Kent
118 C6 **Bitchfield** Lincs
27 K3 **Bittadon** Devon
7 K3 **Bittaford** Devon
121 K8 **Bittering** Norfk
96 D7 **Bitterley** Shrops
34 F8 **Bitterne** C Sotn
100 C6 **Bitteswell** Leics
45 K5 **Bitton** S Glos
49 H2 **Bix** Oxon
281 d6 **Bixter** Shet
100 C4 **Blaby** Leics
202 C3 **Blackadder** Border
8 B4 **Blackawton** Devon
155 J1 **Blackbeck** Cumb
14 C1 **Blackborough** Devon
120 E8 **Blackborough End** Norfk
65 L6 **Black Bourton** Oxon
23 J3 **Blackboys** E Susx
116 B2 **Blackbrook** Derbys
139 G8 **Blackbrook** St Hel
114 B4 **Blackbrook** Staffs
37 J2 **Blackbrook** Surrey
245 J1 **Blackburn** Abers
139 K2 **Blackburn** Bl w D
133 H1 **Blackburn** Rothm
210 C6 **Blackburn** W Loth
180 E5 **Black Callerton** N u Ty
106 B4 **Black Car** Norfk
37 L3 **Black Corner** W Susx
185 G1 **Blackcraig** E Ayrs
228 E8 **Black Crofts** Ag & B
4 E3 **Black Cross** Cnwll
130 F5 **Blackden Heath** Ches
245 L1 **Blackdog** Abers
13 J1 **Black Dog** Devon
12 C6 **Blackdown** Devon
15 J2 **Blackdown** Dorset
176 F8 **Blackdyke** Cumb
142 A5 **Blacker** Barns
142 B7 **Blacker Hill** Barns
51 M4 **Blackfen** Gt Lon
19 G3 **Blackfield** Hants
177 L6 **Blackford** Cumb
220 F5 **Blackford** P & K
30 F2 **Blackford** Somset
31 L5 **Blackford** Somset
140 B6 **Blackford Bridge** Bury
116 B7 **Blackfordby** Leics
19 H8 **Blackgang** IoW
211 G4 **Blackhall** C Edin
170 B3 **Blackhall** Dur
170 B3 **Blackhall Colliery** Dur
200 F5 **Blackhaugh** Border
72 E3 **Blackheath** Essex
51 K4 **Blackheath** Gt Lon
98 B6 **Blackheath** Sandw
107 J8 **Blackheath** Suffk
36 F2 **Blackheath** Surrey
180 C4 **Black Heddon** Nthumb
257 K3 **Blackhill** Abers
269 K5 **Blackhill** Abers
180 D8 **Blackhill** Dur
269 G7 **Blackhill of Clackriach** Abers
14 A4 **Blackhorse** Devon
119 H4 **Blackjack** Lincs
46 E5 **Blackland** Wilts
140 A6 **Black Lane** Bury
149 G7 **Black Lane Ends** Lancs
186 F4 **Blacklaw** D & G
140 C7 **Blackley** Manch

233 H3 **Blacklunans** P & K
80 C7 **Blackmarstone** Herefs
42 E4 **Blackmill** Brdgnd
36 A4 **Blackmoor** Hants
150 D7 **Black Moor** Leeds
44 F6 **Blackmoor** N Som
141 H5 **Blackmoorfoot** Kirk
70 F6 **Blackmore** Essex
71 H1 **Blackmore End** Essex
68 F4 **Blackmore End** Herts
210 E3 **Blackness** Falk
36 B3 **Blacknest** Hants
50 B5 **Blacknest** W & M
71 J3 **Black Notley** Essex
148 E7 **Blacko** Lancs
57 H6 **Black Pill** Swans
146 F8 **Blackpool** Bpool
8 C5 **Blackpool** Devon
13 J7 **Blackpool** Devon
178 C3 **Blackpool Gate** Cumb
210 A5 **Blackridge** W Loth
3 G4 **Blackrock** Cnwll
61 K4 **Blackrock** Mons
139 J5 **Blackrod** Bolton
254 D4 **Blacksboat** Moray
176 D5 **Blackshaw** D & G
140 E2 **Blackshaw Head** Calder
90 D2 **Blacksmith's Green** Suffk
139 L3 **Blacksnape** Bl w D
22 C4 **Blackstone** W Susx
107 K6 **Black Street** Suffk
55 G5 **Black Tar** Pembks
66 F3 **Blackthorn** Oxon
89 H3 **Blackthorpe** Suffk
143 L3 **Blacktoft** E R Yk
245 J3 **Blacktop** C Aber
12 B2 **Black Torrington** Devon
115 L2 **Blackwall** Derbys
4 B5 **Blackwater** Cnwll
49 K7 **Blackwater** Hants
19 H6 **Blackwater** IoW
30 C7 **Blackwater** Somset
194 D5 **Blackwaterfoot** N Ayrs
177 L8 **Blackwell** Cumb
169 H8 **Blackwell** Darltn
132 C5 **Blackwell** Derbys
133 J7 **Blackwell** Derbys
82 F6 **Blackwell** Warwks
82 A1 **Blackwell** Worcs
63 M2 **Blackwellsend Green** Gloucs
43 J2 **Blackwood** Caerph
176 B2 **Blackwood** D & G
198 C4 **Blackwood** S Lans
131 H8 **Blackwood Hill** Staffs
129 J6 **Blacon** Ches
41 G6 **Bladbean** Kent
174 C4 **Bladnoch** D & G
66 C4 **Bladon** Oxon
30 F6 **Bladon** Somset
75 M2 **Blaenannerch** Cerdgn
110 D2 **Blaenau Ffestiniog** Gwynd
61 L5 **Blaenavon** Torfn
78 C7 **Blaen Dyrryn** Powys
75 L5 **Blaenffos** Pembks
42 D3 **Blaengarw** Brdgnd
92 E7 **Blaengeuffordd** Cerdgn
60 C6 **Blaengwrach** Neath
42 D2 **Blaengwynfi** Neath
42 F2 **Blaenllechau** Rhondd
77 H2 **Blaenpennal** Cerdgn
92 C8 **Blaenplwyf** Cerdgn
76 A5 **Blaenporth** Cerdgn
60 D7 **Blaenrhondda** Rhondd
75 M6 **Blaenwaun** Carmth
58 C3 **Blaen-y-Coed** Carmth
61 H5 **Blaen-y-cwm** Blae G
93 H8 **Blaenycwm** Cerdgn
60 D7 **Blaen-y-cwm** Rhondd
45 G7 **Blagdon** N Som
30 B7 **Blagdon** Somset
8 C3 **Blagdon** Torbay
30 B7 **Blagdon Hill** Somset
167 G1 **Blagill** Cumb
138 F6 **Blaguegate** Lancs
239 G8 **Blaich** Highld
237 K6 **Blain** Highld
61 K5 **Blaina** Blae G
232 C2 **Blair Atholl** P & K
220 C7 **Blair Drummond** Stirlg
233 J6 **Blairgowrie** P & K
210 C2 **Blairhall** Fife
221 H7 **Blairingone** P & K
220 E7 **Blairlogie** Stirlg
207 K2 **Blairmore** Ag & B
276 B4 **Blairmore** Highld
254 D8 **Blairnamarrow** Moray
206 F5 **Blair's Ferry** Ag & B
63 K4 **Blaisdon** Gloucs

97 J8 **Blakebrook** Worcs
97 K7 **Blakedown** Worcs
71 H3 **Blake End** Essex
114 F2 **Blakeley Lane** Staffs
130 A5 **Blakemere** Ches
79 L7 **Blakemere** Herefs
7 M3 **Blakemore** Devon
98 C3 **Blakenall Heath** Wsall
63 K5 **Blakeney** Gloucs
122 A3 **Blakeney** Norfk
114 A2 **Blakenhall** Ches
97 K4 **Blakenhall** Wolves
97 J7 **Blakeshall** Worcs
84 C5 **Blakesley** Nhants
168 B1 **Blanchland** Nthumb
17 H1 **Blandford Camp** Dorset
17 G1 **Blandford Forum** Dorset
17 G1 **Blandford St Mary** Dorset
150 B5 **Bland Hill** N York
208 F3 **Blanefield** Stirlg
135 L7 **Blankney** Lincs
209 J7 **Blantyre** S Lans
229 H2 **Blar a' Chaorainn** Highld
241 G4 **Blargie** Highld
229 H2 **Blarmachfoldach** Highld
18 A2 **Blashford** Hants
101 H4 **Blaston** Leics
101 L4 **Blatherwycke** Nhants
156 C5 **Blawith** Cumb
184 F6 **Blawquhairn** D & G
91 J4 **Blaxhall** Suffk
143 H7 **Blaxton** Donc
180 F6 **Blaydon** Gatesd
31 H2 **Bleadney** Somset
44 C7 **Bleadon** N Som
32 C4 **Bleak Street** Somset
40 F3 **Blean** Kent
136 B3 **Bleasby** Lincs
117 J2 **Bleasby** Notts
147 L6 **Bleasdale** Lancs
167 G7 **Bleatarn** Cumb
80 D1 **Bleathwood** Herefs
223 G4 **Blebocraigs** Fife
79 H2 **Bleddfa** Powys
65 K3 **Bledington** Gloucs
67 J6 **Bledlow** Bucks
67 J7 **Bledlow Ridge** Bucks
46 C7 **Bleet** Wilts
212 B6 **Blegbie** E Loth
166 E4 **Blencarn** Cumb
165 G1 **Blencogo** Cumb
35 L8 **Blendworth** Hants
165 G2 **Blennerhasset** Cumb
66 D3 **Bletchingdon** Oxon
37 M1 **Bletchingley** Surrey
85 G8 **Bletchley** M Keyn
113 K5 **Bletchley** Shrops
55 H3 **Bletherston** Pembks
85 K4 **Bletsoe** Beds
48 D2 **Blewbury** Oxon
122 D6 **Blickling** Norfk
134 B8 **Blidworth** Notts
117 G1 **Blidworth Bottoms** Notts
189 L4 **Blindburn** Nthumb
164 F4 **Blindcrake** Cumb
38 A4 **Blindley Heath** Surrey
10 F7 **Blisland** Cnwll
33 L8 **Blissford** Hants
81 G1 **Bliss Gate** Worcs
84 D4 **Blisworth** Nhants
115 H7 **Blithbury** Staffs
176 F8 **Blitterlees** Cumb
82 E8 **Blockley** Gloucs
107 G2 **Blofield** Norfk
107 G1 **Blofield Heath** Norfk
105 K7 **Blo Norton** Norfk
189 G2 **Bloomfield** Border
114 A4 **Blore** Staffs
115 J2 **Blore** Staffs
35 L2 **Blounce** Hants
115 H5 **Blounts Green** Staffs
138 D4 **Blowick** Sefton
83 K8 **Bloxham** Oxon
118 E1 **Bloxholm** Lincs
98 C3 **Bloxwich** Wsall
17 G3 **Bloxworth** Dorset
149 L5 **Blubberhouses** N York
4 E3 **Blue Anchor** Cnwll
29 J2 **Blue Anchor** Somset
52 F6 **Blue Bell Hill** Kent
138 C7 **Blundellsands** Sefton
107 L4 **Blundeston** Suffk
86 C5 **Blunham** Beds
47 H1 **Blunsdon St Andrew** Swindn
97 K8 **Bluntington** Worcs
103 H8 **Bluntisham** Cambs
6 C2 **Blunts** Cnwll
82 D2 **Blunts Green** Warwks

114 D3 **Blurton** C Stke
135 J1 **Blyborough** Lincs
107 J8 **Blyford** Suffk
97 H1 **Blymhill** Staffs
97 J1 **Blymhill Lawn** Staffs
134 C2 **Blyth** Notts
181 K1 **Blyth** Nthumb
199 K4 **Blyth Bridge** Border
107 J8 **Blythburgh** Suffk
201 J3 **Blythe** Border
114 F3 **Blythe Bridge** Staffs
99 G5 **Blythe End** Warwks
114 F3 **Blythe Marsh** Staffs
135 G1 **Blyton** Lincs
223 K4 **Boarhills** Fife
19 K2 **Boarhunt** Hants
53 G7 **Boarley** Kent
140 C4 **Boarsgreave** Lancs
38 E6 **Boarshead** E Susx
139 H6 **Boar's Head** Wigan
66 D6 **Boars Hill** Oxon
66 F4 **Boarstall** Bucks
12 C1 **Boasley Cross** Devon
263 G5 **Boath** Highld
253 H7 **Boat of Garten** Highld
53 J6 **Bobbing** Kent
97 H5 **Bobbington** Staffs
70 D6 **Bobbingworth** Essex
5 L3 **Bocaddon** Cnwll
71 J2 **Bocking** Essex
71 J2 **Bocking Churchstreet** Essex
80 D3 **Bockleton** Worcs
5 K3 **Boconnoc** Cnwll
257 L4 **Boddam** Abers
281 d8 **Boddam** Shet
64 C2 **Boddington** Gloucs
124 F4 **Bodedern** IoA
127 K4 **Bodelwyddan** Denbgs
80 C5 **Bodenham** Herefs
33 L5 **Bodenham** Wilts
80 D5 **Bodenham Moor** Herefs
125 G2 **Bodewryd** IoA
128 C5 **Bodfari** Denbgs
125 G4 **Bodffordd** IoA
108 E4 **Bodfuan** Gwynd
122 C3 **Bodham** Norfk
24 E2 **Bodiam** E Susx
83 K7 **Bodicote** Oxon
10 D7 **Bodieve** Cnwll
5 K4 **Bodinnick** Cnwll
23 L4 **Bodle Street Green** E Susx
5 H2 **Bodmin** Cnwll
105 G4 **Bodney** Norfk
125 G6 **Bodorgan** IoA
4 D5 **Bodrean** Cnwll
40 E6 **Bodsham Green** Kent
5 H3 **Bodwen** Cnwll
99 G4 **Bodymoor Heath** Warwks
251 H2 **Bogallan** Highld
257 J4 **Bogbrae** Abers
196 D4 **Bogend** S Ayrs
212 A5 **Boggs Holdings** E Loth
211 H6 **Boghall** Mdloth
210 C5 **Boghall** W Loth
198 C5 **Boghead** S Lans
267 G4 **Bogmoor** Moray
235 G1 **Bogmuir** Abers
255 M3 **Bogniebrae** Abers
20 F7 **Bognor Regis** W Susx
253 G7 **Bogroy** Highld
185 G6 **Bogue** D & G
6 E1 **Bohetherick** Cnwll
3 L4 **Bohortha** Cnwll
240 A6 **Bohuntine** Highld
2 B1 **Bojewyan** Cnwll
5 H2 **Bokiddick** Cnwll
169 G6 **Bolam** Dur
180 D2 **Bolam** Nthumb
7 K7 **Bolberry** Devon
129 M2 **Bold Heath** St Hel
98 E4 **Boldmere** Birm
181 J6 **Boldon Colliery** S Tyne
18 A6 **Boldre** Hants
168 C7 **Boldron** Dur
134 F2 **Bole** Notts
132 F8 **Bolehill** Derbys
133 G8 **Bole Hill** Derbys
3 H3 **Bolenowe** Cnwll
29 G7 **Bolham** Devon
29 L8 **Bolham Water** Devon
4 C4 **Bolingey** Cnwll
131 J4 **Bollington** Ches
131 H4 **Bollington Cross** Ches
63 L4 **Bollow** Gloucs
37 L6 **Bolney** W Susx
86 B3 **Bolnhurst** Beds
234 F5 **Bolshan** Angus

133 J5 **Bolsover** Derbys
141 G5 **Bolster Moor** Kirk
141 L8 **Bolsterstone** Sheff
161 H5 **Boltby** N York
243 M2 **Boltenstone** Abers
67 J8 **Bolter End** Bucks
139 L6 **Bolton** Bolton
166 E6 **Bolton** Cumb
212 B5 **Bolton** E Loth
152 B5 **Bolton** E R Yk
191 G3 **Bolton** Nthumb
149 K5 **Bolton Abbey** N York
149 K5 **Bolton Bridge** N York
148 D6 **Bolton by Bowland** Lancs
178 B5 **Boltonfellend** Cumb
165 H3 **Boltongate** Cumb
147 J2 **Bolton le Sands** Lancs
165 H2 **Bolton Low Houses** Cumb
165 H2 **Bolton New Houses** Cumb
160 C3 **Bolton-on-Swale** N York
151 H7 **Bolton Percy** N York
147 J2 **Bolton Town End** Lancs
142 C7 **Bolton Upon Dearne** Barns
11 H7 **Bolventor** Cnwll
181 G2 **Bomarsund** Nthumb
113 G7 **Bomere Heath** Shrops
263 G6 **Bonar Bridge** Highld
228 F8 **Bonawe** Ag & B
144 C5 **Bonby** N Linc
75 L4 **Boncath** Pembks
189 G4 **Bonchester Bridge** Border
19 K8 **Bonchurch** IoW
12 F2 **Bondleigh** Devon
147 J6 **Bonds** Lancs
13 G7 **Bonehill** Devon
99 G3 **Bonehill** Staffs
210 D3 **Bo'ness** Falk
98 D2 **Boney Hay** Staffs
208 C3 **Bonhill** W Duns
97 J3 **Boningale** Shrops
189 H2 **Bonjedward** Border
209 M7 **Bonkle** N Lans
234 F7 **Bonnington** Angus
40 D8 **Bonnington** Kent
222 F6 **Bonnybank** Fife
209 L3 **Bonnybridge** Falk
268 F5 **Bonnykelly** Abers
211 J6 **Bonnyrigg** Mdloth
233 M7 **Bonnyton** Angus
132 E8 **Bonsall** Derbys
177 H4 **Bonshaw Tower** D & G
62 D3 **Bont** Mons
110 C7 **Bontddu** Gwynd
93 J3 **Bont-Dolgadfan** Powys
92 E6 **Bont-goch or Elerch** Cerdgn
137 J5 **Bonthorpe** Lincs
77 H2 **Bontnewydd** Cerdgn
125 J7 **Bontnewydd** Gwynd
128 C8 **Bontuchel** Denbgs
43 G7 **Bonvilston** V Glam
111 L3 **Bonwm** Denbgs
57 J6 **Bon-y-maen** Swans
27 J3 **Boode** Devon
49 K1 **Booker** Bucks
113 J6 **Booley** Shrops
201 J4 **Boon** Border
114 C2 **Boon Hill** Staffs
35 G8 **Boorley Green** Hants
170 F7 **Boosbeck** R & Cl
71 K1 **Boose's Green** Essex
11 K3 **Boot** Cnwll
155 M3 **Boot** Cumb
141 G2 **Booth** Calder
135 K7 **Boothby Graffoe** Lincs
118 C5 **Boothby Pagnell** Lincs
143 J3 **Boothferry** E R Yk
131 H3 **Booth Green** Ches
139 L7 **Boothstown** Salfd
141 G2 **Booth Town** Calder
84 F2 **Boothville** Nhants
155 K5 **Bootle** Cumb
138 D8 **Bootle** Sefton
130 E5 **Boots Green** Ches
90 F5 **Boot Street** Suffk
159 H2 **Booze** N York
80 E1 **Boraston** Shrops
9 k2 **Bordeaux** Guern
53 J6 **Borden** Kent
36 B6 **Borden** W Susx
177 G8 **Border** Cumb
149 G3 **Bordley** N York
36 B4 **Bordon Camp** Hants
71 J5 **Boreham** Essex
32 E2 **Boreham** Wilts
24 B5 **Boreham Street** E Susx
69 G7 **Borehamwood** Herts
187 J8 **Boreland** D & G

258 B6 **Boreraig** Highld
96 C2 **Boreton** Shrops
282 g1 **Borgh** W Isls
283 b13 **Borgh** W Isls
278 B4 **Borgie** Highld
175 G5 **Borgue** D & G
274 F3 **Borgue** Highld
89 G6 **Borley** Essex
89 G6 **Borley Green** Essex
89 K3 **Borley Green** Suffk
258 F2 **Borneskitaig** Highld
174 F5 **Borness** D & G
150 E3 **Boroughbridge** N York
38 F2 **Borough Green** Kent
112 E1 **Borras Head** Wrexhm
116 C4 **Borrowash** Derbys
160 F5 **Borrowby** N York
171 H7 **Borrowby** N York
165 H7 **Borrowdale** Cumb
210 D3 **Borrowstoun** Falk
52 F5 **Borstal** Medway
92 D5 **Borth** Cerdgn
188 C3 **Borthwickbrae** Border
188 D3 **Borthwickshiels** Border
109 K4 **Borth-y-Gest** Gwynd
259 G7 **Borve** Highld
282 d6 **Borve** W Isls
282 g1 **Borve** W Isls
283 b13 **Borve** W Isls
147 K1 **Borwick** Lancs
156 E3 **Borwick Lodge** Cumb
156 A6 **Borwick Rails** Cumb
2 B5 **Bosavern** Cnwll
80 F6 **Bosbury** Herefs
5 H1 **Boscarne** Cnwll
10 F4 **Boscastle** Cnwll
17 M4 **Boscombe** Bmouth
33 L3 **Boscombe** Wilts
5 H4 **Boscoppa** Cnwll
20 C6 **Bosham** W Susx
20 D6 **Bosham Hoe** W Susx
54 F7 **Bosherston** Pembks
2 C4 **Boskednan** Cnwll
2 C6 **Boskenna** Cnwll
131 H6 **Bosley** Ches
4 E3 **Bosoughan** Cnwll
151 M4 **Bossall** N York
10 F4 **Bossiney** Cnwll
40 F5 **Bossingham** Kent
28 F1 **Bossington** Somset
130 C6 **Bostock Green** Ches
119 K3 **Boston** Lincs
150 F6 **Boston Spa** Leeds
2 C4 **Boswarthan** Cnwll
5 G6 **Boswinger** Cnwll
2 B4 **Botallack** Cnwll
69 J7 **Botany Bay** Gt Lon
100 B2 **Botcheston** Leics
105 L8 **Botesdale** Suffk
180 F2 **Bothal** Nthumb
48 D4 **Bothampstead** W Berk
134 D5 **Bothamsall** Notts
165 G3 **Bothel** Cumb
15 L4 **Bothenhampton** Dorset
209 J7 **Bothwell** S Lans
68 B6 **Botley** Bucks
35 G8 **Botley** Hants
66 C6 **Botley** Oxon
67 H2 **Botolph Claydon** Bucks
21 L5 **Botolphs** W Susx
40 F8 **Botolph's Bridge** Kent
117 L4 **Bottesford** Leics
143 M6 **Bottesford** N Linc
87 L3 **Bottisham** Cambs
222 F2 **Bottomcraig** Fife
138 F2 **Bottom of Hutton** Lancs
139 K5 **Bottom o' th' Moor** Bolton
140 D3 **Bottoms** Calder
2 B6 **Bottoms** Cnwll
99 H5 **Botts Green** Warwks
6 D3 **Botusfleming** Cnwll
108 D5 **Botwnnog** Gwynd
38 D4 **Bough Beech** Kent
79 G7 **Boughrood** Powys
63 H7 **Boughspring** Gloucs
84 E2 **Boughton** Nhants
104 D3 **Boughton** Norfk
134 D6 **Boughton** Notts
40 D6 **Boughton Aluph** Kent
85 J7 **Boughton End** Beds
39 J3 **Boughton Green** Kent
39 M3 **Boughton Malherbe** Kent
39 J3 **Boughton Monchelsea** Kent
40 D3 **Boughton Street** Kent
171 H7 **Boulby** R & Cl
140 F3 **Boulder Clough** Calder
18 F5 **Bouldnor** IoW
96 C6 **Bouldon** Shrops

191 K3 **Boulmer** Nthumb
55 G4 **Boulston** Pembks
135 J6 **Boultham** Lincs
87 G4 **Bourn** Cambs
118 E7 **Bourne** Lincs
70 D8 **Bournebridge** Essex
98 D6 **Bournebrook** Birm
85 J6 **Bourne End** Beds
85 K3 **Bourne End** Beds
49 L2 **Bourne End** Bucks
68 C6 **Bourne End** Herts
17 L4 **Bournemouth** Bmouth
64 C6 **Bournes Green** Gloucs
53 K2 **Bournes Green** Sthend
98 B8 **Bournheath** Worcs
63 L8 **Bournstream** Gloucs
98 D7 **Bournville** Birm
32 C5 **Bourton** Dorset
44 D6 **Bourton** N Som
47 K2 **Bourton** Oxon
96 D4 **Bourton** Shrops
46 F6 **Bourton** Wilts
83 K1 **Bourton on Dunsmore**
 Warwks
65 J1 **Bourton-on-the-Hill** Gloucs
65 H3 **Bourton-on-the-Water**
 Gloucs
225 H3 **Bousd** Ag & B
177 J7 **Boustead Hill** Cumb
156 D5 **Bouth** Cumb
149 L2 **Bouthwaite** N York
82 B3 **Bouts** Worcs
50 B3 **Boveney** Bucks
33 J7 **Boveridge** Dorset
13 J6 **Bovey Tracey** Devon
68 C6 **Bovingdon** Herts
49 K2 **Bovingdon Green** Bucks
70 D6 **Bovinger** Essex
16 F5 **Bovington** Dorset
16 F4 **Bovington Camp** Dorset
177 K7 **Bow** Cumb
8 B3 **Bow** Devon
13 G2 **Bow** Devon
51 K2 **Bow** Gt Lon
275 c6 **Bow** Ork
168 B6 **Bowbank** Dur
85 H6 **Bow Brickhill** M Keyn
64 B6 **Bowbridge** Gloucs
169 J3 **Bowburn** Dur
19 H6 **Bowcombe** IoW
14 D4 **Bowd** Devon
201 H7 **Bowden** Border
8 C5 **Bowden** Devon
46 D5 **Bowden Hill** Wilts
130 E2 **Bowdon** Traffd
280 B4 **Bower** Highld
45 H4 **Bower Ashton** Bristl
33 H6 **Bowerchalke** Wilts
46 C6 **Bowerhill** Wilts
31 G7 **Bower Hinton** Somset
89 K7 **Bower House Tye** Suffk
280 B3 **Bowermadden** Highld
114 C4 **Bowers** Staffs
53 G1 **Bowers Gifford** Essex
210 E1 **Bowershall** Fife
142 B2 **Bower's Row** Leeds
168 C7 **Bowes** Dur
147 K7 **Bowgreave** Lancs
176 D5 **Bowhouse** D & G
11 H6 **Bowithick** Cnwll
138 E6 **Bowker's Green** Lancs
200 F5 **Bowland** Border
156 F5 **Bowland Bridge** Cumb
140 C6 **Bowlee** Rochdl
80 C5 **Bowley** Herefs
80 C5 **Bowley Town** Herefs
36 D3 **Bowlhead Green** Surrey
141 J2 **Bowling** Brad
208 D4 **Bowling** W Duns
112 F2 **Bowling Bank** Wrexhm
81 J5 **Bowling Green** Worcs
156 D3 **Bowmanstead** Cumb
204 D4 **Bowmore** Ag & B
177 H6 **Bowness-on-Solway** Cumb
156 F3 **Bowness-on-Windermere**
 Cumb
222 E4 **Bow of Fife** Fife
234 D6 **Bowriefauld** Angus
165 K4 **Bowscale** Cumb
202 F5 **Bowsden** Nthumb
157 H3 **Bowston** Cumb
92 D6 **Bow Street** Cerdgn
105 L4 **Bow Street** Norfk
106 D2 **Bowthorpe** Norfk
64 B7 **Box** Gloucs
46 B5 **Box** Wilts
63 K3 **Boxbush** Gloucs
63 L4 **Boxbush** Gloucs

85 K5 **Box End** Beds
89 K7 **Boxford** Suffk
48 B4 **Boxford** W Berk
20 E5 **Boxgrove** W Susx
51 G8 **Box Hill** Surrey
53 G7 **Boxley** Kent
68 D6 **Boxmoor** Herts
11 H2 **Box's Shop** Cnwll
72 E1 **Boxted** Essex
89 K8 **Boxted** Essex
89 G5 **Boxted** Suffk
72 E1 **Boxted Cross** Essex
64 A8 **Boxwell** Gloucs
87 G2 **Boxworth** Cambs
87 G2 **Boxworth End** Cambs
88 E4 **Boyden End** Suffk
41 H2 **Boyden Gate** Kent
115 K4 **Boylestone** Derbys
268 B3 **Boyndie** Abers
269 G4 **Boyndlie** Abers
153 J2 **Boynton** E R Yk
234 F5 **Boysack** Angus
16 C1 **Boys Hill** Dorset
133 G5 **Boythorpe** Derbys
11 L4 **Boyton** Cnwll
91 J6 **Boyton** Suffk
32 F3 **Boyton** Wilts
70 F5 **Boyton Cross** Essex
88 E6 **Boyton End** Suffk
85 H3 **Bozeat** Nhants
154 d6 **Braaid** IoM
91 G2 **Brabling Green** Suffk
40 E7 **Brabourne** Kent
40 E7 **Brabourne Lees** Kent
280 D2 **Brabstermire** Highld
246 E1 **Bracadale** Highld
102 B1 **Braceborough** Lincs
135 K6 **Bracebridge Heath** Lincs
135 J6 **Bracebridge Low Fields**
 Lincs
118 D4 **Braceby** Lincs
148 F6 **Bracewell** Lancs
133 G7 **Brackenfield** Derbys
209 K5 **Brackenhirst** N Lans
165 J1 **Brackenthwaite** Cumb
150 C5 **Brackenthwaite** N York
20 C7 **Bracklesham** W Susx
239 K7 **Brackletter** Highld
84 B7 **Brackley** Nhants
84 C7 **Brackley Hatch** Nhants
49 L5 **Bracknell** Br For
220 E5 **Braco** P & K
267 K5 **Bracobrae** Moray
106 D3 **Bracon Ash** Norfk
237 L2 **Bracora** Highld
237 L2 **Bracorina** Highld
11 M4 **Bradaford** Devon
115 K1 **Bradbourne** Derbys
169 J5 **Bradbury** Dur
84 C5 **Bradden** Nhants
5 K2 **Braddock** Cnwll
114 D1 **Bradeley** C Stke
67 K7 **Bradenham** Bucks
46 E3 **Bradenstoke** Wilts
14 B1 **Bradfield** Devon
73 H1 **Bradfield** Essex
122 F5 **Bradfield** Norfk
132 E1 **Bradfield** Sheff
48 F4 **Bradfield** W Berk
89 H4 **Bradfield Combust** Suffk
130 D7 **Bradfield Green** Ches
73 H1 **Bradfield Heath** Essex
89 H4 **Bradfield St Clare** Suffk
89 H3 **Bradfield St George** Suffk
141 J1 **Bradford** Brad
11 G7 **Bradford** Cnwll
12 A1 **Bradford** Devon
180 C3 **Bradford** Nthumb
203 J6 **Bradford** Nthumb
31 K8 **Bradford Abbas** Dorset
46 B6 **Bradford Leigh** Wilts
46 B6 **Bradford-on-Avon** Wilts
30 B6 **Bradford-on-Tone** Somset
16 C4 **Bradford Peverell** Dorset
27 K4 **Bradiford** Devon
19 K6 **Brading** IoW
115 L2 **Bradley** Derbys
35 K3 **Bradley** Hants
141 J4 **Bradley** Kirk
159 J6 **Bradley** N York
145 G6 **Bradley** NE Lin
114 D7 **Bradley** Staffs
98 B4 **Bradley** Wolves
82 A3 **Bradley** Worcs
112 E1 **Bradley** Wrexhm
113 H2 **Bradley Common** Ches
30 C3 **Bradley Green** Somset
99 H3 **Bradley Green** Warwks

82 A3 **Bradley Green** Worcs
115 H3 **Bradley in the Moors** Staffs
45 J3 **Bradley Stoke** S Glos
117 G5 **Bradmore** Notts
30 E3 **Bradney** Somset
14 A2 **Bradninch** Devon
27 L4 **Bradninch** Devon
131 K8 **Bradnop** Staffs
79 K4 **Bradnor Green** Herefs
15 L4 **Bradpole** Dorset
139 L5 **Bradshaw** Bolton
141 G2 **Bradshaw** Calder
141 G5 **Bradshaw** Kirk
11 M6 **Bradstone** Devon
130 E7 **Bradwall Green** Ches
132 C3 **Bradwell** Derbys
27 J2 **Bradwell** Devon
71 K3 **Bradwell** Essex
85 G7 **Bradwell** M Keyn
107 K3 **Bradwell** Norfk
72 E5 **Bradwell-on-Sea** Essex
72 E5 **Bradwell Waterside** Essex
26 E8 **Bradworthy** Devon
263 H7 **Brae** Highld
281 d4 **Brae** Shet
209 K3 **Braeface** Falk
235 H5 **Braehead** Angus
173 K4 **Braehead** D & G
198 F3 **Braehead** S Lans
243 G5 **Braemar** Abers
261 L4 **Braemore** Highld
274 E2 **Braemore** Highld
240 B5 **Brae Roy Lodge** Highld
207 L4 **Braeside** Inver
233 L4 **Braes of Coul** Angus
267 H4 **Braes of Enzie** Moray
275 e2 **Braeswick** Ork
216 E5 **Braevallich** Ag & B
169 H6 **Brafferton** Darltn
150 F2 **Brafferton** N York
84 F3 **Brafield-on-the-Green**
 Nhants
282 f2 **Bragar** W Isls
69 H3 **Bragbury End** Herts
198 D3 **Braidwood** S Lans
115 L3 **Brailsford** Derbys
115 L3 **Brailsford Green** Derbys
63 K5 **Brain's Green** Gloucs
71 J2 **Braintree** Essex
90 D1 **Braiseworth** Suffk
34 E6 **Braishfield** Hants
149 J7 **Braithwaite** Brad
165 H6 **Braithwaite** Cumb
133 K1 **Braithwell** Donc
142 C4 **Braken Hill** Wakefd
21 L5 **Bramber** W Susx
35 G6 **Brambridge** Hants
116 E4 **Bramcote** Notts
99 L5 **Bramcote** Warwks
35 J5 **Bramdean** Hants
106 F2 **Bramerton** Norfk
69 H4 **Bramfield** Herts
107 H8 **Bramfield** Suffk
90 D6 **Bramford** Suffk
131 H3 **Bramhall** Stockp
150 F7 **Bramham** Leeds
150 C7 **Bramhope** Leeds
49 G7 **Bramley** Hants
141 K1 **Bramley** Leeds
133 K1 **Bramley** Rothm
36 F2 **Bramley** Surrey
48 F7 **Bramley Corner** Hants
49 G7 **Bramley Green** Hants
149 L4 **Bramley Head** N York
41 H4 **Bramling** Kent
13 L3 **Brampford Speke** Devon
86 E1 **Brampton** Cambs
166 F6 **Brampton** Cumb
178 C6 **Brampton** Cumb
135 G4 **Brampton** Lincs
122 E6 **Brampton** Norfk
142 C7 **Brampton** Rothm
107 J7 **Brampton** Suffk
63 J2 **Brampton Abbotts** Herefs
101 H6 **Brampton Ash** Nhants
79 L1 **Brampton Bryan** Herefs
133 J2 **Brampton-en-le-Morthen**
 Rothm
115 H5 **Bramshall** Staffs
34 C7 **Bramshaw** Hants
49 H6 **Bramshill** Hants
36 C4 **Bramshott** Hants
31 G5 **Bramwell** Somset
237 G6 **Branault** Highld
121 G3 **Brancaster** Norfk
121 H3 **Brancaster Staithe** Norfk
169 G3 **Brancepeth** Dur
266 B5 **Branchill** Moray

19 L3 **Brand End** Lincs
66 E2 **Branderburgh** Moray
53 H6 **Brandesburton** E R Yk
90 F3 **Brandeston** Suffk
63 L2 **Brand Green** Gloucs
12 G2 **Brandis Corner** Devon
22 C7 **Brandiston** Norfk
69 G3 **Brandon** Dur
18 B2 **Brandon** Lincs
90 F3 **Brandon** Nthumb
04 F6 **Brandon** Suffk
99 L8 **Brandon** Warwks
04 C5 **Brandon Bank** Norfk
04 C5 **Brandon Creek** Norfk
06 B2 **Brandon Parva** Norfk
51 J1 **Brandsby** N York
44 C8 **Brandy Wharf** Lincs
2 B5 **Brane** Cnwll
71 G2 **Bran End** Essex
17 L4 **Branksome** Poole
17 L4 **Branksome Park** Poole
34 F2 **Bransbury** Hants
35 H4 **Bransby** Lincs
14 E5 **Branscombe** Devon
81 H5 **Bransford** Worcs
18 B4 **Bransgore** Hants
44 E1 **Bransholme** C KuH
96 E8 **Bransley** Shrops
82 C1 **Branson's Cross** Worcs
17 L5 **Branston** Leics
35 K6 **Branston** Lincs
15 L7 **Branston** Staffs
35 L6 **Branston Booths** Lincs
19 J7 **Branstone** IoW
18 B1 **Brant Broughton** Lincs
90 D8 **Brantham** Suffk
64 E5 **Branthwaite** Cumb
65 J3 **Branthwaite** Cumb
44 B2 **Brantingham** E R Yk
43 G7 **Branton** Donc
90 F3 **Branton** Nthumb
50 F3 **Branton Green** N York
02 D5 **Branxton** Nthumb
29 M7 **Brassey Green** Ches
15 L1 **Brassington** Derbys
38 D2 **Brasted** Kent
51 M8 **Brasted Chart** Kent
44 F4 **Brathens** Abers
37 J6 **Bratoft** Lincs
35 J3 **Brattleby** Lincs
29 G2 **Bratton** Somset
46 C8 **Bratton** Wilts
96 E1 **Bratton** Wrekin
12 B4 **Bratton Clovelly** Devon
27 M3 **Bratton Fleming** Devon
31 L5 **Bratton Seymour** Somset
69 K2 **Braughing** Herts
70 B2 **Braughing Friars** Herts
83 M2 **Braunston** Nhants
01 H2 **Braunston** Rutlnd
00 C3 **Braunstone** Leics
27 J4 **Braunton** Devon
62 C7 **Brawby** N York
54 D2 **Brawdy** Pembks
78 D3 **Brawl** Highld
61 H1 **Braworth** N York
49 L3 **Bray** W & M
01 G6 **Braybrooke** Nhants
46 F1 **Braydon** Wilts
64 E8 **Braydon Brook** Wilts
46 E2 **Braydon Side** Wilts
28 B4 **Brayford** Devon
24 B4 **Bray's Hill** E Susx
11 L7 **Bray Shop** Cnwll
55 H2 **Braystones** Cumb
50 C6 **Braythorn** N York
42 F2 **Brayton** N York
49 L3 **Braywick** W & M
49 L4 **Braywoodside** W & M
11 K4 **Brazacott** Cnwll
41 G6 **Breach** Kent
53 H6 **Breach** Kent
68 F3 **Breachwood Green** Herts
13 J4 **Breaden Heath** Shrops
16 B4 **Breadsall** Derbys
63 L7 **Breadstone** Gloucs
79 K4 **Breadward** Herefs
3 G5 **Breage** Cnwll
50 E3 **Breakachy** Highld
62 F1 **Brealangwell Lodge** Highld
63 J6 **Bream** Gloucs
33 L7 **Breamore** Hants
44 C7 **Brean** Somset
82 d4 **Breanais** W Isls
40 F3 **Brearley** Calder
50 D4 **Brearton** N York
82 f3 **Breascleit** W Isls
82 f3 **Breasclete** W Isls

116 D5 **Breaston** Derbys
58 F3 **Brechfa** Carmth
234 F3 **Brechin** Angus
105 J4 **Breckles** Norfk
185 L5 **Breckonside** D & G
61 G2 **Brecon** Powys
131 H2 **Bredbury** Stockp
24 E4 **Brede** E Susx
80 E4 **Bredenbury** Herefs
91 G4 **Bredfield** Suffk
53 J7 **Bredgar** Kent
53 G6 **Bredhurst** Kent
81 L7 **Bredon** Worcs
81 L8 **Bredon's Hardwick** Worcs
81 L7 **Bredon's Norton** Worcs
79 L6 **Bredwardine** Herefs
116 C7 **Breedon on the Hill** Leics
210 C7 **Breich** W Loth
139 L6 **Breightmet** Bolton
143 H1 **Breighton** E R Yk
80 B7 **Breinton** Herefs
46 E4 **Bremhill** Wilts
28 B5 **Bremridge** Devon
39 H5 **Brenchley** Kent
11 L1 **Brendon** Devon
28 D1 **Brendon** Devon
29 J4 **Brendon Hill** Somset
206 D3 **Brenfield** Ag & B
282 d4 **Brenish** W Isls
180 F4 **Brenkley** N u Ty
89 J5 **Brent Eleigh** Suffk
50 F3 **Brentford** Gt Lon
117 K7 **Brentingby** Leics
30 E1 **Brent Knoll** Somset
7 K3 **Brent Mill** Devon
70 B1 **Brent Pelham** Herts
70 E8 **Brentwood** Essex
25 J2 **Brenzett** Kent
25 J2 **Brenzett Green** Kent
115 G8 **Brereton** Staffs
130 F6 **Brereton Green** Ches
130 F6 **Brereton Heath** Ches
115 G8 **Brereton Hill** Staffs
106 B7 **Bressingham** Norfk
106 B7 **Bressingham Common** Norfk
116 A7 **Bretby** Derbys
99 L7 **Bretford** Warwks
82 C6 **Bretforton** Worcs
157 J2 **Bretherdale Head** Cumb
138 F4 **Bretherton** Lancs
281 e5 **Brettabister** Shet
105 J6 **Brettenham** Norfk
89 K4 **Brettenham** Suffk
132 D4 **Bretton** Derbys
129 H7 **Bretton** Flints
70 E3 **Brewers End** Essex
51 J8 **Brewer Street** Surrey
97 K2 **Brewood** Staffs
16 F4 **Briantspuddle** Dorset
70 E2 **Brick End** Essex
69 J5 **Brickendon** Herts
68 E6 **Bricket Wood** Herts
132 F3 **Brick Houses** Sheff
71 H1 **Brickkiln Green** Essex
82 A6 **Bricklehampton** Worcs
154 f2 **Bride** IoM
164 F4 **Bridekirk** Cumb
75 L4 **Bridell** Pembks
12 C4 **Bridestowe** Devon
255 M4 **Brideswell** Abers
13 J5 **Bridford** Devon
41 G4 **Bridge** Kent
156 A6 **Bridge End** Cumb
165 L1 **Bridge End** Cumb
7 K5 **Bridge End** Devon
168 C3 **Bridge End** Dur
71 G1 **Bridge End** Essex
118 F4 **Bridge End** Lincs
50 D7 **Bridge End** Surrey
164 E5 **Bridgefoot** Cumb
87 K7 **Bridge Green** Essex
31 J6 **Bridgehampton** Somset
150 D2 **Bridge Hewick** N York
180 D8 **Bridgehill** Dur
149 L3 **Bridgehouse Gate** N York
19 K3 **Bridgemary** Hants
113 M2 **Bridgemere** Ches
255 K4 **Bridgend** Abers
204 E4 **Bridgend** Ag & B
234 E2 **Bridgend** Angus
42 D5 **Bridgend** Brdgnd
75 L3 **Bridgend** Cerdgn
165 L7 **Bridgend** Cumb
187 G4 **Bridgend** D & G
7 G5 **Bridgend** Devon
223 G5 **Bridgend** Fife
255 H5 **Bridgend** Moray

221 L2 **Bridgend** P & K
210 D4 **Bridgend** W Loth
233 L4 **Bridgend of Lintrathen** Angus
255 L8 **Bridge of Alford** Abers
220 D7 **Bridge of Allan** Stirlg
254 C7 **Bridge of Avon** Moray
254 D4 **Bridge of Avon** Moray
231 G6 **Bridge of Balgie** P & K
233 J3 **Bridge of Brewlands** Angus
254 C7 **Bridge of Brown** Highld
233 H5 **Bridge of Cally** P & K
244 E4 **Bridge of Canny** Abers
233 K4 **Bridge of Craigisla** Angus
175 J3 **Bridge of Dee** D & G
245 L2 **Bridge of Don** C Aber
253 H3 **Bridge of Dulsie** Highld
244 E6 **Bridge of Dye** Abers
221 L3 **Bridge of Earn** P & K
230 F4 **Bridge of Ericht** P & K
244 F4 **Bridge of Feugh** Abers
279 J3 **Bridge of Forss** Highld
243 K4 **Bridge of Gairn** Abers
230 F4 **Bridge of Gaur** P & K
267 M6 **Bridge of Marnoch** Abers
230 B7 **Bridge of Orchy** Ag & B
232 C2 **Bridge of Tilt** P & K
267 H4 **Bridge of Tynet** Moray
281 c6 **Bridge of Walls** Shet
208 C6 **Bridge of Weir** Rens
28 B8 **Bridge Reeve** Devon
11 K2 **Bridgerule** Devon
95 J4 **Bridges** Shrops
80 A6 **Bridge Sollers** Herefs
89 H5 **Bridge Street** Suffk
11 L4 **Bridgetown** Cnwll
29 G4 **Bridgetown** Somset
129 K5 **Bridge Trafford** Ches
45 K4 **Bridge Yate** S Glos
105 J6 **Bridgham** Norfk
97 G5 **Bridgnorth** Shrops
98 B2 **Bridgtown** Staffs
30 D3 **Bridgwater** Somset
153 K3 **Bridlington** E R Yk
15 K4 **Bridport** Dorset
63 H2 **Bridstow** Herefs
148 E8 **Brierfield** Lancs
142 B5 **Brierley** Barns
63 J4 **Brierley** Gloucs
80 C4 **Brierley** Herefs
97 L6 **Brierley Hill** Dudley
170 B5 **Brierton** Hartpl
165 J6 **Briery** Cumb
144 C6 **Brigg** N Linc
123 G6 **Briggate** Norfk
162 F1 **Briggswath** N York
164 E4 **Brigham** Cumb
165 J6 **Brigham** Cumb
153 H5 **Brigham** E R Yk
141 J3 **Brighouse** Calder
19 G7 **Brighstone** IoW
132 E7 **Brightgate** Derbys
66 A6 **Brighthampton** Oxon
132 F1 **Brightholmlee** Sheff
12 E3 **Brightley** Devon
24 C3 **Brightling** E Susx
73 G4 **Brightlingsea** Essex
22 D6 **Brighton** Br & H
4 E4 **Brighton** Cnwll
138 C7 **Brighton le Sands** Sefton
210 B3 **Brightons** Falk
48 B3 **Brightwalton** W Berk
48 B3 **Brightwalton Green** W Berk
48 B3 **Brightwalton Holt** W Berk
90 F6 **Brightwell** Suffk
67 G8 **Brightwell Baldwin** Oxon
48 E1 **Brightwell-cum-Sotwell** Oxon
67 G8 **Brightwell Upperton** Oxon
168 D8 **Brignall** Dur
219 J6 **Brig o'Turk** Stirlg
145 H7 **Brigsley** NE Lin
157 G5 **Brigsteer** Cumb
101 L6 **Brigstock** Nhants
67 G4 **Brill** Bucks
3 G5 **Brill** Cnwll
79 J5 **Brilley** Herefs
80 C2 **Brimfield** Herefs
80 C2 **Brimfield Cross** Herefs
133 H5 **Brimington** Derbys
13 J7 **Brimley** Devon
64 D4 **Brimpsfield** Gloucs
48 E6 **Brimpton** W Berk
48 E6 **Brimpton Common** W Berk
64 C6 **Brimscombe** Gloucs
129 G3 **Brimstage** Wirral
132 F3 **Brincliffe** Sheff

143 J2 **Brind** E R Yk
31 H3 **Brindham** Somset
281 c5 **Brindister** Shet
139 J3 **Brindle** Lancs
97 H1 **Brineton** Staffs
101 J5 **Bringhurst** Leics
81 G4 **Bringsty** Herefs
102 B8 **Brington** Cambs
122 A5 **Briningham** Norfk
117 J1 **Brinkely** Notts
137 G5 **Brinkhill** Lincs
88 C4 **Brinkley** Cambs
99 L7 **Brinklow** Warwks
46 E2 **Brinkworth** Wilts
139 J3 **Brinscall** Lancs
44 E8 **Brinscombe** Somset
44 F6 **Brinsea** N Som
116 D2 **Brinsley** Notts
80 B6 **Brinsop** Herefs
133 H2 **Brinsworth** Rothm
122 A4 **Brinton** Norfk
275 c3 **Brinyan** Ork
178 A8 **Brisco** Cumb
121 L7 **Brisley** Norfk
45 J5 **Brislington** Bristl
40 B7 **Brissenden Green** Kent
45 H4 **Bristol** Bristl
122 B5 **Briston** Norfk
7 G2 **Brisworthy** Devon
140 C3 **Britannia** Lancs
33 L5 **Britford** Wilts
61 J6 **Brithdir** Caerph
110 E7 **Brithdir** Gwynd
52 F7 **British Legion Village** Kent
57 K6 **Briton Ferry** Neath
67 G8 **Britwell Salome** Oxon
8 D4 **Brixham** Torbay
7 G4 **Brixton** Devon
51 J4 **Brixton** Gt Lon
32 E3 **Brixton Deverill** Wilts
84 E1 **Brixworth** Nhants
65 L5 **Brize Norton** Oxon
81 K2 **Broad Alley** Worcs
47 H1 **Broad Blunsdon** Swindn
131 K1 **Broadbottom** Tamesd
20 D6 **Broadbridge** W Susx
37 H4 **Broadbridge Heath** W Susx
82 E7 **Broad Campden** Gloucs
141 H4 **Broad Carr** Calder
33 H5 **Broad Chalke** Wilts
140 C3 **Broad Clough** Lancs
14 A3 **Broadclyst** Devon
208 B4 **Broadfield** Inver
55 K6 **Broadfield** Pembks
247 K4 **Broadford** Highld
39 H5 **Broad Ford** Kent
37 G6 **Broadford Bridge** W Susx
187 K4 **Broadgairhill** Border
89 K3 **Broadgrass Green** Suffk
88 D3 **Broad Green** Cambs
72 C2 **Broad Green** Essex
81 H4 **Broad Green** Worcs
82 A1 **Broad Green** Worcs
202 D2 **Broadhaugh** Border
54 D4 **Broad Haven** Pembks
130 E2 **Broadheath** Traffd
80 F2 **Broadheath** Worcs
14 C2 **Broadhembury** Devon
8 B2 **Broadhempston** Devon
104 B8 **Broad Hill** Cambs
47 G4 **Broad Hinton** Wilts
135 H5 **Broadholme** Lincs
24 F3 **Broadland Row** E Susx
56 C3 **Broadlay** Carmth
48 B6 **Broad Layings** Hants
70 B5 **Broadley** Essex
140 C4 **Broadley** Lancs
267 H4 **Broadley** Moray
70 B5 **Broadley Common** Essex
82 D6 **Broad Marston** Worcs
16 D5 **Broadmayne** Dorset
114 C2 **Broad Meadow** Staffs
35 J2 **Broadmere** Hants
63 J4 **Broadmoor** Gloucs
55 J5 **Broadmoor** Pembks
13 G2 **Broadnymett** Devon
155 K4 **Broadoak** Cumb
15 K3 **Broadoak** Dorset
23 K3 **Broad Oak** E Susx
24 E3 **Broad Oak** E Susx
63 K4 **Broadoak** Gloucs
49 H8 **Broad Oak** Hants
62 F3 **Broad Oak** Herefs
41 G3 **Broad Oak** Kent
139 G8 **Broad Oak** St Hel
129 J7 **Broadoak** Wrexhm
106 F8 **Broad Road** Suffk
71 G4 **Broad's Green** Essex

41 L2	**Broadstairs** Kent	163 G6	**Brompton** N York	144 B2	**Brough** E R Yk	31 H7	**Brympton** Somset

41 L2 **Broadstairs** Kent
63 G6 **Broadstone** Mons
17 K3 **Broadstone** Poole
96 C5 **Broadstone** Shrops
24 F4 **Broad Street** E Susx
70 E4 **Broad Street** Essex
39 L2 **Broad Street** Kent
53 G4 **Broad Street** Medway
47 G7 **Broad Street** Wilts
72 B5 **Broad Street Green** Essex
47 G3 **Broad Town** Wilts
81 H4 **Broadwas** Worcs
69 H3 **Broadwater** Herts
21 K6 **Broadwater** W Susx
97 J7 **Broadwaters** Worcs
56 B3 **Broadway** Carmth
56 C3 **Broadway** Carmth
54 E4 **Broadway** Pembks
30 D7 **Broadway** Somset
107 H7 **Broadway** Suffk
82 C7 **Broadway** Worcs
63 H5 **Broadwell** Gloucs
65 J2 **Broadwell** Gloucs
65 K6 **Broadwell** Oxon
83 K2 **Broadwell** Warwks
16 C5 **Broadwey** Dorset
15 K2 **Broadwindsor** Dorset
12 E1 **Broadwood Kelly** Devon
12 A4 **Broadwoodwidger** Devon
79 L6 **Brobury** Herefs
259 K7 **Brochel** Highld
147 K7 **Brock** Lancs
81 H4 **Brockamin** Worcs
35 J7 **Brockbridge** Hants
106 E7 **Brockdish** Norfk
97 K8 **Brockencote** Worcs
18 D3 **Brockenhurst** Hants
198 D5 **Brocketsbrae** S Lans
90 D2 **Brockford Green** Suffk
90 D2 **Brockford Street** Suffk
84 C3 **Brockhall** Nhants
37 J1 **Brockham** Surrey
64 D2 **Brockhampton** Gloucs
64 F3 **Brockhampton** Gloucs
20 B5 **Brockhampton** Hants
63 H1 **Brockhampton** Herefs
16 D1 **Brockhampton Green** Dorset
141 J5 **Brockholes** Kirk
133 G6 **Brockhurst** Derbys
100 A6 **Brockhurst** Warwks
165 J2 **Brocklebank** Cumb
144 E5 **Brocklesby** Lincs
44 F5 **Brockley** N Som
89 G1 **Brockley** Suffk
88 E6 **Brockley Green** Suffk
89 G4 **Brockley Green** Suffk
166 C3 **Brockleymoor** Cumb
97 K5 **Brockmoor** Dudley
12 B3 **Brockscombe** Devon
48 D6 **Brock's Green** Hants
95 H3 **Brockton** Shrops
95 H6 **Brockton** Shrops
96 D4 **Brockton** Shrops
97 G3 **Brockton** Shrops
114 C5 **Brockton** Staffs
63 G6 **Brockweir** Gloucs
35 K5 **Brockwood Park** Hants
64 C4 **Brockworth** Gloucs
5 G1 **Brocton** Cnwll
114 F7 **Brocton** Staffs
195 G4 **Brodick** N Ayrs
264 F8 **Brodie** Moray
142 D6 **Brodsworth** Donc
259 H3 **Brogaig** Highld
85 J7 **Brogborough** Beds
46 D1 **Brokenborough** Wilts
130 D5 **Broken Cross** Ches
131 H5 **Broken Cross** Ches
46 B8 **Brokerswood** Wilts
129 H3 **Bromborough** Wirral
106 C8 **Brome** Suffk
106 C8 **Brome Street** Suffk
91 G5 **Bromeswell** Suffk
165 G1 **Bromfield** Cumb
96 B8 **Bromfield** Shrops
85 K5 **Bromham** Beds
46 D6 **Bromham** Wilts
141 M7 **Bromley** Barns
97 K5 **Bromley** Dudley
51 L5 **Bromley** Gt Lon
97 G4 **Bromley** Shrops
51 L5 **Bromley Common** Gt Lon
72 F2 **Bromley Cross** Essex
40 C8 **Bromley Green** Kent
95 H3 **Bromlow** Shrops
53 G5 **Brompton** Medway
160 E3 **Brompton** N York

163 G6 **Brompton** N York
96 C2 **Brompton** Shrops
160 B3 **Brompton-on-Swale** N York
29 K4 **Brompton Ralph** Somset
29 G4 **Brompton Regis** Somset
63 J2 **Bromsash** Herefs
81 G8 **Bromsberrow** Gloucs
81 G8 **Bromsberrow Heath** Gloucs
81 M1 **Bromsgrove** Worcs
114 B8 **Bromstead Heath** Staffs
80 F4 **Bromyard** Herefs
80 F4 **Bromyard Downs** Herefs
110 D5 **Bronaber** Gwynd
77 H2 **Bronant** Cerdgn
96 C6 **Broncroft** Shrops
76 B6 **Brongest** Cerdgn
113 H3 **Bronington** Wrexhm
79 G8 **Bronllys** Powys
58 D4 **Bronwydd** Carmth
79 J6 **Bronydd** Powys
112 C4 **Bronygarth** Shrops
56 A3 **Brook** Carmth
34 C8 **Brook** Hants
34 D5 **Brook** Hants
18 F6 **Brook** IoW
40 E6 **Brook** Kent
36 D3 **Brook** Surrey
37 G2 **Brook** Surrey
106 F3 **Brooke** Norfk
101 J2 **Brooke** Rutlnd
145 G8 **Brookenby** Lincs
86 B3 **Brook End** Beds
86 D5 **Brook End** Beds
86 B1 **Brook End** Beds
85 H6 **Brook End** M Keyn
208 C6 **Brookfield** Rens
66 F7 **Brookhampton** Oxon
31 K5 **Brookhampton** Somset
34 C7 **Brook Hill** Hants
128 C6 **Brook House** Denbgs
147 K3 **Brookhouse** Lancs
133 K2 **Brookhouse** Rothm
130 F7 **Brookhouse Green** Ches
131 K2 **Brookhouses** Derbys
25 J2 **Brookland** Kent
130 F2 **Brooklands** Traffd
69 H6 **Brookmans Park** Herts
94 E3 **Brooks** Powys
117 H8 **Brooksby** Leics
41 J2 **Brooks End** Kent
37 H6 **Brooks Green** W Susx
70 E8 **Brook Street** Essex
40 B8 **Brook Street** Kent
89 G5 **Brook Street** Suffk
22 D2 **Brook Street** W Susx
64 B4 **Brookthorpe** Gloucs
104 E4 **Brookville** Norfk
50 B7 **Brookwood** Surrey
86 D6 **Broom** Beds
169 H2 **Broom** Dur
133 J1 **Broom** Rothm
82 C4 **Broom** Warwks
107 G5 **Broome** Norfk
95 K7 **Broome** Shrops
97 K7 **Broome** Worcs
130 D3 **Broomedge** Warrtn
191 G4 **Broome Park** Nthumb
21 K3 **Broomer's Corner** W Susx
21 H3 **Broomershill** W Susx
71 H5 **Broomfield** Essex
39 L3 **Broomfield** Kent
41 G2 **Broomfield** Kent
30 B4 **Broomfield** Somset
112 F7 **Broomfields** Shrops
143 M2 **Broomfleet** E R Yk
121 L6 **Broom Green** Norfk
50 B5 **Broomhall** W & M
180 B6 **Broomhaugh** Nthumb
142 C7 **Broom Hill** Barns
17 K2 **Broom Hill** Dorset
116 F2 **Broom Hill** Notts
191 J6 **Broomhill** Nthumb
97 L8 **Broomhill** Worcs
113 K2 **Broomhill Green** Ches
180 C6 **Broomley** Nthumb
81 G8 **Broom's Green** Gloucs
121 J6 **Broomsthorpe** Norfk
40 D3 **Broom Street** Kent
274 B7 **Brora** Highld
96 F3 **Broseley** Shrops
119 J8 **Brotherhouse Bar** Lincs
167 L3 **Brotherlee** Dur
119 J2 **Brothertoft** Lincs
142 D3 **Brotherton** N York
170 F6 **Brotton** R & Cl
279 J4 **Broubster** Highld
167 J7 **Brough** Cumb
132 D3 **Brough** Derbys

144 B2 **Brough** E R Yk
280 B2 **Brough** Highld
135 G7 **Brough** Notts
281 f5 **Brough** Shet
113 J3 **Broughall** Shrops
281 f3 **Brough Lodge** Shet
167 J8 **Brough Sowerby** Cumb
199 K6 **Broughton** Border
67 K4 **Broughton** Bucks
102 F7 **Broughton** Cambs
129 H7 **Broughton** Flints
34 C4 **Broughton** Hants
139 G1 **Broughton** Lancs
85 H7 **Broughton** M Keyn
144 B6 **Broughton** N Linc
149 G5 **Broughton** N York
162 D8 **Broughton** N York
101 H8 **Broughton** Nhants
83 K7 **Broughton** Oxon
140 B7 **Broughton** Salfd
114 B5 **Broughton** Staffs
42 D7 **Broughton** V Glam
100 C5 **Broughton Astley** Leics
156 C6 **Broughton Beck** Cumb
46 C6 **Broughton Gifford** Wilts
81 M3 **Broughton Green** Worcs
81 L4 **Broughton Hackett** Worcs
156 B5 **Broughton-in-Furness** Cumb
174 C6 **Broughton Mains** D & G
156 B5 **Broughton Mills** Cumb
164 E4 **Broughton Moor** Cumb
65 K6 **Broughton Poggs** Oxon
156 B5 **Broughton Tower** Cumb
223 H1 **Broughty Ferry** C Dund
156 C7 **Brow End** Cumb
158 B2 **Brownber** Cumb
35 J3 **Brown Candover** Hants
138 D5 **Brown Edge** Lancs
114 E1 **Brown Edge** Staffs
129 K6 **Brown Heath** Ches
113 G5 **Brownheath** Shrops
256 F4 **Brownhill** Abers
223 J4 **Brownhills** Fife
98 D2 **Brownhills** Wsall
191 H2 **Brownieside** Nthumb
48 E7 **Browninghill Green** Hants
131 G8 **Brown Lees** Staffs
131 G7 **Brownlow Heath** Ches
164 D6 **Brownrigg** Cumb
177 G8 **Brownrigg** Cumb
98 D5 **Brown's Green** Birm
26 E5 **Brownsham** Devon
64 C6 **Browns Hill** Gloucs
100 B7 **Brownsover** Warwks
7 K4 **Brownston** Devon
90 C3 **Brown Street** Suffk
120 E7 **Brow-of-the-Hill** Norfk
107 K3 **Browston Green** Norfk
163 G4 **Broxa** N York
69 K5 **Broxbourne** Herts
212 F3 **Broxburn** E Loth
210 E4 **Broxburn** W Loth
191 J3 **Broxfield** Nthumb
70 E2 **Broxted** Essex
113 H1 **Broxton** Ches
23 G4 **Broyle Side** E Susx
280 D8 **Bruan** Highld
232 B2 **Bruar** P & K
264 E3 **Brucefield** Highld
207 J7 **Bruchag** Ag & B
129 K7 **Bruera** Ches
65 K3 **Bruern Abbey** Oxon
204 C4 **Bruichladdich** Ag & B
91 H2 **Bruisyard** Suffk
91 H2 **Bruisyard Street** Suffk
143 M6 **Brumby** N Linc
132 B7 **Brund** Staffs
107 G2 **Brundall** Norfk
91 G1 **Brundish** Suffk
91 G1 **Brundish Street** Suffk
2 D4 **Brunnion** Cnwll
95 J6 **Brunslow** Shrops
180 F4 **Brunswick Village** N u Ty
141 L2 **Bruntcliffe** Leeds
149 J6 **Brunthwaite** Brad
100 D5 **Bruntingthorpe** Leics
222 E3 **Brunton** Fife
191 J1 **Brunton** Nthumb
47 K7 **Brunton** Wilts
29 G5 **Brushford** Somset
12 F1 **Brushford Barton** Devon
31 L4 **Bruton** Somset
81 K2 **Bryan's Green** Worcs
17 G1 **Bryanston** Dorset
67 L7 **Bryant's Bottom** Bucks
177 G5 **Brydekirk** D & G
112 D1 **Brymbo** Wrexhm

31 H7 **Brympton** Somset
57 G5 **Bryn** Carmth
130 B5 **Bryn** Ches
42 B3 **Bryn** Neath
95 H6 **Bryn** Shrops
139 H7 **Bryn** Wigan
59 K6 **Brynamman** Carmth
75 J5 **Brynberian** Pembks
57 L6 **Brynbryddan** Neath
110 B4 **Bryn-bwbach** Gwynd
42 F5 **Bryncae** Rhondd
42 D5 **Bryncethin** Brdgnd
109 H3 **Bryncir** Gwynd
57 K5 **Bryn-coch** Neath
108 C5 **Bryncroes** Gwynd
92 D3 **Bryncrug** Gwynd
124 F5 **Bryn Du** IoA
110 D5 **Bryn-Eden** Gwynd
112 A2 **Bryneglwys** Denbgs
112 D3 **Brynfields** Wrexhm
128 E5 **Brynford** Flints
139 J7 **Bryn Gates** Wigan
42 F4 **Bryn Golau** Rhondd
124 F4 **Bryngwran** IoA
62 D5 **Bryngwyn** Mons
79 H5 **Bryngwyn** Powys
75 G4 **Bryn-Henllan** Pembks
76 B5 **Brynhoffnant** Cerdgn
138 E2 **Bryning** Lancs
61 K6 **Brynithel** Blae G
61 J5 **Brynmawr** Blae G
108 D5 **Bryn-mawr** Gwynd
42 D5 **Brynmenyn** Brdgnd
57 H6 **Brynmill** Swans
42 F5 **Brynna** Rhondd
112 B3 **Bryn-newydd** Denbgs
94 D3 **Bryn-penarth** Powys
125 K7 **Brynrefail** Gwynd
125 H2 **Brynrefail** IoA
42 F5 **Brynsadler** Rhondd
111 L2 **Bryn Saith Marchog** Denbgs
125 H6 **Brynsiencyn** IoA
125 J3 **Brynteg** IoA
128 F6 **Bryn-y-bal** Flints
127 G4 **Bryn-y-Maen** Conwy
112 D3 **Bryn-yr-Eos** Wrexhm
246 F4 **Bualintur** Highld
128 E4 **Buarth-draw** Flints
83 J1 **Bubbenhall** Warwks
151 M8 **Bubwith** E R Yk
208 D1 **Buchanan Smithy** Stirlg
269 L6 **Buchanhaven** Abers
221 G2 **Buchanty** P & K
220 C6 **Buchany** Stirlg
219 J8 **Buchlyvie** Stirlg
165 L1 **Buckabank** Cumb
86 D2 **Buckden** Cambs
159 G2 **Buckden** N York
107 G2 **Buckenham** Norfk
14 D2 **Buckerell** Devon
7 L2 **Buckfast** Devon
7 L2 **Buckfastleigh** Devon
222 F7 **Buckhaven** Fife
63 G4 **Buckholt** Mons
32 C6 **Buckhorn Weston** Dorset
69 L8 **Buckhurst Hill** Essex
267 J3 **Buckie** Moray
84 D8 **Buckingham** Bucks
67 L4 **Buckland** Bucks
7 K6 **Buckland** Devon
82 C8 **Buckland** Gloucs
18 E4 **Buckland** Hants
87 G8 **Buckland** Herts
41 J6 **Buckland** Kent
65 M7 **Buckland** Oxon
37 K1 **Buckland** Surrey
27 G6 **Buckland Brewer** Devon
68 A5 **Buckland Common** Bucks
32 C1 **Buckland Dinham** Somset
12 B1 **Buckland Filleigh** Devon
13 G7 **Buckland in the Moor** Devon
6 F1 **Buckland Monachorum** Devon
16 D2 **Buckland Newton** Dorset
16 C6 **Buckland Ripers** Dorset
30 C8 **Buckland St Mary** Somset
7 L5 **Buckland-Tout-Saints** Devon
48 E5 **Bucklebury** W Berk
18 F4 **Bucklers Hard** Hants
90 F6 **Bucklesham** Suffk
129 G7 **Buckley** Flints
82 E2 **Buckley Green** Warwks
130 E3 **Bucklow Hill** Ches
118 A7 **Buckminster** Leics
114 E2 **Bucknall** C Stke

Bucknall - Byfleet 299

136 C6 **Bucknall** Lincs
66 E2 **Bucknell** Oxon
95 J8 **Bucknell** Shrops
267 H3 **Buckpool** Moray
245 K2 **Bucksburn** C Aber
26 F6 **Buck's Cross** Devon
37 G4 **Bucks Green** W Susx
68 D7 **Bucks Hill** Herts
36 B3 **Bucks Horn Oak** Hants
26 F6 **Buck's Mills** Devon
153 K1 **Buckton** E R Yk
95 J8 **Buckton** Herefs
203 H5 **Buckton** Nthumb
102 C8 **Buckworth** Cambs
134 C5 **Budby** Notts
114 B2 **Buddileigh** Staffs
223 J1 **Buddon** Angus
11 J2 **Budd's Titson** Cnwll
11 H1 **Bude** Cnwll
6 C3 **Budge's Shop** Cnwll
14 A2 **Budlake** Devon
203 J6 **Budle** Nthumb
14 C6 **Budleigh Salterton** Devon
23 H3 **Budlett's Common** E Susx
3 K5 **Budock Water** Cnwll
113 L3 **Buerton** Ches
84 D4 **Bugbrooke** Nhants
8 B5 **Bugford** Devon
131 G7 **Buglawton** Ches
5 G3 **Bugle** Cnwll
32 C6 **Bugley** Dorset
152 B4 **Bugthorpe** E R Yk
96 E2 **Buildwas** Shrops
78 E4 **Builth Road** Powys
78 E5 **Builth Wells** Powys
68 B4 **Bulbourne** Herts
33 J5 **Bulbridge** Wilts
118 D6 **Bulby** Lincs
279 H3 **Buldoo** Highld
33 L2 **Bulford** Wilts
33 L2 **Bulford Camp** Wilts
113 J1 **Bulkeley** Ches
99 K6 **Bulkington** Warwks
46 D7 **Bulkington** Wilts
27 G8 **Bulkworthy** Devon
160 F4 **Bullamoor** N York
125 G1 **Bull Bay** IoA
116 B1 **Bullbridge** Derbys
49 L5 **Bullbrook** Br For
69 G6 **Bullen's Green** Herts
63 M3 **Bulley** Gloucs
164 E3 **Bullgill** Cumb
80 C7 **Bullinghope** Herefs
34 F3 **Bullington** Hants
136 A4 **Bullington** Lincs
84 F6 **Bullington End** M Keyn
41 G2 **Bullockstone** Kent
69 H4 **Bull's Green** Herts
107 J4 **Bull's Green** Norfk
89 G7 **Bulmer** Essex
151 L2 **Bulmer** N York
89 G7 **Bulmer Tye** Essex
52 D2 **Bulphan** Thurr
14 E4 **Bulstone** Devon
68 C6 **Bulstrode** Herts
24 D5 **Bulverhythe** E Susx
257 G3 **Bulwark** Abers
116 F3 **Bulwell** C Nott
101 L4 **Bulwick** Nhants
69 L6 **Bumble's Green** Essex
237 J3 **Bunacaimb** Highld
239 K6 **Bunarkaig** Highld
130 A8 **Bunbury** Ches
130 A8 **Bunbury Heath** Ches
251 H3 **Bunchrew** Highld
21 K4 **Buncton** W Susx
248 E6 **Bundalloch** Highld
226 D8 **Bunessan** Ag & B
107 G5 **Bungay** Suffk
119 J1 **Bunker's Hill** Lincs
204 F2 **Bunnahabhain** Ag & B
117 G5 **Bunny** Notts
250 C5 **Buntait** Highld
69 K1 **Buntingford** Herts
106 C5 **Bunwell** Norfk
106 C4 **Bunwell Street** Norfk
115 L4 **Bupton** Derbys
131 L5 **Burbage** Derbys
99 L5 **Burbage** Leics
47 K6 **Burbage** Wilts
79 L3 **Burcher** Herefs
39 G7 **Burchett's Green** E Susx
49 K3 **Burchett's Green** W & M
33 J5 **Burcombe** Wilts
66 E7 **Burcot** Oxon
82 A1 **Burcot** Worcs
97 G4 **Burcote** Shrops
67 K4 **Burcott** Bucks
67 L2 **Burcott** Bucks
152 D3 **Burdale** N York
89 H8 **Bures** Essex
65 K5 **Burford** Oxon
80 D2 **Burford** Shrops
226 D3 **Burg** Ag & B
106 B8 **Burgate** Suffk
36 A5 **Burgates** Hants
68 F1 **Burge End** Herts
22 E3 **Burgess Hill** W Susx
90 F5 **Burgh** Suffk
177 K7 **Burgh by Sands** Cumb
107 K2 **Burgh Castle** Norfk
48 C6 **Burghclere** Hants
266 C2 **Burghead** Moray
49 G5 **Burghfield** W Berk
49 G5 **Burghfield Common** W Berk
51 H7 **Burgh Heath** Surrey
24 C2 **Burgh Hill** E Susx
80 B6 **Burghill** Herefs
137 J6 **Burgh le Marsh** Lincs
122 E6 **Burgh next Aylsham** Norfk
136 D2 **Burgh on Bain** Lincs
123 J8 **Burgh St Margaret** Norfk
107 K5 **Burgh St Peter** Norfk
142 E5 **Burghwallis** Donc
52 F6 **Burham** Kent
20 B3 **Buriton** Hants
113 K1 **Burland** Ches
10 D8 **Burlawn** Cnwll
64 C6 **Burleigh** Gloucs
29 K7 **Burlescombe** Devon
16 E3 **Burleston** Dorset
8 B5 **Burlestone** Devon
18 C3 **Burley** Hants
101 J1 **Burley** Rutlnd
96 B7 **Burley** Shrops
113 K3 **Burleydam** Ches
80 E6 **Burley Gate** Herefs
149 L6 **Burley in Wharfedale** Brad
18 C3 **Burley Lawn** Hants
18 B3 **Burley Street** Hants
149 L7 **Burley Wood Head** Brad
107 H1 **Burlingham Green** Norfk
79 J4 **Burlingjobb** Powys
97 H1 **Burlington** Shrops
113 G6 **Burlton** Shrops
25 L1 **Burmarsh** Kent
83 G7 **Burmington** Warwks
142 F2 **Burn** N York
131 G1 **Burnage** Manch
115 M5 **Burnaston** Derbys
166 C7 **Burnbanks** Cumb
210 A7 **Burnbrae** N Lans
152 C6 **Burnby** E R Yk
142 A8 **Burn Cross** Sheff
21 G6 **Burndell** W Susx
139 L6 **Burnden** Bolton
140 D5 **Burnedge** Rochdl
157 H3 **Burneside** Cumb
160 D5 **Burneston** N York
45 K6 **Burnett** BaNES
188 C4 **Burnfoot** Border
188 F3 **Burnfoot** Border
177 K1 **Burnfoot** D & G
186 E7 **Burnfoot** D & G
188 C6 **Burnfoot** D & G
221 H6 **Burnfoot** P & K
50 A3 **Burnham** Bucks
144 D4 **Burnham** N Linc
121 H3 **Burnham Deepdale** Norfk
69 H4 **Burnham Green** Herts
121 H3 **Burnham Market** Norfk
121 H3 **Burnham Norton** Norfk
72 D7 **Burnham-on-Crouch** Essex
30 D1 **Burnham-on-Sea** Somset
121 J3 **Burnham Overy** Norfk
121 J3 **Burnham Overy Staithe** Norfk
121 J3 **Burnham Thorpe** Norfk
257 L3 **Burnhaven** Abers
186 C7 **Burnhead** D & G
256 C7 **Burnhervie** Abers
97 H3 **Burnhill Green** Staffs
169 G1 **Burnhope** Dur
196 D1 **Burnhouse** N Ayrs
163 H4 **Burniston** N York
140 C1 **Burnley** Lancs
181 H8 **Burnmoor** Dur
213 L6 **Burnmouth** Border
147 G7 **Burn Naze** Lancs
220 C6 **Burn of Cambus** Stirlg
180 E7 **Burnopfield** Dur
178 C7 **Burnrigg** Cumb
149 J3 **Burnsall** N York
234 C3 **Burnside** Angus
234 D5 **Burnside** Angus
222 B5 **Burnside** Fife
266 D2 **Burnside** Moray
210 E4 **Burnside** W Loth
234 C8 **Burnside of Duntrune** Angus
50 D8 **Burntcommon** Surrey
115 L5 **Burntheath** Derbys
72 F2 **Burnt Heath** Essex
48 E4 **Burnt Hill** W Berk
3 K4 **Burnthouse** Cnwll
168 E6 **Burnt Houses** Dur
211 H2 **Burntisland** Fife
23 H2 **Burnt Oak** E Susx
98 D2 **Burntwood** Staffs
98 D2 **Burntwood Green** Staffs
150 C4 **Burnt Yates** N York
12 C6 **Burnville** Devon
30 B7 **Burnworthy** Somset
50 C8 **Burpham** Surrey
21 H5 **Burpham** W Susx
181 G4 **Burradon** N Tyne
190 D5 **Burradon** Nthumb
281 f1 **Burrafirth** Shet
3 H4 **Burras** Cnwll
6 E2 **Burraton** Cnwll
281 e4 **Burravoe** Shet
166 F7 **Burrells** Cumb
233 J7 **Burrelton** P & K
15 H1 **Burridge** Devon
27 K4 **Burridge** Devon
19 J2 **Burridge** Hants
160 C5 **Burrill** N York
143 L6 **Burringham** N Linc
27 L7 **Burrington** Devon
80 B1 **Burrington** Herefs
44 F7 **Burrington** N Som
88 C4 **Burrough End** Cambs
88 C4 **Burrough Green** Cambs
101 G1 **Burrough on the Hill** Leics
157 K7 **Burrow** Lancs
29 G2 **Burrow** Somset
30 E5 **Burrow Bridge** Somset
50 B6 **Burrowhill** Surrey
37 G2 **Burrows Cross** Surrey
56 E6 **Burry** Swans
56 E6 **Burry Green** Swans
56 E5 **Burry Port** Carmth
138 E5 **Burscough** Lancs
138 F5 **Burscough Bridge** Lancs
143 K1 **Bursea** E R Yk
153 H6 **Burshill** E R Yk
19 H2 **Bursledon** Hants
114 D2 **Burslem** C Stke
90 C6 **Burstall** Suffk
15 K2 **Burstock** Dorset
106 C6 **Burston** Norfk
114 E5 **Burston** Staffs
37 M3 **Burstow** Surrey
145 G2 **Burstwick** E R Yk
158 F5 **Burtersett** N York
178 D6 **Burtholme** Cumb
88 F2 **Burthorpe Green** Suffk
165 M1 **Burthwaite** Cumb
4 E4 **Burthy** Cnwll
30 F2 **Burtle Hill** Somset
119 J4 **Burtoft** Lincs
129 H5 **Burton** Ches
129 L7 **Burton** Ches
16 D4 **Burton** Dorset
18 B5 **Burton** Dorset
135 J5 **Burton** Lincs
203 K6 **Burton** Nthumb
55 G5 **Burton** Pembks
30 B2 **Burton** Somset
31 H8 **Burton** Somset
32 D4 **Burton** Wilts
46 B3 **Burton** Wilts
153 H3 **Burton Agnes** E R Yk
15 L4 **Burton Bradstock** Dorset
118 C6 **Burton Coggles** Lincs
83 J5 **Burton Dassett** Warwks
70 D2 **Burton End** Essex
88 D6 **Burton End** Suffk
153 H2 **Burton Fleming** E R Yk
99 H8 **Burton Green** Warwks
129 H7 **Burton Green** Wrexhm
99 L5 **Burton Hastings** Warwks
157 H7 **Burton-in-Kendal** Cumb
148 A2 **Burton in Lonsdale** N York
117 H3 **Burton Joyce** Notts
101 K8 **Burton Latimer** Nhants
117 K8 **Burton Lazars** Leics
150 D3 **Burton Leonard** N York
117 G7 **Burton on the Wolds** Leics
100 E4 **Burton Overy** Leics
118 F3 **Burton Pedwardine** Lincs
145 H2 **Burton Pidsea** E R Yk
142 D2 **Burton Salmon** N York
71 K2 **Burton's Green** Essex
143 L4 **Burton upon Stather** N Linc
115 L6 **Burton upon Trent** Staffs
135 J5 **Burton Waters** Lincs
130 A1 **Burtonwood** Warrtn
129 L8 **Burwardsley** Ches
96 E6 **Burwarton** Shrops
24 B2 **Burwash** E Susx
23 L3 **Burwash Common** E Susx
23 L3 **Burwash Weald** E Susx
88 B2 **Burwell** Cambs
137 G4 **Burwell** Lincs
125 G1 **Burwen** IoA
275 c6 **Burwick** Ork
140 B5 **Bury** Bury
102 F6 **Bury** Cambs
29 G5 **Bury** Somset
21 G4 **Bury** W Susx
86 C8 **Bury End** Beds
70 C3 **Bury Green** Herts
89 G2 **Bury St Edmunds** Suffk
152 B3 **Burythorpe** N York
208 F7 **Busby** E Rens
160 E6 **Busby Stoop** N York
65 J7 **Buscot** Oxon
235 J2 **Bush** Abers
11 J1 **Bush** Cnwll
80 B5 **Bush Bank** Herefs
97 L3 **Bushbury** Wolves
100 E3 **Bushby** Leics
68 E8 **Bushey** Herts
68 F8 **Bushey Heath** Herts
106 E6 **Bush Green** Norfk
89 H4 **Bush Green** Suffk
69 J7 **Bush Hill Park** Gt Lon
81 K8 **Bushley** Worcs
81 K8 **Bushley Green** Worcs
86 C3 **Bushmead** Beds
46 F3 **Bushton** Wilts
166 E2 **Busk** Cumb
135 M3 **Buslingthorpe** Lincs
64 C6 **Bussage** Gloucs
30 E4 **Bussex** Somset
140 D3 **Butcher Hill** Calder
23 J2 **Butcher's Cross** E Susx
45 G6 **Butcombe** N Som
31 H4 **Butleigh** Somset
31 H4 **Butleigh Wootton** Somset
67 K5 **Butler's Cross** Bucks
116 F2 **Butler's Hill** Notts
83 H5 **Butlers Marston** Warwks
91 J5 **Butley** Suffk
91 J5 **Butley High Corner** Suffk
151 M4 **Buttercrambe** N York
213 H6 **Butterdean** Border
168 E5 **Butterknowle** Dur
14 A1 **Butterleigh** Devon
116 C1 **Butterley** Derbys
165 G7 **Buttermere** Cumb
47 M6 **Buttermere** Wilts
114 C2 **Butters Green** Staffs
141 H2 **Buttershaw** Brad
233 G6 **Butterstone** P & K
114 C3 **Butterton** Staffs
131 L8 **Butterton** Staffs
169 K5 **Butterwick** Dur
119 L3 **Butterwick** Lincs
152 F2 **Butterwick** N York
162 C7 **Butterwick** N York
113 L1 **Butt Green** Ches
95 G2 **Buttington** Powys
97 G7 **Buttonbridge** Shrops
97 G7 **Buttonoak** Shrops
19 G2 **Buttsash** Hants
11 K2 **Buttsbear Cross** Cnwll
71 J6 **Butt's Green** Essex
89 K4 **Buxhall** Suffk
89 K3 **Buxhall Fen Street** Suffk
23 H3 **Buxted** E Susx
131 L5 **Buxton** Derbys
122 E7 **Buxton** Norfk
122 D7 **Buxton Heath** Norfk
61 J3 **Bwlch** Powys
112 C1 **Bwlchgwyn** Wrexhm
77 G3 **Bwlchllan** Cerdgn
58 C4 **Bwlchnewydd** Carmth
108 E6 **Bwlchtocyn** Gwynd
112 B8 **Bwlch-y-cibau** Powys
112 B7 **Bwlch-y-Ddar** Powys
76 D5 **Bwlchyfadfa** Cerdgn
94 C4 **Bwlch-y-ffridd** Powys
75 M5 **Bwlch-y-groes** Pembks
57 G5 **Bwlchymyrdd** Swans
94 B8 **Bwlch-y-sarnau** Powys
180 F7 **Byermoor** Gatesd
169 G4 **Byers Green** Dur
83 M4 **Byfield** Nhants
50 D6 **Byfleet** Surrey

79 M6 **Byford** Herefs
86 F7 **Bygrave** Herts
181 G6 **Byker** N u Ty
161 J6 **Byland Abbey** N York
127 K7 **Bylchau** Conwy
130 E6 **Byley** Ches
57 G5 **Bynea** Carmth
189 K5 **Byrness** Nthumb
14 B5 **Bystock** Devon
102 B8 **Bythorn** Cambs
79 L2 **Byton** Herefs
180 C6 **Bywell** Nthumb
36 E6 **Byworth** W Susx

C

27 G6 **Cabbacott** Devon
144 E7 **Cabourne** Lincs
205 H3 **Cabrach** Ag & B
255 H6 **Cabrach** Moray
147 J6 **Cabus** Lancs
261 K6 **Cabvie Lodge** Highld
23 G2 **Cackle Street** E Susx
24 C3 **Cackle Street** E Susx
24 E3 **Cackle Street** E Susx
13 L2 **Cadbury** Devon
28 B7 **Cadbury Barton** Devon
209 G4 **Cadder** E Duns
68 D3 **Caddington** Beds
200 F6 **Caddonfoot** Border
142 E7 **Cadeby** Donc
99 L3 **Cadeby** Leics
13 L1 **Cadeleigh** Devon
23 K3 **Cade Street** E Susx
3 J8 **Cadgwith** Cnwll
222 D6 **Cadham** Fife
130 D1 **Cadishead** Salfd
57 H5 **Cadle** Swans
139 G2 **Cadley** Lancs
47 J5 **Cadley** Wilts
47 K8 **Cadley** Wilts
67 J8 **Cadmore End** Bucks
34 C8 **Cadnam** Hants
144 C7 **Cadney** N Linc
128 E7 **Cadole** Flints
43 H7 **Cadoxton** V Glam
57 L5 **Cadoxton Juxta-Neath** Neath
111 K4 **Cadwst** Denbgs
125 J7 **Caeathro** Gwynd
59 M6 **Caehopkin** Powys
135 K2 **Caenby** Lincs
77 J7 **Caeo** Carmth
42 C3 **Caerau** Brdgnd
43 H6 **Caerau** Cardif
59 M6 **Cae'r-bont** Powys
59 H6 **Cae'r bryn** Carmth
110 C7 **Caerdeon** Gwynd
74 C4 **Caer Farchell** Pembks
124 E4 **Caergeiliog** IoA
129 G8 **Caergwrle** Flints
126 F5 **Caerhun** Conwy
188 C7 **Caerlanrig** Border
44 D1 **Caerleon** Newpt
125 H7 **Caernarfon** Gwynd
43 J4 **Caerphilly** Caerph
94 B5 **Caersws** Powys
76 C4 **Caerwedros** Cerdgn
44 F1 **Caerwent** Mons
128 D5 **Caerwys** Flints
110 E8 **Caerynwch** Gwynd
62 D4 **Caggle Street** Mons
126 C3 **Caim** IoA
283 c8 **Cairinis** W Isls
206 C1 **Cairnbaan** Ag & B
269 J3 **Cairnbulg** Abers
213 K6 **Cairncross** Border
208 A5 **Cairncurran** Inver
217 K5 **Cairndow** Ag & B
210 D2 **Cairneyhill** Fife
267 H4 **Cairnfield House** Moray
172 C5 **Cairngarroch** D & G
255 K3 **Cairnie** Abers
256 F3 **Cairnorrie** Abers
172 D1 **Cairnryan** D & G
267 G5 **Cairnty** Moray
107 L1 **Caister-on-Sea** Norfk
144 E7 **Caistor** Lincs
106 E3 **Caistor St Edmund** Norfk
81 K1 **Cakebole** Worcs
106 B5 **Cake Street** Norfk
89 K7 **Calais Street** Suffk
282 f3 **Calanais** W Isls
19 G6 **Calbourne** IoW
137 G4 **Calceby** Lincs
128 E5 **Calcot** Flints
65 G5 **Calcot** Gloucs

49 G4 **Calcot** W Berk
49 G4 **Calcot Row** W Berk
266 E3 **Calcots** Moray
41 G3 **Calcott** Kent
113 G8 **Calcott** Shrops
150 E4 **Calcutt** N York
65 G8 **Calcutt** Wilts
165 K3 **Caldbeck** Cumb
159 K5 **Caldbergh** N York
87 G4 **Caldecote** Cambs
102 C5 **Caldecote** Cambs
86 E7 **Caldecote** Herts
84 D5 **Caldecote** Nhants
87 G3 **Caldecote Highfields** Cambs
85 K2 **Caldecott** Nhants
66 D7 **Caldecott** Oxon
101 J4 **Caldecott** Rutlnd
85 H8 **Caldecotte** M Keyn
209 K6 **Calderbank** N Lans
155 J2 **Calder Bridge** Cumb
140 E4 **Calderbrook** Rochdl
209 L5 **Caldercruix** N Lans
141 M4 **Calder Grove** Wakefd
197 J3 **Caldermill** S Lans
140 D4 **Caldermore** Rochdl
147 K6 **Calder Vale** Lancs
209 H7 **Calderwood** S Lans
44 F1 **Caldicot** Mons
98 C4 **Caldmore** Wsall
168 F8 **Caldwell** N York
128 F3 **Caldy** Wirral
59 J4 **Caledfwlch** Carmth
4 F6 **Calendra** Cnwll
4 D6 **Calenick** Cnwll
88 D6 **Calford Green** Suffk
275 d2 **Calfsound** Ork
226 D2 **Calgary** Ag & B
265 H8 **Califer** Moray
210 B4 **California** Falk
123 K8 **California** Norfk
7 K4 **California Cross** Devon
116 B7 **Calke** Derbys
259 M5 **Callakille** Highld
219 K5 **Callander** Stirlg
282 f3 **Callanish** W Isls
96 A4 **Callaughton** Shrops
4 C5 **Callestick** Cnwll
247 K7 **Calligarry** Highld
6 D1 **Callington** Cnwll
115 K6 **Callingwood** Staffs
80 C8 **Callow** Herefs
81 J5 **Callow End** Worcs
46 F2 **Callow Hill** Wilts
82 B2 **Callow Hill** Worcs
97 G8 **Callow Hill** Worcs
80 D2 **Callows Grave** Worcs
34 D7 **Calmore** Hants
64 F5 **Calmsden** Gloucs
46 E5 **Calne** Wilts
133 H5 **Calow** Derbys
19 H3 **Calshot** Hants
6 E1 **Calstock** Cnwll
46 F5 **Calstone Wellington** Wilts
122 D5 **Calthorpe** Norfk
123 H6 **Calthorpe Street** Norfk
166 B3 **Calthwaite** Cumb
148 F4 **Calton** N York
115 H2 **Calton** Staffs
130 B7 **Calveley** Ches
132 E5 **Calver** Derbys
113 K4 **Calverhall** Shrops
79 L5 **Calver Hill** Herefs
29 G8 **Calverleigh** Devon
150 B8 **Calverley** Leeds
132 E5 **Calver Sough** Derbys
67 G2 **Calvert** Bucks
84 F7 **Calverton** M Keyn
117 G2 **Calverton** Notts
232 B2 **Calvine** P & K
176 F8 **Calvo** Cumb
199 K6 **Calzeat** Border
63 M7 **Cam** Gloucs
228 B3 **Camasachoirce** Highld
237 L8 **Camasine** Highld
248 F6 **Camas Luinie** Highld
247 G1 **Camastianavaig** Highld
250 E4 **Camault Muir** Highld
25 H3 **Camber** E Susx
49 L6 **Camberley** Surrey
51 J4 **Camberwell** Gt Lon
143 G3 **Camblesforth** N York
180 B2 **Cambo** Nthumb
181 H2 **Cambois** Nthumb
3 G3 **Camborne** Cnwll
87 G3 **Cambourne** Cambs
87 J3 **Cambridge** Cambs
63 L6 **Cambridge** Gloucs
4 A5 **Cambrose** Cnwll

220 E8 **Cambus** Clacks
263 L1 **Cambusavie Platform** Highld
220 D8 **Cambusbarron** Stirlg
220 D8 **Cambuskenneth** Stirlg
209 H7 **Cambuslang** S Lans
243 M4 **Cambus o' May** Abers
199 H5 **Cambuswallace** S Lans
51 H2 **Camden Town** Gt Lon
45 J7 **Cameley** BaNES
10 F5 **Camelford** Cnwll
209 M3 **Camelon** Falk
253 K5 **Camerory** Highld
81 H8 **Camer's Green** Worcs
45 K7 **Camerton** BaNES
164 D4 **Camerton** Cumb
231 G4 **Camghouran** P & K
201 J7 **Camieston** Border
245 K4 **Cammachmore** Abers
135 J3 **Cammeringham** Lincs
263 L2 **Camore** Highld
192 E4 **Campbeltown** Ag & B
181 G4 **Camperdown** N Tyne
186 D7 **Cample** D & G
233 K7 **Campmuir** P & K
91 H4 **Campsea Ash** Suffk
88 C6 **Camps End** Cambs
86 C7 **Campton** Beds
189 J4 **Camptown** Border
54 F3 **Camrose** Pembks
232 B5 **Camserney** P & K
239 H8 **Camusnagaul** Highld
261 H2 **Camusnagaul** Highld
248 A3 **Camusteel** Highld
248 A3 **Camusterrach** Highld
34 C7 **Canada** Hants
156 D7 **Canal Foot** Cumb
55 H4 **Canaston Bridge** Pembks
243 K4 **Candacraig** Abers
137 H6 **Candlesby** Lincs
105 L8 **Candle Street** Suffk
96 C2 **Candover Green** Shrops
199 J5 **Candy Mill** Border
49 G3 **Cane End** Oxon
72 C8 **Canewdon** Essex
17 K2 **Canford Bottom** Dorset
17 L4 **Canford Cliffs** Poole
17 K4 **Canford Heath** Poole
17 K3 **Canford Magna** Poole
90 C2 **Canhams Green** Suffk
280 D2 **Canisbay** Highld
133 H2 **Canklow** Rothm
99 J7 **Canley** Covtry
32 E6 **Cann** Dorset
250 B5 **Cannich** Highld
30 C3 **Cannington** Somset
51 L3 **Canning Town** Gt Lon
98 B2 **Cannock** Staffs
98 D1 **Cannock Wood** Staffs
80 A7 **Cannon Bridge** Herefs
177 L4 **Canonbie** D & G
80 F6 **Canon Frome** Herefs
80 B5 **Canon Pyon** Herefs
84 B5 **Canons Ashby** Nhants
2 E4 **Canonstown** Cnwll
40 F4 **Canterbury** Kent
107 H3 **Cantley** Norfk
96 C2 **Cantlop** Shrops
43 J6 **Canton** Cardif
252 E2 **Cantraywood** Highld
147 M1 **Cantsfield** Lancs
53 G2 **Canvey Island** Essex
135 K6 **Canwick** Lincs
11 J4 **Canworthy Water** Cnwll
239 J8 **Caol** Highld
282 f6 **Caolas Scalpaigh** W Isls
224 D5 **Caoles** Ag & B
239 H5 **Caonich** Highld
39 G4 **Capel** Kent
37 J3 **Capel** Surrey
92 E7 **Capel Bangor** Cerdgn
77 H4 **Capel Betws Lleucu** Cerdgn
125 H3 **Capel Coch** IoA
126 E8 **Capel Curig** Conwy
76 C5 **Capel Cynon** Cerdgn
58 E5 **Capel Dewi** Carmth
76 E6 **Capel Dewi** Cerdgn
92 D7 **Capel-Dewi** Cerdgn
127 G8 **Capel Garmon** Conwy
91 J5 **Capel Green** Suffk
58 E4 **Capel Gwyn** Carmth
124 F4 **Capel Gwyn** IoA
59 K4 **Capel Gwynfe** Carmth
59 G6 **Capel Hendre** Carmth
59 G3 **Capel Isaac** Carmth
58 B2 **Capel Iwan** Carmth

41 H7 **Capel le Ferne** Kent
9 j2 **Capelles** Guern
43 H5 **Capel Llanilltern** Cardif
125 G5 **Capel Mawr** IoA
125 H2 **Capel Parc** IoA
91 J5 **Capel St Andrew** Suffk
90 C7 **Capel St Mary** Suffk
92 D7 **Capel Seion** Cerdgn
92 F8 **Capel Trisant** Cerdgn
109 H2 **Capeluchaf** Gwynd
126 E4 **Capelulo** Conwy
61 L1 **Capel-y-ffin** Powys
125 K6 **Capel-y-graig** Gwynd
129 J5 **Capenhurst** Ches
147 K2 **Capernwray** Lancs
180 C3 **Capheaton** Nthumb
208 D7 **Caplaw** E Rens
91 G2 **Capon's Green** Suffk
187 K2 **Cappercleuch** Border
53 G6 **Capstone** Medway
8 C4 **Capton** Devon
29 K3 **Capton** Somset
233 G7 **Caputh** P & K
11 K8 **Caradon Town** Cnwll
208 E3 **Carbeth Inn** Stirlg
5 G3 **Carbis** Cnwll
2 E3 **Carbis Bay** Cnwll
246 E2 **Carbost** Highld
259 G7 **Carbost** Highld
133 G2 **Carbrook** Sheff
105 J3 **Carbrooke** Norfk
134 C5 **Carburton** Notts
5 H4 **Carclaze** Cnwll
3 K3 **Carclew** Cnwll
117 J3 **Car Colston** Notts
142 E6 **Carcroft** Donc
222 C8 **Cardenden** Fife
95 J1 **Cardeston** Shrops
177 K8 **Cardewlees** Cumb
254 D3 **Cardhu** Moray
43 J6 **Cardiff** Cardif
75 L3 **Cardigan** Cerdgn
88 C6 **Cardinal's Green** Cambs
86 B5 **Cardington** Beds
96 C4 **Cardington** Shrops
5 J1 **Cardinham** Cnwll
172 E8 **Cardrain** D & G
200 C5 **Cardrona** Border
208 B3 **Cardross** Ag & B
172 E8 **Cardryne** D & G
177 G7 **Cardurnock** Cumb
118 D8 **Careby** Lincs
234 E3 **Careston** Angus
55 H6 **Carew** Pembks
55 H6 **Carew Cheriton** Pembks
55 H6 **Carew Newton** Pembks
63 H1 **Carey** Herefs
209 K7 **Carfin** N Lans
201 G2 **Carfraemill** Border
107 H1 **Cargate Green** Norfk
176 C4 **Cargen** D & G
176 C4 **Cargenbridge** D & G
233 H8 **Cargill** P & K
177 L7 **Cargo** Cumb
6 E2 **Cargreen** Cnwll
3 M4 **Cargurrel** Cnwll
202 B5 **Carham** Nthumb
29 H2 **Carhampton** Somset
3 J3 **Carharrack** Cnwll
231 H4 **Carie** P & K
283 c8 **Carinish** W Isls
19 H6 **Carisbrooke** IoW
156 E7 **Cark** Cumb
6 E3 **Carkeel** Cnwll
282 e2 **Carlabhagh** W Isls
4 D4 **Carland Cross** Cnwll
169 G7 **Carlbury** Darltn
102 A1 **Carlby** Lincs
190 B4 **Carlcroft** Nthumb
141 J7 **Carlecotes** Barns
3 G5 **Carleen** Cnwll
160 B7 **Carlesmoor** N York
155 J1 **Carleton** Cumb
166 C5 **Carleton** Cumb
178 A8 **Carleton** Cumb
146 F7 **Carleton** Lancs
149 H6 **Carleton** N York
142 D4 **Carleton** Wakefd
106 B2 **Carleton Forehoe** Norfk
106 C5 **Carleton Rode** Norfk
107 G3 **Carleton St Peter** Norfk
3 K5 **Carlidnack** Cnwll
256 B3 **Carlincraig** Abers
45 K7 **Carlingcott** BaNES
171 G6 **Carlin How** R & Cl
177 L7 **Carlisle** Cumb
4 E2 **Carloggas** Cnwll
199 K2 **Carlops** Border

282 e2 **Carloway** W Isls
142 B5 **Carlton** Barns
85 J4 **Carlton** Beds
88 C4 **Carlton** Cambs
142 A2 **Carlton** Leeds
99 L2 **Carlton** Leics
143 G3 **Carlton** N York
159 J5 **Carlton** N York
161 K5 **Carlton** N York
117 G3 **Carlton** Notts
169 K6 **Carlton** S on T
91 J2 **Carlton** Suffk
107 K5 **Carlton Colville** Suffk
100 F4 **Carlton Curlieu** Leics
88 C5 **Carlton Green** Cambs
161 H7 **Carlton Husthwaite** N York
161 H2 **Carlton-in-Cleveland** N York
134 B3 **Carlton in Lindrick** Notts
135 H8 **Carlton-le-Moorland** Lincs
160 F6 **Carlton Miniott** N York
134 F7 **Carlton-on-Trent** Notts
118 B3 **Carlton Scroop** Lincs
198 D3 **Carluke** S Lans
5 H4 **Carlyon Bay** Cnwll
198 C7 **Carmacoup** S Lans
58 D5 **Carmarthen** Carmth
59 G5 **Carmel** Carmth
128 E4 **Carmel** Flints
125 J8 **Carmel** Gwynd
198 F5 **Carmichael** S Lans
209 G7 **Carmunnock** C Glas
209 H6 **Carmyle** C Glas
234 E6 **Carmyllie** Angus
153 J3 **Carnaby** E R Yk
223 J6 **Carnbee** Fife
221 J6 **Carnbo** P & K
3 H3 **Carn Brea** Cnwll
256 F6 **Carnbrogie** Abers
248 E6 **Carndu** Highld
197 J2 **Carnduff** S Lans
3 K6 **Carne** Cnwll
4 E7 **Carne** Cnwll
4 F3 **Carne** Cnwll
196 F4 **Carnell** E Ayrs
4 D1 **Carnewas** Cnwll
147 K2 **Carnforth** Lancs
248 F7 **Carn-gorm** Highld
74 C6 **Carnhedryn** Pembks
3 G4 **Carnhell Green** Cnwll
245 H2 **Carnie** Abers
3 H3 **Carnkie** Cnwll
3 H4 **Carnkie** Cnwll
4 C4 **Carnkiet** Cnwll
93 L4 **Carno** Powys
238 D4 **Carnoch** Highld
210 D1 **Carnock** Fife
3 K3 **Carnon Downs** Cnwll
268 B6 **Carnousie** Abers
234 E8 **Carnoustie** Angus
199 G4 **Carnwath** S Lans
2 B4 **Carnyorth** Cnwll
99 H7 **Carol Green** Solhll
4 F4 **Carpalla** Cnwll
159 H5 **Carperby** N York
140 B4 **Carr** Bury
133 K2 **Carr** Rothm
194 C3 **Carradale** Ag & B
253 C7 **Carrbridge** Highld
140 E7 **Carrbrook** Tamesd
9 c2 **Carrefour** Jersey
125 G2 **Carreglefn** IoA
141 M3 **Carr Gate** Wakefd
143 K6 **Carrhouse** N Linc
206 E2 **Carrick** Ag & B
217 K8 **Carrick Castle** Ag & B
210 D3 **Carriden** Falk
136 F8 **Carrington** Lincs
211 K7 **Carrington** Mdloth
130 E1 **Carrington** Traffd
5 G3 **Carrismerry** Cnwll
110 E2 **Carrog** Conwy
111 L3 **Carrog** Denbgs
210 A3 **Carron** Falk
254 E3 **Carron** Moray
186 C6 **Carronbridge** D & G
209 K2 **Carron Bridge** Stirlg
210 A2 **Carronshore** Falk
44 E1 **Carrow Hill** Mons
167 J1 **Carr Shield** Nthumb
176 E4 **Carrutherstown** D & G
208 B6 **Carruth House** Inver
33 J5 **Carr Vale** Derbys
169 J7 **Carrville** Dur
227 G8 **Carsaig** Ag & B
234 C4 **Carse Gray** Angus
173 H1 **Carseriggan** D & G
176 C7 **Carsethorn** D & G
51 H6 **Carshalton** Gt Lon

115 L1 **Carsington** Derbys
192 D6 **Carskey** Ag & B
174 D4 **Carsluith** D & G
184 E4 **Carsphairn** D & G
198 F4 **Carstairs** S Lans
198 F4 **Carstairs Junction** S Lans
65 L7 **Carswell Marsh** Oxon
34 C6 **Carter's Clay** Hants
70 D5 **Carters Green** Essex
65 L5 **Carterton** Oxon
180 C8 **Carterway Heads** Nthumb
5 G4 **Carthew** Cnwll
160 D6 **Carthorpe** N York
190 E5 **Cartington** Nthumb
198 E4 **Cartland** S Lans
132 F4 **Cartledge** Derbys
156 E7 **Cartmel** Cumb
156 F5 **Cartmel Fell** Cumb
56 E3 **Carway** Carmth
177 L4 **Carwinley** Cumb
64 B6 **Cashe's Green** Gloucs
33 G8 **Cashmoor** Dorset
66 C5 **Cassington** Oxon
169 K3 **Cassop Colliery** Dur
2 C6 **Castallack** Cnwll
9 j3 **Castel** Guern
126 F6 **Castell** Conwy
62 B8 **Castell-y-bwch** Torfn
157 K6 **Casterton** Cumb
5 J3 **Castle** Cnwll
121 H8 **Castle Acre** Norfk
85 G3 **Castle Ashby** Nhants
283 b13 **Castlebay** W Isls
159 J4 **Castle Bolton** N York
98 F5 **Castle Bromwich** Solhll
118 C7 **Castle Bytham** Lincs
75 H6 **Castlebythe** Pembks
94 E2 **Castle Caereinion** Powys
88 C6 **Castle Camps** Cambs
178 D7 **Castle Carrock** Cumb
209 L3 **Castlecary** Falk
31 L4 **Castle Cary** Somset
46 B3 **Castle Combe** Wilts
116 D6 **Castle Donington** Leics
175 J2 **Castle Douglas** D & G
65 H7 **Castle Eaton** Swindn
169 L3 **Castle Eden** Dur
102 C2 **Castle End** C Pete
142 C3 **Castleford** Wakefd
80 F6 **Castle Frome** Herefs
2 D4 **Castle Gate** Cnwll
157 H4 **Castle Green** Cumb
50 B6 **Castle Green** Surrey
115 M7 **Castle Gresley** Derbys
88 F8 **Castle Hedingham** Essex
200 B6 **Castlehill** Border
280 B3 **Castlehill** Highld
39 H5 **Castle Hill** Kent
90 D6 **Castle Hill** Suffk
208 C4 **Castlehill** W Duns
172 D3 **Castle Kennedy** D & G
217 G8 **Castle Lachlan** Ag & B
54 E7 **Castlemartin** Pembks
209 G7 **Castlemilk** C Glas
74 E6 **Castle Morris** Pembks
81 H7 **Castlemorton** Worcs
187 K7 **Castle O'er** D & G
95 K3 **Castle Pulverbatch** Shrops
120 E6 **Castle Rising** Norfk
168 D1 **Castleside** Dur
140 E3 **Castle Street** Calder
252 D2 **Castle Stuart** Highld
84 F6 **Castlethorpe** M Keyn
144 B6 **Castlethorpe** N Linc
188 E8 **Castleton** Border
132 C3 **Castleton** Derbys
162 B1 **Castleton** N York
43 L5 **Castleton** Newpt
140 C5 **Castleton** Rochdl
16 D7 **Castletown** Dorset
280 A3 **Castletown** Highld
154 c8 **Castletown** IoM
181 J7 **Castletown** Sundld
150 C6 **Castley** N York
105 J4 **Caston** Norfk
102 C4 **Castor** C Pete
57 G7 **Caswell Bay** Swans
194 E1 **Catacol** N Ayrs
131 K5 **Cat and Fiddle** Derbys
63 G6 **Catbrook** Mons
128 F5 **Catch** Flints
2 C5 **Catchall** Cnwll
99 H8 **Catchem's Corner** Solhll
180 E8 **Catchgate** Dur
133 H2 **Catcliffe** Rothm
46 E4 **Catcomb** Wilts
30 F3 **Catcott** Somset
30 F2 **Catcott Burtle** Somset

51 J7 **Caterham** Surrey
123 H7 **Catfield** Norfk
123 H7 **Catfield Common** Norfk
51 K4 **Catford** Gt Lon
138 F1 **Catforth** Lancs
209 G7 **Cathcart** C Glas
61 J2 **Cathedine** Powys
98 F7 **Catherine-de-Barnes** Solhll
141 G2 **Catherine Slack** Brad
35 L8 **Catherington** Hants
15 J3 **Catherston Leweston** Dorset
96 E7 **Catherton** Shrops
19 J2 **Catisfield** Hants
80 F6 **Catley** Herefs
140 C4 **Catley Lane Head** Rochdl
241 H5 **Catlodge** Highld
148 F8 **Catlow** Lancs
178 B3 **Catlowdy** Cumb
87 K7 **Catmere End** Essex
48 C3 **Catmore** W Berk
13 H8 **Caton** Devon
147 K3 **Caton** Lancs
147 L3 **Caton Green** Lancs
13 G7 **Cator Court** Devon
197 G6 **Catrine** E Ayrs
44 D1 **Cat's Ash** Newpt
24 C4 **Catsfield** E Susx
24 C4 **Catsfield Stream** E Susx
31 H5 **Catsgore** Somset
31 J4 **Catsham** Somset
98 B8 **Catshill** Worcs
97 G4 **Catstree** Shrops
192 D6 **Cattadale** Ag & B
150 F5 **Cattal** N York
90 C8 **Cattawade** Suffk
147 K7 **Catterall** Lancs
113 J3 **Catteralslane** Shrops
160 C3 **Catterick** N York
160 B3 **Catterick Bridge** N York
160 B3 **Catterick Garrison** N York
166 B4 **Catterlen** Cumb
245 J7 **Catterline** Abers
151 H6 **Catterton** N York
36 E2 **Catteshall** Surrey
100 C7 **Catthorpe** Leics
89 H7 **Cattishall** Suffk
16 B3 **Cattistock** Dorset
160 E7 **Catton** N York
106 E1 **Catton** Norfk
179 J7 **Catton** Nthumb
153 K6 **Catwick** E R Yk
86 B1 **Catworth** Cambs
64 D5 **Caudle Green** Gloucs
85 K6 **Caulcott** Beds
66 D2 **Caulcott** Oxon
235 G6 **Cauldcots** Angus
219 L8 **Cauldhame** Stirlg
188 F3 **Cauldmill** Border
115 H2 **Cauldon** Staffs
115 H2 **Cauldon Lowe** Staffs
115 L8 **Cauldwell** Derbys
176 B7 **Caulkerbush** D & G
178 B3 **Caulside** D & G
31 L8 **Caundle Marsh** Dorset
97 J7 **Caunsall** Worcs
134 E7 **Caunton** Notts
35 M6 **Causeway** Hants
157 G5 **Causeway End** Cumb
173 K3 **Causeway End** D & G
71 G3 **Causeway End** Essex
199 H6 **Causewayend** S Lans
176 F8 **Causewayhead** Cumb
220 D8 **Causewayhead** Stirlg
257 H7 **Causeyend** Abers
191 H7 **Causey Park** Nthumb
191 H7 **Causey Park Bridge** Nthumb
88 F6 **Cavendish** Suffk
88 F7 **Cavenham** Suffk
66 E2 **Caversfield** Oxon
49 H4 **Caversham** Readg
114 F3 **Caverswall** Staffs
202 A7 **Caverton Mill** Border
143 J2 **Cavil** E R Yk
252 F2 **Cawdor** Highld
136 E4 **Cawkwell** Lincs
151 J4 **Cawood** N York
6 E5 **Cawsand** Cnwll
122 C6 **Cawston** Norfk
100 A8 **Cawston** Warwks
162 D5 **Cawthorn** N York
141 L6 **Cawthorne** Barns
161 K7 **Cawton** N York
86 F3 **Caxton** Cambs
87 G4 **Caxton End** Cambs
86 F3 **Caxton Gibbet** Cambs
80 D1 **Caynham** Shrops

118 B2 **Caythorpe** Lincs
117 J2 **Caythorpe** Notts
163 J6 **Cayton** N York
283 b8 **Ceann a Bhaigh** W Isls
239 L1 **Ceannacroc Lodge** Highld
282 f4 **Cearsiadar** W Isls
63 G6 **Ceciliford** Mons
44 B1 **Cefn** Newpt
127 K6 **Cefn Berain** Conwy
111 H2 **Cefn-brith** Conwy
59 K6 **Cefn-bryn-brain** Carmth
60 C5 **Cefn Byrle** Powys
112 C5 **Cefn Canel** Powys
111 L6 **Cefn Coch** Powys
60 F5 **Cefn-coed-y-cymmer** Myr Td
42 C5 **Cefn Cribwr** Brdgnd
42 C5 **Cefn Cross** Brdgnd
111 J4 **Cefn-ddwysarn** Gwynd
95 G6 **Cefn-Einion** Shrops
59 G6 **Cefneithin** Carmth
78 B6 **Cefngorwydd** Powys
43 K5 **Cefn Mably** Caerph
112 D3 **Cefn-mawr** Wrexhm
61 G7 **Cefnpennar** Rhondd
129 H8 **Cefn-y-bedd** Flints
75 L7 **Cefn-y-pant** Carmth
125 J4 **Ceint** IoA
77 H5 **Cellan** Cerdgn
223 K6 **Cellardyke** Fife
114 F2 **Cellarhead** Staffs
166 C5 **Celleron** Cumb
43 K3 **Celynen** Caerph
124 F1 **Cemaes** IoA
93 H2 **Cemmaes** Powys
93 H3 **Cemmaes Road** Powys
76 A7 **Cenarth** Cerdgn
74 D6 **Cerbyd** Pembks
223 G5 **Ceres** Fife
16 C2 **Cerne Abbas** Dorset
65 G7 **Cerney Wick** Gloucs
125 G5 **Cerrigceinwen** IoA
111 J2 **Cerrigydrudion** Conwy
123 J7 **Cess** Norfk
125 J7 **Ceunant** Gwynd
64 B1 **Chaceley** Gloucs
4 B6 **Chacewater** Cnwll
84 D8 **Chackmore** Bucks
83 L6 **Chacombe** Nhants
82 B6 **Chadbury** Worcs
140 D6 **Chadderton** Oldham
140 D6 **Chadderton Fold** Oldham
116 C4 **Chaddesden** C Derb
97 K8 **Chaddesley Corbett** Worcs
12 B6 **Chaddlehanger** Devon
48 B3 **Chaddleworth** W Berk
65 M3 **Chadlington** Oxon
83 H4 **Chadshunt** Warwks
117 K6 **Chadwell** Leics
114 B8 **Chadwell** Shrops
86 B2 **Chadwell End** Beds
52 A1 **Chadwell Heath** Gt Lon
52 E3 **Chadwell St Mary** Thurr
81 J2 **Chadwick** Worcs
82 F1 **Chadwick End** Solhll
139 G7 **Chadwick Green** St Hel
15 H1 **Chaffcombe** Somset
52 D3 **Chadwell Hundred** Thurr
13 G5 **Chagford** Devon
22 F3 **Chailey** E Susx
103 J3 **Chainbridge** Cambs
39 J4 **Chainhurst** Kent
17 K1 **Chalbury** Dorset
17 K1 **Chalbury Common** Dorset
51 J7 **Chaldon** Surrey
19 H8 **Chale** IoW
19 H7 **Chale Green** IoW
68 C8 **Chalfont Common** Bucks
68 C8 **Chalfont St Giles** Bucks
50 C1 **Chalfont St Peter** Bucks
64 C6 **Chalford** Gloucs
67 H7 **Chalford** Oxon
32 E1 **Chalford** Wilts
68 C2 **Chalgrave** Beds
66 F7 **Chalgrove** Oxon
52 E4 **Chalk** Kent
70 F5 **Chalk End** Essex
49 H3 **Chalkhouse Green** Oxon
15 J1 **Chalkway** Somset
53 J6 **Chalkwell** Kent
7 J6 **Challaborough** Devon
28 B3 **Challacombe** Devon
173 K2 **Challoch** D & G
40 C5 **Challock** Kent
16 B2 **Chalmington** Dorset
68 C2 **Chalton** Beds
86 C5 **Chalton** Beds
20 B4 **Chalton** Hants

50 B3 **Chalvey** Slough
23 H5 **Chalvington** E Susx
40 B6 **Chambers Green** Kent
68 D7 **Chandler's Cross** Herts
81 H7 **Chandlers Cross** Worcs
34 F7 **Chandler's Ford** Hants
86 C4 **Channel's End** Beds
32 B2 **Chantry** Somset
90 D6 **Chantry** Suffk
165 H4 **Chapel** Cumb
222 D8 **Chapel** Fife
150 D8 **Chapel Allerton** Leeds
30 F1 **Chapel Allerton** Somset
10 D7 **Chapel Amble** Cnwll
84 E2 **Chapel Brampton** Nhants
102 F4 **Chapelbridge** Cambs
114 C4 **Chapel Chorlton** Staffs
23 K3 **Chapel Cross** E Susx
85 L6 **Chapel End** Beds
86 B4 **Chapel End** Beds
102 C6 **Chapel End** Cambs
99 J5 **Chapel End** Warwks
88 E7 **Chapel End** Essex
131 L3 **Chapel-en-le-Frith** Derbys
140 B6 **Chapel Field** Bury
119 L6 **Chapelgate** Lincs
83 L3 **Chapel Green** Warwks
99 H6 **Chapel Green** Warwks
142 F3 **Chapel Haddlesey** N York
209 K6 **Chapelhall** N Lans
257 K4 **Chapel Hill** Abers
119 G1 **Chapel Hill** Lincs
63 G7 **Chapel Hill** Mons
150 D6 **Chapel Hill** N York
187 K2 **Chapelhope** Border
177 K4 **Chapelknowe** D & G
95 H8 **Chapel Lawn** Shrops
158 C7 **Chapel le Dale** N York
29 L5 **Chapel Leigh** Somset
131 L3 **Chapel Milton** Derbys
256 C7 **Chapel of Garioch** Abers
172 D6 **Chapel Rossan** D & G
23 L5 **Chapel Row** E Susx
71 J7 **Chapel Row** Essex
48 E5 **Chapel Row** W Berk
156 B6 **Chapels** Cumb
137 K5 **Chapel St Leonards** Lincs
156 D2 **Chapel Stile** Cumb
234 F6 **Chapelton** Angus
27 K5 **Chapelton** Devon
197 K1 **Chapelton** S Lans
139 L4 **Chapeltown** Bl w D
4 E4 **Chapel Town** Cnwll
254 E7 **Chapeltown** Moray
142 A8 **Chapeltown** Sheff
32 D1 **Chapmanslade** Wilts
11 L4 **Chapmans Well** Devon
69 J4 **Chapmore End** Herts
72 C2 **Chappel** Essex
6 B1 **Charaton** Cnwll
15 H1 **Chard** Somset
15 H2 **Chard Junction** Somset
30 D8 **Chardleigh Green** Somset
15 G2 **Chardstock** Devon
63 L8 **Charfield** S Glos
64 D3 **Chargrove** Gloucs
40 B5 **Charing** Kent
40 B5 **Charing Heath** Kent
40 B5 **Charing Hill** Kent
82 E7 **Charingworth** Gloucs
66 A3 **Charlbury** Oxon
45 L5 **Charlcombe** BaNES
46 E4 **Charlcutt** Wilts
83 G4 **Charlecote** Warwks
98 C4 **Charlemont** Sandw
28 B4 **Charles** Devon
36 D2 **Charleshill** Surrey
234 B6 **Charleston** Angus
149 L8 **Charlestown** Brad
245 L3 **Charlestown** C Aber
140 E2 **Charlestown** Calder
5 H4 **Charlestown** Cnwll
131 L1 **Charlestown** Derbys
16 C6 **Charlestown** Dorset
210 E2 **Charlestown** Fife
251 H2 **Charlestown** Highld
260 C5 **Charlestown** Highld
140 B7 **Charlestown** Salfd
89 L5 **Charles Tye** Suffk
131 K1 **Charlesworth** Derbys
30 C3 **Charlinch** Somset
222 E5 **Charlottetown** Fife
51 L3 **Charlton** Gt Lon
34 D2 **Charlton** Hants
68 F2 **Charlton** Herts
83 M8 **Charlton** Nhants
179 J2 **Charlton** Nthumb
48 B1 **Charlton** Oxon

30 D5 **Charlton** Somset
31 K2 **Charlton** Somset
45 K8 **Charlton** Somset
50 D5 **Charlton** Surrey
20 E4 **Charlton** W Susx
32 F6 **Charlton** Wilts
46 D1 **Charlton** Wilts
81 J1 **Charlton** Worcs
82 B6 **Charlton** Worcs
96 D1 **Charlton** Wrekin
64 F2 **Charlton Abbots** Gloucs
31 J5 **Charlton Adam** Somset
33 L6 **Charlton-All-Saints** Wilts
16 C3 **Charlton Down** Dorset
96 D2 **Charlton Hill** Shrops
31 L6 **Charlton Horethorne** Somset
64 D3 **Charlton Kings** Gloucs
31 H5 **Charlton Mackrell** Somset
17 H2 **Charlton Marshall** Dorset
32 B5 **Charlton Musgrove** Somset
66 E4 **Charlton-on-Otmoor** Oxon
17 H2 **Charlton on the Hill** Dorset
47 G7 **Charlton St Peter** Wilts
35 K4 **Charlwood** Hants
37 K3 **Charlwood** Surrey
16 C4 **Charminster** Dorset
15 H4 **Charmouth** Dorset
67 G2 **Charndon** Bucks
66 A8 **Charney Bassett** Oxon
139 H4 **Charnock Green** Lancs
139 H4 **Charnock Richard** Lancs
90 F4 **Charsfield** Suffk
39 K3 **Chart Corner** Kent
48 E7 **Charter Alley** Hants
202 B4 **Charterhall** Border
45 G7 **Charterhouse** Somset
209 L1 **Chartershall** Stirlg
65 L5 **Charterville Allotments** Oxon
40 E4 **Chartham** Kent
40 E4 **Chartham Hatch** Kent
39 K3 **Chart Hill** Kent
68 B6 **Chartridge** Bucks
39 K3 **Chart Sutton** Kent
39 L3 **Chartway Street** Kent
49 J4 **Charvil** Wokham
83 M4 **Charwelton** Nhants
98 D2 **Chase Terrace** Staffs
98 D2 **Chasetown** Staffs
65 K1 **Chastleton** Oxon
11 L2 **Chasty** Devon
148 D7 **Chatburn** Lancs
114 B4 **Chatcull** Staffs
43 K4 **Chatham** Caerph
53 G5 **Chatham** Medway
71 H4 **Chatham Green** Essex
203 K7 **Chathill** Nthumb
81 J3 **Chatley** Worcs
53 G4 **Chattenden** Medway
70 C2 **Chatter End** Essex
103 H6 **Chatteris** Cambs
140 B4 **Chatterton** Lancs
90 C6 **Chattisham** Suffk
189 K3 **Chatto** Border
203 G7 **Chatton** Nthumb
68 D3 **Chaul End** Beds
28 C8 **Chawleigh** Devon
66 C6 **Chawley** Oxon
86 C4 **Chawston** Beds
35 L3 **Chawton** Hants
63 L4 **Chaxhill** Gloucs
49 G3 **Chazey Heath** Oxon
115 G3 **Cheadle** Staffs
131 G2 **Cheadle** Stockp
131 G2 **Cheadle Heath** Stockp
131 G2 **Cheadle Hulme** Stockp
51 H6 **Cheam** Gt Lon
50 B5 **Cheapside** W & M
67 H5 **Chearsley** Bucks
114 D6 **Chebsey** Staffs
49 G2 **Checkendon** Oxon
114 A2 **Checkley** Ches
80 E7 **Checkley** Herefs
115 G4 **Checkley** Staffs
114 A2 **Checkley Green** Ches
88 F4 **Chedburgh** Suffk
44 F8 **Cheddar** Somset
68 A4 **Cheddington** Bucks
114 F1 **Cheddleton** Staffs
114 F1 **Cheddleton Heath** Staffs
30 C5 **Cheddon Fitzpaine** Somset
64 D8 **Chedglow** Wilts
107 H3 **Chedgrave** Norfk
15 L2 **Chedington** Dorset
107 G7 **Chediston** Suffk
107 G7 **Chediston Green** Suffk
64 F5 **Chedworth** Gloucs

30 E3 **Chedzoy** Somset
40 D7 **Cheeseman's Green** Kent
140 C7 **Cheetham Hill** Manch
28 C8 **Cheldon** Devon
130 F5 **Chelford** Ches
116 C5 **Chellaston** C Derb
85 J4 **Chellington** Beds
97 G5 **Chelmarsh** Shrops
95 L5 **Chelmick** Shrops
90 E7 **Chelmondiston** Suffk
132 B5 **Chelmorton** Derbys
71 H5 **Chelmsford** Essex
98 F6 **Chelmsley Wood** Solhll
51 H3 **Chelsea** Gt Lon
52 A6 **Chelsfield** Gt Lon
51 K7 **Chelsham** Surrey
29 L6 **Chelston** Somset
89 K5 **Chelsworth** Suffk
64 D3 **Cheltenham** Gloucs
85 K1 **Chelveston** Nhants
44 F5 **Chelvey** N Som
45 J6 **Chelwood** BaNES
38 B7 **Chelwood Common** E Susx
38 B7 **Chelwood Gate** E Susx
64 E8 **Chelworth** Wilts
65 G8 **Chelworth Lower Green** Wilts
65 G8 **Chelworth Upper Green** Wilts
95 K6 **Cheney Longville** Shrops
68 C7 **Chenies** Bucks
63 G8 **Chepstow** Mons
139 K6 **Chequerbent** Bolton
103 K2 **Chequers Corner** Norfk
46 F5 **Cherhill** Wilts
64 C7 **Cherington** Gloucs
83 G7 **Cherington** Warwks
28 C2 **Cheriton** Devon
35 J5 **Cheriton** Hants
41 G7 **Cheriton** Kent
56 E6 **Cheriton** Swans
13 H4 **Cheriton Bishop** Devon
13 K1 **Cheriton Fitzpaine** Devon
55 G7 **Cheriton or Stackpole Elidor** Pembks
113 L7 **Cherrington** Wrekin
152 F7 **Cherry Burton** E R Yk
87 K4 **Cherry Hinton** Cambs
81 K4 **Cherry Orchard** Worcs
135 L5 **Cherry Willingham** Lincs
50 D5 **Chertsey** Surrey
16 E3 **Cheselbourne** Dorset
68 B6 **Chesham** Bucks
140 B5 **Chesham** Bury
68 B7 **Chesham Bois** Bucks
69 K6 **Cheshunt** Herts
53 J6 **Chesley** Kent
98 B2 **Cheslyn Hay** Staffs
99 G8 **Chessetts Wood** Warwks
50 F6 **Chessington** Gt Lon
129 J6 **Chester** Ches
31 L3 **Chesterblade** Somset
133 G5 **Chesterfield** Derbys
98 E2 **Chesterfield** Staffs
211 L6 **Chesterhill** Mdloth
181 G8 **Chester-le-Street** Dur
169 H1 **Chester Moor** Dur
189 G2 **Chesters** Border
189 H4 **Chesters** Border
87 K3 **Chesterton** Cambs
102 A5 **Chesterton** Cambs
64 E7 **Chesterton** Gloucs
66 E3 **Chesterton** Oxon
97 H4 **Chesterton** Shrops
114 C2 **Chesterton** Staffs
83 H4 **Chesterton Green** Warwks
179 J6 **Chesterwood** Nthumb
40 F2 **Chestfield** Kent
53 J6 **Chestnut Street** Kent
7 K3 **Cheston** Devon
114 A5 **Cheswardine** Shrops
113 M8 **Cheswell** Wrekin
203 G4 **Cheswick** Nthumb
98 E8 **Cheswick Green** Solhll
16 B1 **Chetnole** Dorset
29 H7 **Chettiscombe** Devon
103 L6 **Chettisham** Cambs
32 F8 **Chettle** Dorset
96 F5 **Chetton** Shrops
66 F1 **Chetwode** Bucks
114 A7 **Chetwynd** Wrekin
114 B8 **Chetwynd Aston** Wrekin
88 D3 **Cheveley** Cambs
52 A7 **Chevening** Kent
19 G6 **Cheverton** IoW
88 F3 **Chevington** Suffk
191 K6 **Chevington Drift** Nthumb
29 H7 **Chevithorne** Devon
45 H6 **Chew Magna** BaNES
139 K6 **Chew Moor** Bolton

45 H6 **Chew Stoke** BaNES
45 K5 **Chewton Keynsham** BaNES
45 H8 **Chewton Mendip** Somset
12 E3 **Chichacott** Devon
85 H6 **Chicheley** M Keyn
20 E6 **Chichester** W Susx
16 C6 **Chickerell** Dorset
106 E8 **Chickering** Suffk
32 F4 **Chicklade** Wilts
79 K4 **Chickward** Herefs
35 K7 **Chidden** Hants
36 E4 **Chiddingfold** Surrey
23 J4 **Chiddingly** E Susx
38 D4 **Chiddingstone** Kent
38 E4 **Chiddingstone Causeway** Kent
15 K4 **Chideock** Dorset
20 C6 **Chidham** W Susx
141 L3 **Chidswell** Kirk
48 C4 **Chieveley** W Berk
71 G5 **Chignall St James** Essex
71 G5 **Chignall Smealy** Essex
70 B8 **Chigwell** Essex
70 C8 **Chigwell Row** Essex
34 E3 **Chilbolton** Hants
35 G5 **Chilcomb** Hants
15 M4 **Chilcombe** Dorset
45 J8 **Chilcompton** Somset
99 H1 **Chilcote** Leics
129 J4 **Childer Thornton** Ches
32 D8 **Child Okeford** Dorset
48 A2 **Childrey** Oxon
113 L6 **Child's Ercall** Shrops
82 C7 **Childswickham** Worcs
129 K2 **Childwall** Lpool
68 F5 **Childwick Bury** Herts
68 F5 **Childwick Green** Herts
16 B3 **Chilfrome** Dorset
20 D4 **Chilgrove** W Susx
40 E4 **Chilham** Kent
12 B2 **Chilla** Devon
12 B6 **Chillaton** Devon
41 J4 **Chillenden** Kent
19 H6 **Chillerton** IoW
91 J5 **Chillesford** Suffk
203 G8 **Chillingham** Nthumb
8 B6 **Chillington** Devon
30 F8 **Chillington** Somset
33 G4 **Chilmark** Wilts
40 C7 **Chilmington Green** Kent
65 L3 **Chilson** Oxon
12 A7 **Chilsworthy** Cnwll
11 L1 **Chilsworthy** Devon
68 E3 **Chiltern Green** Beds
31 H7 **Chilthorne Domer** Somset
67 G5 **Chilton** Bucks
13 K2 **Chilton** Devon
169 H5 **Chilton** Dur
41 J6 **Chilton** Kent
48 C2 **Chilton** Oxon
89 H6 **Chilton** Suffk
35 J3 **Chilton Candover** Hants
31 J6 **Chilton Cantelo** Somset
47 L5 **Chilton Foliat** Wilts
30 E3 **Chilton Polden** Somset
88 E6 **Chilton Street** Suffk
30 D3 **Chilton Trinity** Somset
116 E4 **Chilwell** Notts
34 E7 **Chilworth** Hants
36 F2 **Chilworth** Surrey
65 M7 **Chimney** Oxon
49 G7 **Chineham** Hants
69 K8 **Chingford** Gt Lon
131 L3 **Chinley** Derbys
67 J6 **Chinnor** Oxon
179 K4 **Chipchase Castle** Nthumb
114 A5 **Chipnall** Shrops
88 D1 **Chippenham** Cambs
46 D4 **Chippenham** Wilts
68 D6 **Chipperfield** Herts
69 K1 **Chipping** Herts
147 M7 **Chipping** Lancs
82 E7 **Chipping Campden** Gloucs
71 K4 **Chipping Hill** Essex
65 L2 **Chipping Norton** Oxon
70 E6 **Chipping Ongar** Essex
45 L3 **Chipping Sodbury** S Glos
83 L5 **Chipping Warden** Nhants
29 J5 **Chipstable** Somset
38 D2 **Chipstead** Kent
51 H7 **Chipstead** Surrey
95 G4 **Chirbury** Shrops
112 D4 **Chirk** Wrexhm
202 D2 **Chirnside** Border
202 C2 **Chirnsidebridge** Border
47 G7 **Chirton** Wilts
47 K5 **Chisbury** Wilts
31 G7 **Chiselborough** Somset

47 J3 **Chiseldon** Swindn
66 E7 **Chiselhampton** Oxon
188 D4 **Chisholme** Border
51 L5 **Chislehurst** Gt Lon
41 H2 **Chislet** Kent
140 F2 **Chisley** Calder
68 E6 **Chiswell Green** Herts
51 G3 **Chiswick** Gt Lon
87 H6 **Chiswick End** Cambs
131 K2 **Chisworth** Derbys
24 E3 **Chitcombe** E Susx
36 C6 **Chithurst** W Susx
87 K1 **Chittering** Cambs
33 G2 **Chitterne** Wilts
28 B6 **Chittlehamholt** Devon
27 L5 **Chittlehampton** Devon
46 D5 **Chittoe** Wilts
8 A7 **Chivelstone** Devon
27 J4 **Chivenor** Devon
172 E3 **Chlenry** D & G
50 B6 **Chobham** Surrey
34 B2 **Cholderton** Wilts
68 B5 **Cholesbury** Bucks
179 L5 **Chollerford** Nthumb
179 L4 **Chollerton** Nthumb
130 C7 **Cholmondeston** Ches
48 E2 **Cholsey** Oxon
80 B3 **Cholstrey** Herefs
161 J3 **Chop Gate** N York
181 G2 **Choppington** Nthumb
180 D7 **Chopwell** Gatesd
113 J1 **Chorley** Ches
139 H4 **Chorley** Lancs
96 F6 **Chorley** Shrops
98 D1 **Chorley** Staffs
68 D7 **Chorleywood** Herts
68 C7 **Chorleywood West** Herts
114 A2 **Chorlton** Ches
130 F1 **Chorlton-cum-Hardy** Manch
113 G2 **Chorlton Lane** Ches
95 J5 **Choulton** Shrops
129 L8 **Chowley** Ches
87 J7 **Chrishall** Essex
207 L4 **Chrisswell** Inver
103 K4 **Christchurch** Cambs
18 B5 **Christchurch** Dorset
63 H4 **Christchurch** Gloucs
44 D1 **Christchurch** Newpt
46 D3 **Christian Malford** Wilts
129 K6 **Christleton** Ches
67 H8 **Christmas Common** Oxon
44 D7 **Christon** N Som
191 J2 **Christon Bank** Nthumb
13 J5 **Christow** Devon
37 H5 **Christ's Hospital** W Susx
38 D6 **Chuck Hatch** E Susx
13 K6 **Chudleigh** Devon
13 K7 **Chudleigh Knighton** Devon
28 B8 **Chulmleigh** Devon
131 L2 **Chunal** Derbys
139 L2 **Church** Lancs
63 M3 **Churcham** Gloucs
114 A8 **Church Aston** Wrekin
84 D2 **Church Brampton** Nhants
98 C2 **Churchbridge** Staffs
167 J7 **Church Brough** Cumb
115 K5 **Church Broughton** Derbys
3 H8 **Church Cove** Cnwll
49 K8 **Church Crookham** Hants
64 C3 **Churchdown** Gloucs
114 A8 **Church Eaton** Staffs
68 C3 **Church End** Beds
68 C3 **Church End** Beds
85 J8 **Church End** Beds
85 K8 **Church End** Beds
85 L3 **Church End** Beds
86 C3 **Church End** Beds
86 D4 **Church End** Beds
86 D7 **Church End** Beds
67 H5 **Church End** Bucks
87 K4 **Church End** Cambs
102 B8 **Church End** Cambs
102 E6 **Church End** Cambs
103 G7 **Church End** Cambs
70 F3 **Church End** Essex
71 H2 **Church End** Essex
71 K4 **Church End** Essex
72 E8 **Churchend** Essex
51 H1 **Church End** Gt Lon
49 G7 **Church End** Hants
68 E5 **Church End** Herts
69 H1 **Church End** Herts
70 C3 **Church End** Herts
119 H5 **Church End** Lincs
145 L6 **Church End** Lincs
99 H5 **Church End** Warwks
99 H5 **Church End** Warwks
66 A2 **Church Enstone** Oxon

151 H8 **Church Fenton** N York
98 C5 **Churchfield** Sandw
69 K6 **Churchgate** Herts
70 C5 **Churchgate Street** Essex
14 E3 **Church Green** Devon
115 M7 **Church Gresley** Derbys
66 B4 **Church Hanborough** Oxon
98 C1 **Church Hill** Staffs
161 L3 **Church Houses** N York
15 G2 **Churchill** Devon
27 L3 **Churchill** Devon
44 E7 **Churchill** N Som
65 L2 **Churchill** Oxon
81 L4 **Churchill** Worcs
97 K7 **Churchill** Worcs
30 B8 **Churchinford** Somset
17 H6 **Church Knowle** Dorset
135 G4 **Church Laneham** Notts
100 F5 **Church Langton** Leics
99 M8 **Church Lawford** Warwks
130 F8 **Church Lawton** Ches
115 G4 **Church Leigh** Staffs
82 B5 **Church Lench** Worcs
115 J3 **Church Mayfield** Staffs
130 C7 **Church Minshull** Ches
20 E7 **Church Norton** W Susx
100 B7 **Churchover** Warwks
96 C4 **Church Preen** Shrops
95 K3 **Church Pulverbatch** Shrops
30 B7 **Churchstanton** Somset
95 G4 **Churchstoke** Powys
7 K5 **Churchstow** Devon
84 C4 **Church Stowe** Nhants
88 F6 **Church Street** Essex
52 F4 **Church Street** Kent
107 K6 **Church Street** Suffk
95 L4 **Church Stretton** Shrops
145 J8 **Churchthorpe** Lincs
146 F7 **Churchtown** Bpool
10 F7 **Churchtown** Cnwll
132 E7 **Churchtown** Derbys
28 B2 **Churchtown** Devon
154 f3 **Churchtown** IoM
147 J7 **Churchtown** Lancs
143 K6 **Church Town** N Linc
138 D4 **Churchtown** Sefton
43 G4 **Church Village** Rhondd
133 L6 **Church Warsop** Notts
116 D5 **Church Wilne** Derbys
178 F3 **Churnsike Lodge** Nthumb
8 D4 **Churston Ferrers** Torbay
36 C3 **Churt** Surrey
129 K8 **Churton** Ches
141 L2 **Churwell** Leeds
109 H4 **Chwilog** Gwynd
2 D5 **Chyandour** Cnwll
3 G6 **Chyanvounder** Cnwll
3 K3 **Chyeowling** Cnwll
3 G6 **Chyvarloe** Cnwll
94 E3 **Cil** Powys
128 E6 **Cilcain** Flints
76 F3 **Cilcennin** Cerdgn
94 F3 **Cilcewydd** Powys
57 L5 **Cilfrew** Neath
43 H3 **Cilfynydd** Rhondd
75 L4 **Cilgerran** Pembks
59 K3 **Cilgwyn** Carmth
109 J1 **Cilgwyn** Gwynd
76 F4 **Ciliau-Aeron** Cerdgn
57 K4 **Cilmaengwyn** Neath
78 D5 **Cilmery** Powys
58 A2 **Cilrhedyn** Pembks
59 H4 **Cilsan** Carmth
111 G3 **Ciltalgarth** Gwynd
77 L7 **Cilycwm** Carmth
57 L5 **Cimla** Neath
63 K4 **Cinderford** Gloucs
97 L4 **Cinder Hill** Wolves
50 B3 **Cippenham** Slough
64 F6 **Cirencester** Gloucs
160 B3 **Citadilla** N York
51 J3 **City** Gt Lon
42 F6 **City** V Glam
125 H2 **City Dulas** IoA
224 F3 **Clabhach** Ag & B
207 J3 **Clachaig** Ag & B
206 B7 **Clachan** Ag & B
216 B3 **Clachan** Ag & B
228 D6 **Clachan** Ag & B
247 H1 **Clachan** Highld
283 C8 **Clachan-a-Luib** W Isls
224 A2 **Clachan Mor** Ag & B
283 C8 **Clachan na Luib** W Isls
209 G3 **Clachan of Campsie** E Duns
216 B3 **Clachan-Seil** Ag & B
251 H2 **Clachnaharry** Highld
270 D3 **Clachtoll** Highld
233 H3 **Clackavoid** P & K

210 B1 **Clackmannan** Clacks
266 E4 **Clackmarras** Moray
73 J4 **Clacton-on-Sea** Essex
217 H3 **Cladich** Ag & B
82 C3 **Cladswell** Worcs
227 K3 **Claggan** Highld
258 C6 **Claigan** Highld
45 K7 **Clandown** BaNES
35 L7 **Clanfield** Hants
65 L6 **Clanfield** Oxon
13 H2 **Clannaborough** Devon
34 D1 **Clanville** Hants
31 K4 **Clanville** Somset
206 D7 **Claonaig** Ag & B
17 K2 **Clapgate** Dorset
70 C2 **Clapgate** Herts
85 K5 **Clapham** Beds
13 L5 **Clapham** Devon
51 H4 **Clapham** Gt Lon
148 C2 **Clapham** N York
21 J5 **Clapham** W Susx
85 K4 **Clapham Green** Beds
40 D7 **Clap Hill** Kent
156 E2 **Clappersgate** Cumb
15 J1 **Clapton** Somset
45 J8 **Clapton** Somset
44 F4 **Clapton-in-Gordano** N Som
65 H3 **Clapton-on-the-Hill** Gloucs
28 B6 **Clapworthy** Devon
92 D6 **Clarach** Cerdgn
180 E6 **Claravale** Gatesd
55 H3 **Clarbeston** Pembks
55 G3 **Clarbeston Road** Pembks
134 E3 **Clarborough** Notts
88 F6 **Clare** Suffk
175 J2 **Clarebrand** D & G
176 E5 **Clarencefield** D & G
180 B5 **Clarewood** Nthumb
188 F3 **Clarilaw** Border
35 H1 **Clarken Green** Hants
37 J3 **Clark's Green** Surrey
208 F7 **Clarkston** E Rens
263 K2 **Clashmore** Highld
270 D2 **Clashmore** Highld
270 E2 **Clashnessie** Highld
254 E7 **Clashnoir** Moray
221 H3 **Clathy** P & K
221 H3 **Clathymore** P & K
255 L6 **Clatt** Abers
94 B4 **Clatter** Powys
70 F4 **Clatterford End** Essex
29 J4 **Clatworthy** Somset
147 K7 **Claughton** Lancs
147 L3 **Claughton** Lancs
129 G2 **Claughton** Wirral
30 C4 **Clavelshay** Somset
82 E2 **Claverdon** Warwks
44 F5 **Claverham** N Som
70 C1 **Clavering** Essex
97 H5 **Claverley** Shrops
46 A6 **Claverton** BaNES
45 M6 **Claverton Down** BaNES
43 G6 **Clawdd-coch** V Glam
111 L1 **Clawdd-newydd** Denbgs
157 H7 **Clawthorpe** Cumb
11 L3 **Clawton** Devon
136 B1 **Claxby** Lincs
137 H5 **Claxby** Lincs
151 L4 **Claxton** N York
107 G3 **Claxton** Norfk
100 B5 **Claybrooke Magna** Leics
107 K7 **Clay Common** Suffk
100 D8 **Clay Coton** Nhants
133 H7 **Clay Cross** Derbys
83 K5 **Claydon** Oxon
90 D5 **Claydon** Suffk
69 J2 **Clay End** Herts
177 L3 **Claygate** D & G
39 H4 **Claygate** Kent
50 F6 **Claygate** Surrey
38 F2 **Claygate Cross** Kent
51 L1 **Clayhall** Gt Lon
29 J6 **Clayhanger** Devon
98 D3 **Clayhanger** Wsall
29 L7 **Clayhidon** Devon
24 F3 **Clayhill** E Susx
18 D2 **Clayhill** Hants
87 K2 **Clayhithe** Cambs
279 L4 **Clayock** Highld
87 G4 **Claypit Hill** Cambs
63 M6 **Claypits** Gloucs
117 M2 **Claypole** Lincs
137 H4 **Claythorpe** Lincs
141 H2 **Clayton** Brad
142 C6 **Clayton** Donc
22 D7 **Clayton** W Susx
139 H3 **Clayton Green** Lancs
139 M2 **Clayton-le-Moors** Lancs

139 H3 **Clayton-le-Woods** Lancs
141 L5 **Clayton West** Kirk
134 E2 **Clayworth** Notts
236 F3 **Cleadale** Highld
181 J6 **Cleadon** S Tyne
7 G2 **Clearbrook** Devon
63 H5 **Clearwell** Gloucs
63 H5 **Clearwell Meend** Gloucs
169 H8 **Cleasby** N York
275 C6 **Cleat** Ork
168 E7 **Cleatlam** Dur
164 D7 **Cleator** Cumb
164 D7 **Cleator Moor** Cumb
141 L6 **Cleckheaton** Kirk
96 D7 **Cleedownton** Shrops
96 D8 **Cleehill** Shrops
209 K7 **Cleekhimin** N Lans
96 D6 **Clee St Margaret** Shrops
96 C5 **Cleestanton** Shrops
145 J6 **Cleethorpes** NE Lin
96 E7 **Cleeton St Mary** Shrops
44 F5 **Cleeve** N Som
48 F3 **Cleeve** Oxon
64 E2 **Cleeve Hill** Gloucs
82 C5 **Cleeve Prior** Worcs
212 D2 **Cleghornie** E Loth
80 B7 **Clehonger** Herefs
221 K7 **Cleish** P & K
209 L7 **Cleland** N Lans
68 C4 **Clement's End** Beds
52 B5 **Clement Street** Kent
216 E2 **Clenamacrie** Ag & B
47 H6 **Clench Common** Wilts
120 D7 **Clenchwarton** Norfk
268 D4 **Clenerty** Abers
97 L7 **Clent** Worcs
96 F8 **Cleobury Mortimer** Shrops
96 E6 **Cleobury North** Shrops
192 D2 **Cleongart** Ag & B
252 F2 **Clephanton** Highld
187 L6 **Clerkhill** D & G
185 K3 **Cleuch-head** D & G
46 F4 **Clevancy** Wilts
44 E5 **Clevedon** N Som
66 B2 **Cleveley** Oxon
146 F7 **Cleveleys** Lancs
46 E2 **Cleverton** Wilts
31 G1 **Clewer** Somset
122 A3 **Cley next the Sea** Norfk
166 E5 **Cliburn** Cumb
35 K1 **Cliddesden** Hants
99 G4 **Cliff** Warwks
139 L1 **Cliffe** Lancs
52 F4 **Cliffe** Medway
143 G2 **Cliffe** N York
169 G7 **Cliffe** N York
25 G4 **Cliff End** E Susx
52 F4 **Cliffe Woods** Medway
79 J6 **Clifford** Herefs
150 F7 **Clifford** Leeds
82 E5 **Clifford Chambers** Warwks
63 K2 **Clifford's Mesne** Gloucs
41 K2 **Cliffsend** Kent
86 D7 **Clifton** Beds
45 H4 **Clifton** Bristl
116 F4 **Clifton** C Nott
141 J3 **Clifton** Calder
166 C5 **Clifton** Cumb
115 K3 **Clifton** Derbys
142 E8 **Clifton** Donc
138 F2 **Clifton** Lancs
150 B6 **Clifton** N York
180 F2 **Clifton** Nthumb
66 C1 **Clifton** Oxon
140 A7 **Clifton** Salfd
81 J6 **Clifton** Worcs
151 J5 **Clifton** York
99 H1 **Clifton Campville** Staffs
66 D7 **Clifton Hampden** Oxon
85 H5 **Clifton Reynes** M Keyn
100 C8 **Clifton upon Dunsmore** Warwks
81 G3 **Clifton upon Teme** Worcs
41 L1 **Cliftonville** Kent
21 G6 **Climping** W Susx
32 C1 **Clink** Somset
150 C4 **Clint** N York
245 J1 **Clinterty** C Aber
105 L1 **Clint Green** Norfk
201 J6 **Clintmains** Border
93 H1 **Clipiau** Gwynd
123 J8 **Clippesby** Norfk
118 C8 **Clipsham** Rutlnd
100 F7 **Clipston** Nhants
117 H5 **Clipston** Notts
68 B2 **Clipstone** Beds
134 B7 **Clipstone** Notts
148 C7 **Clitheroe** Lancs

113 H6 **Clive** Shrops	46 F6 **Coate** Wilts	42 D5 **Coity** Brdgnd	49 K6 **College Town** Br For
144 E7 **Clixby** Lincs	102 F4 **Coates** Cambs	282 g3 **Col** W Isls	222 D4 **Collessie** Fife
46 E1 **Cloatley** Wilts	64 E7 **Coates** Gloucs	272 E6 **Colaboll** Highld	28 B7 **Colleton Mills** Devon
111 L1 **Clocaenog** Denbgs	135 H3 **Coates** Lincs	4 E3 **Colan** Cnwll	52 B1 **Collier Row** Gt Lon
267 H4 **Clochan** Moray	135 G3 **Coates** Notts	14 C5 **Colaton Raleigh** Devon	69 K3 **Collier's End** Herts
234 D5 **Clochtow** Angus	21 G3 **Coates** W Susx	258 C7 **Colbost** Highld	24 E3 **Collier's Green** E Susx
129 M2 **Clock Face** St Hel	170 E5 **Coatham** R & Cl	160 B3 **Colburn** N York	39 J5 **Colliers Green** Kent
94 F2 **Cloddiau** Powys	169 H6 **Coatham Mundeville** Darltn	166 F6 **Colby** Cumb	39 H4 **Collier Street** Kent
62 C2 **Clodock** Herefs	27 L5 **Cobbaton** Devon	154 b7 **Colby** IoM	169 J1 **Colliery Row** Sundld
32 B2 **Cloford** Somset	64 D4 **Coberley** Gloucs	122 E5 **Colby** Norfk	257 J6 **Collieston** Abers
257 J3 **Clola** Abers	80 B8 **Cobhall Common** Herefs	72 E2 **Colchester** Essex	176 D4 **Collin** D & G
86 B7 **Clophill** Beds	52 E5 **Cobham** Kent	48 D5 **Cold Ash** W Berk	47 K8 **Collingbourne Ducis** Wilts
102 B7 **Clopton** Nhants	50 E7 **Cobham** Surrey	100 E8 **Cold Ashby** Nhants	47 K7 **Collingbourne Kingston** Wilts
90 F4 **Clopton** Suffk	71 G3 **Coblers Green** Essex	45 L4 **Cold Ashton** S Glos	150 E6 **Collingham** Leeds
90 F4 **Clopton Corner** Suffk	33 H6 **Cobley** Dorset	65 H3 **Cold Aston** Gloucs	135 G7 **Collingham** Notts
88 F4 **Clopton Green** Suffk	80 B3 **Cobnash** Herefs	277 K4 **Coldbackie** Highld	80 F3 **Collington** Herefs
89 K3 **Clopton Green** Suffk	9 j2 **Cobo** Guern	158 C2 **Coldbeck** Cumb	84 E4 **Collingtree** Nhants
9 k1 **Clos du Valle** Guern	114 D2 **Cobridge** C Stke	55 J4 **Cold Blow** Pembks	130 A1 **Collins Green** Warrtn
186 D7 **Closeburn** D & G	269 G3 **Coburby** Abers	85 H5 **Cold Brayfield** M Keyn	81 G4 **Collins Green** Worcs
186 D7 **Closeburnmill** D & G	133 H5 **Cock Alley** Derbys	148 C2 **Cold Cotes** N York	234 F6 **Colliston** Angus
154 c7 **Closeclark** IoM	161 K3 **Cockayne** N York	22 E5 **Coldean** Br & H	14 C2 **Colliton** Devon
16 A1 **Closworth** Somset	86 F5 **Cockayne Hatley** Beds	13 J7 **Coldeast** Devon	101 M3 **Collyweston** Nhants
69 H1 **Clothall** Herts	112 E2 **Cock Bank** Wrexhm	140 E2 **Colden** Calder	182 E5 **Colmonell** S Ayrs
129 M6 **Clotton** Ches	82 C5 **Cock Bevington** Warwks	35 G6 **Colden Common** Hants	86 C4 **Colmworth** Beds
100 A6 **Cloudesley Bush** Warwks	243 J2 **Cock Bridge** Abers	91 K3 **Coldfair Green** Suffk	50 C3 **Colnbrook** Slough
80 D7 **Clouds** Herefs	213 G5 **Cockburnspath** Border	103 J3 **Coldham** Cambs	103 H8 **Colne** Cambs
140 E6 **Clough** Oldham	71 K6 **Cock Clarks** Essex	135 L3 **Cold Hanworth** Lincs	148 F7 **Colne** Lancs
140 D3 **Clough Foot** Calder	88 E4 **Cock & End** Suffk	4 B5 **Coldharbour** Cnwll	141 J4 **Colne Bridge** Kirk
141 H4 **Clough Head** Calder	211 L4 **Cockenzie and Port Seton** E Loth	29 J8 **Coldharbour** Devon	148 F7 **Colne Edge** Lancs
163 H4 **Cloughton** N York	139 G3 **Cocker Bar** Lancs	63 H6 **Coldharbour** Gloucs	71 K1 **Colne Engaine** Essex
163 H3 **Cloughton Newlands** N York	139 L3 **Cocker Brook** Lancs	68 F4 **Cold Harbour** Herts	106 D2 **Colney** Norfk
281 d5 **Clousta** Shet	147 J5 **Cockerham** Lancs	48 F3 **Cold Harbour** Oxon	69 G6 **Colney Heath** Herts
233 M1 **Clova** Angus	164 F4 **Cockermouth** Cumb	37 H2 **Coldharbour** Surrey	68 F6 **Colney Street** Herts
26 E6 **Clovelly** Devon	68 E2 **Cockernhoe Green** Herts	32 E2 **Cold Harbour** Wilts	65 G5 **Coln Rogers** Gloucs
200 F6 **Clovenfords** Border	141 K2 **Cockersdale** Leeds	113 K7 **Cold Hatton** Wrekin	65 H3 **Coln St Aldwyns** Gloucs
228 F3 **Clovulin** Highld	57 H6 **Cockett** Swans	113 K7 **Cold Hatton Heath** Wrekin	65 G5 **Coln St Dennis** Gloucs
140 B2 **Clow Bridge** Lancs	168 E6 **Cockfield** Dur	169 L2 **Cold Hesledon** Dur	256 B5 **Colpy** Abers
133 K4 **Clowne** Derbys	89 H4 **Cockfield** Suffk	142 B5 **Cold Hiendley** Wakefd	200 D5 **Colquhar** Border
81 G1 **Clows Top** Worcs	69 H7 **Cockfosters** Gt Lon	84 C4 **Cold Higham** Nhants	10 E8 **Colquite** Cnwll
112 F3 **Cloy** Wrexhm	71 G3 **Cock Green** Essex	213 K6 **Coldingham** Border	26 F7 **Colscott** Devon
239 H1 **Cluanie Inn** Highld	20 E3 **Cocking** W Susx	161 H6 **Cold Kirby** N York	159 L6 **Colsterdale** N York
239 H2 **Cluanie Lodge** Highld	20 E3 **Cocking Causeway** W Susx	114 D5 **Coldmeece** Staffs	118 B6 **Colsterworth** Lincs
11 K4 **Clubworthy** Cnwll	8 D2 **Cockington** Torbay	100 F2 **Cold Newton** Leics	117 J5 **Colston Bassett** Notts
173 J3 **Clugston** D & G	31 G1 **Cocklake** Somset	11 H5 **Cold Northcott** Cnwll	266 C3 **Coltfield** Moray
95 H7 **Clun** Shrops	156 C2 **Cockley Beck** Cumb	71 K7 **Cold Norton** Essex	49 H8 **Colt Hill** Hants
253 G2 **Clunas** Highld	104 F3 **Cockley Cley** Norfk	101 H2 **Cold Overton** Leics	122 F7 **Coltishall** Norfk
95 J7 **Clunbury** Shrops	24 F3 **Cock Marling** E Susx	41 J6 **Coldred** Kent	156 D5 **Colton** Cumb
55 J3 **Clunderwen** Carmth	49 J3 **Cockpole Green** Wokham	13 G1 **Coldridge** Devon	142 B1 **Colton** Leeds
252 E6 **Clune** Highld	4 C4 **Cocks** Cnwll	202 C5 **Coldstream** Border	151 H6 **Colton** N York
239 K6 **Clunes** Highld	96 D6 **Cockshutford** Shrops	21 H3 **Coldwaltham** W Susx	106 C2 **Colton** Norfk
95 K7 **Clungunford** Shrops	113 G5 **Cockshutt** Shrops	80 A8 **Coldwell** Herefs	115 G7 **Colton** Staffs
268 B6 **Clunie** Abers	39 K3 **Cock Street** Kent	257 H4 **Coldwells** Abers	39 G4 **Colt's Hill** Kent
233 H6 **Clunie** P & K	121 L3 **Cockthorpe** Norfk	96 C6 **Cold Weston** Shrops	13 M3 **Columbjohn** Devon
95 H7 **Clunton** Shrops	2 E4 **Cockwells** Cnwll	31 L4 **Cole** Somset	79 H4 **Colva** Powys
222 D8 **Cluny** Fife	14 A6 **Cockwood** Devon	95 H6 **Colebatch** Shrops	175 L4 **Colvend** D & G
45 J7 **Clutton** BaNES	30 B2 **Cockwood** Somset	7 G3 **Colebrook** C Plym	81 H6 **Colwall** Herefs
113 G1 **Clutton** Ches	131 L4 **Cockyard** Derbys	14 B1 **Colebrook** Devon	179 M4 **Colwell** Nthumb
45 J7 **Clutton Hill** BaNES	80 A8 **Cockyard** Herefs	13 H3 **Colebrooke** Devon	115 G7 **Colwich** Staffs
125 K7 **Clwt-y-bont** Gwynd	90 D4 **Coddenham** Suffk	135 K7 **Coleby** Lincs	117 G3 **Colwick** Notts
61 K4 **Clydach** Mons	129 K8 **Coddington** Ches	143 M4 **Coleby** N Linc	42 E6 **Colwinston** V Glam
57 J4 **Clydach** Swans	81 G6 **Coddington** Herefs	99 G5 **Cole End** Warwks	20 F6 **Colworth** W Susx
42 E3 **Clydach Vale** Rhondd	117 L1 **Coddington** Notts	13 H2 **Coleford** Devon	127 G4 **Colwyn Bay** Conwy
208 E5 **Clydebank** W Duns	33 G3 **Codford St Mary** Wilts	63 H5 **Coleford** Gloucs	14 F4 **Colyford** Devon
75 M5 **Clydey** Pembks	33 G3 **Codford St Peter** Wilts	31 L1 **Coleford** Somset	14 F4 **Colyton** Devon
47 G3 **Clyffe Pypard** Wilts	69 G3 **Codicote** Herts	29 L4 **Coleford Water** Somset	7 L7 **Combe** Devon
207 L2 **Clynder** Ag & B	21 H3 **Codmore Hill** W Susx	106 D6 **Colegate End** Norfk	79 L3 **Combe** Herefs
60 B7 **Clyne** Neath	116 C2 **Codnor** Derbys	69 H5 **Cole Green** Herts	66 B4 **Combe** Oxon
109 G2 **Clynnog-fawr** Gwynd	45 L3 **Codrington** S Glos	70 B1 **Cole Green** Herts	48 A6 **Combe** W Berk
79 H6 **Clyro** Powys	97 K3 **Codsall** Staffs	34 F1 **Cole Henley** Hants	17 J3 **Combe Almer** Dorset
14 A4 **Clyst Honiton** Devon	97 J2 **Codsall Wood** Staffs	17 K2 **Colehill** Dorset	36 E4 **Combe Common** Surrey
14 B2 **Clyst Hydon** Devon	125 H3 **Coedana** IoA	69 G4 **Coleman Green** Herts	45 M6 **Combe Down** BaNES
14 A5 **Clyst St George** Devon	42 F4 **Coedely** Rhondd	38 C6 **Coleman's Hatch** E Susx	8 C2 **Combe Fishacre** Devon
14 B2 **Clyst St Lawrence** Devon	44 B2 **Coedkernew** Newpt	113 G5 **Colemere** Shrops	29 L4 **Combe Florey** Somset
14 A4 **Clyst St Mary** Devon	62 D5 **Coed Morgan** Mons	35 L5 **Colemore** Hants	45 L7 **Combe Hay** BaNES
282 g3 **Cnoc** W Isls	112 D1 **Coedpoeth** Wrexhm	97 G4 **Colemore Green** Shrops	13 L8 **Combeinteignhead** Devon
92 E8 **Cnwch Coch** Cerdgn	129 G7 **Coed Talon** Flints	221 K1 **Colenden** P & K	27 K2 **Combe Martin** Devon
11 K7 **Coad's Green** Cnwll	112 E8 **Coedway** Powys	116 C8 **Coleorton** Leics	14 E2 **Combe Raleigh** Devon
133 G4 **Coal Aston** Derbys	76 C6 **Coed-y-Bryn** Cerdgn	46 B5 **Colerne** Wilts	130 C4 **Comberbach** Ches
61 K5 **Coalbrookvale** Blae G	44 D1 **Coed-y-caerau** Newpt	64 E4 **Colesbourne** Gloucs	99 G2 **Comberford** Staffs
198 D6 **Coalburn** S Lans	62 C7 **Coed-y-paen** Mons	8 A5 **Cole's Cross** Devon	87 H4 **Comberton** Cambs
180 D6 **Coalburns** Gatesd	61 J3 **Coed-yr-ynys** Powys	15 J2 **Coles Cross** Dorset	80 C2 **Comberton** Herefs
63 M6 **Coaley** Gloucs	109 K6 **Coed Ystumgwern** Gwynd	86 C4 **Colesden** Beds	30 D8 **Combe St Nicholas** Somset
71 J7 **Coalhill** Essex	60 C5 **Coelbren** Powys	90 C7 **Coles Green** Suffk	15 G4 **Combpyne** Devon
96 F2 **Coalmoor** Wrekin	8 D1 **Coffinswell** Devon	68 B8 **Coleshill** Bucks	115 H4 **Combridge** Staffs
45 K3 **Coalpit Heath** S Glos	85 K3 **Coffle End** Beds	65 K8 **Coleshill** Oxon	83 H5 **Combrook** Warwks
98 C3 **Coal Pool** Wsall	13 M6 **Cofton** Devon	99 G5 **Coleshill** Warwks	131 L4 **Combs** Derbys
96 F3 **Coalport** Wrekin	98 C8 **Cofton Hackett** Worcs	14 C2 **Colestocks** Devon	90 B4 **Combs** Suffk
221 G8 **Coalsnaughton** Clacks	43 J7 **Cogan** V Glam	45 H7 **Coley** BaNES	90 B4 **Combs Ford** Suffk
90 F1 **Coal Street** Suffk	84 F3 **Cogenhoe** Nhants	37 K4 **Colgate** W Susx	30 C2 **Combwich** Somset
222 E7 **Coaltown of Balgonie** Fife	65 M5 **Cogges** Oxon	223 H6 **Colinsburgh** Fife	244 F2 **Comers** Abers
222 E8 **Coaltown of Wemyss** Fife	71 K3 **Coggeshall** Essex	211 H5 **Colinton** C Edin	81 J2 **Comhampton** Worcs
116 D8 **Coalville** Leics	23 K2 **Coggin's Mill** E Susx	207 G4 **Colintraive** Ag & B	55 K3 **Commercial** Pembks
178 F7 **Coanwood** Nthumb	251 J8 **Coignafearn** Highld	121 K6 **Colkirk** Norfk	87 L3 **Commercial End** Cambs
31 G6 **Coat** Somset	243 K4 **Coilacriech** Abers	222 C1 **Collace** P & K	93 H3 **Commins Coch** Powys
209 J6 **Coatbridge** N Lans	219 K5 **Coilantogle** Stirlg	281 d1 **Collafirth** Shet	170 F8 **Commondale** N York
209 K6 **Coatdyke** N Lans	246 E1 **Coillore** Highld	7 L7 **Collaton** Devon	138 C1 **Common Edge** Bpool
47 J2 **Coate** Swindn	240 B2 **Coiltry** Highld	8 C3 **Collaton St Mary** Torbay	164 D6 **Common End** Cumb
		266 C3 **College of Roseisle** Moray	

Common Moor - Cowesby 305

6 A1 **Common Moor** Cnwll
47 G2 **Common Platt** Wilts
130 A5 **Commonside** Ches
115 L3 **Commonside** Derbys
133 G4 **Common Side** Derbys
113 H6 **Commonwood** Shrops
112 F1 **Commonwood** Wrexhm
30 D4 **Compass** Somset
131 J2 **Compstall** Stockp
175 G4 **Compstonend** D & G
8 C2 **Compton** Devon
34 D5 **Compton** Hants
34 F5 **Compton** Hants
97 J6 **Compton** Staffs
36 E2 **Compton** Surrey
48 D3 **Compton** W Berk
20 C4 **Compton** W Susx
47 H8 **Compton** Wilts
32 E7 **Compton Abbas** Dorset
64 F4 **Compton Abdale** Gloucs
46 F4 **Compton Bassett** Wilts
47 K2 **Compton Beauchamp** Oxon
44 E7 **Compton Bishop** Somset
33 H5 **Compton Chamberlayne** Wilts
45 J6 **Compton Dando** BaNES
31 H4 **Compton Dundon** Somset
30 F7 **Compton Durville** Somset
45 H3 **Compton Greenfield** S Glos
45 G7 **Compton Martin** BaNES
31 L5 **Compton Pauncefoot** Somset
16 B4 **Compton Valence** Dorset
83 H5 **Compton Verney** Warwks
210 D1 **Comrie** Fife
220 D3 **Comrie** P & K
229 G2 **Conaglen House** Highld
248 E6 **Conchra** Highld
233 G6 **Concraigie** P & K
147 J4 **Conder Green** Lancs
81 M7 **Conderton** Worcs
65 H2 **Condicote** Gloucs
209 K4 **Condorrat** N Lans
96 B2 **Condover** Shrops
64 B3 **Coney Hill** Gloucs
37 H6 **Coneyhurst Common** W Susx
151 M2 **Coneysthorpe** N York
150 E4 **Coneythorpe** N York
105 J7 **Coney Weston** Suffk
36 B4 **Conford** Hants
11 K6 **Congdon's Shop** Cnwll
99 K2 **Congerstone** Leics
120 F6 **Congham** Norfk
131 G7 **Congleton** Ches
110 D3 **Congl-y-wal** Gwynd
44 E6 **Congresbury** N Som
97 K1 **Congreve** Staffs
176 C5 **Conheath** D & G
253 J1 **Conicavel** Moray
136 D8 **Coningsby** Lincs
87 G2 **Conington** Cambs
102 D6 **Conington** Cambs
142 D8 **Conisbrough** Donc
145 K8 **Conisholme** Lincs
156 D3 **Coniston** Cumb
144 F1 **Coniston** E R Yk
148 F5 **Coniston Cold** N York
149 H2 **Conistone** N York
129 G6 **Connah's Quay** Flints
228 E8 **Connel** Ag & B
197 H8 **Connel Park** E Ayrs
2 F3 **Connor Downs** Cnwll
250 F1 **Conon Bridge** Highld
149 H6 **Cononley** N York
114 F2 **Consall** Staffs
180 D8 **Consett** Dur
159 L4 **Constable Burton** N York
140 B3 **Constable Lee** Lancs
3 J5 **Constantine** Cnwll
10 B7 **Constantine Bay** Cnwll
262 D8 **Contin** Highld
126 F4 **Conwy** Conwy
40 C2 **Conyer** Kent
89 H2 **Conyer's Green** Suffk
24 C6 **Cooden** E Susx
12 A1 **Cookbury** Devon
11 M2 **Cookbury Wick** Devon
49 L2 **Cookham** W & M
49 L2 **Cookham Dean** W & M
49 L2 **Cookham Rise** W & M
82 C3 **Cookhill** Worcs
107 G8 **Cookley** Suffk
97 J7 **Cookley** Worcs
49 G1 **Cookley Green** Oxon
245 J5 **Cookney** Abers
22 F4 **Cooksbridge** E Susx
81 L1 **Cooksey Green** Worcs
73 J3 **Cook's Green** Essex
89 K4 **Cooks Green** Suffk
114 E3 **Cookshill** Staffs
5 J1 **Cooksland** Cnwll
70 F6 **Cooksmill Green** Essex
130 B5 **Cookson Green** Ches
37 H6 **Coolham** W Susx
53 G4 **Cooling** Medway
52 F4 **Cooling Street** Medway
3 G3 **Coombe** Cnwll
3 L3 **Coombe** Cnwll
13 J5 **Coombe** Devon
13 L7 **Coombe** Devon
14 C4 **Coombe** Devon
63 M8 **Coombe** Gloucs
35 K6 **Coombe** Hants
33 K1 **Coombe** Wilts
33 K5 **Coombe Bissett** Wilts
13 L8 **Coombe Cellars** Devon
35 K6 **Coombe Cross** Hants
64 C2 **Coombe Hill** Gloucs
17 G5 **Coombe Keynes** Dorset
8 D2 **Coombe Pafford** Torbay
21 L5 **Coombes** W Susx
79 L3 **Coombes-Moor** Herefs
32 C4 **Coombe Street** Somset
98 B6 **Coombeswood** Dudley
70 C6 **Coopersale Common** Essex
70 C6 **Coopersale Street** Essex
38 D3 **Cooper's Corner** Kent
23 H3 **Coopers Green** E Susx
69 G5 **Coopers Green** Herts
41 J3 **Cooper Street** Kent
139 J6 **Cooper Turning** Bolton
21 J4 **Cootham** W Susx
90 D6 **Copdock** Suffk
72 D3 **Copford Green** Essex
150 D3 **Copgrove** N York
281 e4 **Copister** Shet
86 C5 **Cople** Beds
141 G3 **Copley** Calder
168 D5 **Copley** Dur
140 E8 **Copley** Tamesd
132 C4 **Coplow Dale** Derbys
151 J6 **Copmanthorpe** York
114 C5 **Copmere End** Staffs
147 H7 **Copp** Lancs
11 H2 **Coppathorne** Cnwll
114 E7 **Coppenhall** Staffs
130 D8 **Coppenhall Moss** Ches
2 F3 **Copperhouse** Cnwll
97 G7 **Coppicegate** Shrops
102 D7 **Coppingford** Cambs
40 B5 **Coppins Corner** Kent
13 H2 **Copplestone** Devon
139 H5 **Coppull** Lancs
139 H5 **Coppull Moor** Lancs
37 J6 **Copsale** W Susx
139 K1 **Copster Green** Lancs
99 M5 **Copston Magna** Warwks
41 J3 **Cop Street** Kent
70 B7 **Copthall Green** Essex
98 F7 **Copt Heath** Solhll
150 D2 **Copt Hewick** N York
11 K4 **Copthorne** Cnwll
37 M3 **Copthorne** W Susx
100 B1 **Copt Oak** Leics
121 L4 **Copy's Green** Norfk
34 C8 **Copythorne** Hants
89 K6 **Coram Street** Suffk
52 C2 **Corbets Tey** Gt Lon
9 a3 **Corbiere** Jersey
180 B6 **Corbridge** Nthumb
101 K5 **Corby** Nhants
118 C6 **Corby Glen** Lincs
178 B7 **Corby Hill** Cumb
195 G5 **Cordon** N Ayrs
132 F4 **Cordwell** Derbys
96 E8 **Coreley** Shrops
49 L2 **Cores End** Bucks
30 C7 **Corfe** Somset
17 J6 **Corfe Castle** Dorset
17 J3 **Corfe Mullen** Dorset
96 B6 **Corfton** Shrops
243 J2 **Corgarff** Abers
35 J6 **Corhampton** Hants
39 G5 **Corks Pond** Kent
99 J6 **Corley** Warwks
99 J6 **Corley Ash** Warwks
99 H6 **Corley Moor** Warwks
233 L2 **Cormuir** Angus
89 H7 **Cornard Tye** Suffk
13 G5 **Corndon** Devon
138 E1 **Corner Row** Lancs
155 K4 **Corney** Cumb
169 J4 **Cornforth** Dur
267 M4 **Cornhill** Abers
202 D5 **Cornhill-on-Tweed** Nthumb
140 D3 **Cornholme** Calder
88 D7 **Cornish Hall End** Essex
224 C6 **Cornoigmore** Ag & B
167 K2 **Cornriggs** Dur
168 F2 **Cornsay** Dur
168 F2 **Cornsay Colliery** Dur
262 F8 **Corntown** Highld
42 D6 **Corntown** V Glam
65 K2 **Cornwell** Oxon
7 H3 **Cornwood** Devon
8 B4 **Cornworthy** Devon
239 H8 **Corpach** Highld
122 C5 **Corpusty** Norfk
244 B3 **Corrachree** Abers
5 G5 **Corran** Cnwll
229 G3 **Corran** Highld
238 D2 **Corran** Highld
154 f4 **Corrany** IoM
177 G2 **Corrie** D & G
195 G2 **Corrie** N Ayrs
193 J4 **Corriecravie** N Ayrs
195 G4 **Corriegills** N Ayrs
239 M5 **Corriegour Lodge Hotel** Highld
262 C7 **Corriemoille** Highld
250 C5 **Corrimony** Highld
135 H2 **Corringham** Lincs
52 F2 **Corringham** Thurr
93 G2 **Corris** Gwynd
92 F2 **Corris Uchaf** Gwynd
217 K7 **Corrow** Ag & B
247 K4 **Corry** Highld
12 E3 **Corscombe** Devon
15 L1 **Corscombe** Dorset
64 A2 **Corse** Gloucs
64 B1 **Corse Lawn** Gloucs
46 C5 **Corsham** Wilts
244 F2 **Corsindae** Abers
32 D2 **Corsley** Wilts
32 D2 **Corsley Heath** Wilts
185 J7 **Corsock** D & G
45 K6 **Corston** BaNES
46 D2 **Corston** Wilts
211 G4 **Corstorphine** C Edin
109 L7 **Cors-y-Gedol** Gwynd
234 B3 **Cortachy** Angus
107 L4 **Corton** Suffk
32 F3 **Corton** Wilts
31 K6 **Corton Denham** Somset
229 H2 **Coruanan** Highld
111 L3 **Corwen** Denbgs
16 B5 **Coryates** Dorset
12 B5 **Coryton** Devon
52 F2 **Coryton** Thurr
100 C4 **Cosby** Leics
97 L4 **Coseley** Dudley
97 H2 **Cosford** Shrops
84 F6 **Cosgrove** Nhants
19 L3 **Cosham** C Port
55 G6 **Cosheston** Pembks
231 L5 **Coshieville** P & K
116 E3 **Cossall** Notts
116 E3 **Cossall Marsh** Notts
100 D1 **Cossington** Leics
30 E3 **Cossington** Somset
106 D1 **Costessey** Norfk
116 F6 **Costock** Notts
117 M7 **Coston** Leics
106 B2 **Coston** Norfk
65 M6 **Cote** Oxon
30 E2 **Cote** Somset
130 B6 **Cotebrook** Ches
166 B1 **Cotehill** Cumb
157 G5 **Cotes** Cumb
116 F7 **Cotes** Leics
114 C4 **Cotes** Staffs
100 C7 **Cotesbach** Leics
114 C4 **Cotes Heath** Staffs
30 A5 **Cotford St Luke** Somset
117 H4 **Cotgrave** Notts
256 F8 **Cothal** Abers
117 L2 **Cotham** Notts
30 B4 **Cothelstone** Somset
168 C6 **Cotherstone** Dur
66 C7 **Cothill** Oxon
14 E2 **Cotleigh** Devon
116 D3 **Cotmanhay** Derbys
87 H3 **Coton** Cambs
84 D1 **Coton** Nhants
113 J4 **Coton** Shrops
98 F2 **Coton** Staffs
114 C7 **Coton** Staffs
114 F5 **Coton** Staffs
114 D7 **Coton Clanford** Staffs
114 F5 **Coton Hayes** Staffs
96 B1 **Coton Hill** Shrops
115 K5 **Coton in the Clay** Staffs
115 L8 **Coton in the Elms** Derbys
115 M7 **Coton Park** Derbys
8 B3 **Cott** Devon
34 E2 **Cottage End** Hants
152 F3 **Cottam** E R Yk
139 G1 **Cottam** Lancs
135 G4 **Cottam** Notts
87 J2 **Cottenham** Cambs
158 E4 **Cotterdale** N York
69 J1 **Cottered** Herts
98 D7 **Cotteridge** Birm
102 A5 **Cotterstock** Nhants
100 F8 **Cottesbrooke** Nhants
101 K1 **Cottesmore** Rutlnd
144 D1 **Cottingham** E R Yk
101 J5 **Cottingham** Nhants
149 K8 **Cottingley** Brad
66 E1 **Cottisford** Oxon
90 C2 **Cotton** Suffk
86 B6 **Cotton End** Beds
148 F7 **Cotton Tree** Lancs
255 K6 **Cottown** Abers
256 D8 **Cottown** Abers
256 E4 **Cottown of Gight** Abers
43 G6 **Cottrell** V Glam
6 E2 **Cotts** Devon
113 K8 **Cotwall** Wrekin
114 E4 **Cotwalton** Staffs
5 K3 **Couch's Mill** Cnwll
63 H3 **Coughton** Herefs
82 C3 **Coughton** Warwks
206 A6 **Coulaghailtro** Ag & B
248 F3 **Coulags** Highld
155 H1 **Coulderton** Cumb
244 B3 **Coull** Abers
207 L2 **Coulport** Ag & B
51 J7 **Coulsdon** Gt Lon
46 D8 **Coulston** Wilts
199 H6 **Coulter** S Lans
21 G3 **Coultershaw Bridge** W Susx
30 C3 **Coultings** Somset
161 K7 **Coulton** N York
222 F3 **Coultra** Fife
96 D2 **Cound** Shrops
96 D2 **Coundlane** Shrops
169 G5 **Coundon** Dur
169 G5 **Coundon Grange** Dur
159 G5 **Countersett** N York
33 K2 **Countess** Wilts
72 C1 **Countess Cross** Essex
13 M4 **Countess Wear** Devon
100 D4 **Countesthorpe** Leics
28 C1 **Countisbury** Devon
233 K7 **Coupar Angus** P & K
139 H2 **Coup Green** Lancs
167 G7 **Coupland** Cumb
202 E7 **Coupland** Nthumb
194 C2 **Cour** Ag & B
187 G8 **Courance** D & G
40 E8 **Court-at-Street** Kent
237 K1 **Courteachan** Highld
84 E4 **Courteenhall** Nhants
59 G4 **Court Henry** Carmth
72 F8 **Courtsend** Essex
30 B4 **Courtway** Somset
211 L5 **Cousland** Mdloth
39 G6 **Cousley Wood** E Susx
207 L3 **Cove** Ag & B
213 G4 **Cove** Border
29 G7 **Cove** Devon
49 L7 **Cove** Hants
260 C2 **Cove** Highld
245 L3 **Cove Bay** C Aber
107 K7 **Cove Bottom** Suffk
107 L7 **Covehithe** Suffk
97 K2 **Coven** Staffs
103 K7 **Coveney** Cambs
136 F1 **Covenham St Bartholomew** Lincs
136 F1 **Covenham St Mary** Lincs
97 K2 **Coven Heath** Staffs
99 J7 **Coventry** Covtry
3 K7 **Coverack** Cnwll
3 H5 **Coverack Bridges** Cnwll
159 K5 **Coverham** N York
85 L1 **Covington** Cambs
199 G5 **Covington** S Lans
157 K7 **Cowan Bridge** Lancs
23 K4 **Cowbeech** E Susx
119 H7 **Cowbit** Lincs
42 F6 **Cowbridge** V Glam
132 B5 **Cowdale** Derbys
38 C5 **Cowden** Kent
211 G1 **Cowdenbeath** Fife
38 C5 **Cowden Pound** Kent
38 D5 **Cowden Station** Kent
116 A2 **Cowers Lane** Derbys
19 H4 **Cowes** IoW
161 G5 **Cowesby** N York

06 **Cowesfield Green - Crosshill**

34 B6 **Cowesfield Green** Wilts
37 K6 **Cowfold** W Susx
158 C5 **Cowgill** Cumb
90 C2 **Cow Green** Suffk
45 J1 **Cowhill** S Glos
82 D6 **Cow Honeybourne** Worcs
209 M1 **Cowie** Stirlg
152 E3 **Cowlam** E R Yk
13 L3 **Cowley** Devon
64 D4 **Cowley** Gloucs
50 D3 **Cowley** Gt Lon
66 D6 **Cowley** Oxon
139 J4 **Cowling** Lancs
149 H7 **Cowling** N York
160 C5 **Cowling** N York
88 E4 **Cowlinge** Suffk
141 J4 **Cowmes** Kirk
140 C4 **Cowpe** Lancs
181 H3 **Cowpen** Nthumb
170 B5 **Cowpen Bewley** S on T
19 M2 **Cowplain** Hants
167 K3 **Cowshill** Dur
44 F6 **Cowslip Green** N Som
150 F5 **Cowthorpe** N York
95 J8 **Coxall** Herefs
113 L3 **Coxbank** Ches
116 C3 **Coxbench** Derbys
31 J3 **Coxbridge** Somset
107 H7 **Cox Common** Suffk
11 H3 **Coxford** Cnwll
121 J5 **Coxford** Norfk
97 H6 **Coxgreen** Staffs
39 J3 **Coxheath** Kent
169 J3 **Coxhoe** Dur
31 H2 **Coxley** Somset
141 L4 **Coxley** Wakefd
31 H2 **Coxley Wick** Somset
12 A8 **Coxpark** Cnwll
70 E7 **Coxtie Green** Essex
161 H7 **Coxwold** N York
42 E6 **Coychurch** Brdgnd
196 E7 **Coylton** S Ayrs
242 B1 **Coylumbridge** Highld
42 D4 **Coytrahen** Brdgnd
82 B2 **Crabbs Cross** Worcs
17 L1 **Crab Orchard** Dorset
37 K6 **Crabtree** W Susx
112 E3 **Crabtree Green** Wrexhm
166 F6 **Crackenthorpe** Cumb
11 G3 **Crackington Haven** Cnwll
114 C2 **Crackley** Staffs
99 J8 **Crackley** Warwks
97 G1 **Crackleybank** Shrops
159 H3 **Crackpot** N York
149 H4 **Cracoe** N York
29 K8 **Craddock** Devon
70 C3 **Cradle End** Herts
97 L6 **Cradley** Dudley
81 G6 **Cradley** Herefs
97 L6 **Cradley Heath** Sandw
60 F1 **Cradoc** Powys
6 D4 **Crafthole** Cnwll
67 L3 **Crafton** Bucks
157 G7 **Crag Foot** Lancs
253 K6 **Craggan** Highld
150 B8 **Cragg Hill** Leeds
180 F8 **Craghead** Dur
60 D2 **Crai** Powys
267 K4 **Craibstone** Moray
234 D6 **Craichie** Angus
235 H4 **Craig** Angus
249 H2 **Craig** Highld
197 H8 **Craigbank** E Ayrs
200 B2 **Craigburn** Border
57 J4 **Craigcefnparc** Swans
177 K2 **Craigcleuch** D & G
256 F5 **Craigdam** Abers
216 C6 **Craigdhu** Ag & B
245 G1 **Craigearn** Abers
254 F3 **Craigellachie** Moray
221 K3 **Craigend** P & K
208 D5 **Craigend** Rens
208 A3 **Craigendoran** Ag & B
173 H3 **Craighlaw** D & G
205 H3 **Craighouse** Ag & B
233 H6 **Craigie** P & K
196 E4 **Craigie** S Ayrs
269 G3 **Craigiefold** Abers
175 J3 **Craigley** D & G
57 K4 **Craig Llangiwg** Neath
211 H5 **Craiglockhart** C Edin
211 J4 **Craigmillar** C Edin
112 C4 **Craignant** Shrops
185 J5 **Craigneston** D & G
209 K6 **Craigneuk** N Lans
209 K7 **Craigneuk** N Lans
227 L5 **Craignure** Ag & B
235 H3 **Craigo** Angus
42 E6 **Craig Penllyn** V Glam
222 F5 **Craigrothie** Fife
219 H3 **Craigruie** Stirlg
88 E7 **Craig's End** Essex
234 D7 **Craigton** Angus
245 J3 **Craigton** C Aber
208 E8 **Craigton** E Rens
233 M5 **Craigton of Airlie** Angus
57 K4 **Craig-y-Duke** Neath
60 C4 **Craig-y-nos** Powys
223 L5 **Crail** Fife
189 J1 **Crailing** Border
143 J8 **Craiselound** N Linc
160 C5 **Crakehall** N York
160 F7 **Crakehill** N York
115 H4 **Crakemarsh** Staffs
151 M3 **Crambe** N York
181 G3 **Cramlington** Nthumb
211 G4 **Cramond** C Edin
211 G4 **Cramond Bridge** C Edin
34 E6 **Crampmoor** Hants
130 E6 **Cranage** Ches
114 C4 **Cranberry** Staffs
33 H8 **Cranborne** Dorset
39 J6 **Cranbrook** Kent
39 K5 **Cranbrook Common** Kent
141 M7 **Crane Moor** Barns
105 J1 **Crane's Corner** Norfk
85 J6 **Cranfield** Beds
26 F6 **Cranford** Devon
50 E4 **Cranford** Gt Lon
101 K7 **Cranford St Andrew** Nhants
101 K8 **Cranford St John** Nhants
64 C4 **Cranham** Gloucs
52 C2 **Cranham** Gt Lon
82 D4 **Cranhill** Warwks
139 G7 **Crank** St Hel
37 G3 **Cranleigh** Surrey
89 L1 **Cranmer Green** Suffk
18 F5 **Cranmore** IoW
31 L2 **Cranmore** Somset
101 G4 **Cranoe** Leics
91 H2 **Cransford** Suffk
212 F6 **Cranshaws** Border
154 f2 **Cranstal** IoM
152 F5 **Cranswick** E R Yk
4 C3 **Crantock** Cnwll
118 D2 **Cranwell** Lincs
104 F4 **Cranwich** Norfk
105 K3 **Cranworth** Norfk
216 B5 **Craobh Haven** Ag & B
6 F1 **Crapstone** Devon
216 F7 **Crarae** Ag & B
272 D3 **Crask Inn** Highld
250 E3 **Crask of Aigas** Highld
191 K2 **Craster** Nthumb
79 K8 **Craswall** Herefs
97 K2 **Crateford** Staffs
107 G8 **Cratfield** Suffk
245 G4 **Crathes** Abers
243 J4 **Crathie** Abers
241 G5 **Crathie** Highld
161 G1 **Crathorne** N York
95 K6 **Craven Arms** Shrops
180 D6 **Crawcrook** Gatesd
139 G7 **Crawford** Lancs
186 E2 **Crawford** S Lans
186 C2 **Crawfordjohn** S Lans
34 F4 **Crawley** Hants
65 M4 **Crawley** Oxon
37 L4 **Crawley** W Susx
38 A6 **Crawley Down** W Susx
168 C3 **Crawleyside** Dur
140 B3 **Crawshawbooth** Lancs
245 J7 **Crawton** Abers
72 D3 **Craxe's Green** Essex
159 G6 **Cray** N York
52 B4 **Crayford** Gt Lon
151 J2 **Crayke** N York
122 B5 **Craymere Beck** Norfk
71 H8 **Crays Hill** Essex
48 F3 **Cray's Pond** Oxon
115 L6 **Craythorne** Staffs
29 H8 **Craze Lowman** Devon
49 J3 **Crazies Hill** Wokham
28 E7 **Creacombe** Devon
228 F6 **Creagan Inn** Ag & B
283 c9 **Creag Ghoraidh** W Isls
283 c9 **Creagorry** W Isls
230 B2 **Creaguaineach Lodge** Highld
113 H5 **Creamore Bank** Shrops
84 D1 **Creaton** Nhants
177 H5 **Creca** D & G
80 B6 **Credenhill** Herefs
13 J2 **Crediton** Devon
183 J7 **Creebank** D & G
173 K2 **Creebridge** D & G
30 D5 **Creech Heathfield** Somset
30 C6 **Creech St Michael** Somset
4 F5 **Creed** Cnwll
51 M3 **Creekmouth** Gt Lon
72 D7 **Creeksea** Essex
90 C4 **Creeting St Mary** Suffk
118 D7 **Creeton** Lincs
174 D3 **Creetown** D & G
154 b8 **Cregneash** IoM
154 e5 **Cregny Baa** IoM
79 G5 **Cregrina** Powys
222 E3 **Creich** Fife
43 G5 **Creigiau** Cardif
6 E4 **Cremyll** Cnwll
96 D3 **Cressage** Shrops
132 C5 **Cressbrook** Derbys
55 H5 **Cresselly** Pembks
67 K8 **Cressex** Bucks
71 J3 **Cressing** Essex
191 K7 **Cresswell** Nthumb
55 H5 **Cresswell** Pembks
114 F4 **Cresswell** Staffs
133 K5 **Creswell** Derbys
98 D1 **Creswell Green** Staffs
90 F3 **Cretingham** Suffk
206 A5 **Cretshengan** Ag & B
112 F1 **Crewe** Ches
130 D8 **Crewe** Ches
130 E8 **Crewe Green** Ches
112 D8 **Crew Green** Powys
15 K1 **Crewkerne** Somset
69 J7 **Crews Hill Station** Gt Lon
116 C5 **Crewton** C Derb
218 F2 **Crianlarich** Stirlg
45 H3 **Cribbs Causeway** S Glos
76 F5 **Cribyn** Cerdgn
109 J4 **Criccieth** Gwynd
116 B1 **Crich** Derbys
116 B1 **Crich Carr** Derbys
211 L6 **Crichton** Mdloth
44 F1 **Crick** Mons
84 B1 **Crick** Nhants
78 F6 **Crickadarn** Powys
15 J1 **Cricket St Thomas** Somset
112 D7 **Crickheath** Shrops
61 K3 **Crickhowell** Powys
65 G8 **Cricklade** Wilts
51 G2 **Cricklewood** Gt Lon
142 E3 **Cridling Stubbs** N York
220 F3 **Crieff** P & K
5 G3 **Criggan** Cnwll
112 D8 **Criggion** Powys
141 M4 **Crigglestone** Wakefd
140 C5 **Crimble** Rochdl
269 K5 **Crimond** Abers
104 C3 **Crimplesham** Norfk
82 F5 **Crimscote** Warwks
250 D4 **Crinaglack** Highld
216 B8 **Crinan** Ag & B
209 L7 **Crindledyke** N Lans
106 D2 **Cringleford** Norfk
149 J6 **Cringles** Brad
55 K4 **Crinow** Pembks
2 D4 **Cripplesease** Cnwll
33 J8 **Cripplestyle** Dorset
24 D3 **Cripp's Corner** E Susx
62 F1 **Crizeley** Herefs
251 H6 **Croachy** Highld
10 E8 **Croanford** Cnwll
52 B5 **Crockenhill** Kent
49 H2 **Crocker End** Oxon
20 F5 **Crockerhill** W Susx
13 H4 **Crockernwell** Devon
63 G4 **Crocker's Ash** Herefs
32 E2 **Crockerton** Wilts
185 K8 **Crocketford** D & G
151 K6 **Crockey Hill** York
38 C3 **Crockham Hill** Kent
39 G4 **Crockhurst Street** Kent
72 F2 **Crockleford Heath** Essex
30 D8 **Crock Street** Somset
42 C3 **Croeserw** Neath
74 D6 **Croes-goch** Pembks
76 C6 **Croes-lan** Cerdgn
110 B3 **Croesor** Gwynd
58 D5 **Croesyceiliog** Carmth
62 C7 **Croesyceiliog** Torfn
62 C8 **Croes-y-mwyalch** Torfn
62 C6 **Croes-y-pant** Mons
100 B4 **Croft** Leics
137 J7 **Croft** Lincs
130 C1 **Croft** Warrtn
208 E2 **Croftamie** Stirlg
3 H4 **Croft Michael** Cnwll
165 J1 **Crofton** Cumb
142 B4 **Crofton** Wakefd
47 K6 **Crofton** Wilts
160 D1 **Croft-on-Tees** N York
266 F6 **Crofts** Moray
139 M8 **Crofts Bank** Traffd
267 G4 **Crofts of Dipple** Moray
269 J4 **Crofts of Savoch** Abers
56 F6 **Crofty** Swans
111 K4 **Crogen** Gwynd
227 K7 **Croggan** Ag & B
166 D1 **Croglin** Cumb
262 D2 **Croik** Highld
264 B6 **Cromarty** Highld
210 E2 **Crombie** Fife
253 L6 **Cromdale** Highld
69 J2 **Cromer** Herts
122 E3 **Cromer** Norfk
132 F8 **Cromford** Derbys
45 K1 **Cromhall** S Glos
45 K1 **Cromhall Common** S Glos
282 g4 **Cromor** W Isls
140 E6 **Crompton Fold** Oldham
134 F7 **Cromwell** Notts
197 H6 **Cronberry** E Ayrs
36 B1 **Crondall** Hants
154 e6 **Cronkbourne** IoM
154 d5 **Cronk-y-Voddy** IoM
129 L2 **Cronton** Knows
157 G4 **Crook** Cumb
168 F4 **Crook** Dur
165 G2 **Crookdake** Cumb
139 H6 **Crooke** Wigan
63 J3 **Crooked End** Gloucs
196 E3 **Crookedholm** E Ayrs
47 L4 **Crooked Soley** Wilts
132 F2 **Crookes** Sheff
180 D8 **Crookhall** Dur
202 E5 **Crookham** Nthumb
48 D6 **Crookham** W Berk
49 J8 **Crookham Village** Hants
199 J7 **Crook Inn** Border
157 H6 **Crooklands** Cumb
221 J7 **Crook of Devon** P & K
115 L4 **Cropper** Derbys
83 L6 **Cropredy** Oxon
100 C1 **Cropston** Leics
82 B6 **Cropthorne** Worcs
162 D5 **Cropton** N York
117 H4 **Cropwell Bishop** Notts
117 J4 **Cropwell Butler** Notts
282 h1 **Cros** W Isls
195 K1 **Crosbie** N Ayrs
282 g4 **Crosbost** W Isls
164 E3 **Crosby** Cumb
154 d6 **Crosby** IoM
143 M5 **Crosby** N Linc
138 C8 **Crosby** Sefton
158 C1 **Crosby Garret** Cumb
166 E7 **Crosby Ravensworth** Cumb
164 E3 **Crosby Villa** Cumb
31 K2 **Croscombe** Somset
113 G5 **Crosemere** Shrops
141 H5 **Crosland Edge** Kirk
141 H5 **Crosland Hill** Kirk
44 E8 **Cross** Somset
194 C1 **Crossaig** Ag & B
224 C6 **Crossapoll** Ag & B
62 E3 **Cross Ash** Mons
39 K4 **Cross-at-Hand** Kent
21 H5 **Crossbush** W Susx
164 E3 **Crosscanonby** Cumb
4 B4 **Cross Coombe** Cnwll
122 E4 **Crossdale Street** Norfk
85 L4 **Cross End** Beds
89 G8 **Cross End** Essex
138 D4 **Crossens** Sefton
149 K7 **Cross Flatts** Brad
210 E2 **Crossford** Fife
198 D4 **Crossford** S Lans
11 L5 **Crossgate** Cnwll
119 H6 **Crossgate** Lincs
114 E4 **Crossgate** Staffs
211 L5 **Crossgatehall** E Loth
196 D2 **Crossgates** E Ayrs
210 F1 **Crossgates** Fife
142 B1 **Cross Gates** Leeds
163 J6 **Crossgates** N York
78 F2 **Crossgates** Powys
147 L3 **Crossgill** Lancs
11 M5 **Cross Green** Devon
141 M2 **Cross Green** Leeds
97 K2 **Cross Green** Staffs
89 G4 **Cross Green** Suffk
89 H4 **Cross Green** Suffk
89 K4 **Cross Green** Suffk
55 L2 **Crosshands** Carmth
59 G6 **Cross Hands** Carmth
196 F5 **Crosshands** E Ayrs
55 H4 **Cross Hands** Pembks
116 C2 **Cross Hill** Derbys
222 B7 **Crosshill** Fife
183 J2 **Crosshill** S Ayrs

149 H6 **Cross Hills** N York
196 D3 **Crosshouse** E Ayrs
96 C2 **Cross Houses** Shrops
96 F5 **Cross Houses** Shrops
23 J3 **Cross in Hand** E Susx
76 D4 **Cross Inn** Cerdgn
77 G2 **Cross Inn** Cerdgn
55 J5 **Cross Inn** Pembks
43 G5 **Cross Inn** Rhondd
208 B2 **Cross Keys** Ag & B
43 K3 **Crosskeys** Caerph
46 C5 **Cross Keys** Wilts
279 H2 **Crosskirk** Highld
156 E5 **Crosslands** Cumb
19 H5 **Cross Lane** IoW
97 G4 **Cross Lane Head** Shrops
3 H6 **Cross Lanes** Cnwll
4 C6 **Cross Lanes** Cnwll
151 H3 **Cross Lanes** N York
112 E7 **Crosslanes** Shrops
112 E2 **Cross Lanes** Wrexhm
208 C6 **Crosslee** Rens
141 K3 **Crossley** Kirk
175 J2 **Crossmichael** D & G
61 H2 **Cross Oak** Powys
256 D5 **Cross of Jackston** Abers
115 M2 **Cross o' th' hands** Derbys
37 L6 **Crosspost** W Susx
244 D2 **Crossroads** Abers
245 G5 **Crossroads** Abers
78 D4 **Cross Roads** Powys
106 D8 **Cross Street** Suffk
234 E4 **Crosston** Angus
130 E4 **Cross Town** Ches
62 F3 **Crossway** Mons
78 E4 **Crossway** Powys
63 G8 **Crossway Green** Mons
81 J2 **Crossway Green** Worcs
16 E5 **Crossways** Dorset
75 J5 **Crosswell** Pembks
156 F4 **Crosthwaite** Cumb
138 F4 **Croston** Lancs
122 E8 **Crostwick** Norfk
123 G5 **Crostwight** Norfk
38 F2 **Crouch** Kent
40 D4 **Crouch** Kent
51 J1 **Crouch End** Gt Lon
33 J6 **Croucheston** Wilts
32 B8 **Crouch Hill** Dorset
38 C4 **Crough House Green** Kent
84 A8 **Croughton** Nhants
268 E3 **Crovie** Abers
18 B3 **Crow** Hants
3 G4 **Crowan** Cnwll
38 D7 **Crowborough** E Susx
38 D7 **Crowborough Town** E Susx
29 L3 **Crowcombe** Somset
132 B6 **Crowdecote** Derbys
141 G7 **Crowden** Derbys
12 C3 **Crowden** Devon
35 G6 **Crowdhill** Hants
52 C7 **Crowdleham** Kent
141 J6 **Crow Edge** Barns
67 H7 **Crowell** Oxon
87 G4 **Crow End** Cambs
84 B7 **Crowfield** Nhants
90 D4 **Crowfield** Suffk
90 D4 **Crowfield Green** Suffk
123 G7 **Crowgate Street** Norfk
70 E7 **Crow Green** Essex
213 G4 **Crowhill** E Loth
63 J2 **Crow Hill** Herefs
133 G4 **Crowhole** Derbys
24 D5 **Crowhurst** E Susx
38 B4 **Crowhurst** Surrey
38 B4 **Crowhurst Lane End** Surrey
102 E2 **Crowland** Lincs
89 K1 **Crowland** Suffk
2 E4 **Crowlas** Cnwll
143 K5 **Crowle** N Linc
81 L4 **Crowle** Worcs
81 L4 **Crowle Green** Worcs
48 F1 **Crowmarsh Gifford** Oxon
90 F1 **Crown Corner** Suffk
6 F3 **Crownhill** C Plym
36 E2 **Crownpits** Surrey
106 B3 **Crownthorpe** Norfk
3 G5 **Crowntown** Cnwll
2 B5 **Crows-an-Wra** Cnwll
71 G2 **Crow's Green** Essex
105 J2 **Crowshill** Norfk
6 B1 **Crow's Nest** Cnwll
95 J3 **Crowsnest** Shrops
49 K6 **Crowthorne** Wokham
130 B5 **Crowton** Ches
99 G1 **Croxall** Staffs
144 F8 **Croxby** Lincs
169 H3 **Croxdale** Dur

115 H4 **Croxden** Staffs
68 D7 **Croxley Green** Herts
86 E3 **Croxton** Cambs
144 E5 **Croxton** N Linc
105 H6 **Croxton** Norfk
121 L5 **Croxton** Norfk
114 B5 **Croxton** Staffs
114 B5 **Croxtonbank** Staffs
113 J1 **Croxton Green** Ches
117 L5 **Croxton Kerrial** Leics
252 E2 **Croy** Highld
209 J4 **Croy** N Lans
27 H3 **Croyde** Devon
27 G3 **Croyde Bay** Devon
87 G5 **Croydon** Cambs
51 J6 **Croydon** Gt Lon
241 J5 **Crubenmore** Highld
95 K2 **Cruckmeole** Shrops
95 K1 **Cruckton** Shrops
257 K4 **Cruden Bay** Abers
113 K7 **Crudgington** Wrekin
64 D8 **Crudwell** Wilts
12 C3 **Cruft** Devon
79 H1 **Crug** Powys
10 C7 **Crugmeer** Cnwll
77 J7 **Crugybar** Carmth
94 E7 **Crug-y-byddar** Powys
43 K2 **Crumlin** Caerph
5 L4 **Crumplehorn** Cnwll
140 C7 **Crumpsall** Manch
40 E5 **Crundale** Kent
54 F7 **Crundale** Pembks
55 L5 **Crunwear** Pembks
28 F8 **Cruwys Morchard** Devon
48 B7 **Crux Easton** Hants
16 B3 **Cruxton** Dorset
58 E6 **Crwbin** Carmth
67 L7 **Cryers Hill** Bucks
75 L5 **Crymmych** Pembks
60 B6 **Crynant** Neath
51 J5 **Crystal Palace** Gt Lon
260 A8 **Cuaig** Highld
215 L2 **Cuan Ferry Village** Ag & B
83 H2 **Cubbington** Warwks
4 C3 **Cubert** Cnwll
141 K7 **Cubley** Barns
67 K3 **Cublington** Bucks
79 M7 **Cublington** Herefs
22 D2 **Cuckfield** W Susx
32 C5 **Cucklington** Somset
133 L5 **Cuckney** Notts
119 G7 **Cuckoo Bridge** Lincs
35 M3 **Cuckoo's Corner** Hants
129 J7 **Cuckoo's Nest** Ches
66 F6 **Cuddesdon** Oxon
67 H5 **Cuddington** Bucks
130 B5 **Cuddington** Ches
113 G2 **Cuddington Heath** Ches
147 J8 **Cuddy Hill** Lancs
51 L7 **Cudham** Gt Lon
12 C6 **Cudliptown** Devon
17 L3 **Cudnell** Bmouth
142 B6 **Cudworth** Barns
30 F8 **Cudworth** Somset
139 H3 **Cuerden Green** Lancs
130 A2 **Cuerdley Cross** Warrtn
49 G7 **Cufaude** Hants
69 J6 **Cuffley** Herts
228 F4 **Cuil** Highld
263 G7 **Culbokie** Highld
28 E1 **Culbone** Somset
250 E8 **Culburnie** Highld
251 J3 **Culcabock** Highld
253 G2 **Culcharry** Highld
130 C1 **Culcheth** Warrtn
255 K5 **Culdrain** Abers
248 A4 **Culduie** Highld
89 G1 **Culford** Suffk
166 E5 **Culgaith** Cumb
66 D8 **Culham** Oxon
270 D2 **Culkein** Highld
270 F1 **Culkein Drumbeg** Highld
64 D7 **Culkerton** Gloucs
267 K3 **Cullen** Moray
181 K3 **Cullercoats** N Tyne
245 G3 **Cullerlie** Abers
263 H7 **Cullicudden** Highld
149 J8 **Cullingworth** Brad
215 L2 **Cullipool House** Ag & B
281 e2 **Cullivoe** Shet
252 D3 **Culloden** Highld
14 B1 **Cullompton** Devon
29 J7 **Culm Davy** Devon
96 B7 **Culmington** Shrops
29 K8 **Culmstock** Devon
270 E7 **Culnacraig** Highld
175 J5 **Culnaightrie** D & G
259 J4 **Culnaknock** Highld

90 F5 **Culpho** Suffk
263 G1 **Culrain** Highld
210 D2 **Culross** Fife
196 C8 **Culroy** S Ayrs
256 B5 **Culsalmond** Abers
174 D5 **Culscadden** D & G
173 H4 **Culshabbin** D & G
281 C6 **Culswick** Shet
257 G7 **Cultercullen** Abers
245 K3 **Cults** C Aber
52 D6 **Culverstone Green** Kent
118 D3 **Culverthorpe** Lincs
84 A6 **Culworth** Nhants
209 K4 **Cumbernauld** N Lans
209 K4 **Cumbernauld Village** N Lans
137 J5 **Cumberworth** Lincs
165 K1 **Cumdivock** Cumb
268 E6 **Cuminestown** Abers
202 B2 **Cumledge** Border
177 L8 **Cummersdale** Cumb
176 F5 **Cummertrees** D & G
266 C2 **Cummingston** Moray
197 H7 **Cumnock** E Ayrs
66 C6 **Cumnor** Oxon
178 D8 **Cumrew** Cumb
176 E2 **Cumrue** D & G
178 B8 **Cumwhinton** Cumb
178 C8 **Cumwhitton** Cumb
150 F1 **Cundall** N York
196 D3 **Cunninghamhead** N Ayrs
281 e7 **Cunningsburgh** Shet
222 F4 **Cupar** Fife
222 F4 **Cupar Muir** Fife
132 E5 **Curbar** Derbys
19 J1 **Curbridge** Hants
65 M5 **Curbridge** Oxon
35 H8 **Curdridge** Hants
98 F5 **Curdworth** Warwks
30 C7 **Curland** Somset
48 C4 **Curridge** W Berk
211 G5 **Currie** C Edin
30 E6 **Curry Mallet** Somset
30 F6 **Curry Rivel** Somset
39 L5 **Curteis Corner** Kent
39 J5 **Curtisden Green** Kent
7 L4 **Curtisknowle** Devon
3 H6 **Cury** Cnwll
244 C1 **Cushnie** Abers
30 B5 **Cushuish** Somset
79 J7 **Cusop** Herefs
174 C7 **Cutcloy** D & G
29 J3 **Cutcombe** Somset
140 C5 **Cutgate** Rochdl
263 K2 **Cuthill** Highld
110 B8 **Cutiau** Gwynd
70 E1 **Cutler's Green** Essex
5 J2 **Cutmadoc** Cnwll
6 C3 **Cutmere** Cnwll
81 K2 **Cutnall Green** Worcs
65 G1 **Cutsdean** Gloucs
142 C3 **Cutsyke** Wakefd
133 G5 **Cutthorpe** Derbys
6 D2 **Cuttivett** Cnwll
67 G8 **Cuxham** Oxon
52 F5 **Cuxton** Medway
144 F7 **Cuxwold** Lincs
61 J6 **Cwm** Blae G
128 C2 **Cwm** Denbgs
57 L6 **Cwmafan** Neath
60 F7 **Cwmaman** Rhondd
77 G6 **Cwmann** Carmth
62 B3 **Cwmavon** Torfn
56 E4 **Cwm-bach** Carmth
75 M7 **Cwmbach** Carmth
79 G7 **Cwmbach** Powys
60 F7 **Cwmbach** Rhondd
78 E4 **Cwmbach Llechrhyd** Powys
93 K7 **Cwmbelan** Powys
62 C8 **Cwmbran** Torfn
92 F7 **Cwmbrwyno** Cerdgn
56 E4 **Cwm Capel** Carmth
43 K3 **Cwmcarn** Caerph
62 F5 **Cwmcarvan** Mons
61 K5 **Cwm-celyn** Blae G
93 J1 **Cwm-Cewydd** Gwynd
76 B6 **Cwm-cou** Cerdgn
61 J3 **Cwm Crawnon** Powys
60 F6 **Cwmdare** Rhondd
59 H3 **Cwmdu** Carmth
61 J2 **Cwmdu** Powys
57 H6 **Cwmdu** Swans
58 C3 **Cwmduad** Carmth
57 H4 **Cwm Dulais** Swans
59 K2 **Cwmdwr** Carmth
42 C4 **Cwmfelin** Brdgnd
61 H6 **Cwmfelin** Myr Td
55 L3 **Cwmfelin Boeth** Carmth
43 J3 **Cwmfelinfach** Caerph

75 L7 **Cwmfelin Mynach** Carmth
58 D5 **Cwmffrwd** Carmth
59 L6 **Cwmgiedd** Powys
57 K3 **Cwmgorse** Carmth
57 G3 **Cwmgwili** Carmth
60 C6 **Cwmgwrach** Neath
76 C7 **Cwmhiraeth** Carmth
59 J4 **Cwm-Ifor** Carmth
78 A5 **Cwm Irfon** Powys
58 F5 **Cwmisfael** Carmth
93 J2 **Cwm Llinau** Powys
59 K6 **Cwmllynfell** Neath
58 F6 **Cwmmawr** Carmth
58 B2 **Cwm Morgan** Carmth
42 E3 **Cwmparc** Rhondd
58 C2 **Cwmpengraig** Carmth
110 E2 **Cwm Penmachno** Conwy
61 G7 **Cwmpennar** Rhondd
61 J2 **Cwmrhos** Powys
57 J5 **Cwmrhydyceirw** Swans
76 E6 **Cwmsychbant** Cerdgn
61 K6 **Cwmtillery** Blae G
59 G6 **Cwm-y-glo** Carmth
125 K7 **Cwm-y-glo** Gwynd
62 C3 **Cwmyoy** Mons
93 G8 **Cwmystwyth** Cerdgn
92 E3 **Cwrt** Gwynd
76 E5 **Cwrt-newydd** Cerdgn
61 K4 **Cwrt-y-gollen** Powys
94 E2 **Cyfronydd** Powys
57 K4 **Cylibebyll** Neath
42 C3 **Cymer** Neath
42 F3 **Cymmer** Rhondd
77 M7 **Cynghordy** Carmth
56 E3 **Cynheidre** Carmth
42 C3 **Cynonville** Neath
111 K3 **Cynwyd** Denbgs
58 C3 **Cynwyl Elfed** Carmth

D

8 D1 **Daccombe** Devon
166 B5 **Dacre** Cumb
150 B4 **Dacre** N York
150 B3 **Dacre Banks** N York
167 K3 **Daddry Shield** Dur
84 C7 **Dadford** Bucks
99 L4 **Dadlington** Leics
56 F4 **Dafen** Carmth
105 J2 **Daffy Green** Norfk
52 B2 **Dagenham** Gt Lon
64 E6 **Daglingworth** Gloucs
68 C4 **Dagnall** Bucks
89 L3 **Dagworth** Suffk
183 H3 **Dailly** S Ayrs
8 C2 **Dainton** Devon
223 G4 **Dairsie** Fife
139 K6 **Daisy Hill** Bolton
141 L2 **Daisy Hill** Leeds
283 b11 **Dalabrog** W Isls
216 F5 **Dalavich** Ag & B
175 L3 **Dalbeattie** D & G
115 M5 **Dalbury** Derbys
154 b6 **Dalby** IoM
137 H5 **Dalby** Lincs
151 K2 **Dalby** N York
232 E4 **Dalcapon** P & K
274 B6 **Dalchalm** Highld
240 A1 **Dalchreichart** Highld
220 C4 **Dalchruin** P & K
221 J2 **Dalcrue** P & K
136 E6 **Dalderby** Lincs
14 B5 **Dalditch** Devon
166 D2 **Dale** Cumb
116 D4 **Dale** Derbys
54 C5 **Dale** Pembks
165 J6 **Dale Bottom** Cumb
132 B2 **Dale End** Derbys
149 G6 **Dale End** N York
39 H7 **Dale Hill** E Susx
171 H7 **Dalehouse** N York
196 B2 **Dalgarven** N Ayrs
211 G2 **Dalgety Bay** Fife
197 G8 **Dalgig** E Ayrs
220 D3 **Dalginross** P & K
232 E6 **Dalguise** P & K
278 F5 **Dalhalvaig** Highld
88 E3 **Dalham** Suffk
283 b11 **Daliburgh** W Isls
211 K5 **Dalkeith** Mdloth
266 C5 **Dallas** Moray
91 G4 **Dallinghoo** Suffk
24 B3 **Dallington** E Susx
84 E3 **Dallington** Nhants
150 B2 **Dallow** N York
217 K2 **Dalmally** Ag & B
219 H8 **Dalmary** Stirlg

184 D2 **Dalmellington** E Ayrs
210 F3 **Dalmeny** C Edin
252 D7 **Dalmigavie** Highld
252 E7 **Dalmigavie Lodge** Highld
263 H6 **Dalmore** Highld
208 E5 **Dalmuir** W Duns
237 K6 **Dalnabreck** Highld
231 K1 **Dalnacardoch** P & K
252 F7 **Dalnahaitnach** Highld
231 J1 **Dalnaspidal** P & K
279 H8 **Dalnawillan Lodge** Highld
231 L4 **Daloist** P & K
221 K6 **Dalqueich** P & K
183 J4 **Dalquhairn** S Ayrs
273 H6 **Dalreavoch Lodge** Highld
196 B1 **Dalry** N Ayrs
196 D8 **Dalrymple** E Ayrs
198 C3 **Dalserf** S Lans
192 D5 **Dalsmeran** Ag & B
165 L1 **Dalston** Cumb
51 J2 **Dalston** Gt Lon
176 B2 **Dalswinton** D & G
157 H7 **Dalton** Cumb
176 F4 **Dalton** D & G
139 G6 **Dalton** Lancs
159 K1 **Dalton** N York
160 F7 **Dalton** N York
180 D4 **Dalton** Nthumb
133 J1 **Dalton** Rothm
156 B7 **Dalton-in-Furness** Cumb
169 L1 **Dalton-le-Dale** Dur
133 J1 **Dalton Magna** Rothm
160 D1 **Dalton-on-Tees** N York
133 J1 **Dalton Parva** Rothm
170 B4 **Dalton Piercy** Hartpl
186 C5 **Dalveen** D & G
219 K2 **Dalveich** Stirlg
241 H6 **Dalwhinnie** Highld
14 F2 **Dalwood** Devon
69 H1 **Damask Green** Herts
33 J7 **Damerham** Hants
107 H2 **Damgate** Norfk
105 L6 **Dam Green** Norfk
53 J6 **Danaway** Kent
71 J6 **Danbury** Essex
162 C1 **Danby** N York
162 B2 **Danby Bottom** N York
160 E3 **Danby Wiske** N York
254 F3 **Dandaleith** Moray
211 J5 **Danderhall** Mdloth
131 J6 **Danebridge** Ches
69 J3 **Dane End** Herts
38 E6 **Danegate** E Susx
22 F2 **Danehill** E Susx
100 C3 **Dane Hills** C Leic
105 L2 **Danemoor Green** Norfk
97 G5 **Danesford** Shrops
133 H7 **Danesmoor** Derbys
40 D5 **Dane Street** Kent
40 C7 **Daniel's Water** Kent
268 C5 **Danshillock** Abers
212 C5 **Danskine** E Loth
145 H1 **Danthorpe** E R Yk
82 D2 **Danzey Green** Warwks
115 G6 **Dapple Heath** Staffs
49 K7 **Darby Green** Hants
139 L6 **Darcy Lever** Bolton
61 K3 **Dardy** Powys
61 K4 **Daren-felen** Mons
52 C5 **Darenth** Kent
130 B3 **Daresbury** Halton
142 C6 **Darfield** Barns
133 L4 **Darfoulds** Notts
40 E3 **Dargate** Kent
6 B1 **Darite** Cnwll
53 G6 **Darland** Medway
129 J8 **Darland** Wrexhm
114 D4 **Darlaston** Staffs
98 B4 **Darlaston** Wsall
98 B4 **Darlaston Green** Wsall
150 B4 **Darley** N York
116 B4 **Darley Abbey** C Derb
132 E7 **Darley Bridge** Derbys
132 E7 **Darley Dale** Derbys
98 F8 **Darley Green** Solhll
68 F3 **Darleyhall** Herts
150 B4 **Darley Head** N York
82 F6 **Darlingscott** Warwks
169 H7 **Darlington** Darltn
113 J5 **Darliston** Shrops
134 F5 **Darlton** Notts
98 E2 **Darnford** Staffs
201 H6 **Darnick** Border
93 H3 **Darowen** Powys
268 D6 **Darra** Abers
26 D8 **Darracott** Cnwll
26 D7 **Darracott** Devon
27 H3 **Darracott** Devon

180 E5 **Darras Hall** Nthumb
142 D4 **Darrington** Wakefd
91 K1 **Darsham** Suffk
31 K2 **Darshill** Somset
52 B4 **Dartford** Kent
8 B2 **Dartington** Devon
12 F7 **Dartmeet** Devon
8 C4 **Dartmouth** Devon
141 M5 **Darton** Barns
197 H3 **Darvel** E Ayrs
24 C3 **Darwell Hole** E Susx
139 K3 **Darwen** Bl w D
50 C3 **Datchet** W & M
69 H3 **Datchworth** Herts
69 H3 **Datchworth Green** Herts
139 L6 **Daubhill** Bolton
254 E3 **Daugh of Kinermony** Moray
46 E3 **Dauntsey** Wilts
253 J4 **Dava** Highld
130 C5 **Davenham** Ches
131 H2 **Davenport** Stockp
131 G4 **Davenport Green** Ches
130 F2 **Davenport Green** Traffd
84 B3 **Daventry** Nhants
211 H4 **Davidson's Mains** C Edin
11 G5 **Davidstow** Cnwll
52 E6 **David Street** Kent
187 K5 **Davington** D & G
40 D3 **Davington Hill** Kent
256 D6 **Daviot** Abers
252 D4 **Daviot** Highld
252 D4 **Daviot House** Highld
23 J4 **Davis's Town** E Susx
267 K6 **Davoch of Grange** Moray
139 M8 **Davyhulme** Traffd
98 C3 **Daw End** Wsall
37 K2 **Dawesgreen** Surrey
96 F2 **Dawley** Wrekin
13 M7 **Dawlish** Devon
14 A6 **Dawlish Warren** Devon
127 G5 **Dawn** Conwy
30 B6 **Daws Green** Somset
53 H1 **Daws Heath** Essex
11 K6 **Daw's House** Cnwll
120 A5 **Dawsmere** Lincs
116 F3 **Daybrook** Notts
130 F8 **Day Green** Ches
114 F5 **Dayhills** Staffs
98 B7 **Dayhouse Bank** Worcs
65 K2 **Daylesford** Gloucs
128 D5 **Ddol** Flints
111 K8 **Ddol-Cownwy** Powys
41 L5 **Deal** Kent
164 E5 **Dean** Cumb
7 L2 **Dean** Devon
27 L2 **Dean** Devon
28 C1 **Dean** Devon
33 G7 **Dean** Dorset
34 F4 **Dean** Hants
35 H7 **Dean** Hants
140 C3 **Dean** Lancs
65 M3 **Dean** Oxon
31 L2 **Dean** Somset
52 C5 **Dean Bottom** Kent
188 C4 **Deanburnhaugh** Border
7 L2 **Deancombe** Devon
66 C6 **Dean Court** Oxon
139 K6 **Deane** Bolton
35 H1 **Deane** Hants
33 G7 **Dean End** Dorset
141 L7 **Dean Head** Barns
141 G4 **Deanhead** Kirk
33 G7 **Deanland** Dorset
20 B4 **Deanlane End** W Susx
7 L2 **Dean Prior** Devon
179 J6 **Deanraw** Nthumb
131 G3 **Dean Row** Ches
210 D5 **Deans** W Loth
164 E5 **Deanscales** Cumb
84 E7 **Deanshanger** Nhants
267 G6 **Deanshaugh** Moray
220 C6 **Deanston** Stirlg
39 J3 **Dean Street** Kent
164 E5 **Dearham** Cumb
140 D4 **Dearnley** Rochdl
90 F4 **Debach** Suffk
70 C7 **Debden** Essex
87 L8 **Debden** Essex
70 E1 **Debden Green** Essex
90 E3 **Debenham** Suffk
81 J5 **Deblin's Green** Worcs
210 D5 **Dechmont** W Loth
210 D5 **Dechmont Road** W Loth
66 C1 **Deddington** Oxon
90 C8 **Dedham** Essex
72 H1 **Dedham Heath** Essex
50 B4 **Dedworth** W & M
101 L5 **Deene** Nhants

101 L5 **Deenethorpe** Nhants
141 L8 **Deepcar** Sheff
49 L7 **Deepcut** Surrey
158 C5 **Deepdale** Cumb
158 F6 **Deepdale** N York
102 C2 **Deeping Gate** C Pete
102 C2 **Deeping St James** Lincs
119 H8 **Deeping St Nicholas** Lincs
64 C1 **Deerhurst** Gloucs
64 C2 **Deerhurst Walton** Gloucs
40 C3 **Deerton Street** Kent
81 L6 **Defford** Worcs
60 D2 **Defynnog** Powys
126 F4 **Deganwy** Conwy
216 B5 **Degnish** Ag & B
160 E2 **Deighton** N York
151 K7 **Deighton** York
125 K7 **Deiniolen** Gwynd
10 F5 **Delabole** Cnwll
130 A6 **Delamere** Ches
257 H7 **Delfrigs** Abers
27 K6 **Delley** Devon
253 L5 **Delliefure** Highld
20 D6 **Dell Quay** W Susx
65 M4 **Delly End** Oxon
254 C8 **Delnabo** Moray
254 D4 **Delnashaugh Inn** Moray
263 K5 **Delny** Highld
140 E6 **Delph** Oldham
168 E1 **Delves** Dur
233 H7 **Delvine** P & K
88 F8 **Delvin End** Essex
118 D4 **Dembleby** Lincs
5 G2 **Demelza** Cnwll
142 D7 **Denaby** Donc
142 D7 **Denaby Main** Donc
37 H1 **Denbies** Surrey
128 C6 **Denbigh** Denbgs
222 F3 **Denbrae** Fife
8 B1 **Denbury** Devon
116 C2 **Denby** Derbys
116 C2 **Denby Bottles** Derbys
141 K6 **Denby Dale** Kirk
48 A1 **Denchworth** Oxon
146 E2 **Dendron** Cumb
85 K8 **Denel End** Beds
221 G4 **Denfield** P & K
101 L8 **Denford** Nhants
72 E6 **Dengie** Essex
50 D2 **Denham** Bucks
88 E3 **Denham** Suffk
106 D8 **Denham** Suffk
88 F3 **Denham End** Suffk
50 D1 **Denham Green** Bucks
106 D8 **Denham Green** Suffk
269 J5 **Denhead** Abers
223 H4 **Denhead** Fife
222 F1 **Denhead of Gray** C Dund
189 G3 **Denholm** Border
141 G1 **Denholme** Brad
141 G1 **Denholme Clough** Brad
108 F4 **Denio** Gwynd
19 L1 **Denmead** Hants
245 L1 **Denmore** C Aber
37 J5 **Denne Park** W Susx
91 G2 **Dennington** Suffk
209 L3 **Denny** Falk
209 L3 **Dennyloanhead** Falk
222 D4 **Den of Lindores** Fife
140 E5 **Denshaw** Oldham
245 H4 **Denside** Abers
41 G7 **Densole** Kent
88 F5 **Denston** Suffk
115 H3 **Denstone** Staffs
40 E3 **Denstroude** Kent
158 B5 **Dent** Cumb
102 C6 **Denton** Cambs
169 G7 **Denton** Darltn
23 G6 **Denton** E Susx
41 G6 **Denton** Kent
52 E4 **Denton** Kent
117 M5 **Denton** Lincs
149 L6 **Denton** N York
85 G4 **Denton** Nhants
106 F5 **Denton** Norfk
66 E6 **Denton** Oxon
131 H1 **Denton** Tamesd
104 C3 **Denver** Norfk
191 J3 **Denwick** Nthumb
105 L3 **Deopham** Norfk
105 L4 **Deopham Green** Norfk
88 F4 **Depden** Suffk
88 F4 **Depden Green** Suffk
51 K3 **Deptford** Gt Lon
33 H3 **Deptford** Wilts
116 B4 **Derby** C Derb
27 K4 **Derby** Devon
154 C8 **Derbyhaven** IoM

232 C5 **Derculich** P & K
105 K1 **Dereham** Norfk
61 H6 **Deri** Caerph
11 K2 **Derril** Devon
41 G5 **Derringstone** Kent
114 D7 **Derrington** Staffs
11 L2 **Derriton** Devon
46 D5 **Derry Hill** Wilts
143 L6 **Derrythorpe** N Linc
120 F5 **Dersingham** Norfk
226 E2 **Dervaig** Ag & B
111 L2 **Derwen** Denbgs
59 G4 **Derwen Fawr** Carmth
92 F4 **Derwenlas** Powys
59 H5 **Derwydd** Carmth
101 H6 **Desborough** Nhants
100 B3 **Desford** Leics
267 K4 **Deskford** Moray
203 H6 **Detchant** Nthumb
53 G7 **Detling** Kent
96 F6 **Deuxhill** Shrops
62 F7 **Devauden** Mons
92 F8 **Devil's Bridge** Cerdgn
99 H5 **Devitts Green** Warwks
46 E6 **Devizes** Wilts
6 E4 **Devonport** C Plym
221 G7 **Devonside** Clacks
3 K3 **Devoran** Cnwll
211 L6 **Dewarton** Mdloth
16 E3 **Dewlish** Dorset
141 K3 **Dewsbury** Kirk
141 K3 **Dewsbury Moor** Kirk
112 C8 **Deytheur** Powys
45 G5 **Dial** N Som
36 D5 **Dial Green** W Susx
139 M2 **Dial Hall** Lancs
21 K3 **Dial Post** W Susx
15 K2 **Dibberford** Dorset
18 F2 **Dibden** Hants
18 F2 **Dibden Purlieu** Hants
98 E8 **Dickens Heath** Solhll
106 D7 **Dickleburgh** Norfk
64 F1 **Didbrook** Gloucs
48 D1 **Didcot** Oxon
86 D2 **Diddington** Cambs
96 C6 **Diddlebury** Shrops
62 F1 **Didley** Herefs
20 D3 **Didling** W Susx
46 B2 **Didmarton** Gloucs
131 G1 **Didsbury** Manch
7 K2 **Didworthy** Devon
135 M8 **Digby** Lincs
259 H3 **Digg** Highld
140 F6 **Diggle** Oldham
139 G6 **Digmoor** Lancs
69 H4 **Digswell** Herts
69 H4 **Digswell Water** Herts
76 E4 **Dihewyd** Cerdgn
123 G6 **Dilham** Norfk
114 F3 **Dilhorne** Staffs
86 C2 **Dillington** Cambs
180 A6 **Dilston** Nthumb
32 E1 **Dilton** Wilts
32 D1 **Dilton Marsh** Wilts
80 A4 **Dilwyn** Herefs
139 L4 **Dimple** Bolton
132 F7 **Dimple** Derbys
58 A3 **Dinas** Carmth
10 C7 **Dinas** Cnwll
108 D4 **Dinas** Gwynd
75 G4 **Dinas** Pembks
42 F3 **Dinas** Rhondd
125 H8 **Dinas Dinlle** Gwynd
111 G8 **Dinas-Mawddwy** Gwynd
43 J7 **Dinas Powys** V Glam
31 J2 **Dinder** Somset
80 C7 **Dinedor** Herefs
62 F5 **Dingestow** Mons
129 J2 **Dingle** Lpool
39 K7 **Dingleden** Kent
101 G6 **Dingley** Nhants
262 F8 **Dingwall** Highld
62 F8 **Dinham** Mons
111 J3 **Dinmael** Conwy
244 A4 **Dinnet** Abers
180 F4 **Dinnington** N u Ty
133 K3 **Dinnington** Rothm
30 F8 **Dinnington** Somset
125 L7 **Dinorwic** Gwynd
67 J5 **Dinton** Bucks
33 H4 **Dinton** Wilts
187 H8 **Dinwoodie** D & G
26 E7 **Dinworthy** Devon
30 B6 **Dipford** Somset
49 H7 **Dipley** Hants
194 B3 **Dippen** Ag & B
195 G6 **Dippen** N Ayrs
36 B2 **Dippenhall** Surrey

Dippermill - Duffryn 309

12 B1 **Dippermill** Devon
12 B5 **Dippertown** Devon
267 G4 **Dipple** Moray
182 F2 **Dipple** S Ayrs
7 L3 **Diptford** Devon
180 E8 **Dipton** Dur
179 L6 **Diptonmill** Nthumb
212 B2 **Dirleton** E Loth
167 K2 **Dirt Pot** Nthumb
79 K2 **Discoed** Powys
116 D6 **Diseworth** Leics
160 E8 **Dishforth** N York
131 J3 **Disley** Ches
106 C7 **Diss** Norfk
78 E4 **Disserth** Powys
164 D6 **Distington** Cumb
33 J4 **Ditchampton** Wilts
191 G2 **Ditchburn** Nthumb
31 K4 **Ditcheat** Somset
107 G5 **Ditchingham** Norfk
66 A3 **Ditchley** Oxon
22 E4 **Ditchling** E Susx
113 H8 **Ditherington** Shrops
46 B5 **Ditteridge** Wilts
8 C4 **Dittisham** Devon
129 L2 **Ditton** Halton
52 F7 **Ditton** Kent
88 D4 **Ditton Green** Cambs
96 E5 **Ditton Priors** Shrops
64 E1 **Dixton** Gloucs
63 G4 **Dixton** Mons
11 H3 **Dizzard** Cnwll
140 F6 **Dobcross** Oldham
140 D3 **Dobroyd Castle** Calder
5 L2 **Dobwalls** Cnwll
13 H5 **Doccombe** Devon
251 H3 **Dochgarroch** Highld
36 B3 **Dockenfield** Surrey
157 J7 **Docker** Lancs
121 G4 **Docking** Norfk
80 D4 **Docklow** Herefs
165 J1 **Dockray** Cumb
165 L6 **Dockray** Cumb
7 L6 **Dodbrooke** Devon
70 E7 **Doddinghurst** Essex
103 H5 **Doddington** Cambs
40 B4 **Doddington** Kent
135 H5 **Doddington** Lincs
202 F6 **Doddington** Nthumb
96 E8 **Doddington** Shrops
13 K5 **Doddiscombsleigh** Devon
113 K3 **Dodd's Green** Ches
120 F5 **Doddshill** Norfk
6 C2 **Doddy Cross** Cnwll
84 B3 **Dodford** Nhants
97 L8 **Dodford** Worcs
45 L3 **Dodington** S Glos
30 A3 **Dodington** Somset
129 J7 **Dodleston** Ches
27 K7 **Dodscott** Devon
208 E8 **Dodside** E Rens
115 G4 **Dod's Leigh** Staffs
141 M6 **Dodworth** Barns
141 M7 **Dodworth Bottom** Barns
141 M6 **Dodworth Green** Barns
98 E4 **Doe Bank** Birm
133 J6 **Doe Lea** Derbys
136 D8 **Dogdyke** Lincs
141 J5 **Dogley Lane** Kirk
49 J8 **Dogmersfield** Hants
47 G2 **Dogridge** Wilts
102 D3 **Dogsthorpe** C Pete
14 A3 **Dog Village** Devon
94 C1 **Dolanog** Powys
79 G2 **Dolau** Powys
77 J7 **Dolaucothi** Carmth
109 J3 **Dolbenmaen** Gwynd
114 A5 **Doley** Staffs
93 K3 **Dolfach** Powys
93 H2 **Dol-for** Powys
94 D6 **Dolfor** Powys
126 F6 **Dolgarrog** Conwy
110 D7 **Dolgellau** Gwynd
92 E3 **Dolgoch** Gwynd
58 D2 **Dol-gran** Carmth
273 L7 **Doll** Highld
221 G7 **Dollar** Clacks
221 G7 **Dollarfield** Clacks
79 K2 **Dolley Green** Powys
92 E7 **Dollwen** Cerdgn
28 E5 **Dolphin** Flints
47 K5 **Dolphinholme** Lancs
99 J4 **Dolphinton** S Lans
27 K8 **Dolton** Devon
27 H5 **Dolwen** Conwy
10 D1 **Dolwyddelan** Conwy
92 D5 **Dolybont** Cerdgn
79 J4 **Dolyhir** Powys
112 D7 **Domgay** Powys
202 D5 **Donaldson's Lodge** Nthumb
142 F7 **Doncaster** Donc
142 F7 **Doncaster Carr** Donc
32 F6 **Donhead St Andrew** Wilts
32 F6 **Donhead St Mary** Wilts
211 G1 **Donibristle** Fife
29 K2 **Doniford** Somset
119 H4 **Donington** Lincs
136 D3 **Donington on Bain** Lincs
119 G5 **Donington Southing** Lincs
99 J1 **Donisthorpe** Leics
25 L1 **Donkey Street** Kent
50 B6 **Donkey Town** Surrey
65 J2 **Donnington** Gloucs
81 G8 **Donnington** Herefs
96 D2 **Donnington** Shrops
48 C5 **Donnington** W Berk
20 D6 **Donnington** W Susx
113 M8 **Donnington** Wrekin
97 G1 **Donnington Wood** Wrekin
30 E8 **Donyatt** Somset
37 J5 **Doomsday Green** W Susx
196 C7 **Doonfoot** S Ayrs
196 C7 **Doonholm** S Ayrs
253 L8 **Dorback Lodge** Highld
16 D4 **Dorchester** Dorset
66 E8 **Dorchester** Oxon
99 H3 **Dordon** Warwks
132 F3 **Dore** Sheff
251 G5 **Dores** Highld
37 J1 **Dorking** Surrey
89 J7 **Dorking Tye** Suffk
38 B5 **Dormans Land** Surrey
38 B5 **Dormans Park** Surrey
80 D7 **Dormington** Herefs
82 A4 **Dormston** Worcs
82 F8 **Dorn** Gloucs
50 B3 **Dorney** Bucks
248 D6 **Dornie** Highld
264 B2 **Dornoch** Highld
177 H5 **Dornock** D & G
279 J5 **Dorrery** Highld
98 F8 **Dorridge** Solhll
118 E1 **Dorrington** Lincs
96 B3 **Dorrington** Shrops
114 A3 **Dorrington** Shrops
82 D5 **Dorsington** Warwks
79 K7 **Dorstone** Herefs
67 G4 **Dorton** Bucks
99 G3 **Dosthill** Staffs
124 F5 **Dothan** IoA
15 K3 **Dottery** Dorset
5 L2 **Doublebois** Cnwll
46 C1 **Doughton** Gloucs
154 e6 **Douglas** IoM
198 D7 **Douglas** S Lans
234 C8 **Douglas and Angus** C Dund
198 D6 **Douglas Castle** S Lans
217 K7 **Douglas Pier** Ag & B
234 B6 **Douglastown** Angus
198 E6 **Douglas Water** S Lans
198 D6 **Douglas West** S Lans
31 L2 **Doulting** Somset
275 b4 **Dounby** Ork
272 B7 **Doune** Highld
220 C6 **Doune** Stirlg
182 F3 **Dounepark** S Ayrs
263 G2 **Dounie** Highld
7 G1 **Dousland** Devon
112 E7 **Dovaston** Shrops
116 D1 **Dove Green** Notts
131 L4 **Dove Holes** Derbys
164 E4 **Dovenby** Cumb
41 K7 **Dover** Kent
139 J7 **Dover** Wigan
73 K1 **Dovercourt** Essex
81 K2 **Doverdale** Worcs
115 J5 **Doveridge** Derbys
37 L1 **Doversgreen** Surrey
232 F5 **Dowally** P & K
138 E2 **Dowbridge** Lancs
64 E3 **Dowdeswell** Gloucs
61 G5 **Dowlais** Myr Td
12 D1 **Dowland** Devon
30 E8 **Dowlish Ford** Somset
30 E8 **Dowlish Wake** Somset
11 M4 **Downacarey** Devon
65 G7 **Down Ampney** Gloucs
6 C4 **Downderry** Cnwll
51 L6 **Downe** Gt Lon
64 B7 **Downend** Gloucs
19 J6 **Downend** IoW
45 K3 **Downend** S Glos
48 C4 **Downend** W Berk
223 G1 **Downfield** C Dund
11 K8 **Downgate** Cnwll
11 L7 **Downgate** Cnwll
71 H7 **Downham** Essex
51 K4 **Downham** Gt Lon
148 D7 **Downham** Lancs
202 D6 **Downham** Nthumb
104 C3 **Downham Market** Norfk
64 C3 **Down Hatherley** Gloucs
31 J6 **Downhead** Somset
32 A2 **Downhead** Somset
4 D1 **Downhill** Cnwll
221 K1 **Downhill** P & K
138 D6 **Downholland Cross** Lancs
159 K3 **Downholme** N York
245 K4 **Downies** Abers
128 D4 **Downing** Flints
67 K8 **Downley** Bucks
13 H2 **Down St Mary** Devon
31 K2 **Downside** Somset
31 L1 **Downside** Somset
50 E7 **Downside** Surrey
6 F5 **Down Thomas** Devon
18 D5 **Downton** Hants
33 L6 **Downton** Wilts
118 F5 **Dowsby** Lincs
102 F2 **Dowsdale** Lincs
114 D6 **Doxey** Staffs
191 H2 **Doxford** Nthumb
45 L4 **Doynton** S Glos
43 K4 **Draethen** Caerph
198 C4 **Draffan** S Lans
143 M5 **Dragonby** N Linc
37 H6 **Dragons Green** W Susx
134 E2 **Drakeholes** Notts
97 J7 **Drakelow** Worcs
196 B1 **Drakemyre** N Ayrs
81 L5 **Drakes Broughton** Worcs
12 B8 **Drakewalls** Cnwll
149 J5 **Draughton** N York
101 G8 **Draughton** Nhants
143 H3 **Drax** N York
143 H3 **Drax Hales** N York
83 K1 **Draycote** Warwks
47 J3 **Draycot Foliat** Swindn
116 D5 **Draycott** Derbys
82 E8 **Draycott** Gloucs
97 H5 **Draycott** Shrops
31 G1 **Draycott** Somset
31 J6 **Draycott** Somset
81 K5 **Draycott** Worcs
115 J6 **Draycott in the Clay** Staffs
114 F3 **Draycott in the Moors** Staffs
28 D8 **Drayford** Devon
19 L3 **Drayton** C Port
101 H5 **Drayton** Leics
119 H4 **Drayton** Lincs
106 D1 **Drayton** Norfk
66 C8 **Drayton** Oxon
83 K7 **Drayton** Oxon
30 F6 **Drayton** Somset
97 K8 **Drayton** Worcs
99 G3 **Drayton Bassett** Staffs
67 L5 **Drayton Beauchamp** Bucks
67 K2 **Drayton Parslow** Bucks
66 E7 **Drayton St Leonard** Oxon
149 J4 **Drebley** N York
154 g4 **Dreemskerry** IoM
54 F4 **Dreen Hill** Pembks
58 F6 **Drefach** Carmth
76 C7 **Drefach** Carmth
76 F6 **Drefach** Cerdgn
76 C7 **Drefelin** Carmth
196 C3 **Dreghorn** N Ayrs
41 H7 **Drellingore** Kent
212 B3 **Drem** E Loth
114 E3 **Dresden** C Stke
13 H4 **Drewsteignton** Devon
137 G5 **Driby** Lincs
152 F4 **Driffield** E R Yk
65 G7 **Driffield** Gloucs
64 F7 **Driffield Cross Roads** Gloucs
2 C5 **Drift** Cnwll
155 K3 **Drigg** Cumb
141 K2 **Drighlington** Leeds
227 G2 **Drimnin** Highld
15 K2 **Drimpton** Dorset
238 F7 **Drimsallie** Highld
153 J5 **Dringhoe** E R Yk
151 J6 **Dringhouses** York
89 J3 **Drinkstone** Suffk
89 J3 **Drinkstone Green** Suffk
16 B1 **Drive End** Dorset
69 G3 **Driver's End** Herts
115 G6 **Drointon** Staffs
81 K3 **Droitwich** Worcs
221 L4 **Dron** P & K
133 G4 **Dronfield** Derbys
133 G4 **Dronfield Woodhouse** Derbys
196 E7 **Drongan** E Ayrs
234 A8 **Dronley** Angus
16 E1 **Droop** Dorset
133 H1 **Dropping Well** Rothm
35 J7 **Droxford** Hants
140 D8 **Droylsden** Tamesd
111 K3 **Druid** Denbgs
54 E3 **Druidston** Pembks
229 H1 **Druimarbin** Highld
229 G6 **Druimavuic** Ag & B
206 A5 **Druimdrishaig** Ag & B
237 K4 **Druimindarroch** Highld
206 E4 **Drum** Ag & B
221 J7 **Drum** P & K
198 F5 **Drumalbin** S Lans
270 F2 **Drumbeg** Highld
255 M4 **Drumblade** Abers
172 D6 **Drumbreddon** D & G
248 B5 **Drumbuie** Highld
177 J7 **Drumburgh** Cumb
175 L4 **Drumburn** D & G
208 E5 **Drumchapel** C Glas
231 J4 **Drumchastle** P & K
197 J3 **Drumclog** S Lans
223 G6 **Drumeldrie** Fife
199 K6 **Drumelzier** Border
247 L5 **Drumfearn** Highld
244 F4 **Drumfrennie** Abers
234 C5 **Drumgley** Angus
241 L3 **Drumguish** Highld
254 D5 **Drumin** Moray
184 E3 **Drumjohn** D & G
183 H7 **Drumlamford** S Ayrs
244 E2 **Drumlasie** Abers
177 J8 **Drumleaning** Cumb
192 D4 **Drumlemble** Ag & B
245 H7 **Drumlithie** Abers
173 K6 **Drummoddie** D & G
172 E7 **Drummore** D & G
255 H3 **Drummuir** Moray
250 E5 **Drumnadrochit** Highld
172 E7 **Drumnaglaur** D & G
267 L5 **Drumnagorrach** Moray
185 L7 **Drumpark** D & G
271 G7 **Drumrunie Lodge** Highld
195 L8 **Drumshang** S Ayrs
259 G7 **Drumuie** Highld
253 H7 **Drumuillie** Highld
220 B6 **Drumvaich** Stirlg
221 L5 **Drunzie** P & K
191 K7 **Druridge** Nthumb
129 G6 **Drury** Flints
166 F7 **Drybeck** Cumb
267 J4 **Drybridge** Moray
196 D4 **Drybridge** N Ayrs
63 J4 **Drybrook** Gloucs
201 J6 **Dryburgh** Border
117 M2 **Dry Doddington** Lincs
87 H3 **Dry Drayton** Cambs
3 G4 **Drym** Cnwll
208 E1 **Drymen** Stirlg
257 G3 **Drymuir** Abers
246 F2 **Drynoch** Highld
66 C7 **Dry Sandford** Oxon
59 G5 **Dryslwyn** Carmth
52 E2 **Dry Street** Essex
96 D2 **Dryton** Shrops
268 E3 **Dubford** Abers
90 E1 **Dublin** Suffk
271 L4 **Duchally** Highld
85 L6 **Duck End** Beds
86 E2 **Duck End** Cambs
71 G2 **Duck End** Essex
88 D8 **Duck End** Essex
71 H3 **Duckend Green** Essex
113 H1 **Duckington** Ches
65 M5 **Ducklington** Oxon
86 C4 **Duck's Cross** Beds
87 J7 **Duddenhoe End** Essex
211 J4 **Duddingston** C Edin
101 L3 **Duddington** Nhants
30 C6 **Duddlestone** Somset
38 C7 **Duddleswell** E Susx
96 F6 **Duddlewick** Shrops
202 E4 **Duddo** Nthumb
129 L6 **Duddon** Ches
156 B5 **Duddon Bridge** Cumb
129 M6 **Duddon Common** Ches
112 E4 **Dudleston** Shrops
112 E4 **Dudleston Heath** Shrops
97 L5 **Dudley** Dudley
181 G4 **Dudley** N Tyne
141 J2 **Dudley Hill** Brad
98 B5 **Dudley Port** Sandw
96 E8 **Dudnill** Shrops
17 L3 **Dudsbury** Dorset
68 B5 **Dudswell** Herts
116 B3 **Duffield** Derbys
42 C3 **Duffryn** Neath

255 G4 **Dufftown** Moray
266 D3 **Duffus** Moray
166 F5 **Dufton** Cumb
152 D2 **Duggleby** N York
248 C5 **Duirinish** Highld
247 L6 **Duisdalemore** Highld
239 G8 **Duisky** Highld
61 J5 **Dukestown** Blae G
90 C6 **Duke Street** Suffk
140 E8 **Dukinfield** Tamesd
125 H2 **Dulas** IoA
31 J2 **Dulcote** Somset
14 C1 **Dulford** Devon
232 B5 **Dull** P & K
209 K4 **Dullatur** N Lans
88 C4 **Dullingham** Cambs
88 C4 **Dullingham Ley** Cambs
253 J6 **Dulnain Bridge** Highld
86 D3 **Duloe** Beds
5 M3 **Duloe** Cnwll
29 G5 **Dulverton** Somset
51 J4 **Dulwich** Gt Lon
208 C4 **Dumbarton** W Duns
82 B8 **Dumbleton** Gloucs
176 C4 **Dumfries** D & G
208 E2 **Dumgoyne** Stirlg
35 J2 **Dummer** Hants
41 L2 **Dumpton** Kent
235 G3 **Dun** Angus
231 K4 **Dunalastair** P & K
207 J5 **Dunan** Ag & B
247 J3 **Dunan** Highld
230 E4 **Dunan** P & K
192 E6 **Dunaverty** Ag & B
30 D3 **Dunball** Somset
212 E3 **Dunbar** E Loth
275 G2 **Dunbeath** Highld
228 D8 **Dunbeg** Ag & B
220 D7 **Dunblane** Stirlg
222 D4 **Dunbog** Fife
34 D5 **Dunbridge** Hants
263 G8 **Duncanston** Highld
255 M6 **Duncanstone** Abers
13 K5 **Dunchideock** Devon
83 L1 **Dunchurch** Warwks
84 C5 **Duncote** Nhants
176 C2 **Duncow** D & G
221 L5 **Duncrievie** P & K
20 F3 **Duncton** W Susx
223 G1 **Dundee** C Dund
31 G4 **Dundon** Somset
196 D4 **Dundonald** S Ayrs
261 J2 **Dundonnell** Highld
165 H1 **Dundraw** Cumb
240 B1 **Dundreggan** Highld
175 J5 **Dundrennan** D & G
45 H5 **Dundry** N Som
245 G2 **Dunecht** Abers
210 E2 **Dunfermline** Fife
65 H7 **Dunfield** Gloucs
141 J7 **Dunford Bridge** Barns
40 B3 **Dungate** Kent
197 J3 **Dungavel** S Lans
46 C8 **Dunge** Wilts
132 E2 **Dungworth** Sheff
135 G5 **Dunham** Notts
129 L5 **Dunham-on-the-Hill** Ches
81 L3 **Dunhampstead** Worcs
81 J2 **Dunhampton** Worcs
130 E2 **Dunham Town** Traffd
130 E2 **Dunham Woodhouses** Traffd
135 L4 **Dunholme** Lincs
223 J5 **Dunino** Fife
209 L2 **Dunipace** Falk
232 F6 **Dunkeld** P & K
45 L7 **Dunkerton** BaNES
14 D1 **Dunkeswell** Devon
150 D6 **Dunkeswick** N York
129 J5 **Dunkirk** Ches
40 E3 **Dunkirk** Kent
46 A2 **Dunkirk** S Glos
46 E6 **Dunkirk** Wilts
38 F3 **Dunk's Green** Kent
234 F2 **Dunlappie** Angus
48 C8 **Dunley** Hants
81 H2 **Dunley** Worcs
196 E1 **Dunlop** E Ayrs
251 G7 **Dunmaglass** Highld
5 H1 **Dunmere** Cnwll
210 A1 **Dunmore** Falk
280 B2 **Dunnet** Highld
234 D5 **Dunnichen** Angus
221 J4 **Dunning** P & K
153 J5 **Dunnington** E R Yk
82 C4 **Dunnington** Warwks
151 L5 **Dunnington** York
140 B2 **Dunnockshaw** Lancs

53 G6 **Dunn Street** Kent
207 K4 **Dunoon** Ag & B
253 J2 **Dunphail** Moray
172 E3 **Dunragit** D & G
202 B2 **Duns** Border
132 E5 **Dunsa** Derbys
118 E6 **Dunsby** Lincs
139 L5 **Dunscar** Bolton
185 L6 **Dunscore** D & G
143 G6 **Dunscroft** Donc
170 E6 **Dunsdale** R & Cl
49 H3 **Dunsden Green** Oxon
11 K1 **Dunsdon** Devon
36 F4 **Dunsfold** Surrey
13 J4 **Dunsford** Devon
222 D5 **Dunshalt** Fife
269 H6 **Dunshillock** Abers
133 J7 **Dunsill** Notts
171 K8 **Dunsley** N York
97 J6 **Dunsley** Staffs
67 L6 **Dunsmore** Bucks
148 B6 **Dunsop Bridge** Lancs
68 C3 **Dunstable** Beds
115 K7 **Dunstall** Staffs
81 K6 **Dunstall Common** Worcs
88 E3 **Dunstall Green** Suffk
191 K2 **Dunstan** Nthumb
191 J2 **Dunstan Steads** Nthumb
29 H2 **Dunster** Somset
66 C2 **Duns Tew** Oxon
180 F6 **Dunston** Gatesd
135 L7 **Dunston** Lincs
106 E3 **Dunston** Norfk
114 E8 **Dunston** Staffs
7 H4 **Dunstone** Devon
13 G7 **Dunstone** Devon
114 E8 **Dunston Heath** Staffs
143 G6 **Dunsville** Donc
144 D1 **Dunswell** E R Yk
199 J3 **Dunsyre** S Lans
11 M6 **Dunterton** Devon
65 M2 **Dunthrop** Oxon
64 E5 **Duntisbourne Abbots** Gloucs
64 E5 **Duntisbourne Leer** Gloucs
64 E6 **Duntisbourne Rouse** Gloucs
16 D1 **Duntish** Dorset
208 E4 **Duntocher** W Duns
86 E6 **Dunton** Beds
67 K2 **Dunton** Bucks
121 J5 **Dunton** Norfk
100 C5 **Dunton Bassett** Leics
38 D2 **Dunton Green** Kent
52 E1 **Dunton Wayletts** Essex
259 G2 **Duntulm** Highld
195 L7 **Dunure** S Ayrs
57 G6 **Dunvant** Swans
258 C7 **Dunvegan** Highld
91 L1 **Dunwich** Suffk
131 J8 **Dunwood** Staffs
177 L8 **Durdar** Cumb
3 K5 **Durgan** Cnwll
169 H2 **Durham** Dur
186 C5 **Durisdeer** D & G
186 C5 **Durisdeermill** D & G
141 M4 **Durkar** Wakefd
30 C4 **Durleigh** Somset
35 G7 **Durley** Hants
47 K6 **Durley** Wilts
35 H7 **Durley Street** Hants
41 J2 **Durlock** Kent
41 J4 **Durlock** Kent
80 E7 **Durlow Common** Herefs
140 E4 **Durn** Rochdl
276 F3 **Durness** Highld
256 C6 **Durno** Abers
228 F4 **Duror** Highld
216 F5 **Durran** Ag & B
21 J6 **Durrington** W Susx
33 K2 **Durrington** Wilts
245 G4 **Durris** Abers
63 M7 **Dursley** Gloucs
63 K3 **Dursley Cross** Gloucs
30 D5 **Durston** Somset
17 G1 **Durweston** Dorset
84 D3 **Duston** Nhants
253 H6 **Duthil** Highld
94 F7 **Dutlas** Powys
70 F2 **Duton Hill** Essex
11 L5 **Dutson** Cnwll
130 B4 **Dutton** Ches
87 K6 **Duxford** Cambs
66 A7 **Duxford** Oxon
126 E4 **Dwygyfylchi** Conwy
125 H6 **Dwyran** IoA
245 K1 **Dyce** C Aber
88 E7 **Dyer's End** Essex

56 E5 **Dyfatty** Carmth
110 D8 **Dyffrydan** Gwynd
42 C3 **Dyffryn** Brdgnd
61 G6 **Dyffryn** Myr Td
43 H7 **Dyffryn** V Glam
109 K7 **Dyffryn Ardudwy** Gwynd
93 G7 **Dyffryn Castell** Cerdgn
60 C5 **Dyffryn Cellwen** Neath
118 E7 **Dyke** Lincs
264 F8 **Dyke** Moray
233 K4 **Dykehead** Angus
234 B3 **Dykehead** Angus
210 A7 **Dykehead** N Lans
219 K7 **Dykehead** Stirlg
235 H2 **Dykelands** Abers
233 K4 **Dykends** Angus
256 C3 **Dykeside** Abers
93 J4 **Dylife** Powys
25 L1 **Dymchurch** Kent
63 K1 **Dymock** Gloucs
45 L4 **Dyrham** S Glos
222 E8 **Dysart** Fife
128 C4 **Dyserth** Denbgs

E

98 C8 **Eachway** Worcs
180 D4 **Eachwick** Nthumb
147 H6 **Eagland Hill** Lancs
135 H6 **Eagle** Lincs
135 H6 **Eagle Barnsdale** Lincs
135 H6 **Eagle Moor** Lincs
169 L7 **Eaglescliffe** S on T
164 E5 **Eaglesfield** Cumb
177 H4 **Eaglesfield** D & G
208 F8 **Eaglesham** E Rens
139 L5 **Eagley** Bolton
154 d6 **Eairy** IoM
134 D7 **Eakring** Notts
143 K5 **Ealand** N Linc
50 F3 **Ealing** Gt Lon
178 F7 **Eals** Nthumb
166 C5 **Eamont Bridge** Cumb
148 F6 **Earby** Lancs
139 K3 **Earcroft** Bl w D
97 C5 **Eardington** Shrops
80 A4 **Eardisland** Herefs
79 K5 **Eardisley** Herefs
112 E6 **Eardiston** Shrops
80 F2 **Eardiston** Worcs
103 H8 **Earith** Cambs
202 F7 **Earle** Nthumb
130 B1 **Earlestown** St Hel
49 H4 **Earley** Wokham
106 D2 **Earlham** Norfk
258 F4 **Earlish** Highld
85 G3 **Earls Barton** Nhants
71 L1 **Earls Colne** Essex
81 M3 **Earls Common** Worcs
81 K6 **Earl's Croome** Worcs
96 E8 **Earlsditton** Shrops
99 J7 **Earlsdon** Covtry
23 L3 **Earl's Down** E Susx
223 H7 **Earlsferry** Fife
51 H4 **Earlsfield** Gt Lon
256 E5 **Earlsford** Abers
90 B2 **Earl's Green** Suffk
141 L3 **Earlsheaton** Kirk
100 A4 **Earl Shilton** Leics
90 F3 **Earl Soham** Suffk
132 B6 **Earl Sterndale** Derbys
201 J5 **Earlston** Border
196 D4 **Earlston** E Ayrs
90 D3 **Earl Stonham** Suffk
37 L1 **Earlswood** Surrey
98 E8 **Earlswood** Warwks
62 F8 **Earlswood Common** Mons
20 D7 **Earnley** W Susx
139 G2 **Earnshaw Bridge** Lancs
181 H4 **Earsdon** N Tyne
191 J7 **Earsdon** Nthumb
107 G5 **Earsham** Norfk
151 K4 **Earswick** York
20 F5 **Eartham** W Susx
45 K2 **Earthcott** S Glos
161 J1 **Easby** N York
215 L1 **Easdale** Ag & B
36 D6 **Easebourne** W Susx
100 A7 **Easenhall** Warwks
36 E2 **Eashing** Surrey
67 G5 **Easington** Bucks
169 L2 **Easington** Dur
145 K4 **Easington** E R Yk
203 J6 **Easington** Nthumb
67 G7 **Easington** Oxon
171 H7 **Easington** R & Cl
169 L2 **Easington Colliery** Dur

169 K2 **Easington Lane** Sundld
151 H2 **Easingwold** N York
41 H5 **Easole Street** Kent
233 M6 **Eassie and Nevay** Angus
42 F8 **East Aberthaw** V Glam
7 M5 **East Allington** Devon
28 F5 **East Anstey** Devon
34 E1 **East Anton** Hants
160 C3 **East Appleton** N York
19 K6 **East Ashey** IoW
20 D5 **East Ashling** W Susx
34 F2 **East Aston** Hants
163 H5 **East Ayton** N York
11 K3 **East Bank** Blae G
136 C3 **East Barkwith** Lincs
39 H3 **East Barming** Kent
171 J8 **East Barnby** N York
69 H8 **East Barnet** Gt Lon
212 F4 **East Barns** E Loth
121 K5 **East Barsham** Norfk
122 D4 **East Beckham** Norfk
50 D4 **East Bedfont** Gt Lon
90 C8 **East Bergholt** Suffk
141 J2 **East Bierley** Kirk
121 L7 **East Bilney** Norfk
23 H7 **East Blatchington** E Susx
17 H4 **East Bloxworth** Dorset
181 J6 **East Boldon** S Tyne
18 F4 **East Boldre** Hants
191 G3 **East Bolton** Nthumb
169 J7 **Eastbourne** Darltn
23 K7 **Eastbourne** E Susx
30 D3 **East Bower** Somset
105 J2 **East Bradenham** Norfk
44 D8 **East Brent** Somset
91 K2 **Eastbridge** Suffk
117 J3 **East Bridgford** Notts
168 B6 **East Briscoe** Dur
43 J7 **Eastbrook** V Glam
28 B4 **East Buckland** Devon
14 C5 **East Budleigh** Devon
149 J7 **Eastburn** Brad
152 F4 **Eastburn** E R Yk
50 B2 **East Burnham** Bucks
16 F5 **East Burton** Dorset
68 E8 **Eastbury** Herts
47 M3 **Eastbury** W Berk
168 E2 **East Butsfield** Dur
143 L6 **East Butterwick** N Linc
149 J5 **Eastby** N York
210 E5 **East Calder** W Loth
106 D3 **East Carleton** Norfk
150 B7 **East Carlton** Leeds
101 H5 **East Carlton** Nhants
16 F6 **East Chaldon (Chaldon Herring)** Dorset
48 A1 **East Challow** Oxon
7 L6 **East Charleton** Devon
16 A1 **East Chelborough** Dorset
191 K6 **East Chevington** Nthumb
22 F4 **East Chiltington** E Susx
31 H8 **East Chinnock** Somset
47 H8 **East Chisenbury** Wilts
34 C2 **East Cholderton** Hants
53 L5 **Eastchurch** Kent
50 D8 **East Clandon** Surrey
67 H2 **East Claydon** Bucks
44 E5 **East Clevedon** N Som
31 J8 **East Coker** Somset
64 C6 **Eastcombe** Gloucs
29 L4 **East Combe** Somset
31 K3 **East Compton** Somset
8 C4 **East Cornworthy** Devon
176 F7 **East Cote** Cumb
50 E1 **Eastcote** Gt Lon
84 D4 **Eastcote** Nhants
99 G7 **Eastcote** Solhll
26 D7 **Eastcott** Cnwll
46 F7 **Eastcott** Wilts
151 L7 **East Cottingwith** E R Yk
47 K6 **Eastcourt** Wilts
64 E8 **Eastcourt** Wilts
19 H4 **East Cowes** IoW
143 G4 **East Cowick** E R Yk
160 D2 **East Cowton** N York
181 G4 **East Cramlington** Nthumb
31 L2 **East Cranmore** Somset
17 H6 **East Creech** Dorset
165 K1 **East Curthwaite** Cumb
23 J7 **East Dean** E Susx
63 K3 **East Dean** Gloucs
34 C5 **East Dean** Hants
20 E4 **East Dean** W Susx
8 B5 **Eastdown** Devon
27 L3 **East Down** Devon
134 F4 **East Drayton** Notts
51 J4 **East Dulwich** Gt Lon

45 H5 **East Dundry** N Som
144 D2 **East Ella** C KuH
85 J6 **East End** Beds
86 C4 **East End** Beds
145 G2 **East End** E R Yk
145 H2 **East End** E R Yk
70 B5 **East End** Essex
72 D8 **Eastend** Essex
18 E4 **East End** Hants
48 B6 **East End** Hants
70 C2 **East End** Herts
39 L6 **East End** Kent
53 L4 **East End** Kent
85 J6 **East End** M Keyn
44 F5 **East End** N Som
66 B4 **East End** Oxon
198 F5 **Eastend** S Lans
31 L2 **East End** Somset
90 C8 **East End** Suffk
243 J5 **Easter Balmoral** Abers
45 H2 **Easter Compton** S Glos
252 E2 **Easter Dalziel** Highld
20 F6 **Eastergate** W Susx
209 J6 **Easterhouse** C Glas
211 H6 **Easter Howgate** Mdloth
263 G8 **Easter Kinkell** Highld
250 F3 **Easter Moniack** Highld
99 H7 **Eastern Green** Covtry
245 J3 **Easter Ord** Abers
223 K6 **Easter Pitkierie** Fife
281 d6 **Easter Skeld** Shet
202 B6 **Easter Softlaw** Border
46 F8 **Easterton** Wilts
44 D8 **Eastertown** Somset
47 J8 **East Everleigh** Wilts
39 J3 **East Farleigh** Kent
100 F6 **East Farndon** Nhants
143 K7 **East Ferry** Lincs
210 A6 **Eastfield** N Lans
163 J6 **Eastfield** N York
135 K3 **East Firsby** Lincs
212 C3 **East Fortune** E Loth
142 C1 **East Garforth** Leeds
47 M4 **East Garston** W Berk
168 B3 **Eastgate** Dur
118 F7 **Eastgate** Lincs
122 C7 **Eastgate** Norfk
48 C2 **East Ginge** Oxon
100 E1 **East Goscote** Leics
47 K6 **East Grafton** Wilts
91 J2 **East Green** Suffk
34 B5 **East Grimstead** Wilts
38 B5 **East Grinstead** W Susx
25 H3 **East Guldeford** E Susx
84 C2 **East Haddon** Nhants
48 D1 **East Hagbourne** Oxon
144 E4 **East Halton** N Linc
51 L2 **East Ham** Gt Lon
129 H4 **Eastham** Wirral
129 J3 **Eastham Ferry** Wirral
49 L5 **Easthampstead** Br For
80 A3 **Easthampton** Herefs
66 B8 **East Hanney** Oxon
71 J6 **East Hanningfield** Essex
142 D4 **East Hardwick** Wakefd
105 K6 **East Harling** Norfk
160 F3 **East Harlsey** N York
33 K5 **East Harnham** Wilts
45 H7 **East Harptree** BaNES
169 L7 **East Hartburn** S on T
181 G3 **East Hartford** Nthumb
20 C3 **East Harting** W Susx
32 F5 **East Hatch** Wilts
86 F5 **East Hatley** Cambs
159 L4 **East Hauxwell** N York
234 F8 **East Haven** Angus
49 J5 **Eastheath** Wokham
119 G3 **East Heckington** Lincs
168 F3 **East Hedleyhope** Dur
274 D5 **East Helmsdale** Highld
48 C1 **East Hendred** Oxon
163 G7 **East Heslerton** N York
44 E6 **East Hewish** N Som
23 H4 **East Hoathly** E Susx
17 H5 **East Holme** Dorset
96 D4 **Easthope** Shrops
72 C3 **Easthorpe** Essex
117 J1 **Easthorpe** Notts
31 J2 **East Horrington** Somset
50 E8 **East Horsley** Surrey
203 J6 **East Horton** Nthumb
17 L3 **East Howe** Bmouth
151 K5 **East Huntington** York
30 E2 **East Huntspill** Somset
68 A4 **East Hyde** Beds
28 C2 **East Ilkerton** Devon
48 C3 **East Ilsley** W Berk
13 H1 **Eastington** Devon

63 M6 **Eastington** Gloucs
65 H4 **Eastington** Gloucs
137 G7 **East Keal** Lincs
47 G5 **East Kennett** Wilts
150 E7 **East Keswick** Leeds
209 H8 **East Kilbride** S Lans
12 C3 **East Kimber** Devon
136 F7 **East Kirkby** Lincs
16 F5 **East Knighton** Dorset
28 E6 **East Knowstone** Devon
32 E5 **East Knoyle** Wilts
31 G7 **East Lambrook** Somset
185 K8 **Eastlands** D & G
41 K6 **East Langdon** Kent
100 F5 **East Langton** Leics
229 H4 **East Laroch** Highld
20 D5 **East Lavant** W Susx
20 F4 **East Lavington** W Susx
159 L1 **East Layton** N York
65 J6 **Eastleach Martin** Gloucs
65 J6 **Eastleach Turville** Gloucs
116 F6 **East Leake** Notts
202 D5 **East Learmouth** Nthumb
7 K4 **East Leigh** Devon
7 L3 **East Leigh** Devon
13 G2 **East Leigh** Devon
27 J5 **Eastleigh** Devon
34 F7 **Eastleigh** Hants
121 J8 **East Lexham** Norfk
40 C4 **Eastling** Kent
212 D3 **East Linton** E Loth
36 A5 **East Liss** Hants
48 B2 **East Lockinge** Oxon
143 K7 **East Lound** N Linc
17 G6 **East Lulworth** Dorset
152 E2 **East Lutton** N York
30 B5 **East Lydeard** Somset
31 J4 **East Lydford** Somset
39 H2 **East Malling** Kent
39 H2 **East Malling Heath** Kent
20 C4 **East Marden** W Susx
134 E5 **East Markham** Notts
33 J7 **East Martin** Hants
148 F5 **East Marton** N York
35 L6 **East Meon** Hants
29 H7 **East Mere** Devon
72 F4 **East Mersea** Essex
50 F5 **East Molesey** Surrey
104 E3 **Eastmoor** Norfk
17 H3 **East Morden** Dorset
149 K7 **East Morton** Brad
186 C6 **East Morton** D & G
162 B7 **East Ness** N York
153 L8 **East Newton** E R Yk
19 L4 **Eastney** C Port
81 J7 **Eastnor** Herefs
101 G3 **East Norton** Leics
143 K4 **Eastoft** N Linc
13 J8 **East Ogwell** Devon
86 C1 **Easton** Cambs
177 J7 **Easton** Cumb
13 G4 **Easton** Devon
16 D8 **Easton** Dorset
35 G4 **Easton** Hants
118 B6 **Easton** Lincs
106 C1 **Easton** Norfk
31 H2 **Easton** Somset
91 G3 **Easton** Suffk
48 B4 **Easton** W Berk
46 C5 **Easton** Wilts
46 C2 **Easton Grey** Wilts
45 G4 **Easton-in-Gordano** N Som
85 H3 **Easton Maudit** Nhants
101 M3 **Easton on the Hill** Nhants
47 J7 **Easton Royal** Wilts
32 D7 **East Orchard** Dorset
202 F3 **East Ord** Nthumb
11 L4 **East Panson** Devon
17 M3 **East Parley** Dorset
39 G4 **East Peckham** Kent
11 L3 **Eastpeek** Devon
54 F6 **East Pennar** Pembks
31 K3 **East Pennard** Somset
86 C2 **East Perry** Cambs
7 L7 **East Portlemouth** Devon
8 A7 **East Prawle** Devon
21 J6 **East Preston** W Susx
16 D1 **East Pulham** Dorset
26 F7 **East Putford** Devon
29 L2 **East Quantoxhead** Somset
53 H5 **East Rainham** Medway
169 J1 **East Rainton** Sundld
145 G7 **East Ravendale** NE Lin
121 J6 **East Raynham** Norfk
102 F4 **Eastrea** Cambs
177 H5 **Eastriggs** D & G
150 E7 **East Rigton** Leeds
143 K2 **Eastrington** E R Yk

44 E6 **East Rolstone** N Som
65 J8 **Eastrop** Swindn
160 F2 **East Rounton** N York
121 H6 **East Rudham** Norfk
122 D3 **East Runton** Norfk
123 G6 **East Ruston** Norfk
41 J4 **Eastry** Kent
212 B5 **East Saltoun** E Loth
36 C6 **Eastshaw** W Susx
51 G4 **East Sheen** Gt Lon
48 A4 **East Shefford** W Berk
181 G2 **East Sleekburn** Nthumb
123 K7 **East Somerton** Norfk
134 F1 **East Stockwith** Lincs
17 G5 **East Stoke** Dorset
117 K2 **East Stoke** Notts
32 D6 **East Stour** Dorset
41 H3 **East Stourmouth** Kent
27 L5 **East Stowford** Devon
35 H3 **East Stratton** Hants
41 J5 **East Studdal** Kent
39 L3 **East Sutton** Kent
5 L2 **East Taphouse** Cnwll
27 H5 **East-the-Water** Devon
191 J6 **East Thirston** Nthumb
52 E3 **East Tilbury** Thurr
35 L4 **East Tisted** Hants
136 B3 **East Torrington** Lincs
106 B1 **East Tuddenham** Norfk
34 C5 **East Tytherley** Hants
46 D4 **East Tytherton** Wilts
13 K2 **East Village** Devon
45 J4 **Eastville** Bristl
137 H8 **Eastville** Lincs
96 C4 **East Wall** Shrops
121 G8 **East Walton** Norfk
31 J1 **East Water** Somset
12 F4 **East Week** Devon
117 K6 **Eastwell** Leics
34 C6 **East Wellow** Hants
222 F7 **East Wemyss** Fife
210 C6 **East Whitburn** W Loth
70 B5 **Eastwick** Herts
51 M3 **East Wickham** Gt Lon
55 J6 **East Williamston** Pembks
120 F8 **East Winch** Norfk
34 B4 **East Winterslow** Wilts
20 C7 **East Wittering** W Susx
159 L5 **East Witton** N York
140 E3 **Eastwood** Calder
116 D2 **Eastwood** Notts
53 H2 **Eastwood** Sthend
179 L2 **East Woodburn** Nthumb
103 J5 **Eastwood End** Cambs
48 B6 **East Woodhay** Hants
32 C2 **East Woodlands** Somset
35 M3 **East Worldham** Hants
105 J5 **East Wretham** Norfk
26 D7 **East Youlstone** Devon
83 J2 **Eathorpe** Warwks
130 B7 **Eaton** Ches
131 G6 **Eaton** Ches
117 L5 **Eaton** Leics
106 D2 **Eaton** Norfk
134 E4 **Eaton** Notts
66 C6 **Eaton** Oxon
95 J5 **Eaton** Shrops
96 B5 **Eaton** Shrops
80 B7 **Eaton Bishop** Herefs
68 B3 **Eaton Bray** Beds
96 D3 **Eaton Constantine** Shrops
86 D3 **Eaton Ford** Cambs
68 B3 **Eaton Green** Beds
65 K7 **Eaton Hastings** Oxon
96 C2 **Eaton Mascott** Shrops
86 D3 **Eaton Socon** Cambs
113 L7 **Eaton upon Tern** Shrops
130 C1 **Eaves Brow** Warrtn
99 H6 **Eaves Green** Solhll
162 F6 **Ebberston** N York
33 G6 **Ebbesborne Wake** Wilts
61 J5 **Ebbw Vale** Blae G
180 D7 **Ebchester** Dur
44 D6 **Ebdon** N Som
14 A5 **Ebford** Devon
64 B6 **Ebley** Gloucs
113 H2 **Ebnal** Ches
80 B3 **Ebnall** Herefs
82 E7 **Ebrington** Gloucs
12 C4 **Ebsworthy Town** Devon
48 D7 **Ecchinswell** Hants
213 G5 **Ecclaw** Border
177 G4 **Ecclefechan** D & G
202 B5 **Eccles** Border
52 F6 **Eccles** Kent
140 A8 **Eccles** Salfd
132 F3 **Ecclesall** Sheff
133 G1 **Ecclesfield** Sheff

79 L5 **Eccles Green** Herefs
114 C5 **Eccleshall** Staffs
149 M8 **Eccleshill** Brad
210 E4 **Ecclesmachan** W Loth
123 H5 **Eccles on Sea** Norfk
105 L5 **Eccles Road** Norfk
129 J7 **Eccleston** Ches
139 G4 **Eccleston** Lancs
138 F8 **Eccleston** St Hel
139 G4 **Eccleston Green** Lancs
245 G2 **Echt** Abers
201 L7 **Eckford** Border
133 H4 **Eckington** Derbys
81 L7 **Eckington** Worcs
84 F3 **Ecton** Nhants
132 B8 **Ecton** Staffs
132 B3 **Edale** Derbys
22 C5 **Edburton** W Susx
164 E2 **Edderside** Cumb
263 J3 **Edderton** Highld
41 G2 **Eddington** Kent
200 B4 **Eddleston** Border
209 J8 **Eddlewood** S Lans
38 C4 **Edenbridge** Kent
140 B4 **Edenfield** Lancs
166 D4 **Edenhall** Cumb
118 E7 **Edenham** Lincs
156 F7 **Eden Mount** Cumb
51 K5 **Eden Park** Gt Lon
132 E5 **Edensor** Derbys
218 D8 **Edentaggart** Ag & B
143 G6 **Edenthorpe** Donc
108 E4 **Edern** Gwynd
31 H3 **Edgarley** Somset
98 D6 **Edgbaston** Birm
3 J4 **Edgcombe** Cnwll
67 G3 **Edgcott** Bucks
28 E3 **Edgcott** Somset
64 B5 **Edge** Gloucs
95 K2 **Edge** Shrops
113 J7 **Edgebolton** Shrops
63 H4 **Edge End** Gloucs
122 B5 **Edgefield** Norfk
122 B4 **Edgefield Green** Norfk
139 L6 **Edgefold** Bolton
113 H1 **Edge Green** Ches
83 J5 **Edgehill** Warwks
112 E7 **Edgerley** Shrops
141 H4 **Edgerton** Kirk
140 C3 **Edgeside** Lancs
64 D6 **Edgeworth** Gloucs
28 E8 **Edgeworthy** Devon
8 C2 **Edginswell** Torbay
82 B3 **Edgiock** Worcs
114 A7 **Edgmond** Wrekin
114 A7 **Edgmond Marsh** Wrekin
95 J6 **Edgton** Shrops
51 G1 **Edgware** Gt Lon
139 L4 **Edgworth** Bl w D
258 E6 **Edinbane** Highld
211 J4 **Edinburgh** C Edin
99 G1 **Edingale** Staffs
175 L2 **Edingham** D & G
134 D8 **Edingley** Notts
123 G5 **Edingthorpe** Norfk
122 F5 **Edingthorpe Green** Norfk
202 B2 **Edington** Border
180 E2 **Edington** Nthumb
30 F3 **Edington** Somset
46 D8 **Edington** Wilts
30 F2 **Edington Burtle** Somset
44 D8 **Edingworth** Somset
30 E1 **Edithmead** Somset
101 K2 **Edith Weston** Rutlnd
68 B3 **Edlesborough** Bucks
191 G4 **Edlingham** Nthumb
136 D5 **Edlington** Lincs
178 C7 **Edmond Castle** Cumb
33 J8 **Edmondsham** Dorset
169 G1 **Edmondsley** Dur
117 M8 **Edmondthorpe** Leics
10 D7 **Edmonton** Cnwll
69 J8 **Edmonton** Gt Lon
168 C1 **Edmundbyers** Dur
202 A5 **Ednam** Border
115 L3 **Ednaston** Derbys
232 C5 **Edradynate** P & K
202 C2 **Edrom** Border
113 H5 **Edstaston** Shrops
82 E3 **Edstone** Warwks
80 F3 **Edvin Loach** Herefs
117 G4 **Edwalton** Notts
89 J6 **Edwardstone** Suffk
43 G2 **Edwardsville** Myr Td
59 H2 **Edwinsford** Carmth
134 C6 **Edwinstowe** Notts
86 E7 **Edworth** Beds
80 F4 **Edwyn Ralph** Herefs

234 F2 **Edzell** Angus
234 F2 **Edzell Woods** Abers
57 L6 **Efail-fach** Neath
43 H5 **Efail Isaf** Rhondd
108 F4 **Efailnewydd** Gwynd
112 A6 **Efail-Rhyd** Powys
75 K7 **Efailwen** Carmth
128 D8 **Efenechtyd** Denbgs
187 L7 **Effgill** D & G
50 E8 **Effingham** Surrey
115 K8 **Efflinch** Staffs
13 K2 **Efford** Devon
48 B8 **Egbury** Hants
21 G3 **Egdean** W Susx
139 L5 **Egerton** Bolton
40 B6 **Egerton** Kent
6 F3 **Eggbuckland** C Plym
28 B8 **Eggesford** Devon
68 B2 **Eggington** Beds
115 M6 **Egginton** Derbys
169 L7 **Egglescliffe** S on T
168 C6 **Eggleston** Dur
50 C5 **Egham** Surrey
50 B5 **Egham Wick** Surrey
101 J2 **Egleton** Rutlnd
191 G2 **Eglingham** Nthumb
10 D8 **Egloshayle** Cnwll
11 K5 **Egloskerry** Cnwll
126 F5 **Eglwysbach** Conwy
42 F7 **Eglwys-Brewis** V Glam
113 G3 **Eglwys Cross** Wrexhm
92 F4 **Eglwys Fach** Cerdgn
75 K4 **Eglwyswrw** Pembks
134 E6 **Egmanton** Notts
164 D8 **Egremont** Cumb
129 H1 **Egremont** Wirral
162 E2 **Egton** N York
162 D2 **Egton Bridge** N York
72 D2 **Eight Ash Green** Essex
248 C8 **Eilanreach** Highld
93 H6 **Eisteddfa Gurig** Cerdgn
78 C2 **Elan Village** Powys
45 J1 **Elberton** S Glos
20 F6 **Elbridge** W Susx
7 G4 **Elburton** C Plym
47 H3 **Elcombe** Swindn
48 B5 **Elcot** W Berk
103 G4 **Eldernell** Cambs
64 A1 **Eldersfield** Worcs
208 D6 **Elderslie** Rens
88 B8 **Elder Street** Essex
169 G5 **Eldon** Dur
149 L7 **Eldwick** Brad
245 H6 **Elfhill** Abers
203 K7 **Elford** Nthumb
98 F1 **Elford** Staffs
266 E4 **Elgin** Moray
247 H6 **Elgol** Highld
41 G6 **Elham** Kent
223 J7 **Elie** Fife
190 D4 **Elilaw** Nthumb
124 F3 **Elim** IoA
18 F1 **Eling** Hants
134 D4 **Elkesley** Notts
64 D4 **Elkstone** Gloucs
268 B4 **Ella** Abers
8 D2 **Ellacombe** Torbay
215 L1 **Ellanbeich** Ag & B
141 H4 **Elland** Calder
141 H3 **Elland Lower Edge** Calder
206 A4 **Ellary** Ag & B
115 J3 **Ellastone** Staffs
147 J4 **Ellel** Lancs
212 F7 **Ellemford** Border
164 D3 **Ellenborough** Cumb
139 L7 **Ellenbrook** Salfd
114 C6 **Ellenhall** Staffs
37 G4 **Ellen's Green** Surrey
160 F3 **Ellerbeck** N York
171 J7 **Ellerby** N York
113 K7 **Ellerdine Heath** Wrekin
14 A2 **Ellerhayes** Devon
229 G5 **Elleric** Ag & B
144 A2 **Ellerker** E R Yk
149 H7 **Ellers** N York
151 L7 **Ellerton** E R Yk
160 C3 **Ellerton** N York
113 M6 **Ellerton** Shrops
67 K6 **Ellesborough** Bucks
112 F4 **Ellesmere** Shrops
129 J4 **Ellesmere Port** Ches
29 H2 **Ellicombe** Somset
18 A2 **Ellingham** Hants
107 G5 **Ellingham** Norfk
203 K8 **Ellingham** Nthumb
159 M6 **Ellingstring** N York
86 D1 **Ellington** Cambs
191 K7 **Ellington** Nthumb

86 D1 **Ellington Thorpe** Cambs
32 D2 **Elliots Green** Somset
35 K2 **Ellisfield** Hants
259 H3 **Ellishader** Highld
99 L1 **Ellistown** Leics
257 H5 **Ellon** Abers
166 A4 **Ellonby** Cumb
107 J6 **Ellough** Suffk
144 B2 **Elloughton** E R Yk
63 H5 **Ellwood** Gloucs
103 K2 **Elm** Cambs
81 K2 **Elmbridge** Worcs
87 J7 **Elmdon** Essex
98 F6 **Elmdon** Solhll
98 F7 **Elmdon Heath** Solhll
21 G6 **Elmer** W Susx
51 K5 **Elmers End** Gt Lon
139 G6 **Elmer's Green** Lancs
100 A4 **Elmesthorpe** Leics
71 J6 **Elm Green** Essex
98 E1 **Elmhurst** Staffs
82 A7 **Elmley Castle** Worcs
81 K1 **Elmley Lovett** Worcs
64 A4 **Elmore** Gloucs
63 M4 **Elmore Back** Gloucs
52 B2 **Elm Park** Gt Lon
26 D6 **Elmscott** Devon
90 C6 **Elmsett** Suffk
81 G2 **Elms Green** Worcs
72 F3 **Elmstead Heath** Essex
72 F2 **Elmstead Market** Essex
72 F3 **Elmstead Row** Essex
40 F6 **Elmsted Court** Kent
41 H3 **Elmstone** Kent
64 D2 **Elmstone Hardwicke** Gloucs
152 F4 **Elmswell** E R Yk
89 K2 **Elmswell** Suffk
133 K5 **Elmton** Derbys
271 H6 **Elphin** Highld
211 L5 **Elphinstone** E Loth
245 H2 **Elrick** Abers
173 J5 **Elrig** D & G
179 K6 **Elrington** Nthumb
190 C7 **Elsdon** Nthumb
142 B7 **Elsecar** Barns
70 D2 **Elsenham** Essex
66 D5 **Elsfield** Oxon
144 C5 **Elsham** N Linc
122 B8 **Elsing** Norfk
149 G6 **Elslack** N York
19 K3 **Elson** Hants
112 F4 **Elson** Shrops
199 J4 **Elsrickle** S Lans
36 D2 **Elstead** Surrey
20 D3 **Elsted** W Susx
118 E6 **Elsthorpe** Lincs
169 J6 **Elstob** Dur
139 J1 **Elston** Lancs
117 K2 **Elston** Notts
33 J2 **Elston** Wilts
28 B7 **Elstone** Devon
85 L6 **Elstow** Beds
68 F8 **Elstree** Herts
145 G1 **Elstronwick** E R Yk
147 H8 **Elswick** Lancs
180 F6 **Elswick** N u Ty
87 G3 **Elsworth** Cambs
156 D7 **Elterwater** Cumb
51 L4 **Eltham** Gt Lon
86 F3 **Eltisley** Cambs
140 B5 **Elton** Bury
102 B4 **Elton** Cambs
129 K4 **Elton** Ches
132 D7 **Elton** Derbys
63 K4 **Elton** Gloucs
80 B1 **Elton** Herefs
117 K4 **Elton** Notts
169 L7 **Elton** S on T
129 K5 **Elton Green** Ches
180 C6 **Eltringham** Nthumb
186 E3 **Elvanfoot** S Lans
116 C5 **Elvaston** Derbys
105 G7 **Elveden** Suffk
49 J7 **Elvetham Heath** Hants
212 A4 **Elvingston** E Loth
41 J5 **Elvington** Kent
151 L6 **Elvington** York
28 B4 **Elwell** Devon
170 B4 **Elwick** Hartpl
203 J5 **Elwick** Nthumb
130 E7 **Elworth** Ches
29 K4 **Elworthy** Somset
103 L7 **Ely** Cambs
43 J6 **Ely** Cardif
85 H5 **Emberton** M Keyn
165 G5 **Embleton** Cumb
169 L5 **Embleton** Dur

191 J2 **Embleton** Nthumb
264 C1 **Embo** Highld
31 K1 **Emborough** Somset
264 C2 **Embo Street** Highld
149 H5 **Embsay** N York
18 D2 **Emery Down** Hants
141 K5 **Emley** Kirk
141 K5 **Emley Moor** Kirk
49 J5 **Emmbrook** Wokham
49 H4 **Emmer Green** Readg
133 J4 **Emmett Carr** Derbys
67 H6 **Emmington** Oxon
103 K2 **Emneth** Norfk
103 K2 **Emneth Hungate** Norfk
101 L2 **Empingham** Rutlnd
35 M4 **Empshott** Hants
35 M5 **Empshott Green** Hants
20 B5 **Emsworth** Hants
48 B6 **Enborne** W Berk
48 C6 **Enborne Row** W Berk
96 B4 **Enchmarsh** Shrops
100 C3 **Enderby** Leics
157 H5 **Endmoor** Cumb
114 E1 **Endon** Staffs
114 E1 **Endon Bank** Staffs
69 K7 **Enfield** Gt Lon
69 K7 **Enfield Lock** Gt Lon
69 K7 **Enfield Wash** Gt Lon
47 H8 **Enford** Wilts
45 K2 **Engine Common** S Glos
80 D5 **England's Gate** Herefs
48 F4 **Englefield** W Berk
50 C4 **Englefield Green** Surrey
114 B1 **Engleseabrook** Ches
63 H4 **English Bicknor** Gloucs
45 L6 **Englishcombe** BaNES
113 G5 **English Frankton** Shrops
10 B8 **Engollan** Cnwll
34 D1 **Enham-Alamein** Hants
30 C4 **Enmore** Somset
32 E6 **Enmore Green** Dorset
164 E7 **Ennerdale Bridge** Cumb
4 F3 **Enniscaven** Cnwll
233 G3 **Enochdhu** P & K
226 D3 **Ensay** Ag & B
17 L3 **Ensbury** Bmouth
112 F8 **Ensdon** Shrops
27 K5 **Ensis** Devon
114 E6 **Enson** Staffs
66 A2 **Enstone** Oxon
186 C5 **Enterkinfoot** D & G
161 G2 **Enterpen** N York
97 J6 **Enville** Staffs
283 b12 **Eolaigearraidh** W Isls
63 M5 **Epney** Gloucs
117 H2 **Epperstone** Notts
70 C6 **Epping** Essex
70 B6 **Epping Green** Essex
69 J5 **Epping Green** Herts
70 C6 **Epping Upland** Essex
168 F8 **Eppleby** N York
144 C2 **Eppleworth** E R Yk
51 G6 **Epsom** Surrey
83 H7 **Epwell** Oxon
143 K7 **Epworth** N Linc
143 J7 **Epworth Turbary** N Linc
112 E3 **Erbistock** Wrexhm
98 E5 **Erdington** Birm
38 E6 **Eridge Green** E Susx
38 E6 **Eridge Station** E Susx
206 D4 **Erines** Ag & B
228 D6 **Eriska** Ag & B
104 E7 **Eriswell** Suffk
52 B3 **Erith** Gt Lon
46 D8 **Erlestoke** Wilts
7 J4 **Ermington** Devon
122 D5 **Erpingham** Norfk
40 B3 **Erriottwood** Kent
250 F7 **Errogie** Highld
222 D3 **Errol** P & K
208 D5 **Erskine** Rens
172 B1 **Ervie** D & G
90 F8 **Erwarton** Suffk
78 F6 **Erwood** Powys
160 D1 **Eryholme** N York
128 E8 **Eryrys** Denbgs
2 B5 **Escalls** Cnwll
168 F4 **Escomb** Dur
29 K3 **Escott** Somset
151 K7 **Escrick** N York
58 C3 **Esgair** Carmth
77 G2 **Esgair** Cerdgn
93 G2 **Esgairgeiliog** Powys
77 H7 **Esgerdawe** Carmth
126 F4 **Esgyryn** Conwy
169 G2 **Esh** Dur
50 E6 **Esher** Surrey
150 A7 **Esholt** Brad

191 J6 **Eshott** Nthumb
149 G4 **Eshton** N York
169 G2 **Esh Winning** Dur
250 D4 **Eskadale** Highld
211 K5 **Eskbank** Mdloth
155 L3 **Eskdale Green** Cumb
187 K6 **Eskdalemuir** D & G
164 E7 **Eskett** Cumb
145 K8 **Eskham** Lincs
143 G4 **Eskholme** Donc
168 E6 **Esperley Lane Ends** Dur
147 H8 **Esprick** Lancs
102 A1 **Essendine** Rutlnd
69 H5 **Essendon** Herts
251 H4 **Essich** Highld
98 B3 **Essington** Staffs
257 G6 **Esslemont** Abers
170 D7 **Eston** R & Cl
202 E5 **Etal** Nthumb
46 F7 **Etchilhampton** Wilts
24 C2 **Etchingham** E Susx
41 G7 **Etchinghill** Kent
115 G7 **Etchinghill** Staffs
23 H3 **Etchingwood** E Susx
153 L8 **Etherdwick** E R Yk
105 K1 **Etling Green** Norfk
63 K6 **Etloe** Gloucs
50 B3 **Eton** W & M
50 B3 **Eton Wick** W & M
114 D2 **Etruria** C Stke
241 J5 **Etteridge** Highld
167 K5 **Ettersgill** Dur
130 E7 **Ettiley Heath** Ches
97 L4 **Ettingshall** Wolves
83 G5 **Ettington** Warwks
102 C2 **Etton** C Pete
152 F7 **Etton** E R Yk
187 L3 **Ettrick** Border
188 C1 **Ettrickbridge** Border
187 L3 **Ettrickhill** Border
115 M5 **Etwall** Derbys
96 F5 **Eudon George** Shrops
105 H7 **Euston** Suffk
103 K4 **Euximoor Drove** Cambs
139 H4 **Euxton** Lancs
79 J3 **Evancoyd** Powys
263 G6 **Evanton** Highld
118 E2 **Evedon** Lincs
97 G2 **Evelith** Shrops
263 L2 **Evelix** Highld
79 J3 **Evenjobb** Powys
84 B8 **Evenley** Nhants
65 J1 **Evenlode** Gloucs
168 F5 **Evenwood** Dur
168 F6 **Evenwood Gate** Dur
31 L3 **Evercreech** Somset
152 B7 **Everingham** E R Yk
47 J8 **Everleigh** Wilts
163 H5 **Everley** N York
12 B4 **Eversfield** Devon
85 K8 **Eversholt** Beds
16 A2 **Evershot** Dorset
49 J6 **Eversley** Hants
49 J6 **Eversley Cross** Hants
144 A2 **Everthorpe** E R Yk
86 D5 **Everton** Beds
18 D5 **Everton** Hants
129 H1 **Everton** Lpool
134 D2 **Everton** Notts
177 K4 **Evertown** D & G
80 F5 **Evesbatch** Herefs
82 B6 **Evesham** Worcs
100 D3 **Evington** C Leic
141 L8 **Ewden Village** Sheff
97 G4 **Ewdness** Shrops
51 G6 **Ewell** Surrey
41 H6 **Ewell Minnis** Kent
48 F1 **Ewelme** Oxon
64 E7 **Ewen** Gloucs
42 D6 **Ewenny** V Glam
118 F2 **Ewerby** Lincs
118 F2 **Ewerby Thorpe** Lincs
190 F7 **Ewesley** Nthumb
37 G3 **Ewhurst** Surrey
24 E2 **Ewhurst Green** E Susx
37 G3 **Ewhurst Green** Surrey
129 G6 **Ewloe** Flints
129 G6 **Ewloe Green** Flints
139 K3 **Ewood** Bl w D
140 B4 **Ewood Bridge** Lancs
12 B3 **Eworthy** Devon
36 B1 **Ewshot** Hants
62 D2 **Ewyas Harold** Herefs
12 E2 **Exbourne** Devon
29 G6 **Exbridge** Somset
19 G4 **Exbury** Hants
23 H7 **Exceat** E Susx
160 D5 **Exelby** N York

13 L4 **Exeter** Devon
28 E3 **Exford** Somset
95 L2 **Exfordsgreen** Shrops
82 D4 **Exhall** Warwks
99 K6 **Exhall** Warwks
49 G3 **Exlade Street** Oxon
149 J7 **Exley Head** Brad
13 M5 **Exminster** Devon
14 A6 **Exmouth** Devon
88 C2 **Exning** Suffk
41 G6 **Exted** Kent
14 A5 **Exton** Devon
35 J6 **Exton** Hants
101 K1 **Exton** Rutlnd
29 G4 **Exton** Somset
13 L4 **Exwick** Devon
132 D4 **Eyam** Derbys
83 M5 **Eydon** Nhants
102 E3 **Eye** C Pete
80 C2 **Eye** Herefs
106 C8 **Eye** Suffk
102 E3 **Eye Green** C Pete
117 K8 **Eye Kettleby** Leics
213 L6 **Eyemouth** Border
86 E6 **Eyeworth** Beds
39 L2 **Eyhorne Street** Kent
91 H5 **Eyke** Suffk
86 D3 **Eynesbury** Cambs
52 C6 **Eynsford** Kent
66 B5 **Eynsham** Oxon
15 K4 **Eype** Dorset
259 G6 **Eyre** Highld
41 J5 **Eythorne** Kent
80 B3 **Eyton** Herefs
95 J6 **Eyton** Shrops
112 F8 **Eyton** Shrops
113 G7 **Eyton** Shrops
112 E3 **Eyton** Wrexhm
96 D2 **Eyton on Severn** Shrops
113 L8 **Eyton upon the Weald Moors** Wrekin

F

48 A7 **Faccombe** Hants
161 H2 **Faceby** N York
111 K8 **Fachwen** Powys
140 D4 **Facit** Lancs
133 J7 **Fackley** Notts
113 K1 **Faddiley** Ches
161 L5 **Fadmoor** N York
57 J4 **Faerdre** Swans
57 J4 **Fagwyr** Swans
208 E4 **Faifley** W Duns
45 G4 **Failand** N Som
196 F5 **Failford** S Ayrs
140 D7 **Failsworth** Oldham
92 D1 **Fairbourne** Gwynd
142 D2 **Fairburn** N York
131 L5 **Fairfield** Derbys
25 H2 **Fairfield** Kent
97 L8 **Fairfield** Worcs
65 H6 **Fairford** Gloucs
65 H6 **Fairford Park** Gloucs
175 L3 **Fairgirth** D & G
138 C2 **Fairhaven** Lancs
52 B8 **Fairlands** Surrey
207 L8 **Fairlie** N Ayrs
24 F5 **Fairlight** E Susx
14 C3 **Fairmile** Devon
50 E6 **Fairmile** Surrey
200 F6 **Fairnilee** Border
35 G7 **Fair Oak** Hants
114 B5 **Fairoak** Staffs
49 G6 **Fair Oak Green** Hants
52 D6 **Fairseat** Kent
71 J4 **Fairstead** Essex
120 E7 **Fairstead** Norfk
122 F6 **Fairstead** Norfk
23 G2 **Fairwarp** E Susx
43 J6 **Fairwater** Cardif
27 G6 **Fairy Cross** Devon
121 K5 **Fakenham** Norfk
105 H8 **Fakenham Magna** Suffk
211 M6 **Fala** Mdloth
211 M6 **Fala Dam** Mdloth
200 E2 **Falahill** Border
77 G5 **Falcondale** Cerdgn
84 B6 **Falcut** Nhants
135 L3 **Faldingworth** Lincs
9 f2 **Faldouet** Jersey
63 K8 **Falfield** S Glos
91 G7 **Falkenham** Suffk
210 A3 **Falkirk** Falk
222 D5 **Falkland** Fife
133 G7 **Fallgate** Derbys
209 L1 **Fallin** Stirlg

191 H2 **Falloden** Nthumb
131 G1 **Fallowfield** Manch
179 L5 **Fallowfield** Nthumb
216 F4 **Falls of Blarghour** Ag & B
22 E5 **Falmer** E Susx
3 K4 **Falmouth** Cnwll
188 C5 **Falnash** Border
163 J5 **Falsgrave** N York
179 G2 **Falstone** Nthumb
276 B6 **Fanagmore** Highld
68 C2 **Fancott** Beds
250 E3 **Fanellan** Highld
161 J4 **Fangdale Beck** N York
152 A5 **Fangfoss** E R Yk
226 B3 **Fanmore** Ag & B
261 L6 **Fannich Lodge** Highld
201 J5 **Fans** Border
85 G8 **Far Bletchley** M Keyn
102 D4 **Farcet** Cambs
84 E3 **Far Cotton** Nhants
96 D8 **Farden** Shrops
19 K2 **Fareham** Hants
156 D3 **Far End** Cumb
98 D1 **Farewell** Staffs
97 G8 **Far Forest** Worcs
136 F4 **Farforth** Lincs
63 M7 **Far Green** Gloucs
65 L8 **Faringdon** Oxon
139 G3 **Farington** Lancs
232 F8 **Farkhill** P & K
178 D7 **Farlam** Cumb
45 G5 **Farleigh** N Som
51 K7 **Farleigh** Surrey
46 A7 **Farleigh Hungerford** Somset
35 J2 **Farleigh Wallop** Hants
137 J5 **Farlesthorpe** Lincs
157 H6 **Farleton** Cumb
147 L2 **Farleton** Lancs
132 F7 **Farley** Derbys
115 H3 **Farley** Staffs
34 B5 **Farley** Wilts
88 E4 **Farley Green** Suffk
37 G2 **Farley Green** Surrey
49 H6 **Farley Hill** Wokham
63 M4 **Farleys End** Gloucs
19 M3 **Farlington** C Port
151 K2 **Farlington** N York
96 E7 **Farlow** Shrops
45 K7 **Farmborough** BaNES
70 F5 **Farmbridge End** Essex
64 F1 **Farmcote** Gloucs
97 H5 **Farmcote** Shrops
77 J6 **Farmers** Carmth
65 H4 **Farmington** Gloucs
66 C5 **Farmoor** Oxon
139 G7 **Far Moor** Wigan
3 H4 **Farms Common** Cnwll
116 C8 **Farm Town** Leics
267 K6 **Farmtown** Moray
116 B2 **Farnah Green** Derbys
51 L6 **Farnborough** Gt Lon
49 L8 **Farnborough** Hants
48 B3 **Farnborough** W Berk
83 K5 **Farnborough** Warwks
49 L7 **Farnborough Park** Hants
49 L7 **Farnborough Street** Hants
36 E2 **Farncombe** Surrey
85 H3 **Farndish** Beds
112 F1 **Farndon** Ches
117 K1 **Farndon** Notts
235 G4 **Farnell** Angus
33 G7 **Farnham** Dorset
70 C2 **Farnham** Essex
150 E4 **Farnham** N York
91 H3 **Farnham** Suffk
36 B2 **Farnham** Surrey
50 B2 **Farnham Common** Bucks
70 C2 **Farnham Green** Essex
50 B2 **Farnham Royal** Bucks
52 C5 **Farningham** Kent
141 L1 **Farnley** Leeds
150 B6 **Farnley** N York
141 J5 **Farnley Tyas** Kirk
134 C8 **Farnsfield** Notts
139 L6 **Farnworth** Bolton
129 L2 **Farnworth** Halton
64 D6 **Far Oakridge** Gloucs
241 L3 **Farr** Highld
251 J5 **Farr** Highld
278 B4 **Farr** Highld
251 G7 **Farraline** Highld
14 B4 **Farringdon** Devon
45 J7 **Farrington Gurney** BaNES
156 E4 **Far Sawrey** Cumb
141 K1 **Farsley** Leeds
71 K6 **Farther Howegreen** Essex
39 K4 **Farthing Green** Kent

83 M7 **Farthinghoe** Nhants
41 J7 **Farthingloe** Kent
84 B4 **Farthingstone** Nhants
51 L6 **Farthing Street** Gt Lon
136 E5 **Far Thorpe** Lincs
141 J4 **Fartown** Kirk
141 K1 **Fartown** Leeds
14 E3 **Farway Street** Devon
229 G6 **Fasnacloich** Ag & B
250 B6 **Fasnakyle** Highld
239 G7 **Fassfern** Highld
181 H8 **Fatfield** Sundld
178 C7 **Faugh** Cumb
115 K6 **Fauld** Staffs
210 B6 **Fauldhouse** W Loth
71 J4 **Faulkbourne** Essex
45 L8 **Faulkland** Somset
113 K5 **Fauls** Shrops
40 D3 **Faversham** Kent
150 F1 **Fawdington** N York
180 F5 **Fawdon** N u Ty
190 E3 **Fawdon** Nthumb
131 L7 **Fawfieldhead** Staffs
52 C6 **Fawkham Green** Kent
66 A4 **Fawler** Oxon
49 J2 **Fawley** Bucks
19 G3 **Fawley** Hants
48 B3 **Fawley** W Berk
63 H1 **Fawley Chapel** Herefs
128 F6 **Fawnog** Flints
84 A4 **Fawsley** Nhants
143 L3 **Faxfleet** E R Yk
37 K4 **Faygate** W Susx
138 D2 **Fazakerley** Lpool
99 G3 **Fazeley** Staffs
160 B6 **Fearby** N York
264 C4 **Fearn** Highld
231 K6 **Fearnan** P & K
260 B7 **Fearnbeg** Highld
130 C2 **Fearnhead** Warrtn
260 A7 **Fearnmore** Highld
206 E3 **Fearnoch** Ag & B
97 L2 **Featherstone** Staffs
142 C3 **Featherstone** Wakefd
82 B3 **Feckenham** Worcs
72 C3 **Feering** Essex
159 H3 **Feetham** N York
148 D2 **Feizor** N York
38 B5 **Felbridge** Surrey
122 E4 **Felbrigg** Norfk
38 B5 **Felcourt** Surrey
68 D6 **Felden** Herts
59 G4 **Felindre** Carmth
59 K3 **Felindre** Carmth
76 C7 **Felindre** Carmth
77 G4 **Felindre** Cerdgn
61 J2 **Felindre** Powys
94 E7 **Felindre** Powys
57 H4 **Felindre** Swans
75 J4 **Felindre Farchog** Pembks
76 F4 **Felin Fach** Cerdgn
78 F8 **Felinfach** Powys
56 F4 **Felinfoel** Carmth
58 F4 **Felin gwm Isaf** Carmth
58 F4 **Felin gwm Uchaf** Carmth
78 F4 **Felin-newydd** Powys
161 G5 **Felixkirk** N York
91 G8 **Felixstowe** Suffk
91 H7 **Felixstowe Ferry** Suffk
202 E4 **Felkington** Nthumb
142 B5 **Felkirk** Wakefd
181 G6 **Felling** Gatesd
149 J7 **Fell Lane** Brad
165 J3 **Fell Side** Cumb
85 K4 **Felmersham** Beds
122 E5 **Felmingham** Norfk
20 F7 **Felpham** W Susx
89 J4 **Felsham** Suffk
71 G3 **Felsted** Essex
50 E4 **Feltham** Gt Lon
50 E5 **Felthamhill** Surrey
122 D7 **Felthorpe** Norfk
80 D5 **Felton** Herefs
45 G6 **Felton** N Som
191 H6 **Felton** Nthumb
112 F8 **Felton Butler** Shrops
104 E5 **Feltwell** Norfk
141 J4 **Fenay Bridge** Kirk
148 E8 **Fence** Lancs
133 J3 **Fence** Rothm
169 J1 **Fence Houses** Sundld
160 D4 **Fencote** N York
66 E4 **Fencott** Oxon
137 H7 **Fendike Corner** Lincs
87 K3 **Fen Ditton** Cambs
87 G2 **Fen Drayton** Cambs
119 H7 **Fen End** Lincs
99 G8 **Fen End** Solhll

203 H5 **Fenham** Nthumb
139 K2 **Feniscliffe** Bl w D
139 K3 **Feniscowles** Bl w D
14 D3 **Feniton** Devon
97 H6 **Fenn Green** Shrops
53 G4 **Fenn Street** Medway
115 K2 **Fenny Bentley** Derbys
14 D3 **Fenny Bridges** Devon
83 K5 **Fenny Compton** Warwks
99 K4 **Fenny Drayton** Leics
85 G8 **Fenny Stratford** M Keyn
191 H7 **Fenrother** Nthumb
87 G2 **Fenstanton** Cambs
88 F5 **Fenstead End** Suffk
105 K4 **Fen Street** Norfk
90 E3 **Fen Street** Suffk
114 D3 **Fenton** C Stke
103 G7 **Fenton** Cambs
178 C7 **Fenton** Cumb
118 A1 **Fenton** Lincs
135 G4 **Fenton** Lincs
134 F3 **Fenton** Notts
202 F6 **Fenton** Nthumb
212 B3 **Fenton Barns** E Loth
142 F4 **Fenwick** Donc
196 F2 **Fenwick** E Ayrs
180 C4 **Fenwick** Nthumb
203 H5 **Fenwick** Nthumb
3 L3 **Feock** Cnwll
205 G3 **Feolin Ferry** Ag & B
196 C2 **Fergushill** N Ayrs
258 B6 **Feriniquarrie** Highld
9 k3 **Fermain Bay** Guern
234 D3 **Fern** Angus
42 F2 **Ferndale** Rhondd
17 L2 **Ferndown** Dorset
253 J3 **Ferness** Highld
65 L8 **Fernham** Oxon
81 K3 **Fernhill Heath** Worcs
36 D5 **Fernhurst** W Susx
222 E4 **Fernie** Fife
209 K8 **Ferniegair** S Lans
246 E2 **Fernilea** Highld
131 K4 **Fernilee** Derbys
117 L2 **Fernwood** Notts
150 E4 **Ferrensby** N York
144 B4 **Ferriby Sluice** N Linc
247 L7 **Ferrindonald** Highld
21 J6 **Ferring** W Susx
142 D3 **Ferrybridge** Wakefd
235 H4 **Ferryden** Angus
169 H4 **Ferryhill** Dur
263 K3 **Ferry Point** Highld
56 C3 **Ferryside** Carmth
263 K2 **Ferrytown** Highld
106 B6 **Fersfield** Norfk
240 B7 **Fersit** Highld
241 M3 **Feshiebridge** Highld
50 F7 **Fetcham** Surrey
269 H6 **Fetterangus** Abers
235 G1 **Fettercairn** Abers
66 D2 **Fewcott** Oxon
150 B5 **Fewston** N York
59 H4 **Ffairfach** Carmth
77 K2 **Ffair Rhos** Cerdgn
77 H6 **Ffald-y-Brenin** Carmth
61 K3 **Ffawyddog** Powys
110 D3 **Ffestiniog** Gwynd
128 D6 **Ffordd-las** Denbgs
57 G4 **Fforest** Carmth
62 B3 **Fforest** Mons
57 H5 **Fforest Fach** Swans
57 K4 **Fforest Goch** Neath
76 C5 **Ffostrasol** Cerdgn
129 G8 **Ffrith** Flints
76 C4 **Ffynnonddewi** Cerdgn
128 D3 **Ffynnongroyw** Flints
76 F4 **Ffynnon-Oer** Cerdgn
272 C2 **Fiag Lodge** Highld
51 K6 **Fickleshole** Surrey
64 D1 **Fiddington** Gloucs
30 B3 **Fiddington** Somset
32 D8 **Fiddleford** Dorset
4 D4 **Fiddlers Green** Cnwll
70 C6 **Fiddlers Hamlet** Essex
115 G5 **Field** Staffs
156 E6 **Field Broughton** Cumb
121 M4 **Field Dalling** Norfk
166 B3 **Fieldhead** Cumb
100 B2 **Field Head** Leics
32 C6 **Fifehead Magdalen** Dorset
32 C8 **Fifehead Neville** Dorset
16 E1 **Fifehead St Quintin** Dorset
267 H6 **Fife Keith** Moray
65 K3 **Fifield** Oxon
49 L4 **Fifield** W & M
33 K1 **Fifield** Wilts
33 K2 **Figheldean** Wilts

46 D1 **Filands** Wilts
107 K1 **Filby** Norfk
163 L6 **Filey** N York
85 G5 **Filgrave** M Keyn
65 K6 **Filkins** Oxon
28 B5 **Filleigh** Devon
28 C8 **Filleigh** Devon
135 J3 **Fillingham** Lincs
99 H6 **Fillongley** Warwks
35 K5 **Filmore Hill** Hants
45 J3 **Filton** S Glos
152 D4 **Fimber** E R Yk
234 D4 **Finavon** Angus
104 D2 **Fincham** Norfk
49 J6 **Finchampstead** Wokham
216 D6 **Fincharn** Ag & B
20 B4 **Finchdean** Hants
88 D8 **Finchingfield** Essex
51 H1 **Finchley** Gt Lon
116 A5 **Findern** Derbys
265 G7 **Findhorn** Moray
252 E6 **Findhorn Bridge** Highld
267 J3 **Findochty** Moray
221 H3 **Findo Gask** P & K
245 L4 **Findon** Abers
21 J5 **Findon** W Susx
263 G7 **Findon Mains** Highld
244 D3 **Findrack House** Abers
85 H1 **Finedon** Nhants
101 L4 **Fineshade** Nhants
90 F1 **Fingal Street** Suffk
222 B3 **Fingask** P & K
49 J1 **Fingest** Bucks
160 B5 **Finghall** N York
177 H7 **Fingland** Cumb
197 L7 **Fingland** D & G
41 K4 **Finglesham** Kent
72 F3 **Fingringhoe** Essex
88 D7 **Finkle Green** Essex
141 M7 **Finkle Street** Barns
231 G8 **Finlarig** Stirlg
84 C8 **Finmere** Oxon
230 F4 **Finnart** P & K
90 C2 **Finningham** Suffk
143 H7 **Finningley** Donc
282 e6 **Finsbay** W Isls
82 A1 **Finstall** Worcs
156 E5 **Finsthwaite** Cumb
66 A4 **Finstock** Oxon
275 C4 **Finstown** Ork
268 D5 **Fintry** Abers
209 G2 **Fintry** Stirlg
244 D5 **Finzean** Abers
226 B7 **Fionnphort** Ag & B
282 e6 **Fionnsbhagh** W Isls
157 K4 **Firbank** Cumb
133 L2 **Firbeck** Rothm
152 A3 **Firby** N York
160 C5 **Firby** N York
140 D5 **Firgrove** Rochdl
137 H7 **Firsby** Lincs
34 B4 **Firsdown** Wilts
168 F4 **Fir Tree** Dur
19 J5 **Fishbourne** IoW
20 D6 **Fishbourne** W Susx
169 K4 **Fishburn** Dur
220 F8 **Fishcross** Clacks
20 E6 **Fisher** W Susx
256 B4 **Fisherford** Abers
211 K4 **Fisherrow** E Loth
35 G6 **Fisher's Pond** Hants
147 H6 **Fisher's Row** Lancs
36 E4 **Fisherstreet** W Susx
252 D2 **Fisherton** Highld
196 B7 **Fisherton** S Ayrs
33 G3 **Fisherton de la Mere** Wilts
98 F2 **Fisherwick** Staffs
49 L3 **Fishery Estate** W & M
74 F5 **Fishguard** Pembks
143 G5 **Fishlake** Donc
12 D1 **Fishleigh** Devon
119 J4 **Fishmere End** Lincs
227 J4 **Fishnish Pier** Ag & B
15 J3 **Fishpond Bottom** Dorset
45 J4 **Fishponds** Bristl
140 B6 **Fishpool** Bury
119 K3 **Fishtoft** Lincs
119 K2 **Fishtoft Drove** Lincs
139 H2 **Fishwick** Lancs
246 D2 **Fiskavaig** Highld
135 L5 **Fiskerton** Lincs
117 K1 **Fiskerton** Notts
145 H1 **Fitling** E R Yk
33 K1 **Fittleton** Wilts
21 G3 **Fittleworth** W Susx
103 J1 **Fitton End** Cambs
113 G7 **Fitz** Shrops
29 L5 **Fitzhead** Somset

30 B5 **Fitzroy** Somset
142 C5 **Fitzwilliam** Wakefd
23 H3 **Five Ash Down** E Susx
23 J2 **Five Ashes** E Susx
29 K2 **Five Bells** Somset
80 F6 **Five Bridges** Herefs
129 M4 **Fivecrosses** Ches
30 E6 **Fivehead** Somset
11 J6 **Fivelanes** Cnwll
44 F1 **Five Lanes** Mons
39 G4 **Five Oak Green** Kent
9 e3 **Five Oaks** Jersey
37 G5 **Five Oaks** W Susx
56 E4 **Five Roads** Carmth
39 K3 **Five Wents** Kent
71 J4 **Flack's Green** Essex
49 L1 **Flackwell Heath** Bucks
82 A6 **Fladbury** Worcs
281 e7 **Fladdabister** Shet
132 C6 **Flagg** Derbys
153 K2 **Flamborough** E R Yk
68 D4 **Flamstead** Herts
20 F6 **Flansham** W Susx
141 M4 **Flanshaw** Wakefd
149 J8 **Flappit Spring** Brad
149 G4 **Flasby** N York
131 K6 **Flash** Staffs
258 E6 **Flashader** Highld
68 C7 **Flaunden** Herts
117 K3 **Flawborough** Notts
151 G3 **Flawith** N York
45 G5 **Flax Bourton** N Som
150 E4 **Flaxby** N York
63 K4 **Flaxley** Gloucs
130 A5 **Flaxmere** Ches
29 L4 **Flaxpool** Somset
151 L3 **Flaxton** N York
100 E5 **Fleckney** Leics
83 M3 **Flecknoe** Warwks
134 F5 **Fledborough** Notts
16 C6 **Fleet** Dorset
20 B6 **Fleet** Hants
49 K8 **Fleet** Hants
119 L6 **Fleet** Lincs
19 H3 **Fleetend** Hants
119 L6 **Fleet Hargate** Lincs
146 F6 **Fleetwood** Lancs
42 F7 **Flemingston** V Glam
209 H7 **Flemington** S Lans
89 G1 **Flempton** Suffk
38 E3 **Fletcher Green** Kent
5 J2 **Fletchersbridge** Cnwll
165 G2 **Fletchertown** Cumb
23 G3 **Fletching** E Susx
43 J3 **Fleur-de-lis** Caerph
11 J1 **Flexbury** Cnwll
36 D1 **Flexford** Surrey
164 D4 **Flimby** Cumb
39 H7 **Flimwell** E Susx
128 F5 **Flint** Flints
117 K2 **Flintham** Notts
128 F5 **Flint Mountain** Flints
153 K8 **Flinton** E R Yk
99 H7 **Flint's Green** Solhll
39 J6 **Flishinghurst** Kent
120 F6 **Flitcham** Norfk
85 L8 **Flitton** Beds
85 K8 **Flitwick** Beds
143 L5 **Flixborough** N Linc
143 L5 **Flixborough Stather** N Linc
163 J6 **Flixton** N York
107 G6 **Flixton** Suffk
130 E1 **Flixton** Traffd
141 K5 **Flockton** Kirk
141 L5 **Flockton Green** Kirk
202 E6 **Flodden** Nthumb
259 H2 **Flodigarry** Highld
156 E7 **Flookburgh** Cumb
106 D4 **Flordon** Norfk
84 C3 **Flore** Nhants
190 E5 **Flotterton** Nthumb
23 L5 **Flowers Green** E Susx
90 C6 **Flowton** Suffk
141 L3 **Flushdyke** Wakefd
3 K4 **Flushing** Cnwll
14 C4 **Fluxton** Devon
82 A4 **Flyford Flavell** Worcs
52 F2 **Fobbing** Thurr
267 G4 **Fochabers** Moray
61 H6 **Fochriw** Caerph
143 L4 **Fockerby** N Linc
31 J5 **Foddington** Somset
94 B1 **Foel** Powys
59 G6 **Foelgastell** Carmth
42 C3 **Foel y Dyffryn** Brdgnd
152 A8 **Foggathorpe** E R Yk
202 B3 **Fogo** Border
266 E5 **Fogwatt** Moray

276 B6 **Foindle** Highld
233 J3 **Folda** Angus
115 G4 **Fole** Staffs
99 K7 **Foleshill** Covtry
31 L8 **Folke** Dorset
41 H8 **Folkestone** Kent
118 E5 **Folkingham** Lincs
23 J6 **Folkington** E Susx
102 C5 **Folksworth** Cambs
163 J6 **Folkton** N York
256 C5 **Folla Rule** Abers
150 D5 **Follifoot** N York
12 D3 **Folly Gate** Devon
36 B1 **Folly Hill** Surrey
43 G8 **Fonmon** V Glam
32 F4 **Fonthill Bishop** Wilts
32 F4 **Fonthill Gifford** Wilts
32 E7 **Fontmell Magna** Dorset
32 D7 **Fontmell Parva** Dorset
20 F5 **Fontwell** W Susx
43 G8 **Font-y-gary** V Glam
132 D4 **Foolow** Derbys
52 A5 **Foots Cray** Gt Lon
243 L1 **Forbestown** Abers
168 F8 **Forcett** N York
216 D6 **Ford** Ag & B
67 J5 **Ford** Bucks
133 H4 **Ford** Derbys
7 J5 **Ford** Devon
8 B6 **Ford** Devon
27 G4 **Ford** Devon
65 G1 **Ford** Gloucs
202 E5 **Ford** Nthumb
95 K1 **Ford** Shrops
29 K5 **Ford** Somset
45 H8 **Ford** Somset
115 H1 **Ford** Staffs
21 G6 **Ford** W Susx
33 L4 **Ford** Wilts
46 B4 **Ford** Wilts
12 D4 **Forda** Devon
38 E5 **Fordcombe** Kent
211 G1 **Fordell** Fife
94 F3 **Forden** Powys
71 G4 **Ford End** Essex
8 B2 **Forder Green** Devon
147 J6 **Ford Green** Lancs
88 C1 **Fordham** Cambs
72 D2 **Fordham** Essex
104 C3 **Fordham** Norfk
72 D2 **Fordham Heath** Essex
95 K1 **Ford Heath** Shrops
33 K8 **Fordingbridge** Hants
163 J7 **Fordon** E R Yk
245 G8 **Fordoun** Abers
90 C2 **Ford's Green** Suffk
72 D2 **Fordstreet** Essex
29 L7 **Ford Street** Somset
13 J3 **Fordton** Devon
65 L4 **Fordwells** Oxon
41 G3 **Fordwich** Kent
267 L3 **Fordyce** Abers
114 E7 **Forebridge** Staffs
116 B6 **Foremark** Derbys
9 j4 **Forest** Guern
160 C3 **Forest** N York
148 D5 **Forest Becks** Lancs
190 F7 **Forestburn Gate** Nthumb
131 J5 **Forest Chapel** Ches
51 L2 **Forest Gate** Gt Lon
37 H3 **Forest Green** Surrey
181 G5 **Forest Hall** N Tyne
178 D7 **Forest Head** Cumb
51 K4 **Forest Hill** Gt Lon
66 E5 **Forest Hill** Oxon
167 K4 **Forest-in-Teesdale** Dur
150 D4 **Forest Lane Head** N York
221 G8 **Forest Mill** Clacks
38 C6 **Forest Row** E Susx
19 H5 **Forest Side** IoW
20 C4 **Forestside** W Susx
133 L7 **Forest Town** Notts
234 C5 **Forfar** Angus
221 K3 **Forgandenny** P & K
93 G3 **Forge** Powys
62 B7 **Forge Hammer** Torfn
61 L5 **Forge Side** Torfn
267 H5 **Forgie** Moray
267 H5 **Forgieside** Moray
256 A3 **Forgue** Abers
98 D8 **Forhill** Worcs
138 C6 **Formby** Sefton
106 C4 **Forncett End** Norfk
106 D4 **Forncett St Mary** Norfk
106 D5 **Forncett St Peter** Norfk
89 G2 **Fornham All Saints** Suffk
89 G2 **Fornham St Martin** Suffk
253 H2 **Fornighty** Highld

165 K6 **Fornside** Cumb
265 G8 **Forres** Moray
114 F3 **Forsbrook** Staffs
275 H1 **Forse** Highld
98 E8 **Forshaw Heath** Warwks
278 F7 **Forsinard** Highld
16 C3 **Forston** Dorset
240 C2 **Fort Augustus** Highld
221 J4 **Forteviot** P & K
198 F2 **Forth** S Lans
64 B1 **Forthampton** Gloucs
9 i2 **Fort Hommet** Guern
231 K6 **Fortingall** P & K
9 k1 **Fort le Marchant** Guern
34 F2 **Forton** Hants
147 J5 **Forton** Lancs
113 G8 **Forton** Shrops
15 H1 **Forton** Somset
114 B7 **Forton** Staffs
256 B3 **Fortrie** Abers
263 K8 **Fortrose** Highld
16 D7 **Fortuneswell** Dorset
239 J8 **Fort William** Highld
50 A1 **Forty Green** Bucks
69 J7 **Forty Hill** Gt Lon
90 C3 **Forward Green** Suffk
47 L7 **Fosbury** Wilts
65 K3 **Foscot** Oxon
84 C6 **Foscote** Nhants
119 K5 **Fosdyke** Lincs
119 K5 **Fosdyke Bridge** Lincs
231 L4 **Foss** P & K
65 G5 **Fossebridge** Gloucs
76 E3 **Foss-y-ffin** Cerdgn
143 G5 **Fosterhouses** Donc
70 C5 **Foster Street** Essex
115 K5 **Foston** Derbys
100 D4 **Foston** Lincs
117 M3 **Foston** Lincs
151 L3 **Foston** N York
153 H4 **Foston on the Wolds** E R Yk
136 F2 **Fotherby** Lincs
164 D4 **Fothergill** Cumb
102 B5 **Fotheringhay** Nhants
165 M1 **Foulbridge** Cumb
142 B4 **Foulby** Wakefd
202 E2 **Foulden** Border
104 F4 **Foulden** Norfk
99 H4 **Foul End** Warwks
23 K4 **Foul Mile** E Susx
148 F7 **Foulridge** Lancs
122 A6 **Foulsham** Norfk
200 F3 **Fountainhall** Border
98 F8 **Four Ashes** Solhll
97 H6 **Four Ashes** Staffs
97 L2 **Four Ashes** Staffs
89 K1 **Four Ashes** Suffk
9 j3 **Four Cabots** Guern
112 C7 **Four Crosses** Powys
98 B2 **Four Crosses** Staffs
38 C4 **Four Elms** Kent
31 J4 **Four Foot** Somset
30 C3 **Four Forks** Somset
139 J6 **Four Gates** Bolton
120 A8 **Four Gotes** Cambs
141 L7 **Four Lane End** Barns
130 A7 **Four Lane Ends** Ches
3 H3 **Four Lanes** Cnwll
130 F7 **Fourlanes End** Ches
35 K4 **Four Marks** Hants
124 E4 **Four Mile Bridge** IoA
98 E4 **Four Oaks** Birm
24 F2 **Four Oaks** E Susx
63 K2 **Four Oaks** Gloucs
99 H7 **Four Oaks** Solhll
264 C1 **Fourpenny** Highld
48 E3 **Four Points** W Berk
56 E3 **Four Roads** Carmth
65 K1 **Four Shire Stone** Warwks
179 K5 **Fourstones** Nthumb
39 J7 **Four Throws** Kent
38 F3 **Four Wents** Kent
33 H5 **Fovant** Wilts
257 H7 **Foveran** Abers
5 K4 **Fowey** Cnwll
139 K8 **Fowley Common** Warrtn
39 H4 **Fowlhall** Kent
233 M8 **Fowlis** Angus
221 G2 **Fowlis Wester** P & K
87 J6 **Fowlmere** Cambs
80 D8 **Fownhope** Herefs
208 D6 **Foxbar** Rens
12 C5 **Foxcombe** Devon
50 B7 **Fox Corner** Surrey
64 E3 **Foxcote** Gloucs
45 L7 **Foxcote** Somset
154 c6 **Foxdale** IoM
89 G6 **Foxearth** Essex

52 E5 **Foxendown** Kent
156 B5 **Foxfield** Cumb
46 E3 **Foxham** Wilts
70 E7 **Fox Hatch** Essex
18 E1 **Foxhills** Hants
4 F4 **Foxhole** Cnwll
163 H8 **Foxholes** N York
23 J4 **Foxhunt Green** E Susx
84 C5 **Foxley** Nhants
122 A7 **Foxley** Norfk
46 C2 **Foxley** Wilts
82 B2 **Foxlydiate** Worcs
72 F2 **Fox Street** Essex
115 G2 **Foxt** Staffs
87 H5 **Foxton** Cambs
169 K5 **Foxton** Dur
100 F5 **Foxton** Leics
160 F3 **Foxton** N York
158 F7 **Foxup** N York
130 C6 **Foxwist Green** Ches
96 E8 **Foxwood** Shrops
63 H2 **Foy** Herefs
250 E7 **Foyers** Highld
253 G1 **Foynesfield** Highld
2 F4 **Fraddam** Cnwll
4 E3 **Fraddon** Cnwll
98 F1 **Fradley** Staffs
114 F5 **Fradswell** Staffs
153 J3 **Fraisthorpe** E R Yk
23 H3 **Framfield** E Susx
106 F3 **Framingham Earl** Norfk
106 F3 **Framingham Pigot** Norfk
91 G3 **Framlingham** Suffk
16 B3 **Frampton** Dorset
119 K4 **Frampton** Lincs
45 K3 **Frampton Cotterell** S Glos
64 D6 **Frampton Mansell** Gloucs
63 L5 **Frampton on Severn** Gloucs
119 J3 **Frampton West End** Lincs
90 E3 **Framsden** Suffk
169 H2 **Framwellgate Moor** Dur
148 A8 **Frances Green** Lancs
97 J7 **Franche** Worcs
130 C4 **Frandley** Ches
11 M4 **Frankaborough** Devon
128 F2 **Frankby** Wirral
122 F6 **Frankfort** Norfk
80 C6 **Franklands Gate** Herefs
98 C7 **Frankley** Worcs
78 F4 **Franksbridge** Powys
83 K1 **Frankton** Warwks
38 F6 **Frant** E Susx
269 J3 **Fraserburgh** Abers
73 G3 **Frating** Essex
73 G2 **Frating Green** Essex
19 L4 **Fratton** C Port
6 D4 **Freathy** Cnwll
88 D1 **Freckenham** Suffk
138 E2 **Freckleton** Lancs
132 F5 **Freebirch** Derbys
117 L7 **Freeby** Leics
35 G1 **Freefolk** Hants
115 G3 **Freehay** Staffs
66 B4 **Freeland** Oxon
107 H2 **Freethorpe** Norfk
107 H2 **Freethorpe Common** Norfk
119 L3 **Freiston** Lincs
27 J4 **Fremington** Devon
159 J3 **Fremington** N York
45 J3 **Frenchay** S Glos
12 F5 **Frenchbeer** Devon
51 M8 **French Street** Kent
232 B4 **Frenich** P & K
36 C3 **Frensham** Surrey
138 C6 **Freshfield** Sefton
46 A7 **Freshford** Wilts
18 E6 **Freshwater** IoW
18 E6 **Freshwater Bay** IoW
55 G7 **Freshwater East** Pembks
106 F7 **Fressingfield** Suffk
90 E7 **Freston** Suffk
280 E3 **Freswick** Highld
63 L5 **Fretherne** Gloucs
122 E8 **Frettenham** Norfk
222 D6 **Freuchie** Fife
54 F4 **Freystrop** Pembks
98 C4 **Friar Park** Sandw
38 D6 **Friar's Gate** E Susx
162 C5 **Friars' Hill** N York
16 C5 **Friar Waddon** Dorset
103 K2 **Friday Bridge** Cambs
90 F3 **Friday Street** Suffk
91 H5 **Friday Street** Suffk
91 J3 **Friday Street** Suffk
37 H2 **Friday Street** Surrey
152 D4 **Fridaythorpe** E R Yk
132 C7 **Friden** Derbys
141 G3 **Friendly** Calder

69 H8 **Friern Barnet** Gt Lon
225 G4 **Friesland Bay** Ag & B
135 M3 **Friesthorpe** Lincs
118 B2 **Frieston** Lincs
49 J1 **Frieth** Bucks
116 D2 **Friezeland** Notts
66 B7 **Frilford** Oxon
48 E4 **Frilsham** W Berk
49 L7 **Frimley** Surrey
49 L7 **Frimley Green** Surrey
52 F5 **Frindsbury** Medway
66 F1 **Fring** Norfk
66 F1 **Fringford** Oxon
40 A4 **Frinsted** Kent
73 K3 **Frinton-on-Sea** Essex
234 F5 **Friockheim** Angus
92 D1 **Friog** Gwynd
117 J8 **Frisby on the Wreake** Leics
137 J8 **Friskney** Lincs
137 J8 **Friskney Eaudike** Lincs
23 J7 **Friston** E Susx
91 J3 **Friston** Suffk
116 B1 **Fritchley** Derbys
34 B8 **Fritham** Hants
119 K2 **Frith Bank** Lincs
80 F1 **Frith Common** Worcs
27 H7 **Frithelstock** Devon
27 H7 **Frithelstock Stone** Devon
36 B3 **Frithend** Hants
68 C5 **Frithsden** Herts
119 K2 **Frithville** Lincs
39 K5 **Frittenden** Kent
8 B6 **Frittiscombe** Devon
106 E5 **Fritton** Norfk
107 K3 **Fritton** Norfk
66 D1 **Fritwell** Oxon
149 L8 **Frizinghall** Brad
164 D7 **Frizington** Cumb
63 M6 **Frocester** Gloucs
96 C3 **Frodesley** Shrops
129 M4 **Frodsham** Ches
202 B7 **Frogden** Border
87 H6 **Frog End** Cambs
87 L3 **Frog End** Cambs
132 E4 **Froggatt** Derbys
115 G2 **Froghall** Staffs
33 L8 **Frogham** Hants
41 H5 **Frogham** Kent
7 M6 **Frogmore** Devon
102 D2 **Frognall** Lincs
3 J3 **Frogpool** Cnwll
81 J2 **Frog Pool** Worcs
6 C1 **Frogwell** Cnwll
100 B5 **Frolesworth** Leics
32 C1 **Frome** Somset
16 B2 **Frome St Quintin** Dorset
80 F6 **Fromes Hill** Herefs
128 C6 **Fron** Denbgs
108 F4 **Fron** Gwynd
109 J1 **Fron** Gwynd
94 E4 **Fron** Powys
94 F3 **Fron** Powys
112 C3 **Froncysyllte** Denbgs
111 H4 **Fron-goch** Gwynd
112 C3 **Fron Isaf** Wrexhm
107 K7 **Frostenden** Suffk
168 C3 **Frosterley** Dur
85 J8 **Froxfield** Beds
47 L5 **Froxfield** Wilts
35 L5 **Froxfield Green** Hants
34 F6 **Fryern Hill** Hants
70 F7 **Fryerning** Essex
162 B7 **Fryton** N York
227 J3 **Fuinary** Highld
118 B2 **Fulbeck** Lincs
87 L4 **Fulbourn** Cambs
65 K4 **Fulbrook** Oxon
35 G5 **Fulflood** Hants
30 B5 **Fulford** Somset
114 F4 **Fulford** Staffs
151 K6 **Fulford** York
51 H4 **Fulham** Gt Lon
22 C5 **Fulking** W Susx
28 B3 **Fullaford** Devon
196 C3 **Fullarton** N Ayrs
70 D2 **Fuller's End** Essex
113 H1 **Fuller's Moor** Ches
71 H4 **Fuller Street** Essex
38 E2 **Fuller Street** Kent
34 E3 **Fullerton** Hants
136 E5 **Fulletby** Lincs
83 G6 **Fullready** Warwks
152 A5 **Full Sutton** E R Yk
196 E1 **Fullwood** E Ayrs
50 C2 **Fulmer** Bucks
121 M5 **Fulmodeston** Norfk
136 B4 **Fulnetby** Lincs
119 J6 **Fulney** Lincs

141 J6 **Fulstone** Kirk
145 J8 **Fulstow** Lincs
66 A3 **Fulwell** Oxon
181 J7 **Fulwell** Sundld
139 H2 **Fulwood** Lancs
133 J8 **Fulwood** Notts
132 F3 **Fulwood** Sheff
30 B6 **Fulwood** Somset
106 C4 **Fundenhall** Norfk
20 C5 **Funtington** W Susx
19 J2 **Funtley** Hants
220 C2 **Funtullich** P & K
15 G2 **Furley** Devon
217 G7 **Furnace** Ag & B
56 F4 **Furnace** Carmth
92 E4 **Furnace** Cerdgn
99 H5 **Furnace End** Warwks
22 F7 **Furner's Green** E Susx
131 K3 **Furness Vale** Derbys
70 B2 **Furneux Pelham** Herts
39 M5 **Further Quarter** Kent
84 E6 **Furtho** Nhants
28 C2 **Furzehill** Devon
17 K2 **Furzehill** Dorset
136 E5 **Furzehills** Lincs
19 L2 **Furzeley Corner** Hants
49 L3 **Furze Platt** W & M
34 C7 **Furzley** Hants
30 C7 **Fyfett** Somset
70 E5 **Fyfield** Essex
34 C2 **Fyfield** Hants
66 B7 **Fyfield** Oxon
47 H5 **Fyfield** Wilts
47 H5 **Fyfield** Wilts
33 H6 **Fyfield Bavant** Wilts
163 G2 **Fylingthorpe** N York
36 B6 **Fyning** W Susx
256 D4 **Fyvie** Abers

G

196 E1 **Gabroc Hill** E Ayrs
100 F1 **Gaddesby** Leics
68 D4 **Gaddesden Row** Herts
125 H2 **Gadfa** IoA
196 E6 **Gadgirth** S Ayrs
112 E4 **Gadlas** Shrops
61 J3 **Gaer** Powys
62 F7 **Gaer-llwyd** Mons
125 H5 **Gaerwen** IoA
66 B2 **Gagingwell** Oxon
196 C4 **Gailes** N Ayrs
97 K1 **Gailey** Staffs
168 F7 **Gainford** Dur
135 G2 **Gainsborough** Lincs
88 E8 **Gainsford End** Essex
260 C4 **Gairloch** Highld
239 K6 **Gairlochy** Highld
221 L7 **Gairneybridge** P & K
157 K2 **Gaisgill** Cumb
165 L1 **Gaitsgill** Cumb
201 G6 **Galashiels** Border
147 J5 **Galgate** Lancs
31 K5 **Galhampton** Somset
216 C2 **Gallanach** Ag & B
113 H1 **Gallantry Bank** Ches
222 E8 **Gallatown** Fife
99 J5 **Galley Common** Warwks
71 H6 **Galleywood** Essex
240 F5 **Gallovie** Highld
234 C7 **Gallowfauld** Angus
233 J8 **Gallowhill** P & K
72 D2 **Gallows Green** Essex
81 L3 **Gallows Green** Worcs
49 G3 **Gallowstree Common** Oxon
248 C7 **Galltair** Highld
125 K7 **Gallt-y-foel** Gwynd
49 K8 **Gally** Hants
38 D6 **Gallypot Street** E Susx
7 K6 **Galmpton** Devon
8 D4 **Galmpton** Torbay
150 C1 **Galphay** N York
196 F4 **Galston** E Ayrs
16 E5 **Galton** Dorset
131 L6 **Gamballs Green** Staffs
166 E3 **Gamblesby** Cumb
71 J4 **Gambles Green** Essex
177 H8 **Gamelsby** Cumb
131 K1 **Gamesley** Derbys
86 E5 **Gamlingay** Cambs
86 E4 **Gamlingay Cinques** Cambs
86 E5 **Gamlingay Great Heath** Cambs
159 J6 **Gammersgill** N York
268 E4 **Gamrie** Abers
117 G4 **Gamston** Notts
134 E4 **Gamston** Notts

63 G4 **Ganarew** Herefs
216 D1 **Ganavan Bay** Ag & B
6 C1 **Gang** Cnwll
110 D6 **Ganllwyd** Gwynd
234 F1 **Gannachy** Angus
144 F1 **Ganstead** E R Yk
151 L2 **Ganthorpe** N York
163 H7 **Ganton** N York
69 H7 **Ganwick Corner** Herts
13 K7 **Gappah** Devon
266 F5 **Garbity** Moray
105 K7 **Garboldisham** Norfk
243 J2 **Garchory** Abers
129 H6 **Garden City** Flints
49 K5 **Gardeners Green** Wokham
268 E3 **Gardenstown** Abers
141 L8 **Garden Village** Sheff
281 d6 **Garderhouse** Shet
152 E7 **Gardham** E R Yk
32 C3 **Gare Hill** Somset
207 L1 **Garelochhead** Ag & B
66 B7 **Garford** Oxon
142 B1 **Garforth** Leeds
142 B1 **Garforth Bridge** Leeds
149 G5 **Gargrave** N York
220 B8 **Gargunnock** Stirlg
126 D4 **Garizim** Conwy
106 E6 **Garlic Street** Norfk
174 D5 **Garlieston** D & G
41 K2 **Garlinge** Kent
40 F5 **Garlinge Green** Kent
245 H2 **Garlogie** Abers
268 E5 **Garmond** Abers
169 J4 **Garmondsway** Dur
267 G3 **Garmouth** Moray
96 E2 **Garmston** Shrops
59 J6 **Garnant** Carmth
109 J3 **Garn-Dolbenmaen** Gwynd
157 H3 **Garnett Bridge** Cumb
108 E5 **Garnfadryn** Gwynd
209 H5 **Garnkirk** N Lans
57 H3 **Garnswllt** Swans
61 K5 **Garn-yr-erw** Torfn
282 h3 **Garrabost** W Isls
197 G7 **Garrallan** E Ayrs
3 H6 **Garras** Cnwll
109 L3 **Garreg** Gwynd
167 H2 **Garrigill** Cumb
159 L4 **Garriston** N York
184 F6 **Garroch** D & G
172 D7 **Garrochtrie** D & G
207 H8 **Garrochty** Ag & B
259 H4 **Garros** Highld
158 C5 **Garsdale** Cumb
158 C4 **Garsdale Head** Cumb
46 D2 **Garsdon** Wilts
114 F5 **Garshall Green** Staffs
66 E6 **Garsington** Oxon
147 J6 **Garstang** Lancs
68 E7 **Garston** Herts
129 J3 **Garston** Lpool
204 E4 **Gartachossan** Ag & B
209 J5 **Gartcosh** N Lans
42 C4 **Garth** Brdgnd
62 D8 **Garth** Mons
78 C5 **Garth** Powys
79 J1 **Garth** Powys
112 C3 **Garth** Wrexhm
209 H5 **Garthamlock** C Glas
78 E8 **Garthbrengy** Powys
77 G4 **Gartheli** Cerdgn
94 F3 **Garthmyl** Powys
117 L7 **Garthorpe** Leics
143 L4 **Garthorpe** N Linc
92 E6 **Garth Penrhyncoch** Cerdgn
157 H3 **Garth Row** Cumb
157 H5 **Garths** Cumb
255 K5 **Gartly** Abers
219 H7 **Gartmore** Stirlg
209 K6 **Gartness** N Lans
208 E2 **Gartness** Stirlg
208 D2 **Gartocharn** W Duns
145 H1 **Garton** E R Yk
152 F4 **Garton-on-the-Wolds** E R Yk
274 D5 **Gartymore** Highld
212 D5 **Garvald** E Loth
238 F8 **Garvan** Highld
214 D6 **Garvard** Ag & B
262 C7 **Garve** Highld
105 L2 **Garvestone** Norfk
207 L5 **Garvock** Inver
62 F3 **Garway** Herefs
62 F3 **Garway Common** Herefs
62 F2 **Garway Hill** Herefs
282 g4 **Garyvard** W Isls
32 C4 **Gasper** Wilts
46 C5 **Gastard** Wilts

105 K7 **Gasthorpe** Norfk
70 D4 **Gaston Green** Essex
19 H6 **Gatcombe** IoW
157 J5 **Gatebeck** Cumb
135 G3 **Gate Burton** Lincs
134 B3 **Gateford** Notts
142 E2 **Gateforth** N York
196 D4 **Gatehead** E Ayrs
151 L5 **Gate Helmsley** N York
179 H1 **Gatehouse** Nthumb
174 F4 **Gatehouse of Fleet** D & G
121 L6 **Gateley** Norfk
160 D5 **Gatenby** N York
165 G7 **Gatesgarth** Cumb
189 L2 **Gateshaw** Border
181 G6 **Gateshead** Gatesd
129 L7 **Gates Heath** Ches
234 C6 **Gateside** Angus
208 E7 **Gateside** E Rens
222 B5 **Gateside** Fife
208 B8 **Gateside** N Ayrs
186 C5 **Gateslack** D & G
139 G6 **Gathurst** Wigan
131 G2 **Gatley** Stockp
51 H8 **Gatton** Surrey
201 H6 **Gattonside** Border
78 D2 **Gaufron** Powys
100 F3 **Gaulby** Leics
222 F2 **Gauldry** Fife
233 K5 **Gauldswell** P & K
139 M3 **Gaulkthorn** Lancs
103 K2 **Gaultree** Norfk
113 J2 **Gaunton's Bank** Ches
17 K2 **Gaunt's Common** Dorset
70 E2 **Gaunt's End** Essex
136 C5 **Gautby** Lincs
202 B3 **Gavinton** Border
141 M6 **Gawber** Barns
67 G1 **Gawcott** Bucks
131 H5 **Gawsworth** Ches
141 L3 **Gawthorpe** Wakefd
158 B5 **Gawthrop** Cumb
156 C5 **Gawthwaite** Cumb
71 J6 **Gay Bowers** Essex
83 J4 **Gaydon** Warwks
85 G6 **Gayhurst** M Keyn
158 F5 **Gayle** N York
159 L1 **Gayles** N York
21 J3 **Gay Street** W Susx
84 D4 **Gayton** Nhants
120 F7 **Gayton** Norfk
114 F6 **Gayton** Staffs
129 G4 **Gayton** Wirral
137 H3 **Gayton le Marsh** Lincs
121 G7 **Gayton Thorpe** Norfk
120 E7 **Gaywood** Norfk
88 E2 **Gazeley** Suffk
3 J6 **Gear** Cnwll
282 g4 **Gearraidh Bhaird** W Isls
258 D4 **Geary** Highld
89 J4 **Gedding** Suffk
101 K6 **Geddington** Nhants
117 G3 **Gedling** Notts
119 L6 **Gedney** Lincs
119 L7 **Gedney Broadgate** Lincs
120 A5 **Gedney Drove End** Lincs
119 L6 **Gedney Dyke** Lincs
103 G1 **Gedney Hill** Lincs
131 J1 **Gee Cross** Tamesd
101 L3 **Geeston** Rutlnd
107 H5 **Geldeston** Norfk
42 E3 **Gelli** Rhondd
62 B8 **Gelli** Torfn
128 D7 **Gellifor** Denbgs
43 H2 **Gelligaer** Caerph
43 J3 **Gelligroes** Caerph
57 K4 **Gelligron** Neath
110 C4 **Gellilydan** Gwynd
57 K4 **Gellinudd** Neath
55 J3 **Gelly** Pembks
233 G7 **Gellyburn** P & K
58 A4 **Gellywen** Carmth
175 J3 **Gelston** D & G
118 B3 **Gelston** Lincs
153 H4 **Gembling** E R Yk
98 D1 **Gentleshaw** Staffs
187 L7 **Georgefield** D & G
50 C3 **George Green** Bucks
27 H3 **Georgeham** Devon
28 B6 **George Nympton** Devon
61 J5 **Georgetown** Blae G
2 D4 **Georgia** Cnwll
275 c3 **Georth** Ork
126 C6 **Gerlan** Gwynd
12 B4 **Germansweek** Devon
2 F5 **Germoe** Cnwll
3 M4 **Gerrans** Cnwll
50 C1 **Gerrards Cross** Bucks

171 G8 **Gerrick** R & Cl
89 G7 **Gestingthorpe** Essex
112 B8 **Geuffordd** Powys
130 C4 **Gib Hill** Ches
137 K7 **Gibraltar** Lincs
117 J2 **Gibsmere** Notts
46 B4 **Giddeahall** Wilts
16 F5 **Giddy Green** Dorset
52 B1 **Gidea Park** Gt Lon
12 F5 **Gidleigh** Devon
208 F7 **Giffnock** E Rens
212 C5 **Gifford** E Loth
222 E5 **Giffordtown** Fife
148 D3 **Giggleswick** N York
143 L2 **Gilberdyke** E R Yk
81 J6 **Gilbert's End** Worcs
35 K4 **Gilbert Street** Hants
212 B6 **Gilchriston** E Loth
164 F3 **Gilcrux** Cumb
141 K2 **Gildersome** Leeds
133 L3 **Gildingwells** Rothm
169 J2 **Gilesgate Moor** Dur
42 F8 **Gileston** V Glam
43 J2 **Gilfach** Caerph
42 E4 **Gilfach Goch** Brdgnd
76 D3 **Gilfachrheda** Cerdgn
164 D6 **Gilgarran** Cumb
166 B5 **Gill** Cumb
162 B4 **Gillamoor** N York
3 K6 **Gillan** Cnwll
258 D1 **Gillen** Highld
187 J7 **Gillesbie** D & G
161 K7 **Gilling East** N York
32 D5 **Gillingham** Dorset
53 G5 **Gillingham** Medway
107 H5 **Gillingham** Norfk
160 B2 **Gilling West** N York
280 B4 **Gillock** Highld
131 H7 **Gillow Heath** Staffs
280 D2 **Gills** Highld
39 J7 **Gill's Green** Kent
188 B2 **Gilmanscleuch** Border
211 J5 **Gilmerton** C Edin
220 F2 **Gilmerton** P & K
168 C8 **Gilmonby** Dur
100 C6 **Gilmorton** Leics
178 E5 **Gilsland** Cumb
99 G5 **Gilson** Warwks
149 L7 **Gilstead** Brad
200 F2 **Gilston** Border
70 C4 **Gilston** Herts
70 B4 **Gilston Park** Herts
116 E2 **Giltbrook** Notts
61 L4 **Gilwern** Mons
122 F4 **Gimingham** Norfk
131 J4 **Ginclough** Ches
23 K5 **Gingers Green** E Susx
90 C3 **Gipping** Suffk
119 J2 **Gipsey Bridge** Lincs
196 C3 **Girdle Toll** N Ayrs
141 H1 **Girlington** Brad
281 e6 **Girlsta** Shet
160 E1 **Girsby** N York
86 D5 **Girtford** Beds
174 F4 **Girthon** D & G
87 J3 **Girton** Cambs
135 G6 **Girton** Notts
182 F3 **Girvan** S Ayrs
148 E6 **Gisburn** Lancs
107 K5 **Gisleham** Suffk
90 C1 **Gislingham** Suffk
106 C6 **Gissing** Norfk
14 D3 **Gittisham** Devon
79 J4 **Gladestry** Powys
212 A4 **Gladsmuir** E Loth
57 K5 **Glais** Swans
162 D2 **Glaisdale** N York
234 B6 **Glamis** Angus
110 B1 **Glanaber** Gwynd
54 F3 **Glanafon** Pembks
59 J6 **Glanaman** Carmth
122 A3 **Glandford** Norfk
76 F6 **Glan-Duar** Carmth
75 L6 **Glandwr** Pembks
109 J3 **Glan-Dwyfach** Gwynd
92 F4 **Glandyfi** Cerdgn
61 K4 **Glangrwyney** Powys
42 C3 **Glanllynfi** Brdgnd
94 E5 **Glanmule** Powys
75 K4 **Glanrhyd** Pembks
57 L3 **Glan-rhyd** Powys
190 F3 **Glanton** Nthumb
190 F3 **Glanton Pike** Nthumb
16 C1 **Glanvilles Wootton** Dorset
128 E4 **Glan-y-don** Flints
43 H5 **Glan-y-llyn** Rhondd
93 K6 **Glan-y-nant** Powys
111 H3 **Glan-yr-afon** Gwynd

111 K3 **Glan-yr-afon** Gwynd
126 B4 **Glan-yr-afon** IoA
57 H4 **Glan-yr-afon** Swans
101 M5 **Glapthorn** Nhants
133 J6 **Glapwell** Derbys
79 H7 **Glasbury** Powys
127 K5 **Glascoed** Denbgs
62 C6 **Glascoed** Mons
99 G3 **Glascote** Staffs
79 G5 **Glascwm** Powys
111 H2 **Glasfryn** Conwy
209 G6 **Glasgow** C Glas
125 K6 **Glasinfryn** Gwynd
237 G2 **Glasnacardoch Bay** Highld
247 H6 **Glasnakille** Highld
92 F4 **Glaspwll** Powys
39 J6 **Glassenbury** Kent
174 C7 **Glasserton** D & G
197 L2 **Glassford** S Lans
142 C3 **Glass Houghton** Wakefd
63 L3 **Glasshouse** Gloucs
63 L3 **Glasshouse Hill** Gloucs
149 L3 **Glasshouses** N York
177 H6 **Glasson** Cumb
147 J4 **Glasson** Lancs
166 D3 **Glassonby** Cumb
234 F5 **Glasterlaw** Angus
101 K3 **Glaston** Rutlnd
31 H3 **Glastonbury** Somset
102 C6 **Glatton** Cambs
130 D1 **Glazebrook** Warrtn
139 K8 **Glazebury** Warrtn
96 F5 **Glazeley** Shrops
133 G3 **Gleadless** Sheff
130 F6 **Gleadsmoss** Ches
146 E2 **Gleaston** Cumb
250 F8 **Glebe** Highld
150 D8 **Gledhow** Leeds
175 G5 **Gledpark** D & G
112 D4 **Gledrid** Shrops
89 G5 **Glemsford** Suffk
254 E3 **Glenallachie** Moray
237 K2 **Glenancross** Highld
227 G4 **Glenaros House** Ag & B
154 f4 **Glen Auldyn** IoM
192 D1 **Glenbarr** Ag & B
267 L5 **Glenbarry** Abers
237 H8 **Glenbeg** Highld
253 J6 **Glenbeg** Highld
245 G7 **Glenbervie** Abers
209 J5 **Glenboig** N Lans
237 H8 **Glenborrodale** Highld
217 J7 **Glenbranter** Ag & B
187 G2 **Glenbreck** Border
246 F4 **Glenbrittle House** Highld
198 B7 **Glenbuck** E Ayrs
234 A3 **Glencally** Angus
176 C5 **Glencaple** D & G
249 H2 **Glencarron Lodge** Highld
222 C3 **Glencarse** P & K
229 J5 **Glenceitlein** Highld
242 F7 **Glen Clunie Lodge** Abers
229 H4 **Glencoe** Highld
199 J7 **Glencothe** Border
222 B8 **Glencraig** Fife
185 J5 **Glencrosh** D & G
258 B6 **Glendale** Highld
206 F2 **Glendaruel** Ag & B
221 H6 **Glendevon** P & K
240 C2 **Glendoe Lodge** Highld
222 C3 **Glendoick** P & K
222 D3 **Glenduckie** Fife
221 G5 **Gleneagles** P & K
221 G5 **Gleneagles Hotel** P & K
204 E6 **Glenegedale** Ag & B
248 C7 **Glenelg** Highld
253 K2 **Glenerney** Moray
221 L5 **Glenfarg** P & K
241 M5 **Glenfeshie Lodge** Highld
100 C2 **Glenfield** Leics
238 E7 **Glenfinnan** Highld
239 L6 **Glenfintaig Lodge** Highld
222 B4 **Glenfoot** P & K
218 B4 **Glenfyne Lodge** Ag & B
208 B8 **Glengarnock** N Ayrs
279 K3 **Glengolly** Highld
226 E1 **Glengorm Castle** Ag & B
259 G7 **Glengrasco** Highld
199 J6 **Glenholm** Border
184 F5 **Glenhoul** D & G
233 K3 **Glenisla** Angus
207 J3 **Glenkin** Ag & B
243 M1 **Glenkindie** Abers
254 D6 **Glenlivet** Moray
175 J2 **Glenlochar** D & G
222 B6 **Glenlomond** P & K
172 F3 **Glenluce** D & G
207 H2 **Glenmassen** Ag & B

209 K5 **Glenmavis** N Lans
154 b6 **Glen Maye** IoM
154 f4 **Glen Mona** IoM
259 G8 **Glenmore** Highld
242 C2 **Glenmore Lodge** Highld
229 J1 **Glen Nevis House** Highld
220 F8 **Glenochil** Clacks
100 C4 **Glen Parva** Leics
234 C3 **Glenquiech** Angus
206 D5 **Glenralloch** Ag & B
165 L7 **Glenridding** Cumb
222 D7 **Glenrothes** Fife
232 E8 **Glenshee** P & K
240 F5 **Glenshero Lodge** Highld
207 H3 **Glenstriven** Ag & B
135 K2 **Glentham** Lincs
241 L4 **Glentromie Lodge** Highld
183 K7 **Glen Trool Lodge** D & G
183 J7 **Glentrool Village** D & G
241 J4 **Glentruim House** Highld
135 J2 **Glentworth** Lincs
237 K5 **Glenuig** Highld
229 G5 **Glenure** Ag & B
259 H8 **Glenvarragill** Highld
154 d6 **Glen Vine** IoM
182 F8 **Glenwhilly** D & G
198 D7 **Glespin** S Lans
63 H3 **Glewstone** Herefs
102 C2 **Glinton** C Pete
101 G4 **Glooston** Leics
131 L1 **Glossop** Derbys
191 K5 **Gloster Hill** Nthumb
64 B3 **Gloucester** Gloucs
149 H6 **Glusburn** N York
274 D1 **Glutt Lodge** Highld
4 F2 **Gluvian** Cnwll
66 B3 **Glympton** Oxon
76 B5 **Glynarthen** Cerdgn
112 B4 **Glyn Ceiriog** Wrexhm
60 C7 **Glyncorrwg** Neath
23 G5 **Glynde** E Susx
23 G5 **Glyndebourne** E Susx
112 A3 **Glyndyfrdwy** Denbgs
60 D5 **Glynneath** Neath
43 H4 **Glyntaff** Rhondd
60 C4 **Glyntawe** Powys
76 C7 **Glynteg** Carmth
114 C7 **Gnosall** Staffs
114 C7 **Gnosall Heath** Staffs
101 G4 **Goadby** Leics
117 K6 **Goadby Marwood** Leics
46 F4 **Goatacre** Wilts
217 G7 **Goatfield** Ag & B
24 E3 **Goatham Green** E Susx
31 L7 **Goathill** Dorset
162 E2 **Goathland** N York
30 C4 **Goathurst** Somset
38 D3 **Goathurst Common** Kent
40 D6 **Goat Lees** Kent
112 D5 **Gobowen** Shrops
36 E2 **Godalming** Surrey
91 G2 **Goddard's Corner** Suffk
39 K6 **Goddard's Green** Kent
14 D2 **Godford Cross** Devon
66 F2 **Godington** Oxon
140 E8 **Godley** Tamesd
86 F1 **Godmanchester** Cambs
16 C3 **Godmanstone** Dorset
40 D5 **Godmersham** Kent
31 H2 **Godney** Somset
2 F5 **Godolphin Cross** Cnwll
57 L3 **Godre'r-graig** Neath
33 L7 **Godshill** Hants
19 J7 **Godshill** IoW
115 G5 **Godstone** Staffs
51 K8 **Godstone** Surrey
12 C7 **Godsworthy** Devon
18 B4 **Godwinscroft** Hants
62 C6 **Goetre** Mons
69 J6 **Goff's Oak** Herts
61 L4 **Gofilon** Mons
211 G4 **Gogar** C Edin
92 E7 **Goginan** Cerdgn
109 J3 **Golan** Gwynd
5 K4 **Golant** Cnwll
11 L8 **Golberdon** Cnwll
139 J8 **Golborne** Wigan
141 H4 **Golcar** Kirk
44 D2 **Goldcliff** Newpt
23 J5 **Golden Cross** E Susx
39 G4 **Golden Green** Kent
59 G5 **Golden Grove** Carmth
114 D1 **Goldenhill** C Stke
55 G6 **Golden Hill** Pembks
35 L2 **Golden Pot** Hants
116 C1 **Golden Valley** Derbys
51 H2 **Golders Green** Gt Lon
48 D6 **Goldfinch Bottom** W Berk

Goldhanger - Great Potheridge 31

72 C5 **Goldhanger** Essex
103 L5 **Gold Hill** Cambs
32 D8 **Gold Hill** Dorset
96 C3 **Golding** Shrops
86 B5 **Goldington** Beds
150 E4 **Goldsborough** N York
171 J7 **Goldsborough** N York
98 C5 **Golds Green** Sandw
2 E5 **Goldsithney** Cnwll
41 J3 **Goldstone** Kent
113 M6 **Goldstone** Shrops
50 C7 **Goldsworth Park** Surrey
142 C7 **Goldthorpe** Barns
27 G6 **Goldworthy** Devon
39 K6 **Golford** Kent
39 K6 **Golford Green** Kent
252 F1 **Gollanfield** Highld
159 L6 **Gollinglith Foot** N York
129 H7 **Golly** Wrexhm
29 J3 **Golsoncott** Somset
273 K8 **Golspie** Highld
33 L4 **Gomeldon** Wilts
141 K3 **Gomersal** Kirk
37 G1 **Gomshall** Surrey
117 H2 **Gonalston** Notts
118 B4 **Gonerby Hill Foot** Lincs
281 d5 **Gonfirth** Shet
7 G2 **Goodameavy** Devon
70 F5 **Good Easter** Essex
104 F3 **Gooderstone** Norfk
27 L4 **Goodleigh** Devon
152 D7 **Goodmanham** E R Yk
51 M2 **Goodmayes** Gt Lon
40 D3 **Goodnestone** Kent
41 H4 **Goodnestone** Kent
63 H3 **Goodrich** Herefs
8 D3 **Goodrington** Torbay
140 B3 **Goodshaw** Lancs
140 B2 **Goodshaw Fold** Lancs
13 H8 **Goodstone** Devon
74 F4 **Goodwick** Pembks
34 D2 **Goodworth Clatford** Hants
99 J6 **Goodyers End** Warwks
143 J3 **Goole** E R Yk
143 J4 **Goole Fields** E R Yk
82 B4 **Goom's Hill** Worcs
4 B5 **Goonbell** Cnwll
4 C4 **Goonhavern** Cnwll
4 B5 **Goonvrea** Cnwll
245 G7 **Goosecruives** Abers
12 F4 **Gooseford** Devon
73 H2 **Goose Green** Essex
39 G3 **Goose Green** Kent
39 L6 **Goose Green** Kent
45 K4 **Goose Green** S Glos
21 J3 **Goose Green** W Susx
139 H7 **Goose Green** Wigan
26 D7 **Gooseham** Cnwll
81 L3 **Goosehill Green** Worcs
80 B7 **Goose Pool** Herefs
47 M1 **Goosey** Oxon
147 L8 **Goosnargh** Lancs
130 F5 **Goostrey** Ches
126 D5 **Gorddinog** Conwy
201 K4 **Gordon** Border
200 C8 **Gordon Arms Hotel** Border
256 C4 **Gordonstown** Abers
267 L5 **Gordonstown** Abers
79 J3 **Gore** Powys
211 K6 **Gorebridge** Mdloth
103 J1 **Gorefield** Cambs
72 C3 **Gore Pit** Essex
47 G7 **Gores** Wilts
41 J2 **Gore Street** Kent
9 f3 **Gorey** Jersey
48 F3 **Goring** Oxon
21 J6 **Goring-by-Sea** W Susx
49 G3 **Goring Heath** Oxon
107 L3 **Gorleston on Sea** Norfk
268 D4 **Gorrachie** Abers
5 G6 **Gorran** Cnwll
5 G6 **Gorran Haven** Cnwll
5 G6 **Gorran High Lanes** Cnwll
76 D6 **Gorrig** Cerdgn
92 D7 **Gors** Cerdgn
128 E4 **Gorsedd** Flints
47 H2 **Gorse Hill** Swindn
57 G5 **Gorseinon** Swans
115 M1 **Gorseybank** Derbys
76 E5 **Gorsgoch** Cerdgn
59 G6 **Gorslas** Carmth
63 K2 **Gorsley** Gloucs
63 K2 **Gorsley Common** Herefs
130 B5 **Gorstage** Ches
262 C7 **Gorstan** Highld
129 H7 **Gorstella** Ches
97 G8 **Gorst Hill** Worcs
115 H6 **Gorsty Hill** Staffs
227 L6 **Gorten** Ag & B
250 F7 **Gorthleck** Highld
140 C8 **Gorton** Manch
90 D4 **Gosbeck** Suffk
119 H5 **Gosberton** Lincs
119 G5 **Gosberton Clough** Lincs
71 J1 **Gosfield** Essex
14 C3 **Gosford** Devon
155 J2 **Gosforth** Cumb
180 F5 **Gosforth** N u Ty
31 J4 **Gosling Street** Somset
68 F2 **Gosmore** Herts
97 K4 **Gospel End** Staffs
36 D4 **Gospel Green** W Susx
19 K4 **Gosport** Hants
85 J6 **Gossard's Green** Beds
63 L6 **Gossington** Gloucs
203 G4 **Goswick** Nthumb
116 F5 **Gotham** Notts
64 D1 **Gotherington** Gloucs
30 C5 **Gotton** Somset
39 H6 **Goudhurst** Kent
136 E4 **Goulceby** Lincs
256 D3 **Gourdas** Abers
222 F1 **Gourdie** C Dund
235 K1 **Gourdon** Abers
207 L3 **Gourock** Inver
208 F6 **Govan** C Glas
7 L5 **Goveton** Devon
143 G3 **Gowdall** E R Yk
262 E8 **Gower** Highld
57 G5 **Gowerton** Swans
210 E1 **Gowkhall** Fife
152 A5 **Gowthorpe** E R Yk
153 K6 **Goxhill** E R Yk
144 E3 **Goxhill** N Linc
282 g4 **Grabhair** W Isls
118 E5 **Graby** Lincs
3 H8 **Grade** Cnwll
113 K1 **Gradeley Green** Ches
20 F3 **Graffham** W Susx
86 D2 **Grafham** Cambs
36 F3 **Grafham** Surrey
80 C7 **Grafton** Herefs
150 F3 **Grafton** N York
65 K7 **Grafton** Oxon
113 G7 **Grafton** Shrops
80 D3 **Grafton** Worcs
82 A7 **Grafton** Worcs
81 M4 **Grafton Flyford** Worcs
84 E6 **Grafton Regis** Nhants
101 K7 **Grafton Underwood** Nhants
39 L4 **Grafty Green** Kent
128 F8 **Graianrhyd** Denbgs
126 F5 **Graig** Conwy
128 C5 **Graig** Denbgs
112 A1 **Graig-fechan** Denbgs
53 J4 **Grain** Medway
140 E6 **Grains Bar** Oldham
145 H7 **Grainsby** Lincs
145 K8 **Grainthorpe** Lincs
4 F5 **Grampound** Cnwll
4 E5 **Grampound Road** Cnwll
283 c9 **Gramsdal** W Isls
283 c9 **Gramsdale** W Isls
67 J2 **Granborough** Bucks
117 K4 **Granby** Notts
83 L2 **Grandborough** Warwks
9 e3 **Grand Chemins** Jersey
9 j2 **Grandes Rocques** Guern
232 D5 **Grandtully** P & K
165 H7 **Grange** Cumb
53 G5 **Grange** Medway
222 D2 **Grange** P & K
128 F2 **Grange** Wirral
267 K5 **Grange Crossroads** Moray
17 H6 **Grange Gate** Dorset
265 H7 **Grange Hall** Moray
199 G4 **Grangehall** S Lans
70 C8 **Grange Hill** Essex
132 E8 **Grangemill** Derbys
141 K4 **Grange Moor** Kirk
210 B3 **Grangemouth** Falk
222 D4 **Grange of Lindores** Fife
156 F7 **Grange-over-Sands** Cumb
210 D3 **Grangepans** Falk
170 D6 **Grangetown** R & Cl
181 K8 **Grangetown** Sundld
180 F8 **Grange Villa** Dur
153 H4 **Gransmoor** E R Yk
71 G3 **Gransmore Green** Essex
74 E5 **Granston** Pembks
87 J4 **Grantchester** Cambs
118 B4 **Grantham** Lincs
211 H4 **Granton** C Edin
253 K6 **Grantown-on-Spey** Highld
80 C3 **Grantsfield** Herefs
213 H6 **Grantshouse** Border
130 C2 **Grappenhall** Warrtn
144 D6 **Grasby** Lincs
156 D1 **Grasmere** Cumb
140 E6 **Grasscroft** Oldham
129 J3 **Grassendale** Lpool
165 K2 **Grassgarth** Cumb
88 E7 **Grass Green** Essex
149 H3 **Grassington** N York
133 H6 **Grassmoor** Derbys
134 F6 **Grassthorpe** Notts
34 C3 **Grateley** Hants
115 G5 **Gratwich** Staffs
86 E3 **Graveley** Cambs
69 G2 **Graveley** Herts
98 E5 **Gravelly Hill** Birm
95 H3 **Gravelsbank** Shrops
40 D3 **Graveney** Kent
52 E4 **Gravesend** Kent
282 g4 **Gravir** W Isls
144 A8 **Grayingham** Lincs
157 J3 **Grayrigg** Cumb
52 D3 **Grays** Thurr
36 C4 **Grayshott** Hants
164 C5 **Grayson Green** Cumb
36 D4 **Grayswood** Surrey
170 C5 **Graythorpe** Hartpl
49 G5 **Grazeley** Wokham
142 C8 **Greasbrough** Rothm
128 F2 **Greasby** Wirral
116 E2 **Greasley** Notts
87 L5 **Great Abington** Cambs
101 L8 **Great Addington** Nhants
82 D3 **Great Alne** Warwks
138 C6 **Great Altcar** Lancs
69 K4 **Great Amwell** Herts
166 F8 **Great Asby** Cumb
89 K2 **Great Ashfield** Suffk
170 D8 **Great Ayton** N York
71 H6 **Great Baddow** Essex
46 A2 **Great Badminton** S Glos
71 G1 **Great Bardfield** Essex
86 C5 **Great Barford** Beds
98 D4 **Great Barr** Sandw
65 J4 **Great Barrington** Gloucs
129 L6 **Great Barrow** Ches
89 H2 **Great Barton** Suffk
162 C6 **Great Barugh** N York
180 B3 **Great Bavington** Nthumb
90 F5 **Great Bealings** Suffk
47 K6 **Great Bedwyn** Wilts
73 G3 **Great Bentley** Essex
84 F3 **Great Billing** Nhants
121 G5 **Great Bircham** Norfk
90 D5 **Great Blakenham** Suffk
166 B4 **Great Blencow** Cumb
113 L7 **Great Bolas** Wrekin
50 E8 **Great Bookham** Surrey
2 C4 **Great Bosullow** Cnwll
83 K6 **Great Bourton** Oxon
101 G5 **Great Bowden** Leics
88 D4 **Great Bradley** Suffk
72 B4 **Great Braxted** Essex
90 B5 **Great Bricett** Suffk
67 L1 **Great Brickhill** Bucks
114 D6 **Great Bridgeford** Staffs
84 C2 **Great Brington** Nhants
73 G2 **Great Bromley** Essex
164 E4 **Great Broughton** Cumb
161 J2 **Great Broughton** N York
130 C4 **Great Budworth** Ches
169 J7 **Great Burdon** Darltn
71 G8 **Great Burstead** Essex
161 H2 **Great Busby** N York
70 E3 **Great Canfield** Essex
137 H3 **Great Carlton** Lincs
101 M2 **Great Casterton** Rutlnd
46 B6 **Great Chalfield** Wilts
40 C7 **Great Chart** Kent
114 B8 **Great Chatwell** Staffs
114 D1 **Great Chell** C Stke
87 K6 **Great Chesterford** Essex
46 E8 **Great Cheverell** Wilts
87 J7 **Great Chishill** Cambs
73 J4 **Great Clacton** Essex
141 M4 **Great Cliffe** Wakefd
164 D5 **Great Clifton** Cumb
145 G6 **Great Coates** NE Lin
81 L6 **Great Comberton** Worcs
39 G2 **Great Comp** Kent
178 B7 **Great Corby** Cumb
89 H7 **Great Cornard** Suffk
153 L7 **Great Cowden** E R Yk
65 K8 **Great Coxwell** Oxon
101 H8 **Great Cransley** Nhants
105 G3 **Great Cressingham** Norfk
165 J6 **Great Crosthwaite** Cumb
115 K4 **Great Cubley** Derbys
117 K8 **Great Dalby** Leics
85 H2 **Great Doddington** Nhants
63 G4 **Great Doward** Herefs
121 J8 **Great Dunham** Norfk
70 F3 **Great Dunmow** Essex
33 K3 **Great Durnford** Wilts
70 F2 **Great Easton** Essex
101 J5 **Great Easton** Leics
147 H7 **Great Eccleston** Lancs
162 C6 **Great Edstone** N York
105 L4 **Great Ellingham** Norfk
32 C1 **Great Elm** Somset
8 A3 **Great Englebourne** Devon
84 B4 **Great Everdon** Nhants
87 H4 **Great Eversden** Cambs
47 G2 **Greatfield** Wilts
89 K4 **Great Finborough** Suffk
102 B1 **Greatford** Lincs
105 H1 **Great Fransham** Norfk
68 C5 **Great Gaddesden** Herts
115 G3 **Greatgate** Staffs
102 C6 **Great Gidding** Cambs
152 B5 **Great Givendale** E R Yk
91 H3 **Great Glemham** Suffk
100 E4 **Great Glen** Leics
118 B4 **Great Gonerby** Lincs
86 F4 **Great Gransden** Cambs
86 F6 **Great Green** Cambs
106 F5 **Great Green** Norfk
89 J2 **Great Green** Suffk
89 J4 **Great Green** Suffk
162 D7 **Great Habton** N York
118 F3 **Great Hale** Lincs
70 D3 **Great Hallingbury** Essex
36 A5 **Greatham** Hants
170 C5 **Greatham** Hartpl
21 H4 **Greatham** W Susx
67 K6 **Great Hampden** Bucks
85 G1 **Great Harrowden** Nhants
139 L1 **Great Harwood** Lancs
66 F6 **Great Haseley** Oxon
153 K7 **Great Hatfield** E R Yk
114 F7 **Great Haywood** Staffs
142 F3 **Great Heck** N York
89 H7 **Great Henny** Essex
46 C7 **Great Hinton** Wilts
105 J5 **Great Hockham** Norfk
73 J3 **Great Holland** Essex
72 E1 **Great Horkesley** Essex
69 L1 **Great Hormead** Herts
141 J2 **Great Horton** Brad
67 J1 **Great Horwood** Bucks
142 C6 **Great Houghton** Barns
84 F3 **Great Houghton** Nhants
132 D4 **Great Hucklow** Derbys
153 H4 **Great Kelk** E R Yk
67 K6 **Great Kimble** Bucks
67 L7 **Great Kingshill** Bucks
156 D2 **Great Langdale** Cumb
160 D3 **Great Langton** N York
71 H4 **Great Leighs** Essex
144 E6 **Great Limber** Lincs
85 G6 **Great Linford** M Keyn
89 H1 **Great Livermere** Suffk
132 D5 **Great Longstone** Derbys
169 H1 **Great Lumley** Dur
95 L2 **Great Lyth** Shrops
81 H6 **Great Malvern** Worcs
89 G8 **Great Maplestead** Essex
138 C1 **Great Marton** Bpool
121 H7 **Great Massingham** Norfk
106 C2 **Great Melton** Norfk
128 F2 **Great Meols** Wirral
66 F6 **Great Milton** Oxon
67 L6 **Great Missenden** Bucks
148 C8 **Great Mitton** Lancs
41 K5 **Great Mongeham** Kent
106 D5 **Great Moulton** Norfk
69 K2 **Great Munden** Herts
167 H7 **Great Musgrave** Cumb
112 F7 **Great Ness** Shrops
71 H3 **Great Notley** Essex
62 D5 **Great Oak** Mons
73 J2 **Great Oakley** Essex
101 J6 **Great Oakley** Nhants
68 F2 **Great Offley** Herts
167 G7 **Great Ormside** Cumb
177 K7 **Great Orton** Cumb
150 F3 **Great Ouseburn** N York
100 F6 **Great Oxendon** Nhants
71 G6 **Great Oxney Green** Essex
105 G1 **Great Palgrave** Norfk
39 J4 **Great Pattenden** Kent
86 E2 **Great Paxton** Cambs
138 D1 **Great Plumpton** Lancs
106 F2 **Great Plumstead** Norfk
118 B5 **Great Ponton** Lincs
27 J7 **Great Potheridge** Devon

142 B2 **Great Preston** Leeds
83 M7 **Great Purston** Nhants
102 E7 **Great Raveley** Cambs
65 J4 **Great Rissington** Gloucs
65 L1 **Great Rollright** Oxon
54 F3 **Great Rudbaxton** Pembks
121 L6 **Great Ryburgh** Norfk
190 E4 **Great Ryle** Nthumb
96 B3 **Great Ryton** Shrops
71 G2 **Great Saling** Essex
166 D3 **Great Salkeld** Cumb
88 C8 **Great Sampford** Essex
130 B2 **Great Sankey** Warrtn
98 B2 **Great Saredon** Staffs
129 H5 **Great Saughall** Ches
88 F3 **Great Saxham** Suffk
48 A4 **Great Shefford** W Berk
87 J5 **Great Shelford** Cambs
160 E2 **Great Smeaton** N York
121 L4 **Great Snoring** Norfk
46 D2 **Great Somerford** Wilts
114 A5 **Great Soudley** Shrops
169 J6 **Great Stainton** Darltn
53 J1 **Great Stambridge** Essex
86 C2 **Great Staughton** Cambs
137 H6 **Great Steeping** Lincs
45 J3 **Great Stoke** S Glos
41 K3 **Great Stonar** Kent
25 K3 **Greatstone-on-Sea** Kent
166 D6 **Great Strickland** Cumb
102 E8 **Great Stukeley** Cambs
136 D4 **Great Sturton** Lincs
129 J4 **Great Sutton** Ches
96 C6 **Great Sutton** Shrops
179 L4 **Great Swinburne** Nthumb
66 B1 **Great Tew** Oxon
72 C2 **Great Tey** Essex
27 J7 **Great Torrington** Devon
190 E6 **Great Tosson** Nthumb
72 B5 **Great Totham** Essex
72 C4 **Great Totham** Essex
136 D2 **Great Tows** Lincs
156 C7 **Great Urswick** Cumb
53 K2 **Great Wakering** Essex
89 J6 **Great Waldingfield** Suffk
121 L4 **Great Walsingham** Norfk
71 G4 **Great Waltham** Essex
130 F4 **Great Warford** Ches
52 C1 **Great Warley** Essex
82 A8 **Great Washbourne** Gloucs
13 G5 **Great Weeke** Devon
101 K5 **Great Weldon** Nhants
89 H3 **Great Welnetham** Suffk
90 C7 **Great Wenham** Suffk
180 B5 **Great Whittington** Nthumb
72 D4 **Great Wigborough** Essex
87 L4 **Great Wilbraham** Cambs
33 J4 **Great Wishford** Wilts
122 C7 **Great Witchingham** Norfk
64 D4 **Great Witcombe** Gloucs
81 H2 **Great Witley** Worcs
82 F8 **Great Wolford** Warwks
84 A6 **Greatworth** Nhants
88 D5 **Great Wratting** Suffk
69 G2 **Great Wymondley** Herts
98 C2 **Great Wyrley** Staffs
113 J7 **Great Wytheford** Shrops
107 L2 **Great Yarmouth** Norfk
88 F7 **Great Yeldham** Essex
137 H6 **Grebby** Lincs
154 d6 **Greeba** IoM
128 C6 **Green** Denbgs
156 E6 **Green Bank** Cumb
210 B7 **Greenburn** W Loth
168 F1 **Greencroft Hall** Dur
36 C3 **Green Cross** Surrey
45 H8 **Green Down** Somset
85 K5 **Green End** Beds
86 B2 **Green End** Beds
86 B3 **Green End** Beds
86 C5 **Green End** Beds
87 H4 **Green End** Cambs
87 K2 **Green End** Cambs
87 K3 **Green End** Cambs
102 D6 **Green End** Cambs
102 E8 **Green End** Cambs
69 H1 **Green End** Herts
69 J3 **Green End** Herts
87 G8 **Green End** Herts
65 L3 **Greenend** Oxon
99 H6 **Green End** Warwks
207 L1 **Greenfield** Ag & B
85 L8 **Greenfield** Beds
128 E4 **Greenfield** Flints
239 L3 **Greenfield** Highld
140 F7 **Greenfield** Oldham
49 H1 **Greenfield** Oxon
50 F3 **Greenford** Gt Lon

209 L5 **Greengairs** N Lans
150 B8 **Greengates** Brad
164 F3 **Greengill** Cumb
147 H8 **Greenhalgh** Lancs
29 K6 **Greenham** Somset
48 C6 **Greenham** W Berk
151 G4 **Green Hammerton** N York
179 J2 **Greenhaugh** Nthumb
165 L1 **Green Head** Cumb
178 F6 **Greenhead** Nthumb
98 C1 **Green Heath** Staffs
139 L7 **Greenheys** Salfd
176 F3 **Greenhill** D & G
209 L3 **Greenhill** Falk
81 G5 **Greenhill** Herefs
40 F2 **Greenhill** Kent
198 F6 **Greenhill** S Lans
46 F2 **Green Hill** Wilts
116 C2 **Greenhillocks** Derbys
52 C4 **Greenhithe** Kent
197 G3 **Greenholm** E Ayrs
157 J2 **Greenholme** Cumb
188 F2 **Greenhouse** Border
149 K3 **Greenhow Hill** N York
280 B3 **Greenland** Highld
133 H2 **Greenland** Sheff
49 J2 **Greenlands** Bucks
13 H7 **Green Lane** Devon
82 C2 **Green Lane** Worcs
201 L4 **Greenlaw** Border
176 D4 **Greenlea** D & G
220 E5 **Greenloaning** P & K
141 L7 **Green Moor** Barns
140 A5 **Greenmount** Bury
143 K2 **Green Oak** E R Yk
207 M4 **Greenock** Inver
156 D6 **Greenodd** Cumb
31 J1 **Green Ore** Somset
157 G2 **Green Quarter** Cumb
122 B8 **Greensgate** Norfk
199 H4 **Greenshields** S Lans
180 E6 **Greenside** Gatesd
141 J4 **Greenside** Kirk
84 C5 **Greens Norton** Nhants
72 E2 **Greenstead** Essex
71 K2 **Greenstead Green** Essex
70 D6 **Greensted** Essex
24 D5 **Green Street** E Susx
64 C4 **Green Street** Gloucs
69 G7 **Green Street** Herts
70 C3 **Green Street** Herts
81 K5 **Green Street** Worcs
51 M6 **Green Street Green** Gt Lon
52 C5 **Green Street Green** Kent
90 B5 **Greenstreet Green** Suffk
70 C3 **Green Tye** Herts
81 G8 **Greenway** Gloucs
30 D6 **Greenway** Somset
43 G7 **Greenway** V Glam
81 G1 **Greenway** Worcs
51 K3 **Greenwich** Gt Lon
64 F1 **Greet** Gloucs
80 D1 **Greete** Shrops
136 F5 **Greetham** Lincs
118 B8 **Greetham** Rutlnd
141 G3 **Greetland** Calder
139 J2 **Gregson Lane** Lancs
30 F4 **Greinton** Somset
154 c7 **Grenaby** IoM
85 G3 **Grendon** Nhants
99 H3 **Grendon** Warwks
80 E4 **Grendon Green** Herefs
67 G3 **Grendon Underwood** Bucks
12 C8 **Grenofen** Devon
133 G1 **Grenoside** Sheff
282 e6 **Greosabhagh** W Isls
112 E1 **Gresford** Wrexhm
122 D4 **Gresham** Norfk
258 E6 **Greshornish House Hotel** Highld
121 L8 **Gressenhall** Norfk
121 L8 **Gressenhall Green** Norfk
147 L2 **Gressingham** Lancs
113 M1 **Gresty Green** Ches
168 D8 **Greta Bridge** Dur
177 K5 **Gretna** D & G
177 K5 **Gretna Green** D & G
64 E1 **Gretton** Gloucs
101 K4 **Gretton** Nhants
96 C4 **Gretton** Shrops
160 C7 **Grewelthorpe** N York
91 L1 **Grey Friars** Suffk
150 A1 **Greygarth** N York
143 K6 **Grey Green** N Linc
30 F4 **Greylake** Somset
176 E1 **Greyrigg** D & G

49 H2 **Greys Green** Oxon
164 E5 **Greysouthen** Cumb
166 B4 **Greystoke** Cumb
234 E6 **Greystone** Angus
35 L1 **Greywell** Hants
15 J2 **Gribb** Dorset
143 J1 **Gribthorpe** E R Yk
99 K5 **Griff** Warwks
62 C7 **Griffithstown** Torfn
116 C7 **Griffydam** Leics
36 B4 **Griggs Green** Hants
139 J5 **Grimeford Village** Lancs
133 G2 **Grimesthorpe** Sheff
142 C6 **Grimethorpe** Barns
81 J3 **Grimley** Worcs
183 J1 **Grimmet** S Ayrs
137 G2 **Grimoldby** Lincs
112 E6 **Grimpo** Shrops
139 H1 **Grimsargh** Lancs
145 H5 **Grimsby** NE Lin
84 C4 **Grimscote** Nhants
11 J1 **Grimscott** Cnwll
282 g4 **Grimshader** W Isls
139 L3 **Grimshaw** Bl w D
139 G5 **Grimshaw Green** Lancs
118 D7 **Grimsthorpe** Lincs
145 H1 **Grimston** E R Yk
117 J7 **Grimston** Leics
120 F7 **Grimston** Norfk
16 C4 **Grimstone** Dorset
89 J2 **Grimstone End** Suffk
12 A4 **Grinacombe Moor** Devon
153 J2 **Grindale** E R Yk
97 G3 **Grindle** Shrops
132 E4 **Grindleford** Derbys
148 D6 **Grindleton** Lancs
113 H3 **Grindley Brook** Shrops
132 D4 **Grindlow** Derbys
202 E4 **Grindon** Nthumb
169 K5 **Grindon** S on T
115 H1 **Grindon** Staffs
181 J7 **Grindon** Sundld
179 J5 **Grindon Hill** Nthumb
202 E4 **Grindonrigg** Nthumb
134 E2 **Gringley on the Hill** Notts
177 L7 **Grinsdale** Cumb
113 H6 **Grinshill** Shrops
159 J3 **Grinton** N York
282 g4 **Griomaisiader** W Isls
283 c9 **Griomsaigh** W Isls
224 F3 **Grishipoll** Ag & B
23 G3 **Grisling Common** E Susx
163 K6 **Gristhorpe** N York
105 J4 **Griston** Norfk
275 d5 **Gritley** Ork
46 F2 **Grittenham** Wilts
46 B3 **Grittleton** Wilts
156 C5 **Grizebeck** Cumb
156 D4 **Grizedale** Cumb
100 B2 **Groby** Leics
127 K6 **Groes** Conwy
43 G5 **Groes-faen** Rhondd
108 D4 **Groesffordd** Gwynd
127 K5 **Groesffordd Marli** Denbgs
94 F1 **Groeslwyd** Powys
125 H8 **Groeslon** Gwynd
125 J7 **Groeslon** Gwynd
43 H4 **Groes-Wen** Caerph
283 c10 **Grogarry** W Isls
194 C2 **Grogport** Ag & B
283 c10 **Groigearraidh** W Isls
91 J3 **Gromford** Suffk
128 C3 **Gronant** Flints
38 E6 **Groombridge** E Susx
282 e6 **Grosebay** W Isls
62 E2 **Grosmont** Mons
162 E2 **Grosmont** N York
89 J7 **Groton** Suffk
140 E6 **Grotton** Oldham
9 e3 **Grouville** Jersey
67 M3 **Grove** Bucks
16 D7 **Grove** Dorset
41 H3 **Grove** Kent
134 E4 **Grove** Notts
48 B1 **Grove** Oxon
55 G6 **Grove** Pembks
39 K2 **Grove Green** Kent
39 H5 **Grovenhurst** Kent
51 L4 **Grove Park** Gt Lon
45 K1 **Grovesend** S Glos
57 G5 **Grovesend** Swans
52 C5 **Grubb Street** Kent
260 F2 **Gruinard** Highld
204 D3 **Gruinart** Ag & B
246 E3 **Grula** Highld
227 G4 **Gruline** Ag & B
2 C5 **Grumbla** Cnwll
90 F5 **Grundisburgh** Suffk

281 c6 **Gruting** Shet
229 J6 **Gualachulain** Highld
103 H2 **Guanockgate** Lincs
223 H3 **Guardbridge** Fife
81 J6 **Guarlford** Worcs
232 F5 **Guay** P & K
24 F4 **Guestling Green** E Susx
24 F4 **Guestling Thorn** E Susx
122 B6 **Guestwick** Norfk
139 L3 **Guide** Bl w D
140 D8 **Guide Bridge** Tamesd
181 G2 **Guide Post** Nthumb
86 F6 **Guilden Morden** Cambs
129 K6 **Guilden Sutton** Ches
36 F1 **Guildford** Surrey
53 H6 **Guildstead** Kent
221 L1 **Guildtown** P & K
84 D1 **Guilsborough** Nhants
94 F1 **Guilsfield** Powys
41 J4 **Guilton** Kent
183 J1 **Guiltreehill** S Ayrs
27 K3 **Guineaford** Devon
170 E7 **Guisborough** R & Cl
150 B7 **Guiseley** Leeds
121 M6 **Guist** Norfk
65 G2 **Guiting Power** Gloucs
212 B2 **Gullane** E Loth
89 G4 **Gulling Green** Suffk
2 D5 **Gulval** Cnwll
12 B7 **Gulworthy** Devon
55 J6 **Gumfreston** Pembks
100 F5 **Gumley** Leics
4 E3 **Gummow's Shop** Cnwll
143 H1 **Gunby** E R Yk
118 B7 **Gunby** Lincs
137 J6 **Gunby** Lincs
35 J4 **Gundleton** Hants
39 J7 **Gun Green** Kent
23 J4 **Gun Hill** E Susx
99 H5 **Gun Hill** Warwks
27 L4 **Gunn** Devon
159 G3 **Gunnerside** N York
179 L4 **Gunnerton** Nthumb
143 L5 **Gunness** N Linc
12 B8 **Gunnislake** Cnwll
281 e6 **Gunnista** Shet
102 D3 **Gunthorpe** C Pete
143 K8 **Gunthorpe** N Linc
121 M4 **Gunthorpe** Norfk
117 H3 **Gunthorpe** Notts
107 L4 **Gunton** Suffk
3 G6 **Gunwalloe** Cnwll
29 H4 **Gupworthy** Somset
19 H4 **Gurnard** IoW
131 H5 **Gurnett** Ches
31 K1 **Gurney Slade** Somset
57 L3 **Gurnos** Powys
40 D4 **Gushmere** Kent
33 G8 **Gussage All Saints** Dorset
33 G8 **Gussage St Andrew** Dorset
33 G8 **Gussage St Michael** Dorset
41 K6 **Guston** Kent
281 f2 **Gutcher** Shet
234 E5 **Guthrie** Angus
103 H3 **Guyhirn** Cambs
103 H3 **Guyhirn Gull** Cambs
32 D6 **Guy's Marsh** Dorset
191 J5 **Guyzance** Nthumb
128 C3 **Gwaenysgor** Flints
125 G4 **Gwalchmai** IoA
126 C8 **Gwastadnant** Gwynd
59 J6 **Gwaun-Cae-Gurwen** Carmth
75 K2 **Gwbert on Sea** Cerdgn
2 F3 **Gwealavellan** Cnwll
3 H5 **Gweek** Cnwll
62 D6 **Gwehelog** Mons
78 E6 **Gwenddwr** Powys
3 J3 **Gwennap** Cnwll
3 J7 **Gwenter** Cnwll
128 F6 **Gwernaffield** Flints
62 E6 **Gwernesney** Mons
58 F2 **Gwernogle** Carmth
128 F7 **Gwernymynydd** Flints
112 D1 **Gwersyllt** Wrexhm
128 D3 **Gwespyr** Flints
4 F4 **Gwindra** Cnwll
2 F4 **Gwinear** Cnwll
2 F3 **Gwithian** Cnwll
125 G3 **Gwredog** IoA
61 J7 **Gwrhay** Caerph
111 L2 **Gwyddelwern** Denbgs
58 E2 **Gwyddgrug** Carmth
112 C1 **Gwynfryn** Wrexhm
78 E2 **Gwystre** Powys
127 H7 **Gwytherin** Conwy

112 E3 **Gyfelia** Wrexhm
109 G2 **Gyrn-goch** Gwynd

H

95 K3 **Habberley** Shrops
97 H7 **Habberley** Worcs
140 B1 **Habergham** Lancs
137 J6 **Habertoft** Lincs
36 B6 **Habin** W Susx
144 F5 **Habrough** NE Lin
118 E6 **Hacconby** Lincs
118 D4 **Haceby** Lincs
91 G3 **Hacheston** Suffk
51 H5 **Hackbridge** Gt Lon
133 H3 **Hackenthorpe** Sheff
106 B3 **Hackford** Norfk
160 C4 **Hackforth** N York
113 L2 **Hack Green** Ches
275 c4 **Hackland** Ork
84 F4 **Hackleton** Nhants
41 K4 **Hacklinge** Kent
97 K7 **Hackman's Gate** Worcs
163 H4 **Hackness** N York
30 E2 **Hackness** Somset
51 K2 **Hackney** Gt Lon
135 K3 **Hackthorn** Lincs
166 D6 **Hackthorpe** Cumb
52 C2 **Hacton** Gt Lon
202 B6 **Hadden** Border
67 H5 **Haddenham** Bucks
103 J8 **Haddenham** Cambs
212 B4 **Haddington** E Loth
135 H7 **Haddington** Lincs
107 J4 **Haddiscoe** Norfk
256 E4 **Haddo** Abers
102 C5 **Haddon** Cambs
141 J6 **Hade Edge** Kirk
140 F8 **Hadfield** Derbys
70 B3 **Hadham Cross** Herts
70 B3 **Hadham Ford** Herts
53 H2 **Hadleigh** Essex
89 L6 **Hadleigh** Suffk
89 K7 **Hadleigh Heath** Suffk
81 K2 **Hadley** Worcs
96 F1 **Hadley** Wrekin
115 J7 **Hadley End** Staffs
69 H7 **Hadley Wood** Gt Lon
39 G3 **Hadlow** Kent
23 J2 **Hadlow Down** E Susx
113 H7 **Hadnall** Shrops
88 B6 **Hadstock** Essex
81 L3 **Hadzor** Worcs
39 M5 **Haffenden Quarter** Kent
127 H6 **Hafodunos** Conwy
112 D2 **Hafod-y-bwch** Wrexhm
61 K7 **Hafod-y-coed** Blae G
61 K7 **Hafodyrynys** Caerph
140 C1 **Haggate** Lancs
178 B4 **Haggbeck** Cumb
281 d6 **Haggersta** Shet
203 G4 **Haggerston** Nthumb
27 K2 **Haggington Hill** Devon
209 L3 **Haggs** Falk
80 D7 **Hagley** Herefs
97 K7 **Hagley** Worcs
89 J7 **Hagmore Green** Suffk
136 F7 **Hagnaby** Lincs
137 J4 **Hagnaby** Lincs
136 F6 **Hagworthingham** Lincs
139 J6 **Haigh** Wigan
139 H1 **Haighton Green** Lancs
155 J1 **Haile** Cumb
64 F1 **Hailes** Gloucs
69 K5 **Hailey** Herts
48 F2 **Hailey** Oxon
65 M4 **Hailey** Oxon
23 K5 **Hailsham** E Susx
86 D3 **Hail Weston** Cambs
70 C8 **Hainault** Gt Lon
41 K2 **Haine** Kent
122 E7 **Hainford** Norfk
136 C3 **Hainton** Lincs
149 J8 **Hainworth** Brad
153 H3 **Haisthorpe** E R Yk
54 E5 **Hakin** Pembks
117 H1 **Halam** Notts
210 F1 **Halbeath** Fife
29 H8 **Halberton** Devon
280 B4 **Halcro** Highld
157 H7 **Hale** Cumb
129 L3 **Hale** Halton
33 L7 **Hale** Hants
32 C5 **Hale** Somset
36 C1 **Hale** Surrey
130 F2 **Hale** Traffd
129 L3 **Hale Bank** Halton

130 F3 **Halebarns** Traffd
23 J4 **Hale Green** E Susx
147 G7 **Hale Nook** Lancs
107 H4 **Hales** Norfk
113 M5 **Hales** Staffs
119 K6 **Halesgate** Lincs
115 K3 **Hales Green** Derbys
98 B6 **Halesowen** Dudley
40 F3 **Hales Place** Kent
39 G3 **Hale Street** Kent
72 C8 **Halesville** Essex
107 H7 **Halesworth** Suffk
129 K3 **Halewood** Knows
13 J7 **Halford** Devon
95 K6 **Halford** Shrops
83 G6 **Halford** Warwks
157 H5 **Halfpenny** Cumb
97 J5 **Halfpenny Green** Staffs
160 B5 **Halfpenny Houses** N York
59 J3 **Halfway** Carmth
59 M2 **Halfway** Carmth
133 J3 **Halfway** Sheff
48 B5 **Halfway** W Berk
36 D6 **Halfway Bridge** W Susx
95 H1 **Halfway House** Shrops
53 K4 **Halfway Houses** Kent
141 H3 **Halifax** Calder
208 D8 **Halket** E Ayrs
279 K4 **Halkirk** Highld
128 F5 **Halkyn** Flints
208 C8 **Hall** E Rens
116 D4 **Hallam Fields** Derbys
23 H4 **Halland** E Susx
101 H4 **Hallaton** Leics
45 J7 **Hallatrow** BaNES
178 D7 **Hallbankgate** Cumb
157 K5 **Hallbeck** Cumb
141 L4 **Hall Cliffe** Wakefd
138 E2 **Hall Cross** Lancs
156 B3 **Hall Dunnerdale** Cumb
45 H3 **Hallen** S Glos
85 K6 **Hall End** Beds
86 B7 **Hall End** Beds
133 H8 **Hallfield Gate** Derbys
169 J2 **Hallgarth** Dur
210 A3 **Hall Glen** Falk
98 E7 **Hall Green** Birm
258 C5 **Hallin** Highld
52 F6 **Halling** Medway
136 F3 **Hallington** Lincs
180 B4 **Hallington** Nthumb
139 L5 **Halliwell** Bolton
117 J1 **Halloughton** Notts
81 J3 **Hallow** Worcs
81 J3 **Hallow Heath** Worcs
8 B7 **Hallsands** Devon
69 L5 **Hall's Green** Essex
69 H2 **Hall's Green** Herts
156 A5 **Hallthwaites** Cumb
11 H5 **Hallworthy** Cnwll
199 L5 **Hallyne** Border
114 B2 **Halmer End** Staffs
80 F5 **Halmond's Frome** Herefs
63 K6 **Halmore** Gloucs
20 E5 **Halnaker** W Susx
138 D5 **Halsall** Lancs
84 A7 **Halse** Nhants
29 L5 **Halse** Somset
2 D3 **Halsetown** Cnwll
145 H2 **Halsham** E R Yk
27 J3 **Halsinger** Devon
71 K1 **Halstead** Essex
52 A6 **Halstead** Kent
101 G2 **Halstead** Leics
15 M1 **Halstock** Dorset
29 L3 **Halsway** Somset
165 L3 **Haltcliff Bridge** Cumb
136 D7 **Haltham** Lincs
119 L3 **Haltoft End** Lincs
67 L5 **Halton** Bucks
129 M3 **Halton** Halton
147 K3 **Halton** Lancs
142 A1 **Halton** Leeds
180 B5 **Halton** Nthumb
112 D3 **Halton** Wrexhm
149 J5 **Halton East** N York
137 H7 **Halton Fenside** Lincs
158 F7 **Halton Gill** N York
147 K3 **Halton Green** Lancs
137 H6 **Halton Holegate** Lincs
178 F7 **Halton Lea Gate** Nthumb
6 E2 **Halton Quay** Cnwll
180 B5 **Halton Shields** Nthumb
148 E5 **Halton West** N York
179 G6 **Haltwhistle** Nthumb
107 J2 **Halvergate** Norfk
8 A4 **Halwell** Devon
12 B3 **Halwill** Devon

12 B2 **Halwill Junction** Devon
14 F2 **Ham** Devon
63 K7 **Ham** Gloucs
64 E3 **Ham** Gloucs
50 F4 **Ham** Gt Lon
41 K4 **Ham** Kent
30 D6 **Ham** Somset
31 L1 **Ham** Somset
47 L6 **Ham** Wilts
49 J2 **Hambleden** Bucks
35 K7 **Hambledon** Hants
36 E3 **Hambledon** Surrey
19 H2 **Hamble-le-Rice** Hants
147 G7 **Hambleton** Lancs
142 E2 **Hambleton** N York
147 G7 **Hambleton Moss Side** Lancs
30 F6 **Hambridge** Somset
45 J3 **Hambrook** S Glos
20 C5 **Hambrook** W Susx
32 D5 **Ham Common** Dorset
136 F6 **Hameringham** Lincs
102 C7 **Hamerton** Cambs
81 H6 **Ham Green** Herefs
25 G2 **Ham Green** Kent
53 H5 **Ham Green** Kent
45 G4 **Ham Green** N Som
82 B3 **Ham Green** Worcs
52 F6 **Ham Hill** Kent
209 J7 **Hamilton** S Lans
16 B1 **Hamlet** Dorset
23 K5 **Hamlins** E Susx
21 H5 **Hammerpot** W Susx
51 G3 **Hammersmith** Gt Lon
98 D2 **Hammerwich** Staffs
38 C5 **Hammerwood** E Susx
69 J6 **Hammond Street** Herts
32 D7 **Hammoon** Dorset
281 d7 **Hamnavoe** Shet
23 K6 **Hampden Park** E Susx
70 E1 **Hamperden End** Essex
65 G4 **Hampnett** Gloucs
142 D5 **Hampole** Donc
17 L3 **Hampreston** Dorset
156 F6 **Hampsfield** Cumb
147 J5 **Hampson Green** Lancs
51 H2 **Hampstead** Gt Lon
48 D4 **Hampstead Norrey's** W Berk
150 C4 **Hampsthwaite** N York
102 D4 **Hampton** C Pete
15 G3 **Hampton** Devon
50 F5 **Hampton** Gt Lon
40 F2 **Hampton** Kent
97 G6 **Hampton** Shrops
65 J8 **Hampton** Swindn
82 B6 **Hampton** Worcs
80 D7 **Hampton Bishop** Herefs
64 C7 **Hampton Fields** Gloucs
113 H2 **Hampton Green** Ches
113 H2 **Hampton Heath** Ches
99 G7 **Hampton in Arden** Solhll
97 G6 **Hampton Loade** Shrops
81 K2 **Hampton Lovett** Worcs
83 G4 **Hampton Lucy** Warwks
83 G2 **Hampton Magna** Warwks
82 F2 **Hampton on the Hill** Warwks
66 D4 **Hampton Poyle** Oxon
50 F5 **Hampton Wick** Gt Lon
34 B7 **Hamptworth** Wilts
121 K6 **Hamrow** Norfk
22 F5 **Hamsey** E Susx
51 K7 **Hamsey Green** Surrey
115 H7 **Hamstall Ridware** Staffs
98 D5 **Hamstead** Birm
18 F5 **Hamstead** IoW
48 B6 **Hamstead Marshall** W Berk
168 E4 **Hamsterley** Dur
180 D7 **Hamsterley** Dur
40 C8 **Hamstreet** Kent
31 J4 **Ham Street** Somset
44 H3 **Hamwood** N Som
17 K4 **Hamworthy** Poole
115 K6 **Hanbury** Staffs
81 M2 **Hanbury** Worcs
118 D5 **Hanby** Lincs
88 C6 **Hanchet End** Suffk
114 C3 **Hanchurch** Staffs
171 G7 **Handale** R & Cl
14 B3 **Hand and Pen** Devon
129 J6 **Handbridge** Ches
37 L5 **Handcross** W Susx
131 G3 **Handforth** Ches
130 A7 **Hand Green** Ches
129 L8 **Handley** Ches
133 G7 **Handley** Derbys
71 G6 **Handley Green** Essex

115 H8 **Handsacre** Staffs
98 D5 **Handsworth** Birm
133 H2 **Handsworth** Sheff
49 K1 **Handy Cross** Bucks
114 D3 **Hanford** C Stke
32 D8 **Hanford** Dorset
141 L3 **Hanging Heaton** Kirk
101 G8 **Hanging Houghton** Nhants
33 H3 **Hanging Langford** Wilts
22 D6 **Hangleton** Br & H
21 J6 **Hangleton** W Susx
45 J4 **Hanham** S Glos
113 L2 **Hankelow** Ches
46 E1 **Hankerton** Wilts
23 K6 **Hankham** E Susx
114 D2 **Hanley** C Stke
114 D2 **Hanley** C Stke
81 J6 **Hanley Castle** Worcs
80 F2 **Hanley Child** Worcs
81 J6 **Hanley Swan** Worcs
80 F2 **Hanley William** Worcs
148 F3 **Hanlith** N York
113 G3 **Hanmer** Wrexhm
27 L5 **Hannaford** Devon
137 J4 **Hannah** Lincs
48 D7 **Hannington** Hants
84 F1 **Hannington** Nhants
65 H8 **Hannington** Swindn
65 H8 **Hannington Wick** Swindn
86 C8 **Hanscombe End** Beds
84 F6 **Hanslope** M Keyn
118 E6 **Hanthorpe** Lincs
50 F3 **Hanwell** Gt Lon
83 K6 **Hanwell** Oxon
95 K2 **Hanwood** Shrops
50 E5 **Hanworth** Gt Lon
122 D4 **Hanworth** Norfk
198 E6 **Happendon** S Lans
123 H5 **Happisburgh** Norfk
123 H5 **Happisburgh Common** Norfk
129 L5 **Hapsford** Ches
140 B2 **Hapton** Lancs
106 D4 **Hapton** Norfk
8 A3 **Harberton** Devon
8 A4 **Harbertonford** Devon
40 F4 **Harbledown** Kent
98 C6 **Harborne** Birm
100 B7 **Harborough Magna** Warwks
190 C5 **Harbottle** Nthumb
7 K2 **Harbourneford** Devon
81 M2 **Harbours Hill** Worcs
18 A2 **Harbridge** Hants
33 K8 **Harbridge Green** Hants
83 J3 **Harbury** Warwks
117 K5 **Harby** Leics
135 H5 **Harby** Notts
13 K6 **Harcombe** Devon
14 D4 **Harcombe** Devon
15 H3 **Harcombe Bottom** Devon
149 K8 **Harden** Brad
98 C3 **Harden** Wsall
46 C4 **Hardenhuish** Wilts
245 H3 **Hardgate** Abers
175 K2 **Hardgate** D & G
150 C3 **Hardgate** N York
208 E4 **Hardgate** W Duns
21 H3 **Hardham** W Susx
147 G8 **Hardhorn** Lancs
105 L3 **Hardingham** Norfk
84 E4 **Hardingstone** Nhants
45 L8 **Hardington** Somset
31 H8 **Hardington Mandeville** Somset
15 L1 **Hardington Marsh** Somset
31 H8 **Hardington Moor** Somset
26 D6 **Hardisworthy** Devon
19 G3 **Hardley** Hants
107 H3 **Hardley Street** Norfk
85 H5 **Hardmead** M Keyn
158 F4 **Hardraw** N York
140 B4 **Hardsough** Lancs
133 J7 **Hardstoft** Derbys
19 K3 **Hardway** Hants
32 B4 **Hardway** Somset
67 K3 **Hardwick** Bucks
87 H3 **Hardwick** Cambs
85 G1 **Hardwick** Nhants
106 E5 **Hardwick** Norfk
66 A6 **Hardwick** Oxon
66 E1 **Hardwick** Oxon
133 K3 **Hardwick** Rothm
98 D4 **Hardwick** Wsall
64 A4 **Hardwicke** Gloucs
64 C2 **Hardwicke** Gloucs
81 J8 **Hardwick Green** Worcs
72 D3 **Hardy's Green** Essex

23 K5 Harebeating E Susx
136 F6 Hareby Lincs
149 K8 Hare Croft Brad
50 D1 Harefield Gt Lon
73 G2 Hare Green Essex
49 J3 Hare Hatch Wokham
115 K4 Harehill Derbys
141 M1 Harehills Leeds
191 G2 Harehope Nthumb
188 F2 Harelaw Border
178 B3 Harelaw D & G
180 E8 Harelaw Dur
39 L5 Hareplain Kent
166 E2 Haresceugh Cumb
64 B5 Harescombe Gloucs
64 A5 Haresfield Gloucs
34 F4 Harestock Hants
70 B5 Hare Street Essex
70 D7 Hare Street Essex
69 K1 Hare Street Herts
150 D6 Harewood Leeds
63 G2 Harewood End Herefs
7 J3 Harford Devon
106 C5 Hargate Norfk
132 B4 Hargatewall Derbys
129 L7 Hargrave Ches
85 K1 Hargrave Nhants
88 F3 Hargrave Suffk
88 F3 Hargrave Green Suffk
177 L6 Harker Cumb
90 E8 Harkstead Suffk
99 G1 Harlaston Staffs
118 A5 Harlaxton Lincs
109 K5 Harlech Gwynd
113 H8 Harlescott Shrops
51 G2 Harlesden Gt Lon
133 K4 Harlesthorpe Derbys
8 B6 Harleston Devon
106 E6 Harleston Norfk
89 L3 Harleston Suffk
84 D2 Harlestone Nhants
140 C1 Harle Syke Lancs
142 B8 Harley Rothm
96 D3 Harley Shrops
68 D1 Harlington Beds
142 D7 Harlington Donc
50 E3 Harlington Gt Lon
258 D8 Harlosh Highld
70 C5 Harlow Essex
180 C5 Harlow Hill Nthumb
152 A8 Harlthorpe E R Yk
87 H5 Harlton Cambs
10 B7 Harlyn Cnwll
17 J6 Harman's Cross Dorset
159 L5 Harmby N York
69 H4 Harmer Green Herts
113 H7 Harmer Hill Shrops
50 D1 Harmondsworth Gt Lon
135 K7 Harmston Lincs
96 D3 Harnage Shrops
180 C3 Harnham Nthumb
64 F7 Harnhill Gloucs
70 D8 Harold Hill Gt Lon
54 D4 Haroldston West Pembks
281 f1 Haroldswick Shet
52 C1 Harold Wood Gt Lon
161 L6 Harome N York
68 E4 Harpenden Herts
14 C4 Harpford Devon
153 H3 Harpham E R Yk
121 H6 Harpley Norfk
80 F3 Harpley Worcs
84 D3 Harpole Nhants
279 K5 Harpsdale Highld
49 J3 Harpsden Oxon
135 J2 Harpswell Lincs
140 C7 Harpurhey Manch
131 L5 Harpur Hill Derbys
177 M7 Harraby Cumb
27 K5 Harracott Devon
247 K4 Harrapool Highld
221 H1 Harrietfield P & K
39 L3 Harrietsham Kent
51 J1 Harringay Gt Lon
164 C5 Harrington Cumb
137 G5 Harrington Lincs
101 G7 Harrington Nhants
101 K4 Harringworth Nhants
131 G8 Harriseahead Staffs
165 G2 Harriston Cumb
150 D5 Harrogate N York
85 J4 Harrold Beds
140 F6 Harrop Dale Oldham
50 F1 Harrow Gt Lon
12 A8 Harrowbarrow Cnwll
85 L6 Harrowden Beds
169 H7 Harrowgate Village Darltn
89 H4 Harrow Green Suffk

50 F2 Harrow on the Hill Gt Lon
50 F1 Harrow Weald Gt Lon
87 J5 Harston Cambs
117 L5 Harston Leics
152 C7 Harswell E R Yk
170 B4 Hart Hartpl
180 D2 Hartburn Nthumb
89 G5 Hartest Suffk
38 D6 Hartfield E Susx
86 E1 Hartford Cambs
130 C5 Hartford Ches
29 G5 Hartford Somset
49 J7 Hartfordbridge Hants
71 G3 Hartford End Essex
159 L2 Hartforth N York
32 D7 Hartgrove Dorset
129 L8 Harthill Ches
210 B6 Harthill N Lans
133 K3 Harthill Rothm
132 C7 Hartington Derbys
180 B1 Hartington Nthumb
26 D1 Hartland Devon
26 C6 Hartland Quay Devon
81 J1 Hartlebury Worcs
170 C4 Hartlepool Hartpl
158 D1 Hartley Cumb
39 J6 Hartley Kent
52 D5 Hartley Kent
181 H4 Hartley Nthumb
52 D5 Hartley Green Kent
114 F5 Hartley Green Staffs
49 G7 Hartley Wespall Hants
49 J7 Hartley Wintney Hants
53 H6 Hartlip Kent
162 C4 Hartoft End N York
151 L3 Harton N York
181 J6 Harton S Tyne
96 B5 Harton Shrops
64 A2 Hartpury Gloucs
141 J3 Hartshead Kirk
114 D2 Hartshill C Stke
99 J4 Hartshill Warwks
116 B7 Hartshorne Derbys
190 D3 Hartside Nthumb
165 L8 Hartsop Cumb
170 B3 Hart Station Hartpl
29 K5 Hartswell Somset
84 F5 Hartwell Nhants
150 B3 Hartwith N York
209 M7 Hartwood N Lans
188 D1 Hartwoodmyres Border
52 E6 Harvel Kent
82 C5 Harvington Worcs
97 K8 Harvington Worcs
134 D2 Harwell Notts
48 C1 Harwell Oxon
73 K1 Harwich Essex
139 L5 Harwood Bolton
167 J4 Harwood Dur
190 E8 Harwood Nthumb
163 H3 Harwood Dale N York
139 L5 Harwood Lee Bolton
134 C2 Harworth Notts
98 B6 Hasbury Dudley
36 F3 Hascombe Surrey
100 F7 Haselbech Nhants
31 G8 Haselbury Plucknett Somset
82 F2 Haseley Warwks
82 F1 Haseley Green Warwks
82 F1 Haseley Knob Warwks
82 D4 Haselor Warwks
64 B2 Hasfield Gloucs
54 D5 Hasguard Pembks
138 D6 Haskayne Lancs
90 F5 Hasketon Suffk
133 H5 Hasland Derbys
36 D4 Haslemere Surrey
140 B3 Haslingden Lancs
139 M3 Haslingden Grane Lancs
87 H5 Haslingfield Cambs
130 E8 Haslington Ches
130 E8 Hassall Ches
130 F7 Hassall Green Ches
40 E6 Hassell Street Kent
107 H2 Hassingham Norfk
165 G7 Hassness Cumb
22 D4 Hassocks W Susx
132 D5 Hassop Derbys
36 D4 Haste Hill Surrey
280 D6 Haster Highld
137 J5 Hasthorpe Lincs
40 E6 Hastingleigh Kent
24 E5 Hastings E Susx
30 D7 Hastings Somset
70 C5 Hastingwood Essex
68 A5 Hastoe Herts
169 K2 Haswell Dur

169 K2 Haswell Plough Dur
86 D5 Hatch Beds
30 D6 Hatch Beauchamp Somset
86 B3 Hatch End Beds
50 E1 Hatch End Gt Lon
18 F3 Hatchet Gate Hants
68 E4 Hatching Green Herts
130 A5 Hatchmere Ches
145 G7 Hatcliffe NE Lin
143 G6 Hatfield Donc
80 E3 Hatfield Herefs
69 G5 Hatfield Herts
81 K5 Hatfield Worcs
70 E4 Hatfield Broad Oak Essex
70 D4 Hatfield Heath Essex
71 J5 Hatfield Peverel Essex
143 H6 Hatfield Woodhouse Donc
65 M8 Hatford Oxon
34 D1 Hatherden Hants
12 D2 Hatherleigh Devon
116 E7 Hathern Leics
65 H6 Hatherop Gloucs
132 E3 Hathersage Derbys
132 E3 Hathersage Booths Derbys
113 L2 Hatherton Ches
98 B1 Hatherton Staffs
86 F5 Hatley St George Cambs
6 D2 Hatt Cnwll
131 K1 Hattersley Tamesd
35 K3 Hattingley Hants
257 K4 Hatton Abers
234 C6 Hatton Angus
115 L5 Hatton Derbys
50 E4 Hatton Gt Lon
136 C4 Hatton Lincs
95 L5 Hatton Shrops
97 H3 Hatton Shrops
130 B3 Hatton Warrtn
82 F2 Hatton Warwks
129 K7 Hatton Heath Ches
256 F8 Hatton of Fintray Abers
196 F6 Haugh E Ayrs
137 H4 Haugh Lincs
140 D5 Haugh Rochdl
136 F3 Haugham Lincs
209 G3 Haughhead E Duns
202 F7 Haugh Head Nthumb
89 L3 Haughley Suffk
89 L2 Haughley Green Suffk
255 H4 Haugh of Glass Moray
175 K2 Haugh of Urr D & G
134 D5 Haughton Notts
112 D7 Haughton Powys
96 F4 Haughton Shrops
97 G2 Haughton Shrops
112 F6 Haughton Shrops
113 J8 Haughton Shrops
114 D7 Haughton Staffs
131 J1 Haughton Green Tamesd
169 J7 Haughton le Skerne Darltn
130 B8 Haughton Moss Ches
69 J3 Haultwick Herts
99 G1 Haunton Staffs
9 d1 Hautes Croix Jersey
87 J5 Hauxton Cambs
131 G6 Havannah Ches
20 B5 Havant Hants
79 M4 Haven Herefs
119 H1 Haven Bank Lincs
144 F2 Haven Side E R Yk
19 J5 Havenstreet IoW
142 B5 Havercroft Wakefd
54 F4 Haverfordwest Pembks
88 D6 Haverhill Suffk
155 L7 Haverigg Cumb
70 D8 Havering-atte-Bower Gt Lon
84 F6 Haversham M Keyn
156 E6 Haverthwaite Cumb
170 C6 Haverton Hill S on T
44 F6 Havyat N Som
31 H3 Havyatt Somset
129 H6 Hawarden Flints
81 L5 Hawbridge Worcs
71 J3 Hawbush Green Essex
146 D2 Hawcoat Cumb
76 C6 Hawen Cerdgn
158 F5 Hawes N York
106 E4 Hawe's Green Norfk
81 J3 Hawford Worcs
188 E3 Hawick Border
15 H2 Hawkchurch Devon
88 F4 Hawkedon Suffk
39 K4 Hawkenbury Kent
46 B8 Hawkeridge Wilts
14 C5 Hawkerland Devon
45 M2 Hawkesbury S Glos
99 K6 Hawkesbury Warwks
45 M2 Hawkesbury Upton S Glos

99 J6 Hawkes End Covtry
131 J2 Hawk Green Stockp
191 J4 Hawkhill Nthumb
39 J7 Hawkhurst Kent
23 J4 Hawkhurst Common E Susx
41 H7 Hawkinge Kent
35 M5 Hawkley Hants
28 F5 Hawkridge Somset
165 L1 Hawksdale Cumb
139 M5 Hawkshaw Bury
156 E3 Hawkshead Cumb
156 D3 Hawkshead Hill Cumb
198 D5 Hawksland S Lans
71 G1 Hawkspur Green Essex
113 J5 Hawkstone Shrops
149 G2 Hawkswick N York
141 L7 Hawksworth Leeds
117 K3 Hawksworth Notts
53 J1 Hawkwell Essex
180 C4 Hawkwell Nthumb
49 L7 Hawley Hants
52 C4 Hawley Kent
64 F3 Hawling Gloucs
161 J5 Hawnby N York
149 J8 Haworth Brad
68 B6 Hawridge Bucks
89 G3 Hawstead Suffk
89 H3 Hawstead Green Suffk
169 L2 Hawthorn Dur
35 K4 Hawthorn Hants
43 H4 Hawthorn Rhondd
49 L4 Hawthorn Hill Br For
136 D8 Hawthorn Hill Lincs
118 D6 Hawthorpe Lincs
117 L1 Hawton Notts
151 K4 Haxby York
151 K4 Haxby Gates York
143 J7 Haxey N Linc
143 J7 Haxey Turbary N Linc
38 C4 Haxted Surrey
33 K1 Haxton Wilts
4 F4 Hay Cnwll
4 F6 Hay Cnwll
10 D8 Hay Cnwll
139 H8 Haydock St Hel
45 K8 Haydon BaNES
31 L7 Haydon Dorset
30 C6 Haydon Somset
179 J6 Haydon Bridge Nthumb
47 H2 Haydon Wick Swindn
11 L8 Haye Cnwll
50 E3 Hayes Gt Lon
51 L5 Hayes Gt Lon
50 D3 Hayes End Gt Lon
217 H2 Hayfield Ag & B
131 L2 Hayfield Derbys
96 E1 Haygate Wrekin
120 C7 Hay Green Norfk
234 E7 Hayhillock Angus
2 F4 Hayle Cnwll
98 B6 Hayley Green Dudley
113 L2 Haymoor Green Ches
13 H5 Hayne Devon
29 G7 Hayne Devon
86 B7 Haynes (Church End) Beds
86 B6 Haynes (Northwood End) Beds
86 B6 Haynes (Silver End) Beds
85 L7 Haynes (West End) Beds
79 J6 Hay-on-Wye Powys
74 E7 Hayscastle Pembks
74 E7 Hayscastle Cross Pembks
38 F4 Haysden Kent
69 K2 Hay Street Herts
164 F2 Hayton Cumb
178 C7 Hayton Cumb
152 C6 Hayton E R Yk
134 E3 Hayton Notts
96 C7 Hayton's Bent Shrops
13 H7 Haytor Vale Devon
26 F7 Haytown Devon
22 E2 Haywards Heath W Susx
142 F5 Haywood Donc
80 B8 Haywood Herefs
134 C8 Haywood Oaks Notts
24 C5 Hazards Green E Susx
198 D4 Hazelbank S Lans
16 E1 Hazelbury Bryan Dorset
71 K6 Hazeleigh Essex
49 H7 Hazeley Hants
117 J2 Hazelford Notts
131 H2 Hazel Grove Stockp
140 E7 Hazelhurst Tamesd
98 C1 Hazelslade Staffs
39 H5 Hazel Street Kent
88 D6 Hazel Stub Suffk
222 E3 Hazelton Walls Fife

116 B2	**Hazelwood** Derbys
67 L8	**Hazlemere** Bucks
180 F4	**Hazlerigg** N u Ty
114 F2	**Hazles** Staffs
65 G3	**Hazleton** Gloucs
120 E4	**Heacham** Norfk
35 G4	**Headbourne Worthy** Hants
79 K4	**Headbrook** Herefs
39 L4	**Headcorn** Kent
150 C8	**Headingley** Leeds
66 D5	**Headington** Oxon
168 F7	**Headlam** Dur
210 B7	**Headlesscross** N Lans
82 B2	**Headless Cross** Worcs
36 B4	**Headley** Hants
48 D6	**Headley** Hants
51 G8	**Headley** Surrey
36 B4	**Headley Down** Hants
98 D8	**Headley Heath** Worcs
134 E4	**Headon** Notts
197 L2	**Heads** S Lans
178 C7	**Heads Nook** Cumb
116 B2	**Heage** Derbys
151 G6	**Healaugh** N York
159 H3	**Healaugh** N York
131 K3	**Heald Green** Stockp
30 C6	**Heale** Somset
30 F5	**Heale** Somset
160 B6	**Healey** N York
180 B7	**Healey** Nthumb
140 D4	**Healey** Rochdl
141 L4	**Healey** Wakefd
168 D1	**Healeyfield** Dur
145 G5	**Healing** NE Lin
2 D5	**Heamoor** Cnwll
116 D2	**Heanor** Derbys
27 J4	**Heanton Punchardon** Devon
139 J4	**Heapey** Lancs
135 H2	**Heapham** Lincs
36 B3	**Hearn** Hants
53 J6	**Hearts Delight** Kent
28 C4	**Heasley Mill** Devon
247 K5	**Heast** Highld
133 J6	**Heath** Derbys
142 A4	**Heath** Wakefd
68 A2	**Heath and Reach** Beds
21 J4	**Heath Common** W Susx
132 C7	**Heathcote** Derbys
113 L6	**Heathcote** Shrops
67 L7	**Heath End** Bucks
48 B6	**Heath End** Hants
116 B7	**Heath End** Leics
82 F3	**Heath End** Warwks
99 K1	**Heather** Leics
13 J7	**Heathfield** Devon
23 K3	**Heathfield** E Susx
149 L2	**Heathfield** N York
29 L5	**Heathfield** Somset
66 D4	**Heathfield Village** Oxon
82 C1	**Heath Green** Worcs
176 C3	**Heath Hall** D & G
98 C2	**Heath Hayes & Wimblebury** Staffs
97 H1	**Heath Hill** Shrops
30 F2	**Heath House** Somset
14 F2	**Heathstock** Devon
97 H5	**Heathton** Shrops
97 L3	**Heath Town** Wolves
115 H6	**Heatley** Staffs
130 D2	**Heatley** Warrtn
139 L6	**Heaton** Bolton
149 L8	**Heaton** Brad
147 J4	**Heaton** Lancs
181 G5	**Heaton** N u Ty
131 J7	**Heaton** Staffs
131 H1	**Heaton Chapel** Stockp
131 G2	**Heaton Mersey** Stockp
131 H2	**Heaton Norris** Stockp
138 E5	**Heaton's Bridge** Lancs
52 C7	**Heaverham** Kent
131 H2	**Heaviley** Stockp
13 L4	**Heavitree** Devon
181 H6	**Hebburn** S Tyne
149 J3	**Hebden** N York
140 F2	**Hebden Bridge** Calder
130 C6	**Hebden Green** Ches
69 J3	**Hebing End** Herts
75 L6	**Hebron** Carmth
125 H3	**Hebron** IoA
191 J6	**Hebron** Nthumb
49 H6	**Heckfield** Hants
106 D8	**Heckfield Green** Suffk
72 D3	**Heckfordbridge** Essex
118 F3	**Heckington** Lincs
141 K3	**Heckmondwike** Kirk
46 E5	**Heddington** Wilts
180 D5	**Heddon-on-the-Wall** Nthumb

107 G5	**Hedenham** Norfk
19 H1	**Hedge End** Hants
50 B2	**Hedgerley** Bucks
50 B2	**Hedgerley Green** Bucks
30 D5	**Hedging** Somset
180 C7	**Hedley on the Hill** Nthumb
98 C1	**Hednesford** Staffs
145 F2	**Hedon** E R Yk
49 L2	**Hedsor** Bucks
80 D4	**Hegdon Hill** Herefs
281 d6	**Heglibister** Shet
169 H6	**Heighington** Darltn
135 L6	**Heighington** Lincs
81 H1	**Heightington** Worcs
201 L7	**Heiton** Border
13 H8	**Hele** Devon
14 A2	**Hele** Devon
27 J2	**Hele** Devon
30 B6	**Hele** Somset
11 J2	**Helebridge** Cnwll
28 D8	**Hele Lane** Devon
208 A3	**Helensburgh** Ag & B
196 D5	**Helenton** S Ayrs
3 J6	**Helford** Cnwll
3 J5	**Helford Passage** Cnwll
121 J6	**Helhoughton** Norfk
88 C7	**Helions Bumpstead** Essex
133 K1	**Hellaby** Rothm
10 F8	**Helland** Cnwll
10 F8	**Hellandbridge** Cnwll
48 A6	**Hell Corner** W Berk
11 K5	**Hellescott** Cnwll
106 D1	**Hellesdon** Norfk
2 D3	**Hellesveor** Cnwll
83 M4	**Hellidon** Nhants
148 E4	**Hellifield** N York
23 K5	**Hellingly** E Susx
107 G3	**Hellington** Norfk
191 H7	**Helm** Nthumb
84 B6	**Helmdon** Nhants
141 H5	**Helme** Kirk
90 E4	**Helmingham** Suffk
168 F4	**Helmington Row** Dur
274 D5	**Helmsdale** Highld
140 B3	**Helmshore** Lancs
161 K6	**Helmsley** N York
150 F2	**Helperby** N York
152 E2	**Helperthorpe** N York
118 F3	**Helpringham** Lincs
102 C2	**Helpston** C Pete
129 L4	**Helsby** Ches
137 K5	**Helsey** Lincs
3 G5	**Helston** Cnwll
10 F6	**Helstone** Cnwll
166 C6	**Helton** Cumb
159 K2	**Helwith** N York
148 D2	**Helwith Bridge** N York
107 G1	**Hemblington** Norfk
31 K3	**Hembridge** Somset
68 D5	**Hemel Hempstead** Herts
7 H3	**Hemerdon** Devon
143 H2	**Hemingbrough** N York
136 D5	**Hemingby** Lincs
142 B7	**Hemingfield** Barns
86 F1	**Hemingford Abbots** Cambs
86 F1	**Hemingford Grey** Cambs
90 D4	**Hemingstone** Suffk
116 D6	**Hemington** Leics
102 B6	**Hemington** Nhants
45 L8	**Hemington** Somset
91 G6	**Hemley** Suffk
170 C7	**Hemlington** Middsb
153 H5	**Hempholme** E R Yk
106 E4	**Hempnall** Norfk
106 E5	**Hempnall Green** Norfk
266 B3	**Hempriggs** Moray
88 C7	**Hempstead** Essex
53 G6	**Hempstead** Medway
122 C4	**Hempstead** Norfk
123 H6	**Hempstead** Norfk
64 B4	**Hempsted** Gloucs
121 K5	**Hempton** Norfk
66 C1	**Hempton** Oxon
123 K8	**Hemsby** Norfk
135 J2	**Hemswell** Lincs
135 J2	**Hemswell Cliff** Lincs
142 C5	**Hemsworth** Wakefd
29 L8	**Hemyock** Devon
45 H3	**Henbury** Bristl
131 H5	**Henbury** Ches
202 M4	**Hendersyde Park** Border
7 L5	**Hendham** Devon
94 F4	**Hendomen** Powys
51 G1	**Hendon** Gt Lon
181 K7	**Hendon** Sundld
3 J4	**Hendra** Cnwll
10 E7	**Hendra** Cnwll
42 E5	**Hendre** Brdgnd

128 E6	**Hendre** Flints
62 F4	**Hendre** Mons
57 G4	**Hendy** Carmth
125 G4	**Heneglwys** IoA
22 C4	**Henfield** W Susx
11 M3	**Henford** Devon
40 B8	**Henghurst** Kent
43 J3	**Hengoed** Caerph
79 J4	**Hengoed** Powys
112 D5	**Hengoed** Shrops
89 G2	**Hengrave** Suffk
70 E2	**Henham** Essex
94 D2	**Heniarth** Powys
30 C6	**Henlade** Somset
16 C2	**Henley** Dorset
64 C4	**Henley** Gloucs
95 L5	**Henley** Shrops
96 C3	**Henley** Shrops
30 F4	**Henley** Somset
90 E5	**Henley** Suffk
36 D5	**Henley** W Susx
99 K7	**Henley Green** Covtry
82 E2	**Henley-in-Arden** Warwks
49 J2	**Henley-on-Thames** Oxon
50 B8	**Henley Park** Surrey
24 D5	**Henley's Down** E Susx
52 E5	**Henley Street** Kent
76 C7	**Henllan** Cerdgn
127 L6	**Henllan** Denbgs
55 L3	**Henllan Amgoed** Carmth
44 B1	**Henllys** Torfn
86 D7	**Henlow** Beds
13 J6	**Hennock** Devon
89 H7	**Henny Street** Essex
126 F5	**Henryd** Conwy
75 H6	**Henry's Moat (Castell Hendre)** Pembks
142 F3	**Hensall** N York
179 H6	**Henshaw** Nthumb
164 C7	**Hensingham** Cumb
107 K6	**Henstead** Suffk
35 G6	**Hensting** Hants
32 B7	**Henstridge** Somset
32 B6	**Henstridge Ash** Somset
32 B6	**Henstridge Marsh** Somset
67 J6	**Henton** Oxon
31 H2	**Henton** Somset
81 J4	**Henwick** Worcs
11 K7	**Henwood** Cnwll
66 C6	**Henwood** Oxon
57 J5	**Heol-las** Swans
60 D2	**Heol Senni** Powys
42 E5	**Heol-y-Cyw** Brdgnd
190 F1	**Hepburn** Nthumb
190 E6	**Hepple** Nthumb
180 F2	**Hepscott** Nthumb
140 E2	**Heptonstall** Calder
141 J6	**Hepworth** Kirk
105 K8	**Hepworth** Suffk
54 E5	**Herbrandston** Pembks
80 C7	**Hereford** Herefs
41 L2	**Hereson** Kent
258 F3	**Heribusta** Highld
200 E2	**Heriot** Border
211 G5	**Hermiston** C Edin
188 E7	**Hermitage** Border
16 C1	**Hermitage** Dorset
48 D4	**Hermitage** W Berk
20 B5	**Hermitage** W Susx
141 M7	**Hermit Hill** Barns
58 C3	**Hermon** Carmth
125 G6	**Hermon** IoA
75 L6	**Hermon** Pembks
41 G2	**Herne** Kent
41 G2	**Herne Bay** Kent
41 G2	**Herne Common** Kent
51 J4	**Herne Hill** Gt Lon
39 G3	**Herne Pound** Kent
27 K5	**Herner** Devon
40 E3	**Hernhill** Kent
5 L3	**Herodsfoot** Cnwll
41 J4	**Heronden** Kent
52 D1	**Herongate** Essex
182 E6	**Heronsford** S Ayrs
68 C8	**Heronsgate** Herts
35 K2	**Herriard** Hants
107 K4	**Herringfleet** Suffk
86 B6	**Herring's Green** Beds
88 E1	**Herringswell** Suffk
133 J1	**Herringthorpe** Rothm
181 J8	**Herrington** Sundld
41 G3	**Hersden** Kent
11 J1	**Hersham** Cnwll
50 E6	**Hersham** Surrey
23 L5	**Herstmonceux** E Susx
17 K6	**Herston** Dorset
275 c6	**Herston** Ork
69 J4	**Hertford** Herts

69 K5	**Hertford Heath** Herts
69 K5	**Hertingfordbury** Herts
138 F3	**Hesketh Bank** Lancs
147 M7	**Hesketh Lane** Lancs
165 K3	**Hesket Newmarket** Cumb
139 G4	**Heskin Green** Lancs
170 B3	**Hesleden** Dur
158 F7	**Hesleden** N York
134 C1	**Hesley** Donc
179 J2	**Hesleyside** Nthumb
151 K5	**Heslington** York
151 H5	**Hessay** York
6 C3	**Hessenford** Cnwll
89 J3	**Hessett** Suffk
144 C3	**Hessle** E R Yk
142 C4	**Hessle** Wakefd
147 J3	**Hest Bank** Lancs
90 D2	**Hestley Green** Suffk
50 E3	**Heston** Gt Lon
275 b4	**Hestwall** Ork
129 G3	**Heswall** Wirral
66 E1	**Hethe** Oxon
106 C2	**Hethersett** Norfk
178 B5	**Hethersgill** Cumb
178 B5	**Hetherside** Cumb
113 H2	**Hetherson Green** Ches
202 D7	**Hethpool** Nthumb
169 H3	**Hett** Dur
149 G4	**Hetton** N York
169 K1	**Hetton-le-Hole** Sundld
203 G6	**Hetton Steads** Nthumb
180 D4	**Heugh** Nthumb
243 L1	**Heughhead** Abers
213 J6	**Heugh Head** Border
91 H1	**Heveningham** Suffk
38 D4	**Hever** Kent
157 H6	**Heversham** Cumb
122 D7	**Hevingham** Norfk
4 F5	**Hewas Water** Cnwll
63 H6	**Hewelsfield** Gloucs
149 K8	**Hewenden** Brad
44 E6	**Hewish** N Som
15 K1	**Hewish** Somset
15 H2	**Hewood** Dorset
179 L6	**Hexham** Nthumb
52 B5	**Hextable** Kent
142 F7	**Hexthorpe** Donc
68 E1	**Hexton** Herts
11 L6	**Hexworthy** Cnwll
12 F7	**Hexworthy** Devon
148 F7	**Hey** Lancs
70 F7	**Heybridge** Essex
71 L5	**Heybridge** Essex
72 C5	**Heybridge Basin** Essex
6 F5	**Heybrook Bay** Devon
87 J7	**Heydon** Cambs
122 C6	**Heydon** Norfk
118 D4	**Heydour** Lincs
131 G3	**Heyhead** Manch
138 D2	**Hey Houses** Lancs
224 B6	**Heylipoll** Ag & B
281 d4	**Heylor** Shet
140 E7	**Heyrod** Tamesd
147 H4	**Heysham** Lancs
149 L3	**Heyshaw** N York
20 E3	**Heyshott** W Susx
140 D6	**Heyside** Oldham
32 F2	**Heytesbury** Wilts
65 M2	**Heythrop** Oxon
140 C5	**Heywood** Rochdl
46 C8	**Heywood** Wilts
144 B7	**Hibaldstow** N Linc
142 D6	**Hickleton** Donc
123 J6	**Hickling** Norfk
117 J6	**Hickling** Notts
123 H6	**Hickling Green** Norfk
123 H7	**Hickling Heath** Norfk
40 E4	**Hickmans Green** Kent
41 G3	**Hicks Forstal** Kent
22 D5	**Hickstead** W Susx
82 E6	**Hidcote Bartrim** Gloucs
82 E6	**Hidcote Boyce** Gloucs
142 C4	**High Ackworth** Wakefd
141 M6	**Higham** Barns
133 H7	**Higham** Derbys
38 F4	**Higham** Kent
52 F5	**Higham** Kent
148 E8	**Higham** Lancs
88 E2	**Higham** Suffk
89 L8	**Higham** Suffk
180 D4	**Higham Dykes** Nthumb
85 J2	**Higham Ferrers** Nhants
86 C8	**Higham Gobion** Beds
51 K1	**Higham Hill** Gt Lon
99 K4	**Higham on the Hill** Leics
12 C2	**Highampton** Devon
69 K8	**Highams Park** Gt Lon
180 D2	**High Angerton** Nthumb

172 D5 **High Ardwell** D & G
176 B1 **High Auldgirth** D & G
166 D2 **High Bankhill** Cumb
69 L7 **High Beach** Essex
148 B2 **High Bentham** N York
165 H4 **High Bewaldeth** Cumb
27 L6 **High Bickington** Devon
158 D7 **High Bickwith** N York
157 K7 **High Biggins** Cumb
209 H7 **High Blantyre** S Lans
209 L3 **High Bonnybridge** Falk
156 F3 **High Borrans** Cumb
149 H6 **High Bradley** N York
28 B4 **High Bray** Devon
34 F6 **Highbridge** Hants
30 D2 **Highbridge** Somset
38 A7 **Highbrook** W Susx
38 F5 **High Brooms** Kent
27 J6 **High Bullen** Devon
141 J5 **Highburton** Kirk
51 J2 **Highbury** Gt Lon
31 M1 **Highbury** Somset
191 J4 **High Buston** Nthumb
180 E5 **High Callerton** Nthumb
157 K7 **High Casterton** Cumb
151 M5 **High Catton** E R Yk
48 B7 **Highclere** Hants
18 C5 **Highcliffe** Dorset
168 F7 **High Close** Dur
66 A5 **High Cogges** Oxon
105 K2 **High Common** Norfk
169 G7 **High Coniscliffe** Darltn
178 B6 **High Crosby** Cumb
3 J5 **High Cross** Cnwll
196 D2 **High Cross** E Ayrs
35 L5 **High Cross** Hants
69 K3 **High Cross** Herts
147 G8 **Highcross** Lancs
22 C4 **High Cross** W Susx
82 E2 **High Cross** Warwks
172 E7 **High Drummore** D & G
169 J1 **High Dubmire** Sundld
70 F4 **High Easter** Essex
142 F3 **High Eggborough** N York
160 B6 **High Ellington** N York
31 L3 **Higher Alham** Somset
16 E2 **Higher Ansty** Dorset
138 D2 **Higher Ballam** Lancs
139 G1 **Higher Bartle** Lancs
85 J8 **Higher Berry End** Beds
16 D4 **Higher Bockhampton** Dorset
8 D4 **Higher Brixham** Torbay
14 B3 **Higher Burrowton** Devon
129 M8 **Higher Burwardsley** Ches
113 K8 **High Ercall** Wrekin
15 J1 **Higher Chillington** Somset
26 E6 **Higher Clovelly** Devon
28 F5 **Highercombe** Somset
15 M4 **Higher Coombe** Dorset
131 J3 **Higher Disley** Ches
139 K7 **Higher Folds** Wigan
148 F7 **Higherford** Lancs
8 D1 **Higher Gabwell** Devon
15 L1 **Higher Halstock Leigh** Dorset
148 E8 **Higher Harpers** Lancs
147 H4 **Higher Heysham** Lancs
131 J5 **Higher Hurdsfield** Ches
130 E1 **Higher Irlam** Salfd
15 M3 **Higher Kingcombe** Dorset
129 H7 **Higher Kinnerton** Flints
16 E2 **Higher Melcombe** Dorset
27 K3 **Higher Muddiford** Devon
32 B6 **Higher Nyland** Dorset
140 E5 **Higher Ogden** Rochdl
3 G6 **Higher Pentire** Cnwll
139 G2 **Higher Penwortham** Lancs
148 E2 **Higher Studfold** N York
4 C6 **Higher Town** Cnwll
5 G3 **Higher Town** Cnwll
10 C2 **Higher Town** IoS
6 D4 **Higher Tregantle** Cnwll
139 H2 **Higher Walton** Lancs
130 B3 **Higher Walton** Warrtn
15 G1 **Higher Wambrook** Somset
16 D3 **Higher Waterston** Dorset
17 G2 **Higher Whatcombe** Dorset
139 J3 **Higher Wheelton** Lancs
130 B4 **Higher Whitley** Ches
16 A2 **Higher Wraxhall** Dorset
113 H3 **Higher Wych** Ches
168 F5 **High Etherley** Dur
119 K2 **High Ferry** Lincs
151 M8 **Highfield** E R Yk
180 E7 **Highfield** Gatesd
196 C1 **Highfield** N Ayrs
142 E6 **Highfields** Donc
141 K6 **High Flats** Kirk
71 J2 **High Garrett** Essex

38 C6 **Highgate** E Susx
51 H2 **Highgate** Gt Lon
39 J7 **Highgate** Kent
168 F4 **High Grange** Dur
150 B2 **High Grantley** N York
156 F2 **High Green** Cumb
141 K5 **High Green** Kirk
106 C2 **High Green** Norfk
106 D5 **High Green** Norfk
106 F4 **High Green** Norfk
142 A8 **High Green** Sheff
96 F6 **High Green** Shrops
89 G3 **High Green** Suffk
81 K6 **High Green** Worcs
189 L7 **Highgreen Manor** Nthumb
40 A7 **High Halden** Kent
53 G4 **High Halstow** Medway
30 F4 **High Ham** Somset
164 D5 **High Harrington** Cumb
150 D5 **High Harrogate** N York
169 K2 **High Haswell** Dur
113 K6 **High Hatton** Shrops
191 K5 **High Hauxley** Nthumb
163 G1 **High Hawsker** N York
166 B2 **High Hesket** Cumb
141 L5 **High Hoyland** Barns
144 B1 **High Hunsley** E R Yk
23 H2 **High Hurstwood** E Susx
152 A2 **High Hutton** N York
165 H3 **High Ireby** Cumb
122 C3 **High Kelling** Norfk
161 H6 **High Kilburn** N York
163 J6 **High Killerby** N York
166 C6 **High Knipe** Cumb
168 E5 **High Lands** Dur
131 H6 **Highlane** Ches
133 H3 **Highlane** Derbys
131 J3 **High Lane** Stockp
2 F4 **High Lanes** Cnwll
70 D5 **High Laver** Essex
164 F1 **Highlaws** Cumb
63 M2 **Highleadon** Gloucs
130 D3 **High Legh** Ches
20 D7 **Highleigh** W Susx
170 B8 **High Leven** S on T
97 G6 **Highley** Shrops
45 J7 **High Littleton** BaNES
165 G5 **High Lorton** Cumb
134 F5 **High Marnham** Notts
142 D7 **High Melton** Donc
180 C6 **High Mickley** Nthumb
165 J1 **Highmoor** Cumb
49 H2 **Highmoor** Oxon
49 H2 **Highmoor Cross** Oxon
44 F1 **Highmoor Hill** Mons
169 J2 **High Moorsley** Sundld
64 A3 **Highnam** Gloucs
64 A3 **Highnam Green** Gloucs
181 J8 **High Newport** Sundld
156 F6 **High Newton** Cumb
156 D5 **High Nibthwaite** Cumb
114 B6 **High Offley** Staffs
70 E6 **High Ongar** Essex
114 C8 **High Onn** Staffs
72 E3 **High Park Corner** Essex
184 D2 **High Pennyvenie** E Ayrs
33 K4 **High Post** Wilts
45 H5 **Highridge** N Som
70 F4 **High Roding** Essex
165 K3 **High Row** Cumb
165 L6 **High Row** Cumb
147 M3 **High Salter** Lancs
21 K5 **High Salvington** W Susx
165 G2 **High Scales** Cumb
164 D4 **High Seaton** Cumb
158 F4 **High Shaw** N York
165 H4 **High Side** Cumb
180 E7 **High Spen** Gatesd
41 G2 **Highstead** Kent
40 B3 **Highsted** Kent
168 E3 **High Stoop** Dur
5 G4 **High Street** Cnwll
39 J7 **High Street** Kent
40 E3 **Highstreet** Kent
91 J1 **High Street** Suffk
91 K4 **High Street** Suffk
88 F8 **Highstreet Green** Essex
36 E4 **Highstreet Green** Surrey
176 E3 **Hightae** D & G
98 E7 **Highter's Heath** Birm
170 C4 **High Throston** Hartpl
131 G7 **Hightown** Ches
18 B3 **Hightown** Hants
138 C7 **Hightown** Sefton
98 C1 **High Town** Staffs
89 K4 **Hightown Green** Suffk
136 E5 **High Toynton** Lincs
190 E5 **High Trewhitt** Nthumb

181 G8 **High Urpeth** Dur
210 D2 **High Valleyfield** Fife
179 L5 **High Warden** Nthumb
80 B5 **Highway** Herefs
46 F4 **Highway** Wilts
13 K8 **Highweek** Devon
180 D7 **High Westwood** Dur
115 H5 **Highwood** Staffs
69 G8 **Highwood Hill** Gt Lon
63 H7 **High Woolaston** Gloucs
160 F1 **High Worsall** N York
65 J8 **Highworth** Swindn
156 E3 **High Wray** Cumb
70 C4 **High Wych** Herts
67 L8 **High Wycombe** Bucks
105 G3 **Hilborough** Norfk
133 J8 **Hilcote** Derbys
47 G7 **Hilcott** Wilts
38 E4 **Hildenborough** Kent
38 F4 **Hilden Park** Kent
87 L5 **Hildersham** Cambs
114 E4 **Hilderstone** Staffs
153 J3 **Hilderthorpe** E R Yk
16 C2 **Hilfield** Dorset
104 C4 **Hilgay** Norfk
63 J8 **Hill** S Glos
83 K2 **Hill** Warwks
142 D2 **Hillam** N York
167 H7 **Hillbeck** Cumb
41 G2 **Hillborough** Kent
36 B5 **Hill Brow** Hants
17 K2 **Hillbutts** Dorset
114 B4 **Hill Chorlton** Staffs
115 M2 **Hillclifflane** Derbys
123 H7 **Hill Common** Norfk
29 L5 **Hill Common** Somset
32 E3 **Hill Deverill** Wilts
119 K2 **Hilldyke** Lincs
168 C3 **Hill End** Dur
210 F2 **Hill End** Fife
221 J8 **Hill End** Fife
81 K7 **Hill End** Gloucs
211 H5 **Hillend** Mdloth
209 L5 **Hillend** N Lans
56 D6 **Hillend** Swans
63 H4 **Hillersland** Gloucs
13 G3 **Hillerton** Devon
67 G1 **Hillesden** Bucks
45 M1 **Hillesley** Gloucs
29 L6 **Hillfarrance** Somset
53 H6 **Hill Green** Kent
36 D5 **Hillgrove** W Susx
80 D6 **Hillhampton** Herefs
255 M4 **Hillhead** Abers
8 D4 **Hillhead** Devon
19 J3 **Hill Head** Hants
199 G5 **Hillhead** S Lans
257 K3 **Hillhead of Cocklaw** Abers
98 F1 **Hilliard's Cross** Staffs
279 L3 **Hilliclay** Highld
50 D2 **Hillingdon** Gt Lon
208 E6 **Hillington** C Glas
120 F6 **Hillington** Norfk
19 H5 **Hillis Corner** IoW
100 C8 **Hillmorton** Warwks
140 A2 **Hillock Vale** Lancs
210 F1 **Hill of Beath** Fife
264 C4 **Hill of Fearn** Highld
175 J2 **Hillowton** D & G
97 K8 **Hillpool** Worcs
35 J7 **Hillpound** Hants
115 H8 **Hill Ridware** Staffs
245 K4 **Hillside** Abers
235 H3 **Hillside** Angus
7 K3 **Hillside** Devon
141 J4 **Hill Side** Kirk
81 H3 **Hill Side** Worcs
133 J5 **Hills Town** Derbys
34 D7 **Hillstreet** Hants
281 L4 **Hillswick** Shet
168 C6 **Hill Top** Dur
18 F3 **Hill Top** Hants
141 G5 **Hill Top** Kirk
133 H1 **Hill Top** Rothm
98 C5 **Hill Top** Sandw
142 A4 **Hill Top** Wakefd
281 d8 **Hillwell** Shet
46 E4 **Hilmarton** Wilts
46 C7 **Hilperton** Wilts
46 C7 **Hilperton Marsh** Wilts
19 L3 **Hilsea** C Port
145 H1 **Hilston** E R Yk
34 F6 **Hiltingbury** Hants
202 D3 **Hilton** Border
86 F2 **Hilton** Cambs
167 G6 **Hilton** Cumb
115 L5 **Hilton** Derbys
16 E2 **Hilton** Dorset

168 F6 **Hilton** Dur
264 D4 **Hilton** Highld
170 B8 **Hilton** S on T
97 H4 **Hilton** Shrops
81 L3 **Himbleton** Worcs
97 K5 **Himley** Staffs
157 H5 **Hincaster** Cumb
50 F6 **Hinchley Wood** Surrey
99 L4 **Hinckley** Leics
105 L8 **Hinderclay** Suffk
171 J7 **Hinderwell** N York
112 E5 **Hindford** Shrops
36 C4 **Hindhead** Surrey
139 L1 **Hindle Fold** Lancs
180 C7 **Hindley** Nthumb
139 J6 **Hindley** Wigan
139 J7 **Hindley Green** Wigan
81 K3 **Hindlip** Worcs
122 A5 **Hindolveston** Norfk
32 F4 **Hindon** Wilts
121 L4 **Hindringham** Norfk
105 L3 **Hingham** Norfk
97 J5 **Hinksford** Staffs
97 G3 **Hinnington** Shrops
113 M6 **Hinstock** Shrops
90 C6 **Hintlesham** Suffk
63 K6 **Hinton** Gloucs
18 C4 **Hinton** Hants
79 L7 **Hinton** Herefs
45 L4 **Hinton** S Glos
95 K2 **Hinton** Shrops
96 E7 **Hinton** Shrops
18 C4 **Hinton Admiral** Hants
35 J5 **Hinton Ampner** Hants
45 H7 **Hinton Blewett** BaNES
45 M7 **Hinton Charterhouse** BaNES
82 B7 **Hinton Green** Worcs
84 A7 **Hinton-in-the-Hedges** Nhants
35 J5 **Hinton Marsh** Hants
17 K1 **Hinton Martell** Dorset
82 B7 **Hinton on the Green** Worcs
47 K2 **Hinton Parva** Swindn
30 F8 **Hinton St George** Somset
32 C7 **Hinton St Mary** Dorset
66 A7 **Hinton Waldrist** Oxon
96 E8 **Hints** Shrops
98 F3 **Hints** Staffs
85 J3 **Hinwick** Beds
40 E6 **Hinxhill** Kent
87 K6 **Hinxton** Cambs
86 E7 **Hinxworth** Herts
141 H3 **Hipperholme** Calder
191 J4 **Hipsburn** Nthumb
160 B3 **Hipswell** N York
245 G3 **Hirn** Abers
111 K7 **Hirnant** Powys
181 G2 **Hirst** Nthumb
142 F3 **Hirst Courtney** N York
128 D7 **Hirwaen** Denbgs
60 E6 **Hirwaun** Rhondd
27 K5 **Hiscott** Devon
87 J3 **Histon** Cambs
89 K5 **Hitcham** Suffk
89 K5 **Hitcham Causeway** Suffk
89 K5 **Hitcham Street** Suffk
68 F1 **Hitchin** Herts
51 K4 **Hither Green** Gt Lon
13 G3 **Hittisleigh** Devon
13 G3 **Hittisleigh Cross** Devon
143 K2 **Hive** E R Yk
114 F6 **Hixon** Staffs
41 J3 **Hoaden** Kent
115 J7 **Hoar Cross** Staffs
63 G1 **Hoarwithy** Herefs
41 G2 **Hoath** Kent
39 G6 **Hoathly** Kent
95 H7 **Hobarris** Shrops
29 K5 **Hoccombe** Somset
106 B1 **Hockering** Norfk
134 E8 **Hockerton** Notts
131 J3 **Hockley** Ches
99 H7 **Hockley** Covtry
71 K8 **Hockley** Essex
99 G3 **Hockley** Staffs
82 E1 **Hockley Heath** Solhll
68 B2 **Hockliffe** Beds
104 E6 **Hockwold cum Wilton** Norfk

29 J7 **Hockworthy** Devon	32 E5 **Holloway** Wilts	128 E4 **Holywell** Flints	98 C8 **Hopwood** Worcs
69 K5 **Hoddesdon** Herts	84 D1 **Hollowell** Nhants	181 H4 **Holywell** Nthumb	23 K4 **Horam** E Susx
139 L3 **Hoddlesden** Bl w D	129 L6 **Hollowmoor Heath** Ches	82 E2 **Holywell** Warwks	118 F4 **Horbling** Lincs
177 G4 **Hoddom Cross** D & G	177 L3 **Hollows** D & G	141 G4 **Holywell Green** Calder	141 L4 **Horbury** Wakefd
177 G4 **Hoddom Mains** D & G	61 J6 **Hollybush** Caerph	29 K6 **Holywell Lake** Somset	65 H7 **Horcott** Gloucs
131 G5 **Hodgehill** Ches	196 D7 **Hollybush** E Ayrs	104 E7 **Holywell Row** Suffk	170 B3 **Horden** Dur
55 H7 **Hodgeston** Pembks	81 H7 **Hollybush** Herefs	176 B3 **Holywood** D & G	95 K6 **Horderley** Shrops
113 K6 **Hodnet** Shrops	103 K2 **Holly End** Norfk	176 C3 **Holywood Village** D & G	18 D4 **Hordle** Hants
134 C3 **Hodsock** Notts	81 K7 **Holly Green** Worcs	96 E3 **Homer** Shrops	112 F5 **Hordley** Shrops
52 D6 **Hodsoll Street** Kent	113 J3 **Hollyhurst** Ches	138 D7 **Homer Green** Sefton	56 F4 **Horeb** Carmth
47 H3 **Hodson** Swindn	145 J3 **Hollym** E R Yk	106 F6 **Homersfield** Suffk	76 D6 **Horeb** Cerdgn
133 L4 **Hodthorpe** Derbys	98 D7 **Hollywood** Worcs	157 J5 **Homescales** Cumb	45 H4 **Horfield** Bristl
35 H7 **Hoe** Hants	141 H6 **Holmbridge** Kirk	63 H3 **Hom Green** Herefs	90 F1 **Horham** Suffk
121 M8 **Hoe** Norfk	37 H2 **Holmbury St Mary** Surrey	33 K5 **Homington** Wilts	72 E1 **Horkesley Heath** Essex
35 K8 **Hoe Gate** Hants	5 H4 **Holmbush** Cnwll	54 F5 **Honeyborough** Pembks	144 B4 **Horkstow** N Linc
166 F7 **Hoff** Cumb	114 E6 **Holmcroft** Staffs	82 D6 **Honeybourne** Worcs	83 K6 **Horley** Oxon
40 D4 **Hogben's Hill** Kent	102 D6 **Holme** Cambs	12 E2 **Honeychurch** Devon	37 L2 **Horley** Surrey
89 H4 **Hoggards Green** Suffk	157 H7 **Holme** Cumb	40 F3 **Honey Hill** Kent	31 K4 **Hornblotton Green** Somset
67 K2 **Hoggeston** Bucks	141 H6 **Holme** Kirk	47 G6 **Honeystreet** Wilts	147 L2 **Hornby** Lancs
99 G5 **Hoggrill's End** Warwks	144 A6 **Holme** N Linc	89 J8 **Honey Tye** Suffk	160 B4 **Hornby** N York
25 G4 **Hog Hill** E Susx	160 E6 **Holme** N York	82 F1 **Honiley** Warwks	160 E2 **Hornby** N York
139 J2 **Hoghton** Lancs	134 F7 **Holme** Notts	123 G6 **Honing** Norfk	136 E6 **Horncastle** Lincs
139 J2 **Hoghton Bottoms** Lancs	140 C2 **Holme Chapel** Lancs	106 C1 **Honingham** Norfk	52 B2 **Hornchurch** Gt Lon
115 L2 **Hognaston** Derbys	151 J7 **Holme Green** N York	118 B3 **Honington** Lincs	202 E3 **Horncliffe** Nthumb
137 K5 **Hogsthorpe** Lincs	105 H2 **Holme Hale** Norfk	105 H8 **Honington** Suffk	202 D3 **Horndean** Border
119 K6 **Holbeach** Lincs	80 D8 **Holme Lacy** Herefs	83 G6 **Honington** Warwks	35 L8 **Horndean** Hants
119 K6 **Holbeach Bank** Lincs	79 L4 **Holme Marsh** Herefs	14 E2 **Honiton** Devon	12 C6 **Horndon** Devon
119 K6 **Holbeach Clough** Lincs	120 F3 **Holme next the Sea** Norfk	141 H5 **Honley** Kirk	52 E2 **Horndon on the Hill** Thurr
103 G1 **Holbeach Drove** Lincs	152 E6 **Holme on the Wolds** E R Yk	114 A8 **Honnington** Wrekin	38 A4 **Horne** Surrey
119 L6 **Holbeach Hurn** Lincs	117 G4 **Holme Pierrepont** Notts	41 J2 **Hoo** Kent	28 F2 **Horner** Somset
119 K7 **Holbeach St Johns** Lincs	80 C6 **Holmer** Herefs	97 J8 **Hoobrook** Worcs	71 J6 **Horne Row** Essex
119 L5 **Holbeach St Mark's** Lincs	67 L7 **Holmer Green** Bucks	141 M7 **Hood Green** Barns	89 K7 **Horners Green** Suffk
119 L5 **Holbeach St Matthew** Lincs	164 F1 **Holme St Cuthbert** Cumb	142 B8 **Hood Hill** Rothm	23 G2 **Horney Common** E Susx
133 L5 **Holbeck** Notts	130 E6 **Holmes Chapel** Ches	6 F4 **Hooe** C Plym	68 C8 **Horn Hill** Bucks
133 L5 **Holbeck Woodhouse** Notts	132 F4 **Holmesfield** Derbys	24 C5 **Hooe** E Susx	123 G8 **Horning** Norfk
82 B3 **Holberrow Green** Worcs	23 J4 **Holmes Hill** E Susx	68 F3 **Hoo End** Herts	101 H4 **Horninghold** Leics
7 J5 **Holbeton** Devon	138 E4 **Holmeswood** Lancs	130 D3 **Hoo Green** Ches	115 L6 **Horninglow** Staffs
51 J3 **Holborn** Gt Lon	51 H8 **Holmethorpe** Surrey	146 F8 **Hoohill** Bpool	87 K3 **Horningsea** Cambs
52 F6 **Holborough** Kent	152 B8 **Holme upon Spalding Moor**	103 J5 **Hook** Cambs	32 D3 **Horningsham** Wilts
116 B3 **Holbrook** Derbys	E R Yk	15 G2 **Hook** Devon	121 K6 **Horningtoft** Norfk
133 J3 **Holbrook** Sheff	133 H6 **Holmewood** Derbys	143 J3 **Hook** E R Yk	6 B3 **Horningtops** Cnwll
90 E7 **Holbrook** Suffk	141 G2 **Holmfield** Calder	50 F6 **Hook** Gt Lon	30 E8 **Hornsbury** Somset
116 B3 **Holbrook Moor** Derbys	141 H6 **Holmfirth** Kirk	19 H3 **Hook** Hants	166 C1 **Hornsby** Cumb
99 J6 **Holbrooks** Covtry	197 H7 **Holmhead** E Ayrs	49 H8 **Hook** Hants	166 C1 **Hornsbygate** Cumb
203 G6 **Holburn** Nthumb	145 K3 **Holmpton** E R Yk	55 G4 **Hook** Pembks	27 G6 **Horns Cross** Devon
19 G3 **Holbury** Hants	155 K3 **Holmrook** Cumb	47 G2 **Hook** Wilts	24 E3 **Horns Cross** E Susx
140 A4 **Holcombe** Bury	104 D7 **Holmsey Green** Suffk	95 L2 **Hookagate** Shrops	153 K6 **Hornsea** E R Yk
13 M7 **Holcombe** Devon	23 L2 **Holmshurst** E Susx	81 J7 **Hook Bank** Worcs	51 J1 **Hornsey** Gt Lon
31 L1 **Holcombe** Somset	169 G1 **Holmside** Dur	15 M2 **Hooke** Dorset	51 M7 **Horn's Green** Gt Lon
140 A5 **Holcombe Brook** Bury	166 C1 **Holmwrangle** Cumb	70 E7 **Hook End** Essex	41 G8 **Horn Street** Kent
29 J7 **Holcombe Rogus** Devon	7 K1 **Holne** Devon	114 A4 **Hookgate** Staffs	83 J6 **Hornton** Oxon
84 F1 **Holcot** Nhants	16 C1 **Holnest** Dorset	39 G6 **Hook Green** Kent	47 J2 **Horpit** Swindn
148 D6 **Holden** Lancs	29 G2 **Holnicote** Somset	52 D5 **Hook Green** Kent	281 e3 **Horra** Shet
84 D2 **Holdenby** Nhants	11 L2 **Holsworthy** Devon	83 H8 **Hook Norton** Oxon	7 G1 **Horrabridge** Devon
140 D3 **Holder Gate** Calder	11 L1 **Holsworthy Beacon** Devon	63 K7 **Hook Street** Gloucs	13 H7 **Horridge** Devon
70 F1 **Holder's Green** Essex	17 K2 **Holt** Dorset	47 G2 **Hook Street** Wilts	89 G3 **Horringer** Suffk
96 D5 **Holdgate** Shrops	122 B4 **Holt** Norfk	13 K3 **Hookway** Devon	19 J6 **Horringford** IoW
118 E2 **Holdingham** Lincs	46 B6 **Holt** Wilts	37 L2 **Hookwood** Surrey	139 L5 **Horrocks Fold** Bolton
15 H2 **Holditch** Dorset	81 J3 **Holt** Worcs	51 H7 **Hooley** Surrey	148 C1 **Horrocksford** Lancs
141 G2 **Holdsworth** Calder	112 F1 **Holt** Wrexhm	140 C5 **Hooley Bridge** Rochdl	27 J4 **Horsacott** Devon
12 A1 **Hole** Devon	151 L5 **Holtby** York	7 G2 **Hoo Meavy** Devon	12 A7 **Horsebridge** Devon
131 K1 **Holehouse** Derbys	82 C1 **Holt End** Worcs	53 G4 **Hoo St Werburgh** Medway	23 K5 **Horsebridge** E Susx
63 J2 **Hole-in-the-Wall** Herefs	81 J3 **Holt Fleet** Worcs	129 J4 **Hooton** Ches	34 D5 **Horsebridge** Hants
12 A1 **Holemoor** Devon	138 E6 **Holt Green** Lancs	133 K2 **Hooton Levitt** Rothm	95 J2 **Horsebridge** Shrops
21 K4 **Hole Street** W Susx	17 L2 **Holt Heath** Dorset	142 D6 **Hooton Pagnell** Donc	114 F1 **Horsebridge** Staffs
29 L3 **Holford** Somset	81 J3 **Holt Heath** Worcs	142 D8 **Hooton Roberts** Rothm	97 K1 **Horsebrook** Staffs
151 J5 **Holgate** York	66 F5 **Holton** Oxon	66 C2 **Hopcrofts Holt** Oxon	44 E5 **Horsecastle** N Som
156 E7 **Holker** Cumb	31 L5 **Holton** Somset	132 C3 **Hope** Derbys	3 G4 **Horsedown** Cnwll
121 K3 **Holkham** Norfk	107 H7 **Holton** Suffk	7 K6 **Hope** Devon	102 C2 **Horsegate** Lincs
11 M2 **Hollacombe** Devon	136 B3 **Holton cum Beckering**	129 G7 **Hope** Flints	96 F2 **Horsehay** Wrekin
119 H2 **Holland Fen** Lincs	Lincs	95 G2 **Hope** Powys	88 C5 **Horseheath** Cambs
139 G6 **Holland Lees** Lancs	17 J4 **Holton Heath** Dorset	95 H3 **Hope** Shrops	159 J6 **Horsehouse** N York
73 J4 **Holland-on-Sea** Essex	24 B2 **Holton Hill** E Susx	96 D8 **Hope** Shrops	50 C7 **Horsell** Surrey
275 f1 **Hollandstoun** Ork	145 H7 **Holton le Clay** Lincs	132 B8 **Hope** Staffs	113 G3 **Horseman's Green** Wrexhm
177 J5 **Hollee** D & G	144 D8 **Holton le Moor** Lincs	95 L5 **Hope Bowdler** Shrops	67 J6 **Horsenden** Bucks
91 H6 **Hollesley** Suffk	90 C7 **Holton St Mary** Suffk	70 E3 **Hope End Green** Essex	123 J7 **Horsey** Norfk
8 D2 **Hollicombe** Torbay	41 H5 **Holt Street** Kent	187 L3 **Hopehouse** Border	30 D3 **Horsey** Somset
39 L2 **Hollingbourne** Kent	38 C5 **Holtye** E Susx	266 C2 **Hopeman** Moray	123 J6 **Horsey Corner** Norfk
22 D5 **Hollingbury** Br & H	128 E4 **Holway** Flints	63 J3 **Hope Mansell** Herefs	122 D8 **Horsford** Norfk
67 L2 **Hollingdon** Bucks	32 B8 **Holwell** Dorset	95 J6 **Hopesay** Shrops	150 B8 **Horsforth** Leeds
142 B2 **Hollingthorpe** Leeds	86 D8 **Holwell** Herts	142 B3 **Hopetown** Wakefd	37 J5 **Horsham** W Susx
115 L4 **Hollington** Derbys	117 J6 **Holwell** Leics	80 C5 **Hope under Dinmore** Herefs	81 G4 **Horsham** Worcs
115 G4 **Hollington** Staffs	65 K5 **Holwell** Oxon	151 K5 **Hopgrove** York	122 E8 **Horsham St Faith** Norfk
140 F8 **Hollingworth** Tamesd	167 L5 **Holwick** Dur	150 F4 **Hopperton** N York	136 C6 **Horsington** Lincs
131 G3 **Hollinlane** Ches	16 E5 **Holworth** Dorset	102 D1 **Hop Pole** Lincs	32 B6 **Horsington** Somset
140 B6 **Hollins** Bury	35 M3 **Holybourne** Hants	99 L6 **Hopsford** Warwks	116 C3 **Horsley** Derbys
132 F5 **Hollins** Derbys	97 L7 **Holy Cross** Worcs	97 H4 **Hopstone** Shrops	64 B7 **Horsley** Gloucs
114 F2 **Hollins** Staffs	69 K6 **Holyfield** Essex	115 L1 **Hopton** Derbys	180 D5 **Horsley** Nthumb
131 L6 **Hollinsclough** Staffs	124 D3 **Holyhead** IoA	112 F7 **Hopton** Shrops	190 B6 **Horsley** Nthumb
133 H3 **Hollins End** Sheff	203 J5 **Holy Island** Nthumb	114 E6 **Hopton** Staffs	73 H2 **Horsley Cross** Essex
130 D2 **Hollins Green** Warrtn	133 G6 **Holymoorside** Derbys	105 K7 **Hopton** Suffk	73 G1 **Horsleycross Street** Essex
147 K5 **Hollins Lane** Lancs	49 L3 **Holyport** W & M	96 C7 **Hopton Cangeford** Shrops	132 F4 **Horsley-Gate** Derbys
96 F2 **Hollinswood** Wrekin	190 D5 **Holystone** Nthumb	95 J7 **Hopton Castle** Shrops	188 F2 **Horsleyhill** Border
113 H4 **Hollinwood** Shrops	209 K6 **Holytown** N Lans	95 J7 **Hoptonheath** Shrops	67 J8 **Horsley's Green** Bucks
24 C3 **Holllingrove** E Susx	68 C4 **Holywell** Beds	107 L3 **Hopton on Sea** Norfk	116 C3 **Horsley Woodhouse**
27 L8 **Hollocombe** Devon	87 G1 **Holywell** Cambs	96 E8 **Hopton Wafers** Shrops	Derbys
132 F8 **Holloway** Derbys	4 C3 **Holywell** Cnwll	98 F3 **Hopwas** Staffs	39 H5 **Horsmonden** Kent
51 J2 **Holloway** Gt Lon	16 B2 **Holywell** Dorset	140 C6 **Hopwood** Rochdl	66 E6 **Horspath** Oxon

122 F7 **Horstead** Norfk
22 F2 **Horsted Keynes** W Susx
68 A3 **Horton** Bucks
17 K1 **Horton** Dorset
148 E6 **Horton** Lancs
84 F4 **Horton** Nhants
45 M2 **Horton** S Glos
113 H5 **Horton** Shrops
30 D7 **Horton** Somset
131 J8 **Horton** Staffs
51 G6 **Horton** Surrey
56 E7 **Horton** Swans
50 C4 **Horton** W & M
46 F6 **Horton** Wilts
113 L8 **Horton** Wrekin
30 E7 **Horton Cross** Somset
66 F4 **Horton-cum-Studley** Oxon
113 G2 **Horton Green** Ches
35 G7 **Horton Heath** Hants
148 D2 **Horton in Ribblesdale** N York
52 C5 **Horton Kirby** Kent
139 J5 **Horwich** Bolton
131 K3 **Horwich End** Derbys
27 J5 **Horwood** Devon
138 F5 **Hoscar** Lancs
188 C4 **Hoscote** Border
117 J5 **Hose** Leics
51 M8 **Hosey Hill** Kent
220 E3 **Hosh** P & K
281 e8 **Hoswick** Shet
143 M1 **Hotham** E R Yk
40 C6 **Hothfield** Kent
116 F7 **Hoton** Leics
179 H2 **Hott** Nthumb
113 M1 **Hough** Ches
131 G4 **Hough** Ches
118 A3 **Hougham** Lincs
141 K1 **Hough End** Leeds
129 L2 **Hough Green** Halton
118 B2 **Hough-on-the-Hill** Lincs
86 F1 **Houghton** Cambs
177 L7 **Houghton** Cumb
34 D4 **Houghton** Hants
180 D5 **Houghton** Nthumb
55 G5 **Houghton** Pembks
21 H4 **Houghton** W Susx
85 L7 **Houghton Conquest** Beds
181 H8 **Houghton Gate** Dur
25 G3 **Houghton Green** E Susx
130 C1 **Houghton Green** Warrtn
169 G6 **Houghton le Side** Darltn
169 J1 **Houghton-le-Spring** Sundld
100 E3 **Houghton on the Hill** Leics
68 C2 **Houghton Regis** Beds
121 K4 **Houghton St Giles** Norfk
49 H7 **Hound Green** Hants
201 K4 **Houndslow** Border
29 L5 **Houndsmoor** Somset
213 J6 **Houndwood** Border
50 F4 **Hounslow** Gt Lon
71 G3 **Hounslow Green** Essex
253 G1 **Househill** Highld
141 K4 **Houses Hill** Kirk
257 G6 **Housieside** Abers
208 C5 **Houston** Rens
275 G1 **Houstry** Highld
275 b5 **Houton** Ork
22 D6 **Hove** Br & H
141 H3 **Hove Edge** Calder
117 J2 **Hoveringham** Notts
122 F7 **Hoveton** Norfk
161 L7 **Hovingham** N York
141 M8 **Howbrook** Barns
63 J1 **How Caple** Herefs
143 J2 **Howden** E R Yk
168 F4 **Howden-le-Wear** Dur
280 D4 **Howe** Highld
154 b8 **Howe** IoM
160 E6 **Howe** N York
106 F3 **Howe** Norfk
139 K7 **Howe Bridge** Wigan
71 H6 **Howe Green** Essex
71 K6 **Howegreen** Essex
118 F2 **Howell** Lincs
85 K7 **How End** Beds
268 E6 **Howe of Teuchar** Abers
177 G5 **Howes** D & G
71 G4 **Howe Street** Essex
88 D8 **Howe Street** Essex
78 E3 **Howey** Powys
164 C6 **Howgate** Cumb
211 H7 **Howgate** Mdloth
148 E6 **Howgill** Lancs
191 K3 **Howick** Nthumb
168 E5 **Howle** Dur
113 M6 **Howle** Wrekin
63 J3 **Howle Hill** Herefs

88 B8 **Howlett End** Essex
15 G1 **Howley** Somset
178 C7 **How Mill** Cumb
283 b10 **Howmore** W Isls
189 L2 **Hownam** Border
165 K1 **Howrigg** Cumb
144 D6 **Howsham** N Linc
151 M3 **Howsham** N York
202 D6 **Howtel** Nthumb
53 J6 **Howt Green** Kent
62 E1 **Howton** Herefs
166 B6 **Howtown** Cumb
208 C7 **Howwood** Rens
106 D7 **Hoxne** Suffk
128 F2 **Hoylake** Wirral
142 B7 **Hoyland Common** Barns
142 B7 **Hoyland Nether** Barns
141 L6 **Hoyland Swaine** Barns
20 E3 **Hoyle** W Susx
142 A6 **Hoyle Mill** Barns
159 G7 **Hubberholme** N York
54 E5 **Hubberston** Pembks
119 J3 **Hubbert's Bridge** Lincs
150 C6 **Huby** N York
151 J3 **Huby** N York
12 F7 **Huccaby** Devon
64 C4 **Hucclecote** Gloucs
53 H7 **Hucking** Kent
116 F2 **Hucknall** Notts
141 H4 **Huddersfield** Kirk
81 L4 **Huddington** Worcs
68 C4 **Hudnall** Herts
159 L3 **Hudswell** N York
152 D5 **Huggate** E R Yk
99 L1 **Hugglescote** Leics
67 L7 **Hughenden Valley** Bucks
96 D4 **Hughley** Shrops
10 c3 **Hugh Town** IoS
27 J8 **Huish** Devon
47 H6 **Huish** Wilts
29 J5 **Huish Champflower** Somset
31 G5 **Huish Episcopi** Somset
85 J7 **Hulcote** Beds
67 K4 **Hulcott** Bucks
14 B6 **Hulham** Devon
115 L2 **Hulland** Derbys
115 L2 **Hulland Ward** Derbys
46 C3 **Hullavington** Wilts
71 K8 **Hullbridge** Essex
140 C8 **Hulme** Manch
114 E2 **Hulme** Staffs
130 B2 **Hulme** Warrtn
132 B7 **Hulme End** Staffs
131 G6 **Hulme Walfield** Ches
130 E3 **Hulse Heath** Ches
139 K6 **Hulton Lane Ends** Bolton
18 F6 **Hulverstone** IoW
105 J1 **Hulver Street** Norfk
107 K6 **Hulver Street** Suffk
13 L7 **Humber** Devon
80 C4 **Humber** Herefs
145 J6 **Humberston** NE Lin
100 E2 **Humberstone** C Leic
150 F2 **Humberton** N York
212 A6 **Humbie** E Loth
145 G1 **Humbleton** E R Yk
202 F7 **Humbleton** Nthumb
118 D5 **Humby** Lincs
201 L5 **Hume** Border
179 L4 **Humshaugh** Nthumb
280 E2 **Huna** Highld
140 A2 **Huncoat** Lancs
100 B4 **Huncote** Leics
189 H3 **Hundalee** Border
133 H4 **Hundall** Derbys
168 C6 **Hunderthwaite** Dur
137 G6 **Hundleby** Lincs
119 H1 **Hundle Houses** Lincs
54 F6 **Hundleton** Pembks
88 E5 **Hundon** Suffk
138 E3 **Hundred End** Lancs
78 F4 **Hundred House** Powys
100 F2 **Hungarton** Leics
33 L8 **Hungerford** Hants
29 J3 **Hungerford** Somset
47 M5 **Hungerford** W Berk
47 M4 **Hungerford Newtown** W Berk
139 K6 **Hunger Hill** Bolton
139 G5 **Hunger Hill** Lancs
80 B8 **Hungerstone** Herefs
118 A5 **Hungerton** Lincs
113 L6 **Hungryhatton** Shrops
163 K7 **Hunmanby** N York
83 J2 **Hunningham** Warwks
98 B7 **Hunnington** Worcs
84 E4 **Hunsbury Hill** Nhants
69 L4 **Hunsdon** Herts

150 F5 **Hunsingore** N York
141 M2 **Hunslet** Leeds
166 D4 **Hunsonby** Cumb
120 E3 **Hunstanton** Norfk
168 B1 **Hunstanworth** Dur
113 M2 **Hunsterson** Ches
89 K2 **Hunston** Suffk
20 D6 **Hunston** W Susx
89 K2 **Hunston Green** Suffk
45 J6 **Hunstrete** BaNES
141 J2 **Hunsworth** Kirk
82 B2 **Hunt End** Worcs
28 B1 **Hunter's Inn** Devon
207 K3 **Hunter's Quay** Ag & B
30 E5 **Huntham** Somset
234 D1 **Hunthill Lodge** Angus
86 E1 **Huntingdon** Cambs
107 G8 **Huntingfield** Suffk
32 D5 **Huntingford** Dorset
129 K6 **Huntington** Ches
212 B4 **Huntington** E Loth
79 J4 **Huntington** Herefs
80 B6 **Huntington** Herefs
98 B1 **Huntington** Staffs
151 K4 **Huntington** York
63 L3 **Huntley** Gloucs
255 L4 **Huntly** Abers
35 G3 **Hunton** Hants
39 H3 **Hunton** Kent
160 B4 **Hunton** N York
68 D7 **Hunton Bridge** Herts
105 L5 **Hunt's Corner** Norfk
29 G2 **Huntscott** Somset
129 K3 **Hunt's Cross** Lpool
67 L6 **Hunts Green** Bucks
98 F4 **Hunts Green** Warwks
29 H6 **Huntsham** Devon
27 J6 **Huntshaw** Devon
27 J6 **Huntshaw Cross** Devon
30 D2 **Huntspill** Somset
30 C4 **Huntstile** Somset
30 D4 **Huntworth** Somset
168 F4 **Hunwick** Dur
122 B4 **Hunworth** Norfk
30 F7 **Hurcott** Somset
33 L4 **Hurdcott** Wilts
131 H5 **Hurdsfield** Ches
49 K2 **Hurley** W & M
99 H4 **Hurley** Warwks
49 K2 **Hurley Bottom** W & M
99 H4 **Hurley Common** Warwks
196 E4 **Hurlford** E Ayrs
138 E5 **Hurlston Green** Lancs
18 A4 **Hurn** Dorset
119 M2 **Hurn's End** Lincs
34 F6 **Hursley** Hants
16 F4 **Hurst** Dorset
159 J2 **Hurst** N York
31 G7 **Hurst** Somset
49 J4 **Hurst** Wokham
34 F2 **Hurstbourne Priors** Hants
48 A8 **Hurstbourne Tarrant** Hants
24 D2 **Hurst Green** E Susx
73 G4 **Hurst Green** Essex
148 B8 **Hurst Green** Lancs
51 K8 **Hurst Green** Surrey
97 L4 **Hurst Hill** Dudley
79 L5 **Hurstley** Herefs
22 D4 **Hurstpierpoint** W Susx
79 K5 **Hurstway Common** Herefs
22 D4 **Hurst Wickham** W Susx
140 C2 **Hurstwood** Lancs
275 d5 **Hurtiso** Ork
36 E2 **Hurtmore** Surrey
169 L4 **Hurworth Burn** Dur
169 J8 **Hurworth-on-Tees** Darltn
160 D1 **Hurworth Place** Darltn
168 B6 **Hury** Dur
100 E6 **Husbands Bosworth** Leics
85 J8 **Husborne Crawley** Beds
161 H7 **Husthwaite** N York
8 A5 **Hutcherleigh** Devon
142 F3 **Hut Green** N York
161 G2 **Huthwaite** N York
133 J7 **Huthwaite** Notts
137 K4 **Huttoft** Lincs
202 E2 **Hutton** Border
166 B5 **Hutton** Cumb
152 F1 **Hutton** E R Yk
70 F8 **Hutton** Essex
139 G2 **Hutton** Lancs
44 D7 **Hutton** N Som
160 E3 **Hutton Bonville** N York
163 H6 **Hutton Buscel** N York
160 D7 **Hutton Conyers** N York
153 G5 **Hutton Cranswick** E R Yk
166 B2 **Hutton End** Cumb
159 L5 **Hutton Hang** N York

169 L3 **Hutton Henry** Dur
162 B4 **Hutton-le-Hole** N York
170 E7 **Hutton Lowcross** R & Cl
168 E8 **Hutton Magna** Dur
162 E1 **Hutton Mulgrave** N York
157 J7 **Hutton Roof** Cumb
165 L4 **Hutton Roof** Cumb
161 G2 **Hutton Rudby** N York
161 G7 **Hutton Sessay** N York
151 H5 **Hutton Wandesley** N York
13 M3 **Huxham** Devon
31 K4 **Huxham Green** Somset
129 L7 **Huxley** Ches
129 K2 **Huyton** Knows
155 K5 **Hycemoor** Cumb
64 C6 **Hyde** Gloucs
33 L8 **Hyde** Hants
131 J1 **Hyde** Tamesd
49 H5 **Hyde End** Wokham
68 B7 **Hyde Heath** Bucks
114 E7 **Hyde Lea** Staffs
30 D4 **Hyde Park Corner** Somset
36 E3 **Hydestile** Surrey
135 J6 **Hykeham Moor** Lincs
198 F5 **Hyndford Bridge** S Lans
224 C7 **Hynish** Ag & B
95 H4 **Hyssington** Powys
63 K7 **Hystfield** Gloucs
19 G2 **Hythe** Hants
41 G8 **Hythe** Kent
44 F8 **Hythe** Somset
50 C4 **Hythe End** W & M
155 K5 **Hyton** Cumb

I

16 F1 **Ibberton** Dorset
132 E8 **Ible** Derbys
18 A2 **Ibsley** Hants
99 L2 **Ibstock** Leics
67 J8 **Ibstone** Bucks
48 A8 **Ibthorpe** Hants
162 F1 **Iburndale** N York
48 E7 **Ibworth** Hants
44 D6 **Icelton** N Som
105 G4 **Ickburgh** Norfk
50 D2 **Ickenham** Gt Lon
66 F5 **Ickford** Bucks
41 H4 **Ickham** Kent
68 F1 **Ickleford** Herts
24 F4 **Icklesham** E Susx
87 K6 **Ickleton** Cambs
88 F1 **Icklingham** Suffk
149 G1 **Ickornshaw** N York
86 C6 **Ickwell Green** Beds
65 J3 **Icomb** Gloucs
65 K3 **Idbury** Oxon
12 D1 **Iddesleigh** Devon
13 L4 **Ide** Devon
13 K7 **Ideford** Devon
38 D3 **Ide Hill** Kent
25 G3 **Iden** E Susx
39 J6 **Iden Green** Kent
39 K7 **Iden Green** Kent
149 M8 **Idle** Brad
4 D5 **Idless** Cnwll
83 G6 **Idlicote** Warwks
33 L3 **Idmiston** Wilts
58 D5 **Idole** Carmth
115 M2 **Idridgehay** Derbys
258 F4 **Idrigill** Highld
47 K2 **Idstone** Oxon
66 D6 **Iffley** Oxon
37 K3 **Ifield** W Susx
36 F4 **Ifold** W Susx
18 A5 **Iford** Bmouth
22 F5 **Iford** E Susx
44 F1 **Ifton** Mons
112 E4 **Ifton Heath** Shrops
113 K4 **Ightfield** Shrops
38 F2 **Ightham** Kent
91 J4 **Iken** Suffk
115 J2 **Ilam** Staffs
31 H6 **Ilchester** Somset
190 E2 **Ilderton** Nthumb
51 L2 **Ilford** Gt Lon
30 E7 **Ilford** Somset
27 J2 **Ilfracombe** Devon
116 D3 **Ilkeston** Derbys
107 H6 **Ilketshall St Andrew** Suffk
107 H6 **Ilketshall St John** Suffk
107 H6 **Ilketshall St Lawrence** Suffk
107 G6 **Ilketshall St Margaret** Suffk
149 K6 **Ilkley** Brad
11 K6 **Illand** Cnwll

98 B7 **Illey** Dudley
130 F7 **Illidge Green** Ches
141 G2 **Illingworth** Calder
3 H2 **Illogan** Cnwll
100 F3 **Illston on the Hill** Leics
67 J6 **Ilmer** Bucks
82 F6 **Ilmington** Warwks
30 E7 **Ilminster** Somset
13 H7 **Ilsington** Devon
16 E4 **Ilsington** Dorset
57 G6 **Ilston** Swans
160 B7 **Ilton** N York
30 E7 **Ilton** Somset
194 D3 **Imachar** N Ayrs
144 F5 **Immingham** NE Lin
145 G4 **Immingham Dock** NE Lin
87 J3 **Impington** Cambs
129 K4 **Ince** Ches
138 C7 **Ince Blundell** Sefton
139 J6 **Ince-in-Makerfield** Wigan
262 C6 **Inchbae Lodge Hotel** Highld
234 F2 **Inchbare** Angus
266 F5 **Inchberry** Moray
261 G7 **Incheril** Highld
208 L6 **Inchinnan** Rens
239 K3 **Inchlaggan** Highld
222 D2 **Inchmichael** P & K
240 C2 **Inchnacardoch Hotel** Highld
271 H4 **Inchnadamph** Highld
222 D2 **Inchture** P & K
249 L4 **Inchvuilt** Highld
222 C3 **Inchyra** P & K
4 E3 **Indian Queens** Cnwll
107 J5 **Ingate Place** Suffk
70 F7 **Ingatestone** Essex
141 K6 **Ingbirchworth** Barns
150 C3 **Ingerthorpe** N York
114 F6 **Ingestre** Staffs
135 J3 **Ingham** Lincs
123 H6 **Ingham** Norfk
89 G1 **Ingham** Suffk
123 H6 **Ingham Corner** Norfk
120 B8 **Ingleborough** Norfk
116 B6 **Ingleby** Derbys
161 G3 **Ingleby Arncliffe** N York
170 B7 **Ingleby Barwick** S on T
161 G3 **Ingleby Cross** N York
161 J2 **Ingleby Greenhow** N York
12 E1 **Ingleigh Green** Devon
45 L6 **Inglesbatch** BaNES
65 J7 **Inglesham** Swindn
176 C6 **Ingleston** D & G
168 F6 **Ingleton** Dur
158 B8 **Ingleton** N York
147 L7 **Inglewhite** Lancs
180 C4 **Ingoe** Nthumb
139 G1 **Ingol** Lancs
120 F5 **Ingoldisthorpe** Norfk
137 K6 **Ingoldmells** Lincs
118 D5 **Ingoldsby** Lincs
190 E3 **Ingram** Nthumb
52 D1 **Ingrave** Essex
149 J7 **Ingrow** Brad
157 G3 **Ings** Cumb
45 J3 **Ingst** S Glos
101 M2 **Ingthorpe** Rutlnd
122 D5 **Ingworth** Norfk
82 B4 **Inkberrow** Worcs
168 E3 **Inkerman** Dur
257 G4 **Inkhorn** Abers
48 A6 **Inkpen** W Berk
280 C2 **Inkstack** Highld
46 D6 **Innarsh** Wilts
207 J5 **Innellan** Ag & B
200 D6 **Innerleithen** Border
222 F7 **Innerleven** Fife
172 D2 **Innermessan** D & G
212 F4 **Innerwick** E Loth
266 F3 **Innesmill** Moray
256 A6 **Insch** Abers
241 L3 **Insh** Highld
147 J8 **Inskip** Lancs
147 J8 **Inskip Moss Side** Lancs
27 H5 **Instow** Devon
6 E4 **Insworke** Cnwll
133 H3 **Intake** Sheff
243 H5 **Inver** Abers
264 D3 **Inver** Highld
232 F7 **Inver** P & K
238 B7 **Inverailort** Highld
260 D8 **Inveralligin** Highld
269 J3 **Inverallochy** Abers
272 E8 **Inveran** Highld
217 H5 **Inveraray** Ag & B
247 H2 **Inverarish** Highld
234 C6 **Inverarity** Angus

218 D3 **Inverarnan** Stirlg
260 C3 **Inverasdale** Highld
217 G1 **Inverawe** Ag & B
218 E7 **Inverbeg** Ag & B
235 K1 **Inverbervie** Abers
268 B3 **Inver-boyndie** Abers
261 K3 **Inverbroom** Highld
229 G6 **Invercreran House Hotel** Ag & B
242 B1 **Inverdruie** Highld
211 K5 **Inveresk** E Loth
228 F8 **Inveresragan** Ag & B
242 E5 **Inverey** Abers
250 F7 **Inverfarigaig** Highld
228 E6 **Inverfolla** Ag & B
240 A3 **Invergarry** Highld
220 C2 **Invergeldie** P & K
239 L6 **Invergloy** Highld
263 J6 **Invergordon** Highld
222 F1 **Invergowrie** P & K
238 B2 **Inverguseran** Highld
231 J4 **Inverhadden** P & K
218 E2 **Inverherive Hotel** Stirlg
238 B3 **Inverie** Highld
216 F4 **Inverinan** Ag & B
248 E7 **Inverinate** Highld
235 G5 **Inverkeilor** Angus
210 F2 **Inverkeithing** Fife
268 A6 **Inverkeithny** Abers
207 K4 **Inverkip** Inver
270 E4 **Inverkirkaig** Highld
261 K3 **Inverlael** Highld
240 B7 **Inverlair** Highld
216 D6 **Inverliever Lodge** Ag & B
217 K2 **Inverlochy** Ag & B
244 A7 **Invermark** Angus
255 J4 **Invermarkie** Abers
250 D8 **Invermoriston** Highld
251 H3 **Inverness** Highld
217 J7 **Invernoaden** Ag & B
229 M7 **Inveroran Hotel** Ag & B
234 B4 **Inverquharity** Angus
257 J2 **Inverquhomery** Abers
239 M7 **Inverroy** Highld
228 E3 **Inversanda** Highld
248 F7 **Invershiel** Highld
272 E8 **Invershin** Highld
275 H1 **Invershore** Highld
218 E5 **Inversnaid Hotel** Stirlg
269 L6 **Inverugie** Abers
218 D5 **Inveruglas** Ag & B
241 L3 **Inveruglass** Highld
256 D7 **Inverurie** Abers
12 D3 **Inwardleigh** Devon
72 C3 **Inworth** Essex
283 b9 **Iochdar** W Isls
36 C6 **Iping** W Susx
8 B2 **Ipplepen** Devon
48 F2 **Ipsden** Oxon
115 G2 **Ipstones** Staffs
90 E6 **Ipswich** Suffk
128 F3 **Irby** Wirral
137 J7 **Irby in the Marsh** Lincs
145 G6 **Irby upon Humber** NE Lin
85 H2 **Irchester** Nhants
165 H3 **Ireby** Cumb
157 L7 **Ireby** Lancs
86 C7 **Ireland** Beds
156 B7 **Ireleth** Cumb
167 K3 **Ireshopeburn** Dur
115 M2 **Ireton Wood** Derbys
130 E1 **Irlam** Salfd
118 D6 **Irnham** Lincs
45 K2 **Iron Acton** S Glos
103 K4 **Iron Bridge** Cambs
96 F3 **Ironbridge** Wrekin
82 C5 **Iron Cross** Warwks
185 G7 **Ironmacannie** D & G
37 K2 **Irons Bottom** Surrey
116 A7 **Ironville** Derbys
123 H7 **Irstead** Norfk
178 C6 **Irthington** Cumb
85 J1 **Irthlingborough** Nhants
163 H6 **Irton** N York
196 C3 **Irvine** N Ayrs
279 G3 **Isauld** Highld
281 d3 **Isbister** Shet
281 f5 **Isbister** Shet
23 G4 **Isfield** E Susx
101 J8 **Isham** Nhants
36 B2 **Isington** Hants
97 K7 **Islandpool** Worcs
30 E6 **Isle Abbotts** Somset
30 E6 **Isle Brewers** Somset
104 C8 **Isleham** Cambs
51 K3 **Isle of Dogs** Gt Lon
174 D7 **Isle of Whithorn** D & G
247 L6 **Isleornsay** Highld

176 C4 **Islesteps** D & G
9 k2 **Islet Village** Guern
50 F2 **Isleworth** Gt Lon
116 C6 **Isley Walton** Leics
282 d3 **Islibhig** W Isls
51 J2 **Islington** Gt Lon
101 L7 **Islip** Nhants
66 D4 **Islip** Oxon
282 d3 **Islivig** W Isls
96 E1 **Isombridge** Wrekin
52 E1 **Istead Rise** Kent
35 H4 **Itchen Abbas** Hants
35 H4 **Itchen Stoke** Hants
37 H5 **Itchingfield** W Susx
45 K2 **Itchington** S Glos
122 C5 **Itteringham** Norfk
12 F3 **Itton** Devon
62 F8 **Itton** Mons
165 M2 **Ivegill** Cumb
159 G3 **Ivelet** N York
50 D3 **Iver** Bucks
50 C2 **Iver Heath** Bucks
168 C1 **Iveston** Dur
68 B4 **Ivinghoe** Bucks
68 B3 **Ivinghoe Aston** Bucks
80 B4 **Ivington** Herefs
80 B4 **Ivington Green** Herefs
7 J4 **Ivybridge** Devon
25 J2 **Ivychurch** Kent
32 E6 **Ivy Cross** Dorset
38 F3 **Ivy Hatch** Kent
105 H2 **Ivy Todd** Norfk
40 A2 **Iwade** Kent
32 E8 **Iwerne Courtney or Shroton** Dorset
32 E8 **Iwerne Minster** Dorset
89 J1 **Ixworth** Suffk
89 J1 **Ixworth Thorpe** Suffk

J

139 J3 **Jack Green** Lancs
150 B5 **Jack Hill** N York
14 B3 **Jack-in-the-Green** Devon
34 C3 **Jack's Bush** Hants
116 D1 **Jacksdale** Notts
141 J6 **Jackson Bridge** Kirk
209 G8 **Jackton** S Lans
11 H3 **Jacobstow** Cnwll
12 E2 **Jacobstowe** Devon
50 C8 **Jacobs Well** Surrey
55 H7 **Jameston** Pembks
262 E8 **Jamestown** Highld
208 C3 **Jamestown** W Duns
275 K2 **Janetstown** Highld
280 D6 **Janets-town** Highld
176 E1 **Jardine Hall** D & G
181 H6 **Jarrow** Tyne
38 E7 **Jarvis Brook** E Susx
71 H2 **Jasper's Green** Essex
209 M4 **Jawcraig** Falk
73 H4 **Jaywick** Essex
49 L4 **Jealott's Hill** Br For
160 F4 **Jeater Houses** N York
189 H2 **Jedburgh** Border
55 J5 **Jeffreyston** Pembks
263 K7 **Jemimaville** Highld
9 k4 **Jerbourg** Guern
57 K6 **Jersey Marine** Neath
135 J5 **Jerusalem** Lincs
181 G5 **Jesmond** N u Ty
23 J7 **Jevington** E Susx
62 F5 **Jingle Street** Mons
68 D4 **Jockey End** Herts
130 F5 **Jodrell Bank** Ches
166 B4 **Johnby** Cumb
280 E2 **John o' Groats** Highld
24 D3 **John's Cross** E Susx
235 K2 **Johnshaven** Abers
123 H8 **Johnson's Street** Norfk
54 F5 **Johnston** Pembks
187 K6 **Johnstone** D & G
208 D6 **Johnstone** Rens
187 G7 **Johnstonebridge** D & G
58 D5 **Johnstown** Carmth
112 D2 **Johnstown** Wrexhm
211 K4 **Joppa** C Edin
77 G2 **Joppa** Cerdgn
196 E7 **Joppa** S Ayrs
50 B1 **Jordans** Bucks
74 F5 **Jordanston** Pembks
133 G3 **Jordanthorpe** Sheff
52 B4 **Joyden's Wood** Kent
39 L4 **Jubilee Corner** Kent
142 B7 **Jump** Barns
38 C6 **Jumper's Town** E Susx
179 L7 **Juniper** Nthumb

211 G5 **Juniper Green** C Edin
154 e3 **Jurby** IoM
13 G5 **Jurston** Devon

K

167 J8 **Kaber** Cumb
199 G4 **Kaimend** S Lans
206 F5 **Kames** Ag & B
197 K5 **Kames** E Ayrs
4 C6 **Kea** Cnwll
143 L5 **Keadby** N Linc
137 G2 **Keal Cotes** Lincs
150 E6 **Kearby Town End** N York
139 M6 **Kearsley** Bolton
180 B4 **Kearsley** Nthumb
41 J6 **Kearsney** Kent
157 K6 **Kearstwick** Cumb
159 H3 **Kearton** N York
148 C3 **Keasden** N York
7 J4 **Keaton** Devon
130 B3 **Keckwick** Halton
136 F2 **Keddington** Lincs
137 G2 **Keddington Corner** Lincs
88 E6 **Kedington** Suffk
116 A3 **Kedleston** Derbys
144 F5 **Keelby** Lincs
114 C3 **Keele** Staffs
114 C3 **Keele University** Staffs
85 K6 **Keeley Green** Beds
141 G1 **Keelham** Brad
54 E3 **Keeston** Pembks
46 D7 **Keevil** Wilts
116 E6 **Kegworth** Leics
3 G3 **Kehelland** Cnwll
256 A7 **Keig** Abers
149 J7 **Keighley** Brad
220 F8 **Keilarsbrae** Clacks
221 H2 **Keillour** P & K
243 G5 **Keiloch** Abers
205 H3 **Keils** Ag & B
31 J1 **Keinton Mandeville** Somset
186 C7 **Keir Mill** D & G
179 H8 **Keirsleywell Row** Nthumb
118 D6 **Keisby** Lincs
167 G6 **Keisley** Cumb
280 D4 **Keiss** Highld
267 J6 **Keith** Moray
233 J7 **Keithick** P & K
234 F3 **Keithock** Angus
262 F8 **Keithtown** Highld
148 F7 **Kelbrook** Lancs
207 L7 **Kelburn** N Ayrs
118 D3 **Kelby** Lincs
166 D7 **Keld** Cumb
158 F3 **Keld** N York
162 D5 **Keld Head** N York
162 C5 **Keldholme** N York
143 L7 **Kelfield** N Linc
151 J8 **Kelfield** N York
134 F8 **Kelham** Notts
176 F5 **Kelhead** D & G
12 A5 **Kellacott** Devon
138 E2 **Kellamergh** Lancs
234 C8 **Kellas** Angus
266 D5 **Kellas** Moray
8 B7 **Kellaton** Devon
157 L2 **Kelleth** Cumb
122 B3 **Kelling** Norfk
142 E3 **Kellington** N York
169 K3 **Kelloe** Dur
185 J1 **Kelloholm** D & G
164 C7 **Kells** Cumb
11 M6 **Kelly** Devon
11 L8 **Kelly Bray** Cnwll
101 G7 **Kelmarsh** Nhants
65 K7 **Kelmscott** Oxon
91 J2 **Kelsale** Suffk
129 M6 **Kelsall** Ches
87 G7 **Kelshall** Herts
165 G1 **Kelsick** Cumb
201 M6 **Kelso** Border
133 G7 **Kelstedge** Derbys
136 D2 **Kelstern** Lincs
129 G5 **Kelsterton** Flints
45 K5 **Kelston** BaNES
231 L5 **Keltneyburn** P & K
176 C5 **Kelton** D & G
221 L8 **Kelty** Fife
72 C3 **Kelvedon** Essex
70 E7 **Kelvedon Hatch** Essex
2 B5 **Kelynack** Cnwll
28 B2 **Kemacott** Devon
223 G4 **Kemback** Fife
97 G3 **Kemberton** Shrops
64 E7 **Kemble** Gloucs
64 E7 **Kemble Wick** Gloucs

81 L7 **Kemerton** Worcs
62 D6 **Kemeys Commander** Mons
256 D8 **Kemnay** Abers
40 D6 **Kempe's Corner** Kent
63 K1 **Kempley** Gloucs
63 K1 **Kempley Green** Gloucs
81 J5 **Kempsey** Worcs
65 H7 **Kempsford** Gloucs
82 D1 **Kemps Green** Warwks
35 J1 **Kempshott** Hants
85 K5 **Kempston** Beds
85 K6 **Kempston Hardwick** Beds
95 J6 **Kempton** Shrops
22 E6 **Kemp Town** Br & H
52 C7 **Kemsing** Kent
40 B2 **Kemsley** Kent
53 H6 **Kemsley Street** Kent
25 H1 **Kenardington** Kent
80 B6 **Kenchester** Herefs
65 K6 **Kencot** Oxon
157 H4 **Kendal** Cumb
62 E2 **Kenderchurch** Herefs
45 K3 **Kendleshire** S Glos
42 B5 **Kenfig** Brdgnd
42 C5 **Kenfig Hill** Brdgnd
83 G1 **Kenilworth** Warwks
51 J7 **Kenley** Gt Lon
96 D3 **Kenley** Shrops
260 B8 **Kenmore** Highld
231 L6 **Kenmore** P & K
13 L5 **Kenn** Devon
44 E5 **Kenn** N Som
206 C6 **Kennacraig** Ag & B
11 K6 **Kennards House** Cnwll
2 F5 **Kenneggy** Cnwll
13 J1 **Kennerleigh** Devon
138 D7 **Kennessee Green** Sefton
210 B1 **Kennet** Clacks
255 L6 **Kennethmont** Abers
88 D2 **Kennett** Cambs
13 L5 **Kennford** Devon
105 L6 **Kenninghall** Norfk
40 D6 **Kennington** Kent
66 D6 **Kennington** Oxon
222 F6 **Kennoway** Fife
30 D7 **Kenny** Somset
104 D7 **Kennyhill** Suffk
152 B3 **Kennythorpe** N York
224 C6 **Kenovay** Ag & B
259 G6 **Kensaleyre** Highld
51 H3 **Kensington** Gt Lon
68 C3 **Kensworth Common** Beds
228 F4 **Kentallen** Highld
62 E2 **Kentchurch** Herefs
88 E2 **Kentford** Suffk
131 G8 **Kent Green** Ches
14 C1 **Kentisbeare** Devon
27 L2 **Kentisbury** Devon
27 L2 **Kentisbury Ford** Devon
51 H2 **Kentish Town** Gt Lon
157 G2 **Kentmere** Cumb
13 M6 **Kenton** Devon
50 F1 **Kenton** Gt Lon
180 F5 **Kenton** N u Ty
90 E2 **Kenton** Suffk
180 F5 **Kenton Bankfoot** N u Ty
237 J6 **Kentra** Highld
156 F7 **Kents Bank** Cumb
63 L2 **Kent's Green** Gloucs
34 D6 **Kent's Oak** Hants
24 E4 **Kent Street** E Susx
39 G2 **Kent Street** Kent
112 F5 **Kenwick** Shrops
4 D5 **Kenwyn** Cnwll
139 J8 **Kenyon** Warrtn
276 F3 **Keoldale** Highld
248 E6 **Keppoch** Highld
161 G4 **Kepwick** N York
99 J6 **Keresley** Covtry
130 F6 **Kermincham** Ches
8 B6 **Kernborough** Devon
63 H3 **Kerne Bridge** Herefs
131 J4 **Kerridge** Ches
131 J4 **Kerridge-end** Ches
2 C5 **Kerris** Cnwll
94 E5 **Kerry** Powys
207 J6 **Kerrycroy** Ag & B
134 E7 **Kersall** Notts
14 C6 **Kersbrook** Devon
27 L5 **Kerscott** Devon
89 K6 **Kersey** Suffk
89 K6 **Kersey Tye** Suffk
89 K6 **Kersey Upland** Suffk
282 f4 **Kershader** W Isls
178 B2 **Kershopefoot** Cumb
82 A7 **Kersoe** Worcs
14 C1 **Kerswell** Devon

81 K6 **Kerswell Green** Worcs
2 F4 **Kerthen Wood** Cnwll
90 F6 **Kesgrave** Suffk
107 L6 **Kessingland** Suffk
107 L6 **Kessingland Beach** Suffk
5 G5 **Kestle** Cnwll
4 D3 **Kestle Mill** Cnwll
51 L6 **Keston** Gt Lon
165 J6 **Keswick** Cumb
106 E2 **Keswick** Norfk
137 G4 **Ketsby** Lincs
101 J7 **Kettering** Nhants
106 D3 **Ketteringham** Norfk
233 K7 **Kettins** P & K
89 K5 **Kettlebaston** Suffk
222 E5 **Kettlebridge** Fife
99 G3 **Kettlebrook** Staffs
91 G3 **Kettleburgh** Suffk
69 L3 **Kettle Green** Herts
176 F3 **Kettleholm** D & G
171 J7 **Kettleness** N York
131 K4 **Kettleshulme** Ches
150 B4 **Kettlesing** N York
150 B4 **Kettlesing Bottom** N York
121 L5 **Kettlestone** Norfk
135 G4 **Kettlethorpe** Lincs
275 e2 **Kettletoft** Ork
149 H2 **Kettlewell** N York
101 L3 **Ketton** Rutlnd
50 F4 **Kew** Gt Lon
44 C6 **Kewstoke** N Som
141 M6 **Kexbrough** Barns
135 H3 **Kexby** Lincs
151 L5 **Kexby** York
131 H7 **Key Green** Ches
162 D2 **Key Green** N York
100 E2 **Keyham** Leics
18 D5 **Keyhaven** Hants
145 H3 **Keyingham** E R Yk
22 D4 **Keymer** W Susx
45 K5 **Keynsham** BaNES
86 B3 **Keysoe** Beds
86 B3 **Keysoe Row** Beds
102 A8 **Keyston** Cambs
53 J6 **Key Street** Kent
117 G5 **Keyworth** Notts
30 B6 **Kibbear** Somset
181 G7 **Kibblesworth** Gatesd
100 F4 **Kibworth Beauchamp** Leics
100 F4 **Kibworth Harcourt** Leics
51 L4 **Kidbrooke** Gt Lon
164 E6 **Kidburngill** Cumb
97 J2 **Kiddemore Green** Staffs
97 J8 **Kidderminster** Worcs
66 B3 **Kiddington** Oxon
106 C3 **Kidd's Moor** Norfk
66 D4 **Kidlington** Oxon
49 G3 **Kidmore End** Oxon
174 C7 **Kidsdale** D & G
131 G8 **Kidsgrove** Staffs
159 G6 **Kidstones** N York
56 D3 **Kidwelly** Carmth
228 D7 **Kiel Crofts** Ag & B
189 H7 **Kielder** Nthumb
204 F3 **Kiells** Ag & B
208 C6 **Kilbarchan** Rens
247 K7 **Kilbeg** Highld
206 A6 **Kilberry** Ag & B
208 A8 **Kilbirnie** N Ayrs
207 G5 **Kilbride** Ag & B
215 L8 **Kilbride** Ag & B
216 C2 **Kilbride** Ag & B
266 B4 **Kilbuiack** Moray
116 C2 **Kilburn** Derbys
51 H2 **Kilburn** Gt Lon
161 H6 **Kilburn** N York
100 D4 **Kilby** Leics
206 C6 **Kilchamaig** Ag & B
207 H8 **Kilchattan** Ag & B
214 D5 **Kilchattan** Ag & B
228 C7 **Kilcheran** Ag & B
236 F7 **Kilchoan** Highld
204 B4 **Kilchoman** Ag & B
217 G3 **Kilchrenan** Ag & B
223 H6 **Kilconquhar** Fife
63 K2 **Kilcot** Gloucs
251 G2 **Kilcoy** Highld
207 L3 **Kilcreggan** Ag & B
161 K1 **Kildale** N York
192 F4 **Kildalloig** Ag & B
263 K5 **Kildary** Highld
206 F6 **Kildavaig** Ag & B
207 G5 **Kildavanan** Ag & B
274 B4 **Kildonan** Highld
195 G6 **Kildonan** N Ayrs
274 B4 **Kildonan Lodge** Highld
236 F3 **Kildonnan** Highld

172 D4 **Kildrochet House** D & G
255 J8 **Kildrummy** Abers
149 H6 **Kildwick** N York
206 E3 **Kilfinan** Ag & B
239 M4 **Kilfinnan** Highld
128 C6 **Kilford** Denbgs
55 K5 **Kilgetty** Pembks
183 G3 **Kilgrammie** S Ayrs
62 F7 **Kilgwrrwg Common** Mons
153 G3 **Kilham** E R Yk
202 D6 **Kilham** Nthumb
224 B6 **Kilkenneth** Ag & B
192 D3 **Kilkenzie** Ag & B
192 E4 **Kilkerran** Ag & B
26 D8 **Kilkhampton** Cnwll
133 J3 **Killamarsh** Derbys
57 H6 **Killay** Swans
208 E2 **Killearn** Stirlg
263 J8 **Killen** Highld
169 G6 **Killerby** Darltn
14 A2 **Killerton** Devon
231 G4 **Killichonan** P & K
239 L7 **Killiechonate** Highld
227 G4 **Killiechronan** Ag & B
232 D3 **Killiecrankie** P & K
248 F5 **Killilan** Highld
231 G8 **Killin** Stirlg
150 C4 **Killinghall** N York
157 K5 **Killington** Cumb
28 B2 **Killington** Devon
181 G5 **Killingworth** N Tyne
4 C6 **Killiow** Cnwll
200 F4 **Killochyett** Border
208 B5 **Kilmacolm** Inver
219 K5 **Kilmahog** Stirlg
216 B8 **Kilmahumaig** Ag & B
259 G2 **Kilmaluag** Highld
222 F3 **Kilmany** Fife
196 E3 **Kilmarnock** E Ayrs
216 C7 **Kilmartin** Ag & B
196 E3 **Kilmaurs** E Ayrs
216 C4 **Kilmelford** Ag & B
45 K8 **Kilmersdon** Somset
35 J5 **Kilmeston** Hants
192 E4 **Kilmichael** Ag & B
216 D8 **Kilmichael Glassary** Ag & B
206 B2 **Kilmichael of Inverlussa** Ag & B
15 G3 **Kilmington** Devon
32 C3 **Kilmington** Wilts
32 C4 **Kilmington Common** Wilts
32 C4 **Kilmington Street** Wilts
250 E3 **Kilmorack** Highld
216 D2 **Kilmore** Ag & B
247 K7 **Kilmore** Highld
205 M2 **Kilmory** Ag & B
237 G6 **Kilmory** Highld
193 K4 **Kilmory** N Ayrs
251 J2 **Kilmuir** Highld
258 D7 **Kilmuir** Highld
258 F3 **Kilmuir** Highld
263 K5 **Kilmuir** Highld
207 K3 **Kilmun** Ag & B
204 D2 **Kilnave** Ag & B
198 E3 **Kilncadzow** S Lans
39 H6 **Kilndown** Kent
49 K3 **Kiln Green** Wokham
165 H4 **Kilnhill** Cumb
130 C6 **Kilnhouses** Ches
142 C8 **Kilnhurst** Rothm
216 C3 **Kilninver** Ag & B
180 C7 **Kiln Pit Hill** Nthumb
145 L4 **Kilnsea** E R Yk
149 H2 **Kilnsey** N York
152 F6 **Kilnwick** E R Yk
152 C6 **Kilnwick Percy** E R Yk
214 D5 **Kiloran** Ag & B
194 D5 **Kilpatrick** N Ayrs
62 F1 **Kilpeck** Herefs
143 K2 **Kilpin** E R Yk
143 J2 **Kilpin Pike** E R Yk
223 K6 **Kilrenny** Fife
84 A1 **Kilsby** Nhants
222 C2 **Kilspindie** P & K
172 E7 **Kilstay** D & G
209 J3 **Kilsyth** N Lans
250 E3 **Kiltarlity** Highld
171 G7 **Kilton** R & Cl
171 G7 **Kilton Thorpe** R & Cl
258 F3 **Kilvaxter** Highld
29 L2 **Kilve** Somset
117 L3 **Kilvington** Notts
196 B2 **Kilwinning** N Ayrs
106 B3 **Kimberley** Norfk
116 E3 **Kimberley** Notts
133 H1 **Kimberworth** Rothm
169 H1 **Kimblesworth** Dur
67 J5 **Kimble Wick** Bucks

86 B2 **Kimbolton** Cambs
80 C3 **Kimbolton** Herefs
100 D6 **Kimcote** Leics
17 H6 **Kimmeridge** Dorset
202 E6 **Kimmerston** Nthumb
34 C2 **Kimpton** Hants
68 F3 **Kimpton** Herts
26 E8 **Kimworthy** Devon
273 L2 **Kinbrace** Highld
220 D6 **Kinbuck** Stirlg
223 H3 **Kincaple** Fife
210 B2 **Kincardine** Fife
263 G2 **Kincardine** Highld
244 D4 **Kincardine O'Neil** Abers
233 H7 **Kinclaven** P & K
245 L3 **Kincorth** C Aber
265 G7 **Kincorth House** Moray
241 M2 **Kincraig** Highld
232 E5 **Kincraigie** P & K
232 E5 **Kindallachan** P & K
205 L5 **Kinerarach** Ag & B
65 G2 **Kineton** Gloucs
83 H5 **Kineton** Warwks
222 B3 **Kinfauns** P & K
207 H7 **Kingarth** Ag & B
245 J3 **Kingcausie** Abers
62 E6 **Kingcoed** Mons
135 L1 **Kingerby** Lincs
11 K1 **Kingford** Devon
65 K2 **Kingham** Oxon
176 C4 **Kingholm Quay** D & G
211 J2 **Kinghorn** Fife
222 C7 **Kinglassie** Fife
233 M4 **Kingoldrum** Angus
222 F1 **Kingoodie** P & K
80 B7 **King's Acre** Herefs
6 E5 **Kingsand** Cnwll
67 L6 **Kingsash** Bucks
223 K5 **Kingsbarns** Fife
7 L6 **Kingsbridge** Devon
29 H3 **Kingsbridge** Somset
57 G5 **Kings Bridge** Swans
115 J8 **King's Bromley** Staffs
258 F5 **Kingsburgh** Highld
51 G1 **Kingsbury** Gt Lon
99 G4 **Kingsbury** Warwks
31 G6 **Kingsbury Episcopi** Somset
63 H2 **Kings Caple** Herefs
48 D7 **Kingsclere** Hants
101 M4 **King's Cliffe** Nhants
64 B7 **Kingscote** Gloucs
27 K7 **Kingscott** Devon
82 C3 **King's Coughton** Warwks
195 G5 **Kingscross** N Ayrs
31 H5 **Kingsdon** Somset
41 L5 **Kingsdown** Kent
47 H1 **Kingsdown** Swindn
46 A5 **Kingsdown** Wilts
210 F1 **Kingseat** Fife
67 H6 **Kingsey** Bucks
37 J4 **Kingsfold** W Susx
245 J2 **Kingsford** C Aber
196 E2 **Kingsford** E Ayrs
97 J7 **Kingsford** Worcs
41 L1 **Kingsgate** Kent
81 H8 **Kings Green** Gloucs
89 J3 **Kingshall Street** Suffk
27 K3 **Kingsheanton** Devon
98 D7 **King's Heath** Birm
39 H2 **Kings Hill** Kent
98 C4 **Kings Hill** Wsall
229 L4 **Kings House Hotel** Highld
219 J3 **Kingshouse Hotel** Stirlg
98 F5 **Kingshurst** Solhll
177 G8 **Kingside Hill** Cumb
8 C1 **Kingskerswell** Devon
222 E5 **Kingskettle** Fife
15 K3 **Kingsland** Dorset
80 B3 **Kingsland** Herefs
124 D3 **Kingsland** IoA
68 D6 **Kings Langley** Herts
130 A5 **Kingsley** Ches
36 B3 **Kingsley** Hants
115 G2 **Kingsley** Staffs
36 D5 **Kingsley Green** W Susx
84 E3 **Kingsley Park** Nhants
97 H4 **Kingslow** Shrops
120 D7 **King's Lynn** Norfk
166 E6 **Kings Meaburn** Cumb
35 J8 **Kingsmead** Hants
9 i3 **King's Mills** Guern
139 G7 **King's Moss** St Hel
234 D5 **Kingsmuir** Angus
200 B5 **Kings Muir** Border
223 J5 **Kingsmuir** Fife
99 M7 **Kings Newnham** Warwks
116 C6 **King's Newton** Derbys
40 C7 **Kingsnorth** Kent

98 D7 **King's Norton** Birm
100 F3 **King's Norton** Leics
28 B7 **King's Nympton** Devon
80 B5 **King's Pyon** Herefs
102 F8 **Kings Ripton** Cambs
34 D4 **King's Somborne** Hants
32 B8 **King's Stag** Dorset
64 A6 **King's Stanley** Gloucs
83 L8 **King's Sutton** Nhants
98 D4 **Kingstanding** Birm
13 K7 **Kingsteignton** Devon
132 B5 **King Sterndale** Derbys
63 G1 **Kingsthorne** Herefs
84 E3 **Kingsthorpe** Nhants
87 G4 **Kingston** Cambs
11 L7 **Kingston** Cnwll
7 J5 **Kingston** Devon
14 C5 **Kingston** Devon
16 E1 **Kingston** Dorset
17 J6 **Kingston** Dorset
212 C3 **Kingston** E Loth
18 A3 **Kingston** Hants
19 H7 **Kingston** IoW
41 G5 **Kingston** Kent
21 J6 **Kingston** W Susx
66 B7 **Kingston Bagpuize** Oxon
67 H7 **Kingston Blount** Oxon
32 D3 **Kingston Deverill** Wilts
80 A8 **Kingstone** Herefs
30 E8 **Kingstone** Somset
115 H5 **Kingstone** Staffs
47 K2 **Kingstone Winslow** Oxon
47 L2 **Kingston Lisle** Oxon
22 F5 **Kingston near Lewes** E Susx
116 E6 **Kingston on Soar** Notts
267 G3 **Kingston on Spey** Moray
16 A4 **Kingston Russell** Dorset
30 B5 **Kingston St Mary** Somset
44 E5 **Kingston Seymour** N Som
67 H7 **Kingston Stert** Oxon
144 D2 **Kingston upon Hull** C KuH
50 F5 **Kingston upon Thames** Gt Lon
177 L7 **Kingstown** Cumb
68 F2 **King's Walden** Herts
8 C4 **Kingswear** Devon
245 J2 **Kingswells** C Aber
45 G3 **Kings Weston** Bristl
97 K5 **Kingswinford** Dudley
67 G3 **Kingswood** Bucks
63 L8 **Kingswood** Gloucs
39 L3 **Kingswood** Kent
94 F3 **Kingswood** Powys
45 J4 **Kingswood** S Glos
29 K3 **Kingswood** Somset
51 H7 **Kingswood** Surrey
82 E1 **Kingswood** Warwks
82 E1 **Kingswood Brook** Warwks
79 K4 **Kingswood Common** Herefs
97 J3 **Kingswood Common** Staffs
35 G4 **Kings Worthy** Hants
136 B4 **Kingthorpe** Lincs
79 K4 **Kington** Herefs
45 J1 **Kington** S Glos
82 A4 **Kington** Worcs
46 D3 **Kington Langley** Wilts
32 C6 **Kington Magna** Dorset
46 C3 **Kington St Michael** Wilts
241 K3 **Kingussie** Highld
31 H5 **Kingweston** Somset
257 G3 **Kinharrachie** Abers
176 B5 **Kinharvie** D & G
221 G4 **Kinkell Bridge** P & K
257 J3 **Kinknockie** Abers
211 G5 **Kinleith** C Edin
97 G7 **Kinlet** Shrops
246 E8 **Kinloch** Highld
271 K1 **Kinloch** Highld
277 J5 **Kinloch** Highld
233 H6 **Kinloch** P & K
233 L6 **Kinloch** P & K
219 G6 **Kinlochard** Stirlg
276 C5 **Kinlochbervie** Highld
238 F7 **Kinlocheil** Highld
261 G7 **Kinlochewe** Highld
238 F2 **Kinloch Hourn** Highld
240 F5 **Kinlochlaggan** Highld
229 K3 **Kinlochleven** Highld
237 K6 **Kinlochmoidart** Highld
237 L4 **Kinlochnanuagh** Highld
231 J4 **Kinloch Rannoch** P & K
265 H7 **Kinloss** Moray
127 K4 **Kinmel Bay** Conwy
256 E7 **Kinmuck** Abers
256 F8 **Kinmundy** Abers

204 D7 **Kinnabus** Ag & B
257 H3 **Kinnadie** Abers
232 E4 **Kinnaird** P & K
235 G4 **Kinnaird Castle** Angus
266 E2 **Kinneddar** Moray
245 J8 **Kinneff** Abers
186 F6 **Kinnelhead** D & G
234 F5 **Kinnell** Angus
112 E7 **Kinnerley** Shrops
79 L5 **Kinnersley** Herefs
81 K6 **Kinnersley** Worcs
79 J3 **Kinnerton** Powys
95 J4 **Kinnerton** Shrops
129 H7 **Kinnerton Green** Flints
222 B6 **Kinnesswood** P & K
168 D6 **Kinninvie** Dur
234 B4 **Kinnordy** Angus
117 H5 **Kinoulton** Notts
221 K6 **Kinross** P & K
222 C1 **Kinrossie** P & K
68 E4 **Kinsbourne Green** Herts
113 L3 **Kinsey Heath** Ches
79 L2 **Kinsham** Herefs
81 L8 **Kinsham** Worcs
142 C5 **Kinsley** Wakefd
17 L3 **Kinson** Bmouth
48 A5 **Kintbury** W Berk
264 F7 **Kintessack** Moray
221 L4 **Kintillo** P & K
95 K8 **Kinton** Herefs
112 E7 **Kinton** Shrops
256 E8 **Kintore** Abers
205 G6 **Kintour** Ag & B
226 C7 **Kintra** Ag & B
216 C6 **Kintraw** Ag & B
253 G7 **Kinveachy** Highld
97 J6 **Kinver** Staffs
160 C3 **Kiplin** N York
142 C2 **Kippax** Leeds
219 L8 **Kippen** Stirlg
175 L4 **Kippford or Scaur** D & G
39 G5 **Kipping's Cross** Kent
275 c5 **Kirbister** Ork
106 F2 **Kirby Bedon** Norfk
117 J7 **Kirby Bellars** Leics
107 H4 **Kirby Cane** Norfk
99 J8 **Kirby Corner** Covtry
73 J3 **Kirby Cross** Essex
100 B3 **Kirby Fields** Leics
152 D2 **Kirby Grindalythe** N York
150 E2 **Kirby Hill** N York
159 L2 **Kirby Hill** N York
161 G5 **Kirby Knowle** N York
73 J3 **Kirby le Soken** Essex
162 D6 **Kirby Misperton** N York
100 B3 **Kirby Muxloe** Leics
107 H5 **Kirby Row** Norfk
160 F4 **Kirby Sigston** N York
152 B4 **Kirby Underdale** E R Yk
160 E5 **Kirby Wiske** N York
36 F5 **Kirdford** W Susx
280 C4 **Kirk** Highld
281 e7 **Kirkabister** Shet
174 F5 **Kirkandrews** D & G
177 K7 **Kirkandrews upon Eden** Cumb
177 J7 **Kirkbampton** Cumb
176 C7 **Kirkbean** D & G
143 G5 **Kirk Bramwith** Donc
177 H7 **Kirkbride** Cumb
160 C4 **Kirkbridge** N York
234 D6 **Kirkbuddo** Angus
200 C5 **Kirkburn** Border
152 F5 **Kirkburn** E R Yk
141 K5 **Kirkburton** Kirk
138 E7 **Kirkby** Knows
135 L1 **Kirkby** Lincs
161 H2 **Kirkby** N York
160 D4 **Kirkby Fleetham** N York
136 A8 **Kirkby Green** Lincs
160 C3 **Kirkby Hall** N York
133 K8 **Kirkby in Ashfield** Notts
156 B6 **Kirkby-in-Furness** Cumb
118 E2 **Kirkby la Thorpe** Lincs
157 K7 **Kirkby Lonsdale** Cumb
148 F4 **Kirkby Malham** N York
99 M3 **Kirkby Mallory** Leics
160 C7 **Kirkby Malzeard** N York
162 C5 **Kirkby Mills** N York
162 B5 **Kirkbymoorside** N York
136 D7 **Kirkby on Bain** Lincs
150 D6 **Kirkby Overblow** N York
158 D1 **Kirkby Stephen** Cumb
166 E5 **Kirkby Thore** Cumb
118 E6 **Kirkby Underwood** Lincs
151 H7 **Kirkby Wharf** N York
116 E1 **Kirkby Woodhouse** Notts
211 J1 **Kirkcaldy** Fife

178 C5 **Kirkcambeck** Cumb
175 G4 **Kirkchrist** D & G
172 C1 **Kirkcolm** D & G
197 L8 **Kirkconnel** D & G
175 G3 **Kirkconnell** D & G
176 C5 **Kirkconnell** D & G
173 J3 **Kirkcowan** D & G
175 H5 **Kirkcudbright** D & G
129 H1 **Kirkdale** Lpool
150 F5 **Kirk Deighton** N York
144 C2 **Kirk Ella** E R Yk
198 E4 **Kirkfieldbank** S Lans
175 L2 **Kirkgunzeon** D & G
116 D3 **Kirk Hallam** Derbys
138 E1 **Kirkham** Lancs
151 M3 **Kirkham** N York
141 L3 **Kirkhamgate** Wakefd
151 G5 **Kirk Hammerton** N York
180 B2 **Kirkharle** Nthumb
167 G1 **Kirkhaugh** Nthumb
141 J4 **Kirkheaton** Kirk
180 B3 **Kirkheaton** Nthumb
250 F3 **Kirkhill** Highld
186 E5 **Kirkhope** S Lans
178 D7 **Kirkhouse** Cumb
143 G5 **Kirkhouse Green** Donc
247 H5 **Kirkibost** Highld
233 L6 **Kirkinch** P & K
174 C4 **Kirkinner** D & G
209 H4 **Kirkintilloch** E Duns
115 M2 **Kirk Ireton** Derbys
164 E7 **Kirkland** Cumb
166 F4 **Kirkland** Cumb
185 K5 **Kirkland** D & G
186 F8 **Kirkland** D & G
197 L8 **Kirkland** D & G
165 G3 **Kirkland Guards** Cumb
115 M4 **Kirk Langley** Derbys
170 E6 **Kirkleatham** R & Cl
160 F1 **Kirklevington** S on T
107 L5 **Kirkley** Suffk
160 D6 **Kirklington** N York
134 D8 **Kirklington** Notts
178 B5 **Kirklinton** Cumb
210 F4 **Kirkliston** C Edin
174 D4 **Kirkmabreck** D & G
172 E7 **Kirkmaiden** D & G
169 H4 **Kirk Merrington** Dur
154 d4 **Kirk Michael** IoM
233 G3 **Kirkmichael** P & K
183 J1 **Kirkmichael** S Ayrs
198 C4 **Kirkmuirhill** S Lans
202 E7 **Kirknewton** Nthumb
210 F5 **Kirknewton** W Loth
255 K5 **Kirkney** Abers
209 M6 **Kirk of Shotts** N Lans
166 D3 **Kirkoswald** Cumb
183 G2 **Kirkoswald** S Ayrs
186 D8 **Kirkpatrick** D & G
175 K1 **Kirkpatrick Durham** D & G
177 J5 **Kirkpatrick-Fleming** D & G
142 F6 **Kirk Sandall** Donc
155 L6 **Kirksanton** Cumb
142 E4 **Kirk Smeaton** N York
150 C8 **Kirkstall** Leeds
136 C7 **Kirkstead** Lincs
255 L5 **Kirkstile** Abers
188 C8 **Kirkstile** D & G
156 F1 **Kirkstone Pass Inn** Cumb
280 D2 **Kirkstyle** Highld
142 B3 **Kirkthorpe** Wakefd
256 B6 **Kirkton** Abers
176 C3 **Kirkton** D & G
222 F2 **Kirkton** Fife
248 C6 **Kirkton** Highld
248 E3 **Kirkton** Highld
221 G3 **Kirkton** P & K
200 B5 **Kirkton Manor** Border
233 M5 **Kirkton of Airlie** Angus
234 A7 **Kirkton of Auchterhouse** Angus
252 F2 **Kirkton of Barevan** Highld
222 C1 **Kirkton of Collace** P & K
255 H8 **Kirkton of Glenbuchat** Abers
257 H6 **Kirkton of Logie Buchan** Abers
234 E3 **Kirkton of Menmuir** Angus
234 D7 **Kirkton of Monikie** Angus
256 C5 **Kirkton of Rayne** Abers
245 H2 **Kirkton of Skene** Abers
234 B8 **Kirkton of Strathmartine** Angus
234 B7 **Kirkton of Tealing** Angus
244 D1 **Kirkton of Tough** Abers
269 J3 **Kirktown** Abers
269 K6 **Kirktown** Abers
268 B4 **Kirktown of Alvah** Abers
256 E6 **Kirktown of Bourtie** Abers

245 J6 **Kirktown of Fetteresso** Abers
254 F4 **Kirktown of Mortlach** Moray
257 J6 **Kirktown of Slains** Abers
199 K4 **Kirkurd** Border
275 C4 **Kirkwall** Ork
180 B2 **Kirkwhelpington** Nthumb
202 C7 **Kirk Yetholm** Border
144 E5 **Kirmington** N Linc
136 C1 **Kirmond le Mire** Lincs
207 K3 **Kirn** Ag & B
234 B4 **Kirriemuir** Angus
106 F4 **Kirstead Green** Norfk
177 H4 **Kirtlebridge** D & G
88 D4 **Kirtling** Cambs
88 D4 **Kirtling Green** Cambs
66 D3 **Kirtlington** Oxon
278 C3 **Kirtomy** Highld
119 J4 **Kirton** Lincs
134 D6 **Kirton** Notts
91 G7 **Kirton** Suffk
119 J3 **Kirton End** Lincs
208 C4 **Kirtonhill** W Duns
119 J3 **Kirton Holme** Lincs
144 A8 **Kirton in Lindsey** N Linc
173 K4 **Kirwaugh** D & G
248 D4 **Kishorn** Highld
84 D3 **Kislingbury** Nhants
65 K1 **Kitebrook** Warwks
82 E2 **Kite Green** Warwks
83 L2 **Kites Hardwick** Warwks
11 J3 **Kitleigh** Cnwll
139 H6 **Kitt Green** Wigan
29 K6 **Kittisford** Somset
57 G7 **Kittle** Swans
98 F6 **Kitt's Green** Birm
245 K2 **Kittybrewster** C Aber
35 K4 **Kitwood** Hants
62 F1 **Kivernoll** Herefs
133 K3 **Kiveton Park** Rothm
135 G3 **Knaith** Lincs
135 G3 **Knaith Park** Lincs
32 D6 **Knap Corner** Dorset
50 B7 **Knaphill** Surrey
30 D5 **Knapp** Somset
34 E6 **Knapp Hill** Hants
134 E7 **Knapthorpe** Notts
162 F7 **Knapton** N York
122 F5 **Knapton** Norfk
151 J5 **Knapton** N York
80 B5 **Knapton Green** Herefs
87 G3 **Knapwell** Cambs
150 E4 **Knaresborough** N York
178 F8 **Knarsdale** Nthumb
257 G3 **Knaven** Abers
160 F5 **Knayton** N York
69 H3 **Knebworth** Herts
143 J2 **Knedlington** E R Yk
134 D6 **Kneesall** Notts
87 G6 **Kneesworth** Cambs
117 J2 **Kneeton** Notts
56 E7 **Knelston** Swans
114 E4 **Knenhall** Staffs
105 K7 **Knettishall** Suffk
28 B3 **Knightacott** Devon
83 J4 **Knightcote** Warwks
114 C6 **Knightley** Staffs
114 C6 **Knightley Dale** Staffs
100 D3 **Knighton** C Leic
7 G5 **Knighton** Devon
31 K8 **Knighton** Dorset
17 L3 **Knighton** Poole
79 K1 **Knighton** Powys
30 B2 **Knighton** Somset
114 A3 **Knighton** Staffs
114 B6 **Knighton** Staffs
47 L4 **Knighton** Wilts
80 L1 **Knighton on Teme** Worcs
64 C2 **Knightsbridge** Gloucs
10 F6 **Knightsmill** Cnwll
81 G4 **Knightwick** Worcs
79 K3 **Knill** Herefs
117 L5 **Knipton** Leics
168 E1 **Knitsley** Dur
115 K2 **Kniveton** Derbys
166 F5 **Knock** Cumb
247 L6 **Knock** Highld
267 L5 **Knock** Moray
282 g3 **Knock** W Isls
274 F2 **Knockally** Highld
271 H6 **Knockan** Highld
254 D3 **Knockando** Moray
250 F3 **Knockbain** Highld
263 H8 **Knockbain** Highld
207 K6 **Knock Castle** N Ayrs
279 L4 **Knockdee** Highld
207 J5 **Knockdow** Ag & B

46 B1 **Knockdown** Wilts
183 H4 **Knockeen** S Ayrs
195 G5 **Knockenkelly** N Ayrs
196 D3 **Knockentiber** E Ayrs
52 C4 **Knockhall** Kent
51 M7 **Knockholt** Kent
52 A7 **Knockholt Pound** Kent
112 E7 **Knockin** Shrops
196 E3 **Knockinlaw** E Ayrs
52 C6 **Knockmill** Kent
172 B2 **Knocknain** D & G
154 C5 **Knocksharry** IoM
184 F6 **Knocksheen** D & G
175 J1 **Knockvennie Smithy** D & G
91 K3 **Knodishall** Suffk
91 K3 **Knodishall Common** Suffk
31 G6 **Knole** Somset
45 H2 **Knole Park** S Glos
130 F4 **Knolls Green** Ches
112 F4 **Knolton** Wrexhm
32 F3 **Knook** Wilts
101 H2 **Knossington** Leics
147 G6 **Knott End-on-Sea** Lancs
85 K3 **Knotting** Beds
85 K3 **Knotting Green** Beds
142 D3 **Knottingley** Wakefd
129 J1 **Knotty Ash** Lpool
68 B8 **Knotty Green** Bucks
96 D8 **Knowbury** Shrops
183 H8 **Knowe** D & G
184 F5 **Knowehead** D & G
195 L8 **Knoweside** S Ayrs
45 J5 **Knowle** Bristl
13 H2 **Knowle** Devon
14 B1 **Knowle** Devon
14 B6 **Knowle** Devon
27 J3 **Knowle** Devon
96 D8 **Knowle** Shrops
98 F8 **Knowle** Solhll
29 H2 **Knowle** Somset
14 B3 **Knowle Cross** Devon
177 L7 **Knowlefield** Cumb
148 A8 **Knowle Green** Lancs
50 C5 **Knowle Hill** Surrey
30 E8 **Knowle St Giles** Somset
19 J2 **Knowle Village** Hants
88 F7 **Knowl Green** Essex
49 K3 **Knowl Hill** W & M
17 K1 **Knowlton** Dorset
41 J4 **Knowlton** Kent
138 E8 **Knowsley** Knows
28 E6 **Knowstone** Devon
150 C4 **Knox** N York
39 K5 **Knox Bridge** Kent
95 G8 **Knucklas** Powys
85 H2 **Knuston** Nhants
130 E4 **Knutsford** Ches
114 C2 **Knutton** Staffs
141 G4 **Krumlin** Calder
3 J7 **Kuggar** Cnwll
248 B6 **Kyleakin** Highld
248 B6 **Kyle of Lochalsh** Highld
248 C7 **Kylerhea** Highld
271 H1 **Kylesku** Highld
238 C5 **Kylesmorar** Highld
282 f6 **Kyles Scalpay** W Isls
271 H1 **Kylestrome** Highld
80 E8 **Kynaston** Herefs
112 E7 **Kynaston** Shrops
113 L8 **Kynnersley** Wrekin
80 E3 **Kyre Green** Worcs
80 E3 **Kyre Park** Worcs
80 E2 **Kyrewood** Worcs
29 J6 **Kyrle** Somset

L

9 j3 **La Bellieuse** Guern
282 f4 **Lacasaigh** W Isls
282 g3 **Lacasdal** W Isls
145 G6 **Laceby** NE Lin
67 K7 **Lacey Green** Bucks
130 D5 **Lach Dennis** Ches
170 D6 **Lackenby** R & Cl
88 F1 **Lackford** Suffk
88 F1 **Lackford Green** Suffk
46 C5 **Lacock** Wilts
83 K3 **Ladbroke** Warwks
114 F1 **Ladderedge** Staffs
39 H4 **Laddingford** Kent
119 L1 **Lade Bank** Lincs
4 E5 **Ladock** Cnwll
275 e2 **Lady** Ork
222 E5 **Ladybank** Fife
11 L5 **Ladycross** Cnwll
198 F7 **Ladygill** S Lans
156 B5 **Lady Hall** Cumb

202 D3 **Ladykirk** Border
63 H1 **Ladyridge** Herefs
88 E3 **Lady's Green** Suffk
98 D6 **Ladywood** Birm
81 K3 **Ladywood** Worcs
9 k1 **La Fontenelle** Guern
9 j4 **La Fosse** Guern
185 L5 **Lag** D & G
237 J8 **Laga** Highld
204 F7 **Lagavulin** Ag & B
193 K4 **Lagg** N Ayrs
240 A4 **Laggan** Highld
241 G5 **Laggan** Highld
9 k2 **La Greve** Guern
9 b1 **La Greve de Lecq** Jersey
9 e3 **La Hougue Bie** Jersey
9 h3 **La Houguette** Guern
277 G4 **Laid** Highld
260 E2 **Laide** Highld
236 F3 **Laig** Highld
196 F2 **Laigh Clunch** E Ayrs
196 F3 **Laigh Fenwick** E Ayrs
197 J7 **Laigh Glenmuir** E Ayrs
209 J8 **Laighstonehall** S Lans
52 E1 **Laindon** Essex
272 E6 **Lairg** Highld
141 J1 **Laisterdyke** Brad
166 B4 **Laithes** Cumb
12 C4 **Lake** Devon
27 K4 **Lake** Devon
19 K7 **Lake** IoW
17 J4 **Lake** Poole
33 K3 **Lake** Wilts
104 E6 **Lakenheath** Suffk
36 F4 **Laker's Green** Surrey
103 L4 **Lakesend** Norfk
156 E5 **Lakeside** Cumb
50 D5 **Laleham** Surrey
42 C5 **Laleston** Brdgnd
199 L3 **Lamancha** Border
3 J5 **Lamanva** Cnwll
89 H8 **Lamarsh** Essex
122 E7 **Lamas** Norfk
202 A4 **Lambden** Border
39 H6 **Lamberhurst** Kent
39 G6 **Lamberhurst Down** Kent
213 L7 **Lamberton** Border
51 J3 **Lambeth** Gt Lon
88 E4 **Lambfair Green** Suffk
117 H2 **Lambley** Notts
178 F7 **Lambley** Nthumb
47 L3 **Lambourn** W Berk
70 C8 **Lambourne End** Essex
148 C8 **Lamb Roe** Lancs
37 K3 **Lambs Green** W Susx
54 E3 **Lambston** Pembks
6 A2 **Lamellion** Cnwll
12 B7 **Lamerton** Devon
181 G7 **Lamesley** Gatesd
199 G7 **Lamington** S Lans
195 G5 **Lamlash** N Ayrs
165 L3 **Lamonby** Cumb
5 H2 **Lamorick** Cnwll
2 C6 **Lamorna** Cnwll
4 E6 **Lamorran** Cnwll
5 L2 **Lampen** Cnwll
77 G5 **Lampeter** Cerdgn
55 K4 **Lampeter Velfrey** Pembks
55 G6 **Lamphey** Pembks
164 E6 **Lamplugh** Cumb
101 G8 **Lamport** Nhants
31 L4 **Lamyatt** Somset
11 K1 **Lana** Devon
11 L3 **Lana** Devon
198 E4 **Lanark** S Lans
147 J3 **Lancaster** Lancs
63 G7 **Lancaut** Gloucs
168 F1 **Lanchester** Dur
21 L6 **Lancing** W Susx
9 k1 **L'Ancresse** Guern
87 K2 **Landbeach** Cambs
27 H6 **Landcross** Devon
245 G3 **Landerberry** Abers
34 B7 **Landford** Wilts
275 G2 **Land-hallow** Highld
56 E6 **Landimore** Swans
27 L4 **Landkey** Devon
27 L4 **Landkey Town** Devon
57 J5 **Landore** Swans
6 D3 **Landrake** Cnwll
7 M2 **Landscove** Devon
2 A6 **Land's End** Cnwll
55 G4 **Landshipping** Pembks
11 L6 **Landue** Cnwll
6 E3 **Landulph** Cnwll
88 C2 **Landwade** Suffk
98 C2 **Landywood** Staffs
4 D3 **Lane** Cnwll

11 J5 **Laneast** Cnwll
140 C1 **Lane Bottom** Lancs
49 K1 **Lane End** Bucks
5 H1 **Lane End** Cnwll
35 H5 **Lane End** Hants
52 C4 **Lane End** Kent
148 F6 **Lane End** Lancs
130 D2 **Lane End** Warrtn
32 D2 **Lane End** Wilts
115 L4 **Lane Ends** Derbys
140 B2 **Lane Ends** Lancs
149 H7 **Lane Ends** N York
155 K4 **Lane End Waberthwaite** Cumb
97 K3 **Lane Green** Staffs
134 F4 **Laneham** Notts
167 J2 **Lanehead** Dur
168 E8 **Lane Head** Dur
179 H2 **Lanehead** Nthumb
139 J8 **Lane Head** Wigan
98 B3 **Lane Head** Wsall
147 H7 **Lane Heads** Lancs
149 G7 **Laneshaw Bridge** Lancs
140 B3 **Lane Side** Lancs
12 A3 **Langaford** Devon
30 C5 **Langaller** Somset
117 J4 **Langar** Notts
208 C4 **Langbank** Rens
149 K5 **Langbar** N York
170 D8 **Langbaurgh** N York
148 E3 **Langcliffe** N York
163 G4 **Langdale End** N York
11 K4 **Langdon** Cnwll
167 K4 **Langdon Beck** Dur
19 G2 **Langdown** Hants
222 E6 **Langdyke** Fife
72 E3 **Langenhoe** Essex
86 D7 **Langford** Beds
14 B2 **Langford** Devon
71 K5 **Langford** Essex
44 F6 **Langford** N Som
135 G7 **Langford** Notts
65 K6 **Langford** Oxon
29 K6 **Langford Budville** Somset
32 C5 **Langham** Dorset
72 F1 **Langham** Essex
121 M3 **Langham** Norfk
101 J1 **Langham** Rutlnd
89 K1 **Langham** Suffk
139 L1 **Langho** Lancs
177 L2 **Langholm** D & G
57 H7 **Langland** Swans
201 G6 **Langlee** Border
131 J5 **Langley** Ches
116 D2 **Langley** Derbys
64 E2 **Langley** Gloucs
19 G3 **Langley** Hants
69 G3 **Langley** Herts
39 K3 **Langley** Kent
179 J6 **Langley** Nthumb
65 L4 **Langley** Oxon
140 C6 **Langley** Rochdl
50 C3 **Langley** Slough
29 K5 **Langley** Somset
36 B5 **Langley** W Susx
82 E3 **Langley** Warwks
46 D4 **Langley Burrell** Wilts
68 D7 **Langleybury** Herts
179 J6 **Langley Castle** Nthumb
115 M4 **Langley Common** Derbys
115 M4 **Langley Green** Derbys
72 C3 **Langley Green** Essex
82 E3 **Langley Green** Warwks
87 J8 **Langley Lower Green** Essex
29 K5 **Langley Marsh** Somset
116 D2 **Langley Mill** Derbys
169 H3 **Langley Moor** Dur
169 G2 **Langley Park** Dur
107 H3 **Langley Street** Norfk
87 J8 **Langley Upper Green** Essex
23 L6 **Langney** E Susx
134 B2 **Langold** Notts
11 K5 **Langore** Cnwll
30 F5 **Langport** Somset
119 J2 **Langrick** Lincs
45 L5 **Langridge** BaNES
27 K6 **Langridge Ford** Devon
165 G2 **Langrigg** Cumb
35 L6 **Langrish** Hants
141 K7 **Langsett** Barns
220 D4 **Langside** P & K
20 B6 **Langstone** Hants
44 D1 **Langstone** Newpt
160 C4 **Langthorne** N York
150 C4 **Langthorpe** N York
159 H2 **Langthwaite** N York

152 F3 **Langtoft** E R Yk
102 C1 **Langtoft** Lincs
168 F6 **Langton** Dur
136 D6 **Langton** Lincs
137 G5 **Langton** Lincs
152 B2 **Langton** N York
136 C4 **Langton by Wragby** Lincs
38 E5 **Langton Green** Kent
106 C8 **Langton Green** Suffk
16 B6 **Langton Herring** Dorset
17 H1 **Langton Long Blandford** Dorset
17 K6 **Langton Matravers** Dorset
27 H7 **Langtree** Devon
27 H7 **Langtree Week** Devon
166 D4 **Langwathby** Cumb
274 F3 **Langwell House** Highld
135 L4 **Langworth** Lincs
12 C3 **Langworthy** Devon
5 H2 **Lanivet** Cnwll
5 G4 **Lanjeth** Cnwll
10 F7 **Lank** Cnwll
5 J3 **Lanlivery** Cnwll
3 J3 **Lanner** Cnwll
11 K7 **Lanoy** Cnwll
5 L3 **Lanreath** Cnwll
5 K4 **Lansallos** Cnwll
10 F6 **Lanteglos** Cnwll
5 K4 **Lanteglos Highway** Cnwll
189 G2 **Lanton** Border
202 E6 **Lanton** Nthumb
9 j2 **La Passee** Guern
13 G1 **Lapford** Devon
204 F7 **Laphroaig** Ag & B
97 K1 **Lapley** Staffs
9 a3 **La Pulente** Jersey
82 E1 **Lapworth** Warwks
227 K3 **Larachbeg** Highld
209 M3 **Larbert** Falk
147 H7 **Larbreck** Lancs
256 A5 **Largie** Abers
206 E2 **Largiemore** Ag & B
223 H5 **Largoward** Fife
207 K7 **Largs** N Ayrs
195 G6 **Largybeg** N Ayrs
195 G6 **Largymore** N Ayrs
14 C3 **Larkbeare** Devon
207 L4 **Larkfield** Inver
52 F7 **Larkfield** Kent
198 C3 **Larkhall** S Lans
33 K2 **Larkhill** Wilts
105 K5 **Larling** Norfk
9 f4 **La Rocque** Jersey
9 j2 **La Rousaillerie** Guern
168 C7 **Lartington** Dur
64 B8 **Lasborough** Gloucs
35 K2 **Lasham** Hants
12 B1 **Lashbrook** Devon
39 L5 **Lashenden** Kent
131 H8 **Lask Edge** Staffs
221 K8 **Lassodie** Fife
211 J6 **Lasswade** Mdloth
162 C4 **Lastingham** N York
31 G2 **Latcham** Somset
69 K3 **Latchford** Herts
67 G6 **Latchford** Oxon
72 C7 **Latchingdon** Essex
12 A7 **Latchley** Cnwll
139 K8 **Lately Common** Warrtn
85 G6 **Lathbury** M Keyn
275 G2 **Latheron** Highld
275 G2 **Latheronwheel** Highld
223 H5 **Lathones** Fife
68 C7 **Latimer** Bucks
45 L2 **Latteridge** S Glos
32 B5 **Lattiford** Somset
65 G7 **Latton** Wilts
201 H4 **Lauder** Border
56 B3 **Laugharne** Carmth
135 G4 **Laughterton** Lincs
23 H4 **Laughton** E Susx
100 E5 **Laughton** Leics
118 E5 **Laughton** Lincs
143 L8 **Laughton** Lincs
133 K2 **Laughton-en-le-Morthen** Rothm
11 J1 **Launcells** Cnwll
11 K1 **Launcells Cross** Cnwll
11 L5 **Launceston** Cnwll
66 F3 **Launton** Oxon
235 H1 **Laurencekirk** Abers
175 H2 **Laurieston** D & G
210 B3 **Laurieston** Falk
85 H4 **Lavendon** M Keyn
89 J5 **Lavenham** Suffk
43 J8 **Lavernock** V Glam
178 B6 **Laversdale** Cumb
33 L5 **Laverstock** Wilts

35 G1 **Laverstoke** Hants
82 C8 **Laverton** Gloucs
160 B7 **Laverton** N York
45 M8 **Laverton** Somset
9 j3 **La Villette** Guern
129 J8 **Lavister** Wrexhm
209 L8 **Law** S Lans
231 J7 **Lawers** P & K
73 G1 **Lawford** Essex
29 L4 **Lawford** Somset
221 K2 **Lawgrove** P & K
209 L8 **Law Hill** S Lans
11 L6 **Lawhitton** Cnwll
148 D3 **Lawkland** N York
148 D3 **Lawkland Green** N York
96 F2 **Lawley** Wrekin
114 C6 **Lawnhead** Staffs
68 F3 **Lawrence End** Herts
55 G5 **Lawrenny** Pembks
89 H4 **Lawshall** Suffk
89 H4 **Lawshall Green** Suffk
80 B3 **Lawton** Herefs
282 f4 **Laxay** W Isls
282 g3 **Laxdale** W Isls
154 f5 **Laxey** IoM
91 G1 **Laxfield** Suffk
276 C7 **Laxford Bridge** Highld
281 e5 **Laxo** Shet
143 K3 **Laxton** E R Yk
101 L4 **Laxton** Nhants
134 E6 **Laxton** Notts
149 J7 **Laycock** Brad
72 D3 **Layer Breton** Essex
72 D3 **Layer-de-la-Haye** Essex
72 D4 **Layer Marney** Essex
89 L7 **Layham** Suffk
48 A5 **Layland's Green** W Berk
15 J2 **Laymore** Dorset
50 C1 **Layter's Green** Bucks
152 A7 **Laytham** E R Yk
177 H7 **Laythes** Cumb
170 D6 **Lazenby** R & Cl
166 D3 **Lazonby** Cumb
132 F8 **Lea** Derbys
63 K3 **Lea** Herefs
135 G2 **Lea** Lincs
95 J5 **Lea** Shrops
95 K2 **Lea** Shrops
46 D2 **Lea** Wilts
251 H3 **Leachkin** Highld
200 B2 **Leadburn** Border
118 B1 **Leadenham** Lincs
70 E4 **Leaden Roding** Essex
180 D8 **Leadgate** Dur
180 D7 **Leadgate** Nthumb
186 C3 **Leadhills** S Lans
39 M3 **Leadingcross Green** Kent
132 E4 **Leadmill** Derbys
65 L4 **Leafield** Oxon
68 D2 **Leagrave** Luton
130 D6 **Leahead** Ches
115 G6 **Lea Heath** Staffs
160 F4 **Leake** N York
119 L1 **Leake Common Side** Lincs
162 D1 **Lealholm** N York
162 D1 **Lealholm Side** N York
259 H4 **Lealt** Highld
132 E4 **Leam** Derbys
99 G5 **Lea Marston** Warwks
83 K2 **Leamington Hastings** Warwks
83 H2 **Leamington Spa** Warwks
169 J1 **Leamside** Dur
23 K5 **Leap Cross** E Susx
157 H6 **Leasgill** Cumb
118 E2 **Leasingham** Lincs
169 H4 **Leasingthorne** Dur
50 F7 **Leatherhead** Surrey
150 B6 **Leathley** N York
113 G7 **Leaton** Shrops
96 E1 **Leaton** Wrekin
138 F2 **Lea Town** Lancs
40 C4 **Leaveland** Kent
89 J7 **Leavenheath** Suffk
152 B3 **Leavening** N York
51 L6 **Leaves Green** Gt Lon
158 D5 **Lea Yeat** Cumb
163 K6 **Lebberston** N York
9 i4 **Le Bigard** Guern
9 j4 **Le Bourg** Guern
9 f4 **Le Bourg** Jersey
65 J7 **Lechlade on Thames** Gloucs
204 D3 **Lecht Gruinart** Ag & B
157 K7 **Leck** Lancs
231 K7 **Leckbuie** P & K
34 E3 **Leckford** Hants
84 D7 **Leckhampstead** Bucks

48 B4 **Leckhampstead** W Berk
48 B4 **Leckhampstead Thicket** W Berk
64 D3 **Leckhampton** Gloucs
261 K2 **Leckmelm** Highld
43 J6 **Leckwith** V Glam
152 F7 **Leconfield** E R Yk
228 E7 **Ledaig** Ag & B
67 L3 **Ledburn** Bucks
81 G7 **Ledbury** Herefs
80 F8 **Leddington** Gloucs
80 A5 **Ledgemoor** Herefs
80 A3 **Ledicot** Herefs
271 H5 **Ledmore Junction** Highld
129 H5 **Ledsham** Ches
142 C2 **Ledsham** Leeds
142 C2 **Ledston** Leeds
7 L5 **Ledstone** Devon
142 C2 **Ledston Luck** Leeds
66 B2 **Ledwell** Oxon
27 H2 **Lee** Devon
51 K4 **Lee** Gt Lon
34 D7 **Lee** Hants
112 F5 **Lee** Shrops
96 B4 **Leebotwood** Shrops
113 J6 **Lee Brockhurst** Shrops
146 E2 **Leece** Cumb
52 E2 **Lee Chapel** Essex
67 M6 **Lee Clump** Bucks
67 M6 **Lee Common** Bucks
39 K3 **Leeds** Kent
141 L1 **Leeds** Leeds
2 F4 **Leedstown** Cnwll
130 C7 **Lee Green** Ches
131 K8 **Leek** Staffs
83 G2 **Leek Wootton** Warwks
7 H4 **Lee Mill** Devon
141 L1 **Leeming** Brad
160 D5 **Leeming** N York
160 D4 **Leeming Bar** N York
7 H3 **Lee Moor** Devon
19 J3 **Lee-on-the-Solent** Hants
149 J8 **Lees** Brad
115 L4 **Lees** Derbys
140 E6 **Lees** Oldham
115 L4 **Lees Green** Derbys
101 H1 **Leesthorpe** Leics
37 L2 **Lee Street** Surrey
129 G7 **Leeswood** Flints
222 C3 **Leetown** P & K
130 C5 **Leftwich** Ches
61 K4 **Legar** Powys
137 G3 **Legbourne** Lincs
165 K6 **Legburthwaite** Cumb
201 J4 **Legerwood** Border
9 i3 **Le Gron** Guern
136 B3 **Legsby** Lincs
9 e4 **Le Haguais** Jersey
9 e4 **Le Hocq** Jersey
100 D3 **Leicester** C Leic
100 B3 **Leicester Forest East** Leics
28 C8 **Leigh** Devon
16 B1 **Leigh** Dorset
64 C2 **Leigh** Gloucs
38 E4 **Leigh** Kent
95 H3 **Leigh** Shrops
37 K2 **Leigh** Surrey
139 K7 **Leigh** Wigan
64 F8 **Leigh** Wilts
81 H4 **Leigh** Worcs
53 H2 **Leigh Beck** Essex
46 C3 **Leigh Delamere** Wilts
40 A8 **Leigh Green** Kent
197 J1 **Leigh Knoweglass** S Lans
29 J4 **Leighland Chapel** Somset
53 H2 **Leigh-on-Sea** Sthend
17 K3 **Leigh Park** Dorset
81 H5 **Leigh Sinton** Worcs
98 D3 **Leighswood** Wsall
46 B1 **Leighterton** Gloucs
159 L6 **Leighton** N York
94 F2 **Leighton** Powys
96 E2 **Leighton** Shrops
32 B2 **Leighton** Somset
102 C8 **Leighton Bromswold** Cambs
68 A2 **Leighton Buzzard** Beds
31 M2 **Leigh upon Mendip** Somset
45 H4 **Leigh Woods** N Som
80 B2 **Leinthall Earls** Herefs
80 A1 **Leinthall Starkes** Herefs
95 K8 **Leintwardine** Herefs
100 B5 **Leire** Leics
91 K3 **Leiston** Suffk
233 L6 **Leitfie** P & K
211 J4 **Leith** C Edin
202 B4 **Leitholm** Border

2 E4 **Lelant** Cnwll
145 G1 **Lelley** E R Yk
97 G8 **Lem Hill** Worcs
202 B6 **Lempitlaw** Border
282 g5 **Lemreway** W Isls
69 G4 **Lemsford** Herts
82 B6 **Lenchwick** Worcs
182 E5 **Lendalfoot** S Ayrs
219 J6 **Lendrick** Stirlg
257 L3 **Lendrum Terrace** Abers
40 A5 **Lenham** Kent
40 B5 **Lenham Heath** Kent
250 F6 **Lenie** Highld
202 C5 **Lennel** Border
174 F4 **Lennox Plunton** D & G
209 G3 **Lennoxtown** E Duns
50 A3 **Lent** Bucks
116 F4 **Lenton** C Nott
118 D5 **Lenton** Lincs
122 B7 **Lenwade** Norfk
209 H4 **Lenzie** E Duns
244 C2 **Leochel-Cushnie** Abers
98 E2 **Leomansley** Staffs
80 C3 **Leominster** Herefs
64 A4 **Leonard Stanley** Gloucs
9 b2 **Leoville** Jersey
19 G4 **Lepe** Hants
258 B6 **Lephin** Highld
152 A4 **Leppington** N York
141 K5 **Lepton** Kirk
9 h3 **L'Eree** Guern
5 K3 **Lerryn** Cnwll
281 e6 **Lerwick** Shet
9 h3 **Les Arquets** Guern
191 J4 **Lesbury** Nthumb
9 k3 **Les Hubits** Guern
255 M6 **Leslie** Abers
222 D6 **Leslie** Fife
9 i3 **Les Lohiers** Guern
198 D5 **Lesmahagow** S Lans
9 i4 **Les Murchez** Guern
11 G4 **Lesnewth** Cnwll
9 j4 **Les Nicolles** Guern
9 j2 **Les Quartiers** Guern
9 b3 **Les Quennevais** Jersey
9 i3 **Les Sages** Guern
123 H6 **Lessingham** Norfk
165 H1 **Lessonhall** Cumb
3 K6 **Lestowder** Cnwll
9 i4 **Les Villets** Guern
172 C2 **Leswalt** D & G
9 a2 **L'Etacq** Jersey
68 F7 **Letchmore Heath** Herts
86 E8 **Letchworth Garden City** Herts
48 A2 **Letcombe Bassett** Oxon
48 A2 **Letcombe Regis** Oxon
234 E5 **Letham** Angus
189 J4 **Letham** Border
210 B2 **Letham** Falk
222 E4 **Letham** Fife
235 G6 **Letham Grange** Angus
233 H7 **Lethendy** P & K
255 M7 **Lethenty** Abers
256 E4 **Lethenty** Abers
91 G4 **Letheringham** Suffk
122 B4 **Letheringsett** Norfk
13 G5 **Lettaford** Devon
260 F5 **Letterewe** Highld
248 D7 **Letterfearn** Highld
239 L5 **Letterfinlay Lodge Hotel** Highld
237 L3 **Lettermorar** Highld
261 K2 **Letters** Highld
186 D2 **Lettershaw** S Lans
74 F6 **Letterston** Pembks
253 K7 **Lettoch** Highld
254 B5 **Lettoch** Highld
79 L1 **Letton** Herefs
79 L6 **Letton** Herefs
51 M7 **Lett's Green** Kent
69 H5 **Letty Green** Herts
133 L2 **Letwell** Rothm
223 H3 **Leuchars** Fife
282 g5 **Leumrabhagh** W Isls
282 g4 **Leurbost** W Isls
5 G5 **Levalsa Meor** Cnwll
114 D8 **Levedale** Staffs
70 C2 **Level's Green** Essex
153 H6 **Leven** E R Yk
222 F4 **Leven** Fife
157 G5 **Levens** Cumb
69 K3 **Levens Green** Herts
131 G1 **Levenshulme** Manch
281 d8 **Levenwick** Shet
282 d6 **Leverburgh** W Isls
103 J1 **Leverington** Cambs
68 D5 **Leverstock Green** Herts

119 L2 **Leverton** Lincs
9 j2 **Le Villocq** Guern
90 F7 **Levington** Suffk
162 E4 **Levisham** N York
65 L6 **Lew** Oxon
11 K6 **Lewannick** Cnwll
12 B5 **Lewdown** Devon
22 F5 **Lewes** E Susx
31 K8 **Leweston** Dorset
54 F2 **Leweston** Pembks
51 K4 **Lewisham** Gt Lon
250 F6 **Lewiston** Highld
42 E4 **Lewistown** Brdgnd
79 L4 **Lewis Wych** Herefs
67 H7 **Lewknor** Oxon
11 L2 **Leworthy** Devon
28 B3 **Leworthy** Devon
40 C3 **Lewson Street** Kent
147 J8 **Lewth** Lancs
12 B5 **Lewtrenchard** Devon
72 D2 **Lexden** Essex
30 C4 **Lexworthy** Somset
5 K2 **Ley** Cnwll
52 E7 **Leybourne** Kent
159 K4 **Leyburn** N York
114 B2 **Leycett** Staffs
68 F2 **Leygreen** Herts
68 C6 **Ley Hill** Bucks
139 H3 **Leyland** Lancs
139 H7 **Leyland Green** St Hel
245 G1 **Leylodge** Abers
269 J5 **Leys** Abers
233 K7 **Leys** P & K
53 M5 **Leysdown-on-Sea** Kent
234 F6 **Leysmill** Angus
234 B5 **Leys of Cossans** Angus
80 D2 **Leysters** Herefs
51 K2 **Leyton** Gt Lon
51 K2 **Leytonstone** Gt Lon
11 L6 **Lezant** Cnwll
3 H4 **Lezerea** Cnwll
266 F4 **Lhanbryde** Moray
60 F2 **Libanus** Powys
199 G4 **Libberton** S Lans
211 J5 **Liberton** C Edin
98 E2 **Lichfield** Staffs
98 C8 **Lickey** Worcs
81 M1 **Lickey End** Worcs
98 B8 **Lickey Rock** Worcs
36 D5 **Lickfold** W Susx
12 B6 **Liddaton Green** Devon
228 B3 **Liddesdale** Highld
47 J3 **Liddington** Swindn
132 F4 **Lidgate** Derbys
88 E4 **Lidgate** Suffk
143 G7 **Lidget** Donc
134 C6 **Lidgett** Notts
24 F4 **Lidham Hill** E Susx
85 K7 **Lidlington** Beds
53 G6 **Lidsing** Kent
222 E1 **Liff** Angus
98 D7 **Lifford** Birm
11 M5 **Lifton** Devon
11 M5 **Liftondown** Devon
83 H4 **Lighthorne** Warwks
83 H4 **Lighthorne Heath** Warwks
50 B6 **Lightwater** Surrey
114 E3 **Lightwood** C Stke
113 L3 **Lightwood Green** Ches
112 F3 **Lightwood Green** Wrexhm
100 C8 **Lilbourne** Nhants
190 E1 **Lilburn Tower** Nthumb
114 A8 **Lilleshall** Wrekin
68 E2 **Lilley** Herts
48 C3 **Lilley** W Berk
201 H8 **Lilliesleaf** Border
84 D7 **Lillingstone Dayrell** Bucks
84 D7 **Lillingstone Lovell** Bucks
31 K8 **Lillington** Dorset
17 K4 **Lilliput** Poole
29 L2 **Lilstock** Somset
97 G1 **Lilyhurst** Shrops
139 J4 **Limbrick** Lancs
68 D2 **Limbury** Luton
79 L2 **Limebrook** Herefs
140 B5 **Limefield** Bury
197 K1 **Limekilnburn** S Lans
210 E2 **Limekilns** Fife
209 M5 **Limerigg** Falk
19 G7 **Limerstone** IoW
167 J1 **Limestone Brae** Nthumb
64 A1 **Lime Street** Worcs
31 J6 **Limington** Somset
197 J5 **Limmerhaugh** E Ayrs
107 H3 **Limpenhoe** Norfk
45 M6 **Limpley Stoke** Wilts
51 L8 **Limpsfield** Surrey
51 L8 **Limpsfield Chart** Surrey

116 F1 **Linby** Notts
36 C5 **Linchmere** W Susx
176 C3 **Lincluden** D & G
135 K5 **Lincoln** Lincs
81 J2 **Lincomb** Worcs
7 L6 **Lincombe** Devon
156 F6 **Lindale** Cumb
156 C7 **Lindal in Furness** Cumb
22 E2 **Lindfield** W Susx
36 B4 **Lindford** Hants
141 H4 **Lindley** Kirk
150 B6 **Lindley Green** N York
130 F4 **Lindow End** Ches
80 F2 **Lindridge** Worcs
70 F2 **Lindsell** Essex
89 K6 **Lindsey** Suffk
89 K6 **Lindsey Tye** Suffk
30 E4 **Liney** Somset
18 B2 **Linford** Hants
52 E3 **Linford** Thurr
149 K8 **Lingbob** Brad
170 F7 **Lingdale** R & Cl
79 L2 **Lingen** Herefs
38 B4 **Lingfield** Surrey
130 A2 **Lingley Green** Warrtn
107 G2 **Lingwood** Norfk
258 F3 **Linicro** Highld
64 B1 **Linkend** Worcs
48 A7 **Linkenholt** Hants
24 E2 **Linkhill** Kent
11 L7 **Linkinhorne** Cnwll
211 J1 **Linktown** Fife
266 E4 **Linkwood** Moray
95 J5 **Linley** Shrops
80 F4 **Linley Green** Herefs
96 F4 **Linleygreen** Shrops
210 C4 **Linlithgow** W Loth
190 C5 **Linshiels** Nthumb
272 D8 **Linsidemore** Highld
67 M2 **Linslade** Beds
107 G7 **Linstead Parva** Suffk
178 A7 **Linstock** Cumb
82 B1 **Linthurst** Worcs
141 H5 **Linthwaite** Kirk
213 H7 **Lintlaw** Border
267 K3 **Lintmill** Moray
202 B7 **Linton** Border
88 B6 **Linton** Cambs
115 M8 **Linton** Derbys
63 K2 **Linton** Herefs
39 J3 **Linton** Kent
150 E6 **Linton** Leeds
149 H3 **Linton** N York
191 K7 **Linton** Nthumb
115 M8 **Linton Heath** Derbys
63 K2 **Linton Hill** Herefs
151 G4 **Linton-on-Ouse** N York
18 B2 **Linwood** Hants
136 B2 **Linwood** Lincs
208 D6 **Linwood** Rens
283 C9 **Lionacleit** W Isls
282 h1 **Lional** W Isls
23 J4 **Lions Green** E Susx
36 C4 **Liphook** Hants
114 A5 **Lipley** Shrops
129 G3 **Liscard** Wirral
28 F4 **Liscombe** Somset
6 B2 **Liskeard** Cnwll
36 A5 **Liss** Hants
153 J4 **Lissett** E R Yk
36 A5 **Liss Forest** Hants
136 B3 **Lissington** Lincs
89 G6 **Liston** Essex
43 J5 **Lisvane** Cardif
44 D2 **Liswerry** Newpt
121 J8 **Litcham** Norfk
42 D5 **Litchard** Brdgnd
84 C4 **Litchborough** Nhants
48 C8 **Litchfield** Hants
138 D8 **Litherland** Sefton
87 G6 **Litlington** Cambs
23 J7 **Litlington** E Susx
87 L5 **Little Abington** Cambs
101 L8 **Little Addington** Nhants
173 K5 **Little Airies** D & G
69 G2 **Little Alnshoe** Herts
82 D3 **Little Alne** Warwks
138 C6 **Little Altcar** Sefton
69 K5 **Little Amwell** Herts
158 B1 **Little Asby** Cumb
98 E3 **Little Aston** Staffs
19 G7 **Little Atherfield** IoW
170 D8 **Little Ayton** N York
71 J5 **Little Baddow** Essex
46 A2 **Little Badminton** S Glos
177 J7 **Little Bampton** Cumb
71 G1 **Little Bardfield** Essex
86 D4 **Little Barford** Beds

122 C5 **Little Barningham** Norfk
65 J4 **Little Barrington** Gloucs
129 L5 **Little Barrow** Ches
162 D6 **Little Barugh** N York
180 B3 **Little Bavington** Nthumb
90 F5 **Little Bealings** Suffk
162 F2 **Littlebeck** N York
47 L5 **Little Bedwyn** Wilts
73 G2 **Little Bentley** Essex
69 H5 **Little Berkhamsted** Herts
84 F3 **Little Billing** Nhants
68 B3 **Little Billington** Beds
63 G1 **Little Birch** Herefs
146 F7 **Little Bispham** Bpool
90 C5 **Little Blakenham** Suffk
166 B4 **Little Blencow** Cumb
98 C3 **Little Bloxwich** Wsall
21 G3 **Little Bognor** W Susx
116 A1 **Little Bolehill** Derbys
130 E2 **Little Bollington** Ches
50 E8 **Little Bookham** Surrey
28 E8 **Littleborough** Devon
135 G3 **Littleborough** Notts
140 E4 **Littleborough** Rochdl
41 G4 **Littlebourne** Kent
83 K6 **Little Bourton** Oxon
101 G6 **Little Bowden** Leics
88 D5 **Little Bradley** Suffk
79 K3 **Little Brampton** Herefs
95 J7 **Little Brampton** Shrops
71 K4 **Little Braxted** Essex
234 F3 **Little Brechin** Angus
16 B4 **Littlebredy** Dorset
85 H8 **Little Brickhill** M Keyn
114 D6 **Little Bridgeford** Staffs
84 C3 **Little Brington** Nhants
73 G2 **Little Bromley** Essex
164 E4 **Little Broughton** Cumb
130 B6 **Little Budworth** Ches
251 H1 **Littleburn** Highld
71 G8 **Little Burstead** Essex
87 L7 **Littlebury** Essex
87 K7 **Littlebury Green** Essex
118 D7 **Little Bytham** Lincs
70 E3 **Little Canfield** Essex
137 G3 **Little Carlton** Lincs
134 F8 **Little Carlton** Notts
101 M2 **Little Casterton** Rutlnd
153 H6 **Little Catwick** E R Yk
86 B1 **Little Catworth** Cambs
137 G3 **Little Cawthorpe** Lincs
46 B6 **Little Chalfield** Wilts
68 C7 **Little Chalfont** Bucks
30 C3 **Little Charlinch** Somset
40 B6 **Little Chart** Kent
87 L7 **Little Chesterford** Essex
39 H4 **Little Cheveney** Kent
46 E8 **Little Cheverell** Wilts
87 J7 **Little Chishill** Cambs
73 H3 **Little Clacton** Essex
65 K6 **Little Clanfield** Oxon
164 E5 **Little Clifton** Cumb
145 H6 **Little Coates** NE Lin
81 M6 **Little Comberton** Worcs
24 C5 **Little Common** E Susx
39 G2 **Little Comp** Kent
65 K1 **Little Compton** Warwks
178 B7 **Little Corby** Cumb
89 H7 **Little Cornard** Suffk
47 H8 **Littlecott** Wilts
80 E5 **Little Cowarne** Herefs
65 L8 **Little Coxwell** Oxon
160 C4 **Little Crakehall** N York
101 H8 **Little Cransley** Nhants
105 H3 **Little Cressingham** Norfk
138 C7 **Little Crosby** Sefton
165 H5 **Little Crosthwaite** Cumb
115 J4 **Little Cubley** Derbys
117 K8 **Little Dalby** Leics
63 K4 **Littledean** Gloucs
257 K3 **Little Dens** Abers
63 G1 **Little Dewchurch** Herefs
88 D3 **Little Ditton** Cambs
63 G4 **Little Doward** Herefs
47 M7 **Littledown** Hants
103 L6 **Little Downham** Cambs
152 F4 **Little Driffield** E R Yk
105 H1 **Little Dunham** Norfk
232 F7 **Little Dunkeld** P & K
71 G3 **Little Dunmow** Essex
33 K4 **Little Durnford** Wilts
70 F2 **Little Easton** Essex
116 B3 **Little Eaton** Derbys
105 K3 **Little Ellingham** Norfk
32 B2 **Little Elm** Somset
84 B4 **Little Everdon** Nhants
87 H4 **Little Eversden** Cambs
65 J6 **Little Faringdon** Oxon

160 D4 **Little Fencote** N York
142 E1 **Little Fenton** N York
105 H1 **Little Fransham** Norfk
68 C4 **Little Gaddesden** Herts
62 F2 **Little Garway** Herefs
102 C7 **Little Gidding** Cambs
91 H4 **Little Glemham** Suffk
63 K2 **Little Gorsley** Herefs
86 F4 **Little Gransden** Cambs
117 J3 **Little Green** Notts
32 B1 **Little Green** Somset
136 F2 **Little Grimsby** Lincs
134 E3 **Little Gringley** Notts
162 C7 **Little Habton** N York
70 B3 **Little Hadham** Herts
118 F3 **Little Hale** Lincs
116 D3 **Little Hallam** Derbys
70 D4 **Little Hallingbury** Essex
14 B6 **Littleham** Devon
27 H6 **Littleham** Devon
67 L6 **Little Hampden** Bucks
21 H6 **Littlehampton** W Susx
32 D8 **Little Hanford** Dorset
180 B2 **Littleharle Tower** Nthumb
85 G1 **Little Harrowden** Nhants
66 F7 **Little Haseley** Oxon
153 J7 **Little Hatfield** E R Yk
122 E7 **Little Hautbois** Norfk
54 D4 **Little Haven** Pembks
37 J4 **Littlehaven** W Susx
98 E3 **Little Hay** Staffs
131 K2 **Little Hayfield** Derbys
115 G7 **Little Haywood** Staffs
114 D8 **Little Heath** Staffs
49 G4 **Little Heath** W Berk
8 B2 **Littlehempston** Devon
80 D2 **Little Hereford** Herefs
72 D1 **Little Horkesley** Essex
69 L2 **Little Hormead** Herts
23 G4 **Little Horsted** E Susx
141 J2 **Little Horton** Brad
46 F6 **Little Horton** Wilts
67 J1 **Little Horwood** Bucks
142 C6 **Little Houghton** Barns
84 F3 **Little Houghton** Nhants
191 J3 **Littlehoughton** Nthumb
132 C4 **Little Hucklow** Derbys
139 L7 **Little Hulton** Salfd
48 D4 **Little Hungerford** W Berk
161 G7 **Little Hutton** N York
114 F6 **Little Ingestre** Staffs
85 H2 **Little Irchester** Nhants
153 H4 **Little Kelk** E R Yk
32 C2 **Little Keyford** Somset
67 K5 **Little Kimble** Bucks
83 H5 **Little Kineton** Warwks
67 L7 **Little Kingshill** Bucks
175 K3 **Little Knox** D & G
156 D2 **Little Langdale** Cumb
33 H4 **Little Langford** Wilts
12 A1 **Little Lashbrook** Devon
70 E5 **Little Laver** Essex
130 B4 **Little Leigh** Ches
71 H4 **Little Leighs** Essex
139 M6 **Little Lever** Bolton
85 G6 **Little Linford** M Keyn
31 G6 **Little Load** Somset
66 F4 **Little London** Bucks
103 J4 **Little London** Cambs
23 J3 **Little London** E Susx
70 C1 **Little London** Essex
88 D8 **Little London** Essex
63 L3 **Little London** Gloucs
34 E1 **Little London** Hants
48 F7 **Little London** Hants
150 B7 **Little London** Leeds
119 H7 **Little London** Lincs
119 M6 **Little London** Lincs
136 F5 **Little London** Lincs
120 C7 **Little London** Norfk
94 C5 **Little London** Powys
132 D5 **Little Longstone** Derbys
114 B3 **Little Madeley** Staffs
81 H7 **Little Malvern** Worcs
129 H6 **Little Mancot** Flints
89 G8 **Little Maplestead** Essex
80 F7 **Little Marcle** Herefs
27 J8 **Little Marland** Devon
49 L2 **Little Marlow** Bucks
121 H6 **Little Massingham** Norfk
106 D2 **Little Melton** Norfk
243 K4 **Littlemill** Abers
253 H2 **Littlemill** Highld
62 C6 **Little Mill** Mons
66 F7 **Little Milton** Oxon
68 A7 **Little Missenden** Bucks
41 K5 **Little Mongeham** Kent
133 G7 **Littlemoor** Derbys

30 D4 **Little Moor** Somset
66 D6 **Littlemore** Oxon
167 H8 **Little Musgrave** Cumb
112 F7 **Little Ness** Shrops
129 G4 **Little Neston** Ches
75 G6 **Little Newcastle** Pembks
168 E7 **Little Newsham** Dur
31 G7 **Little Norton** Somset
73 J1 **Little Oakley** Essex
101 K6 **Little Oakley** Nhants
85 J4 **Little Odell** Beds
68 E2 **Little Offley** Herts
114 C8 **Little Onn** Staffs
167 G7 **Little Ormside** Cumb
177 K7 **Little Orton** Cumb
104 C5 **Little Ouse** Cambs
150 F4 **Little Ouseburn** N York
116 B5 **Littleover** C Derb
100 F6 **Little Oxendon** Nhants
99 G6 **Little Packington** Warwks
39 J4 **Little Pattenden** Kent
86 D3 **Little Paxton** Cambs
10 C8 **Little Petherick** Cnwll
138 D1 **Little Plumpton** Lancs
107 G1 **Little Plumstead** Norfk
118 B5 **Little Ponton** Lincs
104 B6 **Littleport** Cambs
104 B6 **Littleport Bridge** Cambs
19 J3 **Little Posbrook** Hants
27 J8 **Little Potheridge** Devon
142 B2 **Little Preston** Leeds
84 B4 **Little Preston** Nhants
130 C6 **Littler** Ches
102 E7 **Little Raveley** Cambs
143 K3 **Little Reedness** E R Yk
150 E5 **Little Ribston** N York
65 J3 **Little Rissington** Gloucs
65 L1 **Little Rollright** Oxon
132 E6 **Little Rowsley** Derbys
121 L6 **Little Ryburgh** Norfk
190 E4 **Little Ryle** Nthumb
96 B3 **Little Ryton** Shrops
166 D3 **Little Salkeld** Cumb
88 C8 **Little Sampford** Essex
49 K6 **Little Sandhurst** Br For
97 L2 **Little Saredon** Staffs
129 J6 **Little Saughall** Ches
88 F3 **Little Saxham** Suffk
262 C8 **Little Scatwell** Highld
87 J5 **Little Shelford** Cambs
82 F2 **Little Shrewley** Warwks
13 L1 **Little Silver** Devon
147 G7 **Little Singleton** Lancs
151 K8 **Little Skipwith** N York
142 E4 **Little Smeaton** N York
121 L5 **Little Snoring** Norfk
45 M2 **Little Sodbury** S Glos
45 L2 **Little Sodbury End** S Glos
34 E4 **Little Somborne** Hants
46 D2 **Little Somerford** Wilts
114 A6 **Little Soudley** Shrops
148 E2 **Little Stainforth** N York
169 K6 **Little Stainton** Darltn
129 J5 **Little Stanney** Ches
86 B3 **Little Staughton** Beds
137 H7 **Little Steeping** Lincs
114 E5 **Little Stoke** Staffs
25 K2 **Littlestone-on-Sea** Kent
90 D3 **Little Stonham** Suffk
100 E3 **Little Stretton** Leics
95 K5 **Little Stretton** Shrops
166 D6 **Little Strickland** Cumb
102 E8 **Little Stukeley** Cambs
114 C5 **Little Sugnall** Staffs
129 J4 **Little Sutton** Ches
96 C6 **Little Sutton** Shrops
179 M3 **Little Swinburne** Nthumb
175 H4 **Little Sypland** D & G
66 A2 **Little Tew** Oxon
72 C2 **Little Tey** Essex
103 L8 **Little Thetford** Cambs
161 G7 **Little Thirkleby** N York
122 B4 **Little Thornage** Norfk
147 G7 **Little Thornton** Lancs
169 L2 **Little Thorpe** Dur
100 C4 **Littlethorpe** Leics
150 D2 **Littlethorpe** N York
88 D5 **Little Thurlow** Suffk
88 D5 **Little Thurlow Green** Suffk
52 D3 **Little Thurrock** Thurr
233 M5 **Littleton** Angus
45 H6 **Littleton** BaNES
129 K6 **Littleton** Ches
175 G4 **Littleton** D & G
17 H2 **Littleton** Dorset
34 F4 **Littleton** Hants
31 H5 **Littleton** Somset
36 E2 **Littleton** Surrey

50 D5 **Littleton** Surrey
46 B3 **Littleton Drew** Wilts
45 H1 **Littleton-on-Severn** S Glos
46 E8 **Littleton Pannell** Wilts
27 J7 **Little Torrington** Devon
72 C5 **Little Totham** Essex
165 H6 **Little Town** Cumb
169 J2 **Littletown** Dur
148 B8 **Little Town** Lancs
130 C1 **Little Town** Warrtn
99 J2 **Little Twycross** Leics
156 C7 **Little Urswick** Cumb
53 K1 **Little Wakering** Essex
87 L7 **Little Walden** Essex
89 J6 **Little Waldingfield** Suffk
121 K4 **Little Walsingham** Norfk
71 H4 **Little Waltham** Essex
52 D1 **Little Warley** Essex
82 A8 **Little Washbourne** Gloucs
144 B1 **Little Weighton** E R Yk
101 K5 **Little Weldon** Nhants
89 H3 **Little Welnetham** Suffk
136 F2 **Little Welton** Lincs
90 C7 **Little Wenham** Suffk
96 E2 **Little Wenlock** Wrekin
31 K5 **Little Weston** Somset
19 K5 **Little Whitefield** IoW
180 B5 **Little Whittington** Nthumb
49 K3 **Littlewick Green** W & M
87 L3 **Little Wilbraham** Cambs
15 K2 **Littlewindsor** Dorset
64 C4 **Little Witcombe** Gloucs
81 H3 **Little Witley** Worcs
66 E8 **Little Wittenham** Oxon
83 G8 **Little Wolford** Warwks
98 C2 **Littlewood** Staffs
51 H6 **Little Woodcote** Gt Lon
67 L3 **Littleworth** Bucks
65 L7 **Littleworth** Oxon
98 C1 **Littleworth** Staffs
114 E7 **Littleworth** Staffs
21 L3 **Littleworth** W Susx
81 K5 **Littleworth** Worcs
82 B3 **Littleworth** Worcs
50 B2 **Littleworth Common** Bucks
88 D6 **Little Wratting** Suffk
85 J2 **Little Wymington** Beds
69 G2 **Little Wymondley** Herts
98 C2 **Little Wyrley** Staffs
113 J7 **Little Wytheford** Shrops
88 F7 **Little Yeldham** Essex
71 G4 **Littley Green** Essex
132 C4 **Litton** Derbys
158 F7 **Litton** N York
45 H8 **Litton** Somset
15 M4 **Litton Cheney** Dorset
282 g4 **Liurbost** W Isls
129 H2 **Liverpool** Lpool
141 J3 **Liversedge** Kirk
13 J7 **Liverton** Devon
171 G7 **Liverton** R & Cl
171 G7 **Liverton Mines** R & Cl
39 L3 **Liverton Street** Kent
210 E5 **Livingston** W Loth
210 D5 **Livingston Village** W Loth
128 E5 **Lixwm** Flints
3 H8 **Lizard** Cnwll
124 D3 **Llaingoch** IoA
94 C7 **Llaithddu** Powys
93 J3 **Llan** Powys
109 L7 **Llanaber** Gwynd
109 G3 **Llanaelhaearn** Gwynd
77 J1 **Llanafan** Cerdgn
78 D5 **Llanafan-fechan** Powys
125 J3 **Llanallgo** IoA
109 G4 **Llanarmon** Gwynd
112 A5 **Llanarmon Dyffryn Ceiriog** Wrexhm
128 E8 **Llanarmon-yn-Ial** Denbgs
76 D4 **Llanarth** Cerdgn
62 D5 **Llanarth** Mons
58 F5 **Llanarthne** Carmth
128 D3 **Llanasa** Flints
124 F2 **Llanbabo** IoA
92 D7 **Llanbadarn Fawr** Cerdgn
94 D7 **Llanbadarn Fynydd** Powys
78 F5 **Llanbadarn-y-garreg** Powys
62 D7 **Llanbadoc** Mons
124 F1 **Llanbadrig** IoA
44 D1 **Llanbeder** Newpt
109 K6 **Llanbedr** Gwynd
61 K3 **Llanbedr** Powys
79 G6 **Llanbedr** Powys
128 D7 **Llanbedr-Dyffryn-Clwyd** Denbgs
125 J4 **Llanbedrgoch** IoA
108 F5 **Llanbedrog** Gwynd
126 E6 **Llanbedr-y-Cennin** Conwy

125 K7 **Llanberis** Gwynd
43 G7 **Llanbethery** V Glam
94 D8 **Llanbister** Powys
42 F7 **Llanblethian** V Glam
55 L2 **Llanboidy** Carmth
43 J4 **Llanbradach** Caerph
93 K3 **Llanbrynmair** Powys
42 F8 **Llancadle** V Glam
43 G7 **Llancarfan** V Glam
62 D6 **Llancayo** Mons
62 D2 **Llancillo** Herefs
63 G3 **Llancloudy** Herefs
92 E5 **Llancynfelyn** Cerdgn
43 J6 **Llandaff** Cardif
109 K6 **Llandanwg** Gwynd
58 A6 **Llandawke** Carmth
125 J5 **Llanddaniel Fab** IoA
58 F5 **Llanddarog** Carmth
77 G1 **Llanddeiniol** Cerdgn
125 K6 **Llanddeiniolen** Gwynd
111 J4 **Llanddderfel** Gwynd
59 L4 **Llanddeusant** Carmth
124 F3 **Llanddeusant** IoA
61 G1 **Llanddew** Powys
56 E7 **Llanddewi** Swans
77 J4 **Llanddewi Brefi** Cerdgn
78 E5 **Llanddewi'r Cwm** Powys
62 D4 **Llanddewi Rhydderch** Mons
55 K4 **Llanddewi Velfrey** Pembks
78 F2 **Llanddewi Ystradenni** Powys
126 F7 **Llanddoget** Conwy
125 K4 **Llanddona** IoA
55 M4 **Llanddowror** Carmth
127 H4 **Llanddulas** Conwy
109 K7 **Llanddwywe** Gwynd
125 J4 **Llanddyfnan** IoA
110 B4 **Llandecwyn** Gwynd
60 F1 **Llandefaelog** Powys
61 H1 **Llandefaelog-Tre'r-Graig** Powys
78 F8 **Llandefalle** Powys
125 K5 **Llandegfan** IoA
112 B1 **Llandegla** Denbgs
79 G3 **Llandegley** Powys
62 C8 **Llandegveth** Mons
108 D5 **Llandegwning** Gwynd
59 H4 **Llandeilo** Carmth
78 F6 **Llandeilo Graban** Powys
78 B8 **Llandeilo'r Fan** Powys
74 D6 **Llandeloy** Pembks
62 E6 **Llandenny** Mons
44 E1 **Llandevaud** Newpt
44 E2 **Llandevenny** Mons
63 G2 **Llandinabo** Herefs
94 B5 **Llandinam** Powys
55 J3 **Llandissilio** Pembks
63 G6 **Llandogo** Mons
42 F7 **Llandough** V Glam
43 J7 **Llandough** V Glam
59 L2 **Llandovery** Carmth
42 E7 **Llandow** V Glam
77 J6 **Llandre** Carmth
92 D6 **Llandre** Cerdgn
75 K6 **Llandre Isaf** Pembks
111 K4 **Llandrillo** Denbgs
127 G4 **Llandrillo-yn-Rhos** Conwy
78 E3 **Llandrindod Wells** Powys
112 D8 **Llandrinio** Powys
126 F3 **Llandudno** Conwy
126 F4 **Llandudno Junction** Conwy
78 B7 **Llandulas** Powys
125 H8 **Llandwrog** Gwynd
59 H6 **Llandybie** Carmth
58 D6 **Llandyfaelog** Carmth
59 H5 **Llandyfan** Carmth
76 B7 **Llandyfriog** Cerdgn
125 H3 **Llandyfrydog** IoA
126 B5 **Llandygai** Gwynd
75 M3 **Llandygwydd** Cerdgn
112 B3 **Llandynan** Denbgs
128 D6 **Llandyrnog** Denbgs
94 F4 **Llandyssil** Powys
76 D7 **Llandysul** Cerdgn
43 K5 **Llanedeyrn** Cardif
57 G3 **Llanedi** Carmth
78 E7 **Llaneglwys** Powys
92 D2 **Llanegryn** Gwynd
58 F4 **Llanegwad** Carmth
125 H1 **Llaneilian** IoA
127 G4 **Llanelian-yn-Rhôs** Conwy
111 L2 **Llanelidan** Denbgs
79 H8 **Llanelieu** Powys
62 C5 **Llanelly** Mons
56 F5 **Llanelli** Carmth
110 D7 **Llanelltyd** Gwynd
61 K4 **Llanelly** Mons

78 E5 **Llanelwedd** Powys
109 L6 **Llanenddwyn** Gwynd
108 E6 **Llanengan** Gwynd
111 G8 **Llanerch** Gwynd
95 H4 **Llanerch** Powys
125 G3 **Llanerchymedd** IoA
94 B2 **Llanerfyl** Powys
124 E3 **Llanfachraeth** IoA
110 E7 **Llanfachreth** Gwynd
124 F5 **Llanfaelog** IoA
108 C6 **Llanfaelrhys** Gwynd
62 E4 **Llanfaenor** Mons
126 B4 **Llanfaes** IoA
61 G2 **Llanfaes** Powys
124 E2 **Llanfaethlu** IoA
109 K5 **Llanfair** Gwynd
94 D2 **Llanfair Caereinion** Powys
77 H5 **Llanfair Clydogau** Cerdgn
128 D8 **Llanfair Dyffryn Clwyd** Denbgs
126 D5 **Llanfairfechan** Conwy
125 J6 **Llanfair-is-gaer** Gwynd
62 D5 **Llanfair Kilgeddin** Mons
75 K5 **Llanfair-Nant-Gwyn** Pembks
125 J5 **Llanfair P G** IoA
127 J5 **Llanfair Talhaiarn** Conwy
94 F8 **Llanfair Waterdine** Shrops
125 H6 **Llanfair-y-Cwmwd** IoA
124 E2 **Llanfairynghornwy** IoA
124 E4 **Llanfair-yn-Neubwll** IoA
55 K3 **Llanfallteg** Carmth
55 K3 **Llanfallteg West** Carmth
92 D7 **Llanfarian** Cerdgn
112 B7 **Llanfechain** Powys
124 F2 **Llanfechell** IoA
128 E7 **Llanferres** Denbgs
124 F2 **Llanfflewyn** IoA
124 F3 **Llanfigael** IoA
76 E7 **Llanfihangel-ar-arth** Carmth
111 J2 **Llanfihangel Glyn Myfyr** Conwy
78 C8 **Llanfihangel Nant Bran** Powys
79 H4 **Llanfihangel-nant-Melan** Powys
79 G2 **Llanfihangel Rhydithon** Powys
44 F2 **Llanfihangel Rogiet** Mons
61 H2 **Llanfihangel Tal-y-llyn** Powys
58 E4 **Llanfihangel-uwch-Gwili** Carmth
92 E8 **Llanfihangel-y-Creuddyn** Cerdgn
111 L8 **Llanfihangel-yng-Ngwynfa** Powys
124 E4 **Llanfihangel yn Nhowyn** IoA
92 E2 **Llanfihangel-y-pennant** Gwynd
109 J3 **Llanfihangel-y-pennant** Gwynd
109 L4 **Llanfihangel-y-traethau** Gwynd
78 F8 **Llanfilo** Powys
62 B4 **Llanfoist** Mons
111 H4 **Llanfor** Gwynd
62 C8 **Llanfrechfa** Torfn
110 B3 **Llanfrothen** Gwynd
61 G2 **Llanfrynach** Powys
128 D8 **Llanfwrog** Denbgs
124 E3 **Llanfwrog** IoA
112 A7 **Llanfyllin** Powys
59 G3 **Llanfynydd** Carmth
129 G8 **Llanfynydd** Flints
75 L6 **Llanfyrnach** Pembks
94 B1 **Llangadfan** Powys
56 D3 **Llangadog** Carmth
59 K3 **Llangadog** Carmth
125 G6 **Llangadwaladr** IoA
112 B5 **Llangadwaladr** Powys
125 H6 **Llangaffo** IoA
58 C5 **Llangain** Carmth
78 C6 **Llangammarch Wells** Powys
42 E6 **Llangan** V Glam
63 G3 **Llangarron** Herefs
61 H2 **Llangasty-Talyllyn** Powys
59 G4 **Llangathen** Carmth
61 K3 **Llangattock** Powys
62 D3 **Llangattock Lingoed** Mons
62 F4 **Llangattock-Vibon-Avel** Mons
112 B6 **Llangedwyn** Powys
124 H4 **Llangefni** IoA
42 D4 **Llangeinor** Brdgnd
125 H6 **Llangeinwen** IoA
77 H3 **Llangeitho** Cerdgn

76 C7 **Llangeler** Carmth
92 C2 **Llangelynin** Gwynd
58 E6 **Llangendeirne** Carmth
57 G4 **Llangennech** Carmth
56 D6 **Llangennith** Swans
61 K3 **Llangenny** Powys
127 H6 **Llangernyw** Conwy
108 E5 **Llangian** Gwynd
57 K4 **Llangiwg** Neath
74 E5 **Llangloffan** Pembks
75 L6 **Llanglydwen** Carmth
126 C4 **Llangoed** IoA
75 L3 **Llangoedmor** Cerdgn
112 B3 **Llangollen** Denbgs
75 J6 **Llangolman** Pembks
61 H2 **Llangors** Powys
62 F6 **Llangovan** Mons
111 G5 **Llangower** Gwynd
76 B4 **Llangranog** Cerdgn
125 H5 **Llangristiolus** IoA
63 G3 **Llangrove** Herefs
62 E2 **Llangua** Mons
79 H1 **Llangunllo** Powys
58 D5 **Llangunnor** Carmth
93 K7 **Llangurig** Powys
111 J3 **Llangwm** Conwy
62 E7 **Llangwm** Mons
55 G5 **Llangwm** Pembks
62 E7 **Llangwm-isaf** Mons
108 C5 **Llangwnnadl** Gwynd
128 D6 **Llangwyfan** Denbgs
125 H4 **Llangwyllog** IoA
77 H1 **Llangwyryfon** Cerdgn
77 H4 **Llangybi** Cerdgn
109 G3 **Llangybi** Gwynd
62 D7 **Llangybi** Mons
57 H5 **Llangyfelach** Swans
128 D7 **Llangynhafal** Denbgs
61 J3 **Llangynidr** Powys
55 M3 **Llangynin** Carmth
76 C6 **Llangynllo** Cerdgn
58 C6 **Llangynog** Carmth
78 E6 **Llangynog** Powys
111 K6 **Llangynog** Powys
42 C4 **Llangynwyd** Brdgnd
61 H2 **Llanhamlach** Powys
42 F5 **Llanharan** Rhondd
42 F5 **Llanharry** Rhondd
62 D8 **Llanhennock** Mons
61 K7 **Llanhilleth** Blae G
125 J6 **Llanidan** IoA
93 L6 **Llanidloes** Powys
108 D5 **Llaniestyn** Gwynd
79 H7 **Llanigon** Powys
92 D8 **Llanilar** Cerdgn
42 E5 **Llanilid** Rhondd
76 D3 **Llanina** Cerdgn
77 H4 **Llanio** Cerdgn
43 J5 **Llanishen** Cardif
62 F6 **Llanishen** Mons
126 C6 **Llanllechid** Gwynd
78 C5 **Llanlleonfel** Powys
62 D7 **Llanllowell** Mons
94 C3 **Llanllugan** Powys
58 C5 **Llanllwch** Carmth
94 D5 **Llanllwchaiarn** Powys
76 E7 **Llanllwni** Carmth
109 H1 **Llanllyfni** Gwynd
56 D6 **Llanmadoc** Swans
42 E7 **Llanmaes** V Glam
44 E1 **Llanmartin** Newpt
94 E5 **Llanmerewig** Powys
42 E7 **Llanmihangel** V Glam
55 M5 **Llanmiloe** Carmth
56 F6 **Llanmorlais** Swans
127 K5 **Llannefydd** Conwy
56 F3 **Llannon** Carmth
108 F4 **Llannor** Gwynd
76 F2 **Llanon** Cerdgn
62 C5 **Llanover** Mons
58 D3 **Llanpumsaint** Carmth
111 M6 **Llanrhaeadr-ym-Mochnant** Powys
74 D6 **Llanrhian** Pembks
56 F6 **Llanrhidian** Swans
126 F4 **Llanrhos** Conwy
127 F7 **Llanrhychwyn** Conwy
124 F2 **Llanrhyddlad** IoA
76 F1 **Llanrhystud** Cerdgn
62 F3 **Llanrothal** Herefs
125 J7 **Llanrug** Gwynd
43 K5 **Llanrumney** Cardif
126 F7 **Llanrwst** Conwy
56 A3 **Llansadurnen** Carmth
59 J3 **Llansadwrn** Carmth
125 K4 **Llansadwrn** IoA
56 C3 **Llansaint** Carmth
57 J5 **Llansamlet** Swans

126 F4 **Llansanffraid Glan Conwy** Conwy
127 J6 **Llansannan** Conwy
42 F6 **Llansannor** V Glam
61 H2 **Llansantffraed** Powys
78 D2 **Llansantffraed-Cwmdeuddwr** Powys
78 F4 **Llansantffraed-in-Elvel** Powys
76 F2 **Llansantffraid** Cerdgn
112 C7 **Llansantffraid-ym-Mechain** Powys
59 H2 **Llansawel** Carmth
112 B6 **Llansilin** Powys
62 E6 **Llansoy** Mons
60 F2 **Llanspyddid** Powys
54 F6 **Llanstadwell** Pembks
56 C3 **Llansteffan** Carmth
78 F6 **Llanstephan** Powys
62 C8 **Llantarnam** Torfn
55 L5 **Llanteg** Pembks
62 D4 **Llanthewy Skirrid** Mons
62 B2 **Llanthony** Mons
62 E4 **Llantilio-Crossenny** Mons
62 C4 **Llantilio Pertholey** Mons
124 F3 **Llantrisant** IoA
62 D7 **Llantrisant** Mons
43 G5 **Llantrisant** Rhondd
43 G7 **Llantrithyd** V Glam
43 G4 **Llantwit Fardre** Rhondd
42 E7 **Llantwit Major** V Glam
112 B3 **Llantysilio** Denbgs
111 G5 **Llanuwchllyn** Gwynd
44 E1 **Llanvaches** Newpt
62 F8 **Llanvair Discoed** Mons
62 D4 **Llanvapley** Mons
62 D4 **Llanvetherine** Mons
62 C1 **Llanveynoe** Herefs
62 C3 **Llanvihangel Crucorney** Mons
62 D5 **Llanvihangel Gobion** Mons
62 E4 **Llanvihangel-Ystern-Llewern** Mons
63 G2 **Llanwarne** Herefs
111 K7 **Llanwddyn** Powys
62 B4 **Llanwenarth** Mons
76 F6 **Llanwenog** Cerdgn
44 D2 **Llanwern** Newpt
58 A4 **Llanwinio** Carmth
125 H8 **Llanwnda** Gwynd
74 F4 **Llanwnda** Pembks
76 F6 **Llanwnnen** Cerdgn
94 B4 **Llanwnog** Powys
42 F3 **Llanwonno** Rhondd
59 K3 **Llanwrda** Carmth
93 G3 **Llanwrin** Powys
78 D3 **Llanwrthwl** Powys
78 B5 **Llanwrtyd** Powys
78 B6 **Llanwrtyd Wells** Powys
94 C3 **Llanwyddelan** Powys
112 C7 **Llanyblodwel** Shrops
58 B6 **Llanybri** Carmth
76 F6 **Llanybydder** Carmth
55 J2 **Llanycefn** Pembks
75 G5 **Llanychaer Bridge** Pembks
77 H6 **Llanycrwys** Carmth
111 G7 **Llanymawddwy** Gwynd
112 C7 **Llanymynech** Powys
124 E3 **Llanynghenedl** IoA
128 C7 **Llanynys** Denbgs
112 F1 **Llan-y-pwll** Wrexhm
78 E3 **Llanyre** Powys
109 H4 **Llanystumdwy** Gwynd
61 H2 **Llanywern** Powys
55 H3 **Llawhaden** Pembks
112 C5 **Llawnt** Shrops
93 K5 **Llawryglyn** Powys
129 H8 **Llay** Wrexhm
125 G3 **Llechcynfarwy** IoA
61 G2 **Llechfaen** Powys
61 H5 **Llechrhyd** Caerph
75 L3 **Llechryd** Cerdgn
124 F4 **Llechylched** IoA
77 H1 **Lledrod** Cerdgn
111 G4 **Llidiardau** Gwynd
77 G7 **Llidiartnenog** Carmth
111 M3 **Llidiart-y-parc** Denbgs
108 F3 **Llithfaen** Gwynd
128 D4 **Lloc** Flints
79 H7 **Llowes** Powys
60 F6 **Llwydcoed** Rhondd
111 K8 **Llwydiarth** Powys
128 C6 **Llwyn** Denbgs
76 E3 **Llwyncelyn** Cerdgn
76 C4 **Llwyndafydd** Cerdgn
94 F3 **Llwynderw** Powys
58 A2 **Llwyn-drain** Pembks
62 C4 **Llwyn-du** Mons

108 F3 **Llwyndyrys** Gwynd
92 D2 **Llwyngwril** Gwynd
56 F5 **Llwynhendy** Carmth
112 C4 **Llwynmawr** Wrexhm
60 F5 **Llwyn-on** Myr Td
55 L4 **Llwyn-y-brain** Carmth
77 G4 **Llwyn-y-groes** Cerdgn
42 F3 **Llwynypia** Rhondd
112 D6 **Llynclys** Shrops
125 G4 **Llynfaes** IoA
128 E6 **Llyn-y-pandy** Flints
127 H4 **Llysfaen** Conwy
76 E3 **Llyswen** Cerdgn
79 G7 **Llyswen** Powys
42 E6 **Llysworney** V Glam
55 H2 **Llys-y-frân** Pembks
60 C1 **Llywel** Powys
132 E2 **Load Brook** Sheff
210 C4 **Loan** Falk
202 E3 **Loanend** Nthumb
211 J6 **Loanhead** Mdloth
176 C2 **Loaningfoot** D & G
196 C4 **Loans** S Ayrs
27 H3 **Lobb** Devon
12 B5 **Lobhillcross** Devon
238 B7 **Lochailort** Highld
227 K3 **Lochaline** Highld
172 D3 **Lochans** D & G
176 C3 **Locharbriggs** D & G
216 E4 **Lochavich** Ag & B
217 J2 **Lochawe** Ag & B
283 c11 **Loch Baghasdail** W Isls
283 c11 **Lochboisdale** W Isls
227 H7 **Lochbuie** Ag & B
248 E4 **Lochcarron** Highld
227 L6 **Lochdon** Ag & B
227 L5 **Lochdonhead** Ag & B
206 B3 **Lochead** Ag & B
219 K2 **Lochearnhead** Stirlg
222 F1 **Lochee** C Dund
239 G7 **Locheilside Station** Highld
251 G4 **Lochend** Highld
283 c8 **Locheport** W Isls
283 c8 **Loch Euphoirt** W Isls
176 B4 **Lochfoot** D & G
206 E1 **Lochgair** Ag & B
222 C8 **Lochgelly** Fife
206 D2 **Lochgilphead** Ag & B
217 K7 **Lochgoilhead** Ag & B
222 D4 **Lochieheads** Fife
266 F3 **Lochill** Moray
253 J4 **Lochindorb Lodge** Highld
270 E4 **Lochinver** Highld
262 B7 **Lochluichart** Highld
176 E2 **Lochmaben** D & G
283 d8 **Lochmaddy** W Isls
260 E6 **Loch Maree Hotel** Highld
283 d8 **Loch nam Madadh** W Isls
222 B7 **Lochore** Fife
194 E1 **Lochranza** N Ayrs
235 J3 **Lochside** Abers
176 C3 **Lochside** D & G
252 F1 **Lochside** Highld
264 C4 **Lochslin** Highld
183 G7 **Lochton** S Ayrs
234 E3 **Lochty** Angus
223 J5 **Lochty** Fife
228 B4 **Lochuisge** Highld
208 B7 **Lochwinnoch** Rens
187 G6 **Lochwood** D & G
5 H3 **Lockengate** Cnwll
176 F3 **Lockerbie** D & G
47 H5 **Lockeridge** Wilts
34 C5 **Lockerley** Hants
44 D7 **Locking** N Som
130 C1 **Locking Stumps** Warrtn
152 F6 **Lockington** E R Yk
116 D6 **Lockington** Leics
113 M6 **Lockleywood** Shrops
51 L6 **Locksbottom** Gt Lon
19 G5 **Locksgreen** IoW
19 H2 **Locks Heath** Hants
162 E5 **Lockton** N York
101 H3 **Loddington** Leics
101 H7 **Loddington** Nhants
7 L5 **Loddiswell** Devon
107 G4 **Loddon** Norfk
87 L3 **Lode** Cambs
98 F7 **Lode Heath** Solhll
15 L4 **Loders** Dorset
99 H6 **Lodge Green** Solhll
36 D6 **Lodsworth** W Susx
142 A3 **Lofthouse** Leeds
159 K8 **Lofthouse** N York
142 A3 **Lofthouse Gate** Wakefd
171 G2 **Loftus** R & Cl
197 H6 **Logan** E Ayrs
156 A4 **Loganbeck** Cumb

210 C6 **Loganlea** W Loth
114 A4 **Loggerheads** Staffs
235 H3 **Logie** Angus
223 G3 **Logie** Fife
253 K2 **Logie** Moray
243 M3 **Logie Coldstone** Abers
256 B4 **Logie Newton** Abers
235 G3 **Logie Pert** Angus
232 E5 **Logierait** P & K
257 G6 **Logierieve** Abers
55 K2 **Login** Carmth
87 H2 **Lolworth** Cambs
259 M6 **Lonbain** Highld
152 C6 **Londesborough** E R Yk
51 H3 **London** Gt Lon
5 G5 **London Apprentice** Cnwll
39 M6 **London Beach** Kent
68 F6 **London Colney** Herts
160 D5 **Londonderry** N York
85 H2 **London End** Nhants
118 C4 **Londonthorpe** Lincs
260 D4 **Londubh** Highld
260 C4 **Lonemore** Highld
45 H5 **Long Ashton** N Som
97 H8 **Long Bank** Worcs
117 L3 **Long Bennington** Lincs
181 G5 **Longbenton** N Tyne
65 J1 **Longborough** Gloucs
16 A4 **Long Bredy** Dorset
98 C7 **Longbridge** Birm
83 G3 **Longbridge** Warwks
32 E3 **Longbridge Deverill** Wilts
84 C2 **Long Buckby** Nhants
177 J7 **Longburgh** Cumb
31 L8 **Longburton** Dorset
8 B3 **Long Cause** Devon
117 J6 **Long Clawson** Leics
132 D8 **Longcliffe** Derbys
8 C3 **Longcombe** Devon
35 G7 **Long Common** Hants
114 D7 **Long Compton** Staffs
83 G8 **Long Compton** Warwks
47 K1 **Longcot** Oxon
67 G5 **Long Crendon** Bucks
17 J1 **Long Crichel** Dorset
177 H7 **Longcroft** Cumb
50 C6 **Longcross** Surrey
95 K2 **Longden** Shrops
95 K2 **Longden Common** Shrops
50 F5 **Long Ditton** Surrey
115 H8 **Longdon** Staffs
81 J7 **Longdon** Worcs
98 D1 **Longdon Green** Staffs
81 J7 **Longdon Heath** Worcs
113 K8 **Longdon upon Tern** Wrekin
13 K4 **Longdown** Devon
3 J4 **Longdowns** Cnwll
143 H2 **Long Drax** N York
133 J5 **Long Duckmanton** Derbys
116 E5 **Long Eaton** Derbys
52 D5 **Longfield** Kent
99 K6 **Longford** Covtry
115 L4 **Longford** Derbys
64 B3 **Longford** Gloucs
50 D4 **Longford** Gt Lon
38 D2 **Longford** Kent
113 L5 **Longford** Shrops
114 A7 **Longford** Wrekin
222 E1 **Longforgan** P & K
212 F7 **Longformacus** Border
191 G6 **Longframlington** Nthumb
129 L5 **Long Green** Ches
81 J8 **Long Green** Worcs
17 L3 **Longham** Dorset
121 L8 **Longham** Norfk
66 B4 **Long Hanborough** Oxon
257 L4 **Longhaven** Abers
119 K2 **Long Hedges** Lincs
191 J8 **Longhirst** Nthumb
63 K3 **Longhope** Gloucs
275 b6 **Longhope** Ork
191 H7 **Longhorsley** Nthumb
191 J3 **Longhoughton** Nthumb
83 K2 **Long Itchington** Warwks
165 J3 **Longlands** Cumb
115 L4 **Longlane** Derbys
100 A8 **Long Lawford** Warwks
64 B3 **Longlevens** Gloucs
141 G3 **Longley** Calder
141 J6 **Longley** Kirk
81 G5 **Longley Green** Worcs
233 L6 **Longleys** P & K
31 G6 **Long Load** Somset
268 D4 **Longmanhill** Abers
67 L4 **Long Marston** Herts
151 H5 **Long Marston** N York
82 K5 **Long Marston** Warwks
166 F5 **Long Marton** Cumb

95 K7 **Long Meadowend** Shrops
89 H6 **Long Melford** Suff
36 B4 **Longmoor Camp** Hants
266 E4 **Longmorn** Moray
131 H5 **Longmoss** Ches
64 C8 **Long Newnton** Gloucs
201 J7 **Longnewton** Border
212 B6 **Long Newton** E Loth
169 K7 **Longnewton** S on T
63 M4 **Longney** Gloucs
212 A4 **Longniddry** E Loth
96 B3 **Longnor** Shrops
132 B6 **Longnor** Staffs
34 F2 **Longparish** Hants
178 A6 **Longpark** Cumb
148 E4 **Long Preston** N York
147 M8 **Longridge** Lancs
114 E8 **Longridge** Staffs
210 C6 **Longridge** W Loth
209 L5 **Longriggend** N Lans
153 H7 **Long Riston** E R Yk
2 D5 **Longrock** Cnwll
114 F1 **Longsdon** Staffs
139 G7 **Longshaw** Wigan
140 D6 **Long Sight** Oldham
113 L4 **Longslow** Shrops
87 H2 **Longstanton** Cambs
34 D3 **Longstock** Hants
55 K5 **Longstone** Pembks
86 F4 **Longstowe** Cambs
106 D5 **Long Stratton** Norfk
84 F5 **Long Street** M Keyn
47 H8 **Longstreet** Wilts
35 M2 **Long Sutton** Hants
119 M7 **Long Sutton** Lincs
31 G6 **Long Sutton** Somset
102 D4 **Longthorpe** C Pete
89 K2 **Long Thurlow** Suffk
166 B6 **Longthwaite** Cumb
114 E3 **Longton** C Stke
138 F3 **Longton** Lancs
177 L5 **Longtown** Cumb
62 C1 **Longtown** Herefs
9 e3 **Longueville** Jersey
96 C4 **Longville in the Dale** Shrops
113 K8 **Long Waste** Wrekin
116 D6 **Long Whatton** Leics
67 J6 **Longwick** Bucks
66 E8 **Long Wittenham** Oxon
180 C1 **Longwitton** Nthumb
175 H3 **Longwood** D & G
96 D2 **Longwood** Shrops
66 A7 **Longworth** Oxon
212 C6 **Longyester** E Loth
57 K5 **Lon-las** Swans
269 J4 **Lonmay** Abers
258 D7 **Lonmore** Highld
6 B4 **Looe** Cnwll
39 L4 **Loose** Kent
13 G2 **Loosebeare** Devon
119 K6 **Loosegate** Lincs
67 K7 **Loosley Row** Bucks
268 A5 **Lootcherbrae** Abers
34 B4 **Lopcombe Corner** Wilts
30 F8 **Lopen** Somset
113 G5 **Loppington** Shrops
190 E5 **Lorbottle** Nthumb
20 C5 **Lordington** W Susx
104 B1 **Lordsbridge** Norfk
53 G6 **Lords Wood** Medway
233 J6 **Lornty** P & K
116 C2 **Loscoe** Derbys
15 L3 **Loscombe** Dorset
266 E2 **Lossiemouth** Moray
113 K5 **Lostford** Shrops
130 D3 **Lostock Gralam** Ches
130 D5 **Lostock Green** Ches
139 H3 **Lostock Hall** Lancs
139 K6 **Lostock Hall Fold** Bolton
139 K6 **Lostock Junction** Bolton
5 J3 **Lostwithiel** Cnwll
274 C6 **Lothbeg** Highld
149 G6 **Lothersdale** N York
274 C6 **Lothmore** Highld
49 L1 **Loudwater** Bucks
116 F7 **Loughborough** Leics
57 G5 **Loughor** Swans
70 B7 **Loughton** Essex
85 G7 **Loughton** M Keyn
96 E6 **Loughton** Shrops
118 E7 **Lound** Lincs
134 D2 **Lound** Notts
107 K4 **Lound** Suffk
13 J7 **Lounston** Devon
116 C7 **Lount** Leics
136 E2 **Louth** Lincs
140 B2 **Love Clough** Lancs

19 M1 **Lovedean** Hants
34 B6 **Lover** Wilts
142 F8 **Loversall** Donc
70 F6 **Loves Green** Essex
160 E3 **Lovesome Hill** N York
55 J5 **Loveston** Pembks
31 K5 **Lovington** Somset
142 C4 **Low Ackworth** Wakefd
180 D2 **Low Angerton** Nthumb
63 M1 **Lowbands** Gloucs
172 C2 **Low Barbeth** D & G
136 A5 **Low Barlings** Lincs
162 C3 **Low Bell End** N York
148 A2 **Low Bentham** N York
157 K7 **Low Biggins** Cumb
157 K2 **Low Borrowbridge** Cumb
132 E2 **Low Bradfield** Sheff
149 H6 **Low Bradley** N York
166 A2 **Low Braithwaite** Cumb
143 K7 **Low Burnham** N Linc
191 J5 **Low Buston** Nthumb
164 C6 **Lowca** Cumb
151 L5 **Low Catton** E R Yk
169 H7 **Low Coniscliffe** Darltn
178 B7 **Low Crosby** Cumb
117 H2 **Lowdham** Notts
169 K8 **Low Dinsdale** Darltn
113 H5 **Lowe** Shrops
142 E3 **Low Eggborough** N York
131 K8 **Low Hill** Staffs
160 B6 **Low Ellington** N York
30 B4 **Lower Aisholt** Somset
16 E2 **Lower Ansty** Dorset
64 B2 **Lower Apperley** Gloucs
66 F3 **Lower Arncott** Oxon
13 K5 **Lower Ashton** Devon
49 H2 **Lower Assendon** Oxon
138 D2 **Lower Ballam** Lancs
79 M4 **Lower Barewood** Herefs
139 G1 **Lower Bartle** Lancs
48 F3 **Lower Basildon** W Berk
37 K5 **Lower Beeding** W Susx
101 L5 **Lower Benefield** Nhants
82 A2 **Lower Bentley** Worcs
97 H5 **Lower Beobridge** Shrops
116 D1 **Lower Birchwood** Derbys
83 L5 **Lower Boddington** Nhants
2 B4 **Lower Boscaswell** Cnwll
36 C2 **Lower Bourne** Surrey
83 H7 **Lower Brailes** Warwks
247 L4 **Lower Breakish** Highld
131 H2 **Lower Bredbury** Stockp
81 J4 **Lower Broadheath** Worcs
79 L4 **Lower Broxwood** Herefs
80 E8 **Lower Buckenhill** Herefs
80 C7 **Lower Bullingham** Herefs
33 K7 **Lower Burgate** Hants
14 B3 **Lower Burrowton** Devon
80 A4 **Lower Burton** Herefs
86 D6 **Lower Caldecote** Beds
63 L7 **Lower Cam** Gloucs
44 D7 **Lower Canada** N Som
83 M3 **Lower Catesby** Nhants
78 E8 **Lower Chapel** Powys
33 G5 **Lower Chicksgrove** Wilts
47 L8 **Lower Chute** Wilts
51 K2 **Lower Clapton** Gt Lon
97 L7 **Lower Clent** Worcs
13 K2 **Lower Creedy** Devon
131 L4 **Lower Crossings** Derbys
141 K6 **Lower Cumberworth** Kirk
57 L3 **Lower Cwmtwrch** Powys
139 K3 **Lower Darwen** Bl w D
85 L2 **Lower Dean** Beds
141 K6 **Lower Denby** Kirk
260 C7 **Lower Diabaig** Highld
23 J5 **Lower Dicker** E Susx
95 L6 **Lower Dinchope** Shrops
95 H6 **Lower Down** Shrops
150 F3 **Lower Dunsforth** N York
80 E6 **Lower Egleton** Herefs
131 L8 **Lower Elkstone** Staffs
115 J3 **Lower Ellastone** Staffs
67 G5 **Lower End** Bucks
85 H7 **Lower End** M Keyn
84 F3 **Lower End** Nhants
85 H3 **Lower End** Nhants
47 J8 **Lower Everleigh** Wilts
19 G4 **Lower Exbury** Hants
41 J5 **Lower Eythorne** Kent
45 G4 **Lower Failand** N Som
35 L4 **Lower Farringdon** Hants
50 E4 **Lower Feltham** Gt Lon
21 G3 **Lower Fittleworth** W Susx
154 c6 **Lower Foxdale** IoM
112 E5 **Lower Frankton** Shrops
54 F4 **Lower Freystrop** Pembks
36 A2 **Lower Froyle** Hants

8 D1 **Lower Gabwell** Devon
263 G2 **Lower Gledfield** Highld
31 G2 **Lower Godney** Somset
97 L5 **Lower Gornal** Dudley
86 C8 **Lower Gravenhurst** Beds
86 D8 **Lower Green** Herts
87 J8 **Lower Green** Herts
38 E5 **Lower Green** Kent
39 G5 **Lower Green** Kent
121 L4 **Lower Green** Norfk
97 K2 **Lower Green** Staffs
88 E2 **Lower Green** Suffk
91 H4 **Lower Hacheston** Suffk
50 E5 **Lower Halliford** Surrey
15 M1 **Lower Halstock Leigh** Dorset
53 J5 **Lower Halstow** Kent
17 K4 **Lower Hamworthy** Poole
40 F5 **Lower Hardres** Kent
79 K3 **Lower Harpton** Herefs
53 H6 **Lower Hartlip** Kent
116 C1 **Lower Hartshay** Derbys
67 J4 **Lower Hartwell** Bucks
114 C4 **Lower Hatton** Staffs
156 B5 **Lower Hawthwaite** Cumb
79 K4 **Lower Hergest** Herefs
66 C2 **Lower Heyford** Oxon
147 H4 **Lower Heysham** Lancs
52 F4 **Lower Higham** Kent
90 E8 **Lower Holbrook** Suffk
112 F5 **Lower Hordley** Shrops
21 G3 **Lower Horncroft** W Susx
140 B1 **Lowerhouse** Lancs
141 J5 **Lower Houses** Kirk
81 H5 **Lower Howsell** Worcs
130 D1 **Lower Irlam** Salfd
116 C3 **Lower Kilburn** Derbys
46 A1 **Lower Kilcott** Gloucs
204 D7 **Lower Killeyan** Ag & B
16 A3 **Lower Kingcombe** Dorset
51 H8 **Lower Kingswood** Surrey
129 H7 **Lower Kinnerton** Ches
44 F6 **Lower Langford** N Som
223 G6 **Lower Largo** Fife
115 G4 **Lower Leigh** Staffs
82 F8 **Lower Lemington** Gloucs
78 C2 **Lower Llanfadog** Powys
27 J5 **Lower Lovacott** Devon
27 L3 **Lower Loxhore** Devon
63 H4 **Lower Lydbrook** Gloucs
79 M2 **Lower Lye** Herefs
43 K4 **Lower Machen** Newpt
62 D1 **Lower Maes-coed** Herefs
17 L2 **Lower Mannington** Dorset
32 C2 **Lower Marston** Somset
63 H6 **Lower Meend** Gloucs
30 B4 **Lower Merridge** Somset
83 L7 **Lower Middleton Cheney** Nhants
31 J2 **Lower Milton** Somset
82 A6 **Lower Moor** Worcs
63 J8 **Lower Morton** S Glos
69 K6 **Lower Nazeing** Essex
82 F3 **Lower Norton** Warwks
32 C6 **Lower Nyland** Dorset
43 J7 **Lower Penarth** V Glam
97 K4 **Lower Penn** Staffs
18 E5 **Lower Pennington** Hants
139 G2 **Lower Penwortham** Lancs
130 E5 **Lower Peover** Ches
140 D5 **Lower Place** Rochdl
67 H4 **Lower Pollicott** Bucks
82 E6 **Lower Quinton** Warwks
53 H5 **Lower Rainham** Medway
90 B7 **Lower Raydon** Suffk
29 J3 **Lower Roadwater** Somset
147 M3 **Lower Salter** Lancs
46 D3 **Lower Seagry** Wilts
70 C4 **Lower Sheering** Essex
85 K6 **Lower Shelton** Beds
49 J3 **Lower Shiplake** Oxon
83 L3 **Lower Shuckburgh** Warwks
65 H3 **Lower Slaughter** Gloucs
141 L3 **Lower Soothill** Kirk
63 K5 **Lower Soudley** Gloucs
41 H7 **Lower Standen** Kent
46 D3 **Lower Stanton St Quintin** Wilts
53 H4 **Lower Stoke** Medway
63 K8 **Lower Stone** Gloucs
98 D3 **Lower Stonnall** Staffs
105 K4 **Lower Stow Bedon** Norfk
17 G3 **Lower Street** Dorset
24 C5 **Lower Street** E Susx
122 F4 **Lower Street** Norfk
88 F5 **Lower Street** Suffk
90 D5 **Lower Street** Suffk
130 C3 **Lower Stretton** Warrtn

15 K3 **Lower Stroud** Dorset
68 D2 **Lower Sundon** Beds
19 H2 **Lower Swanwick** Hants
65 H2 **Lower Swell** Gloucs
83 J7 **Lower Tadmarton** Oxon
14 C2 **Lower Tale** Devon
115 G4 **Lower Tean** Staffs
107 J3 **Lower Thurlton** Norfk
3 G5 **Lower Town** Cnwll
13 G7 **Lower Town** Devon
80 E6 **Lower Town** Herefs
74 F5 **Lower Town** Pembks
11 L7 **Lower Trebullett** Cnwll
3 K4 **Lower Treluswell** Cnwll
83 H6 **Lower Tysoe** Warwks
91 G5 **Lower Ufford** Suffk
13 K6 **Lower Upcott** Devon
35 H7 **Lower Upham** Hants
53 G5 **Lower Upnor** Medway
29 L4 **Lower Vexford** Somset
130 B3 **Lower Walton** Warrtn
16 E3 **Lower Waterston** Dorset
44 E8 **Lower Weare** Somset
84 C3 **Lower Weedon** Nhants
79 K5 **Lower Welson** Herefs
81 L7 **Lower Westmancote** Worcs
17 G2 **Lower Whatcombe** Dorset
32 B2 **Lower Whatley** Somset
130 B4 **Lower Whitley** Ches
63 L7 **Lower Wick** Gloucs
81 J5 **Lower Wick** Worcs
35 K3 **Lower Wield** Hants
23 K6 **Lower Willingdon** E Susx
130 F5 **Lower Withington** Ches
49 K2 **Lower Woodend** Bucks
33 K4 **Lower Woodford** Wilts
16 A2 **Lower Wraxhall** Dorset
81 H6 **Lower Wyche** Worcs
141 J3 **Lower Wyke** Brad
100 F2 **Lowesby** Leics
107 L5 **Lowestoft** Suffk
164 F6 **Loweswater** Cumb
181 G7 **Low Fell** Gatesd
37 L3 **Lowfield Heath** W Susx
208 D2 **Low Gartachorrans** Stirlg
179 L6 **Low Gate** Nthumb
178 C7 **Low Gettbridge** Cumb
157 K3 **Lowgill** Cumb
148 A3 **Lowgill** Lancs
150 B2 **Low Grantley** N York
150 B4 **Low Green** N York
97 H7 **Low Habberley** Worcs
30 F5 **Low Ham** Somset
150 C5 **Low Harrogate** N York
163 G1 **Low Hawsker** N York
166 B2 **Low Hesket** Cumb
152 A2 **Low Hutton** N York
156 D5 **Lowick** Cumb
101 L7 **Lowick** Nhants
203 G5 **Lowick** Nthumb
156 D5 **Lowick Bridge** Cumb
156 D5 **Lowick Green** Cumb
166 C6 **Low Knipe** Cumb
150 B3 **Low Laithe** N York
168 E5 **Lowlands** Dur
62 C7 **Lowlands** Torfn
136 C4 **Low Langton** Lincs
131 K3 **Low Leighton** Derbys
164 F5 **Low Lorton** Cumb
134 F6 **Low Marnham** Notts
203 H6 **Low Middleton** Nthumb
161 L4 **Low Mill** N York
141 J2 **Low Moor** Brad
169 J2 **Low Moorsley** Sundld
156 F6 **Low Newton** Cumb
164 F5 **Low Rogerscales** Cumb
165 G2 **Low Row** Cumb
165 K3 **Low Row** Cumb
178 D6 **Low Row** Cumb
159 H3 **Low Row** N York
172 C2 **Low Salchrie** D & G
144 B5 **Low Santon** N Linc
82 E2 **Lowsonford** Warwks
123 G6 **Low Street** Norfk
52 E3 **Low Street** Thurr
106 D4 **Low Tharston** Norfk
166 D6 **Lowther** Cumb
166 C6 **Lowther Castle** Cumb
153 H4 **Lowthorpe** E R Yk
12 F2 **Lowton** Devon
30 B7 **Lowton** Somset
139 J8 **Lowton** Wigan
139 J8 **Lowton Common** Wigan
139 J8 **Lowton St Mary's** Wigan
210 D2 **Low Torry** Fife
136 E5 **Low Toynton** Lincs
142 B7 **Low Valley** Barns
169 G7 **Low Walworth** Darltn

156 E6 **Low Wood** Cumb
160 F1 **Low Worsall** N York
156 E2 **Low Wray** Cumb
29 G7 **Loxbeare** Devon
36 F3 **Loxhill** Surrey
27 L3 **Loxhore** Devon
27 L3 **Loxhore Cott** Devon
83 G4 **Loxley** Warwks
115 H5 **Loxley Green** Staffs
81 G7 **Loxter** Herefs
44 D7 **Loxton** N Som
36 F4 **Loxwood** W Susx
277 L7 **Loyal Lodge** Highld
100 F6 **Lubenham** Leics
119 M2 **Lucasgate** Lincs
50 B7 **Lucas Green** Surrey
29 G2 **Luccombe** Somset
19 K7 **Luccombe Village** IoW
203 J7 **Lucker** Nthumb
11 M7 **Luckett** Cnwll
89 G8 **Lucking Street** Essex
46 B2 **Luckington** Wilts
46 B4 **Lucknam** Wilts
28 F3 **Luckwell Bridge** Somset
80 B2 **Lucton** Herefs
169 G6 **Lucy Cross** N York
283 c12 **Ludag** W Isls
145 H8 **Ludborough** Lincs
7 J4 **Ludbrook** Devon
55 K4 **Ludchurch** Pembks
141 G3 **Luddenden** Calder
140 F3 **Luddenden Foot** Calder
40 C3 **Luddenham Court** Kent
52 E5 **Luddesdown** Kent
143 L4 **Luddington** N Linc
82 E5 **Luddington** Warwks
102 C6 **Luddington in the Brook** Nhants
136 D2 **Ludford** Lincs
96 C8 **Ludford** Shrops
67 G4 **Ludgershall** Bucks
34 B1 **Ludgershall** Wilts
2 D4 **Ludgvan** Cnwll
123 H7 **Ludham** Norfk
96 C8 **Ludlow** Shrops
30 F8 **Ludney** Somset
32 F6 **Ludwell** Wilts
169 K2 **Ludworth** Dur
69 J1 **Luffenhall** Herts
11 L3 **Luffincott** Devon
212 B3 **Luffness** E Loth
197 H6 **Lugar** E Ayrs
212 D4 **Luggate Burn** E Loth
80 B3 **Lugg Green** Herefs
209 K4 **Luggiebank** N Lans
129 M3 **Lugsdale** Halton
208 C8 **Lugton** E Ayrs
80 D7 **Lugwardine** Herefs
247 J3 **Luib** Highld
80 A7 **Lulham** Herefs
99 H1 **Lullington** Derbys
23 J6 **Lullington** E Susx
45 M8 **Lullington** Somset
45 G6 **Lulsgate Bottom** N Som
81 G4 **Lulsley** Worcs
16 F6 **Lulworth Camp** Dorset
140 F3 **Lumb** Calder
140 C3 **Lumb** Lancs
140 E3 **Lumbutts** Calder
142 D2 **Lumby** N York
209 H5 **Lumloch** E Duns
244 D3 **Lumphanan** Abers
222 B8 **Lumphinnans** Fife
255 K7 **Lumsden** Abers
235 H5 **Lunan** Angus
234 D5 **Lunanhead** Angus
221 K1 **Luncarty** P & K
152 E6 **Lund** E R Yk
143 G1 **Lund** N York
233 L8 **Lundie** Angus
220 C6 **Lundie** Stirlg
223 G6 **Lundin Links** Fife
223 G6 **Lundin Mill** Fife
106 E5 **Lundy Green** Norfk
281 e4 **Lunna** Shet
52 F7 **Lunsford** Kent
24 C5 **Lunsford's Cross** E Susx
138 D7 **Lunt** Sefton
79 M4 **Luntley** Herefs
14 E1 **Luppitt** Devon
7 L4 **Lupridge** Devon
141 M4 **Lupset** Wakefd
157 J6 **Lupton** Cumb
36 D5 **Lurgashall** W Susx
29 G7 **Lurley** Devon
136 F6 **Lusby** Lincs
8 B3 **Luscombe** Devon
7 H5 **Luson** Devon

218 E8 **Luss** Ag & B
258 D5 **Lusta** Highld
13 H6 **Lustleigh** Devon
80 B3 **Luston** Herefs
235 G2 **Luthermuir** Abers
222 E3 **Luthrie** Fife
97 L6 **Lutley** Dudley
13 L7 **Luton** Devon
14 C2 **Luton** Devon
68 E3 **Luton** Luton
53 G5 **Luton** Medway
100 C6 **Lutterworth** Leics
7 H3 **Lutton** Devon
7 K3 **Lutton** Devon
119 M6 **Lutton** Lincs
102 C6 **Lutton** Nhants
29 H3 **Luxborough** Somset
5 H3 **Luxulyan** Cnwll
140 E7 **Luzley** Tamesd
275 H1 **Lybster** Highld
95 J6 **Lydbury North** Shrops
28 B4 **Lydcott** Devon
25 K3 **Lydd** Kent
41 H6 **Lydden** Kent
41 K2 **Lydden** Kent
101 J4 **Lyddington** Rutlnd
29 L4 **Lydeard St Lawrence** Somset
49 H7 **Lyde Green** Hants
12 C5 **Lydford** Devon
31 J5 **Lydford on Fosse** Somset
140 D3 **Lydgate** Calder
140 E4 **Lydgate** Rochdl
95 H5 **Lydham** Shrops
47 G2 **Lydiard Green** Wilts
47 G2 **Lydiard Millicent** Wilts
47 G2 **Lydiard Tregoze** Swindn
138 D7 **Lydiate** Sefton
98 B8 **Lydiate Ash** Worcs
32 B8 **Lydlinch** Dorset
63 J6 **Lydney** Gloucs
55 J7 **Lydstep** Pembks
97 L6 **Lye** Dudley
44 F6 **Lye Cross** N Som
68 B6 **Lye Green** Bucks
38 D6 **Lye Green** E Susx
82 E2 **Lye Green** Warwks
97 G8 **Lye Head** Worcs
32 D2 **Lye's Green** Wilts
66 B8 **Lyford** Oxon
40 F6 **Lymbridge Green** Kent
15 H4 **Lyme Regis** Dorset
40 F7 **Lyminge** Kent
18 E4 **Lymington** Hants
21 H6 **Lyminster** W Susx
130 D2 **Lymm** Warrtn
40 F8 **Lympne** Kent
44 C8 **Lympsham** Somset
14 A5 **Lympstone** Devon
28 C1 **Lynbridge** Devon
28 F2 **Lynch** Somset
241 L3 **Lynchat** Highld
106 C2 **Lynch Green** Norfk
18 D2 **Lyndhurst** Hants
101 K3 **Lyndon** Rutlnd
98 F6 **Lyndon Green** Birm
199 L5 **Lyne** Border
50 C5 **Lyne** Surrey
113 G5 **Lyneal** Shrops
63 J1 **Lyne Down** Herefs
13 K6 **Lyneham** Devon
65 K3 **Lyneham** Oxon
46 F3 **Lyneham** Wilts
178 C4 **Lyneholmford** Cumb
191 K7 **Lynemouth** Nthumb
245 G2 **Lyne of Skene** Abers
275 b6 **Lyness** Ork
122 B7 **Lyng** Norfk
30 E5 **Lyng** Somset
79 K4 **Lynhales** Herefs
28 C1 **Lynmouth** Devon
98 D3 **Lynn** Staffs
114 B8 **Lynn** Wrekin
254 E6 **Lynn of Shenval** Moray
40 B3 **Lynsted** Kent
11 H2 **Lynstone** Cnwll
28 C1 **Lynton** Devon
16 C1 **Lyon's Gate** Dorset
79 L4 **Lyonshall** Herefs
17 J3 **Lytchett Matravers** Dorset
17 J4 **Lytchett Minster** Dorset
280 C4 **Lyth** Highld
138 D2 **Lytham** Lancs
138 D2 **Lytham St Anne's** Lancs
95 L2 **Lythbank** Shrops
171 K8 **Lythe** N York
279 J3 **Lythmore** Highld

M

3 J4 **Mabe Burnthouse** Cnwll
176 C5 **Mabie** D & G
137 J3 **Mablethorpe** Lincs
131 H5 **Macclesfield** Ches
268 C3 **Macduff** Abers
192 E6 **Macharioch** Ag & B
43 K4 **Machen** Caerph
194 D4 **Machrie** N Ayrs
192 D4 **Machrihanish** Ag & B
214 D5 **Machrins** Ag & B
93 G3 **Machynlleth** Powys
56 F5 **Machynys** Carmth
116 A4 **Mackworth** Derbys
211 M4 **Macmerry** E Loth
12 D3 **Maddaford** Devon
221 G3 **Madderty** P & K
33 J2 **Maddington** Wilts
210 B4 **Maddiston** Falk
21 G5 **Madehurst** W Susx
114 B3 **Madeley** Staffs
96 F3 **Madeley** Wrekin
114 B2 **Madeley Heath** Staffs
29 L8 **Madford** Devon
87 H3 **Madingley** Cambs
80 A7 **Madley** Herefs
81 J5 **Madresfield** Worcs
2 C5 **Madron** Cnwll
125 H3 **Maenaddwyn** IoA
126 F6 **Maenan** Conwy
75 J6 **Maenclochog** Pembks
42 F6 **Maendy** V Glam
3 K5 **Maenporth** Cnwll
110 C3 **Maentwrog** Gwynd
76 C3 **Maen-y-groes** Cerdgn
11 H1 **Maer** Cnwll
114 B4 **Maer** Staffs
59 J3 **Maerdy** Carmth
42 E2 **Maerdy** Rhondd
112 D7 **Maesbrook** Shrops
112 D6 **Maesbury** Shrops
112 D6 **Maesbury Marsh** Shrops
44 C2 **Maes-glas** Newpt
55 L2 **Maesgwynne** Carmth
128 E7 **Maeshafn** Denbgs
76 C6 **Maesllyn** Cerdgn
78 D6 **Maesmynis** Powys
78 E5 **Maesmynis** Powys
42 C3 **Maesteg** Brdgnd
59 G5 **Maesybont** Carmth
43 J3 **Maesycwmmer** Caerph
70 D5 **Magdalen Laver** Essex
254 F3 **Maggieknockater** Moray
70 C2 **Maggots End** Essex
23 K5 **Magham Down** E Susx
138 D7 **Maghull** Sefton
44 E2 **Magor** Mons
37 L4 **Maidenbower** W Susx
32 D3 **Maiden Bradley** Wilts
8 D1 **Maidencombe** Torbay
15 G3 **Maidenhayne** Devon
45 H5 **Maiden Head** N Som
49 L3 **Maidenhead** W & M
168 F1 **Maiden Law** Dur
16 B3 **Maiden Newton** Dorset
182 F1 **Maidens** S Ayrs
49 L4 **Maidens Green** Br For
136 F4 **Maidenwell** Lincs
55 G7 **Maiden Wells** Pembks
84 B5 **Maidford** Nhants
84 D8 **Maids Moreton** Bucks
39 J2 **Maidstone** Kent
101 G8 **Maidwell** Nhants
281 e6 **Mail** Shet
44 C1 **Maindee** Newpt
169 J4 **Mainsforth** Dur
234 D3 **Mains of Balhall** Angus
244 E8 **Mains of Balnakettle** Abers
254 B5 **Mains of Dalvey** Highld
235 H1 **Mains of Haulkerton** Abers
255 J6 **Mains of Lesmoir** Abers
176 B7 **Mainsriddle** D & G
95 G6 **Mainstone** Shrops
64 A3 **Maisemore** Gloucs
98 E7 **Major's Green** Worcs
116 B3 **Makeney** Derbys
7 K7 **Malborough** Devon
131 L3 **Malcoff** Derbys
50 F6 **Malden Rushett** Gt Lon
71 K5 **Maldon** Essex
148 F3 **Malham** N York
237 K1 **Mallaig** Highld
237 K1 **Mallaigvaig** Highld
211 G6 **Malleny Mills** C Edin
70 C2 **Mallows Green** Essex
125 G6 **Malltraeth** IoA

93 J1 **Mallwyd** Gwynd
46 D2 **Malmesbury** Wilts
28 D1 **Malmsmead** Devon
113 H2 **Malpas** Ches
4 D6 **Malpas** Cnwll
44 C1 **Malpas** Newpt
63 L2 **Malswick** Gloucs
136 F3 **Maltby** Lincs
133 K1 **Maltby** Rothm
170 B8 **Maltby** S on T
137 J3 **Maltby le Marsh** Lincs
72 E3 **Malting Green** Essex
40 B6 **Maltman's Hill** Kent
152 B2 **Malton** N York
81 H5 **Malvern Link** Worcs
81 H6 **Malvern Wells** Worcs
80 F1 **Mamble** Worcs
62 C6 **Mamhilad** Mons
3 J6 **Manaccan** Cnwll
94 D3 **Manafon** Powys
282 e6 **Manais** W Isls
13 H6 **Manaton** Devon
137 G2 **Manby** Lincs
99 J4 **Mancetter** Warwks
140 C8 **Manchester** Manch
129 H6 **Mancot** Flints
240 A3 **Mandally** Highld
103 K5 **Manea** Cambs
98 E4 **Maney** Birm
169 G8 **Manfield** N York
15 L3 **Mangerton** Dorset
45 K4 **Mangotsfield** S Glos
68 E2 **Mangrove Green** Herts
3 H5 **Manhay** Cnwll
282 e6 **Manish** W Isls
140 E3 **Mankinholes** Calder
129 L5 **Manley** Ches
61 J6 **Manmoel** Caerph
224 C7 **Mannel** Ag & B
47 H7 **Manningford Bohune** Wilts
47 H7 **Manningford Bruce** Wilts
141 J1 **Manningham** Brad
37 K5 **Manning's Heath** W Susx
17 L1 **Mannington** Dorset
73 G1 **Manningtree** Essex
245 K3 **Mannofield** C Aber
55 H7 **Manorbier** Pembks
55 H6 **Manorbier Newton** Pembks
59 J4 **Manordeilo** Carmth
201 K6 **Manorhill** Border
74 F5 **Manorowen** Pembks
51 L2 **Manor Park** Gt Lon
79 M6 **Mansell Gamage** Herefs
80 A6 **Mansell Lacy** Herefs
157 K6 **Mansergh** Cumb
197 J8 **Mansfield** E Ayrs
133 K7 **Mansfield** Notts
133 K7 **Mansfield Woodhouse** Notts
156 D6 **Mansriggs** Cumb
32 D7 **Manston** Dorset
41 K2 **Manston** Kent
142 B1 **Manston** Leeds
17 J1 **Manswood** Dorset
118 B4 **Manthorpe** Lincs
118 E8 **Manthorpe** Lincs
144 A7 **Manton** N Linc
134 C4 **Manton** Notts
101 J3 **Manton** Rutlnd
47 H5 **Manton** Wilts
70 C2 **Manuden** Essex
70 E4 **Manwood Green** Essex
31 L5 **Maperton** Somset
134 E7 **Maplebeck** Notts
68 C8 **Maple Cross** Herts
49 G4 **Mapledurham** Oxon
49 G8 **Mapledurwell** Hants
37 J6 **Maplehurst** W Susx
52 C6 **Maplescombe** Kent
115 K2 **Mapleton** Derbys
38 C3 **Mapleton** Kent
116 D3 **Mapperley** Derbys
117 G3 **Mapperley Park** C Nott
15 L3 **Mapperton** Dorset
82 C2 **Mappleborough Green** Warwks
153 K7 **Mappleton** E R Yk
141 M5 **Mapplewell** Barns
16 E1 **Mappowder** Dorset
4 C5 **Marazanvose** Cnwll
2 E5 **Marazion** Cnwll
113 J2 **Marbury** Ches
103 J4 **March** Cambs
186 E3 **March** S Lans
66 C7 **Marcham** Oxon
113 K5 **Marchamley** Shrops
113 K5 **Marchamley Wood** Shrops

115 J5 **Marchington** Staffs
115 J6 **Marchington Woodlands** Staffs
108 E6 **Marchros** Gwynd
112 E2 **Marchwiel** Wrexhm
18 F2 **Marchwood** Hants
42 D7 **Marcross** V Glam
80 C6 **Marden** Herefs
39 J4 **Marden** Kent
47 G7 **Marden** Wilts
70 E6 **Marden Ash** Essex
39 J5 **Marden Beech** Kent
38 D7 **Mardens Hill** E Susx
39 J5 **Marden Thorn** Kent
69 H3 **Mardlebury** Herts
62 C4 **Mardy** Mons
101 G2 **Marefield** Leics
136 E7 **Mareham le Fen** Lincs
136 E6 **Mareham on the Hill** Lincs
116 C2 **Marehay** Derbys
21 H3 **Marehill** W Susx
23 G2 **Maresfield** E Susx
144 E2 **Marfleet** C KuH
129 H8 **Marford** Wrexhm
57 L7 **Margam** Neath
32 D7 **Margaret Marsh** Dorset
70 F5 **Margaret Roding** Essex
71 G6 **Margaretting** Essex
71 G7 **Margaretting Tye** Essex
41 K1 **Margate** Kent
195 G4 **Margnaheglish** N Ayrs
174 F5 **Margrie** D & G
170 F7 **Margrove Park** R & Cl
104 E2 **Marham** Norfk
11 J2 **Marhamchurch** Cnwll
102 C7 **Marholm** C Pete
125 J3 **Marian-glas** IoA
28 C6 **Mariansleigh** Devon
53 K4 **Marine Town** Kent
244 F2 **Marionburgh** Abers
259 H4 **Marishader** Highld
6 F2 **Maristow** Devon
176 E2 **Marjoriebanks** D & G
30 F1 **Mark** Somset
38 D5 **Markbeech** Kent
137 J4 **Markby** Lincs
30 E2 **Mark Causeway** Somset
38 F7 **Mark Cross** E Susx
116 B4 **Markeaton** C Derb
99 L3 **Market Bosworth** Leics
102 C2 **Market Deeping** Lincs
113 L5 **Market Drayton** Shrops
100 F6 **Market Harborough** Leics
46 E8 **Market Lavington** Wilts
118 A8 **Market Overton** Rutlnd
136 B2 **Market Rasen** Lincs
136 D4 **Market Stainton** Lincs
133 L6 **Market Warsop** Notts
152 D7 **Market Weighton** E R Yk
105 K7 **Market Weston** Suffk
100 B2 **Markfield** Leics
61 J6 **Markham** Caerph
134 E5 **Markham Moor** Notts
222 E6 **Markinch** Fife
150 C3 **Markington** N York
212 C3 **Markle** E Loth
45 K6 **Marksbury** BaNES
19 H5 **Mark's Corner** IoW
72 C2 **Marks Tey** Essex
6 D3 **Markwell** Cnwll
68 D4 **Markyate** Herts
81 H7 **Marl Bank** Worcs
47 J5 **Marlborough** Wilts
80 C4 **Marlbrook** Herefs
98 B8 **Marlbrook** Worcs
82 C5 **Marlcliff** Warwks
8 C2 **Marldon** Devon
23 K4 **Marle Green** E Susx
91 H3 **Marlesford** Suffk
41 G5 **Marley** Kent
41 K4 **Marley** Kent
113 J2 **Marley Green** Ches
180 F7 **Marley Hill** Gatesd
106 C2 **Marlingford** Norfk
54 C5 **Marloes** Pembks
49 K2 **Marlow** Bucks
95 K8 **Marlow** Herefs
49 K1 **Marlow Bottom** Bucks
38 C4 **Marlpit Hill** Kent
24 C4 **Marlpits** E Susx
38 C7 **Marlpits** E Susx
116 D3 **Marlpool** Derbys
32 C7 **Marnhull** Dorset
131 J2 **Marple** Stockp
131 J2 **Marple Bridge** Stockp
142 E6 **Marr** Donc
159 K3 **Marrick** N York
55 L5 **Marros** Carmth

141 G5 **Marsden** Kirk	254 D4 **Marypark** Moray	31 G3 **Meare** Somset

141 G5 **Marsden** Kirk
181 K6 **Marsden** S Tyne
148 F8 **Marsden Height** Lancs
158 F5 **Marsett** N York
149 J8 **Marsh** Brad
67 K5 **Marsh** Bucks
30 C8 **Marsh** Devon
68 F4 **Marshall's Heath** Herts
68 F5 **Marshalswick** Herts
122 D6 **Marsham** Norfk
66 E7 **Marsh Baldon** Oxon
48 B5 **Marsh Benham** W Berk
41 J4 **Marshborough** Kent
95 K5 **Marshbrook** Shrops
145 K7 **Marshchapel** Lincs
43 L5 **Marshfield** Newpt
45 M4 **Marshfield** S Glos
11 G4 **Marshgate** Cnwll
66 F3 **Marsh Gibbon** Bucks
14 B4 **Marsh Green** Devon
38 C4 **Marsh Green** Kent
113 K8 **Marsh Green** Wrekin
103 L2 **Marshland St James** Norfk
133 H4 **Marsh Lane** Derbys
63 H5 **Marsh Lane** Gloucs
138 D4 **Marshside** Sefton
29 H2 **Marsh Street** Somset
15 J3 **Marshwood** Dorset
159 K3 **Marske** N York
170 E6 **Marske-by-the-Sea** R & Cl
139 K7 **Marsland Green** Wigan
130 D5 **Marston** Ches
79 L4 **Marston** Herefs
118 A3 **Marston** Lincs
66 D5 **Marston** Oxon
97 J1 **Marston** Staffs
114 E6 **Marston** Staffs
99 G4 **Marston** Warwks
46 D7 **Marston** Wilts
98 F6 **Marston Green** Solhll
99 K5 **Marston Jabbet** Warwks
31 K6 **Marston Magna** Somset
65 H7 **Marston Meysey** Wilts
115 J4 **Marston Montgomery** Derbys
85 K7 **Marston Moretaine** Beds
115 L5 **Marston on Dove** Derbys
83 M6 **Marston St Lawrence** Nhants
80 D4 **Marston Stannett** Herefs
100 F6 **Marston Trussell** Nhants
63 H3 **Marstow** Herefs
68 A4 **Marsworth** Bucks
47 L7 **Marten** Wilts
130 F4 **Marthall** Ches
123 J7 **Martham** Norfk
33 J7 **Martin** Hants
41 K6 **Martin** Kent
136 B7 **Martin** Lincs
136 D6 **Martin** Lincs
166 B6 **Martindale** Cumb
136 C7 **Martin Dales** Lincs
33 H6 **Martin Drove End** Hants
28 B1 **Martinhoe** Devon
81 K3 **Martin Hussingtree** Worcs
130 C2 **Martinscroft** Warrtn
16 C4 **Martinstown** Dorset
90 F6 **Martlesham** Suffk
90 F6 **Martlesham Heath** Suffk
55 H5 **Martletwy** Pembks
81 H3 **Martley** Worcs
31 G7 **Martock** Somset
130 C6 **Marton** Ches
131 G6 **Marton** Ches
156 C7 **Marton** Cumb
153 J7 **Marton** E R Yk
153 K2 **Marton** E R Yk
135 G3 **Marton** Lincs
170 C7 **Marton** Middsb
150 F3 **Marton** N York
162 C6 **Marton** N York
95 G3 **Marton** Shrops
83 J2 **Marton** Warwks
150 E2 **Marton-le-Moor** N York
50 E7 **Martyr's Green** Surrey
35 G4 **Martyr Worthy** Hants
275 b3 **Marwick** Ork
27 K3 **Marwood** Devon
250 E1 **Marybank** Highld
262 F8 **Maryburgh** Highld
245 J4 **Maryculter** Abers
213 H7 **Marygold** Border
256 E3 **Maryhill** Abers
208 F5 **Maryhill** C Glas
235 H2 **Marykirk** Abers
45 G1 **Maryland** Mons
51 H3 **Marylebone** Gt Lon
139 H6 **Marylebone** Wigan

254 D4 **Marypark** Moray
164 D3 **Maryport** Cumb
172 E7 **Maryport** D & G
12 B6 **Marystow** Devon
12 C6 **Mary Tavy** Devon
235 H4 **Maryton** Angus
244 D4 **Marywell** Abers
245 L4 **Marywell** Abers
235 G6 **Marywell** Angus
160 B6 **Masham** N York
71 G5 **Mashbury** Essex
180 F4 **Mason** N u Ty
157 L7 **Masongill** N York
133 J4 **Mastin Moor** Derbys
70 D5 **Matching** Essex
70 D5 **Matching Green** Essex
70 D5 **Matching Tye** Essex
180 C4 **Matfen** Nthumb
39 G5 **Matfield** Kent
45 G1 **Mathern** Mons
81 G6 **Mathon** Herefs
74 E6 **Mathry** Pembks
122 C4 **Matlask** Norfk
132 F7 **Matlock** Derbys
132 F7 **Matlock Bank** Derbys
132 F8 **Matlock Bath** Derbys
132 F7 **Matlock Dale** Derbys
64 B4 **Matson** Gloucs
165 L6 **Matterdale End** Cumb
134 D2 **Mattersey** Notts
134 D2 **Mattersey Thorpe** Notts
49 H7 **Mattingley** Hants
105 L1 **Mattishall** Norfk
105 L1 **Mattishall Burgh** Norfk
196 F5 **Mauchline** E Ayrs
269 G6 **Maud** Abers
9 e2 **Maufant** Jersey
65 J2 **Maugersbury** Gloucs
154 g4 **Maughold** IoM
250 C4 **Mauld** Highld
85 L7 **Maulden** Beds
166 E7 **Maulds Meaburn** Cumb
160 E5 **Maunby** N York
80 D5 **Maund Bryan** Herefs
29 J5 **Maundown** Somset
107 K1 **Mautby** Norfk
115 H8 **Mavesyn Ridware** Staffs
137 G6 **Mavis Enderby** Lincs
164 E1 **Mawbray** Cumb
139 G5 **Mawdesley** Lancs
42 B5 **Mawdlam** Brdgnd
3 H6 **Mawgan** Cnwll
4 D2 **Mawgan Porth** Cnwll
130 D8 **Maw Green** Ches
4 A5 **Mawla** Cnwll
3 K5 **Mawnan** Cnwll
3 K5 **Mawnan Smith** Cnwll
101 H8 **Mawsley** Nhants
137 J5 **Mawthorpe** Lincs
102 C2 **Maxey** C Pete
99 G6 **Maxstoke** Warwks
40 F6 **Maxted Street** Kent
201 J7 **Maxton** Border
41 J7 **Maxton** Kent
176 C4 **Maxwell Town** D & G
11 J4 **Maxworthy** Cnwll
57 H6 **Mayals** Swans
114 D2 **May Bank** Staffs
183 H1 **Maybole** S Ayrs
50 C7 **Maybury** Surrey
37 H3 **Mayes Green** Surrey
23 K2 **Mayfield** E Susx
211 K6 **Mayfield** Mdloth
115 J2 **Mayfield** Staffs
50 C7 **Mayford** Surrey
63 L3 **May Hill** Gloucs
72 D6 **Mayland** Essex
72 C6 **Maylandsea** Essex
23 K3 **Maynard's Green** E Susx
98 D7 **Maypole** Birm
41 G2 **Maypole** Kent
62 F4 **Maypole** Mons
107 J4 **Maypole Green** Norfk
89 J3 **Maypole Green** Suffk
91 G2 **Maypole Green** Suffk
49 H3 **May's Green** Oxon
50 E7 **May's Green** Surrey
26 C7 **Mead** Devon
45 K7 **Meadgate** BaNES
67 K6 **Meadle** Bucks
169 H3 **Meadowfield** Dur
95 H3 **Meadowtown** Shrops
12 A6 **Meadwell** Devon
157 H4 **Meal Bank** Cumb
164 F2 **Mealrigg** Cumb
165 H2 **Mealsgate** Cumb
150 C8 **Meanwood** Leeds
148 E4 **Mearbeck** N York

31 G3 **Meare** Somset
30 D6 **Meare Green** Somset
30 E5 **Meare Green** Somset
208 F7 **Mearns** E Rens
85 G2 **Mears Ashby** Nhants
99 J1 **Measham** Leics
156 F6 **Meathop** Cumb
153 H7 **Meaux** E R Yk
7 G2 **Meavy** Devon
101 H5 **Medbourne** Leics
26 D7 **Meddon** Devon
134 B5 **Meden Vale** Notts
136 F8 **Medlam** Lincs
147 H8 **Medlar** Lancs
49 K2 **Medmenham** Bucks
180 D7 **Medomsley** Dur
35 K3 **Medstead** Hants
131 K7 **Meerbrook** Staffs
79 L5 **Meer Common** Herefs
70 B1 **Meesden** Herts
113 L7 **Meeson** Wrekin
12 D1 **Meeth** Devon
88 E4 **Meeting Green** Suffk
122 F6 **Meeting House Hill** Norfk
58 B5 **Meidrim** Carmth
94 E1 **Meifod** Powys
233 L6 **Meigle** P & K
186 A3 **Meikle Carco** D & G
209 J8 **Meikle Earnock** S Lans
207 G6 **Meikle Kilmory** Ag & B
232 F7 **Meikle Obney** P & K
233 J7 **Meikleour** P & K
256 C5 **Meikle Wartle** Abers
56 E3 **Meinciau** Carmth
114 E3 **Meir** C Stke
114 E3 **Meir Heath** Staffs
87 H6 **Melbourn** Cambs
116 C6 **Melbourne** Derbys
152 A7 **Melbourne** E R Yk
26 F7 **Melbury** Devon
32 E6 **Melbury Abbas** Dorset
16 B1 **Melbury Bubb** Dorset
16 A1 **Melbury Osmond** Dorset
16 A1 **Melbury Sampford** Dorset
85 K2 **Melchbourne** Beds
16 E2 **Melcombe Bingham** Dorset
12 D4 **Meldon** Devon
180 D2 **Meldon** Nthumb
180 D2 **Meldon Park** Nthumb
87 H6 **Meldreth** Cambs
220 C7 **Meldrum** Stirlg
4 F4 **Meledor** Cnwll
216 C4 **Melfort** Ag & B
234 E4 **Melgund Castle** Angus
128 C3 **Meliden** Denbgs
55 K4 **Melinau** Pembks
93 H4 **Melin-byrhedyn** Powys
60 B6 **Melincourt** Neath
127 G7 **Melin-y-coed** Conwy
94 D2 **Melin-y-ddol** Powys
111 K2 **Melin-y-wig** Denbgs
166 D5 **Melkinthorpe** Cumb
179 G6 **Melkridge** Nthumb
46 C6 **Melksham** Wilts
3 H5 **Mellangoose** Cnwll
48 C3 **Mell Green** W Berk
166 B2 **Mellguards** Cumb
147 M2 **Melling** Lancs
138 E7 **Melling** Sefton
138 E7 **Melling Mount** Sefton
95 G5 **Mellington** Powys
106 B8 **Mellis** Suffk
260 D2 **Mellon Charles** Highld
260 E1 **Mellon Udrigle** Highld
139 K2 **Mellor** Lancs
131 K2 **Mellor** Stockp
139 J2 **Mellor Brook** Lancs
32 B1 **Mells** Somset
107 H8 **Mells** Suffk
166 E3 **Melmerby** Cumb
159 K5 **Melmerby** N York
160 E7 **Melmerby** N York
277 K4 **Melness** Highld
89 G4 **Melon Green** Suffk
15 L3 **Melplash** Dorset
201 H6 **Melrose** Border
275 b6 **Melsetter** Ork
160 B1 **Melsonby** N York
141 H5 **Meltham** Kirk
141 H5 **Meltham Mills** Kirk
144 B2 **Melton** E R Yk
91 G5 **Melton** Suffk
152 B5 **Meltonby** E R Yk
122 A5 **Melton Constable** Norfk
117 K7 **Melton Mowbray** Leics
144 D5 **Melton Ross** N Linc
260 B3 **Melvaig** Highld
112 E8 **Melverley** Shrops

112 E7 **Melverley Green** Shrops
278 E3 **Melvich** Highld
15 G2 **Membury** Devon
269 H4 **Memsie** Abers
234 C4 **Memus** Angus
5 J4 **Menabilly** Cnwll
4 B5 **Menagissey** Cnwll
125 K5 **Menai Bridge** IoA
106 F6 **Mendham** Suffk
90 D2 **Mendlesham** Suffk
90 C3 **Mendlesham Green** Suffk
6 B2 **Menheniot** Cnwll
81 G2 **Menithwood** Worcs
185 K2 **Mennock** D & G
149 L7 **Menston** Brad
220 E7 **Menstrie** Clacks
143 H1 **Menthorpe** N York
67 M3 **Mentmore** Bucks
238 C6 **Meoble** Highld
96 B1 **Meole Brace** Shrops
35 J7 **Meonstoke** Hants
52 D5 **Meopham** Kent
52 D6 **Meopham Green** Kent
52 D5 **Meopham Station** Kent
103 J7 **Mepal** Cambs
86 C8 **Meppershall** Beds
79 K6 **Merbach** Herefs
130 E3 **Mere** Ches
32 D4 **Mere** Wilts
138 E4 **Mere Brow** Lancs
140 C2 **Mereclough** Lancs
98 E4 **Mere Green** Birm
81 L3 **Mere Green** Worcs
130 C5 **Mere Heath** Ches
53 H6 **Meresborough** Medway
39 G3 **Mereworth** Kent
99 G7 **Meriden** Solhll
246 E2 **Merkadale** Highld
17 K3 **Merley** Poole
54 F4 **Merlin's Bridge** Pembks
113 J2 **Merrington** Shrops
54 F7 **Merrion** Pembks
31 G8 **Merriott** Somset
12 D7 **Merrivale** Devon
36 F1 **Merrow** Surrey
17 K2 **Merry Field Hill** Dorset
68 E8 **Merry Hill** Herts
97 K4 **Merryhill** Wolves
100 A2 **Merry Lees** Leics
6 B2 **Merrymeet** Cnwll
40 D7 **Mersham** Kent
51 H8 **Merstham** Surrey
20 E6 **Merston** W Susx
19 J6 **Merstone** IoW
4 D6 **Merther** Cnwll
58 C5 **Merthyr** Carmth
78 D7 **Merthyr Cynog** Powys
43 H7 **Merthyr Dyfan** V Glam
42 D6 **Merthyr Mawr** Brdgnd
61 G6 **Merthyr Tydfil** Myr Td
61 G7 **Merthyr Vale** Myr Td
27 J8 **Merton** Devon
51 H5 **Merton** Gt Lon
105 H4 **Merton** Norfk
66 E3 **Merton** Oxon
28 D7 **Meshaw** Devon
72 C3 **Messing** Essex
143 M6 **Messingham** N Linc
106 F7 **Metfield** Suffk
6 E1 **Metherell** Cnwll
135 L7 **Metheringham** Lincs
222 F7 **Methil** Fife
222 F7 **Methilhill** Fife
3 G5 **Methleigh** Cnwll
142 B2 **Methley** Leeds
142 B3 **Methley Junction** Leeds
256 F4 **Methlick** Abers
221 J2 **Methven** P & K
104 E4 **Methwold** Norfk
104 E4 **Methwold Hythe** Norfk
107 H5 **Mettingham** Suffk
122 D4 **Metton** Norfk
5 G6 **Mevagissey** Cnwll
142 D7 **Mexborough** Donc
280 C2 **Mey** Highld
108 D5 **Meyllteyrn** Gwynd
65 K2 **Meysey Hampton** Gloucs
282 e3 **Miabhig** W Isls
282 e3 **Miavaig** W Isls
63 G3 **Michaelchurch** Herefs
79 K8 **Michaelchurch Escley** Herefs
79 J5 **Michaelchurch-on-Arrow** Powys
43 K5 **Michaelstone-y-Fedw** Newpt
43 J7 **Michaelston-le-Pit** V Glam
10 F6 **Michaelstow** Cnwll

7 K1 **Michelcombe** Devon
35 G3 **Micheldever** Hants
35 G2 **Micheldever Station** Hants
34 D5 **Michelmersh** Hants
90 D3 **Mickfield** Suffk
133 K1 **Micklebring** Donc
171 J8 **Mickleby** N York
142 C1 **Micklefield** Leeds
68 D7 **Micklefield Green** Herts
50 F8 **Mickleham** Surrey
116 A5 **Mickleover** C Derb
149 K7 **Micklethwaite** Brad
165 J1 **Micklethwaite** Cumb
168 B6 **Mickleton** Dur
82 E6 **Mickleton** Gloucs
142 B2 **Mickletown** Leeds
129 K5 **Mickle Trafford** Ches
132 F4 **Mickley** Derbys
160 C7 **Mickley** N York
89 G4 **Mickley Green** Suffk
180 C6 **Mickley Square** Nthumb
269 H3 **Mid Ardlaw** Abers
275 c2 **Midbea** Ork
244 E3 **Mid Beltie** Abers
18 B4 **Mid Bockhampton** Dorset
210 E5 **Mid Calder** W Loth
280 C8 **Mid Clyth** Highld
268 B4 **Mid Culbeuchly** Abers
49 H2 **Middle Assendon** Oxon
66 C2 **Middle Aston** Oxon
66 B2 **Middle Barton** Oxon
177 H4 **Middlebie** D & G
232 C2 **Middlebridge** P & K
31 G8 **Middle Chinnock** Somset
67 H2 **Middle Claydon** Bucks
142 C6 **Middlecliffe** Barns
13 G5 **Middlecott** Devon
64 E6 **Middle Duntisbourne** Gloucs
159 L5 **Middleham** N York
133 H4 **Middle Handley** Derbys
105 K6 **Middle Harling** Norfk
6 B1 **Middlehill** Cnwll
46 B5 **Middlehill** Wilts
96 B5 **Middlehope** Shrops
206 E1 **Middle Kames** Ag & B
82 C6 **Middle Littleton** Worcs
114 B3 **Middle Madeley** Staffs
79 L8 **Middle Maes-coed** Herefs
16 C1 **Middlemarsh** Dorset
115 J3 **Middle Mayfield** Staffs
74 C7 **Middle Mill** Pembks
12 C7 **Middlemore** Devon
40 A7 **Middle Quarter** Kent
136 A2 **Middle Rasen** Lincs
8 D1 **Middle Rocombe** Devon
147 M3 **Middle Salter** Lancs
170 C6 **Middlesbrough** Middsb
165 L2 **Middlesceugh** Cumb
157 J5 **Middleshaw** Cumb
159 K7 **Middlesmoor** N York
30 B6 **Middle Stoford** Somset
53 H4 **Middle Stoke** Medway
169 H4 **Middlestone** Dur
169 H4 **Middlestone Moor** Dur
30 F1 **Middle Stoughton** Somset
141 L4 **Middlestown** Wakefd
63 M6 **Middle Street** Gloucs
5 K2 **Middle Taphouse** Cnwll
201 L4 **Middlethird** Border
224 B6 **Middleton** Ag & B
157 K5 **Middleton** Cumb
132 D7 **Middleton** Derbys
132 E8 **Middleton** Derbys
89 H7 **Middleton** Essex
34 F2 **Middleton** Hants
80 D1 **Middleton** Herefs
147 H4 **Middleton** Lancs
141 M2 **Middleton** Leeds
149 L6 **Middleton** N York
162 D5 **Middleton** N York
101 J5 **Middleton** Nhants
120 E8 **Middleton** Norfk
180 C2 **Middleton** Nthumb
203 H6 **Middleton** Nthumb
221 L6 **Middleton** P & K
140 C6 **Middleton** Rochdl
96 C7 **Middleton** Shrops
112 D5 **Middleton** Shrops
91 K2 **Middleton** Suffk
56 D7 **Middleton** Swans
98 F4 **Middleton** Warwks
83 L7 **Middleton Cheney** Nhants
114 F4 **Middleton Green** Staffs
202 F8 **Middleton Hall** Nthumb
168 B5 **Middleton-in-Teesdale** Dur
91 J2 **Middleton Moor** Suffk
169 K8 **Middleton One Row** Darltn
161 G1 **Middleton-on-Leven** N York

20 F6 **Middleton-on-Sea** W Susx
80 C2 **Middleton on the Hill** Herefs
152 E6 **Middleton on the Wolds** E R Yk
96 E5 **Middleton Priors** Shrops
160 E7 **Middleton Quernhow** N York
169 K8 **Middleton St George** Darltn
96 F6 **Middleton Scriven** Shrops
66 D2 **Middleton Stoney** Oxon
160 B2 **Middleton Tyas** N York
155 H1 **Middletown** Cumb
10 b3 **Middle Town** IoS
44 F4 **Middletown** N Som
95 H1 **Middletown** Powys
83 H6 **Middle Tysoe** Warwks
34 C3 **Middle Wallop** Hants
130 D6 **Middlewich** Ches
34 B4 **Middle Winterslow** Wilts
11 K7 **Middlewood** Cnwll
79 K6 **Middlewood** Herefs
33 K4 **Middle Woodford** Wilts
90 C3 **Middlewood Green** Suffk
197 G4 **Middleyard** E Ayrs
64 B6 **Middle Yard** Gloucs
30 E4 **Middlezoy** Somset
169 H5 **Middridge** Dur
45 M6 **Midford** BaNES
139 G3 **Midge Hall** Lancs
178 E7 **Midgeholme** Cumb
48 E5 **Midgham** W Berk
140 F3 **Midgley** Calder
141 L5 **Midgley** Wakefd
37 J2 **Mid Holmwood** Surrey
141 K7 **Midhopestones** Sheff
36 C6 **Midhurst** W Susx
20 D5 **Mid Lavant** W Susx
201 H7 **Midlem** Border
250 D4 **Mid Mains** Highld
31 H5 **Midney** Somset
207 G7 **Midpark** Ag & B
45 K8 **Midsomer Norton** BaNES
136 E5 **Mid Thorpe** Lincs
277 K4 **Midtown** Highld
137 G8 **Midville** Lincs
131 H3 **Midway** Ches
281 e3 **Mid Yell** Shet
244 A2 **Migvie** Abers
31 L7 **Milborne Port** Somset
16 F3 **Milborne St Andrew** Dorset
31 L6 **Milborne Wick** Somset
180 D4 **Milbourne** Nthumb
46 D2 **Milbourne** Wilts
166 F5 **Milburn** Cumb
45 K1 **Milbury Heath** S Glos
150 F2 **Milby** N York
83 K8 **Milcombe** Oxon
89 J6 **Milden** Suffk
104 E8 **Mildenhall** Suffk
47 J5 **Mildenhall** Wilts
79 K1 **Milebrook** Powys
39 J4 **Milebush** Kent
46 E5 **Mile Elm** Wilts
72 E2 **Mile End** Essex
63 H5 **Mile End** Gloucs
107 G5 **Mile End** Suffk
121 K7 **Mileham** Norfk
22 C5 **Mile Oak** Br & H
39 H4 **Mile Oak** Kent
98 F3 **Mile Oak** Staffs
80 D2 **Miles Hope** Herefs
210 E1 **Milesmark** Fife
140 C7 **Miles Platting** Manch
53 K4 **Mile Town** Kent
202 E6 **Milfield** Nthumb
116 B3 **Milford** Derbys
26 D6 **Milford** Devon
94 D5 **Milford** Powys
114 F7 **Milford** Staffs
36 E2 **Milford** Surrey
54 E5 **Milford Haven** Pembks
18 D5 **Milford on Sea** Hants
63 H5 **Milkwall** Gloucs
9 a1 **Millais** Jersey
36 B5 **Milland** W Susx
36 C5 **Milland Marsh** W Susx
140 F3 **Mill Bank** Calder
165 H5 **Millbeck** Cumb
257 J3 **Millbreck** Abers
256 E3 **Millbrex** Abers
36 C2 **Millbridge** Surrey
85 K7 **Millbrook** Beds
34 E8 **Millbrook** C Sotn
6 E4 **Millbrook** Cnwll
9 c3 **Millbrook** Jersey
140 E7 **Millbrook** Tamesd

131 J2 **Mill Brow** Stockp
245 H2 **Millbuie** Abers
250 F1 **Millbuie** Highld
196 E5 **Millburn** S Ayrs
8 B5 **Millcombe** Devon
107 G3 **Mill Common** Norfk
107 H7 **Mill Common** Suffk
24 E3 **Millcorner** E Susx
263 K5 **Millcraig** Highld
7 L3 **Mill Cross** Devon
115 J1 **Milldale** Staffs
49 J2 **Mill End** Bucks
103 G7 **Mill End** Cambs
63 L7 **Millend** Gloucs
87 G8 **Mill End** Herts
211 K5 **Millerhill** Mdloth
132 C5 **Miller's Dale** Derbys
115 M1 **Millers Green** Derbys
70 E5 **Miller's Green** Essex
209 H5 **Millerston** C Glas
140 D4 **Millgate** Lancs
88 C6 **Mill Green** Cambs
70 F6 **Mill Green** Essex
69 G5 **Mill Green** Herts
119 H6 **Mill Green** Lincs
106 C6 **Mill Green** Norfk
113 L6 **Millgreen** Shrops
98 D3 **Mill Green** Staffs
115 H7 **Mill Green** Staffs
89 J6 **Mill Green** Suffk
89 K4 **Mill Green** Suffk
90 D3 **Mill Green** Suffk
91 H3 **Mill Green** Suffk
79 K5 **Millhalf** Herefs
14 F2 **Millhayes** Devon
147 K2 **Millhead** Lancs
198 B3 **Millheugh** S Lans
23 L6 **Mill Hill** E Susx
69 G8 **Mill Hill** Gt Lon
206 F5 **Millhouse** Ag & B
165 K3 **Millhouse** Cumb
176 F2 **Millhousebridge** D & G
141 K7 **Millhouse Green** Barns
142 C6 **Millhouses** Barns
133 G3 **Millhouses** Sheff
208 C6 **Milliken Park** Rens
55 G4 **Millin Cross** Pembks
152 C5 **Millington** E R Yk
114 C5 **Millmeece** Staffs
157 H6 **Millness** Cumb
220 E4 **Mill of Drummond** P & K
208 C3 **Mill of Haldane** W Duns
155 M6 **Millom** Cumb
11 H3 **Millook** Cnwll
2 F5 **Millpool** Cnwll
11 G8 **Millpool** Cnwll
207 K8 **Millport** N Ayrs
157 G6 **Mill Side** Cumb
39 H2 **Mill Street** Kent
122 B7 **Mill Street** Norfk
90 C1 **Mill Street** Suffk
132 F4 **Millthorpe** Derbys
157 L4 **Millthrop** Cumb
245 J3 **Milltimber** C Aber
243 J2 **Milltown** Abers
255 J8 **Milltown** Abers
5 J3 **Milltown** Cnwll
177 K4 **Milltown** D & G
133 G7 **Milltown** Derbys
27 K3 **Milltown** Devon
244 E3 **Milltown of Campfield** Abers
254 F4 **Milltown of Edinvillie** Moray
244 E3 **Milltown of Learney** Abers
221 L6 **Milnathort** P & K
208 F4 **Milngavie** E Duns
140 D5 **Milnrow** Rochdl
157 H6 **Milnthorpe** Cumb
142 A4 **Milnthorpe** Wakefd
258 B6 **Milovaig** Highld
80 E1 **Milson** Shrops
40 A3 **Milstead** Kent
33 L2 **Milston** Wilts
118 F5 **Milthorpe** Lincs
84 B6 **Milthorpe** Nhants
114 E2 **Milton** C Stke
87 K3 **Milton** Cambs
178 D6 **Milton** Cumb
172 F4 **Milton** D & G
175 L1 **Milton** D & G
116 A6 **Milton** Derbys
248 A3 **Milton** Highld
250 E5 **Milton** Highld
251 G2 **Milton** Highld
263 K5 **Milton** Highld
280 D6 **Milton** Highld
208 B5 **Milton** Inver

52 E4 **Milton** Kent
254 D7 **Milton** Moray
267 K4 **Milton** Moray
44 D6 **Milton** N Som
44 D1 **Milton** Newpt
134 E5 **Milton** Notts
66 C8 **Milton** Oxon
83 K8 **Milton** Oxon
233 H4 **Milton** P & K
55 H6 **Milton** Pembks
31 G6 **Milton** Somset
219 H7 **Milton** Stirlg
208 D4 **Milton** W Duns
16 F2 **Milton Abbas** Dorset
12 A6 **Milton Abbot** Devon
211 H6 **Milton Bridge** Mdloth
68 B1 **Milton Bryan** Beds
31 L3 **Milton Clevedon** Somset
6 F2 **Milton Combe** Devon
67 G6 **Milton Common** Oxon
27 G8 **Milton Damerel** Devon
63 L5 **Milton End** Gloucs
65 H7 **Milton End** Gloucs
85 K4 **Milton Ernest** Beds
129 K7 **Milton Green** Ches
48 C1 **Milton Hill** Oxon
85 G7 **Milton Keynes** M Keyn
47 J7 **Milton Lilbourne** Wilts
84 E4 **Milton Malsor** Nhants
231 H8 **Milton Morenish** P & K
244 C3 **Milton of Auchinhove** Abers
222 E7 **Milton of Balgonie** Fife
208 D1 **Milton of Buchanan** Stirlg
209 H4 **Milton of Campsie** E Duns
251 J3 **Milton of Leys** Highld
243 L4 **Milton of Tullich** Abers
32 D5 **Milton on Stour** Dorset
40 A2 **Milton Regis** Kent
23 J6 **Milton Street** E Susx
65 K3 **Milton-under-Wychwood** Oxon
29 L5 **Milverton** Somset
83 H2 **Milverton** Warwks
114 F5 **Milwich** Staffs
128 E5 **Milwr** Flints
216 F7 **Minard** Ag & B
33 G7 **Minchington** Dorset
64 C7 **Minchinhampton** Gloucs
202 C6 **Mindrum** Nthumb
29 H2 **Minehead** Somset
112 C1 **Minera** Wrexhm
46 F1 **Minety** Wilts
109 L4 **Minffordd** Gwynd
237 K6 **Mingarrypark** Highld
136 F6 **Miningsby** Lincs
11 J8 **Minions** Cnwll
196 C8 **Minishant** S Ayrs
111 G8 **Minllyn** Gwynd
173 K2 **Minnigaff** D & G
41 J2 **Minnis Bay** Kent
268 D4 **Minnonie** Abers
130 D7 **Minshull Vernon** Ches
150 E3 **Minskip** N York
18 D2 **Minstead** Hants
20 D3 **Minsted** W Susx
41 J2 **Minster** Kent
53 L4 **Minster** Kent
180 B7 **Minsteracres** Nthumb
95 J2 **Minsterley** Shrops
65 L5 **Minster Lovell** Oxon
63 M4 **Minsterworth** Gloucs
16 C2 **Minterne Magna** Dorset
16 C2 **Minterne Parva** Dorset
136 C5 **Minting** Lincs
269 J6 **Mintlaw** Abers
188 F2 **Minto** Border
95 K5 **Minton** Shrops
55 H4 **Minwear** Pembks
98 F5 **Minworth** Birm
164 C7 **Mirehouse** Cumb
141 K4 **Mirfield** Kirk
64 D5 **Miserden** Gloucs
43 G2 **Miskin** Rhondd
43 G5 **Miskin** Rhondd
134 D1 **Misson** Notts
100 C6 **Misterton** Leics
134 F1 **Misterton** Notts
15 K1 **Misterton** Somset
73 G1 **Mistley** Essex
73 H1 **Mistley Heath** Essex
51 H5 **Mitcham** Gt Lon
63 K3 **Mitcheldean** Gloucs
4 D4 **Mitchell** Cnwll
186 E7 **Mitchellslacks** D & G
62 F5 **Mitchel Troy** Mons
180 E2 **Mitford** Nthumb
4 B5 **Mithian** Cnwll

114 D8 **Mitton** Staffs
84 B8 **Mixbury** Oxon
141 G2 **Mixenden** Calder
131 L8 **Mixon** Staffs
90 B4 **Moats Tye** Suffk
130 F4 **Mobberley** Ches
115 G3 **Mobberley** Staffs
79 L6 **Moccas** Herefs
127 G4 **Mochdre** Conwy
94 C5 **Mochdre** Powys
173 J5 **Mochrum** D & G
18 B2 **Mockbeggar** Hants
39 H4 **Mockbeggar** Kent
164 K6 **Mockerkin** Cumb
7 J4 **Modbury** Devon
114 E4 **Moddershall** Staffs
125 J2 **Moelfre** IoA
112 B6 **Moelfre** Powys
125 J8 **Moel Tryfan** Gwynd
187 G5 **Moffat** D & G
86 C5 **Mogerhanger** Beds
116 A8 **Moira** Leics
40 D5 **Molash** Kent
246 F6 **Mol-chlach** Highld
128 F7 **Mold** Flints
141 J4 **Moldgreen** Kirk
70 E2 **Molehill Green** Essex
71 H3 **Molehill Green** Essex
152 F7 **Molescroft** E R Yk
180 E2 **Molesden** Nthumb
102 B8 **Molesworth** Cambs
28 E5 **Molland** Devon
129 J5 **Mollington** Ches
83 K5 **Mollington** Oxon
209 J4 **Mollinsburn** N Lans
76 F3 **Monachty** Cerdgn
245 G7 **Mondynes** Abers
90 F3 **Monewden** Suffk
221 J1 **Moneydie** P & K
49 L3 **Moneyrow Green** W & M
185 J5 **Moniaive** D & G
223 J1 **Monifieth** Angus
234 D7 **Monikie** Angus
222 E4 **Monimail** Fife
75 K3 **Monington** Pembks
142 B6 **Monk Bretton** Barns
69 H7 **Monken Hadley** Gt Lon
142 D2 **Monk Fryston** N York
80 E6 **Monkhide** Herefs
177 K7 **Monkhill** Cumb
96 E5 **Monkhopton** Shrops
80 B4 **Monkland** Herefs
27 H6 **Monkleigh** Devon
42 D7 **Monknash** V Glam
12 E2 **Monkokehampton** Devon
181 J4 **Monkseaton** N Tyne
89 K5 **Monks Eleigh** Suffk
37 K5 **Monk's Gate** W Susx
131 G5 **Monks Heath** Ches
48 F7 **Monk Sherborne** Hants
40 F7 **Monks Horton** Kent
29 K3 **Monksilver** Somset
100 A6 **Monks Kirby** Warwks
90 F2 **Monk Soham** Suffk
98 E8 **Monkspath** Solhll
67 K6 **Monks Risborough** Bucks
137 H6 **Monksthorpe** Lincs
70 F2 **Monk Street** Essex
62 D6 **Monkswood** Mons
14 E2 **Monkton** Devon
41 J2 **Monkton** Kent
196 D5 **Monkton** S Ayrs
181 H6 **Monkton** S Tyne
42 D7 **Monkton** V Glam
45 M6 **Monkton Combe** BaNES
32 E3 **Monkton Deverill** Wilts
46 A6 **Monkton Farleigh** Wilts
30 C5 **Monkton Heathfield** Somset
33 H8 **Monkton Up Wimborne** Dorset
15 H3 **Monkton Wyld** Dorset
181 K7 **Monkwearmouth** Sundld
35 K5 **Monkwood** Hants
97 L4 **Monmore Green** Wolves
63 G4 **Monmouth** Mons
79 L6 **Monnington on Wye** Herefs
173 J6 **Monreith** D & G
31 H7 **Montacute** Somset
139 K5 **Montcliffe** Bolton
112 F8 **Montford** Shrops
113 G8 **Montford Bridge** Shrops
255 L8 **Montgarrie** Abers
94 F4 **Montgomery** Powys
140 A7 **Monton** Salfd
235 H4 **Montrose** Angus
9 i3 **Mont Saint** Guern
34 C2 **Monxton** Hants
132 C6 **Monyash** Derbys

256 C8 **Monymusk** Abers
220 F2 **Monzie** P & K
209 J5 **Moodiesburn** N Lans
222 F4 **Moonzie** Fife
150 D8 **Moor Allerton** Leeds
15 K3 **Moorbath** Dorset
136 E6 **Moorby** Lincs
79 L4 **Moorcot** Herefs
17 K1 **Moor Crichel** Dorset
17 L3 **Moordown** Bmouth
130 B3 **Moore** Halton
68 B3 **Moor End** Beds
141 G2 **Moor End** Calder
12 F1 **Moor End** Devon
63 L6 **Moorend** Gloucs
147 G6 **Moor End** Lancs
151 J8 **Moor End** N York
143 H4 **Moorends** Donc
35 G7 **Moorgreen** Hants
69 J2 **Moor Green** Herts
116 E2 **Moorgreen** Notts
132 F5 **Moorhall** Derbys
79 M6 **Moorhampton** Herefs
149 L8 **Moorhead** Brad
141 K2 **Moor Head** Leeds
177 H8 **Moorhouse** Cumb
177 K7 **Moorhouse** Cumb
142 D5 **Moorhouse** Donc
134 E6 **Moorhouse** Notts
51 L8 **Moorhouse Bank** Surrey
30 E4 **Moorland** Somset
30 F3 **Moorlinch** Somset
151 H4 **Moor Monkton** N York
164 D7 **Moor Row** Cumb
165 H1 **Moor Row** Cumb
170 F7 **Moorsholm** R & Cl
32 D7 **Moorside** Dorset
138 E1 **Moor Side** Lancs
147 K8 **Moor Side** Lancs
150 C8 **Moorside** Leeds
136 E8 **Moor Side** Lincs
140 E6 **Moorside** Oldham
40 E7 **Moorstock** Kent
98 C6 **Moor Street** Birm
53 H6 **Moor Street** Medway
5 M2 **Moorswater** Cnwll
142 C5 **Moorthorpe** Wakefd
12 C7 **Moortown** Devon
18 A3 **Moortown** Hants
19 G7 **Moortown** IoW
150 D7 **Moortown** Leeds
144 D7 **Moortown** Lincs
113 K7 **Moortown** Wrekin
263 K3 **Morangie** Highld
237 K2 **Morar** Highld
102 C5 **Morborne** Cambs
13 H1 **Morchard Bishop** Devon
15 J4 **Morcombelake** Dorset
101 K3 **Morcott** Rutlnd
112 D6 **Morda** Shrops
17 H3 **Morden** Dorset
51 H5 **Morden** Gt Lon
80 D7 **Mordiford** Herefs
169 J5 **Mordon** Dur
95 H5 **More** Shrops
29 G6 **Morebath** Devon
189 K1 **Morebattle** Border
147 H3 **Morecambe** Lancs
47 H2 **Moredon** Swindn
261 J1 **Morefield** Highld
41 G7 **Morehall** Kent
7 L4 **Moreleigh** Devon
231 H8 **Morenish** P & K
164 C6 **Moresby** Cumb
164 C6 **Moresby Parks** Cumb
35 G6 **Morestead** Hants
16 F4 **Moreton** Dorset
70 D5 **Moreton** Essex
80 C2 **Moreton** Herefs
67 G6 **Moreton** Oxon
114 B8 **Moreton** Staffs
115 J5 **Moreton** Staffs
129 G2 **Moreton** Wirral
113 J6 **Moreton Corbet** Shrops
13 H5 **Moretonhampstead** Devon
65 J1 **Moreton-in-Marsh** Gloucs
80 E5 **Moreton Jeffries** Herefs
113 J7 **Moretonmill** Shrops
83 H4 **Moreton Morrell** Warwks
80 C6 **Moreton on Lugg** Herefs
83 H4 **Moreton Paddox** Warwks
84 B5 **Moreton Pinkney** Nhants
113 K4 **Moreton Say** Shrops
63 M5 **Moreton Valence** Gloucs
76 B4 **Morfa** Cerdgn
109 K4 **Morfa Bychan** Gwynd
125 H8 **Morfa Dinlle** Gwynd
60 C6 **Morfa Glas** Neath

108 E3 **Morfa Nefyn** Gwynd
43 H5 **Morganstown** Cardif
33 L6 **Morgan's Vale** Wilts
212 C5 **Morham** E Loth
92 D7 **Moriah** Cerdgn
166 E6 **Morland** Cumb
130 F3 **Morley** Ches
116 C3 **Morley** Derbys
168 E5 **Morley** Dur
141 L2 **Morley** Leeds
130 F3 **Morley Green** Ches
106 B3 **Morley St Botolph** Norfk
11 L7 **Mornick** Cnwll
211 H5 **Morningside** C Edin
209 L7 **Morningside** N Lans
106 E5 **Morningthorpe** Norfk
180 F2 **Morpeth** Nthumb
235 H3 **Morphie** Abers
115 J7 **Morrey** Staffs
115 G1 **Morridge Side** Staffs
57 J5 **Morriston** Swans
121 M3 **Morston** Norfk
27 H2 **Mortehoe** Devon
133 J2 **Morthen** Rothm
49 G6 **Mortimer** W Berk
49 G6 **Mortimer Common** W Berk
80 A3 **Mortimer's Cross** Herefs
48 F6 **Mortimer West End** Hants
51 G4 **Mortlake** Gt Lon
166 B3 **Morton** Cumb
177 L7 **Morton** Cumb
133 H7 **Morton** Derbys
19 K6 **Morton** IoW
118 E6 **Morton** Lincs
134 F1 **Morton** Lincs
117 J1 **Morton** Notts
112 D6 **Morton** Shrops
135 H7 **Morton Hall** Lincs
160 D4 **Morton-on-Swale** N York
122 C8 **Morton on the Hill** Norfk
168 F6 **Morton Tinmouth** Dur
2 B4 **Morvah** Cnwll
6 B3 **Morval** Cnwll
248 F7 **Morvich** Highld
96 F4 **Morville** Shrops
96 F4 **Morville Heath** Shrops
26 C7 **Morwenstow** Cnwll
133 H3 **Mosborough** Sheff
196 F3 **Moscow** E Ayrs
97 L4 **Moseley** Wolves
81 J3 **Moseley** Worcs
139 L6 **Moses Gate** Bolton
224 B6 **Moss** Ag & B
142 F5 **Moss** Donc
112 D1 **Moss** Wrexhm
255 K7 **Mossat** Abers
281 e4 **Mossbank** Shet
139 G8 **Moss Bank** St Hel
164 C5 **Mossbay** Cumb
196 D6 **Mossblown** S Ayrs
130 D2 **Mossbrow** Traffd
189 H3 **Mossburnford** Border
175 G1 **Mossdale** D & G
184 D2 **Mossdale** E Ayrs
147 H7 **Moss Edge** Lancs
130 D4 **Moss End** Ches
209 K7 **Mossend** N Lans
164 K5 **Mosser Mains** Cumb
131 H7 **Mossley** Ches
140 E7 **Mossley** Tamesd
188 C3 **Mosspaul Hotel** Border
177 G8 **Moss Side** Cumb
253 G1 **Moss-side** Highld
138 D2 **Moss Side** Lancs
138 D7 **Moss Side** Sefton
267 G4 **Mosstodloch** Moray
174 E4 **Mossyard** D & G
139 G5 **Mossy Lea** Lancs
15 K2 **Mosterton** Dorset
140 C7 **Moston** Manch
113 J6 **Moston** Shrops
130 E7 **Moston Green** Ches
128 E4 **Mostyn** Flints
32 E6 **Motcombe** Dorset
7 H5 **Mothecombe** Devon
166 A5 **Motherby** Cumb
209 K7 **Motherwell** N Lans
51 G5 **Motspur Park** Gt Lon
51 L4 **Mottingham** Gt Lon
34 D5 **Mottisfont** Hants
18 F7 **Mottistone** IoW
140 F8 **Mottram in Longdendale** Tamesd
131 G4 **Mottram St Andrew** Ches

9 j3 **Mouilpied** Guern
129 L5 **Mouldsworth** Ches
232 D3 **Moulin** P & K
22 E6 **Moulsecoomb** Br & H
48 E2 **Moulsford** Oxon
85 H7 **Moulsoe** M Keyn
263 H5 **Moultavie** Highld
130 C5 **Moulton** Ches
119 J6 **Moulton** Lincs
160 C2 **Moulton** N York
84 F2 **Moulton** Nhants
88 D2 **Moulton** Suffk
43 G7 **Moulton** V Glam
119 J7 **Moulton Chapel** Lincs
107 H2 **Moulton St Mary** Norfk
119 K6 **Moulton Seas End** Lincs
4 C4 **Mount** Cnwll
5 K1 **Mount** Cnwll
141 H4 **Mount** Kirk
141 G2 **Mountain** Brad
61 G7 **Mountain Ash** Rhondd
199 K4 **Mountain Cross** Border
40 E5 **Mountain Street** Kent
4 B6 **Mount Ambrose** Cnwll
89 H8 **Mount Bures** Essex
24 D3 **Mountfield** E Susx
263 G7 **Mountgerald House** Highld
4 B5 **Mount Hawke** Cnwll
3 H7 **Mount Hermon** Cnwll
4 E3 **Mountjoy** Cnwll
200 C2 **Mount Lothian** Mdloth
70 F7 **Mountnessing** Essex
63 G8 **Mounton** Mons
131 G8 **Mount Pleasant** Ches
115 M8 **Mount Pleasant** Derbys
116 B2 **Mount Pleasant** Derbys
169 H4 **Mount Pleasant** Dur
23 G4 **Mount Pleasant** E Susx
105 K4 **Mount Pleasant** Norfk
88 E5 **Mount Pleasant** Suffk
82 B2 **Mount Pleasant** Worcs
116 F8 **Mountsorrel** Leics
33 H6 **Mount Sorrel** Wilts
141 G2 **Mount Tabor** Calder
36 E3 **Mousehill** Surrey
2 D5 **Mousehole** Cnwll
176 E4 **Mouswald** D & G
131 G8 **Mow Cop** Ches
189 L2 **Mowhaugh** Border
100 D2 **Mowmacre Hill** C Leic
100 E5 **Mowsley** Leics
240 D7 **Moy** Highld
252 E5 **Moy** Highld
248 D7 **Moye** Highld
75 J3 **Moylgrove** Pembks
205 L8 **Muasdale** Ag & B
245 K5 **Muchalls** Abers
63 G1 **Much Birch** Herefs
80 E6 **Much Cowarne** Herefs
62 F1 **Much Dewchurch** Herefs
30 F6 **Muchelney** Somset
31 G6 **Muchelney Ham** Somset
70 B3 **Much Hadham** Herts
138 F3 **Much Hoole** Lancs
138 F3 **Much Hoole Town** Lancs
5 L3 **Muchlarnick** Cnwll
80 F8 **Much Marcle** Herefs
96 E3 **Much Wenlock** Shrops
52 E3 **Mucking** Thurr
52 E3 **Muckingford** Thurr
16 C4 **Muckleford** Dorset
114 A4 **Mucklestone** Staffs
96 E4 **Muckley** Shrops
137 G3 **Muckton** Lincs
27 K3 **Muddiford** Devon
23 J4 **Muddles Green** E Susx
18 B5 **Mudeford** Dorset
31 J7 **Mudford** Somset
31 J7 **Mudford Sock** Somset
31 G2 **Mudgley** Somset
53 M4 **Mud Row** Kent
208 F4 **Mugdock** Stirlg
246 F1 **Mugeary** Highld
115 M3 **Mugginton** Derbys
115 M3 **Muggintonlane End** Derbys
168 D1 **Mugglesworth** Dur
268 C5 **Muirden** Abers
234 E7 **Muirdrum** Angus
268 C6 **Muiresk** Abers
233 M8 **Muirhead** Angus
222 D6 **Muirhead** Fife
209 J5 **Muirhead** N Lans
197 K5 **Muirkirk** E Ayrs
209 J2 **Muirmill** Stirlg
244 C1 **Muir of Fowlis** Abers
266 D4 **Muir of Miltonduff** Moray

250 F2 **Muir of Ord** Highld
233 G7 **Muir of Thorn** P & K
239 J7 **Muirshearlich** Highld
257 J4 **Muirtack** Abers
221 G5 **Muirton** P & K
250 E1 **Muirton Mains** Highld
233 J6 **Muirton of Ardblair** P & K
158 F3 **Muker** N York
106 D3 **Mulbarton** Norfk
267 G6 **Mulben** Moray
2 C4 **Mulfra** Cnwll
27 J2 **Mullacott Cross** Devon
3 H7 **Mullion** Cnwll
3 H7 **Mullion Cove** Cnwll
137 K5 **Mumby** Lincs
80 F5 **Munderfield Row** Herefs
80 F5 **Munderfield Stocks** Herefs
123 G4 **Mundesley** Norfk
104 F4 **Mundford** Norfk
107 G4 **Mundham** Norfk
72 C6 **Mundon Hill** Essex
40 B6 **Mundy Bois** Kent
165 L4 **Mungrisdale** Cumb
251 H1 **Munlochy** Highld
195 L1 **Munnoch** N Ayrs
80 F7 **Munsley** Herefs
96 C6 **Munslow** Shrops
13 G5 **Murchington** Devon
82 C7 **Murcot** Worcs
66 E4 **Murcott** Oxon
46 D1 **Murcott** Wilts
279 L3 **Murkle** Highld
239 G5 **Murlaggan** Highld
49 H7 **Murrell Green** Hants
234 C8 **Murroes** Angus
103 H2 **Murrow** Cambs
67 K2 **Mursley** Bucks
40 B2 **Murston** Kent
234 C4 **Murthill** Angus
233 G7 **Murthly** P & K
167 G6 **Murton** Cumb
169 K1 **Murton** Dur
181 H5 **Murton** N Tyne
202 F3 **Murton** Nthumb
151 K5 **Murton** York
15 G3 **Musbury** Devon
162 B6 **Muscoates** N York
211 K4 **Musselburgh** E Loth
117 L4 **Muston** Leics
163 K6 **Muston** N York
97 K8 **Mustow Green** Worcs
51 H1 **Muswell Hill** Gt Lon
175 H5 **Mutehill** D & G
107 K5 **Mutford** Suffk
220 F4 **Muthill** P & K
14 B2 **Mutterton** Devon
114 A8 **Muxton** Wrekin
279 L5 **Mybster** Highld
59 L3 **Myddfai** Carmth
113 G6 **Myddle** Shrops
76 E4 **Mydroilyn** Cerdgn
147 K7 **Myerscough** Lancs
3 L4 **Mylor** Cnwll
3 K4 **Mylor Bridge** Cnwll
75 K6 **Mynachlog ddu** Pembks
128 D5 **Myndd-llan** Flints
95 J5 **Myndtown** Shrops
62 F8 **Mynydd-bach** Mons
57 J5 **Mynydd-Bach** Swans
92 F8 **Mynydd Buch** Cerdgn
56 D3 **Mynyddgarreg** Carmth
128 F7 **Mynydd Isa** Flints
126 B6 **Mynydd Llandygai** Gwynd
108 E5 **Mynytho** Gwynd
245 G4 **Myrebird** Abers
189 G6 **Myredykes** Border
49 L7 **Mytchett** Surrey
140 E2 **Mytholm** Calder
140 F3 **Mytholmroyd** Calder
138 D1 **Mythop** Lancs
150 F3 **Myton-on-Swale** N York

N

260 C3 **Naast** Highld
139 J2 **Nab's Head** Lancs
282 d6 **Na Buirgh** W Isls
151 J6 **Naburn** York
40 D6 **Naccolt** Kent
40 F4 **Nackington** Kent
90 F7 **Nacton** Suffk
153 G4 **Nafferton** E R Yk
64 C7 **Nag's Head** Gloucs
63 J4 **Nailbridge** Gloucs
30 B5 **Nailsbourne** Somset
44 F5 **Nailsea** N Som
99 L2 **Nailstone** Leics

64 B7 **Nailsworth** Gloucs
264 D8 **Nairn** Highld
37 L2 **Nalderswood** Surrey
3 G4 **Nancegollan** Cnwll
2 D4 **Nancledra** Cnwll
108 E5 **Nanhoron** Gwynd
128 E5 **Nannerch** Flints
116 E8 **Nanpantan** Leics
4 F4 **Nanpean** Cnwll
2 B5 **Nanquidno** Cnwll
5 H2 **Nanstallon** Cnwll
60 F4 **Nant-ddu** Powys
76 C4 **Nanternis** Cerdgn
58 F4 **Nantgaredig** Carmth
43 H4 **Nantgarw** Rhondd
78 D2 **Nant-glas** Powys
127 K7 **Nantglyn** Denbgs
93 L8 **Nantgwyn** Powys
110 B2 **Nant Gwynant** Gwynd
109 J1 **Nantlle** Gwynd
112 C6 **Nantmawr** Shrops
78 E2 **Nantmel** Powys
109 L2 **Nantmor** Gwynd
126 B7 **Nant Peris** Gwynd
113 L1 **Nantwich** Ches
61 H5 **Nant-y-Bwch** Blae G
58 E5 **Nant-y-caws** Carmth
62 C6 **Nant-y-derry** Mons
42 C3 **Nantyffyllon** Brdgnd
61 K5 **Nantyglo** Blae G
112 C5 **Nant-y-gollen** Shrops
42 D3 **Nant-y-moel** Brdgnd
126 D5 **Nant-y-pandy** Conwy
67 K7 **Naphill** Bucks
81 K5 **Napleton** Worcs
148 E5 **Nappa** N York
83 L3 **Napton on the Hill** Warwks
55 J4 **Narberth** Pembks
100 C4 **Narborough** Leics
104 E1 **Narborough** Norfk
6 C4 **Narkurs** Cnwll
109 H2 **Nasareth** Gwynd
100 F7 **Naseby** Nhants
84 F8 **Nash** Bucks
51 L6 **Nash** Gt Lon
79 K3 **Nash** Herefs
44 D2 **Nash** Newpt
80 E1 **Nash** Shrops
97 H7 **Nash End** Worcs
67 K5 **Nash Lee** Bucks
35 K2 **Nash's Green** Hants
52 D5 **Nash Street** Kent
102 B4 **Nassington** Nhants
64 A6 **Nastend** Gloucs
69 K2 **Nasty** Herts
158 D1 **Nateby** Cumb
147 J7 **Nateby** Lancs
157 H5 **Natland** Cumb
89 L5 **Naughton** Suffk
65 G2 **Naunton** Gloucs
81 K7 **Naunton** Worcs
81 M5 **Naunton Beauchamp** Worcs
135 K8 **Navenby** Lincs
70 D7 **Navestock** Essex
70 E7 **Navestock Side** Essex
274 D5 **Navidale House Hotel** Highld
264 B7 **Navity** Highld
161 L5 **Nawton** N York
89 K8 **Nayland** Suffk
69 L6 **Nazeing** Essex
69 L6 **Nazeing Gate** Essex
18 B4 **Neacroft** Hants
99 J6 **Neal's Green** Warwks
281 e5 **Neap** Shet
115 H2 **Near Cotton** Staffs
156 E3 **Near Sawrey** Cumb
51 G2 **Neasden** Gt Lon
169 J8 **Neasham** Darltn
57 L5 **Neath** Neath
35 M3 **Neatham** Hants
123 G7 **Neatishead** Norfk
77 G2 **Nebo** Cerdgn
127 G8 **Nebo** Conwy
109 H2 **Nebo** Gwynd
125 H2 **Nebo** IoA
105 H2 **Necton** Norfk
270 H2 **Nedd** Highld
180 F2 **Nedderton** Nthumb
89 K5 **Nedging** Suffk
89 L5 **Nedging Tye** Suffk
106 D7 **Needham** Norfk
90 C4 **Needham Market** Suffk
88 E2 **Needham Street** Suffk
87 G1 **Needingworth** Cambs
96 F7 **Neen Savage** Shrops
80 F1 **Neen Sollars** Shrops

96 E6 **Neenton** Shrops
108 E3 **Nefyn** Gwynd
208 E7 **Neilston** E Rens
43 H3 **Nelson** Caerph
148 F8 **Nelson** Lancs
198 E4 **Nemphlar** S Lans
45 G7 **Nempnett Thrubwell** BaNES
167 H2 **Nenthall** Cumb
167 H2 **Nenthead** Cumb
201 L5 **Nenthorn** Border
13 J3 **Neopardy** Devon
22 B4 **Nep Town** W Susx
128 F7 **Nercwys** Flints
204 C5 **Nereabolls** Ag & B
209 H7 **Nerston** S Lans
202 F6 **Nesbit** Nthumb
149 K6 **Nesfield** N York
129 G4 **Ness** Ches
112 F7 **Nesscliffe** Shrops
129 G4 **Neston** Ches
46 B5 **Neston** Wilts
96 E5 **Netchwood** Shrops
131 G4 **Nether Alderley** Ches
33 K1 **Netheravon** Wilts
201 H4 **Nether Blainslie** Border
268 E4 **Netherbrae** Abers
117 J6 **Nether Broughton** Leics
198 C4 **Netherburn** S Lans
15 L3 **Netherbury** Dorset
177 L4 **Netherby** Cumb
150 D6 **Netherby** N York
16 C3 **Nether Cerne** Dorset
176 F2 **Nethercleuch** D & G
31 K7 **Nether Compton** Dorset
83 M2 **Nethercote** Warwks
11 L3 **Nethercott** Devon
27 H3 **Nethercott** Devon
256 E7 **Nether Crimond** Abers
267 G3 **Nether Dallachy** Moray
63 H7 **Netherend** Gloucs
13 L2 **Nether Exe** Devon
24 C3 **Netherfield** E Susx
117 G8 **Netherfield** Leics
117 G3 **Netherfield** Notts
24 D4 **Netherfield Road** E Susx
186 D4 **Nether Fingland** S Lans
143 J7 **Nethergate** N Linc
122 B5 **Nethergate** Norfk
33 K5 **Netherhampton** Wilts
133 H4 **Nether Handley** Derbys
234 B7 **Nether Handwick** Angus
142 C8 **Nether Haugh** Rothm
15 J2 **Netherhay** Dorset
134 E4 **Nether Headon** Notts
116 B2 **Nether Heage** Derbys
84 C3 **Nether Heyford** Nhants
186 F4 **Nether Howcleugh** S Lans
147 K2 **Nether Kellet** Lancs
257 K3 **Nether Kinmundy** Abers
115 H5 **Netherland Green** Staffs
133 K5 **Nether Langwith** Notts
175 J6 **Netherlaw** D & G
245 J5 **Netherley** Abers
176 D1 **Nethermill** D & G
257 G3 **Nethermuir** Abers
51 J7 **Netherne-on-the-Hill** Surrey
141 H4 **Netheroyd Hill** Kirk
132 E4 **Nether Padley** Derbys
208 E7 **Netherplace** E Rens
151 J5 **Nether Poppleton** York
165 K3 **Nether Row** Cumb
99 H1 **Netherseal** Derbys
161 G4 **Nether Silton** N York
95 G8 **Nether Skyborry** Shrops
30 B3 **Nether Stowey** Somset
70 E5 **Nether Street** Essex
46 E6 **Netherstreet** Wilts
141 H6 **Netherthong** Kirk
133 J5 **Netherthorpe** Derbys
234 E4 **Netherton** Angus
13 L8 **Netherton** Devon
97 L5 **Netherton** Dudley
48 A7 **Netherton** Hants
63 G2 **Netherton** Herefs
141 H5 **Netherton** Kirk
209 K8 **Netherton** N Lans
190 E4 **Netherton** Nthumb
66 B7 **Netherton** Oxon
233 H5 **Netherton** P & K
97 G6 **Netherton** Shrops
208 F3 **Netherton** Stirlg
141 L4 **Netherton** Wakefd
82 A7 **Netherton** Worcs
155 H1 **Nethertown** Cumb
280 E1 **Nethertown** Highld
148 C8 **Nethertown** Lancs
115 J8 **Nethertown** Staffs

199 J4 **Netherurd** Border
34 C4 **Nether Wallop** Hants
155 L2 **Nether Wasdale** Cumb
165 K2 **Nether Welton** Cumb
65 J3 **Nether Westcote** Gloucs
99 G5 **Nether Whitacre** Warwks
186 B2 **Nether Whitecleuch** S Lans
67 H4 **Nether Winchendon** Bucks
191 G8 **Netherwitton** Nthumb
253 J7 **Nethy Bridge** Highld
19 G2 **Netley** Hants
34 D8 **Netley Marsh** Hants
13 L3 **Nettacott** Devon
49 G2 **Nettlebed** Oxon
31 L1 **Nettlebridge** Somset
15 L3 **Nettlecombe** Dorset
19 J8 **Nettlecombe** IoW
68 C5 **Nettleden** Herts
135 K4 **Nettleham** Lincs
39 H3 **Nettlestead** Kent
39 H3 **Nettlestead Green** Kent
19 L5 **Nettlestone** IoW
169 H1 **Nettlesworth** Dur
144 E7 **Nettleton** Lincs
46 B3 **Nettleton** Wilts
46 B3 **Nettleton Shrub** Wilts
7 G5 **Netton** Devon
33 K3 **Netton** Wilts
59 K4 **Neuadd** Carmth
93 K8 **Neuadd-ddu** Powys
77 K7 **Neuadd Fawr** Carmth
53 G1 **Nevendon** Essex
75 J4 **Nevern** Pembks
101 H4 **Nevill Holt** Leics
176 C5 **New Abbey** D & G
268 F3 **New Aberdour** Abers
51 K6 **New Addington** Gt Lon
150 B6 **Newall** Leeds
35 J4 **New Alresford** Hants
233 K6 **New Alyth** P & K
102 E3 **Newark** C Pete
275 f2 **Newark** Ork
117 L1 **Newark-on-Trent** Notts
153 G7 **New Arram** E R Yk
209 L7 **Newarthill** N Lans
52 D6 **New Ash Green** Kent
117 L1 **New Balderton** Notts
40 F7 **Newbarn** Kent
52 D5 **New Barn** Kent
69 H7 **New Barnet** Gt Lon
85 G2 **New Barton** Nhants
211 K6 **Newbattle** Mdloth
190 F2 **New Bewick** Nthumb
177 G6 **Newbie** D & G
146 E2 **Newbiggin** Cumb
155 K4 **Newbiggin** Cumb
166 B5 **Newbiggin** Cumb
166 D1 **Newbiggin** Cumb
166 E5 **Newbiggin** Cumb
167 L5 **Newbiggin** Dur
168 F1 **Newbiggin** Dur
159 G4 **Newbiggin** N York
159 H5 **Newbiggin** N York
181 H1 **Newbiggin-by-the-Sea** Nthumb
233 L7 **Newbigging** Angus
234 C7 **Newbigging** Angus
234 D8 **Newbigging** Angus
199 H4 **Newbigging** S Lans
158 C2 **Newbiggin-on-Lune** Cumb
100 B8 **New Bilton** Warwks
133 G5 **Newbold** Derbys
116 C7 **Newbold** Leics
100 B7 **Newbold on Avon** Warwks
82 F6 **Newbold on Stour** Warwks
83 G4 **Newbold Pacey** Warwks
99 M7 **Newbold Revel** Warwks
99 L3 **Newbold Verdon** Leics
136 F8 **New Bolingbroke** Lincs
102 D2 **Newborough** C Pete
125 G6 **Newborough** IoA
115 J6 **Newborough** Staffs
83 M7 **Newbottle** Nhants
181 H8 **Newbottle** Sundld
135 K5 **New Boultham** Lincs
91 G6 **Newbourne** Suffk
84 F7 **New Bradwell** M Keyn
133 G5 **New Brampton** Derbys
169 G2 **New Brancepeth** Dur
210 H4 **Newbridge** C Edin
43 K2 **Newbridge** Caerph
76 F3 **Newbridge** Cerdgn
2 C5 **Newbridge** Cnwll
4 C6 **Newbridge** Cnwll
176 C3 **Newbridge** D & G
34 C7 **Newbridge** Hants

18 F6 **Newbridge** IoW
162 D5 **New Bridge** N York
66 B6 **Newbridge** Oxon
112 D3 **Newbridge** Wrexhm
81 J7 **Newbridge Green** Worcs
62 D8 **Newbridge-on-Usk** Mons
78 E4 **Newbridge on Wye** Powys
128 F6 **New Brighton** Flints
129 G1 **New Brighton** Wirral
116 B2 **New Brinsley** Notts
171 G6 **New Brotton** R & Cl
179 K5 **Newbrough** Nthumb
112 D1 **New Broughton** Wrexhm
106 B5 **New Buckenham** Norfk
13 J2 **Newbuildings** Devon
257 J6 **Newburgh** Abers
269 H4 **Newburgh** Abers
222 C3 **Newburgh** Fife
138 F5 **Newburgh** Lancs
161 J7 **Newburgh Priory** N York
180 E6 **Newburn** N u Ty
139 L6 **New Bury** Bolton
32 B1 **Newbury** Somset
48 C5 **Newbury** W Berk
32 D3 **Newbury** Wilts
51 L1 **Newbury Park** Gt Lon
166 E6 **Newby** Cumb
148 E6 **Newby** Lancs
148 C2 **Newby** N York
163 J4 **Newby** N York
170 C8 **Newby** N York
156 E5 **Newby Bridge** Cumb
177 L8 **Newby Cross** Cumb
178 B7 **Newby East** Cumb
166 E6 **Newby Head** Cumb
268 E5 **New Byth** Abers
177 L8 **Newby West** Cumb
160 E5 **Newby Wiske** N York
62 F4 **Newcastle** Mons
95 G7 **Newcastle** Shrops
76 B7 **Newcastle Emlyn** Carmth
178 C2 **Newcastleton** Border
114 D2 **Newcastle-under-Lyme** Staffs
181 G6 **Newcastle upon Tyne** N u Ty
75 L4 **Newchapel** Pembks
131 G8 **Newchapel** Staffs
38 A5 **Newchapel** Surrey
61 J5 **Newchurch** Blae G
79 L5 **Newchurch** Herefs
19 J6 **Newchurch** IoW
25 K1 **Newchurch** Kent
62 F7 **Newchurch** Mons
79 H5 **Newchurch** Powys
115 J7 **Newchurch** Staffs
148 E7 **Newchurch in Pendle** Lancs
106 D2 **New Costessey** Norfk
164 F2 **New Cowper** Cumb
211 K4 **Newcraighall** C Edin
142 B4 **New Crofton** Wakefd
92 D8 **New Cross** Cerdgn
51 K4 **New Cross** Gt Lon
30 F7 **New Cross** Somset
197 J8 **New Cumnock** E Ayrs
24 E4 **New Cut** E Susx
268 F6 **New Deer** Abers
181 H3 **New Delaval** Nthumb
140 F6 **New Delph** Oldham
50 D2 **New Denham** Bucks
37 J3 **Newdigate** Surrey
84 D3 **New Duston** Nhants
151 K5 **New Earswick** York
116 D2 **New Eastwood** Notts
142 E7 **New Edlington** Donc
266 E4 **New Elgin** Moray
153 J7 **New Ellerby** E R Yk
49 L5 **Newell Green** Br For
51 L4 **New Eltham** Gt Lon
82 C3 **New End** Worcs
24 F2 **Newenden** Kent
102 D3 **New England** C Pete
88 E6 **New England** Essex
63 L2 **Newent** Gloucs
141 L2 **New Farnley** Leeds
129 H3 **New Ferry** Wirral
169 G4 **Newfield** Dur
181 G5 **Newfield** Dur
264 B4 **Newfield** Highld
102 D4 **New Fletton** C Pete
48 E8 **Newfound** Hants
142 C2 **New Fryston** Wakefd
54 D2 **Newgale** Pembks
185 G7 **New Galloway** D & G
122 A3 **Newgate** Norfk
69 J6 **Newgate Street** Herts
223 G5 **New Gilston** Fife
10 b2 **New Grimsby** IoS

113 K2 **Newhall** Ches
115 M7 **Newhall** Derbys
203 K7 **Newham** Nthumb
181 H3 **New Hartley** Nthumb
211 H4 **Newhaven** C Edin
132 C7 **Newhaven** Derbys
23 G7 **Newhaven** E Susx
50 D6 **New Haw** Surrey
55 K6 **New Hedges** Pembks
181 H8 **New Herrington** Sundld
140 E5 **Newhey** Rochdl
121 J4 **New Holkham** Norfk
144 D3 **New Holland** N Linc
171 K8 **Newholm** N York
133 K6 **New Houghton** Derbys
121 H6 **New Houghton** Norfk
209 L6 **Newhouse** N Lans
158 D7 **New Houses** N York
139 H7 **New Houses** Wigan
157 J4 **New Hutton** Cumb
52 F7 **New Hythe** Kent
22 F3 **Newick** E Susx
40 F8 **Newingreen** Kent
41 G7 **Newington** Kent
53 J6 **Newington** Kent
66 F7 **Newington** Oxon
95 K6 **Newington** Shrops
64 B8 **Newington Bagpath** Gloucs
58 E2 **New Inn** Carmth
62 C7 **New Inn** Torfn
95 H8 **New Invention** Shrops
106 E2 **New Lakenham** Norfk
198 E4 **New Lanark** S Lans
144 D2 **Newland** C KuH
156 D6 **Newland** Cumb
143 K2 **Newland** E R Yk
63 H5 **Newland** Gloucs
143 H3 **Newland** N York
66 A5 **Newland** Oxon
28 E3 **Newland** Somset
81 H5 **Newland** Worcs
211 L6 **Newlandrig** Mdloth
188 E7 **Newlands** Border
165 K3 **Newlands** Cumb
180 D7 **Newlands** Nthumb
266 F6 **Newlands of Dundurcas** Moray
138 E5 **New Lane** Lancs
130 C1 **New Lane End** Warrtn
177 K2 **New Langholm** D & G
137 G8 **New Leake** Lincs
269 H5 **New Leeds** Abers
142 A6 **New Lodge** Barns
139 G3 **New Longton** Lancs
172 F2 **New Luce** D & G
2 D5 **Newlyn** Cnwll
4 D3 **Newlyn East** Cnwll
256 F7 **Newmachar** Abers
209 L7 **Newmains** N Lans
51 G5 **New Malden** Gt Lon
70 D4 **Newman's End** Essex
89 H6 **Newman's Green** Suffk
88 C3 **Newmarket** Suffk
282 g3 **Newmarket** W Isls
170 E6 **New Marske** R & Cl
66 D5 **New Marston** Oxon
112 E4 **New Marton** Shrops
245 H7 **New Mill** Abers
188 D4 **Newmill** Border
2 D4 **New Mill** Cnwll
68 A4 **New Mill** Herts
141 J6 **New Mill** Kirk
267 J5 **Newmill** Moray
141 M4 **Newmillerdam** Wakefd
234 C3 **Newmill of Inshewan** Angus
211 G5 **Newmills** C Edin
4 E4 **New Mills** Cnwll
131 K3 **New Mills** Derbys
210 D2 **Newmills** Fife
63 G5 **Newmills** Mons
94 D3 **New Mills** Powys
221 L1 **Newmill** P & K
197 J3 **Newmilns** E Ayrs
18 C4 **New Milton** Hants
73 H1 **New Mistley** Essex
75 H7 **New Moat** Pembks
112 F5 **Newnes** Shrops
71 G5 **Newney Green** Essex
63 K5 **Newnham** Gloucs
49 H8 **Newnham** Hants
86 E7 **Newnham** Herts
40 B4 **Newnham** Kent
84 B3 **Newnham** Nhants
80 E2 **Newnham** Worcs
100 B6 **Newnham Paddox** Warwks
134 D6 **New Ollerton** Notts

98 E4 **New Oscott** Birm
268 F5 **New Pitsligo** Abers
10 C6 **New Polzeath** Cnwll
11 L5 **Newport** Cnwll
17 G3 **Newport** Dorset
143 L2 **Newport** E R Yk
87 L8 **Newport** Essex
63 K7 **Newport** Gloucs
274 F3 **Newport** Highld
19 H6 **Newport** IoW
44 C1 **Newport** Newpt
123 K8 **Newport** Norfk
75 H4 **Newport** Pembks
114 A7 **Newport** Wrekin
223 G2 **Newport-on-Tay** Fife
85 G6 **Newport Pagnell** M Keyn
37 G5 **Newpound Common** W Susx
196 C6 **New Prestwick** S Ayrs
76 D3 **New Quay** Cerdgn
4 D3 **Newquay** Cnwll
72 F2 **New Quay** Essex
106 F1 **New Rackheath** Norfk
79 H3 **New Radnor** Powys
166 B3 **New Rent** Cumb
180 C7 **New Ridley** Nthumb
149 H7 **New Road Side** N York
25 K2 **New Romney** Kent
143 G8 **New Rossington** Donc
92 F8 **New Row** Cerdgn
148 A8 **New Row** Lancs
142 B2 **Newsam Green** Leeds
220 F8 **New Sauchie** Clacks
131 G6 **Newsbank** Ches
256 C5 **Newseat** Abers
147 K8 **Newsham** Lancs
160 E5 **Newsham** N York
168 E8 **Newsham** N York
181 H3 **Newsham** Nthumb
142 B4 **New Sharlston** Wakefd
143 H2 **Newsholme** E R Yk
148 E5 **Newsholme** Lancs
203 K6 **New Shoreston** Nthumb
181 J8 **New Silksworth** Sundld
170 F7 **New Skelton** R & Cl
141 J5 **Newsome** Kirk
118 B4 **New Somerby** Lincs
137 H6 **New Spilsby** Lincs
139 J6 **New Springs** Wigan
201 H6 **Newstead** Border
116 E1 **Newstead** Notts
203 J7 **Newstead** Nthumb
209 K7 **New Stevenston** N Lans
79 L4 **New Street** Herefs
116 D8 **New Swannington** Leics
142 D1 **Newthorpe** N York
116 E2 **Newthorpe** Notts
53 G1 **New Thundersley** Essex
22 D4 **Newtimber** W Susx
135 L2 **Newtoft** Lincs
217 G7 **Newton** Ag & B
86 E6 **Newton** Beds
189 G2 **Newton** Border
42 C6 **Newton** Brdgnd
87 J5 **Newton** Cambs
119 M8 **Newton** Cambs
43 K6 **Newton** Cardif
129 J6 **Newton** Ches
129 L7 **Newton** Ches
129 M4 **Newton** Ches
146 D2 **Newton** Cumb
133 J7 **Newton** Derbys
79 L1 **Newton** Herefs
79 L8 **Newton** Herefs
80 C4 **Newton** Herefs
251 G2 **Newton** Highld
252 D2 **Newton** Highld
263 L6 **Newton** Highld
147 G8 **Newton** Lancs
148 B5 **Newton** Lancs
157 J7 **Newton** Lancs
142 C2 **Newton** Leeds
118 D4 **Newton** Lincs
211 K5 **Newton** Mdloth
266 C3 **Newton** Moray
267 G4 **Newton** Moray
152 D1 **Newton** N York
101 J6 **Newton** Nhants
121 H8 **Newton** Norfk
117 J3 **Newton** Notts
180 C6 **Newton** Nthumb
190 D5 **Newton** Nthumb
198 F6 **Newton** S Lans
209 H6 **Newton** S Lans
98 C4 **Newton** Sandw
112 F4 **Newton** Shrops
29 K3 **Newton** Somset
115 G6 **Newton** Staffs

89 J7 **Newton** Suffk
210 E3 **Newton** W Loth
100 C7 **Newton** Warwks
34 B6 **Newton** Wilts
13 K8 **Newton Abbot** Devon
177 G7 **Newton Arlosh** Cumb
169 H5 **Newton Aycliffe** Dur
170 B5 **Newton Bewley** Hartpl
85 H5 **Newton Blossomville** M Keyn
85 K2 **Newton Bromswold** Nhants
99 K2 **Newton Burgoland** Leics
203 L8 **Newton-by-the-Sea** Nthumb
135 L2 **Newton by Toft** Lincs
6 C2 **Newton Ferrers** Cnwll
7 G5 **Newton Ferrers** Devon
282 C7 **Newton Ferry** W Isls
106 E4 **Newton Flotman** Norfk
211 K6 **Newtongrange** Mdloth
45 G1 **Newton Green** Mons
100 E4 **Newton Harcourt** Leics
140 C7 **Newton Heath** Manch
245 K5 **Newtonhill** Abers
141 M3 **Newton Hill** Wakefd
151 G6 **Newton Kyme** N York
160 B5 **Newton-le-Willows** N York
139 H8 **Newton-le-Willows** St Hel
211 K6 **Newtonloan** Mdloth
67 K1 **Newton Longville** Bucks
208 F7 **Newton Mearns** E Rens
234 F3 **Newtonmill** Angus
241 J4 **Newtonmore** Highld
160 C1 **Newton Morrell** N York
55 G5 **Newton Mountain** Pembks
171 H7 **Newton Mulgrave** N York
222 B5 **Newton of Balcanquhal** P & K
223 J6 **Newton of Balcormo** Fife
151 H4 **Newton on Ouse** N York
162 E4 **Newton-on-Rawcliffe** N York
113 H7 **Newton on the Hill** Shrops
191 H5 **Newton-on-the-Moor** Nthumb
135 G5 **Newton on Trent** Lincs
14 C4 **Newton Poppleford** Devon
66 F1 **Newton Purcell** Oxon
99 H2 **Newton Regis** Warwks
166 B4 **Newton Reigny** Cumb
280 D6 **Newton Row** Highld
13 K3 **Newton St Cyres** Devon
122 E8 **Newton St Faith** Norfk
45 L6 **Newton St Loe** BaNES
27 G8 **Newton St Petrock** Devon
115 M6 **Newton Solney** Derbys
34 E3 **Newton Stacey** Hants
173 K2 **Newton Stewart** D & G
34 B3 **Newton Tony** Wilts
27 J5 **Newton Tracey** Devon
170 D8 **Newton under Roseberry** R & Cl
180 E2 **Newton Underwood** Nthumb
151 M6 **Newton upon Derwent** E R Yk
35 L4 **Newton Valence** Hants
187 H7 **Newton Wamphray** D & G
138 F2 **Newton with Scales** Lancs
61 J5 **Newtown** Blae G
129 M4 **Newtown** Ches
2 F5 **Newtown** Cnwll
11 K6 **Newtown** Cnwll
164 E1 **Newtown** Cumb
166 C6 **Newtown** Cumb
177 L6 **Newtown** Cumb
178 C6 **Newtown** Cumb
185 J1 **Newtown** D & G
131 K3 **Newtown** Derbys
14 C3 **Newtown** Devon
28 D6 **Newtown** Devon
15 L2 **Newtown** Dorset
17 K1 **New Town** Dorset
32 F7 **New Town** Dorset
33 G7 **New Town** Dorset
23 H3 **New Town** E Susx
63 K6 **Newtown** Gloucs
18 D2 **Newtown** Hants
35 J8 **Newtown** Hants
48 C6 **Newtown** Hants
80 B4 **Newtown** Herefs
80 C8 **Newtown** Herefs
80 E6 **Newtown** Herefs
81 G7 **Newtown** Herefs
240 B3 **Newtown** Highld
19 G5 **Newtown** IoW
139 G4 **Newtown** Lancs

101 L7 **New Town** Nhants
190 E6 **Newtown** Nthumb
202 F6 **Newtown** Nthumb
203 G8 **Newtown** Nthumb
17 K4 **Newtown** Poole
94 D5 **Newtown** Powys
61 G7 **Newtown** Rhondd
112 F7 **Newtown** Shrops
113 H5 **Newtown** Shrops
30 C8 **Newtown** Somset
98 C3 **Newtown** Staffs
131 H7 **Newtown** Staffs
139 H6 **Newtown** Wigan
32 F5 **Newtown** Wilts
47 L4 **New Town** Wilts
47 L6 **Newtown** Wilts
81 K4 **Newtown** Worcs
98 B7 **Newtown** Worcs
3 J6 **Newtown-in-St Martin** Cnwll
100 B2 **Newtown Linford** Leics
208 C7 **Newtown of Beltrees** Rens
201 J6 **Newtown St Boswells** Border
100 B3 **Newtown Unthank** Leics
61 J6 **New Tredegar** Caerph
198 D5 **New Trows** S Lans
133 H6 **New Tupton** Derbys
233 L7 **Newtyle** Angus
103 K2 **New Walsoken** Cambs
145 H6 **New Waltham** NE Lin
133 H4 **New Whittington** Derbys
211 M5 **New Winton** E Loth
66 A4 **New Yatt** Oxon
50 D1 **Newyears Green** Gt Lon
216 F5 **Newyork** Ag & B
136 D8 **New York** Lincs
181 H5 **New York** N Tyne
150 B3 **New York** N York
79 L4 **Nextend** Herefs
54 F6 **Neyland** Pembks
154 b6 **Niarbyl** IoM
63 K5 **Nibley** Gloucs
45 K3 **Nibley** S Glos
63 L7 **Nibley Green** Gloucs
29 K7 **Nicholashayne** Devon
56 F7 **Nicholaston** Swans
178 D5 **Nickies Hill** Cumb
150 D4 **Nidd** N York
245 L3 **Nigg** C Aber
264 C5 **Nigg** Highld
45 L5 **Nimlet** BaNES
179 H8 **Ninebanks** Nthumb
47 G2 **Nine Elms** Swindn
80 E2 **Nineveh** Worcs
74 C7 **Nine Wells** Pembks
24 C5 **Ninfield** E Susx
18 F6 **Ningwood** IoW
201 L8 **Nisbet** Border
202 B3 **Nisbet Hill** Border
19 H8 **Niton** IoW
208 E7 **Nitshill** C Glas
52 C7 **Noah's Ark** Kent
52 E1 **Noak Bridge** Essex
70 D8 **Noak Hill** Gt Lon
141 L6 **Noblethorpe** Barns
95 L2 **Nobold** Shrops
84 C3 **Nobottle** Nhants
135 L6 **Nocton** Lincs
107 H3 **Nogdam End** Norfk
66 E4 **Noke** Oxon
54 E3 **Nolton** Pembks
54 D3 **Nolton Haven** Pembks
113 H2 **No Man's Heath** Ches
99 H2 **No Man's Heath** Warwks
6 B3 **No Man's Land** Cnwll
10 C8 **No Man's Land** Cnwll
28 E8 **Nomansland** Devon
34 B7 **Nomansland** Wilts
113 H6 **Noneley** Shrops
41 H5 **Nonington** Kent
157 H6 **Nook** Cumb
178 B3 **Nook** Cumb
51 G5 **Norbiton** Gt Lon
146 F7 **Norbreck** Bpool
81 G6 **Norbridge** Herefs
113 J2 **Norbury** Ches
115 J3 **Norbury** Derbys
51 J5 **Norbury** Gt Lon
95 J5 **Norbury** Shrops
114 B6 **Norbury** Staffs
113 J2 **Norbury Common** Ches
114 B7 **Norbury Junction** Staffs
81 J2 **Norchard** Worcs
130 B4 **Norcott Brook** Ches
146 F7 **Norcross** Lancs
103 L3 **Nordelph** Norfk
140 C5 **Norden** Rochdl

96 F4 **Nordley** Shrops
202 D4 **Norham** Nthumb
141 G3 **Norland Town** Calder
130 B5 **Norley** Ches
18 E4 **Norleywood** Hants
23 G4 **Norlington** E Susx
135 K2 **Normanby** Lincs
143 M4 **Normanby** N Linc
162 C6 **Normanby** N York
170 D7 **Normanby** R & Cl
136 B1 **Normanby le Wold** Lincs
102 D5 **Norman Cross** Cambs
50 B8 **Normandy** Surrey
24 C6 **Norman's Bay** E Susx
14 C2 **Norman's Green** Devon
116 B5 **Normanton** C Derb
117 L3 **Normanton** Leics
118 B2 **Normanton** Lincs
134 E8 **Normanton** Notts
101 K2 **Normanton** Rutlnd
142 B3 **Normanton** Wakefd
33 K3 **Normanton** Wilts
99 K1 **Normanton le Heath** Leics
116 E7 **Normanton on Soar** Notts
117 G5 **Normanton on the Wolds** Notts
134 F6 **Normanton on Trent** Notts
147 G8 **Normoss** Lancs
36 D2 **Norney** Surrey
46 C6 **Norrington Common** Wilts
6 E1 **Norris Green** Cnwll
116 B8 **Norris Hill** Leics
141 K3 **Norristhorpe** Kirk
105 J4 **Northacre** Norfk
68 B3 **Northall** Bucks
160 E4 **Northallerton** N York
121 M8 **Northall Green** Norfk
19 G1 **Northam** C Sotn
27 H5 **Northam** Devon
84 E3 **Northampton** Nhants
81 J2 **Northampton** Worcs
133 K3 **North Anston** Rothm
49 M5 **North Ascot** Br For
66 C1 **North Aston** Oxon
69 H6 **Northaw** Herts
30 D8 **Northay** Somset
34 E6 **North Baddesley** Hants
229 G3 **North Ballachulish** Highld
31 K5 **North Barrow** Somset
121 K4 **North Barsham** Norfk
53 G1 **North Benfleet** Essex
20 F6 **North Bersted** W Susx
212 C2 **North Berwick** E Loth
168 F4 **North Bitchburn** Dur
181 H2 **North Blyth** Nthumb
19 K2 **North Boarhunt** Hants
18 B4 **North Bockhampton** Dorset
102 C2 **Northborough** C Pete
41 K5 **Northbourne** Kent
13 H5 **North Bovey** Devon
46 B7 **North Bradley** Wilts
12 C6 **North Brentor** Devon
32 B3 **North Brewham** Somset
36 E3 **North Bridge** Surrey
24 D2 **Northbridge Street** E Susx
35 G3 **Northbrook** Hants
66 D3 **Northbrook** Oxon
86 F6 **North Brook End** Cambs
27 H3 **North Buckland** Devon
107 H2 **North Burlingham** Norfk
31 K5 **North Cadbury** Somset
135 J4 **North Carlton** Lincs
134 B3 **North Carlton** Notts
143 M1 **North Cave** E R Yk
64 E5 **North Cerney** Gloucs
22 F3 **North Chailey** E Susx
36 E5 **Northchapel** W Susx
33 L7 **North Charford** Hants
191 H2 **North Charlton** Nthumb
51 G6 **North Cheam** Gt Lon
31 M5 **North Cheriton** Somset
15 K4 **North Chideock** Dorset
68 B5 **Northchurch** Herts
152 D8 **North Cliffe** E R Yk
135 G5 **North Clifton** Notts
169 H4 **North Close** Dur
137 G2 **North Cockerington** Lincs
228 E8 **North Connel** Ag & B
42 B5 **North Cornelly** Brdgnd
3 K7 **North Corner** Cnwll
228 C5 **North Corry** Highld
145 J7 **North Cotes** Lincs
11 L4 **Northcott** Devon
14 D1 **Northcott** Devon
29 K8 **Northcott** Devon
4 A6 **North Country** Cnwll
66 D7 **Northcourt** Oxon
107 K5 **North Cove** Suffk

160 D2 **North Cowton** N York
85 H6 **North Crawley** M Keyn
52 A4 **North Cray** Gt Lon
121 J4 **North Creake** Norfk
30 D6 **North Curry** Somset
152 E5 **North Dalton** E R Yk
150 E5 **North Deighton** N York
41 L1 **Northdown** Kent
151 L8 **North Duffield** N York
259 G2 **North Duntulm** Highld
133 G6 **Northedge** Derbys
41 G6 **North Elham** Kent
136 E2 **North Elkington** Lincs
121 L7 **North Elmham** Norfk
142 D5 **North Elmsall** Wakefd
67 H8 **Northend** Bucks
19 L3 **North End** C Port
177 K7 **North End** Cumb
32 D5 **North End** Dorset
145 H2 **North End** E R Yk
153 K7 **North End** E R Yk
71 G3 **North End** Essex
33 J7 **North End** Hants
35 J5 **North End** Hants
116 F8 **North End** Leics
119 H3 **North End** Lincs
137 H2 **North End** Lincs
144 D7 **North End** Lincs
145 J7 **North End** Lincs
144 E3 **North End** N Linc
44 E5 **North End** N Som
85 J2 **North End** Nhants
105 K5 **North End** Norfk
191 G6 **North End** Nthumb
138 C6 **North End** Sefton
21 G6 **North End** W Susx
21 J5 **North End** W Susx
83 J5 **Northend** Warwks
131 G2 **Northenden** Manch
49 L1 **Northend Woods** Bucks
260 B4 **North Erradale** Highld
100 D3 **North Evington** C Leic
71 K7 **North Fambridge** Essex
144 B3 **North Ferriby** E R Yk
98 C7 **Northfield** Birm
245 K2 **Northfield** C Aber
144 C2 **Northfield** E R Yk
102 A2 **Northfields** Lincs
52 D4 **Northfleet** Kent
153 H5 **North Frodingham** E R Yk
33 L8 **North Gorley** Hants
106 E5 **North Green** Norfk
91 G3 **North Green** Suffk
91 J2 **North Green** Suffk
135 K5 **North Greetwell** Lincs
152 C2 **North Grimston** N York
52 F6 **North Halling** Medway
20 B6 **North Hayling** Hants
203 G6 **North Hazelrigg** Nthumb
28 C4 **North Heasley** Devon
37 G6 **North Heath** W Susx
29 J6 **North Hele** Devon
11 K7 **North Hill** Cnwll
50 D2 **North Hillingdon** Gt Lon
66 D6 **North Hinksey Village** Oxon
37 J2 **North Holmwood** Surrey
7 K3 **North Huish** Devon
135 J6 **North Hykeham** Lincs
24 E2 **Northiam** E Susx
86 C6 **Northill** Beds
63 L5 **Northington** Gloucs
35 H3 **Northington** Hants
144 D7 **North Kelsey** Lincs
251 H2 **North Kessock** Highld
144 F4 **North Killingholme** N Linc
160 F5 **North Kilvington** N York
100 D6 **North Kilworth** Leics
18 B3 **North Kingston** Hants
118 F1 **North Kyme** Lincs
153 L2 **North Landing** E R Yk
119 K1 **Northlands** Lincs
65 G4 **Northleach** Gloucs
67 K5 **North Lee** Bucks
160 D7 **North Lees** N York
14 E3 **Northleigh** Devon
27 L4 **Northleigh** Devon
40 F6 **North Leigh** Kent
66 A4 **North Leigh** Oxon
134 F3 **North Leverton with Habblesthorpe** Notts
12 C3 **Northlew** Devon
82 C5 **North Littleton** Worcs
31 H3 **Northload Bridge** Somset
105 L6 **North Lopham** Norfk
101 K3 **North Luffenham** Rutlnd
20 C4 **North Marden** W Susx
67 J3 **North Marston** Bucks
211 K7 **North Middleton** Mdloth

190 E1 **North Middleton** Nthumb
172 D4 **North Milmain** D & G
28 C5 **North Molton** Devon
66 B6 **Northmoor** Oxon
48 E1 **North Moreton** Oxon
234 B4 **Northmuir** Angus
20 E6 **North Mundham** W Susx
134 F7 **North Muskham** Notts
152 D8 **North Newbald** E R Yk
83 K7 **North Newington** Oxon
47 H7 **North Newnton** Wilts
30 D4 **North Newton** Somset
20 B6 **Northney** Hants
63 L7 **North Nibley** Gloucs
48 D8 **North Oakley** Hants
52 C2 **North Ockendon** Gt Lon
50 E2 **Northolt** Gt Lon
128 F6 **Northop** Flints
129 G6 **Northop Hall** Flints
170 C6 **North Ormesby** Middsb
136 E1 **North Ormsby** Lincs
141 K3 **Northorpe** Kirk
118 E8 **Northorpe** Lincs
119 G4 **Northorpe** Lincs
143 M8 **Northorpe** Lincs
160 E5 **North Otterington** N York
31 H3 **Northover** Somset
31 H6 **Northover** Somset
135 L1 **North Owersby** Lincs
141 H2 **Northowram** Calder
15 L1 **North Perrott** Somset
30 D4 **North Petherton** Somset
11 K4 **North Petherwin** Cnwll
105 H2 **North Pickenham** Norfk
81 M4 **North Piddle** Worcs
7 M6 **North Pool** Devon
15 M3 **North Poorton** Dorset
17 H5 **Northport** Dorset
18 B2 **North Poulner** Hants
210 F3 **North Queensferry** Fife
28 C4 **North Radworthy** Devon
118 D2 **North Rauceby** Lincs
122 E4 **Northrepps** Norfk
137 G3 **North Reston** Lincs
150 C6 **North Rigton** N York
18 B4 **North Ripley** Hants
131 H6 **North Rode** Ches
165 H4 **North Row** Cumb
120 E8 **North Runcton** Norfk
146 C2 **North Scale** Cumb
135 G6 **North Scarle** Lincs
181 H2 **North Seaton** Nthumb
181 H2 **North Seaton Colliery** Nthumb
228 E6 **North Shian** Ag & B
181 J5 **North Shields** N Tyne
53 K2 **North Shoebury** Sthend
146 F8 **North Shore** Bpool
102 F3 **North Side** C Pete
164 C5 **North Side** Cumb
170 F7 **North Skelton** R & Cl
145 L8 **North Somercotes** Lincs
160 D7 **North Stainley** N York
167 J7 **North Stainmore** Cumb
52 D3 **North Stifford** Thurr
45 L5 **North Stoke** BaNES
48 F2 **North Stoke** Oxon
21 H5 **North Stoke** W Susx
88 B2 **North Street** Cambs
33 K7 **North Street** Hants
35 K4 **North Street** Hants
40 D4 **North Street** Kent
53 H4 **North Street** Medway
48 F4 **North Street** W Berk
203 K6 **North Sunderland** Nthumb
11 K3 **North Tamerton** Cnwll
12 F2 **North Tawton** Devon
209 K1 **North Third** Stirlg
145 H8 **North Thoresby** Lincs
282 d6 **Northton** W Isls
12 C1 **North Town** Devon
31 J2 **North Town** Somset
49 L3 **North Town** W & M
122 A8 **North Tuddenham** Norfk
180 E5 **North Walbottle** N u Ty
122 F5 **North Walsham** Norfk
35 H2 **North Waltham** Hants
35 M1 **North Warnborough** Hants
29 L5 **Northway** Somset
57 G7 **Northway** Swans
70 D6 **North Weald Bassett** Essex
134 F3 **North Wheatley** Notts
8 C2 **North Whilborough** Devon
130 C5 **Northwich** Ches
45 H6 **North Wick** BaNES
45 H7 **Northwick** S Glos
30 E1 **Northwick** Somset
81 J4 **Northwick** Worcs

45 H7 **North Widcombe** BaNES
136 C2 **North Willingham** Lincs
133 H6 **North Wingfield** Derbys
118 B7 **North Witham** Lincs
104 E4 **Northwold** Norfk
114 D2 **Northwood** C Stke
132 E6 **Northwood** Derbys
50 E1 **Northwood** Gt Lon
19 H5 **Northwood** IoW
113 G5 **Northwood** Shrops
63 L4 **Northwood Green** Gloucs
31 L7 **North Wootton** Dorset
120 E6 **North Wootton** Norfk
31 J3 **North Wootton** Somset
46 B4 **North Wraxall** Wilts
47 H3 **North Wroughton** Swindn
142 E5 **Norton** Donc
23 G7 **Norton** E Susx
64 B2 **Norton** Gloucs
130 A3 **Norton** Halton
86 E8 **Norton** Herts
18 E6 **Norton** IoW
62 F3 **Norton** Mons
44 D6 **Norton** N Som
152 B2 **Norton** N York
84 B3 **Norton** Nhants
133 L5 **Norton** Notts
79 K2 **Norton** Powys
170 B6 **Norton** S on T
133 G3 **Norton** Sheff
95 L7 **Norton** Shrops
96 D2 **Norton** Shrops
96 E6 **Norton** Shrops
97 G3 **Norton** Shrops
89 J2 **Norton** Suffk
57 H7 **Norton** Swans
20 F5 **Norton** W Susx
46 C2 **Norton** Wilts
81 K5 **Norton** Worcs
82 B5 **Norton** Worcs
32 F2 **Norton Bavant** Wilts
114 D5 **Norton Bridge** Staffs
98 C2 **Norton Canes** Staffs
79 M6 **Norton Canon** Herefs
122 B6 **Norton Corner** Norfk
135 H7 **Norton Disney** Lincs
32 C4 **Norton Ferris** Wilts
30 B5 **Norton Fitzwarren** Somset
18 E6 **Norton Green** IoW
45 H6 **Norton Hawkfield** BaNES
70 F6 **Norton Heath** Essex
113 M4 **Norton in Hales** Shrops
114 D1 **Norton in the Moors** C Stke
99 J2 **Norton-Juxta-Twycross** Leics
150 F2 **Norton-le-Clay** N York
82 F3 **Norton Lindsey** Warwks
89 K2 **Norton Little Green** Suffk
45 J6 **Norton Malreward** BaNES
70 E6 **Norton Mandeville** Essex
45 M7 **Norton St Philip** Somset
107 H4 **Norton Subcourse** Norfk
31 G7 **Norton sub Hamdon** Somset
79 L5 **Norton Wood** Herefs
134 F7 **Norwell** Notts
134 E7 **Norwell Woodhouse** Notts
106 E2 **Norwich** Norfk
281 f1 **Norwick** Shet
220 F8 **Norwood** Clacks
133 J3 **Norwood** Derbys
25 K1 **Norwood** Kent
70 E5 **Norwood End** Essex
141 H2 **Norwood Green** Calder
50 E3 **Norwood Green** Gt Lon
37 K2 **Norwood Hill** Surrey
103 H4 **Norwoodside** Cambs
101 G4 **Noseley** Leics
7 G5 **Noss Mayo** Devon
160 C6 **Nosterfield** N York
88 C6 **Nosterfield End** Cambs
248 D6 **Nostie** Highld
65 G3 **Notgrove** Gloucs
42 B6 **Nottage** Brdgnd
6 D3 **Notter** Cnwll
116 F4 **Nottingham** C Nott
16 C6 **Nottington** Dorset
142 A5 **Notton** Wakefd
46 C6 **Notton** Wilts
71 J5 **Nounsley** Essex
81 J2 **Noutard's Green** Worcs
89 H3 **Nowton** Suffk
95 K1 **Nox** Shrops
49 G2 **Nuffield** Oxon
152 C6 **Nunburnholme** E R Yk
116 E1 **Nuncargate** Notts

166 C2 **Nunclose** Cumb
99 K5 **Nuneaton** Warwks
66 E7 **Nuneham Courtenay** Oxon
51 K4 **Nunhead** Gt Lon
153 J6 **Nunkeeling** E R Yk
151 H4 **Nun Monkton** N York
32 B2 **Nunney** Somset
32 B2 **Nunney Catch** Somset
80 D6 **Nunnington** Herefs
161 L6 **Nunnington** N York
190 F7 **Nunnykirk** Nthumb
145 H6 **Nunsthorpe** NE Lin
170 C7 **Nunthorpe** Middsb
151 J6 **Nunthorpe** York
170 D8 **Nunthorpe Village** Middsb
33 K5 **Nunton** Wilts
160 D7 **Nunwick** N York
179 K4 **Nunwick** Nthumb
63 J7 **Nupdown** S Glos
67 L3 **Nup End** Bucks
64 A5 **Nupend** Gloucs
49 L4 **Nuptown** Br For
34 E7 **Nursling** Hants
36 A6 **Nursted** Hants
46 F6 **Nursteed** Wilts
97 J3 **Nurton** Staffs
20 C6 **Nutbourne** W Susx
21 J3 **Nutbourne** W Susx
37 M1 **Nutfield** Surrey
116 E3 **Nuthall** Notts
87 H8 **Nuthampstead** Herts
37 J5 **Nuthurst** W Susx
23 G2 **Nutley** E Susx
35 J2 **Nutley** Hants
140 B4 **Nuttal Lane** Bury
143 G7 **Nutwell** Donc
280 E3 **Nybster** Highld
20 E7 **Nyetimber** W Susx
36 B6 **Nyewood** W Susx
13 G1 **Nymet Rowland** Devon
13 G2 **Nymet Tracey** Devon
64 A7 **Nympsfield** Gloucs
29 L6 **Nynehead** Somset
30 F4 **Nythe** Somset
20 F5 **Nyton** W Susx

100 D3 **Oadby** Leics
53 J6 **Oad Street** Kent
81 J3 **Oakall Green** Worcs
115 G3 **Oakamoor** Staffs
210 E5 **Oakbank** W Loth
12 D3 **Oak Cross** Devon
43 J2 **Oakdale** Caerph
29 L6 **Oake** Somset
97 J3 **Oaken** Staffs
147 K6 **Oakenclough** Lancs
96 F1 **Oakengates** Wrekin
129 G5 **Oakenholt** Flints
169 G3 **Oakenshaw** Dur
141 J2 **Oakenshaw** Kirk
133 H8 **Oakerthorpe** Derbys
76 E4 **Oakford** Cerdgn
29 G6 **Oakford** Devon
29 G6 **Oakfordbridge** Devon
131 H6 **Oakgrove** Ches
101 J2 **Oakham** Rutlnd
114 B1 **Oakhanger** Ches
36 A4 **Oakhanger** Hants
31 K2 **Oakhill** Somset
38 E3 **Oakhurst** Kent
87 H2 **Oakington** Cambs
78 E5 **Oaklands** Powys
63 M4 **Oakle Street** Gloucs
85 K4 **Oakley** Beds
66 F4 **Oakley** Bucks
210 D1 **Oakley** Fife
35 H1 **Oakley** Hants
67 H7 **Oakley** Oxon
17 K3 **Oakley** Poole
106 D7 **Oakley** Suffk
50 A4 **Oakley Green** W & M
93 L6 **Oakley Park** Powys
64 C6 **Oakridge** Gloucs
168 F5 **Oaks** Dur
139 K1 **Oaks** Lancs
95 K2 **Oaks** Shrops
64 E8 **Oaksey** Wilts
115 J5 **Oaks Green** Derbys
178 C4 **Oakshaw Ford** Cumb
35 M5 **Oakshott** Hants
99 J1 **Oakthorpe** Leics
169 K8 **Oak Tree** Darltn
116 C4 **Oakwood** C Derb
179 L5 **Oakwood** Nthumb
37 H3 **Oakwoodhill** Surrey

149 J8 **Oakworth** Brad
40 C3 **Oare** Kent
28 D2 **Oare** Somset
47 H6 **Oare** Wilts
118 D4 **Oasby** Lincs
30 F5 **Oath** Somset
234 D4 **Oathlaw** Angus
50 E6 **Oatlands Park** Surrey
216 D1 **Oban** Ag & B
95 H7 **Obley** Shrops
232 F7 **Obney** P & K
31 L7 **Oborne** Dorset
118 E8 **Obthorpe** Lincs
90 D1 **Occold** Suffk
275 J1 **Occumster** Highld
196 F6 **Ochiltree** E Ayrs
116 C4 **Ockbrook** Derbys
98 B4 **Ocker Hill** Sandw
81 H3 **Ockeridge** Worcs
50 D7 **Ockham** Surrey
237 G6 **Ockle** Highld
37 H3 **Ockley** Surrey
80 E6 **Ocle Pychard** Herefs
153 G2 **Octon** E R Yk
31 H7 **Odcombe** Somset
45 L6 **Odd Down** BaNES
81 L3 **Oddingley** Worcs
65 J2 **Oddington** Gloucs
66 E4 **Oddington** Oxon
85 J4 **Odell** Beds
12 C2 **Odham** Devon
49 H8 **Odiham** Hants
141 J2 **Odsal** Brad
86 F7 **Odsey** Cambs
33 K5 **Odstock** Wilts
99 K2 **Odstone** Leics
83 J2 **Offchurch** Warwks
82 C6 **Offenham** Worcs
131 H2 **Offerton** Stockp
181 J7 **Offerton** Sundld
22 F5 **Offham** E Susx
39 G2 **Offham** Kent
21 H5 **Offham** W Susx
114 B5 **Offleymarsh** Staffs
86 E2 **Offord Cluny** Cambs
86 E2 **Offord D'Arcy** Cambs
90 C5 **Offton** Suffk
14 E3 **Offwell** Devon
47 J4 **Ogbourne Maizey** Wilts
47 J4 **Ogbourne St Andrew** Wilts
47 J4 **Ogbourne St George** Wilts
141 G2 **Ogden** Calder
180 E3 **Ogle** Nthumb
129 K3 **Oglet** Lpool
42 D6 **Ogmore** V Glam
42 C6 **Ogmore-by-Sea** V Glam
42 E4 **Ogmore Vale** Brdgnd
126 C6 **Ogwen Bank** Gwynd
32 D8 **Okeford Fitzpaine** Dorset
12 E3 **Okehampton** Devon
132 E7 **Oker Side** Derbys
13 K7 **Olchard** Devon
84 F1 **Old** Nhants
245 L2 **Old Aberdeen** C Aber
35 J4 **Old Alresford** Hants
270 E2 **Oldany** Highld
185 J3 **Old Auchenbrack** D & G
116 F3 **Old Basford** C Nott
49 G8 **Old Basing** Hants
121 L7 **Old Beetley** Norfk
82 D2 **Oldberrow** Warwks
190 F2 **Old Bewick** Nthumb
136 F6 **Old Bolingbroke** Lincs
49 L5 **Old Bracknell** Br For
150 B7 **Old Bramhope** Leeds
133 G5 **Old Brampton** Derbys
175 J1 **Old Bridge of Urr** D & G
106 B5 **Old Buckenham** Norfk
48 C7 **Old Burghclere** Hants
38 E7 **Oldbury** Kent
98 C5 **Oldbury** Sandw
97 G5 **Oldbury** Shrops
99 J4 **Oldbury** Warwks
63 J8 **Oldbury Naite** S Glos
63 J8 **Oldbury-on-Severn** S Glos
46 B1 **Oldbury on the Hill** Gloucs
161 J5 **Old Byland** N York
143 G7 **Old Cantley** Donc
169 J3 **Old Cassop** Dur
42 D6 **Old Castle** Brdgnd
62 C2 **Oldcastle** Mons
113 G2 **Oldcastle Heath** Ches
95 G4 **Old Churchstoke** Powys
145 H6 **Old Clee** NE Lin
29 J3 **Old Cleeve** Somset
134 C6 **Old Clipstone** Notts
127 H4 **Old Colwyn** Conwy
134 B2 **Oldcotes** Notts

183 G3 **Old Dailly** S Ayrs
117 H6 **Old Dalby** Leics
132 B4 **Old Dam** Derbys
269 H6 **Old Deer** Abers
31 H1 **Old Ditch** Somset
142 E8 **Old Edlington** Donc
169 H5 **Old Eldon** Dur
153 J8 **Old Ellerby** E R Yk
91 H8 **Old Felixstowe** Suffk
149 H8 **Oldfield** Brad
81 J2 **Oldfield** Worcs
102 D4 **Old Fletton** C Pete
32 C1 **Oldford** Somset
63 H3 **Old Forge** Herefs
62 F2 **Old Furnace** Herefs
131 L1 **Old Glossop** Derbys
143 J3 **Old Goole** E R Yk
10 b2 **Old Grimsby** IoS
69 K3 **Old Hall Green** Herts
89 H4 **Oldhall Green** Suffk
122 F5 **Old Hall Street** Norfk
140 D6 **Oldham** Oldham
213 G5 **Oldhamstocks** E Loth
70 C5 **Old Harlow** Essex
72 E3 **Old Heath** Essex
120 F3 **Old Hunstanton** Norfk
102 F7 **Old Hurst** Cambs
157 J5 **Old Hutton** Cumb
4 D6 **Old Kea** Cnwll
208 D4 **Old Kilpatrick** W Duns
69 G3 **Old Knebworth** Herts
106 E2 **Old Lakenham** Norfk
45 K4 **Oldland** S Glos
148 B8 **Old Langho** Lancs
154 f5 **Old Laxey** IoM
119 L2 **Old Leake** Lincs
152 B1 **Old Malton** N York
256 E6 **Oldmeldrum** Abers
142 C1 **Old Micklefield** Leeds
11 M7 **Oldmill** Cnwll
83 G2 **Old Milverton** Warwks
44 C7 **Oldmixon** N Som
90 B3 **Old Newton** Suffk
169 J3 **Old Quarrington** Dur
116 F3 **Old Radford** C Nott
79 J3 **Old Radnor** Powys
256 B6 **Old Rayne** Abers
25 J2 **Old Romney** Kent
22 B6 **Old Shoreham** W Susx
276 C4 **Oldshoremore** Highld
38 F3 **Old Soar** Kent
45 L3 **Old Sodbury** S Glos
118 C5 **Old Somerby** Lincs
161 H6 **Oldstead** N York
84 F7 **Old Stratford** Nhants
97 K6 **Old Swinford** Dudley
157 K2 **Old Tebay** Cumb
160 F6 **Old Thirsk** N York
140 F2 **Old Town** Calder
157 J6 **Old Town** Cumb
166 B2 **Old Town** Cumb
23 K7 **Old Town** E Susx
10 c3 **Old Town** IoS
190 B7 **Old Town** Nthumb
140 B8 **Old Trafford** Traffd
133 H6 **Old Tupton** Derbys
178 B6 **Oldwall** Cumb
56 E6 **Oldwalls** Swans
86 C6 **Old Warden** Beds
28 F6 **Oldways End** Somset
102 B7 **Old Weston** Cambs
280 E6 **Old Wick** Highld
50 C4 **Old Windsor** W & M
40 E4 **Old Wives Lees** Kent
50 C7 **Old Woking** Surrey
84 F7 **Old Wolverton** M Keyn
113 G7 **Old Woods** Shrops
115 J7 **Olive Green** Staffs
187 G1 **Oliver** Border
34 F7 **Oliver's Battery** Hants
281 d4 **Ollaberry** Shet
247 H1 **Ollach** Highld
130 F4 **Ollerton** Ches
134 D6 **Ollerton** Notts
113 L6 **Ollerton** Shrops
77 H4 **Olmarch** Cerdgn
88 C7 **Olmstead Green** Cambs
85 H5 **Olney** M Keyn
279 L3 **Olrig House** Highld
98 E7 **Olton** Solhll
45 J2 **Olveston** S Glos
81 J3 **Ombersley** Worcs
134 D6 **Ompton** Notts
179 H5 **Once Brewed** Nthumb
154 e6 **Onchan** IoM
131 L8 **Onecote** Staffs
89 K3 **Onehouse** Suffk
62 E4 **Onen** Mons

79 M2 **Ongar Street** Herefs	90 E4 **Otley** Suffk	157 K7 **Overtown** Lancs	72 D8 **Paglesham** Essex
95 L7 **Onibury** Shrops	90 F4 **Otley Green** Suffk	209 L8 **Overtown** N Lans	8 C3 **Paignton** Torbay
229 G3 **Onich** Highld	34 F6 **Otterbourne** Hants	47 H3 **Overtown** Swindn	100 A7 **Pailton** Warwks
60 C5 **Onllwyn** Neath	148 F4 **Otterburn** N York	142 A4 **Overtown** Wakefd	23 K3 **Paine's Cross** E Susx
114 B3 **Onneley** Staffs	190 C7 **Otterburn** Nthumb	34 C3 **Over Wallop** Hants	115 G5 **Painleyhill** Staffs
36 E1 **Onslow Village** Surrey	206 E2 **Otter Ferry** Ag & B	99 H5 **Over Whitacre** Warwks	79 G6 **Painscastle** Powys
130 B5 **Onston** Ches	11 H4 **Otterham** Cnwll	133 J5 **Over Woodhouse** Derbys	180 C6 **Painshawfield** Nthumb
116 B2 **Openwoodgate** Derbys	30 C2 **Otterhampton** Somset	66 B1 **Over Worton** Oxon	152 B4 **Painsthorpe** E R Yk
260 B5 **Opinan** Highld	53 H5 **Otterham Quay** Kent	66 E8 **Overy** Oxon	64 C5 **Painswick** Gloucs
266 F5 **Orbliston** Moray	282 C7 **Otternish** W Isls	67 J3 **Oving** Bucks	40 C3 **Painter's Forstal** Kent
258 D7 **Orbost** Highld	50 C6 **Ottershaw** Surrey	20 E6 **Oving** W Susx	208 E6 **Paisley** Rens
137 J6 **Orby** Lincs	281 e3 **Otterswick** Shet	22 E6 **Ovingdean** Br & H	107 L5 **Pakefield** Suffk
30 C6 **Orchard Portman** Somset	14 C5 **Otterton** Devon	180 D6 **Ovingham** Nthumb	89 J2 **Pakenham** Suffk
33 J2 **Orcheston** Wilts	18 F3 **Otterwood** Hants	168 E7 **Ovington** Dur	111 J4 **Pale** Gwynd
62 F2 **Orcop** Herefs	14 C3 **Ottery St Mary** Devon	88 F6 **Ovington** Essex	88 D6 **Pale Green** Essex
62 F2 **Orcop Hill** Herefs	41 G6 **Ottinge** Kent	35 H4 **Ovington** Hants	34 B3 **Palestine** Hants
268 A4 **Ord** Abers	145 H3 **Ottringham** E R Yk	105 J3 **Ovington** Norfk	49 L4 **Paley Street** W & M
244 E2 **Ordhead** Abers	177 J7 **Oughterby** Cumb	180 C6 **Ovington** Nthumb	98 C4 **Palfrey** Wsall
244 A3 **Ordie** Abers	158 F6 **Oughtershaw** N York	19 H3 **Ower** Hants	106 C7 **Palgrave** Suffk
267 G5 **Ordiequish** Moray	164 F3 **Oughterside** Cumb	34 D7 **Ower** Hants	16 F4 **Pallington** Dorset
179 L7 **Ordley** Nthumb	132 F1 **Oughtibridge** Sheff	16 E5 **Owermoigne** Dorset	11 H7 **Palmersbridge** Cnwll
134 D4 **Ordsall** Notts	130 D2 **Oughtrington** Warrtn	95 H5 **Owlbury** Shrops	69 J8 **Palmers Green** Gt Lon
24 F5 **Ore** E Susx	161 J7 **Oulston** N York	133 G2 **Owlerton** Sheff	196 F7 **Palmerston** E Ayrs
80 B2 **Oreleton Common** Herefs	177 H8 **Oulton** Cumb	64 A7 **Owlpen** Gloucs	43 H7 **Palmerstown** V Glam
96 E7 **Oreton** Shrops	142 B2 **Oulton** Leeds	91 G1 **Owl's Green** Suffk	175 K3 **Palnackie** D & G
91 K5 **Orford** Suffk	122 C6 **Oulton** Norfk	49 K6 **Owlsmoor** Br For	174 C2 **Palnure** D & G
130 B2 **Orford** Warrtn	114 B7 **Oulton** Staffs	67 J6 **Owlswick** Bucks	133 J6 **Palterton** Derbys
17 H4 **Organford** Dorset	114 E4 **Oulton** Staffs	135 K2 **Owmby** Lincs	48 F7 **Pamber End** Hants
115 J8 **Orgreave** Staffs	107 L4 **Oulton** Suffk	144 D6 **Owmby** Lincs	48 F7 **Pamber Green** Hants
40 C8 **Orlestone** Kent	107 L5 **Oulton Broad** Suffk	35 G6 **Owslebury** Hants	48 F6 **Pamber Heath** Hants
80 C2 **Orleton** Herefs	122 C6 **Oulton Street** Norfk	142 E5 **Owston** Donc	81 L8 **Pamington** Gloucs
81 G2 **Orleton** Worcs	102 A5 **Oundle** Nhants	101 G2 **Owston** Leics	17 K2 **Pamphill** Dorset
85 G1 **Orlingbury** Nhants	97 K5 **Ounsdale** Staffs	143 K7 **Owston Ferry** N Linc	87 K5 **Pampisford** Cambs
165 J5 **Ormathwaite** Cumb	166 E4 **Ousby** Cumb	145 H1 **Owstwick** E R Yk	31 G2 **Panborough** Somset
170 C7 **Ormesby** R & Cl	88 E3 **Ousden** Suffk	145 J2 **Owthorne** E R Yk	234 E8 **Panbride** Angus
123 K8 **Ormesby St Margaret** Norfk	143 L3 **Ousefleet** E R Yk	117 H5 **Owthorpe** Notts	11 K1 **Pancrasweek** Devon
123 K8 **Ormesby St Michael** Norfk	181 G8 **Ouston** Dur	170 C5 **Owton Manor** Hartpl	43 G7 **Pancross** V Glam
260 D2 **Ormiscaig** Highld	203 J6 **Outchester** Nthumb	104 E3 **Oxborough** Norfk	43 J4 **Pandy** Caerph
211 M5 **Ormiston** E Loth	41 G5 **Out Elmstead** Kent	15 L3 **Oxbridge** Dorset	92 D3 **Pandy** Gwynd
236 F7 **Ormsaigmore** Highld	156 E3 **Outgate** Cumb	136 F4 **Oxcombe** Lincs	111 G5 **Pandy** Gwynd
206 A4 **Ormsary** Ag & B	158 D2 **Outhgill** Cumb	133 J5 **Oxcroft** Derbys	62 C3 **Pandy** Mons
138 E6 **Ormskirk** Lancs	82 D2 **Outhill** Warwks	71 G1 **Oxen End** Essex	93 K3 **Pandy** Powys
168 F1 **Ornsby Hill** Dur	114 B5 **Outlands** Staffs	157 H5 **Oxenholme** Cumb	112 B4 **Pandy** Wrexhm
214 C6 **Oronsay** Ag & B	141 G4 **Outlane** Kirk	140 F1 **Oxenhope** Brad	111 L2 **Pandy'r Capel** Denbgs
275 b5 **Orphir** Ork	145 K3 **Out Newton** E R Yk	156 D5 **Oxen Park** Cumb	127 G6 **Pandy Tudur** Conwy
51 M5 **Orpington** Gt Lon	147 H7 **Out Rawcliffe** Lancs	31 G3 **Oxenpill** Somset	71 H2 **Panfield** Essex
138 D8 **Orrell** Sefton	103 K3 **Outwell** Norfk	64 D1 **Oxenton** Gloucs	48 F4 **Pangbourne** W Berk
139 G7 **Orrell** Wigan	33 K7 **Outwick** Hants	47 L7 **Oxenwood** Wilts	22 D5 **Pangdean** W Susx
139 G6 **Orrell Post** Wigan	37 M2 **Outwood** Surrey	66 D6 **Oxford** Oxon	80 E5 **Panks Bridge** Herefs
154 d4 **Orrisdale** IoM	142 A3 **Outwood** Wakefd	68 E8 **Oxhey** Herts	150 D5 **Pannal** N York
175 J5 **Orroland** D & G	140 B6 **Outwood Gate** Bury	180 F8 **Oxhill** Dur	150 C5 **Pannal Ash** N York
52 D3 **Orsett** Thurr	116 C7 **Outwoods** Leics	83 H6 **Oxhill** Warwks	243 L4 **Pannanich Wells Hotel** Abers
114 C8 **Orslow** Staffs	114 B7 **Outwoods** Staffs	97 K3 **Oxley** Wolves	
117 K3 **Orston** Notts	142 A3 **Ouzlewell Green** Leeds	72 C4 **Oxley Green** Essex	112 D7 **Pant** Shrops
165 H4 **Orthwaite** Cumb	141 G2 **Ovenden** Calder	24 C3 **Oxley's Green** E Susx	128 E4 **Pantasaph** Flints
147 K5 **Ortner** Lancs	87 H1 **Over** Cambs	103 K6 **Oxlode** Cambs	74 F5 **Panteg** Pembks
157 K1 **Orton** Cumb	130 C6 **Over** Ches	189 J3 **Oxnam** Border	5 K1 **Pantersbridge** Cnwll
101 H7 **Orton** Nhants	64 A3 **Over** Gloucs	122 E6 **Oxnead** Norfk	42 E5 **Pant-ffrwyth** Brdgnd
97 K4 **Orton** Staffs	45 HJ **Over** S Glos	50 F6 **Oxshott** Surrey	109 H2 **Pant Glas** Gwynd
102 D4 **Orton Longueville** C Pete	115 L4 **Over Burrows** Derbys	50 E6 **Oxshott Heath** Surrey	93 K4 **Pantglas** Powys
99 J3 **Orton-on-the-Hill** Leics	81 M7 **Overbury** Worcs	141 L7 **Oxspring** Barns	59 G4 **Pant-Gwyn** Carmth
177 K8 **Orton Rigg** Cumb	16 D6 **Overcombe** Dorset	51 K8 **Oxted** Surrey	57 J5 **Pant-lasau** Swans
102 C4 **Orton Waterville** C Pete	31 K7 **Over Compton** Dorset	201 G2 **Oxton** Border	93 J7 **Pant Mawr** Powys
87 H5 **Orwell** Cambs	102 B5 **Over End** Cambs	151 H7 **Oxton** N York	136 C4 **Panton** Lincs
139 K2 **Osbaldeston** Lancs	132 F5 **Overgreen** Derbys	117 G1 **Oxton** Notts	128 B7 **Pant-pastynog** Denbgs
139 K1 **Osbaldeston Green** Lancs	98 F4 **Over Green** Warwks	56 F7 **Oxwich** Swans	93 G3 **Pantperthog** Gwynd
151 K5 **Osbaldwick** York	132 D6 **Over Haddon** Derbys	56 F7 **Oxwich Green** Swans	93 L8 **Pant-y-dwr** Powys
99 L3 **Osbaston** Leics	147 K2 **Over Kellet** Lancs	121 K6 **Oxwick** Norfk	94 E3 **Pant-y-ffridd** Powys
112 D7 **Osbaston** Shrops	66 B3 **Over Kiddington** Oxon	271 L7 **Oykel Bridge Hotel** Highld	57 H3 **Pantyffynnon** Carmth
19 H5 **Osborne** IoW	31 G4 **Overleigh** Somset	256 B6 **Oyne** Abers	61 L7 **Pantygaseg** Torfn
118 E4 **Osbournby** Lincs	115 J8 **Overley** Staffs	57 H7 **Oystermouth** Swans	42 D3 **Pant-y-gog** Brdgnd
129 L6 **Oscroft** Ches	63 G4 **Over Monnow** Mons	64 A8 **Ozleworth** Gloucs	75 K7 **Pantymenyn** Carmth
258 E8 **Ose** Highld	65 L2 **Over Norton** Oxon		128 E6 **Pant-y-mwyn** Flints
116 D7 **Osgathorpe** Leics	130 F5 **Over Peover** Ches		107 G1 **Panxworth** Norfk
135 M1 **Osgodby** Lincs	129 J4 **Overpool** Ches	**P**	164 F4 **Papcastle** Cumb
143 G1 **Osgodby** N York	272 B3 **Overscaig Hotel** Highld		280 E6 **Papigoe** Highld
163 J5 **Osgodby** N York	115 M8 **Overseal** Derbys	282 h3 **Pabail** W Isls	212 D4 **Papple** E Loth
247 H1 **Oskaig** Highld	161 G4 **Over Silton** N York	16 D1 **Packers Hill** Dorset	116 F1 **Papplewick** Notts
226 E4 **Oskamull** Ag & B	40 D4 **Oversland** Kent	116 B8 **Packington** Leics	86 F3 **Papworth Everard** Cambs
115 K3 **Osmaston** Derbys	82 C4 **Overstone Green** Warwks	114 D1 **Packmoor** C Stke	86 F2 **Papworth St Agnes** Cambs
16 D6 **Osmington** Dorset	84 F2 **Overstone** Nhants	83 G2 **Packmores** Warwks	5 H4 **Par** Cnwll
16 D6 **Osmington Mills** Dorset	30 B3 **Over Stowey** Somset	234 C5 **Padanaram** Angus	41 J3 **Paramour Street** Kent
142 A1 **Osmondthorpe** Leeds	122 E3 **Overstrand** Norfk	67 H1 **Padbury** Bucks	139 G5 **Parbold** Lancs
161 G3 **Osmotherley** N York	31 G7 **Over Stratton** Somset	51 H3 **Paddington** Gt Lon	31 J4 **Parbrook** Somset
66 D6 **Osney** Oxon	33 J3 **Overstreet** Wilts	130 C2 **Paddington** Warrtn	37 G6 **Parbrook** W Susx
40 C3 **Ospringe** Kent	130 E4 **Over Tabley** Ches	41 G7 **Paddlesworth** Kent	111 G5 **Parc** Gwynd
141 L4 **Ossett** Wakefd	83 L7 **Overthorpe** Nhants	52 E6 **Paddlesworth** Kent	75 M2 **Parcllyn** Cerdgn
134 E6 **Ossington** Notts	245 J1 **Overton** C Aber	39 G4 **Paddock Wood** Kent	44 E1 **Parc Seymour** Newpt
72 D7 **Ostend** Essex	129 M4 **Overton** Ches	113 H5 **Padolgreen** Shrops	164 E5 **Pardshaw** Cumb
50 F3 **Osterley** Gt Lon	35 G1 **Overton** Hants	140 F8 **Padfield** Derbys	91 G3 **Parham** Suffk
161 K6 **Oswaldkirk** N York	147 H4 **Overton** Lancs	130 C2 **Padgate** Warrtn	186 D7 **Park** D & G
139 L2 **Oswaldtwistle** Lancs	151 J5 **Overton** N York	70 F7 **Padhams Green** Essex	178 F6 **Park** Nthumb
112 D5 **Oswestry** Shrops	80 C1 **Overton** Shrops	140 B1 **Padiham** Lancs	3 H3 **Park Bottom** Cnwll
52 B7 **Otford** Kent	56 E7 **Overton** Swans	149 L4 **Padside** N York	140 E7 **Park Bridge** Tamesd
39 K3 **Otham** Kent	141 L4 **Overton** Wakefd	10 C7 **Padstow** Cnwll	38 E6 **Park Corner** E Susx
39 K3 **Otham Hole** Kent	112 E3 **Overton** Wrexhm	48 F5 **Padworth** W Berk	49 G1 **Park Corner** Oxon
30 F4 **Othery** Somset	112 E3 **Overton Bridge** Wrexhm	169 G4 **Page Bank** Dur	49 K2 **Park Corner** W & M
150 B6 **Otley** Leeds	130 F7 **Overton Green** Ches	20 E7 **Pagham** W Susx	85 K4 **Park End** Beds

63 J5 **Parkend** Gloucs
179 K4 **Park End** Nthumb
38 F4 **Parkers Green** Kent
73 K1 **Parkeston** Essex
90 F8 **Parkeston Quay** Essex
40 D7 **Park Farm** Kent
129 G4 **Parkgate** Ches
165 H1 **Parkgate** Cumb
176 D1 **Parkgate** D & G
24 C4 **Parkgate** E Susx
71 G1 **Parkgate** Essex
19 J2 **Park Gate** Hants
39 L6 **Parkgate** Kent
52 B6 **Parkgate** Kent
150 A7 **Park Gate** Leeds
37 K2 **Parkgate** Surrey
81 L1 **Park Gate** Worcs
70 C2 **Park Green** Essex
90 D2 **Park Green** Suffk
208 E4 **Parkhall** W Duns
27 G6 **Parkham** Devon
26 F6 **Parkham Ash** Devon
116 B1 **Park Head** Derbys
63 H7 **Park Hill** Gloucs
117 J1 **Parkhill** Notts
245 K1 **Parkhill House** Abers
63 G6 **Parkhouse** Mons
57 G7 **Parkmill** Swans
51 G3 **Park Royal** Gt Lon
169 L1 **Parkside** Dur
209 L7 **Parkside** N Lans
129 J8 **Parkside** Wrexhm
17 K4 **Parkstone** Poole
68 F6 **Park Street** Herts
37 H4 **Park Street** W Susx
17 M3 **Parley Green** Dorset
150 F8 **Parlington** Leeds
49 J1 **Parmoor** Bucks
70 B5 **Parndon** Essex
28 B2 **Parracombe** Devon
75 H4 **Parrog** Pembks
164 F3 **Parsonby** Cumb
133 G1 **Parson Cross** Sheff
103 H2 **Parson Drove** Cambs
72 F2 **Parson's Heath** Essex
116 A6 **Parson's Hill** Derbys
208 F5 **Partick** C Glas
130 D2 **Partington** Traffd
137 H6 **Partney** Lincs
164 C6 **Parton** Cumb
22 B3 **Partridge Green** W Susx
62 B3 **Partrishow** Powys
115 K1 **Parwich** Derbys
70 E6 **Paslow Wood Common** Essex
84 F7 **Passenham** Nhants
36 B4 **Passfield** Hants
70 D7 **Passingford Bridge** Essex
102 D3 **Paston** C Pete
123 G4 **Paston** Norfk
114 F6 **Pasturefields** Staffs
12 B3 **Patchacott** Devon
22 D5 **Patcham** Br & H
68 F7 **Patchetts Green** Herts
21 J5 **Patching** W Susx
27 L2 **Patchole** Devon
45 J3 **Patchway** S Glos
149 L3 **Pateley Bridge** N York
72 D4 **Paternoster Heath** Essex
30 F5 **Pathe** Somset
222 E8 **Pathhead** Fife
211 L6 **Pathhead** Mdloth
82 E3 **Pathlow** Warwks
221 K5 **Path of Condie** P & K
70 B2 **Patmore Heath** Herts
183 K1 **Patna** E Ayrs
47 G7 **Patney** Wilts
154 c5 **Patrick** IoM
160 B4 **Patrick Brompton** N York
139 M8 **Patricroft** Salfd
145 J3 **Patrington** E R Yk
145 J3 **Patrington Haven** E R Yk
41 G4 **Patrixbourne** Kent
165 L7 **Patterdale** Cumb
97 J4 **Pattingham** Staffs
84 C4 **Pattishall** Nhants
71 K2 **Pattiswick Green** Essex
96 D4 **Patton** Shrops
2 D5 **Paul** Cnwll
84 D6 **Paulerspury** Nhants
144 F3 **Paull** E R Yk
33 K4 **Paul's Dene** Wilts
45 K7 **Paulton** BaNES
80 F5 **Paunton** Herefs
191 D6 **Pauperhaugh** Nthumb
114 B8 **Pave Lane** Wrekin
85 K4 **Pavenham** Beds
30 D2 **Pawlett** Somset

202 C6 **Pawston** Nthumb
82 E7 **Paxford** Gloucs
202 E3 **Paxton** Border
40 B4 **Payden Street** Kent
14 C2 **Payhembury** Devon
3 H2 **Paynter's Lane End** Cnwll
148 E5 **Paythorne** Lancs
80 A1 **Paytoe** Herefs
22 F7 **Peacehaven** E Susx
132 B4 **Peak Dale** Derbys
132 B4 **Peak Forest** Derbys
119 J8 **Peak Hill** Lincs
102 D2 **Peakirk** C Pete
237 K4 **Peanmeanach** Highld
39 H4 **Pearson's Green** Kent
80 E8 **Peartree Green** Herefs
45 K7 **Peasedown St John** BaNES
116 C2 **Peasehill** Derbys
122 B8 **Peaseland Green** Norfk
48 C3 **Peasemore** W Berk
91 H2 **Peasenhall** Suffk
37 L4 **Pease Pottage** W Susx
37 G2 **Peaslake** Surrey
129 M1 **Peasley Cross** St Hel
25 G3 **Peasmarsh** E Susx
30 E8 **Peasmarsh** Somset
36 E2 **Peasmarsh** Surrey
269 G3 **Peathill** Abers
223 H5 **Peat Inn** Fife
100 D5 **Peatling Magna** Leics
100 D5 **Peatling Parva** Leics
96 C6 **Peaton** Shrops
89 G8 **Pebmarsh** Essex
82 D6 **Pebworth** Worcs
140 F2 **Pecket Well** Calder
129 M8 **Peckforton** Ches
51 J4 **Peckham** Gt Lon
100 A3 **Peckleton** Leics
111 M6 **Pedairffordd** Powys
40 F8 **Pedlinge** Kent
97 K7 **Pedmore** Dudley
30 F4 **Pedwell** Somset
200 B5 **Peebles** Border
154 c5 **Peel** IoM
138 D2 **Peel** Lancs
19 K3 **Peel Common** Hants
41 G7 **Peene** Kent
39 M7 **Peening Quarter** Kent
116 C7 **Peggs Green** Leics
68 E1 **Pegsdon** Beds
180 F2 **Pegswood** Nthumb
41 K3 **Pegwell** Kent
247 H2 **Peinchorran** Highld
259 G5 **Peinlich** Highld
54 F3 **Pelcomb** Pembks
54 F3 **Pelcomb Bridge** Pembks
54 F3 **Pelcomb Cross** Pembks
72 E4 **Peldon** Essex
39 G6 **Pell Green** E Susx
98 C3 **Pelsall** Wsall
98 C3 **Pelsall Wood** Wsall
181 G8 **Pelton** Dur
181 G8 **Pelton Fell** Dur
164 F1 **Pelutho** Cumb
5 L4 **Pelynt** Cnwll
56 F5 **Pemberton** Carmth
139 H7 **Pemberton** Wigan
39 M4 **Pembles Cross** Kent
56 D4 **Pembrey** Carmth
79 M4 **Pembridge** Herefs
55 G6 **Pembroke** Pembks
54 F6 **Pembroke Dock** Pembks
39 G5 **Pembury** Kent
4 D5 **Penair** Cnwll
63 G5 **Penallt** Mons
55 J7 **Penally** Pembks
63 H1 **Penalt** Herefs
5 G6 **Penare** Cnwll
43 J7 **Penarth** V Glam
55 J4 **Penblewin** Pembks
92 E6 **Pen-bont Rhydybeddau** Cerdgn
76 B5 **Penbryn** Cerdgn
58 E2 **Pencader** Carmth
109 G3 **Pencaenewydd** Gwynd
212 A5 **Pencaitland** E Loth
124 F5 **Pencarnisiog** IoA
76 F6 **Pencarreg** Carmth
10 F6 **Pencarrow** Cnwll
61 H2 **Pencelli** Powys
57 G5 **Penclawdd** Swans
42 E5 **Pencoed** Brdgnd
80 E5 **Pencombe** Herefs
63 G2 **Pencoyd** Herefs
63 H3 **Pencraig** Herefs
111 K6 **Pencraig** Powys
2 B4 **Pendeen** Cnwll
60 E5 **Penderyn** Rhondd

55 L5 **Pendine** Carmth
140 B7 **Pendlebury** Salfd
148 D7 **Pendleton** Lancs
81 H8 **Pendock** Worcs
10 E6 **Pendoggett** Cnwll
31 H8 **Pendomer** Somset
43 G6 **Pendoylan** V Glam
42 D5 **Pendre** Brdgnd
93 G3 **Penegoes** Powys
3 K3 **Penelewey** Cnwll
55 J2 **Pen-ffordd** Pembks
43 J2 **Pengam** Caerph
43 K6 **Pengam** Cardif
51 K5 **Penge** Gt Lon
10 F5 **Pengelly** Cnwll
125 H1 **Pengorffwysfa** IoA
6 B2 **Pengover Green** Cnwll
62 C5 **Pen-groes-oped** Mons
127 K4 **Pengwern** Denbgs
3 H7 **Penhale** Cnwll
4 E3 **Penhale** Cnwll
5 J3 **Penhale** Cnwll
6 E4 **Penhale** Cnwll
4 C4 **Penhallow** Cnwll
3 H3 **Penhalurick** Cnwll
3 H3 **Penhalvean** Cnwll
47 H1 **Penhill** Swindn
44 E1 **Penhow** Newpt
24 C4 **Penhurst** E Susx
92 D2 **Peniarth** Gwynd
211 H7 **Penicuik** Mdloth
58 D4 **Peniel** Carmth
127 L7 **Peniel** Denbgs
259 H8 **Penifiler** Highld
192 F3 **Peninver** Ag & B
125 K7 **Penisarwaun** Gwynd
141 K7 **Penistone** Barns
3 K5 **Penjerrick** Cnwll
130 A2 **Penketh** Warrtn
183 G3 **Penkill** S Ayrs
97 L1 **Penkridge** Staffs
11 H3 **Penlean** Cnwll
32 E1 **Penleigh** Wilts
112 F3 **Penley** Wrexhm
57 H5 **Penllergaer** Swans
124 F3 **Pen-llyn** IoA
42 E6 **Penllyn** V Glam
125 G6 **Pen-lon** IoA
110 E2 **Penmachno** Conwy
43 J2 **Penmaen** Caerph
56 F7 **Penmaen** Swans
126 E4 **Penmaenan** Conwy
126 E4 **Penmaenmawr** Conwy
110 C7 **Penmaenpool** Gwynd
43 G7 **Penmark** V Glam
126 C3 **Penmon** IoA
109 K3 **Penmorfa** Gwynd
125 J5 **Penmynydd** IoA
67 M8 **Penn** Bucks
97 K4 **Penn** Wolves
92 F3 **Pennal** Gwynd
268 F3 **Pennan** Abers
76 F3 **Pennant** Cerdgn
111 K5 **Pennant** Denbgs
93 J4 **Pennant** Powys
111 K6 **Pennant-Melangell** Powys
57 G7 **Pennard** Swans
95 J3 **Pennerley** Shrops
13 K2 **Pennicott** Devon
156 C7 **Pennington** Cumb
18 D4 **Pennington** Hants
139 J6 **Pennington Green** Wigan
61 H2 **Pennorth** Powys
68 A7 **Penn Street** Bucks
45 L4 **Pennsylvania** S Glos
156 D6 **Penny Bridge** Cumb
226 F7 **Pennycross** Ag & B
123 G7 **Pennygate** Norfk
227 G7 **Pennyghael** Ag & B
183 H1 **Pennyglen** S Ayrs
133 L4 **Penny Green** Derbys
119 K6 **Penny Hill** Lincs
28 F8 **Pennymoor** Devon
75 L3 **Penparc** Cerdgn
92 D7 **Penparcau** Cerdgn
43 J2 **Penpedairheol** Caerph
62 C6 **Penpedairheol** Mons
62 C6 **Penperlleni** Mons
10 F5 **Penpethy** Cnwll
5 J4 **Penpillick** Cnwll
3 K3 **Penpol** Cnwll
5 K4 **Penpoll** Cnwll
3 G3 **Penponds** Cnwll
10 F7 **Penpont** Cnwll
186 C7 **Penpont** D & G
60 E5 **Penpont** Powys
7 J4 **Penquit** Devon
11 L7 **Penrest** Cnwll

76 B7 **Penrherber** Carmth
75 M4 **Pen-rhiw** Pembks
43 G2 **Penrhiwceiber** Rhondd
57 K3 **Pen Rhiwfawr** Neath
76 C6 **Penrhiwllan** Cerdgn
76 C6 **Penrhiw-pal** Cerdgn
108 F5 **Penrhos** Gwynd
124 D3 **Penrhos** IoA
62 E5 **Penrhos** Mons
59 L6 **Penrhos** Powys
125 K5 **Penrhos garnedd** Gwynd
127 G3 **Penrhyn Bay** Conwy
92 D6 **Penrhyncoch** Cerdgn
109 L4 **Penrhyndeudraeth** Gwynd
126 F3 **Penrhyn-side** Conwy
56 F7 **Penrice** Swans
194 D2 **Penrioch** N Ayrs
166 C4 **Penrith** Cumb
10 B8 **Penrose** Cnwll
166 A5 **Penruddock** Cumb
3 K4 **Penryn** Cnwll
127 J4 **Pensarn** Conwy
81 G2 **Pensax** Worcs
129 G3 **Pensby** Wirral
32 C4 **Penselwood** Somset
45 J6 **Pensford** BaNES
81 L6 **Pensham** Worcs
181 H8 **Penshaw** Sundld
38 E4 **Penshurst** Kent
38 E4 **Penshurst Station** Kent
11 K8 **Pensilva** Cnwll
97 K5 **Pensnett** Dudley
13 H2 **Penstone** Devon
94 C5 **Penstrowed** Powys
5 G5 **Pentewan** Cnwll
125 K6 **Pentir** Gwynd
4 C3 **Pentire** Cnwll
55 J5 **Pentlepoir** Pembks
89 G6 **Pentlow** Essex
89 G6 **Pentlow Street** Essex
120 F8 **Pentney** Norfk
178 B3 **Pentonbridge** Cumb
34 D2 **Penton Grafton** Hants
34 D2 **Penton Mewsey** Hants
125 J4 **Pentraeth** IoA
128 C7 **Pentre** Denbgs
129 H6 **Pentre** Flints
62 C6 **Pentre** Mons
94 C6 **Pentre** Powys
94 E5 **Pentre** Powys
95 G5 **Pentre** Powys
42 E2 **Pentre** Rhondd
112 E7 **Pentre** Shrops
112 D3 **Pentre** Wrexhm
77 G6 **Pentre Bach** Cerdgn
128 F4 **Pentre Bach** Flints
61 G6 **Pentrebach** Myr Td
78 B8 **Pentre-bach** Powys
94 E1 **Pentrebeirdd** Powys
125 H5 **Pentre Berw** IoA
110 D1 **Pentre-bont** Conwy
76 C7 **Pentre-cagel** Carmth
112 A1 **Pentre-celyn** Denbgs
93 J2 **Pentre-celyn** Powys
57 J6 **Pentre-chwyth** Swans
112 D5 **Pentre-clawdd** Shrops
76 D7 **Pentre-cwrt** Carmth
112 B2 **Pentredwr** Denbgs
109 J4 **Pentrefelin** Gwynd
125 H1 **Pentrefelin** IoA
128 F5 **Pentre Ffwrndan** Flints
111 G1 **Pentrefoelas** Conwy
75 L6 **Pentregalar** Pembks
76 C5 **Pentregat** Cerdgn
59 H5 **Pentre-Gwenlais** Carmth
109 L6 **Pentre Gwynfryn** Gwynd
128 E5 **Pentre Halkyn** Flints
95 H7 **Pentre Hodrey** Shrops
127 K5 **Pentre Isaf** Conwy
128 C7 **Pentre Llanrhaeadr** Denbgs
94 E4 **Pentre Llifior** Powys
78 C4 **Pentre-llwyn-llwyd** Powys
92 D8 **Pentre-llyn** Cerdgn
111 J1 **Pentre-llyn-cymmer** Conwy
93 J3 **Pentre-Maw** Powys
42 E6 **Pentre Meyrick** V Glam
62 B6 **Pentre-piod** Torfn
44 B2 **Pentre-poeth** Newpt
76 D4 **Pentre'rbryn** Cerdgn
77 H5 **Pentre'r-felin** Cerdgn
126 F6 **Pentre'r Felin** Conwy
60 D1 **Pentre'r-felin** Powys
127 L7 **Pentre Saron** Denbgs
126 F7 **Pentre-tafarn-y-fedw** Conwy

59 M2 **Pentre ty gwyn** Carmth
116 C1 **Pentrich** Derbys
33 H7 **Pentridge** Dorset
61 K7 **Pen-twyn** Caerph
63 G5 **Pen-twyn** Mons
61 L6 **Pen-twyn** Torfn
43 K2 **Pentwynmaur** Caerph
43 H5 **Pentyrch** Cardif
5 H4 **Penwithick** Cnwll
48 C6 **Penwood** Hants
60 C4 **Penwyllt** Powys
59 H4 **Penybanc** Carmth
78 F2 **Penybont** Powys
112 B6 **Pen-y-bont** Powys
111 L6 **Pen-y-bont-fawr** Powys
75 L4 **Pen-y-bryn** Pembks
60 C4 **Pen-y-cae** Powys
112 D3 **Penycae** Wrexhm
62 E8 **Pen-y-cae-mawr** Mons
108 C6 **Penycaerau** Gwynd
128 D4 **Pen-y-cefn** Flints
62 F5 **Pen-y-clawdd** Mons
43 G4 **Pen-y-coedcae** Rhondd
54 D2 **Pen-y-cwn** Pembks
42 D5 **Pen-y-fai** Brdgnd
128 D5 **Pen-y-felin** Flints
129 G7 **Penyffordd** Flints
125 J8 **Penyffridd** Gwynd
92 D6 **Pen-y-garn** Cerdgn
111 L6 **Pen-y-Garnedd** Powys
61 J1 **Pen-y-genffordd** Powys
108 C5 **Pen-y-graig** Gwynd
42 F3 **Penygraig** Rhondd
59 G6 **Penygroes** Carmth
109 H1 **Penygroes** Gwynd
126 D6 **Pen-y-Gwryd** Gwynd
42 F6 **Pen-y-lan** V Glam
129 G7 **Penymynydd** Flints
126 C8 **Pen-y-pass** Gwynd
62 E5 **Pen-yr-Heol** Mons
60 F6 **Pen-yr-Heolgerrig** Myr Td
125 H2 **Penysarn** IoA
112 B1 **Pen-y-stryt** Denbgs
60 E6 **Penywaun** Rhondd
57 L3 **Penywern** Neath
2 D5 **Penzance** Cnwll
81 L5 **Peopleton** Worcs
130 F5 **Peover Heath** Ches
36 D2 **Peper Harow** Surrey
113 K6 **Peplow** Shrops
70 F5 **Pepper's Green** Essex
68 D3 **Pepperstock** Beds
196 C3 **Perceton** N Ayrs
269 H3 **Percyhorner** Abers
9 i3 **Perelle** Guern
34 B1 **Perham Down** Wilts
29 G2 **Periton** Somset
50 F2 **Perivale** Gt Lon
14 B4 **Perkins Village** Devon
181 G8 **Perkinsville** Dur
134 C5 **Perlethorpe** Notts
3 K3 **Perranarworthal** Cnwll
4 B4 **Perranporth** Cnwll
2 E5 **Perranuthnoe** Cnwll
3 K3 **Perranwell** Cnwll
4 C4 **Perranwell** Cnwll
3 K3 **Perran Wharf** Cnwll
4 C4 **Perranzabuloe** Cnwll
64 E6 **Perrott's Brook** Gloucs
98 D5 **Perry** Birm
98 D5 **Perry Barr** Birm
71 K3 **Perry Green** Essex
70 B4 **Perry Green** Herts
46 E1 **Perry Green** Wilts
15 H2 **Perry Street** Somset
114 C5 **Pershall** Staffs
81 L6 **Pershore** Worcs
86 B2 **Pertenhall** Beds
221 K3 **Perth** P & K
112 E5 **Perthy** Shrops
80 E7 **Perton** Herefs
97 J3 **Perton** Staffs
32 E4 **Pertwood** Wilts
102 D4 **Peterborough** C Pete
79 L7 **Peterchurch** Herefs
245 J3 **Peterculter** C Aber
257 L2 **Peterhead** Abers
169 L2 **Peterlee** Dur
35 M6 **Petersfield** Hants
68 F3 **Peter's Green** Herts
50 F4 **Petersham** Gt Lon
27 H8 **Peters Marland** Devon
43 L5 **Peterstone Wentlooge** Newpt
43 G6 **Peterston-super-Ely** V Glam
63 H2 **Peterstow** Herefs
12 C7 **Peter Tavy** Devon
40 F5 **Petham** Kent
11 K4 **Petherwin Gate** Cnwll

12 C1 **Petrockstow** Devon
85 H4 **Petsoe End** M Keyn
40 E6 **Pet Street** Kent
24 F4 **Pett** E Susx
90 E3 **Pettaugh** Suffk
40 F5 **Pett Bottom** Kent
234 C7 **Petterden** Angus
198 F4 **Pettinain** S Lans
91 G4 **Pettistree** Suffk
29 H6 **Petton** Devon
113 G6 **Petton** Shrops
51 M5 **Petts Wood** Gt Lon
211 J2 **Pettycur** Fife
46 A2 **Petty France** S Glos
257 G7 **Pettymuk** Abers
36 E6 **Petworth** W Susx
23 L6 **Pevensey** E Susx
24 B6 **Pevensey Bay** E Susx
47 H7 **Pewsey** Wilts
49 J2 **Pheasant's Hill** Bucks
81 L3 **Phepson** Worcs
181 H8 **Philadelphia** Sundld
26 D6 **Philham** Devon
200 F7 **Philiphaugh** Border
2 F3 **Phillack** Cnwll
3 L3 **Philleigh** Cnwll
70 F7 **Philpot End** Essex
210 E4 **Philpstoun** W Loth
63 J2 **Phocle Green** Herefs
49 J7 **Phoenix Green** Hants
241 J5 **Phoines** Highld
31 G5 **Pibsbury** Somset
164 D6 **Pica** Cumb
99 G4 **Piccadilly** Warwks
68 D5 **Piccotts End** Herts
142 E6 **Pickburn** Donc
162 D6 **Pickering** N York
34 E2 **Picket Piece** Hants
18 B2 **Picket Post** Hants
99 H7 **Pickford** Covtry
99 H7 **Pickford Green** Covtry
160 E6 **Pickhill** N York
95 K3 **Picklescott** Shrops
130 D4 **Pickmere** Ches
30 B5 **Pickney** Somset
114 A6 **Pickstock** Wrekin
139 L3 **Pickup Bank** Bl w D
27 H3 **Pickwell** Devon
101 G1 **Pickwell** Leics
46 B5 **Pickwick** Wilts
118 D5 **Pickworth** Lincs
101 L1 **Pickworth** Rutlnd
256 D8 **Pictillum** Abers
129 K5 **Picton** Ches
128 D3 **Picton** Flints
160 F1 **Picton** N York
23 G6 **Piddinghoe** E Susx
67 K8 **Piddington** Bucks
84 F4 **Piddington** Nhants
66 F4 **Piddington** Oxon
16 D3 **Piddlehinton** Dorset
16 D3 **Piddletrenthide** Dorset
103 G7 **Pidley** Cambs
169 G7 **Piercebridge** Darltn
275 C1 **Pierowall** Ork
64 C2 **Piff's Elm** Gloucs
180 E1 **Pigdon** Nthumb
82 F3 **Pigeon Green** Warwks
17 K2 **Pig Oak** Dorset
79 L5 **Pig Street** Herefs
132 D7 **Pikehall** Derbys
17 K2 **Pilford** Dorset
70 E7 **Pilgrims Hatch** Essex
135 H1 **Pilham** Lincs
45 G4 **Pill** N Som
6 D2 **Pillaton** Cnwll
6 D2 **Pillatonmill** Cnwll
83 G5 **Pillerton Hersey** Warwks
83 G5 **Pillerton Priors** Warwks
79 J2 **Pilleth** Powys
142 A7 **Pilley** Barns
18 E4 **Pilley** Hants
18 E4 **Pilley Bailey** Hants
44 C2 **Pillgwenlly** Newpt
27 H5 **Pillhead** Devon
147 H6 **Pilling** Lancs
147 G6 **Pilling Lane** Lancs
45 H2 **Pilning** S Glos
25 K4 **Pilot Inn** Kent
132 B7 **Pilsbury** Derbys
15 J3 **Pilsdon** Dorset
102 B2 **Pilsgate** C Pete
132 E5 **Pilsley** Derbys
133 H7 **Pilsley** Derbys
107 H1 **Pilson Green** Norfk
23 G3 **Piltdown** E Susx
27 K4 **Pilton** Devon
101 M6 **Pilton** Nhants

101 K3 **Pilton** Rutlnd
31 K3 **Pilton** Somset
56 E7 **Pilton Green** Swans
148 C7 **Pimlico** Lancs
84 B7 **Pimlico** Nhants
17 H1 **Pimperne** Dorset
119 H6 **Pinchbeck** Lincs
119 G6 **Pinchbeck Bars** Lincs
119 G6 **Pinchbeck West** Lincs
143 G4 **Pincheon Green** Donc
170 D7 **Pinchinthorpe** R & Cl
139 H4 **Pincock** Lancs
138 E5 **Pinfold** Lancs
89 G3 **Pinford End** Suffk
56 D4 **Pinged** Carmth
49 G5 **Pingewood** W Berk
69 H2 **Pin Green** Herts
13 M3 **Pinhoe** Devon
99 H7 **Pinkett's Booth** Covtry
46 B2 **Pinkney** Wilts
99 K7 **Pinley** Covtry
82 F2 **Pinley Green** Warwks
90 E7 **Pin Mill** Suffk
182 F4 **Pinminnoch** S Ayrs
182 F4 **Pinmore** S Ayrs
14 C5 **Pinn** Devon
50 E1 **Pinner** Gt Lon
50 E1 **Pinner Green** Gt Lon
113 K2 **Pinsley Green** Ches
81 M5 **Pinvin** Worcs
182 F5 **Pinwherry** S Ayrs
133 J8 **Pinxton** Derbys
80 C6 **Pipe and Lyde** Herefs
114 A3 **Pipe Gate** Shrops
98 E2 **Pipehill** Staffs
253 G2 **Piperhill** Highld
11 J5 **Pipers Pool** Cnwll
101 J6 **Pipewell** Nhants
27 J3 **Pippacott** Devon
139 H3 **Pippin Street** Lancs
79 G7 **Pipton** Powys
50 B7 **Pirbright** Surrey
50 B7 **Pirbright Camp** Surrey
201 K7 **Pirnie** Border
194 D2 **Pirnmill** N Ayrs
68 F1 **Pirton** Herts
81 K5 **Pirton** Worcs
92 E7 **Pisgah** Cerdgn
49 H1 **Pishill** Oxon
108 E3 **Pistyll** Gwynd
232 B2 **Pitagowan** P & K
269 H3 **Pitblae** Abers
221 J2 **Pitcairngreen** P & K
264 C5 **Pitcalnie** Highld
256 C6 **Pitcaple** Abers
233 M2 **Pitcarity** Angus
64 B5 **Pitchcombe** Gloucs
67 J3 **Pitchcott** Bucks
119 J5 **Pitcher Row** Lincs
96 C3 **Pitchford** Shrops
67 J6 **Pitch Green** Bucks
36 C3 **Pitch Place** Surrey
50 B8 **Pitch Place** Surrey
254 D4 **Pitchroy** Moray
31 L4 **Pitcombe** Somset
42 D6 **Pitcot** V Glam
212 E4 **Pitcox** E Loth
256 B8 **Pitfichie** Abers
256 C3 **Pitglassie** Abers
264 B2 **Pitgrudy** Highld
234 E4 **Pitkennedy** Angus
222 E5 **Pitlessie** Fife
232 D4 **Pitlochry** P & K
256 B6 **Pitmachie** Abers
241 K3 **Pitmain** Highld
256 F6 **Pitmedden** Abers
30 B7 **Pitminster** Somset
234 E5 **Pitmuies** Angus
256 B8 **Pitmunie** Abers
31 G5 **Pitney** Somset
222 C2 **Pitroddie** P & K
223 G4 **Pitscottie** Fife
52 F1 **Pitsea** Essex
140 E7 **Pitses** Oldham
84 E2 **Pitsford** Nhants
68 B4 **Pitstone** Bucks
29 J7 **Pitt** Devon
34 F5 **Pitt** Hants
245 G8 **Pittarrow** Abers
63 L7 **Pitt Court** Gloucs
223 K6 **Pittenweem** Fife
222 D7 **Pitteuchar** Fife
169 J2 **Pittington** Dur
256 C6 **Pittodrie House Hotel** Abers
34 B4 **Pitton** Wilts
38 F3 **Pitt's Wood** Kent
269 H3 **Pittulie** Abers

10 C7 **Pityme** Cnwll
169 H2 **Pity Me** Dur
40 B6 **Pivington** Kent
106 E8 **Pixey Green** Suffk
37 J1 **Pixham** Surrey
209 L5 **Plains** N Lans
10 D6 **Plain Street** Cnwll
96 C4 **Plaish** Shrops
51 L2 **Plaistow** Gt Lon
36 F5 **Plaistow** W Susx
34 C7 **Plaitford** Hants
139 J7 **Plank Lane** Wigan
124 E4 **Plas Cymyran** IoA
48 D6 **Plastow Green** Hants
39 G2 **Platt** Kent
139 J7 **Platt Bridge** Wigan
113 H4 **Platt Lane** Shrops
39 L3 **Platts Heath** Kent
169 H1 **Plawsworth** Dur
38 F3 **Plaxtol** Kent
25 G3 **Playden** E Susx
90 F5 **Playford** Suffk
49 H4 **Play Hatch** Oxon
4 C6 **Playing Place** Cnwll
63 M1 **Playley Green** Gloucs
95 K2 **Plealey** Shrops
209 M2 **Plean** Stirlg
222 C4 **Pleasance** Fife
139 J2 **Pleasington** Bl w D
133 K6 **Pleasley** Derbys
133 K6 **Pleasleyhill** Notts
32 B8 **Pleck** Dorset
70 E2 **Pledgdon Green** Essex
142 A4 **Pledwick** Wakefd
9 j2 **Pleinheaume** Guern
9 a1 **Plemont** Jersey
129 K5 **Plemstall** Ches
179 G6 **Plenmeller** Nthumb
71 G4 **Pleshey** Essex
248 C5 **Plockton** Highld
95 J6 **Plowden** Shrops
95 J3 **Plox Green** Shrops
40 B6 **Pluckley** Kent
40 B6 **Pluckley Station** Kent
40 B6 **Pluckley Thorne** Kent
41 J3 **Plucks Gutter** Kent
164 F3 **Plumbland** Cumb
157 G4 **Plumgarths** Cumb
130 E5 **Plumley** Ches
156 D7 **Plumpton** Cumb
166 C3 **Plumpton** Cumb
22 E4 **Plumpton** E Susx
84 B5 **Plumpton** Nhants
84 D6 **Plumpton End** Nhants
22 E4 **Plumpton Green** E Susx
166 C4 **Plumpton Head** Cumb
51 L3 **Plumstead** Gt Lon
122 C4 **Plumstead** Norfk
122 C4 **Plumstead Green** Norfk
117 G5 **Plumtree** Notts
39 K4 **Plumtree Green** Kent
117 K5 **Plungar** Leics
40 B7 **Plurenden** Kent
16 D2 **Plush** Dorset
11 J6 **Plusha** Cnwll
11 K7 **Plushabridge** Cnwll
76 C5 **Plwmp** Cerdgn
6 F4 **Plymouth** C Plym
7 G4 **Plympton** C Plym
7 G4 **Plymstock** C Plym
14 B2 **Plymtree** Devon
161 K5 **Pockley** N York
152 B6 **Pocklington** E R Yk
119 H7 **Pode Hole** Lincs
31 J6 **Podimore** Somset
85 J3 **Podington** Beds
114 B4 **Podmore** Staffs
73 G4 **Point Clear** Essex
118 F5 **Pointon** Lincs
18 A5 **Pokesdown** Bmouth
11 L4 **Polapit Tamar** Cnwll
270 C6 **Polbain** Highld
6 C3 **Polbathic** Cnwll
210 D6 **Polbeth** W Loth
5 G1 **Polbrock** Cnwll
102 B6 **Polebrook** Nhants
81 J5 **Pole Elm** Worcs
23 K6 **Polegate** E Susx
130 C4 **Polelane Ends** Ches
141 G4 **Pole Moor** Kirk
99 H3 **Polesworth** Warwks
2 B6 **Polgigga** Cnwll
270 D6 **Polglass** Highld
5 G5 **Polgooth** Cnwll
185 H2 **Polgown** D & G
21 H6 **Poling** W Susx
21 H5 **Poling Corner** W Susx
5 J4 **Polkerris** Cnwll

123 G5 **Pollard Street** Norfk
142 F4 **Pollington** E R Yk
228 B2 **Polloch** Highld
208 F6 **Pollokshaws** C Glas
208 F6 **Pollokshields** C Glas
5 G5 **Polmassick** Cnwll
5 J4 **Polmear** Cnwll
210 B3 **Polmont** Falk
237 L4 **Polnish** Highld
5 L4 **Polperro** Cnwll
5 K5 **Polruan** Cnwll
31 H2 **Polsham** Somset
89 K7 **Polstead** Suffk
89 K7 **Polstead Heath** Suffk
216 C7 **Poltalloch** Ag & B
3 J7 **Poltescoe** Cnwll
13 M3 **Poltimore** Devon
211 J6 **Polton** Mdloth
202 A3 **Polwarth** Border
11 J6 **Polyphant** Cnwll
10 C6 **Polzeath** Cnwll
211 H7 **Pomathorn** Mdloth
132 B6 **Pomeroy** Derbys
78 F7 **Ponde** Powys
102 F5 **Pondersbridge** Cambs
69 K7 **Ponders End** Gt Lon
3 J3 **Ponsanooth** Cnwll
155 J2 **Ponsonby** Cumb
3 J7 **Ponsongath** Cnwll
13 G7 **Ponsworthy** Devon
9 e4 **Pontac** Jersey
59 H6 **Pontamman** Carmth
58 E6 **Pontantwn** Carmth
57 K4 **Pontardawe** Neath
57 G4 **Pontarddulais** Swans
58 F4 **Pont-ar-gothi** Carmth
60 C2 **Pont-ar-Hydfer** Powys
59 K4 **Pont-ar-llechau** Carmth
58 E3 **Pontarsais** Carmth
129 G7 **Pontblyddyn** Flints
126 E8 **Pont Cyfyng** Conwy
126 F6 **Pont Dolgarrog** Conwy
94 B5 **Pontdolgoch** Powys
44 C2 **Pont-Ebbw** Newpt
142 C3 **Pontefract** Wakefd
180 E4 **Ponteland** Nthumb
93 G7 **Ponterwyd** Cerdgn
95 K2 **Pontesbury** Shrops
95 K2 **Pontesbury Hill** Shrops
95 K2 **Pontesford** Shrops
112 C4 **Pontfadog** Wrexhm
75 H5 **Pontfaen** Pembks
78 D8 **Pont-faen** Powys
76 B4 **Pontgarreg** Cerdgn
75 K4 **Pontgarreg** Pembks
56 E3 **Ponthenry** Carmth
62 C8 **Ponthir** Torfn
76 A6 **Ponthirwaun** Cerdgn
43 J3 **Pontllanfraith** Caerph
57 H5 **Pontlliw** Swans
61 H6 **Pontlottyn** Caerph
109 H1 **Pontlyfni** Gwynd
56 F3 **Pont Morlais** Carmth
60 D5 **Pontneddfechan** Neath
62 B7 **Pontnewydd** Torfn
62 B6 **Pontnewynydd** Torfn
180 E8 **Pontop** Dur
126 C7 **Pont Pen-y-benglog** Gwynd
77 K2 **Pontrhydfendigaid** Cerdgn
111 G6 **Pont Rhyd-sarn** Gwynd
42 C4 **Pont Rhyd-y-cyff** Brdgnd
42 B3 **Pont-rhyd-y-fen** Neath
77 K1 **Pontrhydygroes** Cerdgn
62 C7 **Pontrhydyrun** Torfn
62 E2 **Pontrilas** Herefs
94 D1 **Pont Robert** Powys
125 J7 **Pont-rug** Gwynd
24 B4 **Ponts Green** E Susx
76 D6 **Pontshaen** Cerdgn
63 J3 **Pontshill** Herefs
61 G5 **Pontsticill** Myr Td
60 D6 **Pont Walby** Neath
76 D7 **Pontwelly** Carmth
56 E3 **Pontyates** Carmth
58 F6 **Pontyberem** Carmth
112 D4 **Pont-y-blew** Wrexhm
129 G7 **Pontybodkin** Flints
42 F5 **Pontyclun** Rhondd
42 D3 **Pontycymer** Brdgnd
75 K5 **Pontyglasier** Pembks
42 F3 **Pontygwaith** Rhondd
75 K5 **Pontygynon** Pembks
110 E1 **Pont-y-pant** Conwy
62 B7 **Pontypool** Torfn
62 C7 **Pontypool Road** Torfn
43 G4 **Pontypridd** Rhondd

74 E7 **Pont-yr-hafod** Pembks
42 D4 **Pont-yr-Rhyl** Brdgnd
43 K3 **Pontywaun** Caerph
3 H3 **Pool** Cnwll
10 b2 **Pool** IoS
150 C6 **Pool** Leeds
17 K4 **Poole** Poole
64 E8 **Poole Keynes** Gloucs
260 D4 **Poolewe** Highld
166 B6 **Pooley Bridge** Cumb
105 L7 **Pooley Street** Norfk
131 H7 **Poolfold** Staffs
80 D5 **Pool Head** Herefs
63 L1 **Poolhill** Gloucs
221 H7 **Pool of Muckhart** Clacks
95 G1 **Pool Quay** Powys
88 F7 **Pool Street** Essex
38 C3 **Pooting's** Kent
35 H2 **Popham** Hants
51 K3 **Poplar** Gt Lon
91 K2 **Poplar Street** Suffk
19 G5 **Porchfield** IoW
106 F3 **Poringland** Norfk
3 H4 **Porkellis** Cnwll
28 F2 **Porlock** Somset
28 F1 **Porlock Weir** Somset
206 B7 **Portachoillan** Ag & B
248 B5 **Port-an-Eorna** Highld
228 D6 **Port Appin** Ag & B
205 G3 **Port Askaig** Ag & B
206 E5 **Portavadie** Ag & B
207 H5 **Port Bannatyne** Ag & B
45 G4 **Portbury** N Som
177 H6 **Port Carlisle** Cumb
204 C4 **Port Charlotte** Ag & B
19 K3 **Portchester** Hants
170 C6 **Port Clarence** S on T
206 F4 **Port Driseach** Ag & B
56 E7 **Port Einon** Swans
204 E7 **Port Ellen** Ag & B
256 D7 **Port Elphinstone** Abers
182 C8 **Portencalzie** D & G
195 K1 **Portencross** N Ayrs
154 b8 **Port Erin** IoM
16 B5 **Portesham** Dorset
267 J3 **Portessie** Moray
154 g4 **Port e Vullen** IoM
54 F4 **Portfield Gate** Pembks
12 A5 **Portgate** Devon
10 D6 **Port Gaverne** Cnwll
208 B4 **Port Glasgow** Inver
267 H3 **Portgordon** Moray
274 D5 **Portgower** Highld
4 D2 **Porth** Cnwll
42 F3 **Porth** Rhondd
3 K6 **Porthallow** Cnwll
5 L4 **Porthallow** Cnwll
42 B6 **Porthcawl** Brdgnd
10 B8 **Porthcothan** Cnwll
2 B6 **Porthcurno** Cnwll
108 D3 **Porth Dinllaen** Gwynd
260 B5 **Port Henderson** Highld
74 D5 **Porthgain** Pembks
2 B6 **Porthgwarra** Cnwll
114 D2 **Porthill** Staffs
4 D6 **Porthkea** Cnwll
43 G8 **Porthkerry** V Glam
3 G6 **Porthleven** Cnwll
109 K4 **Porthmadog** Gwynd
2 C4 **Porthmeor** Cnwll
3 J5 **Porth Navas** Cnwll
4 F6 **Portholland** Cnwll
3 K6 **Porthoustock** Cnwll
5 H5 **Porthpean** Cnwll
4 A5 **Porthtowan** Cnwll
112 F2 **Porthwgan** Wrexhm
58 F5 **Porthyrhyd** Carmth
112 C6 **Porth-y-Waen** Shrops
218 C8 **Portincaple** Ag & B
9 a1 **Portinfer** Jersey
143 K2 **Portington** E R Yk
216 F5 **Portinnisherrich** Ag & B
165 H6 **Portinscale** Cumb
10 D6 **Port Isaac** Cnwll
44 F4 **Portishead** N Som
267 K3 **Portknockie** Moray
245 K4 **Portlethen** Abers
175 L4 **Portling** D & G
4 F7 **Portloe** Cnwll
172 D6 **Port Logan** D & G
6 A4 **Portlooe** Cnwll
264 E3 **Portmahomack** Highld
5 G6 **Portmellon** Cnwll
236 E4 **Port Mor** Highld
4 F7 **Portmore** Hants
171 J7 **Port Mulgrave** N York
228 E6 **Portnacroish** Ag & B
282 h3 **Portnaguran** W Isls

204 B6 **Portnahaven** Ag & B
246 D2 **Portnalong** Highld
282 h3 **Port nan Giuran** W Isls
282 c7 **Port nan Long** W Isls
282 h1 **Port Nis** W Isls
211 J4 **Portobello** C Edin
181 G7 **Portobello** Gatesd
98 B4 **Portobello** Wolves
219 J7 **Port of Menteith** Stirlg
282 h1 **Port of Ness** W Isls
33 L4 **Porton** Wilts
12 A7 **Portontown** Devon
172 B4 **Portpatrick** D & G
10 D6 **Port Quin** Cnwll
228 D6 **Port Ramsay** Ag & B
3 G2 **Portreath** Cnwll
259 H7 **Portree** Highld
154 b8 **Port St Mary** IoM
3 M4 **Portscatho** Cnwll
19 L4 **Portsea** C Port
278 E3 **Portskerra** Highld
45 G1 **Portskewett** Mons
22 C6 **Portslade** Br & H
22 C6 **Portslade-by-Sea** Br & H
172 B3 **Portslogan** D & G
19 L4 **Portsmouth** C Port
140 D3 **Portsmouth** Calder
154 d7 **Port Soderick** IoM
19 L3 **Port Solent** C Port
217 G3 **Portsonachan Hotel** Ag & B
267 M3 **Portsoy** Abers
129 H3 **Port Sunlight** Wirral
34 F8 **Portswood** C Sotn
57 L7 **Port Talbot** Neath
57 J6 **Port Tennant** Swans
236 E7 **Portuairk** Highld
80 B6 **Portway** Herefs
80 C8 **Portway** Herefs
98 B6 **Portway** Sandw
82 C1 **Portway** Worcs
204 B6 **Port Wemyss** Ag & B
173 J6 **Port William** D & G
6 D4 **Portwrinkle** Cnwll
174 D7 **Portyerrock** D & G
13 J3 **Posbury** Devon
96 E3 **Posenhall** Shrops
88 F5 **Poslingford** Suffk
199 L6 **Posso** Border
12 F6 **Postbridge** Devon
67 H7 **Postcombe** Oxon
17 J4 **Post Green** Dorset
40 F7 **Postling** Kent
106 F2 **Postwick** Norfk
244 D4 **Potarch** Abers
5 G5 **Pothole** Cnwll
68 B1 **Potsgrove** Beds
68 C5 **Potten End** Herts
41 H2 **Potten Street** Kent
163 H7 **Potter Brompton** N York
106 D5 **Pottergate Street** Norfk
135 L6 **Potterhanworth** Lincs
135 M6 **Potterhanworth Booths** Lincs
123 J7 **Potter Heigham** Norfk
46 E7 **Potterne** Wilts
46 E7 **Potterne Wick** Wilts
67 L6 **Potter Row** Bucks
69 H6 **Potters Bar** Herts
147 J5 **Potters Brook** Lancs
97 J6 **Potter's Cross** Staffs
68 E6 **Potters Crouch** Herts
39 M4 **Potter's Forstal** Kent
99 K7 **Potters Green** Covtry
23 H3 **Potter's Green** E Susx
69 K3 **Potter's Green** Herts
69 G3 **Pottersheath** Herts
100 B4 **Potters Marston** Leics
115 J4 **Potter Somersal** Derbys
84 E6 **Potterspury** Nhants
257 H8 **Potterton** Abers
150 F8 **Potterton** Leeds
121 L7 **Potthorpe** Norfk
32 D3 **Pottle Street** Wilts
161 G2 **Potto** N York
86 E5 **Potton** Beds
120 F7 **Pott Row** Norfk
72 C3 **Pott's Green** Essex
131 J4 **Pott Shrigley** Ches
11 J1 **Poughill** Cnwll
13 K1 **Poughill** Devon
18 B2 **Poulner** Hants
46 E7 **Poulshot** Wilts
7 M4 **Poulston** Devon
65 G7 **Poulton** Gloucs
129 G2 **Poulton** Wirral
147 G2 **Poulton-le-Fylde** Lancs
65 G7 **Poulton Priory** Gloucs

97 G8 **Pound Bank** Worcs
16 C4 **Poundbury** Dorset
57 G6 **Poundffald** Swans
38 D7 **Poundgate** E Susx
23 H3 **Pound Green** E Susx
88 E4 **Pound Green** Suffk
97 G7 **Pound Green** Worcs
37 L3 **Pound Hill** W Susx
66 F2 **Poundon** Bucks
38 E5 **Poundsbridge** Kent
13 G7 **Poundsgate** Devon
11 H3 **Poundstock** Cnwll
48 C6 **Pound Street** Hants
23 J3 **Pounsley** E Susx
174 C5 **Pouton** D & G
91 H1 **Pouy Street** Suffk
37 L3 **Povey Cross** Surrey
190 F3 **Powburn** Nthumb
13 M5 **Powderham** Devon
15 L3 **Powerstock** Dorset
176 F5 **Powfoot** D & G
81 G6 **Pow Green** Herefs
177 H7 **Powhill** Cumb
81 J5 **Powick** Worcs
221 J7 **Powmill** P & K
16 E5 **Poxwell** Dorset
50 C4 **Poyle** Slough
22 C5 **Poynings** W Susx
31 L6 **Poyntington** Dorset
131 H3 **Poynton** Ches
113 J8 **Poynton** Wrekin
113 J7 **Poynton Green** Wrekin
55 G3 **Poyston Cross** Pembks
89 K4 **Poystreet Green** Suffk
2 F5 **Praa Sands** Cnwll
52 A6 **Pratt's Bottom** Gt Lon
3 G4 **Praze-an-Beeble** Cnwll
3 H7 **Predannack Wollas** Cnwll
113 J5 **Prees** Shrops
147 G6 **Preesall** Lancs
113 J5 **Prees Green** Shrops
112 D4 **Preesgweene** Shrops
113 J4 **Prees Heath** Shrops
113 J4 **Prees Higher Heath** Shrops
113 J5 **Prees Lower Heath** Shrops
190 E4 **Prendwick** Nthumb
76 D6 **Pren-gwyn** Cerdgn
109 K3 **Prenteg** Gwynd
129 G2 **Prenton** Wirral
129 L1 **Prescot** Knows
29 K8 **Prescott** Devon
96 F7 **Prescott** Shrops
112 F7 **Prescott** Shrops
233 J2 **Presnerb** Angus
202 C6 **Pressen** Nthumb
128 C3 **Prestatyn** Denbgs
131 H4 **Prestbury** Ches
64 E2 **Prestbury** Gloucs
79 K2 **Presteigne** Powys
31 K3 **Prestleigh** Somset
139 M6 **Prestolee** Bolton
213 H7 **Preston** Border
22 D6 **Preston** Br & H
13 K7 **Preston** Devon
16 D6 **Preston** Dorset
144 F2 **Preston** E R Yk
64 F7 **Preston** Gloucs
68 F2 **Preston** Herts
40 D3 **Preston** Kent
41 H3 **Preston** Kent
139 G2 **Preston** Lancs
203 K8 **Preston** Nthumb
101 J3 **Preston** Rutlnd
96 C1 **Preston** Shrops
29 K4 **Preston** Somset
89 J5 **Preston** Suffk
8 D3 **Preston** Torbay
46 F3 **Preston** Wilts
47 K4 **Preston** Wilts
82 E2 **Preston Bagot** Warwks
67 G1 **Preston Bissett** Bucks
29 L5 **Preston Bowyer** Somset
113 J6 **Preston Brockhurst** Shrops
130 B4 **Preston Brook** Halton
35 J3 **Preston Candover** Hants
84 B4 **Preston Capes** Nhants
48 F1 **Preston Crowmarsh** Oxon
84 F4 **Preston Deanery** Nhants
82 E2 **Preston Green** Warwks
113 H7 **Preston Gubbals** Shrops
113 G8 **Preston Montford** Shrops
82 F5 **Preston on Stour** Warwks
169 L7 **Preston on Tees** S on T
130 B3 **Preston on the Hill** Halton
79 M7 **Preston on Wye** Herefs

211 L4 **Prestonpans** E Loth
157 H6 **Preston Patrick** Cumb
31 H7 **Preston Plucknett** Somset
41 H3 **Preston Street** Kent
159 K4 **Preston-under-Scar** N York
113 L8 **Preston upon the Weald Moors** Wrekin
80 D6 **Preston Wynne** Herefs
140 B6 **Prestwich** Bury
180 E4 **Prestwick** Nthumb
196 C6 **Prestwick** S Ayrs
67 L7 **Prestwood** Bucks
97 K6 **Prestwood** Staffs
42 E3 **Price Town** Brdgnd
104 B7 **Prickwillow** Cambs
31 H1 **Priddy** Somset
12 B1 **Priestacott** Devon
132 C5 **Priestcliffe** Derbys
132 C5 **Priestcliffe Ditch** Derbys
157 H7 **Priest Hutton** Lancs
197 H3 **Priestland** E Ayrs
141 H3 **Priestley Green** Calder
95 H4 **Priest Weston** Shrops
52 E6 **Priestwood Green** Kent
100 B5 **Primethorpe** Leics
122 B8 **Primrose Green** Norfk
213 H7 **Primrosehill** Border
103 H5 **Primrose Hill** Cambs
133 J8 **Primrose Hill** Derbys
97 L6 **Primrose Hill** Dudley
138 E6 **Primrose Hill** Lancs
202 C7 **Primsidemill** Border
55 K4 **Princes Gate** Pembks
67 K6 **Princes Risborough** Bucks
83 J1 **Princethorpe** Warwks
12 E7 **Princetown** Devon
20 C5 **Prinsted** W Susx
128 C7 **Prion** Denbgs
178 B5 **Prior Rigg** Cumb
96 B8 **Priors Halton** Shrops
83 L4 **Priors Hardwick** Warwks
97 G1 **Priorslee** Wrekin
83 L4 **Priors Marston** Warwks
64 C2 **Priors Norton** Gloucs
47 H1 **Priory Vale** Swindn
79 J6 **Priory Wood** Herefs
42 F6 **Prisk** V Glam
45 K7 **Priston** BaNES
106 C5 **Pristow Green** Norfk
53 J2 **Prittlewell** Sthend
35 L5 **Privett** Hants
27 K3 **Prixford** Devon
4 E5 **Probus** Cnwll
212 B3 **Prora** E Loth
164 F3 **Prospect** Cumb
3 G5 **Prospidnick** Cnwll
268 E3 **Protstonhill** Abers
45 G5 **Providence** N Som
180 D6 **Prudhoe** Nthumb
2 E5 **Prussia Cove** Cnwll
45 J6 **Publow** BaNES
69 K2 **Puckeridge** Herts
30 E7 **Puckington** Somset
45 K4 **Pucklechurch** S Glos
81 K7 **Puckrup** Gloucs
130 E5 **Puddinglake** Ches
129 H5 **Puddington** Ches
28 E8 **Puddington** Devon
105 L5 **Puddledock** Norfk
16 E3 **Puddletown** Dorset
80 D3 **Pudleston** Herefs
141 K1 **Pudsey** Leeds
21 H3 **Pulborough** W Susx
114 A7 **Puleston** Wrekin
129 J7 **Pulford** Ches
16 D1 **Pulham** Dorset
106 D6 **Pulham Market** Norfk
106 E6 **Pulham St Mary** Norfk
63 J8 **Pullens Green** S Glos
96 B2 **Pulley** Shrops
85 L8 **Pulloxhill** Beds
210 E5 **Pumpherston** W Loth
77 J7 **Pumsaint** Carmth
75 G6 **Puncheston** Pembks
15 M5 **Puncknowle** Dorset
23 K3 **Punnett's Town** E Susx
19 M2 **Purbrook** Hants
52 C3 **Purfleet** Thurr
30 D3 **Puriton** Somset
71 K6 **Purleigh** Essex
51 J6 **Purley** Gt Lon
49 G4 **Purley** W Berk
95 G7 **Purlogue** Shrops
46 C5 **Purlpit** Wilts
103 K6 **Purls Bridge** Cambs
32 B2 **Purse Caundle** Dorset
81 K1 **Purshull Green** Worcs
95 J7 **Purslow** Shrops

142 C4 **Purston Jaglin** Wakefd
15 J1 **Purtington** Somset
63 K6 **Purton** Gloucs
63 K6 **Purton** Gloucs
47 G2 **Purton** Wilts
47 G1 **Purton Stoke** Wilts
84 D6 **Pury End** Nhants
65 M7 **Pusey** Oxon
80 E7 **Putley** Herefs
80 F7 **Putley Green** Herefs
63 M5 **Putloe** Gloucs
51 G4 **Putney** Gt Lon
27 H3 **Putsborough** Devon
67 L4 **Puttenham** Herts
36 D2 **Puttenham** Surrey
89 G7 **Puttock End** Essex
16 C6 **Putton** Dorset
84 E6 **Puxley** Nhants
44 E6 **Puxton** N Som
56 E4 **Pwll** Carmth
54 F6 **Pwllcrochan** Pembks
61 L5 **Pwll-du** Mons
111 M1 **Pwll-glas** Denbgs
78 E8 **Pwllgloyw** Powys
108 F4 **Pwllheli** Gwynd
63 G8 **Pwllmeyric** Mons
58 A5 **Pwll Trap** Carmth
42 B3 **Pwll-y-glaw** Neath
126 F4 **Pydew** Conwy
116 D1 **Pye Bridge** Derbys
22 D4 **Pyecombe** W Susx
44 D2 **Pye Corner** Newpt
114 F8 **Pye Green** Staffs
42 B5 **Pyle** Brdgnd
29 L5 **Pyleigh** Somset
31 K3 **Pylle** Somset
103 K6 **Pymoor** Cambs
15 L3 **Pymore** Dorset
50 D7 **Pyrford** Surrey
67 G7 **Pyrton** Oxon
101 J8 **Pytchley** Nhants
11 K2 **Pyworthy** Devon

Q

94 F7 **Quabbs** Shrops
119 H5 **Quadring** Lincs
119 H5 **Quadring Eaudike** Lincs
67 H3 **Quainton** Bucks
43 H3 **Quaker's Yard** Myr Td
180 F8 **Quaking Houses** Dur
281 e7 **Quarff** Shet
34 C2 **Quarley** Hants
116 B3 **Quarndon** Derbys
19 K5 **Quarr Hill** IoW
208 B5 **Quarrier's Village** Inver
118 E3 **Quarrington** Lincs
169 J3 **Quarrington Hill** Dur
130 A6 **Quarrybank** Ches
97 L6 **Quarry Bank** Dudley
266 D3 **Quarrywood** Moray
207 K6 **Quarter** N Ayrs
197 L1 **Quarter** S Lans
97 G5 **Quatford** Shrops
97 G5 **Quatt** Shrops
168 F2 **Quebec** Dur
64 A4 **Quedgeley** Gloucs
104 B7 **Queen Adelaide** Cambs
53 K4 **Queenborough** Kent
31 K6 **Queen Camel** Somset
45 J5 **Queen Charlton** BaNES
28 E7 **Queen Dart** Devon
81 K7 **Queenhill** Worcs
32 C4 **Queen Oak** Dorset
19 J6 **Queen's Bower** IoW
141 H2 **Queensbury** Brad
129 H6 **Queensferry** Flints
112 E6 **Queen's Head** Shrops
209 H6 **Queenslie** C Glas
85 L5 **Queen's Park** Beds
84 E3 **Queen's Park** Nhants
39 H4 **Queen Street** Kent
46 F2 **Queen Street** Wilts
209 J3 **Queenzieburn** N Lans
70 D1 **Quendon** Essex
100 E1 **Queniborough** Leics
65 H6 **Quenington** Gloucs
147 K4 **Quernmore** Lancs
98 D4 **Queslett** Birm
6 C2 **Quethiock** Cnwll
48 E4 **Quick's Green** W Berk
105 L6 **Quidenham** Norfk
35 G1 **Quidhampton** Hants
33 K5 **Quidhampton** Wilts
113 H5 **Quina Brook** Shrops
84 B5 **Quinbury End** Nhants
98 C6 **Quinton** Dudley

84 E4 **Quinton** Nhants
84 F4 **Quinton Green** Nhants
4 D3 **Quintrell Downs** Cnwll
115 H3 **Quixhall** Staffs
213 H6 **Quixwood** Border
12 A3 **Quoditch** Devon
220 E3 **Quoig** P & K
116 F8 **Quorn** Leics
199 G5 **Quothquan** S Lans
275 d5 **Quoyburray** Ork
275 b4 **Quoyloo** Ork

R

39 K4 **Rabbit's Cross** Kent
69 G3 **Rableyheath** Herts
177 G8 **Raby** Cumb
129 H4 **Raby** Wirral
199 K6 **Rachan Mill** Border
126 C6 **Rachub** Gwynd
28 E7 **Rackenford** Devon
21 H4 **Rackham** W Susx
122 F8 **Rackheath** Norfk
176 D4 **Racks** D & G
275 a5 **Rackwick** Ork
115 M4 **Radbourne** Derbys
140 B6 **Radcliffe** Bury
191 K5 **Radcliffe** Nthumb
117 H4 **Radcliffe on Trent** Notts
84 D8 **Radclive** Bucks
65 L7 **Radcot** Oxon
263 J7 **Raddery** Highld
29 J5 **Raddington** Somset
223 H5 **Radernie** Fife
99 J7 **Radford** Covtry
83 H2 **Radford Semele** Warwks
30 B3 **Radlet** Somset
68 F7 **Radlett** Herts
28 C6 **Radley** Devon
66 D7 **Radley** Oxon
70 F6 **Radley Green** Essex
130 B8 **Radmore Green** Ches
67 J7 **Radnage** Bucks
45 K8 **Radstock** BaNES
84 B7 **Radstone** Nhants
83 J5 **Radway** Warwks
114 B1 **Radway Green** Ches
85 K4 **Radwell** Beds
86 E8 **Radwell** Herts
88 C7 **Radwinter** Essex
88 C7 **Radwinter End** Essex
43 H5 **Radyr** Cardif
118 D2 **RAF College (Cranwell)** Lincs
265 H8 **Rafford** Moray
117 H7 **Ragdale** Leics
95 L5 **Ragdon** Shrops
2 D6 **Raginnis** Cnwll
62 E5 **Raglan** Mons
134 F5 **Ragnall** Notts
252 F6 **Raigbeg** Highld
81 K4 **Rainbow Hill** Worcs
138 F7 **Rainford** St Hel
52 B3 **Rainham** Gt Lon
53 H6 **Rainham** Medway
129 L2 **Rainhill** St Hel
129 L2 **Rainhill Stoops** St Hel
131 J4 **Rainow** Ches
140 B7 **Rainsough** Bury
160 E7 **Rainton** N York
134 B8 **Rainworth** Notts
157 K1 **Raisbeck** Cumb
167 G2 **Raise** Cumb
152 C3 **Raisthorpe** N York
222 C2 **Rait** P & K
136 F3 **Raithby** Lincs
137 G6 **Raithby** Lincs
171 K8 **Raithwaite** N York
36 B5 **Rake** Hants
140 E5 **Rakewood** Rochdl
241 J4 **Ralia** Highld
77 G6 **Ram** Carmth
258 B7 **Ramasaig** Highld
3 J4 **Rame** Cnwll
6 E5 **Rame** Cnwll
45 K3 **Ram Hill** S Glos
40 C6 **Ram Lane** Kent
16 A2 **Rampisham** Dorset
146 E3 **Rampside** Cumb
87 J2 **Rampton** Cambs
134 F4 **Rampton** Notts
140 B4 **Ramsbottom** Bury
47 K4 **Ramsbury** Wilts
274 F3 **Ramscraigs** Highld
35 L6 **Ramsdean** Hants
48 E7 **Ramsdell** Hants
65 M4 **Ramsden** Oxon

81 L6 **Ramsden** Worcs
71 H8 **Ramsden Bellhouse** Essex
71 H7 **Ramsden Heath** Essex
102 F6 **Ramsey** Cambs
73 J1 **Ramsey** Essex
154 f3 **Ramsey** IoM
102 F6 **Ramsey Forty Foot** Cambs
102 E6 **Ramsey Heights** Cambs
72 D6 **Ramsey Island** Essex
102 F5 **Ramsey Mereside** Cambs
102 E6 **Ramsey St Mary's** Cambs
41 L2 **Ramsgate** Kent
149 K2 **Ramsgill** N York
168 B1 **Ramshaw** Dur
91 H7 **Ramsholt** Suffk
189 K5 **Ramshope** Nthumb
115 H3 **Ramshorn** Staffs
12 F4 **Ramsley** Devon
36 E4 **Ramsnest Common** Surrey
136 D4 **Ranby** Lincs
134 C3 **Ranby** Notts
136 B4 **Rand** Lincs
64 B5 **Randwick** Gloucs
208 C6 **Ranfurly** Rens
115 K7 **Rangemore** Staffs
45 K2 **Rangeworthy** S Glos
196 E8 **Rankinston** E Ayrs
101 H1 **Ranksborough** Rutlnd
71 H3 **Rank's Green** Essex
139 L3 **Rann** Bl w D
230 D4 **Rannoch Station** P & K
29 G2 **Ranscombe** Somset
134 C2 **Ranskill** Notts
114 D6 **Ranton** Staffs
114 D7 **Ranton Green** Staffs
123 G8 **Ranworth** Norfk
220 D8 **Raploch** Stirlg
275 d2 **Rapness** Ork
30 E7 **Rapps** Somset
175 K5 **Rascarrel** D & G
207 J2 **Rashfield** Ag & B
81 L2 **Rashwood** Worcs
151 G2 **Raskelf** N York
61 J5 **Rassau** Blae G
141 H3 **Rastrick** Calder
248 E7 **Ratagan** Highld
100 B2 **Ratby** Leics
99 J3 **Ratcliffe Culey** Leics
116 E6 **Ratcliffe on Soar** Notts
117 G8 **Ratcliffe on the Wreake** Leics
33 L2 **Ratfyn** Wilts
269 J4 **Rathen** Abers
222 F3 **Rathillet** Fife
148 D4 **Rathmell** N York
210 F5 **Ratho** C Edin
210 F4 **Ratho Station** C Edin
267 J3 **Rathven** Moray
34 E6 **Ratlake** Hants
83 J5 **Ratley** Warwks
41 H4 **Ratling** Kent
95 K4 **Ratlinghope** Shrops
120 B8 **Rattan Row** Norfk
280 C2 **Rattar** Highld
165 K3 **Ratten Row** Cumb
165 L1 **Ratten Row** Cumb
147 H7 **Ratten Row** Lancs
7 L3 **Rattery** Devon
89 K3 **Rattlesden** Suffk
23 K7 **Ratton Village** E Susx
233 J6 **Rattray** P & K
165 L1 **Raughton** Cumb
165 L2 **Raughton Head** Cumb
85 K1 **Raunds** Nhants
133 J1 **Ravenfield** Rothm
155 K3 **Ravenglass** Cumb
81 G4 **Ravenhills Green** Worcs
107 H4 **Raveningham** Norfk
138 C6 **Raven Meols** Sefton
163 H2 **Ravenscar** N York
154 e4 **Ravensdale** IoM
86 B4 **Ravensden** Beds
158 E2 **Ravenseat** N York
133 L8 **Ravenshead** Notts
113 K2 **Ravensmoor** Ches
141 K4 **Ravensthorpe** Kirk
84 C1 **Ravensthorpe** Nhants
99 L1 **Ravenstone** Leics
85 G5 **Ravenstone** M Keyn
158 C2 **Ravenstonedale** Cumb
198 F4 **Ravenstruther** S Lans
159 L1 **Ravensworth** N York
163 G2 **Raw** N York
143 H3 **Rawcliffe** E R Yk
151 J5 **Rawcliffe** York
143 H3 **Rawcliffe Bridge** E R Yk
150 B7 **Rawdon** Leeds
40 B3 **Rawling Street** Kent

Rawmarsh - Riverford 347

142 C8 **Rawmarsh** Rothm
98 C1 **Rawnsley** Staffs
71 J8 **Rawreth** Essex
14 E1 **Rawridge** Devon
140 B3 **Rawtenstall** Lancs
90 B7 **Raydon** Suffk
190 C7 **Raylees** Nthumb
53 H1 **Rayleigh** Essex
15 H3 **Raymond's Hill** Devon
71 H3 **Rayne** Essex
51 G5 **Raynes Park** Gt Lon
88 B2 **Reach** Cambs
140 A1 **Read** Lancs
49 H4 **Reading** Readg
25 G1 **Reading Street** Kent
41 L2 **Reading Street** Kent
166 E7 **Reagill** Cumb
263 K1 **Rearquhar** Highld
117 H8 **Rearsby** Leics
113 L1 **Rease Heath** Ches
279 G3 **Reay** Highld
41 H2 **Reculver** Kent
29 K7 **Red Ball** Devon
55 J6 **Redberth** Pembks
68 E4 **Redbourn** Herts
144 B7 **Redbourne** N Linc
63 G5 **Redbrook** Gloucs
113 H3 **Redbrook** Wrexhm
40 B8 **Redbrook Street** Kent
253 H2 **Redburn** Highld
179 H6 **Redburn** Nthumb
170 E6 **Redcar** R & Cl
175 K2 **Redcastle** D & G
251 G2 **Redcastle** Highld
87 K4 **Red Cross** Cambs
165 H2 **Red Dial** Cumb
210 B3 **Redding** Falk
210 B3 **Reddingmuirhead** Falk
131 H1 **Reddish** Stockp
82 B2 **Redditch** Worcs
88 F4 **Rede** Suffk
106 F6 **Redenhall** Norfk
34 C1 **Redenham** Hants
179 K3 **Redesmouth** Nthumb
235 J2 **Redford** Abers
234 E6 **Redford** Angus
36 C5 **Redford** W Susx
188 C3 **Redfordgreen** Border
42 F4 **Redgate** Rhondd
221 K2 **Redgorton** P & K
105 L7 **Redgrave** Suffk
245 H3 **Redhill** Abers
17 L3 **Red Hill** Bmouth
86 F8 **Redhill** Herts
45 G6 **Redhill** N Som
37 L1 **Redhill** Surrey
82 D4 **Red Hill** Warwks
107 H6 **Redisham** Suffk
45 H4 **Redland** Bristl
275 c3 **Redland** Ork
90 E1 **Redlingfield** Suffk
90 E1 **Redlingfield Green** Suffk
88 D1 **Red Lodge** Suffk
140 C4 **Red Lumb** Rochdl
32 B4 **Redlynch** Somset
33 L6 **Redlynch** Wilts
164 F4 **Redmain** Cumb
81 H2 **Redmarley** Worcs
63 L1 **Redmarley D'Abitot** Gloucs
169 K6 **Redmarshall** S on T
117 L4 **Redmile** Leics
159 J4 **Redmire** N York
245 G8 **Redmyre** Abers
98 C8 **Rednal** Birm
112 E6 **Rednal** Shrops
201 J6 **Redpath** Border
260 B6 **Redpoint** Highld
11 K2 **Red Post** Cnwll
139 H6 **Red Rock** Wigan
55 L4 **Red Roses** Carmth
191 K6 **Red Row** Nthumb
4 A6 **Redruth** Cnwll
46 D6 **Redstocks** Wilts
233 J8 **Redstone** P & K
55 J4 **Redstone Cross** Pembks
114 C1 **Red Street** Staffs
140 B6 **Redvales** Bury
125 J3 **Red Wharf Bay** IoA
44 E2 **Redwick** Newpt
45 H2 **Redwick** S Glos
169 G6 **Redworth** Darltn
87 H8 **Reed** Herts
107 J3 **Reedham** Norfk
143 K3 **Reedness** E R Yk
136 D6 **Reeds Beck** Lincs
140 B3 **Reeds Holme** Lancs
135 L5 **Reepham** Lincs
122 B7 **Reepham** Norfk
159 J3 **Reeth** N York
99 H7 **Reeves Green** Solhll
154 f3 **Regaby** IoM
270 C5 **Reiff** Highld
37 L1 **Reigate** Surrey
163 L7 **Reighton** N York
256 F7 **Reisque** Abers
280 D5 **Reiss** Highld
4 C4 **Rejerrah** Cnwll
3 G4 **Releath** Cnwll
2 F4 **Relubbus** Cnwll
253 J2 **Relugas** Moray
49 J2 **Remenham** Wokham
49 J2 **Remenham Hill** Wokham
116 F6 **Rempstone** Notts
64 E5 **Rendcomb** Gloucs
91 H2 **Rendham** Suffk
91 H4 **Rendlesham** Suffk
208 E5 **Renfrew** Rens
86 B5 **Renhold** Beds
133 J4 **Renishaw** Derbys
191 J3 **Rennington** Nthumb
208 C3 **Renton** W Duns
166 E2 **Renwick** Cumb
123 J8 **Repps** Norfk
116 A6 **Repton** Derbys
251 J3 **Resaurie** Highld
5 G6 **Rescassa** Cnwll
5 G5 **Rescorla** Cnwll
237 L7 **Resipole** Highld
3 G3 **Reskadinnick** Cnwll
263 J6 **Resolis** Highld
60 C6 **Resolven** Neath
218 C5 **Rest and be thankful** Ag & B
213 J6 **Reston** Border
3 K4 **Restronguet** Cnwll
234 D5 **Reswallie** Angus
4 F2 **Reterth** Cnwll
4 F3 **Retew** Cnwll
134 D3 **Retford** Notts
5 G2 **Retire** Cnwll
71 J7 **Rettendon** Essex
4 E3 **Retyn** Cnwll
136 E7 **Revesby** Lincs
7 K7 **Rew** Devon
13 H8 **Rew** Devon
13 M3 **Rewe** Devon
19 H5 **Rew Street** IoW
12 A5 **Rexon** Devon
107 K7 **Reydon** Suffk
105 L2 **Reymerston** Norfk
55 J5 **Reynalton** Pembks
56 E6 **Reynoldston** Swans
11 L7 **Rezare** Cnwll
62 D6 **Rhadyr** Mons
77 L6 **Rhandirmwyn** Carmth
78 D2 **Rhayader** Powys
250 F2 **Rheindown** Highld
128 E5 **Rhes-y-cae** Flints
112 B3 **Rhewl** Denbgs
128 D7 **Rhewl** Denbgs
128 D3 **Rhewl-fawr** Flints
128 D4 **Rhewl Mostyn** Flints
270 E3 **Rhicarn** Highld
276 D5 **Rhiconich** Highld
263 J5 **Rhicullen** Highld
60 D6 **Rhigos** Rhondd
261 G1 **Rhireavach** Highld
273 K7 **Rhives** Highld
43 J5 **Rhiwbina** Cardif
110 D2 **Rhiwbryfdir** Gwynd
43 L4 **Rhiwderyn** Newpt
125 K7 **Rhiwen** Gwynd
42 F4 **Rhiwinder** Rhondd
111 H4 **Rhiwlas** Gwynd
125 K6 **Rhiwlas** Gwynd
112 B5 **Rhiwlas** Powys
43 G5 **Rhiwsaeson** Rhondd
30 C4 **Rhode** Somset
39 H4 **Rhoden Green** Kent
140 C6 **Rhodes** Rochdl
133 L4 **Rhodesia** Notts
40 F6 **Rhodes Minnis** Kent
74 C6 **Rhodiad-y-brenin** Pembks
175 J3 **Rhonehouse** D & G
43 G8 **Rhoose** V Glam
58 C2 **Rhos** Carmth
128 D7 **Rhos** Denbgs
57 K4 **Rhos** Neath
125 G2 **Rhosbeirio** IoA
125 J4 **Rhoscefnhir** IoA
124 D4 **Rhoscolyn** IoA
54 E6 **Rhoscrowther** Pembks
128 F6 **Rhosesmor** Flints
109 G4 **Rhos-fawr** Gwynd
125 J8 **Rhosgadfan** Gwynd
125 G2 **Rhosgoch** IoA
79 H5 **Rhosgoch** Powys
76 F2 **Rhos Haminiog** Cerdgn
75 L4 **Rhoshill** Pembks
108 C5 **Rhoshirwaun** Gwynd
109 H3 **Rhoslan** Gwynd
92 C2 **Rhoslefain** Gwynd
112 D2 **Rhosllanerchrugog** Wrexhm
125 J2 **Rhôs Lligwy** IoA
59 H4 **Rhosmaen** Carmth
125 H4 **Rhosmeirch** IoA
124 E5 **Rhosneigr** IoA
112 E2 **Rhosnesni** Wrexhm
127 G4 **Rhôs-on-Sea** Conwy
112 E1 **Rhosrobin** Wrexhm
56 D7 **Rhossili** Swans
125 J8 **Rhostryfan** Gwynd
112 D2 **Rhostyllen** Wrexhm
125 G2 **Rhosybol** IoA
111 M7 **Rhos y-brithdir** Powys
112 D4 **Rhosygadfa** Shrops
77 H1 **Rhos-y-garth** Cerdgn
111 H4 **Rhos-y-gwaliau** Gwynd
108 D4 **Rhos-y-llan** Gwynd
112 D3 **Rhosymedre** Wrexhm
79 K1 **Rhos-y-meirch** Powys
207 M2 **Rhu** Ag & B
128 C5 **Rhuallt** Denbgs
207 G4 **Rhubodach** Ag & B
130 A7 **Rhuddall Heath** Ches
76 F6 **Rhuddlan** Cerdgn
127 L4 **Rhuddlan** Denbgs
79 G5 **Rhulen** Powys
205 M6 **Rhunahaorine** Ag & B
110 B3 **Rhyd** Gwynd
58 D4 **Rhydargaeau** Carmth
77 G7 **Rhydcymerau** Carmth
81 J6 **Rhydd** Worcs
109 K1 **Rhyd-Ddu** Gwynd
57 K5 **Rhydding** Neath
127 K6 **Rhydgaled** Conwy
110 F1 **Rhydlanfair** Conwy
76 C5 **Rhydlewis** Cerdgn
108 C5 **Rhydlios** Gwynd
111 G2 **Rhyd-lydan** Conwy
76 E6 **Rhydowen** Cerdgn
77 G2 **Rhydrosser** Cerdgn
79 J5 **Rhydspence** Herefs
128 F8 **Rhydtalog** Flints
111 G4 **Rhyd-uchaf** Gwynd
108 E4 **Rhyd-y-clafdy** Gwynd
112 C5 **Rhydycroesau** Shrops
92 D7 **Rhydyfelin** Cerdgn
43 H4 **Rhydyfelin** Rhondd
127 H4 **Rhyd-y-foel** Conwy
57 K4 **Rhydyfro** Neath
125 K6 **Rhyd-y-groes** Gwynd
110 F7 **Rhydymain** Gwynd
62 C5 **Rhyd-y-meirch** Mons
128 E6 **Rhydymwyn** Flints
92 D6 **Rhyd-y pennau** Cerdgn
92 D3 **Rhyd-yr-onnen** Gwynd
110 C3 **Rhyd-y-sarn** Gwynd
127 K3 **Rhyl** Denbgs
61 H5 **Rhymney** Caerph
222 B3 **Rhynd** P & K
255 K6 **Rhynie** Abers
264 C4 **Rhynie** Highld
97 H8 **Ribbesford** Worcs
139 H2 **Ribbleton** Lancs
138 E2 **Ribby** Lancs
139 K1 **Ribchester** Lancs
132 F7 **Riber** Derbys
144 F6 **Riby** Lincs
151 K8 **Riccall** N York
188 F7 **Riccarton** Border
196 E4 **Riccarton** E Ayrs
80 C1 **Richards Castle** Herefs
50 C3 **Richings Park** Bucks
50 F4 **Richmond** Gt Lon
159 M2 **Richmond** N York
133 H3 **Richmond** Sheff
9 i2 **Richmond Fort** Guern
29 L4 **Rich's Holford** Somset
114 E7 **Rickerscote** Staffs
44 F7 **Rickford** N Som
7 L7 **Rickham** Devon
105 L8 **Rickinghall** Suffk
70 D1 **Rickling** Essex
70 D1 **Rickling Green** Essex
68 D8 **Rickmansworth** Herts
188 E1 **Riddell** Border
116 C1 **Riddings** Derbys
27 L8 **Riddlecombe** Devon
149 K7 **Riddlesden** Brad
45 H7 **Ridge** BaNES
17 H5 **Ridge** Dorset
69 G7 **Ridge** Herts
33 G4 **Ridge** Wilts
78 E3 **Ridgebourne** Powys
37 L1 **Ridge Green** Surrey
45 G6 **Ridgehill** N Som
99 J4 **Ridge Lane** Warwks
41 G6 **Ridge Row** Kent
133 H3 **Ridgeway** Derbys
82 B3 **Ridgeway** Worcs
81 G5 **Ridgeway Cross** Herefs
88 E7 **Ridgewell** Essex
23 H3 **Ridgewood** E Susx
85 J8 **Ridgmont** Beds
180 B6 **Riding Mill** Nthumb
52 D6 **Ridley** Kent
179 H6 **Ridley** Nthumb
113 J1 **Ridley Green** Ches
123 G5 **Ridlington** Norfk
101 J3 **Ridlington** Rutlnd
123 G5 **Ridlington Street** Norfk
179 L2 **Ridsdale** Nthumb
161 J5 **Rievaulx** N York
177 J5 **Rigg** D & G
209 K5 **Riggend** N Lans
253 G2 **Righoul** Highld
157 K5 **Rigmadon Park** Cumb
137 H4 **Rigsby** Lincs
198 E6 **Rigside** S Lans
139 J3 **Riley Green** Lancs
115 J8 **Rileyhill** Staffs
11 K7 **Rilla Mill** Cnwll
11 K7 **Rillaton** Cnwll
162 E7 **Rillington** N York
148 D6 **Rimington** Lancs
31 K6 **Rimpton** Somset
145 J2 **Rimswell** E R Yk
75 G7 **Rinaston** Pembks
97 G4 **Rindleford** Shrops
175 H3 **Ringford** D & G
132 F3 **Ringinglow** Sheff
106 C1 **Ringland** Norfk
23 H3 **Ringles Cross** E Susx
39 L2 **Ringlestone** Kent
139 M6 **Ringley** Bolton
23 G5 **Ringmer** E Susx
7 J5 **Ringmore** Devon
13 L8 **Ringmore** Devon
138 F5 **Ring o'Bells** Lancs
254 E3 **Ringorm** Moray
103 H3 **Ring's End** Cambs
107 H5 **Ringsfield** Suffk
107 H6 **Ringsfield Corner** Suffk
68 C4 **Ringshall** Herts
90 B4 **Ringshall** Suffk
90 B5 **Ringshall Stocks** Suffk
101 L8 **Ringstead** Nhants
120 F3 **Ringstead** Norfk
18 A3 **Ringwood** Hants
41 K5 **Ringwould** Kent
2 F5 **Rinsey** Cnwll
2 F5 **Rinsey Croft** Cnwll
23 H5 **Ripe** E Susx
116 C2 **Ripley** Derbys
18 B4 **Ripley** Hants
150 C4 **Ripley** N York
50 D7 **Ripley** Surrey
144 B2 **Riplingham** E R Yk
35 K6 **Riplington** Hants
150 D2 **Ripon** N York
118 E6 **Rippingale** Lincs
41 K5 **Ripple** Kent
81 K7 **Ripple** Worcs
140 F4 **Ripponden** Calder
204 D7 **Risabus** Ag & B
80 D4 **Risbury** Herefs
144 A5 **Risby** N Linc
88 F2 **Risby** Suffk
43 K3 **Risca** Caerph
153 J7 **Rise** E R Yk
38 F7 **Riseden** E Susx
39 H6 **Riseden** Kent
119 H5 **Risegate** Lincs
135 K5 **Riseholme** Lincs
164 D4 **Risehow** Cumb
85 L3 **Riseley** Beds
49 H6 **Riseley** Wokham
90 E2 **Rishangles** Suffk
139 L2 **Rishton** Lancs
140 F4 **Rishworth** Calder
140 A3 **Rising Bridge** Lancs
116 D4 **Risley** Derbys
130 C1 **Risley** Warrtn
150 B2 **Risplith** N York
47 L6 **Rivar** Wilts
71 K4 **Rivenhall End** Essex
41 J6 **River** Kent
36 D6 **River** W Susx
87 L2 **River Bank** Cambs
250 F1 **Riverford** Highld

348 Riverhead - Rushall

38 D2 **Riverhead** Kent
32 C8 **Rivers Corner** Dorset
139 J5 **Rivington** Lancs
28 E6 **Roachill** Devon
84 E5 **Roade** Nhants
106 F4 **Road Green** Norfk
178 C4 **Roadhead** Cumb
198 E3 **Roadmeetings** S Lans
197 H7 **Roadside** E Ayrs
279 L4 **Roadside** Highld
29 J3 **Roadwater** Somset
258 D7 **Roag** Highld
146 D3 **Roa Island** Cumb
183 H2 **Roan of Craigoch** S Ayrs
87 J8 **Roast Green** Essex
43 K6 **Roath** Cardif
188 D3 **Roberton** Border
198 F7 **Roberton** S Lans
24 D3 **Robertsbridge** E Susx
141 J3 **Roberttown** Kirk
55 J4 **Robeston Wathen** Pembks
177 H4 **Robgill Tower** D & G
131 H8 **Robin Hill** Staffs
139 G5 **Robin Hood** Lancs
141 M2 **Robin Hood** Leeds
88 E7 **Robinhood End** Essex
163 G2 **Robin Hood's Bay** N York
6 F2 **Roborough** Devon
27 K7 **Roborough** Devon
129 K2 **Roby** Knows
139 G6 **Roby Mill** Lancs
115 J4 **Rocester** Staffs
54 E3 **Roch** Pembks
140 D5 **Rochdale** Rochdl
5 G3 **Roche** Cnwll
52 F5 **Rochester** Medway
189 M6 **Rochester** Nthumb
53 J1 **Rochford** Essex
80 E2 **Rochford** Worcs
54 E3 **Roch Gate** Pembks
10 C7 **Rock** Cnwll
57 L6 **Rock** Neath
191 J2 **Rock** Nthumb
21 K4 **Rock** W Susx
81 G1 **Rock** Worcs
14 B3 **Rockbeare** Devon
33 K7 **Rockbourne** Hants
177 K6 **Rockcliffe** Cumb
175 L4 **Rockcliffe** D & G
177 K6 **Rockcliffe Cross** Cumb
131 H8 **Rock End** Staffs
8 D2 **Rockend** Torbay
129 H2 **Rock Ferry** Wirral
264 E3 **Rockfield** Highld
62 F4 **Rockfield** Mons
28 D1 **Rockford** Devon
18 B2 **Rockford** Hants
96 C8 **Rockgreen** Shrops
63 K8 **Rockhampton** S Glos
10 F5 **Rockhead** Cnwll
95 G7 **Rockhill** Shrops
81 L1 **Rock Hill** Worcs
101 J5 **Rockingham** Nhants
105 K4 **Rockland All Saints** Norfk
107 G3 **Rockland St Mary** Norfk
105 K4 **Rockland St Peter** Norfk
134 E5 **Rockley** Notts
47 H4 **Rockley** Wilts
140 C3 **Rockliffe** Lancs
207 L1 **Rockville** Ag & B
49 J1 **Rockwell End** Bucks
29 L6 **Rockwell Green** Somset
64 B6 **Rodborough** Gloucs
47 H2 **Rodbourne** Swindn
46 D2 **Rodbourne** Wilts
79 K3 **Rodd** Herefs
190 E2 **Roddam** Nthumb
16 B5 **Rodden** Dorset
168 F3 **Roddymoor** Dur
46 A8 **Rode** Somset
130 F8 **Rode Heath** Ches
131 G6 **Rode Heath** Ches
282 d7 **Rodel** W Isls
113 J8 **Roden** Wrekin
29 J3 **Rodhuish** Somset
113 K8 **Rodington** Wrekin
113 K8 **Rodington Heath** Wrekin
63 L5 **Rodley** Gloucs
150 B8 **Rodley** Leeds
64 D7 **Rodmarton** Gloucs
22 F6 **Rodmell** E Susx
40 B3 **Rodmersham** Kent
40 B3 **Rodmersham Green** Kent
31 H1 **Rodney Stoke** Somset
115 K3 **Rodsley** Derbys
30 C3 **Rodway** Somset
150 E3 **Roecliffe** N York
140 E8 **Roe Cross** Tamesd
69 G5 **Roe Green** Herts
87 G8 **Roe Green** Herts
139 M7 **Roe Green** Salfd
51 G4 **Roehampton** Gt Lon
37 J4 **Roffey** W Susx
273 H7 **Rogart** Highld
36 B6 **Rogate** W Susx
156 E3 **Roger Ground** Cumb
44 B2 **Rogerstone** Newpt
282 d7 **Roghadal** W Isls
44 F2 **Rogiet** Mons
66 F8 **Roke** Oxon
181 K7 **Roker** Sundld
123 J8 **Rollesby** Norfk
100 F3 **Rolleston** Leics
117 K1 **Rolleston** Notts
115 L6 **Rolleston** Staffs
153 K6 **Rolston** E R Yk
44 D6 **Rolstone** N Som
39 L7 **Rolvenden** Kent
39 L7 **Rolvenden Layne** Kent
168 C6 **Romaldkirk** Dur
160 E4 **Romanby** N York
199 K3 **Romanno Bridge** Border
28 C6 **Romansleigh** Devon
40 A7 **Romden Castle** Kent
258 F6 **Romesdal** Highld
17 L1 **Romford** Dorset
52 B1 **Romford** Gt Lon
131 J2 **Romiley** Stockp
52 C6 **Romney Street** Kent
34 D6 **Romsey** Hants
97 H6 **Romsley** Shrops
98 B7 **Romsley** Worcs
206 B8 **Ronachan** Ag & B
46 C7 **Rood Ashton** Wilts
167 L2 **Rookhope** Dur
19 H6 **Rookley** IoW
19 H7 **Rookley Green** IoW
44 D8 **Rooks Bridge** Somset
29 K4 **Rooks Nest** Somset
160 B5 **Rookwith** N York
145 H2 **Roos** E R Yk
146 D2 **Roose** Cumb
146 E2 **Roosebeck** Cumb
86 B4 **Roothams Green** Beds
35 K4 **Ropley** Hants
35 K4 **Ropley Dean** Hants
35 K4 **Ropley Soke** Hants
118 C5 **Ropsley** Lincs
269 K6 **Rora** Abers
95 H3 **Rorrington** Shrops
267 H6 **Rosarie** Moray
4 C4 **Rose** Cnwll
147 H8 **Roseacre** Lancs
28 D6 **Rose Ash** Devon
198 D3 **Rosebank** S Lans
75 J6 **Rosebush** Pembks
11 H3 **Rosecare** Cnwll
4 D3 **Rosecliston** Cnwll
162 C3 **Rosedale Abbey** N York
72 C2 **Rose Green** Essex
89 J7 **Rose Green** Suffk
89 K6 **Rose Green** Suffk
20 E7 **Rose Green** W Susx
272 C7 **Rosehall** Highld
269 G3 **Rosehearty** Abers
23 G4 **Rose Hill** E Susx
140 B2 **Rose Hill** Lancs
113 G8 **Rosehill** Shrops
266 C3 **Roseisle** Moray
23 K7 **Roselands** E Susx
54 F5 **Rosemarket** Pembks
263 K8 **Rosemarkie** Highld
29 L7 **Rosemary Lane** Devon
233 J6 **Rosemount** P & K
4 F2 **Rosenannon** Cnwll
3 K6 **Rosenithon** Cnwll
23 J3 **Roser's Cross** E Susx
5 H3 **Rosevean** Cnwll
3 M4 **Rosevine** Cnwll
2 F4 **Rosewarne** Cnwll
211 J6 **Rosewell** Mdloth
169 L6 **Roseworth** S on T
3 G3 **Roseworthy** Cnwll
166 D7 **Rosgill** Cumb
2 B6 **Roskestal** Cnwll
258 D7 **Roskhill** Highld
3 K6 **Roskorwell** Cnwll
165 K2 **Rosley** Cumb
211 J6 **Roslin** Mdloth
115 L8 **Rosliston** Derbys
207 L2 **Rosneath** Ag & B
175 G6 **Ross** D & G
203 J5 **Ross** Nthumb
129 J8 **Rossett** Wrexhm
150 D5 **Rossett Green** N York
143 G8 **Rossington** Donc
208 D5 **Rossland** Rens
63 J2 **Ross-on-Wye** Herefs
280 C8 **Roster** Highld
130 E3 **Rostherne** Ches
165 H7 **Rosthwaite** Cumb
115 J3 **Roston** Derbys
2 E5 **Rosudgeon** Cnwll
210 F2 **Rosyth** Fife
190 F6 **Rothbury** Nthumb
117 H8 **Rotherby** Leics
38 E7 **Rotherfield** E Susx
49 H3 **Rotherfield Greys** Oxon
49 H3 **Rotherfield Peppard** Oxon
133 H1 **Rotherham** Rothm
84 D4 **Rothersthorpe** Nhants
49 H7 **Rotherwick** Hants
266 F6 **Rothes** Moray
207 H6 **Rothesay** Ag & B
256 D4 **Rothiebrisbane** Abers
267 L6 **Rothiemay** Moray
242 C2 **Rothiemurchus Lodge** Highld
256 C4 **Rothienorman** Abers
100 D1 **Rothley** Leics
180 C1 **Rothley** Nthumb
256 B5 **Rothmaise** Abers
142 A2 **Rothwell** Leeds
144 F7 **Rothwell** Lincs
101 H7 **Rothwell** Nhants
142 A2 **Rothwell Haigh** Leeds
153 G5 **Rotsea** E R Yk
234 B2 **Rottal Lodge** Angus
22 F6 **Rottingdean** Br & H
164 C8 **Rottington** Cumb
176 D3 **Roucan** D & G
19 H7 **Roud** IoW
121 H7 **Rougham** Norfk
89 H3 **Rougham Green** Suffk
114 E4 **Rough Close** Staffs
40 F3 **Rough Common** Kent
148 E7 **Roughlee** Lancs
243 K1 **Roughpark** Abers
136 D6 **Roughton** Lincs
122 E4 **Roughton** Norfk
97 G4 **Roughton** Shrops
38 F3 **Roughway** Kent
72 B6 **Roundbush** Essex
68 F7 **Round Bush** Herts
70 E4 **Roundbush Green** Essex
68 E3 **Round Green** Luton
15 K1 **Roundham** Somset
150 D8 **Roundhay** Leeds
98 C5 **Rounds Green** Sandw
52 E5 **Round Street** Kent
37 G5 **Roundstreet Common** W Susx
46 E6 **Roundway** Wilts
234 B5 **Roundyhill** Angus
15 G4 **Rousdon** Devon
66 C2 **Rousham** Oxon
82 B4 **Rous Lench** Worcs
165 G4 **Routenbeck** Cumb
207 K6 **Routenburn** N Ayrs
153 H7 **Routh** E R Yk
67 J7 **Rout's Green** Bucks
10 F7 **Row** Cnwll
157 G5 **Row** Cumb
166 E4 **Row** Cumb
177 L3 **Rowanburn** D & G
218 E7 **Rowardennan** Stirlg
131 K2 **Rowarth** Derbys
35 H8 **Row Ash** Hants
44 F7 **Rowberrow** Somset
19 G6 **Rowborough** IoW
46 E6 **Rowde** Wilts
12 F3 **Rowden** Devon
126 E5 **Rowen** Conwy
115 K2 **Rowfield** Derbys
178 F6 **Rowfoot** Nthumb
30 C5 **Rowford** Somset
71 H3 **Row Green** Essex
72 F3 **Rowhedge** Essex
37 H4 **Rowhook** W Susx
82 F2 **Rowington** Warwks
132 D5 **Rowland** Derbys
20 B5 **Rowland's Castle** Hants
180 E7 **Rowland's Gill** Gatesd
36 B2 **Rowledge** Surrey
168 E1 **Rowley** Dur
144 B1 **Rowley** E R Yk
95 H2 **Rowley** Shrops
141 J5 **Rowley Hill** Kirk
98 B6 **Rowley Regis** Sandw
62 D2 **Rowlstone** Herefs
37 G3 **Rowly** Surrey
19 K3 **Rowner** Hants
82 B1 **Rowney Green** Worcs
34 E7 **Rownhams** Hants
164 E7 **Rowrah** Cumb
67 K3 **Rowsham** Bucks
132 E6 **Rowsley** Derbys
131 G4 **Rows of Trees** Ches
48 C1 **Rowstock** Oxon
136 A8 **Rowston** Lincs
133 J6 **Rowthorne** Derbys
129 K6 **Rowton** Ches
95 J1 **Rowton** Shrops
95 K7 **Rowton** Shrops
113 K7 **Rowton** Wrekin
50 D6 **Row Town** Surrey
201 L7 **Roxburgh** Border
144 A4 **Roxby** N Linc
171 H7 **Roxby** N York
86 C4 **Roxton** Beds
70 F5 **Roxwell** Essex
169 G6 **Royal Oak** Darltn
138 E7 **Royal Oak** Lancs
113 K3 **Royal's Green** Ches
239 M7 **Roy Bridge** Highld
141 K5 **Roydhouse** Kirk
69 L5 **Roydon** Essex
106 C7 **Roydon** Norfk
120 F7 **Roydon** Norfk
69 L5 **Roydon Hamlet** Essex
142 B5 **Royston** Barns
87 G7 **Royston** Herts
140 D6 **Royton** Oldham
9 e2 **Rozel** Jersey
112 D3 **Ruabon** Wrexhm
224 D5 **Ruaig** Ag & B
4 E6 **Ruan High Lanes** Cnwll
4 E6 **Ruan Lanihorne** Cnwll
3 H7 **Ruan Major** Cnwll
3 J8 **Ruan Minor** Cnwll
63 J3 **Ruardean** Gloucs
63 J4 **Ruardean Hill** Gloucs
63 J4 **Ruardean Woodside** Gloucs
98 C7 **Rubery** Birm
283 c12 **Rubha Ban** W Isls
166 C2 **Ruckcroft** Cumb
80 B7 **Ruckhall** Herefs
40 D8 **Ruckinge** Kent
136 F4 **Ruckland** Lincs
96 C3 **Ruckley** Shrops
161 G1 **Rudby** N York
180 D5 **Rudchester** Nthumb
116 F5 **Ruddington** Notts
63 K5 **Ruddle** Gloucs
5 G4 **Ruddlemoor** Cnwll
63 M3 **Rudford** Gloucs
46 B8 **Rudge** Somset
45 J2 **Rudgeway** S Glos
37 G4 **Rudgwick** W Susx
63 J2 **Rudhall** Herefs
130 D5 **Rudheath** Ches
130 E5 **Rudheath Woods** Ches
71 K6 **Rudley Green** Essex
46 B5 **Rudloe** Wilts
43 K4 **Rudry** Caerph
153 H2 **Rudston** E R Yk
131 J8 **Rudyard** Staffs
189 G2 **Ruecastle** Border
138 F4 **Rufford** Lancs
151 H5 **Rufforth** York
111 K3 **Rug** Denbgs
100 B8 **Rugby** Warwks
115 G7 **Rugeley** Staffs
27 K2 **Ruggaton** Devon
30 C6 **Ruishton** Somset
50 E2 **Ruislip** Gt Lon
267 H5 **Rumbach** Moray
221 J7 **Rumbling Bridge** P & K
107 G7 **Rumburgh** Suffk
168 F4 **Rumby Hill** Dur
10 B8 **Rumford** Cnwll
210 B4 **Rumford** Falk
43 K6 **Rumney** Cardif
30 B6 **Rumwell** Somset
129 L3 **Runcorn** Halton
20 E6 **Runcton** W Susx
104 C2 **Runcton Holme** Norfk
36 C2 **Runfold** Surrey
105 L2 **Runhall** Norfk
107 J1 **Runham** Norfk
107 L2 **Runham** Norfk
29 L6 **Runnington** Somset
71 J6 **Runsell Green** Essex
139 G4 **Runshaw Moor** Lancs
171 J7 **Runswick** N York
233 L2 **Runtaleave** Angus
71 J8 **Runwell** Essex
49 J4 **Ruscombe** Wokham
80 E8 **Rushall** Herefs
106 D6 **Rushall** Norfk
47 H7 **Rushall** Wilts

98 C3 **Rushall** Wsall
89 H3 **Rushbrooke** Suffk
96 C5 **Rushbury** Shrops
69 J1 **Rushden** Herts
85 J2 **Rushden** Nhants
53 K5 **Rushenden** Kent
38 F7 **Rusher's Cross** E Susx
12 B7 **Rushford** Devon
105 J7 **Rushford** Norfk
73 H4 **Rush Green** Essex
52 B2 **Rush Green** Gt Lon
69 G2 **Rush Green** Herts
130 D2 **Rush Green** Warrtn
23 L3 **Rushlake Green** E Susx
107 K6 **Rushmere** Suffk
90 E6 **Rushmere St Andrew** Suffk
36 C3 **Rushmoor** Surrey
79 K3 **Rushock** Herefs
81 K1 **Rushock** Worcs
131 G1 **Rusholme** Manch
130 B7 **Rushton** Ches
101 J6 **Rushton** Nhants
96 D2 **Rushton** Shrops
131 J7 **Rushton Spencer** Staffs
81 J4 **Rushwick** Worcs
169 H5 **Rushyford** Dur
219 K7 **Ruskie** Stirlg
118 E1 **Ruskington** Lincs
156 E5 **Rusland** Cumb
37 K3 **Rusper** W Susx
63 K5 **Ruspidge** Gloucs
71 H4 **Russell Green** Essex
49 H1 **Russell's Water** Oxon
90 F1 **Russel's Green** Suffk
37 K3 **Russ Hill** Surrey
38 E5 **Rusthall** Kent
21 H6 **Rustington** W Susx
163 G6 **Ruston** N York
153 G3 **Ruston Parva** E R Yk
162 F1 **Ruswarp** N York
96 D5 **Ruthall** Shrops
201 K7 **Rutherford** Border
209 G6 **Rutherglen** S Lans
5 G2 **Ruthernbridge** Cnwll
128 D8 **Ruthin** Denbgs
245 K3 **Ruthrieston** C Aber
267 K6 **Ruthven** Abers
233 L5 **Ruthven** Angus
241 K4 **Ruthven** Highld
4 F3 **Ruthvoes** Cnwll
165 H3 **Ruthwaite** Cumb
176 E5 **Ruthwell** D & G
52 A5 **Ruxley Corner** Gt Lon
63 G3 **Ruxton Green** Herefs
112 F7 **Ruyton-XI-Towns** Shrops
180 B4 **Ryal** Nthumb
15 J3 **Ryall** Dorset
81 K7 **Ryall** Worcs
52 F7 **Ryarsh** Kent
67 G6 **Rycote** Oxon
156 E2 **Rydal** Cumb
19 K5 **Ryde** IoW
25 G3 **Rye** E Susx
113 H5 **Ryebank** Shrops
81 H8 **Rye Cross** Worcs
63 J3 **Ryeford** Herefs
25 G3 **Rye Foreign** E Susx
25 H3 **Rye Harbour** E Susx
145 G3 **Ryehill** E R Yk
49 H5 **Ryeish Green** Wokham
81 H8 **Rye Street** Worcs
102 A1 **Ryhall** Rutlnd
142 B5 **Ryhill** Wakefd
181 K8 **Ryhope** Sundld
133 J6 **Rylah** Derbys
135 K4 **Ryland** Lincs
116 F4 **Rylands** Notts
149 H4 **Rylstone** N York
31 J8 **Ryme Intrinseca** Dorset
151 J7 **Ryther** N York
180 E6 **Ryton** Gatesd
162 D7 **Ryton** N York
97 G3 **Ryton** Shrops
99 L6 **Ryton** Warwks
99 K8 **Ryton-on-Dunsmore** Warwks
180 E6 **Ryton Woodside** Gatesd

S

148 D8 **Sabden** Lancs
70 E7 **Sabine's Green** Essex
69 J3 **Sacombe** Herts
69 J3 **Sacombe Green** Herts
169 G1 **Sacriston** Dur
169 J7 **Sadberge** Darltn
194 B4 **Saddell** Ag & B
100 E5 **Saddington** Leics

120 D8 **Saddle Bow** Norfk
22 D5 **Saddlescombe** W Susx
157 G2 **Sadgill** Cumb
87 L7 **Saffron Walden** Essex
55 H6 **Sageston** Pembks
105 H3 **Saham Hills** Norfk
105 H3 **Saham Toney** Norfk
129 K7 **Saighton** Ches
213 K5 **St Abbs** Border
212 F6 **St Agnes** Border
4 B5 **St Agnes** Cnwll
68 F5 **St Albans** Herts
4 D5 **St Allen** Cnwll
9 j3 **St Andrew** Guern
223 J4 **St Andrews** Fife
43 H7 **St Andrew's Major** V Glam
15 L4 **St Andrews Well** Dorset
138 C2 **St Anne's** Lancs
187 G7 **St Ann's** D & G
12 A8 **St Ann's Chapel** Cnwll
7 J5 **St Ann's Chapel** Devon
3 K6 **St Anthony** Cnwll
23 L7 **St Anthony's Hill** E Susx
63 G7 **St Arvans** Mons
128 B5 **St Asaph** Denbgs
42 F8 **St Athan** V Glam
9 c3 **St Aubin** Jersey
5 G4 **St Austell** Cnwll
164 C8 **St Bees** Cumb
5 H4 **St Blazey** Cnwll
5 H4 **St Blazey Gate** Cnwll
201 J7 **St Boswells** Border
9 b3 **St Brelade** Jersey
9 b3 **St Brelade's Bay** Jersey
10 D8 **St Breock** Cnwll
10 F7 **St Breward** Cnwll
63 H6 **St Briavels** Gloucs
54 C5 **St Brides** Pembks
42 D6 **St Bride's Major** V Glam
44 E1 **St Brides Netherwent** Mons
43 H6 **St Brides super-Ely** V Glam
44 C3 **St Brides Wentlooge** Newpt
6 E3 **St Budeaux** C Plym
82 D7 **Saintbury** Gloucs
2 C6 **St Buryan** Cnwll
45 M5 **St Catherine** BaNES
217 J5 **St Catherines** Ag & B
64 B6 **St Chloe** Gloucs
58 A5 **St Clears** Carmth
6 A1 **St Cleer** Cnwll
4 D6 **St Clement** Cnwll
9 e4 **St Clement** Jersey
11 H5 **St Clether** Cnwll
207 G5 **St Colmac** Ag & B
4 E2 **St Columb Major** Cnwll
4 D2 **St Columb Minor** Cnwll
4 E3 **St Columb Road** Cnwll
269 K4 **St Combs** Abers
106 F6 **St Cross South Elmham** Suffk
235 J2 **St Cyrus** Abers
221 G3 **St David's** P & K
74 B7 **St David's** Pembks
4 B6 **St Day** Cnwll
29 K2 **St Decumans** Somset
4 F3 **St Dennis** Cnwll
62 E1 **St Devereux** Herefs
75 K3 **St Dogmaels** Pembks
75 G6 **St Dogwells** Pembks
6 D1 **St Dominick** Cnwll
42 E8 **St Donats** V Glam
46 E6 **St Edith's Marsh** Wilts
10 D6 **St Endellion** Cnwll
4 E3 **St Enoder** Cnwll
4 D5 **St Erme** Cnwll
6 D3 **St Erney** Cnwll
2 E4 **St Erth** Cnwll
2 F4 **St Erth Praze** Cnwll
10 B8 **St Ervan** Cnwll
4 E1 **St Eval** Cnwll
5 G5 **St Ewe** Cnwll
43 H6 **St Fagans** Cardif
269 K6 **St Fergus** Abers
220 B2 **St Fillans** P & K
55 J6 **St Florence** Pembks
11 G3 **St Gennys** Cnwll
127 K4 **St George** Conwy
44 D6 **St Georges** N Som
43 H6 **St George's** V Glam
50 D6 **St George's Hill** Surrey
6 D3 **St Germans** Cnwll
27 J7 **St Giles in the Wood** Devon
11 L4 **St Giles-on-the-Heath** Devon
3 K4 **St Gluvia's** Cnwll

78 D1 **St Harmon** Powys
168 F5 **St Helen Auckland** Dur
164 D4 **St Helens** Cumb
24 E5 **St Helens** E Susx
19 L6 **St Helens** IoW
139 G8 **St Helens** St Hel
51 H5 **St Helier** Gt Lon
9 d3 **St Helier** Jersey
2 E5 **St Hilary** Cnwll
42 F7 **St Hilary** V Glam
14 C1 **Saint Hill** Devon
38 B6 **Saint Hill** W Susx
61 K6 **St Illtyd** Blae G
69 G2 **St Ippollitts** Herts
54 D5 **St Ishmael's** Pembks
10 C8 **St Issey** Cnwll
6 C2 **St Ive** Cnwll
87 G1 **St Ives** Cambs
2 E3 **St Ives** Cnwll
17 M2 **St Ives** Dorset
122 F7 **St James** Norfk
84 E3 **St James's End** Nhants
107 G7 **St James South Elmham** Suffk
6 E4 **St John** Cnwll
9 c1 **St John** Jersey
168 D4 **St Johns** Dur
154 C5 **St John's** IoM
38 E2 **St Johns** Kent
50 C7 **St Johns** Surrey
81 J4 **St Johns** Worcs
27 J5 **St John's Chapel** Devon
167 K3 **St John's Chapel** Dur
103 L1 **St John's Fen End** Norfk
120 C8 **St John's Highway** Norfk
199 G6 **St John's Kirk** S Lans
184 F6 **St John's Town of Dalry** D & G
51 H2 **St John's Wood** Gt Lon
154 e3 **St Jude's** IoM
2 B5 **St Just** Cnwll
3 L4 **St Just-in-Roseland** Cnwll
3 L4 **St Just Lane** Cnwll
256 D5 **St Katherines** Abers
3 K6 **St Keverne** Cnwll
10 E7 **St Kew** Cnwll
10 E7 **St Kew Highway** Cnwll
A3 **St Keyne** Cnwll
5 H2 **St Lawrence** Cnwll
72 D6 **St Lawrence** Essex
19 J8 **St Lawrence** IoW
9 c2 **St Lawrence** Jersey
41 K2 **St Lawrence** Kent
67 M5 **St Leonards** Bucks
17 M2 **St Leonards** Dorset
24 E5 **St Leonards** E Susx
39 H2 **St Leonard's Street** Kent
2 B6 **St Levan** Cnwll
43 H7 **St Lythans** V Glam
10 E7 **St Mabyn** Cnwll
222 C3 **St Madoes** P & K
79 L8 **St Margarets** Herefs
69 K5 **St Margarets** Herts
41 K6 **St Margaret's at Cliffe** Kent
275 c6 **St Margaret's Hope** Ork
107 G6 **St Margaret South Elmham** Suffk
154 d7 **St Marks** IoM
3 J6 **St Martin** Cnwll
6 B4 **St Martin** Cnwll
9 j3 **St Martin** Guern
9 e2 **St Martin** Jersey
221 L1 **St Martin's** P & K
112 D4 **St Martins** Shrops
112 D4 **St Martin's Moor** Shrops
9 c2 **St Mary** Jersey
34 F1 **St Mary Bourne** Hants
8 D2 **St Marychurch** Torbay
42 F7 **St Mary Church** V Glam
52 A5 **St Mary Cray** Gt Lon
42 E6 **St Mary Hill** V Glam
25 K2 **St Mary in the Marsh** Kent
275 d5 **St Mary's** Ork
25 K2 **St Mary's Bay** Kent
44 F5 **St Mary's Grove** N Som
53 H4 **St Mary's Hoo** Medway
62 F4 **St Maughans** Mons
62 F4 **St Maughans Green** Mons
3 L4 **St Mawes** Cnwll
4 E2 **St Mawgan** Cnwll
6 D2 **St Mellion** Cnwll
43 K5 **St Mellons** Cardif
10 B7 **St Merryn** Cnwll
5 G4 **St Mewan** Cnwll
4 F6 **St Michael Caerhays** Cnwll
30 D5 **St Michael Church** Somset
4 D6 **St Michael Penkevil** Cnwll

39 M6 **St Michaels** Kent
80 D2 **St Michaels** Worcs
147 J7 **St Michael's on Wyre** Lancs
107 G6 **St Michael South Elmham** Suffk
10 D7 **St Minver** Cnwll
223 J6 **St Monans** Fife
5 L1 **St Neot** Cnwll
86 D3 **St Neots** Cambs
74 E5 **St Nicholas** Pembks
43 H6 **St Nicholas** V Glam
41 J2 **St Nicholas at Wade** Kent
209 L1 **St Ninians** Stirlg
107 J3 **St Olaves** Norfk
73 H4 **St Osyth** Essex
9 b2 **St Ouen** Jersey
63 G2 **St Owens Cross** Herefs
52 A5 **St Pauls Cray** Gt Lon
69 G3 **St Paul's Walden** Herts
9 b2 **St Peter** Jersey
9 k3 **St Peter Port** Guern
9 i3 **St Peter's** Guern
41 L2 **St Peter's** Kent
86 E1 **St Peter's Hill** Cambs
55 G7 **St Petrox** Pembks
5 L2 **St Pinnock** Cnwll
196 D6 **St Quivox** S Ayrs
3 J8 **St Ruan** Cnwll
9 k2 **St Sampson** Guern
9 i3 **St Saviour** Guern
9 d3 **St Saviour** Jersey
4 F4 **St Stephen** Cnwll
6 E3 **St Stephens** Cnwll
11 L5 **St Stephens** Cnwll
4 F4 **St Stephen's Coombe** Cnwll
10 F6 **St Teath** Cnwll
10 F7 **St Tudy** Cnwll
54 F7 **St Twynnells** Pembks
5 K4 **St Veep** Cnwll
235 G6 **St Vigeans** Angus
5 G2 **St Wenn** Cnwll
63 G2 **St Weonards** Herefs
43 H6 **St y-Nyll** V Glam
229 G5 **Salachail** Ag & B
7 L7 **Salcombe** Devon
14 D5 **Salcombe Regis** Devon
72 D4 **Salcott-cum-Virley** Essex
130 F2 **Sale** Traffd
137 J4 **Saleby** Lincs
81 L4 **Sale Green** Worcs
24 D2 **Salehurst** E Susx
59 H4 **Salem** Carmth
92 E6 **Salem** Cerdgn
227 H4 **Salen** Ag & B
237 K7 **Salen** Highld
139 K1 **Salesbury** Lancs
85 H7 **Salford** Beds
65 L2 **Salford** Oxon
140 B8 **Salford** Salfd
82 C5 **Salford Priors** Warwks
37 L2 **Salfords** Surrey
123 G8 **Salhouse** Norfk
221 J8 **Saline** Fife
33 K5 **Salisbury** Wilts
166 D3 **Salkeld Dykes** Cumb
122 C6 **Salle** Norfk
136 F5 **Salmonby** Lincs
65 G3 **Salperton** Gloucs
86 B5 **Salph End** Beds
209 L6 **Salsburgh** N Lans
114 F6 **Salt** Staffs
164 E2 **Salta** Cumb
149 L8 **Saltaire** Brad
6 E3 **Saltash** Cnwll
263 K6 **Saltburn** Highld
170 F6 **Saltburn-by-the-Sea** R & Cl
117 M6 **Saltby** Leics
155 K3 **Saltcoats** Cumb
195 L3 **Saltcoats** N Ayrs
177 G8 **Salt Cotes** Cumb
138 D2 **Saltcotes** Lancs
22 F6 **Saltdean** Br & H
164 C5 **Salterbeck** Cumb
148 F6 **Salterforth** Lancs
130 C6 **Salterswall** Ches
33 K4 **Salterton** Wilts
137 H1 **Saltfleet** Lincs
137 H2 **Saltfleetby All Saints** Lincs
137 J1 **Saltfleetby St Clement** Lincs
137 H2 **Saltfleetby St Peter** Lincs
45 K5 **Saltford** BaNES
122 B3 **Salthouse** Norfk
98 E5 **Saltley** Birm
44 D2 **Saltmarsh** Newpt

143 K3 **Saltmarshe** E R Yk
129 J6 **Saltney** Flints
162 C6 **Salton** N York
27 H6 **Saltrens** Devon
180 E3 **Saltwick** Nthumb
40 F8 **Saltwood** Kent
21 K6 **Salvington** W Susx
81 K3 **Salwarpe** Worcs
15 K3 **Salwayash** Dorset
82 C3 **Sambourne** Warwks
113 M6 **Sambrook** Wrekin
139 H2 **Samlesbury** Lancs
139 J2 **Samlesbury Bottoms** Lancs
29 K7 **Sampford Arundel** Somset
29 K3 **Sampford Brett** Somset
12 F2 **Sampford Courtenay** Devon
29 K7 **Sampford Moor** Somset
29 J8 **Sampford Peverell** Devon
12 D7 **Sampford Spiney** Devon
275 e3 **Samsonlane** Ork
73 G3 **Samson's Corner** Essex
212 B5 **Samuelston** E Loth
204 C2 **Sanaigmore** Ag & B
2 C5 **Sancreed** Cnwll
152 D7 **Sancton** E R Yk
31 G2 **Sand** Somset
247 M8 **Sandaig** Highld
165 H3 **Sandale** Cumb
142 A4 **Sandal Magna** Wakefd
236 F4 **Sandavore** Highld
130 E7 **Sandbach** Ches
207 K3 **Sandbank** Ag & B
17 K5 **Sandbanks** Poole
267 L3 **Sandend** Abers
51 J6 **Sanderstead** Gt Lon
167 G7 **Sandford** Cumb
13 J2 **Sandford** Devon
17 H4 **Sandford** Dorset
18 B3 **Sandford** Hants
19 J7 **Sandford** IoW
44 E7 **Sandford** N Som
197 L2 **Sandford** S Lans
112 E6 **Sandford** Shrops
113 J5 **Sandford** Shrops
66 D6 **Sandford-on-Thames** Oxon
31 K6 **Sandford Orcas** Dorset
66 B2 **Sandford St Martin** Oxon
41 G8 **Sandgate** Kent
269 H3 **Sandhaven** Abers
172 D5 **Sandhead** D & G
142 C8 **Sandhill** Rothm
16 B2 **Sandhills** Dorset
31 L8 **Sandhills** Dorset
150 E7 **Sand Hills** Leeds
66 E5 **Sandhills** Oxon
36 D3 **Sandhills** Surrey
180 A5 **Sandhoe** Nthumb
216 F7 **Sandhole** Ag & B
152 B8 **Sand Hole** E R Yk
143 L2 **Sandholme** E R Yk
119 K4 **Sandholme** Lincs
49 K6 **Sandhurst** Br For
64 B2 **Sandhurst** Gloucs
39 K7 **Sandhurst** Kent
24 E2 **Sandhurst Cross** Kent
151 L4 **Sand Hutton** N York
160 E6 **Sandhutton** N York
116 E4 **Sandiacre** Derbys
137 K3 **Sandilands** Lincs
130 B5 **Sandiway** Ches
33 K7 **Sandleheath** Hants
66 C6 **Sandleigh** Oxon
32 C6 **Sandley** Dorset
53 G7 **Sandling** Kent
130 F6 **Sandlow Green** Ches
281 c6 **Sandness** Shet
71 H6 **Sandon** Essex
87 G8 **Sandon** Herts
114 E5 **Sandon** Staffs
114 E6 **Sandon Bank** Staffs
19 K6 **Sandown** IoW
6 A3 **Sandplace** Cnwll
68 F5 **Sandridge** Herts
46 D6 **Sandridge** Wilts
120 F5 **Sandringham** Norfk
67 K8 **Sands** Bucks
171 K8 **Sandsend** N York
156 B6 **Sand Side** Cumb
157 G6 **Sandside** Cumb
143 J6 **Sandtoft** N Linc
39 M3 **Sandway** Kent
41 K4 **Sandwich** Kent
166 A6 **Sandwick** Cumb
281 e8 **Sandwick** Shet
282 g3 **Sandwick** W Isls
164 C7 **Sandwith** Cumb
164 C7 **Sandwith Newtown** Cumb
86 D5 **Sandy** Beds

136 E8 **Sandy Bank** Lincs
129 H6 **Sandycroft** Flints
23 K3 **Sandy Cross** E Susx
80 F4 **Sandy Cross** Herefs
187 J7 **Sandyford** D & G
13 K7 **Sandygate** Devon
154 e3 **Sandygate** IoM
54 D5 **Sandy Haven** Pembks
175 M4 **Sandyhills** D & G
147 H3 **Sandylands** Lancs
149 K8 **Sandy Lane** Brad
113 M4 **Sandylane** Staffs
57 G7 **Sandylane** Swans
46 D5 **Sandy Lane** Wilts
112 F3 **Sandy Lane** Wrexhm
13 G4 **Sandy Park** Devon
177 L5 **Sandysike** Cumb
63 G2 **Sandyway** Herefs
277 G3 **Sangobeg** Highld
276 F3 **Sangomore** Highld
130 B2 **Sankey Bridges** Warrtn
81 H2 **Sankyn's Green** Worcs
236 E6 **Sanna Bay** Highld
282 g3 **Sanndabhaig** W Isls
195 G2 **Sannox** N Ayrs
185 K1 **Sanquhar** D & G
155 K2 **Santon** Cumb
154 d7 **Santon** IoM
155 K2 **Santon Bridge** Cumb
105 G6 **Santon Downham** Suffk
100 B5 **Sapcote** Leics
81 G2 **Sapey Common** Herefs
105 J8 **Sapiston** Suffk
102 E8 **Sapley** Cambs
115 K4 **Sapperton** Derbys
64 D6 **Sapperton** Gloucs
118 D5 **Sapperton** Lincs
119 K6 **Saracen's Head** Lincs
280 D7 **Sarclet** Highld
19 H2 **Sarisbury** Hants
42 D5 **Sarn** Brdgnd
108 D5 **Sarn** Gwynd
93 L4 **Sarn** Powys
94 F5 **Sarn** Powys
58 B5 **Sarnau** Carmth
76 B5 **Sarnau** Cerdgn
111 J4 **Sarnau** Gwynd
78 E8 **Sarnau** Powys
112 C8 **Sarnau** Powys
108 E6 **Sarn Bach** Gwynd
79 L5 **Sarnesfield** Herefs
112 D7 **Sarn-wen** Powys
59 H6 **Saron** Carmth
76 C7 **Saron** Carmth
125 H7 **Saron** Gwynd
125 J6 **Saron** Gwynd
68 D7 **Sarratt** Herts
41 H2 **Sarre** Kent
65 L3 **Sarsden** Oxon
34 C2 **Sarson** Hants
168 E2 **Satley** Dur
41 H7 **Satmar** Kent
159 G3 **Satron** N York
28 B6 **Satterleigh** Devon
156 D4 **Satterthwaite** Cumb
49 H2 **Satwell** Oxon
244 F1 **Sauchen** Abers
233 J8 **Saucher** P & K
235 G2 **Sauchieburn** Abers
63 L5 **Saul** Gloucs
134 F2 **Saundby** Notts
55 K6 **Saundersfoot** Pembks
67 J6 **Saunderton** Bucks
27 H3 **Saunton** Devon
137 G6 **Sausthorpe** Lincs
4 C6 **Saveock Water** Cnwll
114 F4 **Saverley Green** Staffs
141 K4 **Savile Town** Kirk
83 L2 **Sawbridge** Warwks
70 C4 **Sawbridgeworth** Herts
163 G5 **Sawdon** N York
116 D5 **Sawley** Derbys
148 D6 **Sawley** Lancs
150 C2 **Sawley** N York
87 K5 **Sawston** Cambs
102 D6 **Sawtry** Cambs
117 L7 **Saxby** Leics
135 K3 **Saxby** Lincs
144 C4 **Saxby All Saints** N Linc
117 J7 **Saxelbye** Leics
90 C3 **Saxham Street** Suffk
135 H4 **Saxilby** Lincs
122 A4 **Saxlingham** Norfk
106 E4 **Saxlingham Green** Norfk
106 E4 **Saxlingham Nethergate** Norfk
106 E4 **Saxlingham Thorpe** Norfk
91 J3 **Saxmundham** Suffk

117 H3 **Saxondale** Notts
88 D3 **Saxon Street** Cambs
91 G2 **Saxtead** Suffk
90 F2 **Saxtead Green** Suffk
90 F2 **Saxtead Little Green** Suffk
122 C5 **Saxthorpe** Norfk
151 G8 **Saxton** N York
22 D4 **Sayers Common** W Susx
161 L8 **Scackleton** N York
134 D2 **Scaftworth** Notts
152 C1 **Scagglethorpe** N York
214 D5 **Scalasaig** Ag & B
143 L2 **Scalby** E R Yk
163 H4 **Scalby** N York
85 L4 **Scald End** Beds
84 E1 **Scaldwell** Nhants
178 B6 **Scaleby** Cumb
178 B6 **Scalebyhill** Cumb
166 E2 **Scale Houses** Cumb
146 E2 **Scales** Cumb
165 K5 **Scales** Cumb
166 B1 **Scalesceugh** Cumb
117 K6 **Scalford** Leics
171 H7 **Scaling** N York
171 H8 **Scaling Dam** R & Cl
281 d7 **Scalloway** Shet
136 E4 **Scamblesby** Lincs
141 G4 **Scammonden** Kirk
228 C1 **Scamodale** Highld
162 F7 **Scampston** N York
135 J4 **Scampton** Lincs
251 H4 **Scaniport** Highld
141 G4 **Scapegoat Hill** Kirk
163 J5 **Scarborough** N York
4 F4 **Scarcewater** Cnwll
133 K6 **Scarcliffe** Derbys
150 E7 **Scarcroft** Leeds
280 C2 **Scarfskerry** Highld
168 D8 **Scargill** Dur
224 D6 **Scarinish** Ag & B
138 D5 **Scarisbrick** Lancs
165 H4 **Scarness** Cumb
105 J1 **Scarning** Norfk
117 J3 **Scarrington** Notts
138 E6 **Scarth Hill** Lancs
151 G8 **Scarthingwell** N York
145 H6 **Scartho** NE Lin
144 B6 **Scawby** N Linc
142 E6 **Scawsby** Donc
142 E6 **Scawthorpe** Donc
161 J6 **Scawton** N York
22 F3 **Scayne's Hill** W Susx
61 H2 **Scethrog** Powys
131 G8 **Scholar Green** Ches
141 J3 **Scholes** Kirk
141 J6 **Scholes** Kirk
150 E8 **Scholes** Leeds
142 B8 **Scholes** Rothm
139 J6 **Scholes** Wigan
142 B3 **Scholey Hill** Leeds
169 H6 **School Aycliffe** Dur
141 H1 **School Green** Brad
130 C6 **School Green** Ches
49 H5 **Schoolgreen** Wokham
15 J2 **School House** Dorset
141 L5 **Scissett** Kirk
74 F5 **Scleddau** Pembks
134 C4 **Scofton** Notts
106 C7 **Scole** Norfk
221 L2 **Scone** P & K
247 H2 **Sconser** Highld
222 F6 **Scoonie** Fife
135 M8 **Scopwick** Lincs
261 G1 **Scoraig** Highld
152 F6 **Scorborough** E R Yk
4 B6 **Scorrier** Cnwll
7 K1 **Scorriton** Devon
147 K6 **Scorton** Lancs
160 C3 **Scorton** N York
122 F7 **Sco Ruston** Norfk
178 B7 **Scotby** Cumb
160 B2 **Scotch Corner** N York
147 J4 **Scotforth** Lancs
114 C2 **Scot Hay** Staffs
135 L4 **Scothern** Lincs
118 C5 **Scotland** Lincs
181 G2 **Scotland Gate** Nthumb
222 C7 **Scotlandwell** P & K
139 J6 **Scot Lane End** Bolton
279 K5 **Scotscalder Station** Highld
177 L4 **Scotsdike** Cumb
180 C2 **Scot's Gap** Nthumb
255 L7 **Scotsmill** Abers
208 F5 **Scotstoun** C Glas
180 F6 **Scotswood** N u Ty
143 M7 **Scotter** Lincs
143 L7 **Scotterthorpe** Lincs
118 D7 **Scottlethorpe** Lincs

143 M7 **Scotton** Lincs
150 D4 **Scotton** N York
160 B3 **Scotton** N York
122 F6 **Scottow** Norfk
118 D4 **Scott Willoughby** Lincs
105 K3 **Scoulton** Norfk
115 H5 **Scounslow Green** Staffs
276 B7 **Scourie** Highld
276 A7 **Scourie More** Highld
281 d8 **Scousburgh** Shet
140 E6 **Scouthead** Oldham
279 K2 **Scrabster** Highld
189 J3 **Scraesburgh** Border
136 F6 **Scrafield** Lincs
190 D4 **Scrainwood** Nthumb
119 L3 **Scrane End** Lincs
100 E2 **Scraptoft** Leics
123 K8 **Scratby** Norfk
151 M4 **Scrayingham** N York
24 D3 **Scrays** E Susx
118 E3 **Scredington** Lincs
137 H6 **Scremby** Lincs
202 F3 **Scremerston** Nthumb
117 J3 **Screveton** Notts
136 E6 **Scrivelsby** Lincs
150 E4 **Scriven** N York
134 C2 **Scrooby** Notts
115 K5 **Scropton** Derbys
136 D8 **Scrub Hill** Lincs
233 K4 **Scruschloch** Angus
160 D4 **Scruton** N York
178 B4 **Scuggate** Cumb
277 L4 **Scullomie** Highld
121 K5 **Sculthorpe** Norfk
143 M5 **Scunthorpe** N Linc
56 E7 **Scurlage** Swans
30 E8 **Sea** Somset
15 K1 **Seaborough** Dorset
114 C3 **Seabridge** Staffs
41 G8 **Seabrook** Kent
181 K6 **Seaburn** Sundld
129 H2 **Seacombe** Wirral
150 E8 **Seacroft** Leeds
137 L7 **Seacroft** Lincs
119 K4 **Seadyke** Lincs
259 H8 **Seafield** Highld
210 D6 **Seafield** W Loth
23 H7 **Seaford** E Susx
138 C8 **Seaforth** Sefton
117 G8 **Seagrave** Leics
46 D3 **Seagry Heath** Wilts
169 L1 **Seaham** Dur
203 L6 **Seahouses** Nthumb
38 E2 **Seal** Kent
36 D1 **Seale** Surrey
170 D6 **Seal Sands** S on T
163 J6 **Seamer** N York
170 C8 **Seamer** N York
195 K2 **Seamill** N Ayrs
123 J6 **Sea Palling** Norfk
144 D6 **Searby** Lincs
40 E2 **Seasalter** Kent
155 J2 **Seascale** Cumb
156 B3 **Seathwaite** Cumb
165 H8 **Seathwaite** Cumb
156 E6 **Seatle** Cumb
165 H7 **Seatoller** Cumb
6 C4 **Seaton** Cnwll
164 D4 **Seaton** Cumb
14 F4 **Seaton** Devon
169 L1 **Seaton** Dur
153 J6 **Seaton** E R Yk
41 H4 **Seaton** Kent
181 H3 **Seaton** Nthumb
101 K4 **Seaton** Rutlnd
181 G4 **Seaton Burn** N Tyne
170 C5 **Seaton Carew** Hartpl
181 H4 **Seaton Delaval** Nthumb
152 B7 **Seaton Ross** E R Yk
181 H3 **Seaton Sluice** Nthumb
15 K4 **Seatown** Dorset
161 J3 **Seave Green** N York
19 L5 **Seaview** IoW
177 G8 **Seaville** Cumb
30 F7 **Seavington St Mary** Somset
30 F7 **Seavington St Michael** Somset
62 C7 **Sebastopol** Torfn
165 K2 **Sebergham** Cumb
99 H2 **Seckington** Warwks
157 L4 **Sedbergh** Cumb
63 H8 **Sedbury** Gloucs
158 F4 **Sedbusk** N York
82 B7 **Sedgeberrow** Worcs
117 M4 **Sedgebrook** Lincs
104 D6 **Sedge Fen** Suffk
169 K5 **Sedgefield** Dur

120 F4 **Sedgeford** Norfk
32 E5 **Sedgehill** Wilts
97 L4 **Sedgley** Dudley
140 B7 **Sedgley Park** Bury
157 H5 **Sedgwick** Cumb
24 E4 **Sedlescombe** E Susx
67 J5 **Sedrup** Bucks
40 B4 **Seed** Kent
46 D6 **Seend** Wilts
46 D6 **Seend Cleeve** Wilts
68 B8 **Seer Green** Bucks
107 G4 **Seething** Norfk
138 D7 **Sefton** Sefton
138 D7 **Sefton Town** Sefton
181 G4 **Seghill** Nthumb
114 D6 **Seighford** Staffs
125 K6 **Seion** Gwynd
97 J4 **Seisdon** Staffs
112 C5 **Selattyn** Shrops
35 M4 **Selborne** Hants
142 F1 **Selby** N York
20 F3 **Selham** W Susx
51 J5 **Selhurst** Gt Lon
201 G7 **Selkirk** Border
63 H2 **Sellack** Herefs
281 e2 **Sellafirth** Shet
2 C5 **Sellan** Cnwll
30 B7 **Sellick's Green** Somset
40 E7 **Sellindge** Kent
40 D4 **Selling** Kent
46 D6 **Sells Green** Wilts
98 D7 **Selly Oak** Birm
23 H6 **Selmeston** E Susx
51 K6 **Selsdon** Gt Lon
64 B6 **Selsey** Gloucs
20 D8 **Selsey** W Susx
38 A6 **Selsfield Common** W Susx
157 H3 **Selside** Cumb
158 D7 **Selside** N York
41 H6 **Selsted** Kent
116 D1 **Selston** Notts
29 G2 **Selworthy** Somset
89 K6 **Semer** Suffk
46 C6 **Semington** Wilts
32 E5 **Semley** Wilts
118 F5 **Sempringham** Lincs
50 C7 **Send** Surrey
50 D7 **Send Marsh** Surrey
43 H3 **Senghenydd** Caerph
2 B6 **Sennen** Cnwll
2 B6 **Sennen Cove** Cnwll
60 D2 **Sennybridge** Powys
134 C2 **Serlby** Notts
161 G7 **Sessay** N York
104 C1 **Setchey** Norfk
18 D3 **Setley** Hants
211 M4 **Seton Mains** E Loth
148 E3 **Settle** N York
152 C2 **Settrington** N York
29 L4 **Seven Ash** Somset
64 F3 **Sevenhampton** Gloucs
47 J1 **Sevenhampton** Swindn
51 M2 **Seven Kings** Gt Lon
38 E2 **Sevenoaks** Kent
38 E3 **Sevenoaks Weald** Kent
60 B5 **Seven Sisters** Neath
64 D4 **Seven Springs** Gloucs
72 D2 **Seven Star Green** Essex
45 G2 **Severn Beach** S Glos
81 K6 **Severn Stoke** Worcs
86 B4 **Sevick End** Beds
40 D7 **Sevington** Kent
88 B7 **Sewards End** Essex
69 K7 **Sewardstonebury** Essex
68 C3 **Sewell** Beds
153 K2 **Sewerby** E R Yk
3 H5 **Seworgan** Cnwll
118 A7 **Sewstern** Leics
161 G2 **Sexhow** N York
65 H1 **Sezincote** Gloucs
282 h1 **Sgiogarstaigh** W Isls
67 G5 **Shabbington** Bucks
97 J2 **Shackerley** Shrops
99 K2 **Shackerstone** Leics
116 C5 **Shacklecross** Derbys
36 D2 **Shackleford** Surrey
140 D3 **Shade** Calder
282 g1 **Shader** W Isls
169 J3 **Shadforth** Dur
107 J6 **Shadingfield** Suffk
40 C7 **Shadoxhurst** Kent
150 D7 **Shadwell** Leeds
105 J6 **Shadwell** Norfk
87 H7 **Shaftenhoe End** Herts
32 E6 **Shaftesbury** Dorset
142 F6 **Shaftholme** Donc
142 B5 **Shafton** Barns
142 B5 **Shafton Two Gates** Barns

139 K7 **Shakerley** Wigan
47 L6 **Shalbourne** Wilts
18 F6 **Shalcombe** IoW
35 L3 **Shalden** Hants
35 L2 **Shalden Green** Hants
13 L8 **Shaldon** Devon
18 F6 **Shalfleet** IoW
71 H1 **Shalford** Essex
36 F2 **Shalford** Surrey
71 H2 **Shalford Green** Essex
114 D5 **Shallowford** Staffs
40 E4 **Shalmsford Street** Kent
84 C7 **Shalstone** Bucks
36 F2 **Shamley Green** Surrey
234 D3 **Shandford** Angus
207 L2 **Shandon** Ag & B
264 D5 **Shandwick** Highld
100 F4 **Shangton** Leics
181 G3 **Shankhouse** Nthumb
19 K7 **Shanklin** IoW
166 D7 **Shap** Cumb
17 H2 **Shapwick** Dorset
30 F3 **Shapwick** Somset
98 F5 **Shard End** Birm
116 D5 **Shardlow** Derbys
97 L2 **Shareshill** Staffs
142 B4 **Sharlston** Wakefd
142 B4 **Sharlston Common** Wakefd
98 E7 **Sharman's Cross** Solhll
53 G4 **Sharnal Street** Medway
85 K3 **Sharnbrook** Beds
140 C3 **Sharneyford** Lancs
100 B5 **Sharnford** Leics
16 D1 **Sharnhill Green** Dorset
139 G1 **Sharoe Green** Lancs
150 D2 **Sharow** N York
68 D1 **Sharpenhoe** Beds
190 D5 **Sharperton** Nthumb
123 H7 **Sharp Green** Norfk
63 K6 **Sharpness** Gloucs
38 B6 **Sharpthorne** W Susx
11 J7 **Sharptor** Cnwll
81 L2 **Sharpway Gate** Worcs
122 A4 **Sharrington** Norfk
97 H7 **Shatterford** Worcs
41 J4 **Shatterling** Kent
132 D3 **Shatton** Derbys
7 G2 **Shaugh Prior** Devon
15 J3 **Shave Cross** Dorset
113 M1 **Shavington** Ches
140 F1 **Shaw** Brad
140 D6 **Shaw** Oldham
47 G2 **Shaw** Swindn
48 C5 **Shaw** W Berk
46 C6 **Shaw** Wilts
113 L8 **Shawbirch** Wrekin
282 f2 **Shawbost** W Isls
113 J7 **Shawbury** Shrops
140 D5 **Shawclough** Rochdl
63 K2 **Shaw Common** Gloucs
190 F3 **Shawdon Hill** Nthumb
100 C7 **Shawell** Leics
34 F6 **Shawford** Hants
140 D4 **Shawforth** Lancs
69 J1 **Shaw Green** Herts
139 G4 **Shaw Green** Lancs
150 C5 **Shaw Green** N York
185 L7 **Shawhead** D & G
150 C3 **Shaw Mills** N York
198 C3 **Shawsburn** S Lans
32 E3 **Shear Cross** Wilts
176 D5 **Shearington** D & G
100 D5 **Shearsby** Leics
30 D5 **Shearston** Somset
12 B1 **Shebbear** Devon
114 B6 **Shebdon** Staffs
279 H3 **Shebster** Highld
208 F7 **Sheddens** E Rens
35 H8 **Shedfield** Hants
132 B7 **Sheen** Staffs
133 G5 **Sheepbridge** Derbys
180 E7 **Sheep Hill** Dur
141 J4 **Sheepridge** Kirk
141 M1 **Sheepscar** Leeds
64 C5 **Sheepscombe** Gloucs
7 G1 **Sheepstor** Devon
12 C1 **Sheepwash** Devon
181 G2 **Sheepwash** Nthumb
45 G4 **Sheepway** N Som
99 J3 **Sheepy Magna** Leics
99 J3 **Sheepy Parva** Leics
70 D4 **Sheering** Essex
53 K4 **Sheerness** Kent
50 D6 **Sheerwater** Surrey
36 A6 **Sheet** Hants
2 D5 **Sheffield** Cnwll
133 G2 **Sheffield** Sheff

49 G5 **Sheffield Bottom** W Berk
22 F2 **Sheffield Green** E Susx
86 C7 **Shefford** Beds
276 B4 **Sheigra** Highld
96 E3 **Sheinton** Shrops
95 K7 **Shelderton** Shrops
98 F6 **Sheldon** Birm
132 C6 **Sheldon** Derbys
14 D1 **Sheldon** Devon
40 D4 **Sheldwich** Kent
40 D4 **Sheldwich Lees** Kent
141 H2 **Shelf** Calder
106 C6 **Shelfanger** Norfk
82 D3 **Shelfield** Warwks
98 C3 **Shelfield** Wsall
82 D3 **Shelfield Green** Warwks
117 H3 **Shelford** Notts
99 L5 **Shelford** Warwks
202 D4 **Shellacres** Nthumb
70 E6 **Shelley** Essex
141 K5 **Shelley** Kirk
89 L7 **Shelley** Suffk
141 K5 **Shelley Far Bank** Kirk
65 L8 **Shellingford** Oxon
70 F5 **Shellow Bowells** Essex
81 G3 **Shelsley Beauchamp** Worcs
81 G3 **Shelsley Walsh** Worcs
85 K2 **Shelton** Beds
106 E5 **Shelton** Norfk
117 K3 **Shelton** Notts
95 L1 **Shelton** Shrops
106 E5 **Shelton Green** Norfk
116 C5 **Shelton Lock** C Derb
114 C4 **Shelton Under Harley** Staffs
95 H4 **Shelve** Shrops
80 C6 **Shelwick** Herefs
70 F8 **Shenfield** Essex
83 J6 **Shenington** Oxon
68 F7 **Shenley** Herts
85 G8 **Shenley Brook End** M Keyn
68 F6 **Shenleybury** Herts
85 G7 **Shenley Church End** M Keyn
79 M7 **Shenmore** Herefs
173 J2 **Shennanton** D & G
98 E3 **Shenstone** Staffs
97 J8 **Shenstone** Worcs
98 E3 **Shenstone Woodend** Staffs
99 K3 **Shenton** Leics
102 F1 **Shepeau Stow** Lincs
69 H2 **Shephall** Herts
4 D4 **Shepherds** Cnwll
51 G3 **Shepherd's Bush** Gt Lon
49 H2 **Shepherd's Green** Oxon
63 L6 **Shepherds Patch** Gloucs
41 H5 **Shepherdswell** Kent
141 J6 **Shepley** Kirk
63 J8 **Shepperdine** S Glos
50 D5 **Shepperton** Surrey
50 D5 **Shepperton Green** Surrey
87 H5 **Shepreth** Cambs
116 E7 **Shepshed** Leics
30 F7 **Shepton Beauchamp** Somset
31 K2 **Shepton Mallet** Somset
31 L4 **Shepton Montague** Somset
39 J3 **Shepway** Kent
170 B4 **Sheraton** Dur
31 L7 **Sherborne** Dorset
65 H4 **Sherborne** Gloucs
45 H7 **Sherborne** Somset
48 F7 **Sherborne St John** Hants
83 G3 **Sherbourne** Warwks
169 J2 **Sherburn** Dur
163 G7 **Sherburn** N York
169 J2 **Sherburn Hill** Dur
142 D1 **Sherburn in Elmet** N York
37 G1 **Shere** Surrey
121 K5 **Shereford** Norfk
34 C6 **Sherfield English** Hants
49 G7 **Sherfield on Loddon** Hants
140 B3 **Sherfin** Lancs
8 A6 **Sherford** Devon
17 H4 **Sherford** Dorset
97 G1 **Sheriffhales** Shrops
151 K3 **Sheriff Hutton** N York
122 D3 **Sheringham** Norfk
85 H6 **Sherington** M Keyn
22 B3 **Shermanbury** W Susx
120 F5 **Shernborne** Norfk
33 G3 **Sherrington** Wilts
46 B2 **Sherston** Wilts
116 F3 **Sherwood** C Nott
209 H6 **Shettleston** C Glas
139 H6 **Shevington** Wigan
139 H5 **Shevington Moor** Wigan

139 G6 **Shevington Vale** Wigan
6 D4 **Sheviock** Cnwll
141 H2 **Shibden Head** Brad
19 H6 **Shide** IoW
202 C5 **Shidlaw** Nthumb
248 F7 **Shiel Bridge** Highld
248 C1 **Shieldaig** Highld
176 D2 **Shieldhill** D & G
210 B4 **Shieldhill** Falk
199 G5 **Shieldhill House Hotel** S Lans
209 K7 **Shields** N Lans
237 J6 **Shielfoot** Highld
234 C4 **Shielhill** Angus
207 L4 **Shielhill** Inver
66 A6 **Shifford** Oxon
97 G2 **Shifnal** Shrops
191 J4 **Shilbottle** Nthumb
169 G5 **Shildon** Dur
208 D7 **Shillford** E Rens
29 H6 **Shillingford** Devon
66 E8 **Shillingford** Oxon
13 L4 **Shillingford Abbot** Devon
13 L5 **Shillingford St George** Devon
32 D8 **Shillingstone** Dorset
86 C7 **Shillington** Beds
190 B4 **Shillmoor** Nthumb
65 K5 **Shilton** Oxon
99 L6 **Shilton** Warwks
106 D5 **Shimpling** Norfk
89 H5 **Shimpling** Suffk
89 H4 **Shimpling Street** Suffk
169 H3 **Shincliffe** Dur
181 H8 **Shiney Row** Sundld
49 H5 **Shinfield** Wokham
86 F6 **Shingay** Cambs
91 J6 **Shingle Street** Suffk
8 B2 **Shinnersbridge** Devon
272 D5 **Shinness** Highld
38 F3 **Shipbourne** Kent
105 J2 **Shipdham** Norfk
44 E7 **Shipham** Somset
8 D2 **Shiphay** Torbay
49 J3 **Shiplake** Oxon
49 H3 **Shiplake Row** Oxon
44 D7 **Shiplate** N Som
149 L8 **Shipley** Brad
116 D3 **Shipley** Derbys
97 H4 **Shipley** Shrops
37 H6 **Shipley** W Susx
37 M3 **Shipley Bridge** Surrey
40 C7 **Shipley Hatch** Kent
107 H5 **Shipmeadow** Suffk
104 C6 **Shippea Hill Station** Cambs
66 C7 **Shippon** Oxon
83 G7 **Shipston on Stour** Warwks
67 J2 **Shipton** Bucks
64 F3 **Shipton** Gloucs
151 H4 **Shipton** N York
96 D5 **Shipton** Shrops
34 B2 **Shipton Bellinger** Hants
15 L4 **Shipton Gorge** Dorset
20 C7 **Shipton Green** W Susx
46 C1 **Shipton Moyne** Gloucs
66 C4 **Shipton-on-Cherwell** Oxon
152 C7 **Shiptonthorpe** E R Yk
65 L3 **Shipton-under-Wychwood** Oxon
67 G7 **Shirburn** Oxon
138 D5 **Shirdley Hill** Lancs
166 E4 **Shire** Cumb
133 K6 **Shirebrook** Derbys
133 G1 **Shiregreen** Sheff
45 G4 **Shirehampton** Bristl
181 H4 **Shiremoor** N Tyne
62 F8 **Shirenewton** Mons
98 D3 **Shire Oak** Wsall
133 L3 **Shireoaks** Notts
40 B8 **Shirkoak** Kent
133 H8 **Shirland** Derbys
96 E4 **Shirlett** Shrops
34 E8 **Shirley** C Sotn
115 L3 **Shirley** Derbys
51 K6 **Shirley** Gt Lon
98 E7 **Shirley** Solhll
80 A3 **Shirl Heath** Herefs
35 H8 **Shirrell Heath** Hants
206 D2 **Shirvan** Ag & B
27 L3 **Shirwell** Devon
27 L3 **Shirwell Cross** Devon
194 E5 **Shiskine** N Ayrs
168 C3 **Shittlehope** Dur
79 M3 **Shobdon** Herefs
18 B2 **Shobley** Hants
13 K2 **Shobrooke** Devon
117 H7 **Shoby** Leics
113 G2 **Shocklach** Ches

113 G2 **Shocklach Green** Ches
53 K2 **Shoeburyness** Sthend
41 K5 **Sholden** Kent
19 G2 **Sholing** C Sotn
164 D5 **Shoose** Cumb
95 K1 **Shoot Hill** Shrops
10 B7 **Shop** Cnwll
26 D7 **Shop** Cnwll
20 E6 **Shopwyke** W Susx
140 D4 **Shore** Rochdl
51 J2 **Shoreditch** Gt Lon
30 C6 **Shoreditch** Somset
52 B6 **Shoreham** Kent
22 C6 **Shoreham-by-Sea** W Susx
202 E4 **Shoreswood** Nthumb
35 J5 **Shorley** Hants
64 F7 **Shorncote** Gloucs
52 E5 **Shorne** Kent
52 E5 **Shorne Ridgeway** Kent
6 B3 **Shorta Cross** Cnwll
23 G3 **Shortbridge** E Susx
36 C2 **Shortfield Common** Surrey
23 H4 **Shortgate** E Susx
98 E5 **Short Heath** Birm
36 A4 **Shortheath** Hants
98 B3 **Short Heath** Wsall
4 C5 **Shortlanesend** Cnwll
196 E4 **Shortlees** E Ayrs
86 B6 **Shortstown** Beds
19 G7 **Shorwell** IoW
45 L7 **Shoscombe** BaNES
106 E4 **Shotesham** Norfk
71 J8 **Shotgate** Essex
90 F8 **Shotley** Suffk
180 D8 **Shotley Bridge** Dur
180 C8 **Shotleyfield** Nthumb
90 F8 **Shotley Gate** Suffk
90 F8 **Shotley Street** Suffk
40 D4 **Shottenden** Kent
36 C4 **Shottermill** Surrey
82 E4 **Shottery** Warwks
83 K6 **Shotteswell** Warwks
91 H6 **Shottisham** Suffk
116 A2 **Shottle** Derbys
116 A2 **Shottlegate** Derbys
169 K5 **Shotton** Dur
169 L3 **Shotton** Dur
129 H6 **Shotton** Flints
180 F3 **Shotton** Nthumb
202 C7 **Shotton** Nthumb
169 K3 **Shotton Colliery** Dur
210 A7 **Shotts** N Lans
129 H5 **Shotwick** Ches
266 D5 **Shougle** Moray
104 D2 **Shouldham** Norfk
104 D2 **Shouldham Thorpe** Norfk
81 J3 **Shoulton** Worcs
39 G7 **Shover's Green** E Susx
114 B2 **Shraleybrook** Staffs
112 F8 **Shrawardine** Shrops
81 J2 **Shrawley** Worcs
50 C3 **Shreding Green** Bucks
82 F2 **Shrewley** Warwks
96 B1 **Shrewsbury** Shrops
33 J2 **Shrewton** Wilts
20 F6 **Shripney** W Susx
47 K1 **Shrivenham** Oxon
105 K5 **Shropham** Norfk
72 E2 **Shrub End** Essex
80 D6 **Shucknall** Herefs
88 C6 **Shudy Camps** Cambs
64 D3 **Shurdington** Gloucs
49 K4 **Shurlock Row** W & M
82 B3 **Shurnock** Worcs
279 J4 **Shurrery** Highld
279 J5 **Shurrery Lodge** Highld
30 B2 **Shurton** Somset
99 G5 **Shustoke** Warwks
13 L2 **Shute** Devon
14 F3 **Shute** Devon
83 J7 **Shutford** Oxon
114 D7 **Shut Heath** Staffs
81 K8 **Shuthonger** Gloucs
84 E5 **Shutlanger** Nhants
13 M6 **Shutterton** Devon
97 K2 **Shutt Green** Staffs
99 H2 **Shuttington** Warwks
133 J5 **Shuttlewood** Derbys
140 B4 **Shuttleworth** Bury
282 f2 **Siabost** W Isls
282 g1 **Siadar** W Isls
100 E6 **Sibbertoft** Nhants
95 K6 **Sibdon Carwood** Shrops
83 H7 **Sibford Ferris** Oxon
83 H7 **Sibford Gower** Oxon
88 F8 **Sible Hedingham** Essex
70 F2 **Sibley's Green** Essex
11 J7 **Siblyback** Cnwll

119 K2 **Sibsey** Lincs
119 K1 **Sibsey Fenside** Lincs
102 B4 **Sibson** Cambs
99 K3 **Sibson** Leics
280 D5 **Sibster** Highld
117 K2 **Sibthorpe** Notts
134 E5 **Sibthorpe** Notts
91 J2 **Sibton** Suffk
89 H3 **Sicklesmere** Suffk
150 E6 **Sicklinghall** N York
30 C5 **Sidbrook** Somset
14 D4 **Sidbury** Devon
96 F6 **Sidbury** Shrops
142 B6 **Sid Cop** Barns
44 E7 **Sidcot** N Som
51 M4 **Sidcup** Gt Lon
164 D4 **Siddick** Cumb
131 G5 **Siddington** Ches
64 F7 **Siddington** Gloucs
81 L1 **Sidemoor** Worcs
122 F3 **Sidestrand** Norfk
14 D4 **Sidford** Devon
20 D7 **Sidlesham** W Susx
20 D6 **Sidlesham Common** W Susx
24 D5 **Sidley** E Susx
14 D5 **Sidmouth** Devon
96 B5 **Siefton** Shrops
13 H7 **Sigford** Devon
153 J6 **Sigglesthorne** E R Yk
42 E7 **Sigingstone** V Glam
65 K5 **Signet** Oxon
48 F6 **Silchester** Hants
117 G8 **Sileby** Leics
155 L6 **Silecroft** Cumb
106 C3 **Silfield** Norfk
77 G5 **Silian** Cerdgn
34 F6 **Silkstead** Hants
141 L6 **Silkstone** Barns
141 L6 **Silkstone Common** Barns
181 J8 **Silksworth** Sundld
118 E3 **Silk Willoughby** Lincs
176 F8 **Silloth** Cumb
163 H4 **Silpho** N York
149 J6 **Silsden** Brad
86 B8 **Silsoe** Beds
32 C5 **Silton** Dorset
211 G7 **Silverburn** Mdloth
157 G7 **Silverdale** Lancs
114 C2 **Silverdale** Staffs
157 G7 **Silverdale Green** Lancs
71 K3 **Silver End** Essex
268 D3 **Silverford** Abers
122 D6 **Silvergate** Norfk
91 H3 **Silverlace Green** Suffk
106 F8 **Silverley's Green** Suffk
84 C6 **Silverstone** Nhants
53 J7 **Silver Street** Kent
31 J4 **Silver Street** Somset
13 M2 **Silverton** Devon
4 B5 **Silverwell** Cnwll
96 E7 **Silvington** Shrops
131 K1 **Simmondley** Derbys
179 K4 **Simonburn** Nthumb
28 D3 **Simonsbath** Somset
29 L7 **Simons Burrow** Devon
140 A1 **Simonstone** Lancs
158 F4 **Simonstone** N York
202 C4 **Simprim** Border
85 H8 **Simpson** M Keyn
54 E3 **Simpson Cross** Pembks
202 C3 **Sinclair's Hill** Border
196 F7 **Sinclairston** E Ayrs
160 E6 **Sinderby** N York
179 K8 **Sinderhope** Nthumb
130 E2 **Sinderland Green** Traffd
49 J5 **Sindlesham** Wokham
116 B5 **Sinfin** C Derb
67 J1 **Singleborough** Bucks
51 L7 **Single Street** Gt Lon
40 C7 **Singleton** Kent
147 G8 **Singleton** Lancs
20 E4 **Singleton** W Susx
52 E5 **Singlewell** Kent
39 K5 **Sinkhurst Green** Kent
244 B1 **Sinnarhard** Abers
162 C5 **Sinnington** N York
81 J3 **Sinton** Worcs
81 J3 **Sinton Green** Worcs
50 D3 **Sipson** Gt Lon
61 J5 **Sirhowy** Blae G
39 K6 **Sissinghurst** Kent
45 K4 **Siston** S Glos
11 L4 **Sitcott** Devon
3 G5 **Sithney** Cnwll
3 G5 **Sithney Common** Cnwll
3 G5 **Sithney Green** Cnwll
40 B3 **Sittingbourne** Kent

97 H5 **Six Ashes** Shrops
61 K6 **Six Bells** Blae G
136 C2 **Sixhills** Lincs
88 B4 **Six Mile Bottom** Cambs
40 F6 **Sixmile Cottages** Kent
33 G7 **Sixpenny Handley** Dorset
9 c2 **Six Rues** Jersey
91 L3 **Sizewell** Suffk
275 d5 **Skaill** Ork
197 G2 **Skares** E Ayrs
245 K5 **Skateraw** Abers
213 G4 **Skateraw** E Loth
259 G7 **Skeabost** Highld
160 B2 **Skeeby** N York
101 G3 **Skeffington** Leics
145 K4 **Skeffling** E R Yk
133 K7 **Skegby** Notts
134 F5 **Skegby** Notts
137 L7 **Skegness** Lincs
264 B1 **Skelbo** Highld
264 B1 **Skelbo Street** Highld
142 D5 **Skelbrooke** Donc
119 K4 **Skeldyke** Lincs
135 J5 **Skellingthorpe** Lincs
131 H3 **Skellorn Green** Ches
142 E5 **Skellow** Donc
141 K5 **Skelmanthorpe** Kirk
138 F6 **Skelmersdale** Lancs
207 K5 **Skelmorlie** N Ayrs
278 B5 **Skelpick** Highld
185 K6 **Skelston** D & G
166 B4 **Skelton** Cumb
143 J3 **Skelton** E R Yk
150 E2 **Skelton** N York
159 K3 **Skelton** N York
170 F7 **Skelton** R & Cl
151 J4 **Skelton** York
156 E2 **Skelwith Bridge** Cumb
137 H5 **Skendleby** Lincs
245 G2 **Skene House** Abers
62 F3 **Skenfrith** Mons
153 G5 **Skerne** E R Yk
277 L4 **Skerray** Highld
276 C6 **Skerricha** Highld
147 J3 **Skerton** Lancs
99 L5 **Sketchley** Leics
57 H6 **Sketty** Swans
57 K5 **Skewen** Neath
151 K2 **Skewsby** N York
122 E6 **Skeyton** Norfk
122 E6 **Skeyton Corner** Norfk
279 H3 **Skiall** Highld
137 H1 **Skidbrooke** Lincs
137 H1 **Skidbrooke North End** Lincs
144 C1 **Skidby** E R Yk
282 h1 **Skigersta** W Isls
29 H5 **Skilgate** Somset
118 A6 **Skillington** Lincs
176 F7 **Skinburness** Cumb
210 B2 **Skinflats** Falk
258 C7 **Skinidin** Highld
48 C6 **Skinners Green** W Berk
171 G6 **Skinningrove** R & Cl
206 E7 **Skipness** Ag & B
177 L2 **Skipper's Bridge** D & G
165 L2 **Skiprigg** Cumb
153 J5 **Skipsea** E R Yk
153 J5 **Skipsea Brough** E R Yk
149 H5 **Skipton** N York
160 E6 **Skipton-on-Swale** N York
151 L8 **Skipwith** N York
153 J7 **Skirlaugh** E R Yk
199 J5 **Skirling** Border
49 J1 **Skirmett** Bucks
152 A4 **Skirpenbeck** E R Yk
166 E4 **Skirwith** Cumb
158 C7 **Skirwith** N York
280 E3 **Skirza** Highld
178 B5 **Skitby** Cumb
67 J6 **Skittle Green** Bucks
247 L4 **Skulamus** Highld
95 G8 **Skyborry Green** Shrops
72 C3 **Skye Green** Essex
253 J6 **Skye of Curr** Highld
149 J4 **Skyreholme** N York
140 E2 **Slack** Calder
140 E6 **Slackcote** Oldham
157 G6 **Slack Head** Cumb
137 K5 **Slackholme End** Lincs
256 F3 **Slacks of Cairnbanno** Abers
64 C5 **Slad** Gloucs
14 D1 **Slade** Devon
27 J2 **Slade** Devon
28 E5 **Slade** Devon
48 E1 **Slade End** Oxon

52 B4 **Slade Green** Gt Lon
97 L2 **Slade Heath** Staffs
133 K2 **Slade Hooton** Rothm
10 E8 **Sladesbridge** Cnwll
81 J8 **Slades Green** Worcs
178 F8 **Slaggyford** Nthumb
148 C5 **Slaidburn** Lancs
141 G5 **Slaithwaite** Kirk
132 E8 **Slaley** Derbys
180 A7 **Slaley** Nthumb
209 M4 **Slamannan** Falk
68 B3 **Slapton** Bucks
8 B6 **Slapton** Devon
84 C6 **Slapton** Nhants
140 D6 **Slattocks** Rochdl
37 L5 **Slaugham** W Susx
46 B4 **Slaughterford** Wilts
101 G4 **Slawston** Leics
36 B3 **Sleaford** Hants
118 E2 **Sleaford** Lincs
166 E6 **Sleagill** Cumb
113 H6 **Sleap** Shrops
113 L8 **Sleapford** Wrekin
69 G5 **Sleapshyde** Herts
272 F8 **Sleasdairidh** Highld
81 J8 **Sledge Green** Worcs
152 E3 **Sledmere** E R Yk
178 C3 **Sleetbeck** Cumb
17 J3 **Sleight** Dorset
168 B8 **Sleightholme** Dur
162 F1 **Sleights** N York
17 H4 **Slepe** Dorset
280 C3 **Slickly** Highld
193 J4 **Sliddery** N Ayrs
247 G3 **Sligachan** Highld
207 K1 **Sligrachan** Ag & B
63 L6 **Slimbridge** Gloucs
114 C5 **Slindon** Staffs
20 F5 **Slindon** W Susx
37 H4 **Slinfold** W Susx
126 B6 **Sling** Gwynd
162 B7 **Slingsby** N York
68 D3 **Slip End** Beds
86 F7 **Slip End** Herts
101 L7 **Slipton** Nhants
115 G8 **Slitting Mill** Staffs
216 C7 **Slockavullin** Ag & B
175 G1 **Slogarie** D & G
122 F6 **Sloley** Norfk
13 H5 **Sloncombe** Devon
137 J5 **Sloothby** Lincs
50 C3 **Slough** Slough
30 C7 **Slough Green** Somset
37 L5 **Slough Green** W Susx
248 E4 **Slumbay** Highld
50 C8 **Slyfield Green** Surrey
147 J3 **Slyne** Lancs
201 K6 **Smailholm** Border
140 D5 **Smallbridge** Rochdl
13 K3 **Smallbrook** Devon
63 H7 **Smallbrook** Gloucs
123 G6 **Smallburgh** Norfk
132 B4 **Smalldale** Derbys
132 C3 **Smalldale** Derbys
22 C5 **Small Dole** W Susx
116 C3 **Smalley** Derbys
116 C3 **Smalley Common** Derbys
116 C3 **Smalley Green** Derbys
37 M2 **Smallfield** Surrey
98 E6 **Small Heath** Birm
25 G1 **Small Hythe** Kent
15 G2 **Smallridge** Devon
114 D2 **Smallthorne** C Stke
168 E8 **Smallways** N York
130 F7 **Smallwood** Ches
147 H6 **Small Wood Hey** Lancs
105 K7 **Smallworth** Norfk
34 E1 **Smannell** Hants
158 C1 **Smardale** Cumb
39 L5 **Smarden** Kent
39 L5 **Smarden Bell** Kent
38 E5 **Smart's Hill** Kent
203 H5 **Smeafield** Nthumb
237 J5 **Smearisary** Highld
30 B8 **Smeatharpe** Devon
40 E7 **Smeeth** Kent
100 E5 **Smeeton Westerby** Leics
150 B3 **Smelthouses** N York
275 G2 **Smerral** Highld
97 J5 **Smestow** Staffs
98 C6 **Smethwick** Sandw
130 F7 **Smethwick Green** Ches
116 B7 **Smisby** Derbys
19 J5 **Smithclose** IoW
81 H5 **Smith End Green** Worcs
178 B6 **Smithfield** Cumb
147 J5 **Smith Green** Lancs
142 A6 **Smithies** Barns

29 J8 **Smithincott** Devon
87 H7 **Smith's End** Herts
70 E3 **Smith's Green** Essex
88 D7 **Smith's Green** Essex
260 C4 **Smithstown** Highld
252 D3 **Smithton** Highld
140 D5 **Smithy Bridge** Rochdl
130 E5 **Smithy Green** Ches
131 G3 **Smithy Green** Stockp
116 C2 **Smithy Houses** Derbys
99 M5 **Smockington** Leics
277 G3 **Smoo** Highld
72 D3 **Smythe's Green** Essex
185 L5 **Snade** D & G
95 J3 **Snailbeach** Shrops
88 C2 **Snailwell** Cambs
163 G6 **Snainton** N York
143 G3 **Snaith** E R Yk
132 B2 **Snake Pass Inn** Derbys
160 C6 **Snape** N York
91 J3 **Snape** Suffk
138 D5 **Snape Green** Lancs
91 J4 **Snape Street** Suffk
51 L1 **Snaresbrook** Gt Lon
99 K2 **Snarestone** Leics
135 L3 **Snarford** Lincs
25 J2 **Snargate** Kent
25 J1 **Snave** Kent
81 L4 **Sneachill** Worcs
95 H5 **Snead** Powys
106 D5 **Sneath Common** Norfk
162 F1 **Sneaton** N York
162 F2 **Sneatonthorpe** N York
135 M4 **Snelland** Lincs
130 F5 **Snelson** Ches
115 J3 **Snelston** Derbys
105 K5 **Snetterton** Norfk
120 F4 **Snettisham** Norfk
116 C8 **Snibston** Leics
64 A1 **Snig's End** Gloucs
190 E5 **Snitter** Nthumb
135 K1 **Snitterby** Lincs
82 F3 **Snitterfield** Warwks
132 E7 **Snitterton** Derbys
96 D8 **Snitton** Shrops
40 B6 **Snoadhill** Kent
79 K7 **Snodhill** Herefs
52 F6 **Snodland** Kent
39 G4 **Snoll Hatch** Kent
141 L7 **Snowden Hill** Barns
69 L1 **Snow End** Herts
82 C8 **Snowshill** Gloucs
106 B7 **Snow Street** Norfk
19 L2 **Soake** Hants
43 H5 **Soar** Cardif
7 K7 **Soar** Devon
60 E1 **Soar** Powys
35 J7 **Soberton** Hants
35 J8 **Soberton Heath** Hants
166 C5 **Sockbridge** Cumb
160 E1 **Sockburn** Darltn
128 C5 **Sodom** Denbgs
112 E3 **Sodylt Bank** Shrops
104 B8 **Soham** Cambs
104 B8 **Soham Cotes** Cambs
282 C7 **Solas** W Isls
54 E4 **Solbury** Pembks
26 E8 **Soldon** Devon
26 E8 **Soldon Cross** Devon
35 K4 **Soldridge** Hants
40 E5 **Sole Street** Kent
52 E5 **Sole Street** Kent
98 F7 **Solihull** Solhll
80 A4 **Sollers Dilwyn** Herefs
80 E8 **Sollers Hope** Herefs
138 F4 **Sollom** Lancs
74 C7 **Solva** Pembks
177 J3 **Solwaybank** D & G
101 G1 **Somerby** Leics
144 D6 **Somerby** Lincs
116 C1 **Somercotes** Derbys
18 B5 **Somerford** Dorset
64 E8 **Somerford Keynes** Gloucs
20 D7 **Somerley** W Susx
107 K4 **Somerleyton** Suffk
115 J4 **Somersal Herbert** Derbys
136 F5 **Somersby** Lincs
103 G7 **Somersham** Cambs
90 C5 **Somersham** Suffk
66 D2 **Somerton** Oxon
31 H5 **Somerton** Somset
89 G4 **Somerton** Suffk
113 J8 **Somerwood** Shrops
21 K6 **Sompting** W Susx
49 J4 **Sonning** Wokham
49 H3 **Sonning Common** Oxon
49 H4 **Sonning Eye** Oxon
112 E2 **Sontley** Wrexhm

18 B4 **Sopley** Hants
46 B2 **Sopworth** Wilts
174 C5 **Sorbie** D & G
279 L4 **Sordale** Highld
225 H3 **Sorisdale** Ag & B
197 G5 **Sorn** E Ayrs
280 C4 **Sortat** Highld
136 D4 **Sotby** Lincs
136 B6 **Sots Hole** Lincs
107 J6 **Sotterley** Suffk
128 F6 **Soughton** Flints
67 L2 **Soulbury** Bucks
166 B5 **Soulby** Cumb
167 H8 **Soulby** Cumb
66 D1 **Souldern** Oxon
85 J3 **Souldrop** Beds
113 K2 **Sound** Ches
267 G5 **Sound Muir** Moray
45 J4 **Soundwell** S Glos
12 D4 **Sourton** Devon
156 B6 **Soutergate** Cumb
121 H8 **South Acre** Norfk
41 H7 **South Alkham** Kent
50 E3 **Southall** Gt Lon
8 B7 **South Allington** Devon
210 A1 **South Alloa** Falk
64 E2 **Southam** Gloucs
83 K3 **Southam** Warwks
20 F3 **South Ambersham** W Susx
19 G1 **Southampton** C Sotn
133 K3 **South Anston** Rothm
50 A5 **South Ascot** W & M
40 C7 **South Ashford** Kent
18 E4 **South Baddesley** Hants
229 H4 **South Ballachulish** Highld
170 C6 **South Bank** R & Cl
151 J5 **South Bank** York
31 K5 **South Barrow** Somset
51 H6 **South Beddington** Gt Lon
11 K4 **South Beer** Cnwll
53 G2 **South Benfleet** Essex
20 F6 **South Bersted** W Susx
18 B4 **South Bockhampton**
Dorset
51 L5 **Southborough** Gt Lon
38 F5 **Southborough** Kent
18 A5 **Southbourne** Bmouth
20 C5 **Southbourne** W Susx
15 K3 **South Bowood** Dorset
143 G5 **South Bramwith** Donc
7 K3 **South Brent** Devon
32 B4 **South Brewham** Somset
17 G4 **Southbrook** Dorset
191 K6 **South Broomhill** Nthumb
105 K2 **Southburgh** Norfk
107 H2 **South Burlingham** Norfk
152 F5 **Southburn** E R Yk
31 K5 **South Cadbury** Somset
135 J4 **South Carlton** Lincs
134 B3 **South Carlton** Notts
144 A2 **South Cave** E R Yk
64 F7 **South Cerney** Gloucs
22 F4 **South Chailey** E Susx
15 H2 **South Chard** Somset
191 H2 **South Charlton** Nthumb
32 B6 **South Cheriton** Somset
169 G5 **South Church** Dur
53 J2 **Southchurch** Sthend
168 E7 **South Cleatlam** Dur
152 D8 **South Cliffe** E R Yk
135 G5 **South Clifton** Notts
137 G2 **South Cockerington** Lincs
42 B5 **South Cornelly** Brdgnd
11 H3 **Southcott** Cnwll
12 D3 **Southcott** Devon
13 H6 **Southcott** Devon
27 H7 **Southcott** Devon
47 H7 **Southcott** Wilts
67 K5 **Southcourt** Bucks
107 K7 **South Cove** Suffk
121 J4 **South Creake** Norfk
141 H5 **South Crosland** Kirk
100 F2 **South Croxton** Leics
152 E6 **South Dalton** E R Yk
52 C5 **South Darenth** Kent
143 H1 **South Duffield** N York
23 G6 **Southease** E Susx
136 E2 **South Elkington** Lincs
142 D5 **South Elmsall** Wakefd
192 E6 **Southend** Ag & B
145 K4 **South End** E R Yk
33 J7 **South End** Hants
81 G6 **South End** Herefs
144 E4 **South End** N Linc
105 K5 **South End** Norfk
47 J4 **Southend** Wilts
53 J2 **Southend-on-Sea** Sthend
165 L3 **Southernby** Cumb

39 L4 **Southernden** Kent
42 D7 **Southerndown** V Glam
176 C7 **Southerness** D & G
260 B5 **South Erradale** Highld
14 C4 **Southerton** Devon
104 C4 **Southery** Norfk
72 B8 **South Fambridge** Essex
48 A3 **South Fawley** W Berk
144 B4 **South Ferriby** N Linc
144 C3 **South Field** E R Yk
209 M4 **Southfield** Falk
52 D5 **Southfleet** Kent
19 J7 **Southford** IoW
69 J8 **Southgate** Gt Lon
120 E5 **Southgate** Norfk
121 J4 **Southgate** Norfk
122 C6 **Southgate** Norfk
57 G7 **Southgate** Swans
38 A4 **South Godstone** Surrey
18 B2 **South Gorley** Hants
181 G5 **South Gosforth** N u Ty
71 G8 **South Green** Essex
72 F3 **South Green** Essex
53 J7 **South Green** Kent
105 L1 **South Green** Norfk
106 D8 **South Green** Suffk
211 G4 **South Gyle** C Edin
71 H7 **South Hanningfield** Essex
20 C3 **South Harting** W Susx
20 B6 **South Hayling** Hants
203 G6 **South Hazelrigg** Nthumb
67 M6 **South Heath** Bucks
23 G6 **South Heighton** E Susx
169 K2 **South Hetton** Dur
142 B5 **South Hiendley** Wakefd
11 L7 **South Hill** Cnwll
31 G5 **South Hill** Somset
66 D6 **South Hinksey** Oxon
26 C6 **South Hole** Devon
37 J2 **South Holmwood** Surrey
52 B2 **South Hornchurch** Gt Lon
31 J2 **South Horrington** Somset
7 K6 **South Huish** Devon
135 J6 **South Hykeham** Lincs
181 J7 **South Hylton** Sundld
86 C6 **Southill** Beds
35 G1 **Southington** Hants
144 D8 **South Kelsey** Lincs
251 H2 **South Kessock** Highld
144 F4 **South Killingholme** N Linc
160 F6 **South Kilvington** N York
100 D7 **South Kilworth** Leics
142 C5 **South Kirkby** Wakefd
13 J7 **South Knighton** Devon
119 G2 **South Kyme** Lincs
14 E4 **Southleigh** Devon
66 B5 **South Leigh** Oxon
134 F3 **South Leverton** Notts
82 C6 **South Littleton** Worcs
105 L7 **South Lopham** Norfk
101 K3 **South Luffenham** Rutlnd
23 G5 **South Malling** E Susx
47 J2 **South Marston** Swindn
51 H8 **South Merstham** Surrey
190 E2 **South Middleton** Nthumb
142 D2 **South Milford** N York
7 K6 **South Milton** Devon
69 G6 **South Mimms** Herts
72 D7 **Southminster** Essex
28 C5 **South Molton** Devon
180 F8 **South Moor** Dur
66 B7 **Southmoor** Oxon
48 E1 **South Moreton** Oxon
234 B5 **Southmuir** Angus
20 E6 **South Mundham** W Susx
134 F8 **South Muskham** Notts
152 D8 **South Newbald** E R Yk
83 J8 **South Newington** Oxon
33 J4 **South Newton** Wilts
133 J8 **South Normanton** Derbys
51 J5 **South Norwood** Gt Lon
37 M1 **South Nutfield** Surrey
52 D2 **South Ockendon** Thurr
86 D2 **Southoe** Cambs
90 E2 **Southolt** Suffk
137 G4 **South Ormsby** Lincs
102 B3 **Southorpe** C Pete
141 L4 **South Ossett** Wakefd
160 E5 **South Otterington** N York
16 B3 **Southover** Dorset
24 B2 **Southover** E Susx
135 L1 **South Owersby** Lincs
141 H3 **Southowram** Calder
37 K1 **South Park** Surrey
15 L1 **South Perrott** Dorset
31 G7 **South Petherton** Somset
11 K6 **South Petherwin** Cnwll
105 G3 **South Pickenham** Norfk

6 E3 **South Pill** Cnwll
7 M6 **South Pool** Devon
15 M3 **South Poorton** Dorset
138 D4 **Southport** Sefton
210 F3 **South Queensferry** C Edin
28 C4 **South Radworthy** Devon
118 D2 **South Rauceby** Lincs
121 J6 **South Raynham** Norfk
131 H1 **South Reddish** Stockp
122 E4 **Southrepps** Norfk
137 G3 **South Reston** Lincs
136 B6 **Southrey** Lincs
65 J6 **Southrop** Gloucs
35 K2 **Southrope** Hants
104 C2 **South Runcton** Norfk
135 G7 **South Scarle** Notts
19 L4 **Southsea** C Port
112 D1 **Southsea** Wrexhm
228 E7 **South Shian** Ag & B
181 J5 **South Shields** S Tyne
138 C1 **South Shore** Bpool
168 E5 **Southside** Dur
137 H1 **South Somercotes** Lincs
150 D3 **South Stainley** N York
52 D3 **South Stifford** Thurr
45 L6 **South Stoke** BaNES
48 F2 **South Stoke** Oxon
21 H5 **South Stoke** W Susx
40 D7 **South Stour** Kent
40 D4 **South Street** Kent
40 F2 **South Street** Kent
52 D6 **South Street** Kent
199 H3 **South Tarbrax** S Lans
12 F3 **South Tawton** Devon
3 G3 **South Tehidy** Cnwll
137 G4 **South Thoresby** Lincs
168 E7 **South Thorpe** Dur
35 K4 **South Town** Hants
107 L2 **Southtown** Norfk
30 D7 **Southtown** Somset
166 B2 **Southwaite** Cumb
107 H1 **South Walsham** Norfk
51 J3 **Southwark** Gt Lon
35 L2 **South Warnborough**
Hants
37 J5 **Southwater** W Susx
37 H5 **Southwater Street** W Susx
31 H2 **Southway** Somset
70 E8 **South Weald** Essex
16 D8 **Southwell** Dorset
117 J1 **Southwell** Notts
67 H7 **South Weston** Oxon
11 J4 **South Wheatley** Cnwll
19 L2 **Southwick** Hants
101 M5 **Southwick** Nhants
30 E2 **Southwick** Somset
181 J7 **Southwick** Sundld
22 C6 **Southwick** W Susx
46 B7 **Southwick** Wilts
45 H7 **South Widcombe** BaNES
100 D4 **South Wigston** Leics
40 D7 **South Willesborough** Kent
136 C3 **South Willingham** Lincs
169 L4 **South Wingate** Dur
133 G8 **South Wingfield** Derbys
118 B7 **South Witham** Lincs
107 K8 **Southwold** Suffk
34 F4 **South Wonston** Hants
107 H2 **Southwood** Norfk
31 J4 **Southwood** Somset
71 K7 **South Woodham Ferrers**
Essex
120 E7 **South Wootton** Norfk
46 B6 **South Wraxall** Wilts
12 F4 **South Zeal** Devon
141 G3 **Sowerby** Calder
160 F6 **Sowerby** N York
141 G3 **Sowerby Bridge** Calder
165 L3 **Sowerby Row** Cumb
147 G7 **Sower Carr** Lancs
28 F6 **Sowerhill** Somset
62 B7 **Sowhill** Torfn
88 D5 **Sowley Green** Suffk
141 G4 **Sowood** Calder
6 F2 **Sowton** Devon
14 A4 **Sowton** Devon
140 F4 **Soyland Town** Calder
122 F5 **Spa Common** Norfk
88 D7 **Spain's End** Essex
119 H7 **Spalding** Lincs
143 J1 **Spaldington** E R Yk
86 C1 **Spaldwick** Cambs
135 G6 **Spalford** Notts
118 E4 **Spanby** Lincs
49 G7 **Spanish Green** Hants
122 B7 **Sparham** Norfk
122 B7 **Sparhamill** Norfk
156 D5 **Spark Bridge** Cumb

166 B5 **Sparket** Cumb
31 K5 **Sparkford** Somset
98 E6 **Sparkhill** Birm
7 H3 **Sparkwell** Devon
121 L8 **Sparrow Green** Norfk
132 B4 **Sparrowpit** Derbys
39 G6 **Sparrows Green** E Susx
34 F4 **Sparsholt** Hants
47 M2 **Sparsholt** Oxon
167 K1 **Spartylea** Nthumb
115 H4 **Spath** Staffs
162 C5 **Spaunton** N York
30 C3 **Spaxton** Somset
239 L7 **Spean Bridge** Highld
21 K3 **Spear Hill** W Susx
34 D5 **Spearywell** Hants
67 K2 **Speen** Bucks
48 C5 **Speen** W Berk
163 L7 **Speeton** N York
129 K3 **Speke** Lpool
38 E5 **Speldhurst** Kent
70 C4 **Spellbrook** Herts
39 H6 **Spelmonden** Kent
65 M3 **Spelsbury** Oxon
141 K3 **Spen** Kirk
49 H5 **Spencers Wood** Wokham
130 F7 **Spen Green** Ches
159 L5 **Spennithorne** N York
169 H4 **Spennymoor** Dur
82 C3 **Spernall** Warwks
13 G3 **Spestos** Devon
81 K4 **Spetchley** Worcs
17 H2 **Spetisbury** Dorset
107 H7 **Spexhall** Suffk
267 G3 **Spey Bay** Moray
253 K6 **Speybridge** Highld
254 E3 **Speyview** Moray
137 G6 **Spilsby** Lincs
203 J6 **Spindlestone** Nthumb
133 J4 **Spinkhill** Derbys
263 J2 **Spinningdale** Highld
133 L6 **Spion Kop** Notts
46 E4 **Spirthill** Wilts
129 H3 **Spital** Wirral
134 C1 **Spital Hill** Donc
135 K2 **Spital in the Street** Lincs
23 G4 **Spithurst** E Susx
212 A4 **Spittal** E Loth
152 B5 **Spittal** E R Yk
279 L5 **Spittal** Highld
202 F3 **Spittal** Nthumb
55 G2 **Spittal** Pembks
233 H7 **Spittalfield** P & K
243 K6 **Spittal of Glenmuick** Abers
233 H2 **Spittal of Glenshee** P & K
189 G2 **Spittal-on-Rule** Border
122 E8 **Spixworth** Norfk
10 C7 **Splatt** Cnwll
11 J5 **Splatt** Cnwll
12 E2 **Splatt** Devon
23 G2 **Splayne's Green** E Susx
43 K6 **Splottlands** Cardif
130 E3 **Spodegreen** Ches
150 E5 **Spofforth** N York
116 C4 **Spondon** C Derb
129 G7 **Spon Green** Flints
106 B4 **Spooner Row** Norfk
105 G1 **Sporle** Norfk
212 E4 **Spott** E Loth
201 J3 **Spottiswoode** Border
84 D1 **Spratton** Nhants
36 B3 **Spreakley** Surrey
13 G3 **Spreyton** Devon
7 G4 **Spriddlestone** Devon
135 K3 **Spridlington** Lincs
209 G5 **Springburn** C Glas
177 K5 **Springfield** D & G
71 H5 **Springfield** Essex
222 F5 **Springfield** Fife
168 F5 **Spring Gardens** Dur
98 B3 **Springhill** Staffs
98 D2 **Springhill** Staffs
175 K1 **Springholm** D & G
196 D3 **Springside** N Ayrs
135 H2 **Springthorpe** Lincs
141 L7 **Spring Vale** Barns
181 G7 **Springwell** Sundld
145 F1 **Sproatley** E R Yk
130 E6 **Sproston Green** Ches
142 E7 **Sprotbrough** Donc
90 D6 **Sproughton** Suffk
202 B6 **Sprouston** Border
106 E1 **Sprowston** Norfk
117 M6 **Sproxton** Leics
161 K6 **Sproxton** N York
112 F5 **Spunhill** Shrops
130 A8 **Spurstow** Ches
15 M4 **Spyway** Dorset

74 D6 **Square & Compass** Pembks
97 G4 **Stableford** Shrops
114 C4 **Stableford** Staffs
132 F2 **Stacey Bank** Sheff
148 E3 **Stackhouse** N York
55 G7 **Stackpole** Pembks
105 L5 **Stacksford** Norfk
140 C3 **Stacksteads** Lancs
7 G4 **Staddiscombe** C Plym
143 L2 **Staddlethorpe** E R Yk
131 L5 **Staden** Derbys
66 F7 **Stadhampton** Oxon
283 b10 **Stadhlaigearraidh** W Isls
166 D2 **Staffield** Cumb
259 H3 **Staffin** Highld
114 E7 **Stafford** Staffs
85 J5 **Stagsden** Beds
141 M7 **Stainborough** Barns
164 D5 **Stainburn** Cumb
150 C6 **Stainburn** N York
118 B7 **Stainby** Lincs
141 M5 **Staincross** Barns
168 E6 **Staindrop** Dur
50 D5 **Staines** Surrey
118 E6 **Stainfield** Lincs
136 B5 **Stainfield** Lincs
143 G5 **Stainforth** Donc
148 E2 **Stainforth** N York
147 G8 **Staining** Lancs
141 G4 **Stainland** Calder
163 G1 **Stainsacre** N York
133 J6 **Stainsby** Derbys
157 H5 **Stainton** Cumb
166 C5 **Stainton** Cumb
177 L7 **Stainton** Cumb
133 L1 **Stainton** Donc
168 D7 **Stainton** Dur
170 B7 **Stainton** Middsb
159 K3 **Stainton** N York
135 L4 **Stainton by Langworth** Lincs
163 H3 **Staintondale** N York
136 C1 **Stainton le Vale** Lincs
146 E1 **Stainton with Adgarley** Cumb
165 H6 **Stair** Cumb
196 E6 **Stair** E Ayrs
142 B6 **Stairfoot** Barns
172 F4 **Stairhaven** D & G
171 H7 **Staithes** N York
181 G2 **Stakeford** Nthumb
147 H6 **Stake Pool** Lancs
19 M2 **Stakes** Hants
32 B7 **Stalbridge** Dorset
32 B7 **Stalbridge Weston** Dorset
123 H6 **Stalham** Norfk
123 H6 **Stalham Green** Norfk
40 B5 **Stalisfield Green** Kent
105 L4 **Stalland Common** Norfk
31 K7 **Stallen** Dorset
145 G2 **Stallingborough** NE Lin
159 G5 **Stalling Busk** N York
114 E4 **Stallington** Staffs
147 G6 **Stalmine** Lancs
147 G6 **Stalmine Moss Side** Lancs
140 E8 **Stalybridge** Tamesd
88 E7 **Stambourne** Essex
88 D7 **Stambourne Green** Essex
102 A2 **Stamford** Lincs
191 J2 **Stamford** Nthumb
129 L6 **Stamford Bridge** Ches
151 M5 **Stamford Bridge** E R Yk
180 C4 **Stamfordham** Nthumb
51 J2 **Stamford Hill** Gt Lon
147 G7 **Stanah** Lancs
69 G5 **Stanborough** Herts
68 B2 **Stanbridge** Beds
17 K2 **Stanbridge** Dorset
149 H8 **Stanbury** Brad
140 B6 **Stand** Bury
209 K5 **Stand** N Lans
210 B4 **Standburn** Falk
97 K2 **Standeford** Staffs
39 L5 **Standen** Kent
39 K7 **Standen Street** Kent
32 D1 **Standerwick** Somset
36 B4 **Standford** Hants
164 D4 **Standingstone** Cumb
64 A5 **Standish** Gloucs
139 H5 **Standish** Wigan
139 H6 **Standish Lower Ground** Wigan
66 B6 **Standlake** Oxon
34 F5 **Standon** Hants
69 K3 **Standon** Herts
114 C4 **Standon** Staffs
69 K3 **Standon Green End** Herts

90 D1 **Standwell Green** Suffk
210 A7 **Stane** N Lans
121 K7 **Stanfield** Norfk
86 D7 **Stanford** Beds
40 F7 **Stanford** Kent
95 H1 **Stanford** Shrops
80 F5 **Stanford Bishop** Herefs
81 G2 **Stanford Bridge** Worcs
113 M6 **Stanford Bridge** Wrekin
48 E4 **Stanford Dingley** W Berk
65 M8 **Stanford in the Vale** Oxon
52 E3 **Stanford le Hope** Thurr
100 D7 **Stanford on Avon** Nhants
116 F7 **Stanford on Soar** Notts
81 G2 **Stanford on Teme** Worcs
70 D7 **Stanford Rivers** Essex
133 J5 **Stanfree** Derbys
170 F7 **Stanghow** R & Cl
102 D4 **Stanground** C Pete
139 L2 **Stanhill** Lancs
121 H4 **Stanhoe** Norfk
199 K7 **Stanhope** Border
168 C3 **Stanhope** Dur
40 C7 **Stanhope** Kent
115 M7 **Stanhope Bretby** Derbys
101 K6 **Stanion** Nhants
97 J8 **Stanklin** Worcs
116 C3 **Stanley** Derbys
180 F8 **Stanley** Dur
133 J7 **Stanley** Notts
221 K1 **Stanley** P & K
97 G6 **Stanley** Shrops
114 E1 **Stanley** Staffs
142 A3 **Stanley** Wakefd
116 C3 **Stanley Common** Derbys
168 F3 **Stanley Crook** Dur
142 A3 **Stanley Ferry** Wakefd
138 F6 **Stanley Gate** Lancs
114 E1 **Stanley Moor** Staffs
64 E1 **Stanley Pontlarge** Gloucs
22 E5 **Stanmer** Br & H
68 F8 **Stanmore** Gt Lon
34 F5 **Stanmore** Hants
48 C3 **Stanmore** W Berk
179 G2 **Stannersburn** Nthumb
89 H4 **Stanningfield** Suffk
141 K1 **Stanningley** Leeds
180 F3 **Stannington** Nthumb
132 F2 **Stannington** Sheff
180 F3 **Stannington Station** Nthumb
79 L3 **Stansbatch** Herefs
88 F5 **Stansfield** Suffk
115 J1 **Stanshope** Staffs
89 G5 **Stanstead** Suffk
69 K5 **Stanstead Abbotts** Herts
89 G5 **Stanstead Street** Suffk
52 D6 **Stansted** Kent
70 D2 **Stansted Mountfitchet** Essex
115 M7 **Stanton** Derbys
82 C8 **Stanton** Gloucs
62 C3 **Stanton** Mons
191 G8 **Stanton** Nthumb
115 J2 **Stanton** Staffs
105 K8 **Stanton** Suffk
116 B6 **Stanton by Bridge** Derbys
116 D4 **Stanton by Dale** Derbys
45 H6 **Stanton Drew** BaNES
47 J1 **Stanton Fitzwarren** Swindn
66 B6 **Stanton Harcourt** Oxon
133 J7 **Stanton Hill** Notts
132 E6 **Stanton in Peak** Derbys
96 B7 **Stanton Lacy** Shrops
132 E7 **Stanton Lees** Derbys
96 D5 **Stanton Long** Shrops
117 G5 **Stanton on the Wolds** Notts
45 K6 **Stanton Prior** BaNES
47 G6 **Stanton St Bernard** Wilts
66 E5 **Stanton St John** Oxon
46 C3 **Stanton St Quintin** Wilts
89 J2 **Stanton Street** Suffk
100 A1 **Stanton under Bardon** Leics
113 J6 **Stanton upon Hine Heath** Shrops
45 J6 **Stanton Wick** BaNES
63 L4 **Stantway** Gloucs
112 F6 **Stanwardine in the Field** Shrops
113 G6 **Stanwardine in the Wood** Shrops
72 D2 **Stanway** Essex
64 F1 **Stanway** Gloucs
72 D2 **Stanway Green** Essex
90 F1 **Stanway Green** Suffk
50 D4 **Stanwell** Surrey

50 D4 **Stanwell Moor** Surrey
85 J1 **Stanwick** Nhants
177 L7 **Stanwix** Cumb
283 b10 **Staoinebrig** W Isls
162 D4 **Stape** N York
17 L2 **Stapehill** Dorset
113 L2 **Stapeley** Ches
115 L7 **Stapenhill** Staffs
41 J4 **Staple** Kent
29 K3 **Staple** Somset
29 J6 **Staple Cross** Devon
24 E3 **Staple Cross** E Susx
37 L5 **Staplefield** W Susx
30 C7 **Staple Fitzpaine** Somset
87 K5 **Stapleford** Cambs
69 J4 **Stapleford** Herts
117 L7 **Stapleford** Leics
135 H8 **Stapleford** Lincs
116 E4 **Stapleford** Notts
33 J3 **Stapleford** Wilts
70 D8 **Stapleford Abbotts** Essex
70 D7 **Stapleford Tawney** Essex
30 B5 **Staplegrove** Somset
30 B6 **Staplehay** Somset
98 B8 **Staple Hill** Worcs
39 K5 **Staplehurst** Kent
19 H6 **Staplers** IoW
40 D3 **Staplestreet** Kent
178 C4 **Staplet** Cumb
79 L2 **Stapleton** Herefs
99 L4 **Stapleton** Leics
169 H8 **Stapleton** N York
95 L3 **Stapleton** Shrops
31 G6 **Stapleton** Somset
30 B8 **Stapley** Somset
86 C3 **Staploe** Beds
80 F7 **Staplow** Herefs
222 E6 **Star** Fife
75 M5 **Star** Pembks
44 E7 **Star** Somset
150 D4 **Starbeck** N York
159 G7 **Starbotton** N York
14 A6 **Starcross** Devon
83 H1 **Stareton** Warwks
132 F7 **Starkholmes** Derbys
140 A5 **Starling** Bury
70 C1 **Starlings Green** Essex
24 D4 **Starr's Green** E Susx
106 E6 **Starston** Norfk
8 B6 **Start** Devon
168 D7 **Startforth** Dur
46 D3 **Startley** Wilts
41 J4 **Statenborough** Kent
130 D2 **Statham** Warrtn
30 E5 **Stathe** Somset
117 K5 **Stathern** Leics
169 L3 **Station Town** Dur
86 C2 **Staughton Green** Cambs
86 C2 **Staughton Highway** Cambs
63 H4 **Staunton** Gloucs
64 A1 **Staunton** Gloucs
117 L3 **Staunton in the Vale** Notts
79 L3 **Staunton on Arrow** Herefs
79 L6 **Staunton on Wye** Herefs
156 E5 **Staveley** Cumb
157 G3 **Staveley** Cumb
133 H5 **Staveley** Derbys
150 E3 **Staveley** N York
8 B2 **Staverton** Devon
64 C2 **Staverton** Gloucs
83 M3 **Staverton** Nhants
46 B6 **Staverton** Wilts
64 C3 **Staverton Bridge** Gloucs
30 E3 **Stawell** Somset
29 J6 **Stawley** Somset
280 E5 **Staxigoe** Highld
163 J6 **Staxton** N York
92 E5 **Staylittle** Cerdgn
93 J5 **Staylittle** Powys
147 G7 **Staynall** Lancs
117 K1 **Staythorpe** Notts
149 L6 **Stead** Brad
159 K8 **Stean** N York
151 K2 **Stearsby** N York
30 C2 **Steart** Somset
71 G2 **Stebbing** Essex
71 G2 **Stebbing Green** Essex
98 E6 **Stechford** Birm
39 L5 **Stede Quarter** Kent
36 C6 **Stedham** W Susx
179 L7 **Steel** Nthumb
38 E7 **Steel Cross** E Susx
210 D1 **Steelend** Fife
188 F7 **Steele Road** Border
155 L6 **Steel Green** Cumb
113 J4 **Steel Heath** Shrops

80 C4 **Steen's Bridge** Herefs
35 M6 **Steep** Hants
19 J8 **Steephill** IoW
140 F3 **Steep Lane** Calder
17 H6 **Steeple** Dorset
72 D6 **Steeple** Essex
46 C7 **Steeple Ashton** Wilts
66 C2 **Steeple Aston** Oxon
66 C2 **Steeple Barton** Oxon
88 D7 **Steeple Bumpstead** Essex
67 H2 **Steeple Claydon** Bucks
102 C7 **Steeple Gidding** Cambs
33 H3 **Steeple Langford** Wilts
86 F6 **Steeple Morden** Cambs
149 J7 **Steeton** Brad
258 D5 **Stein** Highld
180 E6 **Stella** Gatesd
40 F6 **Stelling Minnis** Kent
30 F6 **Stembridge** Somset
5 G3 **Stenalees** Cnwll
185 K4 **Stenhouse** D & G
210 A2 **Stenhousemuir** Falk
136 D3 **Stenigot** Lincs
259 H3 **Stenscholl** Highld
116 B5 **Stenson Fields** Derbys
212 D4 **Stenton** E Loth
282 g3 **Steornabhagh** W Isls
55 K5 **Stepaside** Pembks
51 K3 **Stepney** Gt Lon
131 H2 **Stepping Hill** Stockp
85 K8 **Steppingley** Beds
209 H5 **Stepps** N Lans
91 J3 **Sternfield** Suffk
27 K2 **Sterridge** Devon
46 F7 **Stert** Wilts
88 C3 **Stetchworth** Cambs
69 G2 **Stevenage** Herts
24 C4 **Steven's Crouch** E Susx
196 B3 **Stevenston** N Ayrs
35 H1 **Steventon** Hants
48 C1 **Steventon** Oxon
88 B6 **Steventon End** Essex
85 K4 **Stevington** Beds
85 K6 **Stewartby** Beds
209 G7 **Stewartfield** S Lans
196 E2 **Stewarton** E Ayrs
67 K2 **Stewkley** Bucks
30 D7 **Stewley** Somset
137 G2 **Stewton** Lincs
19 L6 **Steyne Cross** IoW
21 L4 **Steyning** W Susx
54 E5 **Steynton** Pembks
26 C8 **Stibb** Cnwll
121 L6 **Stibbard** Norfk
27 G7 **Stibb Cross** Devon
47 J6 **Stibb Green** Wilts
102 B4 **Stibbington** Cambs
201 L5 **Stichill** Border
5 G5 **Sticker** Cnwll
136 F7 **Stickford** Lincs
12 F4 **Sticklepath** Devon
29 J4 **Sticklepath** Somset
87 K8 **Stickling Green** Essex
136 F8 **Stickney** Lincs
121 L3 **Stiffkey** Norfk
81 G5 **Stifford's Bridge** Herefs
53 J6 **Stiff Street** Kent
39 J4 **Stile Bridge** Kent
31 G3 **Stileway** Somset
283 b10 **Stilligarry** W Isls
151 J7 **Stillingfleet** N York
151 J2 **Stillington** N York
169 K6 **Stillington** S on T
102 D5 **Stilton** Cambs
63 L7 **Stinchcombe** Gloucs
16 D4 **Stinsford** Dorset
95 J3 **Stiperstones** Shrops
98 D7 **Stirchley** Birm
96 F2 **Stirchley** Wrekin
257 L3 **Stirling** Abers
220 D8 **Stirling** Stirlg
86 D2 **Stirtloe** Cambs
149 H5 **Stirton** N York
71 J2 **Stisted** Essex
47 K5 **Stitchcombe** Wilts
3 J4 **Stithians** Cnwll
6 C2 **St Ive Cross** Cnwll
99 J8 **Stivichall** Covtry
136 C6 **Stixwould** Lincs
129 K5 **Stoak** Ches
199 L5 **Stobo** Border
17 H5 **Stoborough** Dorset
17 H5 **Stoborough Green** Dorset
188 B6 **Stobs Castle** Border
191 J7 **Stobswood** Nthumb
71 G7 **Stock** Essex
44 F6 **Stock** N Som
34 D4 **Stockbridge** Hants

198 C6 **Stockbriggs** S Lans
53 H6 **Stockbury** Kent
48 B5 **Stockcross** W Berk
3 K4 **Stockdale** Cnwll
165 L2 **Stockdalewath** Cumb
40 C5 **Stocker's Hill** Kent
101 H4 **Stockerston** Leics
82 A3 **Stock Green** Worcs
63 J1 **Stocking** Herefs
99 J5 **Stockingford** Warwks
84 F5 **Stocking Green** M Keyn
70 C1 **Stocking Pelham** Herts
14 F2 **Stockland** Devon
30 C2 **Stockland Bristol** Somset
38 E5 **Stockland Green** Kent
13 K1 **Stockleigh English** Devon
13 K2 **Stockleigh Pomeroy** Devon
46 E5 **Stockley** Wilts
79 L7 **Stockley Hill** Herefs
30 F7 **Stocklinch** Somset
79 M4 **Stockmoor** Herefs
131 H2 **Stockport** Stockp
141 L8 **Stocksbridge** Sheff
180 C6 **Stocksfield** Nthumb
80 C3 **Stockton** Herefs
107 H4 **Stockton** Norfk
95 G3 **Stockton** Shrops
97 G3 **Stockton** Shrops
83 K3 **Stockton** Warwks
33 G3 **Stockton** Wilts
114 B8 **Stockton** Wrekin
114 E1 **Stockton Brook** Staffs
130 B3 **Stockton Heath** Warrtn
170 B6 **Stockton-on-Tees** S on T
81 G2 **Stockton on Teme** Worcs
151 L4 **Stockton on the Forest** York
64 D4 **Stockwell** Gloucs
97 K3 **Stockwell End** Wolves
115 G7 **Stockwell Heath** Staffs
45 J5 **Stockwood** Bristl
16 B1 **Stockwood** Dorset
82 B3 **Stock Wood** Worcs
147 J4 **Stodday** Lancs
41 H3 **Stodmarsh** Kent
122 B4 **Stody** Norfk
270 D2 **Stoer** Highld
31 J8 **Stoford** Somset
33 J4 **Stoford** Wilts
29 K3 **Stogumber** Somset
30 B2 **Stogursey** Somset
99 K7 **Stoke** Covtry
26 D6 **Stoke** Devon
20 B6 **Stoke** Hants
48 B8 **Stoke** Hants
53 H4 **Stoke** Medway
15 K2 **Stoke Abbott** Dorset
101 H5 **Stoke Albany** Nhants
90 D1 **Stoke Ash** Suffk
117 H3 **Stoke Bardolph** Notts
80 F3 **Stoke Bliss** Worcs
84 E5 **Stoke Bruerne** Nhants
88 E6 **Stoke by Clare** Suffk
89 K7 **Stoke-by-Nayland** Suffk
13 L3 **Stoke Canon** Devon
35 G3 **Stoke Charity** Hants
11 L7 **Stoke Climsland** Cnwll
80 E5 **Stoke Cross** Herefs
50 E7 **Stoke D'Abernon** Surrey
102 A6 **Stoke Doyle** Nhants
101 J4 **Stoke Dry** Rutlnd
80 E7 **Stoke Edith** Herefs
98 F4 **Stoke End** Warwks
33 H5 **Stoke Farthing** Wilts
104 D3 **Stoke Ferry** Norfk
8 C5 **Stoke Fleming** Devon
17 G5 **Stokeford** Dorset
8 C3 **Stoke Gabriel** Devon
45 J3 **Stoke Gifford** S Glos
99 L4 **Stoke Golding** Leics
85 G5 **Stoke Goldington** M Keyn
50 B3 **Stoke Green** Bucks
134 F4 **Stokeham** Notts
67 L1 **Stoke Hammond** Bucks
113 L5 **Stoke Heath** Shrops
81 L2 **Stoke Heath** Worcs
106 E3 **Stoke Holy Cross** Norfk
13 L8 **Stokeinteignhead** Devon
80 E5 **Stoke Lacy** Herefs
66 E2 **Stoke Lyne** Oxon
67 K5 **Stoke Mandeville** Bucks
67 J7 **Stokenchurch** Bucks
51 J2 **Stoke Newington** Gt Lon
8 B6 **Stokenham** Devon
114 D2 **Stoke-on-Trent** C Stke
64 D2 **Stoke Orchard** Gloucs
50 B2 **Stoke Poges** Bucks
81 M2 **Stoke Pound** Worcs

80 C4 **Stoke Prior** Herefs
81 L2 **Stoke Prior** Worcs
27 L4 **Stoke Rivers** Devon
118 B6 **Stoke Rochford** Lincs
49 G2 **Stoke Row** Oxon
30 E5 **Stoke St Gregory** Somset
30 C6 **Stoke St Mary** Somset
31 L2 **Stoke St Michael** Somset
96 D7 **Stoke St Milborough** Shrops
95 K7 **Stokesay** Shrops
107 J1 **Stokesby** Norfk
161 H1 **Stokesley** N York
31 G7 **Stoke sub Hamdon** Somset
67 G7 **Stoke Talmage** Oxon
32 B5 **Stoke Trister** Somset
113 L6 **Stoke upon Tern** Shrops
114 D3 **Stoke-upon-Trent** C Stke
16 E1 **Stoke Wake** Dorset
81 L2 **Stoke Wharf** Worcs
30 C2 **Stolford** Somset
70 E7 **Stondon Massey** Essex
67 J4 **Stone** Bucks
63 K8 **Stone** Gloucs
25 H2 **Stone** Kent
52 C4 **Stone** Kent
133 L2 **Stone** Rothm
31 J4 **Stone** Somset
114 E5 **Stone** Staffs
97 J8 **Stone** Worcs
103 J5 **Stonea** Cambs
30 F1 **Stone Allerton** Somset
45 J8 **Ston Easton** Somset
44 D7 **Stonebridge** N Som
105 J5 **Stonebridge** Norfk
99 G6 **Stonebridge** Warwks
102 F3 **Stone Bridge Corner** C Pete
133 H7 **Stonebroom** Derbys
141 H2 **Stone Chair** Calder
23 K6 **Stone Cross** E Susx
38 D7 **Stone Cross** E Susx
39 G7 **Stone Cross** E Susx
38 E5 **Stone Cross** Kent
40 D7 **Stone Cross** Kent
41 K4 **Stone Cross** Kent
89 G4 **Stonecross Green** Suffk
39 H6 **Stonecrouch** Kent
44 F4 **Stone-edge-Batch** N Som
144 E2 **Stoneferry** C KuH
206 D5 **Stonefield Castle Hotel** Ag & B
39 G7 **Stonegate** E Susx
162 D1 **Stonegate** N York
161 L7 **Stonegrave** N York
81 K5 **Stonehall** Worcs
179 J4 **Stonehaugh** Nthumb
245 J6 **Stonehaven** Abers
143 H6 **Stone Hill** Donc
6 F4 **Stonehouse** C Plym
158 D5 **Stone House** Cumb
64 A6 **Stonehouse** Gloucs
179 G7 **Stonehouse** Nthumb
198 C4 **Stonehouse** S Lans
83 H1 **Stoneleigh** Warwks
113 K1 **Stoneley Green** Ches
86 C2 **Stonely** Cambs
35 M5 **Stoner Hill** Hants
117 L6 **Stonesby** Leics
66 B4 **Stonesfield** Oxon
73 H2 **Stones Green** Essex
38 F2 **Stone Street** Kent
89 K6 **Stone Street** Suffk
89 K7 **Stone Street** Suffk
107 H7 **Stone Street** Suffk
40 E7 **Stonestreet Green** Kent
165 J7 **Stonethwaite** Cumb
266 F3 **Stonewells** Moray
52 D4 **Stonewood** Kent
283 b10 **Stoneybridge** W Isls
97 L8 **Stoneybridge** Worcs
210 C6 **Stoneyburn** W Loth
18 D1 **Stoney Cross** Hants
100 D3 **Stoneygate** C Leic
72 D7 **Stoneyhills** Essex
172 D4 **Stoneykirk** D & G
132 E4 **Stoney Middleton** Derbys
100 B4 **Stoney Stanton** Leics
32 B4 **Stoney Stoke** Somset
31 L3 **Stoney Stratton** Somset
95 J2 **Stoney Stretton** Shrops
245 K1 **Stoneywood** C Aber
209 L2 **Stoneywood** Falk
90 D3 **Stonham Aspal** Suffk
98 D3 **Stonnall** Staffs
49 H1 **Stonor** Oxon
101 G4 **Stonton Wyville** Leics
80 D2 **Stony Cross** Herefs

81 G5 **Stony Cross** Herefs
34 D7 **Stonyford** Hants
133 K6 **Stony Houghton** Derbys
84 F7 **Stony Stratford** M Keyn
98 D1 **Stonywell** Staffs
28 B4 **Stoodleigh** Devon
29 G7 **Stoodleigh** Devon
21 H3 **Stopham** W Susx
68 E2 **Stopsley** Luton
10 C7 **Stoptide** Cnwll
129 G3 **Storeton** Wirral
81 G6 **Storeyard Green** Herefs
138 F6 **Stormy Corner** Lancs
282 g3 **Stornoway** W Isls
81 H5 **Storridge** Herefs
21 J4 **Storrington** W Susx
157 G6 **Storth** Cumb
151 M7 **Storwood** E R Yk
266 E2 **Stotfield** Moray
86 E7 **Stotfold** Beds
96 F6 **Stottesdon** Shrops
100 E3 **Stoughton** Leics
50 C8 **Stoughton** Surrey
20 C4 **Stoughton** W Susx
238 B5 **Stoul** Highld
81 L5 **Stoulton** Worcs
97 K6 **Stourbridge** Dudley
17 G1 **Stourpaine** Dorset
81 J1 **Stourport-on-Severn** Worcs
32 C6 **Stour Provost** Dorset
32 D6 **Stour Row** Dorset
141 M2 **Stourton** Leeds
97 K6 **Stourton** Staffs
83 G7 **Stourton** Warwks
32 C4 **Stourton** Wilts
32 B7 **Stourton Caundle** Dorset
31 G4 **Stout** Somset
281 e8 **Stove** Shet
107 J7 **Stoven** Suffk
200 F4 **Stow** Border
135 H3 **Stow** Lincs
104 C2 **Stow Bardolph** Norfk
105 J4 **Stow Bedon** Norfk
104 B2 **Stowbridge** Norfk
87 L3 **Stow-cum-Quy** Cambs
63 H5 **Stowe** Gloucs
95 H8 **Stowe** Shrops
114 F6 **Stowe by Chartley** Staffs
84 C3 **Stowehill** Nhants
31 L6 **Stowell** Somset
45 H7 **Stowey** BaNES
12 B3 **Stowford** Devon
12 B5 **Stowford** Devon
14 D4 **Stowford** Devon
28 B3 **Stowford** Devon
89 J2 **Stowlangtoft** Suffk
86 C1 **Stow Longa** Cambs
71 K7 **Stow Maries** Essex
90 B3 **Stowmarket** Suffk
65 J2 **Stow-on-the-Wold** Gloucs
40 F7 **Stowting** Kent
40 F6 **Stowting Common** Kent
90 C3 **Stowupland** Suffk
253 J8 **Straanruie** Highld
234 F2 **Stracathro Hospital** Angus
244 F5 **Strachan** Abers
217 H6 **Strachur** Ag & B
106 E8 **Stradbroke** Suffk
46 D8 **Stradbrook** Wilts
88 B3 **Stradishall** Suffk
104 D2 **Stradsett** Norfk
118 B1 **Stragglethorpe** Lincs
117 H4 **Stragglethorpe** Notts
47 L4 **Straight Soley** Wilts
211 J5 **Straiton** Mdloth
183 K2 **Straiton** S Ayrs
256 F7 **Straloch** Abers
232 F3 **Straloch** P & K
115 H4 **Stramshall** Staffs
154 e6 **Strang** IoM
140 B7 **Strangeways** Salfd
63 H2 **Strangford** Herefs
172 C3 **Stranraer** D & G
77 K2 **Strata Florida** Cerdgn
49 G6 **Stratfield Mortimer** W Berk
49 G6 **Stratfield Saye** Hants
49 G7 **Stratfield Turgis** Hants
86 D5 **Stratford** Beds
51 K2 **Stratford** Gt Lon
91 H3 **Stratford St Andrew** Suffk
90 B8 **Stratford St Mary** Suffk
33 K4 **Stratford sub Castle** Wilts
33 J5 **Stratford Tony** Wilts
82 F4 **Stratford-upon-Avon** Warwks
260 C4 **Strath** Highld

270 E4 **Strathan** Highld
277 K3 **Strathan** Highld
197 K2 **Strathaven** S Lans
208 F3 **Strathblane** Stirlg
270 F7 **Strathcanaird** Highld
248 F3 **Strathcarron** Highld
227 K6 **Strathcoil** Ag & B
243 K1 **Strathdon** Abers
223 H4 **Strathkinness** Fife
210 B4 **Strathloanhead** W Loth
241 G5 **Strathmashie House** Highld
222 C5 **Strathmiglo** Fife
262 E8 **Strathpeffer** Highld
232 D4 **Strathtay** P & K
195 G4 **Strathwhillan** N Ayrs
278 E3 **Strathy** Highld
278 E3 **Strathy Inn** Highld
219 J4 **Strathyre** Stirlg
11 J1 **Stratton** Cnwll
16 C4 **Stratton** Dorset
64 E6 **Stratton** Gloucs
66 F2 **Stratton Audley** Oxon
31 L1 **Stratton-on-the-Fosse**
Somset
47 H2 **Stratton St Margaret**
Swindn
106 D4 **Stratton St Michael** Norfk
122 E7 **Stratton Strawless** Norfk
223 J4 **Stravithie** Fife
29 K3 **Stream** Somset
22 E4 **Streat** E Susx
51 J4 **Streatham** Gt Lon
68 D2 **Streatley** Beds
48 E3 **Streatley** W Berk
14 E5 **Street** Devon
147 K5 **Street** Lancs
162 C2 **Street** N York
31 H3 **Street** Somset
99 M7 **Street Ashton** Warwks
112 E4 **Street Dinas** Shrops
23 K3 **Street End** E Susx
40 F4 **Street End** Kent
20 D7 **Street End** W Susx
180 F7 **Street Gate** Gatesd
98 F1 **Streethay** Staffs
151 H6 **Street Houses** N York
160 D3 **Streetlam** N York
116 C2 **Street Lane** Derbys
98 D4 **Streetly** Wsall
88 C5 **Streetly End** Cambs
31 K3 **Street on the Fosse** Somset
95 K6 **Strefford** Shrops
233 J8 **Strelitz** P & K
116 E3 **Strelley** Notts
151 K4 **Strensall** York
81 L7 **Strensham** Worcs
30 D2 **Stretcholt** Somset
8 C5 **Strete** Devon
80 B4 **Stretford** Herefs
80 C4 **Stretford** Herefs
130 F1 **Stretford** Traffd
87 K7 **Strethall** Essex
103 K8 **Stretham** Cambs
20 E5 **Strettington** W Susx
113 G1 **Stretton** Ches
133 H7 **Stretton** Derbys
118 B8 **Stretton** Rutlnd
97 K1 **Stretton** Staffs
115 L6 **Stretton** Staffs
130 C3 **Stretton** Warrtn
99 J1 **Stretton en le Field** Leics
80 E6 **Stretton Grandison** Herefs
83 J1 **Stretton-on-Dunsmore**
Warwks
82 F7 **Stretton on Fosse** Warwks
80 B6 **Stretton Sugwas** Herefs
99 M7 **Stretton under Fosse**
Warwks
96 D4 **Stretton Westwood** Shrops
269 H5 **Strichen** Abers
131 J2 **Strines** Stockp
30 B2 **Stringston** Somset
85 H3 **Strixton** Nhants
63 H7 **Stroat** Gloucs
248 D5 **Stromeferry** Highld
275 b4 **Stromness** Ork
218 F5 **Stronachlachar** Stirlg
207 G3 **Stronafian** Ag & B
271 H4 **Stronchrubie** Highld
207 K3 **Strone** Ag & B
239 J7 **Strone** Highld
239 L6 **Stronenaba** Highld
217 J2 **Stronmilchan** Ag & B
228 C3 **Strontian** Highld
39 L7 **Strood** Kent
52 F5 **Strood** Medway
37 J1 **Strood Green** Surrey
36 F6 **Strood Green** W Susx

64 B6 **Stroud** Gloucs
35 L6 **Stroud** Hants
50 C5 **Stroude** Surrey
53 J1 **Stroud Green** Essex
64 A5 **Stroud Green** Gloucs
118 B5 **Stroxton** Lincs
246 D1 **Struan** Highld
232 B2 **Struan** P & K
137 H3 **Strubby** Lincs
107 G2 **Strumpshaw** Norfk
198 C3 **Strutherhill** S Lans
222 F5 **Struthers** Fife
250 C4 **Struy** Highld
124 F3 **Stryd-y-Facsen** IoA
112 D2 **Stryt-issa** Wrexhm
257 H3 **Stuartfield** Abers
98 D3 **Stubbers Green** Wsall
19 J3 **Stubbington** Hants
140 B4 **Stubbins** Lancs
106 E4 **Stubbs Green** Norfk
32 F8 **Stubhampton** Dorset
133 G4 **Stubley** Derbys
139 H7 **Stubshaw Cross** Wigan
118 A2 **Stubton** Lincs
29 G6 **Stuckeridge** Devon
33 L8 **Stuckton** Hants
148 E2 **Studfold** N York
49 L3 **Stud Green** W & M
68 C4 **Studham** Beds
177 H7 **Studholme** Cumb
17 K6 **Studland** Dorset
82 C2 **Studley** Warwks
46 D4 **Studley** Wilts
82 C2 **Studley Common** Warwks
150 C2 **Studley Roger** N York
150 C2 **Studley Royal** N York
103 L7 **Stuntney** Cambs
23 K4 **Stunts Green** E Susx
114 C5 **Sturbridge** Staffs
135 H2 **Sturgate** Lincs
88 D6 **Sturmer** Essex
32 C8 **Sturminster Common**
Dorset
17 J2 **Sturminster Marshall**
Dorset
32 C8 **Sturminster Newton**
Dorset
41 G3 **Sturry** Kent
144 B7 **Sturton** N Linc
135 H4 **Sturton by Stow** Lincs
134 F3 **Sturton le Steeple** Notts
106 C7 **Stuston** Suffk
151 G7 **Stutton** N York
90 D8 **Stutton** Suffk
131 G3 **Styal** Ches
148 A8 **Stydd** Lancs
267 G4 **Stynie** Moray
134 C2 **Styrrup** Notts
218 D6 **Succoth** Ag & B
81 G5 **Suckley** Worcs
81 G4 **Suckley Green** Worcs
101 L7 **Sudborough** Nhants
91 J4 **Sudbourne** Suffk
118 C3 **Sudbrook** Lincs
45 G2 **Sudbrook** Mons
135 L4 **Sudbrooke** Lincs
115 K5 **Sudbury** Derbys
50 F2 **Sudbury** Gt Lon
89 H7 **Sudbury** Suffk
140 C5 **Sudden** Rochdl
81 J3 **Suddington** Worcs
64 D5 **Sudgrove** Gloucs
163 H4 **Suffield** N York
122 E5 **Suffield** Norfk
113 K8 **Sugdon** Wrekin
114 B5 **Sugnall** Staffs
80 B6 **Sugwas Pool** Herefs
247 J5 **Suisnish** Highld
154 e3 **Sulby** IoM
84 A6 **Sulgrave** Nhants
48 F4 **Sulham** W Berk
48 F5 **Sulhamstead** W Berk
48 F5 **Sulhamstead Abbots**
W Berk
48 F5 **Sulhamstead Bannister**
W Berk
21 J4 **Sullington** W Susx
281 d4 **Sullom** Shet
281 d4 **Sullom Voe** Shet
43 J8 **Sully** V Glam
150 B3 **Summerbridge** N York
4 E4 **Summercourt** Cnwll
121 G4 **Summerfield** Norfk
97 J8 **Summerfield** Worcs
49 H1 **Summer Heath** Bucks
98 D2 **Summerhill** Staffs
112 D1 **Summer Hill** Wrexhm
169 G6 **Summerhouse** Darltn

157 H5 **Summerlands** Cumb
133 G4 **Summerley** Derbys
20 D5 **Summersdale** W Susx
140 B5 **Summerseat** Bury
66 D5 **Summertown** Oxon
140 D6 **Summit** Oldham
140 E4 **Summit** Rochdl
157 L1 **Sunbiggin** Cumb
50 E5 **Sunbury** Surrey
185 K6 **Sundaywell** D & G
204 C3 **Sunderland** Ag & B
165 G4 **Sunderland** Cumb
147 H4 **Sunderland** Lancs
181 K7 **Sunderland** Sundld
169 H3 **Sunderland Bridge** Dur
200 D8 **Sundhope** Border
68 D2 **Sundon Park** Luton
38 D2 **Sundridge** Kent
145 H4 **Sunk Island** E R Yk
50 B5 **Sunningdale** W & M
50 B5 **Sunninghill** W & M
66 D7 **Sunningwell** Oxon
168 F3 **Sunniside** Dur
180 F7 **Sunniside** Gatesd
140 A4 **Sunny Bank** Lancs
169 G4 **Sunny Brow** Dur
116 B5 **Sunnyhill** C Derb
139 K3 **Sunnyhurst** Bl w D
220 D7 **Sunnylaw** Stirlg
66 D5 **Sunnymead** Oxon
47 K8 **Sunton** Wilts
50 F5 **Surbiton** Gt Lon
119 H6 **Surfleet** Lincs
119 J6 **Surfleet Seas End** Lincs
107 G2 **Surlingham** Norfk
72 C3 **Surrex** Essex
122 D4 **Sustead** Norfk
143 L7 **Susworth** Lincs
26 F8 **Sutcombe** Devon
26 F8 **Sutcombemill** Devon
106 B4 **Suton** Norfk
137 G5 **Sutterby** Lincs
119 J4 **Sutterton** Lincs
86 E5 **Sutton** Beds
102 B4 **Sutton** C Pete
103 J7 **Sutton** Cambs
7 K6 **Sutton** Devon
13 G2 **Sutton** Devon
142 E5 **Sutton** Donc
23 H7 **Sutton** E Susx
51 H6 **Sutton** Gt Lon
41 K5 **Sutton** Kent
142 D3 **Sutton** N York
123 H6 **Sutton** Norfk
117 K4 **Sutton** Notts
66 B6 **Sutton** Oxon
54 E4 **Sutton** Pembks
96 C1 **Sutton** Shrops
97 G6 **Sutton** Shrops
112 E6 **Sutton** Shrops
113 L5 **Sutton** Shrops
129 M1 **Sutton** St Hel
114 B7 **Sutton** Staffs
91 G6 **Sutton** Suffk
21 G4 **Sutton** W Susx
52 C5 **Sutton at Hone** Kent
101 G5 **Sutton Bassett** Nhants
46 D3 **Sutton Benger** Wilts
31 J8 **Sutton Bingham** Somset
116 E6 **Sutton Bonington** Notts
120 B7 **Sutton Bridge** Lincs
99 L3 **Sutton Cheney** Leics
98 E4 **Sutton Coldfield** Birm
66 D8 **Sutton Courtenay** Oxon
119 M7 **Sutton Crosses** Lincs
134 D3 **Sutton cum Lound** Notts
116 E6 **Sutton Fields** Notts
66 B5 **Sutton Green** Oxon
50 C8 **Sutton Green** Surrey
112 F2 **Sutton Green** Wrexhm
160 D6 **Sutton Howgrave** N York
133 K7 **Sutton in Ashfield** Notts
149 H7 **Sutton-in-Craven** N York
100 B4 **Sutton in the Elms** Leics
131 H5 **Sutton Lane Ends** Ches
97 G3 **Sutton Maddock** Shrops
30 E3 **Sutton Mallet** Somset
33 G5 **Sutton Mandeville** Wilts
129 L2 **Sutton Manor** St Hel
80 D6 **Sutton Marsh** Herefs
31 K6 **Sutton Montis** Somset
144 E1 **Sutton-on-Hull** C KuH
137 K3 **Sutton on Sea** Lincs
151 J3 **Sutton-on-the-Forest**
N York
115 L5 **Sutton on the Hill** Derbys
134 F6 **Sutton on Trent** Notts
16 D5 **Sutton Poyntz** Dorset

103 H1 **Sutton St Edmund** Lincs
119 L7 **Sutton St James** Lincs
80 C6 **Sutton St Nicholas**
Herefs
34 F3 **Sutton Scotney** Hants
39 K2 **Sutton Street** Kent
83 G7 **Sutton-under-Brailes**
Warwks
161 G6 **Sutton-under-
Whitestonecliffe** N York
151 L6 **Sutton upon Derwent**
E R Yk
39 K3 **Sutton Valence** Kent
32 E3 **Sutton Veny** Wilts
32 E7 **Sutton Waldron** Dorset
130 A4 **Sutton Weaver** Ches
45 H7 **Sutton Wick** BaNES
66 C8 **Sutton Wick** Oxon
137 G4 **Swaby** Lincs
116 A7 **Swadlincote** Derbys
105 G2 **Swaffham** Norfk
87 L3 **Swaffham Bulbeck** Cambs
88 B2 **Swaffham Prior** Cambs
122 F5 **Swafield** Norfk
161 G2 **Swainby** N York
80 B7 **Swainshill** Herefs
106 E3 **Swainsthorpe** Norfk
45 M5 **Swainswick** BaNES
83 J7 **Swalcliffe** Oxon
40 F2 **Swalecliffe** Kent
144 F7 **Swallow** Lincs
135 J6 **Swallow Beck** Lincs
33 G5 **Swallowcliffe** Wilts
49 H6 **Swallowfield** Wokham
133 J3 **Swallow Nest** Rothm
70 F7 **Swallows Cross** Essex
34 E1 **Swampton** Hants
17 K6 **Swanage** Dorset
67 K2 **Swanbourne** Bucks
43 J8 **Swanbridge** V Glam
97 G4 **Swancote** Shrops
130 E5 **Swan Green** Ches
144 C2 **Swanland** E R Yk
52 B5 **Swanley** Kent
52 B5 **Swanley Village** Kent
35 J7 **Swanmore** Hants
116 C8 **Swannington** Leics
122 C7 **Swannington** Norfk
135 J6 **Swanpool Garden Suburb**
Lincs
52 D4 **Swanscombe** Kent
57 J6 **Swansea** Swans
72 C2 **Swan Street** Essex
122 F6 **Swanton Abbot** Norfk
121 M8 **Swanton Morley** Norfk
121 M5 **Swanton Novers** Norfk
53 J7 **Swanton Street** Kent
98 C5 **Swan Village** Sandw
116 C1 **Swanwick** Derbys
19 H2 **Swanwick** Hants
118 D3 **Swarby** Lincs
106 D3 **Swardeston** Norfk
116 B6 **Swarkestone** Derbys
191 H6 **Swarland** Nthumb
191 H5 **Swarland Estate** Nthumb
35 H3 **Swarraton** Hants
149 J6 **Swartha** Brad
156 C7 **Swarthmoor** Cumb
118 F4 **Swaton** Lincs
87 G2 **Swavesey** Cambs
18 D4 **Sway** Hants
118 C7 **Swayfield** Lincs
34 F7 **Swaythling** C Sotn
80 F3 **Sweet Green** Worcs
13 K3 **Sweetham** Devon
38 D7 **Sweethaws** E Susx
39 K4 **Sweetlands Corner** Kent
11 G3 **Sweets** Cnwll
5 J3 **Sweetshouse** Cnwll
91 H3 **Swefling** Suffk
99 K1 **Swepstone** Leics
66 A1 **Swerford** Oxon
130 F6 **Swettenham** Ches
61 K7 **Swffryd** Blae G
39 L4 **Swift's Green** Kent
90 E4 **Swilland** Suffk
138 F1 **Swillbrook** Lancs
142 B2 **Swillington** Leeds
27 L5 **Swimbridge** Devon
27 L5 **Swimbridge Newland**
Devon
65 L4 **Swinbrook** Oxon
141 K2 **Swincliffe** Kirk
150 C4 **Swincliffe** N York
28 B3 **Swincombe** Devon
148 E5 **Swinden** N York
135 H7 **Swinderby** Lincs
64 D2 **Swindon** Gloucs

190 D6 **Swindon** Nthumb
97 J5 **Swindon** Staffs
47 H2 **Swindon** Swindn
153 J8 **Swine** E R Yk
143 J3 **Swinefleet** E R Yk
45 K5 **Swineford** S Glos
85 L2 **Swineshead** Beds
119 H3 **Swineshead** Lincs
119 H3 **Swineshead Bridge** Lincs
275 H1 **Swiney** Highld
100 C7 **Swinford** Leics
66 C5 **Swinford** Oxon
41 G6 **Swingfield Minnis** Kent
41 H6 **Swingfield Street** Kent
89 K6 **Swingleton Green** Suffk
203 K7 **Swinhoe** Nthumb
145 G8 **Swinhope** Lincs
159 J5 **Swinithwaite** N York
80 F7 **Swinmore Common** Herefs
115 J2 **Swinscoe** Staffs
165 H6 **Swinside** Cumb
118 D7 **Swinstead** Lincs
135 L4 **Swinthorpe** Lincs
202 C4 **Swinton** Border
160 B6 **Swinton** N York
162 D8 **Swinton** N York
142 C7 **Swinton** Rothm
140 A7 **Swinton** Salfd
100 C1 **Swithland** Leics
263 G6 **Swordale** Highld
238 B5 **Swordland** Highld
278 C4 **Swordly** Highld
130 D3 **Sworton Heath** Ches
77 J2 **Swyddffynnon** Cerdgn
49 G1 **Swyncombe** Oxon
114 D4 **Swynnerton** Staffs
15 M5 **Swyre** Dorset
112 B6 **Sycharth** Powys
93 L7 **Sychnant** Powys
94 B2 **Sychtyn** Powys
129 G8 **Sydallt** Wrexhm
64 D5 **Syde** Gloucs
51 K4 **Sydenham** Gt Lon
67 H6 **Sydenham** Oxon
12 A7 **Sydenham Damerel** Devon
36 E4 **Sydenhurst** Surrey
121 H5 **Syderstone** Norfk
16 C3 **Sydling St Nicholas** Dorset
48 C7 **Sydmonton** Hants
97 H2 **Sydnal Lane** Shrops
117 K2 **Syerston** Notts
140 D4 **Syke** Rochdl
143 G4 **Sykehouse** Donc
106 E7 **Syleham** Suffk
56 F3 **Sylen** Carmth
281 e5 **Symbister** Shet
196 D5 **Symington** S Ayrs
199 G6 **Symington** S Lans
15 K4 **Symondsbury** Dorset
63 H4 **Symonds Yat** Herefs
150 A8 **Sympson Green** Brad
15 J2 **Synderford** Dorset
76 D4 **Synod Inn** Cerdgn
278 B7 **Syre** Highld
64 F3 **Syreford** Gloucs
84 C7 **Syresham** Nhants
100 D1 **Syston** Leics
118 B3 **Syston** Lincs
81 J2 **Sytchampton** Worcs
84 F2 **Sywell** Nhants

T

130 E4 **Tabley Hill** Ches
66 C3 **Tackley** Oxon
106 C4 **Tacolneston** Norfk
151 G7 **Tadcaster** N York
132 C5 **Taddington** Derbys
65 G1 **Taddington** Gloucs
27 H7 **Taddiport** Devon
48 F6 **Tadley** Hants
86 F5 **Tadlow** Cambs
83 J7 **Tadmarton** Oxon
45 L5 **Tadwick** BaNES
51 G7 **Tadworth** Surrey
61 H5 **Tafarnaubach** Blae G
75 J5 **Tafarn-y-bwlch** Pembks
128 E7 **Tafarn-y-Gelyn** Denbgs
43 H5 **Taff's Well** Rhondd
93 J3 **Tafolwern** Powys
57 L7 **Taibach** Neath
263 L3 **Tain** Highld
280 B3 **Tain** Highld
282 e5 **Tairbeart** W Isls
60 F2 **Tai'r Bull** Powys
70 E3 **Takeley** Essex
70 E3 **Takeley Street** Essex

78 F8 **Talachddu** Powys
128 D3 **Talacre** Flints
14 C3 **Talaton** Devon
54 D4 **Talbenny** Pembks
43 G5 **Talbot Green** Rhondd
17 L4 **Talbot Village** Bmouth
14 C3 **Taleford** Devon
93 K3 **Talerddig** Powys
76 D5 **Talgarreg** Cerdgn
79 G8 **Talgarth** Powys
246 D3 **Talisker** Highld
114 C1 **Talke** Staffs
114 C1 **Talke Pits** Staffs
178 D7 **Talkin** Cumb
260 E6 **Talladale** Highld
187 H2 **Talla Linnfoots** Border
183 K3 **Tallaminnock** S Ayrs
113 G3 **Tallarn Green** Wrexhm
164 F4 **Tallentire** Cumb
59 H2 **Talley** Carmth
102 B2 **Tallington** Lincs
112 D2 **Tallwrn** Wrexhm
277 K4 **Talmine** Highld
58 B3 **Talog** Carmth
77 G4 **Talsarn** Cerdgn
109 L4 **Talsarnau** Gwynd
4 E2 **Talskiddy** Cnwll
125 J4 **Talwrn** IoA
112 F2 **Talwrn** Wrexhm
92 E5 **Tal-y-bont** Cerdgn
126 F6 **Tal-y-Bont** Conwy
109 L7 **Tal-y-bont** Gwynd
126 C5 **Tal-y-bont** Gwynd
61 H3 **Talybont-on-Usk** Powys
126 F5 **Tal-y-Cafn** Conwy
62 E4 **Tal-y-coed** Mons
42 F5 **Tal-y-garn** Rhondd
92 F2 **Tal-y-llyn** Gwynd
109 J1 **Talysarn** Gwynd
61 L6 **Tal-y-Waun** Torfn
93 H3 **Talywern** Powys
139 J7 **Tamer Lane End** Wigan
6 F3 **Tamerton Foliot** C Plym
99 G3 **Tamworth** Staffs
119 L3 **Tamworth Green** Lincs
151 G4 **Tancred** N York
74 E7 **Tancredston** Pembks
38 B3 **Tandridge** Surrey
180 F7 **Tanfield** Dur
180 F8 **Tanfield Lea** Dur
54 F3 **Tangiers** Pembks
47 L8 **Tangley** Hants
20 E5 **Tangmere** W Susx
283 b13 **Tangusdale** W Isls
158 F1 **Tan Hill** N York
275 d4 **Tankerness** Ork
142 A7 **Tankersley** Barns
40 F2 **Tankerton** Kent
280 D6 **Tannach** Highld
245 H6 **Tannachie** Abers
234 D4 **Tannadice** Angus
98 D8 **Tanner's Green** Worcs
90 F2 **Tannington** Suffk
209 J6 **Tannochside** N Lans
132 F7 **Tansley** Derbys
102 B5 **Tansor** Nhants
180 E7 **Tantobie** Dur
170 C8 **Tanton** N York
97 K8 **Tanwood** Worcs
82 D1 **Tanworth in Arden** Warwks
110 C3 **Tan-y-Bwlch** Gwynd
127 J6 **Tan-y-fron** Conwy
112 D1 **Tan-y-fron** Wrexhm
110 C3 **Tan-y-grisiau** Gwynd
76 B5 **Tan-y-groes** Cerdgn
282 d6 **Taobh Tuath** W Isls
49 M3 **Taplow** Bucks
205 L6 **Tarbert** Ag & B
206 D5 **Tarbert** Ag & B
282 e5 **Tarbert** W Isls
218 D6 **Tarbet** Ag & B
238 C5 **Tarbet** Highld
276 B6 **Tarbet** Highld
129 K2 **Tarbock Green** Knows
196 E5 **Tarbolton** S Ayrs
199 H2 **Tarbrax** S Lans
82 B2 **Tardebigge** Worcs
244 B7 **Tarfside** Angus
244 B3 **Tarland** Abers
138 F4 **Tarleton** Lancs
138 E5 **Tarlscough** Lancs
64 D7 **Tarlton** Gloucs
44 D8 **Tarnock** Somset
164 F1 **Tarns** Cumb
156 F4 **Tarnside** Cumb
130 A7 **Tarporley** Ches
28 F4 **Tarr** Somset
29 K5 **Tarr** Somset

17 H2 **Tarrant Crawford** Dorset
32 F8 **Tarrant Gunville** Dorset
32 F8 **Tarrant Hinton** Dorset
17 H2 **Tarrant Keyneston** Dorset
17 J1 **Tarrant Launceston** Dorset
17 J1 **Tarrant Monkton** Dorset
17 H1 **Tarrant Rawston** Dorset
17 H1 **Tarrant Rushton** Dorset
23 G6 **Tarring Neville** E Susx
80 E7 **Tarrington** Herefs
247 J6 **Tarskavaig** Highld
256 F5 **Tarves** Abers
232 F3 **Tarvie** P & K
129 L6 **Tarvin** Ches
129 L6 **Tarvin Sands** Ches
106 D4 **Tasburgh** Norfk
96 F4 **Tasley** Shrops
65 M3 **Taston** Oxon
115 K7 **Tatenhill** Staffs
84 F6 **Tathall End** M Keyn
147 M2 **Tatham** Lancs
136 F3 **Tathwell** Lincs
51 L7 **Tatsfield** Surrey
129 L7 **Tattenhall** Ches
121 J6 **Tatterford** Norfk
121 J5 **Tattersett** Norfk
136 D8 **Tattershall** Lincs
136 C8 **Tattershall Bridge** Lincs
136 D7 **Tattershall Thorpe** Lincs
90 D7 **Tattingstone** Suffk
90 D7 **Tattingstone White Horse** Suffk
15 H1 **Tatworth** Somset
267 H6 **Tauchers** Moray
30 C6 **Taunton** Somset
122 D8 **Taverham** Norfk
70 E3 **Taverners Green** Essex
55 L4 **Tavernspite** Pembks
12 C7 **Tavistock** Devon
12 F3 **Taw Green** Devon
27 K5 **Tawstock** Devon
131 K4 **Taxal** Derbys
217 G3 **Taychreggan Hotel** Ag & B
205 M7 **Tayinloan** Ag & B
63 L3 **Taynton** Gloucs
65 K4 **Taynton** Oxon
216 F1 **Taynuilt** Ag & B
223 H2 **Tayport** Fife
215 L7 **Tayvallich** Ag & B
136 C2 **Tealby** Lincs
181 G7 **Team Valley** Gatesd
247 K6 **Teangue** Highld
263 G6 **Teanord** Highld
157 K2 **Tebay** Cumb
68 C2 **Tebworth** Beds
13 J4 **Tedburn St Mary** Devon
81 M8 **Teddington** Gloucs
50 F5 **Teddington** Gt Lon
80 F3 **Tedstone Delamere** Herefs
80 F3 **Tedstone Wafer** Herefs
170 D6 **Teesport** R & Cl
170 B7 **Teesside Park** S on T
84 D1 **Teeton** Nhants
33 G4 **Teffont Evias** Wilts
33 G4 **Teffont Magna** Wilts
75 L5 **Tegryn** Pembks
117 M8 **Teigh** Rutlnd
12 F5 **Teigncombe** Devon
13 K7 **Teigngrace** Devon
13 L7 **Teignmouth** Devon
188 D4 **Teindside** Border
96 F2 **Telford** Wrekin
46 A7 **Tellisford** Somset
22 F6 **Telscombe** E Susx
22 F7 **Telscombe Cliffs** E Susx
231 J4 **Tempar** P & K
176 E2 **Templand** D & G
11 K7 **Temple** Cnwll
211 K7 **Temple** Mdloth
99 G8 **Temple Balsall** Solhll
76 F4 **Temple Bar** Cerdgn
45 J7 **Temple Cloud** BaNES
32 B6 **Templecombe** Somset
88 D5 **Temple End** Suffk
41 J6 **Temple Ewell** Kent
82 D4 **Temple Grafton** Warwks
65 G2 **Temple Guiting** Gloucs
142 F3 **Temple Hirst** N York
133 H6 **Temple Normanton** Derbys
245 H7 **Temple of Fiddes** Abers
250 F5 **Temple Pier** Highld
166 E5 **Temple Sowerby** Cumb
28 F8 **Templeton** Devon
55 J4 **Templeton** Pembks
168 E1 **Templetown** Dur
86 D4 **Tempsford** Beds
80 E2 **Tenbury Wells** Worcs
55 K6 **Tenby** Pembks

73 H2 **Tendring** Essex
73 H2 **Tendring Green** Essex
73 H2 **Tendring Heath** Essex
104 B4 **Ten Mile Bank** Norfk
73 G3 **Tenpenny Heath** Essex
39 M6 **Tenterden** Kent
71 J4 **Terling** Essex
113 K8 **Tern** Wrekin
113 L5 **Ternhill** Shrops
176 B3 **Terregles** D & G
151 L2 **Terrington** N York
120 C7 **Terrington St Clement** Norfk
104 A1 **Terrington St John** Norfk
98 E8 **Terry's Green** Warwks
39 H3 **Teston** Kent
34 D7 **Testwood** Hants
64 C8 **Tetbury** Gloucs
64 C8 **Tetbury Upton** Gloucs
112 F5 **Tetchill** Shrops
11 L3 **Tetcott** Devon
136 F5 **Tetford** Lincs
145 J7 **Tetney** Lincs
145 J7 **Tetney Lock** Lincs
67 G6 **Tetsworth** Oxon
97 K3 **Tettenhall** Wolves
97 K3 **Tettenhall Wood** Wolves
86 E4 **Tetworth** Cambs
133 J7 **Teversal** Notts
87 K3 **Teversham** Cambs
188 C5 **Teviothead** Border
69 H4 **Tewin** Herts
81 K8 **Tewkesbury** Gloucs
40 B3 **Teynham** Kent
149 M8 **Thackley** Brad
164 F6 **Thackthwaite** Cumb
166 A5 **Thackthwaite** Cumb
21 J3 **Thakeham** W Susx
67 H6 **Thame** Oxon
50 F5 **Thames Ditton** Surrey
52 A3 **Thamesmead** Gt Lon
40 F4 **Thanington** Kent
199 G5 **Thankerton** S Lans
106 D4 **Tharston** Norfk
48 D5 **Thatcham** W Berk
129 L1 **Thatto Heath** St Hel
70 F1 **Thaxted** Essex
160 D5 **Theakston** N York
143 M4 **Thealby** N Linc
31 G2 **Theale** Somset
48 F5 **Theale** W Berk
153 G8 **Thearne** E R Yk
131 G8 **The Bank** Ches
96 E3 **The Bank** Shrops
64 F6 **The Beeches** Gloucs
91 K2 **Theberton** Suffk
115 G6 **The Blythe** Staffs
95 J4 **The Bog** Shrops
82 A4 **The Bourne** Worcs
247 H2 **The Braes** Highld
97 K4 **The Bratch** Staffs
80 C3 **The Broad** Herefs
212 F4 **The Brunt** E Loth
154 e5 **The Bungalow** IoM
64 C4 **The Butts** Gloucs
64 C5 **The Camp** Gloucs
113 H3 **The Chequer** Wrexhm
86 C3 **The City** Beds
67 J7 **The City** Bucks
65 L2 **The Common** Oxon
34 B4 **The Common** Wilts
46 F2 **The Common** Wilts
39 H5 **The Corner** Kent
95 K6 **The Corner** Shrops
154 d3 **The Cronk** IoM
100 E6 **Theddingworth** Leics
137 J2 **Theddlethorpe All Saints** Lincs
137 J2 **Theddlethorpe St Helen** Lincs
196 C1 **The Den** N Ayrs
79 L3 **The Forge** Herefs
40 A6 **The Forstal** Kent
40 D7 **The Forstal** Kent
113 L5 **The Fouralls** Shrops
156 A5 **The Green** Cumb
71 J3 **The Green** Essex
162 D2 **The Green** N York
32 E4 **The Green** Wilts
81 K7 **The Grove** Worcs
37 G5 **The Haven** W Susx
64 B2 **The Haw** Gloucs
170 C4 **The Headland** Hartpl
156 A6 **The Hill** Cumb
49 K3 **The Holt** Wokham
80 C2 **The Hundred** Herefs
28 D8 **Thelbridge Cross** Devon
40 C8 **The Leacon** Kent

67 L6 **The Lee** Bucks
154 e2 **The Lhen** IoM
105 L7 **Thelnetham** Suffk
266 F4 **The Lochs** Moray
106 D7 **Thelveton** Norfk
130 C2 **Thelwall** Warrtn
95 H4 **The Marsh** Powys
122 B6 **Themelthorpe** Norfk
180 F8 **The Middles** Dur
39 J7 **The Moor** Kent
57 H7 **The Mumbles** Swans
209 H8 **The Murray** S Lans
81 K8 **The Mythe** Gloucs
63 G6 **The Narth** Mons
245 G4 **The Neuk** Abers
83 M7 **Thenford** Nhants
46 F5 **Theobald's Green** Wilts
63 L7 **The Quarry** Gloucs
39 M4 **The Quarter** Kent
64 C3 **The Reddings** Gloucs
87 G7 **Therfield** Herts
61 J1 **The Rhôs** Powys
220 D3 **The Ross** P & K
36 C2 **The Sands** Surrey
46 A4 **The Shoe** Wilts
96 F4 **The Smithies** Shrops
87 K5 **The Spike** Cambs
83 G1 **The Spring** Warwks
62 B7 **The Square** Torfn
38 F4 **The Stair** Kent
25 G2 **The Stocks** Kent
36 A3 **The Straits** Hants
46 D7 **The Strand** Wilts
105 H6 **Thetford** Norfk
165 L2 **Thethwaite** Cumb
2 E3 **The Towans** Cnwll
80 C5 **The Vauld** Herefs
97 G2 **The Wyke** Shrops
70 C7 **Theydon Bois** Essex
151 L7 **Thicket Priory** N York
46 B4 **Thickwood** Wilts
136 D5 **Thimbleby** Lincs
161 G3 **Thimbleby** N York
129 G3 **Thingwall** Wirral
161 G6 **Thirkleby** N York
161 G6 **Thirlby** N York
201 H4 **Thirlestane** Border
160 B5 **Thirn** N York
160 F6 **Thirsk** N York
144 F1 **Thirtleby** E R Yk
147 H8 **Thistleton** Lancs
118 B7 **Thistleton** Rutlnd
104 D8 **Thistley Green** Suffk
152 C4 **Thixendale** N York
179 M3 **Thockrington** Nthumb
103 H2 **Tholomas Drove** Cambs
151 G2 **Tholthorpe** N York
55 J5 **Thomas Chapel** Pembks
166 B3 **Thomas Close** Cumb
255 L4 **Thomastown** Abers
82 C3 **Thomas Town** Warwks
105 J4 **Thompson** Norfk
52 E5 **Thong** Kent
159 H5 **Thoralby** N York
134 C5 **Thoresby** Notts
137 J4 **Thoresthorpe** Lincs
144 F8 **Thoresway** Lincs
145 G8 **Thorganby** Lincs
151 L7 **Thorganby** N York
162 C3 **Thorgill** N York
107 J8 **Thorington** Suffk
89 K8 **Thorington Street** Suffk
149 H5 **Thorlby** N York
70 C3 **Thorley** Herts
18 F6 **Thorley** IoW
70 C3 **Thorley Houses** Herts
18 F6 **Thorley Street** IoW
161 H7 **Thormanby** N York
170 B7 **Thornaby-on-Tees** S on T
122 B4 **Thornage** Norfk
84 E8 **Thornborough** Bucks
160 D6 **Thornborough** N York
141 J1 **Thornbury** Brad
12 A1 **Thornbury** Devon
80 E3 **Thornbury** Herefs
45 J1 **Thornbury** S Glos
177 J8 **Thornby** Cumb
100 E8 **Thornby** Nhants
131 K7 **Thorncliff** Staffs
15 J2 **Thorncombe** Dorset
36 F3 **Thorncombe Street** Surrey
86 C5 **Thorncott Green** Beds
19 G7 **Thorncross** IoW
90 D1 **Thorndon** Suffk
12 D4 **Thorndon Cross** Devon
143 H5 **Thorne** Donc
31 H7 **Thorne** Somset
7 M2 **Thornecroft** Devon

27 G7 **Thornehillhead** Devon
150 E7 **Thorner** Leeds
98 D3 **Thornes** Staffs
141 M4 **Thornes** Wakefd
29 K6 **Thorne St Margaret** Somset
50 D3 **Thorney** Bucks
102 F3 **Thorney** C Pete
135 G5 **Thorney** Notts
30 F6 **Thorney** Somset
18 B4 **Thorney Hill** Hants
103 G3 **Thorney Toll** Cambs
30 D6 **Thornfalcon** Somset
31 K8 **Thornford** Dorset
179 H6 **Thorngrafton** Nthumb
30 E4 **Thorngrove** Somset
145 G3 **Thorngumbald** E R Yk
121 G3 **Thornham** Norfk
90 C1 **Thornham Magna** Suffk
90 D1 **Thornham Parva** Suffk
102 B3 **Thornhaugh** C Pete
19 G1 **Thornhill** C Sotn
43 J5 **Thornhill** Caerph
186 C7 **Thornhill** D & G
132 D3 **Thornhill** Derbys
141 L4 **Thornhill** Kirk
219 L7 **Thornhill** Stirlg
141 K4 **Thornhill Lees** Kirk
141 J3 **Thornhills** Calder
153 H3 **Thornholme** E R Yk
17 G2 **Thornicombe** Dorset
202 D6 **Thornington** Nthumb
168 E3 **Thornley** Dur
169 K3 **Thornley** Dur
179 J7 **Thornley Gate** Nthumb
208 F7 **Thornliebank** E Rens
88 E4 **Thorns** Suffk
131 K2 **Thornsett** Derbys
130 F3 **Thorns Green** Ches
165 H5 **Thornthwaite** Cumb
149 L4 **Thornthwaite** N York
234 B6 **Thornton** Angus
141 H1 **Thornton** Brad
84 E8 **Thornton** Bucks
152 A6 **Thornton** E R Yk
222 E7 **Thornton** Fife
146 F7 **Thornton** Lancs
100 A2 **Thornton** Leics
136 D6 **Thornton** Lincs
170 B7 **Thornton** Middsb
202 E4 **Thornton** Nthumb
54 E5 **Thornton** Pembks
138 D7 **Thornton** Sefton
144 D4 **Thornton Curtis** N Linc
129 K5 **Thornton Green** Ches
209 G8 **Thorntonhall** S Lans
51 J5 **Thornton Heath** Gt Lon
129 G3 **Thornton Hough** Wirral
148 F6 **Thornton-in-Craven** N York
158 B8 **Thornton in Lonsdale** N York
160 F4 **Thornton-le-Beans** N York
151 L3 **Thornton-le-Clay** N York
162 E6 **Thornton le Dale** N York
144 D8 **Thornton le Moor** Lincs
160 F5 **Thornton-le-Moor** N York
129 K5 **Thornton-le-Moors** Ches
160 F5 **Thornton-le-Street** N York
213 G4 **Thorntonloch** E Loth
159 G5 **Thornton Rust** N York
160 A5 **Thornton Steward** N York
160 C5 **Thornton Watlass** N York
70 C6 **Thornwood Common** Essex
201 J3 **Thornydykes** Border
165 L6 **Thornythwaite** Cumb
117 K3 **Thoroton** Notts
150 F6 **Thorp Arch** Leeds
115 J2 **Thorpe** Derbys
152 F6 **Thorpe** E R Yk
137 J3 **Thorpe** Lincs
149 H3 **Thorpe** N York
107 J4 **Thorpe** Norfk
117 K2 **Thorpe** Notts
50 C5 **Thorpe** Surrey
106 D7 **Thorpe Abbotts** Norfk
116 E7 **Thorpe Acre** Leics
117 K7 **Thorpe Arnold** Leics
142 D4 **Thorpe Audlin** Wakefd
162 F8 **Thorpe Bassett** N York
53 K2 **Thorpe Bay** Sthend
101 K4 **Thorpe by Water** Rutlnd
133 G1 **Thorpe Common** Rothm
99 H2 **Thorpe Constantine** Staffs
106 F1 **Thorpe End** Norfk
73 H3 **Thorpe Green** Essex
139 H3 **Thorpe Green** Lancs

89 J4 **Thorpe Green** Suffk
142 B8 **Thorpe Hesley** Rothm
142 F5 **Thorpe in Balne** Donc
101 G5 **Thorpe Langton** Leics
169 K5 **Thorpe Larches** Dur
50 C5 **Thorpe Lea** Surrey
135 H4 **Thorpe le Fallows** Lincs
73 J3 **Thorpe-le-Soken** Essex
152 C7 **Thorpe le Street** E R Yk
101 H7 **Thorpe Malsor** Nhants
83 M6 **Thorpe Mandeville** Nhants
122 E4 **Thorpe Market** Norfk
122 D8 **Thorpe Marriot** Norfk
89 J4 **Thorpe Morieux** Suffk
91 L3 **Thorpeness** Suffk
141 M2 **Thorpe on the Hill** Leeds
135 H6 **Thorpe on the Hill** Lincs
106 F2 **Thorpe St Andrew** Norfk
137 J7 **Thorpe St Peter** Lincs
133 K3 **Thorpe Salvin** Rothm
100 F1 **Thorpe Satchville** Leics
169 L6 **Thorpe Thewles** S on T
136 B8 **Thorpe Tilney** Lincs
151 G4 **Thorpe Underwood** N York
101 H7 **Thorpe Underwood** Nhants
102 A7 **Thorpe Waterville** Nhants
142 F2 **Thorpe Willoughby** N York
104 C2 **Thorpland** Norfk
73 G3 **Thorrington** Essex
13 L2 **Thorverton** Devon
68 E4 **Thrales End** Beds
106 C3 **Thrandeston** Suffk
101 M7 **Thrapston** Nhants
165 G3 **Threapland** Cumb
149 H4 **Threapland** N York
113 G3 **Threapwood** Ches
115 G3 **Threapwood** Staffs
115 G3 **Threapwood Head** Staffs
183 J2 **Threave** S Ayrs
63 G3 **Three Ashes** Herefs
37 L3 **Three Bridges** W Susx
4 B5 **Three Burrows** Cnwll
39 K5 **Three Chimneys** Kent
79 G7 **Three Cocks** Powys
57 G6 **Three Crosses** Swans
23 L3 **Three Cups Corner** E Susx
80 F3 **Three Gates** Worcs
123 G7 **Threehammer Common** Norfk
11 J5 **Three Hammers** Cnwll
103 K3 **Three Holes** Norfk
118 E4 **Threekingham** Lincs
39 H7 **Three Leg Cross** E Susx
17 L1 **Three Legged Cross** Dorset
49 H5 **Three Mile Cross** Wokham
4 C6 **Three Milestone** Cnwll
210 E4 **Three Miletown** W Loth
24 C4 **Three Oaks** E Susx
201 G4 **Threepwood** Border
165 K5 **Threlkeld** Cumb
70 D5 **Threshers Bush** Essex
149 H3 **Threshfield** N York
107 J1 **Thrigby** Norfk
167 L6 **Thringarth** Dur
116 D8 **Thringstone** Leics
160 D4 **Thrintoft** N York
87 J6 **Thriplow** Cambs
133 K2 **Throapham** Rothm
103 G2 **Throckenhalt** Lincs
69 J1 **Throcking** Herts
180 E5 **Throckley** N u Ty
82 A5 **Throckmorton** Worcs
17 M3 **Throop** Bmouth
16 F4 **Throop** Dorset
180 D2 **Throphill** Nthumb
190 E5 **Thropton** Nthumb
209 M1 **Throsk** Stirlg
64 D5 **Througham** Gloucs
185 L6 **Throughgate** D & G
12 F4 **Throwleigh** Devon
40 C4 **Throwley** Kent
40 C4 **Throwley Forstal** Kent
116 E5 **Thrumpton** Notts
134 D4 **Thrumpton** Notts
280 D7 **Thrumster** Highld
145 J6 **Thrunscoe** NE Lin
190 F4 **Thrunton** Nthumb
65 L7 **Thrup** Oxon
64 B6 **Thrupp** Gloucs
66 C2 **Thrupp** Oxon
12 B5 **Thrushelton** Devon
117 H8 **Thrussington** Leics
34 C2 **Thruxton** Hants
80 B8 **Thruxton** Herefs
142 D8 **Thrybergh** Rothm
116 C5 **Thulston** Derbys
53 G1 **Thundersley** Essex
100 C1 **Thurcaston** Leics

133 K2 **Thurcroft** Rothm
26 E8 **Thurdon** Cnwll
122 D4 **Thurgarton** Norfk
117 J2 **Thurgarton** Notts
141 L7 **Thurgoland** Barns
100 B4 **Thurlaston** Leics
83 L1 **Thurlaston** Warwks
30 C6 **Thurlbear** Somset
118 E8 **Thurlby** Lincs
135 H7 **Thurlby** Lincs
137 J4 **Thurlby** Lincs
85 L3 **Thurleigh** Beds
7 K6 **Thurlestone** Devon
88 D5 **Thurlow** Suffk
30 C5 **Thurloxton** Somset
141 K7 **Thurlstone** Barns
107 J4 **Thurlton** Norfk
130 F8 **Thurlwood** Ches
100 D2 **Thurmaston** Leics
100 E3 **Thurnby** Leics
123 H8 **Thurne** Norfk
53 H7 **Thurnham** Kent
102 B6 **Thurning** Nhants
122 B5 **Thurning** Norfk
142 C6 **Thurnscoe** Barns
165 K1 **Thursby** Cumb
140 D1 **Thursden** Lancs
121 L5 **Thursford** Norfk
36 D3 **Thursley** Surrey
279 K3 **Thurso** Highld
128 F3 **Thurstaston** Wirral
89 J2 **Thurston** Suffk
140 E6 **Thurston Clough** Oldham
177 K7 **Thurstonfield** Cumb
141 J5 **Thurstonland** Kirk
89 J2 **Thurston Planch** Suffk
107 G3 **Thurton** Norfk
115 L4 **Thurvaston** Derbys
105 L2 **Thuxton** Norfk
158 F3 **Thwaite** N York
90 D2 **Thwaite** Suffk
156 E4 **Thwaite Head** Cumb
149 K7 **Thwaites** Brad
107 G4 **Thwaite St Mary** Norfk
149 K7 **Thwaites Brow** Brad
153 G2 **Thwing** E R Yk
221 J3 **Tibbermore** P & K
186 C6 **Tibbers** D & G
63 M3 **Tibberton** Gloucs
81 L4 **Tibberton** Worcs
113 L7 **Tibberton** Wrekin
187 K2 **Tibbie Shiels Inn** Border
106 C5 **Tibenham** Norfk
133 J7 **Tibshelf** Derbys
152 E5 **Tibthorpe** E R Yk
39 H7 **Ticehurst** E Susx
35 H5 **Tichborne** Hants
101 L2 **Tickencote** Rutlnd
44 F4 **Tickenham** N Som
85 H6 **Tickford End** M Keyn
134 B1 **Tickhill** Donc
96 B5 **Ticklerton** Shrops
116 B6 **Ticknall** Derbys
153 G7 **Tickton** E R Yk
98 E8 **Tidbury Green** Solhll
47 L7 **Tidcombe** Wilts
67 G6 **Tiddington** Oxon
82 F4 **Tiddington** Warwks
46 C4 **Tiddleywink** Wilts
38 F7 **Tidebrook** E Susx
6 C3 **Tideford** Cnwll
6 C3 **Tideford Cross** Cnwll
63 H7 **Tidenham** Gloucs
132 C4 **Tideswell** Derbys
48 F4 **Tidmarsh** W Berk
83 G7 **Tidmington** Warwks
33 J7 **Tidpit** Hants
34 B1 **Tidworth** Wilts
54 E5 **Tiers Cross** Pembks
84 D5 **Tiffield** Nhants
234 E2 **Tigerton** Angus
282 b7 **Tigh a Ghearraidh** W Isls
282 b7 **Tigharry** W Isls
206 F4 **Tighnabruaich** Ag & B
7 L3 **Tigley** Devon
86 B2 **Tilbrook** Cambs
52 D4 **Tilbury** Thurr
88 E7 **Tilbury Green** Essex
88 F7 **Tilbury Juxta Clare** Essex
98 F6 **Tile Cross** Birm
99 H7 **Tile Hill** Covtry
98 F8 **Tilehouse Green** Solhll
49 G4 **Tilehurst** Readg
36 C2 **Tilford** Surrey
37 L4 **Tilgate** W Susx
37 L4 **Tilgate Forest Row** W Susx
31 J4 **Tilham Street** Somset
80 F8 **Tillers Green** Gloucs

221 G7 **Tillicoultry** Clacks
198 D4 **Tillietudlem** S Lans
72 E6 **Tillingham** Essex
80 B6 **Tillington** Herefs
36 E6 **Tillington** W Susx
80 B6 **Tillington Common** Herefs
244 F2 **Tillybirloch** Abers
244 A4 **Tillycairn** Abers
244 E1 **Tillyfourie** Abers
256 F7 **Tillygreig** Abers
221 K6 **Tillyrie** P & K
41 J5 **Tilmanstone** Kent
120 C7 **Tilney All Saints** Norfk
120 C8 **Tilney High End** Norfk
120 C8 **Tilney St Lawrence** Norfk
33 H1 **Tilshead** Wilts
113 J4 **Tilstock** Shrops
113 G1 **Tilston** Ches
130 A7 **Tilstone Bank** Ches
130 A7 **Tilstone Fearnall** Ches
68 B2 **Tilsworth** Beds
101 G2 **Tilton on the Hill** Leics
64 B7 **Tiltups End** Gloucs
70 E2 **Tilty** Essex
136 B7 **Timberland** Lincs
131 H7 **Timbersbrook** Ches
29 G2 **Timberscombe** Somset
149 M5 **Timble** N York
29 H5 **Timewell** Devon
177 K4 **Timpanheck** D & G
130 F2 **Timperley** Traffd
45 K7 **Timsbury** BaNES
34 D6 **Timsbury** Hants
282 d3 **Timsgarry** W Isls
282 d3 **Timsgearraidh** W Isls
89 H2 **Timworth** Suffk
89 H2 **Timworth Green** Suffk
16 E4 **Tincleton** Dorset
178 E7 **Tindale** Cumb
169 G5 **Tindale Crescent** Dur
84 C8 **Tingewick** Bucks
141 L3 **Tingley** Leeds
68 C1 **Tingrith** Beds
12 A5 **Tinhay** Devon
34 E2 **Tinker's Hill** Hants
132 E6 **Tinkersley** Derbys
133 H2 **Tinsley** Sheff
37 L3 **Tinsley Green** W Susx
10 F5 **Tintagel** Cnwll
63 G7 **Tintern Parva** Mons
31 H7 **Tintinhull** Somset
140 F8 **Tintwistle** Derbys
176 D3 **Tinwald** D & G
101 M2 **Tinwell** Rutlnd
28 D2 **Tippacott** Devon
103 K4 **Tipp's End** Norfk
18 C4 **Tiptoe** Hants
97 L5 **Tipton** Sandw
98 B5 **Tipton Green** Sandw
14 C4 **Tipton St John** Devon
72 C4 **Tiptree** Essex
72 C4 **Tiptree Heath** Essex
78 B7 **Tirabad** Powys
206 A6 **Tiretigan** Ag & B
64 B2 **Tirley** Gloucs
61 H6 **Tirphil** Caerph
166 C5 **Tirril** Cumb
129 G7 **Tir-y-fron** Flints
32 F5 **Tisbury** Wilts
37 G4 **Tisman's Common** W Susx
115 K1 **Tissington** Derbys
26 D5 **Titchberry** Devon
19 J3 **Titchfield** Hants
19 J2 **Titchfield Common** Hants
102 A7 **Titchmarsh** Nhants
121 G3 **Titchwell** Norfk
117 J4 **Tithby** Notts
79 L3 **Titley** Herefs
69 G2 **Titmore Green** Herts
51 L7 **Titsey** Surrey
114 D4 **Tittensor** Staffs
121 K7 **Tittleshall** Norfk
81 J1 **Titton** Worcs
130 A7 **Tiverton** Ches
29 G8 **Tiverton** Devon
106 D6 **Tivetshall St Margaret** Norfk
106 D6 **Tivetshall St Mary** Norfk
29 G2 **Tivington** Somset
141 L6 **Tivy Dale** Barns
114 F7 **Tixall** Staffs
101 L3 **Tixover** Rutlnd
281 d9 **Toab** Shet
133 H8 **Toadhole** Derbys
116 B1 **Toadmoor** Derbys
226 F1 **Tobermory** Ag & B

215 L3 **Toberonochy** Ag & B
283 b10 **Tobha Mor** W Isls
256 C5 **Tocher** Abers
267 K3 **Tochieneal** Moray
46 F3 **Tockenham** Wilts
46 F3 **Tockenham Wick** Wilts
170 E7 **Tocketts** R & Cl
139 K3 **Tockholes** Bl w D
45 J2 **Tockington** S Glos
151 G5 **Tockwith** N York
32 D7 **Todber** Dorset
191 G7 **Todburn** Nthumb
68 C2 **Toddington** Beds
82 B8 **Toddington** Gloucs
69 G2 **Todds Green** Herts
82 F8 **Todenham** Gloucs
234 C7 **Todhills** Angus
177 L6 **Todhills** Cumb
169 G4 **Todhills** Dur
140 E3 **Todmorden** Calder
133 K3 **Todwick** Rothm
87 G4 **Toft** Cambs
130 E4 **Toft** Ches
118 E8 **Toft** Lincs
281 e4 **Toft** Shet
83 L1 **Toft** Warwks
168 F5 **Toft Hill** Dur
136 D7 **Toft Hill** Lincs
107 J4 **Toft Monks** Norfk
135 L2 **Toft next Newton** Lincs
121 K6 **Toftrees** Norfk
105 K1 **Toftwood** Norfk
191 K5 **Togston** Nthumb
247 J6 **Tokavaig** Highld
49 H3 **Tokers Green** Oxon
282 h2 **Tolastadh** W Isls
4 F3 **Toldish** Cnwll
29 K4 **Tolland** Somset
32 F7 **Tollard Farnham** Dorset
32 F7 **Tollard Royal** Wilts
142 E6 **Toll Bar** Donc
99 K8 **Tollbar End** Covtry
16 B3 **Toller Fratrum** Dorset
16 A3 **Toller Porcorum** Dorset
151 H3 **Tollerton** N York
117 G4 **Tollerton** Notts
15 L2 **Toller Whelme** Dorset
72 D5 **Tollesbury** Essex
72 D5 **Tolleshunt D'Arcy** Essex
72 D4 **Tolleshunt Knights** Essex
72 C5 **Tolleshunt Major** Essex
16 F3 **Tolpuddle** Dorset
282 h2 **Tolsta** W Isls
3 H5 **Tolvan** Cnwll
51 G5 **Tolworth** Gt Lon
252 E6 **Tomatin** Highld
239 M1 **Tomchrasky** Highld
239 K3 **Tomdoun** Highld
250 B6 **Tomich** Highld
250 F7 **Tomich** Highld
263 J5 **Tomich** Highld
272 F7 **Tomich** Highld
254 D7 **Tomintoul** Moray
83 K3 **Tomlow** Warwks
250 F3 **Tomnacross** Highld
254 D6 **Tomnavoulin** Moray
114 E1 **Tompkin** Staffs
62 C6 **Ton** Mons
62 D7 **Ton** Mons
38 F4 **Tonbridge** Kent
42 D5 **Tondu** Brdgnd
29 L6 **Tonedale** Somset
141 K2 **Tong** Brad
40 C4 **Tong** Kent
97 H2 **Tong** Shrops
116 C7 **Tonge** Leics
40 C4 **Tong Green** Kent
36 C1 **Tongham** Surrey
175 H4 **Tongland** D & G
97 H2 **Tong Norton** Shrops
141 J2 **Tong Street** Brad
277 K5 **Tongue** Highld
118 F7 **Tongue End** Lincs
43 H5 **Tongwynlais** Cardif
57 L5 **Tonna** Neath
43 H4 **Ton-teg** Rhondd
69 J4 **Tonwell** Herts
42 F3 **Tonypandy** Rhondd
42 F4 **Tonyrefail** Rhondd
66 E7 **Toot Baldon** Oxon
70 D6 **Toot Hill** Essex
34 E7 **Toothill** Hants
47 G2 **Toothill** Swindn
51 H5 **Tooting** Gt Lon
51 H4 **Tooting Bec** Gt Lon
160 F7 **Topcliffe** N York
106 F5 **Topcroft** Norfk
106 F5 **Topcroft Street** Norfk

85 L3 **Top End** Beds
143 G4 **Topham** Donc
140 C6 **Top of Hebers** Rochdl
88 E7 **Toppesfield** Essex
139 L5 **Toppings** Bolton
106 D4 **Toprow** Norfk
13 M5 **Topsham** Devon
128 F7 **Top-y-rhos** Flints
194 D5 **Torbeg** N Ayrs
273 H8 **Torboll** Highld
251 H3 **Torbreck** Highld
8 B2 **Torbryan** Devon
239 J7 **Torcastle** Highld
8 B6 **Torcross** Devon
251 G1 **Tore** Highld
5 J4 **Torfrey** Cnwll
206 C6 **Torinturk** Ag & B
135 G4 **Torksey** Lincs
45 M3 **Tormarton** S Glos
194 D4 **Tormore** N Ayrs
252 E2 **Tornagrain** Highld
244 D2 **Tornaveen** Abers
251 G6 **Torness** Highld
169 G4 **Toronto** Dur
227 L5 **Torosay Castle** Ag & B
165 G3 **Torpenhow** Cumb
210 C4 **Torphichen** W Loth
244 E3 **Torphins** Abers
6 E4 **Torpoint** Cnwll
8 D2 **Torquay** Torbay
200 F3 **Torquhan** Border
7 H4 **Torr** Devon
259 K6 **Torran** Highld
209 G4 **Torrance** E Duns
196 D2 **Torranyard** N Ayrs
29 J3 **Torre** Somset
260 E8 **Torridon** Highld
260 D8 **Torridon House** Highld
247 J4 **Torrin** Highld
194 B4 **Torrisdale** Ag & B
278 B4 **Torrisdale** Highld
274 C4 **Torrish** Highld
147 J3 **Torrisholme** Lancs
272 E7 **Torrobull** Highld
245 L3 **Torry** C Aber
210 D2 **Torryburn** Fife
9 h4 **Torteval** Guern
176 D3 **Torthorwald** D & G
21 G6 **Tortington** W Susx
81 J1 **Torton** Worcs
63 L8 **Tortworth** S Glos
259 H7 **Torvaig** Highld
156 C4 **Torver** Cumb
209 M2 **Torwood** Falk
201 G5 **Torwoodlee** Border
134 D2 **Torworth** Notts
247 L1 **Toscaig** Highld
86 E3 **Toseland** Cambs
148 D4 **Tosside** Lancs
89 J3 **Tostock** Suffk
258 B6 **Totaig** Highld
259 G6 **Tote** Highld
259 J4 **Tote** Highld
36 C6 **Tote Hill** W Susx
137 H3 **Tothill** Lincs
18 E6 **Totland** IoW
132 F4 **Totley** Sheff
132 F4 **Totley Brook** Sheff
8 B3 **Totnes** Devon
116 E4 **Toton** Notts
224 F4 **Totronald** Ag & B
258 F7 **Totscore** Highld
51 J1 **Tottenham** Gt Lon
104 C1 **Tottenhill** Norfk
69 H8 **Totteridge** Gt Lon
68 C3 **Totternhoe** Beds
140 A5 **Tottington** Bury
139 L2 **Tottleworth** Lancs
34 D8 **Totton** Hants
49 L4 **Touchen End** W & M
151 G7 **Toulston** N York
30 B4 **Toulton** Somset
264 D4 **Toulvaddie** Highld
39 J3 **Tovil** Kent
5 G5 **Towan** Cnwll
10 B7 **Towan** Cnwll
207 J5 **Toward** Ag & B
207 J5 **Toward Quay** Ag & B
84 D5 **Towcester** Nhants
2 D3 **Towednack** Cnwll
67 H6 **Towersey** Oxon
244 A1 **Towie** Abers
168 E3 **Tow Law** Dur
103 J4 **Town End** Cambs
156 C4 **Town End** Cumb
156 E1 **Town End** Cumb
156 F6 **Town End** Cumb
166 E5 **Town End** Cumb

208 C4 **Townend** W Duns
166 C1 **Towngate** Cumb
102 C1 **Towngate** Lincs
138 E6 **Town Green** Lancs
107 G1 **Town Green** Norfk
141 J7 **Townhead** Barns
156 F2 **Town Head** Cumb
164 E3 **Townhead** Cumb
166 E4 **Townhead** Cumb
176 D1 **Townhead** D & G
148 E4 **Town Head** N York
175 J2 **Townhead of Greenlaw** D & G
210 F1 **Townhill** Fife
169 K3 **Town Kelloe** Dur
12 A7 **Townlake** Devon
139 K7 **Town Lane** Wigan
22 F4 **Town Littleworth** E Susx
139 J8 **Town of Lowton** Wigan
38 E7 **Town Row** E Susx
48 E7 **Towns End** Hants
30 E7 **Townsend** Somset
2 F4 **Townshend** Cnwll
104 F6 **Town Street** Suffk
45 K1 **Townwell** S Glos
202 C7 **Town Yetholm** Border
152 D3 **Towthorpe** E R Yk
151 K4 **Towthorpe** York
151 G7 **Towton** N York
127 K4 **Towyn** Conwy
129 H2 **Toxteth** Lpool
137 G7 **Toynton All Saints** Lincs
137 G7 **Toynton Fen Side** Lincs
137 G7 **Toynton St Peter** Lincs
38 D3 **Toy's Hill** Kent
196 E6 **Trabboch** E Ayrs
196 F6 **Trabbochburn** E Ayrs
3 J6 **Traboe** Cnwll
29 K6 **Tracebridge** Somset
264 D8 **Tradespark** Highld
76 A5 **Traethsaith** Cerdgn
60 E1 **Trallong** Powys
211 L4 **Tranent** E Loth
129 H2 **Tranmere** Wirral
278 F5 **Trantelbeg** Highld
278 F5 **Trantlemore** Highld
180 F2 **Tranwell** Nthumb
59 J5 **Trapp** Carmth
212 D4 **Traprain** E Loth
82 D1 **Trap's Green** Warwks
48 A6 **Trapshill** W Berk
200 D6 **Traquair** Border
49 G5 **Trash Green** W Berk
27 L5 **Traveller's Rest** Devon
148 F8 **Trawden** Lancs
77 J1 **Trawscoed** Cerdgn
110 D4 **Trawsfynydd** Gwynd
42 F3 **Trealaw** Rhondd
138 F1 **Treales** Lancs
4 C4 **Treamble** Cnwll
124 D4 **Trearddur Bay** IoA
258 F6 **Treaslane** Highld
10 C7 **Treator** Cnwll
43 G7 **Tre Aubrey** V Glam
42 F4 **Trebanog** Rhondd
57 K4 **Trebanos** Neath
11 K7 **Trebartha** Cnwll
3 H5 **Trebarvah** Cnwll
10 E5 **Trebarwith** Cnwll
11 J5 **Trebeath** Cnwll
4 D2 **Trebelzue** Cnwll
10 C6 **Trebetherick** Cnwll
29 H4 **Treborough** Somset
4 E3 **Trebudannon** Cnwll
11 L6 **Trebullett** Cnwll
10 E6 **Treburgett** Cnwll
10 B8 **Treburick** Cnwll
11 L7 **Treburley** Cnwll
10 B8 **Treburrick** Cnwll
5 J2 **Trebyan** Cnwll
60 C1 **Trecastle** Powys
11 K6 **Trecogo** Cnwll
12 F2 **Trecott** Devon
74 F5 **Trecwn** Pembks
60 F6 **Trecynon** Rhondd
11 J6 **Tredaule** Cnwll
2 C5 **Tredavoe** Cnwll
61 J5 **Tredegar** Blae G
10 F8 **Tredethy** Cnwll
64 C1 **Tredington** Gloucs
83 G6 **Tredington** Warwks
5 H3 **Tredinnick** Cnwll
5 J2 **Tredinnick** Cnwll
5 M3 **Tredinnick** Cnwll
6 B3 **Tredinnick** Cnwll
10 C8 **Tredinnick** Cnwll
61 H1 **Tredomen** Powys
75 J4 **Tredrissi** Pembks

10 D7 **Tredrizzick** Cnwll
62 D8 **Tredunnock** Mons
61 H1 **Tredustan** Powys
2 B6 **Treen** Cnwll
2 C3 **Treen** Cnwll
5 J4 **Treesmill** Cnwll
133 J2 **Treeton** Rothm
74 E4 **Trefasser** Pembks
125 G5 **Trefdraeth** IoA
61 J1 **Trefecca** Powys
93 L5 **Trefeglwys** Powys
77 H2 **Trefenter** Cerdgn
54 F2 **Treffgarne** Pembks
74 E7 **Treffgarne Owen** Pembks
43 G4 **Trefforest** Rhondd
74 D6 **Treffynnon** Pembks
61 H4 **Trefil** Blae G
77 G4 **Trefilan** Cerdgn
74 D5 **Trefin** Pembks
112 C6 **Treflach Wood** Shrops
112 C8 **Trefnannau** Powys
128 C5 **Trefnant** Denbgs
112 C6 **Trefonen** Shrops
108 F2 **Trefor** Gwynd
124 F4 **Trefor** IoA
10 F5 **Trefrew** Cnwll
126 F7 **Trefriw** Conwy
11 K5 **Tregadillett** Cnwll
63 G5 **Tre-gagle** Mons
125 H4 **Tregaian** IoA
62 E5 **Tregare** Mons
3 K6 **Tregarne** Cnwll
77 J3 **Tregaron** Cerdgn
126 B6 **Tregarth** Gwynd
4 E2 **Tregaswith** Cnwll
10 F5 **Tregatta** Cnwll
5 G2 **Tregawne** Cnwll
11 J5 **Tregeare** Cnwll
112 B5 **Tregeiriog** Wrexhm
124 F1 **Tregele** IoA
10 E7 **Tregellist** Cnwll
4 E6 **Tregenna** Cnwll
2 B5 **Tregeseal** Cnwll
3 K4 **Tregew** Cnwll
60 F6 **Tre-Gibbon** Rhondd
3 J6 **Tregidden** Cnwll
4 F5 **Tregidgeo** Cnwll
5 G5 **Tregiskey** Cnwll
74 D6 **Treglemais** Pembks
11 H3 **Tregole** Cnwll
3 J4 **Tregolls** Cnwll
10 C7 **Tregonce** Cnwll
4 F2 **Tregonetha** Cnwll
4 F6 **Tregony** Cnwll
11 G5 **Tregoodwell** Cnwll
4 F3 **Tregoss** Cnwll
79 H7 **Tregoyd** Powys
5 H4 **Tregrehan Mills** Cnwll
76 D6 **Tre-groes** Cerdgn
5 H2 **Tregullon** Cnwll
10 D7 **Tregunna** Cnwll
11 J6 **Tregunnon** Cnwll
4 D2 **Tregurrian** Cnwll
94 D4 **Tregynon** Powys
58 D5 **Tre-gynwr** Carmth
43 G3 **Trehafod** Rhondd
6 D3 **Trehan** Cnwll
43 H2 **Treharris** Myr Td
10 E6 **Treharrock** Cnwll
10 B7 **Trehemborne** Cnwll
77 G6 **Treherbert** Carmth
42 E2 **Treherbert** Rhondd
6 C2 **Trehunist** Cnwll
11 L6 **Trekenner** Cnwll
10 E5 **Treknow** Cnwll
3 J7 **Trelan** Cnwll
11 H4 **Trelash** Cnwll
4 E4 **Trelassick** Cnwll
5 L4 **Trelawne** Cnwll
128 C4 **Trelawnyd** Flints
3 K6 **Treleague** Cnwll
3 K7 **Treleaver** Cnwll
58 A3 **Trelech** Carmth
58 B3 **Trelech a'r Betws** Carmth
74 B6 **Treleddyd-fawr** Pembks
3 K4 **Trelew** Cnwll
43 H2 **Trelewis** Myr Td
10 E5 **Treligga** Cnwll
10 D6 **Trelights** Cnwll
10 E6 **Trelill** Cnwll
11 K6 **Trelinnoe** Cnwll
4 F4 **Trelion** Cnwll
3 L3 **Trelissick** Cnwll
63 G6 **Trellech** Mons
62 F6 **Trelleck Grange** Mons
128 D4 **Trelogan** Flints
4 E6 **Trelonk** Cnwll
4 F1 **Trelow** Cnwll

3 J6 **Trelowarren** Cnwll
6 B3 **Trelowia** Cnwll
3 M3 **Treluggan** Cnwll
95 G3 **Trelystan** Powys
109 K3 **Tremadog** Gwynd
11 H5 **Tremail** Cnwll
75 M3 **Tremain** Cerdgn
11 J4 **Tremaine** Cnwll
6 B1 **Tremar** Cnwll
6 D3 **Trematon** Cnwll
6 B2 **Trembraze** Cnwll
128 C5 **Tremeirchion** Denbgs
2 C5 **Tremethick Cross** Cnwll
5 G2 **Tremore** Cnwll
128 D4 **Tre-Mostyn** Flints
3 K6 **Trenance** Cnwll
4 D1 **Trenance** Cnwll
10 C8 **Trenance** Cnwll
5 H5 **Trenarren** Cnwll
96 F1 **Trench** Wrekin
49 G3 **Trench Green** Oxon
4 E4 **Trendeal** Cnwll
2 D3 **Trendrine** Cnwll
10 D8 **Treneague** Cnwll
3 H5 **Trenear** Cnwll
11 H5 **Treneglos** Cnwll
2 F4 **Trenerth** Cnwll
5 K4 **Trenewan** Cnwll
10 F6 **Trenewth** Cnwll
11 H4 **Trengune** Cnwll
4 D3 **Treninnick** Cnwll
4 C3 **Trenowah** Cnwll
3 J4 **Trenoweth** Cnwll
31 K7 **Trent** Dorset
114 D3 **Trentham** C Stke
116 E5 **Trentlock** Derbys
135 G3 **Trent Port** Lincs
114 D3 **Trent Vale** C Stke
42 E6 **Treoes** V Glam
42 E2 **Treorchy** Rhondd
10 E7 **Trequite** Cnwll
92 E5 **Tre'r-ddol** Cerdgn
42 F6 **Trerhyngyll** V Glam
6 C3 **Trerulefoot** Cnwll
4 E5 **Tresawle** Cnwll
97 J4 **Trescott** Staffs
2 F5 **Trescowe** Cnwll
4 C3 **Tresean** Cnwll
46 A1 **Tresham** Gloucs
4 E5 **Tresillian** Cnwll
10 F6 **Tresinney** Cnwll
11 H3 **Treskinnick Cross** Cnwll
11 J5 **Tresmeer** Cnwll
11 G4 **Tresparrett** Cnwll
232 B3 **Tressait** P & K
281 d6 **Tresta** Shet
281 f3 **Tresta** Shet
134 F4 **Treswell** Notts
3 G3 **Treswithian** Cnwll
92 E5 **Tre Taliesin** Cerdgn
6 B2 **Trethawle** Cnwll
10 F4 **Trethevey** Cnwll
2 B6 **Trethewey** Cnwll
43 J4 **Trethomas** Caerph
4 F4 **Trethosa** Cnwll
5 H4 **Trethurgy** Cnwll
74 C6 **Tretio** Pembks
63 G2 **Tretire** Herefs
61 J3 **Tretower** Powys
128 F8 **Treuddyn** Flints
11 K6 **Trevadlock** Cnwll
10 F4 **Trevalga** Cnwll
129 J8 **Trevalyn** Wrexhm
10 D7 **Trevanger** Cnwll
10 D7 **Trevanson** Cnwll
2 D5 **Trevarrack** Cnwll
4 E3 **Trevarren** Cnwll
4 D2 **Trevarrian** Cnwll
5 G6 **Trevarrick** Cnwll
3 J3 **Trevarth** Cnwll
55 L4 **Trevaughan** Carmth
58 D4 **Tre-Vaughan** Carmth
2 D3 **Treveal** Cnwll
4 C3 **Treveal** Cnwll
10 F6 **Treveighan** Cnwll
4 B4 **Trevellas Downs** Cnwll
5 L2 **Trevelmond** Cnwll
4 D3 **Trevemper** Cnwll
5 G6 **Treveor** Cnwll
4 E5 **Treverbyn** Cnwll
5 G3 **Treverbyn** Cnwll
3 J5 **Treverva** Cnwll
2 B6 **Trevescan** Cnwll
62 B6 **Trevethin** Torfn
10 F5 **Trevia** Cnwll
6 C1 **Trevigro** Cnwll
3 L3 **Trevilla** Cnwll
4 D4 **Trevilson** Cnwll

4 F4 **Treviscoe** Cnwll
4 F6 **Treviskey** Cnwll
2 D5 **Trevithal** Cnwll
4 E2 **Trevithick** Cnwll
4 F6 **Trevithick** Cnwll
4 D3 **Trevoll** Cnwll
10 B7 **Trevone** Cnwll
112 C3 **Trevor** Wrexhm
2 B6 **Trevorgans** Cnwll
10 C7 **Trevorrick** Cnwll
10 B7 **Trevose** Cnwll
3 G5 **Trew** Cnwll
10 F6 **Trewalder** Cnwll
61 J1 **Trewalkin** Powys
10 F5 **Trewarmett** Cnwll
4 E6 **Trewarthenick** Cnwll
11 G5 **Trewassa** Cnwll
2 F5 **Trewavas** Cnwll
11 J6 **Treween** Cnwll
2 B4 **Trewellard** Cnwll
10 E7 **Trewen** Cnwll
11 J5 **Trewen** Cnwll
3 H5 **Trewennack** Cnwll
55 G7 **Trewent** Pembks
95 G1 **Trewern** Powys
10 E6 **Trewetha** Cnwll
10 E7 **Trewethern** Cnwll
6 B3 **Trewidland** Cnwll
3 K7 **Trewillis** Cnwll
6 B2 **Trewint** Cnwll
11 J6 **Trewint** Cnwll
3 M4 **Trewithian** Cnwll
11 L8 **Trewoodloe** Cnwll
3 H7 **Trewoon** Cnwll
5 G4 **Trewoon** Cnwll
4 D5 **Treworga** Cnwll
4 E7 **Treworlas** Cnwll
11 G4 **Treworld** Cnwll
3 M3 **Treworthal** Cnwll
62 C3 **Tre-wyn** Mons
10 B7 **Treyarnon** Cnwll
20 D3 **Treyford** W Susx
17 L2 **Trickett's Cross** Dorset
178 E5 **Triermain** Cumb
75 G7 **Triffleton** Pembks
11 K4 **Trillacott** Cnwll
169 K4 **Trimdon** Dur
169 K4 **Trimdon Colliery** Dur
169 K3 **Trimdon Grange** Dur
122 F4 **Trimingham** Norfk
91 G7 **Trimley Lower Street** Suffk
91 G7 **Trimley St Martin** Suffk
91 G7 **Trimley St Mary** Suffk
97 H7 **Trimpley** Worcs
56 E4 **Trimsaran** Carmth
70 C4 **Trims Green** Herts
27 J2 **Trimstone** Devon
231 K3 **Trinafour** P & K
61 K7 **Trinant** Caerph
68 A5 **Tring** Herts
67 M4 **Tringford** Herts
68 A4 **Tring Wharf** Herts
234 F3 **Trinity** Angus
9 d2 **Trinity** Jersey
221 G3 **Trinity Gask** P & K
29 G3 **Triscombe** Somset
29 L4 **Triscombe** Somset
239 H8 **Trislaig** Highld
4 D5 **Trispen** Cnwll
191 J7 **Tritlington** Nthumb
4 E3 **Troan** Cnwll
232 E7 **Trochry** P & K
61 H6 **Troedrhiwfuwch** Caerph
76 B6 **Troedyraur** Cerdgn
61 G6 **Troedyrhiw** Myr Td
127 G5 **Trofarth** Conwy
9 c2 **Trois Bois** Jersey
3 G3 **Troon** Cnwll
196 C5 **Troon** S Ayrs
219 H5 **Trossachs Pier** Stirlg
89 H1 **Troston** Suffk
11 J4 **Troswell** Cnwll
81 K4 **Trotshill** Worcs
52 D7 **Trottiscliffe** Kent
36 B6 **Trotton** W Susx
190 B7 **Troughend** Nthumb
140 D3 **Trough Gate** Lancs
156 F2 **Troutbeck** Cumb
165 L5 **Troutbeck** Cumb
156 F3 **Troutbeck Bridge** Cumb
133 H4 **Troway** Derbys
46 B7 **Trowbridge** Wilts
116 E3 **Trowell** Notts
46 B7 **Trowle Common** Wilts
68 D4 **Trowley Bottom** Herts
106 E2 **Trowse Newton** Norfk
150 C8 **Troy** Leeds
32 C2 **Trudoxhill** Somset

30 B6 **Trull** Somset
142 F5 **Trumfleet** Donc
258 C4 **Trumpan** Highld
80 F7 **Trumpet** Herefs
87 J4 **Trumpington** Cambs
50 C5 **Trumpsgreen** Surrey
122 F4 **Trunch** Norfk
147 G7 **Trunnah** Lancs
4 D6 **Truro** Cnwll
11 K5 **Truscott** Cnwll
13 K6 **Trusham** Devon
115 L4 **Trusley** Derbys
137 K3 **Trusthorpe** Lincs
97 J4 **Trysull** Staffs
66 B7 **Tubney** Oxon
8 B4 **Tuckenhay** Devon
97 H5 **Tuckhill** Shrops
3 G3 **Tuckingmill** Cnwll
32 F5 **Tuckingmill** Wilts
18 A5 **Tuckton** Bmouth
4 F5 **Tucoyse** Cnwll
88 E1 **Tuddenham** Suffk
90 E5 **Tuddenham** Suffk
38 F4 **Tudeley** Kent
169 H3 **Tudhoe** Dur
63 H3 **Tudorville** Herefs
108 D4 **Tudweiliog** Gwynd
36 E3 **Tuesley** Surrey
64 B4 **Tuffley** Gloucs
34 F2 **Tufton** Hants
75 H6 **Tufton** Pembks
101 G3 **Tugby** Leics
96 D6 **Tugford** Shrops
203 K7 **Tughall** Nthumb
220 E8 **Tullibody** Clacks
251 H6 **Tullich** Highld
264 D4 **Tullich** Highld
232 F5 **Tulliemet** P & K
256 E5 **Tulloch** Abers
216 F8 **Tullochgorm** Ag & B
240 B7 **Tulloch Station** Highld
232 F8 **Tullybeagles Lodge** P & K
233 J5 **Tullymurdoch** P & K
255 L7 **Tullynessle** Abers
51 J4 **Tulse Hill** Gt Lon
58 F6 **Tumble** Carmth
71 K2 **Tumbler's Green** Essex
136 D7 **Tumby** Lincs
136 E8 **Tumby Woodside** Lincs
231 L4 **Tummel Bridge** P & K
38 F5 **Tunbridge Wells** Kent
177 G3 **Tundergarth** D & G
122 F5 **Tungate** Norfk
45 K7 **Tunley** BaNES
114 D1 **Tunstall** C Stke
145 J2 **Tunstall** E R Yk
40 A3 **Tunstall** Kent
157 K8 **Tunstall** Lancs
160 B3 **Tunstall** N York
107 J2 **Tunstall** Norfk
114 B6 **Tunstall** Staffs
91 H4 **Tunstall** Suffk
181 J8 **Tunstall** Sundld
132 B5 **Tunstead** Derbys
122 F7 **Tunstead** Norfk
131 K4 **Tunstead Milton** Derbys
35 K1 **Tunworth** Hants
80 C7 **Tupsley** Herefs
49 G7 **Turgis Green** Hants
65 G4 **Turkdean** Gloucs
100 F4 **Tur Langton** Leics
46 A6 **Turleigh** Wilts
97 H6 **Turleygreen** Shrops
140 B4 **Turn** Lancs
79 L7 **Turnastone** Herefs
182 F2 **Turnberry** S Ayrs
6 F4 **Turnchapel** C Plym
116 A2 **Turnditch** Derbys
139 J2 **Turner Green** Lancs
23 L3 **Turner's Green** E Susx
82 E2 **Turner's Green** Warwks
38 A6 **Turner's Hill** W Susx
16 F4 **Turners Puddle** Dorset
69 K6 **Turnford** Herts
211 G4 **Turnhouse** C Edin
16 F1 **Turnworth** Dorset
268 C6 **Turriff** Abers
139 L4 **Turton Bottoms** Bl w D
103 G4 **Turves** Cambs
85 J5 **Turvey** Beds
49 J1 **Turville** Bucks
49 H1 **Turville Heath** Bucks
84 B7 **Turweston** Bucks
187 L3 **Tushielaw Inn** Border
115 L6 **Tutbury** Staffs
82 A1 **Tutnall** Worcs
63 G8 **Tutshill** Gloucs
122 E6 **Tuttington** Norfk

11 M7 **Tutwell** Cnwll	23 H3 **Uckfield** E Susx	35 H6 **Upham** Hants	116 C2 **Upper Hartshay** Derbys
134 E5 **Tuxford** Notts	81 K7 **Uckinghall** Worcs	79 M3 **Uphampton** Herefs	64 D3 **Upper Hatherley** Gloucs
275 b3 **Twatt** Ork	64 C2 **Uckington** Gloucs	81 J2 **Uphampton** Worcs	114 C4 **Upper Hatton** Staffs
281 d6 **Twatt** Shet	96 D2 **Uckington** Shrops	44 C7 **Uphill** N Som	142 C8 **Upper Haugh** Rothm
209 J4 **Twechar** E Duns	209 J6 **Uddingston** S Lans	139 G6 **Up Holland** Lancs	96 C7 **Upper Hayton** Shrops
201 H6 **Tweedbank** Border	198 E6 **Uddington** S Lans	208 D8 **Uplawmoor** E Rens	141 J4 **Upper Heaton** Kirk
202 F3 **Tweedmouth** Nthumb	24 F3 **Udimore** E Susx	63 L2 **Upleadon** Gloucs	151 L4 **Upper Helmsley** N York
187 G1 **Tweedsmuir** Border	256 F6 **Udny Green** Abers	170 E6 **Upleatham** R & Cl	79 J4 **Upper Hergest** Herefs
4 B6 **Twelveheads** Cnwll	257 G6 **Udny Station** Abers	40 C2 **Uplees** Kent	84 C3 **Upper Heyford** Nhants
24 C3 **Twelve Oaks** E Susx	47 H3 **Uffcott** Wilts	15 L4 **Uploders** Dorset	66 D2 **Upper Heyford** Oxon
130 F6 **Twemlow Green** Ches	29 K8 **Uffculme** Devon	29 J7 **Uplowman** Devon	80 B4 **Upper Hill** Herefs
118 F7 **Twenty** Lincs	102 B2 **Uffington** Lincs	15 H4 **Uplyme** Devon	52 B5 **Upper Hockenden** Kent
45 L6 **Twerton** BaNES	47 L1 **Uffington** Oxon	20 C4 **Up Marden** W Susx	141 K4 **Upper Hopton** Kirk
50 F4 **Twickenham** Gt Lon	96 C1 **Uffington** Shrops	52 C2 **Upminster** Gt Lon	81 H5 **Upper Howsell** Worcs
64 B3 **Twigworth** Gloucs	102 B3 **Ufford** C Pete	31 J7 **Up Mudford** Somset	131 K7 **Upper Hulme** Staffs
22 C3 **Twineham** W Susx	91 G5 **Ufford** Suffk	49 G8 **Up Nately** Hants	36 F4 **Upper Ifold** Surrey
22 C3 **Twineham Green** W Susx	83 J3 **Ufton** Warwks	14 E1 **Upottery** Devon	65 J7 **Upper Inglesham** Swindn
45 L7 **Twinhoe** BaNES	48 F5 **Ufton Nervet** W Berk	95 K6 **Upper Affcot** Shrops	46 A1 **Upper Kilcott** Gloucs
89 H7 **Twinstead** Essex	194 B5 **Ugadale** Ag & B	263 G2 **Upper Ardchronie** Highld	57 G6 **Upper Killay** Swans
28 D5 **Twitchen** Devon	7 K4 **Ugborough** Devon	97 H7 **Upper Arley** Worcs	217 J2 **Upper Kinchrackine** Ag & B
95 J7 **Twitchen** Shrops	107 J7 **Uggeshall** Suffk	66 F4 **Upper Arncott** Oxon	47 L3 **Upper Lambourn** W Berk
41 H4 **Twitham** Kent	162 F1 **Ugglebarnby** N York	83 L7 **Upper Astrop** Nhants	98 C2 **Upper Landywood** Staffs
12 E7 **Two Bridges** Devon	132 E2 **Ughill** Sheff	48 F4 **Upper Basildon** W Berk	44 F7 **Upper Langford** N Som
132 E7 **Two Dales** Derbys	70 D2 **Ugley** Essex	141 K3 **Upper Batley** Kirk	133 K6 **Upper Langwith** Derbys
99 G3 **Two Gates** Staffs	70 D2 **Ugley Green** Essex	22 B5 **Upper Beeding** W Susx	223 G6 **Upper Largo** Fife
8 C1 **Two Mile Oak Cross** Devon	171 J8 **Ugthorpe** N York	101 L5 **Upper Benefield** Nhants	115 G4 **Upper Leigh** Staffs
27 J2 **Two Pots** Devon	224 F4 **Uig** Ag & B	82 B2 **Upper Bentley** Worcs	45 H6 **Upper Littleton** N Som
68 D6 **Two Waters** Herts	258 B6 **Uig** Highld	278 F5 **Upper Bighouse** Highld	244 F4 **Upper Lochton** Abers
99 J2 **Twycross** Leics	258 F4 **Uig** Highld	133 J8 **Upper Birchwood** Derbys	115 H8 **Upper Longdon** Staffs
67 G2 **Twyford** Bucks	282 d3 **Uig** W Isls	43 H4 **Upper Boat** Rhondd	86 D8 **Upper & Lower Stondon** Beds
35 G6 **Twyford** Hants	259 G7 **Uigshader** Highld	83 L5 **Upper Boddington** Nhants	97 H4 **Upper Ludstone** Shrops
100 F2 **Twyford** Leics	226 D8 **Uisken** Ag & B	92 D5 **Upper Borth** Cerdgn	275 H1 **Upper Lybster** Highld
118 B6 **Twyford** Lincs	280 D7 **Ulbster** Highld	83 G7 **Upper Brailes** Warwks	63 J4 **Upper Lydbrook** Gloucs
121 M6 **Twyford** Norfk	165 L6 **Ulcat Row** Cumb	247 L4 **Upper Breakish** Highld	80 C6 **Upper Lyde** Herefs
49 J4 **Twyford** Wokham	137 H5 **Ulceby** Lincs	80 B7 **Upper Breinton** Herefs	79 M2 **Upper Lye** Herefs
80 C8 **Twyford Common** Herefs	144 E5 **Ulceby** N Linc	81 J4 **Upper Broadheath** Worcs	79 L8 **Upper Maes-coed** Herefs
61 H5 **Twyn-carno** Caerph	144 E5 **Ulceby Skitter** N Linc	117 J6 **Upper Broughton** Notts	141 K7 **Upper Midhope** Sheff
175 G4 **Twynholm** D & G	39 L4 **Ulcombe** Kent	48 D5 **Upper Bucklebury** W Berk	140 F6 **Uppermill** Oldham
81 K8 **Twyning** Gloucs	165 H3 **Uldale** Cumb	33 K7 **Upper Burgate** Hants	81 J1 **Upper Milton** Worcs
81 L7 **Twyning Green** Gloucs	63 M7 **Uley** Gloucs	52 E5 **Upper Bush** Medway	46 E1 **Upper Minety** Wilts
59 L4 **Twynllanan** Carmth	191 J7 **Ulgham** Nthumb	177 L8 **Upperby** Cumb	82 A5 **Upper Moor** Worcs
43 H7 **Twyn-yr-Odyn** V Glam	261 J1 **Ullapool** Highld	86 D6 **Upper Caldecote** Beds	141 K2 **Upper Moor Side** Leeds
62 E6 **Twyn-y-Sheriff** Mons	82 D2 **Ullenhall** Warwks	44 D7 **Upper Canada** N Som	267 G6 **Upper Mulben** Moray
101 L7 **Twywell** Nhants	64 D4 **Ullenwood** Gloucs	18 D1 **Upper Canterton** Hants	96 E5 **Upper Netchwood** Shrops
79 M7 **Tyberton** Herefs	151 H7 **Ulleskelf** N York	83 M3 **Upper Catesby** Nhants	115 G4 **Upper Nobut** Staffs
98 E5 **Tyburn** Birm	100 B6 **Ullesthorpe** Leics	98 B8 **Upper Catshill** Worcs	20 F3 **Upper Norwood** W Susx
57 H3 **Tycroes** Carmth	133 J2 **Ulley** Rothm	78 D7 **Upper Chapel** Powys	132 E4 **Upper Padley** Derbys
111 L7 **Tycrwyn** Powys	80 E5 **Ullingswick** Herefs	30 C5 **Upper Cheddon** Somset	18 D4 **Upper Pennington** Hants
120 A7 **Tydd Gote** Lincs	246 D1 **Ullinish Lodge Hotel** Highld	33 G5 **Upper Chicksgrove** Wilts	67 H4 **Upper Pollicott** Bucks
119 M8 **Tydd St Giles** Cambs	164 E6 **Ullock** Cumb	47 L8 **Upper Chute** Wilts	151 J5 **Upper Poppleton** York
119 M7 **Tydd St Mary** Lincs	156 B4 **Ulpha** Cumb	51 K2 **Upper Clapton** Gt Lon	82 E6 **Upper Quinton** Warwks
20 B6 **Tye** Hants	157 G6 **Ulpha** Cumb	34 D2 **Upper Clatford** Hants	34 D6 **Upper Ratley** Hants
70 D2 **Tye Green** Essex	153 J4 **Ulrome** E R Yk	64 E4 **Upper Coberley** Gloucs	65 J3 **Upper Rissington** Gloucs
71 J3 **Tye Green** Essex	281 e4 **Ulsta** Shet	21 K6 **Upper Cokeham** W Susx	80 E2 **Upper Rochford** Worcs
88 B8 **Tye Green** Essex	71 K5 **Ulting Wick** Essex	115 G2 **Upper Cotton** Staffs	174 E3 **Upper Ruscoe** D & G
141 J1 **Tyersal** Brad	98 E7 **Ulverley Green** Solhll	96 C2 **Upper Cound** Shrops	80 F3 **Upper Sapey** Herefs
139 K7 **Tyldesley** Wigan	156 C7 **Ulverston** Cumb	142 B5 **Upper Cudworth** Barns	46 D3 **Upper Seagry** Wilts
40 F3 **Tyler Hill** Kent	17 K6 **Ulwell** Dorset	141 K6 **Upper Cumberworth** Kirk	85 K6 **Upper Shelton** Beds
67 L8 **Tylers Green** Bucks	185 J1 **Ulzieside** D & G	59 L6 **Upper Cwmtwrch** Powys	122 C3 **Upper Sheringham** Norfk
70 D6 **Tyler's Green** Essex	259 K6 **Umachan** Highld	267 G4 **Upper Dallachy** Moray	83 L3 **Upper Shuckburgh** Warwks
51 K8 **Tylers Green** Surrey	27 L6 **Umberleigh** Devon	41 K5 **Upper Deal** Kent	207 K5 **Upper Skelmorlie** N Ayrs
42 F3 **Tylorstown** Rhondd	271 H2 **Unapool** Highld	85 L2 **Upper Dean** Beds	65 H3 **Upper Slaughter** Gloucs
93 L7 **Tylwch** Powys	157 G4 **Underbarrow** Cumb	141 K6 **Upper Denby** Kirk	63 K5 **Upper Soudley** Gloucs
111 J3 **Ty-nant** Conwy	178 B2 **Under Burnmouth** Border	178 E5 **Upper Denton** Cumb	79 K4 **Upper Spond** Herefs
111 H6 **Ty-nant** Gwynd	141 J1 **Undercliffe** Brad	23 J5 **Upper Dicker** E Susx	41 H7 **Upper Standen** Kent
218 E1 **Tyndrum** Stirlg	96 B1 **Underdale** Shrops	95 L6 **Upper Dinchope** Shrops	86 C3 **Upper Staploe** Beds
112 C3 **Ty'n-dwr** Denbgs	157 K6 **Underley Hall** Cumb	279 H3 **Upper Dounreay** Highld	185 L6 **Upper Stepford** D & G
181 J5 **Tynemouth** N Tyne	39 J4 **Underling Green** Kent	73 K1 **Upper Dovercourt** Essex	106 E3 **Upper Stoke** Norfk
60 E7 **Tynewydd** Rhondd	38 E3 **Under River** Kent	219 L6 **Upper Drumbane** Stirlg	84 C4 **Upper Stowe** Nhants
212 D3 **Tyninghame** E Loth	116 D2 **Underwood** Notts	150 F3 **Upper Dunsforth** N York	33 K7 **Upper Street** Hants
185 K4 **Tynron** D & G	104 D7 **Undley** Suffk	36 E2 **Upper Eashing** Surrey	106 D7 **Upper Street** Norfk
42 F4 **Ty'n-y-bryn** Rhondd	44 E2 **Undy** Mons	263 K7 **Upper Eathie** Highld	123 G7 **Upper Street** Norfk
43 K4 **Ty'n-y-coedcae** Caerph	154 e6 **Union Mills** IoM	80 E6 **Upper Egleton** Herefs	123 G8 **Upper Street** Norfk
125 J3 **Tynygongl** IoA	39 H7 **Union Street** E Susx	131 L7 **Upper Elkstone** Staffs	88 F5 **Upper Street** Suffk
77 J1 **Tynygraig** Cerdgn	133 G4 **Unstone** Derbys	115 J3 **Upper Ellastone** Staffs	90 C5 **Upper Street** Suffk
126 F5 **Ty'n-y-Groes** Conwy	133 G4 **Unstone Green** Derbys	132 B4 **Upper End** Derbys	90 D8 **Upper Street** Suffk
43 G4 **Tyn-y-nant** Rhondd	140 B6 **Unsworth** Bury	34 E1 **Upper Enham** Hants	81 K7 **Upper Strensham** Worcs
85 G6 **Tyringham** M Keyn	165 L1 **Unthank** Cumb	97 H5 **Upper Farmcote** Shrops	68 D2 **Upper Sundon** Beds
98 E6 **Tyseley** Birm	166 B3 **Unthank** Cumb	35 L4 **Upper Farringdon** Hants	65 H2 **Upper Swell** Gloucs
42 C6 **Tythegston** Brdgnd	166 E3 **Unthank** Cumb	64 F4 **Upper Framilode** Gloucs	142 A7 **Upper Tankersley** Barns
131 H4 **Tytherington** Ches	132 F4 **Unthank** Derbys	35 M2 **Upper Froyle** Hants	106 E4 **Upper Tasburgh** Norfk
45 K1 **Tytherington** S Glos	202 F3 **Unthank** Nthumb	258 E6 **Upperglen** Highld	115 G4 **Upper Tean** Staffs
32 C2 **Tytherington** Somset	47 H7 **Upavon** Wilts	31 H2 **Upper Godney** Somset	141 H6 **Upperthong** Kirk
32 F3 **Tytherington** Wilts	16 C2 **Up Cerne** Dorset	86 C3 **Upper Gravenhurst** Beds	133 J4 **Upperthorpe** Derbys
15 H2 **Tytherleigh** Devon	53 H5 **Upchurch** Kent	88 B8 **Upper Green** Essex	143 J7 **Upperthorpe** N Linc
46 D4 **Tytherton Lucas** Wilts	27 K3 **Upcott** Devon	62 D3 **Upper Green** Mons	113 G3 **Upper Threapwood** Ches
68 F6 **Tyttenhanger** Herts	28 D5 **Upcott** Devon	88 E2 **Upper Green** Suffk	36 E6 **Upperton** W Susx
5 J4 **Tywardreath** Cnwll	79 K5 **Upcott** Herefs	48 A6 **Upper Green** W Berk	115 L1 **Upper Town** Derbys
5 J4 **Tywardreath Highway** Cnwll	50 B6 **Updown Hill** Surrey	63 H2 **Upper Grove Common** Herefs	132 F6 **Uppertown** Derbys
126 F4 **Tywyn** Conwy	88 D3 **Upend** Cambs	132 F7 **Upper Hackney** Derbys	168 D3 **Upper Town** Dur
92 C3 **Tywyn** Gwynd	13 L2 **Up Exe** Devon	36 B1 **Upper Hale** Surrey	80 D5 **Upper Town** Herefs
	122 C7 **Upgate** Norfk	50 E5 **Upper Halliford** Surrey	280 D1 **Uppertown** Highld
U	106 B5 **Upgate Street** Norfk	52 E6 **Upper Halling** Medway	45 G6 **Upper Town** N Som
	106 F5 **Upgate Street** Norfk	101 K2 **Upper Hambleton** Rutlnd	89 J2 **Upper Town** Suffk
91 H1 **Ubbeston Green** Suffk	16 A2 **Uphall** Dorset	40 F4 **Upper Harbledown** Kent	59 G6 **Upper Tumble** Carmth
45 G7 **Ubley** BaNES	210 E5 **Uphall** W Loth	40 F5 **Upper Hardres Court** Kent	83 H6 **Upper Tysoe** Warwks
160 C2 **Uckerby** N York	13 K1 **Upham** Devon	79 M4 **Upper Hardwick** Herefs	91 G4 **Upper Ufford** Suffk
		38 C6 **Upper Hartfield** E Susx	

64 F7 **Upperup** Gloucs
47 J3 **Upper Upham** Wilts
53 G5 **Upper Upnor** Medway
234 E8 **Upper Victoria** Angus
32 B1 **Upper Vobster** Somset
83 L6 **Upper Wardington** Oxon
84 F7 **Upper Weald** M Keyn
84 B3 **Upper Weedon** Nhants
23 G4 **Upper Wellingham** E Susx
45 L5 **Upper Weston** BaNES
106 E7 **Upper Weybread** Suffk
81 J5 **Upper Wick** Worcs
35 K3 **Upper Wield** Hants
67 H4 **Upper Winchendon** Bucks
132 F8 **Upperwood** Derbys
33 K3 **Upper Woodford** Wilts
48 E7 **Upper Wootton** Hants
46 A4 **Upper Wraxall** Wilts
81 H6 **Upper Wyche** Worcs
13 L1 **Uppincott** Devon
101 J3 **Uppingham** Rutlnd
17 K1 **Uppington** Dorset
96 D2 **Uppington** Shrops
161 G5 **Upsall** N York
202 D4 **Upsettlington** Border
69 L7 **Upshire** Essex
34 E4 **Up Somborne** Hants
41 H3 **Upstreet** Kent
16 B2 **Up Sydling** Dorset
89 K1 **Upthorpe** Suffk
67 J5 **Upton** Bucks
102 C3 **Upton** C Pete
102 D7 **Upton** Cambs
129 J6 **Upton** Ches
11 H2 **Upton** Cnwll
11 K7 **Upton** Cnwll
165 K3 **Upton** Cumb
7 K6 **Upton** Devon
14 C2 **Upton** Devon
16 E6 **Upton** Dorset
17 J4 **Upton** Dorset
153 J5 **Upton** E R Yk
129 L2 **Upton** Halton
34 E7 **Upton** Hants
47 M7 **Upton** Hants
99 K3 **Upton** Leics
135 H2 **Upton** Lincs
84 D3 **Upton** Nhants
107 H1 **Upton** Norfk
117 J1 **Upton** Notts
134 E4 **Upton** Notts
48 D2 **Upton** Oxon
65 K4 **Upton** Oxon
55 G6 **Upton** Pembks
171 G6 **Upton** R & Cl
50 B3 **Upton** Slough
29 H5 **Upton** Somset
31 G5 **Upton** Somset
142 D5 **Upton** Wakefd
82 D4 **Upton** Warwks
32 E4 **Upton** Wilts
129 G2 **Upton** Wirral
63 K2 **Upton Bishop** Herefs
45 K5 **Upton Cheyney** S Glos
96 E5 **Upton Cressett** Shrops
63 J2 **Upton Crews** Herefs
11 K8 **Upton Cross** Cnwll
86 C8 **Upton End** Beds
35 L1 **Upton Grey** Hants
129 J5 **Upton Heath** Ches
13 K2 **Upton Hellions** Devon
32 F3 **Upton Lovell** Wilts
96 C1 **Upton Magna** Shrops
32 B3 **Upton Noble** Somset
13 L3 **Upton Pyne** Devon
64 B4 **Upton St Leonards** Gloucs
32 E1 **Upton Scudamore** Wilts
81 L4 **Upton Snodsbury** Worcs
2 F3 **Upton Towans** Cnwll
81 K7 **Upton upon Severn** Worcs
81 L2 **Upton Warren** Worcs
20 F4 **Upwaltham** W Susx
87 L1 **Upware** Cambs
103 K3 **Upwell** Norfk
16 C5 **Upwey** Dorset
70 C2 **Upwick Green** Herts
102 E6 **Upwood** Cambs
46 F7 **Urchfont** Wilts
80 C5 **Urdimarsh** Herefs
150 D1 **Ure Bank** N York
169 L7 **Urlay Nook** S on T
130 E1 **Urmston** Traffd
266 F4 **Urquhart** Moray
161 J2 **Urra** N York
250 E1 **Urray** Highld
235 H4 **Usan** Angus
169 G2 **Ushaw Moor** Dur
62 D7 **Usk** Mons

136 A1 **Usselby** Lincs
181 H7 **Usworth** Sundld
130 A6 **Utkinton** Ches
149 J7 **Utley** Brad
13 J3 **Uton** Devon
136 F1 **Utterby** Lincs
115 H5 **Uttoxeter** Staffs
108 B6 **Uwchmynydd** Gwynd
50 D2 **Uxbridge** Gt Lon
281 f2 **Uyeasound** Shet
54 F4 **Uzmaston** Pembks

V

9 k2 **Vale** Guern
124 E4 **Valley** IoA
50 B6 **Valley End** Surrey
10 F6 **Valley Truckle** Cnwll
259 J4 **Valtos** Highld
282 e3 **Valtos** W Isls
52 F2 **Vange** Essex
61 L6 **Varteg** Torfn
281 e3 **Vatsetter** Shet
258 D7 **Vatten** Highld
61 G5 **Vaynor** Myr Td
9 i2 **Vazon Bay** Guern
281 e6 **Veensgarth** Shet
79 H7 **Velindre** Powys
29 K3 **Vellow** Somset
26 E6 **Velly** Devon
11 K1 **Venn** Cnwll
26 F8 **Venngreen** Devon
95 H2 **Vennington** Shrops
14 C4 **Venn Ottery** Devon
13 J3 **Venny Tedburn** Devon
11 L7 **Venterdon** Cnwll
19 J8 **Ventnor** IoW
7 H3 **Venton** Devon
47 M7 **Vernham Dean** Hants
47 M7 **Vernham Street** Hants
95 L7 **Vernolds Common** Shrops
17 L1 **Verwood** Dorset
4 E7 **Veryan** Cnwll
4 F6 **Veryan Green** Cnwll
146 C2 **Vickerstown** Cumb
141 J6 **Victoria** Barns
61 J5 **Victoria** Blae G
5 G3 **Victoria** Cnwll
281 e5 **Vidlin** Shet
266 F3 **Viewfield** Moray
209 J6 **Viewpark** N Lans
52 D6 **Vigo** Kent
9 k3 **Village de Putron** Guern
9 a1 **Ville la Bas** Jersey
9 i3 **Villiaze** Guern
24 D3 **Vinehall Street** E Susx
23 K4 **Vines Cross** E Susx
50 C5 **Virginia Water** Surrey
11 M4 **Virginstow** Devon
32 B1 **Vobster** Somset
281 d5 **Voe** Shet
79 L7 **Vowchurch** Herefs
130 B1 **Vulcan Village** St Hel

W

168 F6 **Wackerfield** Dur
106 D5 **Wacton** Norfk
81 K5 **Wadborough** Worcs
67 H4 **Waddesdon** Bucks
8 C3 **Waddeton** Devon
138 E7 **Waddicar** Sefton
144 B8 **Waddingham** Lincs
148 C7 **Waddington** Lancs
135 K6 **Waddington** Lincs
13 K6 **Waddon** Devon
16 B5 **Waddon** Dorset
10 D7 **Wadebridge** Cnwll
30 D8 **Wadeford** Somset
101 M6 **Wadenhoe** Nhants
69 K4 **Wadesmill** Herts
39 G7 **Wadhurst** E Susx
132 F5 **Wadshelf** Derbys
46 B5 **Wadswick** Wilts
142 F8 **Wadworth** Donc
127 K7 **Waen** Denbgs
128 D6 **Waen** Denbgs
112 C7 **Waen** Powys
112 B8 **Waen Fach** Powys
125 K6 **Waen-pentir** Gwynd
125 K6 **Waen-wen** Gwynd
95 J3 **Wagbeach** Shrops
62 B6 **Wainfelin** Torfn
137 J7 **Wainfleet All Saints** Lincs
137 J7 **Wainfleet Bank** Lincs
137 J8 **Wainfleet St Mary** Lincs

107 G5 **Wainford** Norfk
11 H3 **Wainhouse Corner** Cnwll
52 F5 **Wainscott** Medway
44 E5 **Wain's Hill** N Som
141 G2 **Wainstalls** Calder
158 C1 **Waitby** Cumb
145 H7 **Waithe** Lincs
142 A4 **Wakefield** Wakefd
98 E6 **Wake Green** Birm
101 L3 **Wakerley** Nhants
72 C2 **Wakes Colne** Essex
107 K8 **Walberswick** Suffk
21 G5 **Walberton** W Susx
180 E5 **Walbottle** N u Ty
175 J1 **Walbutt** D & G
178 B6 **Walby** Cumb
31 J2 **Walcombe** Somset
118 E4 **Walcot** Lincs
143 M3 **Walcot** N Linc
95 J6 **Walcot** Shrops
96 D1 **Walcot** Shrops
47 H2 **Walcot** Swindn
82 D4 **Walcot** Warwks
100 C6 **Walcote** Leics
106 C7 **Walcot Green** Norfk
136 B8 **Walcott** Lincs
123 G5 **Walcott** Norfk
159 H6 **Walden** N York
159 H6 **Walden Head** N York
142 E4 **Walden Stubbs** N York
53 G6 **Walderslade** Medway
20 C5 **Walderton** W Susx
15 L4 **Walditch** Dorset
115 J4 **Waldley** Derbys
169 H1 **Waldridge** Dur
91 G6 **Waldringfield** Suffk
23 J3 **Waldron** E Susx
133 J3 **Wales** Rothm
31 K6 **Wales** Somset
136 B1 **Walesby** Lincs
134 D5 **Walesby** Notts
63 H3 **Walford** Herefs
79 M1 **Walford** Herefs
113 G7 **Walford** Shrops
114 C5 **Walford** Staffs
113 G7 **Walford Heath** Shrops
113 M2 **Walgherton** Ches
84 F1 **Walgrave** Nhants
18 E4 **Walhampton** Hants
139 L7 **Walkden** Salfd
181 H6 **Walker** N u Ty
200 D5 **Walkerburn** Border
148 B7 **Walker Fold** Lancs
134 F1 **Walkeringham** Notts
134 F1 **Walkerith** Lincs
69 H2 **Walkern** Herts
80 C5 **Walker's Green** Herefs
98 D7 **Walker's Heath** Birm
222 C7 **Walkerton** Fife
18 C5 **Walkford** Dorset
7 G1 **Walkhampton** Devon
152 F8 **Walkington** E R Yk
133 G2 **Walkley** Sheff
140 C2 **Walk Mill** Lancs
82 B2 **Walkwood** Worcs
2 F4 **Wall** Cnwll
179 L5 **Wall** Nthumb
98 E2 **Wall** Staffs
183 H2 **Wallacetown** S Ayrs
196 C6 **Wallacetown** S Ayrs
22 F5 **Wallands Park** E Susx
129 G1 **Wallasey** Wirral
156 B6 **Wall End** Cumb
80 B4 **Wall End** Herefs
53 J4 **Wallend** Medway
80 F7 **Waller's Green** Herefs
178 B6 **Wallhead** Cumb
97 K5 **Wall Heath** Dudley
180 C5 **Wall Houses** Nthumb
48 F1 **Wallingford** Oxon
51 H6 **Wallington** Gt Lon
19 K2 **Wallington** Hants
86 F8 **Wallington** Herts
98 C3 **Wallington Heath** Wsall
75 G7 **Wallis** Pembks
17 L4 **Wallisdown** Poole
37 H3 **Walliswood** Surrey
281 c6 **Walls** Shet
181 H5 **Wallsend** N Tyne
165 K5 **Wallthwaite** Cumb
96 C5 **Wall under Haywood** Shrops
211 L4 **Wallyford** E Loth
41 L5 **Walmer** Kent
138 F3 **Walmer Bridge** Lancs
140 B5 **Walmersley** Bury
41 H3 **Walmestone** Kent
98 F5 **Walmley** Birm

98 F5 **Walmley Ash** Birm
137 G4 **Walmsgate** Lincs
30 D3 **Walpole** Somset
107 H8 **Walpole** Suffk
120 B7 **Walpole Cross Keys** Norfk
120 B8 **Walpole Highway** Norfk
120 B8 **Walpole St Andrew** Norfk
120 B8 **Walpole St Peter** Norfk
30 E2 **Walrow** Somset
98 C4 **Walsall** Wsall
98 D3 **Walsall Wood** Wsall
140 D3 **Walsden** Calder
99 K7 **Walsgrave on Sowe** Covtry
89 K1 **Walsham le Willows** Suffk
140 A5 **Walshaw** Bury
150 F5 **Walshford** N York
103 K1 **Walsoken** Norfk
199 H4 **Walston** S Lans
69 G1 **Walsworth** Herts
67 K7 **Walter's Ash** Bucks
38 D5 **Walters Green** Kent
43 G7 **Walterston** V Glam
62 D2 **Walterstone** Herefs
40 E5 **Waltham** Kent
145 H7 **Waltham** NE Lin
69 K7 **Waltham Abbey** Essex
35 H7 **Waltham Chase** Hants
69 K7 **Waltham Cross** Herts
117 L6 **Waltham on the Wolds** Leics
49 K4 **Waltham St Lawrence** W & M
71 G1 **Waltham's Cross** Essex
51 K1 **Walthamstow** Gt Lon
102 D3 **Walton** C Pete
178 C6 **Walton** Cumb
133 G6 **Walton** Derbys
150 F6 **Walton** Leeds
100 D6 **Walton** Leics
85 H7 **Walton** M Keyn
79 J3 **Walton** Powys
95 L7 **Walton** Shrops
31 G4 **Walton** Somset
114 D5 **Walton** Staffs
114 D6 **Walton** Staffs
91 G8 **Walton** Suffk
20 D6 **Walton** W Susx
142 A4 **Walton** Wakefd
83 G4 **Walton** Warwks
113 K7 **Walton** Wrekin
64 C1 **Walton Cardiff** Gloucs
55 H2 **Walton East** Pembks
32 C7 **Walton Elm** Dorset
83 L8 **Walton Grounds** Nhants
44 E4 **Walton-in-Gordano** N Som
139 H2 **Walton-le-Dale** Lancs
50 E5 **Walton-on-Thames** Surrey
114 F7 **Walton-on-the-Hill** Staffs
51 G7 **Walton on the Hill** Surrey
73 K3 **Walton on the Naze** Essex
117 G7 **Walton on the Wolds** Leics
115 L7 **Walton-on-Trent** Derbys
44 E4 **Walton Park** N Som
54 D4 **Walton West** Pembks
128 D4 **Walwen** Flints
128 E4 **Walwen** Flints
128 E5 **Walwen** Flints
179 L5 **Walwick** Nthumb
169 G7 **Walworth** Darltn
51 J3 **Walworth** Gt Lon
169 G6 **Walworth Gate** Darltn
54 E4 **Walwyn's Castle** Pembks
15 G1 **Wambrook** Somset
177 H7 **Wampool** Cumb
36 D1 **Wanborough** Surrey
47 J2 **Wanborough** Swindn
68 E3 **Wandon End** Herts
51 H4 **Wandsworth** Gt Lon
107 J7 **Wangford** Suffk
100 D1 **Wanlip** Leics
186 C4 **Wanlockhead** D & G
23 K6 **Wannock** E Susx
102 B3 **Wansford** C Pete
153 G4 **Wansford** E R Yk
39 J4 **Wanshurst Green** Kent
51 L1 **Wanstead** Gt Lon
32 B3 **Wanstrow** Somset
63 K6 **Wanswell** Gloucs
48 B1 **Wantage** Oxon
81 H4 **Wants Green** Worcs
45 L3 **Wapley** S Glos
83 J2 **Wappenbury** Warwks
84 C6 **Wappenham** Nhants
23 K4 **Warbleton** E Susx
66 F8 **Warborough** Oxon
102 F7 **Warboys** Cambs
146 F8 **Warbreck** Bpool
11 H4 **Warbstow** Cnwll

130 D2 **Warburton** Traffd
167 H7 **Warcop** Cumb
53 M5 **Warden** Kent
179 L5 **Warden** Nthumb
98 E5 **Ward End** Birm
86 C6 **Warden Street** Beds
90 B2 **Ward Green** Suffk
85 L8 **Wardhedges** Beds
83 L6 **Wardington** Oxon
130 B8 **Wardle** Ches
140 D4 **Wardle** Rochdl
181 H6 **Wardley** Gatesd
101 H3 **Wardley** Rutlnd
140 A7 **Wardley** Salfd
132 D5 **Wardlow** Derbys
131 J3 **Wardsend** Ches
103 K7 **Wardy Hill** Cambs
69 K4 **Ware** Herts
17 H5 **Wareham** Dorset
25 J1 **Warehorne** Kent
203 J7 **Warenford** Nthumb
203 J6 **Waren Mill** Nthumb
203 H7 **Warenton** Nthumb
69 K4 **Wareside** Herts
86 E4 **Waresley** Cambs
81 J1 **Waresley** Worcs
39 K2 **Ware Street** Kent
49 L4 **Warfield** Br For
8 C5 **Warfleet** Devon
119 H5 **Wargate** Lincs
49 J3 **Wargrave** Wokham
80 B7 **Warham** Herefs
121 L3 **Warham All Saints** Norfk
121 L3 **Warham St Mary** Norfk
179 K3 **Wark** Nthumb
202 C5 **Wark** Nthumb
27 M6 **Warkleigh** Devon
101 K7 **Warkton** Nhants
83 L7 **Warkworth** Nhants
191 K5 **Warkworth** Nthumb
160 E4 **Warlaby** N York
140 E4 **Warland** Calder
5 K1 **Warleggan** Cnwll
46 A6 **Warleigh** BaNES
141 G3 **Warley Town** Calder
51 K7 **Warlingham** Surrey
177 G5 **Warmanbie** D & G
115 M1 **Warmbrook** Derbys
142 B4 **Warmfield** Wakefd
130 D7 **Warmingham** Ches
102 B5 **Warmington** Nhants
83 K5 **Warmington** Warwks
32 E2 **Warminster** Wilts
45 K4 **Warmley** S Glos
142 E7 **Warmsworth** Donc
16 E5 **Warmwell** Dorset
81 K4 **Warndon** Worcs
35 J6 **Warnford** Hants
37 J4 **Warnham** W Susx
37 J4 **Warnham Court** W Susx
21 H5 **Warningcamp** W Susx
37 K5 **Warninglid** W Susx
131 H5 **Warren** Ches
54 F7 **Warren** Pembks
170 D5 **Warrenby** R & Cl
198 F5 **Warrenhill** S Lans
49 K3 **Warren Row** W & M
69 H2 **Warren's Green** Herts
40 B5 **Warren Street** Kent
85 H4 **Warrington** M Keyn
130 B2 **Warrington** Warrtn
211 H4 **Warriston** C Edin
19 H2 **Warsash** Hants
132 B7 **Warslow** Staffs
133 L6 **Warsop Vale** Notts
152 D5 **Warter** E R Yk
152 C6 **Warter Priory** E R Yk
160 B6 **Warthermaske** N York
151 L5 **Warthill** N York
24 B5 **Wartling** E Susx
117 J7 **Wartnaby** Leics
138 E2 **Warton** Lancs
147 K2 **Warton** Lancs
190 E5 **Warton** Nthumb
99 H3 **Warton** Warwks
178 B7 **Warwick** Cumb
83 G2 **Warwick** Warwks
178 B7 **Warwick Bridge** Cumb
178 B3 **Warwicksland** Cumb
275 c3 **Wasbister** Ork
156 B1 **Wasdale Head** Cumb
131 L3 **Wash** Derbys
70 C1 **Washall Green** Herts
5 H1 **Washaway** Cnwll
8 B4 **Washbourne** Devon
30 F1 **Washbrook** Somset
90 D6 **Washbrook** Suffk
29 G7 **Washfield** Devon

159 J2 **Washfold** N York
29 J3 **Washford** Somset
28 E8 **Washford Pyne** Devon
135 L5 **Washingborough** Lincs
181 H7 **Washington** Sundld
21 J4 **Washington** W Susx
98 E5 **Washwood Heath** Birm
48 E6 **Wasing** W Berk
168 D2 **Waskerley** Dur
83 G3 **Wasperton** Warwks
135 M6 **Wasps Nest** Lincs
161 J6 **Wass** N York
29 K2 **Watchet** Somset
47 K1 **Watchfield** Oxon
30 E2 **Watchfield** Somset
157 H3 **Watchgate** Cumb
165 G2 **Watchill** Cumb
8 D2 **Watcombe** Torbay
165 J7 **Watendlath** Cumb
13 H6 **Water** Devon
140 C3 **Water** Lancs
87 K2 **Waterbeach** Cambs
20 E5 **Waterbeach** W Susx
177 H3 **Waterbeck** D & G
121 J4 **Waterden** Norfk
66 D5 **Water Eaton** Oxon
97 K1 **Water Eaton** Staffs
85 L7 **Water End** Beds
86 C5 **Water End** Beds
86 C5 **Water End** Beds
164 F6 **Waterend** Cumb
152 B8 **Water End** E R Yk
88 B7 **Water End** Essex
68 D5 **Water End** Herts
69 G6 **Water End** Herts
115 H1 **Waterfall** Staffs
208 F7 **Waterfoot** E Rens
140 C3 **Waterfoot** Lancs
69 J4 **Waterford** Herts
142 D2 **Water Fryston** Wakefd
11 G6 **Watergate** Cnwll
156 E2 **Waterhead** Cumb
197 G8 **Waterhead** E Ayrs
200 B3 **Waterheads** Border
168 F3 **Waterhouses** Dur
115 H2 **Waterhouses** Staffs
39 H3 **Wateringbury** Kent
64 D6 **Waterlane** Gloucs
10 F7 **Waterloo** Cnwll
133 H7 **Waterloo** Derbys
79 L5 **Waterloo** Herefs
247 K4 **Waterloo** Highld
209 L8 **Waterloo** N Lans
122 E7 **Waterloo** Norfk
233 G7 **Waterloo** P & K
55 G6 **Waterloo** Pembks
17 K4 **Waterloo** Poole
138 C8 **Waterloo** Sefton
29 J8 **Waterloo Cross** Devon
125 J6 **Waterloo Port** Gwynd
19 M2 **Waterlooville** Hants
166 B6 **Watermillock** Cumb
102 C4 **Water Newton** Cambs
98 F5 **Water Orton** Warwks
66 F6 **Waterperry** Oxon
29 J6 **Waterrow** Somset
21 G4 **Watersfield** W Susx
139 L3 **Waterside** Bl w D
68 B7 **Waterside** Bucks
165 H2 **Waterside** Cumb
143 H5 **Waterside** Donc
184 C1 **Waterside** E Ayrs
196 F2 **Waterside** E Ayrs
209 H4 **Waterside** E Duns
139 K6 **Water's Nook** Bolton
258 A1 **Waterstein** Highld
66 F6 **Waterstock** Oxon
54 F5 **Waterston** Pembks
84 C8 **Water Stratford** Bucks
42 B5 **Water Street** Neath
113 K7 **Waters Upton** Wrekin
156 D5 **Water Yeat** Cumb
68 E7 **Watford** Herts
84 B2 **Watford** Nhants
149 L2 **Wath** N York
160 D7 **Wath** N York
142 C7 **Wath upon Dearne** Rothm
104 C1 **Watlington** Norfk
67 G8 **Watlington** Oxon
116 E2 **Watnall** Notts
280 B5 **Watten** Highld
105 K8 **Wattisfield** Suffk
89 K5 **Wattisham** Suffk
15 K4 **Watton** Dorset
152 F6 **Watton** E R Yk
105 J3 **Watton** Norfk
69 J3 **Watton-at-Stone** Herts
105 J3 **Watton Green** Norfk

70 D8 **Wattons Green** Essex
209 K5 **Wattston** N Lans
42 F3 **Wattstown** Rhondd
43 K3 **Wattsville** Caerph
144 B2 **Wauldby** E R Yk
244 E5 **Waulkmill** Abers
57 H6 **Waunarlwydd** Swans
92 D7 **Waunfawr** Cerdgn
125 J7 **Waunfawr** Gwynd
57 G4 **Waungron** Swans
61 J5 **Waunlwyd** Blae G
85 H7 **Wavendon** M Keyn
165 H1 **Waverbridge** Cumb
129 K7 **Waverton** Ches
165 H1 **Waverton** Cumb
153 H8 **Wawne** E R Yk
123 J6 **Waxham** Norfk
145 J2 **Waxholme** E R Yk
41 K2 **Way** Kent
13 H8 **Waye** Devon
15 J1 **Wayford** Somset
15 L3 **Waytown** Dorset
28 F8 **Way Village** Devon
44 D6 **Way Wick** N Som
29 K3 **Weacombe** Somset
65 L6 **Weald** Oxon
50 F1 **Wealdstone** Gt Lon
150 D7 **Weardley** Leeds
44 E8 **Weare** Somset
27 H6 **Weare Giffard** Devon
167 K3 **Wearhead** Dur
30 F5 **Wearne** Somset
158 B2 **Weasdale** Cumb
121 J7 **Weasenham All Saints** Norfk
121 J7 **Weasenham St Peter** Norfk
140 B8 **Weaste** Salfd
98 D8 **Weatheroak Hill** Worcs
130 B5 **Weaverham** Ches
115 J7 **Weaverslake** Staffs
152 E2 **Weaverthorpe** N York
44 D7 **Webbington** Somset
45 K4 **Webb's Heath** S Glos
82 B2 **Webheath** Worcs
80 A7 **Webton** Herefs
256 F5 **Wedderlairs** Abers
149 G6 **Wedding Hall Fold** N York
41 J3 **Weddington** Kent
99 K5 **Weddington** Warwks
46 F7 **Wedhampton** Wilts
31 G1 **Wedmore** Somset
98 C4 **Wednesbury** Sandw
97 L3 **Wednesfield** Wolves
135 G6 **Weecar** Notts
67 K3 **Weedon** Bucks
84 C3 **Weedon** Nhants
84 B6 **Weedon Lois** Nhants
98 F3 **Weeford** Staffs
8 A2 **Week** Devon
27 K5 **Week** Devon
28 C7 **Week** Devon
13 H1 **Weeke** Devon
34 F5 **Weeke** Hants
101 J7 **Weekley** Nhants
11 J3 **Week St Mary** Cnwll
153 G7 **Weel** E R Yk
73 H3 **Weeley** Essex
73 H3 **Weeley Heath** Essex
232 B5 **Weem** P & K
114 E7 **Weeping Cross** Staffs
82 C4 **Weethley** Warwks
104 F5 **Weeting** Norfk
145 K4 **Weeton** E R Yk
138 D1 **Weeton** Lancs
150 C6 **Weeton** N York
150 C8 **Weetwood** Leeds
140 C3 **Weir** Lancs
112 E6 **Weirbrook** Shrops
6 E2 **Weir Quay** Devon
281 d5 **Weisdale** Shet
133 L5 **Welbeck Abbey** Notts
106 B2 **Welborne** Norfk
118 C1 **Welbourn** Lincs
151 M2 **Welburn** N York
160 F2 **Welbury** N York
118 C4 **Welby** Lincs
103 K6 **Welches Dam** Cambs
26 D7 **Welcombe** Devon
191 G6 **Weldon Bridge** Nthumb
100 E7 **Welford** Nhants
48 B4 **Welford** W Berk
82 D5 **Welford-on-Avon** Warwks
101 G5 **Welham** Leics
134 E3 **Welham** Notts
69 G6 **Welham Green** Herts
36 A2 **Well** Hants
137 H5 **Well** Lincs
160 C6 **Well** N York
81 H7 **Welland** Worcs

81 J7 **Welland Stone** Worcs
234 D7 **Wellbank** Angus
68 F1 **Wellbury** Herts
49 L1 **Well End** Bucks
69 G7 **Well End** Herts
83 G4 **Wellesbourne** Warwks
83 G4 **Wellesbourne Mountford** Warwks
68 F2 **Well Head** Herts
52 B6 **Well Hill** Kent
48 D4 **Wellhouse** W Berk
51 M4 **Welling** Gt Lon
85 H2 **Wellingborough** Nhants
121 J7 **Wellingham** Norfk
135 K8 **Wellingore** Lincs
155 K2 **Wellington** Cumb
80 C5 **Wellington** Herefs
29 L6 **Wellington** Somset
96 E1 **Wellington** Wrekin
81 G7 **Wellington Heath** Herefs
80 C6 **Wellington Marsh** Herefs
45 L7 **Wellow** BaNES
18 F6 **Wellow** IoW
134 D6 **Wellow** Notts
69 L3 **Wellpond Green** Herts
31 J2 **Wells** Somset
99 K3 **Wellsborough** Leics
113 M1 **Wells Green** Ches
141 G1 **Wells Head** Brad
121 K3 **Wells-next-the-sea** Norfk
70 F3 **Wellstye Green** Essex
13 L1 **Well Town** Devon
221 G3 **Welltree** P & K
210 E1 **Wellwood** Fife
103 L4 **Welney** Norfk
113 G4 **Welshampton** Shrops
63 H4 **Welsh Bicknor** Herefs
113 H4 **Welsh End** Shrops
112 E5 **Welsh Frankton** Shrops
74 F6 **Welsh Hook** Pembks
63 G3 **Welsh Newton** Herefs
94 F2 **Welshpool** Powys
42 F6 **Welsh St Donats** V Glam
165 K2 **Welton** Cumb
144 B2 **Welton** E R Yk
135 K4 **Welton** Lincs
84 B2 **Welton** Nhants
137 J6 **Welton le Marsh** Lincs
136 E2 **Welton le Wold** Lincs
145 J3 **Welwick** E R Yk
69 G4 **Welwyn** Herts
69 G4 **Welwyn Garden City** Herts
113 H5 **Wem** Shrops
30 D3 **Wembdon** Somset
50 F2 **Wembley** Gt Lon
7 G5 **Wembury** Devon
12 F1 **Wembworthy** Devon
207 K5 **Wemyss Bay** Inver
77 J1 **Wenallt** Cerdgn
87 K8 **Wendens Ambo** Essex
66 E3 **Wendlebury** Oxon
105 J1 **Wendling** Norfk
67 L5 **Wendover** Bucks
3 H5 **Wendron** Cnwll
87 G5 **Wendy** Cambs
10 F7 **Wenfordbridge** Cnwll
107 J8 **Wenhaston** Suffk
102 E7 **Wennington** Cambs
52 B3 **Wennington** Gt Lon
147 M2 **Wennington** Lancs
132 E7 **Wensley** Derbys
159 K5 **Wensley** N York
142 D4 **Wentbridge** Wakefd
95 J5 **Wentnor** Shrops
103 K7 **Wentworth** Cambs
142 B8 **Wentworth** Rothm
141 M7 **Wentworth Castle** Barns
43 H7 **Wenvoe** V Glam
79 M5 **Weobley** Herefs
80 A5 **Weobley Marsh** Herefs
21 H5 **Wepham** W Susx
104 D3 **Wereham** Norfk
97 K3 **Wergs** Wolves
109 K4 **Wern** Gwynd
61 H3 **Wern** Powys
95 G1 **Wern** Powys
112 D4 **Wern** Shrops
131 J1 **Werneth Low** Tamesd
56 F6 **Wernffrwd** Swans
128 F6 **Wern-y-gaer** Flints
102 D3 **Werrington** C Pete
11 L5 **Werrington** Cnwll
114 E2 **Werrington** Staffs
129 K5 **Wervin** Ches
138 E1 **Wesham** Lancs
133 G8 **Wessington** Derbys
42 F8 **West Aberthaw** V Glam
121 G8 **West Acre** Norfk

202 F4 **West Allerdean** Nthumb
7 L6 **West Alvington** Devon
33 K3 **West Amesbury** Wilts
28 E5 **West Anstey** Devon
160 B4 **West Appleton** N York
136 E5 **West Ashby** Lincs
20 D5 **West Ashling** W Susx
46 C7 **West Ashton** Wilts
168 F5 **West Auckland** Dur
163 H5 **West Ayton** N York
30 A4 **West Bagborough** Somset
11 K3 **West Balsdon** Cnwll
61 K6 **West Bank** Blae G
129 L3 **West Bank** Halton
136 C4 **West Barkwith** Lincs
171 J8 **West Barnby** N York
212 E3 **West Barns** E Loth
121 K5 **West Barsham** Norfk
15 K4 **West Bay** Dorset
122 C4 **West Beckham** Norfk
50 D4 **West Bedfont** Surrey
41 G3 **Westbere** Kent
72 D2 **West Bergholt** Essex
15 M5 **West Bexington** Dorset
120 F8 **West Bilney** Norfk
22 D6 **West Blatchington** Br & H
181 J6 **West Boldon** S Tyne
117 M3 **Westborough** Lincs
17 L4 **Westbourne** Bmouth
20 B5 **Westbourne** W Susx
32 C5 **West Bourton** Dorset
141 J2 **West Bowling** Brad
40 E6 **West Brabourne** Kent
105 J2 **West Bradenham** Norfk
148 C7 **West Bradford** Lancs
31 J3 **West Bradley** Somset
141 L5 **West Bretton** Wakefd
117 G4 **West Bridgford** Notts
168 B6 **West Briscoe** Dur
98 C5 **West Bromwich** Sandw
41 K1 **Westbrook** Kent
48 B4 **Westbrook** W Berk
46 D5 **Westbrook** Wilts
188 B3 **West Buccleuch Hotel**
Border
28 B4 **West Buckland** Devon
30 B6 **West Buckland** Somset
159 H5 **West Burton** N York
21 G4 **West Burton** W Susx
84 B8 **Westbury** Bucks
95 J2 **Westbury** Shrops
46 C8 **Westbury** Wilts
32 E1 **Westbury Leigh** Wilts
63 L4 **Westbury on Severn**
Gloucs
45 H3 **Westbury-on-Trym** Bristl
31 H1 **Westbury-sub-Mendip**
Somset
168 E2 **West Butsfield** Dur
143 L6 **West Butterwick** N Linc
138 D2 **Westby** Lancs
50 D6 **West Byfleet** Surrey
172 E8 **West Cairngaan** D & G
107 K1 **West Caister** Norfk
210 D6 **West Calder** W Loth
31 J6 **West Camel** Somset
16 E6 **West Chaldon** Dorset
48 A1 **West Challow** Oxon
7 L6 **West Charleton** Devon
15 M2 **West Chelborough** Dorset
191 J6 **West Chevington** Nthumb
21 J3 **West Chiltington** W Susx
31 G8 **West Chinnock** Somset
47 H8 **West Chisenbury** Wilts
50 D8 **West Clandon** Surrey
41 K6 **West Cliffe** Kent
53 J2 **Westcliff-on-Sea** Sthend
31 H8 **West Coker** Somset
7 L2 **West Combe** Devon
31 L3 **Westcombe** Somset
31 K2 **West Compton** Somset
16 A4 **West Compton Abbas**
Dorset
65 J3 **Westcote** Gloucs
66 B2 **Westcote Barton** Oxon
67 H4 **Westcott** Bucks
14 B2 **Westcott** Devon
28 F6 **Westcott** Devon
37 H1 **Westcott** Surrey
151 L7 **West Cottingwith** N York
47 J6 **Westcourt** Wilts
143 G3 **West Cowick** E R Yk
57 H7 **West Cross** Swans
11 K4 **West Curry** Cnwll
165 K1 **West Curthwaite** Cumb
23 J7 **Westdean** E Susx
20 E4 **West Dean** W Susx
34 B5 **West Dean** Wilts

102 C2 **West Deeping** Lincs
129 J1 **West Derby** Lpool
104 D3 **West Dereham** Norfk
27 J3 **West Down** Devon
33 H2 **Westdown Camp** Wilts
10 F6 **Westdowns** Cnwll
50 D3 **West Drayton** Gt Lon
134 D5 **West Drayton** Notts
280 B2 **West Dunnet** Highld
52 B5 **Wested** Kent
144 C2 **West Ella** E R Yk
85 J4 **West End** Beds
49 L5 **West End** Br For
43 K3 **West End** Caerph
87 G2 **West End** Cambs
177 K7 **West End** Cumb
144 A2 **West End** E R Yk
144 F2 **West End** E R Yk
145 H2 **West End** E R Yk
64 A5 **Westend** Gloucs
34 F7 **West End** Hants
35 K4 **West End** Hants
69 H5 **West End** Herts
69 J6 **West End** Herts
139 L2 **West End** Lancs
150 B8 **West End** Leeds
145 K8 **West End** Lincs
44 F5 **West End** N Som
149 L4 **West End** N York
151 H7 **West End** N York
105 H2 **West End** Norfk
107 K1 **West End** Norfk
48 E2 **West End** Oxon
45 L1 **West End** S Glos
31 L4 **West End** Somset
50 B6 **West End** Surrey
50 E6 **West End** Surrey
49 K4 **West End** W & M
22 B4 **West End** W Susx
32 F6 **West End** Wilts
33 G6 **West End** Wilts
46 E3 **West End** Wilts
49 G6 **West End Green** Hants
179 H6 **Westend Town** Nthumb
40 F7 **Westenhanger** Kent
279 K6 **Westerdale** Highld
161 L2 **Westerdale** N York
251 G5 **Wester Drumashie**
Highld
90 E5 **Westerfield** Suffk
20 F6 **Westergate** W Susx
51 L8 **Westerham** Kent
180 F5 **Westerhope** N u Ty
8 C2 **Westerland** Devon
45 K3 **Westerleigh** S Glos
210 D4 **Wester Ochiltree** W Loth
223 K6 **Wester Pitkierie** Fife
235 G4 **Westerton** Angus
20 E5 **Westerton** W Susx
281 c6 **Westerwick** Shet
51 G6 **West Ewell** Surrey
39 H3 **West Farleigh** Kent
83 M5 **West Farndon** Nhants
112 E6 **West Felton** Shrops
45 K8 **Westfield** BaNES
164 C5 **Westfield** Cumb
24 E4 **Westfield** E Susx
279 J3 **Westfield** Highld
209 J4 **Westfield** N Lans
105 K2 **Westfield** Norfk
210 B4 **Westfield** W Loth
16 D1 **Westfields** Dorset
80 C7 **Westfields** Herefs
233 J6 **Westfields of Rattray**
P & K
53 G6 **Westfield Sole** Kent
23 G6 **West Firle** E Susx
135 K3 **West Firsby** Lincs
163 K6 **West Flotmanby** N York
29 L6 **Westford** Somset
142 B1 **West Garforth** Leeds
167 L3 **Westgate** Dur
143 K6 **Westgate** N Linc
121 L3 **Westgate** Norfk
141 K2 **Westgate Hill** Brad
41 K1 **Westgate on Sea** Kent
122 D7 **Westgate Street** Norfk
48 C2 **West Ginge** Oxon
47 K7 **West Grafton** Wilts
49 H7 **West Green** Hants
33 L5 **West Grimstead** Wilts
37 J6 **West Grinstead** W Susx
142 E2 **West Haddlesey** N York
84 C1 **West Haddon** Nhants
48 D2 **West Hagbourne** Oxon
97 K7 **West Hagley** Worcs
107 J7 **Westhall** Suffk
116 D3 **West Hallam** Derbys

116 C3 **West Hallam Common**
Derbys
144 A4 **West Halton** N Linc
16 C6 **Westham** Dorset
23 L6 **Westham** E Susx
51 K2 **West Ham** Gt Lon
30 F2 **Westham** Somset
20 E5 **Westhampnett** W Susx
133 H4 **West Handley** Derbys
66 B8 **West Hanney** Oxon
71 H7 **West Hanningfield** Essex
33 K5 **West Harnham** Wilts
45 H7 **West Harptree** BaNES
20 C3 **West Harting** W Susx
30 D6 **West Hatch** Somset
32 F5 **West Hatch** Wilts
234 E8 **West Haven** Angus
31 G2 **Westhay** Somset
138 F6 **Westhead** Lancs
104 B2 **West Head** Norfk
98 C7 **West Heath** Birm
48 E7 **West Heath** Hants
274 D5 **West Helmsdale** Highld
48 C1 **West Hendred** Oxon
163 G7 **West Heslerton** N York
44 D6 **West Hewish** N Som
80 D6 **Westhide** Herefs
245 J2 **Westhill** Abers
14 C4 **West Hill** Devon
38 A6 **West Hoathly** W Susx
17 G5 **West Holme** Dorset
31 J3 **Westholme** Somset
80 B5 **Westhope** Herefs
95 L6 **Westhope** Shrops
52 D1 **West Horndon** Essex
83 L5 **Westhorp** Nhants
119 H5 **Westhorpe** Lincs
90 B2 **Westhorpe** Suffk
31 J2 **West Horrington** Somset
50 D8 **West Horsley** Surrey
203 G7 **West Horton** Nthumb
41 H7 **West Hougham** Kent
139 K6 **Westhoughton** Bolton
157 L7 **Westhouse** N York
133 H8 **Westhouses** Derbys
17 L3 **West Howe** Bmouth
29 G4 **West Howetown** Somset
50 F8 **Westhumble** Surrey
221 K2 **West Huntingtower** P & K
30 D2 **West Huntspill** Somset
68 E4 **West Hyde** Beds
50 C1 **West Hyde** Herts
40 F8 **West Hythe** Kent
28 C2 **West Ilkerton** Devon
48 C3 **West Ilsley** W Berk
20 C6 **West Itchenor** W Susx
137 G7 **West Keal** Lincs
47 G5 **West Kennett** Wilts
195 K1 **West Kilbride** N Ayrs
52 C6 **West Kingsdown** Kent
46 A3 **West Kington** Wilts
128 F2 **West Kirby** Wirral
162 F7 **West Knapton** N York
16 D5 **West Knighton** Dorset
32 E4 **West Knoyle** Wilts
203 G5 **West Kyloe** Nthumb
7 J4 **Westlake** Devon
30 F7 **West Lambrook** Somset
70 B3 **Westland Green** Herts
41 K6 **West Langdon** Kent
229 H4 **West Laroch** Highld
20 E3 **West Lavington** W Susx
46 E8 **West Lavington** Wilts
168 F8 **West Layton** N York
116 E6 **West Leake** Notts
202 C5 **West Learmouth** Nthumb
161 G2 **West Lees** N York
13 G1 **West Leigh** Devon
27 H5 **Westleigh** Devon
29 J7 **Westleigh** Devon
29 L5 **West Leigh** Somset
91 K2 **Westleton** Suffk
121 J8 **West Lexham** Norfk
95 J2 **Westley** Shrops
89 G2 **Westley** Suffk
88 C4 **Westley Waterless** Cambs
151 K3 **West Lilling** N York
67 J5 **Westlington** Bucks
199 K3 **West Linton** Border
177 L6 **Westlinton** Cumb
45 M4 **West Littleton** S Glos
48 B2 **West Lockinge** Oxon
16 F6 **West Lulworth** Dorset
152 E2 **West Lutton** N York
31 J4 **West Lydford** Somset
28 C1 **West Lyn** Devon
30 D5 **West Lyng** Somset
120 D7 **West Lynn** Norfk

52 E7 **West Malling** Kent
81 H6 **West Malvern** Worcs
20 C4 **West Marden** W Susx
134 E5 **West Markham** Notts
41 J3 **Westmarsh** Kent
145 H5 **West Marsh** NE Lin
148 F5 **West Marton** N York
32 E6 **West Melbury** Dorset
142 C7 **West Melton** Rothm
35 K6 **West Meon** Hants
35 K5 **West Meon Hut** Hants
35 K5 **West Meon Woodlands**
Hants
72 E4 **West Mersea** Essex
22 E4 **Westmeston** E Susx
180 C6 **West Mickley** Nthumb
69 J4 **Westmill** Herts
69 K2 **Westmill** Herts
15 L3 **West Milton** Dorset
51 J3 **Westminster** Gt Lon
53 K4 **West Minster** Kent
50 E5 **West Molesey** Surrey
30 C5 **West Monkton** Somset
17 L2 **West Moors** Dorset
17 H3 **West Morden** Dorset
201 J5 **West Morriston** Border
149 K7 **West Morton** Brad
31 J6 **West Mudford** Somset
234 A5 **Westmuir** Angus
162 B6 **West Ness** N York
169 K7 **West Newbiggin** Darltn
164 F2 **Westnewton** Cumb
153 K8 **West Newton** E R Yk
120 F6 **West Newton** Norfk
30 D5 **West Newton** Somset
51 J4 **West Norwood** Gt Lon
181 J5 **Westoe** S Tyne
13 J8 **West Ogwell** Devon
45 L5 **Weston** BaNES
114 A1 **Weston** Ches
14 D2 **Weston** Devon
14 E5 **Weston** Devon
16 D8 **Weston** Dorset
129 L3 **Weston** Halton
35 M6 **Weston** Hants
79 L4 **Weston** Herefs
69 H1 **Weston** Herts
119 J6 **Weston** Lincs
149 M6 **Weston** N York
84 B6 **Weston** Nhants
134 F6 **Weston** Notts
95 H8 **Weston** Shrops
96 D5 **Weston** Shrops
112 D6 **Weston** Shrops
114 F6 **Weston** Staffs
48 B4 **Weston** W Berk
80 D7 **Weston Beggard** Herefs
46 B1 **Westonbirt** Gloucs
101 G5 **Weston by Welland** Nhants
35 G3 **Weston Colley** Hants
88 C4 **Weston Colville** Cambs
35 L2 **Weston Corbett** Hants
114 E3 **Weston Coyney** C Stke
84 F3 **Weston Favell** Nhants
88 C5 **Weston Green** Cambs
97 H1 **Weston Heath** Shrops
119 J7 **Weston Hills** Lincs
99 K6 **Weston in Arden** Warwks
85 K8 **Westoning** Beds
44 F4 **Weston-in-Gordano** N Som
68 C1 **Westoning Woodend** Beds
114 B6 **Weston Jones** Staffs
122 C8 **Weston Longville** Norfk
112 F6 **Weston Lullingfields**
Shrops
66 D3 **Weston-on-the-Green**
Oxon
35 L2 **Weston Patrick** Hants
112 D4 **Weston Rhyn** Shrops
82 D7 **Weston Subedge** Gloucs
44 C6 **Weston-Super-Mare** N Som
67 K5 **Weston Turville** Bucks
97 H1 **Weston-under-Lizard** Staffs
63 J3 **Weston under Penyard**
Herefs
113 J5 **Weston-under-Redcastle**
Shrops
83 J1 **Weston under Wetherley**
Warwks
115 M3 **Weston Underwood** Derbys
85 G5 **Weston Underwood** M Keyn
116 C6 **Weston-upon-Trent** Derbys
30 E4 **Westonzoyland** Somset
32 D7 **West Orchard** Dorset
47 H5 **West Overton** Wilts
152 A3 **Westow** N York
11 L4 **West Panson** Devon
245 H4 **West Park** Abers

17 L3 **West Parley** Dorset
39 G3 **West Peckham** Kent
11 L4 **Westpeek** Devon
180 F8 **West Pelton** Dur
31 J3 **West Pennard** Somset
4 C3 **West Pentire** Cnwll
86 C2 **West Perry** Cambs
28 F2 **West Porlock** Somset
30 F6 **Westport** Somset
16 D1 **West Pulham** Dorset
26 F7 **West Putford** Devon
29 K3 **West Quantoxhead** Somset
210 B3 **Westquarter** Falk
43 J7 **Westra** V Glam
13 L2 **West Raddon** Devon
169 J1 **West Rainton** Dur
135 L2 **West Rasen** Lincs
145 G7 **West Ravendale** NE Lin
121 J6 **West Raynham** Norfk
134 D3 **West Retford** Notts
48 E3 **Westridge Green** W Berk
210 B5 **Westrigg** W Loth
65 J8 **Westrop** Swindn
160 F2 **West Rounton** N York
104 D8 **West Row** Suffk
121 H6 **West Rudham** Norfk
122 D3 **West Runton** Norfk
201 K3 **Westruther** Border
103 H4 **Westry** Cambs
212 A5 **West Saltoun** E Loth
13 J2 **West Sandford** Devon
281 e3 **West Sandwick** Shet
159 K6 **West Scrafton** N York
181 G2 **West Sleekburn** Nthumb
123 K7 **West Somerton** Norfk
16 D4 **West Stafford** Dorset
134 F1 **West Stockwith** Notts
20 D5 **West Stoke** W Susx
158 F2 **West Stonesdale** N York
30 F1 **West Stoughton** Somset
32 C6 **West Stour** Dorset
41 H3 **West Stourmouth** Kent
89 G1 **West Stow** Suffk
47 H6 **West Stowell** Wilts
35 H3 **West Stratton** Hants
40 A4 **West Street** Kent
41 K4 **West Street** Kent
52 F4 **West Street** Medway
89 K1 **West Street** Suffk
160 C7 **West Tanfield** N York
5 K2 **West Taphouse** Cnwll
206 D5 **West Tarbert** Ag & B
21 J6 **West Tarring** W Susx
191 H6 **West Thirston** Nthumb
20 C6 **West Thorney** W Susx
133 J4 **Westthorpe** Derbys
117 G6 **West Thorpe** Notts
52 C3 **West Thurrock** Thurr
52 E3 **West Tilbury** Thurr
35 K5 **West Tisted** Hants
136 B3 **West Torrington** Lincs
45 G6 **West Town** BaNES
20 B7 **West Town** Hants
80 B3 **West Town** Herefs
44 F5 **West Town** N Som
31 J4 **West Town** Somset
32 B3 **West Town** Somset
34 C5 **West Tytherley** Hants
103 K1 **West Walton** Norfk
103 K1 **West Walton Highway** Norfk
165 J2 **Westward** Cumb
27 G5 **Westward Ho!** Devon
40 C6 **Westwell** Kent
65 J5 **Westwell** Oxon
40 C5 **Westwell Leacon** Kent
34 C7 **West Wellow** Hants
7 G5 **West Wembury** Devon
222 E8 **West Wemyss** Fife
87 J2 **Westwick** Cambs
168 D7 **Westwick** Dur
44 D6 **West Wick** N Som
122 F6 **Westwick** Norfk
88 C5 **West Wickham** Cambs
51 K5 **West Wickham** Gt Lon
55 H5 **West Williamston** Pembks
120 E8 **West Winch** Norfk
34 B4 **West Winterslow** Wilts
20 C7 **West Wittering** W Susx
159 J5 **West Witton** N York
14 B3 **Westwood** Devon
41 K2 **Westwood** Kent
52 D5 **Westwood** Kent
116 D1 **Westwood** Notts
179 H6 **Westwood** Nthumb
46 A7 **Westwood** Wilts
179 K2 **West Woodburn** Nthumb

48 B6 **West Woodhay** W Berk
99 H8 **Westwood Heath** Covtry
32 C2 **West Woodlands** Somset
143 J7 **Westwoodside** N Linc
35 M3 **West Worldham** Hants
21 K6 **West Worthing** W Susx
88 C5 **West Wratting** Cambs
67 K8 **West Wycombe** Bucks
180 D6 **West Wylam** Nthumb
46 B4 **West Yatton** Wilts
52 D5 **West Yoke** Kent
26 D7 **West Youlstone** Cnwll
53 H5 **Wetham Green** Kent
178 B7 **Wetheral** Cumb
150 F6 **Wetherby** Leeds
89 K3 **Wetherden** Suffk
90 D2 **Wetheringsett** Suffk
71 H1 **Wethersfield** Essex
90 D2 **Wetherup Street** Suffk
114 F2 **Wetley Rocks** Staffs
130 C7 **Wettenhall** Ches
132 B8 **Wetton** Staffs
152 E4 **Wetwang** E R Yk
114 B5 **Wetwood** Staffs
47 K7 **Wexcombe** Wilts
50 C3 **Wexham** Slough
50 C2 **Wexham Street** Bucks
122 C3 **Weybourne** Norfk
36 C1 **Weybourne** Surrey
106 E7 **Weybread** Suffk
106 E7 **Weybread Street** Suffk
50 D6 **Weybridge** Surrey
15 G3 **Weycroft** Devon
279 L3 **Weydale** Highld
34 D2 **Weyhill** Hants
16 C6 **Weymouth** Dorset
84 F8 **Whaddon** Bucks
87 G6 **Whaddon** Cambs
64 B4 **Whaddon** Gloucs
33 L5 **Whaddon** Wilts
46 C6 **Whaddon** Wilts
166 C6 **Whale** Cumb
133 K5 **Whaley** Derbys
131 K3 **Whaley Bridge** Derbys
133 K5 **Whaley Thorns** Derbys
280 D8 **Whaligoe** Highld
148 C8 **Whalley** Lancs
139 L1 **Whalley Banks** Lancs
180 D3 **Whalton** Nthumb
119 K6 **Whaplode** Lincs
103 G1 **Whaplode Drove** Lincs
83 K5 **Wharf** Warwks
148 D2 **Wharfe** N York
147 J8 **Wharles** Lancs
85 J6 **Wharley End** Beds
179 K5 **Wharmley** Nthumb
132 F1 **Wharncliffe Side** Sheff
152 C3 **Wharram-le-Street** N York
130 C6 **Wharton** Ches
80 C4 **Wharton** Herefs
159 L2 **Whashton** N York
157 H6 **Whasset** Cumb
83 G6 **Whatcote** Warwks
99 G3 **Whateley** Warwks
89 L6 **Whatfield** Suffk
15 H1 **Whatley** Somset
32 B2 **Whatley** Somset
45 K3 **Whatley's End** S Glos
24 D4 **Whatlington** E Susx
40 F6 **Whatsole Street** Kent
116 B1 **Whatstandwell** Derbys
117 K4 **Whatton** Notts
173 K5 **Whauphill** D & G
159 H2 **Whaw** N York
4 B6 **Wheal Rose** Cnwll
107 J4 **Wheatacre** Norfk
67 G7 **Wheatfield** Oxon
68 F4 **Wheathampstead** Herts
96 E7 **Wheathill** Shrops
31 J5 **Wheathill** Somset
141 G3 **Wheatley** Calder
36 A3 **Wheatley** Hants
66 E6 **Wheatley** Oxon
169 K3 **Wheatley Hill** Dur
142 F6 **Wheatley Hills** Donc
148 E8 **Wheatley Lane** Lancs
97 J1 **Wheaton Aston** Staffs
112 D1 **Wheatsheaf** Wrexhm
29 G3 **Wheddon Cross** Somset
40 F6 **Wheelbarrow Town** Kent
67 K8 **Wheelerend Common** Bucks
49 J4 **Wheeler's Green** Wokham
39 L4 **Wheeler's Street** Kent
36 E3 **Wheelerstreet** Surrey
130 E7 **Wheelock** Ches
130 E8 **Wheelock Heath** Ches
139 J3 **Wheelton** Lancs

142 C3 **Wheldale** Wakefd
151 L6 **Wheldrake** York
65 H7 **Whelford** Gloucs
68 C6 **Whelpley Hill** Bucks
165 J3 **Whelpo** Cumb
128 F4 **Whelston** Flints
69 J3 **Whempstead** Herts
151 K2 **Whenby** N York
89 G4 **Whepstead** Suffk
90 E7 **Wherstead** Suffk
34 E3 **Wherwell** Hants
132 C4 **Wheston** Derbys
39 G4 **Whetsted** Kent
69 H8 **Whetstone** Gt Lon
100 C4 **Whetstone** Leics
165 G1 **Wheyrigg** Cumb
155 L6 **Whicham** Cumb
85 H8 **Whichford** Warwks
180 F6 **Whickham** Gatesd
12 B3 **Whiddon** Devon
13 G4 **Whiddon Down** Devon
90 D6 **Whight's Corner** Suffk
234 D6 **Whigstreet** Angus
84 C2 **Whilton** Nhants
11 L2 **Whimble** Devon
14 B3 **Whimple** Devon
123 H5 **Whimpwell Green** Norfk
105 K2 **Whinburgh** Norfk
147 H7 **Whin Lane End** Lancs
175 H4 **Whinnie Liggate** D & G
177 J8 **Whinnow** Cumb
257 K5 **Whinnyfold** Abers
169 K7 **Whinny Hill** S on T
19 H5 **Whippingham** IoW
68 C3 **Whipsnade** Beds
13 M4 **Whipton** Devon
132 F3 **Whirlow** Sheff
135 H6 **Whisby** Lincs
117 L8 **Whissendine** Rutlnd
121 K7 **Whissonsett** Norfk
218 C8 **Whistlefield** Ag & B
217 J8 **Whistlefield Inn** Ag & B
49 J4 **Whistley Green** Wokham
129 L2 **Whiston** Knows
85 G3 **Whiston** Nhants
133 J2 **Whiston** Rothm
114 D8 **Whiston** Staffs
115 G2 **Whiston** Staffs
97 H3 **Whiston Cross** Shrops
115 G2 **Whiston Eaves** Staffs
129 L2 **Whiston Lane End** Knows
99 H5 **Whitacre Fields** Warwks
155 K5 **Whitbeck** Cumb
81 G4 **Whitbourne** Herefs
181 K6 **Whitburn** S Tyne
210 C6 **Whitburn** W Loth
129 J4 **Whitby** Ches
171 K8 **Whitby** N York
129 J5 **Whitbyheath** Ches
212 F7 **Whitchester** Border
45 J5 **Whitchurch** BaNES
67 J3 **Whitchurch** Bucks
43 J5 **Whitchurch** Cardif
12 C7 **Whitchurch** Devon
34 F1 **Whitchurch** Hants
63 H4 **Whitchurch** Herefs
48 F3 **Whitchurch** Oxon
74 C7 **Whitchurch** Pembks
113 J3 **Whitchurch** Shrops
15 J3 **Whitchurch Canonicorum** Dorset
48 F3 **Whitchurch Hill** Oxon
16 D5 **Whitcombe** Dorset
95 J5 **Whitcot** Shrops
95 G6 **Whitcott Keysett** Shrops
40 E5 **Whiteacre** Kent
99 G5 **Whiteacre Heath** Warwks
71 J1 **Whiteash Green** Essex
29 K7 **White Ball** Somset
139 L2 **Whitebirk** Bl w D
250 E8 **Whitebridge** Highld
63 G8 **Whitebrook** Mons
257 G8 **Whitecairns** Abers
51 J3 **Whitechapel** Gt Lon
147 L7 **White Chapel** Lancs
82 C7 **White Chapel** Worcs
75 K5 **Whitechurch** Pembks
63 H5 **Whitecliffe** Gloucs
72 C1 **White Colne** Essex
147 L7 **White Coppice** Lancs
211 K5 **Whitecraig** E Loth
63 J6 **Whitecroft** Gloucs
172 F3 **Whitecrook** D & G
2 E4 **Whitecross** Cnwll
3 H6 **White Cross** Cnwll
10 D8 **Whitecross** Cnwll
210 C4 **Whitecross** Falk
81 H8 **White End** Worcs

263 J2 **Whiteface** Highld
194 D3 **Whitefarland** N Ayrs
183 H1 **Whitefaulds** S Ayrs
140 B6 **Whitefield** Bury
28 C4 **Whitefield** Devon
29 K5 **Whitefield** Somset
129 K2 **Whitefield Lane End** Knows
256 C6 **Whiteford** Abers
130 C6 **Whitegate** Ches
49 H8 **Whitehall** Hants
275 e3 **Whitehall** Ork
37 H6 **Whitehall** W Susx
164 C7 **Whitehaven** Cumb
40 C3 **Whitehill** Kent
99 L1 **Whitehill** Leics
36 A4 **Whitehill and Bordon** Hants
268 B3 **Whitehills** Abers
256 A8 **Whitehouse** Abers
206 C6 **Whitehouse** Ag & B
98 E4 **Whitehouse Common** Birm
212 D3 **Whitekirk** E Loth
168 C3 **White Kirkley** Dur
16 D3 **White Lackington** Dorset
30 F7 **Whitelackington** Somset
81 L4 **White Ladies Aston** Worcs
67 K6 **Whiteleaf** Bucks
180 E7 **White-le-Head** Dur
19 J2 **Whiteley** Hants
19 J7 **Whiteley Bank** IoW
131 H4 **Whiteley Green** Ches
50 E6 **Whiteley Village** Surrey
22 D2 **Whitemans Green** W Susx
58 E4 **White Mill** Carmth
253 J1 **Whitemire** Moray
116 F3 **Whitemoor** C Nott
5 G3 **Whitemoor** Cnwll
116 B2 **Whitemoor** Derbys
131 H7 **Whitemoor** Staffs
281 d6 **Whiteness** Shet
71 J3 **White Notley** Essex
65 M4 **Whiteoak Green** Oxon
45 L7 **White Ox Mead** BaNES
34 B6 **Whiteparish** Wilts
137 G4 **White Pit** Lincs
256 F7 **Whiterashes** Abers
70 E4 **White Roding** Essex
280 E6 **Whiterow** Highld
265 G8 **Whiterow** Moray
64 B5 **Whiteshill** Gloucs
23 J4 **Whitesmith** E Susx
139 G3 **White Stake** Lancs
30 D8 **Whitestaunton** Somset
13 K3 **Whitestone** Devon
80 D6 **White Stone** Herefs
13 L4 **Whitestone Cross** Devon
89 K7 **Whitestreet Green** Suffk
152 B2 **Whitewall Corner** N York
49 K3 **White Waltham** W & M
45 L6 **Whiteway** BaNES
64 C5 **Whiteway** Gloucs
148 B6 **Whitewell** Lancs
12 E8 **Whiteworks** Devon
41 J6 **Whitfield** Kent
84 B7 **Whitfield** Nhants
179 H7 **Whitfield** Nthumb
63 K8 **Whitfield** S Glos
179 H7 **Whitfield Hall** Nthumb
14 F3 **Whitford** Devon
128 D4 **Whitford** Flints
143 K3 **Whitgift** E R Yk
114 D6 **Whitgreave** Staffs
174 C6 **Whithorn** D & G
195 G6 **Whiting Bay** N Ayrs
142 B1 **Whitkirk** Leeds
55 L3 **Whitland** Carmth
188 E4 **Whitlaw** Border
196 D6 **Whitletts** S Ayrs
142 E4 **Whitley** N York
49 H5 **Whitley** Readg
133 G1 **Whitley** Sheff
46 C5 **Whitley** Wilts
181 J4 **Whitley Bay** N Tyne
179 L7 **Whitley Chapel** Nthumb
114 C6 **Whitley Heath** Staffs
141 K4 **Whitley Lower** Kirk
38 D3 **Whitley Row** Kent
98 E8 **Whitlock's End** Solhll
63 M5 **Whitminster** Gloucs
17 L1 **Whitmore** Dorset
114 C3 **Whitmore** Staffs
29 J7 **Whitnage** Devon
83 H3 **Whitnash** Warwks
79 J5 **Whitney-on-Wye** Herefs
165 G3 **Whitrigg** Cumb
177 H7 **Whitrigg** Cumb
177 H7 **Whitrigglees** Cumb

366 Whitsbury - Winteringham

33 K7 **Whitsbury** Hants
202 D3 **Whitsome** Border
44 D2 **Whitson** Newpt
40 E2 **Whitstable** Kent
11 K3 **Whitstone** Cnwll
190 F4 **Whittingham** Nthumb
95 K5 **Whittingslow** Shrops
133 H4 **Whittington** Derbys
64 E3 **Whittington** Gloucs
157 K7 **Whittington** Lancs
104 E3 **Whittington** Norfk
112 E5 **Whittington** Shrops
97 J6 **Whittington** Staffs
98 F2 **Whittington** Staffs
99 J4 **Whittington** Warwks
81 K4 **Whittington** Worcs
133 G5 **Whittington Moor** Derbys
84 D6 **Whittlebury** Nhants
139 H3 **Whittle-le-Woods** Lancs
102 F4 **Whittlesey** Cambs
87 K5 **Whittlesford** Cambs
139 L4 **Whittlestone Head** Bl w D
143 M3 **Whitton** N Linc
190 F6 **Whitton** Nthumb
79 J2 **Whitton** Powys
169 K6 **Whitton** S on T
80 D1 **Whitton** Shrops
90 D5 **Whitton** Suffk
47 L4 **Whittonditch** Wilts
180 C7 **Whittonstall** Nthumb
48 C7 **Whitway** Hants
133 K4 **Whitwell** Derbys
68 F3 **Whitwell** Herts
19 J8 **Whitwell** IoW
160 D3 **Whitwell** N York
101 K2 **Whitwell** Rutlnd
151 M3 **Whitwell-on-the-Hill** N York
122 B7 **Whitwell Street** Norfk
116 D8 **Whitwick** Leics
142 B3 **Whitwood** Wakefd
140 D4 **Whitworth** Lancs
113 H4 **Whixall** Shrops
150 F4 **Whixley** N York
168 E7 **Whorlton** Dur
161 G2 **Whorlton** N York
80 D3 **Whyle** Herefs
51 J7 **Whyteleafe** Surrey
63 H7 **Wibdon** Gloucs
141 J2 **Wibsey** Brad
100 B6 **Wibtoft** Warwks
81 H3 **Wichenford** Worcs
40 B4 **Wichling** Kent
18 B5 **Wick** Bmouth
14 E2 **Wick** Devon
280 E6 **Wick** Highld
45 K4 **Wick** S Glos
30 B2 **Wick** Somset
30 F5 **Wick** Somset
42 D7 **Wick** V Glam
21 H6 **Wick** W Susx
33 L6 **Wick** Wilts
81 M6 **Wick** Worcs
88 B1 **Wicken** Cambs
84 E7 **Wicken** Nhants
87 K8 **Wicken Bonhunt** Essex
136 A3 **Wickenby** Lincs
85 K5 **Wick End** Beds
133 J2 **Wickersley** Rothm
89 K6 **Wicker Street Green** Suffk
71 H8 **Wickford** Essex
19 K2 **Wickham** Hants
48 B5 **Wickham** W Berk
71 K5 **Wickham Bishops** Essex
41 H3 **Wickhambreaux** Kent
88 E4 **Wickhambrook** Suffk
82 C7 **Wickhamford** Worcs
90 C2 **Wickham Green** Suffk
48 B4 **Wickham Green** W Berk
48 B5 **Wickham Heath** W Berk
91 G4 **Wickham Market** Suffk
107 J2 **Wickhampton** Norfk
89 G7 **Wickham St Paul** Essex
90 C2 **Wickham Skeith** Suffk
88 F4 **Wickham Street** Suffk
90 C1 **Wickham Street** Suffk
106 B3 **Wicklewood** Norfk
122 D5 **Wickmere** Norfk
44 D6 **Wick St Lawrence** N Som
23 J5 **Wickstreet** E Susx
45 L1 **Wickwar** S Glos
70 D1 **Widdington** Essex
140 D1 **Widdop** Calder
191 K7 **Widdrington** Nthumb
191 J7 **Widdrington Station** Nthumb
13 G7 **Widecombe in the Moor** Devon
6 B3 **Widegates** Cnwll
11 H2 **Widemouth Bay** Cnwll
181 G4 **Wide Open** N Tyne
71 G6 **Widford** Essex
70 B4 **Widford** Herts
47 G1 **Widham** Wilts
19 M2 **Widley** Hants
67 L7 **Widmer End** Bucks
117 G6 **Widmerpool** Notts
51 L5 **Widmore** Gt Lon
129 L3 **Widnes** Halton
14 F3 **Widworthy** Devon
139 H6 **Wigan** Wigan
31 G7 **Wigborough** Somset
14 C4 **Wiggaton** Devon
120 D8 **Wiggenhall St Germans** Norfk
104 B1 **Wiggenhall St Mary Magdalen** Norfk
104 B1 **Wiggenhall St Mary the Virgin** Norfk
88 D6 **Wiggens Green** Essex
132 B7 **Wiggenstall** Staffs
112 E4 **Wiggington** Shrops
68 B5 **Wigginton** Herts
83 J8 **Wigginton** Oxon
99 G2 **Wigginton** Staffs
151 J4 **Wigginton** York
68 B5 **Wigginton Bottom** Herts
148 E4 **Wigglesworth** N York
177 J8 **Wiggonby** Cumb
21 H3 **Wiggonholt** W Susx
151 G6 **Wighill** N York
121 L3 **Wighton** Norfk
97 K4 **Wightwick** Wolves
132 F5 **Wigley** Derbys
34 D7 **Wigley** Hants
80 A2 **Wigmore** Herefs
53 G6 **Wigmore** Medway
135 G5 **Wigsley** Notts
102 A6 **Wigsthorpe** Nhants
100 D4 **Wigston** Leics
100 D3 **Wigston Fields** Leics
100 A5 **Wigston Parva** Leics
134 B3 **Wigthorpe** Notts
119 J4 **Wigtoft** Lincs
165 H1 **Wigton** Cumb
174 C4 **Wigtown** D & G
141 L8 **Wigtwizzle** Sheff
150 D7 **Wike** Leeds
101 H5 **Wilbarston** Nhants
151 M5 **Wilberfoss** E R Yk
103 K8 **Wilburton** Cambs
85 G2 **Wilby** Nhants
105 L5 **Wilby** Norfk
90 F1 **Wilby** Suffk
47 H6 **Wilcot** Wilts
112 F7 **Wilcott** Shrops
44 E2 **Wilcrick** Newpt
132 F5 **Wilday Green** Derbys
131 K6 **Wildboarclough** Ches
86 B4 **Wilden** Beds
81 J1 **Wilden** Worcs
34 D1 **Wildhern** Hants
69 H5 **Wildhill** Herts
209 L8 **Wildmanbridge** S Lans
98 B8 **Wildmoor** Worcs
143 K8 **Wildsworth** Lincs
116 F4 **Wilford** C Nott
113 K3 **Wilkesley** Ches
264 E3 **Wilkhaven** Highld
210 F5 **Wilkieston** W Loth
69 G5 **Wilkin's Green** Herts
136 E7 **Wilksby** Lincs
29 J8 **Willand** Devon
24 C2 **Willards Hill** E Susx
113 L1 **Willaston** Ches
129 H4 **Willaston** Ches
85 G7 **Willen** M Keyn
99 K8 **Willenhall** Covtry
98 B4 **Willenhall** Wsall
144 C2 **Willerby** E R Yk
163 H6 **Willerby** N York
82 D7 **Willersey** Gloucs
79 K6 **Willersley** Herefs
40 D7 **Willesborough** Kent
40 D7 **Willesborough Lees** Kent
51 G2 **Willesden** Gt Lon
27 L4 **Willesleigh** Devon
46 B1 **Willesley** Wilts
29 K4 **Willett** Somset
96 F3 **Willey** Shrops
100 B6 **Willey** Warwks
50 B8 **Willey Green** Surrey
83 L6 **Williamscot** Oxon
42 F4 **Williamstown** Rhondd
69 G1 **Willian** Herts
82 E5 **Willicote** Warwks
70 E5 **Willingale** Essex
23 K6 **Willingdon** E Susx
87 H1 **Willingham** Cambs
135 H3 **Willingham by Stow** Lincs
88 C4 **Willingham Green** Cambs
86 C5 **Willington** Beds
116 A6 **Willington** Derbys
169 G4 **Willington** Dur
39 K3 **Willington** Kent
83 G7 **Willington** Warwks
129 M6 **Willington Corner** Ches
181 H5 **Willington Quay** N Tyne
143 J1 **Willitoft** E R Yk
29 K3 **Williton** Somset
137 J5 **Willoughby** Lincs
83 M2 **Willoughby** Warwks
119 K2 **Willoughby Hills** Lincs
117 H6 **Willoughby-on-the-Wolds** Notts
100 C5 **Willoughby Waterleys** Leics
135 J1 **Willoughton** Lincs
130 B4 **Willow Green** Ches
71 H3 **Willows Green** Essex
45 K5 **Willsbridge** S Glos
12 D6 **Willsworthy** Devon
30 F6 **Willtown** Somset
82 E4 **Wilmcote** Warwks
45 K6 **Wilmington** BaNES
14 F3 **Wilmington** Devon
23 J6 **Wilmington** E Susx
52 B4 **Wilmington** Kent
131 G3 **Wilmslow** Ches
99 G3 **Wilnecote** Staffs
139 K1 **Wilpshire** Lancs
149 K8 **Wilsden** Brad
118 D3 **Wilsford** Lincs
33 K3 **Wilsford** Wilts
47 G7 **Wilsford** Wilts
28 D1 **Wilsham** Devon
141 H6 **Wilshaw** Kirk
150 A3 **Wilsill** N York
39 K6 **Wilsley Green** Kent
39 K6 **Wilsley Pound** Kent
63 H2 **Wilson** Herefs
116 C6 **Wilson** Leics
198 F2 **Wilsontown** S Lans
85 L6 **Wilstead** Beds
102 B1 **Wilsthorpe** Lincs
67 L4 **Wilstone** Herts
67 M4 **Wilstone Green** Herts
164 D8 **Wilton** Cumb
63 H2 **Wilton** Herefs
162 F6 **Wilton** N York
170 D6 **Wilton** R & Cl
33 J4 **Wilton** Wilts
47 K6 **Wilton** Wilts
188 E3 **Wilton Dean** Border
88 B7 **Wimbish** Essex
88 C8 **Wimbish Green** Essex
51 G5 **Wimbledon** Gt Lon
103 J5 **Wimblington** Cambs
130 D7 **Wimboldsley** Ches
17 K3 **Wimborne Minster** Dorset
33 H8 **Wimborne St Giles** Dorset
104 C2 **Wimbotsham** Norfk
87 G5 **Wimpole** Cambs
82 F5 **Wimpstone** Warwks
32 B5 **Wincanton** Somset
136 F6 **Winceby** Lincs
130 C4 **Wincham** Ches
210 E4 **Winchburgh** W Loth
64 F2 **Winchcombe** Gloucs
25 G4 **Winchelsea** E Susx
25 G4 **Winchelsea Beach** E Susx
35 G5 **Winchester** Hants
39 J5 **Winchet Hill** Kent
49 J8 **Winchfield** Hants
68 B8 **Winchmore Hill** Bucks
69 J8 **Winchmore Hill** Gt Lon
131 J6 **Wincle** Ches
133 G1 **Wincobank** Sheff
164 D7 **Winder** Cumb
156 F3 **Windermere** Cumb
83 H7 **Winderton** Warwks
250 F2 **Windhill** Highld
131 J3 **Windlehurst** Stockp
50 A6 **Windlesham** Surrey
10 B7 **Windmill** Cnwll
132 C4 **Windmill** Derbys
23 L5 **Windmill Hill** E Susx
30 D7 **Windmill Hill** Somset
65 J4 **Windrush** Gloucs
267 L4 **Windsole** Abers
50 B4 **Windsor** W & M
64 B7 **Windsoredge** Gloucs
89 H4 **Windsor Green** Suffk
83 G1 **Windy Arbour** Warwks
222 F7 **Windygates** Fife
131 G5 **Windyharbour** Ches
129 G8 **Windy Hill** Wrexhm
22 C3 **Wineham** W Susx
145 J3 **Winestead** E R Yk
148 F7 **Winewall** Lancs
106 C6 **Winfarthing** Norfk
19 J6 **Winford** IoW
45 G6 **Winford** N Som
79 K6 **Winforton** Herefs
16 F5 **Winfrith Newburgh** Dorset
67 L3 **Wing** Bucks
101 K3 **Wing** Rutlnd
169 L3 **Wingate** Dur
139 K6 **Wingates** Bolton
191 G7 **Wingates** Nthumb
133 G6 **Wingerworth** Derbys
68 C2 **Wingfield** Beds
106 E7 **Wingfield** Suffk
46 B7 **Wingfield** Wilts
106 E7 **Wingfield Green** Suffk
41 H4 **Wingham** Kent
41 G6 **Wingmore** Kent
67 L3 **Wingrave** Bucks
134 E7 **Winkburn** Notts
49 L4 **Winkfield** Br For
49 L5 **Winkfield Row** Br For
49 L4 **Winkfield Street** Br For
115 H1 **Winkhill** Staffs
38 D3 **Winkhurst Green** Kent
12 F1 **Winkleigh** Devon
150 C2 **Winksley** N York
18 B4 **Winkton** Dorset
180 E6 **Winlaton** Gatesd
180 E6 **Winlaton Mill** Gatesd
280 D5 **Winless** Highld
112 C7 **Winllan** Powys
147 J6 **Winmarleigh** Lancs
35 G5 **Winnall** Hants
81 J2 **Winnall** Worcs
49 J5 **Winnersh** Wokham
130 C5 **Winnington** Ches
164 D5 **Winscales** Cumb
44 E7 **Winscombe** N Som
130 C6 **Winsford** Ches
28 F4 **Winsford** Somset
27 J3 **Winsham** Devon
15 J1 **Winsham** Somset
115 M7 **Winshill** Staffs
57 J5 **Winshwen** Swans
166 D4 **Winskill** Cumb
35 K1 **Winslade** Hants
46 A6 **Winsley** Wilts
67 J2 **Winslow** Bucks
65 G5 **Winson** Gloucs
34 D8 **Winsor** Hants
156 F4 **Winster** Cumb
132 E7 **Winster** Derbys
168 F7 **Winston** Dur
90 E3 **Winston** Suffk
64 D5 **Winstone** Gloucs
27 J8 **Winswell** Devon
16 D5 **Winterborne Came** Dorset
17 G2 **Winterborne Clenston** Dorset
16 D5 **Winterborne Herringston** Dorset
16 F2 **Winterborne Houghton** Dorset
17 G3 **Winterborne Kingston** Dorset
16 C5 **Winterborne Monkton** Dorset
16 F2 **Winterborne Stickland** Dorset
17 G3 **Winterborne Tomson** Dorset
17 G2 **Winterborne Whitechurch** Dorset
17 H3 **Winterborne Zelston** Dorset
45 J3 **Winterbourne** S Glos
48 C4 **Winterbourne** W Berk
16 B4 **Winterbourne Abbas** Dorset
47 G4 **Winterbourne Bassett** Wilts
33 L4 **Winterbourne Dauntsey** Wilts
33 L4 **Winterbourne Earls** Wilts
33 L4 **Winterbourne Gunner** Wilts
47 G4 **Winterbourne Monkton** Wilts
16 B4 **Winterbourne Steepleton** Dorset
33 J3 **Winterbourne Stoke** Wilts
48 F1 **Winterbrook** Oxon
149 G4 **Winterburn** N York
144 A3 **Winteringham** N Linc

130 E8 **Winterley** Ches
142 B4 **Wintersett** Wakefd
34 B4 **Winterslow** Wilts
144 A4 **Winterton** N Linc
123 K7 **Winterton-on-Sea** Norfk
137 K6 **Winthorpe** Lincs
135 G8 **Winthorpe** Notts
17 L4 **Winton** Bmouth
167 H8 **Winton** Cumb
23 H6 **Winton** E Susx
160 F3 **Winton** N York
162 F8 **Wintringham** N York
102 B7 **Winwick** Cambs
100 D8 **Winwick** Nhants
130 B1 **Winwick** Warrtn
115 M1 **Wirksworth** Derbys
113 J3 **Wirswall** Ches
103 J2 **Wisbech** Cambs
103 J2 **Wisbech St Mary** Cambs
37 G5 **Wisborough Green** W Susx
55 K5 **Wiseman's Bridge** Pembks
134 E2 **Wiseton** Notts
64 D5 **Wishanger** Gloucs
209 L7 **Wishaw** N Lans
98 F4 **Wishaw** Warwks
50 D7 **Wisley** Surrey
136 D5 **Wispington** Lincs
40 B7 **Wissenden** Kent
107 H7 **Wissett** Suffk
104 D4 **Wissington** Norfk
89 J8 **Wissington** Suffk
95 K6 **Wistanstow** Shrops
113 L5 **Wistanswick** Shrops
113 L1 **Wistaston** Ches
130 D8 **Wistaston Green** Ches
131 G5 **Wisterfield** Ches
55 H3 **Wiston** Pembks
198 F6 **Wiston** S Lans
21 K4 **Wiston** W Susx
102 F7 **Wistow** Cambs
100 E4 **Wistow** Leics
142 F1 **Wistow** N York
148 C8 **Wiswell** Lancs
103 J7 **Witcham** Cambs
17 J1 **Witchampton** Dorset
103 K7 **Witchford** Cambs
31 G6 **Witcombe** Somset
71 K4 **Witham** Essex
32 B3 **Witham Friary** Somset
118 D8 **Witham on the Hill** Lincs
135 H7 **Witham St Hughs** Lincs
136 E3 **Withcall** Lincs
22 D5 **Withdean** Br & H
23 L2 **Witherenden Hill** E Susx
28 D8 **Witheridge** Devon
99 J4 **Witherley** Leics
137 H3 **Withern** Lincs
145 J2 **Withernsea** E R Yk
153 K7 **Withernwick** E R Yk
106 F7 **Withersdale Street** Suffk
88 D5 **Withersfield** Suffk
156 F5 **Witherslack** Cumb
5 G2 **Withiel** Cnwll
29 H4 **Withiel Florey** Somset
5 G2 **Withielgoose** Cnwll
64 F4 **Withington** Gloucs
80 D6 **Withington** Herefs
131 G1 **Withington** Manch
96 D1 **Withington** Shrops
115 G4 **Withington** Staffs
130 F5 **Withington Green** Ches
80 D6 **Withington Marsh** Herefs
28 F8 **Withleigh** Devon
139 J3 **Withnell** Lancs
82 B1 **Withybed Green** Worcs
99 L6 **Withybrook** Warwks
29 J3 **Withycombe** Somset
38 D6 **Withyham** E Susx
45 K7 **Withy Mills** BaNES
28 E4 **Withypool** Somset
45 H5 **Withywood** Bristl
36 E3 **Witley** Surrey
90 E5 **Witnesham** Suffk
65 M5 **Witney** Oxon
102 B3 **Wittering** C Pete
25 G2 **Wittersham** Kent
98 D5 **Witton** Birm
107 G2 **Witton** Norfk
123 G5 **Witton** Norfk
169 G2 **Witton Gilbert** Dur
107 J3 **Witton Green** Norfk
168 F4 **Witton le Wear** Dur
168 F4 **Witton Park** Dur
29 K5 **Wiveliscombe** Somset
35 K3 **Wivelrod** Hants
22 E3 **Wivelsfield** E Susx
22 E3 **Wivelsfield Green** E Susx
22 E3 **Wivelsfield Station** W Susx

72 F3 **Wivenhoe** Essex
72 F2 **Wivenhoe Cross** Essex
122 A3 **Wiveton** Norfk
73 H2 **Wix** Essex
82 C4 **Wixford** Warwks
73 H2 **Wix Green** Essex
113 J6 **Wixhill** Shrops
88 E6 **Wixoe** Suffk
85 J8 **Woburn** Beds
85 H8 **Woburn Sands** M Keyn
49 G6 **Wokefield Park** W Berk
50 C7 **Woking** Surrey
49 K5 **Wokingham** Wokham
13 K8 **Wolborough** Devon
51 K7 **Woldingham** Surrey
163 J8 **Wold Newton** E R Yk
145 G8 **Wold Newton** NE Lin
199 H6 **Wolfclyde** S Lans
80 F3 **Wolferlow** Herefs
120 E6 **Wolferton** Norfk
83 M2 **Wolfhampcote** Warwks
233 H8 **Wolfhill** P & K
179 G7 **Wolf Hills** Nthumb
74 F6 **Wolf's Castle** Pembks
54 F3 **Wolfsdale** Pembks
97 K6 **Wollaston** Dudley
85 H3 **Wollaston** Nhants
95 H1 **Wollaston** Shrops
116 E4 **Wollaton** C Nott
13 J6 **Wolleigh** Devon
113 K5 **Wollerton** Shrops
97 L6 **Wollescote** Dudley
115 G7 **Wolseley Bridge** Staffs
168 D3 **Wolsingham** Dur
114 D2 **Wolstanton** Staffs
140 C5 **Wolstenholme** Rochdl
99 L8 **Wolston** Warwks
176 E8 **Wolsty** Cumb
66 D5 **Wolvercote** Oxon
97 K4 **Wolverhampton** Wolves
113 G5 **Wolverley** Shrops
97 J7 **Wolverley** Worcs
48 E7 **Wolverton** Hants
41 H6 **Wolverton** Kent
84 F7 **Wolverton** M Keyn
82 F3 **Wolverton** Warwks
32 C4 **Wolverton** Wilts
48 E7 **Wolverton Common** Hants
62 F7 **Wolvesnewton** Mons
99 L6 **Wolvey** Warwks
99 L5 **Wolvey Heath** Warwks
170 B5 **Wolviston** S on T
161 L6 **Wombleton** N York
97 K5 **Wombourne** Staffs
142 B7 **Wombwell** Barns
41 H5 **Womenswold** Kent
142 E4 **Womersley** N York
62 F5 **Wonastow** Mons
36 F2 **Wonersh** Surrey
13 L4 **Wonford** Devon
12 F4 **Wonson** Devon
35 G3 **Wonston** Hants
49 M2 **Wooburn** Bucks
49 M1 **Wooburn Green** Bucks
49 M1 **Wooburn Moor** Bucks
159 J6 **Woodale** N York
133 J3 **Woodall** Rothm
123 G8 **Woodbastwick** Norfk
134 F4 **Woodbeck** Notts
82 C4 **Wood Bevington** Warwks
117 G2 **Woodborough** Notts
47 G7 **Woodborough** Wilts
14 E3 **Woodbridge** Devon
32 E7 **Woodbridge** Dorset
91 G5 **Woodbridge** Suffk
84 D6 **Wood Burcote** Nhants
14 B5 **Woodbury** Devon
14 B4 **Woodbury Salterton** Devon
64 B6 **Woodchester** Gloucs
40 B8 **Woodchurch** Kent
129 G2 **Woodchurch** Wirral
29 G2 **Woodcombe** Somset
51 J6 **Woodcote** Gt Lon
48 F3 **Woodcote** Oxon
114 B8 **Woodcote** Wrekin
81 L1 **Woodcote Green** Worcs
48 B7 **Woodcott** Hants
63 G7 **Woodcroft** Gloucs
33 G7 **Woodcutts** Dorset
122 B6 **Wood Dalling** Norfk
88 D3 **Woodditton** Cambs
66 D5 **Woodeaton** Oxon
114 C7 **Wood Eaton** Staffs
55 H6 **Wooden** Pembks
85 K6 **Wood End** Beds
86 B2 **Wood End** Beds
103 H8 **Wood End** Cambs
50 E3 **Wood End** Gt Lon

69 J2 **Wood End** Herts
228 B3 **Woodend** Highld
84 B5 **Woodend** Nhants
115 K6 **Woodend** Staffs
210 B5 **Woodend** W Loth
20 D5 **Woodend** W Susx
82 D1 **Wood End** Warwks
99 H4 **Wood End** Warwks
99 J6 **Wood End** Warwks
97 L3 **Wood End** Wolves
136 E6 **Wood Enderby** Lincs
70 E2 **Woodend Green** Essex
33 L6 **Woodfalls** Wilts
26 C8 **Woodford** Cnwll
8 B5 **Woodford** Devon
63 K7 **Woodford** Gloucs
69 L8 **Woodford** Gt Lon
101 L8 **Woodford** Nhants
131 H3 **Woodford** Stockp
51 L1 **Woodford Bridge** Gt Lon
84 A5 **Woodford Halse** Nhants
69 L8 **Woodford Wells** Gt Lon
98 C6 **Woodgate** Birm
29 K7 **Woodgate** Devon
121 K8 **Woodgate** Norfk
121 M8 **Woodgate** Norfk
20 F6 **Woodgate** W Susx
81 M2 **Woodgate** Worcs
51 J1 **Wood Green** Gt Lon
33 L7 **Woodgreen** Hants
66 A5 **Woodgreen** Oxon
136 D6 **Woodhall** Lincs
159 H4 **Woodhall** N York
141 K1 **Woodhall Hill** Leeds
136 C7 **Woodhall Spa** Lincs
67 H3 **Woodham** Bucks
169 H5 **Woodham** Dur
50 D6 **Woodham** Surrey
71 J7 **Woodham Ferrers** Essex
71 K6 **Woodham Mortimer** Essex
71 K5 **Woodham Walter** Essex
97 L3 **Wood Hayes** Wolves
256 E4 **Woodhead** Abers
30 E5 **Woodhill** Somset
181 H1 **Woodhorn** Nthumb
181 H1 **Woodhorn Demesne** Nthumb
141 L1 **Woodhouse** Leeds
116 F8 **Woodhouse** Leics
133 H3 **Woodhouse** Sheff
142 B3 **Woodhouse** Wakefd
116 F8 **Woodhouse Eaves** Leics
131 H7 **Woodhouse Green** Staffs
211 H6 **Woodhouselee** Mdloth
177 L4 **Woodhouselees** D & G
133 H3 **Woodhouse Mill** Sheff
177 K8 **Woodhouses** Cumb
140 D7 **Woodhouses** Oldham
98 D2 **Woodhouses** Staffs
115 J7 **Woodhouses** Staffs
8 D4 **Woodhuish** Devon
103 G8 **Woodhurst** Cambs
22 E6 **Woodingdean** Br & H
141 L3 **Woodkirk** Leeds
256 F7 **Woodland** Abers
7 J4 **Woodland** Devon
8 B1 **Woodland** Devon
168 D5 **Woodland** Dur
40 F7 **Woodland** Kent
182 F4 **Woodland** S Ayrs
13 H3 **Woodland Head** Devon
245 H4 **Woodlands** Abers
142 E6 **Woodlands** Donc
17 L1 **Woodlands** Dorset
18 E1 **Woodlands** Hants
52 C6 **Woodlands** Kent
150 D5 **Woodlands** N York
29 L3 **Woodlands** Somset
49 L3 **Woodlands Park** W & M
47 M4 **Woodlands St Mary** W Berk
31 J3 **Woodland Street** Somset
132 F2 **Woodland View** Sheff
112 F5 **Wood Lane** Shrops
114 C2 **Wood Lane** Staffs
7 L5 **Woodleigh** Devon
142 B2 **Woodlesford** Leeds
131 J1 **Woodley** Stockp
49 J4 **Woodley** Wokham
63 M7 **Woodmancote** Gloucs
64 E2 **Woodmancote** Gloucs
64 E5 **Woodmancote** Gloucs
20 C5 **Woodmancote** W Susx
22 C4 **Woodmancote** W Susx
81 L6 **Woodmancote** Worcs
35 H2 **Woodmancott** Hants
153 G8 **Woodmansey** E R Yk
36 C5 **Woodmansgreen** W Susx
51 H7 **Woodmansterne** Surrey

14 B5 **Woodmanton** Devon
46 B7 **Woodmarsh** Wilts
115 J7 **Woodmill** Staffs
33 H6 **Woodminton** Wilts
41 J4 **Woodnesborough** Kent
102 A4 **Woodnewton** Nhants
116 D1 **Woodnook** Notts
121 M6 **Wood Norton** Norfk
139 G1 **Woodplumpton** Lancs
105 K3 **Woodrising** Norfk
142 B2 **Wood Row** Leeds
97 K8 **Woodrow** Worcs
24 B3 **Wood's Corner** E Susx
113 M5 **Woodseaves** Shrops
114 B6 **Woodseaves** Staffs
47 J4 **Woodsend** Wilts
133 L3 **Woodsetts** Rothm
16 E4 **Woodsford** Dorset
39 G6 **Wood's Green** E Susx
50 B5 **Woodside** Br For
164 D4 **Woodside** Cumb
70 C6 **Woodside** Essex
223 G5 **Woodside** Fife
51 J5 **Woodside** Gt Lon
18 E5 **Woodside** Hants
69 H5 **Woodside** Herts
233 J7 **Woodside** P & K
40 B4 **Woodside Green** Kent
66 C4 **Woodstock** Oxon
75 H7 **Woodstock** Pembks
102 D4 **Woodston** C Pete
123 H7 **Wood Street** Norfk
36 E1 **Wood Street Village** Surrey
133 J5 **Woodthorpe** Derbys
116 F8 **Woodthorpe** Leics
137 H4 **Woodthorpe** Lincs
106 F4 **Woodton** Norfk
147 L7 **Wood Top** Lancs
27 G6 **Woodtown** Devon
138 C5 **Woodvale** Sefton
116 A7 **Woodville** Derbys
114 B5 **Woodwall Green** Staffs
102 E7 **Wood Walton** Cambs
33 H7 **Woodyates** Dorset
28 B1 **Woody Bay** Devon
80 C2 **Woofferton** Shrops
31 H2 **Wookey** Somset
31 H2 **Wookey Hole** Somset
17 G5 **Wool** Dorset
27 H2 **Woolacombe** Devon
41 H5 **Woolage Green** Kent
41 H5 **Woolage Village** Kent
63 H7 **Woolaston** Gloucs
63 H6 **Woolaston Common** Gloucs
30 E3 **Woolavington** Somset
36 C6 **Woolbeding** W Susx
14 D4 **Woolbrook** Devon
29 H4 **Woolcotts** Somset
141 J6 **Wooldale** Kirk
202 F7 **Wooler** Nthumb
13 J1 **Woolfardisworthy** Devon
26 F6 **Woolfardisworthy** Devon
140 B5 **Woolfold** Bury
199 G2 **Woolfords** S Lans
48 E5 **Woolhampton** W Berk
80 E8 **Woolhope** Herefs
16 E1 **Woolland** Dorset
45 J6 **Woollard** BaNES
69 K5 **Woollensbrook** Herts
45 L5 **Woolley** BaNES
102 C8 **Woolley** Cambs
26 D7 **Woolley** Cnwll
133 G7 **Woolley** Derbys
141 M5 **Woolley** Wakefd
131 K1 **Woolley Bridge** Derbys
49 K3 **Woolley Green** W & M
81 M3 **Woolmere Green** Worcs
69 H3 **Woolmer Green** Herts
30 D4 **Woolmerston** Somset
15 J1 **Woolminstone** Somset
39 L6 **Woolpack** Kent
89 K3 **Woolpit** Suffk
89 K3 **Woolpit Green** Suffk
83 L2 **Woolscott** Warwks
13 J2 **Woolsgrove** Devon
180 F5 **Woolsington** N u Ty
95 L4 **Woolstaston** Shrops
117 L5 **Woolsthorpe** Lincs
118 B6 **Woolsthorpe-by-Colsterworth** Lincs
19 G2 **Woolston** C Sotn
7 L5 **Woolston** Devon
7 L6 **Woolston** Devon
95 K6 **Woolston** Shrops
112 D6 **Woolston** Shrops
29 K3 **Woolston** Somset

31 L5 **Woolston** Somset
130 C2 **Woolston** Warrtn
64 D1 **Woolstone** Gloucs
85 G7 **Woolstone** M Keyn
47 L2 **Woolstone** Oxon
8 A2 **Woolston Green** Devon
129 K2 **Woolton** Lpool
48 B6 **Woolton Hill** Hants
90 E7 **Woolverstone** Suffk
46 A8 **Woolverton** Somset
51 L3 **Woolwich** Gt Lon
79 L5 **Woonton** Herefs
80 D3 **Woonton** Herefs
190 F2 **Wooperton** Nthumb
114 A3 **Woore** Shrops
90 F1 **Wootten Green** Suffk
85 K6 **Wootton** Beds
18 C4 **Wootton** Hants
79 L5 **Wootton** Herefs
19 J5 **Wootton** IoW
41 H6 **Wootton** Kent
144 D4 **Wootton** N Linc
84 E4 **Wootton** Nhants
66 B3 **Wootton** Oxon
66 C6 **Wootton** Oxon
112 E6 **Wootton** Shrops
114 C6 **Wootton** Staffs
115 H3 **Wootton** Staffs
46 F3 **Wootton Bassett** Wilts
19 J5 **Wootton Bridge** IoW
85 K6 **Wootton Broadmead** Beds
19 J5 **Wootton Common** IoW
29 G2 **Wootton Courtenay** Somset
15 J3 **Wootton Fitzpaine** Dorset
47 J6 **Wootton Rivers** Wilts
48 E8 **Wootton St Lawrence** Hants
82 E3 **Wootton Wawen** Warwks
81 K4 **Worcester** Worcs
51 G6 **Worcester Park** Gt Lon
97 K6 **Wordsley** Dudley
97 G4 **Worfield** Shrops
17 H5 **Worgret** Dorset
86 B5 **Workhouse End** Beds
164 D5 **Workington** Cumb
134 B4 **Worksop** Notts
136 F4 **Worlaby** Lincs
144 C5 **Worlaby** N Linc
67 L5 **Worlds End** Bucks
19 L1 **Worlds End** Hants
48 C3 **World's End** W Berk
22 E3 **Worlds End** W Susx
44 D6 **Worle** N Som
130 C8 **Worleston** Ches
107 J5 **Worlingham** Suffk
28 D8 **Worlington** Devon
104 D8 **Worlington** Suffk
90 F2 **Worlingworth** Suffk
150 D3 **Wormald Green** N York
62 E1 **Wormbridge** Herefs
104 D1 **Wormegay** Norfk
62 F1 **Wormelow Tump** Herefs
132 C5 **Wormhill** Derbys
80 A7 **Wormhill** Herefs
72 D1 **Wormingford** Essex
66 F5 **Worminghall** Bucks
82 B7 **Wormington** Gloucs
31 J2 **Worminster** Somset
223 G2 **Wormit** Fife
83 K4 **Wormleighton** Warwks
69 K6 **Wormley** Herts
36 E3 **Wormley** Surrey
69 K6 **Wormleybury** Herts
143 G4 **Wormley Hill** Donc
39 M2 **Wormshill** Kent
80 A5 **Wormsley** Herefs
50 B8 **Worplesdon** Surrey
132 F1 **Worrall** Sheff
63 J4 **Worrall Hill** Gloucs
142 A7 **Worsbrough** Barns
142 A7 **Worsbrough Bridge** Barns
142 B7 **Worsbrough Dale** Barns
139 M7 **Worsley** Salfd
139 H7 **Worsley Mesnes** Wigan
122 F6 **Worstead** Norfk
140 C1 **Worsthorne** Lancs
7 H4 **Worston** Devon
148 D7 **Worston** Lancs
41 K4 **Worth** Kent
31 H2 **Worth** Somset
37 L4 **Worth** W Susx
37 M4 **Worth Abbey** W Susx
106 B7 **Wortham** Suffk
95 H2 **Worthen** Shrops
112 F2 **Worthenbury** Wrexhm
121 M7 **Worthing** Norfk
21 K6 **Worthing** W Susx
116 C7 **Worthington** Leics
17 J7 **Worth Matravers** Dorset

62 F5 **Worthybrook** Mons
48 F8 **Worting** Hants
141 M7 **Wortley** Barns
141 L1 **Wortley** Leeds
159 G5 **Worton** N York
46 E7 **Worton** Wilts
106 F6 **Wortwell** Norfk
95 G3 **Wotherton** Shrops
101 M2 **Wothorpe** C Pete
7 H3 **Wotter** Devon
37 H2 **Wotton** Surrey
63 M8 **Wotton-under-Edge** Gloucs
67 G4 **Wotton Underwood** Bucks
85 G7 **Woughton on the Green** M Keyn
52 F6 **Wouldham** Kent
97 H5 **Woundale** Shrops
73 J1 **Wrabness** Essex
27 J4 **Wrafton** Devon
136 B4 **Wragby** Lincs
142 C4 **Wragby** Wakefd
106 C2 **Wramplingham** Norfk
7 K3 **Wrangaton** Devon
142 D5 **Wrangbrook** Wakefd
119 M2 **Wrangle** Lincs
119 M1 **Wrangle Common** Lincs
119 M1 **Wrangle Lowgate** Lincs
29 L7 **Wrangway** Somset
30 D6 **Wrantage** Somset
144 C6 **Wrawby** N Linc
44 F4 **Wraxall** N Som
31 K4 **Wraxall** Somset
147 M2 **Wray** Lancs
156 E3 **Wray Castle** Cumb
50 C4 **Wraysbury** W & M
147 M2 **Wrayton** Lancs
138 E2 **Wrea Green** Lancs
156 B5 **Wreaks End** Cumb
166 B1 **Wreay** Cumb
166 B6 **Wreay** Cumb
36 B2 **Wrecclesham** Surrey
181 G7 **Wrekenton** Gatesd
162 D5 **Wrelton** N York
113 K2 **Wrenbury** Ches
163 H5 **Wrench Green** N York
106 D4 **Wreningham** Norfk
107 K6 **Wrentham** Suffk
141 M3 **Wrenthorpe** Wakefd
95 K3 **Wrentnall** Shrops
143 H2 **Wressle** E R Yk
144 B6 **Wressle** N Linc
86 E5 **Wrestlingworth** Beds
104 D3 **Wretton** Norfk
112 E2 **Wrexham** Wrexhm
97 H8 **Wribbenhall** Worcs
96 E6 **Wrickton** Shrops
139 G5 **Wrightington Bar** Lancs
70 D4 **Wright's Green** Essex
114 B2 **Wrinehill** Staffs
44 F6 **Wrington** N Som
45 K8 **Writhlington** BaNES
71 G6 **Writtle** Essex
96 E1 **Wrockwardine** Wrekin
143 H7 **Wroot** N Linc
149 L8 **Wrose** Brad
52 D7 **Wrotham** Kent
52 D7 **Wrotham Heath** Kent
97 J3 **Wrottesley** Staffs
47 H3 **Wroughton** Swindn
19 J7 **Wroxall** IoW
82 F1 **Wroxall** Warwks
96 D2 **Wroxeter** Shrops
122 F8 **Wroxham** Norfk
83 K7 **Wroxton** Oxon
115 K3 **Wyaston** Derbys
70 F7 **Wyatt's Green** Essex
119 K3 **Wyberton East** Lincs
119 J3 **Wyberton West** Lincs
86 D4 **Wyboston** Beds
113 M2 **Wybunbury** Ches
81 L2 **Wychbold** Worcs
38 C7 **Wych Cross** E Susx
115 K8 **Wychnor** Staffs
35 M3 **Wyck** Hants
65 J3 **Wyck Rissington** Gloucs
168 E7 **Wycliffe** Dur
149 G8 **Wycoller** Lancs
117 K6 **Wycomb** Leics
67 L8 **Wycombe Marsh** Bucks
69 K1 **Wyddial** Herts
40 D6 **Wye** Kent
63 G5 **Wyesham** Mons
117 L7 **Wyfordby** Leics
141 J2 **Wyke** Brad
13 K3 **Wyke** Devon
15 G3 **Wyke** Devon
32 D5 **Wyke** Dorset
96 E3 **Wyke** Shrops

50 A8 **Wyke** Surrey
31 L4 **Wyke Champflower** Somset
162 E7 **Wykeham** N York
163 H6 **Wykeham** N York
99 K7 **Wyken** Covtry
97 H4 **Wyken** Shrops
16 C7 **Wyke Regis** Dorset
112 F6 **Wykey** Shrops
99 L4 **Wykin** Leics
180 D6 **Wylam** Nthumb
98 E4 **Wylde Green** Birm
33 H3 **Wylye** Wilts
117 G6 **Wymeswold** Leics
85 J2 **Wymington** Beds
117 M7 **Wymondham** Leics
106 C3 **Wymondham** Norfk
42 E3 **Wyndham** Brdgnd
16 B3 **Wynford Eagle** Dorset
169 L5 **Wynyard Park** S on T
169 L5 **Wynyard Village** S on T
81 M5 **Wyre Piddle** Worcs
117 G6 **Wysall** Notts
80 C2 **Wyson** Herefs
98 D8 **Wythall** Worcs
66 C5 **Wytham** Oxon
165 K7 **Wythburn** Cumb
131 G2 **Wythenshawe** Manch
165 G5 **Wythop Mill** Cumb
86 F1 **Wyton** Cambs
144 F1 **Wyton** E R Yk
90 B2 **Wyverstone** Suffk
89 L2 **Wyverstone Street** Suffk
118 A5 **Wyville** Lincs

Y

143 M6 **Yaddlethorpe** N Linc
19 G7 **Yafford** IoW
160 E4 **Yafforth** N York
8 C3 **Yalberton** Torbay
39 H3 **Yalding** Kent
166 C5 **Yanwath** Cumb
65 G4 **Yanworth** Gloucs
152 B5 **Yapham** E R Yk
21 G6 **Yapton** W Susx
44 D7 **Yarborough** N Som
19 K6 **Yarbridge** IoW
136 F1 **Yarburgh** Lincs
14 F1 **Yarcombe** Devon
28 D6 **Yard** Devon
98 E6 **Yardley** Birm
84 E6 **Yardley Gobion** Nhants
85 G4 **Yardley Hastings** Nhants
98 E7 **Yardley Wood** Birm
79 J3 **Yardro** Powys
30 B5 **Yarford** Somset
80 E6 **Yarkhill** Herefs
31 H2 **Yarley** Somset
31 L5 **Yarlington** Somset
169 L8 **Yarm** S on T
18 E5 **Yarmouth** IoW
27 L5 **Yarnacott** Devon
46 C7 **Yarnbrook** Wilts
13 H6 **Yarner** Devon
114 D5 **Yarnfield** Staffs
27 K6 **Yarnscombe** Devon
66 C5 **Yarnton** Oxon
80 B2 **Yarpole** Herefs
200 D7 **Yarrow** Border
30 E2 **Yarrow** Somset
200 D7 **Yarrow Feus** Border
200 E7 **Yarrowford** Border
80 A6 **Yarsop** Herefs
102 B4 **Yarwell** Nhants
45 L3 **Yate** S Glos
49 K6 **Yateley** Hants
46 F4 **Yatesbury** Wilts
48 E4 **Yattendon** W Berk
63 J1 **Yatton** Herefs
80 A2 **Yatton** Herefs
44 E6 **Yatton** N Som
46 C4 **Yatton Keynell** Wilts
19 K6 **Yaverland** IoW
15 H4 **Yawl** Devon
135 H1 **Yawthorpe** Lincs
105 K1 **Yaxham** Norfk
102 D5 **Yaxley** Cambs
106 C8 **Yaxley** Suffk
79 M6 **Yazor** Herefs
50 E3 **Yeading** Gt Lon
150 B7 **Yeadon** Leeds
157 H7 **Yealand Conyers** Lancs
157 H7 **Yealand Redmayne** Lancs
157 H7 **Yealand Storrs** Lancs
7 H4 **Yealmbridge** Devon
7 H4 **Yealmpton** Devon
170 E6 **Yearby** R & Cl

164 F2 **Yearngill** Cumb
161 J7 **Yearsley** N York
113 G7 **Yeaton** Shrops
115 K3 **Yeaveley** Derbys
202 E7 **Yeavering** Nthumb
162 F6 **Yedingham** N York
66 A6 **Yelford** Oxon
27 J4 **Yelland** Devon
86 F3 **Yelling** Cambs
100 D8 **Yelvertoft** Nhants
7 G1 **Yelverton** Devon
106 F3 **Yelverton** Norfk
32 B6 **Yenston** Somset
13 H3 **Yeoford** Devon
11 L5 **Yeolmbridge** Cnwll
28 E5 **Yeo Mill** Devon
27 G6 **Yeo Vale** Devon
31 J7 **Yeovil** Somset
31 J7 **Yeovil Marsh** Somset
31 J6 **Yeovilton** Somset
55 H5 **Yerbeston** Pembks
275 b4 **Yesnaby** Ork
190 E4 **Yetlington** Nthumb
31 K8 **Yetminster** Dorset
8 B4 **Yetson** Devon
14 B5 **Yettington** Devon
221 H6 **Yetts o'Muckhart** Clacks
141 H2 **Yews Green** Brad
98 C4 **Yew Tree** Sandw
125 J6 **Y Felinheli** Gwynd
75 L2 **Y Ferwig** Cerdgn
109 G4 **Y Ffor** Gwynd
128 C8 **Y Gyffylliog** Denbgs
85 K2 **Yielden** Beds
97 K7 **Yieldingtree** Worcs
198 E3 **Yieldshields** S Lans
50 D3 **Yiewsley** Gt Lon
111 K3 **Y Maerdy** Conwy
112 D2 **Y Nant** Wrexhm
43 G3 **Ynysboeth** Rhondd
43 J3 **Ynysddu** Caerph
57 J5 **Ynysforgan** Swans
42 F3 **Ynyshir** Rhondd
92 D5 **Ynyslas** Cerdgn
42 F5 **Ynysmaerdy** Rhondd
57 K4 **Ynysmeudwy** Neath
57 J5 **Ynystawe** Swans
60 C4 **Ynyswen** Powys
42 E2 **Ynyswen** Rhondd
43 G3 **Ynysybwl** Rhondd
92 D3 **Ynysymaengwyn** Gwynd
158 F6 **Yockenthwaite** N York
95 K2 **Yockleton** Shrops
143 K3 **Yokefleet** E R Yk
208 E5 **Yoker** C Glas
139 L1 **York** Lancs
151 J5 **York** York
40 E3 **Yorkletts** Kent
63 J5 **Yorkley** Gloucs
49 L7 **York Town** Surrey
113 H7 **Yorton Heath** Shrops
132 D6 **Youlgreave** Derbys
152 B5 **Youlthorpe** E R Yk
151 G3 **Youlton** N York
69 K3 **Youngsbury** Herts
71 H3 **Young's End** Essex
115 J7 **Yoxall** Staffs
91 J2 **Yoxford** Suffk
108 D6 **Y Rhiw** Gwynd
93 G7 **Ysbyty Cynfyn** Cerdgn
110 F2 **Ysbyty Ifan** Conwy
77 K1 **Ysbyty Ystwyth** Cerdgn
128 D5 **Ysceifiog** Flints
92 E4 **Ysgubor-y-Coed** Cerdgn
57 L3 **Ystalyfera** Neath
42 F3 **Ystrad** Rhondd
76 F4 **Ystrad Aeron** Cerdgn
60 D4 **Ystradfellte** Powys
77 L6 **Ystrad Ffin** Carmth
60 B5 **Ystradgynlais** Powys
77 K2 **Ystrad Meurig** Cerdgn
43 J3 **Ystrad Mynach** Caerph
42 F6 **Ystradowen** V Glam
92 F7 **Ystumtuen** Cerdgn
257 G5 **Ythanbank** Abers
256 B4 **Ythanwells** Abers
256 F5 **Ythsie** Abers

Z

13 G2 **Zeal Monachorum** Devon
32 C4 **Zeals** Wilts
4 C4 **Zelah** Cnwll
2 C3 **Zennor** Cnwll
3 J7 **Zoar** Cnwll
116 E6 **Zouch** Notts